THE NEW CAMBRIDGE MODERN HISTORY

VOLUME X

THE ZENITH OF EUROPEAN POWER

1830-70

EDITED BY

J. P. T. BURY

CAMBRIDGE

AT THE UNIVERSITY PRESS

1964

PUBLISHED BY
THE SYNDICS OF THE CAMBRIDGE UNIVERSITY PRESS
Bentley House, 200 Euston Road, London, N.W. 1
American Branch: 32 East 57th Street, New York 22, N.Y.
West African Office: P.O. Box 33, Ibadan, Nigeria

©

CAMBRIDGE UNIVERSITY PRESS
1964

First edition 1960
Reprinted with minor corrections 1964

Printed in Great Britain at the University Printing House, Cambridge
(Brooke Crutchley, University Printer)

CONTENTS

CHAPTER I

INTRODUCTORY SUMMARY *page* 1

By J. P. T. BURY

Fellow of Corpus Christi College and Lecturer in History in the University of Cambridge

CHAPTER II

ECONOMIC CHANGE AND GROWTH

By HERBERT HEATON, *Emeritus Professor of History in the University of Minnesota*

The period, one of improved methods and new institutions. . . . 22
Extension of agriculture 22–3
Enclosure, drainage and fertilisers 24
Improvement of farm equipment and its dependence on capital 25
Operation of the Corn Laws 26
Agricultural prosperity between 1850 and 1873 27
Growth of textile industries 28
Machine production and increase in output of iron, steel and coal . . . 29–31
Transport of goods and materials by road and water 31–2
The coming of the railways 32–4
The golden age of the American sailing ship. Transport by steamship . . . 35
Crossing the Atlantic 36
Improved communications and international trade 36–7
Tariffs and free trade 37–8
Raising of capital necessitated by trade expansion 39
Banks and banking 40–2
Extension of factory system 42–3
Migratory movements of labour 43
Living and working conditions. Limitation of child labour 44–5
Repeal of Combination Laws. Growth of Trade Union movement . . . 45–6
Some tentative conclusions. 1825–50 a period of extraordinary development . 46–7
Improvement of working conditions, 1850–70 48

CHAPTER III

THE SCIENTIFIC MOVEMENT AND ITS INFLUENCE ON THOUGHT AND MATERIAL DEVELOPMENT

By A. R. HALL, *lately Fellow of Christ's College and Lecturer in the History of Science in the University of Cambridge*

1830–70 falls between the formative and modern periods of science . . . 49
The state as patron. Contributions of Western Europe and the U.S.A. . . 50–1
Little co-operation between science and production 51
Influence of scientific attitude on hygiene, farming and chemical industries and on philosophy. The Utilitarian, Positivist and Marxist philosophies . . . 52–5
Interdependence of different branches of science illustrated in exploitation of mathematical analysis 56
Clerk Maxwell and Faraday's theory 57

CONTENTS

The perfecting of spectrum analysis . . . . *page* 58
Thermo-dynamics 59–60
Atomic theory and table of atomic weights 60–2
The theory of valency 62
The periodic law. Mendeléef and Meyer 63
Laboratory synthesis and commercial exploitation 64–5
Pasteur and microbiology 65–6
Opposing schools in experimental physiology 66–7
Geologists and the age of the earth 68
Theory of evolution and its opponents 69–71
Medical and surgical practice 72
Lister's antiseptic system of surgery. Function of the inventor 73–4
The work of Comte and Spencer. Attitude of the Churches . . 74–5

CHAPTER IV

RELIGION AND THE RELATIONS OF CHURCHES AND STATES

By Norman Sykes, *Honorary Fellow of Emmanuel College, Cambridge, and Dean of Winchester*

Ecclesiastical reaction following defeat of Napoleon. Papacy returns to Rome . 76
The Liberal-Catholic movement in France 77–80
Lamennais's appeal to the Pope. The bull *Mirari vos* 78
Ultramontanism and uniform use of Roman liturgy in France 79
The educational struggle; the *Loi Falloux*. The Swiss 'Regeneration' movement . 80
The religious problem in Switzerland. Defeat of the *Sonderbund*. . . . 81
The Oxford Movement 81–3
Disputes in the Church of Scotland. Founding of Free Church of Scotland . 83–4
Re-establishment of Roman Catholic hierarchy in England 84–5
Controversy between Anglicans and Nonconformists concerning state education. 85–6
Ancient universities opened to non-Anglicans. The religious census of 1851 . 87
Doctrine of the Immaculate Conception. Relations between church and state in
  Italy 88
Rise of Louis Napoleon. The Syllabus of Errors 89–93
The General Council 93–9
France's attitude to General Council 97
Council prorogued *sine die*. War between France and Prussia . . . 98
The definition of papal infallibility 98–9
Political aftermath of General Council unfavourable 99–100
The Irish Church and its disestablishment 100–1
Development of social conscience 101
Literary and historical criticism of the Bible 102–3

CHAPTER V

EDUCATION AND THE PRESS

By John Roach, *Fellow of Corpus Christi College, Cambridge*

The aftermath of the French Revolution 104
The role of the state in education 105–6
The spread of liberalism and nationalism 106
Clerical and secular views of education 106–7

CONTENTS

The Liberals and freedom of education . . . . *page* 107
Swiss, German, English and French theorists 108–9
Primary education 109–11
The secondary school and modern studies 111–12
Education and liberal culture 112
The 'public school' system. Growing importance of technical and professional
    training. 113
The universities 114–15
Secondary and higher education in Italy 115
The English universities. Educational history of the U.S.A. 116–17
Education in self-governing colonies and India 117–18
The 'British Indian' system. 118
The education of women 118–19
Adult education 119–20
Mechanics' Institutes, libraries and museums 120
England's lead in the development of the press 121
Abolition of the stamp duty. Unique position of *The Times* . . . 122
Increase in number of newspapers. The French press 123–5
The German and Austrian press 125–7
Connection between press and political parties 127
Censorship. The Russian press 128–9
The American press 129–30
Some comparisons. New techniques 131–2
Growth of news agencies 132–3

CHAPTER VI

ART AND ARCHITECTURE

By NIKOLAUS PEVSNER, *Professor of the History of Art, Birkbeck College,*
University of London

Emancipation from patronage. Artistic lead of England *c.* 1760–*c.* 1800 . . 134–5
The problem of individualism 135
English Victorian architecture 136–7
The Gothic revival and other imitative styles 137–8
The architect a purveyor of façades. Similar developments abroad . . 139
The Neo-Gothic style in Germany, Italy and France 140
Neo-classical style in the U.S.A. Revival of native Renaissance styles. . . 141–2
Inflated size of public buildings 142
A period of design in two, rather than three, dimensions. Consequent poverty of
    sculpture 143
French painting of the period 144–50
The work of Delacroix 145–6
Realism in painting the hall-mark of the period 147
Millet and Courbet 148–9
Industrial revolution exerts little influence on painting. 150
The Pre-Raphaelites 151–3
Impressionism. The late Victorians 154–5

CONTENTS

CHAPTER VII
IMAGINATIVE LITERATURE

By ERICH HELLER, *Professor of German, University College of Swansea,*
University of Wales

The novel dominates the field of literature . . . . *page* 156
The desire to attain a belief; increasing preoccupation with 'psychology' . . 157
Literature as an instrument of exploration 158
Nineteenth-century realism 159–60
Consciousness of the social problems of the age 160
The 'Bildungsroman' 161–2
Decline of the traditional heroic hero 163
The unruly genius of Victor Hugo 164–5
The 'historic' novel. Realism as a mode of presentation 165
The connection between literature and society 166–7
The world of the Russian novelist 168
Comparison between Tolstoy and Dostoevsky 169
Flaubert's realism 170
Realism of the prose and romanticism of the poetry of the period . . . 171
The poetry of the period 172
    French 173–4
    German 174–6
    English 176–8
Baudelaire and Edgar Allan Poe 179–80
Nekrasov and Walt Whitman 180–1
Dramatic writing below level of that reached by the novel and poetry . . 181
German, Austrian and Russian drama 182–4

CHAPTER VIII
LIBERALISM AND CONSTITUTIONAL DEVELOPMENTS

By J. A. HAWGOOD, *Professor of Modern History and Government,*
University of Birmingham

Changes in forms of government 185–6
No continuous advance towards liberal and democratic institutions . . . 186–7
The Marxist challenge to liberalism 188
The first democratic institutions. Fundamental reforms in France, Belgium,
    Great Britain and Germany 189
Constitutional evolution of German states. The revised French charter of 1830 . 190
The Belgian constitution of 1831 191
British parliamentary reform and its influence 192–3
The U.S.A. and Belgium provide models for constitution-makers . . . 194
American influence on German National Assembly 195
The Swiss constitution of 1848. Federal reform and failure in Habsburg Empire . 196–7
The Kremsier draft constitution 197–8
The Italian constitutional dilemma of 1848–9 198–200
The Piedmontese *Statuto* of 1848 and its importance as a national symbol . . 200–1
The Years of Revolution and Reaction 202
The 1850's a period of marking-time and consolidation 203–4
Emancipation of serfs 204

CONTENTS

Liberalism menaced from both Left and Right . . . . . *page* 205–6
Improvements in administrative organisation 206
Tightening up the machinery of the centralised state 207
Lack of any tradition of self-government in Germany and Austria . . . 208
Vicissitudes of the federal idea 208
Its failure in Italy and Austria 209–10
Its revival in Germany and Mexico, and triumph in Canada 210–11
1867 an *annus mirabilis* 211–12

CHAPTER IX

NATIONALITIES AND NATIONALISM
By J. P. T. Bury

Definition of nationality 213
Prospects of nationality in 1832 214–15
The role of France and of Paris and other West European cities before 1848 . 215–16
Irish nationalism 217–18
Nationalism in France. 218
The Schleswig-Holstein problem 219–20
The Pan-Scandinavian movement 220
Separation of Belgium from Holland 221
The Flemish movement 221–2
The Swiss national movement 222–4
Mazzini and Italian nationalism 224–6
German nationalism 226–8
The Polish question reveals the divorce between liberalism and nationalism . 228–9
Nationalism in Eastern Europe 229
Russia's traditional nationalism 230–1
Finland, Latvia and Estonia 231
Slavophiles and Pan-Slavs 232–4
Failure of the Slav Congress in Prague 233
The great Polish emigration of 1831 234
Prussian, Austrian and Russian Poland 235
The Polish rising of 1863. The Lithuanians 236
The Polish poets. Austria the antagonist of national self-determination . . 237
Golden age of literature and scholarship in the Austrian Empire. . . 238
The conflict of nationalities in Hungary 239–40
The Ottoman empire 240
Emergence of the Balkan states 241–3
The Jews 243–4
Progress of nationalism 245

CHAPTER X

THE SYSTEM OF ALLIANCES AND THE
BALANCE OF POWER
By Gordon Craig, *Professor of History, Princeton University*

The diplomatic division of Europe 246
Flexibility of the alliance system illustrated by the Belgian crisis of 1830 . . 247
Palmerston secures acceptance of Belgian independence by the powers . . 248

CONTENTS

Ambiguities of French policy . . . . *page* 249
Reasons for the Eastern powers' acquiescence in the peaceful solution of the
    Belgian problem 250
Widening of the gulf between the Eastern and Western powers. The Near East . 251
The Sultan appeals to Russia. Russo-Turkish Treaty of 1833 252
Affairs of Portugal and Spain. The Quadruple Alliance, the West's answer to
    Unkiar-Skelessi and Münchengrätz 253
Disruptive tendencies in the Anglo-French *entente*. Near Eastern crisis, 1839–40 . 254
Defeat of Mahmud's forces. The four ambassadors meet in Vienna . . . 255
Tsar sends Brunnov to London and drives a wedge between Great Britain and
    France 256
Quadruple Agreement. Isolation of France and danger of war 257
Russia attempts to formalise isolation of France. Metternich's mediation between
    France and the other powers. Straits Convention, 1841 258
Breakdown of the Anglo-French *entente*. France seeks understanding with Austria 259
Anglo-Russian relations more friendly. 259–60
1848 Revolutions threaten balance of power 260
Lamartine's 'Manifesto to the Powers' 261
Peace endangered by Prussia's anti-Russian policy and the revolt of Lombardy
    and Venetia 262–3
Palmerston, Russia, and the Hungarian revolt 264
Threat of Austro-Prussian war. Prussia capitulates at Olmütz. Schleswig-Holstein
    problem 265
Last successful meeting of Concert of Europe. Implications of the balance of
    power 266
Willingness of the powers to maintain peace. The Crimean turning point . . 267
Effects of the Crimean War 268–9
Great Britain's tendency to withdraw from continental affairs 269–70
Alliances and diplomatic alignments cease to be defensive in purpose . . . 271
Inability or unwillingness among statesmen to collaborate 272–3

CHAPTER XI

ARMED FORCES AND THE ART OF WAR: NAVIES

By MICHAEL LEWIS, *lately Professor of History at the*
Royal Naval College, Greenwich

Complete predominance of British navy 274
Extensive and rapid changes in *matériel* 275–6
The new type of fighting force envisaged by Paixhans 276
Early days of steamships 277
Introduction of the screw-propeller 278
The steamship in the Crimean War. The problem of coaling 279
Steam wins the battle with sail in the British navy 280
Transition from wood to iron. French and British hesitations 280–1
End of the wood–iron controversy. Roundshot or shell. The French again
    pioneers 282–3
Whitworth and Armstrong revolutionise gunnery 284
Armour, the answer to the shell. The broadside becoming obsolete . . . 285
Temporary success of the 'ram'. Efficacy of the turret 286
Mine, submarine and torpedo 287
'Commissioned officers', 'warrant officers' and 'men' in the Royal Navy . . 287–300

CONTENTS

Seniority . . . . *page* 288–9
Block in promotion. Unemployed officers. Patronage 289–90
The navy as a full-time profession 290
Introduction of the 'general commission'. The 'active' and the 'retired' list.
    Conditions of entry 291
Senior officers' selection of their own successors. Introduction of entry
    examinations 292
Naval College training of cadets. The spread of commissions 293
Jealousy between 'executive' and engineer officers 294
Evils of impressment. Improvement in conditions of service 294–5
Long-term service established, also fleet reserve. Genesis of the bluejacket . . 296
The seaman's changed status 296–7
The navies of the U.S.A. and France 297–8
Graham's new Register. Formation of Royal Naval Reserve . . . 299
Direction and administration of the Royal Navy. 300–1

CHAPTER XII

ARMED FORCES AND THE ART OF WAR: ARMIES

By B. H. LIDDELL HART

Computing the strength of armed forces by the number of men 302
The flint-lock musket and the percussion system 303
The development of the rifle. Breech-loading 303–5
Development of artillery and machine guns. 306
The French *mitrailleuse* 307
The military use of railways. 308–9
Need for rapid concentration and deployment of forces 309
The electric telegraph 309–10
The Prussian 'General Staff' 310–11
Conscription 312–13
The influence of Jomini and Clausewitz 313–19
The French conquest of Algeria 320
Radetzky's brilliant generalship in the Austro-Italian War of 1848–9 . . 321–2
Ill-management of the Crimean War 322–3
The Italian War of 1859 323
Bismarck observes the military weakness of France and Austria . . . 324
The strategy of the Seven Weeks War of 1866 324–5
Strategic pattern of Franco-Prussian War 325–7
The American Civil War 327–30

CHAPTER XIII

THE UNITED KINGDOM AND ITS WORLD-WIDE INTERESTS

By DAVID THOMSON, *Master of Sidney Sussex College and Lecturer in History in the University of Cambridge*

A rural and agricultural society becomes fundamentally urban and industrial . 331
Increase and shifts in population 331–2
The age of railway construction 332
Trans-Atlantic shipping 332–3

CONTENTS

Coal, iron and cotton . . . . *page* 333
Britain a world power. Modification of political system 334
The two Houses of Parliament 335
Redistribution of constituencies 335–6
Elections and the electorate. Reform Act of 1867 336
Local government reform. Increase in public servants and officials . . . 337
The Civil Service 337–8
Alignments and organisation of political parties 338–9
Cabinet solidarity and collective responsibility. The Queen's memorandum about
    Palmerston 340
Abolition of slavery 341
Improvements in the conditions of factory workers 341–2
Repeal of the Corn Laws 342–4
The Bank Charter Act of 1844 344
Working-class self-help and voluntary organisation 345
The early trade unions. 346
The 'Tolpuddle Martyrs' 346–7
The Chartist movement 347–8
The Co-operative movement 348
Britain's peaceful policy 349
A new conception of Empire and Commonwealth 349
Development in the colonies. Shift in balance of imperial interests . . . 350–1
The quest for markets 351
Self-government the goal of colonial administration 352
Rebellions in Canada; the Durham Report 353–5
Constitutional development of Australia, New Zealand and Cape Colony . . 355
General character of British development epitomised by imperial defence system 356

CHAPTER XIV

RUSSIA IN EUROPE AND ASIA

By J. M. K. VYVYAN, *Fellow of Trinity College, Cambridge*

Survival and recurrence in Russian institutions and thought. 357
The revolt of the Decembrists 358
Political police and censorship as instituted by edicts of 1826 359–60
The State Council 360
The Kochubei Committee of 1826 360–1
The tsar's interest in agrarian reform 361
Increase in local peasant risings. The Polish insurrection (1830) 362
Uvarov, Minister of Education 362–3
Codification of Russian laws 363
Changes in economic policy 364–5
Russia's interest in the strengthening of Prussia and Austria against international
    revolution 365
The revolutionary spirit passes from army and salon to scholar and publicist . 366
Westerners and Slavophiles 366–8
Political controversy under the guise of literary criticism 368
The army the chief field for individual advancement 369
The new emperor Alexander II 369–70
Emancipation of the serfs 370–2
Home-based conspiracy and agitation 373–4

CONTENTS

Nihilism and populism . . . . *page* 374–5
The Polish revolt of 1863. Superficial liberalisation of Finland 376
The local government reform decree (1864) 377
The new judicial system of 1864 377–8
'Peoples' primary schools 378
Attempted assassination of tsar (1866) 378–9
Introduction of universal military service 379
Reform of the Bank of Russia 379–80
Economic conditions following the Crimean War 380–1
Economic failure of the agrarian revolution 381–2
The administration of Siberia 383–4
Alaska ceded to U.S.A. 384
New forward policy at the expense of China 384–5
Pacification of Transcaucasia 385–6
Expeditions against the Khanates of Khiva, Bokhara and Khokand . . . 386–8

CHAPTER XV

THE REVOLUTIONS OF 1848

By CHARLES POUTHAS, *Emeritus Professor in the University of Paris*

Conditions that precede revolution 389
The instigators—intellectuals; their inspiration—France 390
Differing concepts of nationality 391
Significance of the social problem 391–2
Paris Revolution of 24 February 392–4
    Its effect on Europe 394–5
Vienna the source of revolution in Central Europe 395
Liberation of Lombardy and Venetia 396
The rising in Berlin and its consequences 397
Some results of the revolutions 397–8
The ebb-tide of revolution in France 399–400
The effect on Europe 400–3
Election of Louis Napoleon 404
The Prussian Constituent Assembly dissolved 405
The Frankfurt Parliament 405–7
Frederick William of Prussia refuses the German crown 407
End of the political revolution in Italy, Hungary and Austria 408
Revolution comes to a standstill in France and Germany 408–9
Reform of the Germanic Confederation. Humiliation of Prussia . . . 410
Louis Napoleon's *coup d'état* (1851) 411
Results of the revolution 411–15

CHAPTER XVI

THE MEDITERRANEAN

By C. W. CRAWLEY, *Fellow of Trinity Hall and Lecturer in History in the University of Cambridge*

Influence of steamship and railway 416
Extent of the Mediterranean 416–17
Climatic conditions 417
The arrival of the 'tourist' 418

CONTENTS

Relative activity of Mediterranean ports . . . . *page* 418–19
Population of Mediterranean ports 420
The European ports 420–2
The Levantine ports 422–3
The ports of North Africa 424
Rivalries: traditional, trading, dynastic and national 425
Greece becomes independent kingdom. 426
Egypt a disturbing force under Mehemet Ali 426–7
Mehemet Ali and the French capture of Algiers 427
Mehemet Ali's invasion of Syria and Asia Minor 428
The Sultan defeated at Nezib. Settlement imposed by Convention of London
    (1840) 429
French influence in the Levant. Anglo-Russian rivalry a new factor in Mediter-
    ranean politics 430–1
Britain a predominant influence in Mediterranean politics 431
Operation of regular steamship lines 431–2
Demonstrations of British naval power 433
The Suez Canal project 433–40
Chevalier's concept of inter-continental railways and canals 435
Enfantin's belief in a canal connecting the Mediterranean with the Red Sea . 436
English, French and Austro-German groups come to agreement 437
Plan for a railway gains ground 438
De Lesseps obtains formal concession 438–9
De Lesseps issues the prospectus and work is commenced 439
Completion of the canal 440

CHAPTER XVII

THE SECOND EMPIRE IN FRANCE

By PAUL FARMER, *Visiting Lecturer in the Department of History at Smith College,*
Northampton, Massachusetts

Louis Napoleon's early life; his one purpose to restore the Empire . . . 442–3
His failure to secure a revision of the constitution 444
The *coup d'état* of December 1851; the new Constitution (January 1852) . . 445
Restoration of the Empire 446
Napoleon III's supporters of diverse political views 447–8
The logic in his opportunism 448
Two periods in the reign: (1) the period of personal rule 449–53
The functions of the *Corps Législatif* and Senate 450
Encouragement of economic expansion—credit, railways and lowering of tariffs . 451–2
Increasing acceptance of the regime 452–3
(2) The period of unsteady equilibrium 453–65
Internal dissensions over religious issues 453–4
Social and political cleavages consequent on economic expansion . . . 454–5
A resurgence of republicanism. Napoleon veers towards the left . . . 455–6
Rapid increase in foreign investment and industrial production 457
Reasons for economic expansion. Social pre-eminence of the bourgeoisie.
    Changes in the common people 458–9
The world of ideas lags behind economic enterprise 459
The rebuilding of Paris. The new rich 460
Napoleon's aims in foreign policy 461
The Crimean War and the war against Austria (1859) 462–3

CONTENTS

French intervention in Mexico . . . . *page* 464
Napoleon's role in the struggle between Prussia and Austria . . . 464–5
The march of events culminating in Sedan 465
Collapse of Second Empire. Its mark on French history 466–7

CHAPTER XVIII

THE CRIMEAN WAR

By AGATHA RAMM, *Fellow of Somerville College, Oxford*
and the late B. H. SUMNER, *Warden of All Souls College, Oxford*

The background of Russo-Turkish relations 468
Reasons for the war. The dispute over the Holy Places 469
Napoleon's moderation in face of the tsar's insult. Russia recognises probability
    of war, makes further demands on Turkey 470
Russian plans for dismembering the Ottoman empire 471
Turkey complies with an Austrian ultimatum 472
Menshikov's mission 472–3
Turkey rejects the Russian demands 473–4
British and French fleets ordered to Besika Bay. Russian forces occupy line of the
    Danube 474
The Vienna Note. Arrival of Egyptian fleet 475
Russian Foreign Office document leaks out to the press. British and French fleets
    at Constantinople 476
Defeat of Turkish flotilla at Sinope. British and French fleets enter Black Sea . 477
The Western powers declare war. Military operations slow to develop . . 478
Austria occupies Principalities. Crimean peninsula becomes theatre of war . 479
Missed opportunities. Austria signs Franco-British alliance 479–80
Fresh negotiations. Outcry in Britain against conduct of the war. Palmerston
    becomes Prime Minister 481
Decline in Austria's influence. Fall of Sebastopol 482
Sardinia adheres to the Franco-British alliance. Overtures to Sweden . . 483
Palmerston plans bulwarks against Russia, but France makes informal soundings
    for peace 484
Russia accepts terms and armistice declared. Casualty figures . . . 485–6
Press reports of mismanagement result in reorganisation of British army
    administration 486
Effects of the war in France, Russia and Turkey 486–7
The peace congress and the consequent treaty 487–90
Congress turns to affairs of Poland, Greece and Italy 490
Decline in diplomatic prestige of Austria and Russia; they turn towards France . 491
Partition of Turkey postponed 491–2
Russo-British hostility remains 492

CHAPTER XIX

PRUSSIA AND THE GERMAN PROBLEM, 1830–66

By JAMES JOLL, *Fellow and Sub-Warden of St Antony's College, Oxford*

Revival of liberalism throughout Germany 493
Formation of the German Customs Union (*Zollverein*) and the Tax Union
    (*Steuerverein*) 494
Prussian administrative system the envy of liberals throughout Europe . . 495

CONTENTS

Accession of Frederick William IV raises hopes of political unity and a more liberal policy. . . . . *page* 495–6
The political situation in individual states 497
Prussia under the ministry of Count Brandenburg 498
The Habsburg claim to German leadership. Frederick William declines the Imperial crown of Germany 499
Failure of the Frankfurt Assembly 500
Alliance of the Three Kingdoms. Austria's economic plans 501
Failure of Radowitz's Prussian Union plan 502
Prussia's humiliation at Olmütz. Austria fails to gain admission to the *Zollverein* 503
Prussian conservatism. Liberals and the connection between power and sovereignty 504
Prussia's expanding economy. Austria's economic position weakens . . . 505
The war in Italy. Austro-Prussian relations 505–6
Machinery of the German Confederation. The German National Association . 507
William, prince of Prussia, becomes regent 508
Roon's proposals for reforming the Prussian army 509–10
The regent encounters strong parliamentary opposition. The Progressive Party . 510
Bismarck becomes head of the government 511
Bismarck's speech in the Prussian Diet—'by Blood and Iron' . . . 512
Austria's last attempt to assert preponderance in Germany 512–13
Russian goodwill necessary to Prussia 513
William I refuses to attend the Frankfurt Congress of Princes . . . 514
The Schleswig-Holstein question 514–19
Bismarck gambles on French neutrality and secures the alliance of Italy . . 517
Bismarck breaks up the Confederation and prepares for war . . . 518–19
The end of the struggle for supremacy. 519
Formation of the North German Confederation 520–1

CHAPTER XX

THE AUSTRIAN EMPIRE AND ITS PROBLEMS, 1848–67

By C. A. MACARTNEY, *Fellow and Sub-Warden of All Souls College, Oxford*

Difficulties in the customary division of mid-nineteenth-century Austrian history 522
The equation being worked out by 'revolution' and 'reaction' 523
'Reaction' firmly in control of Austria 524
'Historic units' and *Kreise*. Ferdinand succeeded by Francis Joseph . . . 525
Defeat of Hungarians. A new constitution applicable to the entire monarchy (March 1849) 526–7
Lombardy and Venetia kept under military control. The government's plans for Hungary 527
Hungarians proclaim their independence. The repression by Haynau. . . . 528
Settlement of Transylvania and the Southern Slav areas. Bach's influence . 529
Emancipation of the peasants. Judicial and educational reforms. Vigorous attempt to expand industry 530
German becomes the official language 531
Francis Joseph assumes sole political responsibility. A system of complete absolutism 532
Concordat of 1855 places Roman Catholic Church under special protection of the state 533
Easier material existence influences acceptance of absolutism in western half of the monarchy 534

CONTENTS

Economic expansion and growing state expenditure . . . . . . *page* 535
Conditions in Hungary. Continued dissatisfaction 536–8
Prospects of war. The stock-exchange crash of 1857 538
The Italian war (1859). Francis Joseph's retreat from absolutism 539–40
The 'Laxenburg Manifesto' (August 1859). The Hungarian problem . . . 540
The Reinforced *Reichsrath* recommends reconstruction of the monarchy . . 541–2
Concessions made to Hungary. The 'October Diploma' 542–3
Hungary rejects the 'October Diploma' 544
Schmerling's 'February Patent' ill received 545–6
Francis Joseph makes approach to Hungary 547–8
The Austro-Prussian war. Andrássy persuades Francis Joseph to drop federalism 549
Final agreement with Hungary 550–1

CHAPTER XXI

ITALY

By D. MACK SMITH, *Fellow of Peterhouse and Lecturer in History in
the University of Cambridge*

Desire for good government, but complete absence of national consciousness . 552
Sardinia-Piedmont the nucleus for a greater kingdom. Minor insurrections in
1831 553
Austria restores order and the old regime continues 554
Charles Albert of Piedmont-Sardinia 554–7
The neo-Guelph writers 557–8
The influence of Mazzini. Election of Pope Pius IX 558–9
Austria's ill-advised entry into Modena and Ferrara. Insurrection in Palermo . 560
Various rulers grant constitutions. Customs league between the Papal States and
Tuscany 561
Rebellion in Milan precipitates war. Charles Albert compelled to act. . . 562
Charles Albert refuses the collaboration of Garibaldi and is defeated at Custoza
and Novara 563–4
Collapse of the revolution in Naples, Rome and Venice. Italy again becomes
occupied territory 565
Abdication and death of Charles Albert. Victor Emmanuel partially re-establishes
royal authority 566
The passing of the Siccardi laws. Cavour joins the D'Azeglio cabinet. . . 567
Cavour replaces D'Azeglio. His methods 568–9
Piedmont's intervention in the Crimean War 569
Increased clerical opposition. Cavour and Mazzini 570
Cavour's diplomatic duel with Austria. Defeat of Austria at Magenta and Solferino 571
Cavour's resignation and return to power 572
Mazzini's belief in unification of Italy. Garibaldi captures Palermo . . . 573
Naples falls to Garibaldi and Piedmontese troops enter the Papal States. A King-
dom of Italy proclaimed 574
Parliament meets in Turin, February 1861. Death of Cavour 575
Civil war in Sicily. The acquisition of Venice and Rome 576

xvii

CONTENTS

CHAPTER XXII

THE ORIGINS OF THE FRANCO-PRUSSIAN WAR AND THE REMAKING OF GERMANY

By MICHAEL FOOT, *lately Lecturer in Politics in the University of Oxford*

Bismarck not wholly responsible for outbreak of war. Essential difference between Bismarck and Napoleon III . . . . *page* 577–8
Prussia's increase of territory and population. Bismarck's policy of weakening his parliamentary enemies 579
Bismarck's use of the draft Franco-Prussian treaty 580
Napoleon's desire to compensate France for Prussia's gains. The projected purchase of the Grand Duchy of Luxemburg 580–1
Neutrality of Luxemburg to be guaranteed by the powers 582
Napoleon pursues the mirage of an alliance with Austria 583
The projected triple alliance ends in deadlock. Reorganisation of the French army 584
Neither France nor Prussia ready for war. The secret activities of Fleury and Daru 585
Napoleon returns to his plan for a triple alliance. Isabella of Spain takes refuge in France 586
Prince Leopold of Hohenzollern's candidature for the Spanish throne. . . 587–8
Prince Leopold persuaded to accept the Spanish crown 589
France makes two capital mistakes 590–1
Forces at work in the interests of peace 592
France confident of temporary military predominance. 593
Karl Anton in his son's name renounces any claim to throne of Spain . . 594
Gramont proposes a letter of apology to Napoleon from William I . . . 595
Benedetti's interview with William I and Bismarck's published version of the Ems telegram 597
French Cabinet's decision to mobilise 598
France declares war without allies 599
The surrender of Napoleon and fall of the Second Empire. The annexation of Alsace and Northern Lorraine 600
The German Empire is founded 601–2

CHAPTER XXIII

NATIONAL AND SECTIONAL FORCES IN THE UNITED STATES

By D. M. POTTER, *Professor of American History, Yale University*

Sequence of development differs from that of Europe 603
Congress, the Executive and the Supreme Court moving towards nationalism. Growing economic unity 604
Two obstacles to the continued ascendancy of nationalism 605
Two major conflicts during the Jackson administration 606–10
Contrast between North and South 610
Antagonism between seaboard settlements and the interior 611–12
North and West tend to become reciprocal markets and sources of supply . . 612–13
Invention of the cotton gin. Expansion of the plantation system in the South . 613
Four points of conflict between North and South 614–15
Absence of complete sectional unity 615–16
Reactions against slavery 616

CONTENTS

The South unites in defence of slavery. Militant anti-slavery in the North. *page* 617-19
Slavery as a Federal question 620
The annexation of Texas 621
The Mexican war. 622
The Compromise of 1850 and the Kansas–Nebraska Act 623-4
Marked deterioration of Union sentiment 625
Abraham Lincoln becomes President 626-7
Formation of the Confederate States of America. 627
Lincoln's awareness of the importance of voluntary loyalty. 628-30

CHAPTER XXIV

THE AMERICAN CIVIL WAR

By T. HARRY WILLIAMS, *Professor of History, Louisiana State University*

The pivotal event in American history. 631
Man-power of the opposing sides 632
The North's superior economic potential 633
The importance of railways and the blockade of the Southern coast-line . . 634-5
The Confederate cause not a hopeless one 635
Confederate confidence in intervention by European powers 636-7
European powers recognise Confederacy as a belligerent. Lincoln's Emancipation
   Proclamation 637
Overall superiority of the North's diplomacy. Effects of the cotton shortage . 638
English public opinion moves in favour of the North. The *Trent* affair. . . 639
The *Alabama* damage claims. The Laird rams 640
France's ambitions in Mexico 641
Expansion of the North's economic system 641-2
The Republican party's wartime legislation 642-3
Northern war finance and army recruitment. The casualties . . . 644-5
Lincoln's bold exercise of his war powers 646-7
Factions within the major political parties 647
Lincoln's Emancipation Proclamation. The presidential election of 1864 . . 648-9
The Confederate constitution 649
Jefferson Davis and his cabinet 650
Finance, recruitment and states rights in the South 651-3
General strategy of the war 654-5
The command system of the opposing armies 656-7
Results of the war 658

CHAPTER XXV

THE STATES OF LATIN AMERICA

By R. A. HUMPHREYS, *Professor of Latin American History, University of London*

Former Spanish and Portuguese dominions become independent states . . 659
The Brazilian empire 659-63
Brazil's gradual transition to independence 660
The rule of Dom Pedro 663
Chile and the Chilean constitution of 1833 663-4
Economic expansion of the 'forties and 'fifties 665
The presidency of Manuel Montt 665-6
Progressive liberalisation under President Pérez. War with Spain. . . 666
The paralysing problems of Bolivia and Ecuador. 667

CONTENTS

Peru's prosperity and disorder. Venezuela and Colombia . . . . *page* 668–9
United Provinces of the Rio de la Plata 669–70
The Age of Rosas in the 'Argentine Confederation' 669–71
Argentina's constitutional problems and economic development. The police state
    of Paraguay 671–2
The Paraguayan war 673
Monarchy in Mexico followed by an unstable republic and separatist movements 674
Overthrow of Santa Anna. Benito Juárez elected president. 675
Introduction of drastic innovations 675–6
Juárez's struggle with the forces of reaction. His eventual re-election as president 676
British, French and Spanish troops landed. Archduke Maximilian accepts the crown 677
Death of Maximilian; Juárez again president 678
The states of Central America 678–81
Britain's connections with the Mosquito Indians 679–80
The transisthmian canal project; the Clayton–Bulwer Treaty 680
Further friction between Britain and the U.S.A. The colony of British Honduras 681
The negro republic of Haiti and the Dominican republic 682–3
Caudillismo 683
By the 'seventies Latin America is on the threshold of a new age . . . 684

CHAPTER XXVI

THE FAR EAST

By G. F. HUDSON, *Fellow of St Antony's College, Oxford*

The massive political organism controlled by Peking 685–6
Lack of normal diplomatic intercourse with other powers 686
System of trade with Western nations 687
The trade in opium 687–8
Lord Napier as Superintendent of Trade 688–9
The Kowloon episode (1839) 689–90
British expeditionary force invests Nanking. China comes to terms with the
    Treaty of Nanking (1842) 690
Conditions bound to lead eventually to the outbreak of war 691
Provisions of the Treaty of Nanking 692
The International Settlement of Shanghai 693
Foreigners denied freedom of travel. Friction over application of treaties,
    especially the 'right of entry' into Canton 694–5
Activities of Western missionaries 695–6
The rise of the Taipings 696–7
The Taipings declare Nanking their capital. Weakening of their power. . . 698
Their religious fanaticism. Forces raised to combat them 699
Sir George Bonham attempts to make contact with the Taipings. . . . 700
The Small Sword Society seizes Shanghai 700–1
British and French troops enter Canton (1857) 701
American and Russian envoys join the British and French plenipotentiaries.
    Russian encroachments in China 702
Capture of the Taku forts 702–3
The Tientsin treaties concede diplomatic representation and the right of travel.
    Treaty envoys barred admission 703
Treacherous attack on British and French envoys travelling under flag of truce.
    Flight of the Emperor exploited by Russia 704
The regency of the Empress Dowager Tzu Hsi 705

CONTENTS

Final suppression of the Taiping rebellion . . . . *page* 705–6
Repression of Chinese Muslim revolts. The restored empire enters into normal
    diplomatic relations with Western powers 707
The continuance of anti-foreign riots 708
French annexation of Cochin-China and expedition against Korea . . . 709
The Japanese policy of seclusion 710
The Treaty of Kanagawa. The political system of the Tokugawa period . . 711
Attacks on Western nationals result in combined naval action 712
Western powers enforce imperial ratification of their treaties. The Meiji Restoration 713

Index. 715

xxi

EDITORIAL NOTE

Although the July Monarchy in France and the Austrian empire before March 1848 are touched upon at various points in this volume, it may be useful for readers to know that they will be covered more fully in chapters which are to appear in volume IX. Similarly, the history of India from 1840 to 1905 and the development of socialism and social theories are being treated directly in volume XI.

CHAPTER I

INTRODUCTORY SUMMARY

THE prodigious forces discovered and exploited through many decades by the inventive genius and tireless energy of the European peoples seemed in the middle of the nineteenth century to carry them upwards to the very zenith of their power. The states of Europe might subsequently rule over dominions still more extensive, command armies still larger, and possess weapons more terrible by far in their destructive range; yet, as time went on, their supremacy would be increasingly open to challenge from the peoples of other continents. In the years 1830–70, however, it was scarcely questioned. This was a period when the European states were free from serious threat of political dominance by any one among them, and when, prone though they as ever were to shifting antagonisms, they were not more permanently divided into hostile and highly armed camps. Their wars were relatively brief and the loss of life relatively small. Conflict had not yet attained the suicidal proportions of 1914–18, and, although men of vision like Tocqueville and Gioberti could foretell the immense future power of the United States or Russia, it was not until after that first 'world war' that a European statesman would write of the decadence of Europe and a European thinker dilate upon the decline of the West.

This supremacy the European peoples owed above all to their near monopoly of the new skills and machines born of the Industrial Revolution and to the extraordinary and simultaneous increase in their own numbers. These phenomena had become manifest well back in the eighteenth century and had led intelligent men to ponder deeply upon their significance. Malthus had in his *Essay on Population* feared for man's subsistence as early as 1799 and Blake had sung of 'those dark Satanic mills' in his *Milton* only five years after. But such dynamic movements were not to be arrested by the condemnation of poets or by the gloomy prophecies of political economists. In the years after the Napoleonic wars they attained a still greater momentum. Never before had Europe given birth to such teeming populations, and in the forty years from 1830 to 1870 they increased again by more than a quarter (30 per cent). The apogee was attained in the last two of these decades and the multiplication went on in town and country, in east and west, in Brittany as well as in Paris, in Russia as well as in the United Kingdom. 'The fall of the great Roman Empire,' exclaimed Gerard in Disraeli's *Sybil* (1845), 'what was that? Every now and then there came two or three hundred thousand strangers out of the forests, and crossed the mountains and rivers. They come to us every year, and in greater numbers. What are your invasions of the barbarous nations, your Goths and Visigoths, your Lombards and Huns to our Population Returns!'

And just as the barbarian invasions spelt great movements of peoples, so did the arrival of so many infants in the cradles of Europe. Men had always been on the move, as pilgrims or warriors, to trade, or to seek for a living, seasonal or permanent: but now when so many 'strangers' had to be housed, clothed and fed, the pressure of numbers on the means of subsistence was felt as never before. And so, though the movements were, as always, complex, in one place or calling scarcely perceptible, in another almost torrential in their impact, the great tides flowed in two main directions. On the one hand there was the movement within the European continent from country to town, the movement of whole families to man the new factories and work the new machines, a movement which has scarcely since been interrupted and which has resulted in one of the most radical of all the social transformations of the modern age, the divorce between town and country and the heaping up of men in vast urban agglomerations. On the other hand there was the movement away from the Old World, where conscription might bear hardly and where land might be scarce, wages poor, and employment uncertain, to the great undeveloped areas of West and East, the huge shipment of emigrants from northern and western Europe across the Atlantic, and the slower, but ultimately scarcely less significant, eastward trek of Russian *moujiks* and others to Siberia. This exodus across the Atlantic in particular helped to relieve the tensions in the Old World and so to preserve it from further distress and social upheaval. Perhaps of even greater consequence was that it helped with extraordinary rapidity to call the New World into being to redress the balance of the Old. The whole tempo of North American development was vastly accelerated by 'the immigrants continually coming and landing'. The population trebled between 1830 and 1870 and production prodigiously increased. What all this was to mean for the Old World in the twentieth century needs no stressing. Meanwhile this spilling-over of European peoples stamped the New World still more indelibly with the imprint of European ancestry, and was itself a facet of the European supremacy. Moreover, the comings and goings between the two continents, however ostentatious the United States might be in political isolation, went some way to justify the twentieth-century historians who discern an 'Atlantic civilisation' in the making. Did not Walt Whitman see in his poems 'through Atlantica's depths pulses American Europe reaching, pulses of Europe duly return'd'?

What gave this manpower and Europe, with which must be coupled North America, its superior material strength was, however, the Industrial Revolution (ch. II). More men, as the tragic story of Ireland so vividly showed, were useless if society could not employ them. Ireland had no industry and for thousands of Irishmen the choice was to emigrate or starve. But where capital and raw materials abounded, as well as technical skill and inventiveness, there the demand for labour, though fluctuating, was often insistent and immense. So correspondingly was the rise in production, which the French thinkers of the Saint-Simonian school, pioneers in developing the concept of social engineering, rightly emphasised as supremely important in an industrial age. It was they who were among the first to acclaim the engineers and bankers and financiers as the moulders of a new and naturally pacific society (p. 434). It was they who on the continent of Europe helped to promote the railways and to finance the great credit banks of the 1850's and 1860's. It was they who were among the chief (and most picturesque) heralds of the new age in which the Rothschilds extended their empire to South America, and in which the industrialist, the merchant, and the financier as well as controlling the new economy began increasingly to play a direct part in politics, to sit in parliaments in Europe and to undermine the landowner's monopoly of power in Brazil. And what great things the hosts of workers were to accomplish under the direction of these heroes of a new age, the engineers and the contractors and the capitalists, 'wonders far surpassing the Egyptian pyramids, Roman aqueducts and Gothic cathedrals'! Already in 1848 Marx and Engels, in that embittered paean of praise for the achievements of 'the bourgeoisie', the *Communist Manifesto*, could speak of 'the world market', of 'industries that no longer work up indigenous raw material, but raw material drawn from the remotest zones; industries whose products are consumed, not only at home, but in every quarter of the globe', of the creation within the last 100 years of 'more massive and more colossal productive forces' than by 'all preceding generations together. Subjection of nature's forces to man, machinery, application of chemistry to industry and agriculture, steam-navigation, railways, electric telegraphs, clearing of whole continents for cultivation, canalisation of rivers, whole populations conjured out of the ground—what earlier century had even a presentiment that such productive forces slumbered in the lap of social labour?'

In the development of these revolutionary changes England had been pre-eminent. During these years, 1830–70, her industrial and commercial expansion continued unabated. Aided by her natural resources in coal and iron and by her unrivalled naval supremacy and command of sea-routes to all parts of the globe, she had by 1850 'triumphantly established herself as the workshop of the world as well as its shipper, trader and banker' (p. 333). To technical advances, too, she had much to contribute. To these it was largely due that in these forty years her production of iron increased eightfold. More than ever the mid-century was an Age of Iron, when the iron-masters stood behind both the men who used the machines and those who made them, when bridges and public buildings and factories and the first great multiple stores were made of iron, and the wooden ships of the line gave way to fighting ships of iron, thus revolutionising the problems of naval warfare (ch. XI). It was the Englishman Bessemer's process (1856), too, which heralded the coming of the Age of Steel, hitherto almost a precious metal. But these years in which England maintained her pre-eminence were also those of the increasingly rapid diffusion of industry upon the European mainland and in North America, often under the guidance of skilled British labour and entrepreneurs. Wherever this happened the old domestic industries tended to decline and to be replaced by factories. Such a transition was particularly evident in the textile industries, which everywhere, from Normandy to Great Russia, loomed large because of the need for their products, the numbers they employed, the rapidity of their technical improvements and, until the American Civil War, the abundance of cheap supplies of raw cotton. The shift from home to factory was often painful, but generally inescapable. From country to country, however, its rate varied in accordance with the availability of coal and the means to transport it cheaply. Thus it was effected most rapidly in England, Belgium, Germany and the U.S.A., which possessed or were near to coalfields and had established good communications, first by water and then by rail.

Already before 1830 the steamboat had begun to show its utility on rivers and lakes. Now it was to compass the oceans, surpass sail, sound the death-knell of the 'wooden walls' of the old-time navies, and, overcoming some formidable technical problems, provide services which were safe, efficient, regular and economical. Its advent was among other things to bring a new prosperity to Hamburg and Bremen in the north of Europe and to Marseilles in the south; to reanimate the Mediterranean generally and to hasten the realisation of an ancient dream—the building of the Suez Canal (ch. XVI).

Still more revolutionary was the coming of the Railway Age. Hitherto men and goods had always moved most easily and cheaply by water. Now the great continental land masses were to be penetrated by means which were rapid and regular over great distances in a manner undreamt-of before. It was within these forty years, 1830-70, that the initial stages of this revolution were accomplished—the great world envisaged by Tennyson as spinning 'for ever down the ringing grooves of change' had by 1870 built the most important sixth of its railways, the lines centred mainly in Europe and North America (p. 34).

Speed was thus an exhilarating new factor in man's experience—the extraordinary acceleration of movement, already adumbrated, in these years became an accomplished fact, reducing distance, modifying his ways of life and thought and so firing his imagination that already Jules Verne, the father of modern science fiction, could write books with such titles as *From the Earth to the Moon* (1865), *Twenty Thousand Leagues under the*

Sea (1870) and *Round the World in Eighty Days* (1873). Meanwhile men could travel as never before, for pleasure as well as for business, and to the leisurely aristocrat of the Grand Tour there now succeeded the eager tourist with his guide-book, the mountaineer, and the amateur of winter sports. The farmer's horizon widened, for steam-power extended his markets, and from 1850 to 1873, before it showed how vulnerable it could also make him to competition from overseas, contributed to his enjoyment of a new period of prosperity. In the United States the swift building of a great network of communications bound North and West more closely together, accentuating their contrasts with the society of the south, and made the American domestic market the largest unobstructed field of commerce in the world (p. 612). The ocean cable brought into being not only a world market, but also a world ocean freight, once tramp-ships could be directed by a cabled message to their next port of call (p. 37). And the telegraph revolutionised the transmission of news. Intelligence that it had taken days to convey now flashed to its destination in a matter of minutes. The three great news agencies, Havas, Wolff and Reuters, sprang into being, and for the journalist as well as the banker and trader the world was becoming one. History itself was accelerated and the whole time-scale to which statesmen and generals had been wont to work was now transformed.

Only a small part of these immense and rapid advances in material civilisation was directly attributable to contemporary progress in science (ch. III). Developments in organic chemistry were indeed by 1870 affecting society in various ways through the application of its artifices to medicine (anaesthetics and antiseptics), agriculture (fertilisers), manufacture, and war (gun-cotton). But many of the railway engineers, shipbuilders and makers of machines were still trained mostly in the school of empiricism and experience, 'drawing indefinably from the steady accumulation of knowledge since the seventeenth century', and much of the technical skill of the age had little relation to abstract knowledge. The engineer was ordinarily a practical man to whom, however varied his problems, science was an auxiliary rather than a system.

None the less, the pursuit of scientific knowledge had by 1830 attained a genuine autonomy. The scientific amateur had changed or was changing insensibly into the professor, especially in Germany, which was now taking the lead in educational progress, and the professor was a man of university standing with a laboratory and often costly equipment at his disposal. The scientist extended his domain far into space, 'brought millions of years within the scope of his pronouncements' (p. 49), and claimed almost dogmatic certainty for his truths. Pure mathematics developed its modern character, a new astronomy entered into its own, the bases of electrical science were laid and physics was transformed into a unitary study. And, added to all this, there were evolved in western Europe

5

concepts which affected men's social welfare and thinking so deeply as the new theory of energy, which led to the development of thermodynamics, molecular theory and the theories of bacteria and of evolution. No wonder that the scientist had won and secured a prestige which was reflected in a variety of ways: in the growing popular interest in his work and discoveries, in the growing demand for a 'modern' education in which natural sciences as well as modern languages would have a regular part, and in the growing belief of utilitarians, positivists and others that the processes of scientific reasoning could usefully be applied to the study of man in society. Men thus came to speak of the 'science' of political economy, the Saint-Simonians talked of the 'science of production', and philosophy was rechristened 'moral science'. The extreme example of the attempt to transfer to social phenomena the methods proper to mechanistic science came with the deduction by Marx and Engels of economic laws which they believed to determine the whole of history.

Such, in broadest outline, was a part of the vast background to the events of these crowded and sometimes tumultuous years. It is that part in which the eye of the beholder falls upon the highlights that seem to justify a great and confident optimism; in which he sees men who believe that they are captains of their souls and masters of their fate marching surely forward under the banner of Progress. Indeed, the declared aim of the Great Exhibition at the Crystal Palace in London in 1851, the first of many to display and make manifest the material advances of the age, was 'to seize the living scroll of human progress inscribed with every successive conquest of man's intellect'. Men might well feel with the Prince Consort in that year that they were living in 'a period of most wonderful transition, which tends rapidly to accomplish that great end to which indeed all history points—the realisation of the unity of mankind'. Much else there was, too, which might seem to fortify that vision of universal brotherhood, of the onward progress towards 'the Parliament of Man, the Federation of the World'. The liberal and charitable influences released by the intellectual revolution of the seventeenth century and by the political revolution of the eighteenth worked as an ever more powerful leaven in society, goading its conscience and making it freer and more humane. So it was that during these forty years the slave trade was further restricted and slavery itself abolished in many parts of the world, even though in the United States the price of abolition was a prolonged and deadly civil war. So, too, legislators slowly were induced to improve the conditions of workers in factories, the peasants were liberated from feudal bondage in the Habsburg empire, the many millions of Russian serfs were in their turn emancipated, and the areas in which the Jews could enjoy civic rights were gradually extended. As men thus became more equal before the law, the laws themselves became more humane, for the penal code in many countries was revised. And, at the same time, with the extension of the vote and the introduction even of universal manhood suffrage in Switzerland and France, they became more nearly equal in front of the voting urn or ballot box. Gradually, too, tariff barriers were lowered, and its advocates claimed that free trade would also bind the nations more closely together and reduce the causes of war (p. 349). Moreover, though men nevertheless still killed one another in battle, the rules of war were more strictly defined, the idea of neutrality, applicable to a state such as Belgium or a sea like the Black Sea, emerged as a fruitful concept of international law, and the Red Cross was founded to relieve the sufferings of the wounded regardless of their nationality. The Red Cross Society became international, and the growing use of the word 'international' (first coined by Jeremy Bentham) in a wider-than-legal context was itself a development of a new age and the symbol of new aspirations. It was in these years that the International Working Men's Association was founded, that the improvement of the navigation of the Danube was entrusted to an international commission, and that there took place the series of international congresses which led to the establishment of the Universal Postal Union in 1874. Indeed, nationality itself was regarded by some of its finest prophets as but a stepping stone on the way to a United States of Europe (ch. IX).

At the same time the frontiers of the civilisation which thus decidedly on its higher levels emphasised the fraternity and dignity of man were being pushed ever farther afield, advancing sometimes by force and sometimes by peaceful penetration and persuasion. Thus France, by the slow consolidation and extension of her conquest of Algiers in 1830, accomplished what Spain at the height of her power had failed to achieve, and embarked upon an enterprise which would eventually open up a great North African empire to offset her relative decline in Europe (p. 427). Thus in the Far East the doors of the virtually closed worlds of China and Japan were forced asunder with revolutionary consequences for both these states and for the whole area (ch. XXVI). The seclusion of the traditional supreme power of the Far East was fatally breached: Russia seized the opportunity to advance her frontiers to the Amur and beyond the Ussuri to the border of Korea; and in the port of Shanghai, which underwent a phenomenal growth, was established an international settlement of foreign residents that 'became in effect an independent city-republic with its own laws and administration'. When such changes took place it was not long before Japan and Siam were obliged also to 'enter into diplomatic relations on a basis of equality with western states and to grant western merchants and missionaries free access' to all their territory, or before France, establishing herself in Cochin-China, laid the foundations for her dominion in Indo-China. For China the question was no longer whether her 'rulers would be able to prevent the influx of the West, but how they would adapt themselves to the new conditions'. Whereas in the main they sought to 'obstruct in every way possible the forces they no longer dared openly to oppose', in Japan the demands of 'the barbarians' from the West had brought about a revolution and the men who now came to the fore were 'prepared for radical innovations for the sake of national strength and independence'. Having been persuaded by events that it was impossible to oppose western power without learning the secrets of its success, they had become advocates of unrestricted intercourse with the West, ready to seek out knowledge all over the world. The extraordinary success with which they adapted western institutions and techniques to serve their national ends was to be one of the most striking chapters in the history of Asia during the following half-century.

The opening of China was a facet of another, no less notable, development, the shifting of the balance of Great Britain's imperial interests from West to East, from the Atlantic to the Indian Ocean, owing to the growth and consolidation of her trade and power in India, Ceylon, and Burma (p. 350). The consolidation of her power was demonstrated by the continual extension of her Indian territories and, after the mutiny of 1857, by the abolition of the East India Company and the establishment of direct rule under a viceroy. It also involved the critical, and later criticised, decision of 1835 to subsidise an educational system on western lines, in the belief that 'western educated Indians would be assimilated to western ways and that western ideas would filter down through them to the great mass of the people' (p. 118). The consolidation of her trade helped to bring about a remarkable accessory extension of the British colonial empire, for she was led to acquire new or to develop existing territories, trading stations, and commitments all along the route to India or in its vicinity, from the South Atlantic to the Pacific oceans. By 1870 West and South African trading ports had become large colonial possessions, Australia was far more than a convict settlement, and New Zealand, now occupied by white settlers alongside her native Maori inhabitants, had become a dependency of the British Crown.

In this vast epic of European expansion a notable role was played by the missionary as well as the soldier, the administrator, and the trader. These years were among the greatest in the long story of missionary achievement when, for the first time predominantly under the aegis of the Protestant Churches, many intrepid messengers, from the United States as well as from Europe, carried the word of God into what then seemed the utmost parts of the earth, as far as Melanesia in the East and also into the unknown heart of Africa. Their path was often rough, they sometimes caused friction with suspicious rulers, they unwittingly inspired the rebellion of the Chinese Taipings, but in their own way, together with the soldiers and the administrators and the traders, who often took with them the more dubious wares of western civilisation, they too contributed to the great movements which made more dependent upon one another men who spoke different tongues, dwelt in different climates and belonged to societies which were worlds apart in organisation and outlook. For the optimists and the idealists and all those who had an unflinching confidence in man's ability to better himself and control his environment the vista of continuous progress towards the day when the human race would dwell together in unity was beautiful, clear, and infinitely exciting.

But the background to the mid-nineteenth-century scene also had its shadows; and for some thoughtful observers it was these that arrested attention and seemed deep and ominous. In them they saw dark and uncontrollable forces, that threatened to undermine faith, overthrow political order and rend society in two. For such men the French Revolution had let loose a flood of ills and a continuing restless and subversive 'spirit of innovation', while the Industrial Revolution was giving birth to a society as ugly as it was heartless. Man's creative genius had more than ever outstripped his moral capacity. They saw their fellows absorbed as never before by the business of getting and spending, and they saw emerging as patrons of art and as leaders of the new industrial civilisation the new kind of rich men who had no leisure to cultivate the things of the spirit (p. 137), but were mere 'spent ones of a workday age'. They saw their time, too, as an age of doubt and scepticism as well as one that was choked by absorption with material things. The foundations of belief had already been assailed by the eighteenth-century rationalists and their followers, and the institutions that upheld belief derided or attacked by anti-clericals and revolutionaries. Now, when the geologist Lyell overthrew the biblical chronology with his theories of the age of the earth and the antiquity of man, when Darwin replaced the biblical story of special creation by a theory of evolution based upon natural selection, when the new, largely German and 'scientifically' methodical scholarship directly subjected the text of the Bible to critical examination, and when even the divinity of Christ was questioned anew by a writer of the calibre of Ernest Renan, agnosticism penetrated the ancient seats of learning and science itself seemed to join in the assault. The Churches in Europe, for all their expansive vigour in remote climates, were 'facing the most serious and far-reaching challenge to the fundamentals of Christian faith since the thirteenth century' (p. 102). The challenge was indeed met in resounding fashion when, in 1864, Pope Pius IX promulgated his famous Syllabus of Modern Errors, which appeared to be not merely a rejection of certain contemporary scientific theories but also a direct attack on the basic principles of modern society (p. 92). But this war of science and religion encouraged scepticism on the one hand and obscurantism on the other. When, in addition, society was undergoing such swift and sometimes disturbing transformations, it was no wonder that many either knew not what to believe or wished to believe and could not, no wonder that novelists, who now had their splendid noonday, and other writers were concerned with the perplexities of the soul and the search for a seemingly ever more elusive Truth and Reality. 'What ought I to do, and what ought I to believe?' questioned Lord Montacute in Disraeli's *Tancred*, while that great Romantic exile, Herzen, in the remarkable dialogue 'Before the Storm' (of 1848-9) declared 'Universal grief' to be 'the supreme characteristic of our times. A dull weight oppresses the soul of contemporary man; the consciousness of his moral helplessness torments him; the absence of belief in anything whatever causes him to grow old before his time.' If there was unbounded optimism on one side there was equally profound pessimism on the other.

There were further reasons, too, for gloom and anxiety. In the industrial world which was being born, as Carlyle said, 'with infinite pangs', the dark places were sometimes terrifyingly obscure and ugly. Behind the façades, erected by architects who had no concern with social problems and no conception of town planning, lay the slums, next to the 'Palaces of Industry', the hovels of what Tocqueville in 1833 called 'this new Hades' of Manchester, out of which the shortest road was said to be drunkenness. In such places—for Manchester had its parallels, for instance, in Lille— there lived that race of men for whom the new name 'proletariat' had been coined; and it was a melancholy discovery that the conditions in which they had to live and work produced physical and moral debasement and emptiness of mind. Their numbers might increase despite disease and filth, but the quality of the race declined. Moreover, the growth of this 'proletariat' most disquietingly seemed to make two nations where before there had been but one—'Two nations', in Disraeli's famous phrase in *Sybil*, 'between whom there is no sympathy; who are as ignorant of each other's habits, thoughts and feelings, as if they were dwellers in different zones or inhabitants of different planets....' The age-old dumb warfare of the poor against the rich was now threatening to become one on a far vaster scale of labour against capital. The workers in industry, dwelling in towns, were now the potentially disaffected, whereas the peasant, once so prone to revolt, had since his emancipation generally less motive to rebel. Some, who were appalled at these evils of the new industrialism, saw a remedy only in the voluntary building of new societies in which there should be a redistribution of property and some degree of communal ownership—hence the Socialist utopias which were a curious and characteristic product of the time. Others, more practical, hoped and worked with varying degrees of success for gradual mitigation of the evils and reconciliation of the opposing classes through state intervention or the organisation of trade unions and syndicates. Others still, with Marx at their head, propagated the theory of ruthless and inescapable class war between the proletariat and the bourgeoisie. By so doing they injected new venom into the hatreds of society—the wounds of which were later to be kept open and made wider by the bitter dogmas of these new doctrinaires.

'All previous historical movements', proclaimed the *Communist Manifesto*, 'were movements of minorities, or in the interests of minorities. The proletarian movement is the...movement of the immense majority.' It was now that men first began to speak of 'the masses', that Walt Whitman sang 'And mine a word of the modern "*En masse*"', and that to feed and clothe these masses 'mass-production' was on the way. Western society, which had perhaps first acquired the habit of thinking in quantitative terms two centuries earlier, now more than ever reckoned in numbers both in peace and in war. As early as 1833 Tocqueville had written in one of his note-books: 'The century is primarily democratic. Democracy is like a rising tide; it only recoils to come back with greater force, and soon one sees that for all its fluctuations it is always gaining ground. The immediate future of European society is completely democratic.'[1] Democracy, too, meant the rule of the majority, and industrialism was to give a further powerful impetus to the democratic tide. It made wealth more fluid, facilitated the access of new classes to power and acted in various ways as a levelling agent—even the railway appeared to many to be a blind instrument of equality. So, although perhaps men did not yet use the phrase 'the age of the common man', that age appeared to be not far ahead. And in this period beginning after 1815, which was to be historically minded as none before, a period in which historicism even pervaded architecture so that a man would choose in what style of what past age to build his house (p. 138), men also envisaged a transformation of history itself. Already in 1820 Thierry in France was demanding 'a history of citizens, a history of subjects, a history of the people', consideration of 'the destinies of the masses of men who have lived and felt like us'.[2] Michelet in 1846 answered the call in his *Le Peuple*, as, across the Channel in his *French Revolution*, did Carlyle, who foresaw the time when 'History would be attempted on quite other principles; when the Court, the Senate and the Battlefield receding more and more into the background, the Temple, the Workshop and the Social Hearth will advance more and more into the Foreground'.[3] In literature the hero of the novel became a more ordinary, less heroic, character, and Mrs Gaskell, George Sand and many authors besides Dickens wrote works of fiction that were also powerful indictments of social injustice and exposed the wrongs of the poor. At the same time, although the Industrial Revolution and its attendant problems gave little inspiration to the artist, painters like Millet and Courbet could choose farm labourers and stone breakers for subjects,

[1] *Journeys to England and Ireland* (trans. George Lawrence and K. P. Mayer, ed. J. P. Mayer; London, 1958), p. 67.

[2] Cit. Stanley Mellon, *The Political Uses of History* (Stanford, 1958), pp. 10–11.

[3] *Essays*, vol. IV, pp. 84–5 cit. G. M. Trevelyan, *Carlyle: An Anthology* (London, 1953), p. 35.

while the old allegorical and classical and, to some extent, the biblical scenes went out of fashion. After the mid-century realism tended to dominate in art and literature as in many other fields of human activity (chs. VI and VII).

In all this some thinkers found much cause for concern or dislike. In spite of a gradually growing literacy resulting from the introduction of primary schools in many countries, and of many private and public efforts to broaden the basis and opportunities for education, enlightenment and numbers were clearly antithetical—even a progressive thinker like John Stuart Mill feared the tyranny that might be exercised by an unenlightened majority. Many compared the rise of the people to the barbarian invasions. They saw in it a force that on the one hand was impetuous and unpredictable and on the other would ruthlessly sweep aside the things of the mind in order to ensure the comforts of the body. 'Large sections of society', wrote one hostile observer (Jacob Burckhardt), 'would readily give up all their individual literatures and nationality, if it had to be so, for the sake of through sleeping-cars.'[1] This contemporary pessimism was perhaps most comprehensively voiced by another Swiss writer, Amiel, when in 1851 he made the following entry in his *Journal* after reading Tocqueville's celebrated study of *Democracy in America*:

Tocqueville's book has on the whole a calming effect upon the mind, but it leaves a certain sense of disgust behind. It makes one realise the necessity of what is happening around us...but it also makes it plain that the era of *mediocrity* in everything is beginning, and mediocrity freezes all desire. Equality engenders uniformity, and it is by sacrificing what is excellent, remarkable, and extraordinary that we get rid of what is bad. The whole becomes less barbarous, and at the same time more vulgar.

The age of great men is going; the epoch of the ant-hill...is beginning....By continual levelling and division of labour, society will become everything and man nothing....

The statistician will register a growing progress, and the moralist a gradual decline....The useful will take the place of the beautiful, industry of art, political economy of religion, and arithmetic of poetry. The spleen will become the malady of a levelling age.

Finally, another of the greatest movements of the times, 'visceral and profound', as Cournot called it, an essential part of the historical picture and one which provided the foreground with some of its most stirring and heroic scenes, none the less gave more than one comparatively detached observer reasons for deep misgiving. For the principle of nationality, beneficent in many ways, was yet subversive in character and seemingly could triumph only by use of the sword. And nationality too easily degenerated into nationalism, injecting new causes of embitterment and strife into the rivalries of peoples. So it was that men as diverse as Acton

---

[1] *The Letters of Jacob Burckhardt* (trans. and ed. Alexander Dru, London, 1955), p. 143 (20 July 1870).

and Herzen could condemn it as hostile alike to right and freedom and Proudhon see in it a grave obstacle in the way of social progress (p. 245).

Except for the coming of the railway, the years 1830 and 1870, by which this volume is approximately bounded, mark no decisive events or turning points in the movement of populations or in the progress of the Industrial Revolution. But they are most significant dates in the development of the two great movements which were to dominate the political history of Europe in the mid-nineteenth century and they have their importance also in the history of the Roman Catholic Church. 1830 was to initiate a new period of political change, to reveal the growing power of nationality and to open the gates to 'Liberalism', that word so often used and so seldom defined. 1870 was to mark the close of the first great phase of European nationalism, and, by the completion to all intents and purposes of the unification of Germany and Italy, to effect a radical alteration in the balance of European power to the detriment of France. 1830 was also to hasten on the movement in which small but gallant groups of men in various western countries embarked upon the titanic and then fruitless task of liberalising the Roman Catholic Church. 1870 saw the final measure of their discomfiture and witnessed on the one hand the promulgation of the doctrine of papal infallibility and on the other the definitive extinction of the temporal power of the popes save as a purely token sovereignty. Here were movements and events primarily, it is true, European, but ultimately of significance for the history of a whole world that was increasingly sensitive to every major shift in the balance of European power and to every strong breeze of European thought.

But the paths of liberalism and nationalism, which at first appeared to lie side by side, were neither smooth nor easy, and 1830 was, as Victor Hugo said, a revolution stopped half-way. The forces of conservatism were still powerful to obstruct and divide. The municipal revolutions in Italy were swiftly undone and the future of the peninsula was left to depend on 'the slender thread of Franco-Austrian rivalry' (p. 554). The liberal aspirations in Germany were stifled by Metternich's Six Articles (p. 493). The nationalist rising in Poland was ruthlessly suppressed by Russian arms (p. 362), and with the Treaty of Münchengrätz the three eastern powers seemed once again to stand as a solid and irremovable bulwark against any further attempt to disturb the *status quo*; while, as time went on, in France itself, the parent of revolution, the July Monarchy took on a more and more conservative hue. So, many of the hopes aroused in 1830 were disappointed, some even of the promises of 1815 were still unfulfilled, and in the cities of western Europe the political exile was once again a familiar figure. For a while it seemed that order was restored not only in Warsaw but through most of Europe, and there ensued more than a decade (1833–46) of apparent, but superficial, calm. Superficial, for underneath there was in fact an immense activity and an immense preparation, a feverish plotting and an eager theorising and exchanging of ideas. Conservative governments, armed with the machinery of censorship, would strenuously seek to repress dangerous thoughts, but thought, even in Russia, could not for ever be confined in a strait-jacket. So these years and indeed the whole of the mid-century decades saw an immense proliferation of liberal and national sentiments, of liberal and national parties and movements, and the transformation even of a Bonapartist quasi-dictatorship into a liberal empire. In them there would be more experimentation with constitutions, more changes in forms of government, than at any other time between 1790 and 1910–20 (p. 185). In them, in many countries from the United States and United Kingdom in the west to Russia in the east, there would be a remarkable series of liberal reforms, whether effected by the legislative action of elected parliaments or conceded, under fear or threat of revolution, by reluctant despots. Whatever the means by which they were brought into being, they reflected the immense and growing force of public opinion (ch. v). In these years the power of the press and of propaganda was demonstrated as never before. In France journalists had helped to dethrone Charles X in 1830; in 1848 they themselves were carried to the seats of government. These were years in which *The Times* was known as 'The Thunderer', when the reports of war correspondents from the Crimea could help to bring about the reform of the British army, when parties even in conservative Prussia took their names from the *Wochenblatt* and the *Kreuzzeitung*, and when the authority of a paper produced in London by a Russian exile could be acknowledged by the government of the tsar of all the Russias at St Petersburg (p. 370). So it was that about 1870 a French thinker could justly write: 'There is now no European government which does not reckon with opinion, which does not feel obliged to give account of its acts and to show how closely they conform to the national interest, or to put forward the interest of the people as the justification for any increase in its prerogatives.'[1]

Thus during the 1830's and 1840's many charges were being prepared which would disturb the calm, first with minor detonations in 1846 and 1847, and then with the tremendous explosions of 1848–9, the year that marks the great divide in the history of these forty years and that for a brief moment seemed to usher in the springtime of the peoples—'never had nobler passions stirred in the civilised world, never had a more universal impulse (*élan*) of souls and hearts burst forth from one end of Europe to another'.[2] But these revolutions of 1848 (ch. xv)—each of them so distinct, although sharing a common ideology—were revolutions largely

---

[1] A. Cournot, *Considérations sur la marche des Idées*...(ed. F. Mentré, Paris, 1934), vol. II, pp. 234–5.
[2] *Mémoires posthumes de Odilon Barrot* (Paris, 1875), vol. II, p. 83 (cit. L. B. Namier, *The Revolution of the Intellectuals*, p. 4. I have amended Sir Lewis Namier's translation).

of intellectuals and, as Odilon Barrot went on to say, 'all that was to result in failure, because all that was nothing but the pursuit of an impossible ideal'. The intellectuals who were thus unexpectedly carried to power were, many of them, too unversed in affairs to deal with the complex problems of states in social and political turmoil and suffering still from the economic unrest and depression of the 1840's. They pitched their aims too high or lacked the means to carry them out. They were enfeebled by internal divisions: and it now emerged that liberal and national aspirations could conflict as well as coincide. So the forces of order could rally, aided by the fears of growing anarchy, and could weaken and overthrow. Reaction, when it came, was generally swift, and as chill and devastating as a snowstorm in May. Republicanism, now again inextricably associated with revolution, was doomed to an ephemeral existence in an essentially monarchical Europe, while socialism raised such alarm that its more militant adherents were fiercely repressed.

What a contrast there was between the years that preceded and the years that followed the Great Divide! In many ways the years of revolution and their immediate aftermath saw the closing of an old era as much as the opening of a new one. By the time they were over many of the men who had governed Europe in the preceding decades, Melbourne and Peel, Metternich, Guizot, and Louis Philippe, were dead or irrevocably fallen from power. A long period of peace between the great powers, in which all accepted the principle of the balance of power and in spite of their mutual antagonisms and jealousies generally acted in concert for the maintenance of treaties and the restraint of aggression, was now drawing to an end (pp. 266–7). 1848 marked the finish of an age in which society was still largely hierarchical and relatively static, when the peasantry in the Germanic world were still largely subject to feudal dues and checks on individual freedom, when suffrage, if allowed at all, was restricted, and when the full civil and military effects of the building of railways and steamboats were still to be seen. The failure of the revolutions put a term also to the Romantic period of liberalism and nationalism, when the devotees of these movements were largely buoyed up by the ideology of the French Revolution. For all its subsequent echoes that revolution had now virtually exhausted its momentum, and the events which followed were engendered by different ideas.

By contrast, the last two post-revolutionary decades present a more intricate and far more swiftly changing pattern. The immediate reaction was followed by a period of relative political stability and of great economic prosperity and development, in which the chief disturbing event was the Crimean War (ch. XVIII). That war, however, the ninth in the long series of Russo-Turkish conflicts, but very different from its predecessors, was important for many reasons. It was more than a local struggle. It reaffirmed what the crisis of 1840–1 had already made clear, that the

Near Eastern question and the fate of the Ottoman empire was a common concern of the powers and not to be determined by an over-mighty vassal or by Russia alone. It demonstrated the power of new weapons and it dissolved the existing pattern of European relations. The statesmen who now came to the fore on the continental mainland, Napoleon III, Cavour, Gorchakov, Bismarck, had no connection with the Vienna settlement and no interest in upholding it. Rather they were, each for his own particular purpose, ready to take advantage of its undoing or eager to see it undone. When the old European alignments thus became still more fluid and shifting the diplomats and the soldiers were still more important. Complex diplomacy is an integral part of the story of the Crimean War and of the dramatic years that followed. So, too, is the transformation of armies and the parliamentary resistance that their overhaul sometimes entailed. Between 1830 and 1854 alliances had generally been defensive; now they were formed with offensive aims, as in the celebrated secret pact of Plombières between Napoleon III and Cavour in 1858 or in the treaty between Prussia and Italy in 1866. Each of these alliances was shortly followed by 'the impassioned drama' of war. And in the means of war on land there were now demonstrated changes greater than at any previous time in history (ch. XII). Strategical movement was revolutionised by reason of the railway, the range and accuracy of fire-power were immensely increased, and the system of conscription was intensified and given a new and fatal prestige by the reforms and successes of the Prussian army.

It was significant and characteristic that in Prussia it was the conflict over the army that dominated the first years of the reign of William I and that brought Bismarck to power. It was equally characteristic and a presage of the future that Napoleon III, who also clearly saw the need to reform his army, was unable effectively to do so.

Within the short space of sixteen years there were five wars in Europe: in four of them great powers were opposed to one another and in the fifth great powers were also involved. The result was that the map of Europe, which, but for the emergence in 1830 of Belgium and of the diminutive kingdom of Greece and the disappearance in 1846 of the Free City of Cracow, had remained virtually unchanged since 1815, was now drastically modified. The 'miracle' of Italian unification was achieved and what had in 1830 still been little more than a geographical expression had now become a political reality as an independent kingdom claiming rank among the great powers, if only the least (ch. XXI). Still more important, though perhaps less heeded at the time, the vital 'struggle for supremacy in Germany' had been won by Prussia at the expense both of Denmark and Austria (ch. XIX). It was soon followed by the Franco-Prussian war of 1870, whose controversial origins, long classic among the case-histories of diplomacy, are here reconsidered in detail (ch. XXII). Thereby, Germany, whose old loose confederation had already been destroyed by Prussia's victory in 1866, was finally transformed into a unified empire, and to this new power defeated France was forced to surrender her eastern provinces of Alsace and Lorraine. With Britain and Russia both since the Crimean War relatively aloof and preoccupied—a factor which renders the achievements of Bismarck less extraordinary than they have sometimes been made to appear—and France now reeling from the blows of her defeat, the time-honoured principle of the balance of power had been swept aside. In the story of German unification not the least remarkable fact is that the new empire from the moment of its birth acceded to the position of hegemony on the continent of Europe.

All these developments marked the triumph of nationalism (ch. IX) and in part its triumph at the expense of liberalism. In the great reaction that followed 1848–9 the Liberals' strength and faith were weakened. Some were imprisoned and exiled, others voluntarily expatriated themselves, while many of those who were left were convinced that other methods must be used to achieve their aims. They felt the lure of *Realpolitik*, a word apparently first coined in 1853. In Germany, at least, 'sick of principles and doctrines', they thirsted for power that should be embodied in a strong united German national state (p. 504). And so in the end they would be ready to yield to and applaud a man who had ridden roughshod over them in parliament, because by blood and iron he had brought them the power that could be wrested by military success.

All this is a familiar tale, but in recreating or retelling it in the middle of the twentieth century the historian will not only be aware that patient research has modified many of its details. He may also have reason to see it in a different light from that in which it appeared to his predecessors of 1900 or 1910. With the memory or experience of two world wars and the countless and sometimes unspeakable horrors that they engendered he may look more critically at movements which seemed to end in such belligerence, ambition and inhumanity. In reflecting upon German history he can hardly fail to take into account the tremendous consequences of the development of schools of German thought and philosophy partly independent of and antagonistic to the main western stream. He may remember that as early as 1834 Heine wrote that 'The German revolution will not prove any milder or gentler because it was preceded by the Kantian Critique, the transcendentalism of Fichte, or even by the philosophy of nature. These doctrines served to develop revolutionary forces that only wait their time to break forth and to fill the world with terror and with awe.'[1] He can indeed hardly fail to perceive the roots of national socialism growing vigorously throughout the nineteenth century. So, too, the story of the Italian *Risorgimento* may appear in a different perspective, less wholly romantic, less wholly heroic; and mindful of the later rise of

[1] In *Deutschland* (*Sämmtliche Werke*, Hamburg, 1876, vol. v, pp. 264–5), cit. R. d'O. Butler, *The Roots of National Socialism, 1783–1933* (London, 1941), p. 286.

fascist dictatorship the historian may remark, as well as the brilliance of Cavour's statesmanship, the long-term defects of the *connubio* and the unhealthiness of a parliament which initially depended so much on the masterly control of a single, far from scrupulous, individual. He may remember also that, just as civil war in the United States and emancipation in Russia involved huge problems of reconstruction, so too 'the miracle' of political unification in Italy produced a task of adjustment so difficult and painful that there ensued four years of civil war in which the casualties outnumbered 'those in all the battles for national independence put together' (p. 576). On the other hand, the punishments meted out to the Russian Decembrists or to the rebellious subjects (other than Italians and Hungarians) of the Habsburg dynasty, once sternly condemned, may now seem mild indeed by comparison with those that some of the heirs of the revolutionary tradition in central and eastern Europe could cheerfully impose. Any survey of Russian history after forty years of communist rule is likely to stress the elements of continuity, to show how 'the tsarist autocracy and the movements of opposition to it provided many of the moulds of post-revolutionary government and political thought' (ch. xiv, p. 357), and to dwell on the tradition of absolute centralised government on the one hand which was co-existent with a supposedly traditional collectivism on the other. And it may rank high the perspicacity of those nineteenth-century travellers Custine and Haxthausen, who observed 'the association of political authority with bureaucratic or military rank rather than private, local or hereditary status, a common indifference to Western conceptions of liberty...an obsession with Russia's historical status, the sense of national exclusivism linked with a sense of supra-national, indeed universal mission', and 'the confidence in a manifest destiny in Asia owed to a new dispensation distinct from that of the older maritime trading empires' (p. 357). Any survey of Austrian history (ch. xx) forty years after the collapse of the empire may, while not glossing over the defects and blunders of Habsburg rule, recall that in the period of the *Vormärz* it provided the most enlightened and prosperous government in Italy, that in the months immediately following the revolution it carried out the highly complex business of peasant emancipation with remarkable smoothness and efficiency; and that subsequently, partly in consequence of the emancipation and despite the failure to gain admission to the Prussian *Zollverein* or Customs Union, it presided over a great period of economic development, during which Trieste became one of the foremost ports of the Mediterranean and Vienna, like contemporary Paris, began to be adorned with great new imperial monuments. It may also well uphold the view that 'the much abused Compromise' or *Ausgleich* of 1867 'could justify itself historically by continuing to exist for half a century—a remarkable term of life for any settlement in central Europe: because it gave satisfaction to the strongest forces in the field' (p. 534).

As for France, there too, twenty years after the virtual extinction of the Third Republic and one since the demise of the Fourth, the perspective may seem to have altered. After the narrowness of the July Monarchy and the visionary character and disorder of the Second Republic, the Second Empire (ch. xvii), for all its meretricious aspects, stands out as a period of immense and fruitful activity when French society was less rigid than it had been and French economy more flexible than it might be in years to come. And this flexibility was displayed by the emperor himself. The character of that secretive man is likely always to be a matter for speculation; but, however disastrous eventually the hesitations and duplicities of his foreign policy, he must be accorded some measure of admiration for having apparently succeeded in that most difficult feat of political gymnastics, the transformation of a dictatorial into a liberal regime.

The pacific and well-meaning Napoleon III was a protagonist in three of the four great European wars between 1848 and 1871. He also in his Mexican adventure sought to take advantage of a war on another continent which was wholly separate in origin, but had immense significance. The American Civil War (ch. xxiv) was the deadliest of all the conflicts of the mid-nineteenth century in terms of destruction and casualties, and occupies in American history the place accorded to the French Revolution in the history of France. It was also the first of modern wars, because of the use the contestants made of the new means of communication and of new weapons and because it became almost totalitarian in its demands upon society. About the origins of this fratricidal and perhaps not necessarily inescapable conflict historians may long hold differing views, but none can now fail to see how momentous it was, for the future not only of the United States but also of Europe and the world. 'It decided that the United States would remain one nation' and not break up into two or more. 'It unified that nation as it had never been unified before and placed it on the way to become a great world power.' It was thus a triumph for American nationalism over sectionalism (ch. xxiii); but it was also, and this was what made it doubly significant, a triumph for American liberalism and liberalism in general. 'By destroying slavery and by demonstrating that a popular government could preserve liberty during an internal conflict', it has been claimed that it 'vindicated and vitalised the democratic concept everywhere' (p. 657). 'The vital issue was not the survival of one nation, more or less, but the survival of a nation committed to the principle that government of the people, by the people, and for the people should not perish from the earth' (p. 629).

An earlier civil war in nearby Canada, but on a much less spectacular and terrible scale, was also extraordinarily and unpredictably fruitful. Great Britain astonished contemporaries by avoiding in 1832 and 1848 the revolution for which they thought she was ripe, and the peculiar reasons which enabled her highly industrialised society to develop without greater stress and turmoil will always be of interest to historians. But less noticed at the time and of equal importance with the American victory for democracy were the political wisdom and flexibility of outlook which enabled Lord Durham and his aides to devise, and the British government to adopt, a new system of institutional development overseas. The 'changes in colonial policy, which established self-government in the Dominions and gave birth to a new conception of Empire and Commonwealth' with the Durham Report of 1839 as its inspiration, were indeed 'made possible by the growth of economic interests so world-wide that they seemed to be in harmony with universal freedom of the seas and free trade and universal progress' (p. 349). And their effects were to be profound and widely diffused. In accordance with the principles of this new conception men in every inhabited continent would learn to tread the path towards responsible self-government without renouncing their ties of loyalty and affection to the mother-country. Already by the early 1870's Australia, New Zealand and the Cape Colony were following in the way.

'Liberalism', 'nationalism', 'realism', 'industrialism', 'capitalism', 'socialism', such words, along with 'democracy', must inevitably and frequently be used by historians of this period of the zenith of European power. They are convenient labels, they carry with them whole worlds of most powerful ideas and they were constantly on the lips of contemporaries. But they should not be allowed to obscure the infinite richness and variety of life and thought even within the narrow confines of Europe itself. Whatever may be the verdict upon later times, there was no dull uniformity between 1830 and 1870. Within the general framework of European civilisation, helping to weave or to act as foils to its dominant patterns, how many worlds lay juxtaposed, intermingled and overlapping! Within society the old aristocracies and the new, the world of fashion and the *demi-monde*; not a single bourgeoisie or middle class, but middle classes greatly diversified in wealth and status and pursuing a multiplicity of callings; skilled workers, producing the most varied goods from most varied materials, the great majority of whom were employed not in the vast factories of monopolists, but in a multitude of small enterprises with differing conditions of labour and in which regional traditions and standards still counted for much; unskilled labourers and navvies and domestic servants; and beside all these the peasants who held their lands by all manner of tenure, free proprietorship, leasehold, *métayage* and many others, agricultural labourers, serfs and ex-serfs, all of them conserving an infinite variety of customs and costumes and speaking all kinds of dialects. Within the realm of faith the worlds of Protestantism with all its numerous churches and sects, of Roman Catholicism with its monolithic structure of orthodoxy, and of Islam and of the Jews of the dispersion scattered widely from the banking-houses of the West to the ghettos of the East. Within the domain of letters (ch. VII) not only the giants of realism such as Balzac, but the Romantic prophets and poets such as Carlyle and Lamartine and Michelet, the 'deeply religious' genius of a Newman or a Dostoevsky and the men who 'invented and passionately practised' the doctrines of 'pure poetry' and 'Art for Art's sake'. Within the system of states the maritime nations of the West with their colonial empires past and present and their classical heritage; the German peoples in the centre with their memories of empire, their particularism, their frustrations and now their own peculiar *Weltanschauung*; in the south-east the declining and Asiatic Turks; and in the East the 'mighty and still unfathomed' Russian people who had known no Renaissance or Reformation and whose intelligentsia, western-ers and Slavophiles, were even now engaged upon their historic debate concerning their place in Europe, whether they were of it or a people apart with a culture and mission all their own; finally, among them all, the subject peoples 'historic' and 'unhistoric', the 'martyr nation' of Poland whose turbulent history ran so contrary to the main European stream and whose fearless bids in 1831 and 1863 to recover her independence were once again doomed to defeat, and the forgotten communities, from the Provençals in the west to the Estonians in the east for whom, in this historically minded age scholars and poets were beginning to rediscover a past, a language and a culture. And lastly, within each individual state how tenaciously men still in many places clung to the old ways of life and thought, where geography counted for so much and where historical and folk memories went back so far! In the last half-century as historians have sought to rediscover and reinterpret the springs of human action within states, to explain why men voted thus and not otherwise in elections or why economic changes were welcomed in one area and obstructed in another, they have had increasingly to take account of regional dif-ferences and of deep-rooted local or even family traditions and loyalties. What reader, contemplating the infinite complexity of this ever more swiftly changing historical scene and considering the efforts which the men of the mid-nineteenth century, largely impelled by the boundless energy of the European peoples, made to remould their world or to preserve it from upheaval, can fail to be moved by the marvels they accomplished and by the dramas and tragedies of an age that was so significant in the history of mankind?

CHAPTER II

ECONOMIC CHANGE AND GROWTH

EVEN in Britain the Industrial Revolution was not all over by 1830; nor were the agricultural and transport revolutions. Some ways of growing, making, and moving commodities had undergone changes worthy of being deemed revolutionary, especially by Frenchmen. The problems of capital accumulation, of assembling and managing a labour force, of marketing an expanding output, of banking and business practice, and of coping with such phenomena of the business cycle as had been revealed by the boom and collapse of the mid-'twenties were all calling for changes in organisation, methods, voluntary association, and state policies. Thus the economic shape of things to come was clearly visible, provided one looked in the right places, especially in Great Britain. Yet even there nothing was finished, and over the rest of the panorama the picture was one of slow motion or still life.

Apart from the railway, 1830 was no great divide. During the next forty years the methods and organisation already developed were improved, supplemented, or supplanted by important innovations, and spread more widely over western Europe and North America. During the first two decades the pace of expansion and change was at times too fast to be maintained, the consequent depression deep and prolonged, and the transition disastrous to those whose skill was being rendered obsolete. After 1850, however, the new or remodelled institutions worked somewhat better, great new areas of natural resources and of new technology were opened up, while political and social tensions eased after the tumults of 1848. By 1870 the population of Europe was 30 per cent larger than in 1830; that of North America had trebled; and those peoples who could take advantage of the changes in production, transport, and trade had substantially improved their standard of living.

By 1830 agriculture, Europe's largest occupation, was shaking off the worst effects of its painful transition from war to peace. Prices had recovered somewhat; costs had been trimmed by the reduction of rents and interest rates; and land that was hard to till or low in yield had reverted to pasture or waste. The complex story of the next forty years is perhaps best told by examining three aspects: the increasingly commercial character of farming, improvements in methods, and greater dependence on capital.

The pull of the market grew stronger as the number of consumers rose in four decades by almost a third in Great Britain and probably by a quarter in western Europe (excluding France); as the town-dwelling percentage of them climbed from 46 to 55 in England and Wales (if we take 2000 inhabitants as the rural/urban boundary line) and to 30 per cent or more in France, Germany, the Low Countries, Austria, Sweden, and Switzerland; and as improved transport facilities combined with the lowering or removal of tariffs to ease the farmer's way to domestic or foreign markets. Until well after 1850 the European farmer had these markets almost to himself, as imports from other continents were complementary rather than competitive. Often he was not merely pulled to market. He was pushed there by the need to raise money for taxes, rent in regions where tenancy prevailed (for example, in the British Isles), or the annual instalments that were the price of his conversion from serf to emancipated peasant proprietor (for example, in Denmark, south-western Germany, and, after 1861, Russia).

The supply of farm produce was increased by extending settlement and cultivation over the plains of Hungary, Roumania, and southern Russia; by turning expanses of waste land into fertile soil in many western parts of the Continent; but chiefly by raising the productivity of farms already in full use. In the two latter developments British landlords and enterprising farmers played an active part. The former poured money into the improvement of estates or the operation of model farms. They exchanged information through the meetings or the *Journal* of the Royal Agricultural Society (founded in 1838) and of kindred county societies, or in many other publications which described advances in the alliance of 'science with practice'. On the Continent the noteworthy improvers were the large landlords in Germany east of the Elbe, in Denmark, Hungary, and Italy. These men produced grain, livestock, and fine wool for market on what was the counterpart or descendant of the manorial domain. The post-war depression hit them hard, depriving four-fifths of the Prussian Junkers of at least part of their estates; but when it lifted, they resumed the study and imitation of British improvement, and sometimes were pioneers rather than followers.

From the peasant one could expect little innovation and only slow imitation. His holding was too small and scattered for mechanical cultivation. His income left little surplus for capital accumulation, and any spare cash was hoarded or spent in buying more land rather than improving what he had. Borrowing was anathema because of usurious interest rates, and it was not until 1862 that Raiffeisen showed a way of escape by organising his first co-operative bank in a Rhineland village. The little man might change his ways, when it was obviously advantageous but not expensive, within the bounds of the *petite culture* or animal husbandry that he practised and of the unpaid labour supply of the family farm. While such changes may have been more numerous than are recorded in print, it was on the larger farming units that the noteworthy steps were taken to improve agricultural methods.

The first step was the completion in England and the great extension in Germany of the enclosure of open arable fields, common pastures, and waste lands. Most English land worth enclosing had been dealt with before 1830, and by 1870 the redrawing of the rural map was virtually finished. There were now about 250,000 compact farms, nine-tenths of them occupied by tenants and more than half so large that they employed a million labourers, an average of about seven apiece. In Prussia nearly 40,000,000 acres were 'separated', consolidated, and removed from common exploitation between 1821 and 1870, mostly in the eastern region of large estates.

The second step was to build up and maintain soil fertility by using a new effective method of deep drainage and drawing on a better understanding of the function of fertilisers. Drainage 'laid dry' old farms and waste-lands alike. On the former, fields dried out earlier in spring, ploughing and seeding could be done sooner, and manure was no longer washed away. In the latter, whole regions ceased to be worthless when the drains came—fens in Lincolnshire and East Anglia, mosslands in south Lancashire and Scotland, peat bogs and swamps in northern Holland or along the coasts of Germany and the Bay of Biscay. The wastes were then ploughed deeply, heavily manured, and planted. Though the cost of this 'second creation' ran high, rich harvests of grain, roots, and grass justified the outlay, especially when the land was within easy reach of such crowded markets as Lancashire, southern Scotland, or London.

In this making of new fields and improvement of old ones, the use of fertilisers became an exercise in applied science (cf. ch. III, p. 65). Even before Liebig published his *Organic Chemistry in Its Relation to Agriculture and Plant Physiology* (1840) some farmers were using bone dust, Peruvian guano, Chilean nitrates, or 'new and improved artificial manure'. Liebig's list of chemicals present in plants and animals, and hence of essential soil ingredients, was not the last word on the subject, nor, as Lawes and Gilbert at Rothamsted and many others showed by experiments in laboratory or experimental plot, was it always the right one. But it stimulated the use of chemical fertilisers and the vigorous search for supplies. Imports of nitrates and guano mounted rapidly, while potassium salt deposits, found in the Harz Mountains (1852), Alsace, and other parts of Europe, nourished many areas of poor soil, especially in Germany.

Science was less successful in solving the problems of agricultural medicine. Farmers in 1870 were still wellnigh helpless against plagues of sheep foot-rot, hoof and mouth disease, swine fever, and other animal ailments. The turnip crop was ruined by flies in the 'thirties and later; the potato blight of the 'forties was only more severe in Ireland than elsewhere; oidium reduced the French vintage by two-thirds in the 'fifties, and phylloxera began its ravages in the 'sixties. Veterinary science made little real progress until Davaine, Pasteur, Lister, and Koch made possible the bacteriological approach, and the benefits of their work were not enjoyed till after 1870 (cf. ch. III, pp. 65–6). The same is true of those which came from research on the causes of plant disease.

The third step, the improvement of farm equipment, was taken chiefly in Britain and North America. Labour was relatively scarce or costly there, the fields were large enough to be worked by machinery, and inventive ingenuity overflowed from industry to agriculture. At banquets Scots farming enthusiasts drank to the memory of 'that great philosopher and most excellent man, James Watt'. Some of them used steam engines to pull ploughs. The Scots threshing machine moved south to be the target for destruction in the English labourers' uprisings of 1830. Though the Scots harvester found little favour at home, the four models sent to the United States may have caught the eye of Americans looking for something better than a sickle, scythe, or cradle. McCormick patented his reaper in 1834, began to make it in quantity in 1846, exhibited it at the Great Exhibition in 1851, and in field demonstrations convinced English farmers that it could be economically employed. During the next twenty years European and American implement makers offered improved tools and machines for every kind of farm work.

Most of these improvements required heavy investment of fixed or operating capital. The British drainage schemes, for example, cost on an average £4 per acre; the complete conversion of waste-land into fertile farms trebled this figure; and the tenant farmer's operating capital needs were estimated at £4–£8 an acre in 1850. Where the capital came from, how much was taken from the purse or ploughed back from the income of landlord and farmer, and how much was borrowed there is no way of estimating. Drainage projects could be financed by long-term loans from the government or from companies which did the work; but in general no British institutions emerged specifically to supply rural credit. On the Continent the Prussian *Landschaften* continued to provide mortgage loans for the landlord members of these co-operative societies of borrowers. They obtained funds by selling bonds which, being backed by the entire property of all the members, enjoyed the low interest rate of a gilt-edged security. The plan was copied after 1830 in other central European states and found a joint-stock state-subsidised variant in the French *Crédit Foncier*, launched in 1852. But for small landowners and peasants there was virtually no organised aid.

With every improvement in transport and reduction of customs barriers the farmer's market widened. An early picture of a freight-train (1833) shows trucks full of cattle, sheep and pigs. By 1840 eighty steamships were pouring an almost daily stream of Irish livestock, meat, poultry and eggs into British ports. The Belgian farmer followed most closely on the heels of his British counterpart in getting good rail service, but the French farmer had to wait, in some regions till nearly 1870. Only for milk was the farmer slow in gaining access to distant customers. Until about 1870 the railways regarded its long-distance carriage as too trouble-some to merit attention. Meanwhile the effect of tariff changes became evident in Germany after the formation of the *Zollverein*, and in Britain when the customs amendments of 1842, 1846, 1853 and 1860 removed prohibitions, then whittled away duties on foreign animal products. The *per capita* import of these foods in 1870 was about four times that of 1840. While most of the early supplies came from the Continent, the United States jumped into the market in 1842, steadily expanded the volume of shipments, eliminated the early defects of quality, and by 1870 dominated the British import trade in bacon, ham, and cheese.

The marked expansion of animal husbandry did not reduce Europe's dependence on the grains needed for bread and beer. France, Belgium, and England, for example, devoted more than a third of their farm lands to meeting that need. Each country sought to be self-sufficing or took steps to ensure that imports did not depress the domestic price too much. By the early 'thirties these Corn Laws were assuming a common pattern, with a sliding scale of duties. As the home price advanced the duty descended, reaching a nominal figure or even vanishing when famine threatened. In reverse the duty climbed as the price fell, becoming prohibitive long before the price touched an unprofitable level.

The international grain trade was therefore chiefly concerned with supplying the normal deficiency of some countries and the abnormal dearth of others. Belgium and Holland were regular net importers, Denmark and Prussia net exporters, while France oscillated between exports and imports with the size of her harvest. In Britain improved cultivation, when favoured by such good seasons as 1833–6, made the country virtually self-sufficing at moderate prices. But in the bad years 1838–42 bread was scarce and in 1845–7 so also were potatoes. In those 'hungry 'forties' the gap between home production and demand was becoming too wide. Hence Peel's more liberal sliding scale of 1842 and his repeal of the Corn Laws in 1846 were inevitable (cf. ch. XIII, pp. 342–4).

When British farmers defended their costs and corn laws they asked whether free traders wished to force them down to 'that standard which regulates the wages paid to German boors, Polish serfs, and Russian slaves'.[1] These lowly workers produced most of the grain that went into international trade, with Hamburg as the chief outlet for the Elbe basin farms, Danzig for the large harvests of the Vistula valley, and Odessa, supplemented by Taganrog, for the rapidly mounting volume of wheat, wool, leather, and salt beef from the southern Russian farming frontier. By 1840 the Black Sea ports were shipping almost as much grain as Danzig, chiefly to Mediterranean consumers. During the next three decades Russia's total exports more than trebled, establishing her supremacy in the intra-continental trade.

[1] Argument in the protectionist *Farmer's Magazine*, October 1842, p. 308.

All discussions about corn laws voiced the hope, or fear, of a flood of cheap grain from North America. That continent had come to Europe's aid when famine prices were high enough to cover the heavy land and ocean freights and the low duty; but each wave of imports quickly subsided when better harvests reduced prices and raised the tariff. The abolition of the duties in 1846 made little difference to this violently oscillating pattern until after 1870. The waves went higher in the 'sixties, the descent was more gradual, but the troughs were as deep as ever. American wheat was not yet normally abundant or cheap. True, forces were at work to make it both, but they had not yet achieved the necessary combination of large output on cheap or free virgin soil with low inland and ocean freight rates.

The western European farmer, with his high overhead charges and operating expenses, could therefore enjoy that wave of higher prices and prosperity which swept the countryside between 1850 and 1873. Though grain prices rose far less than did those of animal products, the higher yield per acre and the increased number of acres under cultivation produced a satisfactory net income. The price of meats and dairy produce went up between a quarter and a half, and that of wool about three-quarters in spite of a fivefold increase in the supplies from Australia, New Zealand, South Africa, and South America. At scarcely any point did the European farmer have cause in 1870 to fear damaging competition from the outer continents. In one market he was the dangerous competitor, for the spread of beet-sugar production presented a serious challenge to the cane-sugar regions of the world. In 1850 beet fields and sugar factories were spread from northern France to Russia, and may have contributed a seventh of the world's sugar production. By 1870 the output had quadrupled, the fraction was one-third, and both figures were rising rapidly. The price had declined somewhat, while others were rising. Sugar was becoming a necessary for all but the very poor, and the British *per capita* consumption, having trebled in thirty years, reached nearly one pound a week.

'Cotton was the single industry into which industrial revolution had cut really deep by the 'twenties.'[1] During the next four decades the cuts went deeper and wider as more industries in western Europe and North America were influenced by the introduction or improvement of machinery, the harnessing of water or steam power, the enhanced ability to produce metals, the use of coal, and the application of physics or chemistry. New developments were more significant in the heavy capital goods industries—mining, metallurgy, and mechanical engineering—than in those producing lighter consumer goods. Yet the textile industry still loomed large because of the great demand for its products and the large

[1] J. H. Clapham, *Economic History of Modern Britain* (Cambridge, 1926), vol. 1, p. 41.

army of people engaged in making them. The textile mill was therefore everywhere the first evidence of the new industrialism.

It was usually a cotton spinning mill, equipped with the jennies, frames, or mules which had revolutionised yarn-making during the half-century before 1830. Thereafter the mules became self-acting, spindles revolved more rapidly, the hourly output per operator nearly trebled, and the labour cost per pound of yarn was at least halved. A wet flax-spinning process invented in 1825 was quickly adopted by Belfast linen-makers; wool-combing ceased to be a manual task in the 'fifties; and by 1860 waste silk could be made into good yarn. Meanwhile the power loom gradually displaced the hand loom. In 1830 it was efficient and economical only for weaving coarse cottons. By 1850 it would turn out much finer fabrics, was invading the worsted mills in force, but did not fully capture high-grade woollen production till the 'seventies.

The diffusion of British technique did not await the lifting of the bans on emigration of skilled workers (1824) and export of machinery (1843). Some French and Belgian spinning mills were well equipped by 1830, using water power in Alsace and Normandy or small engines in Belgium and northern France where coal was available. In Alsace the power loom had by 1860 almost ousted the hand loom from that most progressive of continental textile regions. Elsewhere, in Switzerland, Germany and Russia, for example, there was similar introduction of spinning machines and importation of cheap British yarns until local production became adequate. In the United States the cotton industry, protected by a tariff that shut out cheap fabrics, grew fivefold between 1830 and 1860. In the latter year it was converting about a fifth of the country's cotton crop into coarse and medium-quality cloths.

The cotton industry was everywhere exceptional in the pace of its growth, its technical change, and its expanding supply of cheap raw material as the United States yield grew from a million bales in 1830 to nearly five million in 1860, and as India and Egypt became minor exporters. Other fabrics felt the fierce competition of cheap cottons, but the woollen manufacturers fought back gamely. They combined cotton warps and fine combed wool to make 'mixed stuffs', light in weight yet 'fancy', approaching good cottons in price and silks in appearance.

A survey of the changes in other industries would be a long catalogue. If the innovation was mechanical it might be an American response to the scarcity of labour, especially skilled, and to the demands of a rapidly expanding domestic market. Sometimes it was an ingenious machine, or a whole battery of them, each designed to turn out a standardised part of a revolver, clock, lock, harvester, sewing machine, door or window frame. British observers in 1853–4 noted the American's 'eager resort to machinery wherever it can be applied', the prevalence of factories in industries still largely served by outworkers and handicraftsmen in Britain, and the 'special purpose machines' for shaping parts in wood or metal.[1] Meanwhile Germany, France and Switzerland were adding their quota to industrial chemistry. British judges at the Paris Exhibition of 1867 were as impressed and alarmed by this fact as by the 'wonderful display' of foreign machines and woollens.

Behind those who used the machines were the men who built them. By the 'thirties the mechanical engineers had heavy- and light-duty machine tools which gave a new degree of speed and precision to metal work. London and Birmingham made a great variety of machines, Manchester was the chief producer of textile equipment, Newcastle of locomotives, and Glasgow of marine engines. In Belgium the Cockerill plant at Seraing was a comprehensive integration of coal mines, blast furnaces, rolling mills, and shops for making engines and equipment of many kinds. In France Le Creusot was a second-rate Seraing, but Germany did not have even a third-rate one till about mid-century. After 1850 the industry made great strides, aided by an increasing supply of lubricants, equipped with better methods for assuring precision, and influenced by the American cult of standardisation.

Behind the machine-makers were the iron-masters. The following table, though based on estimates for the first two lines, gives a rough measure of their achievement.

Output of iron (tons) 1830–70

	U.K.	France	Germany	U.S.A.	World
1830	680,000	270,000	46,000	180,000	1,600,000
1850	2,250,000	400,000	215,000	560,000	4,470,000
1870	5,960,000	1,180,000	1,400,000	1,690,000	12,260,000

This increase in output, about 70 per cent each decade, reflected the improvement and spread of what the French called *le système anglais*. That system comprised the use of coke in place of charcoal for smelting ore and producing brittle iron suitable for castings; then the puddling of liquid cast iron to change it into tough wrought iron which would bend without breaking. Thus equipped, the British industry had quadrupled its output between 1800 and 1830, and its product was the cheapest in Europe. In 1828 Neilson, a Clydeside iron worker, blew hot air instead of cold through the furnace, thereby reducing the fuel bill by a third. This economy, combined with larger furnaces and the tapping of iron deposits in Cumberland and around Middlesbrough, helped to raise production nearly ninefold between 1830 and 1870. Though the price of iron fluctuated with the business curve and the demands of war and railways, the trend was downward, from over £10 per ton in 1825 to £3 in 1866.

Transferred to the Continent, these methods proved most useful where

[1] D. L. Burn, 'The Genesis of American Engineering Competition, 1850–70', in *Economic History*, January 1931, vol. II, pp. 292–311.

coal and ore could be brought together cheaply, as at Seraing and Le Creusot. In many French regions the ore and coal were so far apart and remote from markets that the industry had to await cheaper transport facilities. When these came about 1850 French output trebled in two decades, yet was insufficient to meet all demands. In these same decades Germany made up for a late start by bounding ahead, thanks to abundant cheap fuel from the new Ruhr mines and the railways' need for iron. In the United States the shift to coke made it possible to treble iron production between 1830 and 1850, then to treble it again by 1870.

During those latter years the prospect of cheap abundant steel suddenly grew bright. In 1850 steel was almost a semi-precious metal. Its production was terribly voracious of fuel, slow, and small-scale; hence its use was limited to cutlery, tools, jewellery, and other small articles. The world's output was estimated at 80,000 tons, of which Britain made half. Bessemer's method (1856) offered cheap mass-production. By blowing air through a converter containing liquid iron a ton (or more) of metal could be turned into steel, without using any fuel, in a quarter of an hour. Iron-masters eagerly adopted the process, only to discover that iron containing any trace of phosphorus resisted treatment, and the elimination of that hostile element defied all efforts till 1878. Yet there was sufficient ore of 'Bessemer grade' to permit a rapid expansion in steel production during the 'sixties. In 1870 output was at least eight times the estimate for 1850, and there was a glimpse of the Steel Age as manufacturers put the new metal to all kinds of uses, from railways and ships to milk cans and saucepans.

In 1830 the world's production of coal was probably about 30,000,000 tons, four-fifths of it from British mines. For 1870 the figure was about 220,000,000 tons, of which Britain contributed half, the United States a fifth, and Germany, France, and Belgium together a quarter. The sevenfold increase was at about the same rate as that for iron—between 60 and 70 per cent per decade. The pattern of the market had become clear by 1870. Iron-masters consumed a third of the British output, and manufacturers a quarter. Gas-works and domestic grates burned another quarter, an eighth was exported, while one-twentieth went as fuel to railways and steamships. The British industry was unique in having five coastal coalfields which could deliver their product almost straight into vessels for shipment to such domestic markets as London or for export as ballast and make-weight. Hence exports mounted from 500,000 tons in 1830 to nearly 14,000,000 in 1870.

The exploitation of inland seams depended on cheap water carriage, then on railways, whether to get the coal to market or to bring in raw materials for industries that were best located near the mines. In 1830 Britain and Belgium had the best waterways and by 1850 the best railways. France had more difficulty in providing water and rail services, so that foreign coal was still cheaper to the buyers of a third of her consumption in 1870. In the United States Pennsylvania's anthracite fields were worthless until 'coal and navigation companies' provided canals to the seaboard cities around 1830; but her bituminous coal outcropped on the high banks of streams flowing into the Ohio. It was not only easily mined but could be sent by boat down into the expanding market of the Mississippi valley, or be combined with local supplies of ore and limestone to produce iron in the Pittsburgh area.

Given accessible markets, mines multiplied in such old regions as Belgium and north-east England. New coal beds were discovered, for example, in Pennsylvania and the Donetz basin. During the 'thirties and 'forties a method of sinking shafts through water-logged strata made possible the search for much deeper seams. This search was successful in Britain, the Nord and Pas de Calais, Belgium, and the Ruhr, where the first pit was opened near Essen in 1841. While mining engineers did little to convert coal-hewing from a pick and shovel job to a mechanical operation, they had plenty of other problems: how to free the underground from the menace of flood, suffocation, explosion, and falling roofs; how to extract a larger fraction of the coal; and how to improve its haulage to the surface.

Their achievements were substantial. They made the occupation relatively more productive and less hazardous, for the number of British fatalities remained steady from the mid-'fifties to the early 'seventies, though output rose by four-fifths and the number of miners by three-fifths. But capital and operating costs rose as mines went deeper, while the demand grew rapidly in prosperous times. Consequently the price of coal rose more than the general price level during the third quarter-century and more than doubled when the boom of 1869–73 created a coal famine. In those years productive capacity was hurriedly expanded, as it was in the iron and other heavy industries. By the time the new mines were ready the boom had burst, and the industry faced a serious depression bedevilled by excess capacity.

By 1830 the western world knew the benefits—and the high cost—of good roads, improved river channels, canals, and river steamboats. On the main British turnpikes, now mostly 'macadamised', passengers, mail, and parcels moved at almost ten miles an hour. Though wagons still went at the walking pace of horses, the walking was easier except on the inferior local roads. France, Saxony, Belgium, Switzerland, and north Italy also had good main highways, but poor second- and third-class roads.

In England and the Low Countries, where few places were far from a canal or navigable river, the cost of moving heavy materials had been halved, the volume of traffic increased greatly, and prices tended to become equalised between regions. France was trying to complete its northern network of waterways as well as the links needed in the heart of the country to connect the tributaries or upper reaches of the chief rivers; but the long distances, difficult terrain, defective river courses, great cost, and lack of funds made progress slow and results only moderately satisfactory. In North America the Erie Canal, completed in 1825, and in smaller measure the Canadian canals round the St Lawrence rapids and across the Niagara peninsula, had given a continuous route from the Atlantic to the regions around the Great Lakes.

Finally, the steamboat had revealed its ability to operate on lakes, as well as to carry passengers, mail, and fine cargo on rivers, even upstream against the current. While it was thereby giving new value to the Rhine, Elbe, Vistula, and middle Danube, its greatest promise of service was to the settlers swarming into the vast region drained by the 16,000 miles of the Mississippi and its tributaries.

During the next two or three decades work on roads and waterways continued. German engineers extended the range of river navigation, so that steamboats could go from Rotterdam to Basle by 1840; introduced the steam-tug to haul heavily laden barges; and linked rivers by canals, thereby complementing the natural north–south flow of traffic with an east–west route. The international commission established by the Treaty of Paris in 1856 set out to dredge the Danube, give it a better mouth, and regulate its traffic. French waterways received more attention, though much remained to be done in 1871. In the United States the number of steamboats plying the Mississippi rose from two hundred in 1830 to over a thousand in 1860, thus intensifying the north–south flow of goods.

The opening of the Liverpool–Manchester Railway on 15 September 1830 wed the locomotive to the railed road, with consequences that were in some respects unexpected but mostly encouraging. Passenger traffic became surprisingly heavy, and at twenty miles an hour seemed to abolish time and space. Coal and other freight were moved from one terminus to the other within three hours, in contrast to thirty-six on the waterways. Earnings yielded a steady 8–10 per cent dividend, despite the large capital outlay—over £800,000—and the heavy wear and tear on the early engines.

Given such a lead, there were eager followers in Britain and elsewhere, in fact too many during the little railway boom of 1835–7 and the gigantic one of 1845–7. The following table shows the growth of operating mileage during four decades:

	1830	1840	1850	1870
Europe	60	1,800	14,000	65,000
North America	—	2,800	9,000	56,000
Asia	—	—	200	5,100
South America	—	—	—	1,800
Africa	—	—	—	1,100
Australasia	—	—	—	1,000
World total	60	4,600	23,200	130,000

By 1850 Great Britain had acquired some main and many minor lines. Belgium in 1844 completed the core of its railway plan, with one track from Ostend to the Prussian frontier and another from Antwerp, crossing it at Malines, *en route* for the French border. The French Organic Law of 1842 authorised nine main lines, and by 1850 some parts of them were finished. In the German states about 5000 miles of track were in service. In the United States a boom in the mid-'thirties linked some coastal cities, pushed a few spurs inland, then shared in the general collapse of 'internal improvement' schemes. As the country spent much of the 'forties repairing its damaged credit rating, railway building was largely limited to New England.

During those two decades the railway revealed the kind of service it could render as a common carrier, and the problems of construction, operation, and cost that had to be faced. Passenger service immediately became so popular that the British lines collected two-thirds of their revenue therefrom. This business forced them to increase speed, and by 1850 the best trains were running at 35–40 miles an hour; to expand and improve the cheapest kinds of accommodation; to seek better brakes, signalling and other safety devices; to provide stations, some of them 'ornamental structures of a costly character', and to open refreshment rooms which to those who knew the coaching inns were 'magnificent salons, luxuriously furnished, warmed, and illuminated'. By 1850 fares were less than two-fifths those formerly charged by the coaches, and the duration of journeys had been reduced by two-thirds. Meanwhile the railways had developed fast movement of mail, parcels, livestock, and fish, and were moving heavy materials at rates which not only ruined the road carriers but competed with the waterways.

By 1850 the railway world had explored all ways—private, public, and mixed—of getting its lines built and operated. Private enterprise was the British method, partly because it was the only possible way of financing an innovation, partly because the record of the early companies stimulated sufficient investment, with a heavy over-layer of speculation in boom times, to ensure that capital was forthcoming. There were, however, very few other places where private enterprise was feasible. Distances might be too great, traffic too light, and capital too scarce. Strategic routes might not coincide with trade channels, and in the New World the rails might have to precede settlement, with a long waiting period before traffic developed. Hence governments had to decide whether to build and operate railways themselves, borrowing for construction and meeting deficits out of public revenue; to subsidise private enterprise; or to do both.

Belgium chose public ownership in 1834, as did Austria a little later. France decided on a mixture in 1842. The state would provide the land, prepare the road-bed, and lease it for thirty or forty years to companies. They would raise the construction and operating capital, run the service, borrow from the government if their income was insufficient to pay interest on the bonds, and surrender the lines to the state, when the lease expired, at a fair valuation. North America tried every policy. A few states, chiefly southern, built and operated railroads. Virginia provided two-fifths, later three-fifths of the capital, and claimed the same fractional share of seats on the governing boards. But the commoner practice was the purchase of railroad securities by states, cities, even counties. Massachusetts, for instance, put $5,000,000 into a line that would give Boston a connection with Albany and points west. Then in 1850 Congress made its first railway land grant, and the way was opened for vast subsidies from the public domain.

After mid-century railway construction quickened in Europe and North America and spread to other continents. In the United Kingdom capital, mileage, and net receipts more than doubled. France, having completed its trunk lines by 1859, planned a network of branches. Germany's mileage trebled, that of Austria-Hungary mounted, Italy, Holland, Switzerland, Spain, and Russia entered the picture. Some of this development was stimulated by a French investment bank, the *Crédit Mobilier*, founded in 1852 to raise capital for railways, banks, and other expensive ventures at home or abroad. It secured concessions, including a monopoly and perhaps a subsidy in case revenue was inadequate, from governments which desired railways but lacked funds. Its early successes in France and Austria provoked the Rothschilds to establish the *Creditanstalt für Handel und Gewerbe* in Vienna (cf. ch. xx, p. 535), and other competitors entered the apparently profitable field.

In the United States rails penetrated beyond the Mississippi, and one line spanned the continent in 1869. Trade could now flow between east and west. Canada got its Grand Trunk line, stretching from east of Quebec to western Ontario, also connecting Montreal with the ice-free harbour of Portland, Maine. Australia acquired its first thousand miles during the 'sixties, chiefly in lines running from the capital cities towards the pastoral or grain lands. In Asia, India was the first land to get railways, and in 1870 still almost the only one.

By then the world had built one-sixth of the railways it was eventually to possess. It was the most important sixth, for it transformed the transport system in thickly settled parts of the Old World and showed what benefits railways could confer on large inland continental regions. While strengthening old trade routes, it had carved out new ones, linking regions hitherto disconnected into larger market areas. It had emphasised industrial concentration in favoured spots, and stimulated long-range distribution from railway hubs, whether such old centres as London or such new ones as Chicago. Its construction had been a major influence on capital markets and the movements of the business cycle. In private hands it developed characteristics of monopoly or of competition that was 'imperfect'. There its practices were arousing so much clamour in depressed times against seemingly excessive charges, discriminating treatment of customers, and unsafe or unsatisfactory services, that state regulation was becoming inevitable. In public hands the railway's map and services were influenced by strategic considerations, concepts of national growth or welfare, the pressure of sectional or class interests, the optimism of new countries, and the moods of bond buyers. It had also become a vigorous builder of the national debt.

In 1830 steam vessels were plying on rivers, lakes, and coastal routes or across channels and narrow seas. Their builders were constructing larger ships and improving marine engines, thereby increasing the speed and the certainty with which voyages were performed, lowering operating costs, reducing the fraction of the hull occupied by the power plant and fuel, and expanding that available for passengers and cargo. By mid-century it was elbowing the sailing ship off short runs, especially for the carriage of passengers, livestock, and goods whose bulk was small in proportion to their value. By 1870 it was taking over the short-haul carriage of bulky cargoes as well.

On long ocean routes the steamship faced more serious problems. It must be made as safe as the sailing vessel—not a very high standard; carry sufficient fuel; have enough revenue-earning space to defray heavy construction costs and the high price of 'bought wind'; and do all this in face of the improving and expanding British and American merchant fleets of sailing ships.

The American fleet was especially formidable. Its building costs were far below those of British vessels, thanks to the abundant supply of cheap timber. It had ships for every purpose. The packet liners maintained regular transatlantic services throughout the year, carrying cabin passengers for 'thirty guineas, wines included', fine freight at £2 a ton, mail and bullion, but few steerage passengers. Below them were 'regular traders', which shuttled back and forth laden with general cargoes and often crowded with immigrants on the westward run; great bluff-bowed flat-floored freighters designed especially for the cotton traffic; and hundreds of tramps ready to go anywhere. In 1845 there was added the clipper, stream-lined, speedy, and welcome wherever a quick passage was wanted —to California gold in 1849, Australian gold in 1851, then the Crimea in the war years. It was the most brilliant product of that golden age of the American wooden sailing ship which saw the total tonnage grow fourfold between 1830 and 1860.

It was also the last product, for the golden age was ending. The advantage of cheap timber was vanishing with the coastal forests; some labour, operating, and overhead costs rose; and few clippers made any profit. Meanwhile Quebec and the Canadian maritime provinces learned to make their cheap timber into serviceable vessels. In Europe ship-builders improved designs, some of them using cheap iron for the hull's frame, then for its shell. Finally, the steamship burst out of its narrow range of operations. By 1838 the question no longer was whether any steamship could cross the North Atlantic at one jump, but which would be the first to do it. On 23 April the *Sirius* and the *Great Western* reached New York; by the year's end there had been ten such arrivals; and all made the crossing in about half the time taken by the best packets.

These journeys were, however, only the end of the beginning. For at least a decade the steamship had a poor record for safety. Its crew was large, its revenue-earning space small. Its construction cost might equal that of three or four large packets, yet it delivered only as much service—six transatlantic round trips if all went well—as did two of them. Consequently a regular service, even on a fortnightly time-table, needed a line of at least four vessels. Cunard was able to establish such a line between Liverpool, Halifax, and Boston in 1840 only because of a generous mail subsidy. Until he started his second service, from Liverpool to New York, in 1848, the packets still ran the only regular traffic to that port. In 1856 less than 4 per cent of the passengers arriving there came by steamship.

During the 'fifties and 'sixties the steamship became more safe, efficient, and economical. As iron hulls gained in popularity larger vessels could be built. The propeller supplemented, then supplanted, the paddle-wheel. The compound engine reduced coal consumption by half, thereby increasing the available cargo space and making the ocean-going cargo steamship a potential commercial success. Meanwhile passenger vessels improved at every point: in size and horse-power, speed, cargo capacity, cabin and steerage accommodation. By 1870, therefore, the sailing ship had lost the cream of the North Atlantic traffic and was losing it on all other ocean routes except the Australian. It still dominated the long hauls of heavy crude cargoes, of which there was so much that the world's sailing tonnage did not begin to decline till about 1880.

While every advance in transport made postal services quicker, government action made them cheaper. The British reforms of 1840 set a worldwide pattern: a uniform low charge for delivery in any part of the country, paid by the sender instead of the recipient through purchase of a stamp. Within a quarter of a century most countries had followed this lead, and a series of international conferences led to the establishment of the International Postal Union (1874). Meanwhile domestic and international telegraph services developed from the pioneer work of British and North American railways and telegraph companies in the 'forties. In 1851 a cable from Dover to Calais provided the first of many links with the Continent, where private or state telegraphic services quickly spread as far as Moscow and the Mediterranean. A wire spanned North America in 1861. Ocean cables reached New York in 1866, Calcutta in 1870, and Australia in 1871.

The economic results of improved communications were far-reaching. After a big initial increase, the number of letters delivered in the United Kingdom rose 5 per cent year after year. For those engaged in distant trade the long wait for letters which had bedevilled the making of decisions was reduced by half or more with the coming of the railway and steamship, then almost abolished once wires were available. Shipping movements, demand, supply, prices, and prospects could be known almost instantaneously. The Dover–Calais cable allowed the London and Paris stock exchanges to compare prices hour by hour. Liverpool could keep an eye on Bombay, New York, New Orleans, and Chicago, and they on it. For stocks and the great staple commodities a world market was in the making; so was a world ocean freight market once tramp-ships could be directed by a cabled message to their next port of call.

The total effect of improved transport and communication was an enhanced mobility of persons and goods. Meanwhile the general trend of national policies lowered or removed those obstacles which lay across the paths of international commerce. Inter-state free trade, guaranteed by the federal constitution, continued to be an incalculable boon to the expansion of settlement and trade inside the United States. Its benefits soon became evident in Germany, when the *Zollverein* merged seventeen states and more than 20,000,000 people into a customs union. Its attraction was not overlooked in the discussion that led to Canadian confederation in 1867.

The fate of international trade policies was in the hands of three countries: the United Kingdom, which is estimated to have accounted for a third of the world's exports and imports in 1840; France with about 10 per cent; and the United States with 8 per cent.[1] Any liberalisation of their policies depended on a politically overpowering will for it, and on the ability to afford the loss of customs revenue or to find a substitute. France lacked the will and probably the ability. Manufacturers and farmers unitedly opposed all legislative attempts to lower tariffs, and Napoleon III got his Anglo-French commercial treaty in 1860 only by using his treaty-making power in secret negotiations.

In the United States the northerners' will to high protection had overreached itself in the Tariff of Abominations (1828). The 'Compromise Tariff' of 1833 therefore inaugurated a vacillating trend toward lower duties which lasted till the Civil War. As revenue, especially from land sales, mounted rapidly, there was less need for customs receipts. In the booming 'fifties protectionist sentiment was so torpid that the few Americans and Canadians who desired a reciprocal treaty got their way (1854). For a dozen years the products of forest, farm, fishery, and mine passed across the border as if it were not there.

It was Britain's changes in policy that were most important to the

---

[1] *Encyclopaedia of the Social Sciences* (1932), vol. VIII, p. 194.

world's economy. There the popular will was deeply divided, especially when the depression of 1837–42 drove men into organised offensive or defensive campaigns. While merchants and many manufacturers demanded free trade, farmers clung to protection—though some landlords were deserting them—shipowners to the Navigation Laws, the colonial interests to the preferences on grain, lumber, and sugar. The government, heavy-laden with national debt and faced with seventeen deficits in twenty-eight years (1815–42), was in no position to make heroic cuts in customs duties, which contributed 38 per cent of the revenue, or in excise levies on domestic products, which contributed 37 per cent.

The dismantling of a system which combined protection, revenue and preference had to be done in instalments (see ch. XIII, pp. 342–5). Huskisson had made a good start in the 'twenties, but the rest had to be left to Peel and Gladstone. Peel found in the income tax (1842) a source of revenue that would partly replace the money lost by reducing duties. The Irish famine forced his hand on the Corn Laws, and the Navigation Laws were suspended to let foreign ships bring emergency grain. In 1849 that suspension became permanent, except for coastal journeys, and these were thrown open in 1854. Gladstone carried on the cleaning of the slate so vigorously that by 1870 only seventeen dutiable imports remained, of which five (sugar, tea, wine, spirits, and tobacco) contributed nine-tenths of the customs revenue, as they had done in the 'thirties. Total net imports had risen about 400 per cent since the early 'thirties, but the revenue therefrom only 30 per cent. In the earlier period that revenue represented a levy of about 35 per cent on the imports; in the later it was below 10 per cent.

Though no other country went so far, there was much movement in the same direction. Some actions were unilateral; for example, the Belgian repeal of Corn Laws in 1850 and the Dutch and *Zollverein* paring of tariffs after 1845. Others were reciprocal concessions embodied in a trade treaty, such as the Cobden-Chevalier pact of 1860. By this treaty Britain admitted virtually all French wares duty-free and cut hard the rates on wine and brandy. France swept away her prohibitions on some British goods and scaled down her rates. In addition, each signatory accorded 'most favoured nation' treatment to the other. If France by treaty granted more favourable terms to another nation than Cobden had secured, these would immediately be extended to British goods. As treaties signed by France with ten other European states and by Britain with seven contained some lower duties, the area of reduced tariffs spread wider with each pact.

Even without such tariff changes international trade would have expanded greatly, because of the spread of railway construction, the advancing industrialisation of France, Germany, and the United States, the rising tide of migrant capital and labour to the New World, and the opening of new areas of investment and enterprise on both sides of the Pacific. An international economy on a world-wide scale was in the making. The available statistics, though defective, suggest that world trade rose by 40 per cent during the 'thirties and a similar amount in the 'forties, then jumped 80 per cent in the 'fifties (partly because of a marked increase in prices) and nearly 50 per cent in the 'sixties. British commodity exports rose less than 25 per cent each decade until 1850, then jumped 90 and 60 per cent respectively during the next two. Imports behaved similarly, always exceeding exports, and the gap grew ever wider. But such invisible exports as the earnings of the merchant marine, commercial and banking houses, and overseas investments, made up the deficiency and left something over. This surplus was £7,000,000 or less per annum until the early 'fifties, but thereafter rose rapidly to nearly £40,000,000 in the late 'sixties, and almost twice that figure in the boom years 1868–73. By leaving it abroad, the British investment stake overseas was expanded from perhaps £110,000,000 in 1830 to £700,000,000 in 1870.[1]

The new ways of making and moving goods called for far more capital in buildings and equipment than hitherto, in addition to more 'floating capital'. Where the initial need was relatively small and subsequent accumulation possible, enterprise could remain in the hands of one-man businesses, family, or partnership firms. These units accounted for most of the expansion in manufacturing, mining, shipping, wholesale and retail trade, and fought a long, though often losing, battle in banking. Family resources were mobilised, active or silent partners sought, profits and interest ploughed back into the business. The task was not easy, as there was a big depression every decade with smaller ones in between. The price of failure ran high, since all the property of all partners in Britain and North America, but only of active partners in France, could be seized by creditors.

The alternative, corporate enterprise, had by 1830 shown its usefulness in raising the large sums needed at home for turnpikes, canals, docks, water and gas supplies, banks, insurance, and the pioneer railways, and for developing such faraway resources as land settlement and pastoral production in Australia. During the next forty years it continued along those lines. The promotion of joint stock companies and the underwriting of their securities became the special business of investment banks. Governments gave companies legal personality by decrees in France and Belgium, private acts in Britain, and legislative charters in the United States. After 1840 private incorporation was supplemented by general laws which allowed any group to form a company merely by registering a

---

[1] See Albert H. Imlah, 'Real Values in British Foreign Trade', in *Journal of Economic History*, vol. VIII, pp. 148–51; 'The Terms of Trade of the United Kingdom', *ibid.* vol. X, pp. 170–194; and 'British Balance of Payments and Export of Capital', in *Economic History Review*, second series, vol. V, pp. 234–7.

statement of its name, address, objective, capital structure, directors, and other relevant facts. Limited liability was offered soon afterwards, for instance in Britain by laws of 1856–62, to any company willing to publish certain financial statements.

Joint stock promotion came in waves with every up-swing of the business cycle, only to subside when the tide turned, leaving much wreckage and some evil odour. A third of the 5000 limited liability companies registered in London (1856–65) failed to come to life; a third of the others did not have a fifth birthday, and more than half vanished before their tenth. The continental creations in the 'fifties and 'sixties had a similar mixed record.

While a new breed of bankers concerned itself with long-term investment needs, the old school continued to receive deposits, transfer money from person to person, and make short-term commercial loans, chiefly by discounting bills of exchange. In rapidly expanding economies or periods many commercial banks of the early nineteenth century were far from adequate for their task. The search for stronger banks, for cautious policies, or for restraints on rash ones, therefore concerned bankers and governments alike.

In 1832 a British Rothschild declared: 'This country is in general the Bank for the whole world. I mean that all transactions in India, in China, in Germany, in Russia, and in the whole world are all guided here and settled through this country.'[1] Yet during six of the next ten years parliamentary committees considered ways of improving the British banking system. Its base, consisting of hundreds of private banks in London and the provinces, was weakened by widespread failures in 1815 and 1825, then strengthened when acts of 1826 and 1833 permitted the establishment of joint-stock banks, such as flourished in Scotland. By 1841 there were over a hundred of these in England and Wales, some well supplied with capital and Scots managers; also over three hundred private ones, including such ancient firms as Child or Hoare, and such relative upstarts as Rothschild or Baring; and an increasing number of branches after the Scots pattern. During the next three decades branches multiplied, thus adding to the resources, the diversification of risks, the centralisation of reserves, and the belief, not always justified, that the soundness of a bank was proportionate to its size.

At the head of the 'system' was the Bank of England, which in 1826 had been given permission to set up provincial branches. Yet though here, as in London, it competed with old private or new joint-stock banks, it could not be just one among many. It gradually became a central bank, in which the others deposited funds and to which they could turn when the calls for credit exceeded their resources. In crises their need might be terribly urgent and the Bank their place of last resort. At such times

[1] Quoted in *The Penny Magazine*, 1837, p. 185.

the Bank might ration customers, discriminate between high- and low-grade collateral security, or refuse aid. In the 'forties it tried another device. It raised the 'Bank Rate' on loans—for example, from 3½ per cent in early 1847 by five steps to 8 per cent in October, and later in the crises of 1857 and 1866 to 10 per cent. Any unseasonal raising of the rate was a warning, while a series amounted to an application of brakes and a change into reverse gear. Since the Bank had no monopoly of credit supply and no control over the harvest or the general behaviour of the national or world economy, it had to make the best of its power to cope with 'hazards which the wisest cannot foresee nor the most unremitting attention prevent' in a world where 'there usually comes round every five or seven years a period of failing and distress which may produce loss'.[1]

On the Continent commercial credit was provided by a few central banks, of which the Bank of France was the chief; by purely local institutions; and by that small group of powerful family banking houses—the Hopes, Rothschilds, Mallet *frères*, Hottinguers, Oppenheims, Foulds, and the like—which discounted bills, dealt in merchandise, and underwrote government loans from their strongholds in Paris, Amsterdam, Frankfurt, or Vienna. When the upheavals of 1848 wrecked many weak or over-ambitious banks, the need for better substitutes, then for investment banks, led to an outcrop of new joint-stock banks, especially in France. The *Crédit Mobilier* and its rivals scattered similar banks over the Continent; for example, the *Bank für Handel und Industrie* in Darmstadt (1853), which played a large part in the industrial and railway boom in Germany.

In North America Congress wrecked the promise of a central bank by refusing to renew the charter of the Second Bank of the United States in 1836. As it made no provision for a national banking policy or note issue till 1863, service had to be provided by private bankers and merchant-bankers, or by banks incorporated under state laws which usually forbade the establishment of branches. The task of providing both short-term commercial and long-term mortgage credit was beyond the means of these 'unit' banks. They were damned if they did not provide both, but risked bankruptcy if they did. Emotionally and politically hostile attitudes toward 'monopoly', 'money power', 'paper aristocrats', and 'Shy-locks' made the building of a good banking system a long labour of pain and sorrow on a foundation shaken by violent alternations of boom and depression.

In every western land there was concern over the tendency of banks to issue too many notes when making loans in prosperous times. Argument and bitter experience led to the decision that note issue should be concentrated in a central bank and strictly regulated. The Bank of France

---

[1] A Baring view of the business cycle, quoted in R. W. Hidy, *The House of Baring in American Trade and Finance* (Cambridge, Mass., 1949), p. 130.

in 1848 regained that monopoly, with a maximum limit to its issue. Holland and Russia had never moved from a regulated monopoly. British policy was embodied in the Bank Charter Act of 1844. The issue of each bank (except the Bank of England) was frozen at its current figure and would be wiped out if the bank changed status, while no new bank could issue notes. The Bank of England would thus ultimately become the sole bank of issue. It could issue 'fiduciary' notes worth about £14,000,000 on the security of loans to the state; also some to replace a fraction of those which other banks forfeited; but beyond that potential £20,000,000 every note must be backed in full by precious metal.

This plan had the defects of its virtues. It was honest but inelastic. On three occasions—1847, 1857, and 1866—crisis could not be stemmed or controlled merely by raising the bank rate. Nor could panic-stricken clients be helped unless the government gave the Bank permission to break the law and issue unbacked notes. In 1847 and 1866 the news that permission had been granted was sufficient to allay the panic. But the crisis of 1857 hit so suddenly and so hard, with news of mutiny in India, of virtually every bank in the United States closed, and of disaster at almost every point in between, that illegal notes—less than £1,000,000 in all—had to be used. That venial sin saved some firms or postponed their doom, which was as much as could be expected in a moment when 'all the bubbles, blunders, and dishonesties of five years' European exuberance and experiments in credit were tested or revealed'.[1]

While the business world wrestled with its problems, labour tried to adjust itself to changes in opportunities and conditions of employment. Of these the most noteworthy was the transfer to the factory of occupations hitherto carried on in or around the home. The textile industry was the outstanding example, because of the large number of men, women, and children it employed. In Great Britain, as perhaps in some continental lands, they comprised the third largest occupation, after agricultural labourers and domestic servants, accounting for more than 10 per cent of the working population in 1841 and 1851. In 1830 spinners, a few weavers, and most cloth-finishers were factory-employed. During the next forty years most of the remaining domestic processes were transferred to the mill in Britain, but the transition came later in many parts of the Continent.

Preoccupation with textiles obscures two other important aspects of the labour picture. In the first place, many occupations did not move far, even in Britain, from the home or small workshop. London, Paris, and every other large city swarmed with a vast variety of small producing units and outworkers. The clothing, footwear, baking, small metal-wares, and luxury goods industries were their strongholds. Birmingham, Sheffield, Solingen, the Lyons silk and Swiss watch regions were dominated

[1] J. H. Clapham, *Economic History of Modern Britain*, vol. II, p. 370.

by them. Prussia in 1843 had fewer apprentices and journeymen than masters, and three-fourths of France's 5,000,000 industrial workers in 1850 were outside what was called *la grande industrie*. If the 'workers of the world' in 1848 had answered Marx's call to unite, only a small minority would have been factory proletarians. On the Continent that would still have been largely true in 1870.

In the second place, mining, smelting, building, shipbuilding, and occupations which used much power, fuel, or space for their stills, boilers, vats, and tanks never had been, and could not be, operated on the domestic plan. Now their centralised producing units grew in size and numbers; also in variety as new industries emerged to make machines, engines, iron ships, coal-gas, fertilisers, cement, rubber, paper, and heavy chemicals. As employers these occupations grew greatly in importance. The number of British coal-miners rose nearly threefold between 1841 and 1871, of iron producers nearly sixfold, of machine and engine builders tenfold. By 1871 the combined labour force in mining, quarrying, metal production, engineering, and ship-building almost equalled that of cloth-makers. It was virtually a male preserve, calling for new skills as well as old, earning higher wages than most other occupations, but more vulnerable to unemployment because of violent fluctuations in the demand for its products.

Wherever he worked, the wage-earner's material welfare was determined by the dwelling and environment in which he lived, the conditions under which he did his job, and the size, regularity, and purchasing power of his wages. There was little he could do about the first, whether he stayed in his birthplace or joined the stream of migrants moving from village or farm to town, from rural counties to mining and manufacturing regions, from country to country, or from Europe to America and the Antipodes. That migration accounted for nearly half the 16 per cent growth of population in ten English industrial counties between 1831 and 1841. Only half the adults living in London and Sheffield in 1851 had been born there, and only a quarter of those in Manchester, Glasgow, Liverpool, or Bradford. The Irish loomed large in the movement, comprising a tenth of the population of England and Wales in 1851. On the Continent seasonal or permanent migrations were also marked: of country weavers into Lille or Lyons, of Swiss, French, and Germans into the Mulhouse mills, of German peasants or handicraftsmen into Berlin or the Saxon, Rhineland, and Silesian towns. Beyond that was the great trek across the Atlantic, chiefly of British, German, and Scandinavian origin till the 'seventies.

In no country was the provision of homes regarded as a public duty, and few employers felt any obligation to house their workers. The job was left to private builders, who had to keep one eye on what the tenant could pay and the other on construction and maintenance costs, taxes, interest rates, and land rents. Scattered evidence suggests that rents in

English industrial towns ranged between 2s. and 4s. 6d. for working-class houses. To get a reasonable net return from them a housing unit must not cost much more than £100. Given that limit and also the restricted supply of land, rows of back-to-back houses, courtyard dwellings, and blocks of tenements were the best that could be provided by an industry which lacked the economies of large-scale production, cheap credit, and public subsidies.

The wider problem of streets, sewers, water, and general public health was harder to solve. Large towns, and many small ones, had generally killed more men than they bred. Now there were more towns and some were much larger. Smoke was thicker and more acrid, streams and wells were more polluted, cesspools and privies more numerous, collection and disposal of sewage more difficult. The perennial summer outbreaks of typhus, dysentery, and other diseases were heavier in their toll, as were the cholera scourges of 1831–2, 1848, and later years.

The sanitary reform crusaders had plenty of ammunition. But since the problem could not be tackled by private enterprise, it was necessary to create a combination of public concern, new or improved methods, heavy fixed capital outlays, national policies, and local authorities endowed with adequate powers to plan, tax, and spend. Consequently public health had to jostle with many other issues for legislative attention, and was dealt with spasmodically. Though Britain took some steps in the 'forties and others in the 'fifties, little progress had been made by 1870, save in a few alert towns. The death-rate was about the same as in 1840 and in some towns was about twice that for the country at large. Conditions were no better in other lands, and improvements came slowly. In the New World, as in the Old, man made the city, but found it very hard to make a good job of it.

Working conditions, the second influence on the wage-earner's welfare, became a topic of violent controversy in 1830 when Richard Oastler's letters to the *Leeds Mercury*, denouncing the employment of children for long hours, started the agitation for a ten-hour working day. This demand hastened the next step beyond the rudimentary factory acts of 1802, 1819, and 1825. The law of 1833 covered nearly all textile mills, forbade the employment of children under nine, limited persons between nine and thirteen to a forty-eight-hour working week, and required some attendance at school; fixed a weekly maximum of sixty-nine hours for those between thirteen and eighteen years, with no night work; included some health and safety precautions; and appointed four full-time factory inspectors.

Each subsequent decade improved and widened the range of regulation (see ch. XIII). By 1870 there were few industrial establishments in which rules concerning minimum age, maximum hours for males under eighteen and all females, health and safety were not being enforced by inspectors.

Though men were still untouched by law, they were influenced indirectly wherever their work depended on female or juvenile co-operation, and by the increasing insistence on safety precautions. The shop assistant, farm labourer, industrial outworker, domestic servant, and office employee remained outside the pale long after 1870.

That was where most workers on the Continent and in North America were in 1870. The British agitation of the 'thirties stirred some interest and a little action there. A Prussian decree of 1839 ordered children out of mines and mills and fixed a ten-hour day for young persons; but no inspectors were appointed till 1853. None were appointed in France till 1883. In the United States half a dozen eastern states had by the early 'fifties fixed a minimum age and maximum hours, including a ten-hour day for men; but the laws were easy to evade or lacked machinery for enforcement. Only after the Civil War did Massachusetts in 1866 lead the way to better provisions.

Factory acts were intended to care for women and young people because they could not look after themselves. Men were supposed to be able to protect and advance their own welfare in selling their labour. That they might do this as members of a union was by 1830 regarded in Britain as inevitable, regrettable, and perhaps dangerous. The repeal of the Combination Laws (1824) and the amendment of 1825 had recognised that unions were not illegal; but they were not yet legal personalities with power to own property (including funds), and some of their actions, such as molesting, obstructing, and inducing breaches of contract, were still unlawful. Nearly half a century elapsed before laws of 1867–76 gave them legal personality and the right to do collectively things which would be legal if done by an individual. Elsewhere the ban on labour association was lifted later: in Massachusetts (1842), Saxony, the North German Federation, France, and Belgium during the 'sixties; but legal recognition and the right of peaceful picketing, or even of striking, were slow in coming.

Whatever the law, local societies, clubs, or unions of skilled workers existed in 1830, especially in Britain and the United States. During the 'thirties, when Messiahs stalked the western world preaching deliverance from long hours, middle-class governments, private property, competition, and alcohol, there were British plans for a nation-wide union of workers of every kind and occupation; but these collapsed because of impracticable programmes, bad leadership, lack of solidarity or discipline within, employers' resistance, and the depression of 1836–42 (see ch. XIII).

After the uproars subsided the 'New Model' emerged with the Amalgamated Society of Engineers in 1851. It was a national fusion of more than a hundred local unions, or branches, of engineers, machinists, and other trained skilled metal-workers. Control of local finance and policy was put in the hands of the central executive. The officials were primarily administrators and organisers, whose task was to settle disputes peacefully wherever possible. The union was also a friendly society, giving aid in time of sickness and unemployment as well as industrial strife. It eschewed the secret-society methods of many earlier unions, welcomed publicity, and persistently reminded the public that it was a peaceful concern, with no desire for Utopia or class war.

The New Model worked well, was copied by other skilled crafts, dispelled some middle-class mistrust and gained some recognition from employers. By 1870 collective bargaining had in a few cases got as far as the use of conciliation and arbitration machinery. As the years 1850–73 were relatively prosperous, union membership in Britain rose from perhaps 100,000 in the 'forties to possibly more than a million in 1873. In the 'sixties the German 'Radical' unions, formed by Max Hirsch (1868), gathered in skilled artisans and pursued policies akin to those of the British model, while the first socialist unions appeared, devoted to more exciting programmes inspired by Lassalle or Marx. In the United States craft unions, already widely scattered over the industrial centres, grew in strength, joint action, and successful demands for the eight-hour day and the use of the union label on goods made by their members. But there, far more than in Europe, the collapse of the boom turned advance into rout.

By 1870, therefore, wage-earners were on the right track. As wage-spenders they also were headed in the right direction. There had been lingering traces of utopianism in the objectives of the Rochdale Equitable Pioneers' Society, founded in 1844; but none in such working principles as the provision of capital at a fixed rate of interest by the members, the sale of pure food for cash at market prices, and the return of any net surplus to the pocket from which it had come, as a dividend on purchases. This second New Model worked well as it went on from retailing groceries to milling flour, making clothes, and establishing a Co-operative Wholesale Society (1863) which supplied goods to more than a hundred retail societies in the northern industrial regions. By 1870 those societies had 80,000 members and the figure was rising rapidly.

Thus the industrial worker evolved institutions for his protection. But in 1870 they were still small in range, size, and geographical area, even in Britain, with unskilled and low-paid workers as yet untouched, and on the Continent their influence was negligible. Consequently the wage-earner's income was affected far more by his personal qualifications and conduct, by trends in production and productivity, and by changes in the demand for his labour, his money wages, and in price levels than they were by the things his union, his 'co-op', or even his government did for him.

Though the nature of some of these influences has already been examined, measurement of their effect is difficult for lack of satisfactory figures. Yet a few tentative conclusions emerge. In the first place, until western

Europe could depend on substantial supplies of food from Russia and North America, harvest variations affected the general welfare directly through price movements and indirectly by their influence on the business cycle. Good seasons and lower food prices helped to pull the economy out of depression, bad ones did much to push it back. This factor was far from having lost its influence in 1870.

In the second place, the task of accumulating and maintaining an unprecedented amount of fixed capital equipment introduced a relatively new factor into the distribution and use of income. In an age that knew not planned investment, the 'capitalist classes', as Lord Keynes once remarked, 'were allowed to call the best part of the [income] cake theirs and were theoretically free to consume it, on the tacit underlying condition that they consumed very little of it in practice. The duty of "saving" became nine-tenths of virtue and the growth of the cake the object of true religion.'[1] If labour received less cake than it could have consumed, capital ploughed back much of its share in further investment. This increased the demand for goods and labour, first to build and equip factories, railways, and ships, then to operate them. The growing population therefore found employment, and if the new plants were better equipped or organised, the expanded production and greater productivity were reflected sooner or later in lower prices or higher wages, or both.

This development was not painless. It destroyed enterprises which clung to old methods, organisation, or equipment, as hand-loom weavers and coach-drivers were well aware. Nor was it steady, for investment generated over-enthusiastic bouts of competitive energy followed by over-pessimistic lethargy and excess capacity. In intensity and duration the depression of 1836–42 competes with later rivals for the title of 'the Great Depression'. The lamentations of those and other gloomy years have given the second quarter of the century an evil reputation. Yet the measurable achievements suggest that as a whole the period was 'one of extraordinary development, perhaps the most rapid rate of development of domestic resources throughout the whole of Britain's economic history';[2] and a similar reappraisal might be possible for Belgium, France, Germany, and the United States. Higher productivity raised British real wages between 1830 and 1850, though probably more by reducing prices than by lifting money payments.

The third quarter's reputation is much better, perhaps too good. The demand for consumer goods and still more for capital goods rose high. In the first flush of gold rushes and new gold, it outran supply so much that prices rose far ahead of wages until the collapse of the boom in 1857 checked them. Thereafter wholesale prices oscillated around 25 per cent, and retail prices about 13 per cent, above the 1850 level. Wages caught

---

[1] J. M. Keynes, *The Economic Consequences of the Peace* (London, 1919), p. 17.
[2] W. W. Rostow, *British Economy of the Nineteenth Century* (Oxford, 1948), p. 19.

up with prices by 1860, then continued to rise until 1873. Real wages therefore rose markedly after 1860: in Britain by 15 per cent in 1870 for those in full employment and by 25 per cent in 1873; and in France by 18 per cent in 1870.

It may not be true, in spite of *Punch* cartoons, that coal-miners drank champagne in 1871–3; but certainly many wage-earners were getting more cake as well as tea, cocoa, meat, sugar, rice, and fats. They might return home a little earlier for the evening meal, as trade union pressure was chipping the working week from sixty (or more) hours down toward fifty-five, with a Saturday half-holiday. If they lived in Britain the public health service was beginning to make their living environment a bit better; the factory inspectors had gained much experience in making the working place less unhealthy; parliament had given them a vote in 1867 and in 1870 it finally insisted that the children it had shut out of the factories must go to school. Things had moved since the Hungry 'Forties.

CHAPTER III

THE SCIENTIFIC MOVEMENT AND ITS INFLUENCE ON THOUGHT AND MATERIAL DEVELOPMENT

IN the mid-nineteenth century the pursuit of scientific knowledge at last attained true autonomy and independence. Emerging as a consistent discipline with experiment and observation as its sanctions and mathematics as its logic, science[1] extended its province far into space, and brought millions of years within the scope of its pronouncements. Emancipated from the limitations imposed by formal reasoning and dogmatic theology, an unquestionable force of certainty was claimed for scientific truths such as had never before been granted to any products of the intellect; and though only a small part of the swift advance in material civilisation that was made in this period can be directly attributed to contemporary progress in science, vast accretions of potential power were being built up. The formative period of modern science in which its character, its methods and its problems were established may be said to have ended about 1830; the modern age, with the technical ascendancy of science, to have begun about 1870. The interval is both classical, in that it contains the fulfilment of much that had been originated earlier, and transitional, because the beginning of recent science lies within it. Without abrupt discontinuity there was a remodelling of activity, a displacement of some guiding concepts of scientific thought by others. A single individual, like James Clerk Maxwell, might in one investigation add a coping-stone to the fabric of Newtonian celestial mechanics, while in another he helped to lay the foundations of the new theoretical physics. The doctrine of universal gravitation received its fullest vindication in 1845–6 from the discovery of the planet Neptune in accordance with theoretical predictions, when Newton's optical theories had already been shaken by the newer theory of wave-motion. Even Darwinism, with its revolutionary impact upon biological studies, imposed not less but greater application to the problems which the older naturalists had sought to solve.

The increasing authority of science was reflected in a variety of ways and was not without consequence for the structure of the scientific movement itself. In the more advanced countries of Europe it was demanding more favourable attention within the educational system, above all in the

---

[1] 'Science' is here used in the sense of the rational correlated knowledge of natural phenomena. The invention of the railway locomotive is properly described as a technological invention: but the electric telegraph, which made rapid railway communication possible, can properly be described as a scientific invention.

49

universities. In Italy the academic standing of scientific research had never been wholly lost after the Renaissance; in Germany it was deliberately re-created after the defeat of Napoleon; France and Britain tardily followed the German example of reform. With the increasing ramification and complexity of research the scientific amateur changed insensibly into the professor, as large laboratories, expensive apparatus, and protracted labour became the concomitants of serious work. Laboratory training and instruction in research became normal features of higher scientific teaching. An exemplary institution, such as the chemical laboratory of Justus von Liebig at Giessen, was cited as a model by those who protested against the academic administration which paid insufficient tribute to the outstanding experimental talent of William Thomson or Claude Bernard. Inevitably the state was called upon to reform education and to provide financial support for a more generous organisation of science. As early as 1809 the Berlin Academy of Science had been incorporated in the university of that city; the new University of London, and the reforms in the older universities of England initiated after the Royal Commission of 1850, gave new scope for the teaching of scientific subjects; and Napoleon III was inspired by Pasteur to recognise the enhanced needs of science. With the state as patron and architect of new institutions the importance of the great national academies, founded in the seventeenth century, was correspondingly diminished. To some extent they were supplanted by another organisation, the scientific association. Of these the earliest were the German Scientific Association, founded by Lorenz Oken in 1822, and the British Association for the Advancement of Science, which met for the first time at York in 1831. The scientific association, besides being a response to the widespread interest in the more practical aspects of scientific knowledge in countries affected by the Industrial Revolution, was also intended to strengthen the scientific movement by placing it upon a broader basis of understanding and goodwill. About 1830, British science suffered from apathy and a sense of inferiority, and when, after the collapse of 1871, the like feeling prevailed in France, there too a National Association was brought into being.

The progress of science was still mainly in the hands of the four great nations of western Europe, each of them associated with one of the great conceptual achievements of the period—the theory of bacteria (France), thermodynamics (Germany), evolution (Britain) and molecular theory (Italy). Notable, but scattered, contributions came from eastern Europe, and the Academy of Science of St Petersburg kept the limited number of Russian savants in touch with the West. But beyond western Europe the most promising seat of scientific endeavour lay in the United States of America, whose universities were being gradually adapted to the German pattern, and were enriched by the growing number of young students who had profited by the experience which could only be obtained in

European laboratories. The most celebrated American scientist of the period, Louis Agassiz of Harvard, was a Swiss *émigré*, but the first experiments on anaesthesia (1844), and Willard Gibbs' theoretical work on thermodynamics thirty years later, were America's gifts to Europe.

Here, too, there were changes in the foci of scientific interest. French science, in the time of Lavoisier, Laplace and Cuvier, had held an intellectual ascendancy which was lost after 1830. In the development of physics the empirical genius of Britain reappeared with fresh vigour, but still more remarkable were the consistently high level and fertility of German science. No branch of research was left unimproved by its efforts; German universities attracted men of all nations, and the German language became a major means of scientific communication, while Clausius, Helmholtz, Liebig or Ludwig by their theoretical investigations determined the course of their respective sciences.

Overcoming her initial backwardness, her lack of colonies and mercantile marine, Germany had by 1870 risen to the first rank of manufacturing countries, partly through her achievements in pure science and its technological application. Generally, however, the distance between laboratory and factory and field was still too great to permit effective co-operation between science and production. Since 1830 an increase of population, a greater facility for communication, and a larger volume of commerce had been brought about by many factors of which science was but one. Technical skill, such as the pioneers eulogised by Smiles possessed, had little relation to abstract scientific knowledge. The railway engineers, the ship-builders, and the machine-makers upon whom this new civilisation rested were men trained in the school of empiricism and experience, drawing indefinably from the steady accumulation of scientific knowledge since the seventeenth century. To the practical engineer who was now using accurate methods of survey to lay out a track, hydrodynamical researches to perfect the design of screw propellers, or the Bashforth electric chronograph for the improvement of artillery, science came as an aid rather than as a system. Though science was accelerating the rate of exploitation of inventions, it offered few directly, and even at the close of the period a new type of scientific inventor—Bessemer, Siemens, or Armstrong—was only beginning to impinge upon the basic industries. Precise control of operations by such means as accurate timing, pyrometry, and sampling was still a novelty. Waste from coke-ovens and gasworks, blast-furnaces and acid-towers polluted the neighbourhood of industrial centres and the economy of operation varied widely between one region and another. Conversely the scientific mind turned more naturally to the problems suggested in the logic of its own evolution than to those arising out of economic activity. Faraday's metallurgical researches offer an unusual instance to the contrary, while later Pasteur's life-work— the elimination of diseases afflicting the grape-vine, domestic animals, and man—had a directly utilitarian significance. Here there was a field of research in which the area of contact between science and craft was already broad. In others the organisation to enable industry to profit from scientific progress was inadequate, though it already existed in technical colleges, like the great French École Polytechnique, mining schools and many private undertakings. In 1850 Prince Albert, echoing Bacon, could speak of science as discovering the laws of power, motion and transformation, by which the Almighty governs his creation, and of industry as applying them to the abundant raw materials which knowledge alone renders valuable; to a later generation the Great Exhibition of 1851 is conspicuous as the culmination of empirical technology. Science seems as yet to have entered only into the heavy-chemical industry (there were no synthetic manufactures), the preparation of a long list of vegetable products (including rubber and collodion), and the new arts of photography and electric telegraphy, to which the dynamo and arc-lamp may be added as curiosities. The displacement of coal and iron by oil and steel is not even hinted at in the manufactures of 1851.

Yet in a minor degree most aspects of life were revealing the influence of the scientific attitude by 1870. Better hygiene helped to reduce infant mortality and the incidence of epidemic disease; the outbreaks of cholera ravaging Europe from 1831 to as late as 1893 strikingly emphasised the socio-medical importance of clean water supplies and of rational sanitary legislation. Agricultural science had begun to filter into farming as the problem of soil fertility was taken up with some success. A few new ventures in commerce had sprung from scientific discoveries or owed their success directly to the adoption of scientific principles. The traditional chemical industries had been transformed by greater demands for alkalis, mineral acids and dyestuffs which only the use of novel processes and materials enabled them to satisfy. In addition new chemical preparations were gradually coming into use: artificial fertilisers, aniline dyes, nitro-explosives, chloroform, carbolic acid were the fruit of laboratory experiment, showing moreover, in the generally long interval between discovery and its useful application, the isolation in which research was still conducted. The synthetic-chemical industry, in which both Perkin, the discoverer of the first aniline dye, and Hofmann, his master (whom the Prince Consort had brought from Germany to teach the new organic chemistry) were engaged, from the first required scientific management. Disinterested research in organic chemistry had forged the links which bound these new manufactures to the gas-light industry which had been founded in the older empirical fashion at the opening of the century. Between 1830 and 1870 methods were worked out in the laboratory to give the coal-gas its highest luminous value, to remove impurities and utilise these by-products in other industries. Ammonia, with benzol and other ingredients of coal-tar, was becoming an important article of commerce, but still, outside

Germany, practice lagged far behind theory.[1] The preparation of rubber, gutta-percha and hydraulic cement are other examples of manufactures which were recognised, in the 1851 Exhibition, as being of some importance, as a result of a combination of elementary science and technical skill. The electric-telegraph industry was born of the discoveries of Oersted and Faraday and was developed by scientists of distinction, like Wheatstone, Siemens and Thomson, who also possessed a strong practical talent. High technical ability was needed to overcome the difficulties that increased with the length of the wires, and to design the delicate instruments which, again, only scientific instrument-makers could manufacture. These firms, also, found their business expanding soon after the middle of the century, as the profitable uses for measuring and analytical equipment of all sorts were exploited—perhaps the surest indication of the incipient spread of science into industry. Where there was no strong technological tradition already entrenched, science was serving the needs of entrepreneurs who were far-sighted enough to appreciate its potentialities. Yet the opportunities to carry out the detailed investigations by which scientific principles are made to serve useful ends were still limited, though less severely in Germany than elsewhere.

Rationalisation in industry had begun. Rationalism in philosophy, with a distinct tendency to admire and emulate the works of science, is an older movement that may be traced back to Helvetius, Locke and Descartes. The current was widened and deepened by the nineteenth-century philosophers of the utilitarian school, Jeremy Bentham, the elder and the younger Mill. Rationalists were impressed by the success of mechanistic science in explaining the phenomena of nature (the *natural* philosophers had not generally been deflected thereby from the accepted canons of religion and morality), which they transmuted into such doctrines as the dependence of ideas upon the nature of sense-perceptions received, and, although most of the facts and illustrations that could usefully be drawn from exact science had already been absorbed before this period, the model of scientific reasoning was still before their eyes. The utilitarian, like the scientist, withdrew his attention from final causes in order to apply himself to immediate concerns—the nature of human behaviour and the derivation of the greatest benefits from social organisation. Bentham's doctrine of utility, like Helvetius' hedonism, demanded that the measure of efficiency be applied to the state and the individual. The question: how can society most efficiently ensure general and individual happiness? has a scientific ring. Significantly, the subject which the utilitarians themselves developed, political economy, was becoming known as a 'science'; the mechanism of society was being subjected to the same type of precise (and, increasingly, mathematical) analysis that had

---

[1] In 1870 the Bradford gasworks was paying £800 per annum for the disposal of its wastes; in 1878 it was offered £10,000 per annum for the purchase of the same materials.

triumphed in physical inquiries. Thus Malthus had stated his famous proposition in an exact numerical form (1798); he was not content merely to declare that populations tend to increase faster than their means of subsistence. And the student of the actual, rather than the ideal, state was naturally led to conclude that his own reflections, as well as the policies of those charged with government, could only be founded surely upon a discussion of a mass of facts concerning population, trade or justice collected with scientific rigour and detachment. The administration of the state was indeed not an art but a science. Of the influence of these doctrines on the business of government during the mid-nineteenth century, when they became a part of the general consciousness and the subject of political dispute, of the standard of efficiency as applied to law, finance and economic policy this is not the place to speak. If the changing structure of society was the deep cause of the changing character of government, political philosophies whose evolution had in turn been moulded by the influence of scientific thought suggested the forms which social pressure assumed.

Admiration for science as a purely intellectual fabric is made explicit in the positive philosophy of Auguste Comte, for whom the scientific was the only type of certain knowledge. For him physical science had risen to the third or positive state of learning, devoid of all theological and metaphysical complexion, in which understanding a phenomenon meant a knowledge of its relations to all other phenomena, under generalised laws. Comte urged the study of the history of science as revealing the progress of the sole true learning in comparison with which the history of philosophy was but a record of man's dreams and aberrations. His conception, grandly organic, assembled all intellectual achievement into a single corpus of knowledge of an ascending order of complexity, the laws of the more complex sciences resting upon the laws of the less, from the most general and abstract theorems of mathematics to biology and finally the study of human society. His own endeavour was to elevate sociology to the positive state, to educe the laws of human behaviour with their verification in history and psychology, and to make an exact science of the natural history of man by the use of those methods which had been defined in physical science. And for J. S. Mill, as for Comte, the application of this perfected system of thought and investigation to philosophy or 'moral science' was not prohibited by the very different character of its problems and ends. 'The proper study of mankind' might become positive, propounding universal and demonstrative truth, if 'the same process through which the laws of many simpler phenomena have by general acknowledgment been placed beyond dispute,...be consciously and deliberately applied to those more difficult enquiries.'[1] Following Comte in striking out a new course in sociology, parallel to

[1] John Stuart Mill, *A System of Logic* (7th edn, London, 1868), vol. II, p. 414.

that upon which he believed the physical sciences to be already defini- tively entered, Mill sought to draw the broad lines of a scientific deductive logic in moral and social thinking.

Within the positivist philosophy, Comte, the author of a religion of humanity in which material benefactors replaced the hierarchy of saints, emphasised the moral element in human life. Other minds looked to a happier future ushered in by technological versatility and mechanical social adjustments. Evolution, in society as in science, was the dominant concept of the latter part of the period. Liberals eagerly sought to accelerate the progress they believed to be inevitable. Socialism also developed an evolutionary interpretation of the broad course of history. In its earliest stages socialism had an idealist adumbration inherited from the French Revolution, but in the hands of Marx and Engels, despite the legacy of Hegel, it became the most extreme of rationalist doctrines. The weight of science (or rather, positivism) in Marxist philosophy is best seen in the particular theses by which the general dialectic was supported. In *Das Kapital* Marx deduced laws that had determined the development of the existing economic order, and would equally bring about its dis- solution. In the economic interpretation of history—very different from the rigorous historiography that another facet of the influence of science was helping to create—similar laws are given a wider range, while Engels utilised recent anthropological findings to buttress the socialist theory of the archaic evolution of society from its primitive institution, the family. In human affairs Marx's deterministic laws resembled Newton's laws of motion; if they were correct they admitted no intervention of chance or genius. Laplace had boasted that given the mass and motion of the particles in the universe, its destiny was infinitely calculable; in the same spirit Marx maintained that in the ownership of the means of production the whole history and structure of a society, even to its arts and sciences, was determined. Mechanistic sociology had followed upon mechanistic science.

While philosophers were interpreting the astonishing triumphs of science in their various ways, the organic growth of natural knowledge was con- tinuing, its stages not always confirming the assertions of those who tried to extract the quintessence of scientific thought for use in other disciplines. Fundamental assumptions were called in question, and the tendency was towards less rather than greater determinism. The complexity of nature belied the more dogmatic utterances of an earlier period. The unforeseen importance of an unconsidered dimension—time—began to work upon the structure of both physical and biological theory, giving the latter especially renewed interest and power. The interdependence of the various branches of science (accurately discerned by Comte) became yearly more evident, the effect being to increase rather than lessen the fragmentation of research. Studies on the frontiers between the sciences, in theoretical physics, physical chemistry and biochemistry, were more intensively cultivated, and helped to strengthen the internal consistency of science by causing the same concepts (such as those of thermodynamics, or atomism) to prevail in all or many of its branches.

The further exploitation of mathematical analysis was a prime instance of this process. Pure mathematics developed its modern character in this period. While existing modes of mathematical thought were extended—masters of an earlier age (Cauchy in France, Gauss in Germany) remaining active to the 'fifties—not less importance attaches to profound innovations. Hamilton of Dublin laid the foundations of the theory of operators and vectors; the Russian Lobatchevsky, the two Bolyais in Hungary, and the German Riemann initiated the study of geometries based upon non-Euclidean postulates; Hamilton, Grassmann, and Boole were pioneers of non-commutative algebras. The last-named, in the *Laws of Thought* (1854), has a claim to be the father of modern symbolic logic. These were all heterodox offshoots from the main stem of mathematics, comparatively little regarded, and apparently of the most highly speculative nature. Yet it was to this type of mathematics that theoretical physics returned at the end of the century. Meanwhile contemporary physics was bringing mathematical analysis from the branches such as mechanics and optics in which it was already established to the study of gases and electricity. A vital movement of research from the macrophysical problems of celestial mechanics to the microphysical problems of the structure of matter required a new type of mathematical equipment which was created by the use of statistical methods put into exact form in Gauss's work on probability (*c.* 1800). For instance, in the investigations of Maxwell, Boltzmann and others into the kinetic theory of gases, it was not possible to observe or calculate the motion of a single molecule, but by means of complex statistical calculations it was possible for its probable motion to be inferred from the known properties of the mass. The non-physical sciences partly owed their emergence from a purely descriptive stage to the adoption of similar procedures. Mendel's interpretation of his experiments on the hybridisation of plants (published in 1869, but ignored till 1900), which established the primary laws of genetics, is of a truly statistical type though the mathematics involved are elementary; and so, less precisely, is Darwin's hypothesis of natural selection.

Before considering the progress of theoretical physics it is necessary to mention the empirical discoveries. Michael Faraday stands out in the nineteenth century as an experimenter of unsurpassed genius. Following-up Oersted's observation (1820) of the magnetic field surrounding a conductor, Faraday at last obtained the converse effect in 1831, when he detected the changing electro-motive force in a conductor lying across a changing magnetic field. After this the other leading phenomena of induction were rapidly revealed and his fame was assured. By 1850 the bases of electrical science were secure; new concepts such as potential, dielectric capacity and resistance were firmly defined in spite of the lack of delicate instruments and metrology which continued until long after Faraday's death in 1867. Much of this painstaking investigation was pursued in Germany, and is immortally linked with the name of Ohm. Of the industrially useful properties of electricity, heating and electrolysis had been known since the beginning of the century. The intraconversion of electrical and mechanical energy had been demonstrated. With this the electric telegraph, long projected, became a practical proposition, taken up rapidly by the railways before 1850, and soon made available for public use. In 1858 the first abortive transatlantic link was attempted. Since an efficient design of electric motor and generator could not spring at once from first principles, the consumption of electric power was still tiny in 1870. The distributive and other technical merits of electricity in industry were not obvious, and to many, including Joule of Manchester, whose experiments (1840–50) gave the quantitative relations between electrical and other forms of energy, heat-engines seemed considerably more economic.

The theoretical interpretation of the empirical work in electricity was of the first importance both in the purest scientific sense and in the applications which in turn flowed from it. Faraday was no great mathematician; instead he framed a vivid imagery of the play of electro-magnetic forces. His picture demanded an ether, an elastic medium of transmission in which the 'lines of force' became lines of strain. Although etherial hypotheses were very old, physicists had tended to gloss over the problem of the action of a force (such as gravity) at a distance across empty space, about which Newton himself had been discreetly silent. It was revived more acutely (about 1820) by the victory of the wave theory of light, for a vacuum could not be supposed to undulate. Faraday's ether seemed, however, unable to submit to the quantitative treatment that was necessary, or to yield the comprehensive generalisations embracing the phenomena of magnetism, electricity and light that were sought.[1] More conventional mathematical hypotheses also failed. At last, starting from Faraday's ideas and admitting to the Royal Society that Faraday's theory was 'the same in structure as that which I have begun to develop', Clerk Maxwell demonstrated mathematically in papers published between 1864 and 1868 that as a line of force spreads outwards from a centre of disturbance it travels as an electromagnetic wave, with the electric and magnetic components at right angles as they are in a conductor, having a velocity equal to that of light. Maxwell concluded that light is in fact such an electro-magnetic wave, so that a single ether with a given set of properties could in his equations be used to account for the propagation of all such forces. Certain consequences followed from the theory which

[1] The action of a magnetic field upon light was demonstrated by Faraday in 1845.

could be, and were, experimentally verified; finally in 1887 Herz detected the electro-magnetic waves created by a spark-discharge.

The study of radiations was becoming an established department of physics as the physical similarity of the causes of the physiological sensations of light and heat was worked out. Radiations outside the visible spectrum could be brought under the scope of Maxwell's theory. Faraday and others were experimenting on discharges within vacuum-tubes at high potentials—the first step to atomic physics. But the main advance in this period was towards the perfection of spectrum analysis. The primary observation that incandescent elements emit characteristic bright lines in their spectra was about a century old when the researches of Bunsen and Kirchhoff (c. 1855) gave to spectroscopy a firm position in analytical technique. Somewhat grander possibilities were disclosed by Foucault's identification (1849) of some of the bright lines in the spectra of elements with the Fraunhofer *dark* lines in the spectrum of the sun. The coincidence of these lines was accounted for a decade later by Kirchhoff and others in an hypothesis derived from thermodynamical reasoning (since confirmed by electron theory) showing that light of the appropriate frequencies was absorbed by elements present in the sun's periphery. As in the laboratory the spectroscope took its place beside the balance, so in the observatory it became an indispensable instrument of precision, second in importance in modern times to the giant reflecting telescope of which the prototype, with a 72-inch metallic mirror, was set up by Lord Rosse at Parsonstown, Ireland, in 1845. Spectroscopy revealed the composition of many stars as well as that of the sun, their temperature and their proper motions. The big telescope and its adjuncts brought in a new astronomy whose exponents became increasingly confident in their own opinions on the past and future of the universe. Astrophysics faced, cosmically, the same questions about the nature and history of matter which were becoming the most important subjects of physical inquiry.

In this, and other ways to be mentioned later, science was led to declare its own universal chronology. Whatever the hypothesis, whether it was assumed that the cosmos had been wound up in some great act of creation, or had evolved mechanistically in accordance with one of the possible variants of the nebula hypothesis, it seemed certain that it was not static, but was undergoing a steady process of equipartition of energy which must end in a motionless state of uniform temperature. Ultimate stagnation was stated by Thomson to be an inevitable consequence of the operation of thermodynamical laws as early as 1852; it was a doctrine that religious beliefs might rather suggest than oppose. The physical time-scale as then calculated (notably, in ignorance of radio-active phenomena) was far too brief to accommodate the vast epochs of slow transformation of species which evolutionary biology required, and which the geologists also were not disposed to deny, and these differences remained in dispute.

But by whatever means the duration of the solar system was computed, the attempt is important for its recognition of a limit in science, the irreversibility of a one-way process. Other limits imposed by the pattern of nature and not by logical or experimental inadequacies were being discovered, the first to be clearly apprehended being absolute zero, the ultimate degree of cold (1848). Of wider significance was the limitation or conservation of energy.

The term 'energy' has already been used in contexts where it is strictly anachronistic, since the exactly defined concept was unknown before 1851. At the beginning of the period the physics of heat was in confusion, for conventional opinion, including that of the strong French school, favoured the material theory which considered heat as an impalpable fluid flowing down temperature gradients; the kinetic theory, whose clearest evidence was the unlimited quantity of heat produced by mechanical friction, had failed to command general assent. The issues were hard fought in the decade 1840–50, which saw the complete triumph of thermodynamics. The development of the principle of the conservation of energy must be distinguished from that of the general kinetic theory. In 1824 a French engineer, Sadi Carnot, had examined the efficiency with which motive power could be obtained from a source of heat, taking as his example a perfect heat-engine in which work is done by the expansion and contraction of a gas without loss. By proving that otherwise a finite quantity of heat can be made to do infinite work, Carnot showed that the 'motive power' obtainable from heat is independent of all considerations save the difference in temperature of the two bodies between which heat is transferred—for example the boiler and condenser of a steam-engine. Carnot's principle did not commit him to the kinetic theory, which, however, he expressed in unpublished notes of 1830, and it became better known in a material form. The material theory failed to explain how work was done by an expanding gas; the kinetic theory could not be established till it had been demonstrated that the heat lost by the gas was not latent but had been *converted* into mechanical energy. The conversion of energy at constant equivalencies was investigated experimentally by Mayer (1842) and Joule (from 1843): after the first complete and satisfactory account of thermodynamics due to Helmholtz (1847), Clausius, Rankine and Thomson elaborated the framework of mathematical equations, which were firmly embodied in physical science. The two so-called Laws of Thermodynamics are really derivable from Carnot's principle (and indeed from the *reductio ad absurdum* of perpetual motion): the energy within a closed system is constant and becomes unavailable when the system reaches equilibrium, and it cannot be conserved by any means of reversing the natural flow of heat from a hot body to a cold.

Thermodynamics was partly called into existence by the study of the working steam-engine, but the science had hardly begun to have a return effect upon technology before the end of the period. It is interesting also that despite this link, much was owing to two Germans who were primarily physiologists, Mayer and Helmholtz. A new theory of energy was in the general consciousness, and was necessary to the progress of several departments of science. Even so, the pioneers of thermodynamics were granted but cursory attention before 1847; indifference was probably due partly to logical difficulties arising from the strange general concept of energy (for which no name then existed in the vocabulary of science) and the confusion between the two theories of heat, partly also to the technical delicacy of experiments to demonstrate precise equivalence. But by 1870 physics had been transformed into a unitary science, the study of a single dynamism in nature in which the phenomena of mechanics, electricity, heat and light were parallel manifestations of a single duality, matter and energy. If the universe was a closed system—and such was the assumption—then the general deduction of a single irreversible sequence and of a final state in which the processes of nature would cease through the equipartition of energy was inevitable. Physics seemed able to foretell the doom of creation.

Through thermodynamics (soon applied to the study of chemical reactions), electro-chemistry and other points of contact the physical or kinetic and the chemical or atomistic investigations of nature were brought to meet and gradually amalgamate. The revival of atomic theory by Dalton (1808) in a quantitative form had no immediate influence upon physics and even at the opening of this period many chemists doubted whether it was more than a convenient fiction. The mathematical physicist was gradually induced to take a particulate view of matter in treating (for instance) the properties of a gas in accordance with the empirical laws of Boyle and Charles, and thermodynamical ideas also prompted a return to Bernoulli's early kinetic theory of gases (1738). In the following decade experimental investigations substantiated it further. Statistical methods in mathematics provided a suitable technique for theoretical study, and predictions based upon the theory were found to be confirmed. By 1862 'the theory of gases being little bodies flying about', as Maxwell described it, had been raised at least to the level of a probable hypothesis by his own labours and those of Helmholtz and Clausius. But a unification of physical and chemical atomic theory, necessary for the full validity of either, was still prevented by the fact that certain constants, which could be determined independently by physical and chemical methods, showed a puzzling discordance. This was removed only when, after 1860, chemists accepted the force of Avogadro's molecular hypothesis. Since 1845 attempts, little regarded, had been made to calculate the probable velocities and masses of the individual 'atoms' (really molecules) of gases. Events between 1860 and 1870 made it certain that during the next period of science the main task of chemistry would be to penetrate the mechanisms by which the fundamental particles are linked into molecules, which are the units of compound substances, while physics would be occupied in an examination of their properties and behaviour.

The consolidation of atomic theory had been the chief concern of inorganic chemists since 1830, by which time the list of common elements was complete. Analytical chemistry was already sufficiently advanced, and being steadily refined, so that it was normally possible to determine the *proportions* of the elements in a compound; the problem was to discover what these proportions signified in terms of relative *numbers* of atoms, and this required a knowledge of their relative *weights*. Moreover it was soon realised that all the atoms of one element in a compound are not necessarily included in a single group, but may be divided among two or more having independent linkages with the other elements in the combination, and therefore the pattern of the linkages became important. As Dalton's theory conceived of the atom as the normal free unit of matter, experimental results became conflicting when elements were investigated in the gaseous state and in combination, since the particles of most gases are not atoms, but molecules; and Dalton had been unable to suggest any reliable means of ascertaining whether combinations of atoms were simple (one-to-one) or complex (one-to-two; two-to-two, etc.). Amidst these difficulties the work of measuring atomic weights and ascribing atomic formulae resembled a complicated piece of cryptography which could command slight confidence. However, the Swedish chemist Berzelius compiled a table of atomic weights which compares tolerably with those now accepted; he also introduced the symbolism of modern chemistry and derived correctly the formulae of many of the simpler organic compounds. He gave currency to an electro-chemical hypothesis which shows the influence of contemporary physics, supposing that the atoms of each element (and atomic groups, or radicals) were endowed with a characteristic charge, so that their affinities were a result of differences in polarity. But the methods in use were devious and depended largely on making analogies with the simplest compounds. Many chemists regarded the whole matter of atomic weights as speculative, and distrusted the use of numerical formulae which varied according to the opinions of the user. Even towards the middle of the century it was by no means certain that the whole atomic theory would not collapse under the weight of its own inconsistencies.

The confusion was naturally greatest with respect to the more complex organic compounds in which the molecules are composed of many atoms of different elements. Early organic analyses had been made by Lavoisier, and Dalton had attempted some application of his theory to organic substances. It was recognised that they consist very largely of the four elements carbon, hydrogen, nitrogen and oxygen; methods of estimating the proportions of the elements in combination were improved by

Berzelius and Liebig, the phenomena of isomorphism and isomerism[1] were known. As the molecules of the three gases are bi-atomic, the atomic weights in use varied by a factor of two (C = 6 or 12; O = 8 or 16). Electrochemical dualism imposed a somewhat arbitrary pattern on the notions of the processes by which more complex compounds are synthesised in the laboratory from the less. While theory was in doubt, empirical work proceeded. The first great triumph was Wöhler's synthesis of urea, an excretory product, in 1828. This seemed a trenchant blow against the vitalist belief that biological substances could never be artificially prepared. More interesting from the point of view of theory were the chains of compounds discovered during the next ten years in which a stable radical served as a peg to which other atoms or groups could be attached. A pattern was emerging; it seemed that 'in inorganic chemistry the radicals are simple; in organic chemistry they are compounds, that is the sole difference' (Dumas and Liebig, 1837). The number of preparations synthesised was growing enormously; some were to prove useful.

Within the next twenty years the growing mass of detailed research outgrew the generalisations which chemical theory was capable of framing. Dualism and the simple radical theory proved inadequate; elaborations of the latter, due on the one hand to the French school (Dumas, Gerhardt, Laurent), and to the German (Liebig, Wöhler, Wurtz, Hofmann), with which English organic chemistry was closely allied, on the other, were inconclusively argued. Through the perplexing alternations of the theory of combination and the confusion of atomic weights it is possible to see that the problems at issue—the pattern of atomic structure within the molecule, and the reasons why certain arrangements only are possible or stable—were being visualised with greater clearness. The theory of valency, originated by the English chemist Frankland in 1852 and largely perfected by Kekulé, a German who worked for a time in London, had by 1865 classified the elements numerically according to their combining-powers, that is, according to the number of hydrogen atoms with which an atom of the element enters into combination. In that year Kekulé also gave the famous ring-formula for benzene, showing the multiple bonds between the six carbon and the six hydrogen atoms within the molecule. This first step in 'molecular architecture' was soon extended to other so-called 'aromatic' compounds.

Valency offered another useful criterion for the determination of atomic weights. At the Karlsruhe Conference (1860), summoned to resolve the doubts still obscuring this fundamental of chemical theory, it had been impossible to reach a satisfactory convention; but the Italian Canizzaro had revived with new force the molecular hypothesis of his countryman

[1] The same number of atoms, similarly arranged, producing the same crystalline form in two substances; the same proportions of the same elements producing two chemically distinct substances

Avogadro, which was further promulgated by Meyer in an important work of 1864. With the concept of the molecule, not the atom, as the least free particle of matter discrepancies were removed and atomic theory was placed upon a secure quantitative foundation. The atomic weights derived by inorganic methods could now be reconciled with those that the organic chemist had accepted, and, as already mentioned, chemical atomism was by the same adjustment brought to agree with the kinetic theory of physics.

The first three-dimensional molecular patterns, worked out by Le Bel and van t'Hoff, fall just outside this period, though their history begins in 1848 with Pasteur's discovery of optical isomers, two substances of identical composition but with different properties and forming crystals which are mirror-images of each other. Pasteur had already attributed this phenomenon to an asymmetry of atomic arrangement. The notion of spatial chemistry was not sympathetically received, and endeavour to discern some logical order in the table of the elements also awaited its full vindication after 1870. Early attempts to correlate properties and atomic weights inspired by some obvious family likenesses, such as that of Newlands in 1865, were treated with contempt. The reasoned and demonstrative statements of the periodic law made by Mendeléef and Meyer (1869–71) subdued scepticism, which was finally overcome through the isolation of the elements whose existence Mendeléef had predicted. Theoretical explanation of the law was awaited for more than a generation, and came from the development of atomic physics. As these last instances suggest, pragmatism was strong among even the chemical theorists of the time. This was only in part due to a healthy reluctance to frame hypotheses, for numerous 'laws' and 'types' of combination were announced and rejected, arising rather from an excessive preoccupation with the synthetic aspect of chemical technique. Organic chemistry had become the largest and most important branch of the science, but while organic chemists were acquiring greater operative powers for transforming substances and constructing molecules, they were in danger of losing sight of the fundamental study of matter which was the intellectual justification of their work.

The new artifices of organic chemistry were already affecting society in their applications to medicine, manufacture and war. The raw materials of the old chemical industry had been salt, alum, vitriols, and a great variety of vegetables used in the preparation of dyes and drugs. From wood, coal, nitrates and sulphur organic chemistry fabricated a variety of natural and artificial products. Although some large industries such as tanning and pottery-making continued their traditional processes untouched by science, techniques borrowed from chemistry were becoming more usual. Electrolysis, from which the plating industries grew up, had been discovered by Davy in 1807; catalysis, which has effected economies by speeding industrial reactions, by Berzelius in 1836. With the theory of radicals the modern pattern of laboratory synthesis and commercial exploitation begins to emerge, though the earlier workers were comparatively little interested in the useful properties of the many thousands of substances they examined. Delays in application were due less to this factor than to the ignorance and conservatism of those who ought to have cherished improvements. Chloroform was discovered in 1831; its use as an anaesthetic by Simpson in Edinburgh followed sixteen years later. Carbolic acid was discovered in 1834; its power to prevent putrefaction was vaguely known, but its systematic use as an antiseptic waited thirty years. Sodium salicylate was prepared in 1860; the useful medicament aspirin was marketed only in 1899. On the whole the most useful adaptations from science were those which gave scope to an inventor and a patent. Thus the peaceful uses of cellulose began with the mercerisation of cotton (1857) and the invention of celluloid (1869). Gun-cotton had already been discovered in 1846. Through industry, science offered to the lower middle-class, whose purchasing power was becoming enormous in the manufacturing state, substitutes for commodities like silk which nature could never provide in vast quantity: wood-pulp paper (c. 1860) instead of rag, which made the mass newspaper possible, margarine instead of butter (this last becoming a manufacture in the late 1870's). These were new articles for which the market was open among the poor, and there were others whose sale justified the scientific treatment of manufacture, such as the brewing of beer. There were many more whose methods and products were capable of improvement, had taste or habit not kept demand at a low level. The soap industry, for example, only grew to the factory scale with domestic plumbing and a fresh attitude to hygiene. For the same reason, while Gregory's powder and the black draught continued as household remedies, there was little change in the pharmaceutical branch of the chemical industry. Pharmacy was coming under the control of a few manufacturing drug-houses which naturally followed the leadership of the medical profession, but the great transformation of the pharmacopoeia, which owes much to the chemical research of this period, took place after it. Yet it was in a futile attempt to synthesise quinine that Perkin accidentally came across the first aniline dye, mauve (1856). In a short time the aniline-dye industry rose to a considerable magnitude, its activity thereafter stimulating renewed investigation. Given the clue, other synthetic dyestuffs were rapidly prepared; alizarin, the pigment of the madder plant, was synthesised in 1869, and indigo in 1870. Vegetable dyes were variable, expensive and restricted, and their cultivation was quickly ruined. The synthetic dyes, combining a wider range of unblended colours with more exact control, offered an opportunity to the textile industry which at first was used with more acumen than taste.

Towards the middle of the period it became possible to extend the empirical revolution in agricultural techniques which had begun in England a century before by applying chemical and physiological knowledge to the cultivation of plants. The nitrogen cycle and the photosynthetic formation of sugar were already partly understood. Pioneers like Wiegmann, Sprengel and Boussingault had already established the necessity for restoring to the soil mineral constituents taken up by the plant, the doctrine which the more popular writings of Liebig on agricultural chemistry disseminated. The first artificial fertilisers to be used were phosphates, manufactured from 1842, but later found in 'basic slag' from the phosphoric iron-ores used in the Bessemer and open-hearth steel processes. Ammoniacal liquors from gasworks were also taken to the fields before they were sold to the dye factories, but popular theory paid insufficient attention to the presence of nitrogen in the soil. Nitrates from the Chile beds were not used in quantity until after 1870. Fortunately the burden of supporting a larger population was not to descend wholly on agricultural science, since Europe had for many years consumed grain, and was now consuming other foodstuffs, from the American continent where farming methods were mechanically progressive and scientifically primitive.

Many problems of plant nourishment, especially that of nitrogen fixation from the atmosphere, could be understood only through the progress of microbiology, which began as a science in close association with organic chemistry and chemical industry. Pasteur, whose genius was responsible for nearly all the advance in this direction during the period, passed on from a study of the tartaric acids to the processes of fermentation in general, which could be regarded as a series of chemical reactions now that the composition of sugar, alcohol and acetic acid were known. Wine-makers and brewers were saved much loss by his investigation of ferments and his method of arresting degeneration by a gentle heat (pasteurisation). Pasteur was a strong vitalist in science, indeed his only difference with his friend Claude Bernard was on this point, and his philosophy determined the nature of his work, with its portentous influence. Fermentation occurs only in the presence of yeast, known since 1838 to consist of a mass of minute vegetable cells, and Pasteur vehemently opposed the mechanical or inorganic hypothesis of the ferment's action put forward by Berzelius and Liebig (a crude version of the theory which has been adopted since the discovery of enzymes); for him the synthesis of alcohol was inseparable from the life-process of the yeast. From this he went on to make a far-reaching analogy between fermentation and putrefaction, which was universally believed to take place spontaneously in dead organic matter. Pasteur asserted that nothing could putrefy unless living agents were introduced into it, an assertion which provoked sharp controversy and was demonstrated (from 1859) by experiments in which putrefiable materials were kept wholesome in heat-sterilised vessels protected from contamination by air-borne dust.

Pasteur's victory was hastened by his practical success in combating silk-worm disease and the phylloxera of the vineyards about 1865, but the great age of bacteriology in which the name of Koch is joined with that of Pasteur opened after 1870. The germ-theory of disease, justified by Pasteur's experiments on putrefaction, was a magnificent gift to humanity. Philosophically, however, vitalism had been a retarding influence in medical science since at the points where scientific inquiry was most necessary it interjected into orderly notions of cause and effect a mysterious and unanalysable life-force which was supposed to mark an absolute distinction in nature. In the mid-nineteenth century there was a reaction, and of the leaders of experimental physiology only Müller was a vitalist; in Germany Ludwig and Schwann, in France Magendie and Bernard, inclined to the opposite school. With the more forceful means of research offered by chemistry and powerful achromatic microscopes they applied themselves to the detailed examination of mechanisms: the tracing of a stimulus through the nervous system to the consequent muscular contraction or glandular secretion; the rendering available of food for the restoration of tissues and conversion into energy. Some problems demanded a finer technique for uncovering structures and testing their functions, such as Bell's and Magendie's work on sensory and motor nerves; empiricism was coming into its own. Others required a wider scientific perspective. Helmholtz's excellent study of sense-perception, combining physics and anatomy, is an example of this, but more striking still were Bernard's researches on metabolism which led him to one of the great early achievements of biochemistry. In 1846 he demonstrated the function of the pancreatic juice in splitting neutral fats into fatty acids and glycerine; in 1857 he isolated the carbohydrate glycogen, the form in which sugar is stored in the liver. He was also the first to recognise internal secretions and to examine their control through the nerves.

The discovery of glycogen broke down an old distinction between plant physiology, in which substances such as cellulose are built up from their inorganic constituents, and animal physiology, which was regarded as destructive, by showing that the animal body is also capable of synthesis. Apart from the theoretical and medical significance of these researches, they induced consideration of the body as an integrated organism whose parts are interrelated and their functions balanced. The nervous system could be seen not merely as the means of communication with the environment and of effecting volitions, but as the mechanism by which the temperature, secretions and general working of the body are regulated. The discovery and synthesis of the highly complex substances prepared by the body and on which its activities depend was begun. The old metaphysical problems of the nature of life were thrust farther back by science, as long chains of mechanism, each in itself subject to the normal laws of causality, were revealed.

At an even finer level of detail physiology faced the problems of the growth and viability of living tissue, which were brought within the general compass of cell theory, whose development sprang from the removal of technical limitations. About 1830 the achromatic microscope became a practicable instrument giving high magnification and good resolution; ten years later methods of staining sections, and towards 1870 microtomes for cutting them, were introduced. For centuries particular aspects of these problems had been discussed in embryology, and the egg as a special kind of cell retained its importance in cytology, though as yet the mechanism of inheritance (to which the theory of evolution gave fresh importance) was beyond investigation. Knowledge of cellular structure was more highly developed for plants than for animals when in 1831 the botanist Robert Brown discovered the nuclei of cells, and Schleiden in 1838 represented the plant as a community of cells. Schwann (1839) further generalised the theory and laid down the concept of the cell as the universal unit in the animal and vegetable kingdoms. The observation of cell-division followed soon after, and the distinction of the parts of the cell itself by von Mohl and Nägeli. Histology had its own complexities; from work on unicellular organisms and the discovery of many different types of cell it gradually became apparent that no simple theory of these structural units was possible. Virchow, moreover, stressed (1858) the importance of pathological cells in disease, and like Pasteur and others who advocated the theory that micro-organisms were the cause of disease, argued strongly against spontaneous generation. When the classical definition of the cell, and the modern scope of cell theory in physiological thought were given by Schültze in 1861, the difficulties encountered in a biological doctrine of discontinuous structure seemed at least as great as those which faced atomic theory in physical science. And though the cruder notions of vitalism had disappeared by 1870, in cytology and microbiology the mysteries of the living state were still almost as obscure as they had been on the organic scale to the older physiologists.

The progress of experimental biology, standing apart from the main line of development of natural history, took place mainly in France and Germany. The English contribution was a formative concept growing directly out of the study of natural history which deflected and enriched every branch of biology. The memoirs by Darwin and Wallace, read to the Linnean Society in 1858, in which the theory of evolution by natural selection was first expounded, followed by the publication of the *Origin of Species*, appeared as a cataclysmic break with all sound thinking. It is now obvious that the scientific propositions which mid-Victorian Englishmen greeted with horror and alarm because they reflected upon the unique dignity of man and the literal truth of the Bible as a revelation of divine actions were the counterparts of the idea of progress which filled their thoughts with complacency. The study of history had endowed the concept of change, development, elaboration and specialisation with a central interest and adopted most naturally the metaphor of *growth*; the historical contrast between the contemporary state of civilisation and that of the past inspired a sense that the growth of arts, sciences and manufactures had been beneficent and would endure. This assumption was rejected only by a minority of romantics who, like Carlyle and Ruskin, distrusted the scientific movement and its fruits. The dynamic view of history impinged upon the cognate study of society, and upon science. It suggested that a static account of things as they are, incomplete because it ignores their coming into being and their passage into futurity, is even more vitally deficient because it ignores the very fact that what is observed is fluid and transitory. The introduction of time as a dimension in physics and astronomy has already been mentioned, and biology demanded a similar reform of its principles.

In one branch indeed, palaeontology, the obstinate retention of the static picture of the universe in deference to biological theory subjected the evidence to such violence of interpretation that geologists seem to have followed Darwin's lead almost with relief. The hypothesis that fossils were relics of the flood or tests of man's credulity was already threadbare in 1830, and geology was in any case assigning to the earth an age of the order of 100,000,000 years. The main techniques of the science had been worked out, the succession of strata and formations determined, and many parts of the world surveyed. Lyell, whose *Principles of Geology* (1830–3) was the authoritative treatise of the time, adopted the empirical principle that in renouncing early catastrophic theories of the formation of the earth's crust its configuration should be attributed solely to the same slow processes of elevation and depression, deposition and erosion, that operate still. Yet, following Cuvier, the father of palaeontology, who had ascribed the disappearance of extinct species to successive catastrophes, he controverted all theories that living ones had originated from those found only in fossilised remains, directing his arguments particularly against Lamarck. The earth had a history of evolution, but each species was an immediate creation.

The doctrine of the orthodox naturalist was simple. At the creation there were an original pair of each distinct species, which by breeding in pure lines had populated the earth with its extant flora and fauna. The grounds for this belief were not solely theological, but rested upon the concept of species which it had been a main task of the previous century to define. The members of a species formed a homogeneous group, distinguished according to precisely selected characteristics which, in the perfected system of the Swedish naturalist Linnaeus, mainly referred to the reproductive mechanism; the species again were grouped in genera, orders and higher classes. Linnaeus had recognised the necessary artificiality of any taxonomy, and thought that possibly the orders represented only created pairs, the species having diverged within them. But these cautions were lost upon many of his successors who ignored the vagueness of specific distinctions and exaggerated the criterion of interfertility as the touchstone of common specific descent. As Wallace remarked, the concept of species had become circular when it was founded on principles which were themselves justified as corresponding to the natural idea of species. That the principles were convenient, but indefensible as determinants of the whole logic of botany was not widely appreciated in 1859, and the obvious scientific argument against any theory of evolution was that plants or animals having a common ancestor, though evolving along diverging paths, must be interfertile: since distinct species were not, by definition, interfertile they could not share a common descent.

The concept of biological evolution was older than Darwin. To Linnaeus varieties, and possibly species, which always breed true, had evolved from a common stock. Erasmus Darwin in 1794, the French zoologist Lamarck in 1802, had emphasised the dynamic aspect of nature but, in finding the cause of divergent change in a plastic power of the organism to pass on to its posterity its own adaptations—the inheritance of acquired characteristics—they overstrained credulity. Herbert Spencer, preferring Lamarck to Lyell, was already developing the philosophy of evolution before 1859. In the intervening half-century the accumulation of the geological evidence with its enormous extension of the period of time in which evolutionary processes could be supposed to have been effective and the ascendancy of the historical outlook helped to prepare the way for Darwin; even more influential, however, was the mechanism of evolution which he developed. This postulated that organisms do not inherit parental modifications acquired in life, but found that the individuals of each generation do differ slightly among themselves: minute and random variations occur (which Darwin assumed to be of a genetical, that is, inheritable character), assisting or impeding the individual in the normal activities and functions of its species. Darwin adopted Malthus' law that populations increase faster than the means of their subsistence, inevitably causing a high mortality in each generation which only the fittest survive. The mid-nineteenth-century community well understood competition and the destruction of the feeble. Those individuals and their progeny that are best adapted to fill a given place in nature become specialised and diverge in type from their fellows, who either become extinct or are likewise adapted to some other manner of life. The operation of natural selection is frequently compared by Darwin to the artificial selection carried out by the breeder who allows only those individuals in each generation to reproduce which most nearly conform to the ideal type he has in mind, and who has by this means produced races of domestic animals of distinctive characteristics none of which closely resemble the wild species. Thus it was difficult for him to escape altogether the implications of teleology, though consciously he struggled against them, for it seems to be postulated that nature must purposefully adapt organisms to suit most efficiently each niche in the creation.

Darwin conceived his hypothesis of evolution early in his career as a naturalist, the long gestation of the *Origin of Species* being spent in the amassing of the detailed evidence upon which it could be represented as a plausible and consistent theory. He was well aware of the temerity of his thought and the strength of the opposition it would encounter. The marshalling of materials continued in successive volumes of which *The Descent of Man* (1871) was the most famous. The survey of the whole of natural history for this new purpose was a tremendous undertaking, and Darwin's genius is most surely revealed in the skill with which he handled a subject in which almost every word had been written from a point of view diametrically opposed to his own. To an astonishing extent he was forced to rely upon his own observations and experiments to provide him with the answers to the novel questions he proposed. He had to re-create the method of biological inquiry before he could expect a reform to follow from his theory. The comparative development of single structures; the sexual physiology of plants; behaviour in animals; the geographical distribution of species; the selective mechanism of inheritance; ecology and palaeontology in many of their aspects—all these were branches of science which Darwin originated in their modern form almost *de novo*, and welded into a harmonious synthesis. In particular he paid great attention to artificial selection, a subject which science had neglected in spite of its considerable economic importance in agriculture, learning the secrets of London pigeon-fanciers and comparing these morphologically very distinct races with the almost indistinguishable separate species of the naturalist. The study of genetics, however, was in such a primitive state that no conclusive argument could be offered against the orthodox criticism, and Darwin's somewhat loose reasoning on these problems has been unfavourably contrasted with Mendel's precise experiments on inheritance ten years later. On the whole perhaps the state of ignorance was more propitious for the theory of evolution than otherwise. Darwin anticipated many other objections raised by his critics, such as the preservation of the purity of incipient species in the natural state, or the problematic usefulness of a rudimentary and imperfect organ. These were among the least compelling portions of the *Origin of Species*, whose strength lay rather in the broad generalising power of the theory, for a great deal of work remained to be done in comparative and developmental studies before the course of evolution of the higher animals and plants could be adequately traced. Evolutionary modification of the cells of which the organism is composed is, of course, the necessary foundation for any sound doctrine of evolution, but though this might have been realised in 1860, the progress of cytology is in fact scarcely reflected in the early literature of Darwinism.

The furious tide of criticism and the scornful ridicule which greeted the *Origin of Species* are well known. The conflict was bitter, yet short in relation to the momentous issues involved, penetrating as they did to the roots of Christian civilisation. Among naturalists Hooker and Huxley were immediately converted to Darwin's view, and Lyell brought the geologists. Scientists generally had accepted Darwinism before the close of the period, but the initial criticism by such men as Agassiz, Owen and Sedgwick was by no means wholly occasioned by prejudice. There was enough weakness in parts of Darwin's argument for scientific scepticism to be reasonable, some of the early rejoinders being based upon the same type of argument that in more recent times has given rise to the declaration that Darwinism is outmoded. If the older sceptics clung to the more romantic philosophy of nature of which vitalism was also a manifestation, others like Kölliker in Germany attacked Darwin's theory not because it was evolutionary—various hypotheses of evolution, it was declared, were conceivable—but on account of its teleology, the lack of evidence of transitional forms, and the weak substantiation of its assumptions concerning inheritance. The palaeontological testimony for evolution had indeed hardly been declared in 1870, and the anthropological history of man was almost entirely unexplored. For the mass of Darwin's opponents who followed the leadership of Bishop Wilberforce it was the light which was reflected by his ideas upon the literal interpretation of scripture and the intricate metaphysical problems of the human soul which was most obnoxious. The hostility to science aroused in the Papacy by discussion of the Copernican cosmology had long been dormant and among Protestant peoples faith in science and religion had framed a single philosophy in which the inspiration to a deeper veneration of the Creator was constantly urged as an incentive to the study of nature. This harmony was now disrupted. In 1864 Pius IX plainly announced in the *Syllabus* of modern errors the firm opposition of the Roman Catholic faith to the modern trend of civilisation, condemning liberalism, rationalism, and the influence of science (cf. ch. IV, pp. 90–3). From this position there was no retreat, but the Protestant Churches, having generally accepted and developed the scientific study of scriptural language and history that was already beginning in Germany before 1859, gradually came to terms with Darwinism. The shock of the conflict between science and religion was profound, and it was the authority of religion, rather than science, that emerged weakened from it. Darwin himself was an agnostic; the simple piety of Faraday was to become increasingly uncommon in men of science.

The medicine of the mid-nineteenth century was still far removed from experimental and theoretical biology, though towards the end of the period it was being suggested that it should rise from being an art to the status of a science. General practice altered little; the stethoscope and clinical thermometer were invented, but the physician continued to prefer the old art of diagnosis to the use of instruments. Many of the most nauseous and useless concoctions were banished from the pharmacopoeia, and some vegetable drugs of real effect, such as opium and digitalis, chemistry prepared in purer forms. As remedies from which a confident action against a specific disease could be expected were few (they included the administration of quinine against ague or malaria, and of mercury against syphilis), the patient had most to hope from a strong constitution aided by restoratives, with some attention to the relief of painful symptoms. Probably the training of medical men was more thorough in 1870 than in 1830, and they were certainly required to learn more general science. Hospitals were appalling places of death where the chances of the poor for surviving disease and childbirth were much less than those of richer people who could be treated at home. The rebuilding of these almost medieval institutions largely took place after this period. The care of the sick among Roman Catholic peoples remained, as always, in the hands of nursing orders. In Protestant states it had fallen to an abysmally low level. The first attempts to train respectable nurses were made in Germany and France; Florence Nightingale had studied the new methods before reorganising British military medicine during the Crimean War. What was needed here was not so much science as common sense and hygiene, but the administration of few hospitals had been reformed by 1870. The same statement is true of urban life, which at the best was unclean and at the worst was unimaginably squalid, though the state began to assume some responsibility after the first British Public Health Act of 1848. Very little science, in the intellectual sense, entered into the movement to provide towns with pure water, sewage disposal, public baths and decent workmen's dwellings, which was inspired rather by the false theory that bad smells cause disease, charitable disgust at the animal lives of the lowest stratum, and experience that the better districts could not hope to escape the epidemics of the slums. Plague had gone with the black rat; in cleaner towns typhus and cholera accounted for fewer lives, though the origins and means of transmission of these diseases were unknown.

Operative surgery, on the other hand, benefited more directly by advances in organic chemistry. Its worst horrors were removed by the introduction of ether as an anaesthetic by Morton and Wells in the U.S.A. (1844), and of chloroform by Simpson in 1847. These pioneers had to withstand much professional and religious obscurantism and the early methods were very imperfect. The instruments and techniques employed in obstetrics and the small number of possible operations such as amputation and lithotomy were already highly developed, and the need for speed had made the best surgeons skilful. Little improvement was possible in this respect even with the aid of anaesthetics, for a limit to the surgeon's action was still fixed by the very strong probability that the wound would become infected by gangrene or a septic condition. As mortality in surgical cases was normally of the order of 50 per cent, surgery was a last resort until Lister introduced his antiseptic system at Glasgow in 1865. Lister had been converted to the germ-theory of disease, and himself repeated a number of Pasteur's experiments on putrefaction, devoting his leisure for the remainder of his life to the study of micro-organisms. His practice was designed to eliminate them from every possible source of infection by the use of carbolic acid on instruments, the patient, the operators' hands, the dressings, and even the air itself, by means of a spray. Immediate success attended his experiments, gradually forcing his colleagues to follow the same procedures, and after 1870 giving surgery a scope and security hitherto inconceivable.

Lister's discovery is a fine example of the process of scientific invention by one who was not himself a creative scientist. Disturbed in his early medical experience by the sepsis which was then the inescapable accompaniment of surgery, he made a comparison between suppuration of tissues and putrefaction of dead matter. In Pasteur's researches he found a theory to account for the latter and in organic chemistry a powerful agent to hinder it. By experiment the details of his method were brought to perfection. The stages by which a reasoned application was effected in chemical industry or electrical engineering were not dissimilar, and whereas before 1830 technological and medical improvements were the result of accident or trial-and-error experimentation, since 1870 they have been largely the fruit of design. Perhaps the most decisive years of change in this respect were those between 1855 and 1865. Science, aware of its material as well as its philosophic purpose since the seventeenth century, only came within reach of making the former real in the mid-nineteenth. This did not involve any great modification in the nature of pure research because discovery and application were normally separated by a long interval, but it did mean that the function of the inventor was most important if material progress was to be advanced by science, and it was the lack of this scientifically experienced intermediary which had caused industrial progress to remain mainly in the hands of sheer empiricists up to about 1855. The early inventors, stealing a little primitive science (such as the principle of the steam-engine) and imitating in automatic machinery the actions of human weavers and spinners, had created the ugly society of the Industrial Revolution. Their clumsy genius was still strong—by 1851 they were using cast-iron for every suitable and unsuitable purpose—but as it had lost contact with science it was receiving no new inspiration. Its vision was limited to coal, iron and steam until the intervention of the scientific inventor between 1855 and 1870 brought in fresh materials and methods. The deflection at first was slight, and it cannot be supposed that conditions in, for example, an alkali works or a phosphorus-match shop were better than in a textile mill. The credit for alleviating the lot of labour must go to the humanitarian movement and the social legislation which it championed with increasing success from 1833 onwards. Moreover, improvements in the standard of living of the peoples owed less to science than to cheap bread and tariff reform. In England, for example, between 1830 and 1850 wages remained fairly stationary, while the cost of living showed a general tendency to fall. From 1850 to 1870 real wages were rising in trend, once prices ceased to mount steeply following the collapse of the 1857 boom (ch. II, pp. 47–8). The worst tenements, the longest hours, the sharpest starvation were gone or going. The crude death-rate did not show much sign of decreasing, however, being stable at slightly over 22 per thousand, though this was always less than the mortality in France or Belgium in spite of the large French peasant population. The colder and less densely peopled Scandinavian countries were far healthier, the death-rate in Denmark falling from 20·3 in 1840 to 19 in 1870—a little less, perhaps, than the level in the English countryside at the same date. Significant improvements in health as in manufacturing techniques were achieved by science only after 1870.

The part of the inventor in techniques was played in the history of thought by such men as Comte and Spencer; and their function was not merely to elucidate the intellectual and philosophical implications of scientific knowledge, for just as an invention may provoke a fundamental investigation in science, so Spencer (for instance) stimulated biologists to examine the principles of their studies more carefully. Such men have not been highly esteemed by historians of either science or philosophy, but their ideas, in spite of some deficiency of fact and logic, have passed into the general consciousness. The Positivist school was never dominant; nevertheless, the acceptance of science as embracing a type of knowledge peculiarly exact, rigorous and practical has passed into language. As men adopted the idea of progress, as at last they began to see their own world as richer and more learned than that of Rome, they also became convinced that it was the scientific mind especially which had brought this happy state to be, and trusted increasingly to its benevolent powers for the future. Popular interest in science turned from descriptive natural history, astronomy and drawing-room marvels to the constructive sciences of electricity and chemistry. Positively, science meant knowledge and power. Nothing is more formidable than the doctrine which was already being taught that life is plastic and that science does not submit to disease, labour and humility as pillars of creation. Negatively, that which did not fall within the province of science was not knowledge and was therefore arbitrary or conventional. Against this thesis the Roman Catholic Church had set itself firmly by 1870, defining the limits which scientific pronouncements might not transgress; the Protestant Churches, though not yet routed by Darwinism, were less successful in maintaining that moral laws are as certain and clear as those of science. It is often supposed by those who overlook the import of the development of toleration, rationalism and free-thinking, that the theory of evolution came as an abrupt and single shock to traditional religion, whereas in fact the denial of other authority, though a deduction which many early scientists personally refused to draw, is intrinsic in the scientific method. Darwin did not invent the doctrine that science follows the simplest hypothesis, and the crude argument from Providence which he expelled from natural history had long been rejected in physical science and serious philosophy. Materialism, in the strictest sense the belief that all the phenomena of the universe, including man, are reducible to the physicist's reality of matter and energy; perception of the inconsistency between a literal reading of Old Testament chronology and the considered verdicts of science; critical examination, in the *Leben Jesu* of D. F. Strauss (1836) and the works of the Tübingen school, of the historical authenticity of the Gospels; all this was building the mid-nineteenth-century crisis of religion long before 1859 (cf. ch. IV, pp. 101–2). If in England and America free speculation, which had formerly been cautious, broke forth suddenly in the reviews during the 'sixties and 'seventies, anti-clerical scepticism had been a touch-stone of liberalism in Catholic Europe since the time of Voltaire. Yet Darwinism acted as a catalytic concept in the conflict of loyalties which it aroused, and which was all the greater because Protestant theology had tended to assert that its dogmas were defensible by reason alone and did not rest upon blind faith. It was the last blow to the final authority of Scripture, but it by no means filled the last loop-hole in the scientific claim to omniscience, for there were many more subtle refuges to which the plea for the necessity of Design might retire. Science was increasingly demonstrating that the operation of chance, as conceived by a statistician, does not produce sheer confusion, and that at least the existing universe with its existing species was not the immediate, immutable product of creation. Similarly, in formal philosophy the influence of Darwin extended far beyond that of Herbert Spencer in making biology stand in relation to nineteenth-century thought as mechanics had to that of the late seventeenth. But the adjustment of the moral and ethical image of man as a being not degenerate, but progressively evolving from *Pithecanthropus erectus* through primitive society to civilisation, had scarcely begun in 1870. In this the new sciences of psychology and anthropology have played a vital part.

CHAPTER IV

RELIGION AND THE RELATIONS OF CHURCHES AND STATES

'A FREE church in a free state.' The maxim of Cavour, which was to become the most influential principle of the relations of church and state in Europe during the latter half of the nineteenth century, had too much novelty to win its way easily to general acceptance. The French Revolution indeed had shaken altars no less than sceptres within the sphere of its direct conquests and even beyond; and had broken the traditional association of church and state. Consequently in England, where *émigrés* from across the Channel, both clerical and lay, were received with sympathy, the clergy of the established church, as portrayed in the novels of Jane Austen, assumed a new character and importance as commissioned officers in the army of the church militant against Jacobinism and atheism. A contemporary French historian, Professor A. Latreille, indeed has fortified this interpretation by arguing that the principles of 1789 were a portent of the modern conflict of the totalitarian state with Christianity. 'Thence came the demand for total obedience, comparable to a religious obedience, to the State and the Law, and thence the fanatical determination, in case of resistance, to secure the triumph of the principles necessary for social order.'[1] If the meaning of the French Revolution were to involve the translation of the maxim of Gambetta, 'Clericalism—there is the enemy', into 'Christianity—there is the enemy' then the nature of the ecclesiastical reaction which followed the defeat of Napoleon may be more easily understood, if not exculpated. In France the restored Bourbon monarchy espoused the closest possible alliance with the church: altar and throne were to be indissolubly bound together; whilst to Rome itself and to the Papal States the Papacy returned in the baggage train of the victorious allies. Even in England there seemed at first to be no visible breach in the traditional policy of denying to dissenters from the established church, whether Popish or Protestant, civil equality with their conformist brethren. But by 1830 the cracks which the settlement of 1815 had papered over were beginning to show themselves again; and signs were evident that a regime of repression could not obliterate the effects of 1789. In 1828 in England the repeal of the Test and Corporation Acts marked the victory of the Protestant dissenters, though these statutes had not been enforced for nearly a century and though their repeal was only the first step in a sustained campaign for

[1] A. Latreille, *L'Église catholique et la révolution française* (2 vols. Paris, 1946–50), vol. 1, p. 83.

complete civil equality and for the removal of remaining restrictions. More significant was the grant in the following year of Roman Catholic emancipation; whilst 1828 also had seen the foundation of University College, London, the first educational institution of university status to eschew a religious basis and to provide a purely secular education. In July 1830, moreover, there came the revolution in Paris which manifested a markedly anti-clerical character. In face of these episodes, the established churches on both sides of the Channel had to work out a new theory and practice of their relationship with the state and to erect new defences against liberalism.

Perhaps the most influential of the attempts to readjust ideas to circumstances was the Liberal-Catholic movement in France, initiated by Lamennais and gathering to its support Lacordaire, Montalembert and Gerbet. It seems probable indeed that this owed much of its inspiration and inception to a parallel tendency in Belgium, where a Liberal-Catholic circle had centred in the Archbishop of Malines, Mgr de Méon, and was led by his vicar-general, Engelbert Sterckx, himself later to become archbishop and cardinal. But the fame of the 'School of Malines' was soon eclipsed by that of France. By 1830 indeed the unpredictable genius of Lamennais had already accomplished the first of a series of *volte-faces* by his conversion from an ardent royalist to an equally devoted liberal. 'Men tremble before liberalism; make it Catholic and society will be reborn';[1] such became the maxim of his new policy. In 1828 he had published *Des Progrès de la révolution et de la guerre contre l'église*; in which he had urged upon the Gallican church the duty of demanding freedom from the dying regime of Bourbon royalism, and liberty to reorganise its internal constitution, and especially the education of its clergy, in order to prepare for an alliance with liberalism. The anti-clerical disturbances of 1830 seemed at first to presage ill for this new evangel; but in October Lamennais and his disciples launched in Paris a daily newspaper, *L'Avenir*, in the first number of which Lamennais demanded the union of religion and liberty: 'God and liberty—unite them.' The only alternative, however, to alliance with the state was reliance on the Papacy; and the programme of these reformers depended upon support by Rome against the opposition of the French episcopate, which not unnaturally took alarm at the demand for four freedoms: freedom of education (involving the end of the monopoly enjoyed by the state-controlled Napoleonic university), freedom of the press (involving the abolition of the censorship), freedom of association (both for workers in industry and for the formation of religious communities), and freedom of worship (including the right of every church to exercise discipline over its own members). Accordingly everything waited upon the decision of Rome; pending which Lamennais founded the *Agence générale pour la défense de la liberté*

[1] E. D. Forgues, *Lamennais: correspondance inédite* (Paris, 1863), vol. II, p. 106.

religieuse, whilst the right to form religious communities was exercised by the Capuchins of Aix and the Trappists of Milleray, and an *École libre* was opened in Paris in defiance of the University. This indeed was a far greater menace than *L'Avenir*; this was 'Catholic Action'; and as enemies both at home and abroad began to close in upon the reformers, Lamennais took the bold steps in November 1831 of suspending his newspaper and of appealing to the Pope himself for an investigation and report on his principles. Unfortunately for the reformers, Gregory XVI had nothing save his name in common with Gregory VII; nor would his position have permitted, even if his personal policy had suggested, the affronting of civil princes in order to rally a reformed episcopate to Lamennais' standard. When therefore Lamennais, Lacordaire and Montalembert reached Rome in December to advocate their cause in person, they did not secure an audience with the Pope until 15 March following, and then only of fifteen minutes' duration and of a general and desultory character.

On their way home, at Munich, where they were entertained by the famous Catholic confraternity of Görres, Döllinger, Schelling and Baader, they were overtaken by the bull *Mirari Vos* of 15 August 1832, which sounded the death-knell of their hopes. Gregory XVI had done more than disavow the reformers; he had condemned the principles of their campaign. The bull denounced the demand for an end of the Concordat; it repudiated the suggestion that the church needed regeneration and reform or that it should ally itself with revolutionary liberalism; it condemned indifferentism; it fulminated particularly against the chief error of indifferentism, namely freedom of conscience; and it denounced freedom of the press. It was cold comfort that the covering letter from Cardinal Pacca explained that, though the encyclical repudiated liberal catholicism, it refrained from actually specifying *L'Avenir* or the names of its editors out of consideration for their past services to the Papacy.

The effects of the bull were far-reaching; for though Lamennais at first submitted, his recantation was transient; and within two years a further fulmination from Rome, *Singulari Nos* of 7 July 1834, condemned specifically his *Paroles d'un croyant* as containing 'propositions which were respectively false, calumnious, rash, inducing to anarchy, contrary to the Word of God, impious, scandalous, and erroneous'. But, though liberal catholicism lost thereby its leader, his followers, Lacordaire and Montalembert, continued to uphold its standard, not without considerable influence and even success. Indeed, the July Monarchy witnessed the Indian summer of the movement; on the one hand by the apologetic Lenten conferences of Lacordaire in Notre Dame, by the revival of religious orders both for men and women, and by the formation of an association for the laity, the Society of St Vincent de Paul; and on the other hand by a remarkable outburst of missionary enterprise in Syria, India, Siam and China, ennobled particularly by the heroic martyrdoms of the mission in Indo-China. It was ironical therefore that the most permanent element of Lamennais' legacy should be, not the liberal catholicism which was his most ardent enthusiasm, but an ultramontane tendency which was to vanquish the Liberal-Catholic spirit in its Gallican home. Perhaps the paradox was well summarised in the contrasting fortunes of *L'Avenir* and *L'Univers*. Not of course that Louis Veuillot, the editor of *L'Univers*, was the most important and characteristic figure of the Ultramontane reaction; though he may have been its most skilful populariser. Another of the ironies of fortune lay in the circumstance that Dom Guéranger, who as a young man had joined the circle of Lamennais, was to become, as abbot of the restored Benedictine house at Solesmes, the principal agent of a liturgical revival, which culminated in the uniform adoption throughout the church in France of the Roman Liturgy. Two years after Guéranger's appointment at Solesmes in 1837, the bishop of Langres, Mgr Parisis, whose diocese after 1801 had embraced parts of five former dioceses and therewith five varying liturgies, enforced the uniform use of the Roman Liturgy; and the process of reducing the area of liturgical differences progressed gradually to the final stage in 1875 when the diocese of Orléans, three years after the death of Bishop Dupanloup, likewise adopted the Roman Rite. Not least amongst the architects of the Ultramontane conquest of Gallicanism was the studious author of the series of *Institutions Liturgiques*, Abbot Guéranger, whom Pius IX playfully called Dom Guerroyer.

For a period, however, the Liberal-Catholic standard fluttered bravely. Montalembert's campaign for freedom of Catholic education and for the emancipation of instruction from the monopoly of the Napoleonic University, waxed stronger and more formidable. The farcical penalty of a fine of 100 francs which was the outcome of his prosecution before the house of peers for the foundation in Paris of an *École Libre* in 1831, emboldened him to publish in 1843 *Du Devoir des catholiques dans la question de la liberté d'enseignement*, in which he inaugurated his battle for freedom of education at all levels. His influence was seen in the introduction in 1844 of a government bill for education which failed, however, because unacceptable to the episcopate, whereupon Montalembert by organising a Committee for the Defence of Religious Freedom, prepared for a nation-wide political contest. In the educational field 'the sons of the Crusaders' had openly challenged 'the sons of Voltaire'. The success of this appeal was seen in the return at the general election in 1846 of 140 deputies pledged to support its demands for freedom of Catholic education, a portent of which the administration was compelled to take cognisance. Accordingly a new bill was introduced in 1847, diminishing though not abolishing the control by the University over voluntary schools. The controversy aroused thereby was continuing when the 1848 revolution occurred; and was not settled until the *Loi Falloux* was passed in 1850. This statute, thanks to the reaction provoked by the excesses of 1848, was a victory for the Church, though bearing marks of compromise necessary to command the support on the one side of Montalembert and Bishop Dupanloup and on the other of Thiers, and was therefore denounced by Catholic extremists like the editor of *L'Univers*, and by Victor Hugo from a far different standpoint. The law abolished the University monopoly; substituted for the *Conseil Royal de l'Université* a new *Conseil Supérieur de l'Instruction Publique* in which the eight University members constituted a minority flanked by nineteen others who included four bishops, two Protestant ministers and one rabbi; in each department a new *Conseil Académique* for the local supervision of education was set up with authority to grant the certificate of competence (*brevet de capacité*) as the indispensable professional qualification for teaching; schools were recognised as either public, that is state-controlled, or voluntary; and in the latter the right of state inspection was confined to hygiene and health; whilst members of religious congregations were allowed to teach provided they possessed the certificate. Substantially therefore Catholic action had achieved a considerable victory for the principles of liberal catholicism; within a year of the passing of the *Loi Falloux* over 250 new educational establishments were opened, mainly by religious orders. Nor was it without significance that, as in England, popular education had become the battleground for contention between church and state.

Meantime Switzerland had been affected by the successive winds of political and religious doctrine which had blown themselves out in France. Since the overspreading of the French Revolution into its territory, Switzerland had experienced an aggravation of the traditional religious differences dividing its cantons into Catholic and Protestant, by the penetration of the revolutionary maxims of a secular society and of the cult of reason. After Napoleon's defeat the old order had been restored; and had suffered likewise the first challenge to its authority when the Revolution of 1830 in France revived the doctrines of liberalism. The Swiss 'Regeneration' movement achieved perhaps its greatest success in the sphere of public education (cf. ch. v, pp. 108 ff.); reforming the primary schools from top to bottom, establishing training colleges, and also founding universities at Zürich and Berne. Through these educational measures the spirit of liberalism spread widely, arousing enthusiasm in some cantons and alarm in others; and leading to the conclusion of concordats in seven liberal cantons to safeguard their new constitutions and in five other cantons to defend their old status. Indeed, the religious issue was to prove once more a divisive factor. Even in Zürich, the home of Zwingli, the reforms in the primary schools provoked opposition, and the appointment to the university of a liberal theologian, D. F. Strauss, led to a rising in rural districts in 1839, which spread to the city itself and installed a new civil administration recruited from conservative churchmen. Furthermore, Lucerne in 1841 communicated its new constitution to the Pope and made bold to try the experiment of a democratic form of government allied with the Catholic church.

The stage was therefore set for conflict between Radicals and Conservatives;[1] and the *casus belli* once more centred in the religious problem. Friction in Aargau between the Radical government and a section of the Catholic minority led to disturbances in Muri and to the consequent dissolution of the monasteries. Both within the other Swiss cantons and outside the Confederation, however, this secularisation of the monasteries evoked vehement Catholic opposition. Moreover the conflict now was not the traditional rivalry of Protestant and Catholic cantons, but between a new militant ultramontanism and freethinking. In 1844 the Great Council of Lucerne invited the Jesuits to undertake theological teaching in its seminary; and this defiant *riposte* to the dissolution of the Aargau monasteries had repercussions throughout the Confederation. The Radicals accepted the challenge and organised an anti-Jesuit campaign. Oratorical extremes were succeeded by armed clashes; and in order to protect themselves the Catholic cantons of Lucerne, Uri, Schwyz, Unterwalden, Zug, Fribourg and Valais concluded a defensive alliance, known as the *Sonderbund*. When the question of this pact came before the Federal Diet, the accession of St Gallen to the Radical camp gave this party a majority which was used to demand the dissolution of the *Sonderbund* as incompatible with the federal pact and the prohibition by the Confederation of the admission of the Jesuit Order. These events were the prelude to civil war in 1847, in which the *Sonderbund* was decisively defeated. The chief European powers, indeed, considered themselves vitally interested in the internal affairs of Switzerland, but their desires to mediate were frustrated by the unexpectedly speedy defeat of the *Sonderbund*; and their attention was then diverted to the more far-reaching revolutions of 1848 in other states, so that the Swiss were left to work out in peace the adjustments to their federal constitution necessitated by the civil war. The new constitution was characterised by a spirit of moderation and reconciliation; and the relationship of church and state in Switzerland was to remain peaceful until the Old Catholic schism, following upon the proclamation of papal infallibility in 1870.

'Men tremble before Liberalism; make it Catholic and Society will be reborn.' Such was the maxim of Lamennais in 1830. For Newman and the leaders of the Oxford Movement in England the exact contrary was the true remedy for a fell disease. Indeed, the English ecclesiastical historian Gwatkin dismissed the movement in a sentence as 'the backwash

---

[1] For the nationalist aspect of this conflict, see ch. IX, pp. 222–4.

of the Reform bill'.[1] Although the liberalism against which Newman proclaimed war to the knife was predominantly religious, the religious issue had arisen from the political. Before Newman left England in 1832 he had commented on the French 1830 revolution that he 'believed that it was unchristian for nations to cast off their governors and much more sovereigns who had the divine right of inheritance'. Similarly the advent of the Whigs to power in England had raised 'the vital question... how were we to keep the church from being liberalised?'; and if during his absence 'it was the success of the liberal cause which fretted him inwardly', it was the scheme of Irish church reform espoused and carried by the Whigs which provoked Keble's Assize sermon on National Apostasy.[2] The gentle author of *The Christian Year* indeed had canvassed the freeholders of his rural parish to refuse their votes to a candidate who supported the first reform bill. It was in an atmosphere of panic therefore that the Tractarian revival was born. Amongst churchmen there was a widespread fear lest Grey's advice to the episcopate to set their house in order should be the prelude to disestablishment and disendowment. The recently emancipated Dissenters and Roman Catholics might well desire the former; whilst Jeremy Bentham coveted the latter as a means of financing his National Mechanics' Institute. Consequently the fabulously wealthy dean and chapter of Durham, with the counsel of Bishop van Mildert, resolved to sacrifice some of their revenues to found a university there, in the hope of saving something from the anticipated ruins of confiscation. In these circumstances the prime objective of the Tractarian movement was to furnish a *raison d'être* for the Church of England if the cataclysm of disestablishment came suddenly upon it. In the first of the *Tracts for the Times*, addressed to the clergy, Newman pointedly asked: 'Should the government and country so far forget their God as to cast off the church, to deprive it of its temporal honours and substance, *on what* will you rest the claim of respect and attention which you make upon your flocks?... the question recurs, on *what* are we to rest our authority when the state deserts us?' The answer was plain: 'the real ground on which our authority is built—our Apostolical descent'.

With the enunciation of this remedy, the Oxford Movement passed from politics to religion. There its first principle was to combat liberalism by asserting the dogmatic basis of Christianity. 'My battle', avowed Newman in his *Apologia pro vita sua*, 'was with liberalism; by liberalism I meant the anti-dogmatic principle and its developments.... Such was the fundamental principle of the Movement of 1833.' Before its rise the dominant influence within the established church had been that of the Evangelicals, who had rekindled the flame of personal religion and developed new patterns of pastoral work. Nor had their importance been

---

[1] H. M. Gwatkin, *Church and State in England to the Death of Anne* (London, 1917), p. 384.
[2] J. H. Newman, *Apologia pro vita sua* (1913 edn, Oxford), pp. 131, 134, 140.

unrecognised in political matters. Their leaders had played a foremost part in the campaign for the abolition of slavery, which reached its climax in the very year of 'National Apostasy' by the vote of £20,000,000 for the emancipation of slaves; the efforts of Shaftesbury had resulted in that same year, 1833, in a Factory Act to restrict the hours of child labour in industry; and evangelical clergy and laity had combined to encourage missionary enterprise in regions so widely separated as India and Newfoundland. The Oxford Movement was to provide both a corrective and a complement to the evangelical revival by its doctrine of the church, the ministry and the sacraments. In the first of the *Tracts*, the doctrine of an exclusive validity of episcopal ministries had been laid down. 'All we who have been ordained clergy, in the very form of our ordination, acknowledged the doctrine of the Apostolical Succession. And for the same reason we must necessarily consider none to be *really* ordained, who have not *thus* been ordained.' This principle, enunciated as a defence against disestablishment, became one of the most potent ecclesiastical shibboleths in England and beyond. Behind the protracted controversies which these doctrines evoked, the Oxford Movement worked a pervasive and far-reaching religious revival; its revival of patristic studies, its emphasis on holiness of life and its strongly moralistic tradition, its restoration of the discipline of auricular confession and absolution, and of religious orders, and its ceremonial and liturgical interests: all wrought a change in the general standards of thought and practice amounting to a revolution. Not even the presence in its early stages of a headstrong Rome-ward element, nor the spectacular secessions to Rome in 1845 of Newman and in 1851 of Manning, deprived it of its self-confidence and success, thanks to the steadiness of Pusey and Keble

In its challenge to the state, however, the Oxford Movement spoke in muffled tones compared with contemporary events in the Church of Scotland, where church and state came into open and dramatic conflict. The dispute arose from local exercise of the right of private patronage of churches; which, though disallowed by the Act of Union of 1707, had been brought back by the united parliament in 1712 and during the eighteenth century had spread considerably. In 1834 the General Assembly of the Church of Scotland reaffirmed the right of heads of households in a parish to exclude by a majority vote an unacceptable presentee; and this was acted upon in Auchterarder in the same year, and followed in 1837 in Marnoch. Meantime the former quarrel had been the subject of litigation; in which the court of session upheld the patron's authority, and the House of Lords on appeal limited the presbytery's right of rejection to proved charges of heresy, ignorance or immorality. This decision, though legally impeccable, did not touch the difficult issue of the impossibility of harmonious relationship between a minister forced by a private patron upon a parish antipathetic to him. Moreover, Thomas Chalmers, the leader of the campaign for asserting the rights of the church, exercised a growing influence in the General Assembly; and by 1840 he had reached the conclusions that 'Scottish patronage is a system not to be regulated but destroyed', and that it represented 'that great Erastian controversy in which all states and churches have a common interest'. Therefore in 1842 the General Assembly carried a resolution for the abolition of private patronage with a threat of secession if its wishes were not granted; and accompanied this by a declaration calling 'the Christian people of this kingdom and all the churches of the Reformation throughout the whole world, who hold the great doctrine of the sole Headship of the Lord Jesus over his Church, to witness that it is for their adherence to that doctrine...that this Church is subject to hardship, and that the rights so sacredly pledged and secured to her are put in peril'.[1] The queen's administration finding these resolutions unacceptable, the threat was executed on 24 May 1843 when the Free Church of Scotland was founded by 474 seceding ministers, with the astonishing result that within four years this church had raised £1,250,000 and built 654 churches. The contemplation of this dramatic and successful defiance of Leviathan by the kingdom of fairies moved a modern commentator, not otherwise markedly sympathetic to the claims of the church, to record his surprise

that more attention should not have been paid to the remarkable analogy between the Oxford movement and the Disruption of 1843 in the established church of Scotland. Each was essentially an anti-Erastian movement. It was against an all-absorptive state that each group of men was contending. There is a striking temporal parallel between the two movements. That of Oxford in the narrower sense begins in 1833 and ends with the conversion of Newman in 1845; that of which Chalmers was the distinguished leader, begins in 1834 with the abolition by the General Assembly of lay patronage and ends in 1843 with the secession of those who refuse to accept what they term an invasion of the peculiar province of the church by the state. In each case, as was well enough admitted by contemporaries, the attempt was made...to work out a doctrine of the church which, neglecting the state, gave the church the general organization of a perfect society.[2]

As with the liberal catholicism of Montalembert, the Church of Scotland had fortified protest with action; and in both cases Leviathan had not prevailed.

A lesser example of successful defiance of the state by the church occurred in England in 1851 with the restoration of a territorial Roman Catholic hierarchy instead of the system of government by vicars apostolic. In 1850 Pius IX had resolved on this change, which was heralded by a flamboyant pastoral letter by the new archbishop of Westminster, Nicholas Wiseman, which in turn aroused the slumbering No Popery alarms of English public opinion. The situation was not improved by Lord John

[1] H. Watt, *Thomas Chalmers and the Disruption* (Edinburgh, 1943), pp. 227, 243, 257–8.
[2] H. J. Laski, *Studies in the Problem of Sovereignty* (New Haven, 1917), pp. 112–13.

Russell's 'Open Letter to the Bishop of Durham', denouncing this 'insolent and insidious action' on 4 November 1850; and there survived until 1930 a nonagenarian Anglican prelate who remembered how on 5 November 1850 the Pope took the place of Guy Fawkes, when he himself took part at York in the burning of a life-size effigy bearing the legend 'Oh, No, Pio No No'![1] Unfortunately the demonstrations were not confined to such schoolboy ebullitions; for Russell piloted on to the statute book an Ecclesiastical Titles Act, voted by large majorities despite the opposition of Bright and Gladstone, which prohibited the assumption of territorial titles by the Roman prelacy. Notwithstanding, the reorganisation of the Roman Catholics proceeded according to plan; the penalties of the act were not enforced; and Gladstone in his first administration was quietly to draw its teeth.

Meantime the strife between the established church and the Nonconformists, which accompanied the struggle for complete civil equality, after achieving its primary objectives in the grant of marriage and burial rights to the Dissenters, concentrated on education. The second generation of the nineteenth century indeed saw a gradual transformation of the educational system by the intrusion of the state into what had previously been a field of voluntary enterprise. The year 1833 saw the first governmental grant to education, when the sum of £20,000 was voted for division between the 'National Society for promoting the education of the poor in the principles of the established church' and its rival the 'British and Foreign School Society', in proportion to the number of schools under their respective direction. With the steady increase of state subvention (for by 1850 the annual amount had risen to £125,000), and therewith of state intervention (symbolised by the creation in 1839 of a committee of the privy council on education, which was replaced in 1856 by an Education Department under a Vice-President of the Council), there developed a severe clash of opinion between the established and the free churches concerning the use of public funds in support of schools teaching a denominational formulary. At first indeed the Nonconformists held fast to their traditional principle of voluntaryism, thus expressed by Edward Baines in 1843: 'it is not the province of a government to educate the people; and the admission of the principle that it is its province would lead to practical consequences fatal to civil and religious liberty.'[2] But the accumulating evidence of the inability of churches and other voluntary societies to provide the means necessary for a nation-wide system, and the increasing interest in education evinced by the state, led to a change of position. By the middle of the century the Dissenters were in favour of state education, provided it were either secular or at least non-denominational; whilst the Anglicans, being in possession of by far the largest

[1] G. F. Browne, *The Recollections of a Bishop* (London, 1915), p. 7.
[2] R. W. Dale, *History of English Congregationalism* (London, 1907), p. 659.

number of primary schools, refused to hand them over for either of these purposes. In Gladstone's first administration the Forster Education Bill of 1870 brought the conflict to an issue; by its proposals to continue the voluntary schools (notwithstanding their predominantly Anglican complexion), to increase the state grant which they enjoyed, and to supplement them by the erection of board schools where necessity required. The religious issue was met by the Cowper–Temple clause which provided for non-denominational religious instruction in the new board schools, with permission for parents to withdraw their children from even this instruction on grounds of conscience. The act was a compromise and, like the *Loi Falloux*, it represented a substantial victory for the established church; and therefore drew the criticism of radical Free-churchmen, such as Dale of Birmingham who declared that 'not even at the bidding of a liberal ministry will we consent to any proposition which under cover of an educational measure, empowers one religious denomination to levy a rate for teaching its creed and maintaining its worship'.[1] The act did not resolve the interconfessional rivalry therefore, but introduced a further element of discord by accepting a dual system of schools; thereby perpetuating the controversy between Anglicans and Freechurchmen which was to bedevil public education for a further three-quarters of a century.

It is easy to dismiss the protracted history of disputes concerning education and the respective rights therein of churches and states, whether in France or in England, as an unusually virulent symptom of *odium theologicum*. But though the accidents of the controversies may appear trivial, the substance was of importance, as the emergence of the modern totalitarian state has emphasised. Moreover the recent echoes from the past in B. L. Manning's history of *The Protestant Dissenting Deputies*,[2] with its denunciation of 'the woodenness of Gladstone and the maliciousness of Forster', its scornful contempt for 'the self-opinionated Gallios of the Board of Education', and its concluding verdict that 'the seeds of clerical and anti-clerical struggles hitherto unknown in England, were sown by the ex-Quaker Forster and watered by Whitehall agnostics', suggest that in matters of religious education the discovery of that magic elixir which maketh men to be of one mind in an house may yet have eluded the English genius for pragmatic compromise. On the other hand, a singular example of this characteristic was seen in the Dissenters' Chapels Act of 1845, by which twenty-five years' actual possession was declared a legal warrant for the continuing enjoyment by Unitarians of churches, manses and endowments, originally bequeathed for the propagation of orthodox Protestant Trinitarian doctrine (and so adjudged in a series of judicial decisions concerning particular cases), which had devolved on Unitarian congregations during the eighteenth century. Rarely

[1] A. W. W. Dale, *Life of R. W. Dale of Birmingham* (London, 1928), p. 275.
[2] B. L. Manning, *op. cit.* (Cambridge, 1952), p. 353.

could the omnicompetence of the British parliament have been more strikingly displayed than in its determination of a theological issue without regard to the terms of trust deeds or the intentions of pious founders, in the interest of practical politics. More commendable were the gradual steps to open the ancient universities to non-anglicans, typified by the removal of restrictions on their admission to the B.A. degree at Oxford and Cambridge in 1854 and the M.A. two years later; and the process was virtually completed by Gladstone's University Tests' Act of 1871, which threw open to non-anglicans all offices in the universities of Oxford, Cambridge and Durham, with the exception of specifically clerical fellowships, headships of houses and divinity professorships. This statute opened the way also for the return of the Free-church theological colleges to the universities, to the mutual profit of church, state and academy.

The diversity of English religious life constituted, however, a marked obstacle to generalisation and summary. Whilst the Methodists suffered a severe setback during the first half of the century, thanks to an epidemic of internal divisions and secessions, culminating in the Fly Sheet controversy of 1844–8 and the consequent expulsion of about 57,000 persons, the Congregationalist and Baptist churches made the first moves towards closer association by the formation of their respective Unions in 1831, and the English Presbyterians effected the reorganisation essential to their recovery from the landslide of their eighteenth-century predecessors into Unitarianism. In the novelty of the religious census of 1851, the Church of England was recorded as possessing 14,077 churches with accommodation for 5,317,915 persons; followed by the Methodists (in their various separate groups) with 11,007 churches with accommodation for 2,194,298 persons; whilst the Independents had 3244 churches providing 1,067,760 sittings. The Roman Catholics, in addition to the reconstitution of their diocesan episcopate, had greatly strengthened their numbers by Irish immigration and by the vigorous proselytism of Wiseman, who was succeeded as archbishop of Westminster in 1865 by the convert from Anglicanism, Manning. The dramatic transformation of the Roman Catholic community from the 'race that shunned the light' described by Newman to the vigorous, aggressive church fostered by Manning is most graphically depicted in the autobiography of Bishop W. B. Ullathorne, whose long life from 1806 to 1899 spanned this historic century of expansion and consolidation.

Meantime, however, the accession of Pius IX to the Papacy in 1846 heralded a generation of strife in the relations between church and state in various European countries. The portent of his election (which evoked the remark of Metternich that he had reckoned with everything save a liberal Pope) rekindled hope among the Liberal Catholics that at last their cause would enjoy the championship of the apostolic see. But the liberalism of Pio Nono was distinctly diluted, proceeding from the goodness of his heart rather than the conviction of his head; and even its pristine manifestations, as reflected in an amnesty for political prisoners, a commission of inquiry into the necessary reforms in the administration of the Papal States and the nomination of a council of state and a ministry, were destined to perish in the rude shocks of 1848 (cf. ch. XXI, p. 565). For the revolutions of that year affected Rome also; where a republic was proclaimed, causing the flight of the pope to Gaeta, whence he returned in 1849 by the agency and under the continuing protection of French troops, dispatched by Louis Napoleon to outbid Austria and to secure for himself the prestige of defender of the church. The papal flirtation with liberalism was ended. Moreover, during his exile the pontiff had besought the especial protection of the Virgin Mary; and at Candlemas 1849 he circularised the episcopate as to the state of Catholic opinion concerning the elevation of the belief in her Immaculate Conception to the status of a dogma of faith. The suggestion had the enthusiastic support of the Jesuits, and the theological acumen of Professor Perrone of the Collegium Romanum elaborated the distinction between *patent* and *latent* tradition, justifying the latter as sufficient for the definition of a doctrine. On 8 December 1854 Pius IX formally defined and proclaimed 'that the doctrine which teaches that the most blessed Virgin Mary in the first moment of her conception, by a special gift of grace from almighty God, ...was preserved pure from all taint of original sin, is revealed by God'.[1] Equally important with the content of the definition was the manner of its promulgation; for although inquiries had been made of the episcopate, and about 150 bishops present in Rome in November 1854 had debated the question at four meetings, the actual proclamation was made without the prior concurrence of a general council.

During the decade separating the definition of the Immaculate Conception from the issue of the Syllabus of Errors, the relations between church and state, particularly in Italy, grew steadily worse. Not only was Piedmont–Sardinia secularising ecclesiastical property and controlling public education, but its foreign policy was pregnant with difficulties for the Papacy. In 1859 the alliance between Napoleon III and Cavour was the prelude to the expulsion of Austria from the Lombard plain, the annexation of the central duchies, the expedition of Garibaldi to Sicily and south Italy, and the extinction of the Papal States, reserving to the apostolic see only the city of Rome, and even this only by grace of the French garrison's prolongation of its precarious occupation (cf. ch. XXI, pp. 571–4). In an attempt to extricate himself from so equivocal a situation, Napoleon III concluded the September Convention of 1864; by which, in return for Victor Emmanuel's promise to establish the capital of Italy elsewhere than at Rome, which should be guaranteed to the Papacy, the

[1] C. Mirbt, *Quellen zur Geschichte des Papsttums und des römischen Katholizismus* (5th edn, Tübingen, 1934), p. 447.

emperor undertook to withdraw permanently his garrison. But the departing French troops had gone no farther than Città Vecchia when a further threat to the papal possession of Rome developed, and they returned hurriedly to prop up the surviving fraction of the temporal power. It was amid such portents of revolution and rebellion that the pope resolved to launch upon the world a comprehensive catalogue of erroneous principles and opinions, formally censured by ecclesiastical authority.

The origin of the Syllabus may probably be traced to a proposal of the future Leo XIII, then bishop of Perugia, at a council at Spoleto in 1849 that Pius IX should issue a list of contemporary errors relating to the authority of the church and the rights of property. In 1851 the new monthly Jesuit magazine, the *Civiltà Cattolica*, advocated the addition of the errors of rationalism and semi-rationalism; in 1854 a papal commission of theologians began work on the preparation of the scheme; whilst in 1860 Bishop Gerbet of Perpignan (a former disciple of Lamennais!) issued an *Instruction pastorale sur diverses erreurs du temps présent*, which contained eighty-five false opinions. A further papal commission was appointed to conflate these several suggestions; and meantime Montalembert's activities had supplied further subjects for condemnation. The fortunes of liberal catholicism indeed during and after 1848 had fluctuated severely. Whereas at first in France the revolution had appeared to inaugurate the desired union of catholicism and republicanism (as country *curés* blessed the ubiquitous planting of trees of liberty, three bishops were members of the constituent assembly, and Lacordaire was elected by popular suffrage for Marseilles), the June days darkened the situation, especially when the archbishop of Paris was rewarded for his adhesion to the regime by death during the tumults. Accordingly most Liberal Catholics welcomed the rise of Louis Napoleon. Political liberalism, however, was now postponed to the distant and half-hearted experiment of the liberal empire (cf. ch. XVII, pp. 456-7); and liberal catholicism could not hope to find the atmosphere of the Second Empire congenial. Its champions had perforce to look abroad for the triumph of their principles. It was at a Catholic congress in 1863 at Malines (where the Liberal-Catholic movement had enjoyed its first Spring and early Summer) that Montalembert once more raised his standard. He congratulated Belgium on having understood 'the new situation of public life' and having accepted the reciprocal independence of the spiritual and temporal powers; and observed that just as Catholics had nothing to regret in the old order, so they had nothing to fear from the new. Indeed, the history of Belgium since 1830 had justified the alliance of the Liberal-Catholic group led by Sterckx with the political democrats to produce the Constitution of 1831; and Cardinal Sterckx was still directing the policy of the Belgian episcopate until his death in 1867. Montalembert was at pains to make his meaning explicit by affirming his acceptance of religious liberty with the attendant risk of heresy and by equating religious persecution with political: 'The Spanish inquisitor who said to the heretic: "the truth, or death", is as odious to me as the French terrorist who said to my grandfather, "liberty and fraternity, or death".' Moreover, he uttered a panegyric on liberty. 'By liberty I mean complete liberty, not political liberty without religious liberty; I mean quite simply modern liberty, democratic liberty, founded upon the common law and upon equality and regulated by reason and justice. For my part I frankly confess that I see an immense step forward in this solidarity between Catholicism and public liberty.'[1] Such an unequivocal adoption of Cavour's maxim of a free church in a free state and of democratic liberty without qualification earned for him a formal delation to Rome by Bishop Pie of Poitiers, who pressed for an explicit censure of his opinions by name. Pius IX, however, whilst avowing in respect of liberty of conscience that the church could never admit or approve it in principle but only as a matter of expediency, declined to pronounce a personal censure on Montalembert, and reserved the condemnation of his principles for the forthcoming compendium of errors. In regard to the acceptance of freedom of conscience as an expedient, whilst disapproving it as matter of principle, an article in the *Civiltà Cattolica* of 6 December 1863 on the Malines congress was reported to reproduce not only the ideas but the words of the pope himself; particularly 'the distinction between the thesis and the hypothesis which is the fundamental theme in the article, is no mere idea, it is also a formula presented by the Holy Father with whom the editors have talked at length on this subject'.[2]

The *Syllabus Errorum* with an attendant encyclical, *Quanta Cura*, was issued on 8 December 1864. The encyclical began by recalling that Pius IX had previously condemned the monstrous portent of the opinions of the age, and must now repeat his censure in respect of other depraved and profligate opinions, which flowed from these errors and corrupted both individuals and society. First was the application to civil society of the principle of naturalism and the doctrine that civil society should make no distinction between the true religion and false beliefs; which St Augustine had denounced as a liberty leading to perdition; and which led to such societies being governed only by natural force and public opinion. Next the error of socialism and communism was reprobated, as denying the divine origin of the family and the exclusive right of the church to direct the education of the young, and therefore being hostile to the clergy, who were considered enemies to useful knowledge and the progress of civilisation. Further, these erroneous opinions subjected the church to the state, regarded ecclesiastical law as binding only if enforced by temporal sanc-

---

[1] E. Lecanuet, *Montalembert* (Paris, 1910–12), vol. III, p. 353.
[2] Louis Baunard, *Histoire du Cardinal Pie, évêque de Poitiers* (Paris, 1887), vol. II, pp. 218–19.

tions, secularised church property and revenues, and denied the independent sovereignty and authority of the church. The encyclical concluded with a warning against deniers of the divinity of Christ and with an exhortation to prayer and invocation of the Virgin Mary.

The Syllabus or Collection of Modern Errors embraced eighty propositions. The first two sections condemned pantheism, naturalism and absolute rationalism in seven propositions, followed by a further seven in condemnation of moderate rationalism. Such ancillary errors as denial of revelation or assertion that it was progressive in character, denial of the biblical prophecies and miracles and the assertion that the Bible contains myths, were reproved. Four propositions relating to indifferentism and latitudinarianism were next censured, including the beliefs that salvation is procurable through any religion and that protestantism is an equally sound version of Christianity as catholicism. A single comprehensive condemnation sufficed for socialism, communism and secret societies, including Bible societies and free church societies. Twenty propositions relating to the nature, rights and authority of the church were arraigned, specifically the denials that the church is a perfect society, that the catholic religion is the only true religion, and that the church has any temporal power, either direct or indirect. Seventeen erroneous propositions concerning civil society were reproved; including the opinions that the civil power had the right to concern itself with religion and morals; that the state should control education; and that church and state ought to be separated. A further nine concerning natural and Christian ethics were condemned, particularly the belief that ethics and morals can be maintained without the basis and sanctions of revealed religion, and the maxim favoured by many states of neutrality or non-intervention in ecclesiastical matters. Ten propositions relating to Christian marriage were reproved; including the denial of the sacramental character of marriage, the assertion of the legitimacy of divorce and generally the belief that matrimonial cases are a matter for civil magistrates. Two propositions anathematised erroneous opinions about the temporal power of the Papacy, which held it to be unnecessary for the liberty and well-being of the apostolic see. Finally, four articles condemned false opinions concerning contemporary liberalism; that it was no longer expedient that catholicism alone should have the position of an established religion; that in Catholic states immigrants of other beliefs should enjoy religious toleration; that liberty should be granted to all citizens to propagate their own religious beliefs; and that the Roman Pontiff can and ought to be reconciled to and come to terms with progress, liberalism and modern civilisation.

Immediately a controversy arose concerning the interpretation of these two documents. The Encyclical was one of a series of papal pronouncements against modern errors; the Syllabus a brief compendium and summary of various propositions taken from previous papal allocutions and with references to thirty-two utterances of Pius IX; and both were accompanied by a covering letter from the cardinal secretary of state Antonelli to the episcopate. 'The Pope has already in encyclicals and allocutions condemned the principal errors of this most unhappy age. But all of you may not have received all the pontifical acts. Therefore the Pope wished a Syllabus of these errors to be drawn up for the use of all the catholic bishops, that they may have before their eyes the pernicious doctrines that he has proscribed.'[1] Taken at its face value, the Syllabus seemed to be a direct assault on the basic principles of modern society and to constitute a decisive rebuttal of all attempts of Liberal Catholics to effect their reconciliation. As such the Ultramontanes welcomed the papal pronouncements with acclamation. But was this the correct interpretation? Or could they bear a comparatively innocuous meaning? Bishop Dupanloup published a pamphlet, *La Convention du 15 septembre et l'encyclique du 8 décembre*, in which, accepting the distinction between the thesis and the hypothesis—a point well understood amongst theologians and also mentioned in the *Civiltà Cattolica*—he observed that the papal document declared the thesis, that is the absolute principles which ideally should govern a Christian society; but that this did not exclude the practical recognition and even acceptance *de facto* by the Papacy of the hypothesis, namely the practical compromises necessitated by an evil and gainsaying generation. All that Pius IX therefore had done was to recall the absolute principles of Christianity, which might be forgotten in prospect of the immediate makeshifts and compromises of the present situation. Thus, whilst Rome could not approve religious toleration and freedom of conscience as a universal ideal and absolute right, it could allow a *modus vivendi* with actual states which had enacted this in their constitution. So the Papacy could accept what was good in modern civilisation whilst repudiating what was evil; it was not progress or civilisation as such which were condemned, but a certain progress and a certain civilisation. The relief accorded to Catholic consciences by Dupanloup's exegesis was seen in the fact that many bishops expressed their gratitude to him, and the pope himself thanked him for his work. In similar vein Newman in England argued that 'as to the Syllabus, it has no connection with the Encyclical except that of date. It does not come from the Pope;...and it is not a direct act of the Pope, but comes to the bishops from Cardinal Antonelli, with the mere coincidence of time, and as a fact, each condemnation having only the weight which it had in the original papal document in which it is to be found. If an Allocution is of no special weight, neither is the condemnation of a proposition which it contains.'[2] To these troubled clerical voices there was added later that of a freethinking Frenchman, Émile Ollivier, chief minister of Napoleon's short-lived liberal

---

[1] J. B. Bury, *A History of the Papacy in the Nineteenth Century* (London, 1930), pp. 8–9.
[2] W. Ward, *The Life of John Henry, Cardinal Newman* (London, 1912), vol. II, p. 101.

empire, who likewise interpreted the documents of 1864 as of little importance, and particularly minimised the significance of the Syllabus.

On this interpretation, the scattered episcopate would need to engage in considerable historical research in order to be sure of the exact meaning and degree of authority attaching to each censured proposition. For example, they would need to discover that the condemnation of Free Church societies referred only to certain societies founded by Italian clergy of the Piedmontese kingdom which were concerned with the internal politics of Italy. Again, the condemnation of state control of education related only to the law of Piedmont abolishing clerical control of the instruction of youth, and the censure of the principle of non-intervention had reference to the political acts of aggression by Piedmont against the Papal States and the abstention by other European Catholic powers from the defence of the Papacy. Thus also the final resounding proposition was taken from an allocution of 1861 in which the pope specified certain anti-Catholic tendencies with which he could not compromise.

If the Liberal Catholic interpretation were correct, it must be allowed that what Dom Cuthbert Butler wrote of the final proposition, is true of all: 'as a piece of indexing, this proposition, thus out of its context, was singularly unfortunate'.[1] For assuredly the pope had chosen an unfortunate means of drawing the attention of all the bishops to various of his previous utterances, by abstracting them from their context and setting them forward apparently as succinct, authoritative statements of principle. Moreover, the purpose of circulating the Syllabus was stated in the covering letter to be that all the bishops would not have read all these separate papal pronouncements. To what end was the pith of them circulated without any of the qualifying and restrictive interpretations of their context, and in a form necessitating considerable investigation to establish their relevance and purport?

Two days before the publication of the Syllabus, Pius IX confided secretly to the cardinals of the Congregation of Rites that he had been considering the summoning of a General Council, and invited their counsel. Twenty-one replied; of whom only two were definitely opposed, six gave a qualified approval, whilst the majority accorded unqualified support; and a great number and variety of subjects for consideration were suggested. Accordingly, in March 1865 a Commission of five cardinals was nominated to prepare for the project; and in April a confidential letter was sent to thirty-four selected bishops (including Dupanloup and Manning), whose answers were mostly favourable, though the bishop of Orléans wished for postponement, whilst eight prelates included papal infallibility amongst their suggested subjects for discussion. On 26 June 1867, therefore, the pope formally announced his intention to convoke a General Council. By this time Dupanloup, and a majority of French Liberal

[1] Cuthbert Butler, *The Vatican Council*... (London, 1930), vol. I, p. 70.

Catholics, had swung round in favour of a council. They even professed confidence that it would pronounce in favour of their minimising interpretation of the Syllabus, and be a powerful influence towards a constitutional papal monarchy by emphasising the importance of the episcopate. In reply to the papal allocution an address was signed by 500 bishops, welcoming the proposal, and couched in language described as 'flamboyant, effusive and even adulatory. But Pio Nono was a very old man, and in a wonderful way the object of catholic affection, sympathy, admiration and enthusiasm.'[1] Preparations were now accelerated by the setting up of five commissions to deal respectively with matters of faith and doctrine, ecclesiastical discipline and canon law, religious orders and regulars, oriental churches and foreign missions, and politico-ecclesiastical affairs and the relations of church and state. Amongst theologians and canonists invited to Rome as consultors was the most learned conciliar historian of the Roman church, C. J. Hefele (later a member of the council as bishop of Rottenburg); and on 28 June 1868 the bull of summons was published, fixing the date of assembly for 8 December 1869, and referring to a wide and varied agenda of subjects for deliberation, without any specific mention of papal infallibility.

This official reticence did not mean that the definition of this new dogma was not already a matter of widespread discussion and controversy. On 8 February 1869 the *Civiltà Cattolica* described catholic opinion in France as desiring the council to define the Syllabus so as to remove doubts about its interpretation, to carry the definition of papal infallibility by acclamation, and to proceed further to proclaim the dogma of the Assumption of the Virgin Mary. It seems probable that the article was a deliberate *ballon d'essai*. Its importance was generally recognised; and provoked a reply in a remarkable series of articles in the *Augsburger Allgemeine Zeitung* by Ignatius von Döllinger, the doyen of the Roman Catholic school of church history at Munich, which were later published with additional matter, as a volume entitled *The Pope and the Council*, over the pseudonym of Janus. The significance of Döllinger's learned survey of the historical evidence could hardly be overstated. The fame of the Catholic school of history at Munich, including also J. A. Möhler and Hefele, had been one of the glories of the Roman church; and the mordant articles of Döllinger showed that the new proposal would not command the assent of some of its most erudite scholars. In *The Pope and the Council* there was nothing of the opportunism which weakened French liberal catholicism; though from the latter quarter indeed there appeared *Du Concile général et de la paix religieuse* by the dean of the Catholic theological faculty of the Sorbonne, Mgr Maret, which advocated the position taken in the famous decree *Frequens* of the Council of Constance, declaring the superior authority of a General Council over the Papacy and the

[1] Cuthbert Butler, *op. cit.* vol. I, p. 86.

desirability of such councils being held decennially. Both Maret and Dupanloup, however, before leaving France for the Council, issued a declaration of their adhesion and submission to whatever the assembly should finally decree.

In summoning the council, the pope had been faced by the difficult question whether invitations should be sent to Roman Catholic sovereigns. Papal relations with Victor Emmanuel evidently forbade his being invited; and this decision carried the corollary that no other Catholic rulers should be asked to send official representatives. This break with tradition provoked suspicion and criticism among the chancelleries of Europe, whilst by no means solving the problem of the relations of the civil powers to the council. For the assembly and continuance of the prelates depended upon the presence of Napoleon III's troops in Rome; if they were withdrawn, the Italian government would march into the city, and the council would be automatically suspended. Moreover, the position of Napoleon himself was delicate; growing Franco-Prussian tension demanded a close association with Italy; whilst Catholic opinion at home demanded the continued withholding of Rome from Victor Emmanuel. The south German Catholic state of Bavaria was anxious to promote joint diplomatic action by the chief European powers in regard to the programme of the council. Austria was hesitant, however, and Prussia unwilling; but, as Bismarck pointed out, France had the fate of the assembly entirely in its hands. In England Gladstone, the prime minister, was eagerly interested in the ecclesiastical question, closely allied with Lord Acton and sympathetic towards the anti-infallibilists, whereas his foreign secretary Lord Clarendon was briefed from the opposite standpoint by Odo Russell, the British representative in Rome, who in turn was plied with arguments by Manning, whom the pope dispensed from the oath of secrecy imposed upon the Conciliar fathers in order that he might prevent action on the part of Great Britain. In such a delicate diplomatic situation, although the assembly of the council had been unimpeded by political pressure, the course of its proceedings might at any time imperil the uneasy equilibrium.

From the organisation of its procedure such difficulties might arise in various ways. The very intricacies of managing the business of an assembly attended at its first congregation by 679 persons were formidable; and the provisions made in the bull *Multiplices Inter* of 2 December did not escape criticism. This document vested the right of proposing questions for deliberation by the council in the pope, whose decision was to be final upon suggestions submitted by the bishops. The council was to have as the basis of discussions in its general congregations a series of *schemata* drawn up by the preparatory theological and canonical commissions; and if after such discussion they needed revision, the task was to be committed to four deputations, each of twenty-four bishops, chosen by secret ballot. When revised, they were to be debated again in general congregation; and the final approval was to be given at a public session, where, after the bishops had voted *placet* or *non placet*, the pope solemnly proclaimed them. The first excitement occurred in the election of the deputation on Faith; preparatory to which a list of twenty-four names was circulated by Cardinal de Angelis to all the bishops, in honour of the Blessed Mary of the Immaculate Conception. When these twenty-four zealous infallibilists were elected to this vitally important deputation, to the exclusion of all anti-infallibilists, the latter felt themselves to have been tricked. This was hardly a promising overture to the council.

Worse, however, was to follow. The first *schemata* were all so roughly handled as to need drastic revision, and by this time it had become evident that the conciliar programme was badly out of order. From 25 February to 8 March therefore no general congregations were held, ostensibly in order that improvements might be made in the acoustic properties of that part of St Peter's used for the conciliar meetings, but actually to seek some way out of the procedural deadlock. This was found by the issue of new regulations; *schemata* were to be distributed to the bishops for their consideration and for submission of amendments in writing, prior to discussion in congregations. The appropriate deputations, after examining these written amendments, could then revise the *schemata* and submit them for oral discussion. It would still be possible for further amendments to be made during the debates; but the most important and controversial regulation was that by which closure could be applied to a debate in general congregation if ten bishops made a written request to this end and if the council by a simple majority voted for closure. Ninety bishops signed a protest against this method of procedure, and the ruling raised the delicate issue as to whether moral unanimity, as distinct from a numerical majority, was essential for a dogmatic definition. There was an evident difference between the application of the closure and the sufficiency of a majority vote in temporal legislatures, whose enactments could be repealed by subsequent assemblies, and the solemnity and unanimity requisite for the final acceptance by a general council of a dogmatic definition, which would remain irrevocable and irreversible. By this time the minority was deeply suspicious of the tactics of the majority and increasingly sensitive to anything bearing an appearance of a further entrenchment on its own rights.

On 21 January, moreover, there had been circulated the scheme Concerning the Church which touched all the nerve-centres of contemporary relations between church and state. It was a lengthy document, the first ten chapters of which defined the doctrine of the church, the two following dealt with the Roman primacy (but did not include the question of papal infallibility as distinct from the *magisterium*) and with the temporal power of the Papacy, and the last three with the relations of church and state. Although the subsequent insertion of a definition of papal infallibility became the principal, and even the sole, topic of conciliar discussion and diplomacy, at first interest centred in the chapters defining the relations of church and state. In these the ideal of the recognition of the church by the state was reaffirmed; the right of the Papacy to pronounce on and to censure the actions of the temporal power in accordance with the Christian revelation was asserted; and the *schema* claimed for the church the control of education, the exemption of its ministry from military service, the right to set up without restraint religious orders and to acquire and hold property and revenues. Amongst some Catholic states, the claim implicit in this section of the project *De Ecclesia* that the spiritual power possessed an indirect authority over the temporal caused considerable perturbation; and the question of a concerted diplomatic *démarche* to the pope was raised again.

Evidently the crux of this issue was the attitude of France, where on 2 January 1870 Ollivier had become First Minister. Ollivier was an unwavering champion of non-intervention in the affairs of the council; but the foreign minister, Count Daru, a friend of several leading Liberal Catholics was anxious to intervene; and the leakage of *De Ecclesia* to the press provided the occasion. On 20 February therefore, with the assent of the emperor, but without informing Ollivier, Daru sent a dispatch to the French ambassador for presentation to Cardinal Antonelli; but on the following day, when he reported his action to the council of ministers, orders were sent to delay presentation until they had had an opportunity of considering its terms. After revision and considerable toning-down from Ollivier, the memorandum was approved on 23 February. It was not an ultimatum; but a reminder to the Papacy that the issues raised by implication in *De Ecclesia* were an object of anxious concern to civil powers and an exhortation to the council to walk circumspectly in framing decrees on practical questions concerning the relations of church and state. Even so, if supported emphatically, this warning might have been effective. But Ollivier, increasingly convinced of the fundamental unwisdom of any overt act, set himself to win support from his ministerial colleagues and the emperor for his own policy of strict non-intervention, whilst Daru vainly canvassed the chancelleries of Europe for active support. On 19 March Antonelli's reply was dispatched, which underlined the distinction between thesis and hypothesis, reaffirmed the authority of the Papacy to censure the actions of civil powers, and dismissed Daru's fears as illusory. Faced by this retort courteous, which had not receded an iota from the words of *De Ecclesia*, the French administration resolved simply to iterate its former sentiments but without further diplomatic pressure. Moreover, on 11 April Daru resigned; and the telegram sent from Paris to Rome announcing this event succinctly summarised its importance: 'Daru resigns, Ollivier takes his place, Council free.'[1] The hope and

[1] E. Ollivier, *L'Église et l'état au concile du Vatican* (Paris, 1877), vol. II, p. 225.

threat of positive action by France had vanished. Henceforth the council could follow its own course.

The diplomatic episode indeed had been of greater importance in regard to the definition of papal infallibility than to the menaced rights of the civil power. For on 6 March it was announced that a *schema* on infallibility would be introduced for discussion in general congregation, and its text was distributed. Even so, with other *schemata* claiming priority of debate, it was doubtful when the new document would obtain attention. Accordingly a series of petitions to the pope were organised, praying him to accord precedence to the definition of infallibility; and these were followed by counter petitions from the minority. Pius IX acceded to the former requests and henceforth gave absolute priority to this question. On 13 May therefore the formal debate began, covering fifteen days, during which sixty-five bishops spoke; and forty more names had been entered when on 3 June a petition of 150 bishops for the application of the closure was carried, which in turn was followed by a protest from eighty bishops. The detailed consideration of the several sections followed from 6 June to 4 July and on 13 July the council took its penultimate vote on the *schema* defining the papal magistracy (*magisterium*) and infallibility, in which 451 bishops voted *placet*, eighty-eight *non-placet* and sixty-two gave conditional approval (*placet juxta modum*). After further consideration by the appropriate deputation and some not unimportant alterations, the revised definition was carried on 16 July, and the public conciliar session for the final vote and promulgation of the dogma was appointed for 18 July. On that date therefore, nature co-operating in the solemnities of the day by the incidence of a thunderstorm, 533 *placets* were recorded against two *non-placets*; and the constitution *Pastor Aeternus* was promulgated. Fifty-five bishops had departed from Rome after sending a letter to the pope explaining the reasons for their absence from the final session. On 19 July war was declared between France and Prussia; on 20 September Italian troops took possession of Rome, and on 20 October the pope prorogued the council *sine die*.

The definition of the papal magistracy and infallibility was thus carried without its attendant sections *De Ecclesia*, into which *schema* it should have fitted and of which it was a constituent element. Its first chapter defined the Petrine primacy, its second the perpetuity of this primacy in the Roman pontiffs, and its third declared the power and nature of the papal magistracy. It affirmed that 'this power of jurisdiction of the Roman Pontiff, which is truly episcopal, is immediate', that all, both pastors and people, are bound to submit to it in all things, including matters of government and discipline; and that this magistracy is so far from 'being of any prejudice to the ordinary and immediate power of episcopal jurisdiction, by which bishops, who have been set by the Holy Ghost to succeed and hold the place of the apostles, feed and govern each his own flock as true pastors, that this their episcopal authority is really asserted, strengthened and protected by the supreme and universal Pastor.'[1]

The fourth chapter defined the infallibility; 'that the pope, when he speaks *ex cathedra* to define a doctrine regarding faith or morals to be held by the universal church, is possessed of that infallibility bestowed by Christ on his church, and therefore such definitions of the Roman Pontiff are irreformable of themselves and not from the consent of the church.'[2]

The definition as promulgated was a compromise between the desires of a majority of bishops for a stronger and of a minority for a weaker document. In regard to the papal magistracy, the minority wished to omit 'truly episcopal' and to explain 'ordinary and immediate power'; and in respect of the infallibility to insert either 'and supported by the witness of the churches' (*et testimonio ecclesiarum innixus*) or 'not excluding the bishops' (*non exclusis episcopis*), in order to associate formally the authority of the church with papal prerogative. They failed to secure any of these modifications; instead, after the penultimate vote on the *schema* and before its final acceptance by the council, the infallibility definition was altered by the addition of the words in relation to papal definitions: 'not however by the consent of the church' (*non autem ex consensu Ecclesiae*). On the other hand the careful definition of the conditions of the exercise of the prerogative of infallibility, that the pope should speak *ex cathedra* and that his pronouncements should be confined to the spheres of faith and morals, were more restrictive than some of the majority had desired. The prorogation of the council as a result of international events prevented further consideration of the rest of the *schema De Ecclesia* and therewith a possible definition of the respective spheres and degrees of authority of Papacy and episcopate.

The political aftermath of the council indeed was unfavourable. On 1 November the pope placed the king and government of Italy under the ban of the church for their invasion of Rome; and refused all offers of compromise, including the law of guarantees, which offered all reasonable concessions short of renunciation of Rome as Italy's capital. This dissension remained unhealed until the concordat with Mussolini in 1929. In France the collapse of Napoleon III's regime, the Paris Commune and the

---

[1] 'Tantum autem abest, ut haec Summi Pontificis potestas officiat ordinariae ac immedi-atae illi episcopalis jurisdictionis potestati, qua episcopi, qui positi a Spiritu Sancto in Apostolorum locum successerunt, tanquam veri pastores assignatos sibi greges, singuli singulos pascunt et regunt, ut eadem a supremo et universali Pastore asseratur, roboretur ac vindicetur.' C. Mirbt, *Quellen*, pp. 463–4.

[2] 'Docemus et divinitus revelatum dogma esse definimus: Romanum Pontificem, cum ex cathedra loquitur, id est, cum omnium Christianorum Pastoris et Doctoris munere fungens pro suprema sua Apostolica auctoritate doctrinam de fide vel moribus ab universa Ecclesia tenendam definit, per assistentiam divinam, ipsi in beato Petro promissam, ea infallibilitate pollere, qua divinus Redemptor Ecclesiam suam in definienda doctrina de fide vel moribus instructam esse voluit; ideoque ejusmodi Romani Pontificis definitiones ex sese, non autem ex consensu Ecclesiae, irreformabiles esse.' *Ibid.*

protracted division between monarchists and republicans sowed the seeds of a fierce harvest of hostility between church and state. The emergence of Prussia as the dominant power in the German empire and the *Kulturkampf* of Bismarck against Rome presented the Papacy with its most acute conflict. Ecclesiastically, however, the Vatican definition secured easy general acceptance. The French Liberal Catholics were weakened fatally by internal divisions between anti-infallibilists and inopportunists; the former alone opposing the dogma on the ground of the contrary evidence of history, whilst the latter merely argued for the inopportuneness of its present definition. Moreover, the inopportunist bishops had relied on diplomatic intervention by Napoleon III's administration to save them from direct opposition to the wishes of Pius IX; and when this hope was frustrated, their ineffectiveness was manifest. A few prelates east of the Rhine, notably Hefele, Schwarzenberg, Haynald and Strossmayer, held out for varying periods before publishing the decrees and requiring their acceptance; but the most determined resistance came from the German universities of Munich, Bonn and Prague, culminating in the excommunication of professors Döllinger and Friedrich. From this there followed the Old Catholic schism which spread over to Switzerland and the Netherlands. But the dissidents were insignificant in numbers, though influential in erudition.

In Great Britain the affairs of the Church of Ireland, which had caused both ecclesiastical and political trouble throughout the period, came to a head in 1869. During the 1830's the payment of tithes to the Protestant Church of Ireland by Roman Catholics had provoked a protracted and bitter dispute, and the resultant act of 1838 had fixed a tithe rent charge on landlords, which involved the clergy in the loss of one-quarter of their ancient revenues. Before this problem had been thus settled, the Church Temporalities Act of 1833, the result of the report of a royal commission on the revenues of the Irish church published in 1832, had reduced the number of sees by amalgamation, and in so doing had provoked Keble's protest against National Apostasy, which Newman regarded as the proper beginning of the Oxford Movement. The grant of Roman Catholic emancipation in 1829 was bound indeed to lead to an increasing demand from Irish Roman Catholics for the disestablishment of the Church of Ireland; though the controversies about education during the middle of the century delayed the assault on the church. What could not have been anticipated, however, was that disestablishment would be effected by Gladstone, whose early views had demanded the maintenance of the establishment both in Ireland and England. The agitation of Cardinal Cullen, Sir John Gray, and Mr W. J. O'Neil Daunt was to be expected; but the conversion of Gladstone in 1865 to the principle of disestablishment and his avowal in 1867 of his intention to discharge 'a debt of civil justice, the disappearance of a national, almost a world-wide reproach, a condition indispensable to the success of every effort to secure the peace and contentment of that country', sounded the death-knell of the Irish establishment.[1] In 1869, despite the opposition of the episcopate and clergy of the Church of Ireland, the act of disestablishment and disendowment was carried; though its protagonist had made no practical provisions for the reconstitution of the disestablished church. The measure was certainly a portent of the change of mind on the part of the whilom author of 'The State in its relations with the Church'; and there was evidence to suggest that Gladstone was even beginning to contemplate in the abstract the possibility of a victory of the Nonconformist campaign for the like separation of church and state in England. The Irish episode encouraged his Free-church supporters in their persistent demand for disestablishment in England; but no further success was to attend their efforts until the Welsh church disestablishment act of 1914.

The churches during this period became much more keenly interested in social questions, and as a result developed a Christian social conscience. Indeed the 'condition-of-the-people' question became one of their major preoccupations. In France the intimate relationship between liberal catholicism and social questions was writ in such large letters in the career of Lamennais that he who ran might read; and his principles influenced many of his followers. Ozanam and his Society of St Vincent de Paul were active in good works, mainly of an ameliorative character in relation to individuals, whilst Buchez became the theorist of Catholic democracy. In 1848 a group of French Catholics associated with *L'Ère nouvelle*, a journal founded by Lacordaire and continued by Mgr Maret, upheld the principles of a Catholic social order. The victory of conservatism by the establishment of the Second Empire, however, gave little opportunity for the spread of their doctrines. In Germany Ketteler represented a moderate social catholicism and Döllinger was aware of the existence of social problems and of the need for sympathetic study by Catholic clergy and laity. In England a school of Christian socialism developed from the teaching and practical experiments of F. D. Maurice, for whom competition was antichristian, whilst co-operation was the divine law of the universe. He taught that socialism must be christianised if it was to remain true to its ideals and realise them in practice, whilst the church must accept the fundamental principle of co-operation. His own practical experiments in socialism failed; but he was a prophet born out of due time, and one of the seminal thinkers of his age. With the close of the Vatican Council, however, one generation was passing and another taking its place. Lacordaire had died in 1860, and Montalembert was to follow in 1870; and new problems and new men were to occupy the stage during the last generation of the nineteenth century.

Behind all the controversies concerning church and state, education and

[1] J. Morley, *Life of Gladstone* (London, 1903), vol. II, p. 257.

even social questions, moreover, the churches were facing the most serious and far-reaching challenge to the fundamentals of the Christian faith since the thirteenth century, thanks to the rapid discoveries in the various natural and applied sciences and to the movement of higher and lower criticism of the Bible. From the side of science Lyell's *Principles of Geology* in 1830 and his *Evidence of the Antiquity of Man* in 1863 overthrew the biblical chronology of creation worked out by Ussher; whilst Darwin's *Origin of Species* in 1859 set forth the revolutionary theory of evolution by natural selection in place of the biblical story of special creation. In 1865 E. B. Tylor's *Researches into the Early History of Mankind* raised new problems of anthropology and of the comparative study of religion. But if the impact of these studies upon religion was indirect (though not the less disturbing for that), the assault of literary and historical criticism of the Bible itself was direct and revolutionary. In regard to the Old Testament, the pioneer work of Eichhorn in the eighteenth century was followed in the nineteenth by Ewald's *History of the People of Israel* (1843), which interpreted the patriarchal period of the Hebrews as mythical and regarded Moses as the first historical figure; whilst De Wette argued that Deuteronomy belonged to the reign of Josiah, and Kuenen's *Religion of Israel* (1869) carried the process farther by contending that polytheism was the original Hebrew faith which survived until the exile. These theories were consummated by Wellhausen's *History of Israel* (1878), which elaborated the critical hypotheses concerning the Old Testament writings, placing the eighth-century prophetic books as the earliest and relegating much of the Pentateuch to a late date in Hebrew history. A faint anticipation of these theories had been set forth in England by H. H. Milman's *History of the Jews* (1830), which sought to prepare educated opinion for the shocks to come from Germany. More serious were the critical onslaughts on the New Testament. D. F. Strauss's *Leben Jesu*, translated by George Eliot in 1846, presented the gospels not as historical biographies but as mythical embodiments of spiritual truth. The author insisted that the religious value of the gospels was independent of their authenticity as historical documents. When the Tübingen school led by F. C. Baur sought to defend the substantial historicity of the New Testament by interpreting it, in accordance with Hegelian principles, as the result of a conflict between Judaistic and Gentile Christianity, which culminated in the evolution of catholicism, little comfort was derived by the orthodox. E. Renan's *Vie de Jésus* (1863) further disturbed traditional convictions. It was amidst this confusion and overturning of long-established opinions concerning the nature of revelation, the historical character of the Bible and the relationship of Christianity to science and to the comparative study of religions, that the churches entered into the last generation of the nineteenth century. The story of their gradual acceptance of the discoveries of science on the one hand and of the principles of biblical criticism on the other belongs to a later stage than the present narrative. Compared, however, with these far-reaching and fundamental issues, the strife between churches and states sinks into secondary place. Furthermore, the nineteenth century was witnessing contemporaneously the greatest missionary expansion of Christianity since the early centuries of its history; and this was chiefly the work of the non-Roman churches, particularly in the United States. Viewed against this vaster stage the quarrels of churches and states in the original Respublica Christiana of the European continent fade even farther into the background of old, unhappy, far-off things and battles long ago.

CHAPTER V

EDUCATION AND THE PRESS

EDUCATION, like every other department of European life, had been deeply affected by the French Revolution and its aftermath. All the European states had seen ancient institutions tumbled to the ground, ancient conceptions swept away; the only exceptions were Russia, remote in its eastern plains, and Great Britain, which in this, as in so many other ways, pursued its own course. In France, out of the debris of the old order had arisen the secular state-controlled 'University', founded by Napoleon in 1808 to direct secondary and higher education; nothing was done by the state for primary education until after the Restoration. In Germany academic learning took the place occupied in the other civilised countries of the West by political and economic life; there was nothing in other lands to compare with the German belief in education. In Prussia, in particular, the great revival after 1807 had produced the University of Berlin (1810), which set the standard of all nineteenth-century university work. The *Gymnasium*, or secondary school, was developed out of the old Latin school, and primary education was fostered on lines suggested by the Swiss teacher and theorist, Pestalozzi. When peace returned after 1815, there was a widespread interest in education, expressed both by statesmen and by theorists, in all European countries. Everywhere there was much to be done, more especially in the backward countries like Italy, the eastern provinces of the Habsburg empire, and Russia, and considerable efforts were made, though political reaction was often harmful to educational advance. As the century went on, educational policy was influenced in Europe itself by the urge towards national unity and the advance of democracy. In the wider world new prospects of expansion were opened by the growth of the United States and the British self-governing colonies, and by European penetration into other continents. At the same time, although the European world was becoming immensely larger, it was also, through the development of railways, steamships, and telegraphs, being reduced to a single projection, so that men had a far greater mastery of the world in which they lived. If the results at which they aimed were to be achieved, wider educational opportunities were necessary for every level of the population. In consequence the years between 1830 and 1870 saw both a great expansion of the activities of schools and universities in their traditional forms and the provision of greater facilities for the training of technicians, of adults, and of women. There were also striking developments in other methods of forming and influencing opinion, the most important of which was, of course, the newspaper press, which at this time assumed something like its modern form.

The problem which dominated the educational history of all European countries was that of the proper role of the state. To what extent should it intervene, and to what ends? What was to be its relationship with the churches and with private individuals who might, either corporately or individually, cherish independent aims and ideals of their own? France and the German states stood at one end of the scale and England at the other. Matthew Arnold, in his writings on European educational systems, was never tired of comparing the disorder of English methods, which left almost everything to private individuals and groups, with the ordered and regular state direction which he found in Germany or France, Holland or Switzerland. At the beginning of this period (1830–70) state intervention was not popular in England; yet, although most of the changes introduced were due to private effort, even there the state was taking an increasing share in the direction of educational policy. Both in France and in Prussia state control of education was one expression of the national sovereignty affirmed in the first by the revolution of 1789 and renascent in the second in the great period of reform after Jena. Many Frenchmen thought that the state would fail in its mission if it renounced its position as the promoter of education. A state system of education, Guizot wrote in his *Memoirs*, was imposed upon France by her 'history and national genius. We desire unity—the state alone can give it; we have destroyed everything, —we must create anew.'[1] Fichte had placed his hopes for the future of Germany in a new national system of education. The task of the state, Germans believed, was to elicit, by means of its educational system, the natural forces within itself, and to promote the realisation of the moral ideal by the advancement of culture and the careful training of its citizens. This conception was not limited to absolutist and militarist states like Prussia. In Switzerland, after the overthrow of the old oligarchic cantonal constitutions in 1830, the Liberals showed a great interest in education because they believed it to be the nerve-centre of democratic citizenship, the chief means of raising the level of national life. Consequently it was the duty of the state to help its citizens to make the most of themselves.

If this was to be the purpose of state control, it followed naturally that the education given by the state should serve the state's own purposes. Thus the government of Napoleon III closely controlled French education, and dismissed professors, such as Michelet the historian and Mickiewicz the Polish poet and Slavonic scholar, who were unfriendly to it. Similarly the government of Frederick William IV of Prussia imposed the Regulation of 1854 on the elementary schools to counteract the danger of modern ideas and to keep the schools loyal to the established system in church

[1] F. Guizot, *Memoirs to Illustrate the History of my Time* (trans. J. W. Cole; London, 1860), vol. III, p. 23.

and state. The most extreme form of this control was in Russia under Nicolas I (1825-55) when a Minister of Education defined the spirit of Russian education as that of 'Orthodoxy, Autocracy, Nationality' (cf. pp. 230 and 363). Yet the institutions, founded by the state to train its own officials, achieved results very different from those intended by statesmen and rulers. When under Alexander II (1855-81) the universities were allowed more freedom, they were producing a new educated class which, unlike the earlier cultured aristocracy, had no assured position in Russian national life. Hostile to the government and divided from the masses, the Raznochintsi, 'men of no class', were a potentially revolutionary force. In western countries, too, the policies of reactionary governments were unable to check the tendencies which made this the great age of academic liberalism. Professors and students played an important role in both the German and Italian revolutions of 1848. In Germany, especially, the universities transcended the barriers of states and religions, and were forcing-houses of liberal and national sentiment. The 'Göttingen Seven', professors of that university who were dismissed for protesting against the violation of the constitution by Ernest Augustus of Hanover (1837), were German heroes in their own day (cf. ch. XIX, p. 494). In Switzerland the growth of liberalism after 1830 was closely bound up with the spread of education, and, after the *Sonderbund* war, one of the signs of closer federal unity was the establishment of a federal technical university, the Zürich *Polytechnikum*, opened in 1855. But national sentiment was also a cause of educational conflict where nationalities overlapped. Much of the rivalry between Czech and German in Bohemia, or between Magyar and Slovak in Hungary, was fought out in the schools. The same is true of Pole and Russian. After the rising of 1830 Polish education was suppressed in the Russian borderlands, and after the rising of 1863 in the 'Congress' kingdom itself (cf. pp. 236 and 376).

Since the role of the state in education expanded rapidly between 1830 and 1870, conflicts could not fail to arise with individuals and associations, the most important of which was the church. The spread of education could hardly have occurred so rapidly without the state's assistance; yet, as the sphere of the state grew, there was necessarily less room for new experiments or new ideas. State intervention meant the growth of state 'systems'. In many lands, particularly in Germany, teaching programmes and policy were closely tied to the requirements of state service, and a large proportion of secondary school and university students aimed at government employment, for which the official examinations were a necessary qualification. The more bureaucratic educational institutions became, the greater the danger of a dull and stagnant uniformity, the less the scope for individual initiative. The danger was the greatest where the public system was the most efficient and the most extensive. Froebel's kindergarten was banned in Prussia, that Mecca of nineteenth-century educationalists (1851), and in nearby Denmark, where popular education had made considerable progress, Bishop Grundtvig and his followers felt that freedom and spontaneity were lacking. Another danger implicit in the growth of state education lay in the immense increase of the power which the state wielded over its citizens. A sharp conflict arose between the claims of the secular and of the spiritual worlds. This conflict was not inevitable. In many countries—in the German states, in Austria, in the Scandinavian lands—state and church worked harmoniously together in primary education, which had a definitely confessional character. In England there was little direct clash between religious and secular principles. This was replaced by the quarrels of 'church' and 'chapel', the Church of England and the dissenting sects, which left their deep mark on the Education Act of 1870, the root of the modern system of national education. In many countries, however, the conflict was joined directly between the claims of the Christian church, more especially the Church of Rome, and a secular view of education. The schools question was one of the main points at issue between the Roman Catholic church and the new Italian state. It was one of the causes of the *Sonderbund* war in Switzerland, and it dragged on as a source of trouble after 1848. The most complete surrender made by the state to the claims of the church was the Austrian Concordat of 1855, the climax of a policy inspired by fear of revolution (cf. ch. xx, p. 533).

The attitude of the Liberals towards the problem of the state, the church, and the school varied very much from country to country, according to the local situation. In France Catholics struggled for years against the monopoly of secondary education held by the University, until the *Loi Falloux* of 1850 gave to private persons—or, in effect, to the church—the right to open secondary schools freely (cf. ch. iv, p. 80). Many Liberals, like Lamartine, had opposed the monopoly of the University, and Montalembert, the Catholic leader, had based his policy on an appeal to civil and religious liberty. In Belgium dislike of the state monopoly of primary education under Dutch rule had been an important cause of the revolution of 1830, after which a policy of complete educational freedom had been adopted. Yet the educational question broke down the alliance between Catholics and Liberals, the latter perceiving that educational freedom meant in fact clerical dominance. In 1834 both parties set up universities, the Catholics at Malines, transferred in 1835 to Louvain, and the Liberals at Brussels. The primary-school law of 1842 was favourable to the church, but the secondary-school law of 1850 strengthened the control of the state and was strongly disliked by the Catholic party. In Holland the elementary-school system, set up during the Napoleonic period (1806), gave only unsectarian religious teaching; moreover, primary education was a state monopoly, and permission to open private schools was only very sparingly granted. On one side it was argued that it was the duty of the state to provide undenominational education everywhere and to continue the existing system; on the other that such a system overrode individual and parental rights. The question divided the Liberals; some supported educational freedom, but the fear of clerical influence was strong enough to impose severe restrictions on the grant of freedom of education in the Constitution of 1848. The state monopoly was finally broken by the law of 1857, but this satisfied neither the orthodox Protestants nor eventually the Catholics. In fact the respective claims of the state, the individual, and the group proved everywhere more difficult to satisfy than was envisaged by the Liberal theory of personal freedom.

The concern of politicians and men of affairs with educational problems was matched by the attention given to them by theorists; both alike show the increasing part which education was coming to play in European thought and consciousness. One of the leaders of the preceding half-century, the Swiss, Johann Heinrich Pestalozzi, had died in 1827, but his belief that the potentialities of the child must be brought out by the orderly development, through his own activities, of his powers and instincts, remained a strong force in popular education. One of Pestalozzi's contemporaries in Switzerland was Philipp Emanuel von Fellenberg, who had set up, on his estate at Hofwyl, a series of schools, each offering to different classes of society an education appropriate to their position. His work attracted much attention from foreign observers, and he was actively at work until his death in 1844. Among the many German thinkers who were influenced by Pestalozzi were Johann Friedrich Herbart (1776–1841) and Friedrich Wilhelm August Froebel (1782–1852). Herbart set out to form a science of education based on a comprehensive view of psychology and ethics which laid great stress on the importance of teaching method. His ideas gained much support among university teachers in Germany who were concerned with educational theories, and were later much studied in America and England. Froebel was a pioneer of better methods of educating small children. He taught that they should be shown the interconnections between things and stimulated to creative activity through play, and for this purpose he invented a series of 'gifts' and 'occupations' to develop their capacities. The 'gifts' consisted in blocks of varying shapes from which figures could be constructed, the 'occupations' in the making of mats, clay and paper models, and so on. The former were to teach the child to assimilate, the latter were to teach him to express himself. The first school for small children based on these ideas was founded in 1837, and received the name *Kindergarten*. Froebel was frowned upon by the Prussian government, as already mentioned, and his work was influential rather in England and America than in Germany.

Both in France and England the major political and social theorists were concerned with educational problems. The English Utilitarians of

1830, with their belief in 'the greatest happiness of the greatest number', were naturally deeply interested in them. Both Jeremy Bentham and James Mill had written on the subject, the latter, in particular, showing the greatest confidence in the results which education could achieve. Another important English thinker of a later date was Herbert Spencer (1820–1903). Profoundly influenced by the new scientific ideas, he insisted on the importance of psychology and stressed that the education of the child must be in harmony with the natural stages in the evolution of his mind, and also with the successive stages in the evolution of human civilisation. He strongly emphasised the value of scientific knowledge, which alone could train human beings in the skills necessary for complete living. In France Auguste Comte (1798–1857) was also demanding a 'positive' education which should be in conformity with the needs of modern times, and should be based on the teaching of the sciences in their relationship to one another. The earlier French Socialist schools of thought, which followed Charles Fourier and Henri de Saint-Simon, both stressed the importance, alike for society and for the individual, of bringing out the child's natural aptitudes, and the Saint-Simonians, at least, helped to diffuse a general interest in popular education.

In practical achievement Germany took the lead, alike in the universities, in secondary and technical schools, and in primary education. Travellers from all over Europe and beyond testified their admiration of what had been done. The American, Horace Mann, Secretary of the Massachusetts State Board of Education, writing in the 'forties, considered that Prussia, Saxony, and some of the western and south-western German states stood foremost in the education of the people. The French observer, Victor Cousin, had already, in 1831, called Prussia 'that classic land of barracks and schools, of schools which civilise the people and of barracks which defend them'.[1] There, and in the German states generally, education was compulsory, but the provision of the Prussian Constitution of 1850 that it should be gratuitous had not been carried out. In Austria the government had made great efforts, and in the western provinces of the Habsburg empire a very high proportion of children went to school. However, there were serious deficiencies in the provisions made for popular education, and the level of attainment was much lower than in north Germany. The Elementary School Law of 1869 made more generous provision for the training of teachers and extended the period of school attendance to eight years.

Great advances were made by Germany's neighbours, the Swiss, the Scandinavians, and the Dutch. The primary schools of Holland were praised by Mann and by Cousin, and by English observers like Dr Kay (Sir James Kay-Shuttleworth) and Matthew Arnold. Arnold also, writing

---

[1] Victor Cousin, *De l'instruction publique dans quelques pays de l'Allemagne...* (3rd edn, Paris, 1840), vol. I, p. 26.

in the 'sixties, called the schools of the more advanced Swiss cantons among the best in Europe; there had been a rapid growth of the cantonal systems after 1830, and, in general, education had been made compulsory. The Scandinavian countries made considerable strides, often in the face of great difficulties. In all of them the state undertook to establish and control a general system of primary schools, covering the whole country, including the sparsely populated rural districts. This was done in Sweden in 1842 and in Norway in 1860; in more thickly peopled Denmark, the state system, which dated from 1814, was improved by a law of 1856. In all three states education had been made compulsory. The Scandinavian lands also produced some interesting educational ideas of their own. In Denmark, Kristen Kold (1816–70), a disciple of Bishop Grundtvig, developed the 'Free Schools' on more unfettered lines than the state system. Sweden took the lead in recognising gymnastics as a necessary part of school training, and the most important educational thinker of Finland, Ugo Cygnaeus (1810–88), was a pioneer of manual training in schools.

In the politically advanced states of western Europe general literacy was a necessary adjunct of advancing democracy. In addition, the demand for better education was the demand of an age of increasing technical complexity. Those who used and controlled machines needed more 'book-learning' than their peasant ancestors. Another contributory influence was that of humanitarianism, the desire to help the less fortunate members of society, which was also expressed, for instance, in English factory legislation. Not only was popular education something bestowed from above; it was also, to some extent, the result of a demand from below. Leaders of the English working class, such as Robert Owen and the Chartist, William Lovett, were deeply concerned with these problems, and in France there was a belief among the workers that education was the key to the betterment of their conditions and a desire that it should be both free and compulsory. Neither in France nor in England had this goal been generally attained by 1870. So far as methods are concerned, the great vogue of the mutual, or Lancasterian, system, whereby the master taught monitors, who taught the other children, was over by the 'thirties. In 1837 the French Society for Elementary Instruction undertook an inquiry, and found that the weaknesses of the system were recognised in many different countries. A comprehensive primary-school organisation came into existence much earlier in France than in England. The Education Law of 1833 ordered each commune to have a school and each department to have a college for training teachers. When Matthew Arnold visited France in 1859 his judgment was favourable; the level reached was low, but the increase of national well-being was bound to push it higher. It was also in 1833 that the English government made its first grant to the two societies, the Church of England 'National' Society and the undenominational 'British' Society. These grants were gradually increased in size, but progress was checked by the introduction, in 1862, of a system of paying grants according to examination results. No general law was passed until Forster's Education Act of 1870, which preserved the existing denominational schools and supplemented them by new schools supported out of the rates. The Scottish parish schools had a fine history dating from the seventeenth century; they earned the praise of Mann, and were perhaps unique in that they aimed at preparing students for the university, which they entered at a lower age than in England. The statutory system, which was insufficient to meet all the country's needs, had been supplemented by many voluntary schools of various kinds; most of these came into the reorganised state system set up by the Scottish Education Act of 1872.

In southern and eastern Europe, in comparison, conditions were deplorable and illiteracy widespread. The newly united Italian kingdom grappled at once with the problem, which was most serious in the south, by the law of 1859, and a real improvement was made, but 72 per cent of the population were still illiterate in 1871.[1] In the eastern provinces of Austria and in Hungary education was also very backward. The 1869 Hungarian census showed 63 per cent illiterates and 9·7 per cent who could read but not write.[2] The problem was most immense in Russia. Nothing was really attempted until the reforms of Alexander II in the 'sixties, when the liberation of the peasantry brought the question to the fore (cf. ch. xiv, p. 378). The *Zemstva*, or District Councils, set up in 1864, did good work, but their task was hardly begun in 1870.

In its higher levels education was forced, by the advance of science, to meet new requirements. The pre-eminence of the classical disciplines came under attack. One demand was for general secondary education of a wider scope which should give a larger place to science and the modern languages; another demand was for technical training for industry because an industrial civilisation required an ever-increasing supply of trained technicians in the senior ranks as well as a higher standard of general literacy in the lower. Alike in classical, in modern, and in technical studies German institutions were efficiently organised. The Prussian *Gymnasium* was meant to give an all-round education based on the classics. In 1834 it was finally made impossible for anyone who had not passed the *Gymnasium* Leaving Certificate to enter the universities, which were the road to state service. There were certain differences in emphasis between the systems of the different German states, but there was a broad likeness between all of them; the Austrian system had originally imposed a much more limited curriculum, but it was effectively reformed in 1849. During this period the *Realschulen*, giving a thorough training on the basis of

[1] Benedetto Croce, *History of Italy, 1871–1915* (Eng. trans.; Oxford, 1929), p. 57.
[2] Scotus Viator (R. W. Seton-Watson), *Racial Problems in Hungary* (London, 1908), p. 207.

modern subjects, had been growing in importance: they had originated in the early part of the century, and were regulated by law in Prussia in 1832 and also in 1859, when the courses of the *Realschulen* of the first grade were made parallel with those of the *Gymnasia*. Similar developments were to be found in other countries, through the institution either of courses in modern subjects (Belgian Secondary Schools Law of 1850) or of separate modern schools (Dutch Law of 1863).

Both in France and in England the curricula of the secondary schools were purely classical and little had been done to promote modern studies. In England the deficiencies of the traditional course were stressed by publicists like Herbert Spencer and T. H. Huxley, and, towards the end of the 'sixties, public interest was being aroused in the problem. In 1870 a Royal Commission was set up to consider scientific instruction and the advancement of science. In France a system of 'bifurcation' between literary and scientific studies had been introduced in 1852, but it was not a success, and in 1865 a plan for 'special scientific instruction' was introduced into the schools in its place. The French schools, the *collèges royaux* or *lycées* and the *collèges communaux*, formed part, with the faculties, of the Napoleonic University. Until 1850 private schools, or, in effect, church schools, could not exist without prior licence; when they were permitted, they tended to revolve in a different orbit from that of the state schools, with little contact between the two. However, the state maintained its control over degrees, and the school course led everywhere to the *baccalauréat*, which was a state examination. Consequently there were critics, as in Germany, where similar conditions existed, who complained that schoolboys were made to work much too hard, and that examinations, especially those for the higher professional schools, pressed far too hardly upon them. Strictly professional studies played an important part in higher education, and, once a student left school, he entered his training for a definite career. As a result, the link between formal education and liberal culture which, in other countries, was forged primarily by the universities was, in France, associated rather with the final years of the secondary school course. One example of this French conception of studies was the important part played by philosophy in the final *lycée* year.

The French *lycées*, Matthew Arnold thought, gave an admirable education at moderate cost. In England there was nothing to compare with the comprehensive system of public instruction which they provided. There were, he argued, a few great schools where the standard was very high, but, for the great mass of the middle class, nothing effective was being done, with the result that they were nearly the worst educated in the world. Arnold's plea for the state organisation of secondary education went unheeded for a generation. There was no government control and no general system; apart from many unsatisfactory private schools, there were only the ancient grammar schools, many of them inefficiently or even corruptly run, and the much smaller group of 'public schools', mostly consisting of boarding schools, which had largely developed out of them. It was during this period that the 'public school' system took its modern shape, both through the reorganisation of older schools by men like Thomas Arnold, Headmaster of Rugby (1828–42), and through the foundation of many new ones. But, although the recommendations of the Taunton Commission of 1864–7 checked abuses of grammar school endowments, England was still behind her neighbours in 1870.

Technical and professional training was also growing in importance everywhere. In Germany large numbers of technical schools had been set up, often humble in their origin and not well co-ordinated. Gradually they came to form a hierarchy according to the level of the education which they offered, one strong external influence being that of the Zürich *Polytechnikum*, which became the model for the German technical universities. Towards 1870 some of the leading technical institutions, such as those of Karlsruhe (1825), Dresden (1828), and Stuttgart (1829) were moving towards university rank, but the full development of technical universities came after 1870. However, in the years 1868–72, the German higher technical schools had already a yearly average of some 3500 pupils.[1] France had its *École Centrale des Arts et Manufactures*, founded in 1828, and other lower-grade schools, but England was far behind. The Prince Consort was deeply interested, and wished to set up an institution at South Kensington on the site purchased from the profits of the 1851 Exhibition. This was never done, but the site became the headquarters of the Science and Art Department, an offshoot of the Board of Trade, founded in 1853. This did something by making grants to encourage science teaching, but its operations were not extensive, and a government inquiry of 1868 revealed England's weaknesses.

One special type of professional instruction which was much extended everywhere at this time was the Training College for elementary school teachers, or Normal School. Here again the Germans were pioneers, and the training colleges were one main source of the progress of popular education in Germany. The most prominent figure in the Prussian elementary education of his day was F. A. W. Diesterweg (1790–1866), who was head of the Berlin college from 1832 until his supersession in 1847. The Swiss training colleges were also highly praised by English observers. Their most prominent leader was Johann Jakob Wehrli (1790–1855), who had worked under Fellenberg at Hofwyl and was head of the Kreuzlingen college (1834–53). One of his leading principles was the combination of manual labour with ordinary classroom instruction. In England the Committee of the Privy Council on Education, set up in 1839, failed to

---

[1] J. Conrad, *The German Universities for the Last Fifty Years* (Eng. trans. Glasgow, 1885), p. 188.

establish a national Normal School because of the religious difficulty, but their secretary, Dr Kay, established a successful school at Battersea in 1840, which was later transferred to the 'National' Society. An earlier effort had been that of David Stow at Glasgow (1836). In England, official policy after 1846 was to create a large body of trained teachers by instituting a pupil-teacher system.

At the top of the education ladder stood the university. This was one of the fundamental institutions of European life, and all the different universities shared much in common. The great model institutions of the time, where modern standards of research and scholarship were being developed, were the German universities. In the eighteenth century the three professional faculties of Theology, Law, and Medicine had ranked higher than the fourth faculty of Philosophy, but in the nineteenth century that faculty, the home of independent study for its own sake, became the most important part of these universities, which aimed, as a whole, to be laboratories for scientific research. German professors were pre-eminently scholars and original investigators, and university study concentrated more and more on detailed scholarship. Significant of the general trend was the growth of the 'seminar' or small class in which advanced work was done under the guidance of the professors. Both to them and to their students the goal was the pursuit of learning for its own sake. The great names in German science and learning were to be found in the universities as they were not at this time in England. It was in Germany that scientific research was first organised and linked with education; Müller in physiology, Gauss in mathematics, Liebig in chemistry, were all university teachers (cf. ch. III, p. 50).

The universities of Austria, of German Switzerland, of Holland, and of Scandinavia followed, in general, the German type of organisation. In the German lands of the Austrian crown the same progress had not been made as in the other German states. Particularly before 1848 the Austrian universities, like the schools, were bound to a strict routine. *Gymnasium* teachers and university professors alike were forced to keep to the state-permitted texts. The faculties were supervised by Directors of Studies who watched over both professors and students. The emphasis was not on independent thought, but on learning by rote; there were too many examinations and too many restrictions. Even after 1849 the spirit of the regime was unfavourable to academic freedom, though the Austrian universities had some distinguished men among their teachers. Two major schemes for extending higher education which came to nothing were Bishop Grundtvig's plan for a great Scandinavian university, and the project of establishing a federal university in Switzerland, which failed to overcome cantonal and religious jealousies. However, new cantonal universities were founded at Zürich (1833) and Berne (1834), and in 1835 Basle, the ancient university of German Switzerland, was reorganised.

Only in France was there no real university life in the sense in which it was known in other states. The old foundations had been swept away by the Revolution, and Napoleon had created separate faculties of Theology, Law, Medicine, Science, and Letters. The first had been opposed by the Roman Catholic Church, and the Roman Catholic Theological Faculties fell into disuse; the second and third were merely professional schools; the last two merely provided examining boards or lecture courses for a floating group of casual listeners. Guizot, Minister of Public Instruction (1832–6), wished to set up real universities with a full course of instruction and a true corporate existence, but his scheme came to nothing; the same fate befell a later scheme of Victor Cousin to set up a university at Rennes (1840). The faculties remained scattered over the country, often in isolation from one another; it was impossible for them to have any real corporate sense or to become genuine centres of learning. In contrast to them, however, there was one important centre of higher scholarship in Paris, the *Collège de France*, which enjoyed a wide freedom. Among its professors were distinguished men like Michelet, Cuvier, Ampère, and Berthelot; it had no prescribed course and prepared for no examinations. Under Napoleon III the Minister Duruy was anxious to improve higher education; in 1868 he organised the *École Pratique des Hautes Études* as a centre for research work in history, mathematics, and natural sciences. Strictly professional studies played a larger part in higher education in France than in other countries; the pre-eminent institutions of this type continued to be the *École Polytechnique*, training men for the civil and military engineering services of the state, and the *École Normale Supérieure*, training men for the higher posts in secondary education.

The French had reformed secondary and higher education in Italy during the Napoleonic period, but the advances which had been made were lost, after 1815, through the rigidity of the censorship and the strength of clerical influence. The Normal School at Pisa, founded on the model of the *École Normale Supérieure*, was closed; the Tuscan government reopened it in 1846, but there were no pupils left in it in 1862. There were numerous universities, of which Naples and Bologna were the best known, but the atmosphere prevented the development of new studies and crushed out independent thought. The Education Law of 1859 made the new Italian state and the local authorities jointly responsible for secondary and higher education; it also required a definite entrance standard for the universities and introduced greater strictness into their examinations. However, as in primary education, the path of progress was long and stony. Matthew Arnold, in his *Schools and Universities on the Continent* (1868), pointed out that very few students were reading literary or scientific subjects at the universities; the great majority were to be found in the professional faculties of medicine and law. The increased severity in examinations ordained by the law of 1859 had not been carried out. The authorities were slack and indulgent, and there was laxity and want of discipline on the part both of professors and students.

The English universities stood rather apart from those of other European nations; they aimed at producing well-educated gentlemen, while the German universities aimed at producing scholars and officials. They did not give professional training; they did little to foster research, aiming at nothing more than the course for the first degree, which, though exacting for honours, had a low pass-standard. In Matthew Arnold's opinion they were no more than higher schools. Their riches and the limitation of their privileges to members of the Established Church meant that they came under severe attack from reformers, many of whom wished to sweep away the collegiate system, and to exalt professorial teaching on German lines, or according to the practice of the Scots universities, which had their own independent, more egalitarian traditions. Yet the older English universities, for all their conservatism, had a real tradition of their own, of education as a corporate experience, as a preparation for life, a tradition which had its own value, and which was gradually brought into line with the conditions of the time. Oxford and Cambridge were not finally freed from religious tests until 1871. By that time the foundation of new universities, which were often free from such tests, was well under way, the most important of them being the University of London, chartered in 1836, which was, however, purely an examining body at the centre of a number of independent colleges. Other new institutions were Durham University, chartered in 1837, and Owens College, Manchester (1851), the germ of the modern Manchester University. All these foundations were the result not of state action but of private initiative.

The general educational history of the United States is a striking illustration of the adaptation of European ideas to a new environment. The most advanced area was New England and the most backward the South, which was, in addition, seriously set back by the Civil War. The general tendency in elementary and secondary education was towards a public, non-sectarian system, which was one aspect of the extension of democratic ideas. As an English critic of 1856 wrote: '...the loose, free tone of equality seems to cry aloud in the common schools—the same tone the hoarser echo of which rises afterwards on the platform and around the ballot box.'[1] During the second quarter of the century there were long struggles in the northern states for and against the system of free, tax-supported, state-controlled, and non-sectarian elementary education. Such schools were bitterly opposed by many ecclesiastical and propertied interests, but the question had been settled in principle in the northern states by 1850, an important landmark being the Pennsylvania Free School Law of 1834. In secondary education the same demand for public schools under public control led to the rise of the Public High Schools,

[1] *Saturday Review* (London), 8 November 1856, vol. II, p. 616.

the first of which had been created at Boston in 1821, though the privately controlled 'academies' were still very strong at the end of the period. In higher education the impulse towards state control led to the foundation of state universities in the southern and western states, though these were to become really important much later. This was the great period of the small denominational college, generally poor and struggling, and often with too many local competitors. Nevertheless, as settlement extended, so colleges of this type spread with it, and they did important civilising work on the frontier. At the end of the Civil War the level of American higher education was low, even in the old colleges of the east, such as Harvard, Yale, and Princeton. Their courses were elementary and their curricula old-fashioned. However, about 1870, great reforms were beginning, with new foundations such as Cornell University (1868) and new academic leaders such as Charles W. Eliot, who became President of Harvard in 1869. An important source of progress was the example of Germany, for it was to German universities that American students usually went for foreign study. European ideas also influenced the growth of the common schools through the work of reformers like Horace Mann of Massachusetts and Henry Barnard of Connecticut and Rhode Island. The latter spread new ideas through his *American Journal of Education*, founded in 1855; one of the former's achievements was to found the first state Normal School for primary teachers at Lexington (Mass.) in 1839.

English educational ideas were very widely extended during this period both in the self-governing colonies and in India. In the former, the general shape of the English system was reproduced, except in Lower Canada where French ideas were strong. Most of the self-governing colonies organised some system of elementary education either before 1870 or very soon after. As in England denominational rivalries played a large part. In New South Wales and Victoria there was conflict between the advocates of a national and of a denominational system. In the Canadian provinces there was sharp rivalry between the churches in higher education, Bishop John Strachan, for instance, fighting a long, but finally unsuccessful, battle to keep the later Toronto University under Anglican control. Another article of export was the English 'public school', which found imitators in Australia, New Zealand, and South Africa. A far different, and far greater, problem was that of India. At the beginning of the period there was much discussion whether the English authorities should support the traditional learning of the East or introduce education on western lines. The critical decision was taken in 1835 in favour of the latter course.[1] The famous Minute drawn up by T. B. Macaulay had something to do with the decision, but there were other important advocates of the same

[1] The background to this decision has been a subject of controversy. For a discussion of the problem see K. A. Ballhatchet, 'The Home Government and Bentinck's Educational Policy' in *Cambridge Historical Journal*, vol. x, no. 2 (1951), pp. 224-9.

course, officials like C. E. Trevelyan, liberal Hindu thinkers like Ram Mohan Roy, and missionary educators like Alexander Duff, who had founded the 'General Assembly's College' at Calcutta in 1830. The decision was based upon the belief that western-educated Indians would be assimilated to western ways, and that western ideas would filter down through them to the great mass of the people. The policy, in fact, ignored the depth of the differences between East and West—for instance, the clash between school training and home influences. Sir Charles Wood's Despatch of 1854 planned a complete system based on grants-in-aid from the government, and the first universities, which were purely examining bodies like the University of London, were opened in 1857. The faults of the British Indian system were numerous. Too little attention had been paid to primary education, though this was an enormous problem, and means were strictly limited. The secularised British schools made little appeal to the Muhammedans, who distrusted a system of education divorced from their religion. The type of education given was too purely literary and contained too little of scientific and technical disciplines, which the Indians needed. A graver political criticism is that the British 'Raj' gave very few opportunities to the classes whom it had educated, and thus fostered discontent with itself. Nevertheless, the British had done remarkable work in India in a short time. It is interesting to compare the situation in the Dutch East Indies where the chief emphasis had been on schools for resident Europeans. However, even for them, secondary education was only beginning after 1860. The natives could get a western education only by entering European schools, and this was difficult for them to do. Not much had been done for primary education. In fact, the Dutch colonies were half a century behind British India, though more progress was made after 1864.

Apart from their wider geographical extension, the traditional European systems of education were also being extended in their homelands to touch new sections of the population. One important aspect of this expansion during the second half of the century was the public education of women, involving their claim to a proportionate share in general educational advantages. Of the great European nations, the most backward here were the French. The Minister Duruy in the 'sixties promoted extension courses for girls, but state secondary schools did not come till the 'eighties. In Germany there were secondary schools but none beyond that level. In England more had been done, though the movement was only beginning. The Christian Socialists—F. D. Maurice, Hughes, Kingsley, and their friends—were concerned with the foundation of Queen's College, London (1848). Two of its early pupils, Frances Mary Buss and Dorothea Beale, were important respectively in the growth of girls' day schools and girls' boarding schools. However, in the 'sixties, only some 2 per cent of the endowments of secondary education were appropriated to girls' schools.

The next step was university education. In London, Bedford College, which already had twenty years of history, was incorporated in 1869, and in 1870 University College opened its doors to women. At Cambridge the two older womens' colleges date from 1869 and 1871. In Scandinavia girls' secondary schools had been set up, and in 1870 girls were given the right to be admitted as university students in Sweden. In view of the general condition of the country, Russia had also made great progress. The first *Gymnasia* for women had been set up in 1858; in 1873 there were some 190 secondary schools of different grades for them and by that date they were making their way into the universities.[1] The greatest progress, however, was that of the United States. Early pioneers were Mary Lyon and her school at Mount Holyoke (1837–49) and Emma Willard and her school at Troy (1821–38). Oberlin College, opened in 1833, gave equal opportunities to women from the start, and the first of them graduated in 1841. Antioch College, opened in 1853, followed the same example. By 1870 several of the state universities in the western states had been opened to women. In the eastern states the tendency was towards the foundation of separate colleges, the key date here being the opening of Vassar College in 1865.

Adult education had attracted much interest in England. Many 'Mechanics' Institutes' had been founded, though these generally failed to attract the real working-class. The 'Christian Socialists' were doing useful work in the 'fifties, and in 1867 James Stuart began the lectures in northern towns which were one of the roots of the University Extension Movement. Another example of this desire to touch the adult masses is to be found in the Peoples' High School Movement in Denmark, inspired by Bishop Grundtvig (1783–1872). The fundamental influences on his mind were those of Christianity, patriotism, and Scandinavian mythology. He had been impressed on his visits to England in 1829–31 by the freedom of English education and the intensity of its corporate life. After his return home he elaborated a new theory of education which aimed at arousing the Danish people and giving them a new sense of freedom and community. He attacked traditional education as dead and mechanical, and wished to replace it by education for life, the clash of mind on mind instead of the imparting of dead information. He thought that childhood was too early for this to be achieved, and that real education of this sort could not be carried out till after the age of 18. His own schemes, for instance, for a great Scandinavian university, were not successful, but, in the crisis through which Denmark passed in the mid-nineteenth century, the high-water mark of which was the war of 1864 with Austria and Prussia, his ideas were adapted by others to the needs of the time. The first

[1] C. Hippeau, *L'Instruction publique en Russie* (Paris, 1878), pp. 245–6; see also Alfred Rambaud in *Revue des Deux Mondes* (Paris), 15 March 1873, vol. CIV, p. 327. Rambaud's and Hippeau's figures differ slightly.

Peoples' High School was opened in the border province of Schleswig in 1844, and the movement gradually spread, its chief practical leader being Kristen Kold, who really brought the idea into touch with the life of the peasantry. The schools gave winter courses to the peasant farmers. They had no utilitarian aims, no examinations and no fixed syllabus. Their purpose was to quicken the spirit and to strengthen national sentiment. Their achievement was to raise the standards of the peasantry, both morally and in practical life.

The Danish Peoples' High Schools stand at the junction between formal education and more general cultural influences on opinion. Another movement which appealed to adults was the Lyceum Movement in the United States, which offered lecture courses, both for instruction and for amusement. At their height, in the 'fifties and 'sixties, they attracted lecturers like Emerson, Greeley of the *New York Tribune*, and Agassiz the scientist. Another powerful influence on opinion was provided by the growth of free lending libraries. There had, of course, long been learned libraries and subscription libraries of various kinds, but at this time an attempt was made, in England and the United States, to bring books to people who could not buy them or pay fees for borrowing them. In both countries the public library movement began about the middle of the century, and, by 1870, was still only in its first beginnings. In England something had been done by the Mechanics' Institutes. The first legal provision was 'Ewart's Act' of 1850 which allowed boroughs to establish libraries and museums if they wished, but gave no permission to spend money on books. The act is named after its main promoter in Parliament, William Ewart, but most of the work of collecting information and statistics had been done by Edward Edwards, who became the first librarian of the Manchester library, the first opened under the act. In 1855 another act allowed the levy of a penny rate to be spent on books. A parliamentary return of 1870 showed that there were, in 1868, fifty-two libraries in existence, containing about 500,000 books.[1] In the United States the earliest efforts were to set up libraries in school districts. The first state to legislate in this way was New York in 1835, and it was followed by many others, but the plan was not generally a success, one reason being that the unit of administration was too small. The scheme which was ultimately successful was similar to the English plan of allowing towns to establish rate-supported libraries. The pioneer was Boston, which got power to set up a public library in 1848, the library itself being opened in 1854. The first state to pass a general law was New Hampshire in 1849, followed by Massachusetts in 1851, and by three other states before 1870. At that date the public library system was at its strongest by far in Massachusetts which had, in 1872, eighty-two libraries with some 565,000 volumes.

---

[1] *Libraries and Museums: Abstract of Return...*, H.C. 168 (1870), LIV. The figures have been summarised by J. J. Ogle in *The Free Library* (London, 1897), pp. 38–9.

Naturally the most powerful and widespread of all methods of influencing opinion was the newspaper and periodical press. It was a great weapon in the hands of national leaders and political reformers; both Cavour and Bismarck, for instance, appreciated its importance. The freedom of the press was one of the primary Liberal demands, and, in the more progressive countries, oppressive restrictions were, to a great extent, swept away, while rapid communications meant that the press had a range of action unknown before. With the spread of popular education the newspaper could appeal to a far wider public, and astute publicists, like Girardin of the Paris *Presse* and Bennett of the *New York Herald*, saw that through cheapness lay the path to vast influence over classes too poor to buy the existing high-priced papers. If, in education, the palm must be given to Germany, then in the development of the press England led the world, both in business efficiency and in public standing. It was an age in England of family proprietorships, constituting 'a little aristocracy of high ideals and great stability of character'.[1] The greatest of these families were the Walters of *The Times*, but the Levy Lawsons of the *Daily Telegraph* and the Taylors of the *Manchester Guardian* belonged to the same type. All through the period the press was rising in social estimation. The older Bohemian traditions of journalism were being outgrown, and, by 1870, many of the most promising young men from the universities were writing for the press. In general, independence had been achieved of everyone but the public—and the advertisers. Many of the most prominent politicians of the time, such as Brougham, Palmerston, and Aberdeen, attempted to influence the press, but the relationship was much more equal than in earlier days because the papers were stable enough not to need government support. 'The usefulness and influence of the best conducted paper in the country, it was remarked in 1852, would be at once destroyed if the fact came to be known that that paper had been bought by the Government.'[2]

Earlier traditions of government control linger just into the period. Two prominent Radical journalists were prosecuted in 1831 by Lord Grey's government for inciting disturbances among the country labourers —Richard Carlile, who was sentenced to two years' imprisonment, and William Cobbett, who was acquitted—but in general the attitude of the law officers was that free discussion was not to be feared, a point of view which thereafter predominated. An important change was made in the law by Lord Campbell's Libel Act of 1843, which allowed the plea that publication was true and in the public interest. This increased freedom of the press from official interference was, however, still freedom for the few for, with the paper duty and the stamp and advertisement taxes, a daily paper cost sevenpence. Henry Hetherington defied the law in 1831

---

[1] G. Binney Dibblee, *The Newspaper* (London, n.d.), p. 100.
[2] A. Aspinall, *Politics and the Press, c. 1780–1850* (London, 1949), p. 372.

with an unstamped *Poor Man's Guardian*, and there were many convictions in the next few years for this offence in the 'Battle of the Unstamped'. The novelist Bulwer led a movement in Parliament against the so-called 'Taxes on Knowledge', and, as a result, the advertisement tax was reduced in 1833, and in 1836 the newspaper stamp was reduced to one penny, though the unstamped papers were crushed out of existence by a stricter enforcement of the law. One very successful cheap publication of this time, the *Penny Magazine* (1832), printed only general information and not political news. The 'Taxes on Knowledge' were finally abolished between 1853 and 1861, the crucial date being the abolition of the newspaper stamp in 1855, which at last made it possible to develop a cheap press.

Like the press of France and unlike that of Germany, the English press tended towards centralisation in the capital. Its greatest newspaper was *The Times*, which in this period reached its apogee of relative importance. In 1854 its circulation of 55,000 was nearly three times that of the five other leading London dailies together. In the John Walters II and III the paper had enlightened proprietors. In Thomas Barnes (1817–41) and John Thadeus Delane (1841–77) it had two outstanding editors. Among its leader-writers were men of the stamp of Edward Sterling, Henry Reeve and Robert Lowe. In politics the 'Thunderer', as it was popularly known, was independent, its constant aim being to lead the opinion of the substantial middle classes. It maintained close relations with leading politicians, one of its most famous successes being the publication, in December 1845, through Lord Aberdeen, of the news that Peel meant to repeal the Corn Laws. *The Times*' greatest successes, however, were scored during the Crimean War, when the revelations of inefficiency made by its correspondent, W. H. Russell, had much to do with the fall of Lord Aberdeen's government (cf. ch. XVIII, p. 481). One reason for the strong position of *The Times* was its care for the best and earliest news. In 1838 a service of special couriers had been arranged to carry news from the East. Difficulties made by the French government led *The Times* temporarily to reroute its service through Trieste and Austria to get the news in time (1845).

After the repeal of the stamp duty *The Times* had to face much sharper competition, and lost its relative pre-eminence. Several of the old highly priced papers did not survive the change. The *Daily News*, founded in 1846, came down to the new popular price of one penny in 1868; its greatest success was the war-reporting of Archibald Forbes in the Franco-Prussian War of 1870–1. Another old paper, the *Standard*, had come down to a penny in 1858. But *The Times*' most successful competitor was the *Daily Telegraph*, founded in 1855 and controlled by J. M. Levy, who made it the first London penny paper. Vigorously written and served by such able journalists as G. A. Sala and Edwin Arnold, it was, in 1870, selling between 175,000 and 190,000 copies, as against the 70,000 or less of

The Times. This enormous increase in the numbers of the newspaper-reading public is illustrated by the calculation that in 1865 the number of copies printed by London papers alone was six times as great as the total circulation of all papers in the United Kingdom twenty-five years earlier.[1] The changed conditions after 1855 also brought about a revolution in the provincial press. A number of new dailies were set up, the most important of them being the *Scotsman*, edited from 1848 to 1876 by Alexander Russel, and the *Manchester Guardian*, both of which were old-established bi-weeklies which became dailies in 1855. England also possessed the most highly developed periodical press in the world, ranging from the great quarterlies to weeklies such as the *Spectator*, controlled from 1861 by R. H. Hutton and Meredith Townsend. The most remarkable English periodical of this period was the *Saturday Review*, brilliantly edited from 1855 to 1868 by John Douglas Cook, with an able list of contributors, most of them young men on their way to success in the professions.

In France press questions had been one of the matters of dispute which brought on the revolution of 1830, in which also the newspapers had played a large part. The revised charter of 1830 guaranteed the freedom of the press. The preventive censorship was abolished and the cautionary payment which newspapers had to make reduced. In the France of the day, the press was a great power, and there was a close connection between journalism, literature, and politics, for instance in the career of Thiers, which did not exist in England. The French press, even more than that of England, was centralised in the capital. The 'doyen' of the Paris papers was undoubtedly the *Journal des Débats*, controlled by the Bertin family. It represented the upper middle classes, and its general point of view was Orleanist. Among its distinguished authors were Saint-Marc Girardin, de Sacy, and Prévost-Paradol, and a number of its writers were members of the French Academy. A parallel position among French periodicals was held by the *Revue des Deux Mondes*, of which François Buloz became chief editor in 1831. Many of the great names of French literature of the time wrote in its pages. An important branch of the press in France was the Catholic press. *L'Avenir* (1830), of which Lamennais was chief editor, preached the union of Catholicism and popular rule, but Lamennais was condemned by the Vatican in 1832 (cf. ch. IV, p. 78). Very important subsequently was *L'Univers* (1836), later edited by Louis Veuillot, which was at the height of its power in the early years of the Second Empire, but was suppressed by the government in 1860. However, Veuillot was allowed to revive it in 1867.

In its early years the July Monarchy came under heavy attack from both legitimist and republican papers. Prominent among the left-wing journals were the *National* of Armand Carrel and the *Tribune* of Armand Marrast,

[1] 'The Modern Newspaper', '*The Times*' *Printing Number* (London), 29 October 1929, p. x.

the latter of which was in constant trouble with the authorities. Finally, in 1835, the government tightened up the press laws. Trouble was constant until the collapse of the regime. Clandestine republican papers circulated, and, in press trials, sometimes the government and sometimes the opposition were successful. In 1843 the opposition gained the support of the new *Réforme*, which was primarily interested in social change. Similar demands were put forward in *L'Atelier* (1840), which deserves mention as a paper for the working class conducted by working men.

Meanwhile, behind the scenes, a great transformation was taking place in the business aspect of French newspapers. Like the older English papers, those which have been mentioned were all expensive and limited in their appeal. It was clear that cheaper papers would be able to tap new levels of the population. The pioneers here were Dutacq and Émile de Girardin, who established, in 1836, the *Siècle* and the *Presse* respectively, at an annual subscription which was half that of the older papers. Both quickly gained large circulations, aided by the vogue of the *roman-feuilleton*, or serial novel, of which Balzac, George Sand, the elder Dumas, and Eugène Sue were prominent writers, and in the use of which the older papers were forced to copy the younger. Girardin had been influenced by English examples, and he proposed to cover costs by a greater development of advertising than was usual in the French press. Even so, all through the century, the French press made less use of advertisements than the English. Girardin must stand very high among those who regarded the newspaper primarily as a business enterprise, a side of newspaper production which became more and more important as the century went on.

The revolution of 1848 swept away all restrictions on the press, and there was a flood of new publications, representing the most divergent views. The provisional government, which took over power on Louis Philippe's fall, represented the views of the *National* and the *Réforme* (cf. ch. xv, p. 390). However, the extremism of many of the papers led to the restoration of restrictions as soon as the heyday of revolution was over. Cautionary payments (1848) and stamp duties (1850) were reimposed, along with other hampering measures. Finally, after the *coup d'état* of Louis Napoleon, the press was put into much tighter leading-strings. The press law of 1852 forced a newspaper to obtain an authorisation before it could appear. The preventive censorship was not restored, but was replaced by a system of 'warnings', leading to the suspension and then to the suppression of the paper, a system which in fact made the editors of newspapers censor themselves, and which was copied in other countries. The result of these stringent rules was to reduce the number of Paris newspapers. In the provinces official control was even stricter, and it was difficult to get an opposition paper printed at all. In Paris, however, the opposition press was dominant, though Napoleon III had much more press support than Charles X had had. Théophile Gautier, Sainte-Beuve, and Mérimée wrote for the *Moniteur Officiel*, and the other government papers could depend on good circulations, and on such able journalists as Granier de Cassagnac and de la Guéronnière.

Since political journalism was difficult and dangerous, writers turned to less serious subjects. A landmark here is the foundation, by Hippolyte de Villemessant, of the *Figaro* (weekly from 1854, daily from 1866) which was concerned, at first, not with politics, but with Paris gossip and the news of the boulevards. Villemessant carried even farther than Girardin the idea of the press as a great industry. Another development leading in the same direction was Moïse Millaud's *Petit Journal* (1863), published at one *sou*. This meant that, whereas Girardin and Dutacq had appealed to the lower middle class, Millaud was appealing to the poor. Such an appeal meant more advanced methods in publicity and sales, but it was successful, and the *Petit Journal* was soon selling about 250,000 copies, and on special occasions far more. In 1866 the *Siècle*, with 44,000 copies, had the largest circulation of the ordinary dailies.

Meanwhile, after 1860, the lot of the political press had been eased. Several new papers were founded, among them the *Temps* in 1861, and in 1868 the system of authorisations and warnings was swept away. A flood of new papers then appeared bitterly critical of the government, the most famous of them being Henri Rochefort's *Lanterne*, with the opening sentence of its first number: 'France contains, according to the Imperial Almanac, thirty-six million subjects, not counting the subjects of discontent.' Clashes between the government and the press went on right up to the end of the Empire, among the most celebrated being the Baudin trial, in which Gambetta scored a great triumph at the expense of the regime (1868).

In Germany, as in France, the development of the press was considerably affected by political factors. The influence of the July Revolution of 1830 caused no permanent change in the existing policy of governmental repression, which was strengthened by the Six Articles of 1832 (cf. ch. xix, p. 493). In general, the policy of German governments was to keep the newspapers few in number and limited in content. Such Liberal newspapers as the *Rheinische Zeitung*, founded at Cologne in 1842 and edited for a time by Karl Marx, were quickly suppressed. The greatest of German papers, the Augsburg *Allgemeine Zeitung*, suffered under Bavarian censorship, and was also closely watched by Austria. In 1832 its owner, Cotta, was warned to print no more of the contributions of its Paris correspondent, the poet Heine. From Vienna Metternich kept a careful eye on both the home and foreign press. The periodical press, which was left more liberty by the censor and which allowed more room for discussion, was also important, though prominent Liberal journals, such as F. W. A. Held's *Lokomotive* (1843), clashed with the censorship and were suppressed. The controversies, in which Heine took a prominent part, over the literary group 'Young Germany', led the Bund in 1835 to condemn this new, supposedly revolutionary school of writers.

The localised nature of German life meant that there was no one great centre like London or Paris, and newspapers were influential chiefly in their own regions. Technically the German press was backward, being severely limited by the burdensome and capricious censorship. One of the most advanced papers was the *Kölnische Zeitung*, whose owner, Joseph Du Mont, installed the first steam-press in Germany in 1833. In the 'forties the *Kölnische Zeitung* and the *Allgemeine Zeitung* both had circulations of about 8000 copies. The Berlin *Vossische Zeitung*, which had been selling less than 10,000 in 1840, had doubled its circulation by 1847.

The 1848 revolutions brought with them the freedom of the press. Everywhere there was an immense, almost febrile, expansion. At the beginning of 1848 there were seventy-nine newspapers in Austria; at the end of the year there were 388, 306 of them being political dailies. Many of the new foundations were short-lived; some of them, however, had permanent importance like the Berlin papers, the *National-Zeitung* and the reactionary *Neue Preussische Zeitung*, commonly known as the *Kreuzzeitung*, the organ of the circle to which Bismarck belonged.

The victory of reaction in 1849–50 brought a sharp check. In Austria cautionary payments were restored, a system of official warnings introduced and official authorisations made necessary. As a result, there was a sharp decline in the number of papers published, and many of those were under government control. Greater freedom was allowed after the laws of 1862 and 1863. In 1864 came the foundation of the *Neue Freie Presse*, which became Austria's leading newspaper. Meanwhile Prussian policy had followed much the same course, the *Kölnische Zeitung* being forced, for instance, in 1855, to change its editor under threat of having its concession withdrawn.

However, despite all these difficulties, the press had on balance improved its position. Its business enterprise and technical equipment were growing, and it profited from the general interest in politics during the 'sixties. In addition, it exploited the *feuilleton* on the French model. The capitalistic side of newspaper development was becoming more prominent, a pioneer being August Zang, who founded the Vienna *Presse* in 1848, a paper which was sold at a cheap price and managed with profit as a primary aim. An important new growth was the *Frankfurter Zeitung*, which began, under another name, as a paper providing business information, in 1856, and became one of the leading newspapers in western Germany. This more extensive business development was reflected in government policy. The chief weapon after 1848 was not the censorship, but the withdrawal of concessions and the forfeiture of cautionary payments which struck at the business interests of the proprietors.

Although greater freedom was allowed after 1860, newspapers were still under close state control. Both the Austrian and the Prussian governments closely controlled their own press, and spread their influence as far as they could over the newspapers of other states. Their methods too were much the same: a Press Bureau to direct newspaper policy and the publication of an official 'Correspondence', stating the official point of view, which was circulated to the newspapers. In Prussia this system, which was initiated by Manteuffel during the 'fifties, was inherited by Bismarck. From his early days the latter had realised the importance of the press, and throughout his career devoted great attention to it. He used it, for instance, as a weapon in the struggle against France. One means of financing his policy was provided by the notorious 'Reptile Fund', endowed from the Hanoverian crown properties.

The period between 1850 and 1870 was one of close connections between the press and the growing political parties. The existing newspapers were sharply attacked from a Socialist point of view by Lassalle in a speech in 1863,[1] and the following years saw the beginnings of a Socialist press. At much the same period a Catholic press was also growing up. After 1870, however, the business side of newspaper enterprise became more and more important. Circulations in general were rising. Critics of the press were beginning to point out the importance of the business factor, and newspapers were being criticised for their subservience to dishonest financial interests. Newspapers were becoming more complex; the emphasis was shifting from argument and the expression of opinion to the objective reporting of news. A significant change was the increasing importance of advertisements. In fact, Germany was treading, somewhat in arrear, the path which had already been traced out by France and England.

In the smaller liberal countries of Europe the press also played an important role. In Switzerland the struggles between Liberals and Conservatives were fought out between rival newspapers. In Sweden in the 'thirties the government of King Charles John fought the Liberal papers, at the head of which stood Lars Hierta's *Aftonbladet*, though the government gave up the struggle after the outbreak of a riot caused by the condemnation of a Liberal editor in 1838. At the same time liberalism was becoming articulate in the press in Denmark, and this also led to difficulties with the government. The Danish Constitution of 1849 guaranteed the freedom of the press. Another development of the 'thirties and 'forties in Denmark and Norway was a press catering for the peasants. In Belgium, as in France, press questions had played an important part in the 1830 revolution, and the Belgian Constitution of 1831 guaranteed the freedom of the press. During the Second Empire Belgium became a

---

[1] Ferdinand Lassalle, 'Die Feste, die Presse und der Frankfurter Abgeordnetentag', *Gesamtwerke* (Leipzig, n.d.), vol. I, pp. 107–55.

place of refuge for French *émigré* journalists, and their attacks on Napoleon III led to serious difficulties with the French government. The matter was raised at the Congress of Paris (1856) by the French representative, Walewski, though the attitude of the Belgian government was firm and nothing came of the incident.

In countries without a free press the influence of refugee journalists was very important. The greatest of them was Giuseppe Mazzini, who had already written for several papers before he left Italy in 1831. Of his many publications in exile the most important were the six numbers of his *Young Italy* (1832–4) (cf. ch. IX, p. 224). In Italy itself at that time the severity of the censorship allowed only scientific and literary periodicals to survive, although there was much to be read between the lines in the literary discussions. The free political press began in Piedmont. In 1847 a modification of the censorship permitted the freer expansion of newspapers; one of the new foundations was Count Cavour's *Risorgimento* which served as a spring-board for his political ideas. The Piedmontese Constitution of 1848 granted the freedom of the press, which was more or less maintained after it had been swept away in the other states of Italy by the triumph of counter-revolution in 1849 over the Liberal principles of 1848. In his appreciation of the power of the press Cavour resembled Bismarck; it is noteworthy that, during the latter part of his life, he gained a hearing for his point of view in France through the *Revue des Deux Mondes*, the editor of which, Buloz, was a Savoyard by birth. The appearance of an effective press elsewhere in Italy came only after unification had been achieved. It was a natural result of Italian history that the Italian press, like the German and unlike the French and English, developed on decentralised lines.

In Russia, under Tsar Nicolas I, the censorship was administered with extreme harshness (cf. ch. XIV, p. 359). In 1848 a special committee was set up to watch the press in addition to the ordinary censors. On the accession of Alexander II this committee was abolished and new magazines were allowed to appear. These monthly magazines were of a high standard, and long continued to be of very great importance, because they suited the conditions of a country without political life. The great problems of reform which faced the country in the 'fifties and 'sixties gave rise to much press comment, and the press, despite the trammels which hampered it, gained a new importance. An important figure was another exile, Alexander Herzen. His fortnightly *Bell*, first published in London in 1857, was smuggled into Russia and wielded great power during these crucial years, though it lost influence after the Polish rising of 1863 (cf. ch. XIV, p. 370). It was in Alexander II's reign that the daily newspapers first became important, though, as yet, circulations were very small. After 1862 government policy tended to become stricter. In 1865 new censorship rules were introduced. These maintained preventive censorship in the provinces, but made the papers of St Petersburg and Moscow free to adopt a system of 'warnings' similar to that of France. The rules were strictly enforced, but nevertheless the press had some authority as the exponent of such public opinion as there was. Its chief personality was Michael Katkov, editor of the *Moscow News*, who was becoming in the 'sixties the chief exponent of nationalist and autocratic ideas. James Bryce considered him worthy to be ranked, as an editor, with Delane and J. D. Cook, or with the Americans, Greeley and Gordon Bennett. One characteristic of the Russian press was the backwardness of the provincial papers, which still lay under preventive censorship, and the predominance of the press of St Petersburg and Moscow.

In the United States the possibilities of a cheap press were realised at much the same time as in France. Before 1830 the existing papers were too expensive for any but the minority. The first to appreciate the future of cheap newspapers was Benjamin Day, who, inspired by the success of the English *Penny Magazine*, brought out the *New York Sun* in 1833, ignoring politics and concentrating on sensational news and police-court reports. In 1835 James Gordon Bennett started the *New York Herald* on the same lines, though his ideas were broader than those of Day, and he was a pioneer in the use of new techniques such as the telegraph. His conduct of his paper was strictly individual, even flamboyant, and his alleged salacity and inclusion of objectionable advertisements led to a 'moral war' on him in 1840 by the other New York papers. However, the *Herald*, like the *Sun*, was a great success—in 1849 Bennett's paper was selling 33,000 copies—and similar papers, such as the *Philadelphia Public Ledger* (1836) and the *Baltimore Sun* (1837), were founded in other cities. All of them had certain characteristics in common. They were preoccupied with getting the news as early as possible; with their large circulations and large advertising revenues they had much greater resources at their command than the old papers. They were generally free from political patronage. They exaggerated the unusual and sensational elements in the news.

The next developments of the cheap press were on rather different lines. In 1841 Horace Greeley founded the *New York Tribune*. He wished to run his paper without the objectionable features of the Bennett journalism. His connections with politics were close, first as a Whig and later as a Republican, and he was a great editorial propagandist, an enthusiast for new causes—Fourier's principle of Association, Women's Rights, and, most important of all, the Abolition of Slavery. His greatest influence was exercised through the weekly *Tribune*, which, by 1860, was selling 200,000 copies a week, and historians have stressed the importance of his paper in turning public opinion against slavery. One of his assistants was Henry J. Raymond, who, in 1851, founded the *New York Times*. He saw that there was room for a newspaper which should avoid Bennett's vulgarity and Greeley's preoccupation with unpopular causes. The tone of the new paper was balanced, moderate, and always self-possessed. An interesting comment on the growing complexity of press finance is that Raymond's venture was backed by $100,000, while Greeley had launched the *Tribune* with $2000 ten years earlier.

Meanwhile the older tradition of a political press in close connection with party groups—one example being the *Globe*, the organ of President Jackson's 'Kitchen Cabinet'—had survived, but had become less important. The primacy of the Washington papers passed away as the country grew larger, and the newer type of journalism, which was until the Civil War centred on New York, was better able to meet the more varied demands which were being made on the press. In periodical literature the United States was backward, and had little of importance before the 'fifties. The Abolitionist press, whose leading figure was William Lloyd Garrison of the Boston *Liberator* (1831–65), must not be forgotten. Abolitionist papers were sometimes excluded from the mails, printing offices were destroyed and editors were assaulted, at least one of them, Lovejoy, of Alton (Ill.), being murdered (1837), facts which show the limitations imposed by a democracy on the expression of unpopular opinions.

American journalism was greatly stimulated by the Civil War. The papers, with the *New York Herald* at the head, made immense efforts to cover the news. The craft of the war correspondent was developed further, and in the Franco-Prussian War of 1870–1 American journalists were also prominent. On the home front there was much editorial criticism of Lincoln's administration, and many official complaints about the leakage of news. The events of the war gave the public a greater taste for news than ever, and circulations mounted rapidly, the expansion being especially felt by the papers of the interior cities. This decentralisation of the American press was one of the changes which introduced a new period. Bennett and Greeley both died in 1872, and the new generation saw a decline in party connections and an increasing emphasis on news as against editorial comment. Of the New York papers the *Sun* was selling 100,000 copies and the *Herald* 95,000 in 1872. All over the country the press was expanding, American newspapers increasing in number by one-third during the 'sixties. At the end of the period the papers of the interior, such as Joseph Medill's *Chicago Tribune*, had become more important. In Samuel Bowles of the Springfield (Mass.) *Republican* they had one of the leading journalists in the United States. Since his paper had become a daily in 1844, he had steadily built up a national reputation as an independent journalist. In the younger generation of New York editors the leading men were Charles A. Dana and E. L. Godkin. The former, who had been Greeley's right-hand man on the *Tribune*, gained control of the *New York Sun* in 1868, and carried it to new prosperity by introducing a more sprightly style of writing and by concentrating on stories of 'human interest'. The latter, an Englishman and a Utilitarian, founded the weekly *Nation* in 1865. A pioneer among weekly journals of opinion in the United States, the *Nation* never gained a large circulation, but it had great influence on the leaders of American thought.

Some comparisons may now be attempted between the countries which have been discussed. It was thought in 1870 that the London papers gave more news than the New York papers with the Paris papers a bad third. In all three countries the press had become highly capitalised, though in each its development had taken an individual course. The American papers gave more news of a sensational type than the English, and the English more prominence to editorial comment than the American, but both were primarily presses of information, giving first place to the news-report and the advertisement. The French press, on the other hand, was a press of opinion. The difference is summed up by a critic of 1882: 'The English reader wants to know what is going on in the world; the French reader wishes to be informed of what some celebrated politician thinks of what is passing in France.'[1] In general, the German press was less advanced than any of these. An English judgment of 1889 was that, whereas thirty years earlier the press of both France and England had been highly developed, that of Germany had been very backward, its news outdated, and its commercial enterprise nil, though it had made great progress in the intervening period.[2] Once again the expansion of European ideas and techniques is important. By 1870 such countries as Egypt in the Near East and Japan in the Far East were advancing towards a press in their own languages. Already in India, small and poor as the papers were, a real beginning had been made. The first vernacular newspaper had appeared in 1818; by 1875 there were 254 in many different languages.

All through the period the press was gaining command of new techniques. One fruit of this was the growth of the illustrated press. The *Illustrated London News* appeared in 1842; the Paris *L'Illustration* and the Leipzig *Illustrierte Zeitung* a year later. Advance in the related field of caricature had been made possible through the development of lithography. In France Charles Philipon created *Caricature* and *Charivari*, which ridiculed Louis Philippe (1831). *Punch* in London came ten years later, and the German papers later in the 'forties, the Munich *Fliegende Blätter* in 1845 and the Berlin *Kladderadatsch* in the year of revolutions, 1848. The most fundamental improvement of all, however, was the steady advance in printing which made it possible to deal with far larger circulations. In 1846 Richard Hoe's four-cylinder rotary press for the *Philadelphia Public Ledger* printed 8000 copies per hour, though on one side only, and in 1848 *The Times* introduced a similar Applegath machine. In 1861

[1] Joseph Reinach in *Nineteenth Century* (London, September 1882), vol. xii, p. 349.
[2] Sidney Whitman, *Imperial Germany* (London, 1889), p. 282.

the Hoe machines were first adapted to take stereotype plates, which meant that numerous plates could be cast from the type instead of printing direct from the type itself. In 1868 *The Times* introduced the Walter press, the first modern rotary press fed by a continuous web of paper, with a speed of 12,000 complete, or 'perfected', copies per hour. At much the same time similar advances were being made in France by Hippolyte Marinoni, who worked first for Girardin at the *Presse* and then, in the later 'sixties, for the *Petit Journal.* Next to printing advance came the speeding up of communications by railway, steamship, and telegraph. So far as the last was concerned, the American papers were pre-eminent in early days. Greeley in 1851 expressed his opinion that they used the telegraph a hundred times more than the English papers. *The Times*, for all its care for early news, was conservative here, feeling that the telegraph was expensive and inaccurate. However, the Crimean War proved that the new invention was indispensable.

One great result of the coming of telegraphic news was the growth of the news agencies, organisations for collecting and selling news to the press and to business interests. Clearly this centralised much of the business of news-collecting, and made it possible for the press to rely on much larger news-resources, though the agency could never replace the skilled special correspondent of the greater papers. The earliest of the agencies was the French Havas agency which began as a translation bureau, and in 1840 organised a pigeon service between London, Brussels, and Paris. It made use of the new means of communication as they developed, and in 1856 took over a large advertising agency, which gave it control over a large part of French newspaper advertising and thus of a stable source of income. In 1849 Bernhard Wolff founded a telegraphic bureau in Berlin which grew into the great German news agency. In 1851 another German Jew, Julius Reuter, came to England, and opened an agency in London. In October 1858 he persuaded the London papers, except *The Times*, to give his service a trial, and won an established position with them. Very soon afterwards *The Times* also began to make use of his news. One of Reuter's great successes was to report the murder of President Lincoln two days ahead of anyone else in Europe. His expansion into Germany led him into conflict with the Wolff agency, which had the strong backing of the Prussian government. Finally, in 1870, the three great agencies agreed on a division of territory. Wolff was to control central and eastern Europe, Reuter the British empire and the Far East, Havas the French empire and the Latin countries. In England itself the collection of news was made not by Reuter but by the Press Association, formed in 1868 under the leadership of John Edward Taylor of the *Manchester Guardian* by the provincial papers, which worked in close co-operation with Reuters. The provincial papers had been very dissatisfied with the services of the private telegraph companies, and when these

were, at this time, taken over by the state, they made independent arrangements of their own. Co-operative agencies, owned by the papers they
served, also developed in the United States. The New York papers, eager
to get the earliest European news, formed an Association in 1848 for the
collection of foreign news. This became the New York Associated Press,
which adopted a more definite form of organisation in 1856. After the
formation, through amalgamations, of the Western Union Telegraph
Company in 1855, arrangements for co-operation between the two bodies
were made. The tendency of the New York association towards monopoly
led to combination by the western papers among themselves. The Western
Associated Press, chartered in 1865, after a period of struggle with the
New York organisation, made an agreement with it in 1867, and subsequently the country was divided between groups of co-operating associations. In 1866 the transatlantic cable was finally completed. In 1870
India was put in direct telegraphic communication with England. The
world, from the journalist's point of view, was becoming a new unity,
and his work was to be done under new conditions. The European system
had taken another great step towards mastering the earth.

CHAPTER VI

ART AND ARCHITECTURE

IN the arts of building, painting and sculpture, the nineteenth century starts about 1760. Before that date in most countries art had been a need of the church or the pleasure of court and nobility. From that date the artist, like the writer, began to emancipate himself from patronage. Art became the pursuit of self-reliant, socially emphatically independent men. 'The unacknowledged legislators of the world', is what Shelley called the artists, and Schiller ranks the bard with the king; 'for both walk on the summits of mankind'. The social break is best remembered in this country by Dr Johnson's letter to Lord Chesterfield, written in 1755:

> Is not a Patron, my Lord, one who looks with unconcern on a man struggling for life in the water, and, when he has reached ground, encumbers him with help? The notice which you have been pleased to take of my labours, had it been early, had been kind, but it has been delayed till I am indifferent, and cannot enjoy it,...till I am known, and do not want it.

It is characteristic that this remarkably early declaration of liberty should have been written in England. For socially, politically, philosophically, England was the leading country of Europe in the eighteenth century. That this was so in art and architecture too, is less known. It might be denied on the strength of the supreme aesthetic qualities of Watteau's or Tiepolo's paintings or the South German and Austrian churches and palaces of the Rococo. But if the later eighteenth century is looked at as a preface to the nineteenth, then it will be recognised beyond any doubt that from road making and canal making, from factory construction (of iron as early as 1792) and bridge construction to the arts of architecture and painting England was ahead at least until the closing years of the century. Eighteenth-century painting on the continent had been chiefly of religious and mythological or otherwise classical subjects, in England of portraits. Now J. H. Mortimer competed for a prize endowed by the Society of Arts, not with a composition from the life of Alexander the Great, but with one representing Edward the Confessor, and William Hamilton painted for Alderman Boydell *The Abdication of Mary Queen of Scots*, that is to say a scene from national, not from Greek and Roman history. In 1760 Hayman painted the *Victory of Quiberon Bay* and *Clive receiving the Homage of the Nabob*, and in 1770 West his celebrated *Death of General Wolfe*, that is scenes from contemporary, not from long-past history. De Loutherbourg's Methodist preacher surrounded by a crowd of listeners dates from 1777, Copley's *Brook Watson and the Shark* from 1778. They are not history painting at all, but sensational contemporary reportage. And on the side of imaginative painting, visitors to the exhibitions could now derive that gruesome pleasure which in past centuries had been aroused by a *Temptation of St Anthony* or a *Martyrdom of St Agatha*, from Fuseli's *Nightmare*, shown in 1782, and depicting a woman thrown back on her bed in agony with her bosom bare and a huge ghostly mare peering in through the bed curtains. At the same moment when Fuseli was thus replacing religious by secular sensation (Goya in the *Caprichos* was to follow soon), Blake replaced a mythology familiar to all members of the educated classes by a private mythology of his own. His Urizens and Luvahs and Loses remained inaccessible to the public. They are entirely individual expressions, and wherever an artist or art as a whole puts the individual before the group, class, nation, or whatever the superordinate unity may be, work of high personal character may result, but the social well-being of art and artist are in danger. Here lies for the art historian one of the basic problems of the nineteenth century.

It was not a completely new problem. The Dutch Republic in the seventeenth century, under a middle-class hegemony, the most conspicuous before that of the nineteenth century, had known similar conditions. The fate of Seghers, and of Rembrandt and Frans Hals in their old age is a foreboding of the fate of Blake, of Corot, of Cézanne, of van Gogh. Another parallel between the nineteenth century and the Holland of Rembrandt's age is that both are remembered not for their contributions to the Grand Manner, but for the more intimate arts of landscape, portrait, still-life and genre painting. Here, once more, England led the way. Her chief contributions from about 1760, when Reynolds and Gainsborough were mature artists, to at least the years about 1800, when Crome, Girtin, Turner and Constable set to work, were to portrait and landscape painting. The intimacy of Reynolds's Nelly O'Brien, of so many Gainsborough portraits, of the works of Stubbs and of Zoffany was unmatched on the continent, and so were the observation of nature and the self-abandon in nature (and in native British nature at that) of the landscape painters in oil and water-colours.

The same qualities which appear in their works and those of the portrait painters led the English (at a yet earlier date) to give up the grand formality of French and Italian gardens and replace it by the free asymmetrical layouts known as picturesque. Their freedom—accepted as a corollary of English political freedom—and their naturalness impressed the continent enormously, more perhaps than any other English innovation in art and architecture. In a subtle way they prepared the ground for an architectural style equally free and asymmetrical and picturesque, that is the style predominant in most private and much public architecture of the mid and the later nineteenth century. As to the architecture of 1760 and after,

English leadership appears again. It shows itself here in the early abandonment of one accepted taste. The imitation of Palladio's serene classicism, it is true, went on to 1830 and after, but the essential new facts of about 1760 are the discovery of the real Greek Doric and its occasional adoption by certain architects and clients, and the fashion for Gothic. Here and there yet other styles were imitated, Chinese, Moorish, Hindoo. Conversely an architect like Sir John Soane could evolve his highly personal style, so remarkably independent of period precedent, only at a moment when a self-conscious selection of style had become possible and variety was replacing uniformity.

Variety of style, what Pugin called the 'Carnival of Architecture',[1] is the hallmark of architecture for the whole nineteenth century. Yet 1830 marks a clearly definable boundary. Conditions in 1830 and the following decades are here analysed first and foremost in England, because England was specially important in architecture, on account of her great prosperity, the wide range of public and private building that went on, and the religious movements which acted as an equally potent stimulus to church building. The most notable individual building of the period between 1830 and 1870 from our present point of view is no doubt the Crystal Palace. But the Crystal Palace, like the iron-framed factories, the quite numerous iron-framed office buildings put up in the 1850's and 1860's, and the bridges, from the Clifton Suspension Bridge designed in 1829 to the Firth of Forth Bridge begun in 1883, was not the work of an architect. These buildings were mostly due to civil engineers, a profession which had separated itself during the early nineteenth century from that of the architect; and the designer of the Crystal Palace, Joseph Paxton (1801–65), was a gardener, horticultural expert and amateur inventor. Some architects and critics could see that iron and glass held the promise of a new style in architecture. Sir George Gilbert Scott (1811–78) for instance, perhaps the most successful architect of the period, wrote that 'this triumph of modern metallic construction opens out a perfectly new field for architectural development',[2] but it never occurred to him that this field might be his. Discrepancies between thought and performance are always a sign of weakness. In Victorian architecture they occur everywhere and point to a disturbed balance for which there were many reasons. Architects could not absorb the new materials and techniques, let alone create them, as they had done in the Middle Ages, because architecture as an art had changed its function together with all other arts.

A new class of patrons made new demands. They were a class neither trained in the subtleties and elegances of Georgian taste nor provided with leisure to acquire them. They were for the first time in history patrons

---

[1] *An Apology for the Revival of Christian Architecture in England* (London, 1841), p. 2.
[2] *Remarks on Secular and Domestic Architecture, Present and Future* (2nd edn, London, 1858), p. 109.

altogether short of leisure. The rich man as a hard worker was a new type. Art and architecture to please him had to be of a new kind: eloquent, speaking in rather a loud voice, seeking rather elementary effects, but at the same time sufficiently remote from everyday considerations to fortify their claim to being something special, select, worth while, and worth money. This situation is as evident in painting as it is in architecture. As to architecture, the everyday surroundings in the cities were grim; grim the factories, and grim the miles of uniformly drab housing. Work was a duty, art a superadded ornament. 'Ornamentation is the principal part of architecture', taught Ruskin.[1] The 'great principle' of architecture was in Scott's words 'to decorate construction'.[2] Both definitions ignore planning, that is creation in space, whether the exterior space of a town or a quarter, or the interior space of the rooms of a building. The architect is the designer of façades.

Here lies one explanation of Pugin's 'Carnival of Architecture'. Another is that to distinguish between a Grecian and a Gothic façade is so much easier for the busy layman than to distinguish between the aesthetic values of varieties of proportions, of mouldings and similar details. A third is the rapid growth of all factual knowledge, including archaeological knowledge, throughout the nineteenth century. The nineteenth century believed in the provable fact, in scientific accuracy, in the accumulation of data. In terms of architecture that meant volume after volume of measured drawings of Gothic churches in Spain, of the brick buildings of north Germany, of the palace architecture of Tuscany, of the cathedral antiquities of England, of window tracery, capitals and much besides. Architects, confined to the decoration of construction and working for clients impressed by knowledge more than sensitivity, drew freely on these innumerable publications, and so the history of nineteenth-century architecture, as presented in the few textbooks and handbooks devoting any space to it, is a history of the styles imitated. As such it is not without interest.

At the beginning, up to about 1830, churches were mostly classical but could also be Gothic. For private houses the same two styles were available (as they had been in the late eighteenth century). Public buildings were exclusively classical. The first public building in England to disown the rules of Georgian taste was the new Houses of Parliament, for which the competition of 1835 stipulated Gothic or Elizabethan, as the two national styles of England. Gothic won; and Gothic received a further strengthening from the fervently propounded theories of A. W. N. Pugin (1812–52), a convert to Rome, the equally fervent, if more verbose and therefore more popular theories of John Ruskin (1819–1900), and the

---

[1] *Architecture and Painting* (1853), Addenda to Lectures I and II. Libr. Edn, vol. XII (London, 1904), p. 83.
[2] *Remarks on Architecture*, p. 221.

ecclesiological movement started by the Cambridge Camden Society in 1839 and championed in the volumes of *The Ecclesiologist*. Gothic became thus established in England as the Christian style *par excellence*. Norman or Romanesque remained relatively rare. Archaeological research gave Gothic churches of the 1840's and after an earnestness absent from the efforts of the late Georgians. The churches of George Gilbert Scott may be dull, but they are competent. Originality such as can be found in the ecclesiastical architecture of William Butterfield (1819–1900) was rare and not usually welcome. Restraint and a certain unction seemed to belong to church design. The more robust if coarser virtues of Victorian architects and clients appear in secular commissions. In public buildings, besides the Gothic and the Elizabethan a third style was admitted, the Italian Palatial, first established by Charles Barry (1795–1860), the architect of the Houses of Parliament, in the Travellers' and Reform Clubs in London. In freer, more open and more lustily decorated *Cinquecento* forms this style became a serious competitor to Gothic for town halls and other official buildings. For private houses Gothic was recommended only by the staunchest Gothicists but Elizabethan and Jacobean were highly popular, as was a debased Italian style which Professor Robert Kerr called Rural Italian.[1] They were all three asymmetrical and picturesque, and displayed broken skylines and restless all-over ornamentation. Add to these accepted styles of the mid-nineteenth century the French Renaissance with its tall pavilion roofs, which reached England in the late 1850's (and the United States about the same time) and we have all that is needful for a general picture of English architecture in the mid-Victorian era. There were some critics who complained of the absence of an original style in the nineteenth century, but Scott for instance wrote: 'Eclecticism is a principle of the highest value';[2] Professor Kerr asserted: 'Our age has a very notable style of its own, the style of instinct superseded by learning';[3] and Ruskin in his irritable and pompous manner formulated the same thought as follows: 'We want no style of architecture. . . . The forms of architecture already known are good enough for us, and far better than any of us. . . . A man who has the gift, will take up any style that is going. . .and be great in that. . .'.[4] His conclusion is that the choice should lie between the Pisan Romanesque, the Early Gothic of Tuscany, Lombardy and Liguria, the Venetian Gothic, and the English Earliest Decorated. As we have seen, the accepted choice was more catholic and less consistent, but choice it was all the same. 'In what style of architecture shall you build your house?' is the first sentence of Kerr's chapter on architectural style.

[1] *The Gentleman's House* (London, 1864).
[2] *Remarks on Architecture*, p. 266.
[3] *The Gentleman's House*, p. 358.
[4] *The Seven Lamps of Architecture* (London, 1849), 'The Lamp of Obedience', pp. 4–5.

This attitude is still with us to this day, though the gradual creation of an original style of the twentieth century has reduced its dangers. Its worst danger in its heyday was the almost total lack of interest amongst architects in the most burning problems of building, which were social rather than aesthetic problems, and problems of planning rather than of façade embellishment. How could the precipitously growing working classes of the cities be housed? Tenement houses built specially for them, after a promising start in the 1840's, became hideously grim in the hands of the Baroness Burdett Coutts, the Peabody Trust and similar philanthropic or profit-making institutions—grimmer visually, though no doubt more hygienic, than the slums of cottages had been which they were to replace. Factories were not designed by professional men and were placed in no planned relation to houses. Schools were sombre, open spaces inadequate, amenities confined to church halls, chapel halls, and public houses. It should have been for the architects and their professional representatives, the Royal Institute of British Architects, to point to these deficiencies and remedy them. But nothing of this sort happened. The architect remained the purveyor of façades.

If this was true of England, it was true of all other nations. The picture just painted of the architectural development in Great Britain between 1830 and 1870 is in no essential way different from that of developments in France, Germany, Italy, the Netherlands and the other European countries, or indeed the United States of America in the same period. Accents are not everywhere placed in exactly the same positions, and certain *nuances* are to be found only or predominantly in certain countries, but the general character and the main course of events were international.

Everywhere, including Russia, the 1830's saw the Neo-Greek style in firm possession of the academic fields of building activity. A building like the Moscow Gate (1833–8) at Leningrad, by Vassili Petrovich Stassow (1769–1848), a hexastyle Greek Doric triumphal arch with columns not of stone, but of cast iron, might have been erected in any country.

Gothic, on the other hand, was nationally more diversified, in strength as well as forms. England, undeniably, was leading. It is a characteristic fact that English architects won both the international competitions for St Michael's, the principal church of Hamburg in 1844, and for the new cathedral at Lille in 1855. But in Germany Gothic achieved almost the same leading position for church building as in England. Goethe in his youth was the first to appraise its true greatness and character. The Romantics, Wackenroder, Schlegel and others, worshipped it. Karl Friedrich Schinkel (1781–1841), the greatest German architect of the first decades of the nineteenth century, used it as enthusiastically and as originally as he used Neo-Greek. It received a public triumph, when in 1840 the *Domverein* was founded at Cologne to complete the gigantic fragment of the cathedral in accordance with the original plans discovered in 1814 and 1816. E. F. Zwirner (1802–61) was made *Dombaumeister*, and from 1842 to 1880 the huge building rose above the roofs of the medieval city. Yet Gothic was not in sole possession of the field of church architecture in Germany. It had a competitor in what was called the Round-arched Style (*Rundbogenstil*), a style mixed of elements of the Early Christian and the Italian Romanesque, which was established at the same time by Schinkel and his successor Persius (1805–45) in Prussia and by Gärtner (1792–1847) and others in Munich. In England it had only a passing popularity in the 1840's. In Germany it was adapted even to the building of a railway station (Munich, 1847–9, by Bürklein), and in and around Hanover to schools, museums, banks and other edifices. It was indeed perhaps more suitable in the secular field than the bristly Gothic. Yet right to the end of the period and beyond, some of the most spectacular public buildings chose a Gothic dress, notably the town halls of Vienna (1872) and of Munich (1874) and the Houses of Parliament at Budapest (1885–1902).

The Romance nations reacted differently. They knew nothing like the Anglo-German passion for Neo-Gothic. In Italy the Gothic style had never succeeded in acclimatising itself, not even in the thirteenth and fourteenth centuries. So the revival also was late and weak, and it is characteristic that the first example of *goticismo* was built under English influence by the architect of one of the best Neo-Greek buildings in Italy: the so-called Pedrocchino of 1837 at Padua by Giuseppe Japelli (1783–1852) the architect of the celebrated Café Pedrocchi with its Doric porches (1816–31).

That France did not take kindly to the Gothic Revival, may at first appear stranger. However, it can perhaps be said that just because France had created the Gothic style in the twelfth century and developed it to its logical conclusion in the thirteenth, she could instinctively not agree to its use for purely picturesque purposes. The best Neo-Gothic church of Paris, Ste Clotilde (1840), is the work of Franz Christian Gau of Cologne (1790–1853). But a real understanding of Gothic principles survived— more so than in England. That is proved by the fact that some French architects were ready in the middle of the century to make intelligent and unashamed use of the new metallic building materials. In England, we have seen, these were used extensively, more extensively perhaps than in France, but only by a few outsiders. In France Henri Labrouste (1801–75) proudly exhibited his iron construction at the Library of Ste Geneviève (1844–50) and then the Bibliothèque Nationale (1868). At the same time L.-A. Boileau (1812–96) built the church of St Eugène with iron piers and iron rib-vaulting (1854–5). England possesses nothing so radical.

Nor does America. Down to the middle of the nineteenth century and after, the United States seem indeed at first glance merely to repeat the pattern of England. Most large-scale public building was Neo-Classical, more even than in England, State Capitols everywhere and the big structures of the administration at Washington. Architects such as William Strickland (1787–1854) are, if anything, superior to their opposite numbers in England. The leading churches on the other hand, for instance Holy Trinity, New York (1839–46), by Richard Upjohn (1802–79) and St Patrick's Cathedral, New York (1850–79), by James Renwick (1792–1863), are Gothic, and commercial architecture makes thorough use of iron. In this America seems to have gone beyond England. There is evidence that the first façades of office buildings made completely of iron and glass, without any outer stone encasement, belong to New York and the 1830's and 1840's.[1] Naturally, to a country in which skilled craftsmanship was so scarce, any system of prefabrication, that is of building parts made in a factory and only assembled on the site had much to recommend itself.

In American design also it is certain factory-made comforts which show the country to be ahead of Britain: such as Pullman trains and their convertible compartments, and bathrooms in private houses and hotels. The hotel in fact owes much to America. In England the Regency type of hotel, a kind of country-house-cum-assembly-rooms remained until it was replaced by the modern type in the 1860's. In the United States this appears already in Isaiah Rogers's (1800–89) Tremont Hotel at Boston in 1828–9 with 'its elaborate battery of water closets, and the bathrooms with running water in the basement'.[2] The decorative style used in this and other hotels, however, remained consistently Classical.

So much for the Classical and the Gothic components of the phase here under discussion. In England, as we have seen, the 1830's added to them the Italian High Renaissance and the Elizabethan-Jacobean which was then still called the native Renaissance. The best examples of the *Quattrocento* and *Cinquecento* revival on the Continent belong to Germany. At Munich it began as early as Leo von Klenze's (1784–1864) Odeon of 1816 and was carried on in Gärtner's State Library of 1831. The high-water marks of this Neo-Renaissance, however, are the works of Gottfried Semper (1803–79) at Dresden, the first Opera House of 1838–41 and the State Gallery of 1847, forming incidentally with two older buildings a fine and picturesque piece of urban planning—a rarity in the nineteenth century. The revival of native 'Renaissance', that is the sixteenth-century styles of northern countries, began in France at the same time as in England. In both countries it was moods of national pride which led to an appreciation of the somewhat showy architecture of their sixteenth centuries. The key-dates in France are the extension to the Paris Town Hall begun in 1836 and the far more spectacular and influential extensions of the Louvre begun in 1851 by L. Visconti (1791–1853) and continued by

[1] See N. Pevsner, *Pioneers of Modern Design* (Penguin Books, 1959), ch. 5.
[2] T. Hamlin, *Greek Revival Architecture in America* (Oxford, 1944), pp. 112 ff.

H.-M. Lefuel (1810–81). A curiously early and solitary case of this revival of the French Renaissance, the style of the Loire châteaux, is the large new palace at Schwerin in north Germany begun by Demmler in 1844. Other countries also tended to revert to their native forms of 'Renaissance', Germany characteristically enough immediately after the Franco-Prussian War, and—to give one more example—Russia, where a slowly growing Byzantine revival and a renewed sympathy with Russian forms of the sixteenth and seventeenth centuries is to be noticed. Showiness and pomposity, which are so eminently High-Victorian in England, also began to tinge the more purely classical designs from the 1840's and 1850's onwards. In France from such façades as J.-L. Duc's (1802–79) Palais de Justice, begun in 1841, there originated that style which the Americans later on christened the *Beaux Arts* style, that is the accepted style of the Paris Academy. In America itself the completion of the Capitol at Washington by Thomas U. Walter (1804–87) between 1855 and 1865 with a huge dome (of cast-iron) and extensive colonnades is characteristic of the same tendency. It culminated at the end of the century in such vast and empty monuments as that to King Victor Emanuel II in Rome, begun in 1885 by Sacconi.

The vastness of such buildings is in itself characteristic of the nineteenth century. Larger cities needed larger town-halls, larger populations altogether larger public offices. So national and municipal administration and also care for education, care for the sick, and other services all called for buildings as large as the palaces of Baroque rulers, and as these edifices multiplied in the metropolitan cities they caused a general inflation of building sizes. The monument for all posterity, it seems, of that megalomania of the nineteenth century is Joseph Poelaert's truly splendid Palais de Justice at Brussels (1862–83). Here in crushingly solid stone the proudest dreams of Piranesi are left far behind. That this should be a building in the land of Rubens is significant. England in accordance with the restraint of the national character has little more of this Neo-Baroque than occasional theatre interiors. The most refined example of Neo-Baroque is to be found at Paris in the Opéra by Charles Garnier (1825–98) begun in 1861.

A great deal of the external effect of the Opéra depends on its position at the intersection of several of the new boulevards and avenues of Paris. These new, long, wide, straight, tree-planted thoroughfares are the most famous contribution of our period to town-planning. They are bold, very logical and very impressive—wholly in the absolutist traditions of the Paris of Louis XIV, and indeed due to the absolutism of Napoleon III and his Prefect of the Seine Department, Baron Haussmann (1809–91). The straightness of the boulevards recommended itself for defence in case of civil war, but it was without any doubt also welcome aesthetically. London has nothing like these sweeping axes. Holborn Viaduct, Victoria

Street and Shaftesbury Avenue are ridiculous in comparison. Yet, socially the Paris boulevards were just as ineffectual as was the absence of any major planning in London. The slums of the vast tenements and narrow sunless courtyards remained unchanged behind the new spectacular façades.

Nineteenth-century architecture, as we have seen, was entirely a matter of façades, that is of designing in two rather than three dimensions. Here also lies the reason why the century did so badly in sculpture and so exceedingly well in painting. Sculpture works in volumes and spaces, painting on the flat wall or canvas. It is no accident that one remembers so few names of sculptors working between 1830 and 1870, and that a chapter on the arts of these decades is complete without any. Whom should one mention in England? Alfred Stevens of course (1817–75), who was far from successful, then Thomas Woolner (1825–92) and Alexander Munro (1825–71), the two who started as Pre-Raphaelites, and then John Bell (1811–95) and J. H. Foley (1818–74) who were most popular and had their share in the decoration of the Albert Memorial. Their opposite numbers in Germany were Ernst Rietschel (1804–61) and perhaps August Kiss (1802–65) whose *Amazon* Sir Matthew Digby Wyatt in 1851 called 'probably the noblest work of art now existing'. The French contribution is aesthetically more worth while than that of the other nations—with François Rude's (1784–1855) dramatic groups, Louis Barye's (1796–1875) animals and the lively and graceful Neo-Rococo nudes and groups of the younger J. B. Carpeaux (1827–75). Carpeaux's is the only work where the voluptuousness desired by wealthy Victorian clients and supplied by the less scrupulous but most highly paid artists goes with high artistic quality.

On the whole it can be said that a divorce between what is officially or socially successful and what is aesthetically good is one of the chief characteristics of nineteenth-century art. Nor has this situation much changed during the first half of our century, as any comparison between Academy exhibitions and the art discussed by serious critics of contemporary work shows. It has been said before that this cleavage appeared for the first time in Holland in the seventeenth century. The pioneer and experimenter had to be satisfied with the garret, and silk and velvet came to the man of superficial glamour, or cheap naturalism. In France also in the Rococo period the Chardins were obscured by the Bouchers, though not as completely. What then was new in the Victorian age? Two things chiefly. What had been exceptional and rare became now usual everywhere. And, whereas in the seventeenth and eighteenth centuries at least some of the greatest artists had been amongst the socially successful, aesthetic conscience now fades out of accepted art. The new situation appears with perfect clarity in France, and as French painting is without any doubt the most important in Europe during the nineteenth century, it must now for the decades here under consideration be analysed in as much detail as space will allow.

By 1830, Jacques-Louis David, exponent of classical painting, had been dead some five years. When he was young, he had belonged to the revolutionary Convention, painted trenchant portraits of martyrs of the Revolution—*Marat assassinated in his Bath*—and voted for the abolition of the Académie de Peinture et de Sculpture as the privileged body in art during the *ancien régime*. He then turned to Napoleon and glorified him and his empire in vast, classically aloof compositions. With the Restoration he had to leave Paris and died at Brussels. The academy was now revived as the Académie des Beaux Arts, one part of the Institut de France, and enjoyed privileges as useful as the old. It staffed the École des Beaux Arts, distributed prizes including the coveted Prix de Rome, and managed the selection of works of art for the Salon. In the academy by 1830 the leading personality was Jean Auguste-Dominique Ingres (1780–1867). He had in his youth adhered to romantic ideals, but his impeccable draughtsmanship had soon turned to classical subjects. The older he grew, the more did his rule tend to be narrow in its high-mindedness. His career is closely paralleled by that of Peter von Cornelius (1783–1867) in Germany who also had started as a romantic rebel against academic conventions and become the academic tyrant of 1830 and after. Like Ingres he upheld drawing as against colour, precision as against rapidity of execution, and subjects from the accepted fields of history, religion or mythology as against the subjects which for new reasons the young painters passionately preferred.

Who were they, and what did they want to achieve? They belonged to the generation born about the end of the eighteenth century, Théodore Géricault (1791–1824), Eugène Delacroix (1798–1863), Camille Corot (1796–1875) in art; in literature Victor Hugo (born in 1802), and in music Hector Berlioz (born in 1803). The meaning of the revolt is more familiar in literature and music than in art. The scandal at the first night of Hugo's *Hernani* (1830) will be remembered as will the preface to his *Cromwell* (1827) with its emphasis on nature, truth and inspiration, on violent contrasts, local colour, the characteristic rather than the beautiful, and on drama as the leading art of the modern age. Berlioz at the Conservatoire in the 'twenties was in permanent revolt. In 1827 he composed an overture to *Waverley*, in 1828–9 eight scenes from *Faust*, and in 1830 he came out with a cantata, *The Death of Sardanapalus*. The *Fantastic Symphony* followed with its sensational scenes, and *Harold in Italy*.

Géricault leapt into fame with his *Raft of the Medusa* (1819), a ferociously dramatised report of a recent shipwreck with all its horrors duly underlined. He also painted the Epsom Derby, cavalry officers on prancing horses, and shockingly true-to-life faces of madmen and mad women portrayed in an asylum. He worked with excessive concentration; his handling of his brushes was fast, and his life was fast too. Ingres called him an enemy of 'sound honest painting', and blamed him for corrupting public taste.[1] Amongst the most important early works of Eugène Delacroix (1798–1863) are *Marino Falieri*, the *Death of Sardanapalus*, the *Murder of the Bishop of Liége* (from *Quentin Durward*), a set of lithographic illustrations to *Faust*, and the *Massacre of Scio* and *Liberty on the Barricades*. Clearly, inspiration came to these French romantics of 1830 from Britain and Germany, from Byron and Scott and the early Goethe, and from contemporary events.

Delacroix's was the highest intellect amongst all nineteenth-century painters. His journals and his letters are an incomparable source of information on the mood of the second romanticism, the romanticism of 1830, after the profounder, more monumental, more disciplined, more Christian romanticism of the first third of the century. For Delacroix, Rubens was the Homer of painting. No earlier romantic painter would have agreed.[2] 'The father of warmth and enthusiasm', is what Delacroix calls him.[3] He is fascinated by Rubens's 'verve which is both of the blood and of the head'. 'He dominates you, he overwhelms you with so much freedom and boldness', he writes.[4] In such passages he speaks for himself, his own character and art. But there are others apparently in complete contradiction, expressing admiration for Mozart, for Racine, for Raphael. There are, he says, artists 'who are not in control of their genius but who are controlled by it' and others 'who follow their natural bent but are also in command of it'.[5] A man of genius, he says in one place, knows no rules, in another (very much later, it is true) his definition of genius is 'a man of superior rationality'.[6] This conflict between theory and performance is worth remembering as typical of the successful artist of the nineteenth century. Another example has been pointed out before, in the person of Sir George Gilbert Scott. Delacroix was indeed successful, even if never popular nor the founder of a school. The same conflict between character and ambition is reflected in Delacroix's social attitude. He was dark and romantic looking, musical, and elegantly dressed, carried on a liaison with a niece of the Empress Josephine, and for twenty years pined for acceptance by the academy. But at the same time he called the public 'this stupid herd',[7] and wrote to a civil servant friend, who warned him

---

[1] A. J. Boyer d'Agen, *Ingres d'après une correspondance inédite* (Paris, 1909), p. 28.

[2] But the first to write with fervour about Rubens had been J. J. Wilhelm Heinse in his *Letters from the Düsseldorf Gallery*. They were written in 1776–7; Heinse was born in 1746, Fuseli in 1741, Goethe in 1749. So they belong to the German *Sturm und Drang* and are amongst those pointers to the nineteenth century of which more has been said above.

[3] *Journal*, ed. A. Joubin (Paris, 1950), vol. ii, p. 95 [1853].

[4] *Questions sur le Beau* (in *Œuvres Littéraires*, ed. Cris, Paris, 1923, vol. i, p. 31) and *Journal*, vol. iii, p. 307 [1860].

[5] *Journal*, vol. ii, p. 456 [1856].

[6] *Journal*, vol. ii, p. 372 [1855].

[7] *Journal*, vol. ii, p. 318 [1855].

against showing paintings which were too revolutionary or daring: 'The whole universe will not prevent me from seeing things in my own manner.'[1]

What was his manner? It was developed from an admiration of Géricault and from study at the Louvre. Delacroix was proud of being essentially self-trained, a pride which appears again and again amongst mid-nineteenth-century painters and expresses their distrust of steady traditions. The decisive event, however, in Delacroix's formative years was his discovery of Constable's art, which was represented by three pictures in the *Salon* of 1824. Delacroix was showing his *Massacre of Scio* and immediately before the opening repainted large parts of it to open up the surfaces, get rid of all heaviness of modelling and colour and give it that sketchiness which Constable had developed to represent a never halting life in nature. From that date Delacroix's brush also assumed that dashing rapidity. 'When he was in front of his canvas', said Gautier, 'he forgot his classical views, his impetuous painter's temperament got the upper hand and he roughed out one of his feverish and impassioned sketches.'[2] Delacroix was the first to formulate what had already been Constable's problem and became later that of the Impressionists: to keep in the final painting the freshness of the first sketches and yet endow it with a completeness and consistency necessarily absent in the early stages. Delacroix was a ferocious worker. 'We will work till our last gasp', he wrote at the age of fifty-five. 'What else is there to do except get drunk when the time comes when reality no longer equals one's dreams?'[3] His *œuvre* is vast in number and wide in range. His early subjects from romantic literature have already been mentioned. 'Remember certain passages of Byron if you wish for eternal inspiration', he wrote in his diary at twenty-six.[4] The *Liberty on the Barricades* of 1830 is a rare if characteristic excursion into the politics of the day. After 1830 such excursions ceased and literary subjects also became much rarer. The Bible on the other hand continued to offer subjects to Delacroix, and he may well be called the last for a long time who could paint *Jacob wrestling with the Angel*, or *The Lake of Gennesaret*, or *The Good Samaritan*. An artist younger than he, an artist born in the nineteenth and not the eighteenth century, could not have done it. Religious painting returned as a possibility—if a rare one—only at the very end of the nineteenth century in Gauguin and in the twentieth in Rouault and Nolde. The mid-nineteenth century was not religious and not enthusiastic. It was too realistic for that. It is eminently characteristic in this context that Delacroix himself, after 1830, looked for justification of the tempestuous scenes he wanted to paint in surroundings more real, more probable than those of Byron and the Bible. He found them on a

[1] See E. A. Piron, *Eugène Delacroix, sa vie et ses œuvres* (Paris, 1865), p. 71.
[2] *Histoire du romantisme*, reprinted from *Le Moniteur*, 17 November 1864.
[3] *Correspondance générale de E.D.*, ed. A. Joubin (Paris, 1937), vol. III, p. 180 [1853; letter to George Sand].
[4] *Journal*, vol. I, p. 99 [1824].

journey to Morocco which he undertook in 1831. What he saw here of heat and violence, or dreamt he might have seen, provided him with subjects for the rest of his life: battle scenes with sheiks, slaves and rapes of women, and lion-hunts glowing with ruby reds and emerald greens set against hot browns and an occasional passage of blue and dashed off with a vehemence which European painting had not seen since Rubens. But what in Rubens had been the *Rape of the Sabine Women* and the *Calydonian Boar* was now made to appear contemporary. Thus far Delacroix, after 1830, gave way to realism.

Realism is the hall-mark of the mid-century decades. It is what corresponds in art to the great developments of science and technology, to the *Origin of Species* and the Crystal Palace. In French painting realism appears in many guises, in Paul Gavarni's (1804–66) lithographs of Parisian life, in Honoré Daumier's (1808–79) political and social caricatures and his brilliantly vivid oil sketches—the theatre (*Le Drame*), a washerwoman and her child, a third-class carriage—in J. L. E. Meissonnier's (1815–91) pedantically and meticulously painted and immensely popular Louis XV and Louis XVI genre scenes and his contemporary battle scenes, in the exquisitely limpid early landscapes of Corot, and in the great art of the painters of Barbizon in the Forest of Fontainebleau. Camille Corot (1796–1875) is another of the untutored artists of the nineteenth century. 'Nobody has taught me anything,' he wrote towards the end of his life, and 'I struggled with nature quite alone, and this is the result', and 'Nature must be interpreted with naïvety'.[1] This naïvety which was indeed one of the most engaging qualities in the personal character of the much beloved 'père Corot' gives his small and unpretentious Italian landscapes painted in the 'twenties their freshness and spontaneity. They are the French parallel to Cotman's contemporary water-colours. Corot's more popular nymphs in misty glades belong to his later years—one instance among many of a slackening of tensions in the course of the careers of nineteenth-century artists. Baudelaire, the most sensitive art critic of the 1840's and 1850's, places Corot 'at the head of the modern school', with the proviso, however, that if Rousseau would exhibit more, that supremacy might be doubtful.[2]

Théodore Rousseau (1812–67) can be regarded as the chief of the school of Barbizon. His robust art of landscape painting is visibly influenced by Constable's. It can hardly be said that he or the older landscape painters of the school break new ground. But they established the English innovations of the first and second thirds of the century for the Continent, and handed them on to the Impressionists of the last third. More important from the point of view of this survey is Jean-François Millet (1814–75), who in 1849 also settled down at Barbizon. Millet

---

[1] Quoted from *Corot, raconté par lui-même...*, vol. I (Geneva, 1946), pp. 84 and 88.
[2] Salon of 1845. Quoted from *Variétés critiques*, ed. Cris (1924), vol. II, p. 216.

discovered the farmer and the farm labourer for the nineteenth century. No painter since Bruegel had taken the worker on the land as seriously as Millet. He was not aware himself that—chiefly by means of his low horizons which make his figures appear of more than human stature—he monumentalised his subjects and that often, for instance in the famous *Angelus*, he sentimentalised them too. Baudelaire was the only critic perspicacious enough to see that: 'His peasants are pedants who think too much of themselves.... Whether they are harrowing, sowing, pasturing their cows, or tending their animals they always seem to be saying: It is we the poor and disinherited of the earth who make it fertile. We are fulfilling a mission, exercising a priestly vocation.'[1] It is typical that Millet was anxious not to be mistaken for a socialist.[2] Proudhon's '*Qu'est-ce que la propriété*' appeared in 1840, his *Philosophie de la misère* in 1846. Henceforth realism in art—the exposure of life as it really is—might easily join forces with socialism.

Such was the case of Gustave Courbet (1819–77), the chief representative in painting of the second half of our period. Delacroix, more than twenty years older, had still the burning fire of romanticism, Corot still its poetry. Courbet was proud of being 'without ideals and without religion'. Thus in his irritating way, he stated on his notepaper heading: 'Gustave Courbet, Master Painter, without ideals and without religion'.[3] Courbet is in painting what the English High Victorian buildings are in architecture: robust, self-confident and gross. 'I am the first and only artist of this century', he said of himself.[4] He was a big fat man, with a roaring laugh, who used to beat the table with his fist to show approval or disapproval and to consume innumerable *chopes* of beer while at work. He was proud of never having had any other intention with women than to enjoy them; among his paintings are characteristically enough some which are unashamedly pornographical, and many which are elaborately suggestive. In French literature the counterpart of Courbet is the much younger Zola, rather than the contemporary Flaubert. Like so many of the other progressive artists of the nineteenth century Courbet was essentially self-taught. 'A pupil of nature' he called himself. The chief works of his early maturity, the 1850's, deserve individual notice. They begin with the *Stonebreakers*, painted when he was thirty-one. He wrote of them: 'I have invented nothing. I saw the wretched people in this picture every day as I went on my walks.'[5] But the fact remains that, if he has not invented, he has arranged. The attitudes of the old man and his young mate form themselves into an easily discerned composition and the paint possesses a rich and substantial old-masterliness. The result is

[1] *Variétés critiques*, vol. I, p. 172 [Salon of 1859].
[2] A. Sensier, *J. F. Millet* (English edn, London, 1881), pp. 93 and 157.
[3] Quoted from *Courbet. Raconté par lui-même...*, vol. I (Geneva, 1948), p. 21.
[4] *Ibid.* p. 28.
[5] *Ibid.* p. 96.

life on the land as monumentalised as Millet's, though without sentimentality. The *Stonebreakers* was accompanied in the Salon of that same year by the *Funeral at Ornans*, a picture 9½ ft. by more than 21 ft., deliberately primitive in composition, which showed a large number of figures all standing stock-still and mostly bolt-upright. They are painted with the greatest truth. No piety or tenderness seems to move the participants.

M. Courbet's Studio, which followed it a few years later, is of about the same size as the *Funeral*. It formed the programmatic centrepiece of the special pavilion at the International Exhibition of 1885 which Courbet put up for his work and called '*Realism*'. In the middle the painter himself is seen busy at a canvas with a landscape. A farmer's boy and a nude model, with her clothes scattered demonstratively on the floor, watch him; for everybody can understand Courbet's work. On the left are his other models, a huntsman, a poor Irishwoman in rags, a Jew, a gravedigger, a prostitute and various others; on the right appear Baudelaire representing poetry, Proudhon representing socialism and, among many others, two couples representing *Fashionable Love* and *Free Love*.

To the same years belong the *Bathers*, two heavily built women in a thickly wooded landscape, one exposing the back of her naked body—'the vulgarity and pointlessness of the conception are abominable' Delacroix wrote of it[1]—then the *Girls on the Banks of the Seine*, two young women lazily and voluptuously stretched out by the river, and *The Hammock*, where a woman of similar fleshiness shows a little too much of her legs and her breasts. It is a revelation of the animal nature of man. The brutal vigour of Courbet's paint and the solidity of his modelling matched his programme to perfection. They enabled him to create some of the most powerful landscapes and seascapes of the nineteenth century. Next to one of Courbet's rocky river gorges a Corot looks flimsy and so does a Monet. But often, especially in those later works in which he introduces stags and deer, everything is spoiled by his lack of refinement and the vulgarity of his taste. Everything—except success. It is just these least discriminating of his pictures which have become popular in reproductions. Courbet remains the interesting and rare case of a great painter with bad taste. Just like some of his nudes, some of his landscapes were painted to rouse cheap emotions. Courbet could not understand that Daumier, whom he felt to be his brother in revolt, could choose to remain in the background. When Daumier in 1870 refused the Legion of Honour Courbet embraced him with delighted approval but blamed him because Daumier had not refused it 'with *éclat*'. Courbet did everything with *éclat*, the *éclat* with which, in his stodgier and more respectable way, Sir George Gilbert Scott endowed St Pancras Station. Courbet's idea, Sainte-Beuve tells us in 1862, was 'to look on vast railway stations as new churches for painting, and to cover the big walls with a thousand subjects...

[1] *Journal*, vol. II, p. 18.

picturesque, moral, industrial...; in other words the saints and miracles of modern society'.[1]

Nothing came of this dream, and there are no paintings by Courbet celebrating industry and commerce. More generally speaking, the Industrial Revolution and the age of the railways have not left much of a mark on contemporary painting. Wright of Derby's smithies are Caravagesque compositions of figures in violent artificial light. Turner's *Rain, Steam and Speed; the Great Western Railway* of 1844 is an atmospheric not a social study. The same is true of Karl Blechen's (1798–1845) *Rolling Mill*, an impressionist sketch, and of Adolf Menzel's (1813–1900) *Berlin-Potsdam Railway* of 1847. But Menzel was also the first major painter to take as his subject the interior of a factory. His *Rolling Mill*, a picture 5 ft. by more than 9 ft., shows the steamy, smoky atmosphere under the vast glass roofs and the workmen—not monumentalised in any way—as they deal with the white hot molten metal pouring out. The date of the picture is 1875.

Menzel's career is interesting from our present viewpoint. He was a man of brilliant talent, and his early sketchy pictures are influenced by Blechen and typical of that pre-Impressionism which is the German parallel to Constable and Bonington—landscapes near Berlin, or a corner of a church with the pastor in the pulpit, or a room with the white curtains blown by a breeze and the sun fully shining in. Concurrently, however, Menzel worked on a series of wood engravings to illustrate Kugler's *Life of Frederick the Great*. He applied himself to this task with immense industry and gathered all available information on the multifarious paraphernalia of Prussian life in the eighteenth century. The engravings are accurate in every detail, and their success made Menzel embark on some oil paintings of subjects from the life of the king. The first of these dates from 1850. Here are realism and historicism, those hallmarks of the nineteenth century, at their most meticulous. The technique is similar to that of Meissonier in his pictures of Rococo fops. In his late years Menzel adopted the same technique for many-figured scenes from contemporary society. *The Supper at the Imperial Palace* of 1878 and the *Piazza d'Erbe at Verona* of 1884 are *tours de force* of keenly observed and painstakingly rendered detail—always entertaining and never pedantic.

The sparkle of his technique, grounded in his early impressionism, distinguishes Menzel from his English counterpart, William P. Frith (1819–1909). *Ramsgate Sands* of 1854, *Derby Day* of 1858, and *Paddington Station* of 1862 are too familiar to need description here. They made Frith famous all over Europe, and he could place below his name on the title-page of his autobiography: 'Chevalier of the Legion of Honour, Member of the Royal Academy of Belgium, Member of the Academies of Stockholm, Vienna and Antwerp.'

[1] *Courbet. Raconté par lui-même...*, vol. I, p. 164.

Belgian honours were especially valued at the time. For Antwerp had become a centre of academic art in Europe. It was here in the hands of Wappers (1803–74), Gallait (1810–87), and de Keyser (1813–87) that a kind of melodramatic history painting was developed which took the place from about 1830 onwards of the noble but anaemic art of the neo-classical cartoon or painting. The Belgians—and Paul Delaroche (1796–1856) in France—are like so many Delacroixs with the genius of their prototype watered down and his *brio* tempered.

Wishing to become a history painter, Ford Madox Brown (1821–93) went to study under Wappers in Antwerp. Then, however, after some time in Paris, he visited Rome, and here he came under the influence of Overbeck, the surviving Nestor of the German romantics of the early years of the century. The outcome of this was his *Chaucer at the Court of Edward III* painted in 1847. The picture with its Gothic arched top and its colourfully painted figures in the costumes of the fourteenth century is entirely Pre-Raphaelite in style, though painted several months before the formation of the Brotherhood. Its founders, chiefly Rossetti, Holman Hunt and Millais, were all younger than Brown, and Rossetti became Brown's pupil for a short time during the crucial winter of 1847–8. The aims of the Brotherhood are set down in their short-lived journal *The Germ*. Here we read a doctrine which is in every respect but one a mere translation of that of the German romantics. 'Without the pure heart nothing can be done worthy of us', wrote F. G. Stephens. And: 'exaggerated action,...false sentiment, voluptuousness, poverty of invention' must be rigorously avoided. 'An entire adherence to the simplicity of nature' is to be aimed at, 'and direct attention to the comparatively few works which art has yet produced in this spirit'. They were to be looked for in the Italy of before Raphael and also, or even more, in the Netherlands and Germany of Memling and Dürer. Hence the extremely attractive, humble and angular drawings and paintings of 1848 and the following years by Holman Hunt, Millais and Rossetti. They seem the very opposite of all that at the same moment Courbet and Millet and Daumier were doing. Yet the hallmark of the mid-nineteenth century is firmly impressed on the Pre-Raphaelites as well. Truth was their watchword, but truth not interpreted in the sense of the *Nazarenes*. 'Truth demands from the painter of a historical picture that he should make himself thoroughly acquainted with the character of the times and habits of the people which he is about to represent...[and] consult the proper authorities for the costume...architecture, vegetation or landscape, or accessories.' Menzel could have written that. In fact it is by Ford Madox Brown.

Now Brown, older than the others and never strictly speaking a member of the Brotherhood himself, remained faithful to the principles of *The Germ* to the end, whether he painted Wyclif or Cordelia or one of his sharply green landscapes closely rendered with fine pointed brushes. His most personal contribution is one also demanded by *The Germ* (in an article by J. L. Tupper). *The Germ* says that to find worth-while subjects artists should go not only to the past but also to the 'great lessons of piety, truth, charity, honour, gallantry' in our own time. Today's heroes should appear in today's paintings. We should hate Nero, but we should also hate 'an underselling oppressor of workmen'. How Courbet would have agreed, and how different his heroes of our time, say his *Stonebreakers*, look from, for instance, John Brett's *Stonebreaker* painted seven years after—a healthy pretty boy in a tightly packed sunny landscape. Madox Brown began to paint *The Last of England*, illustrating the departure of emigrants for Australia, in 1852 and *Work* in the same year. Among his late pictures are *John Dalton collecting Marsh-gas* and *Crabtree discovering the Transit of Venus*. *Work* is the most important document of social reform in European painting of its time. It would take too long here to describe properly its contents and the significant attitudes and action of its nearly twenty figures. Since Hogarth no one had attempted to crowd so much meaning on to a moderate-sized canvas. The scene is Hampstead, painted with entire accuracy. Carlyle and F. D. Maurice are portraits at once recognisable. They represent brain-work, as the navvies represent work of the strong arm and the ragged flower-vendor those who have never learnt to work. Then there are the poor fatherless slum children in tatters, the idle young lady and the well-meaning woman distributing tracts. The tract is called *The Hodman's Haven or Drink for Thirsty Souls*. The navvies prefer ale and have a right to. Other inscriptions on posters and so on remind the reader—or, rather, the spectator—of the Working Men's College (which had been founded by Maurice in 1854 and where Rossetti taught for a while) and the Boys' Home in the Euston Road.

A literary subject indeed, one that can only be fully appreciated with a key or guide! But then the same is true of Courbet's *Studio* and Menzel's *Supper at the Palace*. The Pre-Raphaelites objected fiercely to the superficially theatrical genre pictures with subjects chosen at random from poetry or fiction, which were so highly popular in Victorian days, the pictures described by Dickens in *Bleak House* as follows: 'One stone terrace (cracked), one gondola in distance, one Venetian senator's dress complete, richly embroidered white satin costume with profile portrait of Miss Jogg the model, one scimitar superbly mounted in gold, with jewelled handle, elaborate Moorish dress (very rare), and Othello.'[1] The Pre-Raphaelites objected even if the execution was done with the utmost care. 'Frith beastly', writes Brown in May 1851.[2] Their own *Lears* and *Dantes*

[1] Cf. Ruskin's diatribe in *Pre-Raphaelitism* (1853) against idealities of chivalry fitted out with Wardour Street armour, or eternal scenes from *Gil Blas*, *Don Quixote* and the *Vicar of Wakefield*. Libr. Edn, vol. XII, p. 351.
[2] F. M. Hueffer, *Ford Madox Brown* (London, 1896), p. 78.

and *Ladies of Shalott* combined accuracy with a new dedication and earnestness—at least in the early years of the movement.

After a few years the Pre-Raphaelite group disintegrated, as all such groups of young artists have a way of doing, and the founders went in opposite directions. Holman Hunt (1827–1910) remained entirely a Pre-Raphaelite. To paint *The Scapegoat* he had to go to Palestine in 1854 so that his Dead Sea might be the correct Dead Sea—a most curious aberration of realism—and to paint *May Day at Oxford* he had, though an old man then, to climb Magdalen Tower every morning at five. The results are so close to nature in their detail and so over-focused that they cease entirely to be realistically convincing. They would be reminiscent of the modern photographer's cobbles and pebbles and unretouched large portrait heads, if it were not for their vile, obtrusive, shadowless colours, heather-purples, absinthe greens and so on. Dante Gabriel Rossetti's (1828–82) colours in his later works are hotter and richer but equally repulsive. The languid voluptuousness of his figures is in no way compatible with the preachings of *The Germ*, though very tame if compared with the full-blooded sensuality of Courbet. Even so, it had to be purified and translated into cool blues and greys to become universally popular in the works of Burne-Jones. But Burne-Jones's more refined art belongs to the late Victorian era.

Finally there was John Everett Millais (1829–96). He changed from a P.R.B. to a P.R.A., that is from being a Pre-Raphaelite Brother to being the President of the Royal Academy, and in later life painted *The North West Passage* and *Soap Bubbles* rather than *Christ in the House of his Parents* and *Ophelia*. His is the most interesting case in England of the conflict in one man between the worlds of conscientious art and social success. G. F. Watts (1817–1904) is another example. He started in a vigorous Venetian manner, strong and warm, and ended with large, vapid illustrative *machines* such as the celebrated *Mammon* and *Love and Life*, and *Time, Death and Judgement*.

Titles did a good deal in High Victorian days to attract success. Just as laymen found it easier to distinguish between Italianate and Gothic than between the managing of proportions in one façade as against another, so they preferred to look at a picture of two dogs if it was called *High Life and Low Life*, or a picture of a stag if it was called *The Monarch of the Glen*, than at good pictures pure and simple. These two titles are taken at random from the *œuvre* of Sir Edwin Landseer (1802–73). Others are *Alexander and Diogenes*, *A Distinguished Member of the Humane Society* (a St Bernard dog) and *Dignity and Impudence*.

In France a popular picture, the picture of the year, was less likely to be literary. The English painter to be successful appealed to sentiment, the French to the senses. Men like Cabanel (1823–89) and Bouguereau (1825–1905) went on painting their seductive nudes year in year out.

Cabanel's *Birth of Venus*, spread out voluptously on a sea of cardboard, appeared at the Salon in 1863 and was at once bought by Napoleon III, as Queen Victoria had bought Frith's *Ramsgate Sands* and knighted Landseer.

In the same year in which Cabanel's *Venus* was the sensation of the Salon, Manet had painted his *Olympia* which was rejected by the Salon. The antagonism between popularly accepted art and the art of Manet and his friends who, a little later, gathered around him under the banner of Impressionism, was even more strident than it had been in the middle of the century. 'An almost childish ignorance of the first elements of drawing', 'a deliberate manifestation of inconceivable vulgarity', 'this Olympia, a kind of female gorilla', 'this yellow-bellied odalisk', 'art which has sunk to such a low level doesn't deserve to be condemned'—these are only a few of the press comments on Manet's *Olympia* when the picture was shown in 1865.[1]

But Manet, who was born in 1832, belongs only with his earliest work to the period here considered, and the Impressionists belong scarcely at all. In 1870 Degas was 36 years old, Monet and Renoir 30. The art of Impressionism, subtle, fleeting, exceedingly sensitive and exceedingly superficial in that true sense of the word which indicates that all phenomena are regarded purely as they affect the eye, is decidedly of the late nineteenth century. The same turn towards refinement and an isolation of the aesthetic aspects of art from all others appears in English architecture and design, the two arts in which, thanks chiefly to William Morris and Norman Shaw, England carried on her leadership beyond the confines of this chapter. Morris was born in 1834, Norman Shaw in 1831. Morris's style and his theories of social reform, also characteristic in their particular form of the Late as against the High Victorian era, were developed, it is true, in the 1860's, but they began to spread only when his firm received its first big commissions—such as the dining room of 1867 designed for the Victoria and Albert Museum—and when he began to lecture publicly in 1877. Norman Shaw's mature style begins with the New Zealand Chambers in Leadenhall Street in the City. This was designed in 1871. The daintiness of its bay windows, the freshness and independence of period precedent of its wide ground-floor oriels, the playful and original way in which motifs are interwoven—all this is in a complete contrast to the heavy, pompous, respectable and gloomy office buildings of the preceding High Victorian decades. Four years later, at Bedford Park near London, the first of all garden suburbs was built, in just as convincing a contrast to the mid-Victorian housing of Kensington and Bayswater. Again, two years later, William Morris in the earliest of his lectures compared the London of the Middle Ages with its 'pretty, carefully whitened houses' with the London of his day consisting entirely

---

[1] A. Tabarant, *Manet et ses œuvres* (Paris, 1947), pp. 107–8.

of 'hideous hovels, big, middle-sized and little'. In the same lecture Morris recommended that ancient work should be studied but not imitated or repeated, advocated 'simplicity of life', and 'cleanliness and decency' in the things we surround ourselves with in our houses, and ended with a hope 'that the world should sweep away all art for a while. . .that it might yet have a chance to quicken in the dark'.[1] Now let us compare with these revolutionary words, what the new painters have to say, Whistler in 1885 and Monet in 1889. Here is Whistler: 'Art. . .is a goddess of dainty thought—reticent of habit, abjuring all obtrusiveness, proposing in no way to better others',[2] and here Monet: 'He wished he had been born blind and then suddenly gained his sight or that he could have begun to paint without knowing what the objects were that he saw before him.'[3] This detachment from everything material, everything literary, every-thing moral is just as revolutionary as the architecture of Norman Shaw and the theories of Morris. All these tendencies can only be understood as the outcome of a quickened sensitivity and recovered aesthetic integrity: the late as against the mid-nineteenth century.

[1] 'The Lesser Arts', Collected Works, vol. XXII, pp. 11, 15, 20.
[2] Ten o'clock (London, 1888), p. 8. The address was delivered in 1885.
[3] J. Rewald, The History of Impressionism (New York, 1949), p. 408.

CHAPTER VII

IMAGINATIVE LITERATURE[1]

IT is characteristic of this period of literature that, with exceptional vigour, it both provokes and defeats large historical generalisations. For its writers show an exceedingly high degree of historical self-consciousness and debate their problems in terms of 'the needs of the age', believing that theirs is an age which calls for radically new insights, approaches and departures of the mind. On the other hand, this feeling is but a symptom of the dissolution of all naïvely held common beliefs, a negative fact which makes it hard to find for the epoch any positive common denominator. Is it a scientifically minded, materialistic, positivistic age? Yes, it is the age of Comte, Feuerbach, Darwin, Marx and Herbert Spencer. Yet it is also romantic, idealistic and anxiously waiting upon the spirit of man and his cultural possessions. Its intellectual history would certainly be badly out of focus if no mention were made of Carlyle, Emerson, Ruskin, Matthew Arnold, the Austrian writer Adalbert Stifter, the Swiss historian Jacob Burckhardt. Is it an age estranged from religion? Certainly. Yet religious feelings run high, and not only feelings. There are such profound and dramatic religious thinkers as Kierkegaard and Cardinal Newman, and there is, in literature, the deeply religious genius of Dostoevsky. Is it a prosaic age? Very likely; yet it is also the age which invented and passionately practised the doctrine of 'pure poetry', and which revelled in the emotional abandon of Richard Wagner's music. Is it an age which believes in the innate power of man to embark on a voyage of infinite progress? It would no doubt be easy to answer in the affirmative were it not for the eager reception given—and by no mean hosts—to the metaphysical pessimism of Schopenhauer. It seems impossible to portray the age on a canvas of limited dimensions.

However, one generalisation can be made which is likely to prove fruitful for our understanding of the intellectual character of the epoch: the novel dominates the literary scene. This is clear not only in retrospect; it was recognised at the time. A contributor to the *Prospective Review* wrote in 1849 that 'the novel is now what the drama was in the reigns of Elizabeth and James I'; and when the same journal said in 1850 of the novel that it was 'the vital offspring of modern wants and tendencies', it certainly spoke not only for England but for almost the whole world of letters.[2]

---

[1] The author wishes gratefully to acknowledge the help given him by the late Mr E. K. Bennett, President of Gonville and Caius College, Cambridge.

[2] Pp. 37 and 495. Cit. Kathleen Tillotson, *Novels of the Eighteen-Forties* (Oxford, 1954), a book to which I am indebted for several quotations and illuminating suggestions.

Bagehot, reviewing in 1858 the course of the English novel from Walter Scott to George Eliot, hit upon yet another trend which was noticeable also outside the English literary scene: 'The desire to attain a belief, which has become one of the most familiar sentiments of heroes and heroines, would have seemed utterly incongruous to the plain sagacity of Scott, and also to his old-fashioned art.'[1] In other words, the novel has a history: from the simple epic narrative which takes for granted that a human being responds in a universally established and plainly comprehensible manner to certain situations and events, it moves towards an ever-subtler delineation of the inner life, which is felt to be too complex to permit epic simplicity. Nietzsche once enumerated some of the qualities of mind ideally suited to the purposes of the new novelist: he must be endowed with subtle and bold senses, must be inquisitive to the point of cynicism, logical because he is disgusted with the muddle of life, a conqueror of riddles, a friend of the Sphinx. A far cry indeed from Scott's 'plain sagacity'! We catch a glimpse of the extremities of this development by comparing James Joyce's *Ulysses* (1922) to that of Homer. The ancient hero travels through time and space, exploring the outer world; the modern Ulysses stays in town and in one day braves the adventures lying in wait for him in his own soul. The whole distance from Homer to James Joyce seems all but condensed into the few decades of our period. Walter Scott, who died in 1832, is, in this sense, still close to Homer; yet there is but a short way from Dostoevsky, who died in 1881, to James Joyce, or from George Eliot to Proust.

This increasing preoccupation with 'psychology' is, of course, related to the 'desire to attain a belief' which, according to Bagehot, had become 'one of the most familiar sentiments of heroes'. In the epic and the older type of novel beliefs did not enter the plot because they formed the clear background which threw up in relief the meaning of actions, events and sentiments. It was only with the blurring of that background that the search for meaning could itself become part of the story. The world of the old beliefs was a 'cosmos', the fundamental order of which was established once and for all. Many strange and exciting things could happen in this world, but whatever happened fell into its place. In the new world there were no preordained places. They had to be discovered in the souls of individual men and women; and the search turned out to be endless, with every new discovery brought into question by a still subtler suspicion. For in the algebra of the human soul one belief lost does not equal one doubt acquired; it equals an infinity of possible truths and untruths. John Stuart Mill described this situation well, even while he attributed its causes rather arbitrarily to two men, when in 1867 he wrote: 'By Bentham, beyond all others, men have been led to ask themselves in regard to any ancient or received opinion, Is it true? and by Coleridge, What is

---

[1] Walter Bagehot, *Literary Studies*, vol. II (London, 1858), p. 160.

the meaning of it?'[1] And the question asked by the hero of Disraeli's *Tancred* (1847) could well serve as a motto to many works of the period: 'What ought I to believe?'

With the gradual weakening and eventual collapse of the framework of fundamental beliefs about the meaning of life, literature was irresistibly tempted to modify its own meaning and function. It could no longer be content to provide higher entertainment or moral examples; it became itself an instrument of exploration, a tool in the search for truth. The early German romantics, above all Friedrich Schlegel, knew that this would happen, and even believed that it should. It is Schlegel's voice that speaks through Carlyle writing in 1833: 'Poetry, it will more and more come to be understood, is nothing but higher Knowledge; and the only genuine Romance (for grown persons) Reality.'[2] And at the end of our period the following was written: 'We should conceive of poetry worthily, and more highly than it has been the custom to conceive of it.... More and more mankind will discover that we have to turn to poetry to interpret life for us, to console us, to sustain us. Without poetry, our science will appear incomplete; and most of what now passes with us for religion and philosophy will be replaced by poetry.' The author of this is, of course, Matthew Arnold.[3] Was such 'replacement' not, for instance, carried out by 'Mark Rutherford' (William Hale White)—who said of Wordsworth that he had done for him 'what every spiritual reformer has done—he recreated my Supreme Divinity'?[4] Before the nineteenth century no statement of this kind is likely ever to have been made about a lyrical poet.

The exploratory character of literature, the conviction that it is 'higher Knowledge' and dedicated to 'Reality' expresses itself, on one level, as 'realism' in the commonly accepted sense of the term. The name suggests that now, for the first time in history, literature concerned itself with the 'real'. To accept this claim would be to pander to an illusion and Nietzsche was undoubtedly right in saying that 'realism in art is an illusion.... All the writers of all the ages were convinced that they were realistic'.[5] In truth, the realist writer is only, like any other writer at any other time, fascinated by certain aspects of reality, and uses the selective scheme of his fascination for the aesthetic ordering of his chosen materials. For we seem to get to know one thing at the price of losing sight of another; and however wide our interests, the sharp edge of our perception in one sphere is but in contrast to the bluntness of our sensibility in another. What then is it, Nietzsche went on to ask, that distinguishes

---

[1] *Dissertations and Discussions* (London, 1867), p. 403.
[2] Carlyle, 'Essay on Diderot', first published in *Foreign Quarterly Review* (1833), reprinted in *Critical and Miscellaneous Essays* (London, 1839). Cf. Jakob Minor, *Friedrich Schlegel 1794–1802: seine prosaischen Jugendschriften* (Vienna, 1906), vol. II, p. 200.
[3] *Essays in Criticism*, Second Series (London, 1915), p. 2.
[4] *Autobiography of Mark Rutherford* (London, n.d.), p. 19.
[5] F. Nietzsche, *Gesammelte Werke* (Musarion edn, Munich, 1922), vol. XI, p. 80.

modern realism? He arrived at an answer much in keeping with at least one form of the belief that the new literature should be 'Knowledge'. The new writers were possessed, Nietzsche thought, by the desire to know and understand reality in an analytical and almost scientific manner; and thus, he said, 'the artists of our century willy-nilly glorify the scientific beatitudes'.[1]

This indeed marks a distinctive quality of nineteenth-century realism. For neither the 'realistic' subject-matter of the great realistic novels nor the brave contemplation of the 'seamy side of life' is new. Chaucer is exquisitely 'realistic' and the eighteenth century has given us considerable literary documents of life as it was lived, enjoyed or bungled, by people in the unheroic and unspectacular regions of existence. Dickens, in his Introduction of 1841 to *Oliver Twist*, believed he had to prepare the readers of his realistic novel for a shock: '...there are people of so refined and delicate a nature, that they cannot bear the contemplation of these horrors. Not that they turn instinctively from crime; but that criminal characters, to suit them, must be, like their meat, in delicate disguise....' But 'the stern and plain truth' of the 'horrors' which he promised would have seemed mild indeed to a Jacobean audience used to John Webster, Cyril Tourneur and John Ford; and Dickens's 'realistic frankness' in the face of the unromantic and indelicate might even have been judged as not entirely free from prudery by readers accustomed to the straightforwardness of Fielding's *Tom Jones*. No, the presentation neither of horrors nor of 'realistic' indelicacies breaks new literary ground. But what might strike readers of the past as new in nineteenth-century realism is the particular passion which is at work in the books of Stendhal, Balzac, Flaubert, Tolstoy or Dostoevsky (although not, or hardly at all, in the English novels of this period, with the exception of George Eliot). It is the passion of understanding, the desire for rational penetration and imaginative appropriation, the driving force towards the resolution of the mystery of living.

Baudelaire noticed how strange it was that Balzac's fame as a realist writer should rest on his power of detached observation. It was the quality, in Balzac, of passionate ardour and visionary zeal which struck Baudelaire—a quality which distinguishes him from Dickens with whom he has often been compared.

Indeed, how tedious would be Balzac's elaborate descriptions if they were not alive with the zeal for absolute imaginative possession of the things so described; how cheap would be Stendhal's melodramas if the emotions were merely evoked without being completely controlled by the analytical intelligence and made transparent by the master-eye which sees through it all with rational irony! And Dostoevsky's genius is closely allied to the spirit of detection, his singular greatness being due to the fact

[1] *Ibid.* vol. x, pp. 284–5.

that the light by which he searches is also the fire by which he is consumed. Nor is it beside the point—the point of his art as a novelist—that Tolstoy repeatedly declared 'Reason, that is good'. For the apparent quietness and equipoise of Tolstoy's prose (some critics have even called it 'idyllic') is yet vibrant with the pugnacious enthusiasm of rational understanding.

Thus it would seem that nineteenth-century realism is a more complex phenomenon than its usual definitions suggest. On the other hand, it is of course clear that it has to do with the radical changes in the nature of society which are conveniently summed up as 'capitalism' and 'Industrial Revolution'. More than ever before, man now lived in a world which was, blatantly and noisily, made by himself. The domains of 'civilisation' and 'nature' fell apart. Both the quick accumulation of wealth and the sudden exposure to destitution appeared to be the probable fortunes awaiting an ever greater number of people; and while the lives of men were over-crowded with 'stuff', the relations between men themselves, and between them and the mass-produced 'things', were rendered ever more prob-lematical and 'abstract'. With the 'natural' privileges of birth and in-herited status retreating before the skill of making money, life became ever more strenuously competitive, things assumed ever more the charac-ter of commodities, and human worth was ever more definable in terms of finance. This is what Karl Marx meant when he spoke of the 'abstract' nature of human relationships within capitalism, of man's 'self-alienation' in the midst of a world which was dominated by 'things' to the point of being finally itself transformed into a negotiable object.

The relevance of this to the contemporary literature is obvious. There is hardly a writer of any importance whose work does not reflect, in fascination for, or revulsion from it, or both, this major theme of the age. *Hard Times* (1854)—the very title of one of Dickens's novels reflects the overpowering (and often overpowered) consciousness of the social and spiritual problems of the age, a consciousness which is an almost all-pervasive element in the English literature of the period. If an English journal in 1832 complained that 'no one talks of literature in these stormy and changeful times...no attention is paid to anything but speculations on reform and change of rulers',[1] then, within a decade or so, it had be-come all but impossible to pay attention to literature without being talked to about reforms. On every level of immature sentiment or mature moral intelligence utterance is given—in the words of Mrs Gaskell's preface to *Mary Barton* (1848)—'to the agony which...convulses this dumb people'. The English novel is as problem-ridden as society itself, and obsessed with the identical problems. However, more important than the note of social indignation within many novels is the fact that sometimes, as, for instance, in Dickens's *Dombey and Son*, the critique of society becomes the novel itself, is embodied in it and truly assumes its form.

[1] *Athenaeum*, 12 May 1832, p. 307.

Balzac's great endeavour to depict, in a long series of novels, the human comedy, revolves around the theme of the essential falseness of human relationships in a world dominated by thoughts of money and power; and Flaubert's *Madame Bovary* (1857) exposes the heart's corruption, brought about by the discrepancy between ideas about life, vaguely and unauthentically inherited from the past, and the reality of living. Such doubts about the possible attainment of true authenticity amid the universal betrayal of traditional human values gives the genre 'Bildungsroman'—the novel which has as its central subject the gradual integration of one individual character—a new twist.

The literary archetype of the 'Bildungsroman' is Goethe's *Wilhelm Meister* (1795 and 1829) which exercised an inescapable spell over the German romantics as well as the German realists. They could hardly think of a novel save in the image of *Wilhelm Meister* and its ostensible theme (ostensible because it is by no means easy to extract a thematic design from so labyrinthine an architecture). This theme was the ultimate reconciliation between a man and a world; and the only two considerable novels in German in our period, Gottfried Keller's *Der grüne Heinrich* (1854 and 1879) and Adalbert Stifter's *Der Nachsommer* (1857), are undoubtedly cast in the mould of Goethe's work. Yet already with Goethe the antagonistic pair, individual and world, although finally persuaded by the poet to come to terms with one another, are of remarkably unequal stature. While the hero has a convincing (and convincingly autobiographical) existence, the world is an eccentric and hazy entity—as hazy as the 'common good' to which also Goethe's other hero, Faust, in the end redeemingly dedicates his soul, all but damned in its powerful subjectivity. Even where the grip on the world is more realistic, as it is, for instance, with Keller, it takes two versions of *Der grüne Heinrich*, separated by a quarter of a century, to decide on the true nature and outcome of the feud. If we add that in Stifter's *Nachsommer*, one of the most beautiful creations of this period, the 'world' in which the hero's education is accomplished is no longer the world at all, but a secluded and carefully guarded province of humanity, it will be clear that the 'Bildungsroman' was bound to undergo a radical change in an age which made the relationship between the self and the world problematical to the point of unsteadying the very notion of the integrity and authenticity that the individual might possibly achieve in it. Small wonder then that the term 'realistic novel', which rightly suggests a concern of the writer with the 'real', the external world, is almost synonymous with 'psychological novel' suggesting introspective preoccupation with the inner life. Where the traditional beliefs of society are thinned out into mere conventions and are no longer *felt* to be true, an unbridgeable gulf is fixed between them and the inner truths of individual existence. True authenticity becomes then a disturbing and hardly realisable demand. The question of reconciliation between such a world and such selves hardly arises, and the individual is compelled to embark on the chimerical chase after 'self-realisation'—chimerical, because there no longer exists a valid model of an ideal self. The 'Bildungsroman' turns into the record of this chase, more often than not with a hero who exemplifies this subtle form of moral falseness, its dangers and its virtual inevitability.

This theme and this kind of hero enter into the novel, never to leave it, with Benjamin Constant's *Adolphe* (1816), the story of a young man who is driven to do what 'ought' not to be done, and is incapable of feeling what 'ought' to be felt. And although reminiscences of the traditional 'Bildungsroman' may be found in some of the English novels of the period, in Dickens's *David Copperfield* (1850), Thackeray's *Pendennis* (1850), George Eliot's *Mill on the Floss* (1860) and *Middlemarch* (1872), the genre is most vigorously and influentially alive through its most 'transformed character': Julien Sorel of Stendhal's *Le Rouge et le noir* (1830), who was to become the prototype of the 'inauthentic' hero—'inauthentic' because 'life' provides no place for a superior being ('un esprit supérieur'), as Taine described Julien. A genius is destined to remain an outsider in a spiritually corrupt society and to be, in his own way, corrupted himself in his state of alienation. The romantic imagination would have conceived a hero of this kind simply as an example of greatness uncomprehended by a dull world. Stendhal's realistic sensibility is profounder: society is, at the deepest level, *successful* in denying integrity to genius. This is what gives finality and completeness to Stendhal's critique. Julien Sorel, a 'napoleonic' youth, of socially inferior parentage, sets out on his career by seeking the black robe of the Church which was to open for him the doors of the world to richer feasts of power than would the red uniform of the Army, and ends by being guillotined for attempting to murder his one-time mistress who interferes with his ambitious marriage plans. The melodramatic plot is transfigured by Stendhal's art into one of the subtlest works of literature, a work which has remained the classical example of the psychological novel. This kind of falsity was to occur again and again as the dominant theme of this genre. Balzac's social cosmos, phosphorescent with disorder, is over-populated by a race of villains and frauds, driving home the lesson that goodness is synonymous with failure. Flaubert's *Madame Bovary* (1857) *is* the denial of authenticity, while his *L'Éducation sentimentale* (1869), the title of which promises a 'Bildungsroman', is in fact the reverse: not integrity and reconciliation, but moral disintegration is the outcome of subjective complexity and idealistic enthusiasm in contemporary society.

The theme persists in many variations and on many different levels throughout the psychological novel. In a different setting and with strong romantic overtones, it is yet central to Lermontov's *A Hero of our Times* (1840), a book which holds a distinguished place in the distinguished history of the Russian novel. In the novels of George Meredith (1828–1909) the theme recurs repeatedly, often treated in the vein of sophisticated comedy. It is raised to the height of religious passion in Dostoevsky's *Crime and Punishment* (1866).

We seem to have arrived at yet another possible generalisation about the literature of our period: in a large and representative portion of it the 'hero' becomes increasingly unheroic. True, from Stendhal and Carlyle to Nietzsche the heroic hero is again and again the object of yearning, romantic worship and metaphysical expectation, but the central figure of the great realistic novels hardly ever justifies the traditional name. It tends to become a mere technical term; and the heroic hero declines for the very reason which accounts for the emergence of the realistic, analytical, psychological novel itself. This took the place of the more 'poetical' forms of narrative because 'life' had ceased to lend itself to condensed poetical expression. To the new writers life appeared no longer as something given and definite, but as in a state of indefinite flux, in process of being made—and made by men themselves. Hence it constantly invited a new understanding, and yet constantly evaded it, protracting the search for meaning and the true interpretation over the pages of ever more voluminous books. For where there is no given and generally accepted order, anything—literally any thing, any thought, dream, or whim—may help to reveal the elusive truth. In such a world there can be no real hero. The traditional hero enacts his destiny in the face of a given world, a world which makes or breaks him; the new 'hero', on the other hand, is either on the brink of becoming the entrepreneur, the industrialist, of his own world and soul, or else of being submerged by the waves of historical circumstance. There is a kind of inner logic by which extremely disparate works can be identified as belonging to the same period: Stendhal's *Le Rouge et le noir* with its profound critique of the heroic ideal; the same writer's *La Chartreuse de Parme* (1839) with its ironical reflections upon the actual reality of a heroic occasion, the battle of Waterloo; Thackeray's *Vanity Fair* (1848), the novel challengingly introduced as 'A Novel without a Hero' (in accordance with the author's conviction, expressed in a letter, that, by its very nature, a novel should 'convey as strongly as possible the sentiment of reality as opposed to a tragedy or poem, which may be heroical');[1] and Tolstoy's *War and Peace* (1865–9), the epic of men and women at the mercy of the mysterious forces of history.

Of course this is by no means true of every work produced in the period. In English literature, an important exception is the works of the Brontë sisters, above all Emily Brontë's *Wuthering Heights* (1847), a sanctuary of elemental passions, unaffected by the analytical, ironical, reforming, moralising, or rationalising temper of the literary world around. And if,

---

[1] May 1851, *Letters* (London, n.d.), vol. II, p. 773.

reading a novel of this time, we chance upon words like these: 'Delight is to him...who against the proud gods and commodores of this earth, ever struck forth his own inexorable self ', we may rightly wonder whether we are not, having left behind the main stream of the age, adrift in an unfamiliar ocean of timelessness and timeless heroic adventure. We are reading in fact what may well be the strangest of all literary masterpieces, the New Englander Herman Melville's *Moby Dick* (1851), the epic of Ahab, a whaleship captain, pursuing in the South Seas the white whale Moby Dick with all the passion, fascination and hatred of an 'inexorable self ' at grips with an inexorable destiny and doom. In this novel, told against the background of a realistic setting meticulously and even pedantically described, realism for once merges, in a deeply stirring, if not wholly successful, manner with a heroic grandeur and symbolic immediacy which seems of another age, the age of Homer or of Shakespeare.

Further, by way of 'exception', there is, above all, the unruly genius of Victor Hugo—unruly because he defies all categories of historical classification and apprehension. In terms of literary history, he is an eccentric who yet occupies a central position in the literature of France; an enemy of classicism who became a classical, if somewhat belated, exemplar of romanticism. The heyday of European romanticism was certainly over when Hugo in 1830 took the Paris stage by storm, and shattered its seemingly invincible classical conventions with his *Hernani*, to repeat and strengthen his success with *Ruy Blas* in 1838. Although 'romanticism' is one of the most elusive (and most pervasive) characters in literary history, resisting every attempt to catch it in a categorical net, it yet has a forceful and distinguished 'personality'—and Hugo is certainly one of its incarnations. Reading Stendhal's *Le Rouge et le noir* after Hugo's *Notre-Dame de Paris* (1831)—two almost contemporaneous novels —is like awakening from a lurid dream to the sober precision of daylight; and this despite the fact that it is easy to find many romantic ingredients in the realist's work. Still, the medieval setting of Hugo's novel, the architectural mysticism of the Gothic cathedral, passion expressed and not analysed, virtues and vices embodied in distinct figures, not debating their claims within the same persons, the flow and eloquence of rhetorical diction assailing the imagination with calculated melodrama and macabre images, paralysing rather than stimulating the critical intelligence—all this romantically relegates *Notre-Dame de Paris* to a place far removed from the literary centre of the period. Yet Hugo has a kingdom of his own, if somewhat impoverished in literary status, and in it he towers majestically, through the sheer force of his poetical ability, power of language and imaginative inventiveness, above many a minor caterer for the romantic requirements of the day. Among the latter, Alexandre Dumas *père* (*Les Trois Mousquetaires*, 1844; *Le Comte de Monte-Cristo*, 1845) and, on a considerably higher literary level, Prosper Mérimée (*La*

Chronique du règne de Charles IX, 1829; and, in a different vein, *Carmen*, 1845) are the most popular. Nevertheless, even in so romantic a writer as Hugo the spirit of the times in the end asserted itself: while an exile from Louis Napoleon's France in Guernsey he wrote, among other novels, *Les Misérables* (1862) in which the heroic-romantic manner of story-telling is incongruously, but vigorously, made to serve the unheroic and unromantic social preoccupations of the time.

Hugo's *Notre-Dame de Paris* is the most spectacular survival in our period of the genre 'historical novel', which only just before had held a dominant position by virtue of the power and influence of its inaugurator, Walter Scott. Indeed, it would be tempting to assume that the historical novel, as an upshot of the romantic discovery of the past (the German romantic Novalis's *Heinrich von Ofterdingen*, 1802—is the first truly literary manifestation of the genre) must of necessity be romantic. This assumption might draw support from the realist Flaubert's trespass upon romantic territory, a literary misdeed which happened to take the form of a historical novel, *Salammbô* (1862); yet it would have to be abandoned if confronted with Thackeray's *Henry Esmond* (1852), Dickens's *The Tale of Two Cities* (1859), Adalbert Stifter's *Witiko* (1864–7) and above all Tolstoy's *War and Peace* (1865–9), a historical novel which many regard, with good reason, as the greatest achievement of literary realism in the nineteenth century. Indeed, realism, as a mode of presentation, invades not only history but another apparent preserve of the romantic sensibility: the 'natural life', the 'rural idyll'. It is interesting to observe how, with the growing interest in 'the people', the romantic affection for simple and unsophisticated modes of living in town and country merges with the social and political preoccupations of the new realism, finally to be superseded by the latter; how the 'pure Present', romantically admired in the lives of humble folk, is transformed into 'the claims of the Future' which Disraeli, in his novel *Sybil* (1845) saw 'represented by suffering millions'; how the romantically tinged and highly individualistic exploits of George Sand's earlier novels (*Indiana*, 1831; *Valentine*, 1832; and *Lélia*, 1833) give way to the socialist enthusiasm of her later works (*Le Meunier d'Angibault*, 1845; and *Le Péché de Monsieur Antoine*, 1847); not to mention the distance from the almost idyllic and sentimental to the more sternly realistic which Dickens travelled between *The Old Curiosity Shop* (1841) and *Bleak House* (1853) or *Hard Times* (1854), between *Christmas Books* (1843–8) and *Little Dorrit* (1857).

This change of mood in the writer's dealings with the poor expresses itself in a variety of literary styles, yet their common denominator is realistic observation and the absence of romantic sentimentality. It takes the form of satire in the Russian Gogol's *Dead Souls* (1842), a work designed after the model of Dante's *Divine Comedy*, but with its first part (and only the first part exists) more reminiscent, in its plotless and rambling explorations of the social scene, of Dickens's *The Pickwick Papers* (1836–7) from which, however, it differs in almost every other respect: through the violence of its satire which is yet shot through with mystical elements, and through the aggressive caricatures of its almost Jonsonian 'humours', the whole yet issuing into the prophecy of future national glory. In Dostoevsky's *Poor Folk* (1845), which made its author famous in his country ('A new Gogol has arisen!' cried a Russian poet when he first read the manuscript), the realistic temper is infused with poignant pity and compassion. The Swiss pastor Albert Bitzius, who wrote under the name of Jeremias Gotthelf (*Der Bauernspiegel*, 1837; *Uli der Knecht*, 1841; *Uli der Pächter*, 1849), combines his very great gifts as a realistic writer with didactic zeal, conservatively upholding the truth of religion against the revolutionary appeals of his time. On the other hand, Turgenev's book with the deceptively jovial title of *A Sportsman's Sketches* (1847–52), a collection of stories about the life of peasants, and one of the masterpieces of Russian realism, is alleged to have had a spectacular political effect (if so, certainly not against the author's intention) in persuading one of its readers that serfdom had to be abolished. This reader was the future Tsar Alexander II.

Contemplation of the indisputable excellence of the Russian realistic novel is bound to put the reader on guard against two widely held views. The first, shared by many a literary historian, concerns the connection between literature and society. The realistic novel, it is maintained, is the literary form typical of the social, if not political, predominance of the middle classes, the artistic correlative of the arrival of an industrialised and industrialising bourgeoisie as the power socially and intellectually in control of affairs. In the light of this theory, the strength of English and French realism is then compared with the embryonic state of realistic literature in 'backward' Germany. Set against the mature social and political consciousness of Stendhal, Balzac, Dickens, for instance, the literature of 'Young Germany' is politically immature and socially confused: even at its most 'provincial', the English realistic novel is decisively superior to its German counterpart. If we compare, say, Anthony Trollope's *The Warden* (1855) or *Barchester Towers* (1857) with Gustav Freytag's *Soll und Haben* (1855) or Otto Ludwig's *Zwischen Himmel und Erde* (1856) we shall be struck, in the Englishman's work, by a note of literary assurance and quiet competence, by a vitality and spontaneity of the imagination which is absent from the German works, or if perceptible at all, certainly to a considerably lesser degree. And before the 'doubting' women of Mrs Gaskell or George Eliot, the 'Young-German' Gutzkow's *Wally die Zweiflerin* (1835) dwindles to the status of a jejune and dilettante literary exercise. On a higher level, Immermann's *Münchhausen* (1838) will hardly bear comparison with the all but contemporary *Pickwick Papers*; and is it not revealing, a sociologically minded critic may ask, that Immermann, one of Germany's most talented realists, should choose as his hero the mendacious baron of the 'tall tale'? Is he not a symbol of the lack of social reality? And what are Spielhagen's *Problematische Naturen* (1860) to the problematical natures of the contemporaneous French novel?

In support of the same argument the literary historian could evoke the American scene to show how the experimental nature and unsettledness of American society is reflected in the exotic flights and literary self-consciousness of its writers. It may indeed be due to the (as yet indefinite) character of America's social existence that her literary imagination, in all its incipient realism, tends to dwell in outlandish and fantastic spheres (Washington Irving, James Fenimore Cooper, and Edgar Allan Poe) or in the realm of timeless heroic passion (Herman Melville) or seek its roots in a novel brand of nature-mysticism and pantheistic transcendentalism, cultivated by the New Englanders, Ralph Waldo Emerson and Henry David Thoreau, in their 'Lake District', the Massachusetts countryside, with—from a European point of view—surprisingly out-of-date idealistic determination. And how self-conscious, by the side of the European realists, is the realism of Nathaniel Hawthorne, marred occasionally by allegorical and symbolical contrivances even in his greatest achievement, *The Scarlet Letter* (1850)! Eventually, this sociological theory of literature may be reinforced by the fact that one of the best-known American writers of the period immediately following, the remarkable, pessimistic and didactic buffoon and humorous sage Mark Twain, wrote two masterpieces whose heroes are children, *The Adventures of Tom Sawyer* (1876) and *Huckleberry Finn* (1884). For is not childhood farthest removed (except passively—and Huckleberry Finn is not at all like Oliver Twist) from social actuality, and closest to that elemental quality in life which will for ever make it an ageless adventure?

Yet even in America our theory would come up against a major hurdle; for it was in America that a new poetic voice began to speak—a 'realist' voice: that of Walt Whitman. And it would come to grief when encountering the Russian realist novel, and the fact that 'backward' Germany, more than England or France, was the model of 'advanced' Europe for the Russian intelligentsia, those prolific critics of their own sadly retarded country, whose 'westernising', indeed 'Germanising', efforts certainly contributed to the powerful efflorescence of Russian realism—in a social milieu of feudalist survivals, lingering serfdom and only the most timid beginnings of bourgeois capitalism.

The other common assumption which is brought into question by the Russian literature of this period concerns the essential 'otherness' of the Russian soul and mind. It is a double-edged belief, at work both in the criticisms and perhaps still more in the apologetics indulged in by the West towards Russian realities. Of course, Russian literature is Russian, but it would be hard to state with any precision the difference which sets it off from, say, English literature in a more 'essential' manner than English literature differs from that of France. If the concept of Europe is to make any intellectual or literary sense, it would be impossible to exclude from it such writers as Turgenev and Tolstoy, and it would certainly be incomplete without the 'uniquely Russian' Dostoevsky. Russian literature reflects, often in a dramatically heightened and spiritually more poignant way, the social, moral and religious perplexities which are common to Europe as a whole. The prototypes of Turgenev's intellectual world, for instance, are not mythical figures of the steppes, but Hamlet and Don Quixote—two European literary heroes to whom he devoted his celebrated essay of 1860; and his novel *Fathers and Sons* (1862) with its pessimistically detached and artistically accomplished treatment of the conflict between two generations easily finds its place within a European pattern, establishing itself in it still more firmly on account of its preoccupation with the problems of unbelief, materialism and austere intellectualism. If Turgenev was the first Russian to be received by the West as a great novelist, this was because his manner of writing had great affinities to that cultivated in Paris, and not because he was essentially less 'Russian' than Tolstoy or Goncharov.

Even Dostoevsky—is he more 'Russian' than the rest of Russian novelists? Perhaps only in the sense in which Emily Brontë is less 'English' than Dickens. Indeed, Dostoevsky is 'strange', but he is a stranger also in his own literary home. The profound difference, for instance, between him and Tolstoy has become a classical subject of critical speculation and literary philosophising. And Dostoevsky is doubly bewildering because in the sphere of political and quasi-political thought and activity he amply shares, in his own manner, the interests and aspirations of the contemporary Russian intelligentsia, while all his major novels take place in a world in which there is no room whatever for political remedies or collective solutions. His world is indeed as much a social world as any which is presented in European realist literature, and Dostoevsky is as skilful as Dickens or Balzac at dramatising its conflicts in mystery, suspense and detection, but every human relationship in it is inextricably entangled with the promise of salvation or the threat of damnation. His creatures are certainly made of flesh and blood, but in their flesh and blood divine anxiety and the passion of spiritual fulfilment are incarnate. Compared to him, Tolstoy is, despite the serene acceptance of life which informs *War and Peace*, puritanical: 'life' is one thing, ultimate moral and religious demands are another. Hence Tolstoy is undoubtedly the greater artist by any purely aesthetic or literary standards, and has his assured place—perhaps the highest—in the history of the European realist novel. Therefore, too, Tolstoy wished, after his religious conversion in 1880, to abandon literature, denouncing it as a deeply immoral concern.

Such a puritanically religious disavowal of art would have been meaningless to Dostoevsky. With him it is religion itself which takes shape in his books: *Crime and Punishment* (1866), *The Idiot* (1868), *The Possessed* (1871–2) and in the greatest of all, *The Brothers Karamazov* (1880). For his religion is not a religion of communal work, or transcendental felicity; it is a religion of flesh and blood and ecstasy and suffering. Both Tolstoy and Dostoevsky are great psychologists, but their psychologies are different. Tolstoy probes the hidden motives and motivations of human behaviour, revealing the subtle interplay of natural impulses, social conventions and earthly ambitions. Dostoevsky's psychological insight, on the other hand, leaves us, when all the probing is done, and done most penetratingly, with a psychologically indissoluble core of mystery from which every person acts out his part in a cosmic drama. And from this drama there is no dispensation. Dostoevsky's Saviour has not come to set man free from pain, but to sanctify it in all its cruelty and sordidness. Religious rapture, therefore, is expressed in Dostoevsky's works not through the mystical contemplation of pure spirit, but through man embracing the earth—the soil in all its impurity.

With Dostoevsky every human situation, even the seemingly most trivial, may find itself at the crossroads between Heaven and Hell—a location very different from that which the majority of realist writers would allot to human affairs; and it may well be that the undercurrent of spiritual pessimism, so clearly perceptible in most of the outstanding works of European realism, can be ascribed to the failure to share Dostoevsky's sacramental vision of the world. On the other hand, the very uniqueness of Dostoevsky's spirituality may give to it the occasional note of shrillness and hysterical over-emphasis, so different from the perfectly controlled poetic vitality of Tolstoy's *War and Peace*, that masterpiece which defies the faculty of critical appraisal by giving the appearance of being neither smaller nor larger than life, but just as large as life itself, thus setting the reader wondering whether this is not too large for a work of art. It certainly is the rarest example of a rarely achieved equilibrium between the artistic imagination and the actuality of living, an equilibrium so complete that no room is left for tragedy or melodrama, satire or sentimentality, caricature or moral purpose— ingredients hardly ever completely absent from the novel of the period. However, Tolstoy himself was unable to maintain this balance. Already upon his next work, *Anna Karenina* (1875–7), there fell the shadows of that despair which marks the beginning of his flight from literature into the life of religion.

At another extreme of the Russian novel, realistic pessimism and melancholy humour come into their own—and so suggestively and successfully that the hero of Goncharov's *Oblomov* (1868), the story of an utterly purposeless life, became the great symbolic character of a 'lost generation', a Hamlet who 'cannot care less', a Faust who 'cannot be bothered'. A pessimistic literary observer might see significance in the fact that the history of the realistic and psychological novel in our period begins with *Le Rouge et le noir*, that subtle and ruthless critique of society, its feelings and its ideals, and ends with the epic of Oblomov, who thinks life not worth the effort of rising from his bed.

Such an observer was Nietzsche. He had never heard of Oblomov, but he guessed his existence. Planning a book on 'European nihilism' (a book he never wrote), he intended to base its first chapter on an analysis of the literature of realism. This was to show, as a posthumous note suggests, how 'between 1830 and 1850 the romantic faith in love and in the future turned into the craving for nothingness'.[1] From his notes it would appear that foremost in his mind was Flaubert. And there is little doubt that with Flaubert a latent nihilistic disposition in realism emerges into the open. For the 'realistic' sense of reality, which possessed so many minds in the nineteenth century, lured him ever farther towards the rational conquest of the human world only to prove to him its absolute meaninglessness. Psychological truthfulness and faithful representation, the great virtues of realism, are, for Flaubert, nothing but the conventional surface of his literary enterprise. At its heart is the hatred of reality and the desire to conquer it. Even the 'reality' of the person who does the writing seemed to him at times a mere obstacle to the ultimate rational and aesthetic triumph. If only the human subject could be reduced to nothing but observing, understanding and writing; if only the real object could be transmuted into nothing but words! Reality ought to be dissolved by insight and style! Yet again and again, as we can see from his correspondence, Flaubert was dismayed by the undue resistance offered by the meaningless world. After the 'realistic' labour of *L'Éducation sentimentale* he said: 'Beauty is incompatible with modern life, and this is the last time I will have anything to do with it. I have had enough.'[2] It seemed that no purity of style, however hygienically contrived, could prevail against the infection that realism was bound to contract by dealing with reality at all. Perhaps the immaculate victory over reality could be achieved only by writing, as Flaubert once said, 'a book about nothing at all, a book without any external connection, and which would support itself entirely by the internal force of style'.[3]

This, clearly, would no longer be realism. But these words of the realist Flaubert are relevant to a type of poetry which is the most original poetic creation of our period, and the suspicion that 'beauty is incompatible with modern life' is certainly one of the motives determining the course of poetry from romanticism to an ever more radical insistence on the

[1] *Gesammelte Werke* (edn cit.), vol. XIX, p. 384.
[2] *Œuvres complètes de Gustave Flaubert*, vol. V (Paris, 1929), p. 260.
[3] *Ibid.* vol. II (Paris, 1923), p. 345.

'purity' of the poetic sphere. The extreme antithesis of reality and poetry is the most characteristic feature of the literary history of the epoch so that, while the realist novel strives to come to ever closer grips with the 'real' world, lyrical poetry seeks to settle in fields which are at the farthest possible remove from 'life'. At the beginning there seemed still some hope of reconciliation: in 1826 Alfred de Vigny, the French romantic poet, wrote in the introductory essay to his *Cinq-mars*: 'In our troubled and contradictory hearts we should find two needs which seem opposed to each other, but which—to my way of thinking—blend together in a common source: one is the love of the *true*, the other the love of the *fabulous*.'[1] The opposition is by no means new. It is at least as old as Plato, who attacked, in the name of truth, the misleading fabrications of poetic fancy. But what is new is that the opposing forces should become entrenched in the field of literature itself. For the two loves of de Vigny inspire the two main literary trends of the age: realism and romanticism; and if he still hoped for a reconciliation, then at the end of our period the poetry and life of his fellow-countryman Rimbaud stood as symbols of the incompatibility of the poetic with the real.

While 'realism' is, on the whole, the appropriate formula for the prose literature of the epoch, its poetry is predominantly 'romantic'. To give any precise definition of 'realism' is difficult enough, but it seems to be of the essence of 'romanticism' that it is indefinable. It is an aroma rather than an entity; it is not in the shape of a deed but in the state of a soul vaguely reflected in action, not in the syntax and grammar of an utterance but in its intonation and cadence. Romantic practice throughout Europe has certainly not been entirely faithful to the programme of the German legislators of the movement. For this programme embraced, in its vast intellectual ambition, every conceivable contradiction of the human mind; and yet historically Friedrich Schlegel was not so wrong in proclaiming that thenceforward all poetry was to be romantic poetry.[2] This has proved true in so far as almost all poetry since has been in 'romantic' opposition to the prosaic ways of the world—an opposition expressed not through a system of opinions but through a mode of imaginative responses. Thus the main source and theme of romanticism can better be stated negatively: it is the estrangement of the imagination and of the nobler passions of the mind, indeed, of mind itself, from 'reality'. This is also one of the great themes of the philosophy of the romantic period from Fichte to Marx. Hegel already wrote of 'mind mourning over the loss of its world', then 'rising above it' and finally 'creating, out of its own pure self, its true nature'. 'In such an epoch', Hegel added, 'absolute art emerges.'[3] In saying this, he prophesied that 'absolute poetry' which is the climax of

[1] *Cinq-mars* (ed. M. Revon, Paris, n.d.), p. xxx.
[2] Cf. Jakob Minor, *op. cit.* vol. II, pp. 220–1.   [3] *Werke*, vol. II (Berlin, 1832), p. 529.

the story of romanticism. Rimbaud was to lament its tragic failure in *Une Saison en enfer* (1873): 'I have created all feasts, all dramas. I have tried to invent new flowers, new stars, new flesh, new languages. I believed I had acquired supernatural powers. Well, I must bury my imagination and my memories!...I who called myself seer and angel, exempt from all morality, I am brought back to earth, with a duty to pursue, and rugged reality to embrace!'[1] It was a near-contemporary of Hegel, the German romantic poet Clemens Brentano, who, some thirty years before Rimbaud, anticipated this particular outcome of the romantic cult of the creative imagination. 'We have nourished nothing but the imagination', he said, 'and this, in its turn, has all but devoured us.'[2]

A brief survey of the poetry written between, roughly, 1830 and 1870 is bound to confine itself, with one or two exceptions, to France, England and Germany. The classical poet of Russia, Pushkin, and the Italian Leopardi belong, with their main poetic work, to the preceding period. And of the three countries mentioned, it is France which contributes to the history of romantic poetry its most concentrated chapter. In Germany and England the 'classics' of romanticism had had their day. Goethe—whose poetry, despite his hostility to the romantic ideologues, partakes of the essence of romanticism—died in 1832. Novalis's short life had ended in 1801, and *Des Knaben Wunderhorn* of Arnim and Brentano, which, with its devotion to the lyrical spontaneity of the folk-song, is the most characteristically German of romantic enterprises, was published in 1805–8. In England, Coleridge and Wordsworth had practically ceased to write poetry; Keats, Shelley and Byron were dead. In France, however, where the classical model of literature had established itself with a persuasiveness and exclusiveness which it lacked in the rest of Europe, romanticism arrived with some delay, assisted partly by the fascination the German romantic theorist August Wilhelm Schlegel had for Madame de Staël. It was her *De l'Allemagne* (1810) which spread the new literary gospel of Germany among the French intelligentsia. Once accepted, romanticism enjoyed a more radically consistent career in France than anywhere else. Perhaps it was the logicality of the French mind—the very heritage of classicism—which allowed the romantic passion of poetry to play itself out so unrestrainedly that ultimately it could set up its reign of poetic terror over such men as Baudelaire, Rimbaud and Mallarmé.

If the early German romantics created the idea of romanticism and furnished it with all the profundities and paraphernalia of philosophical speculation, it was the French romantic poets who, more than any others, provided the popular imagination with the rich, if vague, picture of romantic practice. The literary history of France during our period reads like

[1] *Œuvres* (Paris, 1950), p. 198.
[2] C. Brentano, *Gesammelte Schriften* (Frankfurt a. M., 1855), vol. IX, p. 423 (written in April 1842, a few months before his death).

a complete inventory of romantic equipment. In Alphonse de Lamartine's *Méditations poétiques* (1820) and *Nouvelles Méditations* (1823) a young man wanders through woods and mountains listening to the song of birds and the promptings of his lonely heart. In his *Les Harmonies poétiques et religieuses* (1830) God and Nature are one. Passions of angels and men, divine and human love meet in *La Chute d'un ange* (1838) and *Jocelyn* (1836). The tragic loneliness of the great, be they prophets of God or poets among men, is the pessimistically recurring theme of Alfred de Vigny: Moses (in *Poèmes antiques et modernes*, 1836), Christ (in *Les Destinées*, 1864), and the Poet (in the play *Chatterton*, 1835, and in *Journal d'un poète*, 1867) share a common agony, the agony of the spirit deserted and victimised by God and the world. In Alfred de Musset's life (1810–57) and writing the turbulent affairs of love and spirit are arranged against a background of exotic and ominous beauty, dandyism mingles with despair, Byronic irony with melancholy, delicate health is raised by spiritual yearning to the *mal du siècle*, and night is the time for poetry: *Les Nuits* (1840) is Musset's most celebrated cycle of poems. With Gérard de Nerval (1808–55) poetry enters into the romantic alliance with madness, the subconscious mind bursts the boundaries of the dream and invades with its emblems of enigmatic beauty the daylight of verse; some of Nerval's poems point backward to Coleridge and forward to the symbolists.

Théophile Gautier (1811–72) marks an important point in the history of romantic poetry: the point where the poetic self, after all the excesses of private and subjective outpourings, avenges itself upon a hostile world by setting up an autonomous world of poetry. In the preface to his novel *Mademoiselle de Maupin* (1835), Gautier pronounces the dogma of Art for Art's sake. In calling for absolute obedience to the laws of this independent sphere, Gautier adds the classical virtue of form to the romantic code, and Greek and Roman antiquity to the romantic explorations of the Old Testament and the Middle Ages. With the establishment of a poetic world in its own right, a new objectivity becomes possible and necessary. The poet need no longer devote himself, in a poetically sterile world, to the poetic affections of his own soul and heart; a new world, poetical throughout, offers itself to his contemplative gaze. Gautier's doctrine, exemplified in his volume of poems *Émaux et camées* (1852), became the inspiration of the Parnassian movement which had its centre in *Le Parnasse contemporain*, a journal of contemporary poetry which appeared between 1866 and 1876. Although several poets, among them Leconte de Lisle and José-Maria de Hérédia, gave distinction to the Parnassus, the name of Gautier may rely for survival on his own considerable poetic achievement and, perhaps still more safely, on Baudelaire's dedicating to him *Les Fleurs du mal*. For Baudelaire was the most important lyrical poet of the period under review.

In the middle of the century, however, the question who were the greatest poets, would have been answered without much hesitation: Victor Hugo in France, Heinrich Heine in Germany, Alfred Tennyson in England. What we have said about Hugo the novelist could be repeated of Hugo the poet: he is both exceptional and typical. Moreover, no other poet can teach us better the degree of caution required in handling the almost useless yet indispensable concept 'romanticism'. For it could be said that his is both the most and the least romantic among the great romantic reputations. Not for Victor Hugo the blue flowers of insatiable yearning, the spiritual seclusion of inwardness and tuberculosis, the mingled contempt and timidity in the face of the world. Small wonder that Alfred de Musset denied him altogether the title of poet! What could be less romantic than his seemingly boundless vitality, his greatly satisfied appetite for 'life', his regarding the unutterable and ineffable as mere tributaries to swell the mighty river of his eloquence? On the other hand, is there anything more romantic than his desire to enlarge the domain of poetry by conquering for it ever new and ever more foreign land, as in his early *Odes et ballades* and in *Les Orientales* (1829); or the intense exploration of his own feelings, passions and beliefs in volumes such as *Les Feuilles d'automne*, *Les Chants du crépuscule*, *Les Voix intérieures*, *Les Rayons et les ombres* (1831–40), or his highly subjective reaching-out for ultimate mysteries in his *Les Contemplations* (1865), or his aspiration to render in a vast epic the whole history of the spirit of man: *La Légende des siècles* (1859–83)? Also, he was the most broadly comprehensible and therefore the most effective anti-classical innovator, experimenting with new images, new metres and new rhythms, and the most romantic of romantics in crediting poetry with prophetic powers, indeed in believing that the voice of the poet was so similar to the voice of God that the one might easily be taken for the other.

In his amazing versatility and eloquence, his power to blur the distinction between pose and sincerity, his political excitability, his talent to irritate and to divide literary judgment, Victor Hugo has his equal in Heinrich Heine (1797–1856), the *enfant terrible* of German romanticism, with whom he also shares the experience of exile: as Victor Hugo writes *Les Châtiments* (1853), his satires against Louis Napoleon, in Guernsey, so Heine satirises from Paris the political conditions of Germany in his *Deutschland—ein Wintermärchen* (1844). Already his first collection of poems, *Das Buch der Lieder* (1827), had established Heine's fame, which spread with the ease and smoothness of his verse and the infectious suggestiveness of his rhythms. No doubt Heine has a claim to greatness; it can be safely based on the immensity of his talent. It would be less safe to base it on his genius; if he has it, then his is the bewildering case of talent getting in the way of genius. He brilliantly succeeds in creating the impression of superficiality and irresponsibility, but he does not always silence the suspicion that he may in fact be superficial and irresponsible.

Nevertheless, the suspicion would be unjust. Heine deeply feels the conflict of the romantic sensibility: the intelligence refusing to co-operate with the emotions. But with Heine, poetry is not, as with the true romantics, the means of appeasing the conflict. On the contrary: he makes the lack of co-operation between the two faculties the very method of his poetry. Emotion and intelligence are kept apart and then suddenly brought face to face in a devastatingly ironical *dénouement*. Hence Heine, like hardly another poet of his time, can render to perfection the emotional simplicity of folk-song and folk-ballad in a kind of pastiche which is so brilliantly executed that it transcends itself and occasionally even its model. At times he sustains the tone of naïveté without the slightest ironical interference, although more often he uses his gift for superior mockery, not in order to discredit the sentimental, but, in a cunning manœuvre of face-saving, in order to retain for it a measure of poetic respectability. Whatever are the merits of this technique, it has certainly endeared Heine to a large reading public whom he wittily allows to enjoy lyrical banalities with a clear intellectual conscience.

Heine develops his method to still higher degrees of virtuosity in such volumes as *Atta Troll* (1847) and *Romanzero* (1851), in which his irony becomes ever more aggressive, his rhyming ever more self-consciously outrageous, and the quality of his poetry ever more intriguing. 'And what person of any importance is not something of a charlatan?' he once asked,[1] and the question reveals his scandalous honesty as well as reflects upon the character of his age. Heine's 'charlatanry', however, acquires the attributes of a force of nature in the poems he wrote in his last years, between 1853 and 1856, when, lying in his 'mattress-grave' in Paris, tortured by pain, and every day expecting to die, he contemplates life, agony and death still in the same poetic vein, angry, playful and mocking, like foam at the foot of a cliff.

It is by no means an accident that of all the German poets of this period only Heine has gained a secure place in the literary consciousness of the world. He represents the cosmopolitan extreme of the peculiar romantic tension between the demands of the great world and the concerns of individual souls or small communities, a tension which, at its other pole, brought about a revival of forgotten national literatures, such as Provençal in whose resurrection the poet Frédéric Mistral played an outstanding part. Heine, in his turn, certainly adjusted the folk-song idiom of the late German romantics, their village moons and forest whispers and river gurgles, to metropolitan tastes, just as he europeanised German prose. Compared to him, even such exquisite poets as Eichendorff, Mörike and Annette von Droste-Hülshoff are provincial. Yet this need not necessarily speak for the world or against the province. The best romantic poetry is, by virtue of its linguistic intimacy, untranslatable, and the biggest noises

[1] *Werke in einem Band* (Salzburg, 1954), p. 40.

are certainly not the purest poetic sounds. World-wide reputations in lyrical poetry are usually world-wide misunderstandings based on hearsay.

In a strictly poetic sense Mörike, for instance, may be one of the finest poets of the period if we believe that poetry may reveal a possible perfect congruity between the natures of a thing, a feeling, a thought, and a word. It is this which, again and again, strikes the reader of Mörike's *Gedichte* (1838), many of which maintain, without aping it, the spirit of Goethe's lyrical genius. And some of Eichendorff's *Gedichte* (1837) are not less successful in their unassuming declaration of the romantic love for moon, mountains, woods and meadows. More obviously complex than Mörike (and he is fundamentally by no means simple) is the poetry of Annette von Droste-Hülshoff, whose earlier poems were published between 1837 and 1844. Her myopic pictures of the details of nature are vibrant with the anxiety of a soul fearing the loss of its world, and the simultaneous presence of religious strength, morbidity and exquisiteness of language in *Das geistliche Jahr* (1851) almost suggests the world of Baudelaire. Very different is Nikolaus Lenau, yet another embodiment of the romantic idea of the unhappy poet, sublimely agonised and ending in madness. His poetic-dramatic or semi-epic heroes are, characteristically, *Faust* (1836), *Savonarola* (1837) and *Don Juan* (1844), but his real talent is lyrical, and some of his nature-poems are, by virtue of their intensity and poignancy, considerable achievements in the genre. He is enchanted with the gentle dying away of all things—'Ich liebe dieses milde Sterben'; and much of German poetry during this period is under the same melancholy spell. It is the poetry of poets who know that they can neither rival their master, Goethe, nor escape the power of his vision and idiom.

England's poetry at this time is certainly wider in power and scope, though not necessarily greater. Its centre is comfortably occupied by Tennyson, the Victorian Poet Laureate, a truly representative writer, above all in the sense of having supplied a wide public, whose standard of poetic profundity and subtlety were not over-exacting, with a highly respectable and aesthetically convenient idea of 'the poet'. While the poets of France intensively searched for the meaning poetry could have in an unpoetical age and, pelican-like, tore out their hearts in order to feed the starving spirit of the race, Tennyson is content to give poetic decorum to an undecorous world. His fire is not of the volcano; it is of the fireplace, and gently warms the surface of the soul. Yet if there is not much he has to say, he says it with a very fine sense of language and lyrical precision. As with so many other poets of the period, his strength lies in the brief and exact lyrical utterance, in 'the short swallow flights of song', instanced by his *Poems* of 1842. Again like many other poets, he is less fortunate where he is lured into competition with the 'epic spirit' which had been so successfully appropriated by the contemporary novel. Thus he largely fails in the attempt, renewed throughout his career, to render in *Idylls* the legendary and heroic world of King Arthur, unable as he is fully to integrate his lyricisms into the narrative, and his allegorical moralising into the body of poetry. *The Princess* (1847) and *Enoch Arden* (1864) are, despite their formal and decorative merits, likely to remain Victorian curiosities, brave defeats of the Muse in taking the spirit of poetry on long journeys, despite its preference for living in the brief moment of lyrical exaltation. However, in his intensely personal and confessional poem *In Memoriam* (1850), written on the death of a friend, he rises to the standard of poetic seriousness set by the preceding epoch.

Second to Tennyson, but not quite so secure in the esteem of the Victorians, is Robert Browning, the romantic hero of Wimpole Street. Thence he abducted, and took as his wife, Elizabeth Barrett, whom he (and not only he) judged to be a great poetess. Indeed, her *Sonnets from the Portuguese* (1850), more so than *Aurora Leigh* (1856), show genuine if delicate poetic gifts, marred only by that preciousness and extravagance with which the age punished so many of its minor poets for their self-conscious deviations from sober living. Robert Browning himself became a controversial figure; understandably in so far as he was either a defective genius or a bad poet of great ingenuity. Though lacking the poetical courtesy of Tennyson, he was capable of writing swiftly-moving lyrics; but he seldom aimed at the melodious smoothness which was accepted as natural to poetry. His rhythms and rhymes are often harsh, crude and unobliging, and he dares to have ideas and provoke thought. Yet he never quite succeeds in quelling uneasiness: is the inner purpose firm enough to justify the unorthodox display? Is the thought profound enough to reward the effort of thinking? His chosen form was the unactable lyrical drama or the 'dramatic monologue'. It is a form best suited to his literary temperament in which egocentricity is coupled with the desire for objective comprehensiveness. Examples of this genre are *Paracelsus* (1835), *Pippa Passes* (1841), and the three volumes of *Dramatic Lyrics* (1842), *Men and Women* (1855) and *Dramatis Personae* (1864), in which many a figure from the Bible and the Italian Renaissance springs into a somewhat over-produced and over-managed existence. His longest and most sustained attempt to bestow poetic life upon his philosophy is *The Ring and the Book* (1868-9), at the centre of which is the problem of evil. In so far as evil remains 'a problem', and a problem which vastly exceeds the philosophical melodrama it engenders, this work is Browning's most original and distinguished failure.

The most romantic contribution to English poetry in this period—romantic in the exotic choice of a Persian model, and not less in the manner of its adaptation—is Edward Fitzgerald's *The Rubaiyat of Omar Khayyám* (1859). Fitzgerald might have remained unknown, had he not been discovered by the literary and artistic circle around D. G. Rossetti, whose theories go beyond the Parnassian 'Art for Art's sake', heading, as they do, for 'Life for Art's Sake'. Art is the vehicle of Truth, and therefore has to shun the aesthetic over-refinements of virtuosity. In poetry as well as painting Rossetti aimed at that bold simplicity which he found in Italian painting before Raphael, an ideal of which, as a poet, he hardly reached more than the colourful haze of its enveloping atmosphere. One of his followers was William Morris, a man of many artistic trades, whose poetry, medievalising in its subject-matter (*The Defence of Guinevere*, 1858) or Chaucerian in its technique (*The Earthly Paradise*, 1868–70), practically came to an end in his later life when he devoted himself to the task of social reform, the urgency of which had been impressed upon him by Ruskin. Coventry Patmore, also connected with the group and best known through his verse-novel *The Angel in the House* (1854–6), went in a very different direction: towards an ever-firmer attachment to the Roman Catholic Church; and as his spirituality deepened, he became, as for instance in *The Unknown Eros*, a remarkable, and remarkably independent, poet.

To complete this sketch of English poetry, we may set against the largely academic virtues of Matthew Arnold, whose critical insight was more acute than his poetic genius, the highly unacademic and unvirtuous verse of Algernon Charles Swinburne, whose first (and best) poetry appeared at the close of our period: *Atalanta in Calydon* (1865) and *Poems and Ballads* (1866). He has remained a controversial poet although the controversy is no longer concerned with the shock he administered to those of his contemporaries who identified poetry with the niceties of a domesticated fancy. Swinburne outraged them with the blatant eroticism of his themes and the pagan sensuality of his rhythms. He did not recollect emotions in tranquillity but appeared to assemble words for a debauch. The outrage, of course, has become irrelevant; since Swinburne's day poetic taste has not only grown accustomed to his themes, but almost lost interest in themes altogether. Poems are not made of ideas, said Mallarmé, they are made of words. This is a critical sentiment which has come to dominate the appreciation of poetry; and because Swinburne seems to dwell 'exclusively and consistently among words', as T. S. Eliot said,[1] he meets with a less condescending interest now than most other Victorian poets. Yet Mallarmé's dictum must not be taken too literally; however boisterous and intense a poet's verbal expressiveness, ultimately the substance expressed will matter more. In weight of substance Swinburne hardly stands comparison with Baudelaire, whom he acknowledged as a master, and by whose poetry, more than by life itself, he appears to have been initiated into the depths of sensual excess.

Baudelaire's *Les Fleurs du mal* (1857) are nourished by the purest and truest substances of the romantic soil. Here the opposition of spirit and reality, of word and flesh, of 'idéal' and 'spleen', is maintained so radically that the tension becomes unbearable, resolving itself in language

---

[1] *Selected Essays* (London, 1932), p. 327.

which comprehends and assimilates both the sublimity and the degradation, the beatitude and the anger. The formal perfection and superb workmanship seem to bear out the fruitfulness of the dogma of 'Art for Art's sake'—of the poet who cares only for the excellence of his craft; yet the poems prove that this ideal can only be realised if the poet cares in fact for much more than his art. And Baudelaire is concerned with good and evil, seemingly sacrificing good in a single-minded pursuit of evil. But *Les Fleurs du Mal* would not be the great poetry it is if it did not announce through its very beauty the one hope of salvation surreptitiously upheld by a soul which fears that it is damned. It is as if God were to be persuaded, by the poetic saintliness of the celebrant, divinely to pervert the course of the satanic celebration. This rare combination of aesthetic exquisiteness and spiritual intensity has made Baudelaire the classical poet of modern poetry. It was he who first took the squalor and dialect of city life into a poetic sphere as radiant and lucid as that of Racine, and he who first endowed the boredom of metropolitan dissipation with true, if negative, spiritual significance.

The American poet and writer Edgar Allan Poe might well have remained a peripheral figure, had he not been transfigured by Baudelaire (who translated his *Tales of Mystery and Imagination*) into the patron-saint of modern French poetry. It was Poe's insistence upon the need for brevity—a 'long poem' seemed to him a contradiction in terms—as well as upon the banishment of all non-poetic matter, didactic or instructive, which endeared him to Baudelaire and many French poets after Baudelaire. While Poe enjoyed only a moderate reputation among his literary fellow-countrymen—Emerson called him 'jingle-man'[1] and Lowell 'three-fifths genius and two-fifths sheer fudge'[2]—he was hailed by the French as the quintessentially 'pure poet'. 'There are some facts in the physical world which have a really wonderful analogy with others in the world of thought',[3] Poe wrote, and it was observations of this kind which confirmed Baudelaire's belief, inspired originally by E. T. A. Hoffmann, in a universe held together by a mysterious system of communications, *correspondances*, so that colours, for instance, were intimately related to tastes, sounds to aromas, and images to states of the soul. Life was 'a forest of symbols', with their branches touching one another and setting off a whispered chorus of intimations. Thus Poe had a share in Baudelaire's great gift to poetry: to have bestowed upon metaphors and poetic symbols a new sense of immediacy and associative power, and added to poetic language the dimension which was to be so keenly explored and exploited by the symbolist movement and such poets as Verlaine, Rimbaud and Mallarmé.

---

[1] William Dean Howells, recounting a conversation with Emerson, in *Literary Friends and Acquaintances* (New York, 1901), p. 63.
[2] J. R. Lowell, *A Fable for Critics* (Boston, 1848), p. 78.
[3] *The Works of Edgar Allan Poe* (Edinburgh, 1875), vol. III, p. 354.

In the history of poetry Baudelaire marks the crossroads at which romanticism, in its distrust of reality, chooses the road which leads to the absolute denial of the 'real'. At the close of our period Baudelaire's *correspondances*, which still point towards a mystical unity of everything that is, can be freely manipulated by the poet because the imagination is no longer limited by any significant and independent reality. If there is to be any significant world, it has not only to be re-experienced and re-named; it has to be re-created in totality. Rimbaud, whose prose-poems, *Les Illuminations* (written in or before 1873) owe something of their poetic technique to Baudelaire's *Les Petits Poèmes en prose*, already believed that the poet had to become a *voyant*, a seer; but he meant much more than the word usually implies. In order to 'see', the poet had systematically to derange his senses which, in their ordered state, can convey to him nothing but a senseless world. Soon words themselves threatened to become too 'real' to be of any poetic use: poetry (Mallarmé's, for instance) was to approach the point where words would have to be replaced by immaculate and esoteric hieroglyphs, akin to music and uncontaminated by 'real' meanings. This is the romantic journey's end, anticipated, as we have seen, even by the despairing realist Flaubert.

Only two major poets of the period travel in a different direction and at great distance from the main stream of romanticism: the Russian Nekrasov and the American Walt Whitman. Both are the 'true democrats' among an aesthetic aristocracy, and were therefore accused of being 'non-poetical'. Turgenev said of Nekrasov that 'poetry never so much as spent a night in his verse',[1] and Emerson of Whitman: 'I expect him to make the songs of the nation but he seems contented to make the inventories.'[2] 'Romantic' is Nekrasov's love of folk-song, but with him it is not, as it is with the Germans, the song of a dreamily nostalgic people; it is more like the popular ballads of the street-singers: brutal, melodramatic and outrageous. *The Thief* (1846), *The Pedlars* (1861) and *Frost the Red-Nosed* (1863)—the very titles announce a kind of poetry very different from *Des Knaben Wunderhorn*. His longest work, a satire in the folk-song manner, which he wrote in the 1870's, is called *Who is Happy in Russia?*, while 'Everybody should be happy in America' might serve as an alternative title for Walt Whitman's *Leaves of Grass* (1855). And Whitman's poetic ideal: 'the dialect of common sense', is certainly shared by Nekrasov. Sympathy is the main inspiration of both the Russian and the American, the difference being that Nekrasov's is sympathy with a suffering people, and Whitman's with the anticipated joy of a nation setting up its community of freedom. *Leaves of Grass* was written at about the same time as *Les Fleurs du mal*—reason enough for caution in general-

---

[1] Cit. D. S. Mirsky, *A History of Russian Literature* (London, 1949), p. 228.
[2] John Burroughs in his journal of December 1871, cit. Edmund Wilson, *The Shock of Recognition* (2nd edn, London, 1956), p. 277.

ising about literary periods, and for wonder at the vast distance which separates the houses of poetry. Nevertheless, Whitman's boisterous, vital, lyrical oratory, dedicated to the soul of the people, is, in the century's literary history, a lonely voice amidst multitudes of romantic loneliness.

Solitude was the predominant condition of literature even in its reception. More and more the 'reading public' consisted of individuals engaged in the lonely pursuit of printed words. Not even so small a group as the family circle, which listened to the reading aloud of the novels of Scott or Jane Austen or Dickens, could possibly keep up with the writers' increasing complexities and intimacies. When people assembled to enjoy the finer pleasures of art, it was music which drew them together. The literary word had become too finely spun to exert a collective spell. 'Le théâtre c'est un terrain banal', André Gide once said.[1] He was not only summing up the nineteenth-century situation in which theatrical robustness seemed no longer compatible with depth, but also hinting at a prerequisite of great drama: that the author should be united with his audience in a profound yet broadly comprehensible (and, therefore, in a sense, 'banal') common interest. For only then is his audience an audience, and not a number of individuals more suitably approached in their privacy. More than any other literary medium the drama needs for its health a common readiness to believe in the immediate significance of the strong and simple deeds and passions. And precisely this was lacking in our period, as is shown both by the novel, with its increasing analytical probing, and by poetry, with its ever more determined withdrawal from life. No representative stage could be built in the vacuum which was left between the extremes of realistic psychology and romantic inwardness. England, it has been said, had no dramas because it had hardly any buildings in which to perform them. It may equally be correct to say that it had no theatres because it had no dramas. Even where there was no scarcity of theatres as, for instance, in France, dramatic writing, though undoubtedly more plentiful, fell far below the level of excellence reached by the novel and by poetry. Scribe, with hundreds of well-contrived plays to his credit, as well as Augier and Dumas *fils*, moralising with theatrical skill on the contrasts and entanglements between the humble front-parlours and the ostentatious drawing-rooms of society, have hardly any literary existence left once the names of Stendhal and Baudelaire are mentioned. Even the apparently invincible Victor Hugo, after having romantically succeeded with his Spanish cloaks and daggers in *Hernani* and *Ruy Blas*, was eventually driven off the stage when his *Les Burgraves* collapsed as noisily in 1843 as *Hernani* had triumphed in 1830. Only Musset's experiments with the form of drama (and he

---

[1] In a conversation quoted by Walter Benjamin in *Schriften* (Frankfurt a. M., 1955), vol. II, p. 299.

intended them to be read rather than acted) achieve the distinction of his poetry: the hardly actable play *Lorenzaccio* (1834), whose hero romantically pursues self-realisation and 'identical being' by becoming an assassin, and the short comedies and 'proverbs', sophisticated in their sentimentality, extravagant in their playfulness, and romantic in their pensive humour.

Again, the Russian contribution comes from writers who need not rely for their reputation on the theatre, although Gogol's *Revizor* (*The Government Inspector*, 1836) was one of his great achievements in social satire, one which, like his *Dead Souls*, by far transcends the usually narrow artistic limits of the genre. And Turgenev's comedies (*A Month in the Country*, 1850, and *The Provincial Lady*, 1851) are, with their psychological niceties and their device to introduce 'atmosphere' as one of the main *dramatis personae*, akin to the dramatic essays of Musset and anticipate the trappings (if not more) of the genius of Chekhov. The Russian drama just before and just after our period too is represented by non-dramatists—Pushkin and the later Tolstoy—while during the period itself it is Ostrovsky who, by virtue of his Scribe-like fertility and dramatic resourcefulness, dominates the Petersburg stage with his un-Scribe-like realism poetically redeemed only in his *Thunderstorm* (1860).

Weightier than either the French or the Russian (not to mention the negligible English) contribution is the German and Austrian drama. It has in Grillparzer and Hebbel dramatic poets of high purpose, rare single-mindedness and great artistic integrity. In Grillparzer's uneven and almost pathologically pessimistic genius the 'classical' impulses of Goethe's and Schiller's epoch mingle with the theatrical fancy and sentimentality of the 'baroque' tradition of Vienna. And from the Habsburgs' Austria it is not far to Spain: Lope de Vega and Calderon are almost as close to Grillparzer's mind as Goethe and Schiller. Although Grillparzer is too pessimistic to write great tragedy, too sentimental to write great comedy, and too introspective to write great drama, his work is nevertheless pervaded by the sense and taste of dramatic greatness. Only with his last plays does he belong to our period, and he fell silent when his comedy *Weh' dem, der lügt* (1838) failed to please the public. After his death in 1872 three plays were found in his drawers, among them *Ein Bruderzwist im Hause Habsburg*, his most successful bid, by virtue of the character of Rudolf II, for the highest honours of drama.

Grillparzer said of himself that his true roots were in the 'ghost-and-fairy-land of the Leopoldstadt Theatre',[1] the home of the Vienna 'Volksstück', the popular comedy interspersed with music and song. And it was in the Leopoldstadt, that provincial enclave in the middle of the Habsburg metropolis, that the theatre then lived its most spontaneous life, uninhibited by dramatic theories and high literary ambitions. No one had ever

---

[1] *Beiträge zur Selbstbiographie* (1846) in *Sämtliche Werke* (Stuttgart, 1887), vol. xv, p. 200.

worried there about Diderot or Lessing. 'Time you did something for posterity' said a friend once to Johann Nestroy, the most prolific supplier of the Leopoldstadt stage, a truly profound wit and man of those letters that are awkwardly written in the heart of a people. 'For posterity?', Nestroy replied, 'what has posterity done for me?'[1] But in writing, producing and acting for his own day his satirical, exuberant, fantastic comedies, full of those traps of language in which the pompous illusions of life are caught and of which only true characters can wriggle themselves free, he has, together with his older contemporary Ferdinand Raimund, given Vienna a kind of domestic Elizabethan stage, and himself survived with a vigour denied to many a serious dramatist of his time.

For instance, to Friedrich Hebbel, whose *Judith* (1840) Nestroy parodied and whose dramatic work, despite its seriousness and literary importance, may fall victim to that unkind process of time which, regardless of other merits, relentlessly punishes any discrepancies in art between substance and intention. Hebbel attempted the impossible: he undertook not only to write great poetic drama but also, by intense philosophical digging, to unearth once more the foundation on which alone, in his opinion, great poetic drama could be erected: a comprehensive mythology or systematic metaphysical interpretation of life and the world. His diaries, prefaces and essays in dramatic theory—often fascinating—bear testimony to his intellectual passion. 'Art is the realisation of philosophy',[2] he said, and the philosophy which his dramas are meant to realise is an uneasy compound of Schopenhauer's metaphysical pessimism and Hegel's eschatological historicism (although a witness to the reality of the *Zeitgeist*, he may have arrived at these ideas without any substantial help from the philosophers themselves). Individual existence is itself tragic, for it is, for Hebbel as for Schopenhauer, the result of a necessary but ultimately self-defeating emancipation from the wholeness of life. Thus his theory of tragic guilt is a secular variant of the doctrine of the Fall: to be is to be guilty. Therefore some of Hebbel's heroes and heroines are doomed not because of a tragic flaw in their character, or an involvement in active guilt, but simply because of the most original of sins: the sin of being. Hebbel presents this sin dramatically by endowing his creatures with an excessive quality of being: the heroine of *Agnes Bernauer* (1855) is innocent but surpassingly beautiful, Siegfried in *Die Nibelungen* (1862) is good but surpassingly strong—excesses which render the tragic outcome inevitable. Yet their doom must have a dramatic meaning—

---

[1] An anecdote about Nestroy, based verbatim on the saying of one of his characters in *Der Schützling* (*The Protégé*), act I, scene 2: 'Was hat denn die Nachwelt für mich getan? Nichts! Gut, das nämliche tu ich für sie!' ('What has posterity done for me? Nothing! Well then, I shall do the same for it!') Johann Nestroy, *Sämtliche Werke* (Vienna, 1926), vol. VII, p. 116.

[2] Preface (1844) to *Maria Magdalena* (*Werke*, ed. Th. Poppe, vol. VIII, Berlin, n.d., p. 75).

and at this point Hegel's historical optimism takes over from Schopenhauer's pessimism: the undoing of the hero is meaningful because it is a sacrifice on the altar of historical necessity, change and progress: Siegfried's death ushers in a higher state of peace and good-will among men, Agnes Bernauer's horrible end gives rise to a firmer rule of law and order in the state, the murderous love-and-hate struggle between *Herodes und Mariamne* (1850) opens the dialectical gate for the entrance of Christianity into a pagan world.

Hebbel complicates still further his metaphysical structure of historically hopeful gloom by insisting upon yet another element, reminiscent more of Kant than of Hegel or Schopenhauer: the tragic consequences which follow upon the violation of the individual's sacred autonomy: the Nibelung cataclysm comes about through the deceitful disregard of Brünhilde's individuality, Herodes's love for Mariamne spells disaster because it is blind to the autonomous right of her person—a theme which dominates with still greater force the drama of *Gyges und sein Ring* (1854).

With the burden of such philosophical thought upon his plays, Hebbel's shortcomings are less surprising than the considerable measure of his success. Like his contemporary Richard Wagner (both were born in 1813), he was obsessed with 'the problem of the drama' in an age which lacked any spontaneous sense of the dramatic significance of life. Yet by following the heroic-poetic manner, evolved by poets who knew little of Hebbel's central concern, he was bound to assert his intention against the natural pull of the medium, without ever quite resolving his problem in a truly appropriate form. For under the pressure of this problem, genuine enough in itself, the chosen form deteriorated into a convention which not even the heat of his mind could quicken into convincing life. Incomparably more legitimate and ultimately more poetic is the 'unpoetic' work of Georg Büchner who produced his two despairingly nihilistic dramas as early as 1835 and, probably, 1836: *Dantons Tod* and *Woyzeck*.

It was left to the Norwegian writer Ibsen to give to the epoch's problems, so 'undramatic' in terms of the inherited conventions of great drama, their authentic dramatic form. Some of Hebbel's themes pointed already in the direction of Ibsen's later plays while, with some historical logic, the great 'naturalist' wrote his two best-known poetic dramas: *Brand* (1866) and *Peer Gynt* (1867), at the close of our period. Soon afterwards, however, he was to conquer, with dramatic masterpieces of poetic realism, a theatre which for so long had known hardly anything but the feeble survivals of the '*drame bourgeois*' and the rear-guard of the poetic-heroic drama in retreat. As far as the period itself is concerned, it is the measure of its failure dramatically to *speak* its uneasy mind that its greatest theatrical achievements lie outside the province of literary history: in the operas of Verdi and Richard Wagner.

CHAPTER VIII

LIBERALISM AND CONSTITUTIONAL DEVELOPMENTS

EIGHTEEN-THIRTY, the 'revolution stopped half-way', and eighteen-forty-eight, the 'turning point at which modern history failed to turn', are the principal landmarks of this period during which the forms of government of states changed perhaps more sharply and in more interesting and varied ways than at any other time between the revolutionary decade of the 1790's and the ten years that shook the world between 1910 and 1920.

In a brief period of some forty years between 1830 and 1871 France experimented with a semi-liberal 'bourgeois monarchy', a radical Second Republic, a semi-authoritarian prince-presidency, an authoritarian Second Empire (see ch. XVII), a so-called 'liberal empire', an ultra-radical Paris Commune and an (at first) ill-defined Third Republic. Great Britain passed two parliamentary reform acts (cf. ch. XIII, pp. 335 and 336), abandoning the 400-year-old forty-shilling franchise in the counties and sweeping away the rotten and pocket boroughs, and in 1870 was on the eve of adopting that secret ballot which the dreaded Chartists had demanded as one of their 'Six Points' in 1839. Prussia, after a false dawn of liberalism when Frederick William IV became king in 1840 (like that in Italy when Pius IX was elected pope in 1846), saw a united Diet called for the first time in 1847, initiated a constitutional regime in 1848 and, after briefly adopting universal manhood suffrage, settled down at last as a mildly limited monarchy (though with a distinctly undemocratic class franchise) under the constitution of 1850—which was to last until the year 1918 (see ch. XIX *passim*). Austria, on the other hand, recoiled in 1851 from her first experience as a constitutional state (Hungary's 1848 constitution had been eradicated even earlier), and, after the experiments of the *Diploma* of 1860 and the *Patent* of 1861 had failed, achieved compromise if not stability in the *Ausgleich* of 1867 (see ch. XX). The rest of Germany, under the leadership of a more forward-looking Prussia, was unified as a quasi-federation of states, several of which had reserved to them powers enjoyed by no state of the American Union, while Prussia herself managed to retain a dominating position in the German Second Reich such as neither Virginia nor Massachusetts had carved out, despite the part these states had played in the struggle for independence. Italy, too, was unified, and, in becoming so, rejected federalism in favour of the general adoption of the unitary and (for its day) liberal Piedmontese *Statuto* of 1848 (see ch. XXI). Switzerland in 1848 (as later in 1874) refashioned her form of government in the direction of a truer federalism and a real democracy, and became (like the United States once again after 1865 and Great Britain, too, after 1867 and 1872) an inspiration to other countries and peoples seeking to marry effective government to free institutions.

On the other side of the account Spain suffered from continuous disorders, and neither her authoritarian nor her liberal forces could bring to her the blessings of stable or wise government. Mexico, equally troubled, abandoned the unitarism of Santa Anna for the federalism of Juarez in 1856, but her hard-won republican institutions suffered a temporary setback in the 1860's under the blows of foreign intervention, while the United States, her potential protector against European adventurers, was preoccupied with internecine warfare (see ch. xxv). The United States experienced, in this civil war of South versus North, her own greatest crisis of federalism, and the Confederate constitution of 1861 challenged for a time many of the hallowed principles of the federal constitution of 1787, until, by the defeat of the South in 1865, the Union was restored on an even stronger basis than before (see ch. xxiv). The Poles, despite two heroic rebellions against their oppressors in 1831 and in 1863 (and an abortive rising in 1846), failed to recover any part of their lost independence or liberties. Russia, unregenerate under Nicholas I (1825–55), turned at last toward tentative reforms in the 1860's (cf. ch. xiv, pp. 369–80), but did not go on to achieve a truly constitutional regime or a national legislature until the twentieth century. The decay of the Ottoman empire was as yet unchecked by even the smallest effort at reform, while China, supine under the decadent Manchu emperors, seemed fully to justify Alfred Tennyson's gibe of the year 1842: 'Better fifty years of Europe than a cycle of Cathay.'

The two decades stretching from the first British Reform Act of 1832 to the proclamation of the Second French Empire in 1852 constitute the period of most rapid advance in the direction of democracy, as defined by Tocqueville's *Democracy in America* and John Stuart Mill's *Representative Government*, of the whole nineteenth century; during the six months ending in June 1848 its progress seemed irresistible, and its complete achievement everywhere only a matter of time.

But events from the middle of 1848 onwards reversed that seemingly inevitable trend in country after country. The Chartist fiasco in April set Great Britain in the mould of 'finality' for the greater part of a generation; the bloodshed of the 'June Days' in Paris finally frightened the French middle classes out of their radicalism and threw them into the arms of a lesser Napoleon (cf. ch. xv); Custoza and Novara stopped the onward march of Charles Albert of Sardinia toward that throne of a liberal and united Italy which had so recently seemed within his grasp. In Prague,

Windischgrätz dispersed the Pan-Slav Congress and shut down the Bohemian revolution; in Frankfurt the newly assembled National Parliament was sidetracked from the pursuit of democracy to participate in a German chauvinistic 'crusade' against Denmark—which even the arch-radical Karl Marx applauded with the rest from his sniper's nest at Cologne. The picture was the same everywhere—in Vienna, in Hungary, in Croatia, in Poland—while the tide of revolution had turned back even before it had reached the boundaries of an unregenerate Russia and a moribund Spain.

The forces of revolutionary radicalism fought on sporadically through 1849—in Baden and Saxony, in Hungary and in Rome—and even in 1850 and 1851 in a few places, but Louis Napoleon's *coup d'état* of 1851 in France (which spared the universal franchise only because he and his like were no longer afraid of it as a disruptive force, and even found a use for it as an instrument of reaction) was a sign to all the world that a great liberal age was over. When he restored the French empire as Napoleon III in 1852 the door seemed doubly barred and bolted to those forces which had grown from such small beginnings in 1776 and 1789 to shock the western world on two occasions (in January 1793 and in February 1848) in a way in which it had not been shocked since the executioner had held up the severed head of Charles I of England in Whitehall on 30 January 1649.

A sincere radical who had campaigned against the *Sonderbund* in Switzerland in 1847, or subscribed to a reform banquet in Paris in 1848, or stood defiantly on the ramparts of beleaguered Rome in 1849, or chased 'butcher' Haynau through the streets of London in 1850, or cheered the exiled Kossuth in New York in 1851, might well have been in the depths of despair by 1852, for the prospects for his ideals, recently so bright, now appeared in sombre colours everywhere.

The forty years stretching from the revision of the French Constitutional Charter to the establishment of the unified German *Reich* of 1871 thus constitute an epoch in the development of constitutional forms in Europe and the world which is by no means one of continuous advance toward more liberal and more democratic institutions. It is true that in 1831 there was still no really democratic form of government existing anywhere on a nation-wide scale, whereas by 1871 there were several, while many more had democratic features and implications; nevertheless, the progress of the two preceding decades was by no means maintained during the 1850's and 1860's. Indeed, from about 1849 to about 1859 a phase of reaction set in during which a good deal of ground was lost. The advance began again in the latter year, but it was more tentative and cautious than immediately before the reaction. Their former optimism and enthusiasm had, in large measure, gone out of liberals and democrats after their chastening experiences of the 'fifties, and they now had to watch their countries receive constitutions from the hands of those whom they regarded as anything but democrats, or acquire a long-sought and much-prayed-for political unification on bases they considered unsound and illiberal. Often they swallowed their disappointment—like the Prussian liberals who gave Bismarck his bill of indemnity in 1866 (cf. ch. XIV, p. 520), and the Italian liberals who fell in with the schemes of the Machiavellian Cavour—and made the best of this rather less brave new world than that of which they had dreamed; but to many of them the process was permanently embittering.

Meanwhile new forces and new doctrines had arisen to challenge classical nineteenth-century liberalism. The utopian and other socialists had already fired some small salvoes, and it was the turn of the big guns. Co-author of *The Communist Manifesto* in 1847 and an incisive contemporary critic of the liberals of 1848, Karl Marx had mercilessly pilloried their mistakes in his newspaper at Cologne and in his articles printed by Horace Greeley in the *New York Herald*. Moreover, he had before 1870 produced the first volume of his *magnum opus*. Although *Das Kapital* was as yet little known and even less read, it presented, embedded in its pages for those who could ferret it out, a complete alternative to the philosophy of liberalism that had hitherto held the progressive field. The old struggle between autocratic princes and peoples imbued with liberal principles struggling to secure a fuller share in the government of their countries, was, in the system of Marx, replaced by the even more bitter economic struggle between the exploiting and the exploited classes of society, which would end, in his view, in the seizure of power by the latter and the creation of a truly classless and completely egalitarian community, owning the instruments of production and all the products of its toil in common. This was not the Utopia of John Stuart Mill, for all the mild socialism of his latter years!

Yet this new doctrine of the class struggle, this post-liberal dogmatism, had nowhere affected practical politics or constitution-making even by the end of these forty years. It is true that some of the men of the Paris Commune of 1871 were unconscious or semi-conscious Marxists, in that they had seen the 'June Days' of the revolution of 1848 in France as the revolt and the suppression of an urban proletariat demanding the right to work as well as simply the right to vote, and like Marx had drawn their conclusions (albeit more muddled and less systematised than his) therefrom. But the Paris Commune was at the most an ultra-radical episode on a purely local scale. It led to no nation-wide movement and created no national instrument of government. It did not even discover a new technique of revolution as the Russians were to do in their 'rehearsal' revolution of 1905 with their councils of soldiers and workers. The Commune was created and run mainly by disillusioned radicals and socialists many of whom had been forced into exile or into underground conspiracy during the Second Empire. They were, in spirit and outlook, much more akin to the Jacobins of 1793 than to the Bolshevists of 1917.

Those countries which in earlier centuries had given a lead in establishing and safeguarding the liberty of the individual in the state, began to concentrate in the nineteenth century upon giving to the individual citizen the liberty to express himself and to make his own views felt in local and central government. The sum of the individual citizens in the state, known collectively as 'the people', came to express themselves through what are known as democratic institutions only about the middle of the nineteenth century. These at first existed only in France between 1848 and 1851, under the Second Republic before the *coup d'état*, and in Prussia between 1848 and 1850. In Switzerland they have existed continuously since 1848. They were not very evident elsewhere, except in a few of the newer states of the American Union (such as Iowa and Wisconsin), until very much later.

The so-called 'legitimist' constitutions of which the French Charter of 1814 had been the prototype—for the Spanish constitution of 1812 and the Norwegian of 1814 were suspect as being revolutionary in origin and as owing too much to French constitutional experiments of the 1790's—were a step forward from unadulterated absolutism, but they were anything but liberal and were deliberately anti-democratic in intention. Nobody was satisfied with them other than the small groups of moderate conservatives who had devised them. The reactionaries (represented in France by the 'Ultras' of the White Terror) did not find them reactionary enough and the various shades of radicals thought them too reactionary. Under fire from all sides as they were, it is remarkable that they survived until the 1830's. It only needed the example of France to show the way for a whole series of states in western and central Europe to revise their legitimist constitutions in a more liberal direction, while a number of states which had not as yet been given constitutions at all now received instruments of government of a legitimist or post-legitimist type.

The forces of liberalism in Europe were heartened within the short span of three years by genuine and fundamental reforms in the governments of France (in 1830), of Belgium (in 1831) and of Great Britain (in 1832), while the lesser states of Saxony and Kurhessen (in 1831), Brunswick (in 1832) and Hanover (in 1833) in Germany were given new constitutions before Metternich, in the *Schluss-Protokolle* of 1834, put a stop through the machinery of the *Bund* to any further constitution-granting until he and his system were to disappear from the scene in 1848 (cf. ch. xv, p. 396). Several of these constitutions (like that of Saxony) were to last for nearly a century, but, by way of exception, that of Hanover (issued by King William IV in 1833), though it was a very mild piece of legitimist constitutionalism, was withdrawn after only four years by King Ernest Augustus

—the wickedest of Queen Victoria's 'wicked uncles'—on his accession in 1837. The 'constitution' he issued in 1840 was a mere affirmation and reiteration of the king's unique authority in the state and of the subordinate position of the estates, and is even more conservative than had been the French Charter of 1814, preamble and all. Ernest Augustus was able to put the clock back in Hanover in a way Charles X had failed to do in France, an index of the extent to which the liberal and democratic ideal had taken hold of France and of the small headway it had as yet made in Germany. The German states were, in fact, still a generation behind France in their constitutional evolution before 1848, which made it necessary for them to attempt to make up so much ground so rapidly during the years of revolution. In some cases (as in Prussia) they were to make very substantial progress—though by no means all of it was maintained—between 1847 and 1850, but in others (as was the case with Austria and the Habsburg realm generally) their inoculation during those years still did not successfully 'take', and a fresh start had to be made a decade later.

The revised French Charter of 1830—in which sovereignty was taken away from the monarch though not yet clearly given to the people, but in which the autocratic preamble was suppressed—was far less directly copied in other countries than had been the Charter in its original version of 1814. This was because it had in 1814 represented the limit of the concessions which a monarch of the period was prepared to make, whereas by 1830 the people in many countries were demanding a much wider actual share in government and a much more complete recognition of their importance in the state than even Louis Philippe was willing to admit them to. That is why Victor Hugo called 1830 'a revolution stopped halfway'[1] and the romantics and radicals criticised the July Monarchy no less bitterly than they had attacked the regime of the Restoration. Nowhere was the Charter of 1830 nailed to the mast as a banner of progress as had been the Spanish constitution of 1812. Other countries and peoples which copied it all sought to improve upon it, to do what Louis Philippe had left undone, and what his French critics continued to tell him he ought to do. Adolphe Thiers went into opposition on the refrain of 'the King should reign but he should not govern',[2] a position that had been accepted by King William IV in England and by the new King Leopold I in Belgium, but which Louis Philippe—and Guizot—found it very difficult indeed to accept. Under a constitution which gave him great scope for parliamentary manipulation and for packing the chambers with his henchmen, the Citizen King could not resist the temptation of

[1] V. Hugo, 'Journal des idées et des opinions d'un révolutionnaire de 1830', in *Philosophies Mêlées* (Paris, 1841), p. 158.

[2] *Le National*, 20 February 1830, cit. Duvergier de Hauranne, *Histoire du gouvernement parlementaire* (Paris, 1857–71), vol. x, p. 405.

trying to play the part of George III. Less lucky than that monarch, he was to lose his throne as a result.

From a liberal point of view France after 1831 compared unfavourably with Belgium after the southern Netherlands broke away from the Kingdom of Holland, to which they had been arbitrarily and somewhat crudely joined in 1815 under the terms of the Vienna settlement. Suddenly, as a result of the Belgian revolution, there came into existence in 1831 a 'model' state, presided over by a truly model king, who accepted all the implications of limited monarchy and who recognised without quibble or reservation the sovereignty of the people. The Belgian constitution of 1831 (which still remains in force, virtually unchanged) completely out-bid the revised French Charter and practically every other European constitution of its day. Only across the Atlantic did there exist—in the shape of that United States constitution so warmly described in Alexis de Tocqueville's *Democracy in America* (first published in 1835)—a form of government possessing competing attractions for the liberal-minded citizen of the older continent; but many more conservative Europeans—especially if they were devotees of Mrs Elizabeth Trollope and Mr Charles Dickens—had very serious doubts indeed about the applicability of the institutions of the country of Andrew Jackson and the Spoils System, of 'Cannibal Phil' and the Know-Nothings, of the 'Workies' and the 'Locofocos', to their more genteel civilisation.

The Belgian constitution of 1831 rapidly replaced the Spanish constitution of 1812—except in the remoter backwoods of Latin Europe and Latin America—as the beacon-light for liberals and radicals who did not stand so far to the left (and there were very few in the 1830's who did) that they wanted to overthrow all monarchies and replace them by republics. Wherever a strictly limited constitutional monarchy was the ideal—there stood the Belgium of King Leopold as a shining example. Hers was the constitution that 'had everything'—the sovereignty of the people clearly recognised, a monarch and a dynasty owing their position to having taken an oath to honour the constitution, a bicameral legislature, both houses of which were completely elected by the people, an independent judiciary, a clergy paid by the state but independent of it, and a declaration of the rights of the citizen firmly based on the principles of 1776 and 1789, yet in a number of respects containing improvements upon these. It is true that this paragon of a constitution was not democratic (though it contained nothing that would prevent democratic features from being added later) and was hard (though not as hard as the American) to amend, but it contained so many features that were either unique or very much better than anything to be found elsewhere—including Great Britain, from which the Belgian constitution-makers had borrowed so many ideas and practices—that it is only to be wondered at that it was not more extensively copied than it was. In the revolutionary constitution-making period of 1848, however, it was very influential: in Germany, in Italy, in Scandinavia, and elsewhere.

The British Parliamentary Reform of 1832 aroused as much interest in the world as the Belgian constitution of 1831 and was equally seminal, though in a different way and for different reasons. It had long been realised on the continent of Europe that Great Britain possessed a limited monarchy and had managed to protect the liberty of the citizen from arbitrary governmental action to a remarkably successful extent. Voltaire, Montesquieu and many other continental commentators had discussed these features nearly a century earlier and the repressive measures occasionally adopted in the days of William Pitt and Lord Liverpool had not shaken the Continent's faith in the essential reality of British liberty. But nobody had quite succeeded in explaining how Great Britain managed to do it. With an extremely inactive central government (except in foreign affairs) and with local affairs run by part-time amateurs, with a negligible army, no bureaucracy worthy of the name, and—most remarkable of all— 'governed without police' (not to mention the ubiquitous secret police without which continental rulers imagined they could not survive), Great Britain was the wonder and also the despair of foreign constitution-makers. They were forced to the conclusion that her institutions (except to a limited and piecemeal extent) were 'not for export' and were incapable of logical definition.

Not only were Great Britain's political institutions hard to explain and harder to copy, but they were, to the liberals of the continent of Europe of the 1830's, in a way irrelevant to their needs. The hard-won (but very tentative) first Reform Act of 1832 increased the number of voters in British elections by some 50 per cent, but Great Britain's electoral franchise had, even before 1832, been the widest in the world outside some of the new republics of the American continent. The Swedish constitution of 1809, the Spanish of 1812, the Norwegian of 1814, the Dutch of 1815, the revised French Charter of 1830, and the Belgian constitution of 1831 itself (or the electoral laws passed under their provisions) all prescribed narrower franchises than even the old unreformed British system of the forty-shilling freehold and of all but the rottenest of the rotten boroughs. France of the Charter of 1814 had under 100,000 voters out of a population of 29 millions; Belgium in 1831 enfranchised only 46,000 people out of over 4 millions, and even by 1848 there were only 79,000 voters in that country. The Reform Act of 1832, therefore, widening a 400-year-old county franchise that was already wider than anything as yet dreamed of in the philosophy of most foreign reformers, and sweeping away pot-walloper, scot and lot, burgage, corporation and freeman borough franchises, the significance of which was but vaguely understood by them, was not much of a direct inspiration to the outside world. What attracted more notice was the legislative activity of the first reformed Parliament (despite the fact that it was, by and large, in the hands of the same governing classes as before) and the turning by Great Britain to an intensive programme of law reform and codification (to which Jeremy Bentham and his school had pointed the way in voluminous writings, read more assiduously on the Continent than at home). In the space of a generation this was to transform many of her institutions and permit her to catch up administratively with the multitudinous changes wrought by an Industrial Revolution which had, before 1830, all but engulfed Great Britain's governmental machine. Foreigners were also interested in Parliament and its procedure, and how it maintained its legislative supremacy; they were interested in the cabinet system and how it synthesised the different functions of government; they were interested in the party system and how it avoided permanent fragmentation even when Tories changed into Protectionists and then into Conservatives, when the Radicals split off from Whigs and Peelites evolved into Liberals, and when Gladstone, 'the rising hope of the stern unbending Tories' of 1832, metamorphosed himself into the greatest Liberal prime minister of the second half of the nineteenth century.

The 'reception' of the reformed British constitutional system on the Continent was also hindered during the 1830's and 1840's by the lack of any up-to-date commentary upon it comparable in authority and readability to that of Montesquieu a century earlier, or to Tocqueville's new work on the American constitution. Rotteck and Welcker's *Staatslexikon* (1834–49) was merely descriptive, and it was not until 1857 that Rudolf von Gneist was to publish his influential *Das englische Verfassungs- und Verwaltungsrecht* or until 1867 that Walter Bagehot was to write so lucidly on *The English Constitution*.

What the Continent did notice was the continuing discontent in Great Britain herself at the meagre extent of the constitutional changes of the 1830's and the repeated statements on the part of some leading politicians that these reforms were 'final'. The rebellions in Canada of 1837 also did nothing to endear the British system to the rest of the world, and the full implications of the very liberal Durham Report of 1839 were neither understood nor worked out until some years later. The growing Chartist agitation was a clear indication that something was still rotten in the state of Great Britain. Her new young Queen and her equally young and inexperienced consort (a minor German prince from the same family as Leopold of Belgium) were as yet virtually unknown quantities in the situation. Great Britain could, in 1847, have been heading for another constitutional crisis which might disrupt her political life for a generation, for all that the outside world could tell. For such reasons Great Britain was less of an inspiration to the liberals and radicals who made and led the revolutions of 1848 than she might perhaps have been, and certainly less than was Belgium.

By contrast, the United States of America, from 1835 onwards, was rapidly becoming almost a cult among some continental liberals, who had escaped the poisoned arrows of Mrs Trollope and Charles Dickens and whose countrymen were not waging a 'literary war' with the Americans. In France Lafayette, that great champion of everything American and traditional symbol of friendship for the United States, lived long enough to see the torch taken up by Tocqueville. In Germany Rotteck and Welcker—who were also active politicians—reserved their highest praises for the American constitution, and returned emigrants like Professor Tellkampf expressed their unbounded enthusiasm for it in speeches and pamphlets. On a more popular level the lively and exciting novels of the Austrian writer Carl Postl ('Charles Sealsfield') romanticised for readers throughout German-speaking Europe the course of western settlement and life on the American frontier, with its freedom and lack of conventions or social caste. In this generation, men who wanted to found a utopia thought of going first to the United States or the western wilderness beyond her borders. Robert Owen and his sons went from New Lanark to New Harmony in Indiana; Karl Follen and his brother, leaders of the Men in Black of Giessen (*Giessener Schwarzen*), went to Missouri. Nobody thought of setting up a utopia in the land of Disraeli's 'two nations', any more than in that of Ernest Augustus and the seven martyrs of Göttingen.

During the decades of 'finality' in the Germany of Metternich, in Guizot's France and in Lord John Russell's Great Britain, the American example made much headway in Europe, so that when the pent-up forces of radical reform were released by the revolutionary outbreaks of January, February and March 1848, it was to the United States and to Belgium that some constitution-makers eventually looked. If they wanted a purely unitary government or to limit a monarchy without overturning it, they tended to turn toward Belgium. This was the case in Denmark, for example, and even in Holland. If they wanted a republic, or to create a federal government, whether monarchical or republican, they were powerfully attracted toward the United States. President Polk in his annual messages of December 1847 and 1848 took the opportunity of lecturing Europe on the advantages of the American system, and his representatives abroad, such as Andrew Jackson Donelson (nephew as well as namesake of the former President) who was Minister to Prussia and was also accredited to the Frankfurt provisional central government in 1848, underlined this theme at every opportunity. Donelson wrote to Anton von Schmerling (then head of the Frankfurt provisional government) on 25 July 1848:

The idea of Unity from which this German movement springs is that on which the American states have ever acted. They began their independence by the organisation of a federal power strong enough to repel foreign aggression. Under this system they have passed through three wars and after the experience of three-fourths of a century, it may confidently be asserted that they possess not a citizen who would not regard the dissolution of the Union as the greatest calamity that could befall his country.[1]

Aiding and abetting this good work, the representative of the Frankfurt government in the United States, Friedrich von Roenne (who had previously been Prussian Minister there, and whose pro-American views were well known),[2] peppered the ministries of the provisional government and the committees of the National Assembly with advice concerning how things were done in the United States and how profitably Germany could copy the political and economic institutions of that country. On 10 January 1849, for example, he quoted at considerable length a speech by Daniel Webster on the theme that power was with the people, but they could not exercise it in masses or *per capita* but only by their representatives. Even before returning to the United States he had, in a speech in Berlin (later printed as a pamphlet[3]) on 28 April 1848, when seeking election to the Frankfurt National Assembly, strongly urged the example of America's federal union as a model for a monarchical German *Bundesstaat*. Thanks to these and other efforts, the example of the United States was, indeed, on almost everybody's lips at Frankfurt during the constitution-making days of 1848 and 1849. A Swedish observer, Maximilian Schele de Vere (who had been in the service of Prussia), wrote from that city on 23 July 1848 to Robert T. Hunter, then a member of the United States House of Representatives, that 'The American name, I am glad to find, has never stood higher; everywhere are works and pamphlets in Book-stores and on centre tables in our institutions, and almost every orator points to them as a glorious example'.[4]

Small wonder was it that the federal constitution that finally emerged in 1849 from the deliberations of the German National Assembly owed a great deal, both in structure and in spirit to the United States' constitution of 1787. It created a true *Bundesstaat*, and the main difference between the two constitutions was the substitution of an hereditary monarchical head of the state for an elected president. In a number of ways it improved upon the American constitution and nowhere was it markedly inferior to it. After the Frankfurt constitution was wrecked by the refusal of Frederick William IV of Prussia to accept the headship of the new federal *Kleindeutschland*, the constitution remained an ideal. Bismarck borrowed freely (though without acknowledgment) from it in devising a federal constitution for the North German Confederation in 1867 and in extending

---

[1] MS. in Bundesarchiv in custody of City of Frankfurt-am-Main, Akten des Reichs Ministerium der Auswärtigen Angelegenheiten, v. 13. 120.

[2] See J. A. Hawgood: 'Friedrich von Roenne—a German Tocqueville' in *University of Birmingham Historical Journal*, vol. III, no. 1 (1951), pp. 79–94.

[3] No. 100 in P. Wentzcke, *Kritische Bibliographie der Flugschriften zur deutschen Verfassungsfrage, 1848–51* (Halle a. S., 1913).

[4] *Correspondence of Robert T. Hunter*, ed. C. H. Ambler in Annual Report of the American Historical Association, 1916, vol. II, p. 91.

this to serve the needs of the second German *Reich* of 1871, and again in 1919 the makers of the Weimar constitution of the first German republic made use of the Frankfurt constitution. Even the West German Federal Republic is in its debt to some extent.

Other experimenters in federal constitution-making went to the well of American experience in 1848 and 1849. The Swiss, after the defeat of the forces of disruption and of a narrow particularism in the *Sonderbund* war of 1847, turned their loose and inadequate confederation of 1815 into a true *Bundesstaat* in the new constitution of 1848. Borrowing to a lesser extent from France (they adopted the universal manhood suffrage of the Second Republic) and from Belgium (though they kept their weak 'directorial' executive, and of course retained their hallowed republican institutions) they helped themselves to whatever appealed to them in the American constitution. In particular they followed Section IV of that instrument in giving teeth to the federal government for interfering wherever necessary in the affairs of the separate cantons. Nevertheless, the reserved powers of the cantons were most meticulously defined and protected, rather more carefully indeed than those of the American states. That vagueness which had resulted in the rise of claims to state sovereignty and of nullification in John C. Calhoun's South Carolina and elsewhere, and which had caused the 'internal improvements' and 'United States Bank' controversies (cf. ch. XXIII, pp. 604–10), was studiously avoided. This bargain between twenty-two cantons made use of, but also improved upon, the earlier bargain between the thirteen states. Had the United States possessed in 1848 as tightly drawn a federal constitution as did Switzerland, it is possible that the constitutional crisis of the 'fifties and the temporary break-up of the Union in 1861 might not have occurred.

Yet Switzerland, in contrast to the U.S.A., did not set up a Supreme Court to act as a constitutional watchdog over federal legislation, for when the powers of the Federal Tribunal were extended in 1874 it could invalidate only cantonal ordinances as unconstitutional. Nevertheless, at one bound (even without the significant improvements that were to be added in 1874) the Swiss form of government leaped in 1848 to the forefront of those which were to provide encouragement to liberals and democrats throughout the world, and provided a valuable example to all countries feeling the need for a federal system. Like the Belgian constitution of 1831 it has remained in force ever since. Switzerland has never since 1848 turned her back on the universal manhood suffrage she then adopted—in a year that saw the Chartists and their 'Six Points' (of which universal manhood suffrage was one) discredited and set aside by a highly disapproving Great Britain.

Another experiment with federal institutions during the years of revolution was to meet with a less happy fate. On the face of it the Austrian empire—indeed the whole Habsburg monarchy—would seem to have been perhaps riper than any other country for the blessings of federalism. A multi-national state, composed of provinces and crown lands of strikingly different traditions and needs, Austria had much to learn from the American and the Swiss examples—even if the Magyars of the Kingdom of Hungary, over-anxious to keep down their 'subject races', had proceeded with precipitate haste from their 'ten points' of reform to devise a purely unitary constitution early in 1848, and to present this to their monarch as a *fait accompli*. In the Austrian half of the monarchy a genuine attempt at a federal solution to all the difficulties of governing such a state was made. Although the Slav elements in the empire eventually broke away and refused further collaboration in the work of the Austrian Reichstag which first met on 22 July 1848 (just as they had refused to collaborate from the beginning in the work of the Frankfurt Constituent Assembly, which had originally intended to comprehend the Austrian crown lands in a *Grossdeutsch* federal state), this great assembly, assuming constituent functions, went on to produce at the beginning of 1849 the remarkable Kremsier draft constitution (cf. ch. xx, p. 524). This constitution, again borrowing freely but by no means slavishly from the United States and Switzerland, might, had it been adopted, have altered the destinies of the Habsburg monarchy, for, if it had succeeded in Austria, the Hungarian crown lands might well have eventually been drawn in on a basis of reasonable equality (one with another and with the Austrian lands), and whether or not the Habsburg dynasty could have continued to rule over it, a great and viable federation might have arisen to bind together the lands of the Danube valley in a political system that did justice to their geographical and economic interdependence. Josef Redlich said of the Kremsier draft constitution of 1849 that, measured both by moral and intellectual standards, this document was the only great political monument of the common will for the state which in Imperial Austria the people had created through their own representatives,[1] and R. W. Seton-Watson saw in it 'the living proof that the nations of Austria were in that age capable of working out their political salvation';[2] but, unlike the Frankfurt constitution, it was to be still-born. Banished to the remote Moravian town of Kremsier by the emperor and his reactionary advisers, the Austrian constituent Diet was dissolved and its constitution rejected by them in favour of a unitary, illiberal and entirely inadequate one of their own devising issued on 9 March 1849. Even this was a piece of window-dressing on the part of the ingenious Prince Felix von Schwarzenberg, for its 'representative' legislature was never to meet. It was abandoned on 31 December 1851 in favour of a return to naked absolutism for nearly a decade.

[1] *Das Österreichische Staats- und Reichsproblem* (Leipzig, 1920–6), vol. i, p. 323.
[2] Introduction to English translation of C. Tschuppik, *The Reign of the Emperor Francis Joseph* (London, 1930), p. xx.

The Kremsier constitution would have recognised religious freedom within the Austrian empire; it would have protected minorities and safeguarded the rights of the individual; it proclaimed absolute national equality and provided a federal legislature in which all the nationalities would have been adequately represented. The emperor would have been required to accept the position of a limited monarch under this constitution, but under it, also, the Habsburg dynasty might have been able to prolong its rule beyond the debacle of 1918. Perhaps the Kremsier constitution was too idealistic even for that age of idealists, but it provided the polyglot Austrian monarchy with its last real chance of modernising itself and maintaining its place in a changing world.

In the Italy of 1848 and 1849 it is difficult to discern definite trends amidst the welter of constitutional experiment. But one aim was clear: the removal of the Austrians to beyond the Alps. As with Machiavelli when he wrote *The Prince*, the thought uppermost in the patriotic Italian mind was 'To all of us this barbarian dominion stinks'. National independence was as important as free institutions to the Italians and it was, indeed, in Italy that national and liberal feeling achieved their closest co-ordination at this time. In France, with national independence and national (if not 'natural') frontiers long since achieved, the nation as 'the popular will organised by the state' stood against and overthrew an insufficiently liberal king; in Germany and in the Habsburg monarchy nationalism and liberalism often stood in each other's way and cancelled each other out, as when the National Assembly that was making a liberal constitution at Frankfurt stepped aside from its task to collaborate with Prussia in the bullying of Denmark, or when the Magyars secured free institutions for themselves in Hungary while denying them to the 'subject nationalities' of the kingdom (cf. ch. IX, pp. 239–40). Gradually in Germany and much more rapidly in Austria and Hungary, the liberal impetus was to be blotted out by an insatiable nationalism, which made use of the Hegelian concept of the 'state as god' to prepare the way for a solution of the German problem by blood and iron. In parts of Italy alone a fervent nationalist could remain a good liberal in and after 1848. He was not required (as was his French counterpart) either to accept the dictatorship of Louis Napoleon Bonaparte or to pursue his liberalism in exile or underground; he was not, as were so many good German, Austrian and Hungarian liberals, driven to emigrate to America in the 1850's. In Italy Giuseppe Mazzini typified both the national and the liberal ideal, and after he had been driven from the Roman republic by French arms in 1849 he was able temporarily to collaborate with the monarchical government of Piedmont–Sardinia to drive both the French and the Austrians out of Italy, but he remained a republican to the last. Charles Albert's constitution of 1848 was just sufficiently liberal to be acceptable to the men who had founded the Young Italy movement in the 1830's. They were not asked to accept a return to a purely arbitrary monarchical government (such as was reinstated in Austria after 1851) or to one presenting only a sham façade of liberalism (as in France after the *coup d'état* or in Prussia under the constitution of 1850). This was what gave such strength to the Italy of Victor Emmanuel and Cavour, and it was a lesson not entirely lost sight of by Bismarck when—after brutally crushing the liberal opposition of the Progressive Party in Prussia in 1862—he asked for a bill of indemnity, produced universal manhood suffrage out of his helmet for the North German Confederation in 1867 and borrowed so much from the Frankfurt constitution of 1849 in devising a federated German empire in 1871.

The history of Italian unification (ch. xxi) is a noteworthy example of the use and the discarding of a variety of constitutional forms and concepts in the process of pursuing the one overriding objective of political unity and independence. Before 1848 several competing constitutional solutions to the Italian problem held the field. In 1815 Italy had still been 'a geographical expression' and had no constitutions in the modern sense in any of the states, principalities and provinces within her traditional boundaries. A virtual *tabula rasa* had existed for her thinkers and men of action of the succeeding two generations. Even as late as the abortive outburst of unrest against her more arbitrary rulers in 1820 and 1821 all that had been demanded by the revolutionaries in Piedmont at one end of the peninsula and in Naples at the other was the adoption of the Spanish constitution of 1812. This somewhat faded copy of the first French revolutionary constitution of 1791 was by then entirely inadequate for Italy's (as indeed it was also for Spain's) needs, and few of the Italians who demanded its proclamation had read it. It was as the current symbol of the aspirations of a people struggling to free itself from monarchical tyranny and foreign occupation that it had its long popularity in Latin Europe, though Latin America had already before 1821 begun to aspire to higher things. Even as late as 1848 the benighted Neapolitans, cut off from the main stream of European political thought during the obscurantist dictatorship which had persisted since the restoration of the *ancien régime* in the kingdom in 1815, once more demanded the Spanish constitution of 1812, and it was proclaimed there yet again —though never properly put into force. At the same time the Sicilians went back to their 'British-type' constitution of the same year (1812), an interesting if somewhat rustic exercise in putting Britain's institutions of the day on paper.

Apart from these somewhat antiquarian touches, Italians were remarkably realistic about their constitutional dilemma in 1848. Mazzini and Young Italy had, ever since 1831, favoured a unitary republic for Italy; the neo-Guelphs wanted a monarchical federation under the presidency of the pope, and Gioberti's influential *Del Primato morale e civile degli*

Italiani, published in 1843, gave direction and crystallisation to this idea; then came Balbo's *Delle Speranze d'Italia* in 1844 to advocate a crusade led by Piedmont–Sardinia against Italy's oppressors. For a short time between 1846 and 1848 when many Italians believed (with Metternich) that Pius IX really was a liberal pope, the federal and monarchical solution of the *Primato* appeared to hold the field. Even Mazzini announced that he would support papal leadership of a united and independent Italy. The craven attitude of Pius IX in the early months of 1848, and his subsequent 'surrender' to the Austrians, entirely wrecked the neo-Guelph cause (even Gioberti himself was to desert it in 1851), while the courageous action of that hitherto not very liberal or idealistic monarch, Charles Albert of Piedmont–Sardinia, in attacking the Austrians in Lombardy and pinning them down within their quadrilateral of fortresses, immediately switched the loyalties of large numbers of Italian liberals and nationalists everywhere to the views of Balbo—which had, of course, also powerfully influenced Charles Albert himself.

The *Statuto* which Charles Albert so providentially proclaimed on 4 March 1848, three weeks before he declared war and more than a week before Metternich was to be dismissed from office in Vienna, allowed national and liberal feelings to focus on to one objective and one solution of the Italian problem. It was not much of a constitution (as constitutions went in 1848), being far less liberal than that of the Second French Republic and in some ways even than the revised French Charter of 1830. It was indeed a sort of compromise between 1830 and 1814 with some British influence (such as a responsible 'parliamentary' ministry) and some Belgian (particularly in the sphere of protecting the rights of the citizen). American federalism was irrelevant to Piedmont's needs in 1848, but the system of permanent legislative committees for the examination of proposed laws that had grown up in the United States was adopted and written into the *Statuto*—though of course these had been given no formal sanction by the American constitution. The electoral law of (1848 provided for in the *Statuto*) was anything but democratic, for it enfranchised barely $2\frac{1}{2}$ per cent of the population of Piedmont–Sardinia in a year which saw universal manhood suffrage adopted in both France and Switzerland. On the subject of the sovereignty of the people the framers of the *Statuto* sat squarely on the fence. It was not made by a popularly elected assembly or even submitted to the representatives of the people for their approval; it was simply given by a hitherto autocratic monarch to his subjects, although he did consent to swear to maintain the constitution once it was in force. In somewhat (perhaps deliberately) equivocal language the king was declared to hold his throne 'by the grace of God and by the will of the Nation'. By great good fortune (for the House of Savoy at least) no special machinery for amending the *Statuto* was devised; it could therefore be amended at any time by ordinary legislation duly passed by the two chambers and assented to by the king. Because of this it was possible, when the time came, to stretch and stretch it again to extend by stages over the whole of Italy. It was also possible in the course of time to introduce a more democratic franchise and to liberalise the Italian state (as it was to be called after 1859) in a number of other ways after unification was achieved. A weakness of the *Statuto*, not to be discerned until much later, was that it could equally easily be twisted into the instrument of a fascist dictatorship (and Benito Mussolini, after 1922, never troubled formally to repeal it, though he ignored whatever parts of it he could not adapt to his needs).

This Piedmontese *Statuto* thus became the new symbol of Italian national self-expression in the constitutional field and Italian patriots flocked to the standard of the House of Savoy. Federalism and republicanism were alike forgotten for the time being during the 1850's. Manin (in 1855) and eventually Mazzini himself joined Gioberti in their support of Victor Emmanuel and Cavour. The National Society, supported by patriots of all types, was formed in 1856 to unite 'Italy without adjectives', and—it may be added—without too many doctrinaire liberal scruples.

Lacking that somewhat mystical approach to the problems of state-making which complicated political life for most Germans before Bismarck—and for more than a few of them since his day—the Italians, true compatriots of Machiavelli, used whatever political instruments and constitutional devices were, in their eyes, best fitted to secure for them the speediest possible national independence and unity. That Italy was to emerge in 1870 as a unified country with a somewhat archaic and inadequate monarchical constitution, a potpourri of early nineteenth-century ideas mostly borrowed from abroad and sometimes mistranslated, did not seem to worry Italians very much after their initial enthusiams for secular republics and papal federations had faded in the clear light of disillusionment during the years of revolution. Even Napoleon III's somewhat belated and half-hearted attempts to bribe them into accepting a weak federation of all Italy, *including* Nice and Savoy, was to be rejected by Italians in favour of a strong unitary monarchy without Nice and Savoy (if such had to be the price) and even—for the time being—without Rome. Italy's liberals and patriots were perhaps the most hard-headed to be found anywhere in Europe during those difficult years of revolution and counter-revolution which started with the smokers' riots in Milan on 1 January 1848 and ended (for the time being) with Garibaldi's march on Rome in 1860. Even Garibaldi had been forced to see his birthplace, Nice, pass under French sovereignty in the sacred cause of Italian unification, beside which nothing else could really matter.

The cause of the Italian revolutionaries thus weathered the storms and stresses of 1848 far better than did that of the revolutionaries in France, in Germany or in the Habsburg monarchy. This was in part because the crowing of the Gallic cock on 24 February 1848 had not been needed to awaken the unsleeping liberal patriots of Italy, whose revolutionary movement was already nearly two months old by then.

The Swiss, too, retained stability in a tumultuous year by getting their crisis over early, and the Belgians (like the British) were able to hold back revolution from their borders by having anticipated many of the reforms that Frenchmen and Germans still had to obtain (cf. pp. 191 and 196). The 'cabbage-garden revolution' in Ireland fizzled out as damply as did the Chartist demonstration in London, and the throne of Queen Victoria was not even faintly rocked. King Leopold I continued his discreet rule, working as easily with the Liberals who came (very conveniently) into power in 1847 as he had with the Liberal-Catholic coalitions between 1831 and 1846. Because revolution did not come to these fortunate countries in 1848, reaction did not set in there afterwards, as it did in Germany, France, Austria, Hungary and parts of Italy. Britons, Belgians and Swiss could afford to feel superior about the Years of Revolution and the Years of Reaction and to welcome their exiles with humiliating impartiality. Prince Metternich and Karl Marx were both received (though in slightly different circles) in London, and allowed to remain in Britain as long as they wished, whereas the 'liberal' Second French Republic had expelled Marx. The Citizen King, hardly a more popular figure in England than had been the Austrian Chancellor, was permitted to reside and to die there undisturbed. Britain had not yet been roused to a state of moral indignation by such campaigns as those of Gladstone against the Neapolitan prisons and the Bulgarian atrocities, and it needed the appearance of a 'hyena' in man's clothing to disturb the hearty phlegm of the employees of Messrs Barclay and Perkins' Brewery in the direction of a physical force demonstration (in 1850) against recent Habsburg tyranny and sadism in Hungary (see ch. xx). But this had been so savage that it had even faintly shocked the tsar of all the Russias, Nicholas I, himself.

The Years of Revolution form a major watershed in nineteenth-century history. Even at the time men were everywhere conscious that they marked the end of an epoch. People living in central Europe from 1848 onwards began to speak of 'The Period before March' (or in German, more succintly, *Vormärz*) rather in the way that after 1914 (and more particularly after 1918) they spoke of 'pre-war'. 'In the 1850's as in the 1920's men looked back across a great divide.'[1]

In the field of politics and government this was more evident than perhaps in any other sphere of human endeavour. Most of the men and some of the ideals that had dominated the *Vormärz* scene had disappeared or were in retirement. In England Lord Melbourne died in 1848, Sir Robert Peel in 1850 and the duke of Wellington in 1852; in the United States

---

[1] R. C. Binkley, *Realism and Nationalism, 1852–1871* (New York, 1933), p. 124. Cf. ch. x, pp. 267 f.

John Quincey Adams, Albert Gallatin, John C. Calhoun, Daniel Webster and Henry Clay all breathed their last between 1848 and 1852; in France the Second Republic died, and with it much of the liberalism of such men as Lamartine and Tocqueville; Metternich had fallen in 1848 never to return to office, and even his successor as champion of Austria's autocratic hegemony in Germany, Schwarzenberg, was to die in April 1852; in distant Mexico General Santa Anna, that stormy petrel who had disturbed her politics and her foreign relations for thirty years, went finally into eclipse after 1850 and into his last period of exile in 1855. Although only one dynasty (that of Orléans in France) lost its throne in the Years of Revolution, there were a number of enforced or voluntary abdications and a host of new royal faces appeared on coins (and on postage stamps, which were just coming into general use) in consequence—in Bavaria, in Hanover, and in Piedmont–Sardinia, for instance—while the king of Holland died in 1848 and the king of Denmark in 1849.

Among ministers, at embassies and in parliaments the 1850's also had to welcome new faces. Men such as Gladstone and Disraeli in Britain, Lincoln in the United States, Bismarck in Germany, were now well on the way to the leadership of affairs that they were to achieve in the 1860's, whereas before 1850 they had all still been minor if promising figures. There were of course a few notable survivors from *Vormärz*, such as Pope Pius IX, King Frederick William IV, and in Naples King 'Bomba', while the inextinguishable Lord Palmerston was to rise again to political eminence after his fall from grace at the end of 1851 and to live until 1865, and the course of Nicholas I had still a few years to run.

The 1850's was a period of marking time, even in those countries which had seen substantial reforms during the Years of Revolution and where the clock had not been turned back again. Despite the enthusiastic atmosphere surrounding the Great Exhibition of 1851 it was a decade remarkable neither for social nor for political reform in Great Britain. The two crises of the Crimean War and the Indian Mutiny absorbed much political energy there. The United States, working out the uneasy compromise of 1850, ran into greater and greater difficulties and the deadlock on the slavery issue produced such ugly incidents as the Civil War in Kansas and John Brown's raid (cf. ch. XXIII, pp. 624–5); a series of undistinguished incumbents of the White House—the 'dough-face' Presidents Fillmore, Pierce and Buchanan—provided inadequate and uninspiring leadership in this time of stress; only to the westward of the embattled North and South was the land relatively bright, with new communities and new political institutions being born in young states or territories such as Iowa, Wisconsin, Utah, California, Minnesota and Oregon. Denmark had received a constitution, of a modern type at last, in 1849, but her political life was bedevilled by the apparently insoluble Schleswig-Holstein problem and by the hostility of Germans and Danes both within and outside the Duchies (cf. ch. IX, p. 219); Sweden and Norway retained their joint king and their respective, but by now somewhat illiberal, constitutions of 1809 and 1814, and were not to see any significant reforms until the 'sixties. Prussia, humiliated at Olmütz, was still licking her wounds; the dawn of her 'New Era' (and even then it was a false one) did not come until 1858. In the Netherlands that ministerial responsibility implicit in the new and relatively liberal constitution of 1848 was not to be achieved in practice until the 'sixties. Things were not going too well in the new Balkan countries of Greece and Serbia, while the Danubian principalities, placed in 1856 under a collective guarantee of the powers, saw their first, 'falsified', elections annulled in 1859 and not a glimmer as yet of free or democratic institutions. Anarchy and chaos continued in Spain (as it did in many parts of liberated Latin America) throughout the decade. In Russia Nicholas I held back the deluge until his death in 1855 and his successor released only a trickle of reforms or promises until the first floodgate was opened by the emancipation of the serfs in 1861 (see ch. XIV, p. 369 ff.).

While not in any way therefore a decade remarkable for political progress—and indeed, as has been seen, there was a return to autocracy and dictatorship in France, in the Habsburg lands and in parts of Italy and Germany, the 1850's were at least a period which saw the consolidation of certain important gains of previous decades and of the Years of Revolution. Outside Russia and Spain the remnants of serfdom and of feudalism had been swept aside wherever they had persisted until 1848 (see ch. XV). Even in the Habsburg lands no attempt was made during the reaction presided over by Schwarzenberg to rescind the economic emancipation of the peasants. Indeed, all classes recognised that this emancipation had been much overdue, and although political emancipation and the vote was not yet given (except in France and Switzerland) to the peasant and the farm labourer, economic freedom—even when it temporarily brought misery and maladjustment, as it often did—was a necessary pre-requisite to political enfranchisement; otherwise the latter would have proved less than useless to its recipients. Nevertheless, a time-lag of several generations between economic and political emancipation seemed still to be the order of the day. Servile status had long since disappeared in Great Britain, but the farm labourer was not to get the vote (and then not in every case) until 1885; Prussia abolished serfdom early in the nineteenth century, but the constitution of 1850 accorded only a most limited three-class franchise, heavily weighted in favour of the class of land and property owners; even France waited for universal male suffrage until 1848 and Switzerland, that cradle of peasant freedom and self-expression, had a very restricted franchise in most of its cantons and in its confederate legislature until 1848; a number of the American states (though none of the newly created ones) retained very restricted franchises

—on which voting in federal elections was also based—up to the Civil War, quite apart from the exclusion of negro slaves and 'Indians not taxed' as being without political existence.

As had been the case between 1834 and 1848, the years stretching from 1850 to 1865 (and even more distinctly the decade of the 1850's) appear as an interlude between two eras of concentrated reform and political advance. But there was to be a big difference between the reform era of the late 1860's and that of the late 1840's in that few if any of the progressive changes wrought by governments or peoples in the later period were to be undone. The last quarter of the nineteenth century was also to be a period of remarkable if not always steady progress in the direction of liberal and democratic government. No era of reaction comparable to the 1850's was to recur until the 1930's were to see the rise or the consolidation of dictatorships in Italy, in Germany, in Russia, in Spain and elsewhere, although all these countries had previously enjoyed—if in some cases only briefly or intermittently—the blessings of free and more or less democratic government.

It is much more difficult to disentangle or describe in general terms the many threads of political reform of the 1860's than the simpler patterns of reaction, frustration and 'finality' of the 1850's. Perhaps the most notable theme is a last attempt to realise in full the principles of classical liberalism. John Stuart Mill gave *Liberty* and *Representative Government* their classic interpretations at the beginning of the decade and wrote his authoritative description of *Utilitarianism* in 1863. Because he chose to write an historical description rather than a vindication of utilitarianism it was not evident immediately that he had himself departed from the traditional utilitarian position and had taken more than a step in the direction of that 'collectivism' which A. V. Dicey later discerned as having been in the ascendant from the 1860's onward in influencing 'law-making opinion'.[1] Ferdinand Lassalle's Workers' Programme (*Arbeiter-Program*) had already appeared in Germany in 1862, and five years later Karl Marx's *Das Kapital* first saw the light of day. The battle was thus joined between the new ideology and the old even before the 1870's began. The liberal impulse was still to achieve great things before it was finally spent, but liberalism no longer held the field as the creed of all progressive and forward-looking men and women. It was, indeed, menaced from two directions. Not only were the new socialism and the International Working Men's movement (founded in 1864) challenging it from the left, but a renovated, up-to-date type of conservatism, already practised by such men as Disraeli in England, was seeking to outbid it from the right. In addition, the surrender of liberalism to the force of nationality

[1] A. V. Dicey, *The Relation between Law and Public Opinion in England during the Nineteenth Century* (London, 1905).

(and more particularly to its more chauvinistic manifestations) in the various new National-Liberal parties which sprang up during the late 'sixties and the 'seventies seriously weakened its appeal. Directly it became a middle-of-the-road creed, willing to 'do business' with such men as Bismarck and Cavour, it was felt, by a growing number of people who had hitherto given it unswerving loyalty, to have prostituted itself. No longer could it offer more to the people than could the new conservatism— Disraeli's reform act of 1867 was a case in point—but it had lost its starry-eyed innocence in the rough and tumble of the years of revolution and reaction. Intellectuals had been forced to become men of affairs, and in the course of their new experiences they often had to make the same compromises and strike the same corrupt bargains as did the professional politicians and diplomats they had despised for doing exactly that.

A second trend of the 'sixties, reflecting the growing complexity of managing and running the modern state, was an improvement in administrative organisation and in the quality of administrators. France and Prussia already had efficient civil services, bequeathed to them by the reforms of Napoleon I and of Stein, and recruited from persons trained in their admirable if rigid educational systems. Great Britain lagged behind in the sphere of state-sponsored education, and her civil service was recruited on a most haphazard basis before the 1870's, but in Great Britain too the 'merit system' (first introduced into the Civil Service of the East India Company, and passed on to the British government in India by it in 1858) was gaining ground, and the reform of the curriculum of the older universities, coupled with the foundation of new ones, in London— to which John Stuart Mill and Walter Bagehot were sent—in Manchester and elsewhere, was beginning to bear fruit (cf. ch. v, p. 116, and ch. XIII, pp. 337–8). In the United States the spoils system was still too recent a phenomenon, and too useful a political tool, to have been seriously menaced by reformers, and indeed the most corrupt period in the whole history of American politics and in the federal administration was that immediately after the end of the Civil War. But even there the Liberal Republicans under Carl Schurz and Horace Greeley, crying 'turn the rascals out!', attacked the graft of the Grant administration at Washington and of the Democratic 'Tweed Ring' in New York, while the territory of Wyoming gave the vote to women in 1869 and a woman, Victoria Claflin Woodhull, ran for President against Grant and Greeley in 1872 on an 'equal rights' ticket.

In the United States there was relatively little danger before 1865 that liberty might be destroyed and liberal institutions assailed by the destruction of free local government; the chief danger lay rather in the exploitation of the autonomy left to the separate states under the federal constitution and in so extensive a vindication of states' rights that the Union might fall apart and the nation disintegrate (cf. ch. XXIII). The same danger had existed in Switzerland before 1848. It existed to a critical degree when South Carolina seceded from the Union in 1860. It is true that in the period of reconstruction after 1865 the pendulum was made to swing too far in the opposite direction in some of the defeated southern states during the years of 'carpet-bag' and 'scalawag' rule, but this was a temporary aberration (cf. p. 629). In some of the leading states of Europe, on the other hand, the period of reaction of the 1850's (which happened to coincide with the coming of the Industrial Revolution) produced a tightening up of the machinery of the centralised state that threatened even the most tenuous forms of local self-expression with extinction. In the Habsburg realm the old provincial system had already been destroyed in 1848, and now the 'system' of Bach pulverised the *Kreis* into a number of *Bezirke*, so that 'county' followed 'province' into the discard, and nothing above the status of 'district' remained. Schmerling's attempt to reverse this trend and to restore a measure of the lost local autonomy in 1860 was to be abandoned (cf. ch. xx, pp. 544–8). In Prussia, too, local government (which at least was efficient and honestly administered) was made more autocratic when any element of popular choice for the office of *Landrat* was removed and when appointment to that office became purely a unilateral act of the central government. In France the Second Empire like the First exalted the powers of the prefects and made them petty tyrants in their respective departments. Even in Great Britain the long-overdue reform and liberalisation of the institutions of local government in rural areas had not yet fulfilled the promise of the Municipal Corporations Act of 1835; the Local Government Board was not created until 1871 and big reforms did not come until the 1880's and 1890's.

Yet liberals were clear-sighted enough to realise, even when they were living under the shadows of dictatorships, that, if local government did not provide channels for the expression of popular opinion and choice, there was little hope of its restoration or extension at the centre. With great courage the French political scientist E. Laboulaye published arguments along these lines in his work *Le parti libéral, son programme et son avenir* (1863), and also in another book of the same year, *L'État et ses limites...*, both of which appeared in what (for a liberal) was still a discouragingly authoritarian period of the Second Empire. Meanwhile Rudolf von Gneist's important book on British constitutional law which had appeared in 1857 had also stressed the importance of free local institutions in building up liberty of the subject and training the citizen in public affairs.

France was to return under the Third Republic to a more liberal interpretation of local government (though she did not sacrifice her strictly centralised administration in favour of a 'federation of local bodies', as the Paris Commune of 1870 had demanded), but Austria and Prussia were not even then moved to accord to their citizens adequate means of securing political experience and education at a local level. The failure of the democratic way of life to 'take' in Imperial Germany and in the Habsburg empire, even after universal manhood suffrage and parliamentary government of a more or less responsible type had been introduced, can in part be ascribed to this failure to liberalise local government. Even the ultra-liberal Weimar Republic of 1919 in Germany and the democratic Austrian Republic set up at the same time were both to suffer from the heritage of political inexperience of their citizens, bequeathed to them by the two empires they succeeded. That dictatorships were so easily established in these two countries in 1933 and 1934 respectively is evidence of the same lack of any real traditions of self-government in either. The dictatorship set up in Italy in 1922, on the other hand, gained its opportunity rather from the decay of parliamentary government and the corruption of politics at the centre, although it was also able to play upon the ignorance and credulity of a population with an inadequate standard of literacy, but with an intense interest in politics.

A third and most interesting trend of the period of the 1860's was the eclipse and then the partial recovery (after 1865) of the federal idea. Already well-established in its modern form for over half a century on the other side of the Atlantic Ocean, by the time of the Years of Revolution in Europe it had, as has been seen, exercised a powerful influence on the thinking and constitution-making of the Swiss, the Germans and the Austrians in 1848 and 1849, though only in Switzerland were effective federal institutions to be maintained during the decade of reaction. In Latin America (cf. ch. xxv), where several hopeful attempts at wide regional federations had been made in the early days of independence an era of acute fragmentation and of centralism had set in; yet Mexico, which had started out as a federal state under the first republican constitution of 1824, but reverted to centralism in the new constitution of 1836, at last got rid of that inveterate centralist Santa Anna in 1855 and produced a fresh and truly federal constitution in 1857, which was to last (more honoured, it must be admitted, in the breach than in the observance) until 1917—excluding the interlude of the empire of Maximilian between 1864 and 1867. But the re-federalisation of Mexico was the one notable exception to a distinct trend away from federalism until the Northern victory and the re-establishment of the American Union on its former broad basis in 1865 had restored faith in the federal solution to the problem of states less homogeneous than were France, Belgium and—Ireland always excepted—the British Isles.

It is, in a way, one of the great mysteries of political science that federal institutions, with all their obvious advantages, were not more widely received in Europe and in the Americas during the middle years of the nineteenth century during which struggles for national existence, independence and integration were the order of the day. It has already been seen how the selfishness of the Magyars banned federalism from the kingdom of Hungary in 1848 and how the obtuseness of King Frederick William IV and the Emperor Francis Joseph in 1849 rendered abortive two very promising federal experiments which might have helped to save their respective dynasties from eventual extinction. The peculiar situation in Italy made federalism less attractive than a unitary solution because federalism meant weak government and lack of sufficient resolution to expel the Austrians and the more reactionary native rulers, whereas the expansion of unitary Piedmont gave promise—which was to be spectacularly fulfilled—of speedy and nation-wide independence and unification. In addition, by identifying himself with schemes for an Italian federation, Napoleon III aroused quite understandable suspicions in the Italian mind, which never really trusted this alien sympathiser. The 'Confederation of Plombières', which modelled a government for Italy on that of the despised German *Bund*, was completely transparent, and Napoleon III's next ingenious plan, the fourfold Italian state proposed at Villafranca, drove Cavour from office and appalled all good Italians by envisaging the perpetuation of Austrian rule in north Italy (cf. ch. XVII, p. 463). When revolutionary constituent assemblies in Parma, Modena, Tuscany and the Romagna had all four elected Victor Emmanuel of Savoy as their king, Cavour was able to return to office in time to defeat Napoleon's last despairing effort (in 1860) to use federalism as a weapon to keep Italy weak and supine. All the indefatigable emperor was able to salvage from the wreck was the postponement by ten years of the incorporation of the city of Rome in the new Italian kingdom which Italians had 'made by themselves'. No wonder federalism remained an unpopular political concept in the minds of all good Italians—even of such good Italian liberals and political thinkers as Benedetto Croce and Guido de Ruggiero! When Ruggiero wrote 'Federalism has never brought success to its votaries in France, from the Girondins to the Communards, and has only served to emphasise by their utter discomfiture the fundamentally centralised political and administrative structure of the French state,'[1] it is clear from the context that he thought very much the same about federalism and its votaries in Italy.

Federalism having been repudiated in Austria in 1849, it was briefly and half-heartedly revived during the 'reform' period of the October *Diploma* of 1860 and 1861, but the February *Patent* of 1861 restored centralism and the *Ausgleich* of 1867 (following the surrender to Deák and the Magyar chauvinists in 1865) substituted the notorious dual monarchy for a truly federal Habsburg state (see ch. XX). A last effort, in the shape of Schaeffle's 'fundamental article' of 1871, to reintroduce

[1] In *The History of European Liberalism* (trans. R. G. Collingwood; London, 1927), p. 205.

the federal idea to the extent at least of giving autonomy to Bohemia, was quickly abandoned under pressure both from Vienna and from Budapest. From that point onward the Habsburg empire was doomed. The partial revival of federalism planned by the Archduke Francis Ferdinand was to come far too late—and far too near to Sarajevo.

Prussia had learned a bitter lesson in 1850, when she was forced by Schwarzenberg at Olmütz to consent to the restoration of the old ineffective German Confederation of 1815, and to play second fiddle to Austria once again in a disunited Germany. It was the humiliation of Olmütz and his bitter experiences as Prussian representative in the restored *Bundestag* at Frankfurt between 1851 and 1859 that converted Otto von Bismarck from the reactionary, blinkered, Prussian Junker politician of 1848 and the *Kreuz-Zeitung* to the far-seeing German statesman of 1867, who turned to a modified federalistic solution for Germany's problem of unification, and devised (partially on the basis of the still-born Frankfurt Constitution of 1849) a constitutional plan that unified North Germany under Prussia's domination, and extended this unification to the southern states (with Austria excluded) in 1871 (cf. ch. XXII). Yet the *Bund* of 1867 and the *Reich* of 1871 were both incompletely federal (on account of the dominating position of Prussia in both, and of the minor privileges thrown in as a sop to the three states south of the River Main in 1871) just as they were—despite universal manhood suffrage—incompletely democratic. The new empire inherited Prussia's difficulty in admitting full parliamentary control over the army, and was to solve (or rather to shelve) this problem by the unsatisfactory *Septennat* of 1874, while Bismarck could not resist retaining the irresponsible executive which his conservative background made him believe essential. The rulers of the Second *Reich* left until too late the decision to turn it into a liberal empire, and six weeks after William II's declaration of 30 September 1918 a republic had been proclaimed in Germany. The timing was no better than had been Napoleon III's *Sénatus-Consulte* fixing the Constitution of the Empire of 21 May 1870 in France. The Republic was established *de facto* in France on 4 September 1870!

Bismarck's federal scheme was less complete than that of the Frankfurt constitution of 1849, or even that of the 'Plan of the Princes' of 1863. It has been called an attempt to weld together the *Bundesakte* (of 1815) and the Frankfurt constitution, but it also contained many of his own ideas. Where he obtained his notions of federal government from has long interested investigators. Treitschke opined that 'Bismarck was in his youth a friend of Motley, the talented American historian. Motley wrote a book on the United Netherlands, and from this Bismarck acquired a theoretical knowledge of Federalism',[1] but in fact Bismarck is likely to

---

[1] H. von Treitschke, *Politik*, vol. II (Leipzig, 1897), Bk. 3, p. 312, cit. and trans. by H. W. C. Davies, *The Political Ideas of H. von Treitschke* (London, 1914).

have profited in 1867 and 1871 more from his correspondence with Motley on the subject of federal government in the United States than from reading *The Rise of the Dutch Republic*. Motley wrote to Bismarck in 1866: 'I believe you were one of the very few Europeans who ever cared to know my opinion (which was that of every loyal American) and who thought that an American might possibly know something about his country...I shall refrain from giving you advice as to how to deal with Schleswig-Holstein.'[1] Bismarck also had read Robert von Mohl, Constantin Frantz and other mid-nineteenth-century writers on federalism, and the debt of his final draft of the North German constitution of 1867 to the 'preliminary draft' of Max Duncker, who had been one of the architects of the Frankfurt constitution of 1849, is believed to have been considerable.[2] The German constitutions of 1867 and 1871 were, indeed, de-liberalised versions of that of 1849 in many respects. Bismarck was incapable of an honest and equitable appreciation of the principles of federalism—as also, of course, of liberalism.

In general, however, the greatest triumphs of federalism (after its restoration throughout the United States in 1865) were outside Europe. The Mexican federal republic was restored in 1867 and in that same year the federated Dominion of Canada was established by the British North America Act. Owing a great deal to the American constitution, the Canadian nevertheless profited from some of its mistakes, and (like the Swiss) gave the central government relatively stronger powers than had been accorded to it at Philadelphia in 1787. The separate territorial members of the dominion were called 'provinces' instead of states, and residual powers were left to the dominion government. Bismarck, had he wished, or had he been well enough informed, might have learned much from the British North America Act of 1867 about preserving a strong central government, with adequate powers, in a federation. But then Australia (in 1900) and South Africa (in 1909) were not to learn all that could have been learned from the Canadian example and Canadian experience.

In 1867—a sort of *annus mirabilis* of constitutional change and reform (not all of it in a definitely liberal or democratic direction)—came also the Second British Reform Act, the introduction of ministerial responsibility in the Netherlands (the Swedish constitution had been liberally and the Danish illiberally revised in 1866), the first modern Austrian constitution effectively to be put into force (but it was hardly a democratic one) and the 'Meiji Restoration' in Japan (cf. ch. xxvi, p. 713), whereby the young emperor Mutsohito freed himself from the control of the Tokugawa

[1] *J. L. Motley and his Family*, ed. S. and H. St John Mildmay (London, 1910), pp. 246–7.
[2] See H. Triepel, in his essay *Zur Vorgeschichte der Norddeutschen Bundesverfassung* (in the *Festschrift Otto Gierke zum Siebzigsten Geburtstag*, Weimar, 1911, pp. 589–640).

Shogunate and initiated a remarkable renaissance, which was to produce in time (and with the aid of the famous German jurist Rudolf von Gneist) the western-type 'theocratic-patriarchal' Japanese constitution of 1889; but only after priority had been given to the creation of a Prussian-type army and a British-type navy—for the Age of Blood and Iron had now begun, and that of Speechifying and Majorities was over.

Whether in fact speechifying and majorities were 'the mistake of 1848' as Bismarck averred, or blood and iron the mistake of 1862, 1867 and 1871, is a matter still open to debate.

CHAPTER IX

NATIONALITIES AND NATIONALISM

THE years round about 1830 were momentous for the progress of a cause little regarded in 1815, the cause of nationality. About the same time the word 'nationality' was first used as a term with a special political significance. It was accepted by the Académie Française in 1835. In 1834 a Russian, Pletkov, spoke of it (*Narodnost*) as a new word of unclear meaning; it was rapidly becoming current in Czech and Italian and had for some time been known in Germany (*Nationalität* or *Volkstum*) and England. To define it was not easy. In the 'sixties the Frenchman Buchez commented that the word had had a prodigious success, although people did not know whence it came and perhaps because they did not know what it meant. And he added 'It means not only the nation, but also the something in virtue of which a nation continues to exist even when it has lost its autonomy'.[1] Political scientists have since essayed elaborate definitions, but it may well be that Buchez's vague formula is as good as any and that it was precisely because of its vagueness that the word had become so popular: 'Each theorist, each party, each country was able to read into it what it wished, what justified its own aspirations.'[2] For liberals it implied liberty and a degree of popular sovereignty—thus Mazzini could speak of 'the progressive principle which constitutes British nationality';[3] for conservatives the maintenance of native traditions and an established order of society; for others a community spiritually bound by a common heritage of language and culture or one linked by bonds of blood or a special relationship to a homeland. Some saw in the movement of nationalities a step towards universal brotherhood, while others gave their allegiance to the nation-state as a supreme and final entity. The dominant emphasis might vary from decade to decade and from East to West; but, whatever it was, here was a word which quickly became charged with emotional content and, with its fellows 'nation' and 'nationalism', connoted a dynamic force of immense potentiality.

Already by 1830 the cause of nationality was fully equipped. Philologists and historians, poets and journalists, had played their part in rekindling the national spirit of Greek and Serb. Exiles, voluntary or perforce, had quickened the Philhellenism or pro-Belgian feeling of

---

[1] *Traité de politique et de science sociale*, vol. I (Paris, 1866), p. 75 n. Cit. G. Weill, *L'Europe du XIXe. siècle et l'idée de nationalité* (Paris, 1938), p. 6.

[2] G. Weill, *ibid.*

[3] 'The Nationalist Question in Switzerland', in *Lowe's Edinburgh Magazine*, May 1847.

Frenchmen and Englishmen. The symbols, so potent in rousing popular enthusiasm, needed only to be adapted from the armoury of the French Revolution—the tricolour, the national song or anthem, the national costume, the national festivals, the National Guards. The fundamental concepts underlying the cause, the attributes which helped to give it its appeal, had almost all been worked out or invented by the pioneers of nationalist thought or action in the later-eighteenth and early-nineteenth centuries. In the years 1830–70 they were reiterated and diffused with such effect as to transform political thinking and to remould the European map. A tenet largely unacceptable to the ruling circles of 1815 was widely held or had to be reckoned with in 1860. A leading English political writer, John Stuart Mill, could then declare that it was 'in general a necessary condition of free institutions that the boundaries of governments should coincide in the main with those of nationalities'.[1] By 1862 Lord Acton could describe the theory of nationality as the most attractive of subversive theories at the present time 'and the richest in promise of future power'.[2] By 1871 that power had been demonstrated in the unification of Italy and Germany.

The successes of nationality achieved by the early 'thirties had modified the distribution of sovereignty, thereby infringing two important principles, the sanctity of the treaties of 1815 and the integrity of the Ottoman empire. But the breaches were limited, the principles were still adhered to in the main by the great powers concerned and the Concert of Europe still subsisted (see ch. x). The story of the Serbians, the Roumanians and the Greeks had demonstrated that no subject nationality was likely to win political freedom unaided; while that of Greece and Belgium, areas of particular strategic importance, had shown that frontiers would still be determined primarily by the interests of the great powers. Much then would depend on how far a power or group of powers would further the efforts of nations struggling to be free.

By 1832 the outlook was unpromising. England's intervention in Belgium had been governed by fear of French expansion, and her intervention in Greece had aimed to check Russia as much as to champion the Greeks. That aim once achieved, she preferred narrowly to restrict the infant Greek kingdom and to keep the remainder of Turkey-in-Europe intact. Thus Greek patriots were unsatisfied and dreamed for decades of liberating the Greeks beyond the frontiers and of the 'Great Idea' of reviving a Greek empire at Constantinople. But it was not ideological sympathy that moved British governments. Although her institutions became more liberal after 1832 and she was increasingly looked to as an ensample and champion of liberalism, England's main principles of

---

[1] *Considerations on Representative Government* (Oxford University Press, 'World's Classics' edn, 1924), p. 384.
[2] *History of Freedom and other Essays* (London, 1922), p. 273.

foreign policy continued to be the preservation of peace, existing treaties, and the balance of power (see ch. x, p. 267).

The events of 1830–1 showed also that little could be expected of Russia. So long as her conservatism buttressed that of Prussia and Austria, so long as she deprived the Poles of such liberties as they had enjoyed in the Congress Kingdom, so long might Russia seem to nationalists through-out Europe to be a formidable adversary. Yet such a view was susceptible to qualification. She had aided the Greeks and the Serbs as a protector of co-religionists and to further her designs on Turkey. Much might depend on whether Russia was satisfied with her gains by the Treaty of Adrianople in 1829, or whether she wished to proceed with the break-up of Turkey-in-Europe.

It was, however, above all to France that liberals and nationalists had looked in 1830–1. But their hopes that France would once again take up the sword as an emancipator of oppressed peoples were disappointed. Louis Philippe and his advisers well knew that she was unfit to go crusad-ing or to face a new European coalition. The 'historic' subject nationalities thus had little to hope for from governments: still less could the little-known, forgotten, 'unhistoric' peoples expect their claims to be coun-tenanced. They must all prepare to work out their own salvation.

This was what their leaders sought to do, and not without optimism, which was encouraged by the intellectual climate of the western liberal countries and perhaps by the diagnosis of shrewd observers that Austria, the chief obstacle, the great multi-national state, was but a colossus with feet of clay. Already in 1831 Victor Hugo had declared that everywhere there could be heard 'the dull sound of revolution,...pushing out under every kingdom its subterranean galleries from the central shaft which is in Paris'.[1] Whatever the attitude of their governments, such cities as London, Brussels, Berne, Zürich, Geneva, and above all Paris, served as nurseries of nationalism in the years before 1848. It was in London that Mazzini, *par excellence* 'the Italian in England', spent the larger part of his long exile. It was in Paris that the great Polish poet Adam Mickiewicz lectured and wrote. It was to Paris that rich Roumanian *boyars* sent their sons. These cities of the West gave asylum to refugees from many lands, Germans, Italians, and above all Poles, and their relative freedom of press and association provided admirable opportunities for propaganda. Thus Paris was an international capital, and the sympathies of large-hearted men and women in many countries, the meeting of exile with exile, the comings and goings of refugees and the founding of newspapers and associations gave the nationalism of the 'thirties and 'forties a strong cosmopolitan flavour.

Nor were these cities passive hosts. 'Friends of Poland' and 'Friends

---

[1] *Œuvres complètes de Victor Hugo, Poésie* ('Feuilles d'Automne'), vol. II (Paris, 1880), pp. 239–40.

of Italy' followed on the Philhellenes of the 'twenties. Literary figures such as Michelet and Browning, Quinet and Swinburne were won for the cause of nationalities, or at least of some particular nation. Moreover, literature itself was a powerful inspiration. French writers in particular combined literary power with political appeal. Lamennais' *Paroles d'un croyant* (1833–4), with its fervent denunciation of the 'oppressors of the nations', went through many editions, and Lamartine's *Histoire des Girondins* (1847) was read as eagerly in Dublin, Athens, Budapest and Bucharest as it was in Paris. In this sense France seemed to be cast for the role of 'mediator and interpreter among the nations'. Moreover, her dead and living prophets were such that many still believed she would again become the great liberator. Small wonder that the Russian Herzen recalled how he entered Paris 'with reverence, as men used to enter Jerusalem and Rome'.[1] Small wonder that in 1848 expectation rose to fever-pitch and that the Second French Republic was immediately invested with the character of a romantic and fearless crusader.

But the view of Paris as the Mecca of exiles and of France as the only true paladin must be qualified. There were Italians who distrusted their neighbour and Germans who reacted violently against her. Moreover, the studies of German scholars, above all of Herder (1744–1803), had given an impetus to a linguistic nationalism, not necessarily associated with liberalism, whose effect was far-reaching in central and eastern Europe (cf. ch. xv, p. 391). Herder had also initiated the idea of 'Volkstum' or folk-nation, an organic historical group, which replaced the traditional concept of the state, and this idea was developed by influential writers of the nineteenth century. Through their influence and the prestige of her universities Germany came to be a rival centre of attraction, and the men who fell under their spell tended to think of nationality in terms of language and power rather than of community of purpose and free institutions.

Such are some of the more conspicuous features in the background to the movement of nationalities in the 'thirties and 'forties. In the foreground, nationalism as a mood is widely discernible. It may be seen in the nation-state with a long history, such as France; in the nation-state newly emerged, such as Belgium; in the loose federations—such as Germany and Switzerland—which aspired to closer union; in the historic temporarily subject nations, such as Poland; and even among those which were only beginning to recapture a lost cultural heritage.

In Great Britain it would be difficult to speak of a nationalist 'movement'. Such nationalism as existed manifested itself in a continued insular pride, in dislike of the traditional foe notwithstanding the *ententes* or alliances of the days of Louis-Philippe and Napoleon III, in the popularity of Lord Palmerston, in the activities of individuals who promoted colonial

[1] Cit. E. H. Carr, *The Romantic Exiles* (Penguin edn, 1949), p. 32.

expansion and settlement despite the Little Englandism of Whitehall, and in the egoism of Irish landlords and of increasingly powerful and wealthy industrial and commercial interests. But the British government had real nationalist 'movements' to contend with in Ireland, whose wrongs had moved Hugo and were likened to their own by the Czechs.[1]

The Act of Union of 1801 abolishing the Dublin parliament and giving Ireland representation at Westminster had proved a bitter disappointment, since Irish interests were still subordinated to English. Eventually, in 1840, Daniel O'Connell, 'the Liberator' of the Catholic emancipation struggle, decided to revive agitation for repeal of the act and founded what was soon called the Loyal National Repeal Association. Two years later some young lawyers, the nucleus of what became a 'Young Ireland' party, independently founded *The Nation*, a weekly, which aimed 'above all, to direct the popular mind and the sympathies of educated men of all parties to the great end of Nationality...which will not only raise our people from their poverty, by securing to them the blessings of a DOMESTIC LEGISLATURE, but inflame and purify them with a lofty and heroic love of country—a Nationality of the spirit as well as of the letter'. For men such as John Pigot, one of the youngest of the group, 'this matter of nationality' was, as he wrote in 1847, 'a sacred religion; and I mean the word in its highest sense'.[2] At first welcome and unexpected allies for O'Connell, they eventually broke with a repeal association which had deteriorated in the hands of his son, and founded a new organisation, the Irish Confederation, in 1847. But it split upon policy, whether to act constitutionally or by violence, and endured for only eighteen months. In 1848, when revolution in France encouraged even the more cautious to urge their supporters to arm and drill and to plan their own uprising, the government naturally took stringent measures. Extra troops were sent over; John Mitchel, a foremost advocate of insurrection, was tried for sedition and condemned to deportation; and in July the Habeas Corpus Act was suspended. These events provoked the conspirators into premature action which ended in fiasco. It was hoped to base a widespread insurrection upon Kilkenny and Tipperary, to hoist the green banner and declare an Irish Republic; but the rebel troops were unready and few responded to the call. In fact Young Ireland, like so many other movements which attained notoriety in 1848, was the work of intellectuals, ill-prepared and ill-organised. Unsupported by the influential hierarchy, these men had little touch with the mass of hunger-stricken peasantry, to whom subsistence and religion mattered more than politics. As one

[1] The first demonstration of Scottish nationalism in 1853 was too slight to enlarge upon here. Reference to it may be found in Sir Reginald Coupland, *Welsh and Scottish Nationalism—A Study* (London, 1954).
[2] Cit. Denis Gwynn, *Young Ireland and 1848*, p. 112.

of them confessed, 'The Confederates know no more of Ireland than the Cockneys do'.[1]

For a while after this debacle the country was 'deader than at any period since 1800'.[2] But the men of 1848 did not abandon hope. After a decade they renewed their activities, and from the United States, or in Ireland itself, began in 1858 to organise the Irish Republican Brotherhood or Fenians, a secret society which aimed at reverting to Wolfe Tone's methods of well-prepared conspiracy in order to destroy British rule by force. This was, in keeping with most nationalist endeavours of the 'fifties and 'sixties, a more realistic design than the 1848 plan of carrying the country on a wave of enthusiasm: but it was mis-timed. The Fenians came too late to exploit Great Britain's embarrassments during the Crimean War and the Indian Mutiny. Their outrages advertised their cause and induced Gladstone to conciliate Irish opinion by disestablishing the Irish church (see ch. IV, pp. 100–1), but they hardly shook British rule. Indeed, until the rise of Sinn Fein, perhaps the most important aspect of Irish nationalism lay in the great transatlantic emigration which had begun in the 'thirties and which attained huge proportions in the 'forties and 'fifties. The Irish nationalists concentrated in the United States were a more massive political force than the Poles of the Polish Great Emigration dispersed through many countries of Europe. They strengthened existing anti-British feeling in the U.S.A. and their money and sympathy provided nationalists in Ireland with powerful backing. The U.S.A. replaced France as the land to which such Irishmen looked for inspiration and aid.

In France the nationalism of the mid-century, born of defeat and the wish to continue to play the part of a great nation, manifested itself in periodic xenophobia and in the recurrent desire for the overthrow of the 1815 treaties and for a vigorous foreign policy (see chs. X and XVII). In these years it was still part of the revolutionary tradition and its main standard-bearers were men of the left who regarded themselves as the true heirs of the great revolution. But, self-contained within frontiers which were largely natural, envied by Treitschke because she had neither an Ireland nor a Poland, France was little affected by ambitions to link up with supposedly kindred nationalities. Michelet might wish her to collaborate especially with her Latin 'sisters', Italy and Spain, and kinship of language and culture may have been a powerful argument in support of French designs on Belgium or for assisting the Roumanians, but there was no Pan-Gallicism and all that Latin co-operation produced was the Latin Monetary Union of 1865. Vocal though they might be, French nationalists affected policy but little before 1848.

In the lesser states of northern and western Europe nationalism also acquired significance. Among the Scandinavian peoples the study of

---

[1] Thomas F. Meagher to Gavan Duffy, cit. Denis Gwynn, *Young Ireland and 1848*, p. 152.   [2] *Ibid.* p. 466.

folk-lore, history, and philology, made each more conscious of its distinctness from the others. It fostered a more sturdy national consciousness, especially among Norwegians and Danes. In Norway, although this was almost wholly linguistic and literary in expression, it was a necessary prelude to eventual political separation from Sweden. In Denmark, the chief sufferer in the Napoleonic wars, it stimulated a vigorous response to a new challenge. Denmark had lost Norway to Sweden. She now found her hold over Schleswig and Holstein menaced by the penetration of nationalist German influences. Her reaction to the danger was closely bound to the desire to end absolutism, and this raised delicate constitutional issues.

Schleswig and Holstein were, according to Royal Letters Patent of 1846, independent states having nothing in common with Denmark except the person of their sovereign, who was duke in each. Holstein, the southernmost, was a member of the Germanic confederation and its people were almost wholly German. Schleswig, with its considerable Danish, mainly peasant, population, had for so long been linked to the Danish crown that emotionally the Danes regarded it as an indissoluble part of their inheritance. An incident in 1842, when a deputy was evicted from the Schleswig Estates for insisting upon his right to address them in Danish, deeply stirred Danish opinion. In the next two years several associations were founded for the defence of Danish interests, and the Danish liberals became a National Liberal party which pressed for the incorporation of Schleswig in Denmark. They triumphed in 1848: a new king, Frederick VII, was persuaded to abolish absolutism and the news of the February Revolution in Paris, arousing nationalist enthusiasm in Copenhagen still further —'Denmark to the Eider' (the river boundary between Schleswig and Holstein) was the slogan of the day—led to the formation of a new radical and nationalist ministry which declared that Schleswig would be united with Denmark by a common liberal constitution. The German majorities in the Estates of the duchies immediately retorted by declaring them independent and requesting their formal admission into the Germanic confederation. The Frankfurt Assembly met this request and asked Prussia to send troops to their support: thus Denmark's Liberal Nationalists involved their country in a war which lasted intermittently for nearly three years and was ended only by the intervention of the great powers (ch. x, p. 265). The Treaty of London of 1852 marked a return to something like the *status quo*: the integrity of the Danish monarchy was reaffirmed, the special position of the duchies was recognised, and the vexed question of the succession to the reigning duke (for Frederick VII had no heir and the duchies were subject to Salic law) appeared to have been satisfactorily settled.

But this compromise pleased neither Danish nor German nationalists. Before long tension revived and in 1863 the Danes, who had consistently rejected proposals that the frontier should be determined by plebiscite, attempted to effect that closer union with Schleswig which they had failed to achieve in 1848. Once again a new king, Christian IX, was forced to approve a new constitution which separated Schleswig from Holstein and bound it more nearly to Denmark. Once again German reactions were violent, and this time the cards were so cunningly played by Bismarck as eventually to secure both duchies for Prussia. This time there was no effective outside intervention because the western powers could not agree upon any effective common action (see ch. XIX). The tenacity of Denmark's nationalists had thus brought nemesis upon her: the Prussian government ignored the provision for a plebiscite made in the Treaty of Prague (1866) and she lost both duchies in perpetuity except for northern Schleswig, which she recovered when at long last a plebiscite was held in 1920.

The war of 1864 also tested the reality of the wider northern nationalism known as Scandinavianism or the Pan-Scandinavian movement. Although the Romantic movement had made Norwegians, Danes, and Swedes more conscious of their differences, a number of intellectuals had emphasised the broad similarities of history, tradition, and culture, and suggested that closer intellectual interchanges and political friendship would enable the North to play a greater part in Europe. Scandinavianism was the consequence, in some sense a retort, albeit a feeble one, to Pan-Germanism and Pan-Slavism. It had a strong appeal to students in all the Scandinavian universities, and to the National Liberals in Denmark, and the notion of Scandinavian solidarity was sufficiently compelling for 5000 Swedish troops to be sent to protect the Danish island of Fünen in 1848. But Russia frowned on any idea of wider co-operation and Scandinavianism never obtained any firm hold in Sweden or Norway. In 1863–4 the Swedish king, Charles XV, who sympathised with it, was eager to help Denmark, but his government made so many conditions that in the end nothing was done. And the number of Swedes and Norwegians who volunteered to fight for the Danes was significantly small. 'The Scandinavian movement burst like a soap bubble. It had been difficult to maintain the union already existing between Sweden and Norway; still less could there be any reasonable hope of extending it.'[1]

In the Netherlands the situation differed in many ways. Although Pan-Germans cast covetous eyes on Holland, there was no debatable territory such as the duchies to cause a Dutch–German problem, and the main linguistic issue which developed was one internal to Belgium. But there was a certain broad similarity in that nationalist feeling was at its peak in Holland and Belgium, just as in Denmark and the duchies, immediately before and after the breach which finally separated them.

In Holland the Dutch had shared their king's resentment at the Treaty

[1] C. Hallendorf and A. Shuck, *A History of Sweden* (trans. Mrs L. Yapp; London, 1929), p. 377.

of XVIII Articles and had supported him when he had thrown his army into the balance in order to obtain more equitable terms of separation from Belgium. But when he persistently refused to recognise the modified territorial settlement prescribed by the Treaty of XXIV Articles of November 1831, although it was more favourable to Holland, and although the great powers were resolved to maintain it, his subjects began to weary of a policy which kept considerable forces under arms and involved heavy taxation. By 1839, when at last he accepted the treaty, such nationalism as existed found vent not so much in denunciation of Belgium as in demands for constitutional revision which would give the elected representatives of the people a greater share in the direction of policy.

The Belgians, on the other hand, aggrieved by the Treaty of XXIV Articles, had protested vigorously against the loss of East Limburg, Maestricht and what had become the new Grand Duchy of Luxemburg. In 1839, when the Belgian Chamber was called upon to ratify the agreement, the representatives of the surrendered territories recorded their opposition in moving terms which anticipated those of the deputies of Alsace and Lorraine in 1871. For a while a nationalism of an irredentist character continued to exist. But before long most Belgians accepted the inevitable consequences of the determination of the great powers, the danger of invasion, and the restrictions upon an adventurous foreign policy imposed by a condition of guaranteed neutrality. For the surrendered populations this was the easier because the Dutch and Luxemburg administrations were mild, while in Belgium national pride found compensation in the development of free institutions, and in the rapid growth of industrial and economic power (see ch. 11 and p. 191).

Within Belgium, however, a separate problem arose which was in part a legacy of the Dutch connection, in part a product of the Romantic impetus given to linguistic and historical studies. Whereas French had long been the dominant tongue, William I had insisted on making Dutch the official language. At the same time a linguistic and literary movement had begun among the Flemings of which Jan Frans Willems (1793–1846) was the protagonist. Poet, philologist and publicist, he assiduously proclaimed the greatness of the Flemish language and literature and inspired a small but devoted band of disciples. Once launched, the movement grew, aided by many popular writers in the 'thirties and 'forties. The Flemish lion from the shield of the counts of Flanders was adopted as 'the symbol of the Flemish government' and a new patriotic song, 'The Lion of Flanders' was widely sung. When Hendrik Conscience (1812–83) prefaced the first edition of his *Lion of Flanders* (1839), with the words: 'There are twice as many Flemings as there are Walloons. We pay twice as much in taxes as they do. And they want to make Walloons out of us, to sacrifice us, our old race, our language, our splendid history, and all that we have inherited from our forefathers', the possibility of political implications became clear. It was not, however, until 1856 that the government appointed a commission to inquire into the 'Flamingants' grievances. Its recommendations were so sympathetic to them that they served as their platform for years to come. They urged that Flemish should be used in all business between the Flemish provinces and the central government, in the schools in Flanders, in Ghent university, and in the law-courts upon the request of a defendant. They proposed that a Flemish Academy should be created to protect Flemish culture, and that the army should be divided into Flemish- and French-speaking regiments. In spite of such findings, however, political opinion was not much stirred: the Liberals who were in power most of the time before 1870 had little sympathy for the 'Flamingants' and saw no need to make concessions. The movement remained primarily intellectual without any specific political organisation of its own. Its leaders aimed, not at separatism, but at making Belgium into a bilingual state, urging that national unity did not depend upon unity of speech. In this they might well cite the arresting example of Switzerland.

Switzerland, to be sure, before 1848 had a national problem so grave that it could be resolved only at the price of civil war; but it was not provoked or exacerbated by any rivalry of languages within or without. Pan-Germans might lay claim to German-speaking Switzerland as well as to Holland and Denmark, and individual German-Swiss might feel the pull of Germany, but there was no practical dilemma of colliding nationalisms as in Schleswig. The Swiss national movement was an attempt to solve the problem of the political and economic structure of the state, and it was embittered by confusion with a religious conflict. Essentially it was concerned with an internal question, though neighbouring great powers sought to intervene.

The Diet and Vorort created by the Federal Pact of 1815 had, like the Diet of the Germanic Confederation, proved cumbersome and ill-fitted to prevent either foreign interference or domestic obstruction from particularist interests. These, indeed, were dominant; and the cantons' jealousy for their own political sovereignty was matched only by the almost medieval chaos of the country's economic arrangements, its coinage, weights and measures, customs, tolls and postal services. Swiss nationalists, then, like German, sought a more effective central government and a more rational and unified economic system, better fitted to the needs of a country in which industrialisation was beginning to make rapid strides. The effervescence of 1830–1, which had led several cantons to adopt liberal institutions, encouraged the liberal-nationalists and radicals to campaign for a revision of the Federal Pact and the conversion of the federation of states (*Staatenbund*) into a federal state (*Bundesstaat*) on liberal lines. The revisionist proposals in the early 'thirties were, however, frowned on by Metternich, and bitterly opposed by the more conservative, predominantly Catholic and rural, cantons. In consequence they came to nothing. But vigorous party strife continued, and the radicals spread their ideas both through the press and at the shooting festivals which they organised.

A crisis arose in 1844 when Lucerne's Great Council agreed to entrust the direction of the seminary for priests and the ministry in part of the town to the Jesuits. Legitimate though it was, this action looked like a retort to earlier anti-clerical measures in Aargau. Such conduct by a leading canton could not, in the tension of the time, remain a purely cantonal issue, and what had originally been a quarrel between disbelievers and Ultramontanes[1] turned into a nation-wide struggle in which eventually (1845) the seven Catholic cantons formed a defensive league or *Sonderbund*, while the anti-Jesuit movement led to election victories which gave the radicals an absolute majority in the Diet. Thereupon the radicals were eager to fulfil their programme. A majority of the Diet, representing over 80 per cent of the population and over 90 per cent of its wealth,[2] was induced to vote both for the dissolution of the *Sonderbund*, on the grounds that it contravened the Federal Pact, and for the revision of the pact itself. When the *Sonderbund* refused to disband, civil war resulted. Once again Metternich and his conservative friends were eager to intervene, but the radical victory was so swift and thorough—the war lasted less than a month—that their desires were frustrated. The government of the Confederation pointed out that the powers had no legal right to mediate or to prevent Switzerland from amending her constitution as she thought fit. As has been said of one of the Swiss notes, 'there was a new tone of self-reliance in the document'; in 'foreign policy the *Sonderbund* War meant Switzerland's final release from tutelage, and complete national independence'.[3] The military triumph of the nationalists in 1847 made possible the Federal constitution of 1848. This established a more unified state with a permanent executive, which alone had the right to direct foreign policy and control customs, and which had appreciable powers of supervision over the home policy of the cantons. The transformation was facilitated by the moderation both of General Dufour, whose humanity in the campaign against the *Sonderbund* made reconciliation easier for the defeated cantons, and of the radical leaders in rejecting the temptation to create a unitary state and to override the historic traditions of cantonal autonomy in the interest of doctrinaire principles. It was exemplified by the ban on any new capitulations with foreign powers for the hire of Swiss mercenary troops and on the acceptance by any civil or military officers of the reformed Confederation of rewards of money or honour from foreign governments. The magnitude of the achievement

---

[1] Cf. ch. IV, p. 81.

[2] J. Halperin in *The Opening of an Era: 1848* (ed. F. Fejtö, London, 1948), p. 61.

[3] E. Bonjour, H. S. Offler, G. R. Potter, *A Short History of Switzerland* (Oxford, 1952), p. 267.

was not impaired by the radicals' failure to fulfil their dream of a federal university and federal training colleges for teachers from which 'a new Helvetic spirit' might be disseminated; for, although the Swiss in the main preferred to leave education to their cantonal authorities, they 'now stood united in face of the outer world, as a people with a fully developed national feeling'.[1]

Since Switzerland at that time was, as Ochsenbein said, a replica of Europe in miniature, the rest of Europe had followed the *Sonderbund* struggle with passionate interest. Nowhere was this more so than in Italy and Germany, to many of whose exiles the Swiss gave shelter.

After the collapse of the Carbonari movements and the 1830-1 risings it was Mazzini, the Genoese whose state had been merged in Piedmont, who most insistently preached the cause of Italian unity. His revolutionary society, 'Young Italy', founded in July 1831 at Marseilles, was the chief agency through which he sought to educate his compatriots. The deeds of the Risorgimento are recounted elsewhere (see ch. XXI); here it is possible only to say something of the ideas and writings which helped to inspire Italian nationalism and contributed to the development of the concept of nationality itself. Mazzini's fundamental ideas were set out in *Young Italy*, the society's newspaper of the same name, and developed in his prolific subsequent writings. Independence, unity, and liberty, this last to be secured through a republic, must be the triple goal. Through the republic the nation would be made, and by the nation Mazzini explained that he meant 'the totality of citizens speaking the same language, associated together with equal political and civil rights in the common aim of bringing the forces of society...progressively to greater perfection'.[2] For him nationalism was never divorced from liberalism, although its basis was partly linguistic. That basis might lead him to say 'Sicily, Sardinia, Corsica and the smaller islands between them and the mainland... belong undeniably to you...'; but he recognised limits and believed in natural frontiers—for Italy the 'sublime and undeniable' frontiers from the mouth of the Var to the mouth of the Isonzo. 'As far as this frontier your language is spoken and understood: beyond this you have no rights.'[3] His conception of Italian nationality was not exclusive and his dominant ideal was the recreation of the moral unity of mankind. 'Unity of man was to overcome the dispersion of modern man in an industrialised mass civilisation....Unity of nation was to bind all the free individuals of democracy into a community of liberty and equality....Unity of mankind was to assure the peace and collaboration of all nations....Rome was to be the symbol of this threefold unity.'[4] Where France had failed

---

[1] E. Bonjour, H. S. Offler, G. R. Potter, *op. cit.* p. 274.
[2] *Scritti editi ed inediti di Giuseppe Mazzini*, vol. III (Imola, 1907), p. 64.
[3] *Ibid.* vol. LXIX (Imola, 1935), pp. 61-2.
[4] Hans Kohn, *Prophets and Peoples* (New York, 1952), p. 82.

—and he held that she had failed greatly in not supporting the Italians in 1830—Italy would show men how to use their new-won freedom aright.

Characteristically undaunted after the failure of Young Italy's revolutionary attempt in Piedmont in 1833, Mazzini founded a still more ambitious society called 'Young Europe', which met on 15 April 1834 to draw up a pact of fraternity, a kind of holy alliance of the youth of the nations to fight for liberty, equality, and fraternity. 'To constitute humanity so as to enable it through a continuous progress as quickly as possible to discover and apply the law of God': that, he declared, was the mission of Young Europe: 'Every people has its special mission, which will co-operate towards the general mission of Humanity. That mission is its Nationality. Nationality is sacred.'[1] Like Young Italy, Young Europe was soon involved in unsuccessful revolutionary activity; it was subdivided into national communities which soon quarrelled and the Swiss authorities were obliged to suppress it in 1836 and to expel its members. But, although both societies were doomed to failure, and Young Europe in particular was a typically utopian product of romantic internationalism, they set an example which was imitated far and wide, from the groups calling themselves Young Ireland and Young Serbs in the nineteenth century to the Young Turks or Young Chinese of the twentieth.

Mazzini's were not the only works of the 'thirties and 'forties to proclaim Italy's national destiny. Gioberti's *Moral and Civil Primacy of the Italians* (1843) was notable not only because it espoused a federal instead of a unitary solution of Italy's national problem and forecast a new role for the Papacy, but because it spoke in such exalted terms of Italy's function as the creative and redeeming nation, the eldest son in a patriarchal household with all that son's rights and privileges. Poets such as Berchet, known as the Italian Tyrtaeus, and Gabriel Rossetti, both exiles in England, Mameli, author of the famous hymn *Fratelli d'Italia*, Giuseppe Giusti and many more wrote stirring patriotic songs; the operas of Verdi such as *I Lombardi* (1843) and *Ernani* (1844) occasioned patriotic demonstrations; Machiavelli and Dante were rediscovered as prophets of Italian independence, and history knew a new vogue with the writings of men such as Manzoni (1785–1873), Carlo Troya (1784–1858), Cesare Balbo (1789–1853), Michele Amari (1806–89) and others, of whom it has been said: they 'had two things in common: serious, diligent research and enthusiasm for the Italian cause...most of these works...went in a short time through several editions. History studied...with such eagerness was ...itself a sign that Italians were conscious of, or at least eager to discover, the moral unity of their history.'[2] Mazzini's advertised distrust of France, Gioberti's desire to avoid revolution or 'the most sad or most shameful

---

[1] *Scritti editi ed inediti di Giuseppe Mazzini*, vol. IV (Imola, 1908), pp. 9, 11.
[2] D. Pettoello, *An Outline of Italian Civilisation* (London, 1932), pp. 419–20.

expedient of foreign help',[1] and the self-confidence resulting from so much patriotic literature contributed, too, to the prevalent feeling that Italy could work her own salvation. The Italian movement in 1848, like its German counterpart, had nothing specifically French about it; 'it was the Roman ideal of Mazzini and Gioberti which was the source of the patriotic ideology which impelled the university students to join the volunteer battalions hurled against the 'Tedeschi'.[2] The events of the 'thirties and 'forties gave a great impetus to Italian nationalism but removed it considerably farther from its Napoleonic source; and France's inaction in 1848–9 meant a further weakening of French influence.

The great parallel to Italy of an historic nation with a splendid cultural tradition seeking effective political unity was Germany. The words nation and nationality might be sometimes applied to individual German states by contemporaries;[3] but what they described is better met by the term particularism. Essentially German political nationalism aimed at the creation of a strong German national state. This was an ideal which attracted men of all kinds: its strongest advocates were among those whose states had been mediatised; it appealed to conservatives as well as to liberals; they differed over the means rather than the ends.

The German Confederation of 1815 was as unsatisfactory a political force as the Swiss. The nature of men's discontent with it was well expressed in 1847 by a conservative Bavarian nobleman. The German people, he declared, had attained its majority:

The nation demands a share in public administration....One reason for discontent is universally diffused....This is the impotence of Germany among other States.... Austria asserts herself far too little because she is lacking in internal strength;... Prussia...is only admitted on sufferance among the great Powers...while the rest of Germany for ever plays a minor part as a mere camp-follower. No one will deny that it is hard...to be unable to say abroad: 'I am a German'—not to be able to pride himself that the German flag is flying from his vessel, to have no German consul in cases of necessity, but to have to explain, 'I am a Hessian, a Darmstädter, a Bückeburger; my Fatherland was once a great and powerful country, now it is shattered into eight and thirty splinters.'[4]

Two main strands of influence, sometimes separate, sometimes merging, sometimes conflicting, helped to give German nationalism its strength and colouring. One derived from the French Revolution and Napoleon; the other from a native cultural tradition of which Herder was the most brilliant champion. He had collected German folk poetry and urged the

---

[1] *Del Primato Morale e Civile degli Italiani*, ed. G. Balsamo-Crivelli, vol. III (Turin, 1946), p. 291.

[2] C. Vidal, 'La France et la question italienne en 1848', in *Études d'Histoire moderne et contemporaine*, vol. II (1948), p. 169.

[3] For example, *The Examiner* (1832), p. 488, col. 1.

[4] *Memoirs of Prince Chlodwig of Hohenlohe Schillingsfuerst* (ed. F. Curtius, trans. G. W. Chrystal; London, 1906), vol. I, p. 41.

Germans to cultivate their own language. He had, as has been seen, conceived the idea of the 'folk-nation', and had declared that the German national spirit required German territorial unity. This new note was accentuated by many writers during and after the Napoleonic wars. Fichte (1762–1814) anticipated List when he advocated economic self-sufficiency, and Görres foreshadowed later Pan-German claims when he demanded the formation of a greater Germany which would include Denmark. Jahn (1778–1852), who extolled Arminius as a national hero, was the precursor of Quinet's professor[1] who in 1842 described Germany's political objective as a return to the Treaty of Verdun; just as the anti-French patriotic songs of Arnim and Arndt (1769–1860) anticipated those of Becker and Schneckenburger in 1840 when war with France again seemed imminent (see ch. xix). Adam H. Muller (1779–1829) also was the ancestor of a long line of nationalists who glorified war as investing states with personality and giving them outline and solidity. The nationalist trend had been further strengthened by the philosophy of Hegel (1770–1831), who represented the Germanic spirit as that of a new world in process of becoming, exalted the state based on power, and discerned in Prussia its best exemplar, as well as by the jurists, Savigny (1778–1861) and others, who interpreted German law as something derived from the whole past of the nation, from its innermost being and its history.

By 1830, then, there already existed a considerable body of nationalist literature, significant because of the prestige of some of its authors and because it rejected many ideas derived from France and attempted to put something which was regarded as peculiarly German in their place. The reaction against the recent conqueror and hereditary foe (*Erbfeind*), as Görres first described France, was thus intellectual as well as material, and it was profound. Fed by Romantic yearnings for power and by legends of the superior creativeness of the German, it lent to German nationalism an exclusiveness not indeed peculiar to it, but which expressed itself earlier there and as brutally as anywhere. German nationalists turned their backs on France and scorned the Slavonic peoples in the East. Their attitude implied a rejection of the universal values of western civilisation. Thus, paradoxically, in an age when Germany was producing great classical scholars, other Germans were belittling the classical heritage. As Fichte had rejoiced in what he described as the refusal of the ancient Germans to accept the protection of the Roman empire in order that they might remain 'pure Germans', so in the 'forties learned 'Germanisten' were seeking to purge away corruption by substituting German for Roman law throughout the German lands.

The nationalist note was also sounded in economic writings, notably by Friedrich List (1789–1846). List attacked economic liberalism as

---

[1] E. Quinet, *Allemagne et Italie* (December 1842), in *Œuvres complètes*, vol. vi (Paris, 1857), p. 233.

materialist and cosmopolitan and urged the need for a planned national economy—nationality he claimed as the distinctive character of his system and protective tariffs he deemed essential until Germany was fitted for the ultimate goal of universal free trade. But List's views of economic necessity or advantage went far beyond tariff walls. He wished the *Zollverein*, which he called 'one of the most important attributes of German Nationality', to extend 'over the whole coast from the mouth of the Rhine to the frontier of Poland including *Holland* and *Denmark*'.[1] Both these naturally Germanic countries would enter the German Confederation, which would then obtain 'what it is now in need of, namely fisheries and naval power, maritime commerce and colonies'. Moreover, he conceived it to be Germany's mission to lead in world affairs, to civilise wild and barbaric countries, and to populate those still uninhabited. Thus the Pan-German was transcended by the imperialist. Such dreams were not unique—in 1849, for instance, Prince Chlodwig of Hohenlohe-Schillingsfuerst was urging that Rhodes, Cyprus and Crete should be won from the Turk and peopled with German immigrants: 'We shall thereby obtain a splendid outlet for thousands of the proletariat, we shall gain a seaboard and a mercantile navy, marines and sailors. Nor must Syria and Asia Minor be forgotten.... German Consulates, filled by efficient men, are among the most pressing tasks of the Imperial Executive.'[2]

Attempts to realise such visions still lay far in the future. But in 1848 and 1849 the enthusiasm for the Danish war and the treatment of the Poles both showed how firm a hold nationalism had gained. German liberals, especially in the south and west, had shown much sympathy for the Poles since 1830 and in the spring of 1848 the *Vorparlament* at Frankfurt resoundingly declared Poland's restoration a 'holy duty of the German nation'. But this resolution was of no more practical value than the similar declarations of the French National Assembly six weeks later. There was indeed a brief Polish-Prussian honeymoon (cf. p. 397), favoured on the Prussian side by the belief that war with Russia was imminent and that Prussia would then need the fullest co-operation of her Polish subjects. The Prussian government announced a 'national reorganisation' of the Grand Duchy of Posen (Poznan) and seemed ready to sponsor some measure of Polish autonomy. But the effervescence and uncertainties of the following weeks speedily brought the two peoples into armed conflict and, once Russian intervention in Germany was no longer to be feared, German affection rapidly cooled. Nationalism in the sense of the will to dominate prevailed over liberal-nationalism with its belief in self-determination, and in the Frankfurt Assembly at the end of July only 101 out of 575 deputies voted that the partition of Poland was a shameful wrong which should be righted by the re-establishment of Polish indepen-

---

[1] *The National System of Political Economy* (trans. Sampson S. Lloyd; London, 1904), p. 143.   [2] *Op. cit.* vol. I, pp. 52–3.

dence. The majority, who upheld Prussia's right of conquest and claim to civilise an inferior people, and were willing to sanction a proposed partition of Posen wholly disadvantageous to the Poles, included several who called themselves liberals. The divorce between liberalism and nationalism became manifest and German liberalism was dangerously weakened in the process (see p. 397).

The picture thus far presented by the growth of nationality in western and western-central Europe is relatively simple and self-contained. In eastern Europe, however, it is infinitely more complex because of the variety of peoples involved and their conflicting aspirations.

The great multinational empires, Russia, Austria, and Turkey, were each faced with nationalist movements of varying intensity. In Russia and Turkey the movements were geographically peripheral, affecting Turkey's Balkan subjects and Russia's non-Russian western lands from Finland to the Ukraine. For Austria, however, they were central and directly threatened the empire with disintegration from which it was rescued only by Russian intervention. This intervention was the most striking demonstration in the nineteenth century of the solidarity of conservative powers menaced by revolutionary liberalism and nationalism. The Austrian empire survived; the Russian empire crushed the Poles when they once again revolted in 1863; but Turkey, although bolstered by the western powers in her greatest crisis between 1840 and 1870, had subsequently to make significant concessions to Balkan nationalism. Apart from the new Roumanian state the nationalist ferment in these vast areas left the European map unchanged. Great struggles had, however, taken place and great issues had been raised. Among peoples whose very existence had been forgotten, such as the Estonians and the Bulgars, national feelings had begun to stir. But, significant as they were for the future, the movements of non-historic peoples did not seriously endanger the existing state system. It was the stubbornness of the historic nationalities, such as the Poles and the Hungarians, which presented the gravest challenges to the established order. The nationalism of these and the other greater subject-peoples had proved itself a potent force, which would have been still more formidable but for the internal divisions and mutual rivalries that enabled the Habsburgs, for example, to play off Croat against Magyar and the Russians to bid for the support of the Polish peasantry against the Polish landed nobility. Moreover, it had accentuated the antagonisms of the leading historic peoples within the two empires— of Magyars against Germans and of Poles against Russians. But by 1870 those antagonisms had been very differently resolved. In the Habsburg empire the German elements were not strong enough to dominate indefinitely both Magyars and Slavs and so, with the *Ausgleich* of 1867, the former Magyar enemy was taken into partnership (see ch. xx). In the

Russian empire, on the other hand, the ruthless attempt to obliterate Polish nationalism after 1863 rent the two leading Slav peoples still farther asunder and appeared to doom the one to limitless subordination. It also added one more to the many queries raised by the national movements—What of the Slavs? Could they be united more easily than the Latins? Was Pan-Slavism the reflection of a formidable force, a new and mighty super-nationalism or something as insubstantial as Scandinavianism? And, above all, what were the designs of the greatest Slav state? Was Russia never to harness nationalism to her own chariot?

In fact Russia was the only one of the three empires which could be said to have a nationalism of its own. This was in part the product of an old tradition, handed down by those who wished to preserve an Orthodox and holy land from the corruption of western ideas, and strengthened by the spread of western liberalism and by the shock received by autocracy from the Decembrist rising. At the same time, the national spirit, roused by the invasion and defeat of Napoleon, was further quickened by the fresh shock of Polish revolt. In consequence, although the government for the most part had little sympathy with the extravagant notions of some nationalists and Pan-Slavists, official policy and the objectives of the Slavophiles, in these years the chief intellectual defenders of the old tradition, to some extent coincided. Officially nationalism was reflected in a russifying policy which was largely maintained during the reign of Nicholas I, relaxed during the first years of Alexander II, and reintroduced after the Polish revolt of 1863 (see ch. xiv). Initially this naturally bore most hardly upon the lands recently in revolt, Russian Poland and the hitherto largely polonised lands of Lithuania and White Russia. There administration was entrusted to Russian officials, the University of Vilna was closed, the Russian language was made obligatory for official business, and large estates were confiscated and transferred to Russian ownership. The Lithuanian Statute was abrogated in Lithuania proper and in 1842 the name Lithuania disappeared as an administrative term, when the 'government' was divided into three departments. The educational aspect of this policy was part of the aim of Count Uvarov, Minister for Education from 1833 to 1849, to develop native Russian culture. It was he who, in a famous memorandum, declared that instruction should be based on 'the truly Russian and conservative principle of orthodoxy, autocracy and nationality (*Narodnost*)' (see ch. xiv, p. 363). In 1835 the first chairs in Slavonic languages and literature were established; and under his patronage the Slavophile review *Moskvityanin* was founded in 1841.

Russification, however, while it cowed Russian Poland and Lithuania for a generation, did not eradicate Polish culture. The Baltic German nobility, whose influence was powerful at St Petersburg and who were determined to maintain their Germanic culture as well as their social and economic privileges, resisted it strongly; and it only temporarily checked an incipient nationalism among the Ukrainians, shifting its centre for a while from Kiev to Lwow in Austrian Galicia. It is indeed arguable that russification succeeded most under the guise of religion: as in 1839 when some of the Orthodox in communion with Rome, known as the Uniates, were induced to rejoin 'the ancestral all-Russian Church'; or as in 1836 when the establishment of an Orthodox see at Riga was followed by the conversion of many Latvian and Estonian peasants.

The application of russifying policies was always governed primarily by considerations of defending the autocracy from the dangers of revolutionary subversion and political separatism. Thus the Ukrainian nationalists of the secret society of SS. Cyril and Methodius, founded in 1846, were severely dealt with because they opposed autocracy and serfdom and hoped for a democratic confederation of all Slav peoples. On the other hand, the primarily literary nationalisms of the northern Baltic countries developed unhindered, for they constituted no obvious political or social danger. In these lands literary movements led to an increasing use of the vernacular and to the appearance of the Finnish national epic, the *Kalevala*, in 1835, and the first Estonian epic, the *Kalevipoeg*, in 1857. But in the semi-autonomous Grand-Duchy of Finland, politically and socially much the most advanced of the three nations, the linguistic struggle was one between Finnish and Swedish, which, after long years of Swedish rule, was in 1830 still the dominant tongue. The 'Finnomen', or champions of Finnish speech, were the counterpart of the 'Flamingants' of Belgium, seeking equality for their own language. They achieved their goal in 1863 when a language ordinance placed Finnish on an equal footing with Swedish in all matters pertaining to the Finnish-speaking part of the population. The Russians could afford to humour the Finnomen in such an issue. Indeed, it is a striking measure of the difference in the histories of Poland and Finland, despite the similarities of their status before 1830, that in 1863, the year in which the Poles revolted again and were once more ruthlessly repressed, the Finns obtained their language ordinance and their Diet was summoned for the first time for fifty years, while in 1864 a separate Finnish unit of money was introduced (cf. ch. xiv, p. 376).

If Finnish nationalism thus seemed innocuous, so did those of the smaller, largely peasant, communities of Estonia and Latvia. Their very existence was partly obscured by the periodic tension between the dominant German and Russian cultures: 'even in the 'sixties none of the Baltic Germans believed in any future for the Latvian and Estonian tongues, much less in any political future of the Baltic peoples'.[1] Yet within less than a century the linguistic movements of these peoples and of the Finns had broadened into vigorous political nationalisms which added three new states to the European community.

[1] R. Wittram, *Baltische Geschichte* (Munich, 1954), p. 199.

The Slavophile movement, which with its successor Pan-Slavism represented the intellectual aspect of Russian nationalism, was a growth of the 'thirties and 'forties (see ch. xiv). It borrowed much, often without acknowledgment, from western, especially German, thought and literature. Its adherents had no close organisation or clearly defined political aim, but, just as much German Romantic writing extolled the uniqueness of German civilisation compared with that of the West, so they glorified the uniqueness of Russia and announced that she too had a mission, 'to transcend nationality by becoming the archetype of universal humanity'.[1] Profoundly religious, deeply conservative and suspicious of a governmental machine centred at St Petersburg, they represented in their own way a fervent popular nationalism. It cannot be shown that they had any direct influence upon Russian foreign policy, but their debates with their rationalist opponents, the westerners, marked a fascinating phase of Russian intellectual history, and they encouraged the growth of another scarcely less amorphous but strongly nationalist movement, namely Pan-Slavism.

Although there were men in Russia in the 'thirties and 'forties, such as Pogodin and Tyutchev, who have sometimes been classified as Pan-Slavs, Pan-Slavism as a movement originated among the Slavs of the Austrian empire and was inspired by two Lutheran Slovak scholars, Jan Kollar (1793-1852) and Josef Šafarik (1795-1861). Their main concern was to effect a cultural revival and to make their fellow Slavs aware that they had a common cultural heritage. But the works of both aroused passionate enthusiasm, less for their scholarship than for the visions of Slav greatness which they evoked.

Thus Kollar, whose 'Daughter of Sava' has been called the national bible of early Pan-Slavism, lamented that he would not see the 'great age of Slav dominion' when the sciences would flow through Slav channels, and Slavonic dress, manners and song would be fashionable on the Seine and on the Elbe. Thus, too, Zagreb patriots were enthralled when they saw the map in Šafarik's *Slav Ethnography*, and were astonished to see that the Slav nation was spread so far. To such enthusiasts, from Croatia to the Ukraine, the free and equal union of all Slavs appeared as a new and splendid ideal. Apart from scholars' dreams, many Austrian Slavs wished for an opportunity to exchange ideas on current politics. Their chance came in 1848, when, partly by way of riposte to German and Magyar pressures, a Slav Congress was called in Prague. 341 delegates assembled in June amid scenes of rejoicing and expectation: 'The new Slav tricolor blue, white and red was everywhere seen; shouts of "Slava" replaced the usual "Heil" or "Vivat"...the Slovak song "Hej Slovane" became a demonstrative assertion of Slav national vitality.'[2] A Slav mission to spread freedom and

---

[1] E. H. Carr, '"Russia and Europe" as a Theme of Russian History', in *Essays presented to Sir Lewis Namier* (ed. R. Pares and A. J. P. Taylor, London, 1956), p. 371.
[2] Hans Kohn, *Pan-Slavism. Its History and Ideology* (Notre Dame, 1953), p. 71.

enlightenment was proclaimed and the delegates considered sending a petition to the Austrian emperor, drafting a manifesto to the Slav world, and appealing to the European nations to arrange a general congress for the settlement of international disputes. The whole episode was highly characteristic of 1848. The sponsors hoped that the congress would be the first of a series: but it was the first and last for many years, because the Whitsun rising in Prague and the subsequent repression brought it to an untimely end. It has sometimes been called a Pan-Slav conference, but this is a misnomer, for, apart from the Austrian Slavs, there were only a few delegates from Prussian Poland and only two from Russia. And for all the expressions of good-will and unity it failed to agree upon any serious problems at issue between Slav and Slav.

In fact the Slav world was hopelessly divided. There was the religious division between the Roman Catholics, such as the Poles, Czechs, and Croats, and the Orthodox led by Russia; there was something of a dividing line between the Slavs within the Habsburg empire and those outside it; and there were divisions between those within. Except perhaps in the Balkans, the lesser Slav peoples on the whole profoundly distrusted Russia's expansionist ambitions and her absolutism. At the same time within the Austrian empire Slovak nationalism conflicted with Czech, the Ruthenians detested the Poles, and Slovenes and Serbs preferred to develop their own individuality rather than merge it within a larger South Slav union. Ambitious Serbs or Croats dreamed of a Greater Serbia or a Greater Croatia which they would dominate.

But the fiasco of 1848 did not mean the disappearance of Pan-Slavism as an ideal, either revolutionary, as with the exiled adventurer Bakunin, who regarded the overthrow of the Habsburgs and the establishment of a federation of free and equal Slav republics as an essential condition of general revolution, or conservative, as with the Pan-Slavs in Russia. After the death of Nicholas I, in the greater intellectual freedom of Alexander II's reign, the question of Russia's mission, the idea that she was the natural leader not merely of the Orthodox but still more of fellow Slavs was increasingly canvassed in Russia and it was to Russia that the centre of Pan-Slav ambitions shifted. And in the 'fifties, and still more the 'sixties, the disappearance of the earlier generation of Slavophils, the emancipation of the peasants, and the unification of Italy and Germany all encouraged the champions of the Slavs against the West to become more stridently materialist and nationalist. This was all the more understandable because of Russia's great development since 1830. As Hans Kohn has said, 'By 1860 the educated Russian felt that European culture was part of his heritage, that Russian intellectual life was in its full development, that Russia was, not only in size and population, the first country of Europe'.[1] So in 1867 Russian Pan-Slavs organised a new

---

[1] *Ibid.* p. 130.

Slav conference, in Moscow this time, and Pan-Slav propaganda, conducted by powerful journalists such as Katkov (1818–87), made considerable headway, gained influential converts, even in the imperial family, and had a forceful protagonist in Ignatyev, Russian ambassador at Constantinople from 1864 to 1877. After the *Ausgleich* of 1867 had dashed the hopes of the Austro-Slavs, Russian Pan-Slavs could hope to win their sympathies, and, significantly, the Moscow congress was attended by eighty-four delegates from Austria-Hungary, including several Czechs. The Pan-Slavs, moreover, made a special bid to act as patrons of the Serbs and Bulgars. But not until after 1870 were they able to exercise any real influence upon Russian foreign policy.

If further proof were needed of the unreality of any dream of a voluntary union of all Slavs under Russian leadership it would be provided by the Poles, many of whom, like their poet Krasinski, regarded Russia as the embodiment of evil, and spoke of the Russians contemptuously as 'Asiatics'. They were conspicuous absentees from Moscow in 1867. The course of Polish history, already so contrary to the main stream of European development, also affords the greatest exception to the chronicle of nationalist victories of the mid-nineteenth century. Whereas Italians, Germans, Hungarians and Roumanians all triumphed to a greater or lesser extent, Poland by 1870 seemed farther than ever from the recovery of national independence.

Partitioned between three great states, the Poles were split anew by the great emigration of 1831. Nearly ten thousand fled to western Europe, mainly to France. Although in Poland as in Hungary the nobles and gentry commonly regarded themselves alone as the nation, the emigrants included workers and peasants and middle-class folk who shared the national pride and were ready to fight and suffer for Poland. They soon fell into two main groups, the aristocratic, eventually headed by Prince Adam Czartoryski in Paris, and the democratic, represented by the short-lived 'National Committee' of the historian Joachim Lelewel, by the Community of the Polish People in England, and other bodies. Socially their aims were very different and each looked to different means to effect Poland's rebirth. While all vainly hoped that some government would allow the formation of a Polish legion, Czartoryski and his friends put their main trust in diplomacy, whereas the democrats, Mazzini-like, looked rather to secret societies and fresh insurrections.

Their revolutionary efforts, no more successful than Czartoryski's diplomacy, merely worsened the lot of their fellow-countrymen at home. The 1830 revolt had led both to a period of repression in Russian Poland and to an intensification of the germanising policy begun by Prussia in the Grand Duchy of Posen in 1825. The 1833 attempt to raise Galicia likewise strengthened the germanising tendencies of Austrian administration; while the rising of 1846, which demonstrated that the peasantry for the most part prized freedom from serfdom above freedom from the Habsburgs, ended in the disappearance of the surviving vestige of Polish territorial independence, the nominally autonomous Free City of Cracow, and its incorporation in the Habsburg empire. The consequences of 1848 were similar. Although the Polish cause gained widespread advertisement in the assemblies and on the battlefields, although Polish exiles fought in every revolutionary or national army, advertisement and fighting were without avail for Poland herself. The conflict of German and Pole after their brief fraternisation widened the gulf between the two nations and led to a renewal of germanisation in Posen; while in Galicia disturbances following upon similar hopes of autonomy provoked the bombardment of Cracow and Lwow and induced the Austrian authorities to encourage the growing anti-Polish national consciousness of the Ruthenians. Thereafter there was to be insurrection only in Russian Poland, which had not stirred in 1848. The Poles of Austria and Prussia, convinced by bitter experience that revolt was hopeless, preferred to work for national consolidation through the maintenance of their national culture, and through social and economic reform, and looked to legal and parliamentary machinery for the defence of their rights (see ch. xx).

A similar tendency developed in Russian Poland where Alexander II's new policy of conciliation led to a general amnesty and the creation of an Agricultural Society and a Warsaw Academy of Medicine. Moderate men like the Marquis Wielopolski believed that through co-operation with the Russian government it would be possible to reconstruct Poland's ill-balanced society, return to the constitutional status of 1815 and strengthen the country economically and politically. But emigrants like Mieroslawski, for all the setbacks of 1848, remained unrepentant insurrectionists; and, when the aristocratic wing of the emigration was discredited through failure to secure consideration of the Polish question by the great powers at the Congress of Paris in 1856 (cf. ch. xviii, p. 490), they began once more to come into their own. There were good reasons why Russian Poland should now be their chosen ground. The change in Russian policy had aroused great expectations there and caused something of an intellectual ferment. A new generation remembered little of the horrors of 1830-1 and was readily fired by Mieroslawski's secret agents and the tales of the returning exiles, while the resurrection of Italy in 1859-60 led many a young Pole to dream of emulating the deeds of Garibaldi. To such enthusiasts the tsar's concessions were negligible and co-operation with the conqueror a contemptible course. After a great demonstration in Warsaw in February 1861, however, Alexander sanctioned several administrative and educational reforms and appointed Wielopolski to supervise their introduction. This conciliatory policy might for a while have succeeded, had not the Poles unwisely raised the demand for the return of the eastern border-lands lost in 1772. Such a request was inadmissible for any Russian government, since these provinces were regarded generally in Russia as integral parts of the Russian state. The tsar's refusal aggravated the situation, and in January 1863 a conscription decree provoked the long-threatened rising. Yet the outbreak found the revolutionaries divided, there was no single political or military direction and the great mass of the people, the peasantry, were largely apathetic in spite of the democrats' efforts to court them. 'Only in the cities, among the young officials and the sons of officials as well as in the artisan class, and in the country among the lower gentry, was the sentiment for war hearty and general.'[1] In these circumstances, and when the great powers were too divided to intervene effectively on Poland's behalf, the result was a foregone conclusion. The rising was followed by repression even more ruthless than that of 1830–1, and in resuming its russification policy the Russian government was widely supported by Russian opinion. The 'Kingdom' of Poland became the 'Vistula Territory'. Russian became the official language of administration and its teaching was made compulsory even in village schools, while religious instruction in Polish was forbidden. At the same time the Russian land-reform policy aimed at convincing the Polish peasant that the tsar was his only friend. Such vestiges of self-government as had hitherto distinguished Russian Poland now disappeared. After the great disillusionment of 1863 a new generation of Poles would follow the example of their compatriots in Posen and Galicia and settle down to a programme of 'organic work' such as had already been gaining favour before the rising. Land reform, the consequential ample supply of emancipated peasant labour, and railways, enabled them to develop industrially and capture many Russian markets.

The Lithuanians, whose fortunes were inextricably bound up with those of the Poles, suffered likewise. Such cultural revival as they had experienced before 1830 contained no hint of an eventual struggle for a national independence apart from that of a free Poland. They had rebelled alongside the Poles in 1830 and in 1863 many again answered the Polish call. But they too were divided. A new element, the Populists, emerged who, as well as championing social reform, envisaged action independent of Warsaw. When the revolt started they set up their own committee at Vilna to administer Lithuania. When the revolt collapsed russification was intensified under the ruthless rule of Muraviev. All printing of Lithuanian books in Latin characters was forbidden. Roman Catholic parochial schools were closed and colonies of 'Old Believers' were imported to strengthen the Russian elements in the country. The failure of the revolt meant a grave setback for a national cultural movement which had grown independently and had in no wise caused the outbreak. It had repercussions also in the Ukraine where, although the Ukrainians had been deaf to Polish appeals, the Russians seized the opportunity to

[1] *The Cambridge History of Poland* (*1697–1935*), (Cambridge, 1941), p. 378.

try and stamp out a cultural nationalism which might conceal separatist leanings.

The Polish rising of 1863 was not followed by any great new exodus. The phase of heroic exile was over. The Great Emigration of 1830 had played its part for more than a generation but had achieved no concrete gain. Yet spiritually it had been of immense importance, for it had inspired a great and ardently nationalist literature. 'It proved to be neither the politicians nor the secret agents nor the diplomats of the Emigration who saved Poland, but the poets.'[1] In his *Books of the Polish Nation* (1832) and other poems in prose and verse Mickiewicz developed the new concept of his country's Messianic role among the nations, the great martyr in the cause of human freedom: the same theme was the inspiration of Krasinski's (1812–59) stirring poem 'Dawn' (1843); while Słowacki (1809–49) taught his fellow-countrymen that they must die nobly for the day of ultimate regeneration. These and other lesser writers in exile became the veritable moral leaders of divided Poland. Their works found their way into the homeland in spite of censors and customs officials and contributed to maintain a spiritual unity which transcended artificial boundaries and defied the efforts at germanisation and russification by the ruling states.

The Habsburg empire, the second of the great eastern European powers, remained throughout the great upholder of the ancient principle of dynastic property in countries and the great antagonist of national self-determination. There was no Austrian nationalism in the sense that there was a nationalism of the French or the Danes: but the Germans and the Magyars, the Italians and the Poles, the four leading historic peoples of the empire, felt strongly that they were superior and the non-historic subject peoples inferior beings. The antipathies thus expressed were often returned with interest and were intensified by the growth of national sentiment during the 'thirties and 'forties. What Grillparzer had written in 1830, 'The Hungarian hates the Bohemian, the Bohemian hates the German, and the Italian hates them all',[2] was still truer in 1848–9. It enabled the authorities in Vienna to continue to apply the ancient maxim of 'divide and rule', notably in the great crisis of 1848–9, which shook the empire to its foundations (see chs. xv and xx). Had it not been for the problem of the subject races, the dynasty's continued control of the armed forces except in Hungary, and Russia's readiness to intervene, the break-up of Habsburg power between the four master peoples might have been accomplished at that time; for not only did the Magyars and Italians bid for independence, but the Poles were eager to recreate the nucleus of an independent Poland and the Austrian Germans felt a strong pull towards *Anschluss* or incorporation in a Greater Germany.

[1] *Ibid.* p. 320.
[2] Cit. Oscar Jászi, *The Dissolution of the Habsburg Monarchy* (Chicago, 1929), p. 11.

The nationalism of the Habsburg peoples contained an admixture of western liberal influences, especially in the leading cities such as Vienna, Budapest and Prague. This was reflected in the growth of a political press, which included such notable papers as Karel Havliček's *Prague News* (1846) and Lajos Kossuth's *Pesti Hirlap* (1841), of societies with political aims, such as the Czech Repeal Association (so called after O'Connell's Irish organisation), and in the demands for local autonomy and for measures of political and social reform which would curtail the privileges of a predominantly feudal aristocracy and give some share of power to the lesser gentry and middle classes. It was this more-or-less national liberalism which provoked the mainly urban revolutions of March 1848 and produced the spate of constitutional demands with which the Vienna government was subsequently faced. But the liberal constitutional cause was soon bedevilled by the problems of nationalism.

The government of Metternich had maintained a lofty indifference towards the cultural renaissance which affected almost every people of the empire, leading each to cherish and develop its own tongue and to glorify its own past. Paradoxically then, the 'thirties and 'forties, so often simply dismissed as politically reactionary, were for Magyars and many Austrian Slavs a golden age of literature, scholarship, and linguistic development. Poets like Petöfi (1823–49) in Hungary, historians such as Palacky (1798–1876) in Bohemia, and philologists such as Ljudevit Gaj (1809–72) whose *Short Outline of Croat-Slovene Orthography* (1830) paved the way for the development of the modern unified Serbo-Croatian language, were men of whom any people might be proud. But the political effect of their activities was to increase national pride, sensitivity, and exclusiveness, and to stimulate conflicting claims. The enmity of Czech and Pole or Pole and Ruthene was, however, overshadowed by still greater national problems which partly transcended frontiers. On the one hand there was the possible danger of being crushed between the upper and the nether millstones of a great new Germany and of a formidable absolutist Russia. On the other there was the existing evil of Magyar intolerance.

The first danger was most clearly seen by the Czechs, who, like the Poles of Posen, had no wish to be swallowed up in a Great Germany. Bohemia with Moravia and Austrian Silesia had been included in the German confederation in 1815 without reference to the Bohemian estates; but all that had happened since had accentuated the Czechs' feeling of separateness. Accordingly, when in 1848 their historian Palacky was invited to be a deputy to the German National Assembly in Frankfurt, he refused on the grounds that he was a member of a nation 'which never regarded itself nor was regarded by others...as part of the German nation' and because the Germans would inevitably seek to 'undermine Austria ...whose preservation, integrity and consolidation' was essential as a bulwark against Russian expansion, not only for his own people, but for the whole of Europe.[1] What he and Slavs who thought like him wanted was equality within, not separation from, the Austrian empire—its transformation, not necessarily upon a strictly ethnic basis, into a federation in which the Slavs would play the part befitting their numbers and abilities (cf. ch. xx, pp. 523–4). They were Austro-Slavs, whose hostility to the Magyars also made them the readier to support the central government, which had promised increased autonomy and reform.

The exclusive character of Magyar nationalism was indeed one of the factors which enabled Vienna to triumph in the end. Despite the antiquity of her institutions Hungary had never fully become a nation in the western sense. In a population of eleven millions the dominant Magyars numbered only five millions. Nobles and intellectuals of Slovak or other non-Magyar origin such as Kossuth and Petöfi might be wholly magyarised, but for the most part the ruling Magyar nobility had failed to assimilate their largely peasant non-Magyar subjects or to reconcile them to their rule. In the 'thirties and 'forties the coincident growth of nationalism among the subject peoples and among the Magyars themselves naturally increased a tension already overt—the linguistic legislation of 1843–4 which made Magyar compulsory in official business and public instruction had, for instance, caused violent recriminations between Magyars and Croats and done much to further the Illyrian or Yugo-Slav cause in Croatia.

In the spring of 1848 a change could be hoped for. There were young democrats in Pest who won the sympathies of Serbs and Roumanians and 'realised that a Hungarian Constitution would only be practicable if it . .took into account the particular interests of each of Hungary's various nationalities'.[2] The spontaneous risings of Serbs in some south Hungarian towns in March were not at first specifically anti-Magyar, and from Novi-Sad Serbs concerned mainly with the abolition of feudalism sent a friendly delegation to Pest. Again, while the Roumanians of Transylvania protested against the decision of the Diet of Kolozsvár (at which they were not represented) to vote for union with Hungary, they were ready to accept it once the emperor had assured them that the new Hungarian government would protect their nationality by special legislation, set up Roumanian schools and employ the Roumanian language in all branches of administration. Only the Croats, who had long enjoyed a certain autonomy, were from the first uncompromisingly hostile.

But Kossuth and the new men in power did not appreciate the strength of the new nationalism of the subject peoples or understand how closely it was bound up with the desire for autonomy. They thought that they should be good Hungarians, just as Alsatians and Bretons were good Frenchmen, content with the grant of civil rights, and when a Serbian

---

[1] Cit. Hans Kohn, *Pan-Slavism. Its History and Ideology*, p. 6.
[2] F. Fejtö (ed.), *The Opening of an Era: 1848*, p. 322.

delegation asked for autonomy it was refused. The consequence was a revolt of Hungarian Serbs which, backed by the Orthodox church, became increasingly nationalist and led to the setting up of a Serbian National Assembly in May. Nevertheless the lesson was lost upon Kossuth and his colleagues. In August, in the Hungarian Parliament, Baron Wesselenyi vainly pleaded for the introduction of the Roumanian statute promised by the emperor. Kossuth denounced the Roumanians as leading conspirators against Hungary and firmly rejected the grant of any special position to Roumanian, Serb, or Slovak, because it would endanger the unitary state and Magyar predominance.[1] Thus inevitably the subject peoples came to side with Vienna against Budapest. But this did not bring them autonomy, once Vienna achieved control or was confidently swinging back to absolutism. With the overthrow of the Hungarians in August 1849 the experiment of a unitary Austrian empire was launched and despite cultural concessions to various nationalities a new period of progressive germanisation was inaugurated. In Transylvania even the Saxons lost their old autonomy and the Roumanians waited in vain for the fulfilment of the imperial promises of 1848. A few years later Russia could complain bitterly of Austrian ingratitude: already this was something well known within the Habsburg empire, where the disappointed complained that 'the nationalities which support the Government suffer and those that oppose it are rewarded'.[2] But disappointment was for many softened by material benefits in the prosperous 'fifties; and when the fortunes of the empire once again were jeopardised by defeat in war and by financial difficulties the dogged nationalism of the Hungarians was strong enough to force upon the emperor the Compromise or *Ausgleich* of 1867. This finally extinguished the hopes of Austria's Slav nationalists, for it established the joint Austro-Hungarian supremacy which endured until the empire fell.

In the Ottoman empire, the third and weakest of the great eastern powers, nationalism had begun to operate in three ways. It stimulated the Balkan Christians to a new desire for freedom from the Muslim yoke; it led them to rebel against the religious and secular hellenisation which had resulted from the control of administration and religious life by the Phanariot Greeks; and, as everywhere among subject peoples, it entailed a rebirth of cultural life, a rediscovery of past history and the gradual differentiation of one little-known Balkan people from another. But since these nations were relatively small and materially weak it also raised the question how far they could hope for complete autonomy and whether liberation from Turkey must not involve domination by Russia or Austria, Turkey's European neighbours by land.

---

[1] He had, however, initially been prepared to consider the Croats as a separate nation and even to consider discussing with them their eventual secession.

[2] Cit. Count Lutzow, *Bohemia, An Historical Sketch* (London, Everyman edn, 1920), p. 348.

The history of Greece, Serbia, and Montenegro had by the 'thirties suggested that autonomy was a practical end where it was aided by geography. The history of the Principalities, however, suggested that elsewhere it might be more difficult to achieve, for, although since 1821 their Roumanian inhabitants had been allowed native instead of Greek hospodars or governors, the Treaty of Adrianople of 1829 had established a Russian military occupation which lasted until 1834 and a protectorate which was effective until the Crimean War. Yet neither Russian nor Turkish power prevented the growth of a national consciousness. As early as 1835 the British Consul in Bucharest had written of 'the desire of the whole people' for union under a foreign prince, 'one neither Russian nor Greek'.[1] This desire was strengthened by the education of well-to-do young Roumanians in western Europe, especially France, and by the growth of native institutions such as the Academy of Jassy, founded in 1835. In 1846, moreover, the abolition of customs barriers between the two Principalities was, as in Germany (see ch. XIX), an economic forerunner of political union. But this goal was attainable only after Russia, who with Turkey intervened to suppress the short-lived liberal and social revolutions of 1848 and whose troops again occupied the Principalities at the outset of the Crimean War (see ch. XVIII), had been seriously crippled.

Russia's defeat in that war had the paradoxical consequence of weakening Turkey, whose preservation from Russian encroachments had been the main object of the western powers. The great powers now took a more direct interest in the Balkans, and a pretension to a kind of collective tutelage supplanted Russia's claim to exclusive protectorate over her coreligionists (see p. 488). The achievement of Roumanian ambitions was facilitated, Montenegrin independence was confirmed, and the Crimean War together with the Italian War of 1859 encouraged other Balkan peoples to bolder designs for emancipation, aggrandisement, and the partition of Turkey-in-Europe.

For the Roumanians self-help and French support were the decisive factors. After 1848 many Roumanian liberals had returned to France where their national cause found powerful advocates in men such as Michelet, Quinet, Cousin, and eventually Napoleon III himself. Napoleon welcomed opportunities to display his genuine sympathy with the cause of nationality and to strengthen French prestige in the Near East (see ch. XVIII). His government canvassed the idea of union at the Paris Congress of 1856, and, although it was momentarily unsuccessful, French influence encouraged the development of a situation in which the unionist forces could triumph. In 1859 both Principalities elected the same native prince, Alexander Cuza, and the powers, preoccupied by the imminence of war between France and Austria (see ch. XVII), were obliged to accept the *fait accompli*. But few native princes had been wholly satisfactory, and in

[1] Cit. R. W. Seton-Watson, *A History of the Roumanians* (Cambridge, 1934), p. 213.

241

1866, when the powers were once more preoccupied by the prospect of war between two of them (see chs. XVII, XIX), the Roumanians again seized their opportunity. They forced the now unpopular Cuza to abdicate, and chose a foreign prince, Charles of Hohenzollern, to be their ruler. At the same time their national assembly substituted the name Roumania for that of the United Principalities. Once again the powers reluctantly bowed to the *fait accompli*. Although nominal Turkish suzerainty continued until 1878 a new nation state had come into being; in doing so it had at least partly demonstrated the truth of the lesson already apparent in 1830–1, that a subject nationality could achieve statehood only with the aid of some great power. At the same time, like Greece, it was a nation state with an irredenta. Already in lectures as early as 1843 Michael Kogalniceanu, later one of free Roumania's statesmen, had claimed as his country all the territories inhabited by Roumanians.

By 1870 the political climate had also perceptibly changed elsewhere in the Balkans. In 1862 Great Britain had ceded the Ionian Islands to Greece, and Palmerston had justified the action as 'a natural arrangement' owing to their nearness to Greece and their 'identity of race and of language and religion'.[1] In Serbia, where men aspired to make their country the Piedmont of the Balkans, Prince Michael, one of the ablest and wisest of the Obrenoviches, had in 1867 secured the evacuation of the Turkish garrisons and won such prestige that Greeks and Bulgars looked to him for support. By allying with Greece and Montenegro and winning recognition from Bulgarian revolutionaries as potential ruler of a great South Slav federation which would include Bulgars as well as Serbs he anticipated the grand alliance of Balkan Christian peoples which was the prelude to the first Balkan war of 1912. But the great war of liberation did not materialise in the nineteenth century, for Michael was assassinated in 1868 and his successors lacked both his ability and his boldness. Nevertheless the restlessness of the Greeks and the advances made by the Serbs and Roumanians could seem to justify those who believed that the heirs of Turkey in Europe would be not Austria and Russia, but the Balkan peoples themselves.

The re-emergence of the Bulgarians gave further support to such a view. They were a peasant people for long so much hellenised that until the publication of the work of the Slovak scholar Venelin (1802–39), described on his tomb at Odessa as the 'Awakener of Bulgaria', 'even the most celebrated scholars…knew very little of the Bulgarian language'.[2] As with so many other 'unhistoric' peoples, early Bulgar nationalism expressed itself chiefly through the founding of schools and development of education in the vernacular. But it also took the form of a demand for

---

[1] Palmerston to Queen Victoria, 8 December 1862, cit. E. Prevelakis, *British Policy towards the Change of Dynasty in Greece* (Athens, 1953), p. 86.

[2] R. W. Seton-Watson, *Rise of Nationality in the Balkans* (London, 1917), p. 81.

a national church independent of the Greek Patriarchate at Constantinople, and when the Turks, acting upon the principle of divide and rule, eventually agreed and set up an independent Bulgarian exarchate in 1870, bitter Greek hostility was aroused. At the same time revolutionary secret societies in the manner of the Italian Carbonari, Greek Hetairia, or Serb Omladinu, sprang up, and Bucharest and Novi-Sad became the headquarters of Bulgarian exiles who dreamed of recreating a great Bulgaria or Southern Slav federation. It was, however, clear that the visions of a great Greece and a great Bulgaria were incompatible. If the Balkan peoples were to be Turkey's heirs they were only too likely to fall out over the heritage.

One people must finally be mentioned which, having had no fatherland in modern history, might seem to have small claim to be regarded as a nation. The Jews, who numbered rather more than three millions in 1830 and about seven millions in 1870,[1] had long been a predominantly European people by domicile, but they were still in many places despised and persecuted. Throughout these forty years the majority, from two-thirds to three-quarters, lived a life apart in the great Yiddish-speaking Pale of Poland and western Russia. By comparison their numbers in individual western European countries were insignificant—but it was from the West that there had sprung those principles of humanitarianism and enlightenment which most powerfully operated for the improvement of their lot. They were excluded altogether from Spain until 1869, liable to expulsion from a Swiss canton such as Basle until 1866, and in parts of Italy confined to the ghetto again after the fall of Napoleon—in Piedmont, for instance, until 1848 and in Rome for most of the time until 1870. In the Danubian principalities, where their numbers increased considerably during the years 1830–70 owing to overcrowding in the Russian Pale, they were subjected to bitter persecutions, and in the Russian empire they were obliged to live within the Pale and debarred from any professions but those of artisan and trader. But by 1830 there were many parts of western Europe such as the Netherlands, France, and various German states, in which they enjoyed religious freedom and equal rights of citizenship; some in which Jewish families like the Rothschilds already wielded conspicuous financial and political influence.

This emancipation had revolutionary consequences for the Jewish communities concerned, since it led to their secularisation and assimilation to the other citizens of the states in which they were domiciled, and to the gradual supersession of Yiddish—until the end of the eighteenth century the language of the majority of European Jews—by the vernacular tongues. This change and the accompanying movement to improve Jewish education occasioned bitter controversy, for Yiddish was a bulwark of Jewish

[1] These figures are derived from A. Ruppin, *The Jews in the Modern World* (London, 1934), p. xvii.

separateness and orthodoxy, and by the stricter Jews the mixing of Jewish children with Gentiles in state schools and the adoption of the Gentile custom of preaching in the vernacular were regarded as anathema. The processes of assimilation, the absorption of foreign learning and alien traditions, resulted in a partial disintegration of the old, closely knit Jewish communities. In compensation, however, wealthy emancipated Jews who remained loyal to their people and religion could intervene or organise as never before on behalf of their less fortunate fellows. Thus when thirteen Jews were charged with the ritual murder of a Capuchin friar and his assistant at Damascus in 1840, Sir Moses Montefiore and Adolphe Crémieux, supported by the British and French governments, secured their release. Sir Moses, moreover, went on to obtain from the Porte a *hatti humayun* abolishing the peculiar disabilities of the Jews in Turkey and placing them on an equality with its other non-Muslim subjects. 'For the first time since the fall of Jerusalem', wrote a Jewish author, 'Israelites of different nations took counsel and action together for general defence against a common peril. The latent national consciousness sprang into overt existence, and the New Israel of modern times was born...before 1840 what corresponded to Zionism was mainly religious and only unconsciously national.'[1] On the other hand, failure to secure from the papal government the release of Edgar Mortara, a Jewish child abducted in 1858, suggested the need for permanent bodies to defend Jewish interests. So there came into being the Board of Delegates of American Israelites (1859–78) in the U.S.A., modelled upon the long-established (1760) Board of Deputies of British Jews, and in Europe in 1860 the more important Alliance Israélite Universelle, whose aim was 'to work actively everywhere on behalf of the emancipation and the moral progress of Israelites and to lend efficient aid to all who suffer from the fact of being Israelites'. By 1870 these bodies had done much useful work, and despite continued persecutions in Roumania the lot of the Jews had much improved in many parts of Europe, including even Russia. Meanwhile some had found relief elsewhere. There was a significant movement of Jews to the U.S.A., particularly from Germany and the Habsburg empire in and after 1848, some because of their part in the revolutions, some in flight from renewed anti-semitic outbreaks or because they were fired by the 'On to America' (*Auf! nach Amerika!*) movement launched in Prague in April 1848, some because they were disillusioned and weary of the Old World (*europamüden*), and some lured by Californian gold. Trivial in comparison, but of great interest in view of later Zionism, were a few settlements in Palestine and the various projects of individual writers and associations, especially in England, urging a restoration of the Jewish people to their biblical homeland.

[1] J. Jacobs, 'The Damascus Affair of 1840 and the Jews of America', in *Publications of the American Jewish Historical Society*, no. 10 (1902), p. 120.

Between 1830 and 1870 nationalism had thus made great strides. It had inspired great literature, quickened scholarship and nurtured heroes. It had shown its power both to unify and to divide. It had led to great achievements of political construction and consolidation in Germany and Italy; but it was more clearly than ever a threat to the Ottoman and Habsburg empires, which were essentially multi-national. European culture had been enriched by the new vernacular contributions of little-known or forgotten peoples, but at the same time such unity as it had was imperilled by fragmentation. Moreover, the antagonisms fostered by nationalism had made not only for wars, insurrections, and local hatreds —they had accentuated or created new spiritual divisions in a nominally Christian Europe. The movement towards cosmopolitanism encouraged by eighteenth-century enlightenment and by many of the principles of the French Revolution was arrested by the self-isolation of German nationalism and by the revulsion of Slavophiles and Pan-Slavs against the West: and the new cleavages were deepened as peasant emancipation and universal suffrage enabled nationalists to harness the masses in their cause. For the Romantics before 1848 the true brotherhood of a universal republic of liberated nations had not seemed a fantastic dream. But, despite the multiplication of peace societies, the growth of international socialism, and practical devices of international co-operation such as the Red Cross, the story of nationalism since 1848 had made such a goal infinitely remote. Bismarck and Cavour had shown what could be achieved by *Realpolitik*, and the urge to dominate and expand had become more insistent as nationalism itself became more exclusive, populations expanded and industrial power showed its strength. Nationalism and the cause of nationalities had immensely gained in impetus. They promised to be the basis and driving force of future states, but Acton was not alone among contemporaries in viewing them with disquiet and in believing the theory of nationality to be a retrograde step in history. Proudhon, regarding the course of events from a very different angle, saw in it a grave obstacle to social progress, Herzen, whom Kohn calls 'one of the few Russians who fully valued individual liberty and the freedom of the West', denounced exclusive nationalism as a principal obstacle to the development of universal liberty; and Emile de Laveleye, a shrewd Belgian publicist, declared that it filled him with anxiety and sometimes with anguish: 'It mocks at treaties, tramples on historic rights, puts diplomacy in disarray, upsets every situation...and to-morrow perhaps will unleash accursed war.'[1]

[1] *Revue des Deux Mondes*, 1 August 1866.

CHAPTER X

THE SYSTEM OF ALLIANCES AND THE BALANCE OF POWER

THE result of the revolutions of 1830 was to divide Europe into two opposing diplomatic combinations and, in most European questions in the years immediately following the risings of 1830, the eastern powers—Russia, Austria and Prussia—were to be found ranged against Great Britain and France. This separation, as Palmerston noted in 1836, was 'not one of words but of things, not the effect of caprice or of will, but produced by the force of circumstances. The three and the two think differently and therefore they act differently.'[1]

The differences were largely matters of political principle and method. The eastern courts were bound together by a common belief in autocratic government and a common fear of a resurgence of the revolutionary principles of 1789 and 1793. They took a completely static view of the organisation of Europe and believed that changes in the political and social structure of the Continent, or of its member states, must be resisted lest the whole edifice fall in ruins. In addition, since they regarded all movements for constitutional reform, or—in the case of subject nationalities—for national self-determination, as 'revolutionary', they claimed for themselves the right to intervene in the internal affairs of the smaller states of Europe in order to extirpate these heresies before they spread. The western powers, on the other hand, stood for liberal and constitutional government, rejected the theory of intervention advanced by the reactionary governments of eastern Europe and, whenever it was within their power to do so, encouraged and protected other constitutional regimes.

It would be a mistake, however, to regard the two opposing combinations as cohesive and mutually exclusive leagues; and certainly if we view the years which stretched between the revolutions of 1830 and the outbreak of the Crimean War as a whole, it would appear that the powers ignored their ideological differences as often as they observed them. If, for instance, co-operation with France was 'the axle' upon which Lord Palmerston's policy turned,[2] that statesman had no compunction about concluding agreements with the eastern powers in moments when he considered the French to be acting in a manner which jeopardised British interests or menaced the peace of Europe; while, on the French side,

[1] Viscount Melbourne, *Papers*, ed. L. C. Sanders (London, 1889), p. 339 (Palmerston to Melbourne, March 1836).
[2] R. W. Seton-Watson, *Britain in Europe, 1789–1914: A Survey of Foreign Policy* (Cambridge, 1937), p. 169.

Louis Philippe showed a growing desire—once his regime was firmly established—to seek an accommodation with the eastern powers even at the expense of his *entente* with England. In much the same way, the Austrian chancellor, Metternich, was impelled on occasion, through fear of the Near Eastern policy of Tsar Nicholas of Russia, to discuss with Britain means of restraining him; while the tsar, when irritated by the Baltic ambitions of his Prussian ally, was quite capable of co-operating with Britain to defeat them. There was, in short, despite the ideological division of the great powers, enough free play in the European system to permit diplomatic alignments to shift as new problems arose; and this was not the least important reason why the years 1830–54 were years of peace, and years in which the territorial balance of power established at Vienna in 1815 was maintained.

The flexibility of the system of alliances is ideally illustrated by the first serious diplomatic crisis of this period, that caused by the revolution of the Belgian provinces in 1830. This dispute, which began in an atmosphere of menacing hostility between the eastern and western groups of powers, was solved in the end, after many shifts of position, by the concerted action of the five powers; and it is still considered to be one of the notable victories gained by the Concert of Europe in the nineteenth century.

In August 1830 the long smouldering resentment of the inhabitants of the Belgian provinces against their forced union with the Dutch burst into flames; a sudden rising in Brussels was followed by revolutionary disturbances throughout the land; a provisional government was formed on 26 September; and in the first week of October this body began to deliberate on various draft declarations of independence. These events constituted a clear violation of the treaties of 1815, which had prescribed the perpetual union of the Low Countries and had justified this decision by the necessity of erecting a barrier against future French aggression; and they could not help but be a matter of concern to the great powers. The king of the Netherlands confidently expected that the eastern powers at least would intervene on his behalf; and it is known that the emperor of Russia was eager to do so. In Vienna Metternich also felt that intervention was the only way of preventing 'the universal shipwreck of Europe';[1] while in Berlin, although Frederick William III was betraying the indecision which always affected him in moments of crisis, his soldiers seemed ready to act and were indeed holding staff talks with the Russians.

In face of this threat, the western powers acted with commendable dispatch. Late in September, the veteran Talleyrand arrived in London as the new French ambassador. In his first conversations with the king and the

---

[1] Cit. Heinrich Ritter von Srbik, *Metternich: der Staatsmann und der Mensch* (Munich, 1925), vol. I, p. 660.

duke of Wellington, he warned that intervention in the Low Countries by eastern forces would lead to prompt retaliation and that only a firm insistence upon the principle of non-intervention would prevent war. Wellington agreed and immediately circularised the other courts, urging them to refrain from action until representatives of the five powers had held friendly conversations in London concerning the future of the Belgian provinces.

The eastern powers accepted this invitation to conference reluctantly and probably only because Metternich and his opposite number in St Petersburg, Nesselrode, thought that the discussions might persuade Wellington to join the eastern powers in a campaign to restore the authority of the king of the Netherlands. It was not, however, Wellington with whom they had to deal. Before the London Conference had an opportunity to apply itself seriously to the difficulties in the Low Countries, the Wellington government had fallen from office; and Palmerston, Foreign Secretary in the new Grey cabinet, had become the chief British negotiator.

It has been suggested that the new Foreign Secretary was animated by the desire to destroy Holland's economic threat to Britain by detaching the Belgian provinces from her.[1] As a matter of fact, Palmerston privately regretted the Belgian revolt, for he believed that the continued union of the Low Countries 'would have been most advantageous to the general interests of Europe'.[2] He was realist enough to believe, however, that the independence movement had gone too far to be reversed; while, as an Englishman, he had no desire to see the troops of another great power in an area which had always been of special interest to his country. He eagerly joined with the French, then, in insisting that the principle of non-intervention be observed by all powers, urging simultaneously that the powers should accept the fact of Belgian independence under conditions which would, as far as possible, repair the breach in the system of 1815.

He was aided in this endeavour by the sudden rising of the Russian Poles against their suzerain in November (cf. ch. xiv, p. 362), an event which absorbed the military energies of Russia, diverted the attention of Metternich and the Prussians toward the situation in their own Polish provinces and made all three powers more amenable to peaceful solutions in the West. By 20 December Palmerston was consequently able to secure the assent of all members of the conference to Belgium's independence. This victory, however, eliminated only one of many problems that had to be solved. The new state had to be provided with definite boundaries and with a ruler; the disposition of the so-called barrier fortresses had to be decided; and the Belgians and the Dutch had to be persuaded to accept the conference's decisions. Moreover, as the threat from the east became less

---

[1] Srbik, *Metternich*, vol. i, p. 659.
[2] Herbert C. F. Bell, *Lord Palmerston* (London, 1936), vol. i, p. 119.

serious, the attitude of the French became less reasonable. Talleyrand now argued that public opinion in France would not be satisfied unless Louis Philippe were granted some compensation for the admirable restraint he had shown; and the Paris government began to indulge in manœuvres which indicated that they desired a Belgian ruler who would be subservient to French interests.

Angered by what seemed to be bad faith on the part of the French, Palmerston reacted as he was to react on many future occasions in his dealings with Paris, with an abrupt resort to threats and menaces. The vigour with which he rejected Talleyrand's claims and his evident willingness to make a common front with the eastern powers convinced the French plenipotentiary that retreat was necessary; and on 20 January 1831 Talleyrand joined the other members of the conference in signing a protocol which, by delineating the boundaries of Belgium and Holland and establishing Belgium as a neutral state under the permanent guarantee of the powers, constituted a kind of self-denying ordinance for France, as for the other signatories. But the French government hesitated to ratify this protocol, and, in addition, became involved in an elaborate intrigue to secure the throne of Belgium for Louis Philippe's son, the duc de Nemours. This double policy increased Palmerston's irritation and led him to intimate plainly that Britain was fully prepared to go to war to prevent any part of Belgium from falling to the French. The British, he said in a private letter at this time, occupied the position of 'impartial mediators between France on the one hand, and the three other Powers on the other,...as long as both parties remain quiet, we shall be friends with both; but...whichever side breaks the peace, that side will find us against them'.[1]

These admonitions seem to have produced their desired effect. With the advent of the moderate Casimir Périer government to power in Paris, the co-ordination of Anglo-French policy was largely restored; and, after the Belgian National Assembly had elected Leopold of Saxe-Coburg as their future ruler, the two powers succeeded in persuading the other members of the conference to agree on a definitive settlement for submission to the Belgians and the Dutch. The ambiguity of French policy was, it is true, not yet at an end. When the Dutch king sent his armies into Belgium in August and when the conference authorised Anglo-French intervention to expel him, the French troops showed a stubborn reluctance to leave the country after their mission had been accomplished; and the British Foreign Secretary was once more forced to resort to threats, and to say ominously that 'the French must go out of Belgium or we have a general war and war in a given number of days'.[2] Once again, however,

[1] Sir Henry Lytton Bulwer and the Hon. Evelyn Ashley, *The Life of Henry John Temple, Viscount Palmerston* (London, 1870–76), vol. II, p. 39.
[2] *Ibid.* pp. 109–10.

the French gave way, abandoning even the hope that they might be able to dictate to the Belgians which of the barrier fortresses should be demolished. Moreover, this was the last flicker of French resistance and on 15 November 1831 they joined with the other powers in the famous treaty by which Belgium was accepted as a member of the European state system. The ratifications of this document were not completed until May 1832, and the Dutch king did not accept the loss of Belgium until April 1839, his prolonged resistance being made possible by the refusal of the eastern courts to join in coercive measures against him. But by the end of 1831 the Belgian dispute had ceased to constitute a diplomatic problem, although there was a flurry of indignation in December 1832 when an Anglo-French force bombarded the citadel of Antwerp and forced the Dutch to surrender that stronghold to the Belgian king.

The successful avoidance of war during this crisis had been possible, in the first instance, because of the determined collaboration of Britain and France, and it is not too much to say that the *entente cordiale*, which was to last, with some interruptions, until the very eve of the revolutions of 1848, was consummated in the negotiations of 1830 and 1831. At the same time, the limitations of that *entente* were clearly set forth by Palmerston in his frequent warnings to Paris; and it was unfortunate for the July Monarchy, in another crisis ten years later, that its statesmen did not remember Palmerston's conduct in the Belgian dispute. As for the eastern powers, they quite clearly regarded the separation of the Low Countries as a dangerous weakening of the barrier against France. Distracted by troubles in their border districts, however, they could not act to support their opinions, and, in the end, they decided that concerted action with Britain and France was preferable to a solution imposed by the western powers alone. The disagreeable necessity which confronted them was probably eased by Palmerston's constant disavowal of partisan or national objectives and his ability to portray conference decisions as actions taken 'for European objects and to maintain peace and preserve the balance of power'.[1]

The acquiescence of the eastern powers was doubtless influenced also, however, by the restraint displayed by Britain and France in the Italian and Polish affairs. During the troubles in Italy which followed the risings in Parma, Modena and the Romagna in 1831[2] there were many heated parliamentary speeches and not a few incautious ministerial pronouncements in Paris; but in the end the Casimir Périer government decided that support of the revolutionaries was inexpedient and that—in view of Metternich's determination to restore order in the Peninsula—insistence upon the principle of non-intervention would be dangerous. In this

[1] C. K. Webster, *The Foreign Policy of Palmerston, 1830–1841* (London, 1951), vol. I, p. 158.
[2] Cf. ch. XXI, pp. 553–4.

policy of caution the French were encouraged by the British government; and Metternich was permitted to carry out his police action without serious opposition. Similarly, in the Polish question, although Louis Philippe considered the possibility of mediation between the tsar and the rebels, he was dissuaded by Palmerston, who took his stand on the treaties of 1815, refused to give more than formal sympathy to the Polish cause and won the praise of the wife of Russia's ambassador in London for his 'very loyal conduct towards Russia during the struggle in Poland'.[1] The prudent behaviour of the western powers had the effect of diminishing the latent hostility of the two European groups; and it is interesting to note that in October 1831 an ambassadorial conference in Paris could agree on a protocol which recommended a general reduction of European armaments and spoke in glowing terms of the 'happy restoration of agreement among the Powers'.[2]

These signs of reconciliation were, however, misleading, and, in the course of 1832 and 1833, the gulf between the eastern and western powers widened sharply. The measures adopted by the tsar to punish the Poles (see chs. IX and XIV) angered public opinion in the West; and Metternich's encouragement of the repressive measures adopted by the lesser German courts in their campaign against political agitation contributed to the same result. Simultaneously, the dispatching of a French army of observation to Ancona in Italy in 1832 awakened all of Metternich's suspicions of France's desire for aggrandisement. But perhaps the most important factor in dividing Europe into two opposed camps was the turn of events in the Near East (see ch. XVI, p. 428).

In the latter part of 1831 Mehemet Ali, the pasha of Egypt, who had long aspired to extend his control over Palestine, Syria and Arabia, manufactured a dispute with the pasha of Lebanon and sent an army under his son Ibrahim to invest Acre. Sultan Mahmud II, after trying vainly to adjudicate the quarrel, declared Mehemet a rebel and set out to crush him. In the subsequent campaigns, however, which lasted throughout 1832, his forces suffered a series of disastrous defeats; and by December the Egyptians were threatening to overrun all Asia Minor and to take Constantinople itself.

The Egyptian advance was a matter of concern to all powers with interests in the Levant; and the Austrian government for one—regarding Mehemet Ali simply as a rebel who must be suppressed—sought to promote collective action by the powers to preserve the integrity of the Ottoman empire. Metternich's attempts in this direction, however, aroused no enthusiasm in Paris, where the government enjoyed cordial relations with Mehemet and was more interested in mediation between

[1] Bell, *Palmerston*, vol. I, p. 169.
[2] Alfred Stern, *Geschichte Europas seit den Verträgen von 1815 bis zum Frankfurter Frieden von 1871* (Stuttgart, 1905), vol. IV, pp. 223–5.

the sultan and his vassal than in any coercive action; and, while they were received more warmly in London, they had no tangible effect there either. At this stage in his career, Palmerston was still undecided concerning the policy best designed to promote British interests in the Near East, and, while he was inclined to agree that collective action was desirable, he wished London rather than Vienna to be the centre of conversations between the great powers, a condition that was quite unacceptable to Metternich, who always longed to restore Vienna as the diplomatic capital of Europe.[1]

While the unrewarding discussions between Vienna and London were proceeding, the sultan, in his extremity, turned to Russia for aid; and, in February 1833, to the dismay of the western powers, Russian troops disembarked on the shores of the Bosporus and the Russian fleet anchored at Constantinople. This Russian intervention was the decisive factor in effecting peace between the belligerents in May, on terms that left Mehemet Ali in possession of Syria, Adana and Tarsus. But the Russian action had an even more alarming result. Before the tsar's forces withdrew, a new treaty was signed between Turkey and Russia at Unkiar Skelessi on 8 July 1833. This document, while confirming existing treaties between the two powers, announced that for eight years Russia and Turkey would be mutually bound to defend each other's dominions in the event of aggression from without. By a separate article, however, Turkey was freed from the obligation of sending naval and military aid to Russia in time of war, provided she would close the Dardanelles to armed vessels, 'not allowing any foreign vessels to enter therein on any pretext whatever'.

Unkiar Skelessi provided a European sensation, since it appeared to give Russia a preferential position at the Porte. In London, Palmerston professed publicly to be scornful of the document, but he joined with France in a spirited but fruitless attempt to prevent ratification of the treaty, and there can be little doubt that he feared that it would make Turkey a Russian satellite or promote her speedy partition. At the same time, he was furiously indignant with Metternich, accusing him of having been privy to the tsar's intentions and of having misled the British government. This was perhaps unjust, since the evidence seems to indicate that the treaty was an unpleasant surprise to Vienna.[2] But western suspicion of Austrian and Russian policy was now fully inflamed, and received apparent confirmation in September 1833 when Nicholas met the Emperor Francis and Metternich at Münchengrätz. At this meeting, the tsar apparently sought to reassure the Austrians concerning his intentions in the Near East, but the talks covered other subjects as well. Before they were finished, the eastern partners had agreed on future measures of repression

[1] Webster, *Palmerston*, vol. I, pp. 290, 296–9, 300.
[2] *Ibid.* pp. 306, 310. See, however, G. H. Bolsover, 'Lord Ponsonby', *Slavonic Review*, vol. XIII (1934–5), p. 102 and note 31.

to be employed against the Poles and the German liberals, and they had concluded a formal alliance which recognised the right of any sovereign to summon the aid of the eastern powers if threatened by revolution. This pronouncement seemed to herald a new offensive against the liberal west, and the British and French governments drew together to oppose it.

They found an opportunity to make an effective rejoinder in the Iberian Peninsula. It is unnecessary here to go deeply into the political complications of the Iberian countries; but it can be noted briefly that, since 1831, Britain and France had been lending encouragement and disguised military aid to the efforts of the young Portuguese queen Maria to regain her throne, which had been seized in 1828 by her uncle Dom Miguel. In July 1833—roughly at the same time that the Russians were negotiating the Treaty of Unkiar Skelessi—a Portuguese fleet under the command of a British admiral captured the bulk of Miguel's naval forces and, a few weeks later, Maria's armies entered Lisbon and deposed him. Within a week of these events, King Ferdinand VII of Spain died, leaving the throne to his infant daughter, with his wife Christina as regent. This settlement was, however, immediately challenged by Ferdinand's brother, Don Carlos, who raised the standard of revolt and joined forces with the Portuguese pretender, Dom Miguel. Since Pedro and Miguel were both men of unrelieved reactionary views, and since they enjoyed the sympathy of Metternich, the young queens became perforce identified, in the popular mind, with the cause of liberalism, although there was little in their politics to justify this.

In any event the French and British governments extended their protective mantle over the Spanish queen, as over the Portuguese; and Palmerston decided to use this popular cause as the basis for a diplomatic gesture designed to answer, and defy, the pronouncements of Unkiar Skelessi and Münchengrätz. Thanks to his initiative, Britain and France in April 1834 converted their understanding with the two queens into a Quadruple Alliance, which dramatically set forth the western powers' intention of preventing the application of Metternich's theory of intervention in the peninsula. This, Palmerston boasted, would 'serve as a powerful counterpoise to the Holy Alliance of the East', for 'the moral effect in Europe of a formal union of the four constitutional states of the West...must be by no means inconsiderable'.[1]

This combination did have the happy effect of discouraging adventures by other powers in Spain and Portugal, and although disorders and civil war continued for years, the cause of the queens was ultimately triumphant. The Quadruple Alliance seemed also to confirm that rigid division of Europe between east and west which had first become apparent in 1830. In actuality, however, the fluidity that characterised the diplomatic alignments of this period continued. The Anglo-French *entente*, for

[1] Webster, *Palmerston*, vol. I, p. 397.

instance, was much less intimate than enthusiasts for the Quadruple Alliance supposed. Indeed, within a month of the signature of that alliance Louis Philippe was closeted with Prince Esterhazy, the confidant of Metternich, and was suggesting that he had adhered to the alliance reluctantly and that he would be better pleased by a permanent arrangement with Austria.

This *démarche* of the king's, which he was to repeat periodically for the next five years—although never receiving the encouragement he desired—was doubtless animated by his growing conservatism and by his keen desire to be accepted as an equal by his royal colleagues on the Continent. But Louis Philippe was not alone in his growing dislike of the Anglo-French *entente*. The basic weakness of that combination, as Raymond Guyot has pointed out in *La première entente cordiale*, was that there was no real community of economic interest between the two nations. French industrialists complained angrily about the menace of British competition and demanded tariff schedules which were received with dismay and indignation across the Channel. British and French trading interests fought bitterly in Greece and in Spain and in more remote markets in Africa and the Pacific. These things inevitably affected the official relations of the two countries. In 1837 Palmerston was grumbling that the ruling motive in France was 'jealousy of the commercial prosperity of England and a desire to arrest the progress of that prosperity';[1] and, the following year, when tariff negotiations between the two countries failed to reach any tangible result, his ambassador in Paris warned the French government that 'two nations cannot continue to be united politically unless they are bound directly together by the bond of commercial affairs'.[2] The British Foreign Secretary continued to believe in the political advantages of union with France and reminded his envoys abroad that 'it is of great importance to us, not only to be well with the French government, but to appear to all Europe to be so';[3] but he was conscious both of the forces driving the two countries apart and of the manœuvres of the French king and realised that he might have to revise his attitude toward the eastern powers at any time.

These disruptive tendencies in the *entente*—and the fact that they were not entirely unappreciated in the eastern capitals—had a marked effect upon the alignment of the powers during the Near Eastern crisis of 1839 and 1840. This affair, like the earlier one of 1833, had its origins in the ambitions of Mehemet Ali, who clearly regarded his settlement of 1833 with the sultan as a mere truce and who, in May 1838, told the consuls in Alexandria that he meant to declare his independence. Sultan Mahmud, on his part, was eager to settle the old score with Mehemet, and it was, in fact, Mahmud who took the initiative in opening hostilities in April

[1] Webster, *Palmerston*, vol. i, p. 455.   [2] Guyot, *Entente cordiale* (Paris, 1926), p. 149.
[3] Webster, *op. cit.* vol. i, p. 414.

1839. The sultan's forces, however, were no more effective in their new campaign than they had been previously. In June, the flower of Mahmud's army was routed at Nezib; in July the whole of his fleet deserted to the enemy; and at the end of the year Mehemet Ali seemed once more to be in a position to make of the Ottoman empire what he pleased.

Long before this dangerous stage had been reached, the great powers had begun to move. In London, for instance, Palmerston betrayed none of the indecision which had marked his conduct in the earlier crisis. Between 1833 and 1839 successful experiments in steam navigation both on the Red Sea and the Euphrates had greatly enhanced the importance of the overland routes to India in British eyes, and this fact had strengthened Palmerston's determination that neither Russia nor Mehemet Ali, whom he came to regard increasingly as a client of France, should be allowed to dominate them. As the outbreak of hostilities neared, it was his desire to arrange a concerted *démarche* of the powers which would not only check the Egyptian pasha but would replace the Treaty of Unkiar Skelessi with a general guarantee of Turkish integrity. In the late spring of 1838 and throughout the summer months he strove to persuade the other powers that it was necessary to concert a policy before an act of aggression should be committed. Both the Austrians and the French seemed ready to co-operate, but Palmerston received no encouragement from St Petersburg. With his customary forthrightness, he bombarded the Russian capital with notes, on one occasion going so far as to warn that 'Europe never would endure that the matter should be settled by the single independent and self-regulated interference of any one power', a clear intimation that Britain would resist unilateral action taken on the basis of the Treaty of Unkiar Skelessi. After reading this despatch to Nesselrode, the British ambassador reported that that minister had answered that Russia regarded Unkiar Skelessi more as a burden than as anything else.[1] Russia remained, however, unresponsive to all suggestions of a '*concert préalable*' throughout the year 1838.[2]

Once the fighting had begun it was Metternich who seized the initiative, seeing once more an opportunity of drawing the European Concert to Vienna. In May 1839 he began talks with the four ambassadors in Vienna and established what was in fact a continuing conference on the eastern crisis. It was this body which—after the crushing defeats suffered by the sultan's forces in June and July—despatched the instructions that formed the basis of the famous collective note of 27 July, presented to the sultan by the representatives of the five powers in Constantinople, informing him that the powers were preparing to intervene and urging him to make no concessions to Mehemet Ali until they had made their

[1] *Ibid.* vol. II, pp. 592–5.
[2] See Philip E. Mosely, *Russian Diplomacy and the Opening of the Eastern Question* (Cambridge, Mass., 1934), pp. 67–92.

wishes known. Metternich's prompt action doubtless heartened the Turkish government, at a time when it was shaken by military disaster and by the sudden death of Mahmud II, and encouraged it to continue its resistance. But it led also to a surprising move on the part of the tsar. For, at the beginning of August, Nicholas made it clear that the collective *démarche* had been made without his approval and that, while accepting it, he utterly rejected the suggestion that Vienna should be the centre of future discussions on the eastern question. This news, and the tsar's apparent anger at Austria's participation in what he seemed to regard as an anti-Russian demonstration, was an overwhelming disappointment to Metternich and, suffering from what appeared to be complete nervous collapse, he retired to his estates.

Nicholas, however, had no desire to play a lone hand in the Near East. He was impressed by the British warnings of the previous year, and realised that unilateral action on his part might precipitate war with Great Britain. Moreover—as Nesselrode had already intimated—he had come to regard Unkiar Skelessi as a burdensome arrangement and one which the Turks themselves would repudiate if they were assured of British support; and, in the circumstances, he was prepared to abandon it in favour of any arrangement which would retain that closure of the Straits which was so advantageous to Russian interests. Finally, the tsar saw an opportunity of driving a wedge between Britain and France and of isolating the country which he persisted in regarding as the chief breeding ground of revolution and disaffection in Europe. Accordingly, in September 1839 he sent one of his ablest diplomatists, Baron Brunnov, to London to convince Palmerston of Russia's willingness to co-operate in finding a method of stopping Mehemet Ali and maintaining the integrity of the Turkish empire.

In Palmerston's eyes Russia's willingness to give up Unkiar Skelessi outweighed all other considerations; and he and the Russian envoy had little trouble in framing the outlines of a Near Eastern settlement which provided for coercive action to force Mehemet Ali to give up most of his gains and—once hostilities were terminated—for an international agreement closing both the Bosporus and the Dardanelles to the warships of all powers. As Palmerston and Brunnov neared agreement, the Austrian and Prussian envoys in London secured the right to participate in the talks and indicated that their governments would support the terms agreed on. At the same time, Palmerston loyally communicated the substance of the conversations to the French ambassador, hoping to secure French collaboration in the projected intervention of the powers.

His wishes in this regard were not, however, satisfied. French public opinion was enthusiastic about Mehemet Ali's military victories and neither the Soult government nor the Thiers government which succeeded it in March 1840 was willing to antagonise boulevard sentiment by depriving the Egyptian pasha of his gains. Thiers, moreover, refused to believe that the other powers could unite in effective coercive measures against Mehemet, and he was encouraged by Francophil elements in England—some of them close to the cabinet—to believe that England would never abandon France. He therefore resisted all proposals from the Foreign Office.

Conversations between the great powers and debates within the British cabinet continued throughout the first six months of 1840. Palmerston, however, was now determined that, if France would not co-operate, it was important 'for the interests of England, the preservation of the balance of power and the maintenance of peace in Europe' that the other powers act without her. If they failed to do so, he argued, Russia might renew the Treaty of Unkiar Skelessi; and the result would be 'the practical division of Turkey into two separate states—one the dependency of France and the other a satellite of Russia, in both of which our political influence will be annulled and our commercial interests sacrificed'.[1] The Foreign Secretary made it clear to his cabinet colleagues that, unless his views were accepted, he would resign, an event which would certainly have precipitated the fall of the Whig government. In the end he had his way and, on 15 July 1840, was able to sign a Quadruple Agreement with the representatives of the eastern powers.

This agreement, which was based on the terms already agreed to by Palmerston and Brunnov, was the decisive turning point in the Near Eastern crisis; and it is unnecessary here to go into details concerning the manner in which the four powers executed it and forced Mehemet Ali to retire to his Egyptian dominions. It should be noted, however, that for three months after the conclusion of the Agreement the peace of Europe hung in the balance, for public opinion in Paris was exasperated by the isolation of France, and there was angry talk of war against England and—rather illogically—of an assault across the Rhine. The situation was aggravated by Thiers' reluctance to face facts and withdraw from a position which was untenable, by Palmerston's indifference to the susceptibilities of his former allies[2] and by the sultan's desire to use the support of the powers to crush Mehemet Ali utterly and to force his deposition. The fall of the Thiers government in October, however, and some skilful diplomacy on the part of Metternich, which forced the dismissal of the sultan's more intransigent advisers, alleviated the tension and opened the way for a settlement which returned to the sultan what he had lost in 1833, while leaving Mehemet Ali secure in Egypt.

Before the crisis was completely liquidated there were manœuvres on the part of single powers which throw some interesting light on the nature

---

[1] Seton-Watson, *Britain in Europe*, p. 205.
[2] Webster (*Palmerston*, vol. II, pp. 695–737) has nothing but admiration for his subject's tactics. See, however, Seton-Watson, *Britain in Europe*, pp. 213, 220–2.

of the European alliance system in the first half of the nineteenth century. Late in 1840, for instance, Nicholas I asked the British ambassador whether Great Britain would 'object to record and establish by some act the alliance which...happily existed between the four Powers to serve as a security against any efforts that France might make to awaken revolutionary feelings in Europe, or against, perhaps, a revolutionary war'.[1] This invitation to formalise the isolation of France by written or verbal agreement was embarrassing; and Palmerston hastened to decline it. This he did in a courteous dispatch in which—while emphasising Britain's intention of continuing 'to watch attentively and to guard with care the maintenance of the Balance of Power', and while stating that 'an attempt of one nation to appropriate to itself territory which belongs to another nation' would constitute 'a derangement of the existing balance'—he explained the constitutional difficulties which prevented the British government from entering into 'engagements with reference to cases which have not actually arisen'.[2]

It is instructive to note that, while this exchange was taking place, Metternich was working at cross-purposes with the tsar. The Austrian chancellor had never been entirely happy about the agreement of July 1840, and he seems to have suspected both Palmerston and the tsar of desiring war with France. To prevent that, Metternich's biographer has written, 'he was determined if the worst came to the worst to secede from the concert of July, to draw Prussia with him and to conclude a separate agreement with France'.[3] Metternich was never forced to go that far; but throughout the critical months he used his influence at London and Paris and at Constantinople and Alexandria to promote moderate solutions; and if France was able to find her way back to the concert and to give her assent to the so-called Straits Convention of 13 July 1841 which terminated the long crisis, this was due in large part to the success with which Metternich, aided by the Prussians, mediated between her and the other powers.

Palmerston's willingness to turn against France in the Near Eastern crisis of 1839–40 and Metternich's policy in the last stages of that crisis reveal how little the ideological differences of the powers were apt to influence their attitudes when issues arose which affected their interests, or the maintenance of peace and the balance of power. It is not too much to say that, by the 1840's, the division between the 'liberal powers' and the 'reactionary powers' had broken down completely. Certainly in the years that followed the eastern settlement Britain's official relations with Russia and France's official relations with Austria seem on the whole

---

[1] Clanricarde to Palmerston, 22 December 1840. Quoted in F. S. Rodkey, 'Anglo-Russian Negotiations about a "Permanent" Quadruple Alliance', *American Historical Review*, vol. XXXVI (1930–1), p. 343.

[2] Palmerston to Clanricarde, 11 January 1841. *Ibid.* pp. 345–6.

[3] Srbik, *Metternich*, vol. II, p. 80.

to have been more untroubled than the relations of the western powers with each other. It is true that between 1841 and 1846, when Peel was Prime Minister in England and Lord Aberdeen was at the Foreign Office, every effort was made to restore the *entente cordiale* with France. But despite the close relations between Aberdeen and Guizot, who was Louis Philippe's chief minister in these years, the two countries were involved almost continuously in contention. A dispute between British and French missionaries in Tahiti led to bitter exchanges between the London and Paris press in 1842; rivalry between the two countries' diplomatic representatives in Greece caused relations to deteriorate to a point where the French king complained to the Austrian ambassador in Paris of 'the unfortunate tendency of the British government at all times to support revolutions and thus disturb the peace of Europe';[1] and finally, shortly after Palmerston's return to the Foreign Office in 1846, the *entente* broke down completely in a wave of British indignation over the marriage of Louis Philippe's son, the duc de Montpensier, to the Spanish Infanta, a marriage which appeared to violate previous French promises and to threaten a French hegemony in the Peninsula.

Fully aware of the political disadvantages of isolation, the French government redoubled its efforts to reach an understanding with Austria. In May 1847 Guizot sent a special agent to Vienna to conduct negotiations with Metternich; and, when this *démarche* was accepted with cordiality, he followed it up with a letter in which he wrote: 'France is now disposed and suited to a policy of conservatism. She has long attained her objects and occupied her place....A policy of *entente* is therefore natural to us and founded on the facts.'[2] Metternich was at this time preoccupied with the upsurge of revolutionary agitation in Germany, in Switzerland and, especially, in Italy (see chs. XIX and XXI); and, although he was never entirely convinced of the genuineness of the French conversion to conservatism,[3] he welcomed a collaboration which might be used to protect the Vienna settlement from the troubles rising against it. Thus, the new *entente* came into being, although—as events were to prove—too late to have an effect upon the course of European developments.

Meanwhile Anglo-Russian relations had become more friendly than they had been since the days of the alliance against Napoleon. The tsar had not been rebuffed by Palmerston's answer to his proposals of alliance in 1840 and he persisted in his efforts to secure British friendship. In 1844, indeed, he paid a visit to England, talked with Peel and Aberdeen about the state of Turkey, assured them that he would do everything in his power to maintain the *status quo* and urged them to consider the necessity of an Anglo-Russian understanding concerning the policy to be followed if that

---

[1] Seton-Watson, *Britain in Europe*, p. 235.
[2] A. J. P. Taylor, *The Italian Problem in European Diplomacy, 1847–1849* (Manchester, 1934), p. 25.   [3] *Ibid.*

proved to be impossible. Apart from this, he insisted that there was no reason for the hostility which had existed between the two countries in the past. 'Years ago,' he said to Peel, 'Lord Durham was sent to me, a man full of prejudices against me. Merely by contact with me, his prejudices were all driven to the winds. And that is what I hope to bring about with you, and generally in England. I hope to dissipate those prejudices by personal intercourse.'[1]

Professor Seton-Watson has suggested[2] that, if the personal contact established by the tsar during this visit had been maintained, the misunderstandings which led to the Crimean War in 1854 might have been averted. This is a hypothesis which it is, of course, impossible to prove. There can be no doubt, however, that the new *rapprochement* between Russia and Great Britain was a more effective diplomatic combination than the tentative *entente* between Austria and France and that it was instrumental in preserving the balance of power and the general peace during the storm that now descended on Europe.

The revolutions of 1848 (ch. xv) were the most serious threat that had yet developed to the treaty structure and the balance of power that had been established in 1815. The paralysis of Austria and Prussia, the sudden transformation of France from a liberal-conservative monarchy to a radical republic, and the awakening of the national aspirations of the peoples of Italy, Germany, Hungary, Poland and Schleswig-Holstein opened a dismal prospect to the two powers on Europe's periphery, and it is not surprising that they should have felt a common interest in preventing, as far as possible, the chaos and disruption that they feared. Shortly after receiving the news of the revolutions in Vienna and Berlin, Nicholas was writing to Queen Victoria and arguing that only the 'intimate union' of Russia and Britain could 'save the world';[3] and, in answer to a similar communication from Nesselrode, Palmerston wrote on 11 April 1848 to his ambassador: 'Assure Count Nesselrode that our feelings and sentiments towards Russia are exactly similar to those which he expresses to you towards England. We are at present the only two Powers in Europe (excepting always Belgium) that remain standing upright, and we ought to look with confidence to each other.'[4]

It would perhaps be an exaggeration to speak in terms of Anglo-Russian co-operation during the revolutionary disturbances, for the two powers

[1] *Memoirs of Baron Stockmar*, ed. by F. Max Müller (London, 1873), vol. ii, pp. 109–10. See also Vernon J. Puryear, *England, Russia and the Straits Question, 1844–56* (Berkeley, Cal., 1931), pp. 40–74.

[2] Seton-Watson, *Britain in Europe*, p. 236.

[3] *The Letters of Queen Victoria*, ed. by A. C. Benson and Viscount Esher (London, 1907), vol. ii, p. 196.

[4] Evelyn Ashley, *Life and Correspondence of Henry John Temple, Viscount Palmerston* (London, 1879), vol. ii, p. 79.

went their separate ways and were not always in complete harmony. But their objectives were similar; each desired to prevent the local disturbances from precipitating a general war which would upset the careful arrangements of 1815 and destroy the balance of power; and each was careful not to interfere with the methods used by the other to accomplish this end.

British policy, once more under the capable direction of Palmerston, was in the first instance inspired by the desire to restrain ambitious designs on the part of the new republican government in France. It is true that the Foreign Minister of that government, the poet Lamartine, had, as early as 27 February, declared that 'the republican form of government had neither changed the position of France in Europe, nor its loyal and sincere intentions of preserving friendly relations with the powers that wish, as she does, the independence of nations and the peace of the world'.[1] But on 4 March, in a long 'Manifesto to the Powers', he announced that 'the Treaties of 1815 legally no longer exist in the eyes of the French Republic', although he added in the same breath that 'their territorial clauses are a fact admitted by her as basis and starting point in relations with other nations' and, furthermore, that 'the French Republic will not start war against anyone'.[2]

Palmerston recognised in this curious effusion a desire to appease boulevard sentiment without committing France to dangerous adventures. The policy which he adopted—and which was in fact outlined before the 'Manifesto to the Powers'—was similar to that adopted in 1830: he would restrain Europe from attacking France provided France refrained from attacking Europe. The revolutions in Vienna and Berlin in March removed any possibility of a campaign against the new republic; but the attitude of friendship assumed from the outset by the British was not without effect in persuading the French government to exercise caution and moderation in the months that followed.

This was all the more important since there were other forces at work which sought to persuade the republic to participate in a general attack upon the *status quo*. The revolution of 18 March in Berlin, for instance, led certain German liberals, including Max von Gagern and the new Prussian Foreign Minister, Heinrich von Arnim, to conceive an elaborate plan whereby Prussia would take advantage of the rising of the Poles in Posen to liberate all of Poland, deliberately challenging Russia to a war and, in the enthusiasm which such a conflict would arouse, forging a new united Germany under Prussian leadership. The supporters of this project believed that Great Britain would preserve a benevolent neutrality while their designs were carried out; but they desired the aid and collaboration

---

[1] Alphonse de Lamartine, *Trois mois de pouvoir* (Paris, 1848), p. 68.
[2] *Ibid.* pp. 69 *et seq*. See L. B. Namier, '1848: The Revolution of the Intellectuals', *Proceedings of the British Academy*, vol. xxx (1944), pp. 35–6.

of France. Accordingly, on 23 March, Arnim invited the French government to join in a public declaration of alliance, the object of which would be to reconstruct Poland, and he asked further that France send a naval squadron into the Baltic whenever Prussia should consider it necessary.

This scheme—which is interesting primarily as an illustration of the dangerous possibilities inherent in the European situation at the time—came to nothing, in large part because of the restraint exercised by the tsar, who was careful to make no move which might give support to the German war party, and by the French government, which decided not to commit its fortunes to a Prussian government whose stability it distrusted. But the attitude of both Russia and France was probably influenced by the determined intervention of Palmerston in this affair. On 30 March Stratford Canning, passing through Berlin, had talked with Frederick William IV and with his new Foreign Minister; and the king had urged him to dissuade Arnim from plans which would certainly involve Prussia in war with Russia. Canning reported this to London, and Palmerston immediately despatched a stern warning to Berlin, urging the Prussian government 'to abstain from any proceeding which could justly be considered by Russia as aggressive'.[1] The tone of this despatch destroyed Arnim's illusions concerning Britain's benevolence towards his plans; and it seems also to have encouraged the king—who had until now been so cowed by the victory of revolution that the tsar had contemptuously labelled him 'the king of the streets'[2]—to take a firmer line with his ministers. By May, Frederick William was threatening to abdicate if any anti-Russian policy was adopted, and the Arnim scheme was dead.

A much more serious threat to the peace had meanwhile arisen in Italy, where, encouraged by the collapse of the Metternich regime, the populations of Lombardy and Venetia had risen in revolt and were being supported by the king of Sardinia, who aspired to be the liberator of Italy from Austrian domination. Here again Palmerston intervened as peacemaker, although his policy was less obviously successful and was never fully understood either by his sovereign or by his own party. Initially, his objective was to persuade the Austrian government to give up her Italian provinces, not because he had any enthusiasm for Italian unity, or because he wished to weaken the Austrian empire—indeed, he always maintained that a strong Austria was indispensable to the balance of power and the 'political independence and liberties of Europe'[3]—but rather because he was sure that Austria could not put down the disaffection in Italy and that an attempt to do so would invite French intervention and lead to war. In May and June the Austrian government was willing

---

[1] Namier, *loc. cit.* pp. 63–4.

[2] Heinrich Ritter von Srbik, *Deutsche Einheit* (Munich, 1935–42), vol. I, p. 331. See also Rudolf Stadelmann, *Soziale und politische Geschichte der Revolution von 1848* (Munich, 1948), pp. 55–6.

[3] See, for instance, Bell, *Palmerston*, vol. II, p. 14.

at least to discuss the possibility of freeing Lombardy, but the intransigence of the provisional government at Milan blocked any agreement; and, in July, the Austrian victory at Custoza and the forced evacuation of Lombardy by Piedmontese troops changed the situation radically. For both the Milanese government and that of Piedmont now began to consider a direct appeal for armed intervention by France—an event which would undoubtedly precipitate a general war.

The French government was not anxious to go to war, but, as General Cavaignac admitted, 'if...there came a popular appeal for assistance from the Italian people...no government established here would long be able to resist the demand'.[1] It was necessary, therefore, to find some substitute form of action which would be acceptable to French public opinion and which would make intervention unnecessary. This was now supplied by Palmerston who proposed joint Anglo-French mediation between Austria and Piedmont on the basis of a previous Austrian suggestion that Lombardy might be joined to Piedmont. The French government grasped this suggestion eagerly, and the crisis passed. Palmerston's association with France was later described by his sovereign as 'a most iniquitous proceeding', but it is clear that 'he had provided the French government with the only possible excuse for not going to war',[2] and there is much justification in his own boast in the House of Commons that the mediation had 'contributed to the maintenance of peace in Europe'.[3]

Apart from this, the joint mediation cannot be described as successful, for the Austrian government, now under the energetic leadership of Prince Felix Schwarzenberg, refused to make any concessions whatever and insisted not only on holding Lombardy but on instituting the most brutal of repressive measures in the rebellious province. In the circumstances, there was little that Palmerston could do but maintain his close association with France and hope that the disorders in Italy would come to an end as quickly as possible. Tension mounted once more in the spring of 1849, when the king of Piedmont was so misguided as to reopen his war with Austria and so unfortunate as to suffer another disastrous defeat at Novara. It was clear now that, if Austria imposed unreasonable terms upon the defeated sovereign, French intervention might yet become a possibility, despite the apparently pacific intentions of the new French president, Louis Napoleon. Palmerston, therefore, redoubled his efforts to make the Austrians see reason; and, since his personal relations with Schwarzenberg made objective discussion impossible, he instructed his ambassador in Paris to approach Baron Hübner, the Austrian leader's confidential agent, and to convince him that Britain's only desire was to see 'Italy pacified as soon as possible'.[4] This and the increasing activity of French agents in Italy helped to convince Schwarzenberg that it would

---

[1] Taylor, *The Italian Problem*, p. 138. [2] *Ibid.* p. 218.
[3] Hansard, 3rd series, vol. CII, p. 216. [4] Taylor, *The Italian Problem*, p. 230.

be wise not to humiliate Piedmont needlessly; and peace was finally signed at Milan in August 1849, ending the dangerous situation and restoring in Italy the territorial arrangements of 1815.

Throughout this affair Palmerston had acted with a studied disregard for Italian national aspirations; and his guiding motive had always been defence of the balance of power. This determined his attitude also in the face of events taking place in eastern Europe, and especially in Hungary, where the revolutionary government of Kossuth was attempting to assert its independence of Vienna. Whatever his private sympathies may have been for the rebels, Palmerston could not approve of a revolt which, if successful, would weaken Austria as the bulwark of order in central Europe, and he rejected all advances from Kossuth's representatives with the argument that he had 'no knowledge of Hungary except as one of the component parts of the Austrian Empire'.[1] The decisive role in restoring Hungary to order was played by the Russian government, which sent troops to the aid of Francis Joseph's armies. It is important to note, however—especially in view of Palmerston's spirited protests against Austrian persecution of the rebels once their cause was broken—that the British Foreign Secretary not only raised no objections to the original Russian intervention but actually encouraged it. In April 1849, indeed, he was telling the Russian ambassador in London that Russia must act in aid of Austria, but must then 'finish as quickly as possible', advice which Baron Brunnov correctly interpreted to mean that the British Foreign Secretary desired Russia to assume responsibility for maintaining the balance of power in eastern Europe.[2]

That Russia was fully prepared to do this is shown, not only by her role in the Hungarian revolt, but also by the policy she observed in German affairs in 1849 and 1850. Here the careful balance arranged in 1815, whereby the bulk of the German states were loosely organised in such a way as to serve as a buffer between the contiguous territories of the great powers, had been overthrown by the events of March 1848; and the assembly of liberal politicians at Frankfurt had striven manfully through the rest of that year to create a unified German empire out of the ruins of the old Germanic confederation. Their experiment had failed, because of the rapid recovery of Austria and Prussia and because of the Prussian king's scornful refusal, in April 1849, to accept the imperial crown which the Frankfurt Parliament had offered him (see ch. xv, p. 407). These events had reassured the tsar, who had no desire to see a united Germany on his western flank; but almost immediately he had cause for greater concern. For, on the basis of a plan conceived by Josef Maria von Radowitz, Frederick William IV attempted in 1849 to unite the German princes in a league under his leadership, a league, moreover, which would

---

[1] Charles Sproxton, *Palmerston and the Hungarian Revolution* (Cambridge, 1919), p. 46.
[2] Seton-Watson, *Britain in Europe*, p. 266.

exclude Austria from membership, while seeking friendly relations with her. The Austrian government, not unnaturally, objected to this project; throughout 1849, while it was still preoccupied with events in Italy and Hungary, it did everything in its power to sabotage Prussian negotiations with the other princes; and in 1850, Schwarzenberg, whose *Gewaltnatur*—as Friedjung has written—'drove him to decisions by force',[1] bluntly confronted Prussia with a choice between abandonment of the project or war.

The year 1850 was one of growing crisis between the two German great powers, and by late summer war seemed quite possible, for neither Schwarzenberg nor Radowitz was in a mood to back down. At this juncture in what was probably the most serious of the war threats produced by the revolutions of 1848, Russia intervened. In June the tsar warned Frederick William that changes in European treaties that were made without the approval of the co-signatories must be considered as acts of aggression;[2] and, after this almost classic definition of the balance-of-power philosophy, he threw his weight behind the Austrian objections. Whether the tsar's forces were capable of intervening effectively in an Austro-Prussian war is a doubtful question;[3] but there is no doubt that the tsar's stand was decisive. It gave the reactionary court party in Berlin additional arguments with which to convince the king to jettison Radowitz and his plan; and, at Olmütz in November 1850, Prussia capitulated to Austrian demands and allowed the German settlement of 1815 to be restored.

In the solution of this question Great Britain played no part. In the last troublesome international complication to arise from the revolutions, however, the British government took the lead, with the tacit approval of Russia, in promoting a settlement designed to leave the balance of power undisturbed. This was the protracted dispute caused by the revolt of the duchies of Schleswig and Holstein against the Danish crown and by the subsequent intervention of Prussian and German Federal troops in their behalf. As early as June 1848 Nesselrode and Palmerston agreed that they had no desire to see the balance of forces in the Baltic disturbed by a German victory; and, although it meant opposing liberal sentiment in Germany and the duchies, Palmerston undertook the difficult task of mediation, as the best means of avoiding the possibility of a Russo-Prussian war. Two years of incessant negotiation, with three spells of fighting and three armistices, had passed before the Prussian king was persuaded to sign a treaty which, in accordance with British and Russian desires, restored the *status quo*; and even when that result had been achieved the British and Russian governments felt it advisable to seek a definitive

[1] Heinrich Friedjung, *Oesterreich von 1848 bis 1860* (Stuttgart, 1908 and 1912), vol. II, pp. 30–1.
[2] Leopold von Gerlach, *Denkwürdigkeiten* (Berlin, 1892), vol. I, p. 491.
[3] See, for instance, Theodor Schiemann, *Geschichte Russlands unter Kaiser Nikolaus I*, vol. IV, pp. 226–32.

settlement of the status of the duchies in a Five Power Conference which met in London in 1851 and 1852.

That conference is not without significance, for it was the last successful meeting of the Concert of Europe in the long period of peace which had begun in 1815. Only two years after it had completed its labours, war came at last between the great powers, and, when it came, forces were released which eventually destroyed that balance of power which had been so jealously guarded by Russia and Great Britain during the revolutionary years.

In view of the number and the nature of the crises which filled the years from 1830 to 1854, it may seem surprising that this was a period of continual peace. It has been suggested above that this was partly due to the very nature of the system of diplomatic alignments, to that fluidity which enabled single powers to shift their position and their influence at crucial moments when war threatened. Yet the more one contemplates the changing combinations of the period, the more one is apt to be impressed by other factors which made this fluidity possible, and indeed necessary. The truth of the matter seems to be that, despite the deep ideological divisions of the powers, there was a remarkable consensus of opinion among them.

With the exception of France, who seldom dared admit her uniqueness, all powers accepted the balance of power: that is to say, they accepted the territorial arrangements laid down at Vienna in 1815 and they agreed with the broader principle that no state should obtain aggrandisement without the consent of the others. Acceptance of the balance, moreover, implied certain other things. It implied a high degree of restraint on the part of single powers; it implied a respect for existing treaties; and it implied a willingness—in moments when members of the system were led by ambition or indiscretion to seek unilateral aggrandisement—to participate in concerted action to restrain them.

In their dealings with each other in the pre-Crimean period, the great powers observed these rules of behaviour. There can be little doubt that open support of the Polish rebels in 1830 or of the kingdom of Piedmont in 1848 would have been accepted with enthusiasm by liberal opinion in France and England; but the governments of the two countries preferred to refrain from policies which might have embroiled the whole European system. It is possible that the tsar could, without serious opposition from the other powers, have exacted a higher price for his aid to Turkey in 1833, but Nicholas always shrank back from anything that could be regarded as unilateral aggrandisement and, if he thought of the dismemberment of the Ottoman empire, he always did so in terms of equitable partition among the powers, based on prior agreement among them. Throughout this period, also, treaties were accorded a degree of respect which they have not enjoyed in more recent years; and the most striking feature of the dispute over the occupation of the Republic of Cracow by Austria in 1846 is the surprised indignation with which this action was greeted by European opinion in general and the frantic efforts made by Metternich to compose legal arguments with which to justify it.[1]

Finally, there was a general willingness on the part of the powers to participate in efforts to maintain peace and the balance of power. This is especially notable in the case of Great Britain, whose geographical position and world-wide interests made her connection with the European system more tenuous than that of the continental states and who had, in the 1820's, seceded from the conference system established in 1814 and 1815. Yet, even at the moment of that secession, Castlereagh had expressed Britain's readiness to play her part in European affairs when the balance of power was threatened; and this promise was reiterated, and acted upon, continually in the years 1830–54. The essential nature of Great Britain's tie with the continental system was clearly recognized in Palmerston's note to the tsar in January 1841; and it was defined again in 1852 by Lord John Russell when he said in the House of Commons:

We are connected, and have been for more than a century, with the general system of Europe, and any territorial increase of one Power, any aggrandisement which disturbs the general balance of power in Europe, although it might not immediately lead to war, could not be a matter of indifference to this country and would, no doubt, be the subject of conference, and might ultimately, if that balance was seriously threatened, lead to war.[2]

National self-restraint, respect for the public law as defined in treaties, and willingness to enforce its observance by concerted action were, then, the conditions which made possible the maintenance of peace and the balance of power in the period 1830–54. The most notable thing about the Crimean War which broke out in 1854 was that it destroyed those conditions.

The origins and the course of the Crimean War are discussed elsewhere in this volume (ch. XVIII) and may be passed over here. Yet it is important to note that that curious conflict marks a significant turning point in European history. Behind it lay forty years of peace; before it stretched fifteen years in which four wars were fought by the great powers of Europe, with the result that the territorial arrangements of the Continent were completely transformed.

That this was true was due primarily to the fact that the Crimean War destroyed the old consensus that had existed between the powers and radically changed their attitude toward the existing distribution of forces on the Continent. As an American historian has written, 'there remained

---

[1] Metternich, *Nachgelassene Papiere*, ed. by Richard Metternich-Winneburg (Vienna, 1880–4), vol. VII, pp. 276 *et seq.*   [2] Hansard, 3rd series, vol. CXIX, p. 552.

in 1857 no great political force irretrievably committed to the preservation of things as they then stood'.[1] In the case of France, the war had released her ruler from the inhibitions from which he had suffered, or the restraints which he had observed, in his early years of power. In 1853 Napoleon III had referred to himself as 'a man carried by the force of a new principle to the exalted level of the old dynasties'. The new principle was that of the plebiscite but beyond this was the principle of nationalities;[2] and, when his victories in the east had confirmed his popularity and his power, Napoleon became increasingly intent upon securing a general rearrangement of the map upon national lines. In the case of Austria, whose very existence was bound up with the maintenance of the 1815 settlement, new and dangerous tendencies were also apparent. Conscious of the universal indignation and distrust which Austrian diplomacy during the war had inspired in the other courts, and perhaps fearing reprisals, the Austrian government increased its efforts to consolidate its position and influence in Germany, using methods which were in complete violation of the practices of collaboration with Prussia which had been honoured since 1815 and undermining the foundations of the federal system which it had been at such pains to restore in 1850. And Prussia, too, was left feeling insecure at the end of the war and, because insecure, more inclined to consider the advantages of an adventurous foreign policy. This feeling was encouraged by the reluctance with which the other powers had invited Prussian participation in the peace conference at Paris in 1856, a reluctance which seemed to reflect doubts concerning Prussia's right to be considered a great power; it was encouraged by Austrian tactics in the German confederation; and it was encouraged most of all by a growing disinclination on the part of the liberal opposition in Prussia to support an army unless that army were employed to solve the German question. Not until 1862 did the leader appear who was to transform Prussia from an upholder to an opponent of the old balance of power, but the forces which were to determine Bismarck's policy were already at work and, even in 1856, he was writing: 'In the not too distant future, we shall have to fight for our existence against Austria and...it is not within our power to avoid that, since the course of events in Germany has no other solution.'[3]

But the most striking effect of the Crimean War in changing the attitude of the powers towards the existing order is to be seen in the case of the two powers who had been the staunchest defenders of the balance of power and who, indeed, when the revolutions of 1848 had prostrated Europe, had maintained it by their joint efforts. The damage inflicted by the war in Russia and the grave need for internal reforms in the Russian empire convinced statesmen in St Petersburg that the active foreign policy of the

[1] R. C. Binkley, *Realism and Nationalism 1852–71* (New York, 1935), p. 179.
[2] *Ibid.* p. 165.
[3] Bismarck, *Die gesammelten Werke* (2nd edn, Berlin, 1924 *et seq.*), vol. II, p. 142.

past must, at least temporarily, be discontinued. Nesselrode, now at the end of his long career, admitted this when he spoke of 'the almost absolute necessity of devoting ourselves to domestic matters and the development of our moral and material resources'.[1] This in itself was a significant change, for under Nicholas I Russia had been the strong support of the existing treaty structure, and she had, moreover, by her close association with Austria and Prussia, prevented the German dualism from degenerating into open antagonism and war. The projected change in Russian policy, then, clearly threatened to weaken the cause of European order.

The Russian government, however, was now less willing to support that order. Humiliated by her defeat in the war and, even more, by the loss of Bessarabia and of her rights upon the Black Sea, Russia had in fact become a revisionist power; and for the next fifteen years the new emperor, Alexander II, had only one objective in foreign policy: to free his country from the shameful conditions imposed by the Peace of Paris in 1856. The weakness of the country and the pressure of internal events made any immediate attempt to achieve this end impossible—Russia's policy was perforce that described in 1856 by Nesselrode's successor, Gorchakov, in the words: 'Russia is not sulking; she is silently biding her time'[2]—but the objective was not lost to view. Indeed, it produced a new strain of opportunism in Russian policy, for Russian statesmen were willing now to consider agreements with other revisionist powers, who promised to support Russia's Black Sea claims if she would not interfere with their designs elsewhere.

The existing balance of power and the public law of Europe were jeopardised also by a growing tendency on the part of Great Britain to withdraw from continental troubles. For the English people the Crimean War had been a frustrating and inconclusive conflict which had brought little glory to British arms. In the period that followed there was a general desire to avoid risks that might lead to a new conflict. This did not mean, immediately, that Britain would abstain from intervention in continental disputes. Indeed, it was generally believed that her position as a great power implied a moral obligation to make her opinion known in European affairs. As Tennyson had written:

> As long as we remain we must speak free
> Though all the storm of Europe o'er us break.
> No little German state are we
> But the one voice of Europe; we must speak.[3]

Unfortunately, it proved difficult to base an effective foreign policy upon a desire to avoid risks and an insistence upon the right to preach to Europe;

[1] *Lettres et Papiers du Chancelier Comte de Nesselrode*, vol. XI, p. 112, cit. Christian Friese, *Russland und Preussen vom Krimkrieg bis zum Polnischen Aufstand* (Berlin, 1931), p. 11.
[2] Friese, *Russland und Preussen*, p. 23.   [3] 'The Third of February, 1852.'

firmness of purpose was hard to maintain when 'conscience and reason [were] at internal war';[1] and Europe was soon diverted by the spectacle of British statesmen taking determined, and even belligerent, positions in diplomatic crises and then retreating precipitately and awkwardly when serious resistance developed. This was especially notable during the Polish revolt of 1863 and the German attack upon Denmark in 1864 (see ch. XIX, p. 515), and Britain's policy of 'menaces never accomplished and promises never fulfilled'[2] in those crises weakened both her reputation and her influence.

This was clearly realised in England itself and, in 1864 in a notable debate in the House of Commons, representatives of all parties joined in attacking the principles which had animated Palmerston's diplomacy since 1830. While the Radicals, led by Richard Cobden, urged that the time had come to apply the philosophy of *laissez-faire* to foreign policy, the Tories argued that Britain's national interest lay overseas rather than in Europe and that the theory of the balance of power was 'founded on the obsolete traditions of an antiquated system'.[3]

There was general agreement at the end of this debate that Britain must base her policy exclusively on the principle of non-intervention, and this, indeed, became the shibboleth of all ministries between 1865 and 1870. But this was not the non-intervention enunciated by Castlereagh and practised by Canning and Palmerston, in accordance with which Britain would refrain from intervening in the domestic concerns of other nations but would always reserve the right of freedom of action if other powers refused to obey the same rule. Non-intervention as practised in the years 1865-70 was interpreted to mean almost complete abstention from continental affairs, and this at a time when attacks on the old territorial balance were becoming frequent occurrences. 'There was a time when they interfered with everything', a French observer wrote, 'and they have finished by not wishing to interfere with anything.'[4] The statement is accurate. Not only did Britain play a negligible role in European affairs in these years, but, as if to give legal expression to her new isolation, the House of Commons, in March 1868, deleted from the Mutiny Bill that traditional phrase which stated, as one of the reasons for the existence of a British army, the necessity of preserving the balance of power of Europe.

The new fears, resentments and hesitations of the powers in the post-Crimean years produced an atmosphere admirably suited to the new breed of statesmen who appeared now on the European stage—the Gorchakovs, Cavours and Bismarcks who, unlike their predecessors, had no personal

---

[1] *North British Review*, vol. XXXVIII (1863), pp. 493-4.
[2] The phrase is Disraeli's. Hansard, 3rd series, vol. CLXXVI, p. 731.
[3] *Ibid.*
[4] *Revue des deux mondes*, vol. LXIV (1 July 1866), p. 248.

connection with the Vienna settlement and were completely unresponsive to the ideals associated with it, who were proud of their 'realism' and lack of sentimentality, and who found it easy to justify breaches of law by appeals to the natural egoism of states. This is not the place to follow in any detail the steps by which they carried out their designs, but it is at least worth noting that, in their hands, diplomacy became an instrument, not for the preservation of peace, but for the promotion of war. There is no better way of illustrating this than by considering the character and purpose of the alliances they concluded.

In the years before 1854, alliances and diplomatic alignments were generally defensive, and were concluded to protect the partners from the threat of such things as revolution or an attempt by another power or group of powers to extend its influence in such a way as to disrupt the balance of power. The Anglo-French *entente* in 1830, the association of the three eastern courts, the Quadruple Alliance of 1834, Britain's association with the eastern powers in 1840 and even the 'permanent' Quadruple Alliance proposed by Nicholas I in 1840 were combinations of this nature.

In the period after 1856, however, alliances and diplomatic 'understandings' were generally concluded for an aggressive purpose, either to secure the collaboration of the partners in a projected war against a third party or to facilitate the designs of one of the partners by assuring him of the benevolent neutrality of the other. The Pact of Plombières, concluded between Cavour and Napoleon III in 1858, is perhaps the best example of this new type of alliance, and the nature of the compact is best described in Cavour's own words:

The Emperor began by saying that he had decided to support Sardinia with all his forces in a war against Austria provided the war should be undertaken for a non-revolutionary cause, and could be justified in the eyes of diplomacy, and even more in the eyes of the public opinion of France and Europe.

The search for this cause presented the principal difficulty.... The Emperor came to my aid and we put our heads together and went through the whole map of Italy looking for this cause of war which was so difficult to find. After having traversed without success the whole Peninsula we arrived almost with certitude at Massa and Carrara and found what we had sought with such ardour.[1]

Plombières was perhaps the first deliberate war-plot in the nineteenth century, but it was by no means an isolated case. A secret treaty of March 1859, concluded between France and Russia, provided for Russian neutrality in the event of a French war against Austria and for Russian troop movements to divert Austrian forces, while France in return promised her assistance in efforts to revise the treaty of 1856. And there was no essential difference between the Plombières pact and the famous Italo-Prussian alliance of 8 April 1866, for not only was the latter agreement predicated

---

[1] *Il Carteggio Cavour–Nigra* (Bologna, 1926), vol. I, p. 103. Quoted in Binkley, *Realism and Nationalism*, pp. 203–4.

on the assumption of war but it contained a provision for the invalidation of the treaty if war had not begun within three months of the exchange of signatures.

The designs of the realists and the operation of their alliances might, of course, have been frustrated if the Concert of Europe had remained an effective instrument and had been able to record successes similar to those of 1830, 1841 and 1852. But, although attempts were made, in the great crises which occurred after 1856, to summon the concert, there were few meetings of the five powers and only one—the conference on the Luxemburg dispute of 1867—that succeeded in averting a war. In general, the statesmen of the period seemed to lack the ability, or the will, to collaborate. An international congress might have prevented the war of 1859 but failed to meet because of British suspicion of Russian and French motives and Austria's refusal to participate if the kingdom of Sardinia were permitted to attend. A conference of the powers did meet in 1864 to try to restore peace between Denmark and the German powers, but it failed utterly in its purpose, and Disraeli was, on the whole, justified in saying of it: 'It lasted as long as a Carnival and, like a Carnival, it was an affair of masks and mystification. Our Ministers went to it as men in distressed circumstances go to a place of amusement—to while away the time, with a consciousness of impending failure.'[1]

Britain's growing isolation after 1865 further weakened the possibility of collaborative action in the interests of peace, because it became increasingly clear that she was unwilling to accept the kind of responsibility and assume the kind of commitments which would restrain the continental realists. When the German powers were approaching war in 1866, Lord Clarendon resisted suggestions of British mediation, pointing out that 'neither English honour nor English interests are involved',[2] and the failure of a conference to meet before the conflict broke out was probably due in part to the pains Clarendon took to convince the chancelleries of Europe that Britain could not undertake to enforce the decisions of any conference by military means.[3] Even in the case of the Luxemburg conference, the British government was most reluctant to participate; and, when the Grand Duchy had been placed under the collective guarantee of the great powers, and the conference had completed its labours, the European courts were disagreeably surprised to learn that Britain would not attempt to enforce the guarantee if it were violated by another signatory power.[4] This seemed to make a mockery of the public law; and, in the face of this attitude on the part of a power which in the years

[1] Hansard, 3rd series, vol. CLXXVI, p. 743.
[2] Seton-Watson, *Britain in Europe*, p. 468.
[3] See *Les origines diplomatiques de la guerre de 1870–1. Recueil de documents publié par le Ministère des Affaires étrangères* (Paris, 1910 *et seq.*), vol IX, p. 94, n.
[4] For the British declarations on the guarantee, see Hansard, 3rd series, vol. CLXXVII, pp. 1922 *et seq.*, vol. CLXXXVIII, pp. 148 *et seq.*

1830–54 had been the strongest advocate of concerted action, it is not surprising that the Concert of Europe was an ineffective instrument in the post-Crimean period, and that, having failed to avert wars, its sanction was not even sought to legitimise the territorial changes effected by them.

The failure of the concert was, of course, merely the reflection of the disappearance of that consensus to which reference has been made above. After 1856 there were more powers willing to fight to overthrow the existing order than there were to take arms to defend it. That fact alone made inevitable the destruction of the balance of power which had been contrived so painfully at Vienna and maintained with such care for almost half a century.

CHAPTER XI

ARMED FORCES AND THE ART OF WAR: NAVIES

URING the 250 years immediately preceding 1830, the navies of the world did not greatly change in their material composition and in the technical requirements of their personnel. If Drake's men had found themselves in Nelson's *Victory*, they would, without prolonged training, have sailed and fought her with considerable efficiency. During these centuries, therefore, the development of *matériel* and personnel need not constantly engage the historian's attention. On the other hand, the use of navies as instruments of national policy, and the consequent campaigns waged at sea, loom too large to be disregarded.

After 1830, however, the emphasis is exactly reversed. Now the great seafaring nations are no longer in endemic conflict, and the nations most usually at war are not the seafaring nations. So 'operations' fall naturally into the background, and, though fleets are still used as instruments of policy, that use is more indirect, less primarily warlike. There now occurs, however, a series of unparalleled revolutions in *matériel* which, extending inevitably to personnel, profoundly alters the whole nature of navies. Though Nelson's men could have gone back two-and-a-half centuries without trouble, they would have been utterly bemused if called upon to go forward only a quarter of that period.

It is, therefore, the great evolutions in the ships themselves, their propulsion, weapons and equipment, and in their men which must be the main concern here. It is in the period from 1830 to 1870, indeed, that those changes were at their quickest and most bewildering, and in their results most decisive. The navies of 1830 were still, in essence, the navies of Nelson and Villeneuve: those of 1870 were already, in most respects, those of Fisher and von Tirpitz.

Further, at no other period in modern times has one navy so predominated in men's minds over its rivals. Britain's recent victory over her old sea-competitors, France and Spain, had been singularly decisive, while the newcomers in the race—Prussia, Japan, the U.S.A.—though destined later to take up the challenge, were as yet, navally speaking, in their infancy. Hence—in prestige even when not in sheer power—the Royal Navy, throughout the period, overshadowed all its rivals. No other nation was so situated that it regarded its fleet as its main weapon, whether for attack or defence, or even for the maintenance of the *status quo*. Priority of place, therefore, must go here to the Royal Navy, for to no other country was sea-power of even comparable importance.

Two lines, then, will be investigated: first, the vast and rapid changes in *matériel* which invaded all the world's navies—perhaps the greatest revolution in all naval history; nothing less than the application of modern science and invention to the armed sea-forces: and second, a corresponding and almost equally radical change in the personnel of navies, especially in that paramount one, the Royal Navy.

The changes in *matériel* cover all that pertains to warships, and may be divided into four main subheadings, namely *propulsion*—the change from sail to steam; *basic material*—the change from wood to iron; *offence*—the revolution in the gun; and *defence*—the introduction of armour. These four, acting quickly and often interacting, revolutionised both ships and men.

That all came so quickly and simultaneously is not surprising. The common cause is the marked acceleration of technical skill which began in the latter part of the eighteenth century, leading to improvements of all kinds, but mainly perhaps in machine-making tools. But this new technology, especially in Britain, which led the way, was mainly confined to industry. Indeed, for a long time it was not applied at all to the art of war, so that, though Britain secured a long lead in industrial development based upon machinery, she held no such advantage where her naval forces were concerned.

The reason for this, too, is plain. Britain lacked any overriding motive for making naval changes. Her old 'wooden walls', with their masts, sails, and broadsides of smoothbore guns, had been allotted an important task in the nation's policy, and had been altogether successful. It was only natural that the British, people and government alike, should feel that the Royal Navy, which had served them so long and so well, stood in no need whatever of drastic improvements.

Doubtless this was partly prejudice. Yet it was not prejudice alone which made Britain refuse to take the lead which might have been expected. There were two reasons which acted as brakes upon precipitate change. First, she held an immense lead in existing naval *matériel*. Why, then, deliberately sacrifice it by rendering her great navy obsolete? If the changes meant, as well they might, that she would have to start again at scratch alongside her potential enemies, why bring on the evil day a moment before it was necessary?

The other reason is often forgotten by those who accuse successive British governments of mere ostrichism. Many of these novelties were—then—far from perfect. It is easy to be wise after the event. Ultimately they proved themselves, and became thoroughly reliable. But the men of the 'twenties, 'thirties and 'forties could not be expected to sense a reliability which was not there. What they did see was much less reassuring: that iron, in nature, will not float; that the vast inefficient engines of the day were prone to cease turning altogether; that the earlier experiments with new guns, powders and projectiles led to shocking tragedies in explosions and conflagrations. The problem, thus viewed, seems almost to justify the governments in their caution. The old 'wooden wall', so long Britain's first and principal weapon of war, certainly had this cardinal quality of reliability: to tamper with it by introducing admittedly less reliable apparatus was not—at any rate until the authorities were quite sure of the need—a justifiable risk.

Those very considerations which restrained Britain acted in exactly the opposite direction elsewhere, especially in France. There the old methods had been far from successful. She had repeatedly fought Britain with them, and had failed. Here, then, was the most cogent motive for experimenting—the urge of failure. France, therefore, will be found in the van of the new movement. The young American people, too, had special motives for entering the experimental lists. It was not that their battleships had been unsuccessful, like those of France—they had none. Their seagoing navy in their last war with Britain (1812–15) was very small—twenty-two ships, all cruisers. As new competitors for sea-power, they thought it only sensible not to compete at all in the old naval types, now obsolescent. The obvious short cut, should they ever want to take it, lay in that same policy which Britain herself dreaded—starting from scratch in the new race. In the 'sixties, too, the spur of actual war was added, with the Southern States so much the weaker in naval resources that only a tremendous effort of improvisation with new and half-tried weapons could possibly turn the scale. This was courageously attempted; and, though it failed, it forced the North to retaliate with equal enterprise. Here was the most fertile possible soil for rapid development.

The man who was more responsible than any other for the long sequence of material revolutions was a French artillery officer, Henri Joseph Paixhans. Setting to work as early as 1809 upon his startling ideas, over the next twenty years he conducted experiments and published pamphlets which had the profoundest influence upon the future.[1] He advocated a perfectly new fighting force, designed for a completely new system of tactics—a large number of relatively small (and therefore cheap) ships, steam-driven, built of iron and armoured, and armed with a collection of heavy guns, uniform in weight and bore, firing heavy, hollow, explosive shells. He described in minute and convincing detail the success of the experiments made with such projectiles against the old ships; he revealed quite openly that the devastating results which he claimed were accepted as facts by the Ministry of Marine; and he loudly proclaimed his conviction that his projects, if accepted, would, swiftly and decisively, reverse the long tale of French defeats and British victories. Across the Channel his works were read with acute anxiety, and the Admiralty, though still

[1] *Nouvelle Force Maritime* (Paris, 1822) and *Expériences...sur une arme nouvelle* (Paris, 1825), etc.

unwilling to move, watched the shipbuilding and rearmament policy of France with growing suspicion. There was a longish pause, for Paixhans, far ahead of his time, was not heeded for a while. Yet it is clear, though no one realised it then, that his work was an amazingly prophetic blue-print of all that followed.

Of the great transitions, the first in time was the change in propulsion, in motive-power from sail to steam. It was made inevitable by the eighteenth-century improvements in the steam-engine. In all sea-use, whether for trade or war, the absence of 'free movement' in sailing ships—their inability, that is, to move at will in any direction—involved at best an immense waste of time, at worst serious danger. Most of all, this limita-tion was felt in enclosed waters, where there was no room to tack, and where ships and fleets might spend days and even weeks entirely immobi-lised. In the trading world where, even then, time was money, and engine-breakdown, though aggravating, would not necessarily prove fatal, there was no valid reason why free movement, once more possible, should not be restored at once. So steam invaded merchant-ships before warships. Its earliest use was to tow ships into the open sea: the first steamers were mostly tugs. But by 1830 steam was being used, as well, for pleasure-boats and even, in moderation, as auxiliary motive-power in merchantmen when the wind was contrary or absent.

Such advantages, however, touched warships too. To be wind-bound, either in harbour or in the crisis of action, might be decisively dangerous. Thus here, too, steam could not be long excluded; at first, again, to pro-vide towage, but soon to add to a ship's manœuvrability in action. The earliest of all steam warships was American—Fulton's queer twin-hulled *Demologos* of 1814. The first Royal Navy steamer was the paddle-tug *Monkey*, purchased, with evident reluctance, in 1821. In 1822 the *Comet* and her sisters were built for the navy; but it is characteristic of authority's attitude towards them that their names were omitted from the contem-porary Navy List.[1] The first to be so honoured were the *Lightnings* of 1827—paddle-tugs like the rest: even by 1830 there were no others. This was the considered policy of the country, and in 1828 Melville, then First Lord of the Admiralty, officially voiced it: 'Their Lordships feel it their bounden duty to discourage to the utmost of their ability the employment of steam vessels, as they consider the introduction of steam is calculated to strike a fatal blow at the naval supremacy of the Empire.'[2] Britain might accept the tug for its obvious time-saving qualities, but she would not have a finger laid upon her beloved sail-of-the-line.

Progress, however, would not wait upon the First Lord and his old-world views. Across the Channel the fire-eating Paixhans fulminated,

---

[1] The *official* Navy List, that is, published regularly 'By Authority' since 1814.
[2] Minute to Colonial Department, quoted in Sir J. H. Briggs, *Naval Administration* (London, 1897), p. 9.

and, in Britain in 1830, the progressive Sir James Graham, with 'Nelson's' Hardy as his naval adviser, succeeded Melville. More important, the perfection of the screw-propeller removed at last the real gravamen from the Admiralty's objections.

Here, too, was something more than mere prejudice. In all ages of naval warfare there has been a certain conflict between power to move freely and fast, and power to hit hard: between mobility and punch. Long ago, in the days of the oar, mobility was in the ascendant. There was free movement, but hitting power was severely limited. Here lay the great weakness of the oared galley—it had no place for many or heavy guns. In the sixteenth and seventeenth centuries all countries, failing to secure both, had followed the English in discarding free movement altogether in favour of heavy gunfire, adopting as their standard the high-sided sailing-ship with its broadside of effective artillery. This shelved the problem: it did not solve it. Nor, so far, had steam done so. It could confer a mobility greater than ever before, but the cumbrous paddles which transmitted it and the monstrous boxes which protected them masked much of the broadside, and detracted materially from its weight.

The screw, however, did no such thing, and its development in the early 'thirties by Sir Francis Pettit Smith in England and Captain John Ericsson in America went far towards providing a solution, and persuading the Admiralty to allow steam to invade its inviolate 'wooden walls'.

Even so, their Lordships were not to be stampeded. The screw having made great progress in all merchant navies—and some fighting navies, such as the American, where Ericsson's *Princeton* was laid down in 1842— they instituted in 1845 a series of official tests to decide, once and for all, the rival merits of screw and paddle. They prepared two sloops, of equal tonnage and engine-power; one the *Alecto* (paddle), the other the *Rattler* (screw). These competed first in ordinary steaming races, which the *Rattler* won. But the paddle's many friends remained unconvinced. In towing at any rate, they asserted, their favourite must win. So the sloops were attached stern to stern and worked up to full steam ahead. The end of that strange tug-of-war found the *Rattler* towing her rival stern-first at two-and-a-half knots. The screw's victory was complete.

During the next four years the Admiralty allowed some old battleships to be fitted with exceedingly low-powered auxiliary engines; not because they were convinced, but because the French were experimenting along these lines. During the 'forties the mantle of Paixhans had fallen upon the shoulders of Labrousse, another progressive officer. As early as 1841 he proposed a line-ship driven by screw: and though he too met with opposition, France was able to launch in 1850, to the designs of the great French *Directeur du Matériel*, Stanislas Dupuy de Lôme, the *Napoléon*, in other respects old-fashioned but fitted from the start with an auxiliary screw. Thus challenged, Britain replied in 1852 with the *Agamemnon*, also screw-driven though equally old-fashioned otherwise.

The Crimean War caught both France and Britain with almost all their line-ships still sail-propelled, though they could be towed into action, if necessary, by steam tugs. The war was no good school for experiment because the Russians refused throughout to be lured into fleet actions. Yet the fighting did convince everyone that steam-power had come to stay. In the sea bombardment of Sebastopol on 17 October 1854, for instance, though but little credit accrued to the Allies, or damage to the enemy, the two out of ten British and three out of eleven French battleships which could steam were clearly more valuable, and less vulnerable, than the rest: and in an action of smaller ships at Odessa the steamers did much the better.

Yet this did not convince the Admiralty that sail must go. Rather, they concluded, ships must have both propellents—full-rig for ordinary cruising and auxiliary steam for emergencies. There was common prudence here, too. If the sailing-ship was tactically weak, lacking free movement, she was strategically very strong, possessing one strategic advantage unequalled before or since. She was pre-eminent in 'sea-endurance', enjoying a radius of action, independent of outside assistance, greater than either the oared galley before her or the steamship which followed. Unlike the former, her broad beam and deep draught left plenty of space for provisioning: unlike the latter, she required no fuel-space for her propellent, the wind. The early steamer, however, needed not only coal, but coal in vast quantities relative to the power developed; and she had to have it wherever she might be. This involved one, or both, of two costly accessories—tremendous fleets of colliers constantly in attendance, or widely-spread coaling-stations, also, ultimately, demanding many colliers. At first Britain had neither: nor could she venture upon a wholesale change to steam without them. Those continental nations whose naval occasions seldom took them far from home might, perhaps, risk it, but not so Britain, with her world-wide imperial commitments. She must first face, and solve, her coaling problem. So once again it was France, with her smaller oceanic interests, who set the pace.

In 1859 she produced *La Gloire* (5600 tons), also designed by Dupuy de Lôme, which, though called a frigate, was, for that day, an immense steam-battleship, and a great advance on anything preceding it. Once more Britain must respond, and she did so with the *Warrior* (1860), perhaps the most revolutionary warship ever built, containing all sorts of novel features to which reference will later be made. Here must be recorded only her great size—9200 tons—and her complete set of screw-machinery. But—she remained a full-rigged sailing-ship.

Britain's naval policy in the 'sixties becomes harder to defend: she lagged behind. She had her dilemma—one horn her coal problem, the other her rivals' steam progress. But she was slow to escape from it, clinging overfondly to sail. She had to pay the penalty, and it was heavy. H.M.S. *Captain*, of nearly 8000 tons, was laid down in 1867, not without many misgivings, at the earnest solicitation of the forceful, but far from orthodox Captain Cowper Coles. She contained all the most modern improvements—even turrets—which made her very heavy: yet she had a dangerously low freeboard—in the event, under seven feet. Then, to crown all, she was not only full-rigged: she also had her rigging stopped off at a flying deck, set high to avoid interference with her guns. The accumulated instability thus produced proved suddenly fatal when she encountered a gale off Spain in September 1870. Failing to recover from a heavy roll, she turned right over, drowning Coles himself and all but eighteen of her company. Instantly a strong reaction set in, not only against full-rig, but against any rig at all. The resulting ship, the *Devastation* (see p. 286), carried nothing but one small signalling mast. It was thus, just as the period ends, that steam won its long battle with sail. Later, masts and yards reappeared, but no seagoing battleship thereafter carried anything like full-rig.

The tables were now turned. The warship had forged ahead of the merchantman. Figures for the latter show that, even in 1870, the great bulk of Britain's total shipping remained sail-propelled. In that year, out of some $5\frac{2}{3}$ million tons, over $4\frac{1}{2}$ million were under sail—a proportion of more than four to one in sail's favour.[1] Yet Britain had moved farther towards steam than any of her competitors: and this was sound policy, for, on the long view, the change to steam was almost pure gain to her. Sail involved masts, and the United Kingdom did not, and never could, supply that commodity indigenously—a fact which had, several times in the past, brought her face to face with disaster.[2] But coal she could produce, ample for all her needs; and in turning from Scandinavia to Wales for her basic supplies, she covered one of the most vulnerable chinks in her armour.

The transition in basic material from wood to iron requires less description. It began later, ended earlier, and met with rather less conservative obstruction because it was more patently inevitable. What happened was that wood, even carefully seasoned oak, constantly invited to bear the new weight of ever heavier objects, began to reach the limits of its natural

[1] W. S. Lindsay, *History of Merchant Shipping*, vol. IV (London, 1876), p. 646. Comparison with other leading countries is instructive:

Country	Sail	Steam	Total	Proportion Sail to Steam
United Kingdom	4,506,318	1,111,375	5,617,693	4 to 1
British Possessions	1,440,682	90,759	1,531,441	16 to 1
U.S. (Registered)	1,324,256	192,544	1,516,800	6 to 1
France	917,633	154,415	1,072,048	6 to 1
Holland	474,463	24,942	499,405	19 to 1
Norway	1,008,800	13,715	1,022,515	50 to 1

[2] R. G. Albion, *Forests and Sea-Power* (Harvard, 1926), *passim*.

strength. The larger guns and, especially, the vast turning engines set up in ships a series of local strains, unevenly distributed throughout their frames, which racked them beyond endurance. Even iron strutting, reinforcing the overstrained parts, proved unsatisfactory: iron and wood did not happily consort together. The basic material must be of homogeneous texture, and that must be iron.

Again the merchants led the way: their problem was relatively simple. Trade demanded fast roomy ships, to carry large engines and heavy goods in hold. Nor were they likely to be fired upon—an important factor, as will shortly be seen. So iron was being used for trading craft—mostly small—as early as 1815, though as a material for warships it had reached only the discussion stage in the 'twenties—Paixhans' small-ship fleet was to be of this metal. In the 'thirties it made great progress in commercial shipbuilding, and in 1839 I. K. Brunel dared to lay down the first iron liner, the *Great Britain*. In that year, too, the East India Company acquired two iron-built gunboats, one of which, the *Nemesis*, proved very successful in the China War; and in 1840 the *Dover* (Packet) became the first iron ship in the Royal Navy. The U.S.A. followed, laying down in 1842 the *Princeton*. It must have looked, just then, as though the new material would carry all before it, especially when, in 1843, the Admiralty, with unusual enterprise, ordered six iron paddlewheel frigates.

But there came a reaction, due, for once, not to official caution but to unofficial—indeed, uninformed—conservatism. The cry was, 'hands off our Wooden Walls', and the Admiralty had to bow to the storm. An artillery trial, held in 1849, led to an adverse report on the splinter-effect of gunfire on iron hulls. Maybe the wood 'interest' was exerting undue influence here. But the immediate result was decisive: the iron frigates were relegated to the status of unarmed transports; and in that capacity one of them earned tragic immortality—the *Birkenhead*, lost off South Africa in 1852. Yet suspicions are perhaps dangerous, for France, experimenting along similar lines (again rather ahead of Britain) came at about the same time to much the same conclusions and also reverted to wood. Here Russia took the lead: just as Britain and France were retreating, she began, in 1850, to order from England a series of iron gunboats.

The next advance also came from Russia. At Sinope, in November 1853, her Black Sea squadron, with its new shell-firing guns, annihilated a Turkish wooden fleet. The western powers, notably Britain, were slow in assimilating the lessons of this significant incident: yet there was thereafter a growing school of thought which questioned the finality of the 1849 report. For Sinope revealed a somewhat overlooked characteristic of wood which, once shellfire won the day, would surely develop into a fatal weakness. Iron will not burn: wood will. It was possibly fortunate that the Russians refused fleet action when war came, for not one allied ship was built of iron.

After the war France once more took the lead. In 1858 she laid down *La Gloire*, already mentioned. Her hull was not of iron, it is true, but she was armoured; and that decided Britain. Her reasoning was, for once, highly logical. She was already *almost* convinced that the future lay with iron. There was the Sinope argument of combustibility, and the 'weight' argument of engines and guns. But now the last straw was being added, and it was very weighty indeed. If wood was barely strong enough to sustain the required engines and guns, how could it possibly sustain yet another and even heavier weight—armour? So the British laid down the *Warrior* and armoured her, as they had to do: but, going one better than their rivals, they boldly built her entirely of iron.

Thus, quite suddenly, came the end of the wood–iron controversy. Other countries instantly followed Britain's lead. After 1861 no battleship was built of anything but iron until, in 1885, mild steel took its place.

On the long view, 'wood to iron' was as beneficial to Britain as was 'sail to steam'. Several times, in 'wooden' days, Britain had been brought to the verge of disaster by the shortage of home-grown ship-timber. But, once iron displaced it, that particular danger departed for ever. There was incomparably more iron under the surface of Britain than there were oak-trees on it.

The accompanying improvements in offence, in the gun, were no less revolutionary. The smooth-bore, roundshot-firing, cast-iron pieces had had a long innings, with no basic changes in the weapons themselves, though some not inconsiderable improvements in their mountings. There was, in fact, no essential difference in manufacture or mechanism between the newest of the pieces which went down in the *Mary Rose* in 1545 and a standard ship-gun of three centuries later. Nor was the latter appreciably improved in either range or accuracy. The principal reason for this apparently curious stagnation was, again, lack of inducement to change. This was particularly true in Britain. Tactical experience, as interpreted by all her greatest fighters, had taught them to seek the closest possible action, and so to pound the enemy as to induce in him the will to surrender. Under such conditions long ranges and accuracy were of quite secondary importance. This attitude was epitomised by Nelson himself. Hearing that a friend was sending him a man who had an idea about aiming guns, he wrote: 'As to the plan,...I shall of course look at it, or be happy, if necessary, to use it: *but I hope we shall be able, as usual, to get so close to our enemies that our shot cannot miss the object.*'[1] The italics are not Nelson's; but the sentiment, among all British officers of his day, was universal and unchallenged.

What changed all this at last was the replacement of the solid roundshot by the hollow shell filled with explosive or incendiary material. Here

[1] Nelson to Capt. Berry. *The Dispatches and Letters...of Nelson*, ed. Sir N. H. Nicolas (London, 1844–6), vol. IV, p. 292.

again, not unexpectedly, the French were the pioneers. To them the solid shot had proved no infallible battle-winner. Paixhans again was in the van. The guns he advocated were shell-throwers: not mortars, already old in use, which lobbed over shells at short ranges, but ordinary low-trajectory guns. Nor were there to be exceptions: all solid shot was to be abolished, and one standard pattern of shell substituted. There were no half-measures about Paixhans. He got his way, but at first only in part. The voice of public opinion was raised against the explosive and incendiary shell. Such arms, Paixhans himself admitted, were regarded as 'odieuses'. Such humanitarianism is highly creditable (though another motive may have been intermingled with it—uncertainty of the shell's reliability). Whatever the reason, however, the evil day was postponed: in 1829 his idea of standardisation was adopted, but it was not until 1837 that shellfire was accepted in principle.

This was the signal for cataclysmic changes. Britain was far behind: she had not even standardised her armaments. But now, having discovered that not only France, but also Denmark, Holland, Russia and Sweden were adopting these novelties, she was forced into action. Fortunately, she had by then acquired a gunnery centre where experiment, practice and training were possible. It was situated in H.M.S. *Excellent*, in Portsmouth harbour, started in 1830, and made a permanent institution in 1832. But Britain, like her rivals, did not go all the way: she adopted two types, standardising both—the old-fashioned solid-shot long gun, and the newfangled short shell-firer. This was not mere conservatism. Unquestionably the old gun still retained three paramount advantages— much longer range, considerably greater accuracy and far higher penetration than the shell-gun as it then was.

For the shell was still only a hollow roundshot. It was formidable enough against the old ship, with unprotected wood as its only defence; and this the world learnt from Sinope in 1853. But iron material, with quite a thin layer of the new armour (even then the subject of experiment) would no doubt have been a good enough answer to the globular shell. What the war experience of the Crimean campaigns taught—and this was their principal contribution to the progress of arms—was that the shell itself was capable of immense improvement: which, when it came, led almost instantly to both the modern gun and the modern shell. These two revolutionised all, remedying the old shell's weaknesses and creating a weapon far longer-ranged, more accurate and more penetrating than had ever existed before.

Progress here came almost too late to allow of trial in the Crimean War, though, towards the end, the British did produce the Lancaster, which fired a projectile designed to rotate, not by means of rifled grooves in the barrel, but by a lengthwise twist in a barrel itself slightly oval. It was too crude: but in the same year there appeared a gun which emphatically was not—an even more significant revolution in gunnery than the *Warrior* was in ship-construction.

The great names here are Whitworth and Armstrong. The former introduced into gunmaking the essentially modern quality of precision: where, earlier, men had worked in fractions of inches, Whitworth was thinking in terms of thousandths, and even ten-thousandths, thus translating gunfounding and gunnery from the realm of somewhat airy art to the status of very exact science. Armstrong was essentially the inventor. His was the gun of 1855 which was the first truly modern weapon. It fired an elongated cylindrical shell, designed to rotate on its long axis by the rifling in the barrel; but it was also revolutionary in its structure. It discarded the old principle of casting in one piece, and adopted that since followed in all later artillery. It was a built-up mechanism, made of different components—an inner barrel of forged iron, reinforcing cylinders on the outside, and, between the two, a jacket of long iron bars, wound at white heat to form a spiral cylinder, and shrunk on the inner barrel. It was also a breech-loader. But here it was comparatively unsuccessful, the breech-closing apparatus being its weakest feature. Thus, though the rest of Armstrong's ideas were adopted, the new guns which emerged remained muzzle-loaders. It was the French who made the key-invention here—the principle of the 'interrupted thread'. Indeed, Britain at this point fell some years behind her rivals, being almost the last of the naval powers to re-adopt the breech-loader, in 1880.

In defence, armour was the inevitable sequel to the Armstrong gun. Indeed, the lesson had been there for the learning since 1788, when Sir Samuel Bentham, commanding a Russian squadron, had destroyed a superior Turkish fleet in the Black Sea by lobbing incendiary shells at it. The lesson was that the shell meant *fire*, the age-old enemy of wooden ships: and that at all costs it must be kept out. Paixhans, in his day, showed that he realised it, by advocating, even in the 'twenties, both iron material and armour. But he did not convert his countrymen to his way of thinking. Nor were other pioneers more successful. As early as 1842 the U.S. Congress had appropriated money to build a shot-and-shell-proof steamer, which, however, was never completed; and, in France in the following year, Labrousse had proposed, in vain, a fast iron frigate with an armoured bridge. All had to wait, in fact, until the second exposition of the shell's peculiar power at Sinope in 1853.

Even then Britain hung back; but not so France, presided over by Napoleon III, himself a considerable artillery expert. His 'floating batteries', hurriedly ordered, were just ready to be tested under war conditions, at the bombardment of Kinburn on 17 October 1855. They were small cut-down wooden vessels, lined with iron plates fastened to a 17-inch wall of timber, and they answered their limited purpose admirably. The Russian roundshot bounced off them; their shells burst on impact and left barely a scar. It was clear from that single encounter that armour was the answer to shell. But that was only the beginning of the great battle now developing. Defence was momentarily in the ascendant: here was the challenge to offence to catch up. Just as the floating battery was the immediate result of the old shell fired from the old smooth-bore one-piece cannon, so the new shell, fired from the new built-up gun, was the immediate result of the floating battery. So, of course, it has gone on ever since, this see-saw strife between thrust and parry.

The British seemed unimpressed even by the evidence of Kinburn. Though they produced similar floating batteries, as in duty bound, indeed improving them a little by bolting the armour-plates on to iron hulls, they would not take the next logical step—to apply the armour principle to capital ships. But the French, as ever more logical, produced *La Gloire*, extending all round her water-line a belt of 4¾-inch armour-plate. The British, though they might ignore Kinburn, could not ignore the existence across the Channel of a battleship which they could not sink. So they replied with the *Warrior*, thus regaining the lead; for, as we saw, her construction was of iron where her rival's was of wood.

By 1860, then, the great struggle of gun v. armour—attack v. defence—was joined. Its results soon eliminated all surviving features of the old ship. First, it was found impossible to clothe the whole of a big ship with armour thick enough to keep out the shells from the new guns. The only answer was to erect some sort of 'citadel' or strong-point wherein to collect all the ship's essentials. This instantly affected that 350-year-old institution, the broadside. Once the 'citadel' or 'casemate' idea was accepted, the unarmoured bow and stern must be cleared of all guns and engines, and left only to confer sufficient buoyancy. Hitting-power must be concentrated in the central armed part: while, as compensation for the inevitable reduction in their numbers, guns must be much larger, with heavier projectiles.

For another reason, too, the broadside was becoming obsolete. It had always had one characteristic weakness—a severely limited field of fire. Its guns all pointed (with but slight deviations) in one direction—at right angles to the ship's course. To fire, therefore, one had to aim with the whole ship, altering course, not towards the enemy, but half away. With the new manoeuvrability and far fewer guns this seemed intolerably inefficient. The guns must be mounted to move independently of the ship, traversing the greatest possible arc—ideally, 360 degrees.

It was the 'citadel' principle combined with the 'mobile gun' idea which, in the 'sixties, produced the 'turret'—a heavily armoured, revolving casemate which, while affording the guns protection, would also introduce all-round fire. It is this which gives such significance to the first encounter, in Hampton Roads on 9 March 1862, between two armoured ships, Ericsson's *Monitor* and the Confederates' *Merrimac*.

Both were, essentially, freaks, designed and built in great haste to fight rather than to steam, and both were correspondingly unseaworthy. The *Merrimac* was merely a large floating—but fixed—casemate, clad in four inches of iron over twenty-two inches of wood, armed with ten guns only, mostly smooth-bore, and a formidable ram. The *Monitor* was simply a revolving turret which floated—just: her freeboard was two feet—clothed in eight-inch armour, and carrying a pair of enormous—eleven-inch—smooth-bore guns. In itself the encounter was strangely indecisive: ship-damage and casualties were negligible, though the ships engaged in close fight for four hours. Nor is this surprising, for the new defensive armour was here pitted against the old offensive gun. The action's importance lies rather in its influence on the development of two weapons.

The first was the ram. Both ships possessed one, and, on 8 March the *Merrimac* had sunk the North's wooden sloop *Cumberland* with hers. In doing so, however, she left it in her victim: which was the reason, perhaps, why, when she struck the *Monitor* next day, she did no damage. The *Monitor* also tried to ram, but narrowly missed. The evidence of the weapon's efficacy against iron was thus extremely slender. Yet it made a great impression, which seemed to be confirmed four years later when, on 20 July 1866, off Lissa in the Adriatic, the enterprising Austrian admiral Tegetthoff drove his flagship at full speed into one of the best of the Italian ships, the armoured *Re d'Italia*, piercing her armour, tearing a hole which measured 300 square feet, and sinking her instantly. Thus by 1870 the ram was at the height of its popularity. That soon faded, however—as soon as the new attack caught up with defence and revealed the weapon's fatal limitation, its negligible range. It was certainly deadly, yet useless when faced by a gun capable of sinking its carrier long before it could close.

The more lasting lesson of Hampton Roads was the efficacy of the turret and the all-round fire-power which it conferred. This was not a purely American invention, since Captain Coles's plans for the first British turret-ship, *Prince Albert*, had been approved before news of Hampton Roads reached Britain; and it had not won a complete victory even by 1870. It was still competing with another development of the casemate principle known as the 'central battery'. But its victory was in sight, for in 1869 Britain laid down the warship with which this account will close. The turret-battleship *Devastation*, designed by Coles's rival, Sir E. J. Reed, and completed in 1873, was such a combination of all that was new as to justify for her the title of 'first modern battleship'.

So vanished the 'line' ship of 1830, propelled by sail alone, built only of wood and possessed of no other protection whatever; with its broadside of many nearly-fixed, smooth-bore, cast-iron cannons firing solid, non-exploding roundshot, the heaviest of which seldom weighed more than 32 pounds or did any damage beyond 400 yards. Here instead was a monster of four times the tonnage, moved only by steam-driven propellers; of all-iron frame, protected by a ten-inch armour-belt; with revolving turrets clad in fourteen-inch armour and housing four thirty-five-ton built-up, mechanically operated, rifled guns, each of which discharged a cylindrical rotating shell, armour-piercing and explosive, weighing 700 pounds and capable of inflicting heavy damage at 4800 yards, and of carrying nearly 10,000 yards. The one was essentially a *Victory*; the other, in essentials though not in details, a *Dreadnought*.

Those characteristic modern weapons, the mine, the submarine and the torpedo, cannot receive detailed treatment here because they became really formidable only after 1870. Yet all first appeared before that date. The floating mine, laid defensively, but not tested by use, in Kiel Harbour in 1848, was first seriously exploited by Russia, in the Baltic in 1855. Brun's submarine, *Le Plongeur*, was launched in 1863, and the first fatal submarine casualty was the Federal *Housatonic*, sunk in 1864 by one of the South's diminutive semi-submersibles called 'Davids'. Already, too, intrepid Americans on both sides were taking suicidal risks with primitive torpedoes lashed to spars or towed at an angle behind light craft. The earliest 'fish' torpedo, even, first thought of in Austria, was developed by Whitehead in 1866.

It is significant that all these novelties were first exploited, even when not initiated, outside Britain: and for the same reason as before. All were, at first, the weapons of lesser sea powers, wishing to secure the coveted command of the sea without the expense of maintaining vast fleets and elaborate ships. All were calculated to take the enemy's major pieces by a judicious sacrifice of pawns. In every case, therefore, Britain held back at first, but, in the interests of self-preservation, had in the end to follow, sometimes to catch up, and, occasionally, to lead.

Nelson and his predecessors handled comparatively simple weapons in comparatively simple ships. The naval profession in their day was not, indeed, entirely unscientific, but the basic qualifications required in it were still almost entirely such abstractions as valour, leadership, discipline, devotion and experience: not technical knowledge of highly specialised and complicated installations. This was still so in 1830.

By 1870, however, the ships and their contents had become miracles of complex mechanisms, all of which someone on board must understand and work. So personnel obviously had to change with *matériel*. Yet it had a harder—because a double—task to face: while acquiring the new specialised, scientific knowledge, it must lose none of its old abstract qualities. As the great American Farragut said, iron in the ships was less important than iron in the men.

Up to 1815 there remained, in the British service, the time-hallowed division of all personnel under the big headings of 'commissioned officer', 'warrant officer', and 'men' (or, as we should now say, 'ratings').

Between these grades were steps great and high, and not often surmounted. The commissioned officers were by far the most important, both in status and authority. They were all 'executive' (that is, responsible for 'command', whether in peace or war) and 'military' (that is, the prime participants in all the fighting). And they were the only officers who were. They included all admirals, captains, commanders and lieutenants, and no others. Already the grade of sub-lieutenant (so-called since 1860, but first established as a substantive grade under the name of 'mate' in 1840) was emerging, and the grade of midshipman was fully established. But these latter were not commissioned officers. They were, officially, ratings, yet not in practice so treated, being really commissioned officers in embryo. The warrant-officer group—the 'departmental' officers—was larger than at present because it contained not only men like boatswains, gunners and carpenters (now 'Special Duty Officers', though essentially the same as they were), but also all those 'branch' officers—as pursers, surgeons, chaplains and instructor officers—who are now appointed by 'commission'. That important branch, the engineers, was non-existent. All the rest were ratings, from whom the captain of a ship was entitled to select a number to act as petty officers: but even these were, strictly speaking, only locally and temporarily promoted.

By 1830 this arrangement had changed but little. Between 'commission' and 'warrant' there still loomed that high and seldom-mounted step. The very uniforms, the very buttons worn by each category were quite different. The unique prestige of the commissioned officers in the hierarchy of ship life remained unshaken.

The whole corps of commissioned officers was still essentially a privileged class—almost a social clique or club—jealously guarding its rights; very exclusive; even harder to enter, probably, than it had been during the great wars, when sheer demand for quantity sometimes watered down the 'quality'. But now, when few were required, the still universal practice of 'interest', or 'protection', tended to close the doors against all but those whom the members themselves regarded as socially suitable— that is, their own relatives and friends. There was thus a great tendency towards naval heredity—a characteristic always prone to appear in old fighting services. The constant recurrence of certain surnames in mid-nineteenth-century navy lists reveals this as pre-eminently the epoch of 'naval families'.

Yet, during the 'thirties and 'forties, the profession was distinctly precarious, offering neither constant employment nor a decent competence upon retiring. The average officer was, indeed, much more often out of employment than in it. Even the principles of rank and seniority were not theoretically recognised, though the latter was strictly—too strictly— applied in the upper categories. It was still the rule that, on being 'posted captain', every man took his place upon the ladder of seniority, nevermore to pass, or be passed by, a fellow-officer. This and three other factors —the late great wartime expansion with its legacy of a very overcrowded navy list, the keeping of so few ships in commission, and the absence of any proper system of retirement—all rendered inevitable a formidable block in promotion. By the early 1840's, when things were at their worst, septuagenarians were commanding fleets, and captains and lieutenants, all old in proportion, were officering ships; while aspirants for commissions—mates and midshipmen—often obtained no commission at all, remaining, if they stuck it, to become old and soured men. This was doubly unsatisfactory. While over-old men were employed, those in their prime were too often overlooked, and, while waiting, had perforce to find other occupation. Hence the phenomenon of officers serving under foreign flags, like Abney Hastings (Greece) and Sir Charles Napier (Portugal), or serving in private employ, like McClintock (elucidator of Franklin's fate) and the brothers Allen (explorers of the Niger). Pleasanter symptoms of the same complaint, too, appear in men like Marryat, Chamier and Howard, who could find ample time between commissions to write novels about their first love, the navy.

Such a state of things furnished an ideal seed-bed for patronage. 'Interest' was still the prerequisite of success, and even of employment. During the wars most officers had ultimately obtained work, because so many ships were in commission. One used interest—then—to obtain a good command: but now it needed a very potent interest to obtain employment at all. In this somewhat sinister atmosphere, in fact, the right *kind* of interest became all-important, and it is instructive—but not easy—to see what that kind was. For juniors—up to lieutenants—it was essential to be 'protected' by admirals or captains, whose influence still, in practice, filled up most of those vacancies. But even here the very great might sometimes unexpectedly stoop to reward some lucky junior, especially if he were of a 'naval family'. In 1841, for instance, Captain Thomas B. Sulivan received the following *official* communication from the Board of Admiralty itself: 'As a special mark of their Lordships' approbation of your services on the Brazil station, My Lords have been pleased to promote your son...to the rank of Commander....'[1] This was pure 'naval' interest —the best kind; for its recipients usually justified their promotion, as young Sulivan certainly did. Yet it shows clearly how deep-rooted was the practice, and how unquestioningly it was accepted at all levels.

Captains and higher officers had to be protégés of more political personages. The First Lord was probably the safest of all, for he was the immediate fount of appointments. Otherwise parliamentary interest was the best. This unhealthy influence grew gradually weaker after the first Reform Bill, but only gradually. Captain Sir William Dillon, for example, though a capable officer, went from 1819 to 1835 without employment

[1] From the original in the possession of Vice-Admiral Norton A. Sulivan, C.V.O.

of any kind, even though, throughout the period, he had the active interest both of the duke of Sussex, whose equerry he was, and of the 'Sailor Prince', the duke of Clarence himself. Yet, despite such advantages, he failed, even when Clarence became, in 1827, the (last) holder of the resuscitated office of Lord High Admiral. He succeeded in the end, and was given a ship, but only after his royal backer had been reigning monarch for five years. Dillon, naturally embittered, quotes cases of officers preferred to himself, and makes the reason for their preference sufficiently clear. Their 'protectors', being in Parliament, were able to strike something very much like a bargain with the dispensers of employment, having somewhat to trade in exchange for services rendered![1]

That such a system, based so frankly upon nepotism and patronage, should produce such good results is surprising to the twentieth-century mind. That the material *was* good is sure: what is harder to judge is how much better it might have been had more competitive methods obtained. As it was, however, the officer-personnel remained, as before, confined to the governing classes; and, as the successive Reform Bills gradually enlarged those classes, so—but always a little later—was the commissioned-officer class itself enlarged.

The excessive age of all officers naturally did not pass unnoticed, and was often deplored. But no real remedy was devised until it became intolerable; until, that is, war-clouds began to gather, and the test of active service loomed large. The remedies were to hand, and had long been clear to thoughtful men. The main one was for authority to admit at last that the navy was a whole-time profession, and, therefore, that the naval officer should be cared for all the time: not only when employed but also both when unemployed and when not required any more. Up till 1860 the strictly official view—fortunately not always put strictly into practice—was that an officer was only such when actually employed. As a practical expedient, it is true, he had for long been 'retained' between-whiles: otherwise he would simply not be available when wanted. So the institution of half-pay was already there, though on a distinctly mean scale. But that was all. The obligation to give him *retired* pay remained unrecognised, though a very few lucky individuals received it as an act of grace. This is not surprising. The idea of pensioning the part-time labourer belongs rather to the 1940's than the 1840's.

These two cognate principles—the right of a naval officer to more or less continuous employment while serving, and to be retired with adequate after-care when no longer required—won recognition at almost the same time, and, in so doing, revolutionised the profession.

Government at last acknowledged him as its permanent servant in 1860, when it made an unspectacular change in the wording of the commission which it gave him. Hitherto, each time he was employed he

[1] Navy Records Society, vol. XCVII, pp. 446 ff.

had received a document known as a 'ship commission', appointing him to a specified post in a specified ship for a specified time: for example, he was still, technically, plain John Smith, Captain (*pro tempore*) of a named warship: not, in his own right and all the time, Captain Smith, R.N.

Now, however, all was changed. By a quiet, unpublicised order-in-council he was to have—what his descendant still has —a 'general commission', valid during his whole tenure of the rank he had reached. Now he was appointed 'Captain [or Commander, or Lieutenant] *in Her Majesty's Fleet*'. The difference is all-important. The first left his employment casual: the second made him a whole-timer.

The other change is a corollary of the first. Now that he is accepted as a permanent employee he must be allowed—indeed, where necessary, ordered—to retire (with proper provision for his support) when his time comes. It was this absence of ordered retirement, principally, which had caused the great post-war block: for so long as no officer retired, but merely (if not required) ceased to be employed, only one event ever withdrew him from the promotion scramble—his death. This is why in 1840 the first twenty captains on the list had been captains in 1806 and the senior commander had been one for forty-six years; while in 1841 the senior lieutenant died, having been for sixty-three years a lieutenant!

The remedy again was simple—to split the list into two parts, 'active' and 'retired': to retain as 'active' all likely to be employed again, and to 'retire' all not likely. This could be done, without injustice. Such octogenarian officers were never employed: they were merely keeping promotion from their juniors. By a series of big 'retirements'—especially those of 1847, 1851 and 1864—the axe fell, and a healthy flow of promotion was at last established. But only in 1870 were 'Active' and 'Retired' Lists published separately. By that year, then, the old part-time post-holder had vanished, and the modern whole-time rank-holder had come.

Meanwhile, changes just as decisive were happening at the other end of his career—his entry and preliminary training. For centuries the would-be officer had gone first to sea as the protégé of some captain. This 'captain's servant' method had indeed been the only one until, in 1676, Samuel Pepys inaugurated an entry which would now be called 'Admiralty Nomination'. But even Pepys's scheme did not touch the great majority of candidates for executive command, who continued to enter as captain's servants until 1794, when the name—but not its essential nature—changed to 'First Class Volunteer'. In such a set-up nepotism and interest played their foreordained part, contributing materially to the retention of the caste system.

The small minority not entered by arrangement with individual officers —called, in Pepys's day, 'Volunteers-per-Order', or, familiarly 'King's Letter Boys'—survived throughout the eighteenth century. Their representatives in 1829 were the eighty students of the Royal Naval College,

Portsmouth, who were still the only people in the profession in whose original appointment the Admiralty had any say. By 1830 the College was almost at its last gasp as a training-place for youngsters. Serving admirals and captains never liked it: it cut right across one of their most cherished vested interests—the right to select their successors. The Admiralty itself, however, usually supported the College students, partly because it had selected them, but mainly because nowhere else was there any theoretical instruction at all. And it was, paradoxically enough, just this necessity for such instruction, born of the new technical specialisation, which killed the College as a training establishment. In 1829, to meet this very need, older officers, hitherto totally untrained in any modern sense, were admitted to the courses along with the boys; and, eight years later, ousted them altogether. Thereafter, for a few years, all volunteers went straight to sea.

This change was not quite so retrogressive as it sounds, in either training or entry: for, with it, the Admiralty introduced some theoretical training at sea by providing a regular supply of university-trained naval instructors; and, on the entry side, almost at the same time (January 1838), an examination for *all* volunteers, College-trained and officer-chosen alike, was unobtrusively introduced. It was the thin end of the wedge because, though the examination itself was at first a mere farce, its very existence implied the examiner's—that is, the Admiralty's—right to fail a candidate, and therefore, in the last resort, to select him. In 1839 an examination—this one a reality—was instituted for the next grade, the midshipman, so that thereafter the Admiralty had secured the right to select all but the youngest of the 'young gentlemen'. Thereafter the senior officers' vested interest died hard, whittled down gradually by a long series of small cuts, two only of which occur in or before 1870. In 1848 the government restricted the number of nominations that each senior officer could make: next, in 1870, it ordained that the number of nominations was to be twice the number of vacancies, the final result to be determined by examination. This 'limited competition' was a great blow to officer-nomination, for now it was no longer certain that the officers' choices would ever be admitted. It was a long step towards the inevitable concept of open competition, having its counterpart in similar rules governing the army and the civil service. But the fight went on into the present century, and terminated in complete victory for the state only in 1913.

Meanwhile, training too had advanced, as it had to in face of the revolution in *matériel*. In 1857 the policy of putting all volunteers—after 1843 known officially as naval cadets—untrained into seagoing ships was completely reversed: all, now, were to start in a training ship. The *Illustrious*, first selected for the purpose, soon gave way (1859) to the *Britannia*, which, after several experiments, cast permanent anchor in the Dart in 1863.

Here the U.S.A. led Britain by many years. In 1845 the energetic Secretary of the Navy, George Bancroft, established at Annapolis the naval academy which still flourishes there. He was going far beyond the practice of Britain, for Portsmouth had never trained more than a fraction of her officers; nor, even, was the *Britannia* so theoretically 'educational' as Annapolis, though perhaps more practically 'naval'. It was only when the colleges of Osborne (1903) and Dartmouth (1905) were founded that, for the first time, all British cadets received their initial training on shore.

Meanwhile the old college at Portsmouth persevered with its new (but older) scholars. As specialisation grew, the courses multiplied, and the dockyard buildings became too small to hold them. In the late 1860's the number of pensioners in Wren's great hospital at Greenwich was dwindling, partly through the absence of wars and wounds but mainly because they were being granted out-pensions in lieu of residence. Thus, when the hospital was closed in 1869, the R.N. College, Portsmouth, could be transferred thither. This move, made in 1873, gave the navy, for the first time, a centralised home for the theoretical study of naval science.

Within the brief bounds, then, of our period the whole process of entry and training was revolutionised. In 1830 the system was as it had been in Pepys's day: for all but the very few, entry by interest; practical training afloat, but theoretical training—nowhere. By 1870 the necessity of specialisation had established, in most essentials, the modern system.

All, so far, has concerned only the 'executive' or 'military' officers— the admirals, captains and lieutenants. These, moreover, were in 1830 the *only* officers whose status was established by virtue of the king's commission: the only *commissioned* officers. Between them and all the others—all appointed by 'warrant'—was fixed a great gulf, both 'service' and social. Yet, here again, by 1870 a tremendous change had occurred: the jealously guarded privilege of appointment by commission had escaped from the exclusive clique which monopolised it, and spread to other branches—masters, for instance, paymasters, surgeons, chaplains, naval instructors and, perhaps most significant of all, engineers.

The masters—the navigating experts—led the way when, in 1832, their more senior representatives came to be appointed by commission. A like privilege came to paymasters, surgeons and chaplains in 1843, and to naval instructors in 1861. The position of the engineers was different, and —for some time—difficult. They went afloat, naturally, only with their steam-engines, and were first officially established only in 1837, when no engineer was a commissioned officer. In the reform of 1843 they were overlooked, but the most senior received commissions in 1847; and thereafter, as their numbers and technical qualifications grew, they rose in rank and status, albeit a good deal more slowly than they hoped. In 1870 the most senior engineer ranked with a senior captain.

Throughout our period the executive and the engineer officers were recruited from different social strata, and much of the jealousy which admittedly existed between them was due to this fact. The newcomers, essentially technicians, were playing a considerable part in widening the class-basis of all officers, and both were aware of it. The engineer could not but feel that he had a big future in an all-steam navy: the executive could not but fear it. So, for the rest of the century, the one pressed upwards while the other strove to keep him down. It was perhaps no accident that, from 1847 to 1903, the navy continued to call its senior engineers, not captains (or admirals), but 'inspectors [or chief inspectors] of machinery afloat'. None the less, this infiltration into the once exclusive territory of the 'naval families' is symptomatic of the times. It was one direct result of the new technical age, and it made an irreparable breach in the stronghold of privilege.

The same general causes influenced the nature of the men and their terms of service. Hitherto Britain's naval personnel had been essentially part-timers: almost all seamen, but by no means necessarily fighting seamen. There was not in 1830—and never had been—any form of long-term service in the navy. The majority were merchant-seamen *and* man-of-warsmen, the former in peacetime, the latter in war. The transition from one to the other had been accomplished, mainly, by the operation of the impressment system, not dead even in 1830, though well past its prime. It was a bad system, often and justly censured, and it was at its worst during the revolutionary and Napoleonic wars, because these crises, longer and larger than preceding ones, had stretched Britain's sea-personnel to breaking-point, and beyond. Long before they ended, the whole seafaring population had proved numerically insufficient. As a result, non-seamen had perforce been imported into the navy in order to complete crews: which expedient, in its turn, showed up the faults of the impressment system. Leaving things too late, and then using unwise and unfair methods, the state obtained, at great cost, only the dregs of the land population.

The root trouble was that the naval service was too unattractive to entice volunteers. This created a vicious circle. Impressment involved forcible detention: many thus coerced would escape if they could: free men's shore-leave was therefore impossible, so that the ships became virtual prisons. But free men are not prone to volunteer for prison: so they must be forcibly recruited—pressed.

Another evil was that impressment allowed the government to ignore ordinary economics. Shipowners, always subject to competition, had to maintain current standards of living and wages: but the government, with forcible recruitment behind it, did not. When war came, the average seaman was not unpatriotic; but, as between the two services, the prospects offered him were fantastically unequal: in the merchant service, relative comfort and safety, and *very* good pay (for in wartime he was a commodity in short supply, with both merchant and Admiralty in the market); in the crown's service, wounds and death, gross overcrowding and quite uneconomic pay, iniquitously doled out: in a merchantman, no forcible abduction, no imprisonment; in a warship, both—his imprisonment supplemented with brutal and brutalising punishments. There were never nearly enough volunteers: the wonder was that there were any.

Thoughtful men such as William Pulteney (in 1786), Captain Marryat (in 1822) and many others were often suggesting possible or partial remedies. No one contemplated abolishing the whole press system: that reform, unaccompanied by others, would have been impossible, since war-crews had to be found—the men themselves admitted that. But two suggestions were made: first, that all seamen should be registered, so that the great naval burden might be distributed evenly among them; and second, that named limits should be put upon the length of any man's service. There were also suggested better pay, a better system of payment, and the institution of regular pensions. Such reforms would have rendered the naval seaman's life more bearable, and, by removing some of the scarcely credible hardships, improved voluntary recruitment. But they remained suggestions.

The situation grew better after 1815, but only because, the war being over, many seamen could be discharged. No conscious cure was attempted. Impressment was not abolished—indeed, in principle, has never been abolished. Yet, unconsciously, the first—rather obvious—step was taken towards breaking the vicious circle. Beginning from 1797, when the men forced its hand, government gradually improved both the pay (and its disbursement) and the general living conditions in H.M. ships. These measures, combined with the smallness of the peacetime demand, enabled the royal service gradually to compete with the merchant service, naturally and economically, so that its wants could be supplied by voluntary recruitment. The government always realised that, other things being equal, the volunteer was more valuable than the conscript: at last that desirable state of things was happening.

This position had been reached by 1830, but it was a precarious one. Most of the navy's seamen were now volunteers: but still only because the demand was small, not because the problem was solved. It was not until 1836 that Sir James Graham, after some years at the Admiralty, at length secured the long-discussed reforms—registration and limited service (five years maximum).

Thus the worst features of impressment disappeared. Voluntary recruitment, for the first time in British history, became the norm. But what would happen when, or if, an emergency arose? Such appeared imminent in the early 'fifties, and the question had to be faced.

The answer was long-term service, one of the most important events in British naval history. In 1853, and only then, Britain did what France had done nearly a century earlier, and what Pepys had begun to do for English officers nearly two centuries before—inaugurated the new profession of naval rating. Now at last a man could join the Royal Navy and make a full career of it, knowing beforehand all his conditions of service—the time, the pay, the pension.

This new and excellent scheme arose, ostensibly, out of difficulties, real and anticipated, in manning the fleet for the Crimean War. Yet the reform was overdue for another reason, and, war or no war, must have come. That reason was—as before—the impact of science upon the navy, with its ever-pressing need for training and specialisation. Hitherto a seaman had been invited—often compelled—to oscillate between the two branches of the sea-service—a practicable movement because the difference between them was comparatively small, and he could master the rudiments of the war-part in a reasonable time. Henceforward, however, the war-part would become so complex that he must be encouraged to make a career out of the navy alone. It had, indeed, ceased to be an economic proposition to haul men in as required, retain them for a bare year or two, and thereafter turn them off without ceremony. Now, once acquired, they must be trained. Moreover, this specialising process was evidently in its infancy: it would grow with the years. So long-term service was established; and, with it, a fleet reserve, into which ratings would pass when their service term was over. The scheme had its teething troubles. Memories of the bad old days still lingered among seamen, and at first their response was far from good. But a regard for their interests was potentially there, and in the end they responded. Here is the genesis, surprisingly modern, of that well-loved, that most institutional figure, the British bluejacket—'blue' because the state, putting him for the first time into official uniform, chose to perpetuate that colour (as well as that cut of jacket and bell-bottomed trousers) which chanced just then to be the fashion.

The new name coincided with an immense change of status. Hitherto, seamen had been a race apart—rough, uncouth, apparently callous: at sea held down, and often broken, by an iron discipline; on shore, where they were rarely allowed, behaving like escaped lunatics: yet simple men, warm-hearted and intensely loyal to each other: a race who kept themselves to themselves, mistrusting landsmen and, by a natural corollary, mistrusted—even vaguely feared—by landsmen. Under such conditions a seaman did not normally leave the sea: no landsman would employ him. This only served to isolate him the more, and to keep alive the mutual suspicions, bred of mutual ignorance. 'Once a seaman always a seaman' was a saying as true as it was old. But when 'pressed man' became 'volunteer' everything changed. The old bad discipline could be relaxed. Already an Act of 1847 had modified the more sanguinary eighteenth-century enactments, and given to courts martial, for the first time, discretionary powers to award a mitigated sentence. Other acts followed, all superseded in 1866 by the Naval Discipline Act, under which, with trifling alterations, the navy is governed today. Thereafter flogging—most symbolic of the old order—quickly died out. The act forbade more than four dozen strokes: the Admiralty, in various Instructions, discouraged courts martial from ordering it, and made execution of sentence dependent upon their express sanction. In 1871 it was 'suspended' in peacetime, and in 1879 at all times. This is characteristically British: to this day it remains 'suspended', not abolished.

Simultaneously, while shedding the more undesirable traits which a bad system had fostered, the bluejacket contrived to retain the more endearing ones—his simplicity, loyalty and warm-heartedness. Thereupon, with remarkable suddenness, the nation's attitude to him completely changed. It had always loved the navy, recognising it as its first line of defence. It even professed to love its sailors—generically; but not as individuals. These it had only known as madcap rum-swillers who lit their pipes with pound notes, or bought gold-watches and fried them. But now the curse of over-much strong drink was itself removed by reductions in the rum issue. In 1824 the rum-ration was cut from $\frac{1}{4}$ pint rum $+\frac{3}{4}$ pint water twice daily, to the same quantity once daily, tea being substituted for the evening issue. In 1826 the ration was increased by one-fifth, and the evening issue reintroduced. In 1850 the existing ration was halved again, the evening issue stopped, and all hands given a monetary allowance 'in lieu'. Jack Tar came ashore not only much more regularly, but also with much less inducement to drown his woes, so that people, getting to know him, liked what they knew. Thus, from being almost a pariah he became almost a pet. Moreover, he was no longer compelled to face dangers and hardships afloat: he volunteered. So he became, generically at any rate, a hero. He was taken unreservedly to the people's heart. Before he knew where he was, he found himself prime favourite of music-hall and light opera—the 'lively little man in navy-blue', the 'Jack Ahoy whom all our hearts adore'. And, to his everlasting credit, it did not turn his head.

In examining conditions in other countries we must make a firm distinction between impressment as a method—the forcible and inequitable recruitment of seamen for war-service—and impressment as a principle—the right of any sovereign state to summon its own citizens to defend it in time of peril. For while the method was confined almost exclusively to Britain the principle was, and is, wellnigh universal. It is in fact the conscription or 'direction' of today, and has never been abolished anywhere when danger really threatened. Thus the U.S.A. can claim, with proper pride, that they never had the former. Indeed, their naval effort never having been commensurate with Britain's, it was unnecessary. Nor did they have to tighten, to the point of brutality, its concomitant prison-discipline. During the long wars, therefore, when British impressment was at its peak, naval conditions in the United States compared favourably with Britain's, and many British seamen deserted to American ships, being thereby largely responsible for the war of 1812–15. Otherwise, the traditional discipline was much the same, the U.S.N. having unconsciously absorbed that of its parent, the R.N.

But, by the 'thirties and 'forties, when Britain's strain was eased, the reverse probably became true. Herman Melville, whose influence certainly helped to persuade Congress to abolish flogging in 1850, attributed this, in the main, to the rawness of contemporary American officers, whom he compares unfavourably with those of Britain.[1] But even America could not escape the *principle* of forcible recruitment, and the 'drafting' system of the Civil War was essentially this. It remains true, however, that the American seaman never, like his British brother, swung so violently from one extreme to another, so that, when the reaction came, Jack Tar's amazing metamorphosis was not reproduced. As the individual enlisted man had never been so suspect, so he has never been so universally idealised.

The French managed better and more logically. They had to, for they suffered throughout from one serious weakness—a chronic shortage of all seamen, naval or mercantile. So, from 1769, they organised nine divisions of trained seamen-gunners, some 10,000 strong, who were essentially long-service men. This was over and above their *Inscription maritime*, which was much the same thing, in full operation, as the oft-advocated but never-achieved British Register of Seamen; and this they retained throughout. The irresponsible regime of the Terror, however, abolished the seamen-gunners, gratuitously throwing away this great advantage, and paying a terrible price therefor in inefficiency and insubordination. But later governments soon realised this, and by 1830 had a system which was already practically conscription, especially after 1835 when the '*Levée permanente*' was instituted. This called up all seamen automatically as they reached the age of twenty, and so provided a constant pool of trained naval men, in spite of small overall numbers. In 1839, for instance, the active *Inscription maritime* totalled only 45,000, of whom 18,000 were, at the moment, in warships and the rest in merchantmen. But, though by 1844 the effective *Inscription maritime* still stood only at 46,000, no less than 55,517 seamen had actually done their naval training since 1835. Moreover, British officers in touch with French personnel during the Crimean War were greatly impressed by both its efficiency and the system which produced it.

Other countries never had recourse to the British impressment method, at least on anything like the same scale. It was patently bad, and, their

---

[1] Samuel Leach, *A Voice from the Lower Deck* (London, 1844), and H. Melville, *White Jacket* (1850). Both view proceedings through lower-deck eyes, the Briton frankly pro-American, the American equally pro-British.

total sea-efforts being so much smaller, they had no need for it. Rather, they followed, on the whole, a policy similar to that employed in the recruitment of their armies. Those who, like the U.S.A., could manage to do so, adopted the voluntary principle; but the 'military' powers, mainly those of Europe, followed the French example of bringing their naval recruitment into line with, indeed making it a part of, their military policy of conscription.

Meanwhile, in Britain, Graham's new Register contained, by 1839, 167,013 names. There were also 21,450 apprentices, almost all of whom would become seamen, making in all nearly 190,000 'in the pool'. But, of these, probably no more than 4 per cent had served in the navy. There would also be, it was realised, another serious drain on naval seamen if war came. The privateer system was still universally recognised, and, in an average year during the Napoleonic War, some 47,000 potential man-of-warsmen had been lost through this alone. Unwillingness to face so dangerous a depletion was a prime reason why Britain favoured the abolition of the whole privateering business; and this was duly achieved by international agreement in the Declaration of Paris of 1856; very soon, that is, after the introduction of long-term service.

This—after its teething troubles—met Britain's immediate needs. But it posed another problem—a corollary. The French had now, in their *Levée permanente*, a true reserve, based upon conscription. Could Britain devise one on the voluntary basis which now obtained in her navy itself? It was a question which had to be answered because now, for the first time, the Royal and Merchant navies, ceasing to draw upon a common source of supply, were setting out as separate entities along diverging roads. No more, upon emergency, could authority hustle unwilling, un-war-trained seamen into the fleet—the new ships and their fitments were too highly technical for that. Nor would the fleet reserve, however excellent in quality, provide the quantity for any major expansion. There was only one answer, and, fortunately, it was quickly found. The Royal Naval Reserve was formed: for ratings in 1859; for officers in 1861. This in effect reforged the old link between Royal and Merchant navies. But the new was infinitely more equitable than the old. As the naval men were volunteers, so were the naval reserve men—merchant officers and seamen, or fishermen, who, while continuing their normal callings, volunteered to spend a few weeks annually acquiring at least the rudiments of the new, complex war technique. It was a brilliant success, not only in itself, but as providing a model for that other great wartime source of supply, the Royal Naval Volunteer Reserve, founded by Act of Parliament in 1903.

The rise in prestige of the British bluejacket is partly responsible for one great difference still existing between the Royal Navy and its continental neighbours. Originally all powers—Britain included—recruited mainly from sea-board provinces: the press indeed could by law operate only in the sea-shires, and its right of seizure was confined to seafaring persons. There has been but little change in continental recruitment areas: but in Britain the new long-term voluntary profession became attractive, and honourable *per se*. In the 'fifties and 'sixties men began, in increasing numbers, to join the navy from all parts of the island, until its personnel ceased—not entirely, yet relatively to other lands—to be territorially confined at all.

The officers too were affected, though less so. Here the prestige of the service, by virtue of its great record, had been high enough, even in the eighteenth century, to induce good men to join it from inland manor house and rectory, as well as from the halls of the governing class. During the nineteenth century these widening tendencies grew, until it would be difficult today to indicate on a map which shires provide the bulk of the officers. But in France and other continental countries where the army always held pride of place, the navy has tended to remain provincial, and in prestige somewhat below the army. In Britain it is neither.

To carry through such revolutionary changes, of personnel and *matériel* alike, another revolution—in administration and direction—was essential: and it took place, again almost exactly within our period. Between 1832 and 1872 the Royal Navy acquired its modern government—the new Admiralty.

Till 1832 direction and administration had been all but separate things, the Admiralty being responsible for the former, the Navy Board for the latter. Such machinery had often creaked ominously. It was barely adequate for the simple Old Navy: it could never have sufficed for the New. In 1832 Sir James Graham amalgamated the two, making each subordinate member of the new board individually responsible for a single administrative department to a chief himself responsible to Parliament—the First Lord. This led to much greater administrative efficiency; but at first it went too far—it nearly destroyed the Admiralty's original function of direction. For the First Lord, now always a civilian and a political figure, though he obtained admirable technical advice from his naval subordinates, found them too busy with their respective departments to advise him effectively on more general policy. This at times—notably during the Crimean War—led to the unhappy situation of a First Lord interfering too much, and—in a literal sense—ill-advisedly, with the admiral afloat: and it almost led to the abolition of the office of First Lord itself during the early 'sixties, and again during the troubled tenure of Hugh Childers (1868–71). But, just in time, the right balance was achieved. The undoubted advantage of strict departmental responsibility was maintained, as it had to be. Without a Second Sea Lord, responsible for the intricacies of personnel, and a Third Sea Lord (after 1869 called Comptroller), responsible for *matériel*, the baffling problems and crises of that transitional age could scarcely have been tackled. But when George

Goschen, in 1872, put administration and direction in their modern perspective, he created in effect the modern Admiralty. His three 'principles' were: 'supremacy of the First Lord', 'personal responsibility of the other members to the First Lord', and 'utilisation of the full Board as a general council of advice'.[1] Thus direction and administration, like *matériel* and personnel, had their great revolutions after 1830, and had all but assumed their modern shape by 1870.

[1] Sir Oswyn Murray, 'The Admiralty' (*Mariner's Mirror*, 1938, vol. XXIV, no. 4, p. 476).

CHAPTER XII

ARMED FORCES AND THE ART OF WAR:
ARMIES

THE forty years from 1830 to 1870 saw a greater change in the means of warfare, both on land and sea, than during the whole previous span of modern history—or of all previous history. Most of the change was concentrated, at least in the sense of being demonstrated, within the last decade of the period. The technical, tactical, and strategical developments during the wars of this decade foreshadowed the operational trend, and social form, of warfare in the next century. Some of the new trends also exemplified the remarkable influence of two great military thinkers of the nineteenth century, Jomini and Clausewitz, whose main works appeared in the 'thirties.

For many centuries the strength of armies was reckoned in number of men, with merely a distinction between cavalrymen and infantrymen— 'horse' and 'foot', as the two branches, or arms, were customarily described. Subject to that distinction, of respective mobility, it was the most suitable way of computing their material strength before the advent of firearms, and it remained a reasonable form of reckoning so long as firearms were effective only at very short range, while still so inaccurate and slow-loading that the opponent had a good chance, especially if mounted, of coming to close quarters without being shot down. Even so, the volley-fire of infantry armed with the flint-lock musket became sufficiently effective with good training to put a strong curb on cavalry charges, and in the Napoleonic wars the cavalry arm was palpably a diminishing force. At the same time, field artillery played an increasingly important part in Napoleon's later battles, through improved tactical employment in concentrated numbers, so that it became more necessary in a reckoning of strength to count 'guns' as well as 'horse and foot'. But after Napoleon's fall, artillery suffered a relapse while the cavalry did not recover its power—although there was no proportionate decline in its prestige—so that the infantry became, increasingly, the preponderant arm in power as well as in numbers.

It was still reasonable in 1830 to reckon the strength of armies in number of men. But it was no longer a reasonable or safe way of computation by 1870 owing to the immense, and uneven, qualitative development of infantry firearms, and to a lesser extent of artillery. During the next forty years the artillery weapon made faster progress than the infantryman's individual weapon, but the development of the machine-gun, a portable automatic firing weapon, fully maintained the power of 'small arms'. It thus became an absurdity to reckon quantitatively by the number of men, infantry or cavalry. Yet even in the first great war of the twentieth century it was still customary to measure the comparative strength of armies in X-thousand 'rifles' and Y-thousand 'sabres'—so persistent is the grip of traditional habits of thought.

In 1830 the standard infantry firearm was still the flint-lock musket with a smooth bore, loaded from the muzzle end, a ramrod being used to push the round leaden bullet and its cartridge down the barrel. The process of loading was so cumbrous that the rate of fire was rarely more than two rounds a minute, and often less. Only a very good shot could hit a man at more than fifty yards' distance, and the effectiveness of the musket beyond such short range depended on volleys by a close-ranked line of soldiers. Although muskets with a rifled bore had come to be adopted to some extent for the skirmishing light troops, their spiral grooves and tendency to become fouled made loading even slower—the process taking nearly two minutes—while their accuracy was only a little better than the smooth-bore musket's. It is doubtful whether the infantry-man's firearm of the early nineteenth century was superior to the medieval-archer's long-bow which had an effective range of 200–300 yards with more accuracy, and could shoot at about four times as fast a rate as the smooth-bore musket.

The first important development in the nineteenth-century firearm was the percussion musket, using a fulminate priming-powder, which developed from the experiments of a Scottish minister, the Rev. Alexander Forsyth, at the start of the century. His invention aroused some brief interest in government circles and he was invited to pursue his experiments in London, at the Tower. But the conservatively minded Board of Ordnance soon achieved his dismissal, thus quenching the chance of providing the British army with a firearm superior to the flint-lock during the 'Great War' against Napoleon. Shortly after the war the work of other private experimenters made the percussion system more practicable by the use of a copper cap for the detonator. But it was not until 1834 that the military authorities were moved to try it, and not until 1840 that the British army was re-equipped with percussion muskets. After much public pressure the government made a meagre award of £1000 to Forsyth—the payment arriving just after he died! The principal value of the percussion-lock was in achieving an immense reduction in the number of misfires, especially in wet weather.

The next important developments were in the rifled musket. Unless the bullet fitted the bore tightly it lost power and accuracy—through windage, and wastage of the propulsive gases—but if it fitted tightly loading was very slow. The solution was sought in devising a bullet which, while small enough to slide down the barrel easily, could be made to expand into the grooving when fired and thus fill the bore completely. Various methods of producing the expansive effect were evolved. The earliest to be put into use was worked out in 1826 by a French officer, Delvigne, and attracted wide attention when a battalion of *Chasseurs d'Afrique* was armed with his rifle in the Algerian campaign of 1838. In England, Captain Norton had conceived a more promising method in 1823, and this was improved in design by Mr Greener in 1835. It was rejected by the British military authorities, but aroused more interest in France, where in 1847 Captain Minié produced a further improvement of this design that was accepted by the French army. This was adopted in 1851 by the British army—which paid Minié £20,000 for it, and gave Greener a belated reward of £1000 for 'the first public suggestion of the principle of expansion'. Minié's bullet was initially conoidal but later made cylindro-conoidal. This pointed and elongated bullet had a hollow base with an iron cup inserted—which, when the charge was fired, was forced into the cavity in the bullet, thus expanding the base to fit the grooves of the rifle.

The shape of the bullet, in combination with its expansion to fit the grooved bore, produced a great increase of accuracy and of effective range. At 400 yards' range it scored more than 50 per cent in hits, of rounds fired on a target, compared with less than 5 per cent by the percussion musket, which had been adopted only ten years earlier. Even at ranges up to 800 yards, marksmen achieved about 40 per cent in hits. The Minié rifle was first used in war during the 1852 campaign in South Africa against the Kaffirs, and it was then found effective in dispersing small bodies of Kaffirs at ranges up to 1300 yards. But the reliability of the Minié did not match its performance—owing particularly to the weakness of the bullet and the deepness of the grooves—and an improved pattern was produced by the small-arms factory at Enfield. This new 'Enfield' rifle was used in the Crimean War along with the Minié, and then superseded it, becoming the final advance in the muzzle-loading firearm.

For another big advance had already been made abroad with the development of a breech-loading rifle, the 'needle-gun' produced by Johann Nikolaus von Dreyse in 1836 and adopted by the Prussian army in 1841. This rifle had a bolt-action of door-bolt kind, as with the rifles in general use a century later. On pulling the trigger, a striker that had a long and sharp needle-like point was driven, by a spiral spring, through the base of the paper cartridge containing the gunpowder to strike a percussion disc at the forward end and thus ignite the charge. It had a number of defects—the needle was apt to break or bend, and there was a large escape of gas at the breech, which tended to diminish the propulsive power and to cause rust in the rifle's action. But although its effective range was shorter than the later types of muzzle-loading rifle, its rate of fire was about three times as fast—seven shots a minute instead of two.

Above all, it enabled the men to load and fire while lying flat on the ground, thus being a much smaller target for the enemy. The value of the new Prussian weapon was demonstrated in the conflicts with Denmark in 1848 and 1864, and still more against the Austrians in 1866 (cf. p. 325).

The military authorities of most countries tended, as usual, to dwell on the particular defects of the 'needle-gun' rather than on the general advantages of breech-loading, and conservatism was reinforced by economy. But they were stirred to a greater interest in the potentialities of this system. Between 1857 and 1861 four types of breech-loading carbine (a short rifle feasible for use by mounted troops) were experimentally introduced in the British army for cavalry. The four years' duration of the American Civil War provided increasing proof of the advantage of this system, and an increasing proportion of the troops were equipped with breech-loading weapons (cf. ch. XXIV, p. 631). A stronger spur was applied to European armies by the battle successes of the Prussians. In 1866 the French army adopted a breech-loading rifle developed by Antoine Alphonse Chassepot, which was first used in battle at Mentana the next year, where it caused havoc among Garibaldi's troops. In the war of 1870 the Chassepot rifle proved much superior to the German needle-gun, although the technical advantage which the French army had thus achieved was offset by its faults in strategy, tactics and organisation (cf. p. 325). Meanwhile the British army adopted in 1864 a breech-loading rifle designed by an American, Jacob Snider, which was used with striking effect in the Abyssinian campaign of 1868. It was replaced three years later by the Martini–Henry rifle—Martini being another American, who designed the firing action. But although the value of the further advance to a repeating, magazine-feeding rifle was strikingly demonstrated in the later stages of the American Civil War (see ch. XXIV, p. 631), there was a long interval before the European armies adopted rifles of this type— the German in 1884, the French in 1885, the Austrian in 1886, and the British in 1888.

A significant accompaniment of the development in infantry firearms was the increasing limitation of cavalry action. In the Crimean War the cavalry were still able to carry out their traditional role, although at heavy cost. In the American Civil War they were soon reduced to fighting dismounted in battle, and thus to the intermediate mobile role of mounted infantry. The lesson was ignored by European armies, but soon repeated and reinforced by the experience of the Franco-Prussian War of 1870. Even with the now obsolete needle-gun, a single volley by the German infantry shattered the charge of the French cavalry at Sedan. Yet tradition and sentiment had such a dominating influence, swamping a sense of reality, that European armies maintained a large mass of cavalry for more than half a century, and during the 1914–18 war their leaders continued to indulge in vain dreams of repeating the decisive cavalry charges and pursuits of earlier times.

Progress in artillery was not so fast as with the infantry firearm, but during the Crimean War a number of smooth-bore guns were converted into rifled guns, with striking effect in the siege of Sebastopol. Their advantage in range and precision was so marked as to give a strong impetus to the development of guns that should be not only rifled but breech-loading. By 1870 rifled guns were in general use, but the muzzle-loading type was still preferred in most armies. The British tried a breech-loading type in the China campaign of 1860, and it received good reports from the users, but the prejudice against the innovation was so strong that it was rejected in favour of an improved muzzle-loader—which was retained until 1886. Yet in the Franco-Prussian War of 1870 the German artillery was equipped with breech-loading guns while the French were still muzzle-loaders. In analysis of the battles it is clear that this difference of equipment, coupled with superior artillery tactics, gave the Germans a decisive tactical advantage, which outweighed the superiority of the French Chassepot rifle over the German infantry's needle-gun.

The German artillery broke up French infantry attacks at distances of more than a mile—a range too long for the French to use their Chassepot rifles effectively. The Germans, when attacking, were at first so eager to close with the enemy that they would not wait until their own artillery had prepared the way. Thus, particularly in the great battle of Gravelotte–Saint Privat, they forfeited the potentially decisive advantage provided by their superiority, in quality and quantity, of artillery. On the left wing at Saint Privat the Prussian Guard withered under the unshaken fire of the French riflemen, losing a third of its strength, while part of the right wing near Gravelotte was thrown into disorder and fled in panic—although the irresolute and incompetent conduct of the French commander, Marshal Bazaine, eventually retrieved the day for the Germans. But the German infantry learned patience with experience, and the effect of the strategic manœuvre which trapped Marshal MacMahon's army at Sedan was sealed by an enveloping ring of 600 guns, which shattered all break-out attacks by the French, and forced the surrender of an army of 80,000 at a cost to the victor of barely one-tenth of that number.

A more revolutionary type of weapon which made its appearance in the 'sixties was the machine-gun, a weapon producing a stream of shots in rapid succession or simultaneously by a mechanical arrangement of the lock. Attempts to develop such a weapon had been made during previous centuries, usually on a multi-barrelled design. But the first to prove significantly effective was the Gatling gun, which profited from recent developments in breech-loading, and appeared during the American Civil War. Invented by Richard Gatling of Chicago, it was a form of revolving rifle with six or ten barrels—set around an axis and firing in turn when brought into position by the revolving mechanism, so that an almost continuous stream of bullets could be maintained by turning the crank-handle quickly. It was intended as a reinforcement to the fire of the infantry, and at similar ranges.

Meanwhile the French artillery were looking for a weapon that would produce the shower effect of the old case-shot at ranges greater than had been possible with this kind of ammunition—so that it could be fired from positions out of reach of the enemy's rifle fire. Working with this aim —in Napoleon III's private arsenal at the Château de Meudon—Commandant Reffye developed from a Belgian design a *canon à balles*, or *mitrailleuse*, intended for use at ranges from 1500 to 2700 yards. Outwardly it resembled an ordinary field gun, with a wheeled carriage, limber, and four-horse team to draw it. But the gun-barrel was a casing for twenty-five rifle-barrels, with a screw-attached compound breech containing the firing mechanism, and chambers holding twenty-five cartridges apiece. With this a rate of five rounds—125 shots—a minute could be attained. The *mitrailleuse* was adopted by the French army in 1867, and a large number were produced during the next few years. But secrecy was considered of such paramount importance that the men intended to handle the new weapon were given no information or practice before the outbreak of war in 1870, and when used in action most of the crews had not even seen it fired. A worse result of such fatally mistaken secrecy was that the commanders under whom the new weapons were placed distributed them piecemeal for close-quarter action with the forward troops, instead of massing them and firing from positions well back, as intended.

Secrecy had succeeded only in producing an inefficient handling of the new weapon. It did not prevent, but fostered, the spread of rumour that the French had something of this kind up their sleeve. Thus the Germans were quick to spot it, and quashed the threat by turning a concentration of artillery fire on to each of the scattered *mitrailleuses* that appeared in exposed positions, knocking them out one by one. This nullification of the French *mitrailleuse* not only deflated the high hopes which it had raised, but led soldiers everywhere to jump to the conclusion that the fault lay in the weapon itself rather than in the way it had been used. Even when much improved types of machine-gun were developed— automatic firing, small enough to be portable, and easily concealable— the general run of military opinion persisted in regarding machine-guns as of little value, and was ready to dismiss the claims made for them by scornful reference to the failure of the *mitrailleuse* in 1870. Nearly half a century later, none of the armies that went to war in 1914 had more than two such weapons per thousand men. Yet that handful soon dominated the battlefields, and produced a prolonged state of deadlock.

This brief excursion into the next half-century, and projection of its lines of progress, may help to make clearer the significance of the 1830–70 period as the start of a new era in warfare. Moreover, the great development of fire-power during this period was matched, and even exceeded, in results by that which took place in other technical means.

Foremost of these was the railway and its military use as an aid to strategical movement. In Europe its effect was exerted during this period mainly in assisting the offensive, as was demonstrated in the way it enabled the Prussians to achieve an opening advantage, by quick enveloping deployment, over the Austrians in 1866. But in North America its effect on the course of the Civil War was mainly in impeding the offensive —through fostering an encumbering accumulation of numbers at the forward end of the railway line, and thereby making commanders acutely sensitive to any threatened interruption of the flow of supplies to railheads.

The military bearing of this new means of transportation was first appreciated in Prussia. It had been pointed out by several men of vision there as early as 1833—before any railway had been built in that country. The most influential prophet was Friedrich List, the economic theorist. Born in Württemberg, he became an enthusiast for railways during his political exile in the United States, and after his return to Germany in 1832 he devoted much of his time to a press campaign for the development of railways. He argued that a railway network would aid both the political unification of Germany and its defensive strength—enabling it to profit by its central position, hitherto a source of danger, for rapid switching of forces to counter invasion on either side. That idea, defensively inspired, was fulfilled in the subsequent construction of German railways, and given an offensive turn in operational application by Moltke thirty years later.

Moltke had taken a keen interest in railways at an early stage of his career. In 1839, on returning from his advisory mission with the Turkish army, he invested his savings in the new Hamburg–Berlin railway—of which he became a director. The thoroughness with which he studied the technical side is shown in an essay he wrote in 1843 on the principles of laying out and working a railway, while his grasp of the strategic possibilities is indicated in a letter of the following year, to one of his brothers, in which he significantly remarked: 'While the French Chambers are still engaged in discussing the matter, we have laid down three hundred miles of railway, and are working at two hundred more.'[1] In 1846—the year of List's death—the first large-scale movement of troops on record was carried out, as a test exercise, by a Prussian army corps. In 1857 Moltke was appointed Chief of the General Staff, and immediately applied a spur to the military use of railways. He argued, as List had done, that a strategic railway network was required to meet Prussia's two-front risks, and would be the best means towards an effective solution of the problem arising from her precarious situation. Hence he pressed the claims of

[1] *Letters of Field-Marshal Count Helmuth von Moltke to His Mother and His Brothers* (trans. C. Bell and K. W. Fischer; London, 1891), vol. II, p. 138.

strategy to have a deciding voice in civil plans for railway construction. From that time onwards, such plans were usually referred to him, and he gave close attention to all points of detail likely to be of military significance.

The first important operational use of railways was in the Italian war of 1859—when Austria attacked Piedmont, which was supported by a strong French force under Napoleon III (see p. 323). Although Prussia abstained from intervening, Moltke took the opportunity of testing the plans for the rapid transportation and concentration of the Prussian forces. The benefit of the important improvements then made was seen when the Prussians invaded Austria in 1866, and again in the invasion of France in 1870. These two wars brought out the tremendous advantage of a well-developed railway network for the quick concentration and deployment of armies. They changed all previous conceptions and calculations of the basic factors in strategy—force, space, and time. In 1866 the Prussians started their mobilisation later than the Austrians, but were able to use five lines of railway to bring up their forces from the various parts of Prussia, while the Austrians had only one line running forward from Vienna, and did not use that effectively. Moltke succeeded in deploying the Prussian armies on the frontiers of Bohemia and Saxony, and pushing through the Bohemian mountain passes, before the Austrians had completed their concentration in Moravia and begun to advance into Bohemia. Thus the Prussians managed to reach a good strategical position, despite the risks entailed by their delayed mobilisation and wide-flung initial deployment.

The Prussian success in 1866, reinforced by victory over France in 1870, made so deep an impression on the military world that speed of assembly and deployment at the outset came to be regarded as the main key to victory. Thus strategic planning became geared to the time-table—above all, the railway time-table. That trend produced a habit of thought which was to have a fatal effect in precipitating war in 1914, and nullifying the hope of negotiating a settlement of the crisis. It also obscured the paralysing effect on strategy liable to arise from dependence on anything so fixed as a railway line, and so inelastic in transport capacity. The wars of 1866 and 1870 in Europe both ended so quickly, and so successfully for the attacker, as to obscure the inherent drawbacks of such dependence on an inflexible means of strategic movement. The drawbacks were strikingly exposed in the far more prolonged civil war in America, but the lessons received much less attention in European military circles and schools.

A similar recoil-effect occurred with the application of the electric telegraph to military purposes as a means of intercommunication. That effect was manifested very early—in the Crimean War, the first war in which it was used. Its advantages were quickly appreciated by governments, and their military advisers, as a means of keeping in touch with the commanders in the field. But in the view of the commanders themselves the disadvantages bulked larger—the British commander complaining that the new means of long-distance communication 'upset everything', and the French commander that he was 'at the paralysing end of an electric cable'. In the American Civil War the paralysing tendency became even more predominant. Nevertheless, this means of quick long-distance communication was of great value, when wisely used, in co-ordinating the action of the armies that were operating in different theatres, so widely spread. In the war of 1866 the telegraph enabled Moltke to direct most of the movements of the Prussian armies from his office in Berlin, and he did not move up to the front until almost the eve of the decisive battle, of Königgrätz—while on reaching the front he found it harder to keep informed of the situation than at his desk in Berlin. His long-range control had worked well on the whole because he wisely confined it to broad strategic directions and left the executants a large measure of freedom. When General Headquarters moved up close to the front it was dependent, as in the past, on messages carried by mounted liaison officers.

That condition still prevailed in 1870, for although seven field telegraph detachments had been mobilised nothing was done during the crucial frontier battles to lay a linking wire between Moltke's position and the army headquarters, two of which were quite close. The omission appears to have been due partly to a fear that such a wire might be tapped by the enemy, but even more to a desire that the initiative of army commanders should not be weakened by the feeling that they were tied to a wire. For Prussian military doctrine gave more emphasis than any other to the cultivation and uncurbed use of initiative by subordinate commanders.

The possibility of combining such initiative with harmonious co-operation towards the common goal was largely due to the Prussian system of staff organisation and training. In the struggle against Napoleon the military reformers Scharnhorst and Gneisenau, developing the earlier ideas of Massenbach, had created the nucleus of a 'General Staff' with functions wider and responsibility greater than those of former staff assistants to a commander—who were usually little more than gallopers to carry his orders, or clerks to deal with administrative detail. In the Prussian system the General Staff was to be the collective brain of the army. It was to formulate tactical doctrine, prepare operational plans in peace as well as in war, and provide expert advisers for the field commands, both high and low. Such staff officers would share responsibility with the actual commanders, besides relieving them of the detailed planning. They would apostolically interpret the concepts of the General Staff to the commander, and the commander's decisions to his subordinate executants. Where he was not present, they could use their own discretion and give orders in his name which overrode those issued in circumstances that had changed. Such intelligent variation of orders, to the point of nominal disobedience, depended on the development of a common doctrine and habit of thought in dealing with problems. The spread of such a common doctrine was helped by the practice of sending General-Staff officers back to regimental duty at intervals.

The Prussian staff system was consolidated, and its military educational basis developed, during the half-century following Waterloo. In 1821 the General Staff was detached from the War Ministry and made a separate advisory organ, but still subordinate to the Ministry. That measure temporarily diminished its influence, although potentially giving it more independence. Its power did not grow until the later stages of the war of 1864 against Denmark, and then fortuitously—when hitches in the campaign led to the Chief of the General Staff, Moltke, being sent to act as chief of staff to the commander of the field army. The successful results produced a change in the fighting leaders' view that the General Staff was merely a superfluous group of 'backroom boys'. At the start of the war of 1866 it was given direct control of the field armies, and Moltke replaced the War Minister as the prime military adviser to the king. The paramount position of the General Staff was confirmed by the victorious war of 1870 against France. This led other armies to reorganise and develop their staff organisation and training on similar lines.

Thus the conduct of warfare became more orchestral than in the past, when the issue was often decided by the individual ability of the respective field commanders, and their art counted for more than corporate technique. The intellectual discipline and common habit of thought developed by the General Staff system produced a higher level of functional efficiency, but also tended to a uniformity and conventionality of thought that hindered the recognition of changing conditions and the adoption of new ideas.

Another, and worse, sequel of the paramount position gained by the General Staff was to foster the military concept, a product of the specialist's narrow view, that military victory was an end in itself, to which political considerations and aims should be secondary and subordinate, at least until the enemy was crushed. That concept and claim came to the fore as soon as Moltke gained control of the Prussian Army's operations. It produced clashes with Bismarck, when he sought to limit the military aims and bring about an early peace in 1866, and again in 1870. Subsequently the increasing influence of the General Staff powerfully contributed to the tendency for military considerations to dictate policy which had such fateful consequences two generations later.

The recruiting and organisation of armies during this period showed no such revolutionary change as occurred in the technical means of fire, movement, and communication. But there was an increasing systematisation, especially in the application of conscription, which had such an important and far-reaching influence not only in the military field but also in social and political ways that it amounted to a revolution—or at least completed that which had spasmodically started with the wars of the French Revolution.

It might have been no more than a spasm but for Prussian military policy and theory, together with the effect of Prussia's dramatic military successes half a century after Waterloo. In France, conscription was cast off with Napoleon, since it had become the people's greatest grievance under his rule. Through it they had been bled white, and its abolition was one of the main points in the new constitution. In other continental countries the conscript system nominally continued in force, and even in France was soon revived, but with such extensive modification and permission for substitution that it became in practice little more than a supplement to standing armies mainly composed of men who voluntarily undertook a long-service engagement. In France, for example, there were only 120,000 conscripts in 1866 among the army's total establishment of 400,000.

But in Prussia the system was maintained as the real basis of the army, and short-service conscripts continued to be the largest component. The Prussian people were the more easily persuaded to accept its continuance since it was associated in their minds—unlike those of the French people —with liberation from Napoleon's tyranny.

The Prussian Army Law of 1814 laid down the rule of compulsory service for all men between the ages of seventeen and fifty, and although the rule was not fully applied in practice the principle was thus constitutionally consolidated. In 1860 the growing possibility of war with Neo-Napoleonic France led to its extension in practice. The annual intake was increased from 40,000 to 63,000—for three years' active duty and four years' reserve service. That raised the effective strength of the army and its immediate reserves from 200,000 to 440,000. The change met great opposition, and led to a prolonged struggle between the king, guided by Bismarck, and parliament (see ch. XIX, pp. 509–20). The people in general became reconciled to the new law only after the victories of 1866 and 1870 —which also swung the other continental countries into line with the Prussian system.

The consequences were multiple and far-reaching. When armies became bigger in scale, wars tended to become more comprehensive in scope. They imposed greater demands on industry, which became more closely geared to military needs. Armies became less manageable, and this handicap, in conjunction with the greater quantity of trained man-power available in reserve, tended to make wars longer in duration. War became less politically controllable—at all stages, from inception to completion. In the first place, universal conscription tended to precipitate war, as the dramatic calling-up of the nations' men from their civil jobs produced a state of excitement and disturbance prejudicial to diplomatic efforts to avert a conflict, and also because the machinery of mass mobilisation and deployment was so dependent on keeping rigidly to time-table. That effect was very clearly seen in the outbreak of war in 1914. Moreover, once a war broke out under these conditions, its widened embrace coupled with mass emotion hindered any limitation of aim or action, making a negotiated settlement far more difficult than in wars waged by professional forces under the control of statesmanship. Thus the effects of war became much worse, and more damaging to all concerned, as war became more 'total'.

Moreover, although conscription had the appearance of being democratic, it provided autocratic rulers, hereditary or revolutionary, with more effective and comprehensive means of imposing their will, not only in war but in peace. Once the rule of compulsory service in arms was re-established for the young men of a nation, it was an all too easy transition for a government to bring the whole population into a state of servitude. Totalitarian tyranny is the natural offspring of total war.

That reflection prompts an examination of the trend of military theory during the incubatory period in the nineteenth century, and of its influence on the development of the quantitative ideas, unlimited aims, and unbridled violence of action which in combination produced the 'total war' of the next century.

The nineteenth century saw two outstanding military theorists, Jomini and Clausewitz. Born almost at the same time, nearly ten years before the French Revolution, both began to have an influence as young men, during the Napoleonic wars. But their principal works were published, and their influence thus greatly extended, in the 1830's. Their thought and writings moulded the minds and doctrines of the next generation of soldiers, who conducted the wars of the 'sixties—and in Clausewitz's case the influence extended, with increasing effect, to successive generations after 1870.

Jomini, born in 1779, was of Swiss origin. Like many ardent students of war he was of unmilitary parentage. But the outbreak of revolution in Switzerland rescued him from a bank-clerk's stool in Paris and gave him military opportunity—to command a battalion when aged only twenty-one. The peace of Lunéville ended that first opportunity, and brought him back to a civil job, but gave him leisure for reflection on the experience and for military thinking of wider scope. At twenty-five, in 1804, he produced an ambitious text-book, his *Traité des grandes opérations militaires*. It attracted the attention of Marshal Ney, who invited Jomini to accompany him on the campaign of 1805 as a volunteer aide-de-camp. Later that year Napoleon also read the book and was so impressed that he gave Jomini a colonel's commission in the French army, appointing him to his own staff for the campaign against Prussia the next year. Jomini's services were rewarded by a barony and promotion to general of brigade. But his rapid advancement and growing influence aroused jealousy, particularly on the part of Napoleon's chief of staff, Berthier—who, in 1813, blocked Jomini's further promotion. The emperor of Russia had earlier made a bid for his services, and now renewed it, offering him a lieutenant-general's commission, which Jomini accepted. After the fall of Napoleon in 1815 Jomini gave offence to his new employers and their allies by his strenuous efforts to save his old patron, Ney, from execution. Jomini then went back to military writing, but was soon recalled to become military tutor to the tsarevitch, and then did much to develop staff education in Russia. On retirement in 1829 he settled in Brussels, where he produced his famous *Précis de l'art de la guerre*, for two generations the most esteemed of all books on war.

It still remains a remarkably clear definition of the various types of war, and exposition of the differences which should affect the conduct of each type. Jomini was not blinded by the post-Napoleonic worship of unlimited force regardless of the end, and of the dividend. He pointed out that in wars where a profit was sought offensive operations should be proportioned to the end proposed. And he significantly remarked in comment on Napoleon's later career: 'One might say that he was sent into this world to teach generals and statesmen what they ought to avoid.'[1]

Jomini praised Napoleon for breaking away from the old point-winning convention, and for perceiving that 'the first means of doing great things was to strive, above all, to dislocate and ruin the enemy army; certain that states and provinces fall of themselves when they have no longer organised forces to cover them'.[2] But with the Russian and Spanish campaigns stamped on his memory, Jomini emphasised that the pursuit of this object must be governed by the conditions. His own moderate view was that 'the excessive abuse which Napoleon made of this system does not destroy the real advantage that it offers, so long as one knows how to put a limit on one's successes, and to set one's enterprises in harmony with the respective condition of the neighbouring armies and nations'.[3] If European military thought had continued under the influence of Jomini, the nations would hardly have pursued mutual destruction so thoughtlessly in 1914–18.

But the stalemate which developed after the opening moves would still have been probable. For Jomini's teaching failed to set in correct focus the basic conditions of mobile war, or point out the requirements as clearly as Bourcet and Guibert, the two leading military thinkers of the late eighteenth century, had done in the theory they had developed—and which Napoleon had so brilliantly applied in his earlier campaigns.

[1] *Précis de l'art de la guerre* (Paris, 1838), vol. 1, p. 58.
[2] *Ibid.* p. 201.   [3] *Ibid.* p. 202.

Jomini defined 'the fundamental principle of war' as comprising:

1. Carrying by strategic combinations the mass of the forces of an army successively on the decisive points of a theatre of war, and as far as possible upon the enemy's communications without endangering one's own.

2. Manœuvring in such a manner as to engage this mass against fractions only of the enemy's army.

3. Directing equally...by tactical manœuvres the mass of one's forces upon the decisive point of the battlefield, or upon that part of the enemy line that it is important to overwhelm.

4. Contriving that these masses are not only brought to bear upon the decisive point, but that they are brought into action with energy and as a whole, in such a way as to produce a simultaneous effort.[1]

That simple definition contained a profound truth, but was too simple to convey the truth adequately. Moreover, in Jomini's elaboration of it he put the emphasis on massed instead of on surprise effect; on geometry instead of on mobility. The error became more perceptible in his concise definition of the principle as 'the art of putting into action the maximum possible forces at the decisive point'.[2] By the dropping out of that key word, the adverb 'successively', the vital idea of fluid concentration is lost from sight, and is replaced by the picture of a concentrated mass—which can be met by a concentrated enemy.

His *Précis de l'art de la guerre* failed to bring out the fundamental truth that a point only becomes decisive when its condition permits the attacker to gain a decision there. For this to be possible it must be a weak point relatively to the force concentrated against it. The real art of war is to ensure or create that weakness. Distraction in one form or another is the most effective instrument, and mobility is its mainspring.

But Jomini was little concerned either with generating mobility or with immobilising the enemy. He was too interested in the form of operations to see the need of injecting the vital fluid into them. He filled pages in discussing bases of operation, zones of operation, lines of operation, fronts of operation, objective points, strategic points, manœuvre lines, interior lines, eccentric and concentric operations—all with an abundance of geometric diagrams. He showed the properties, advantages, and disadvantages of each. But he did not give due reflection to the fact that an advantageous line of operation depends for its effect on the enemy being unable to block it—which depends on distraction. Nor did he give due weight to the moral weight of the unexpected.

In justice to Jomini one should point out that his mathematical treatment of war was characteristic of the age, and that he did not press it to such extremes as other writers.

He saw the fallacy of 'making war trigonometrically', and pointed out that 'the nature of the country, the lines of rivers and mountains, the moral state of the armies, the spirit of the people, the capacity and energy of the

---

[1] *Ibid.* pp. 157–8.　　　　　　　　[2] *Ibid.* p. 254.

chiefs, are not measured by angles, diameters, and peripheries'. He gave examples to show that Napoleon had successfully violated such formulae, and remarked 'the explanation is simple, it is that war is an impassioned drama, and by no means a mathematical operation'.[1]

Yet by his fondness for geometrical terms and diagrams, as well as his inattentiveness to mobility, he unintentionally distorted the outlook of his pupils. In his exposition the mathematical aspect of strategy obscured the psychological basis of war. Despite his own good sense, based on personal experience, he made strategy appear a science of lines and points to pupils who lacked his experience of war.

Worse still, he focused their eyes on a single objective point. His teaching shows no sign that he had recognised the vital significance of Bourcet's argument that every plan ought to have branches, so that if one line is blocked by the enemy, another may be instantly developed to serve the same purpose. No theory of war could be adequate which overlooked that principle. For war is a two-party affair. Thus, to be practical, any theory must take account of the opposing side's power to upset your plan. The best guarantee against their interference is to be ready to adapt your plan to circumstances, and to have ready a variant that may fit the new circumstances. To keep this elasticity while still keeping the initiative, the best way is to choose a line originally which offers alternative objectives.

The drawbacks of Jomini's teaching were illustrated in the American Civil War. The most studious general in either army was Halleck, whose mind had been nourished on Jomini. Yet in practice Halleck proved perhaps the most ineffective pedant who ever commanded armies, a general whose paralysing hand produced stalemate wherever he directed. Another pupil was Sherman, and it can be seen that his knowledge of text-book lore at first handicapped him in comparison with Grant, a man of unlettered and unfettered common sense. Sherman's development was delayed until he had gradually freed his mind from theoretical bonds, and learned from experience to pursue the unexpected instead of the orthodox. Then, his superior intellect enabled him to produce and practise a theory of his own which decided the war, and in which, significantly, his strategic aim was to place the enemy 'on the horns of a dilemma' by having alternative objectives. But there was a final irony in the fact that Sherman's war-winning manœuvre through Georgia and the Carolinas against Lee's rear was delayed through Halleck's influence—an influence exerted upon the side of what is miscalled 'sound strategy'.

When the next great war came, in Europe, Jomini's influence had been to a large extent supplanted. Not through profitable attention to the lessons of the American Civil War, which were foolishly ignored, but through the greater growth of another writer's influence. For the victories of 1866 and 1870 were gained under the direction of Clausewitz's dis-

[1] *Traité des grandes opérations militaires* (Paris, 1804), vol. III, pp. 274–5.

ciples in the Prussian General Staff, and this striking testimony to the value of his theories quickly made their influence paramount everywhere. His classic work *On War* (*Vom Kriege*) shaped military and even political thinking throughout the world in the succeeding generations. By that dual effect Clausewitz had perhaps a greater effect on the world than any of its executive rulers during that time. Unhappily it moulded both military and political thought in a form that in some vital respects was deforming.

His book was by far the most profound study of war that had been published anywhere, apart from the Chinese classic of Sun Tzu about 500 B.C.—which was more lucid and in some respects more profound. That Clausewitz's great work, so full of valuable thought, had predominantly ill effects was partly, but not wholly due, to the way it was misinterpreted by shallower minds. It was the product of twelve years' intensive thought; if its author had lived longer he might have reached wiser and clearer conclusions. There are ample indications that, as his thinking progressed, he was being led towards a different view—penetrating deeper. Unhappily, the process was cut short.

Clausewitz was born in 1780, the year after Jomini. He was steeped in war before he had time for education. For he entered the army at the age of twelve, gaining a commission at the siege of Mainz two years later. He used the opportunity to develop his own education, and in 1801 gained admittance to the Berlin Academy for Officers, where he became a favourite pupil of Scharnhorst. In 1809 he became one of Scharnhorst's assistants in the reform of the Prussian army and its training after its defeat by Napoleon. In 1812 he joined the Russian army, thus participating in the campaign which ended in Napoleon's fateful retreat from Moscow. Early in 1815 he rejoined the Prussian army and was chief of staff to Thielmann's corps during the Waterloo campaign. In 1818 he was made director of the Prussian War School, where he remained for twelve years. His work here was mainly administrative, but he devoted his spare time to a fresh and deeper study of military theory, and an effort to think out a philosophy of war. Returning to more active duty in 1830, as chief of staff to the army on the Polish frontier, he fell a victim to cholera the following year. It was only after his death that his writings on war were published, by his widow.

They were found in a number of sealed packets, bearing the significant and prophetic note—'Should the work be interrupted by my death then what is found can only be called a mass of conceptions not brought into form...open to endless misconceptions.'[1] Misinterpretation has been the common fate of most prophets and thinkers in every sphere. It must be admitted, however, that Clausewitz invited misinterpretation more

---

[1] Note dated 10 July 1827—printed immediately after his widow's Preface in the first edition, 1832.

than most. A student of Kant at second hand, he had acquired a philosophical mode of expression, and his theory of war was expounded in a way too abstract for ordinary soldier-minds, essentially concrete, to follow the course of his argument—which often turned back from the direction in which it was apparently leading. Impressed yet befogged, they grasped at his often vivid leading phrases, seeing only their surface meaning and missing the deeper current of his thought.

Clausewitz's greatest contribution to the theory of war was in emphasising the psychological factors. Raising his voice against the geometrical school of strategy, then fashionable, he showed that the human spirit was infinitely more important than operational lines and angles. He discussed the effect of danger and fatigue, the value of boldness and determination, with deep understanding. Moreover, he appreciated and emphasised the importance of surprise and the moral effect of the unexpected. 'It lies', he declared, 'more or less at the foundation of all undertakings, for without it the preponderance at the decisive point is not properly conceivable.'[1] That is a phrase which his later disciples would have done better to remember than many which stuck in their minds.

It was his oversights, however, which had the greater effect on the subsequent course of history. He was too continental in outlook to understand the meaning of sea-power. He was too little concerned with the development of weapons—and, on the very threshold of the mechanical age, declared his 'conviction that superiority in numbers becomes every day more decisive'.[2] Such a dictum gave reinforcement to the instinctive conservatism of soldiers in resisting the possibilities of the new form of superiority which mechanical invention increasingly offered. It also gave a powerful impulse to the universal extension and permanent establishment of the method of conscription—as a simple way of providing the greatest possible numbers. This, by its disregard for psychological suitability, meant that armies became more liable to panic, and sudden collapse.

In his operational teaching there is much valuable guidance, but in some important respects it is misguiding and narrowing. A significant example lies in his dictum—'there is no more imperative and no simpler law for strategy than to keep the forces concentrated—no portion is to be separated from the main body unless called away by some urgent necessity. On this maxim we stand firm.'[3] It shows only too clearly that he regarded strength as a matter of solidity, and had missed the essential point of the Napoleonic system. He still thought in terms of *physical concentration* instead of *potential unity*. Indeed, there is no sign throughout his book that he had grasped the value of Napoleon's elastic

---

[1] Book III, ch. ix, para. 1.   [2] Book v, ch. iii, para. 2.
[3] Book III, ch. xi, para. 1.

grouping and wide distribution as a means to distraction of the enemy's concentration and a prelude to a suddenly concentrated blow against a weakened part of the enemy's position or forces.

The worst effect of Clausewitz's views came through his metaphysical exposition of the idea of 'absolute' warfare. By taking the logical extreme as the theoretical ideal, he conveyed the impression, to superficial readers, that the road to success was through the unlimited application of force. Thereby a doctrine which defined war as 'only a continuation of state policy by other means'[1] led to the contradictory end of making policy the servant of strategy. Moreover, Clausewitz contributed to the subsequent decay of generalship when in an oft-quoted passage he wrote—'Philanthropists may easily imagine that there is a skilful method of disarming and overcoming the enemy without great bloodshed, and that this is the proper tendency of the Art of War....It is an error which must be extirpated.'[2] Clausewitz was reacting against the extremely careful and force-conserving leaders of the late eighteenth century whose cautious manœuvring had been disrupted by Napoleon's quickness in bringing on a battle. Unfortunately Clausewitz's corrective arguments would henceforth be cited by countless blunderers to excuse, and even to justify, their futile squandering of life in bull-headed assaults.

An even more disastrous dictum of his was that—'to introduce into the philosophy of war a principle of moderation would be an absurdity. ...War is an act of violence pushed to its utmost bounds.'[3] That declaration served as a foundation for the self-exhausting absurdity and futility of 'total' war in the twentieth century. The principle of force without limit and without calculation of cost is the negation of statesmanship. A state which expends its strength to the point of exhaustion bankrupts its own policy.

That hard truth of experience had been appreciated earlier, in the Age of Reason which followed the devastating Thirty Years War. Clausewitz himself recognised it, for in the development of his argument he emphasised that to pursue the logical extreme entailed that 'the means would lose all relation to the end, and in most cases the aim at an extreme effort would be wrecked by the opposing weight of forces within itself'.[4] He provided the clue to his own apparent inconsistency when he explained that—'Reasoning in the abstract, the mind cannot stop short of an extreme...but everything takes a different shape when we pass from abstractions to reality.'[5] In the course of his writings, drafted over a period of some fourteen years, he brought out many of the limitations that he had come to see as his study extended. But his qualifying passages made less impression than the dramatic phrases in which he defined the logical extreme, and depicted it as the ideal.

[1] Book I, ch. i, sec. 24.　　　[2] Book I, ch. i, sec. 3.　　　[3] *Ibid.*
[4] Book VIII, ch. iii, sec. B.　　　[5] Book I, ch. i, sec. b.

It proved fateful for humanity that one of his earliest disciples, Moltke, became the directing mind in Prussia's victorious campaigns of 1866 and 1870. This brought an immense extension of Clausewitz's influence. Henceforth his gospel was accepted everywhere as true—and wholly true. All soldiers were quick to swallow it, although few were capable of digesting it.

Much of the harm might have been avoided but for the fatal cholera germ that intervened to deprive him of the chance of reformulating his theory in accord with the evolution of his thought, and taking greater care against the misinterpretation of his original concept of 'absolute' war. His death, before he could revise his treatise, left the way open to 'endless misconceptions' far in excess of his anticipation—for the general adoption of the theory of unlimited war went far to wreck civilisation. The teaching of Clausewitz, taken without understanding, largely influenced both the causation and the character of the first world war. Thereby it led on, all too logically, to the second world war.

It was not until the 'sixties that the new technical means and less-new concepts began to exert an important influence on the course of wars. But there is a misjudgment in the view later prevailing among military students that the fifty years following Waterloo were a barren period— a view epitomised in the statement of one distinguished military historian that 'War-weary Europe was practically sterile from a military point of view'.[1] The most fertile phase of nineteenth-century military thought, signalised by the writings of Jomini and Clausewitz, came when Europe was most war-weary. The wars of the period also provide evidence that military art did not decay, nor tactical progress cease, so completely as came to be assumed by writers and historians in the later part of the century.

In the French conquest of Algeria, Bugeaud displayed a dynamic energy and mobility comparable with Napoleon's, while developing a technique aptly fitted to the differing conditions of irregular warfare. France had, in 1830, sent an expeditionary force to occupy Algiers, but it ran into trouble when trying to establish control of the interior. The massive French columns, cumbrously organised and equipped on European lines, were continually harassed and frequently trapped by nimble native forces under the inspiring and skilful leadership of Abd-el-Kader, the amir of Mascara. But a break in the clouds came in 1836 when Bugeaud, given a subordinate command in western Algeria, carried out swift offensive thrusts with flying columns, lightly equipped and self-contained for supplies—which they carried on horses, mules and camels, instead of in wagons. In 1840 Bugeaud was made Governor-General of Algeria, and applied the new technique more extensively, chasing Abd-el-Kader's

[1] A. F. Becke, *Introduction to the History of Tactics, 1740–1905* (London, 1909), p. 38.

forces from place to place, and disrupting their sources of maintenance, while strengthening French control of the territory gained by building a network of roads. His operations were a conscious application of a theory he had evolved in reflection, particularly from study of Roman practice, and his account of them became a classic treatise on colonial warfare for later generations of French soldiers.

Another notable demonstration of the military art, in a European setting, was provided by the Austrian commander, Field-Marshal Radetzky, in the Italian War of 1848–9—when he shattered the first of the three big efforts to eject the Austrians from Italy. Profiting by the revolution in Vienna and the revolt of the Hungarians, an Italian rising started in Milan (17 March 1848), and quickly spread throughout Lombardy and Venetia. King Charles Albert of Sardinia advanced eastward to its support with the Piedmontese army, while papal and Neapolitan forces moved up, bringing the Italian strength up to nearly 100,000. At that moment the Austrian army, of 70,000, was scattered in many small garrisons, and in Milan Radetzky had barely 10,000 troops. Evacuating Milan, to evade being trapped, he retreated to the historic Quadrilateral of fortified towns (Mantua–Peschiera–Verona–Legnago) between the Mincio and the Adige. Here, while awaiting reinforcements, he succeeded in repelling the attacks of the Piedmontese forces, although Peschiera fell to them. When reinforced, and while keeping the Piedmontese in check, he turned eastward and annihilated the papal and Neapolitan forces established astride his line of communication, near Vicenza. Next, he cleared the Brenta valley. Then he turned back against the Piedmontese, and pierced their front at Custoza by a quick concentration of superior force on one sector. Swiftly following up his victory, Radetzky chased the Piedmontese back into their own territory and reoccupied Milan on 4 August.

The continuance of civil war in Austria and Hungary encouraged the Italian patriots to make a fresh bid for independence in 1849, and in March the Piedmontese army—reorganized and strengthened—advanced afresh on Milan, with some 80,000 men. This time Radetzky had nearly as large a force available. But he again evacuated Milan, and moved south-eastward, giving the appearance of retreating towards Piacenza. Then he suddenly wheeled westward to Pavia, crossed the Ticino on the 20th, and turned the Piedmontese right flank, driving a wedge between their main army and the force intended to cover its flank. Thrown off balance, the Piedmontese fell back over the Ticino, but their attempt to block Radetzky's northwestward thrust across their rear was nullified by another quick by-passing move on his part—which forced them to fall back northward, to Novara, on the 22nd. Next day, Radetzky again moved north-westward, to block their line of retreat, following a mistaken report that they had already withdrawn westward. In consequence, only his right wing hit the Piedmontese position at Novara—and with only one of his four corps against the whole of the enemy's main army, the situation looked perilous for some hours. But the danger was diminished by the dislocating and paralysing effect already achieved, and in the afternoon the other corps arrived successively, reinforcing the attack while developing a strong threat to the enemy's flank, and line of retreat. The effect was decisive and that night Charles Albert abdicated in favour of his son, Victor Emmanuel, who was granted an armistice on lenient terms—this enabled the Austrians to crush the renewed revolt in their Italian provinces and then to release troops for the task of restoring control in the central parts of the empire.

The energy and rapidity that Radetzky had showed in these campaigns was the more remarkable as he was eighty-two years old. But his ardent interest in military art and theory had kept him mentally fresh during many years of frustration in pressing his ideas of army reform, so that he proved capable of exploiting the opportunity that at last came to him in old age.

The more usual performance, and consequence, of elderly commanders was seen five years later, in the Crimean War—one of the most ill-managed campaigns in modern history (see also ch. XVIII, pp. 478–83). Its only enduring interest and value for study of the art of war is in providing abundant examples of 'how *not* to do it'—tactically and logistically. The original British commander-in-chief, Lord Raglan, and all save one of his divisional commanders were nearing seventy years of age. So was the Russian commander-in-chief, Menshikov. The French commanders were not so old, and their tactical performance was not so bad; but it was far from brilliant. The generals, on both sides, were mostly of the 'pipeclay and polish' school that had become paramount in a long period of peace. The barrack square constituted the bounds of their horizon, and precision in close-order drill was regarded as the standard test of professional efficiency. The British troops had very little training in field exercises, and their commanders no experience in handling large formations. The Russians, with more opportunity, still handled them in parade-ground style, and moved about the battlefield in a densely massed way that took no account of improvement in firearms. Moreover, most of their troops were still armed with smooth-bore muskets.

The administrative organisation was even worse than the tactical handling, and much more damaging—to both sides. The Allied expedition to capture Sebastopol, Russia's only naval base in the Black Sea, was launched with scanty knowledge of the geographical conditions. It was assumed that the Crimea, being a peninsula, could be easily isolated by using the Allied fleets to dominate the isthmus with their guns—until the belated discovery that the sea on either side of the isthmus was much too shallow for the ships to close within range of it. The British brought sufficient horses to mount their cavalry and draw their artillery, but no transport to carry their food and ammunition supplies. When the landing, in mid-September, failed to bring about the speedy fall of the fortress, the expeditionary force was found lacking in almost all requirements for a prolonged winter campaign. The field hospitals were soon appallingly overcrowded, and before the end of the year less than half the British force was fit for service. The French loss from sickness was even higher than the British, although hidden by a more strictly controlled press. The Russian losses were much heavier still, while drafts sent to the Crimea to fill gaps in the ranks suffered so greatly on the long winter journey that two-thirds of the men died on the way from sickness or hunger.

It was the all-round incompetence in this first important European war since 1815 which led later students to take the too sweeping view that the whole fifty years between Waterloo and Prussia's success in 1866 was a period of sterility and decay in warfare.

That impression was not redeemed by the second Italian War, of 1859, when Napoleon III with a French army 150,000 strong backed the Piedmontese in a fresh effort to liberate Italy from the Austrians. Yet in some respects the campaign showed notable developments in means and methods. Both sides made use of railways in the mobilisation and assembly of their forces, while the French after deployment in Piedmont used one of the lines there in switching their weight from the right flank to the left for a blow against the Austrian right flank near Magenta—a plan inspired by Jomini, whose advice had been sought by Napoleon III. The French army, too, profiting by the lessons of the Crimean War, had organised large transport echelons to carry reserve supplies of ammunition for each corps, and to maintain supplies from France. They also introduced new rifled cannon, which gave them an advantage over the Austrians, still armed with smooth-bore cannon.

But the conduct of operations did not match these improvements. While Napoleon showed much energy at the start, the French moves were slow and poorly co-ordinated. The French won the Battle of Magenta, on 4 June, but they did not succeed in exploiting their success, and the Austrians withdrew safely to the Quadrilateral—although their fumbling conduct of operations had allowed their opponents more openings and opportunities than in Radetzky's day.

The French were tardy in following up the withdrawal, and Napoleon's attention was distracted by the threatening Prussian mobilisation on the Rhine. Meanwhile the young emperor, Francis Joseph, assumed supreme command of the Austrians—who now took the offensive, on 24 June, just as the French were moving forward to the Mincio. Thus the two armies collided head-on, in a way that neither had expected, and this encounter battle at Solferino became a 'soldier's battle'—of hard fighting and confused generalship. In the afternoon the Austrians broke off the battle and retired across the Mincio, but the French had suffered almost as heavily, and were in no condition to press their advantage. Thus

Napoleon, with the shadow of Prussian invasion looming in his rear, was glad to make a compromise peace. But the 'battle honours' of Magenta and Solferino were more than offset by the way that the military weaknesses of France as well as of Austria had been made clear to watchful eyes in Prussia. Bismarck could now more confidently guide Prussia's policy towards challenging Austria's primacy in the German sphere, and then, with a united Germany under her own leadership, tackling France. Moltke and Roon, the War Minister, also profited from long-range observation of the 1859 campaign in preparing Prussia's forces for the prospective conflicts. Moltke wrote an account of that war; it was the first official staff history published in any army and set a new standard in military scholarship.

The technical and tactical features of the wars of 1866 and 1870 have already been surveyed (pp. 305–11). Strategically, the main feature of the 'Seven Weeks War' in 1866 was the extraordinary width of the Prussians' deployment, their main force of 250,000 troops being extended over a front of 270 miles—in order to cover Silesia as well as Berlin, to make supply easier, and to save time by using all available railways. Such a wide extension meant that the ratio of force to space was very low, and would have been hazardous in face of a mobile and dynamic opponent—all the more since the Austrians, who were equal in numbers, could reckon on direct reinforcement by a Saxon force of 25,000 and indirect aid from Bavaria and other German states—Württemberg, Hesse-Darmstadt, Hanover and Hesse-Kassel—whose total forces amounted to a further 150,000 men.

But Moltke, with good reason, felt that he could count on the Austrians being neither mobile nor dynamic, and that their allies could be kept in check by a relatively small detachment from his forces. He also reckoned on the three Prussian armies being able to push through the frontier mountain belt quickly, converging inward, and then concentrating on a shorter front in northern Bohemia. In this calculation he was disappointed, owing to loss of time caused by the king's unwillingness to appear the aggressor, and during the delay the Austrian army moved forward into Moltke's intended concentration area, where it deployed on a forty-mile front. Moreover, a mistaken deduction that the Austrians intended to invade Silesia led the Prussian crown prince, on the left wing, to move his army south-eastwards to shield this projecting province—thereby extending the marching front again just as it was closing in.

The Austrian commander-in-chief, Benedek, did not take advantage of the opportunity offered by this expansion, even when the crown prince's army got into difficulties in its advance through the mountain defiles. Instead, Benedek became paralysed by the extending threat to his own flank and rear. All he did was to concentrate his forces more closely —like a hedgehog rolling itself up into a ball—thus forfeiting the potential counter-offensive advantage of his central position, while making it easier for the Prussians to envelop him in the static position which he took up on an eight-mile front near Königgrätz. Here Prince Frederick Charles's army, in the Prussian centre, ran into danger of defeat by attacking prematurely and alone on 3 July, but the risk incurred by such impetuosity was redeemed by Prussian energy, and the arrival of the crown prince's army on the Austrian flank, in the afternoon, decided the issue of the battle—and of the war.

The brief campaign had been a triumph for Moltke's strategy, and while the result owed much to effects he had not planned, it was greatly influenced by his flexibility in adapting his plan to circumstances—so that blunders by the executants were redeemed and even converted into advantages. It is evident, however, that the Prussians also owed much to the technical and tactical advantage provided by their breech-loading rifle against opponents who were still armed with a muzzle-loading rifle. The Austrian losses, apart from men taken prisoner, were three times as heavy as the Prussian—25,000 against 9000—even though the Prussian infantry, as the attackers, had to expose themselves far more. Most significantly, in the one battle won by the Austrians, the frontier fight at Trautenau, they lost nearly five times as many men as the Prussian corps they drove off the battlefield.

The strategic pattern of the Franco-Prussian war of 1870 was broadly similar to that of 1866, and became more similar as operations developed. Moreover, the outcome was more clearly due to a superiority in strategy and mobility—the product of superior leadership, staffwork, and training. For in this war the weapon-balance was more even, as the German advantage in artillery was offset by the French advantage in small arms. But this time, Moltke's strategy was backed by a superiority of numbers, since the forces of the other German states were now added to Prussia's strength. Thanks to skilful staff planning and rail organisation, a total of some 380,000 men (in three armies) were mobilised and transported to the forward zone in eighteen days—compared with five weeks in 1866—while three more corps, with a further 90,000, were brought up as soon as rail transport was available (they were initially kept back as a safeguard against Austrian intervention). The French mobilisation broke down in such confusion that large numbers of reservists were late in arriving at the front and, worse still, many units assembled there were temporarily immobilised by lack of their transport and supplies. Barely 200,000 were assembled at the start of operations, and only a fraction of these were brought into action early, although the total was later brought up to 300,000. By then the situation had turned adversely to the French, whose best chance of success had lain in dislocating the German deployment before it was completed. Loss of time, increased by hesitant leadership, forfeited the qualitative advantage which the French hoped to gain from their higher proportion of professional troops.

As in 1866, Moltke's strategy did not go 'according to plan', yet was turned to decisive advantage through the combination of his flexibility and the executants' initiative with the inherent value of wide manœuvre—in outflanking resistance and producing surprise effect. He had intended to fight the decisive battle on the Saar, using the concentrated weight of the three German armies to crush the heavily outnumbered French. This plan went astray: partly owing to an excess of independent initiative—and insubordination—among German subordinate commanders; partly owing to the paralysis their action induced in the French higher command; and partly owing to the fog of war. The French paralysis developed from the news that the German Third Army (under the Prussian crown prince) on the extreme left near the Rhine, had crossed the frontier and driven back a small French detachment near Weissemburg. Pushing on, the four corps of the Third Army enveloped and defeated the flank corps of the French right wing, before the rest of it came into action. In this Battle of Wörth, on 6 August, the greatly outnumbered French troops fought with a gallantry that deserved a better fate—and a better higher command.

The German higher command, however, was now groping in the fog of war, and jumped to the conclusion that the French army as a whole was withdrawing westward over the Moselle—which was momentarily Napoleon III's decision, although quickly cancelled under pressure of telegrams from Paris that such a withdrawal would shake the people's confidence. On the assumption that the French were in general retreat, Moltke allowed the Third Army, instead of wheeling inwards, to continue advancing along a southerly circuit to the Moselle—well outside the focal centre of the next phase of the campaign. That wide flanking advance became a decisive asset in the next phase but one.

Meanwhile the bulk of the German forces, sweeping south of Metz in an imagined pursuit over the Moselle towards the Meuse, collided with the flank of the main French forces—in position just west of Metz. This unexpected collision, and the Germans' consequent turn northward, produced the two blundering battles of Vionville (16 August) and Gravelotte (18 August), in which the two sides fought facing their own rear. The Germans built up to a three-to-two superiority in numbers, but the issue was tactically a draw and the German losses heavier than the French. Strategically, however, the Germans gained an advantage because the French withdrew within the Metz defences and stayed there. Their commander, Bazaine, had made no attempt to seize the fine opportunity for a counterstroke when the Germans were off balance and dispersed after the unexpected flank collision on the 16th.

Marshal MacMahon, who had been assembling a freshly improvised army of four corps on the Marne, at Chalons, was now politically pushed into advancing to the aid of Bazaine. It proved a fatal move in face of such mobile and flexibly handled opponents, accustomed to marching fifteen miles a day whereas the French averaged only five or six when moving in large formations. The German Third Army, still marching westwards along an open path, now wheeled north on to the flank and rear of MacMahon's army, which had already been headed off by part of the German forces moving on from Metz. Trapped against the Belgian frontier, near Sedan, MacMahon's army was compelled to surrender on 2 September, with 82,000 men. That decided the issue of the war—after five weeks of campaign. With one French field army shut up under guard in Metz and the other in prisoners' cages, the Germans were left with an open path to Paris.

Even so, the raw levies raised by the Republican government of *Défense Nationale*, which now replaced Napoleon III, succeeded in prolonging the war for six months, in a way very upsetting to German calculations. But in later years it was the quick run of victory culminating at Sedan which remained in the minds of the military world, rather than the surprisingly protracted sequel. Soldiers everywhere assumed that future great wars would be decided as quickly as in 1866 and 1870—and worked on that assumption. They would have been wiser to have paid more attention to the lengthy last phase, and also to the four years' Civil War in America. For this foreshadowed the future of war more truly—although Moltke is said to have discounted it as a case of 'two armed mobs chasing each other around the country, from which nothing could be learned'.

The American Civil War was the first large-scale war of the industrial age, and also the first between modern democracies (see ch. XXIV). The course of operations was greatly influenced by the development of railways, the invention of the magnetic telegraph, and the increasing dependence on large-scale manufacture or import of arms and other supplies. No less important was the multiplied spread of newspapers, which exerted a powerful influence on public opinion, and thus on democratically elected governments. The sum effect was to increase the economic target, and also the moral target, while making both more vulnerable. This in turn increased the incentive to strike at the sources of the opponent's armed power instead of at its shield—the armed forces.

For a time, the significance of these developments was obscured because the Southern Confederacy—a relatively primitive organism owing to its loose agrarian nature—was far less vulnerable than a highly industrial society. The Confederate will had no fixed seat, and its various focal points were mostly remote—although the Confederate states had established their capital in Richmond, Virginia, the will to war was strongest in South Carolina, which had taken the lead in seceding from the Union. That was far distant from the Union forces, and comfortably sheltered.

The Union armies' one asset for striking at such distant targets was the wideness of the fronts, which allowed much scope for penetrating manœuvre, and with it was coupled a potential aid in the new railroad network. But the potentiality of this was reduced by the fixity of its routes, which fostered the normal tendency of operations to run on narrow and straightforward lines. Moreover, the increased ease of supply that railroads provided led commanders to build up increased numbers of troops at the railhead, without pausing to consider the hampering effect on their own power of manœuvre. Thus the first result of the new means of strategic movement was, paradoxically, to reduce strategic mobility. The railroad fostered the expansion of armies—it could forward and feed many more than could operate effectively. It also tended to inflate their wants and demands, so that they became more closely tied to the railhead, or to a coastal base.

Tactical mobility, too, was increasingly restricted—by the growing development of firepower during the war. The smooth-bore musket, still standard at the outset, was gradually replaced by a muzzle-loading rifle, of greater accuracy, and before the war ended the advent of a breech-loader quickened the rate of fire of such troops as were equipped with it. The increasing fire effect produced a recourse to the trench and the breastwork for protection even in field operations, and the combination gave defence a greater advantage over attack than ever before.

The double check on mobility was demonstrated in the repeated frustration of the Union forces in their efforts to overcome the numerically weaker Confederate forces which barred the path to Richmond. When a seaborne flank approach was tried in the spring of 1862, this more promising move succeeded no better, after the landing, than the direct overland approach attempted both previously and subsequently. Moreover, the initially more skilled and more skilfully handled Confederate forces, although brilliantly countering the Union offensives, suffered similar checks in each northward thrust into Union territory. It was by their threats to Washington and the Union forces' communications that the Confederates achieved most—in the negative way of upsetting their opponents' advances, and thus relieving the pressure. But their chances of breaking the Union's will to continue the war faded with the repulse at Gettysburg of Lee's invasion of Pennsylvania in 1863—although this did not solve President Lincoln's problem of how to win the war, nor clear the Union forces' path to Richmond. So long as their main efforts were confined to the narrow bounds of the Virginian theatre, where the offensive was cramped, they courted frustration.

A better prospect was open in the wide western theatre of war, hitherto regarded as a side-show. In April 1862 a naval squadron under Farragut slipped past the forts guarding the mouth of the Mississippi, and thereby produced the bloodless surrender of New Orleans. On 4 July, the day of Lee's retreat from Gettysburg, a Union army under Grant achieved, after four unsuccessful attempts, the capture of Vicksburg, the keypoint on the middle stretch of the Mississippi. That victory gave the Union control of this great artery, and deprived the Confederacy of reinforcements and supplies from the Trans-Mississippi states.

Grant then turned eastward and drove back the Confederate army blocking the Chattanooga gateway into Georgia—'the granary of the Confederacy'. After this success, he was called to Washington in the spring of 1864 to take over supreme command of the Union forces. But his renewal of the direct southward advance on Richmond was no more successful than his predecessors' efforts, and even more costly. Each successive move was checked by Lee. By the end of that summer, mounting losses had brought the Union forces and people to the end of their endurance. War-weariness became so intense and widespread as to produce rapidly growing support for immediate peace and acceptance of the Confederacy's demand for independence. Lincoln himself lost hope of being re-elected President in the autumn. But in September Sherman, Grant's successor in the western theatre, captured Atlanta—the capital of Georgia—by a skilful series of manœuvres. In these, he repeatedly lured the Confederates to attack him, foiled their attacks by a technique of quick field fortification, and from each costly failure to pierce his mobile shield drew the strategic advantage of a fresh vantage point gained, against weakened opposition. His exhilarating, and economically gained, success was the main factor in restoring Lincoln's position and securing his re-election.

In the course of this advance to Atlanta, and after its capture, Sherman's main difficulties had come from dependence on a long-stretched line of rail supply, and its liability to interruption by mobile raiding forces. Such raids had hamstrung previous Union offensives. An acute appreciation of the problem led Sherman to try a new and bold solution. The enemy had struck him through his rail communications; he would strike at theirs, while immunising himself. He saw that to regain and secure mobility he must free himself from dependence on a fixed line of supply—which meant that his troops must be self-contained for supplies, carrying the necessary minimum with them and supplementing it by foraging the countryside through which they passed. So after reducing transport to the minimum, he cut loose from his own rail lines of supply and marched eastward through Georgia, destroying the Confederacy's supply system at the source and cutting the lines which fed its main army, under Lee, in Virginia.

After reaching the sea at Savannah, and there reopening his own communications, by sea, Sherman turned northward—marching through South Carolina towards Lee's rear, and depriving the Confederacy of its chief remaining ports. In seeing the unchecked progress of this deep strategic thrust the people of the Confederate states lost faith in the optimistic assurances of their leaders and press. Loss of faith led to loss of hope, and then in turn to loss of the will to continue the struggle. By mid-March, when Sherman was driving through North Carolina, Grant was able to tell him that Lee's army 'is now demoralised and deserting very fast, both to us and to their homes'[1]—though Grant's own army was still immobilised in the trench lines round Petersburg and Richmond where it had been brought to a state of stalemate the previous summer. This indirect approach to the opponents' economic and moral rear was decisive in producing the Confederacy's collapse, and Lee's surrender, three weeks later.

Had European soldiers during the next half century studied the American Civil War as closely as they did the 1870 war, they would have better understood the basic conditions of strategic and tactical mobility, and suffered less from wishful thinking, than they did in 1914. (In 1940, the Germans' military success owed much to a study of Sherman's campaigns, and the application of methods deduced from it.)

They might have learnt, also, to expect and prepare for a long war, even if hoping for a short war; to reckon with economic and social factors, to broaden military studies accordingly, to facilitate the economic and psychological mobilisation of the nation, and to give more attention to new inventions which might offer a possibility of turning the scales in a protracted war. And they might have seen the danger of seeking immediate military gains without regard to the political disadvantages, and to the long-term interests of their nations. Their eyes might even have been opened to the mutual destructiveness of a long and unlimited war between the nations of Europe, with their closely interwoven fabric, and to the danger that a recklessly conducted 'European Civil War' would wreck European civilisation—or, at least, jeopardise its future.

[1] Grant's letter of 16 March 1865—printed in full in *Memoirs of General William T. Sherman* (New York, 1875), vol. II, pp. 311–12.

CHAPTER XIII

THE UNITED KINGDOM AND ITS
WORLD-WIDE INTERESTS

ETWEEN 1830 and 1870 the internal development of the United
Kingdom passed through two phases, dividing roughly at 1850. By
the middle of the century Great Britain (but not Ireland) had been
transformed from a society that was predominantly rural and agricultural
to one predominantly urban and industrial. In the first two decades
social and political conflicts arose between the landed and agricultural
interest on one hand and the growing commercial and industrial interests
on the other. They arose over such issues as the reform of the electoral
and parliamentary system, reorganisation of poor relief and of municipal
government, free trade and factory legislation. The decades 1830–50 also
saw the rise and temporary failure of such working-class movements as
Chartism and trade unionism, born of the growth of industrialism during
these years. By the time of the Great Exhibition of 1851, it was clear
that at almost every point the commercial and industrial interests had
gained what they wanted, and that the efforts of the working classes to
claim that freedom of action and association which the rising class of
merchants and manufacturers succeeded in claiming for themselves, had
been severely checked. The two decades after 1851 brought consolidation
and extension of the advantages gained by the new ruling classes; a
remarkable growth of overseas trade and investment as well as of total
national wealth; and a multitude of legislative measures adjusting the
political and administrative system to the needs of the new society of
towns and factories. From this growth in national wealth and in legislative protection the working classes gained considerable benefits. They
succeeded in establishing trade unions and voluntary organisations which
laid the basis for their future power in the state.

Behind these conflicts and shifts of power lay the constant factor of
immense and rapid expansion: expansion of population, of production,
of trade and investment. Between 1831 and 1871 the population of the
whole United Kingdom (constituted in 1801 by the union of Ireland with
Great Britain) grew from roughly 24 to nearly 32 millions. This increase
was almost equal to the total numbers of people who had inhabited England and Wales in 1800, and it was a continuation of the immense growth
in population which had been happening since the middle of the eighteenth
century. The increase varied between the different parts of the United
Kingdom. The population of England and Wales grew steadily and sharply
in these years, and that of Scotland grew steadily but less sharply. The

331

population of Ireland increased until 1845 and then, mainly because of massive emigration and famine, decreased equally sharply until the end of the century. Thus Great Britain grew during the first two decades from 16½ millions to more than 21 millions, and then to more than 26 millions by 1871; but the population of Ireland rose from roughly 7 millions in 1831 to a peak figure of 8½ millions in 1845, and then fell to less than 5½ millions by 1871. More than 2 million people emigrated from the United Kingdom during the first two decades, and more than another 3½ millions during the second two decades. Most of them went to the American continent, and probably not more than 1 million returned. Within the British Isles themselves there was also considerable movement of people, from Ireland to Scotland and England, from Scotland to England, and from countryside to town within each. This great mobility was in part cause and in part effect of the rapid industrialisation.

Within the United Kingdom the distribution and occupations of people were, in consequence, changing equally rapidly. In 1871 agriculture still, as in 1831, employed more men and women than any other industry, though after 1831 it soon ceased to be true that half the families of Great Britain lived by work on the land or by trades and industries which served countrymen. Agriculture directly employed 275,000 families in Great Britain in 1831, and throughout the period the numbers employed remained almost stationary. It was not that agriculture declined but that the proportion of people making a living out of industry, trade and the occupations of transport and communication, immensely increased.

The years between 1830 and 1850 were the great age of railway and steamship construction and, partly in consequence, were a time of expansion in the heavy industries, mining and textiles. When the duke of Wellington, in September 1830, attended the opening of the new Manchester and Liverpool railway, he witnessed the first great triumph of the steam locomotive: its acceptance as the best means of traction by rail. Between 1825 and 1835 fifty-four Railway Acts of all kinds went through Parliament. The first boom in railway construction came in the years 1836–7, when thirty-nine more bills for new lines in Great Britain were passed and 1000 miles were added to the railroads of the country. After a second boom in the years 1844–7, some 6600 miles of line were in use by the end of 1850. By 1870 the total had increased to 15,620 miles, leaving relatively little more to be constructed. The lines were consolidated and amalgamated into a system, and the telegraph developed mainly as an adjunct of the railways. In 1840 Sir Rowland Hill introduced the penny post. In the same year the Cunard Steamship Line was founded, and twelve years later it was running a weekly service from Liverpool to New York. Between 1827 and 1848 the total tonnage of British shipping, both sail and steam, rose from 2½ to 4 million tons, and to 5 million tons by 1860. In 1850 nearly 60 per cent of the world's ocean-going tonnage was

British, and the tonnage of all shipping entered and cleared from ports in the United Kingdom (exclusive of coastal trade and of trade between Britain and Ireland) rose from more than 6 million tons in 1834 to more than 14 million tons in 1847. It suffered a setback after the commercial crisis of that year, and then rose to more than 36½ million tons by 1870. This is perhaps the most vivid index of how much the prosperity of Britain had come to depend on overseas trade.

The output of British coal mines rose from 30 million tons in 1836 to 57 million tons in 1851, and to 110 million tons by 1870. By the middle of the century probably half the world's production of pig iron took place in Great Britain, and a quarter of that output came from the west of Scotland. It was, however, an age of coal and iron rather than of steel (cf. ch. II, pp. 29–31). Although the discoveries of Bessemer, Siemens, Thomas and Gilchrist had by the end of this period perfected the making of steel, its widespread use came only after 1870. But by 1871 more than three-quarters of a million people were employed in the metal, engineering and shipbuilding trades, and more than 300,000 in coal-mines. British exports of coal, iron and steel increased correspondingly. During the four decades the value of exports of coal rose from £184,000 to £5,638,000, and of iron and steel from little more than £1,000,000 to over £23,500,000. Engineering and the industries devoted to making machines remained small-scale until after the middle of the century; then there grew up a large engineering and machine-tool industry.

It was as much the Age of Cotton as the Age of Coal and Iron, and because its raw material had to be imported the industry was even more closely linked with overseas trade. Already in 1830 three-quarters of the raw cotton came from the United States; and in 1849 the total import was as high as 346,000 tons, estimated to be worth about £15,000,000. The following year the exports of cotton yarn and cotton goods (mainly cloth, hosiery and lace) were worth more than £28,250,000, and by 1870 cotton exports were worth £71,416,000. In 1851 more than half a million people were employed in the cotton industry alone, and textiles as a whole employed well over one million people. Textiles were the industry most representative of the Age of Machinery and Power. From the beginning of the period, cotton was the pre-eminent factory industry, and the other textile manufacturers, in wool and flax and silk, before long organised their workers in larger factories. Mechanisation was slow throughout the period, and production still depended on cheap labour and long working hours.

The effect of economic change in these four decades was that by 1850 Great Britain had triumphantly established herself both as 'the workshop of the world' and as the shipper and trader of the world. For the next two decades she enjoyed the great advantages and profits which this position opened up to her enterprise and labour. Her interests, become world-wide, were soon to be deeply and seriously affected by formidable rivals whose industrialisation had meanwhile taken place. The greatest of these were Germany and the United States. But until the decade after 1870 she continued to harvest very rich rewards, as the impetus of her growth and productivity carried her forward. Between 1850 and 1870 her imports trebled in value from £100,000,000 to £300,000,000. Her total exports increased from £71,000,000 to nearly £200,000,000. The gap between imports and exports was much more than bridged by her 'invisible exports' in the form of shipping, banking and insurance services. Her great accumulations of capital were partly invested abroad, so that by 1870 her overseas investments amounted to probably £700,000,000. In 1830 they had been only £110,000,000. She became in every sense of the term a world power.

The domestic history of the United Kingdom in these years was dominated by the consequences of these basic demographic and economic developments. The classes which benefited most from them were on the one hand the mine-owners and mill-owners, shippers and traders, bankers and financiers, and all the subsidiary businessmen connected with so vast a growth in production and commerce; on the other, the fast-growing masses of urban workers who, by finding employment in these industries, escaped the fate of their fellows in Ireland. There, rapid growth of population combined with a shortage of land and a lack of large-scale industrialisation to produce extreme poverty and famine. British landowners and farmers, though they benefited from greater mechanisation and the application of more scientific methods, and from the growing home market for foodstuffs, did not so directly share in the rich profits and boundless prosperity of the mid-Victorian era. Although the decline of British agriculture did not become apparent until the 'seventies, the conditions which made it vulnerable were created before 1850.

Even before Great Britain became predominantly an industrial state the political system, which had evolved on the assumption that land was the most important form of wealth, had been fundamentally challenged and modified. This challenge was the movement for parliamentary and municipal reform, and these modifications were the Reform Acts of 1832 and the Municipal Reform Act of 1835. Once these changes had been made, the way was open for a long series of other modifications which still further destroyed the previously overwhelming preponderance of the landed interest. They included the abolition of the Navigation and the Corn Laws, a sequence of free-trade budgets under Sir Robert Peel and W. E. Gladstone, and the Representation of the People Act of 1867. In aggregate these modifications shifted the whole balance of political power and transformed the electoral and parliamentary systems. The state as well as society underwent great and permanent changes in these decades.

The admission of the growing commercial and industrial classes to a larger share of political power was achieved only to a moderate extent by the Reform Acts of 1832, and no effort was made to destroy the hegemony of the landed and agricultural interests. The property qualification for members of the House of Commons, imposed in 1710, was left intact except in Scotland, so that county members had to own a landed estate of £600 a year and borough members a landed estate of £300 a year. In 1838 the qualifications were extended to include personal as well as real property, and there were several well-established devices for evading the requirements of the law. No such qualifications were required in Scotland after 1832, but it was 1858 before the qualification disappeared in the rest of the United Kingdom. The heavy cost of contesting elections and the non-payment of members ensured that the great majority of parliamentary representatives remained, as they had been before 1832, men of independent means, often country gentlemen and members of aristocratic families.

The House of Lords had already, before 1832, become much larger and in many respects more broadly representative of the nation as a whole than it had normally been in the eighteenth century. Its average size throughout the previous century had been 220, and most peers had represented the landed interest. As a result of the lavish creations of peerages by the younger Pitt and his successors, the House of Lords by 1837 numbered 456 and included large numbers of service chiefs and administrators, wealthy businessmen and manufacturers. This insertion, alongside the landed aristocracy, of representatives of new forms of wealth and social power was achieved in the lower house by the Reform Acts, and became of significant proportions only after the Act of 1867.

The major change effected by the Act of 1832 was the redistribution of constituencies. The House of Commons consisted, as before, of 658 seats. But whereas the number of county members had been 188 it now became 253, and instead of 262 boroughs returning 465 members, there were now only 257 borough constituencies and 399 borough members. The Universities of Oxford and Cambridge and Trinity College, Dublin, each returned two representatives. The disfranchisement of fifty-six smaller boroughs and the reduction of thirty others to one-member constituencies was a blow to the influence of the landowners and borough-mongers who had in practice controlled the electoral power of these boroughs. The increase of county representation by sixty-five members strengthened the direct territorial interest at the expense of the oligarchical system of nomination, influence and corruption. At the same time, the creation of twenty-two new boroughs with two members each, and of twenty more with one member, gave more power to the manufacturing and commercial interests which enjoyed this new enfranchisement in the urban areas of the midlands and the north. London was left under-represented as compared with other urban areas. The great era of borough proprietors was brought to an end by the bill: but through the retention of many boroughs with small electorates and the extension of the vote in counties to tenants-at-will of small substance, opportunities were preserved for considerable electoral influence and corruption. Nearly fifty boroughs and well over sixty members still depended on the influence of great peers and land-owners in England and Wales alone. There were still some forty peers and a few commoners who could virtually nominate a representative to the House of Commons. In large and popular constituencies the amount of money spent on electioneering could be very great; and it seems likely that although corrupt practices changed in character they hardly diminished in extent. Indeed, with a tendency for more seats to be contested, there were more occasions for expenditure. In the five elections between 1832 and 1847 on average more than half the 401 constituencies were actually contested: a high proportion as compared with elections before 1832. When ballot was still not secret (until 1872) and when electors mostly regarded the vote as a property right which entitled them to profits at election-time, there could not be much decline either in pressure and inti-midation or in bribery and other forms of corrupt persuasion.

The electorate, numbering less than 500,000 before 1832, was increased by about half by the Act of 1832. It rose to well over one million by 1867, mainly because the total population increased, and the value of money fell. The Reform Act of 1867 further extended the electorate of England and Wales to nearly two millions, and the corresponding Acts for Scotland and Ireland in the following year added another 260,000 voters to the registers. But the Act of 1867 increased the urban electorate much more than the rural, for it more than doubled the borough electorate (from 514,000 to 1,203,000), whilst it increased that of the counties from 543,000 to only 792,000. Thereafter in England and Wales the boroughs, for the first time in history, had collectively more voters than the counties. They had for long had more representatives in the Commons, so an old disparity was removed. At the same time the Act redistributed forty-five seats by taking away one member from boroughs of less than 10,000 inhabi-tants and transferring them partly to the counties and partly to the larger towns. The Act thus served as a political reflection of the growth of urbanisation and industrialisation during these decades. Its effect was to increase the middle-class vote in the counties, and (by establishing household suffrage in towns) to extend the vote to the artisans and most well-to-do industrial workers. Like the first Reform Act, it produced little immediate change in the social composition of the Commons: middle-class men were still chosen as representatives. But the House of Commons as a whole was henceforward subject to wider and more popu-lar pressure, and party organisation made such influence more direct and effective.

By the middle of the century the system of local government was also radically reformed. The Poor Law Amendment Act of 1834 set up Boards of Guardians elected by the ratepayers. These boards assumed responsibility, hitherto borne by the parish vestries and Justices of the Peace, for the care of the poor. They worked under the general direction and instructions of a new central authority, the Poor Law Commissioners. Parishes were grouped into unions for the purpose of maintaining workhouses, and by 1840 six-sevenths of the population lived in areas covered by poor-law unions. The following year town government was overhauled by the Municipal Reform Act. In most boroughs the old closed corporations had remained in power. Again reform was based on the twin principles of locally representative bodies and tighter central control. Henceforth borough councils elected by the ratepayers became the regular form of municipal government. They worked through certain paid officials, at least a town clerk and a borough treasurer. They had power to make by-laws and exercised control over the new police, municipal property, and such aspects of finance as the collection of local rates. The floating of loans required approval from the Treasury. The electorate of the councils included all householders who had occupied their properties for at least three years and had paid the poor rate. It was normally narrower than the parliamentary electorate and narrower than that for the election of Poor Law Guardians: but it was wide enough to include most of the wealthier merchants and industrialists of the large towns. In 1848, when the recurrence of cholera and the efforts of Edwin Chadwick drew public attention to the desperate needs of the towns for minimal safeguards of public health, a central Board of Health was created on the lines of the Poor Law Commissioners, with certain powers to create local boards. At last, in the 'sixties, local authorities were compelled to appoint sanitary inspectors and to undertake the provision of sewers, water supply and refuse disposal. In 1870 the Education Act set up locally elected school boards. Thus the recurrent features of local government were a multiplication of locally elected bodies for separate functions, and in consequence a great complication of authorities; but also an increasing activity, by public authorities of diverse kinds, local and central, on behalf of the welfare of the population.

As administration became more extensive, more elaborate and more technical, there was increasing reliance on expert, paid officials. Inspectors of prisons and factories, town clerks and treasurers, doctors and commissioners, constituted a growing class of public servants and officials. Central government, too, encountered the need for a larger number of more carefully chosen civil servants. In 1853 Sir Charles Trevelyan and Sir Stafford Northcote published their *Report on the Organisation of the Permanent Civil Service*. On the model of the new Indian Civil Service, instituted by Macaulay in the Government of India Act of that year (cf. ch. VIII, p. 206), they urged recruitment exclusively by competitive examination, conducted by one central board, in place of the previous system of recruitment by patronage and by departmental tests: and organisation of the civil service into two levels or grades. An Order in Council of 21 May 1855 set up a Civil Service Commission, empowered to arrange with the heads of departments the conditions of entry into their respective departments. 'Limited competition among selected candidates, not "open" competition among all comers, with final responsibility for appointments remaining with the heads of departments—these were the key-notes of the 1855 reform.'[1] In 1870 Gladstone, by another Order in Council, abolished patronage, adopted the principle of recruitment by 'open competition', and introduced the two-class organisation. The ideal of an efficient and unified service was not yet achieved in 1870, but a basis for it now existed.

The four decades between 1830 and 1870 were a period of first Whig and then Liberal hegemony, broken by short but important interludes of Conservative government. The three Reform Acts of 1832 were passed by Whig ministers, under pressure from Radical agitation in the country and against strong opposition from the Tories. The Representation of the People Acts of 1867 and 1868 were passed by a Conservative government, led by Benjamin Disraeli and Lord Derby, under both Liberal and Radical pressure in parliament and country. Between the two dates the nature and alignments as well as the organisation of political parties underwent great changes. The personalities of Lord Melbourne and Sir Robert Peel dominated the party contests of the first two decades, those of Lord Palmerston and W. E. Gladstone the last two. Party alignments were confused during the first two by the issue of free trade: and although the Whigs for the most part supported the free-trade agitation led by Richard Cobden and John Bright on behalf of the manufacturing and commercial interests, it was Peel, a Conservative, who in 1846 split his party by repealing the hated Corn Laws. They were confused during the last two decades by the resistance of Lord Palmerston to parliamentary reform; because although the Liberals in general favoured it, it was in the end Disraeli, a Conservative, who once again 'dished the Whigs' by passing the Act of 1867.

Yet, throughout the period of confusion, divisions between the parties were hardening upon other issues, and the organisation of parties for both electoral contest and parliamentary debate was greatly elaborated. After 1832 a fairly well contrasted division of political issues could be presented to the electorate; and at first the contrast was even exaggerated, because the Tories regarded the Reform Act as much more radical than it was whilst the Radicals were bitterly disappointed with its moderation. Thus the Whigs, with the support of the Radicals, stood for such measures of reform as the abolition of slavery, reform of the system of poor-

[1] Edward Hughes, 'Civil Service Reform, 1853–5', in *History*, vol. XXVII, p. 76.

law and municipal government, and free trade; whereas the Tories, re-created into the Conservative Party by Peel and accepting the Reform Act as a *fait accompli*, emerged as the defenders of the landed interest, the Church and Parliament against further radical change. Peel's Tamworth Manifesto of 1834 became the charter of this cautious but more liberal conservatism implying, in his words, 'a careful review of institutions, civil and ecclesiastical, undertaken in a friendly temper, combining with the firm maintenance of established rights the correction of proved abuses and the redress of real grievances'. The existence of a larger electorate and the technical requirements of electoral registration gave an impetus to more elaborate local party organisation in the country, and centrally led to the formation of the Conservative Carlton Club in 1832 and of the Liberal Reform Club in 1836. Unlike previous political clubs, which had been social centres in which politics had gradually taken hold, these were from birth designed to be political party organisations combining the functions of central office and national headquarters, and concerned primarily with problems of registration and the conduct of elections. From this time onwards the whole apparatus of more modern party organisation developed. Party funds, managers and whips existed already: now local constituency associations, registration committees and election agents began to be added. In 1867 appeared the National Union of Conservative and Constitutional Associations, followed ten years later by the National Liberal Federation. The great parties became nation-wide organisations. They were in structure combinations of local associations, although they differed greatly in the extent to which their programmes were framed by the parliamentary leaders and the central office, or by opinion expressed through the national federation.

These stronger and more elaborate organisations prepared the way for the decisive party majorities of the years after 1868. But most ministries of the four previous decades enjoyed only precarious majorities. Governments were unstable and party allegiances shifted. The parties in Parliament were moved less by their own constituency associations than by the large and independent associations which grew up so spectacularly in these years: the Anti-Corn Law League, the Chartist Associations, and the many other propagandist societies born of the radical technique of popular agitation. The political life of the period represents a transition stage in the development of parties. The force of public opinion had become powerful and active: party cohesion in Parliament was growing. But these two major factors in the development of Victorian Britain remained disjointed one from the other and it was only after 1868, when parties were prompted to strike their own roots deeper into the constituencies, that the classical pattern of two-party rivalry could emerge under the leadership of Gladstone and Disraeli.

A somewhat similar disjointedness existed between the parliamentary parties and the ministries. Cabinet posts were still filled predominantly by peers rather than commoners, in the tradition of the eighteenth century and of Pitt. It was more common for the Prime Minister to be a peer than to be a commoner, and if the Chancellor of the Exchequer was always a commoner the Foreign Secretary was nearly always a peer. The House of Lords, still serving a more focal purpose in parliamentary life than in later decades, was throughout predominantly Conservative: yet most of the time there was a Whig or Liberal majority in the Commons. The two Houses played a more equal part, both in parliamentary debate and in control of the ministries, than in the twentieth century. Relations between ministers and the monarch were likewise on a flexible and ill-defined footing. The supremacy of the Prime Minister in relation to his colleagues and the principles of cabinet solidarity and collective responsibility were by now generally accepted. But their full implications had not been worked out. Queen Victoria expected to play an independent and active role in government, especially in such matters as foreign and military affairs; and until the end of this period the complexity and fluidity of party politics left her with some room for choice and for influencing the formation of cabinets. She succeeded in preserving the power of dissolution as a royal prerogative, and would not pledge herself to accept her Prime Minister's advice about it. Her famous memorandum to Lord John Russell about Palmerston, shortly before Palmerston was abruptly dismissed for expressing approval of the *coup d'état* by Louis Napoleon in France, is a classical statement of the conception of constitutional monarchy which she succeeded in asserting during these decades.

She requires: 1. That he [Lord Palmerston] will distinctly state what he proposes in a given case, in order that the Queen may know as distinctly to *what* she has given her Royal sanction. 2. Having *once given* her sanction to a measure, that it be not arbitrarily altered or modified by the Minister; such an act she must consider as failing in sincerity towards the Crown, and justly to be visited by the exercise of her Constitutional right of dismissing that Minister. She expects to be kept informed of what passes between him and the Foreign Ministers before important decisions are taken, based upon that intercourse; to receive the Foreign Despatches in good time, and to have the drafts for her approval sent to her in sufficient time to make herself acquainted with their contents before they must be sent off.[1]

The British Constitution in these years preserved enough aristocratic influence and enough royal power to keep the parliamentary system in its traditional ways. Whilst political parties were still finding new strength and new foundations in popular opinion, these traditional elements made it possible for democratic forces, as well as the new purposes of the industrial and commercial classes, to find some satisfaction in the political system without violent upheaval and without dislocation of government

[1] Queen Victoria to Lord John Russell, 12 August 1850 (*Letters of Queen Victoria*, ed. A. C. Benson and Viscount Esher, London, 1908; vol. II, p. 264). And see the memorandum by Baron Stockmar, on which the queen's was based, *ibid.* vol. II, p. 238.

and administration. Strong humanitarian and philanthropic movements succeeded in getting important measures through the reformed parliament. One of the first acts of the reformed parliament was to abolish slavery throughout the British empire. The slave trade had been made illegal within the empire since 1807, and an Abolition Society, headed by Sir Thomas Fowell Buxton and Zachary Macaulay, pressed for the abolition of slavery itself. In 1833 Lord Stanley, backed by Buxton, steered through parliament his Act 'for the abolition of slavery throughout the British colonies'. The British taxpayer provided £20,000,000 which might be paid in compensation to the slave-owners: and the sum of £18,669,401 was so paid. The colonies chiefly affected were the West Indies, British Guiana and Mauritius. The economy of these territories was seriously affected by the change, but by the end of these decades the development of crops other than sugar and the introduction of Indian coolies did something to restore their economy.

Another reform which philanthropic and humanitarian movements sponsored in the reformed parliament was improvement in the conditions of industrial workers at home. Several Factory Acts had already been passed between 1802 and 1819, and their effect was to ban the employment of children in cotton mills for more than 12 hours a day between the ages of 9 and 16, and to prohibit the employment of children under 9. Child labour in other than cotton mills, and the conditions of adult labour, remained unrestricted. The Factory Act of 1833 extended regulation to all types of textile factory. It imposed the limit of an 8-hour day for children between 9 and 13, and of a 12-hour day for young people between 13 and 18, with some exceptions for silk factories. Children of the protected age-groups were to attend school for at least 2 hours each day. Factory inspectors, responsible to the Home Office, were appointed to enforce the law. Thus three important new principles were established; more general regulation, compulsory education, and impartial inspection and enforcement. The Act also began the long agitation for the 10-hour day for adults, an agitation which Short Time Committees maintained until 1847. The Ten Hours Bill of that year was defeated in operation by the obstructiveness of employers and by legal interpretation, but in 1850 compromise was reached in the Ten-and-a-Half Hours Act. Meanwhile tireless individual philanthropists like Robert Owen and Lord Shaftesbury collaborated with Edwin Chadwick and other Radical reformers to improve, by similar regulation, the lot of boy chimney-sweeps, lunatics and prisoners. Much was done by the force of good example, such as Robert Owen's reorganisation of his own factory at New Lanark in the early years of the century and Lord Shaftesbury's work for the farm labourers on the estates which he inherited from his father in 1851. More could be done by parliamentary agitation. Public conscience was stirred, and the way was prepared for more extensive state regulation of economic life.

A Mines Act of 1842 extended regulation and inspection to coal mines, and prohibited employment of women and girls underground. A Factory Act of 1844 secured the fencing of machinery and other restrictions, and in 1845 calico-printing was added to the list of protected industries. In 1860 the protection given by the factory acts was extended to women and children employed in the bleaching and dyeing trades. In 1864 the definition of 'factory' was widened to include 'any place in which persons work for hire', and such trades as the pottery and match industries were brought under regulation. Three years later small workshops, foundries, glass-works and blast-furnaces were likewise covered. By the end of the period it was widely accepted that industry should in such ways be subject to regulation by the state in the interests and for the welfare of its employees. It was also increasingly realised that, far from improvements in working conditions hampering business and trade, production could even be increased, as Robert Owen had maintained, when workers were not debilitated by excessive hours of labour and bad conditions.

Whilst the state in these ways increasingly regulated industrial life, its old regulation of trade was being demolished. Since the first volume of Adam Smith's *Wealth of Nations* had appeared in 1776 there had been demands for freer trade and a simplification and reduction of duties on imports and exports. This movement grew immensely in strength after 1830, and in 1836, with corn very dear, the first Anti-Corn-Law Association was founded by the London Radicals. But Lancashire of the cotton mills was destined to be the real home and power-house of the free trade movement. Raw cotton had to be imported, and cotton goods constituted a very high proportion of British exports. The prosperity of Lancashire very obviously depended directly upon foreign trade: and it seemed particularly monstrous that foreign trade should be impeded by corn laws designed primarily to keep the price of food high. In the 1830's Richard Cobden, himself a calico manufacturer, became the leading parliamentary spokesman of this interest. Soon he was joined by John Bright, the son of a Rochdale mill-owner. Although they wanted free trade in general, it was both natural and expedient first to concentrate the attack upon the hated Corn Laws. On this issue the conflict between the agricultural interest and the manufacturing and commercial interests reached its height. In 1838 new Anti-Corn-Law Associations were formed. Being supported by the rich class of manufacturers, they had large funds at their disposal for public meetings and printed propaganda. Soon their publications were filled with denunciations of the crimes of landlords, the game laws, and the selfishness of the farmers. The agitation for the Ten Hours Bill, backed in the 1840's by the Church of England, was in part a reprisal of the landed interest. One rich class fought another, each appealing for the support of working-class opinion even before it was enfranchised.

On 28 January 1839 *The Times* declared in favour of free trade. It had been attacking the new Poor Law system, and now it turned its fire against the Corn Laws, arguing that the sliding scale of duties produced constant fluctuations in the price of corn and so did not benefit even the farmers. The local associations combined, in the same year, to form the national Anti-Corn-Law League, with its headquarters in Manchester. John Bright was himself a Quaker, and nonconformists in general began to back the League. With the Church of England supporting the agitation for factory regulation there was competition between the churches in demanding social improvement, just as there was competition between the landed and the industrial interests, each eagerly detecting motes in the eyes of the other. The principles of free competition, applied to agitation for social reforms, seemed as likely to produce beneficial results as the Manchester free-traders contended it would produce in economic life and in international relations. In such conditions it was possible for 'Cobdenism' to become what a century later would be called an 'ideology': a complete philosophy of human behaviour and, in the minds of its most fanatical disciples, almost a religion. In mass meetings, pamphlets and the press the arguments against the Corn Laws and in favour of general freedom of trade were propagated with great intensity and fervour.

The impact of this kind of strenuous popular agitation on political parties and on the functioning of the parliamentary system has already been noted. At some moments (as in 1842) the movement became revolutionary in character, linked up with Chartism, and popular feeling became inflamed against the government. By 1843 its weekly publication, *The League*, reached a circulation of 20,000 and twenty-four mass meetings were held in Covent Garden Theatre, so spreading the movement to the capital. As it spread to the country districts, rick-burning and agrarian unrest spread with it. From the summer of 1844 onwards the Anti-Corn-Law League perfected the method of purchasing land and distributing it as freehold property to League sympathisers, so securing them a vote as forty-shilling freeholders. Despite good harvests in 1842, 1843 and 1844, it grew in strength. In 1845 the harvest was less good, and a devastating disease ruined the potato harvest. Since potatoes rather than corn were the staple diet of Ireland, this brought famine to that country. The League demanded the immediate and complete repeal of the laws which kept out imported corn. Confusion prevailed among both parties. Peel resigned but Lord John Russell failed to form a minority government. Peel formed a new cabinet, little different from the old, and tackled the overhaul of the whole fiscal system. The duty on maize was at once completely abolished. A greatly reduced sliding scale of duties on wheat, oats, barley and rye was substituted for the scale of 1842, and from the beginning of 1849 they were to be subject only to a fixed nominal duty of one shilling a quarter. He halved the duties on butter, cheese, hops and preserved fish, and permitted the free importation of all other foodstuffs. To compensate the farming interests for this loss of protection, he proposed to lighten their burdens in local finance and to lower duties on the import of manufactured goods. His previous budgets of 1842 and 1845 had practically abolished duties on the import of raw materials. He now completed the process of turning England into a free-trade country. The famine in Ireland was met partly by emigration on an immense scale, and partly by extensive measures of public and private charitable relief. The Navigation Laws, which even Adam Smith had defended on the grounds that 'defence, however, is of much more importance than opulence',[1] had been designed to protect British shipping in much the same way as the Corn Laws had been intended to protect farming. In 1849 they too were abandoned, involving no loss to British shipping interests because these already enjoyed so great a natural superiority in the world. So, by the middle of the century, duties remained only for reasons of revenue and not for purposes of protection.

The whole controversy was conducted in exaggerated terms, with inflated hopes and fears on both sides. The price of corn did not in fact fall after repeal, though repeal possibly prevented its rising. Nor were the Corn Laws the only or necessarily the major factor controlling the cost of living. The underlying truth was that Great Britain had by now reached the point of becoming an industrial and commercial state, whose interests lay predominantly in cheap food and cheap raw materials; and both technologically and in total productivity for export she was so much ahead of all her competitors that she had nothing to fear from foreign competition in world markets. Now that large and cheap supplies of corn were becoming available from Russia, Germany and North America, it was at least for some time to come more profitable for her to import such supplies and pay for them with export of manufactures and with commercial services. But these advantages were not to last much longer than another two decades, and as competition in world markets intensified so protective measures were eventually to be restored. The error of the most ardent champions of free trade was to assume that a policy which was undoubtedly to British advantage for one generation would necessarily remain equally appropriate for ever.

Peel's great ministry lasted from 1841 to 1846, and was a climax of Tory reform. Its other achievements included the Bank Charter Act of 1844 which anchored sterling to the gold standard. It fixed the relationship between the Bank of England and the other joint-stock banks which had now proved their success. Since 1826 joint-stock banks had been permitted to issue notes outside a radius of sixty-five miles from London; and since 1833 had been permitted within this radius. Financial crises, resulting from rash expansions of credit during the railway boom

---

[1] *An Inquiry into the Nature and Causes of the Wealth of Nations*, ed. E. Cannan (5th edn, London, 1930), vol. I, p. 429.

of the middle 1830's, led to demands for the restriction of such issues. Accordingly the Act of 1844 separated the Banking Department of the Bank of England from its Issue Department, limited its fiduciary issue of notes to £14,000,000 and required nearly all notes additional to that sum to be backed by a reserve of bullion or coin. New banks would not be permitted to issue notes, and other existing banks could not increase their issue (see ch. II, pp. 40–1). Another act of the same year regulated the operation of joint-stock companies. Peel's budgets succeeded in overhauling and simplifying the whole fiscal system, and in reducing the burden of customs and excise duties and the charges on the national debt.

Whilst the enterprising classes of manufacturers and merchants were in these ways staking out a new place for themselves in the state and for their interests in the shaping of national policy, the working classes were by no means inactive. By 1830 there was already a vigorous tradition of self-help and of radicalism among the town workers. Radical ideas spread in the years after 1815, despite the repressive measures of frightened governments. The Political Unions took some part in the agitation for the Reform Bill, just as the labours of men like Francis Place succeeded, in 1824, in securing the repeal of the most oppressive features of the Combination Acts. Whilst social distress during the post-war years stirred working-class feelings, the growth of industrialism made possible a remarkable spread of labour organisations. The disguise of friendly societies, previously used to mask trade union activities, could now be dropped. New unions were formed with open constitutions and published books of rules. They succeeded in making many local bargains about conditions of work, wages and apprenticeship. The chief features of the next two decades were the alliance between radicalism and the new socialism expounded by Robert Owen, and the collaboration of both with working-class movements and organisations. If by 1850 their concrete achievements amounted to relatively little, they had at least disseminated and demonstrated the principles of working-class self-help and voluntary organisation. And by 1870 organised labour asserted its position as a force of crucial importance in the state, whilst some of the demands of the Chartists had either been granted or were increasingly accepted as desirable in a democratic society.

Radicals were bitterly disappointed with the moderation of the Reform Acts of 1832; and the harsh operation of the new poor law in its early years stirred up working-class grievances. Between 1832 and 1850 social unrest found expression in the drive for more general trade union organisation, in the political agitation of the Chartist movement, and in the Co-operative movement. Many of the leaders of these movements felt that success depended on creating a sense of solidarity and strenuous self-help amongst the working classes and on exerting pressure on the governing classes and the industrial employers. The free-trade movement was, from this point of view, a rival and a diversion, in that it encouraged expectations of prosperity through legislative and fiscal reforms, and emphasised some conflict of interests between industrial and agricultural workers. On the other hand, as already suggested, it similarly emphasised a conflict of interest between two sections of the rich and powerful classes. But the demand for cheap food was more compelling than demands for the vote and for annual elections: and by the middle of the century there was a striking contrast between the complete success of the free-trade agitation and the failure of Chartism as well as of efforts to bring about a more general union of trade unions. Of the main working-class movements of these two decades, only the Co-operative movement made much headway.

Chartism, indeed, received some of its impetus from the early failures of trade unionism. In 1829 John Doherty formed a General Union of Operative Spinners, and the next year he founded the National Association for the Protection of Labour. It flourished mainly in the textile industries and extended its affiliations to societies in pottery, mining, hat-making and engineering. It had little driving force and achieved little before it withered away. But amongst the larger labour organisations was the Builders' Union, and it soon took the lead with more than 40,000 members. In 1833 it adopted the teaching of Robert Owen, recently returned from America with a scheme for co-operative production by which capitalism could be abolished, and the building trade taken over by a Grand National Guild: and in 1834 it became the nucleus of the Grand National Consolidated Trades Union, aiming at combining all trade unions into a national organisation. This included agricultural labourers and women workers hitherto little touched by trade unionism. The culmination of such associations as Owen's Grand National Moral Union of the Productive Classes of the United Kingdom and his Society for Promoting National Regeneration (both formed in 1833) was the Grand National Consolidated Trades Union. Unlike them, it was confined to trade unionists. The various co-operative and propagandist societies which proliferated in these years had no place in it, and Owen himself did not at first join it. It marked the climax of several abortive attempts to achieve a 'general union', seeking unity of action, though not uniformity of organisation, among the many existing trade-union bodies. But its plan was too ambitious for the stage of development reached by unionism. Its projects were too visionary to succeed in the face of ruthless employers and a hostile government. It suffered a fatal blow when six agricultural labourers of Tolpuddle in Dorsetshire were convicted of administering unlawful oaths and sentenced to transportation for seven years. Their purpose had been to form a friendly society of agricultural labourers and establish some contact with the Grand National Consolidated. Their savage punishment produced extensive protests, organised by a 'London Dorchester Committee' headed by William Lovett. But the government refused to lighten the sentence, and henceforth fear of the law drove many workers out of unionism. The Grand National Consolidated collapsed. The 'Tolpuddle Martyrs' were pardoned four years later, but their fate remained a stern deterrent to unionist activities. In most trades national organisation vanished, and even the Builders' Union broke up into its constituent trades. In the 1840's the miners set up a National Association, and in 1845 a further attempt at a 'general union' met with only temporary success. A pattern for the future was laid only in 1851, when the Amalgamated Society of Engineers was created with centralised control, high contributions and benefits and national scope. Skilled workers in particular succeeded in forming stable unions, such as the Amalgamated Society of Carpenters and Joiners in 1861; and in 1868 the Trades Union Congress was formed. From then onwards trade unionism spread and flourished.

Meanwhile, the failures of the 1830's gave impetus to the tide of discontent and agitation which produced Chartism. In 1836 William Lovett formed the London Working Men's Association of respectable and self-educated London artisans. Two years later he and Francis Place drew up the 'People's Charter' of six points which became the programme of reforms on which a majority of the radical and working-class movements could unite. It called for universal male (but not female) suffrage; equal electoral districts; removal of the property qualification for members of Parliament; payment of members of Parliament; secret ballot; and annual general elections. The last point—the only demand of the Chartists never subsequently obtained—was the most radical of all and would, if gained, have transformed the whole character of the parliamentary system. A House of Commons subject to annual elections would have been an instrument of direct democracy, and the nature of parliamentary responsibility (and so of ministerial responsibility) would have been completely changed.

The Birmingham Political Union of 1816, now revived by the banker and currency-reformer Thomas Attwood, sponsored the Charter and called for a National Petition on its behalf. So, too, did the reformers of Leeds headed by the stormy Feargus O'Connor, whose paper the *Northern Star* became the official Chartist organ. On the tripod basis of London, Birmingham and Leeds, the Chartists organised mass-meetings and nation-wide popular agitation. Highly inflammatory orators, like J. R. Stephens, Bronterre O'Brien and Richard Oastler, aroused popular enthusiasm for the 'Charter', which was soon regarded as a panacea for all social ills. The climax of the movement was the National Convention which in the spring of 1839 met in Westminster Palace Yard and organised a monster petition to Parliament. But the movement was deeply divided between the moderates, led by Lovett and his southern followers, and the violent groups led by O'Connor and O'Brien and their northern followers. There was a tang of civil war in the air in July when, after the Convention had moved to Birmingham, the petition with nearly a million and a quarter signatures was rejected by the House of Commons. Riots and local strikes, and even an insurrection in South Wales, followed the rejection. But the firmness of the government and the solid sense of the working-class artisans discouraged violence. A National Charter Association was formed to keep the movement alive. A second petition was presented, and again rejected, in 1842; and yet a third, with many forged signatures, was presented in 1848. Chartism after 1839 was more violent in tone but less solid in strength. It revived in times of bad harvests and more acute social distress, but it never again attained its original impetus. It was killed partly by reviving trade and greater prosperity. But it was the first effective and spontaneous working-class organisation; it drew the attention of all classes to the urgency of social reforms; it stirred the conscience of Victorian England and shook its hardening complacency; and it left a deep and permanent mark on English history.

The ideals of voluntary co-operation for production, to replace the system of competitive private enterprise for individual profit, were extensively canvassed in the years after 1815: and most actively by Robert Owen and his followers. They founded the Co-operative and Economical Society in 1821, and similar co-operative experiments were made in various places. They suffered by the general collapse of unionism in 1834, and Owenism thereafter lost ground. But such experiments in co-operative villages as Queenwood lasted into the eighteen-forties, and in 1844 the 'Rochdale Pioneers' founded a successful co-operative store. It was based on democratic control by its members as consumers, and gave members a 'dividend on purchases'. In 1854 they also formed the Rochdale Co-operative Manufacturing Society, so extending their principles to production as well as retail trading: and a decade later set up the Co-operative Wholesale Society, which was followed by its counterpart in Scotland in 1868–9. Industrial and Provident Societies Acts, passed in 1852 and 1862, greatly facilitated their progress: and they received considerable help from both the trades unions and the Christian Socialists. By the 1870's the principles were being rapidly extended to other sectors of economic life, and co-operative collieries, textile mills and banks were set up. The movement was the most speedily and conspicuously successful of all the working-class movements of these years.

The two decades before 1868 were an era of immense national prosperity and of solid middle-class predominance. Radical agitation for secret ballot and extension of the franchise went on. Violent controversy arose over the startling theories of Charles Darwin, whose *Origin of Species* appeared in 1859. But the acute social tensions of the previous two decades had passed away. Working-class agitation subsided. The domestic legislation that was passed was less violently controversial. Under the leadership of Lord Palmerston foreign affairs predominated. The rise of Napoleon III in France, the excitement of the Crimean War, the American Civil War and the domination of European affairs by Bismarck, absorbed public attention. These issues of foreign policy, dealt with elsewhere in this volume (chs. XVII and XVIII), need concern us here only so far as they were connected with imperial developments.

Under Palmerston Britain welcomed every movement of suppressed nationalities to achieve self-government.[1] She kept a watchful eye on the expansion of rival powers, especially of Russia, and the only important European war in which she took part in this period was against Russia. She tried by means of commercial treaties, of which the most important was the Cobden Treaty with France in 1860, to free her trade with Europe. Her policy was peaceful because war—even a civil war like that in America between 1860 and 1865—interfered with trade and damaged her industrial production. One of the most persuasive arguments brought forward by Cobden and Bright in favour of free trade was that it would eliminate some of the main causes of war and bind nations together by bonds of mutual interest. Britain's interests, in short, were not thought of as in conflict with those of other countries. Because they were world-wide, and because freedom of trade and movement would remove impediments to the realisation and working of the natural harmony of interests among peoples, the expansion and the prosperity of Britain were steps towards the general progress of the world. It was a blissful and comfortable belief, but also a sincere and dynamic faith.

These ideas which shaped British commercial and foreign policy likewise revolutionised her colonial policy. The momentous changes in colonial policy, which established self-government in the Dominions and gave birth to a new conception of Empire and Commonwealth, were made possible by the growth of economic interests so world-wide that they seemed to be in harmony with universal freedom of the seas and free trade, and with universal progress. The expansion of trade, whether with the colonies or with other countries, had repercussions on the development of emigration and oversea investment; and both were closely connected with the growth of railways and shipping, and with the development of the idea of colonial self-government. Underlying all was the quest of a rapidly expanding industrial production for correspondingly expansive markets and sources of supply. What enabled Englishmen to pursue this quest on a more completely world-wide scale than ever before was the dramatic improvement in means of transport and communication: especially of railways, steamships and telegraph.

Already by 1840 a service of steamship lines linked Britain with her colonies and spheres of interest in the Indian Ocean; but the Mediterranean route still involved transport overland from Alexandria to Suez and Aden, and the bulk of the eastern trade still went by sail round the

---

[1] But for Palmerston's attitude towards the Hungarian revolution in 1848–9, see p. 264.

Cape, taking between six and eight months on the way. By then, too, steamship lines ran from the Cape to Australia. In 1870 the British Indian Telegraph Company laid the first successful direct cable linking England with Bombay: and from Bombay it ran to Singapore, and thence on to Australia. Railways in the oversea colonies were slower to develop. By 1853 Canada had only some 200 miles of line, and Australia virtually none. India's railways developed only in the 1860's and were financed almost entirely by British capital. The colonies were transformed from remote outposts and bases, difficult of access, into a much more closely knit network of economic interests: and this integration of their economic development with that of Great Britain took place *pari passu* with a greater readiness to loosen the political controls and commercial regulations which hitherto had been regarded as the natural bonds of empire. Yet the economic status of the colonies was at first broadly maintained, even whilst their political status changed. They were to remain sources of raw materials and markets for English goods; and this division of labour between England and her colonies was not merely maintained but extended during these years, as the influx of English capital joined the flow of English manufactures. 'Increasing concentration upon a few staple products for export, large capital imports in the shape mainly of capital goods, a high rate of investment, full employment despite heavy immigration, profit inflation and rising property values; this was the common pattern of economic activity in the colonies.'[1]

This development of the colonies tended, after about 1850, to change the focus of British oversea capital investment, and even to narrow its geographical range. Before then capital flowed out to the whole world, but little of it to the colonies: during the third quarter of the century, it concentrated increasingly on the colonies. In 1850 about one-third of England's overseas investment (of some £225,000,000) was in America, and the rest mainly in Europe. By 1870 more than £75,000,000 of it had been sunk in Indian railways alone, and probably a quarter of the total was invested in loans to colonial governments.

Between 1830 and 1870 the oversea interests of the United Kingdom were transformed in two ways: they became for the first time really world-wide in extent, and they ceased to be predominantly commercial in character. The old colonial empire, which broke up when the thirteen American colonies achieved their independence, had consisted mostly of contiguous territories in North America and had centred mainly on the North Atlantic. Imperial connections with Canada and the West Indies, and close economic connections with the United States of America, kept British interests anchored there still. But the balance of imperial interests had shifted, meanwhile, from the Atlantic to the Indian Ocean, where the growth and consolidation of British trade and power in India, Ceylon

[1] *Cambridge History of the British Empire* (Cambridge, 1929–36), vol. II, p. 754.

and Burma were creating a vast new eastern empire. In consequence, Britain was acquiring extensive new interests in the South Atlantic and the Pacific Oceans. Cape Colony and a chain of islands and west African ports formed stepping-stones on the routes between the North Atlantic region and the Indian Ocean. The map of British possessions in 1830 looks like a sketchy outline of the shape of things to come. By 1870 the West African ports and trading-posts had grown into large colonial possessions, Livingstone had explored central Africa, the Cape had become the spring-board for immense expansion northwards, and on the western shores of the Indian Ocean lay a corresponding chain of British possessions. In the South Pacific, what had been mere footholds in southern Australia and northern New Zealand were fast becoming a solid continent under British control. It was expected, after the Suez Canal was opened in 1869, that the new possibility of the much quicker Mediterranean route to India would at once destroy the value of the older 'all-red' route round the Cape. But the Cape long retained those advantages which it held at the end of this period, and which an official of the Colonial Office stated thus: 'It is clear of the Suez complications, almost equally distant from Australia, China, India, Gibraltar, the West Indies and the Falklands, the best sanatorium for troops from the East, and the best depot for reliefs, a good and cheap market for provisions, and a repairing place for large ships.'[1]

The expansion of trade and the quest for markets were still important impulses behind these developments. But now other motives and impulses were no less strong than the purely commercial. The industrial revolution, which reached its phase of most rapid expansion of output in these decades, demanded not merely colonial markets but world markets. Britain's policy of free trade meant the death of that colonial policy which had also been mercantilist policy, and the repeal of the Navigation Laws half-way through this period denoted a new assessment of the commercial value of colonial territories. They were valued as foundations of a world-wide trade. To open and to keep open the supplies and the markets of the world for British manufactures was regarded as more important than the securing of special commercial advantages in scattered colonial possessions. They were valued as points of strategic advantage and strength, for securing the 'freedom of the seas'; as offering opportunities for investors, missionaries and emigrants; as providing national prestige in an era of intensifying nationalist rivalries. The aggregate of such advantages outweighed the more purely commercial motives of the old mercantilism.

Abandonment of mercantile commercialism as the unifying policy of colonial expansion and administration left, for a time, a vacuum. At the beginning of the period there was no coherent policy about colonies, and the most influential schools of thought regarded them as an encum-

---

[1] *Cambridge History of the British Empire*, vol. II, p. 591.

brance to be shed as soon as possible. But during the next generation a new and positive policy of empire emerged, involving the systematic use of colonial lands for organised emigration and investment, and the establishment of responsible self-government as the goal of colonial administration. Optimistic liberalism, which based its faith in free trade on the dogma that there was a natural harmony of interests among producers and consumers as well as among nations, applied the same ideas to colonial affairs. Instead of control exerted from London, there should be a timely concession of self-government to the colonists: and self-interest, operating through the natural harmony of interests among free peoples, would prove a stronger cement of empire than the artificial regulation of their trade or long-distance political direction by the mother country. Given freedom of trade and freedom of the seas, and given, too, the immense lead of the United Kingdom in industrial production, the colonies could also enjoy the freedom of self-government. The 'open door', even in British colonies, was a small price to pay if it secured an 'open door' everywhere else: so long as British manufactures could, with little competition, profit from every opening.

In 1798 Jeremy Bentham had urged the French, 'Emancipate your Colonies', and the early radicals, partly influenced by the experience of American independence, were opposed to colonialism as a part of the old order which they condemned. But in the 1830's there grew up a group of younger radical reformers who saw in the enlightened planning and administration of colonial settlements both an outlet for the rapid growth of population in the United Kingdom (which gloomy prophets like Malthus predicted would lead to general impoverishment) and an opportunity for creating new communities on more rationalistic foundations. John Stuart Mill, Charles Buller, Edward Gibbon Wakefield and Lord Durham shared this belief. The extensive migrations of the middle decades of the century, combined with a sequence of urgent colonial problems, afforded them the chance to carry their principles into operation. Through their achievements the principles of responsible self-government were extended to all the overseas territories settled by people from Britain, and the concept of 'Dominion status', one of the most creative and fertile concepts produced by nineteenth-century Britain, made possible a new ideal of imperial cohesion founded not on control and restriction but on independence and freedom. The administration of India, the largest portion of the empire, was also reorganised by these radical reformers: and through the reforms of the Indian civil service effected by Macaulay in 1853, new standards of efficiency and integrity were introduced which in their turn influenced, as has been described above (p. 337), the administrative system of the United Kingdom itself. The Indian penal code, introduced in 1860, was also drawn up by Macaulay on the basis of the ideas of Bentham and James Mill.

The younger radicals first turned their attention to Australia, and Wakefield worked out a plan for its systematic colonisation. He proposed that the government should sell land at a high figure and, with the profit, organise the immigration of the labourers needed to cultivate the land. So would the United Kingdom unload its surplus population to the advantage of a new and prosperous colony. Bentham prepared for him the plan of a joint-stock colonisation society, which was duly formed. It was backed by J. S. Mill, George Grote and Sir William Molesworth. Although Wakefield's ingenious scheme was only partially carried out, the agitation of his society stimulated a new interest in the fortunes and future of Australia and New Zealand. Immigration was assisted partly by proceeds from the sale of land and partly by grants from the British government, and the hitherto slow trickle of migrants quickened during the 1830's. Transportation of convicts was stopped for New South Wales in 1840, but was resumed for Western Australia between 1850 and 1868. In 1837 Wakefield founded the New Zealand Association to promote his idea, and a New Zealand Land Company was formed two years later. Settlement took place amidst the greatest confusion, but in 1840, by the Treaty of Waitangi, the British crown acquired the sovereignty of New Zealand.

Meanwhile rebellion in Canada attracted the attention of the radicals, and by 1838 it seemed clear that the division instituted by the Canada Act of 1791, between the predominantly British settlement of Upper Canada and the mainly French settlement of Lower Canada, could no longer be preserved. The English-speaking minority of Lower Canada had grown by immigration, but bad feeling between the two national groups produced constitutional deadlock between the French majority of the elected Assembly and the British Governor and Council. For different reasons— the conflict between the executive controlled by the old Loyalist families and the Assembly dominated by the newer and poorer immigrants— a similar deadlock appeared in Upper Canada. At the end of 1837 rebellions broke out in both provinces. Lord John Russell introduced a law suspending the constitution of Lower Canada, and in 1838 Lord Durham was sent out as High Commissioner with wide powers, and as Governor-General of all the North American provinces (including Nova Scotia, New Brunswick, Prince Edward Island and Newfoundland, as well as Upper and Lower Canada). He was accompanied by Buller and Wakefield, and his mission was regarded as the test case for Whig and Radical statesmanship in colonial affairs. The following year Durham produced his *Report on the Affairs of British North America* which has justly become the charter of British Commonwealth development.

The Report contrived to deal not only with the immediate political and constitutional problems of Canada, but also with the broader colonial issues of public lands, migration and settlement, and future political self-government and unification. Its two essential recommendations were the reunion of Upper and Lower Canada and the grant of responsible government. By reunion Durham meant complete fusion and not federation; and he regarded this as the necessary prelude to self-government. Like John Stuart Mill, he regarded some degree of national unity as essential to self-government and aimed 'to settle, once and for ever, the national character of the province'. This would be achieved by complete hegemony of British over French, so eliminating for ever 'some idle and narrow notion of a petty and visionary nationality'. He looked to a united Canada to serve as the nucleus for a future federation of the whole of the British territories in North America. By responsible government he meant making the executive authorities of the provinces responsible directly to the legislative assemblies, instead of to the London government. 'It is difficult', he wrote, 'to understand how any English statesman could have imagined that representative and irresponsible government could ever be combined.' He argued that responsible government would itself preserve the unity of the empire, by making it a community of free peoples: but he made important concessions to the wish of the government to preserve some control by proposing a distinction between the domestic affairs of the provinces in which they would enjoy complete self-determination, and certain reserved subjects still controlled by the government in London. The latter included 'the constitution of the form of government, the regulation of foreign relations and of trade with the mother country, the other British colonies and foreign nations, and the disposal of the public lands'. The Governor, still made responsible to London, was to look for 'no support from home in any contest with the legislature except on questions involving strictly Imperial interests'.

In 1840 Upper and Lower Canada were united, and the problem of establishing responsible government was left to be worked out in practice by subsequent governors-general. In 1846–8 instructions were sent first to the Governor of Nova Scotia, and then to the Governor-General of Canada, that they should act on the advice of ministers acceptable to the representative legislatures. Between 1847 and 1853 Lord Elgin, who was Durham's son-in-law, gradually established the conventions by which the executive submitted to the consent of the legislative assembly on all domestic matters. In 1867 the British North America Act opened the door for the federation of all the provinces, except Newfoundland, and the process was completed by 1873. Within a generation Canada had moved from discontent and disunity to self-government and national cohesion. But the change was not easy. In 1846 Canadian corn-growers lost the preferential treatment they had enjoyed in the United Kingdom market, and it was three years before the Navigation Laws, which confined their export trade to British markets, were repealed. Had Elgin not succeeded in making the Reciprocity Treaty with the United States in 1854, the drift of Canada away from Britain might well have become more pronounced. The western expansion of the new Dominion was slow and difficult. In 1869 it purchased the vast area of the Hudson Bay Company between Lake Winnipeg and the Rockies, and in the following year established the new province of Manitoba. The Canadian Pacific Railway, the vital link between the western provinces and the eastern, encountered many obstacles and it was 1885 before the first train ran from Montreal to the Pacific.

The progress of Canada towards responsible government served as a model for the constitutional development of Australia, New Zealand and Cape Colony. In 1851 New South Wales, Victoria, South Australia and Tasmania were invited to draft their own constitutions as self-governing colonies. The constitutions were accepted and legalised by Act of Parliament in 1855. As in Canada, self-government was followed by expansion into more of the continent, much stimulated by the discovery of gold fields in New South Wales and Victoria. In 1859 Queensland became a separate colony, but Western Australia remained small and undeveloped until the discovery of gold in 1890. Between 1850 and 1870 the total population of Australia increased fourfold, from less than half a million to nearly two millions. In 1852 New Zealand was divided into six provinces, each with an elected council. The government of the whole colony was vested in a Governor, a nominated Council, and an elected House of Representatives. From 1857 until 1870 the country was plagued by the Maori Wars, and it was 1876 before British troops could be withdrawn completely and New Zealand became a united Dominion enjoying self-government. In 1870 her population was still only a quarter of a million. Cape Colony received responsible government in 1872, having had a Legislative Assembly since 1854.

In 1865 the Colonial Laws Validity Act declared that laws passed by colonial legislatures should be void only in so far as they were clearly repugnant to an Act of the British Parliament, or to an Order or Regulation made under such an Act, which was designed to apply to the colony. This was, in effect, a general assurance of internal self-government to all the colonial legislatures, and a formal removal of the doubts cast by judgments in the courts of South Australia upon the validity of colonial legislation which conflicted with English law. It meant that within its own sphere a colonial legislature was sovereign, and that it was subordinate only to the Imperial Parliament. It was the 'charter of colonial legislative independence'. The process of abandoning Durham's proposed restrictions had already begun. By Acts of 1840 and 1852, control of the unoccupied lands of Canada had been turned over to the provinces. In 1858 the Canadian legislature succeeded in imposing a tariff on English goods. By 1870 the process of establishing complete Dominion autonomy had substantially begun: and it was to continue until the formal recognition of it in the Statute of Westminster in 1931.

But this pattern of development so clearly set for the white settlements of Canada, Australia and New Zealand was by no means universal in the empire. Some of the older colonies, such as Barbados, Bermuda and the Bahamas, kept their ancient representative constitutions but did not gain responsible government. Jamaica, which had previously had an elective legislature, lost it. Most of the colonies acquired by conquest or concession after 1814 were not given representative institutions of the old type. In India, after the Mutiny of 1857–8, the government of the East India Company came to an end, and was replaced by direct rule of the crown. In the empire as a whole it was as likely that direct colonial administration would continue as that the principles of responsible self-government would spread from the favoured white settlements. In so diversified an empire, diversification of methods of government seemed, indeed, more appropriate than a rigid assimilation to any single pattern.

The general character of British development, both at home and overseas, during these years is epitomised in the system of imperial defence which was devised by 1870. These decades saw the change-over in the navy from sail to steam, from wood to iron, and from shot to shell (cf. ch. XI). The new types of ship and gun demanded greater technical skill and therefore more expensive training. Expenditure on the navy roughly doubled during this period. Except for the strong garrison in India, the imperial army came to be concentrated at home. This was made possible by the existence of rapid steam transport, and advisable by the threatening situation in Europe. The reorganisation of the army achieved by Edward Cardwell after 1868 produced a more efficient as well as a more democratic fighting force than the army which had fought the Crimean War. Growing realisation that Britain's world-wide interests and territories required a coherent scheme of imperial defence won acceptance for the strategic principles laid down in classical form by Sir John Colomb in 1867.[1] They were significantly based on the thesis that trade is the link of empire. In war the function of the navy should be to blockade enemy ports and keep open the vital sea routes linking the naval and commercial bases of the empire; so destroying enemy trade whilst securing British trade. The role of the army would be to garrison India, protect home ports and oversea naval bases, and under cover of naval protection serve as the spearhead of attack on enemy territories. This was clearly the defence system best suited to the needs of a maritime commercial empire; and it was characteristic that it should be but a modernisation of the doctrines of Chatham and Wellington. The changes which had made Britain rich in new ways had also made her vulnerable in new ways. But by inventive adaptation of traditional institutions and principles to new needs, she might yet hope to be strong as well as rich.

[1] J. Colomb, *The Protection of our Commerce and the Distribution of our War Forces considered* (London, 1867).

CHAPTER XIV

RUSSIA IN EUROPE AND ASIA

THE contribution to the twentieth-century Russian revolution made by the condition of Russia in the mid-nineteenth century is all the more clearly revealed as the character of the society which the revolution has established becomes increasingly certain and perceptible. Even a generation ago the institutions of tsarist Russia, like the efforts of the autocracy to conserve them, could appear no more than obstacles or incentives to its overthrow in favour of the liberal democracy which was often still regarded as the world-wide objective of political reform. Similarly the tendencies towards spiritual collectivism, indeed social absolutism, shared so generally by Russian reformers of distinct and even opposed schools long before the advent of Marxism in Russia, could still be counted as aberrations from the course of liberal development. But by now we can perceive that the tsarist autocracy and the movements of opposition to it provided many of the moulds of post-revolutionary government and political thought. A historical revision is therefore gaining ground in the West in which the evidence of survival and recurrence in Russian institutions and thought is a directing factor.

Such evidence is most conspicuous, perhaps, in the tradition of absolute centralised government at one extreme, co-existent with a village collectivism reputedly, if not in fact, traditional at the other. But the western interpreter will also observe, as did his more acute predecessors at the time,[1] the association of political authority with bureaucratic or military rank rather than private, local, or hereditary status, a common indifference to western conceptions of liberty for either moral or economic ends, an obsession with Russia's historical status, the sense of national exclusivism linked with a sense of supra-national, indeed universal mission, the confidence in a manifest destiny in Asia owed to a new dispensation distinct from that of the older maritime trading empires, the reluctant debt to Germany for the principle of national economics, and for models of militarism and technology—besides the education of German philosophy which the Russian intelligentsia digested and transformed.

The course of Russian history through which these national characters endured is demarcated by the reigns of tsars. This was due partly to the peculiar dependence of Russian political and economic society on government and the dependence of the government on the autocrat himself, and

---

[1] For example, Marquis A. de Custine, *La Russie en 1839* (4 vols. Paris, 1843), and Baron A. von Haxthausen, *Studien über die inneren Zustände, das Volksleben und insbesondere die ländlichen Einrichtungen Russlands* (3 vols. Hanover, 1847).

partly because the tsars' reigns were often punctuated by violent beginnings and violent ends. Thus on the death of Alexander I in 1825 the succession of his brother Nicholas I was delayed and confused by doubts over the heir and was marked by the bloody mutinies of the Decembrists; Nicholas died during the Crimean War when a contemporary wrote that his only choice was between abdication and death;[1] his son, Alexander II, was assassinated by terrorists a quarter of a century later. The second of these crises, culminating in the insurrection of 14 (o.s.)/26 (n.s.) December 1825,[2] was the first outburst of comprehensive revolutionary thought and action in Russia. Although its leaders were 'young colonels' of the twentieth-century type with the doctrines of eighteenth-century *philosophes*, this had been no mere epilogue to Alexander I's schizophrenic regime. As Lenin wrote in words regularly quoted by Soviet historians, 'the Decembrists aroused Herzen. Herzen developed revolutionary agitation.'[3] And Herzen himself, the foremost Russian publicist of the century, founded, in his *Development of Revolutionary Ideas in Russia*, the traditional liberal interpretation of early nineteenth-century Russian history which accepted the Decembrists as forerunners and martyrs.

The first administrative act of the Emperor Nicholas had been to arrange for the investigation and trial of the Decembrists on a vast scale intended for purposes of political intelligence as well as a political demonstration. The execution of only five would-be regicide conspirators and the deportation of the remainder to act as a civilising leaven in Siberia hardly deserved the condemnation it received from liberal historians sympathetic to a revolutionary tradition which has outlived their standards of mercy. All the more since the conditions of exile, whether in the initial period of nominal hard labour or subsequent resettlement, bore no resemblance to those inflicted on common criminals, prisoners of war or political convicts, in particular Polish nationalists, who made up an average rate of 5000 deportees to Siberia annually between 1800 and 1850.[4]

This clemency was prudent, not magnanimous; the emperor did not mean to demoralise the nobility by his treatment of the political heretics among them. In consequence his reputation as a brutal martinet was modified and also the suspicion of his militarist ambitions held by even the loyal serving nobility. In fact, Nicholas developed as tsar into a severe but conscientious autocrat, and his reputation of competent majesty became an important factor in European as well as Russian history, disguising until the Crimean War the decline in comparative military

---

[1] T. Schiemann, *Geschichte Russlands unter Kaiser Nikolaus I* (Berlin, 1904-19), vol. IV, p. 374.

[2] The difference between the Russian ('old style') and the western or Gregorian ('new style') calendar in the nineteenth century is that the latter is in advance by twelve days.

[3] *Sobranie Sochineniya*, vol. XV (1937 edn), p. 469.

[4] G. Kennan, *Siberia and the Exile System* (2 vols. New York, 1891), vol. I, pp. 78 ff., which remains the best description of Siberia as a penal colony.

power and national cohesion of the regime of 'parade Tsarism', which was so dependent upon his personality, and through which he more or less successfully influenced the affairs of the whole continent. His prestige was such at its zenith that when he visited England in 1844, Queen Victoria marvelled that she could breakfast with '*this* greatest of all earthly Potentates', although significantly she accepted the common western opinion that his magnificence relied upon domestic oppression.[1] But his iron demeanour did not deceive his entourage. He had neither brilliance nor serenity as a qualification for leadership, and his associates detected a highly strung rather than a powerful character behind his abrupt decisions.

Nicholas began his reign not as a political doctrinaire but as a soldier succeeding to a military command in poor order, and he was therefore ready to apply the lessons of the Decembrist revolt towards expedient reforms as well as checks upon revolutionary infection from Europe. Yet even before the shock of the revolutions of 1830, the administrative pattern of the regime was determined by two famous repressive controls, the edict reinstituting and fortifying the political police, which had flourished informally during the previous reign, and the censorship edict, both issued in 1826. The former entrusted to the new institution 'all dispositions and information in higher police matters' and control in particular over 'state criminals', the supervision of foreigners and religious dissidents (*raskolniki*), and the investigation of correspondence. 'Department III' of the Imperial Chancellery was to be distinct from the existing gendarmerie or semi-military police and from the ordinary provincial police, which was recruited and controlled locally. Although it consisted of only forty officials, by the end of Nicholas's reign its control through a web of undeclared agents was legendary. It formalised the Russian tradition of police administration, and its extra-legal action 'according to administrative procedure' (*po administrativnom poryadke*, a famous phrase in Russian history) could lead to detention, deportation, or attachment of property, without judicial process. Moreover, it served as an agency of cultural and even moral control, partly outside the law and partly within the scope of the censorship decree. The latter *ukaz*, equally representative of this era, introduced a system of censorship, revised in 1828 and lasting with minor modifications until 1865. Obscurantist though this was, there are parallels to its operation in Russian and other administrative practice at different times. It was often laxly applied—and much of the comment in the golden age of liberalism now looks ingenuous. The prohibition common in the contemporary European autocracies upon publications held to disparage religion, monarchy, or the legitimate government was extended to historical studies insufficiently intolerant of past revolutions,

---

[1] *The Letters of Queen Victoria*, ed. A. C. Benson and Viscount Esher (London, 1908), vol. II, pp. 12 ff.

to philosophical works other than text-books, and even to medical publications if they 'weakened faith' in the immortality of the soul. The machinery was preventive, administered through boards of officials in literary centres, supervised by the Ministry of Education but subject to frequent intervention by the tsar or the Imperial Chancellery. It was also a function of the censorship until 1828 to control style and language and in the 1830's it came to be used as an instrument of official nationalism. On the other hand, the assault on philosophy apparently followed the tsar's own conviction that such studies stimulated or covered political speculation, and the consequence was the closure of some university faculties. But Nicholas had no use for the independent clerical persecutors of the universities who had flourished at the end of Alexander's reign; the chief of these were dismissed, while the leading religious extremist of the right, the Archimandrite Photius, lost favour. The evangelical movement, for long encouraged by Alexander I, was even more suspect, and its principal agency, the Bible Society, which propagated vernacular versions of the gospels, was dissolved.

The repression of any spontaneous movement was stimulated by a report on the Decembrist conspiracy, which recommended change but concluded that the demand for change had resulted from excessive freedom of thought and education. Through the report a Decembrist influence can be traced in many of the reforms which Nicholas considered in the first phase of his reign. Some of its more superficial recommendations were actually carried out, while deeper changes, in particular the consolidation of the noble class and agrarian reform, were repeatedly touched upon but not solved. The same early mood of the regime was shown in the 'great' Kochubei committee appointed in December 1826 to investigate the existing system of government and to decide 'what is right for today, what must not be retained, and by what it is to be replaced'.

The autocratic machinery which was thus to be revised acted at the higher levels largely by *ad hoc* methods and continued to do so, as the proliferation of lesser committees during the next half century was to show. The State Council was rather a nominated quasi-legislature than a cabinet; it prepared the budget and revised the draft legislation presented to it with the tsar's approval by ministers, but the procedure was often by-passed by decrees (*ukazy*) emanating direct from the Imperial Chancellery which had equal force of law. Departmental ministers commonly dealt direct with the tsar, while the Committee of Ministers set up in 1805 overlapped the State Council. Nor was there any significant primacy among ministers even when, as in the case of Kochubei, and after him Gorchakov, the Chairman of the State Council was also Chairman of the Council of Ministers and bore the title of Chancellor of the Empire. Meanwhile the Senate had become no more than a supreme court. Indeed, the only vital organ of government was the tsar's own

Chancellery, which there was no question of reforming; and the most important institutions of Nicholas's reign were established as new departments of the Chancellery. Such were the third department, the department for codification of the laws, and (1838) the department for reform of state peasant status and state lands. Provincial government, which the committee reviewed but left unchanged, was centralised through the governors of fifty provinces (*gubernii*), and the governors-general in Siberia and in some frontier and colonial territories. These were notoriously understaffed, and, in case of emergency or cumulative scandal in administration, a commissioner (*revizor*) would be sent from St Petersburg to report or act on the situation, whether a small provincial town was involved or a vast territory like Siberia. It was characteristic that Nicholas's most trusted representatives were usually army officers, whether it was a famine or a riot which led to their mission.

The Kochubei committee was also charged to consider the agrarian problem which, like slavery in contemporary America, impended upon all political thought and action. Out of a total population of some 45 millions in Russia proper in 1815, about 21 millions were serfs attached to the land and owned as personal property by some 200,000 hereditary nobles, or by a few of the 500,000 officers and officials qualified by their lifetime noble grade, while another 15 millions were state- or crown-owned peasants with varying but exiguous rights. So far minor experiments in reform—emancipating peasants of the non-Russian Baltic provinces without land and, licensing elsewhere in Russia voluntary agreements between master and peasant for emancipation with land—had produced at most a moral impact on the Russian social system. The degree of the tsar's own reluctant conversion was expressed in his words to Kiselev in 1834, that his duty was to prepare for the transformation of serf law by his successor. But further piecemeal reforms, aimed against the treatment of the peasant as detachable from his land, were obstructed in committee by Grand Duke Constantine, and then came the European revolutions of 1830 bringing more general revulsion against concessions to liberal sentiment.

The tsar's interest in agrarian reform survived, however, until 1848. From 1833 onwards reforms were carried out in the status, tenure, taxation, recruiting and local self-government of the state peasants, and their free status was specifically affirmed. In 1838 a department of state lands was created under Count Kiselev, the tsar's most active subordinate in the agrarian committees of the 'thirties and 'forties. But the reforms achieved by these committees were of more indirect than direct significance. In 1833 the public sale of serfs was forbidden, and in 1842 an edict revised the law of 1802 in order to encourage landlords to emancipate their serfs with land, by creating a class of 'free' peasants temporarily 'bonded' for further services. In 1844 the emancipation of domestic serfs without land was allowed, but not until 1858 was the abuse to which this led corrected by effectively preventing the transfer of peasants from the land to domestic service. Between 1840 and 1848 edicts dealt with the right of peasants to buy their freedom when their master sold his estate. This right was made subject to agreement with their master, thus avoiding recognition of the peasants' tenure as prescriptive. Indeed, it was not until 1848 that the right of the privately owned peasant to possess chattels even was established by edict. All these enactments applied to Russia as a whole. In addition, in western Ukraine the governor-general, Bibikov, began in the 'forties to enforce a register of serfs' maximum duties to their largely Polish masters, but when the system expanded to affect Russian nobles it came to a stop.

The reformers were influenced by several motives: cosmopolitan misgivings over serfdom as a social evil, a growing belief (as much the result of practical experiment as of the influence of English classical economics) in the superior profitability of mobile wage labour, and apprehensiveness at the possibility of agrarian revolution from below. The increase in local peasant risings, endemic in Russia, appeared ominous; official figures showed increases of over 50 per cent in each decade of Nicholas I's reign, from 148 in the years 1826–35 to 474 in the six years before emancipation, while recorded murders of landlords or bailiffs numbered some 300 in the thirty-five years before 1861. The unrest was perhaps due as much to premature rumours of imminent liberation, which piecemeal reforms and imperfect secrecy stimulated, as to exasperation at the delay. It reinforced both the opposition of conservatives to emancipation and the liberals' belief in the urgency of change.

This unrest originated almost exclusively in purely Russian conditions. The coincidence of riots and mutinies during the cholera epidemic in Russia in 1830–3 with political convulsions in Europe was, contrary to government suspicions, almost certainly fortuitous. The only region susceptible to western currents of revolutionary optimism was Poland. Here the effective grievance was the nationalist one of the nobility and intelligentsia. When insurrection broke out in Warsaw on 7/19 November 1830 the viceroy retreated with the Russian garrison, and the Polish army, a separate entity, won some early successes. The course of the subsequent war brought no credit, however, to Russian arms or to Polish politics; the Russians did not gain a decisive victory in the field until May 1831, but there was no effective prolongation of guerilla resistance because the interest or sentiment of the semi-servile Polish peasantry had never been engaged by the patriots. The revolt ended in hundreds of executions and thousands of expropriations and left both sides irreconcilably embittered.

In Russia proper the alarm of 1830 ended the experimental period of Nicholas's reign, whereupon cultural repression became more systematic. The system is associated with the name of Count Uvarov, Minister of Education from 1833 to 1849, although he never ranked among the tsar's closest advisers. Regarded by contemporaries as a renegade humanist, it was as a bureaucrat rather than a genuine doctrinaire that Uvarov proposed in 1832 his 'triple formula' of 'orthodoxy, autocracy and nationality'.[1] This became the official ideology, with the emphasis on autocracy, and survived into the last years of tsarism. Both divine right and supremacy over the orthodox church were attributed to the tsar in the basic law of the empire, issued in 1832, while the subordinate place of nationality was defined by Uvarov in 1847: 'Russian nationality (*narodnost*)', he explained, 'must express unconditional devotion to orthodoxy and autocracy.'[2]

In the task of control educational policy was of minor importance compared to police regulation and censorship. The expansion of universities was checked, although Uvarov was responsible for one new foundation at Kiev, which, as a Great Russian institution, challenged the cultural separatism of the historic Ukrainian city. Here and elsewhere courses in philosophy were limited, and those in mathematics favoured on account of their supposed military value; faculty appointments were entrusted to the state, students put in uniform and state supervisors of their conduct and discipline introduced, while entry to universities or secondary schools by 'other ranks' than the nobility was impeded. For study abroad the age limit was lowered, and in general foreign travel was restricted by a passport system. Yet, given its objects and methods, the regime's cultural policy was not barbarous. Uvarov was a good patron to the Academy of Sciences and under his aegis some of the great series of official Russian publications in the fields of archaeology, geography and documentary history were begun.

Equally consistent with conservative autocracy was the vaunted semi-codification of Russian laws, the last service of the veteran Speranskii. It comprised a collection of all legislation since 1649 (published in 45 volumes in 1830) and the *Svod*, an extract of still valid laws (published in 15 volumes in 1832) to serve as a quasi-code. Yet this did not establish the rule of law, as some historians have pretended, even if it eased the later judicial reform.[3] It was an academic operation, no more a legislative one than the monumental Neo-Byzantine dynastic buildings of the reign were in essence public works. The churches and palaces for which the tsar was responsible reflected rather the high morale of the dynasty and its orderly extravagance which was also largely responsible for the lavish cosmopolitan standards of St Petersburg society. These contrasted with Nicholas's personal ostentation of soldierly austerity and also, as foreigners frequently observed, with the depth and expanse of surrounding Russian poverty.[4]

[1] Cf. ch. x, p. 230. The Russian word *narodnost* has no English equivalent. It is less positive than 'nationalism' and nearer to the German *Volkstum*.

[2] M. Lemke, *Ocherki po istorii russkoi tsenzury* (St Petersburg, 1904), p. 186.

[3] P. P. Gronski, 'Le Centenaire du Code des Lois Russes', pp. 400, 406 in *Le Monde Slave* (Paris, 1932).

[4] E.g. R. Bremner, *Excursions in the Interior of Russia* (London, 1839), vol. i, pp. 340-3.

Some virtues as well as vices of conservatism were shown also in economic policy. A contemporary German economist observed that if any country was suited to 'autarky' it was Russia,[1] and in fact the 1822 tariff, only slightly modified during more than a quarter of a century, altogether prohibited a large range of imports, particularly textiles and metals. But nationalist economics was not a dogma and in 1852 a revolution in tariff policy occurred; Polish competition was accepted by the abolition of the customs frontier and in 1857 Russia entered a period of freer trading than any major state besides Great Britain was practising; yet the revenue was maintained. Meanwhile Kankrin, the finance minister from 1823 to 1844, had revalued the currency. By 1843 a 'silver rouble' had been established at three-and-a-half times the value of the old paper rouble and the new currency in its paper issue did not depreciate by as much as 25 per cent in the next quarter of a century.

Economic progress had made no more than scratches or pockets in the surface of agrarian Russia, yet the turnover in foreign trade in 1853, the last full year before the Crimean War, was, at 250 million roubles, nearly double that of 1825.[2] Raw cotton imports and the productivity of factory labour in textiles[3] had nearly doubled, and in the early 1850's Russia had about 1700 machine-operated looms.[4] In 1855 she was producing nearly as much pig iron—over 250,000 tons—as Germany,[5] though by primitive methods. In the 1840's Haxthausen could write that Moscow, not the show place of industry, 'from being a residence of the nobility' had 'become a factory town'.[6] But factory organisation meant not mechanisation, but merely the first step from domestic industry, which was simultaneously increasing both on private estates and in towns; little more than half a million Russians were classified as factory workers in 1860. Meanwhile, the estimated population grew during Nicholas I's reign from 53 to 71 millions, but contemporary estimates indicate no commensurate increase in grain harvests, irrespective of the new wheat exports from the Black Sea ports.[7]

The Russian bureaucracy was not wholly in favour of the rise of the factory system. Some still saw a future for domestic industry and were encouraged by foreign and other experts who thought Russia might escape the 'proletarian cancer' of the West.[8] But the tsar took a simpler mercantilist view of *raison d'état* and encouraged industry by establishing a council of manufacturers, granting direct monetary aid to producers,

---

[1] W. Kosegarten, in appendix to Haxthausen, *op. cit.* vol. III, p. 533.

[2] P. Khromov, *Ekonomicheskoe Razvitie Rossii v XIX–XX vekakh*. Tables on pp. 439, 453. Figures are adjusted to 1840 rouble values.

[3] *Ibid.* pp. 65, 439.   [4] *Ibid.* p. 55.   [5] *Ibid.* p. 62.

[6] *Op. cit.* vol. I, p. xiii.

[7] Khromov, *op. cit.* pp. 436–8.

[8] M. Tugan-Baranovskii, *Russkaya Fabrika v proshlom i nastoyashchem* (St Petersburg, 1898), pp. 297, 359.

founding model industrial enterprises and technical and agricultural schools, and patronising industrial exhibitions. In the crucial question of railway building he was, however, hesitant. The first line of 27 km. from St Petersburg to Tsarskoe Selo was built by private enterprise in 1838; in 1843 the railway from Warsaw to the Austrian frontier was undertaken by the state and from 1847 to 1851 that from St Petersburg to Moscow, in each case at increasing cost per mile. As elsewhere, railway construction in Russia set a new rate of economic expansion. This was closely linked with the demographic changes, particularly the mobility of labour, which followed the abolition of serfdom and like this belong to a new era.

The Russian political system was regarded by the tsar as his share in the international policy of counter-revolution pursued by the three eastern European courts and stabilised for fifteen years in the Münchengrätz agreement of 1833 (see ch. x, pp. 252–3). How dynasts believed that the ideological conflict transcended frontiers is shown by an authoritative appreciation drafted in 1839.[1] This explained that the focus of revolution was France, and that Britain, too, was interested in 'spreading in this direction her political influence and...the constitutional forms by which she is governed'. Russia's interest was to strengthen Austria and Prussia 'in the terrible struggle...against an adversary who attacks them daily'. The international links of revolution were confirmed by the events of 1848–9 (see especially ch. xv). In Russia regular news kept the intelligentsia in a state of political excitement while rumours of the foreign upheavals seem to have stimulated even the endemic peasant unrest. The tsar took up the challenge in a manifesto addressed to the world at large in March 1848, which ended with the words: 'Take heed, ye peoples, and submit [sc. to your rulers] for God is with us.' Admonitions and eventual intervention abroad were accompanied by a more searching repression of dangerous thoughts in Russia. Censorship passed to a committee and Uvarov lost his office, perhaps partly because he defended the universities against restrictions on their numbers as well as on their courses. There was, in fact, no revolutionary agitation or conspiracy, but in 1849 the extremist Petrashevskii discussion group to which Dostoevskii belonged was broken up. Action was also taken against the independent right, the so-called Slavophiles, partly because revolution and nationalism were still confounded in the minds of European autocrats, partly to check propaganda against the Baltic German minority who were so valuable to the Russian army and administration, and partly to protect the tsar's brother sovereigns from Russian xenophobic outbursts which wars and rumours of wars had stimulated.

[1] This memorandum, prepared by the leading Russian diplomatist Brunnow for the instruction of the heir to the throne, is summarised in S. S. Tatishchev's *Vneshnaya Politika Imperatora Nikolaya Pervago* (St Petersburg, n.d.), pp. 25 ff.

This reaction was hardly the 'terror' depicted by some historians, but it is significant that a moderate liberal later reported to Nicholas's successor that 'nihilism owes its origin and development primarily to the repressive measures operating from 1849 to 1855'.[1] In fact these measures brought to a peak the repressive policy which the autocracy and its critics had made the most important issue in Russia after serfdom. The control of dangerous thoughts was not new, but at this juncture it established tsarism as the symbolic enemy of the European left, while inside Russia it interacted with a new and profoundly important political literature which bore the germs of several schools of thought and action besides nihilism. This literature owed more to the general ideas than the political impulses of Europe, where its significance was underrated until its influence on the reception and eventual processing of Marxism in Russia became apparent.

The intellectual efflorescence culminating in the stupendous achievement of Pushkin had found political expression in the Decembrist movement. When this was broken the revolutionary spirit passed from officers' messes and salons to a new generation of dilettante scholars and publicists, the future 'men of the forties'. Two schools emerged, the 'westerners' and the 'easterners' or Slavophiles whose literary debate systematised and circulated ideas already current in inchoate form. Its starting point was the publication in 1836 of P. Chaadaev's 'Philosophical Letter', the burden of which was the nullity of Russian culture. 'We belong', Chaadaev wrote, 'to those nations who...exist only to teach the world some serious lesson.'[2] Geography and the Byzantine church had separated Russia from creative European culture, her response to Peter the Great's offer of civilisation had been negligible, and more recent contact with the West had led to disaster—the Decembrist revolt. The only hope was to 'retrace the whole course of human experience'.[3] The effect of this 'gunshot in a dark night',[4] as Herzen called it, in rallying a 'western' school was gradual, but the Slavophiles took up the challenge and thus confirmed the main agenda of Russian political thought for at least a generation.

The opposition between westerners and Slavophiles was more formal than fundamental, since both were liable to change their ground and their personal relations were often close. Both had their training in the German philosophical systems of Hegel and Schelling but, while this rationalised the historical traditionalism of the Slavophiles, for the westerners Hegel

---

[1] P. A. Zaionchkovskii, 'Zapiski K. D. Kavelina o nigilisme', in *Istoricheskii Arkhiv*, vol. v (1950), p. 341.

[2] P. Chaadaev, *Sochineniya i pisma* (ed. M. Gershenson, Moscow, 1913), p. 81.

[3] *Ibid.* p. 79.

[4] The phrase is in his *Byloe i Dumy* (ed. Shcherbun, Minsk, 1957), vol. i, p. 378. This is an autobiography of the first importance in Russian social and intellectual history, of which there is an English translation by Constance Garnett (London, 1908).

was, in Herzen's famous words, the 'algebra of revolution'.[1] Indeed, when blended with French Utopian socialism, this grounding turned the more forceful, Herzen, Belinskii, and Bakunin, towards Hegelianism of the left and contact with the contemporary German school which led from Feuerbach to Marx. A. I. Herzen (1811–70) was an eclectic humanist of immense literary powers who had no use for Russian national character or institutions until he emigrated in 1847, when he became disgusted in turn by bourgeois democracy and by the centralising character of 'Jacobin' revolution. Y. V. Belinskii (1811–47), the most influential inside Russia of contemporary publicists, had glorified the tsarist state during his Hegelian phase more explicitly than the Slavophiles, and in opposition to their idea of the unpolitical nation. Although he later wrote as a champion of personality it was less the spontaneous personality cherished by western liberals than personality seeking or forced to realise itself in a 'just' and 'free' society under the leadership of the intelligentsia which it was his major task to expand and vitalise. M. Bakunin (1814–76) was even less consistent. His permanent vein of anarchism was expressed in 1847 in his famous phrase 'the passion for destruction is a creative passion'. But during his imprisonment after his part in the German revolutions of 1848 he wrote a confession in which he went as far as any Slavophile in morbid nationalism and xenophobia.[2] Later, in Siberia, before he escaped to Europe to struggle with Marx for control of international socialism, he privately advocated a kind of protofascist dictatorship to be exercised by Muraviev, the governor-general in Irkutsk.

On the other side the Slavophiles substituted the Russian *narod* for the German *Volk*, and without borrowing the idea of the transcendental state, which did not harmonise with their clerical sympathies, transposed German historicism into terms of a mystical Russian nationality. Russian history was for them strictly autonomous, Peter the Great was an apostate, the universal Russian mission was to be realised through the national character, more Christian than that of the Latin West, with its virtue of humility exemplified in the individual, and its spiritual collectivism exemplified in the characteristic institutions of the village commune (*mir*) and craftsmen's co-operative (*artel*) as well as in the national church and the dissenting sects. The two most respected Slavophiles were less prolific than the westerners. The literary reputation of I. V. Kireevskii (1806–56) rested on two essays and his friend Khomyakov (1804–60) wrote primarily as a lay theologian. Their influence was personal and epistolary, for

---

[1] A. I. Gertsen (i.e. Herzen), *Polnoe sobranie sochinenii i pisem* (ed. M. K. Lemke, 22 vols., St Petersburg, 1906 onwards), vol. XIII, p. 16. Cf. Herzen's tribute to Hegel's influence in his 'Diletantizm v nauke' published in the periodical *Otechestvennye Zapiski* in 1843 (*Polnoe Sobranie*, vol. III, p. 191).

[2] Its motives and sincerity have been questioned. See E. H. Carr, *Michael Bakunin* (London, 1937), pp. 211–16.

instance on Y. F. Samarin (1819–76), who took a prominent official part in the reform of serfdom, and on the Aksakovs (K. S., 1817–60, and I. S., 1823–86), whose cultural revivalism led to an ostentatious hatred of the new creation of St Petersburg and therewith of the whole apparatus of contemporary Russian government. All these were opponents of Uvarov's system who condemned serfdom hardly less severely than the westerners as an aberration of Russian history, and favoured the revival of the *Zemskii Sobor*, the old Muscovite assembly of estates. Even those Slavophiles most amenable to the government, such as Shevyrev and Pogodin, turned reformers during the Crimean War. Perhaps the most revealing index of the three great ideological interests in the middle of the century is their conception of the village commune. To the westerners it was a stage in all European society which the West had outlived but which might enable Russia to bypass bourgeois capitalism on the way to socialism. To the Slavophiles it was a unique and precious phenomenon of Slav culture. To Uvarov it was an irreplaceable fiscal institution devised by Peter the Great.

The greater literary names appear on the fringe only of the political controversy. As Pushkin (1799–1837) was killed before the issue had been joined, his intellectual inheritance was claimed by both parties. He had contacts with the Decembrists but was no admirer of western *laissez-faire* democracy, finding greater human dignity in the food-producing Russian serf than in the proletarian English mill-hand. The works of N. V. Gogol (1809–52) were satires of acceptance rather than revulsion, and his later explicit defence of serfdom provoked a bitter denunciation by Belinskii which circulated among the reformist intelligentsia as a kind of secret manifesto. In the next generation, Ivan Turgenev (1818–83) was intimately associated with the westerners, but not of their party, and his political influence on their side was, like Tolstoi's in the same period, a formidable by-product of his undidactic novels.

Political controversy was forced by censorship into the disguise of literary criticism, and Russian periodicals, multiplying nearly fourfold between 1800 and 1850, served as a substitute for debate and agitation. Journals like the *Notes from the Fatherland* and the *Contemporary* which Belinskii used, and the *Muscovite* (*Moskvityanin*) of the Slavophiles, reached both the higher bureaucracy and the unemployed nobility and formed in a real sense the political education of both the reformers of Alexander II's reign and the next more revolutionary generation of the intelligentsia. As the political ferment spread, more nobles became conscious of the problem of their own class. Although relieved of the former obligation of service, only the more boorish failed to serve the central government for a few years, either in the army or as civilians. Thereafter they too often retired to St Petersburg, Moscow or even a provincial capital, visiting their estates for long holidays rather than residence, letting their demesne and putting their serfs on *obrók* (that is, commuting their labour services for cash payment). There were progressive farming landlords, but they were exceptions. There was no country life on the western grand scale. Indeed the same estates seldom lasted through several generations, and there was consequently lacking that sense of home and local particularism which has elsewhere helped to bind class to class whatever the degree of exploitation. Moreover, while the nobility remained politically stagnant their numbers, standard of living and pressure on the agrarian economy rose. Types of the consequent frustration appear in Turgenev's novel *Rudin* and Goncharov's febrile or resigned *Oblomov*.

The army continued the chief field for individual advancement, and not only for the nobility since, owing to the very large recruitment of officers from other ranks, as distinct from the cadet schools, it was the main road to the hereditary ennoblement carried by the higher grades of the service hierarchy. Socially too, it had much the same status as in Prussia whence it had long drawn much of its doctrine. Since 1812 it had been the real basis of Russia's international influence, although critics abroad pointed to its corruption and questioned its ability to deploy or supply its paper establishment of about half a million men, not counting Cossacks or the army of a hundred thousand tied up in the Caucasus. Its prestige, raised by success against Persia and Turkey in the late 1820's, was lessened by the persistence of the Caucasus guerilla (see below, pp. 385–6), but restored by the triumph against the Hungarian insurgents in 1849 (see ch. xv, p. 407).

The military legend was so important that a change of course was generally seen as the natural consequence of failure in the Crimean War (ch. xviii), and the death of Nicholas I on 18 February/2 March 1855 appeared as a presage of both these things. Russia's exhaustion was recognised by all classes. For a few years she was to have a more normal political history in which administrative policy, public opinion, and even economic developments showed a coherent if agitated pattern.

The new emperor, Alexander II, known to pre-Soviet history as the 'Tsar Liberator', had grown up to accept and serve his father's ideal of military autocracy. But, not strained to the tension of Nicholas's puritanical egoism, he was ready to embrace reform when it appeared in the shape of *raison d'état*. Early signs of coming change were shown by the usual gauge of domestic policy, the censorship. Then on the conclusion of peace, the emperor issued a manifesto, dated 18/30 March 1856, containing the words: 'May everyone under the equal protection of laws equally just for all enjoy the well earned fruits of his labours.' Taken throughout Russia as an announcement of the approaching end of serfdom, this was followed by explanations intended to damp both impatience and opposition. Among these was the tsar's speech to the Moscow nobility on 30 March/11 April, in which Alexander observed that 'it is better to abolish serfdom from above than to await the time when its abolition would begin from below without action on our part'.

The importance of this statement lay in the tsar's personal commitment to reform and in the way it involved the serf-owning nobles in the task. There were various motives for a policy which gave unusual recognition to initiative outside the government. It acknowledged the conservative view that the resignation of a fundamental property right should be voluntary, and it tended to obscure the state's responsibility for the financial operation which the reform would evidently entail. The serf owners were therefore wary, and while the emperor gave further proof of liberal intentions, nothing came of soundings of the provincial corporations of nobles by the Ministry of the Interior. The bureaucracy itself had no plan, but varying proposals were submitted by independent individuals. The crucial questions were generally seen to be the amount of land to be held by a freed serf, the rate at which emancipation should proceed, and the compensation for the serf-cum-land owner. Conservatives thought immediate emancipation would lead to anarchy, liberals could not see how the financial problem of compensation could be solved. Early in 1857 recourse was had to the common tsarist expedient of a 'secret committee' at the highest level, and discussion of a plan for emancipation without land submitted by the nobility of the Lithuanian provinces led to the issue of the decisive 'reskript' of 20 November/2 December. This called on the three provinces to amend their proposals to provide for the allotment of land; moreover, the nobility of other provinces were invited to form committees to elaborate similar plans.

The rescript of 20 November was the true administrative beginning of reform, marking the peak of reconciliation between the government and reformist public opinion, and between the different schools into which such opinion was divided. The leading radical spokesmen were now Herzen in London and Chernyshevskii in St Petersburg. Herzen's serious influence began with the publication in London in 1857 of *Kolokol* (*The Bell*). This famous periodical published as anonymous documents most of the leading plans and statements of the Russian left. Although nominally banned, it circulated widely in Russia and its authority was recognised by the government itself. It demanded emancipation of the serfs with land, and freedom of the press, reforms which even most Slavophiles favoured, and which publicists such as Chernyshevskii could at least regard as outweighing all others. Indeed the latter wrote in *Sovremennik* (*The Contemporary*) no less enthusiastically than Herzen of the tsar's initiative in the November rescript. But this truce did not last. Chernyshevskii was a new phenomenon in Russian politics, a *raznochinets* (that is, of 'other rank' than noble), like Belinskii, but an economist rather than a man of letters, an ascetic socialist and a critic of 'liberalism'. He shared Herzen's belief in the adaptability of Russian co-operative institutions to socialism, but his faith in 'the people' had no conscious historic or romantic basis such as made common ground between Herzen and the Slavophiles. It was the dogma of a nineteenth-century democratic positivist, soon impatient both with Herzen's tolerance of reform from above and with the delay in its accomplishment. The relaxation of censorship for a time allowed even serfdom to be discussed directly. But the Russian journals could not be as specific as *Kolokol* and so Chernyshevskii's and his disciple Dobrolyubov's criticisms on the eve of reform were generally conducted in the conventional literary disguise of which the latter's article on Goncharov's *Oblomov* is a famous example.

Meanwhile the preparation of reform revealed wide differences in the provinces. Where the land was rich, high compensation was demanded for its alienation; where labour could obtain good wages in industry, a high ransom was required for manumission. Less predictable was the liberalism of a western type in the proposals of some provinces, particularly Tver where for some years there was a movement for a constitutional central government. In general both conservative and liberal nobles showed resentment towards the bureaucracy and this is held by liberal Russian historians to have stimulated besides constitutionalism a new move towards oligarchy as the reaction of the right to autocratic reforms. Indeed it was due to the progressive members of the court and civil service, above all Rostovtsev and N. Milyutin, that the reform took shape. And when Rostovtsev died it was the determination of the tsar which overrode obstruction in the main ('secret') committee and the Council of State.

The reform statute was promulgated on 19 February/3 March 1861. It affirmed the immediate freedom of the peasant's person and the permanence of his future land allotment. Within two years a contract was to be negotiated between landlord and peasant with the assistance of 'peace mediators' drawn from the nobility in each province. This would fix the size of the allotment according to scales prescribed for different regions, and would end all responsibilities and jurisdiction of the landlord. At the same date domestic serfs without land were to be free of service. But the landed peasant was still to perform *barshchina* (that is, boon work) on an estate run on this basis and pay *obrók* (that is, body rent) on an estate run on commuted services. He was to have a 'temporarily bonded' status with *barshchina* at a rate of only 40 days a year for men, or about a quarter of the previous average, but he could commute *barshchina* for *obrók* after three years; and this situation was to last until he redeemed his allotment. Redemption was obtained by a down payment of one-fifth of the valuation of the land, generally an inflated one owing to the method of calculation. This was to be paid through the village commune and was followed by annuities usually of 6 per cent. The peasants' payments were to continue for 49 years but the landlord was to get the capital sum at once in negotiable state bonds paying 5 per cent. Redemption was finally enforced in 1881, and until 1870 the peasant could not refuse an allotment. But he could accept one of a quarter the standard size, a so-called 'orphan's share', without any obligations, and many did this, renting the extra land they needed more cheaply than by paying dues for it.

The peasants on imperial estates had had their status of personal freedom equated with that of state peasants since 1858. The land allotments and annuity payments of both groups were settled by 1866 on a far more generous basis than applied to private serfs; indeed their holdings were enlarged. To the peasants outside the Russian agrarian system the principle of emancipation with land was also later extended. In Siberia private serfdom was virtually non-existent, in Poland it was already legally extinct, but a decree giving them explicit proprietorship was issued in 1864 to benefit the peasants as against the more nationalist landlords. In Transcaucasia, particularly Georgia, where it was held important to conciliate the landlords, the opposite policy was applied between 1864 and 1867.

For all categories of peasants a new system of rural administration was introduced. The village commune took over some of the landlords' rights with more than all his duties. Through the *starost* (elder), elected by the heads of households, it was responsible for old and new tax and annuity payments, minor police duties and emergency relief. The *starshina* (headman) of a *volost* (canton), elected by the elders of a number of villages grouped together, had larger police functions, including the apprehension of runaways, and control of local migration. To the responsibilities of both *mir* and *volost* was added that of providing courts of first instance for the judgment of minor disputes and misdemeanours by customary law. Over the peasants' life and property, particularly in a commune of periodically redistributed holdings, the power of these communal institutions was therefore very great. Their grip on each 'soul', as one of the taxpayers for whom the *mir* was collectively responsible, was hardly less jealous than the landlord's had been, while they could recommend deportation to Siberia of a reputedly vicious ne'er-do-well and frequently did so.[1]

What the 20 million or so privately owned peasants gained from the laws of 19 February/3 March 1861 was in effect a minimum of civil rights—freedom to contract, to sue, to marry, to trade, to manufacture, to own property. But, on the average, unlike the state peasants, they were to receive less land than they had tilled before. In spite of the remarkable fairness of the 'peace mediators' supervising the contracts, the regional scales led to average reductions for the whole of Russia of 20 per cent on holdings which, in view of labour service obligations, had not been big

[1] *Polnoe Sobranie Zakonov*, vol. XLII, no. 447649.

enough to take up half the peasants' time hitherto. Such peasants had therefore solid grievances besides the disappointment of the fantastic visions of benefit which the typical *muzhik* had entertained, besides the provisional continuance of reduced *barshchina* or *obrók*, and besides their prejudice against paying at all for land which they felt they had already owned even when their masters had owned them. There was indeed some basis for this prejudice in that land was being valued at the capitalisation of labour services, not at market price. The consequence of disillusionment was a severe outbreak of agrarian disturbances in 1861–3.

These events strengthened the radicals' hostility to the statute. The opposition inside and outside Russia was also rallied by the first violent measures taken in 1861 against the reviving activity of the Polish nationalists whom it represented as fellow victims with the Russian peasants. For the first time for over 35 years home-based conspiracy and agitation began and was never again to subside under tsarism. The first and therefore epoch-making illegal publication was the *Velikorus* (*Great Russian*), three issues of which appeared in St Petersburg in the autumn of 1861. It appealed for the removal of the dynasty as incompatible with constitutional government or a just agrarian settlement. It was followed by the more pregnant manifesto 'To the young Generation' (*K molodomu pokoleniyu*), printed by Herzen and smuggled into Russia. This called for 'revolution in aid of the people' (*Na pomoshch narodu*), proposed the formation of propaganda cells in the peasantry and the army, and added to the liberal programme of a representative democracy, nationalisation of land for the village commune's use. Of particular interest was its emphasis on co-operative institutions and the quasi-Slavophile faith in the Russian genius and mission to escape the sequence of history which Chaadaev had maintained must be 'retraced'. Still more extreme was the programme of 'Young Russia' (*Molodaya Rossiya*) (1862), written by Zaichnevskii in the Moscow prison. Yet Zaichnevskii's division of society into haves and have-nots, his plan for an economy based on agrarian communes and public ownership of factories, belonged to the main stream of Russian social thought; even his emphasis on the need for a 'bloody and ruthless revolution' and his rejection of marriage as an institution were only slightly futurist.

Some of the threads leading to this agitation were gathered into the first *Zemlya i Volya* (Land and Liberty) organisation, whose programme was mostly the work of Herzen's collaborator Ogarev. It was the most substantial bridge between the Russian underground and the emigration in the 1860's and the first real conspiracy since the Decembrists. It planned a pyramidal organisation of local cells, and managed to affiliate, at least nominally, a serious proportion of the revolutionary-minded youth. The moving spirit, S. Serno-Solovevich, was arrested in 1862, but his successors soon described themselves as the 'Russian central national committee' and in 1863 brought out two issues of a sheet called *Svoboda* (*Freedom*). The society petered out in 1864 after internal disagreement over a plan to start a peasant revolt in Russia in support of the Polish nationalist revolt. One independent group connected with it decided on such action in the Volga region but they were arrested. Theirs was the so-called Kazan conspiracy of students and some young officers whose leaders were shot in 1864.

The active underground opposition was small, but its feats are highly important in the prehistory of the Russian revolution. It was winning converts and encouraging the mood of sacrifice or competitive fanaticism which produces terrorists. Most of these would be found among students whose formidable political tradition was even then being moulded in an atmosphere of liberal sympathy. This they won by their demonstration in St Petersburg in 1861 against the inadequacy of the peasant reform when they were beaten up by police and cossacks, and by the suspension of their university courses which followed. But in other quarters there was a revulsion against such a mood; even liberal sympathisers blamed revolutionary saboteurs for the great conflagrations in St Petersburg and elsewhere in 1862, and the word 'nihilism' was coming into use to denounce the left since Turgenev had applied it to his new model revolutionary Bazarov in the novel *Fathers and Children* (1862). The idea of nihilism became still more significant when a new writer, Pisarev (1840–68), acknowledged in the *Russkoe slovo* (*Russian Word*) Turgenev's imputation which the left as a whole rejected. Pisarev carried on Belinskii's mission of vitalising the intelligentsia as an educational leaven. Moreover, he made the characteristic Russian renunciation of aesthetic values, he accepted the antithesis of class interests, and his obsession with the social function of materialist science in Russia was prophetic, and probably influential. The nihilist whom Pisarev acknowledged was an ascetic radical carrying his rationalism to the extreme of scrapping all religious, political and humanist values in order to think out social duty *a priori*. Socialism is part of the nihilist answer in Chernyshevskii's novel *Chto delat?* (*What is to be done?* (1863), whose hero, Rakhmetov, became an even more popular model than Bazarov to Russian youth. The ultimate ethical and political imperative characteristic of Russian thought at the time, the relief of suffering, is explicit in Pisarev's writings and Chernyshevskii's as in Belinskii's, Tolstoi's and Dostoevskii's. But, as the irrational element in revolutionary propaganda gained ground, particularly under Bakunin's influence in the later 'sixties, the licence to transform values led to confusion of ends and means. The puritan strain survived, but nihilism and anarchism merged with terrorism in action as well as reputation. The later type of nihilist is standardised in Dostoevskii's novel *The Devils*, founded on the career of Nechaev, a protégé of Bakunin, whose conspiracy was sprung in 1869 by a murder inside his gang.

The other new tendency in political thought, populism (*narodnichestvo*), drew largely upon Slavophile ideology. The *narodniks* did not appear as a political party until the 'seventies, but the idea of seeking a source both of revelation and power in the peasant masses dates traditionally from Herzen's injunction to the students locked out of St Petersburg university in 1861: '*V Narod!*' '[Go] To the People!' Some of the common ground of the 'men of the 'forties' was restored in combining the old Slavophile prejudice against western inspiration with the belief that Russian communal institutions might form a means of socialisation from below. The overlapping of populism and nihilism appears in the comprehensive sympathies of a Herzen or a Chernyshevskii and in most of the underground effusions of the 1860's. Indeed, a member of one of these groups deposed that what he feared was a liberal revolution which would 'push Russia into western forms of life'.[1] Moreover, a populist slant was given to the nihilists' utilitarian contempt for aesthetic values through a spreading sense of guilt at the contrast of culture and labour. This humanist heresy, endemic in Russia, was most fully expressed on the left by P. Lavrov (1823–1900), the second emigré publicist of importance in the line from Herzen to Lenin. A repentant intelligentsia was succeeding the 'repentant nobility';[2] to it belonged individuals as remote from the nihilists in spirit as Tolstoi and in politics as Dostoevskii.

The revolutionary underground, stigmatised as 'nihilists', and already calling themselves 'democrats', were the bitter leaven of Russian politics and soon gained, through propaganda or terrorism, the only real initiative outside the imperial court and chancellery. In contrast the 'liberals' were neither homogeneous nor organised. They included such personalities as the progressive Slavophile Samarin and the 'westerner' Kavelin, who had worked together on agrarian reform, and probably the great majority of educated and semi-educated Russians in the 1860's. Constitutional government was what they hankered after; it was disillusionment in this that caused the later drift to populism. With few exceptions liberals greeted the emancipation edict as the beginning of a new dispensation. Its defects they attributed to the '*reaktsiya*' (reaction) and the '*camarilla*' within the government, which by the spring of 1861 had got rid of the chief architects of reform, the Minister of the Interior, Count Lanskoi and his more famous deputy N. Milyutin.

The only active liberal opposition to the first stage of reform came from the nobility of Tver province. In 1862 they expressed doubt of the government's competence to carry out a reform programme, and their wish to resign all fiscal and occupational privileges of nobility; they appealed for a central representative government. The province's 'peace mediators'

---

[1] Quoted by F. Venturi, *Il populismo russo* (2 vols. Turin, 1952), vol. I, p. 546.
[2] *Kayushchëesya Dvoryanstvo*, the well-known phrase which Lavrov's contemporary Mikhailovskii originated when the phenomenon itself was already out of date.

went even further, declaring their intention of 'following the people's wishes' rather than departmental instructions, and incurred a prison sentence as a result. But this incident was a flash in the pan and, in general, Russian liberals settled down to a critical acceptance of the further course of reform from above.

Circumstances helped to conciliate them temporarily, namely the gradual easing of agrarian tension, the nihilist threat to civil order, and above all the patriotic reaction to the Polish revolt of 1863 (see also ch. IX, p. 236). This took the form of widely dispersed guerilla operations whose early success was favoured by the Russian strategic concentration. United even, the Poles would have had no chance, but this time there were two parties, 'reds' and 'whites', the former with a social and the latter with a national motive only. To non-Polish peasants in particular the 'white' *szlachta* (land-owning nobility) had less to offer than the Russians, who promised land reform. When the end came in 1864 the inter-faction killings outnumbered the 400 Russian capital sentences. Besides executions, deportations, confiscations and fines far exceeded the retribution in 1831. There followed a still more intense subjection of the Polish language and culture, while, to split the Poles horizontally, an agrarian reform more liberal than the Russian was introduced. In Russia itself public indignation was exploited in domestic politics by the autocracy and the press. The ascendancy began of the pseudo-liberal and future Pan-Slav editor, M. Katkov, who became a mouthpiece or mentor of the autocracy for more than two decades.

In Finland, by contrast with Poland, Alexander II's reign had brought a superficial liberalisation.[1] Finland, since the grand-duchy's incorporation in the empire, had been administered by a bureaucracy with high respect for national law and custom although there had been no immunity from the tsarist political system, and the Diet as an institution had been ignored. But, in accordance with a promise on his accession, Alexander II summoned the Diet in 1863 and in 1869 established its quinquennial convocation as a fundamental law. This did not make Finland a constitutional monarchy, and if the Finns remained placid, it was rather because they had no historical background of national sovereignty and above all because the element of inter-Slav jealousy and antipathy did not exist. But the relationship became less happy when Pan-Slavism later turned totalitarian and intolerant of minorities.

The liberals' movement to the right after the Polish revolt and the settling down of the agrarian reform made 1864 propitious for the next stage of reform. Most of the legislation which followed, like the emancipation decree, represented a compromise between the tsar's inclination towards the most radical changes compatible with the inviolability of the autocracy, and the conservatism of the diehard nobility. To explain this

[1] Cf. ch. IX, p. 231.

there is no need of the theory that an 'oligarchical' opposition was in existence. The autocracy feared to demoralise rather than to challenge the nobility as a class. The momentum for further reform came from the assumed need to harmonise institutions with the results of emancipation, from the motive of *raison d'état* in modernising Russia according to western practice, and that of winning over moderate opinion against the revolutionary left. Behind it all was the genuine atmosphere of nineteenth-century political optimism seeping through the cracks in autocracy and Russian nationalist superstition.

The decree of January 1864 introducing the *Zemstvo* or local government reform integrated the peasant institutions of the *mir* and *volost* into a system of elective government at the *uyezd* (district) and *gubernya* (province) level. Three separate bodies of rural and town property owners and of electors chosen by peasant cantons respectively elected the district assemblies and the latter nominated delegates to their provincial assembly. The assemblies only met for a few days annually to supervise paid executives whom they appointed for a three-year term. The *zemstvos* took over the responsibility for communications, famine relief, and hospitals, formerly ineffectively exercised by the assemblies of nobles, and in addition supervised local trade and agriculture, prisons, and, above all, education. Even Lenin called them a 'fragment of a constitution'.[1] They were introduced gradually in groups of provinces at a time. In the first two years about two-fifths of the district representatives were nobles and two-fifths peasants, in the indirectly elected provincial assemblies three-quarters were nobles and the peasants and townsmen were almost equal. This formal co-operation of classes did amount to a revolution although critics of every shade continued to call it hollow. In 1863 the draft reform had provided for a brief annual meeting of a central assembly of *zemstvo* representatives to co-operate with the State Council. But, as political tension lessened, appeasement of constitution seekers was dropped, and the autocracy resisted the intermittent attempts of the *zemstvos* to organise nationally. They were made juridical persons in private law instead of administrative entities, intercourse between provincial *zemstvos* was forbidden, and the overriding authority of provincial governor and Ministry of the Interior was such that they could not even publish their edicts without permission. They therefore exercised rather than satisfied the political instincts of Russian society, but their practical achievement went far. Virtually all rural primary schools, many secondary and girls' schools, and all medical services in the countryside were owed to them.

The second major reform after emancipation was the new judicial system introduced at the end of 1864. The old class courts and closed hearings, with their indefinite reference or remission to other tribunals under administrative control, were replaced by an unusually simple hierarchy

---

[1] *Sochineniya* (2nd edn), vol. v, p. 80.

of open courts with full publicity and an independent judiciary. The country was divided into judicial circuits in which courts of first instance delivered final judgment with the participation of a jury. In non-jury cases there was an appeal to 'judicial chambers' with wider circuits. The sole higher court of appeal—on points of law only—was the Senate. Petty offences were dealt with by 'justices of the peace', elected, but irremovable like the higher courts' judges whom the executives appointed in the first instance.

The judicial reform was based on studies of western procedure. Communist historians explain this uncompromising 'bourgeois' modernity by the exigencies of incipient capitalism; liberal critics have found a grave discrepancy from cosmopolitan jurisprudence in the treatment of the peasants. For the cantonal courts established in 1861 remained in being and used distinct customary law for peasants' cases instead of the public and private law of the *Svod* (see above, p. 363). The argument that peasants were thus classified as an inferior order found confirmation in that corporal punishment was retained for them despite the law of 1863 which abolished it otherwise, even in the army. The independence of the courts was, however, demonstrated in 1878 by the audacious if misdirected acquittal of Vera Zasulich, who had shot and wounded a police chief as a reprisal on behalf of the revolutionary underground. And, even more than the courts, the new Russian bar won an early reputation for intrepidity and learning.

A third reform in 1864 was the law providing for 'peoples' primary schools' which could be established by private individuals or public bodies. Controlled by the educational committees of the *zemstvos*, they were to provide 'useful' and religious teaching, with Russian as the sole medium of instruction even in national minority areas. A new establishment for secondary schools was introduced separately which nominally removed class restrictions on entry and followed the usual European division between 'grammar' and 'modern'. The secondary education of girls had been brought under the ministry's control in 1862 but initiative and responsibility remained with independent societies. Two other educational reforms were the nominal decontrol of university faculties in 1863, of little practical significance, and the new censorship law of 1865. In principle preventive censorship was replaced by the sanction of prosecution in the courts of responsible editors for infringements of the law, but authority was retained to prohibit books or periodicals which disregarded official warnings. This system imitated contemporary French methods, but as always the letter of the rules counted less than fluctuating policy, and the liberal mood of the early 1860's was unable to survive the onset of revolutionary terrorism.

The attempted assassination of the tsar on 4/16 April 1866 did not open a new phase of underground activity, but it was a shocking discouragement to liberals and a handle to the critics of reform. The government's counter-measures harked back to the theory that education was the root of revolution and the liberal minister Golovnin was replaced by D. Tolstoi, regarded as a champion of reaction. The burden of Tolstoi's restrictions on schools, universities, and press, has perhaps been exaggerated. Most important was the limitation of science teaching and encouragement of the classics. The connection so alleged between positivist science and doctrinaire politics, iconoclastic or utopian, has not been disproved, least of all in Russia, although there the autocracy's challenge doubtless stimulated such a development. But the reaction in educational and censorship policy together with ministerial changes towards the right did not alter the plan of reform. The extension of modern institutions implied no relaxation of autocratic control, and the risk of multiplying centres of disaffection seemed less urgent than completion of the plan. So in 1870 the transformation of local government was extended to the towns, their administration being brought into line with the *zemstvo* system, following a Prussian model. The multiple differentiation of urban classes was abandoned with respect to civil, and nominally also political rights, but the electorate of all ratepayers was divided into 'colleges' by property qualifications so that the richer inhabitants had a larger representation in the town *duma*. Like the *zemstvo*, the town administration chosen by the *duma* lacked coercive powers and was made subservient to the provincial governor or, in provincial capitals, the Ministry of the Interior.

The last major act in the 'era of reform' was the introduction of universal military service, the work of D. A. Milyutin, whose brother had played so large a part in the peasant emancipation. On becoming Minister of War in 1861 he reduced the peasants' term of selective service from 25 to 16 years. In 1874 he fixed compulsory service for all classes at six years with the colours followed by nine in the reserve, exemption being confined mainly to the sole breadwinners of families. The reform was part of a wide military reorganisation which ranged from the general staff to cadet schools and recruiting areas, and had efficiency as much as or more than liberalisation in view.

The 'great reforms' left the executive power untouched in authority and virtually so in privilege and organisation. In 1861 the need for co-ordination brought a new body, the Council of Ministers (*Sovet Ministrov*) into being, but like its surviving predecessor, the Committee of Ministers, it failed to take root. This it seems, was due to the quasi-constitutional inhibition in Russia against consolidating high policy independently of the sovereign. Indeed the nearest the autocracy came to shedding any privilege was perhaps in the law of 1862 prescribing the annual publication of accounts of state income and expenditure. But that belonged rather to the series of financial reforms beginning with the creation of the Bank of Russia (1861) 'for stimulating industry and trade'. This institution was to operate for these purposes as a discount bank with several state bank functions added. Other measures provided for central control and publication of the accounts of provincial and local governments, and in 1863 abolished liquor concessions in favour of an excise tax which maintained revenue from the same abundant source.

These changes, together with the liberal tariff of 1857-71 (see p. 364), reflected the autocracy's belief that a new political era meant a new economic one. It was upon the 'merchant' class, not the suspect intelligentsia, that authority smiled as representative of this new era. Their service to the state had already been recognised in the last reign by the grant of the rank of 'honourable citizenship' just below the orders of hereditary nobility, and in the provincial towns they were acquiring some social influence. Still the pattern of a new natural prosperity remained elusive. The steepening curve of expansion in the first decade of Alexander II's reign runs through two financial crises, setbacks in major industries owing to raw materials or labour shortages, and, above all, to the secular curse of erratic and deficient harvests, which the abolition of serfdom at first accentuated. It was not until the 1870's that the Russian economic revolution ceased to appear experimental.

The surge in enterprise following the Crimean War is most obvious in foreign trade, the mechanisation of the textile industry and, above all, railway building. Between 1799 and 1853, 72·1 million roubles had been invested in joint-stock companies; between 1855 and 1860 the figure was 317 millions, and of this 177 millions went into railways which meanwhile doubled their mileage. After 1858 symptoms of the world depression appeared in Russia, though peculiar ones. There was a drop in bank deposits owing to railway speculation, and a shortage of money followed by a decline in some branches of production.[1] Then in 1860 industry picked up again and in the ensuing decade the rise in output shown by an index of high authority is some 60 per cent, from 8 to 13 in terms of a 1913 level of 100, compared to a rise from 8 to 11 in the United States and 14 to 18 in Germany in the same decade.[2] According to Lenin's figures of labour productivity in factories selected as significant this increased nearly 20 per cent between 1864 and 1870.[3] There were forty-two factories employing a thousand or more hands as early as 1866, and of 160,000 workers in the cotton industry over 94,000 were then employed in factories.[4] Not only had capitalist industry taken root but the economic revolution had extended to foreign trade. Between 1860 and 1870 exports rose in value from 181 to 359 million 'credit' roubles, and imports from 159 to 336

[1] According to the finance minister Bunge, quoted by Khromov, *op. cit.* p. 214.
[2] *Vierteljahrshefte für Konjunkturforschung*, 1953, *Sonderheft* 31, p. 180.
[3] *Sochineniya* (2nd edn), vol. III, p. 355 and appendix, p. 471.
[4] M. Tugan-Baranovskii, *Geschichte der Russischen Fabrik*. But the latter suggested a simultaneous and even relative increase in domestic industry—a defiance of the Marxist laws of development which incurred Lenin's censure.

millions.[1] Meanwhile state expenditure rose by over a third including the service of railway loans, while ordinary income increased more than proportionately from 329 to 460 million silver roubles. To the latter figure alcohol excise contributed more than a third at 164 millions, poll tax and peasants' other dues a fifth at 98 millions and customs less than a tenth at 43 million roubles.[2]

Railways were the chief material achievement, their total length increasing from 1626 km. in 1860 to 10,731 km. in 1870. The high cost of the earlier St Petersburg–Moscow line (above, p. 365) led the government in 1857 to grant a concession to a foreign company largely backed by French capital and so to begin a fateful connexion between Russian economic and strategic planning and the Paris money market. The concession system was continued in the 1860's, with variable economic success. Indeed, the government had to strain the budget not only to provide guarantees and advances for this private sector, but to supplement it by more state building. The railways gained labour from the agrarian reform which relaxed the control of seasonally migrant and landless peasants. Their mortality as navvies was shocking by contemporary western standards, but unchecked, for there was no protective legislation even in factories until the 1870's. But the emancipation struck another industry adversely: the ascribed (*pripisnye*) peasants in the Ural mines and foundries began to drift westwards so that the output of pig iron declined and did not recover till 1870. Meanwhile the most advanced Russian industry, cotton textiles, sagged owing to material shortage, as the American Civil War cut Russian imports by two-thirds. The demand for alternative supplies tripled the price of Turkestan raw cotton, but it was a coincidence that in the same decade the Russians conquered the Central Asian khanates where it grew; another half-century of planned autarky was needed before Russia became independent of American cotton.

As significant as the vicissitudes of incipient industrialisation was the economic failure of the agrarian revolution. The grain harvest in 1861 was officially estimated at 216 million Russian quarters; in 1865 it had fallen to 182 and after reaching 282 in 1870 it fell again to 219 million in 1871.[3] Then in the decade after 1870 the average grain production per head increased compared to the middle 'sixties (21·8 *puds* against 19·3 in 1864–6) and the increase continued slowly with accelerating mechanisation until 1913.[4] But this did not bring security against intermittent famine.

It was mainly by commercialising land and mobilising labour that

---

[1] Khromov, *op. cit.* Appendix (Statistical Tables, pp. 434–545), p. 453. The 'credit' (paper) rouble fluctuated during the decade, falling to 68 per cent of the silver rouble in 1866, but in 1860 and 1870 it was at only a slight discount.

[2] *Ibid.*, from Tables 25*a* and 26*a*, pp. 495, 517.

[3] *Ibid.*, from Table 4, p. 452.

[4] *Ibid.*, table on p. 168. 1 *pud* = 16·4 kg.

emancipation conduced to increased productivity, particularly in the Ukraine and other black earth regions where the allotments of land to the peasants under the 1861 law fell as low as 1·2 *desyatin* (say 1·3 hectares) per head, and tended to be sold by them as too small for subsistence farming. The same process occurred to a lesser extent all over European Russia, for in thirty-six provinces the *otrezki* ('cuttings-off' from pre-reform holdings) averaged over 18 per cent.[1] It was the uneconomic size of this holding and the burden of taxation and redemption that put the weaker peasant into the hands of a more fortunate, efficient or usurious fellow member of his commune. Hence the famous 'differentiation of the village' into the arbitrarily defined classes of *kulak*, *sredniyak* (middle peasant) and *bedniyak* (poor peasant) on which Marxist historiography lays such stress. It was not only of land still tied to the commune, however, but often of free land bought or rented from noble landlords that a *kulak* built up his holding. Noble land began to change hands at once not only as a result of previous indebtedness. In 1860 62 per cent of all serfs and 53 per cent of all agricultural land was pledged to the banks—a circumstance which had its effect on the timing and terms of the reform. But, their property having been undervalued by the banks or overvalued by the reform settlement, the landlords had to transfer to their creditors only 248 out of the 543 millions received in redemption payments. Not much of the surplus, however, seems to have gone back into their estates; they had tasted cash and were not on the whole a rural class of agricultural improvers with local attachments. So the marketability of land led to further sales instead of high farming, some 5 per cent of noble land being disposed of in the first decade of the reform and 30 per cent by the early 1890's.

One of the tremendous consequences of the agrarian and economic revolution was the integration of Russian Asia, hitherto almost as separate as if it were composed of overseas dependencies. There were four sectors of Russian consolidation and advance beyond Europe: Siberia, the Far East, the Caucasus and central Asia. For Siberia and to a lesser extent the Far East and, eventually, central Asia the abolition of serfdom in Europe and the consequent diffusion of Great Russians and Ukrainians, began a demographic change of the same order as the peopling of the North American middle and far west half a century earlier. The railways furthered this process towards the end of the century after having contributed earlier to the strategic assimilation of Turkestan. Caucasia had been finally pacified before the railway line reached Rostov-on-Don but then the new communications by land and sea brought Russian settlers to

---

[1] M. Lyashchenko, *Istoriya Narodnovo Khozyaistva S.S.S.R.*, vol. I, p. 590. This figure, arrived at by averaging percentages, is statistically unsatisfactory. But the alternative estimates, as low as 4 per cent for the whole of European Russia, given by other authorities convey a more false impression.

replace over 250,000 Circassians who had fled to Turkey after the collapse of their resistance.

Siberia was still primarily a penal colony when Speranskii was sent in 1819 as inspector and governor-general to reform its administration. The skeleton military or police occupation of nearly five million square miles had as a backbone a ribbon of agricultural settlement on the intermittent black earth zone between the forest and the steppe, through which ran the transcontinental road. Here and in patches along the rivers lived perhaps one-and-a-half million legal or illegal immigrants or their descendants comprising convicts, exiles, pensioned soldiers, persecuted sectaries, free or directed peasants.[1] As the importance of the natives' fur tribute had decreased, the government lost interest in maintaining the old centralisation. So, despite the new problems set by a growing and increasingly self-conscious population, there was little check on the governors besides the characteristic system of petitions to St Petersburg from the governed.

Speranskii set out to restore the dependence on St Petersburg and to broaden the basis of local authority. The territory was divided between two governments-general at Tobolsk and Irkutsk and at each level of the reorganised administration the senior official was to be moderated by a council. This was a return to the 'collegiate' system and to the indigenous Russian illusion that group control of authority need not represent the public. The councillors were officials and the only elective element was in larger towns and at the lowest (*volost* or 'township') level outside. This stimulation of a low-grade officialdom is generally blamed for the failure of the reform; it remained for the *zemstvo* institutions, when they spread to Siberia in the 1880's, to take its place. Meanwhile if the practically undiminished powers of authority became less oppressive this was by reason not of local controls but of improved personnel and supervision from St Petersburg, and also of Speranskii's new social and economic policy.

In treating the native question Speranskii aimed at assimilation in the long run: inside the areas of Russian settlement this was furthered by more stringent measures against slavery, seeing that there was virtually no colour bar; outside them indirect rule gave Russian imperialism the comparatively good name which it enjoyed in Asia until systematic russification began towards the end of the century.

Speranskii's influence was, however, most effective in economic policy where his western *laissez-faire* principles led to the repudiation of state monopolies and direction, and the encouragement of private enterprise, particularly internal free trade in grain. Meanwhile moderation of the penal system which Siberia stood for to the outside world was negligible,

---

[1] A. G. Rashin, *Naselenie S.S.S.R. za 110 Let* (Moscow, 1956), p. 68. But there were 3½ millions in 1859. See F. Lorimer, *The Population of the U.S.S.R.* (Geneva, 1946), App. 1, p. 208.

though it came to be more humanely administered. The flow of penal immigrants besides runaway peasants continued undiminished but the quality of such recruits as the Decembrists and Polish nationalists tended to offset that of the criminal element. Deportees were classified as *katorzhennye*, who were condemned to *katorga* or penal servitude, and *poselentsy* (settler convicts); both were deported in chained columns, while *ssilniye* (exiles) were merely banished from Europe and *dobrovoltsy* were volunteers generally consisting of convicts' wives and families. After the reforms the first two categories had to be condemned by a court, and they normally went for life, but of the thousands of *ssilniye* most were peasants or vagrants banished by communes, and only a few were the victims of 'administrative procedure'.[1] The annual influx of exiles and deportees fluctuated between some 7000 in the 1840's to 18,000 in the 1850's, and it was not recorded as distinct from surreptitious peasant immigration until this was decontrolled in 1881.

Siberia had not expanded since the conquest of Kamchatka in the early eighteenth century. To the south there was a fluid frontier from the nominal marches of Europe as far as Chinese-administered Mongolia and thence a recognised boundary with the Manchu empire as far as the Amur, whose whole basin, however, was attributed to China by the Treaty of Nerchinsk (1689). Far to the north-eastward, Alaska was administered independently by the Russian America company founded in 1799. In course of time the authorities in St Petersburg began to find the return from the company's fur trade uneconomic and concluded also that Alaska was too great a strategic liability. So overtures for cession were made to the U.S.A. after the Crimean War, and the territory was finally sold for 7,200,000 dollars in 1867.

To another school of Russian statecraft Alaska could have served as a bridge between the two great nations of the future, Russia and America. So thought Count Muraviev, the formidable eccentric who became governor-general in Irkutsk in 1847.[2] The development of the intercontinental contact as a front against British sea-power in the Pacific was one of the motives of the new forward policy at the expense of China which Muraviev initiated, but the opportunity which the progress of British imperialism offered to the Russians was more significant than the excuse. China's opium war with Britain, followed by her treaty concessions to the western powers and then by the Tai ping rebellion, destroyed both the superstitious respect for the Manchu empire which had so long kept its frontiers with Siberia intact and also the *morale* and some of the military force which might have helped to defend them. The Russians had on the whole accepted their exclusion from navigation in the Amur and other restrictions on intercourse with China dating from the Treaty of Nerchinsk, and the geography of the river's outlet and of Sakhalin beyond it was unknown

[1] G. Kennan, *loc. cit.*   [2] See above, p. 367.

to Europe until Nevelskoi reached these waters from the Baltic and in 1850 hoisted the Russian flag at the future Nikolaevsk. Muraviev then proposed an armed Russian sortie down the river but the plan was approved only after much hesitation;[1] it had to contend with the theory that forcing a way into the Pacific, like freeing the outlet into the Mediterranean from the Black Sea, might let the maritime powers in as well as letting the Russians out. In fact Muraviev's demonstration in 1854 was unopposed by the Chinese and unchallenged by the British; the Chinese could not claim to exercise *de facto* administration north of the river and in 1858 their local commander concluded a treaty with Muraviev ceding the whole left bank to Russia together with the right bank below the River Ussuri. Meanwhile a diplomatic plenipotentiary, Admiral Putyatin, reached Tientsin independently in 1858 where he obtained for Russia all the commercial and capitulatory rights exacted by the western powers, together with the extra privilege of commercial access to Kashgar. In 1860 a supplementary treaty confirmed the territorial cessions and added the rest of the future Ussuri province. In its southern bay Russian naval forces landed and founded, also in 1860, the port of Vladivostock, the future terminus of the Trans-Siberian railway which outflanked northern Manchuria and confronted northern Japan. The Japanese had disputed the ownership of Sakhalin since Nevelskoi charted it and Putyatin had claimed it in the middle 'fifties, but after a condominium lasting from 1867 to 1875 the Russians acquired the whole island in exchange for the Kuriles. In both the Amur province and Sakhalin the strategic commitment was supported immediately by forced immigration. Convicts on the expiry of sentences of *katorga* were sent as exiles to the former territory and so-called Amur and Ussuri 'Cossack' settlements were formed by drafted troops, while the island itself became a *katorga* settlement. The knout had followed the flag.

At the opposite end of Asia, in the Caucasus, a resistance movement was developing which absorbed the surplus military energy of Russia for a generation, and in its evocation of frontier romance and mountain glamour was a powerful element in Russian literary as well as military history.[2] Muridism, a species of Moslem zealotry, reached the Caucasus in the 1820's when it blended with xenophobia and a tradition of political freedom.[3] A kind of theocracy (*imamat*) was superimposed on a small confederation of clan-like societies centring on the Avars of western Daghestan with links or sympathetic agitation among many distinct peoples from the Caspian almost to the sea of Azov. The first leader (*imam* or *murshid*), Kazimullah, declared a holy war in 1829, but after

---

[1] M. Tatischev, *Imperator Alexander II* (St Petersburg, 1903), vol. I, pp. 127, 273 ff.

[2] The foremost examples are the novels: Lermontov's *Hero of our Time* (*Geroi nashevo vremeni*) and Tolstoi's *Hajji Murat*. Much of Pushkin's and Lermontov's Caucasian inspiration recalls the influence of the Alps on Shelley and Byron.

[3] J. Baddeley, *The Russian Conquest of the Caucasus* (London, 1908), pp. 230 ff.

some brilliant military successes he was killed in 1832. It was the third *murshid*, Shamyl, who became a world-renowned guerrilla leader and was able to defeat Russian regular troops off and on, not merely in ambush but in defensive battles, for nearly a quarter of a century. His forces were not dispersed until he was himself captured in 1859, and then the Circassians continued more desultory resistance until 1864, when they committed themselves to mass emigration. The subsequent pacification was, however, rapid. Before the end of the 1860's the first railway in Transcaucasia, from the Black Sea to Tiflis, was being built, and such was the state of public security and the government's enlightenment in these matters that the high-level exploration of the central Caucasus had been begun by the classical school of English travellers with Alpine guides. Meanwhile the striking force of the Russian army and the *élite* of the staff were freed for other tasks.

These tasks were in central Asia. The sector of advance was the great enclave between the Caspian and the T'ian shan mountains in the centre of which lay the geopolitical objective of Russia, the three renowned but decrepit and constantly feuding states of Khiva, Bokhara and Khokand. Southward the first effective boundary was beyond the Afghan political frontier in the natural barrier of the Pamirs and the Hindu Kush. This continuation of the Himalayas the British in India had not yet reached, but their progress had not lost momentum and it was still uncertain whether, and if so where, the two empires would meet. On the Russian side an approach to India through Turkestan had been a vision of Peter the Great's and more recently a plan of the Emperor Paul's; on the British side it was a strategist's nightmare which contributed no less than the Near Eastern question to maintaining Anglo-Russian antagonism as a major theme of European diplomacy and faded only towards the end of the century.

Until the middle of the century Russian administration stopped at the Ural and Siberian 'Cossack lines' which ran up the Ural River past Orenburg to its head and thence eastward to Semipalatinsk and the Chinese frontier. But the Russians had consolidated their hold over the nomads of the steppe and desert zone across the line. The next step was therefore to probe through the desert into the oases where, in competition with the British reconnoitring from the Punjab, Russian explorers, savants and diplomatic agents at least held their own. This 'great game in Asia'[1] reflected a fluid political situation from the Indus to the Aral sea in which the three doomed khanates and the uneasy kingdom of Afghanistan were able to play off their great neighbours against each other. Then came the years of crisis from 1838 to 1842. The alternate British successes and disasters from the defence of Herat to the inconclusive military demonstration in Afghanistan in 1842 had repercussions north of the Oxus. Meanwhile

[1] See H. W. C. Davis, 'The Great Game in Asia', *Proc. British Academy*, vol. XI (1927), p. 19.

the first Russian military venture to be aimed at the khanates for over a century had been made and failed.

This was the expedition against Khiva undertaken by the governor-general of Orenburg, Perovskii, in 1839. There was ample standing provocation in slave raiding, violence to caravans, and irregular and exorbitant tolls. Perovskii's declared object was 'to strengthen in this part of Asia the lawful influence to which Russia has a right and which can alone assure the maintenance of peace'.[1] But there was also an admitted desire to frustrate British political and commercial prospects, both of which the Russians overestimated. Perovskii's expedition had to turn back half way; the single bound was too long for a force of all arms of 5000 men. Still, the Russians lost little prestige through this retreat in contrast to the British in Afghanistan, and in 1842 a treaty with Khiva secured most of their requirements.

The decisive step towards territorial expansion was taken during the middle 1840's. On the western route the posts of Turgai and Irgiz were established in 1845, and in 1847 the estuary of the Syr Darya (Jaxartes) was seized and a fort placed at Aralsk. In 1853 Ak Mechet (renamed Perovsk) was taken by siege from the Khokandis and already in the same year two armed steamers, brought in pieces from Orenburg by the desert route now made passable for vehicles, were patrolling up-river. Meanwhile on the eastern flank Kopal, opposite Lake Balkhash, was occupied in 1847 and in 1853 the outpost of Vernoe was founded as an agricultural colony, several thousand state peasants and so-called 'cossacks' being drafted as settlers. In 1862 the Russians were ready to join the heads of the two southward approaches to form their new front—the *Novokokandskaya liniya*. This was done between 1862 and 1864 when the first oasis town of Turkestan, and, also for operational reasons, Chimkent beyond it, were taken from the Khokandis, whereas a premature and almost certainly unauthorised attack on the greater city of Tashkent failed.

Then in 1864 came the Russian chancellor Gorchakov's premature circular which purported to explain and justify the Russian advance and to announce its termination. The argument was that to safeguard her frontier Russia had been obliged to include the intractable and generally nomad peoples who were harrying the populations under her protection and that this process had been unfortunately cumulative. But the Issik Kul–Syr Darya line was final. 'In adopting this line we obtained a double result, on one side the country...is fertile and wooded...on the other it gives us for immediate neighbours the settled agricultural and trading peoples of Khokand.' It was the point 'where interest and reason demand that we should arrive and command us to stop'. Such was probably a genuine expression of the tsar's policy, but the independent logic of military operations, if not the ambitions of generals, caused it to be

[1] Sir H. Rawlinson, *England and Russia in the East* (London, 1875), pp. 149–50.

overtaken by events.[1] Clashes with the Khokandis gave Chernaev another chance in 1865, when almost certainly against orders Tashkent was stormed and annexed, the seat of government of Turkestan being placed there in 1867 under a general statute of administration. In 1868 reckless provocation by the emir of Bokhara gave one of Chernaev's successors, Kaufmann, an excuse to attack and occupy Samarkand and, after defeating the emir's troops, he signed treaties with the rulers of both Bokhara and Khokand, giving the respective emirate and khanate the status of protectorates. Of the oases states only Khiva remained to be reduced in 1873.

Russian expansion at its second peak in 1860 onwards did not meet the same strategic competition from British India as earlier. But the spate of published correspondence in this golden age of Blue Books on foreign policy shows how the practical repudiation of the Gorchakov circular and the conquest of Khiva were verbally contested and how far the strategic frontier of the middle Oxus was diplomatically consolidated by the British. On the whole the Russians tended to respect this last ditch of British influence until the testing incident at Penjdeh in 1885. Even Sir H. Rawlinson, whom Russian historians have treated as an alarmist russophobe,[2] regarded the conquest of central Asia as a triumph of civilisation over barbarism and saw no threat to India beyond competition from an 'Asiatic Russia...possessing within itself a germ of vitality and vigour that will enable it to replenish rather than exhaust the parent stem'.[3] Already in 1865 he had rightly emphasised the intended integration of the region with Russia, pointed out that the annual turnover of Russian trade with the khanates was nearly a million sterling and—with some prescience —that the Russians might 'convert Central Asia into an exclusively cotton-producing country'.[4] In 1868, he later noted, a Russian government coal mine near Chimkent was producing 5000 tons a year for the Aral steamers, and other private mines were richer. So Russia's manifest destiny was now obvious and no longer that of the primitive empire earlier denounced by British propagandists.[5] But imperial policy in Turkestan began and remained a straight military and economic colonialism. There was to be no colour bar, russification was encouraged and race was merely a provisional class indicator, not a barrier. Yet administrative practice in Tashkent never came within the ambit of that new Russian imperial ideology, Pan-Eurasian rather than Pan-Slav, which belongs essentially to the period between the disappointment over Constantinople in 1878 and the defeat by Japan in 1905.

[1] See O. Hoetzsch, *Russisch-Turkestan und die Tendenzen der heutigen russischen Kolonialpolitik* (Schmollers Jahrbücher, Jhrg. 37–8), vol. I, p. 388. The argument of operational necessity comes out in the best brief military survey of the conquest: Graf M. Yorck von Wartenburg, *Das Vordringen der Russischen Macht in Asien* (Berlin, 1900), pp. 21 ff.
[2] For example, Nechkina, *Istoriya S.S.S.R.*, vol. II, p. 588.
[3] Rawlinson, *op. cit.* p. 195.   [4] *Ibid.* p. 199. See p. 381 above.
[5] J. H. Gleason, *The Origins of Russophobia in Great Britain* (Cambridge, Mass., 1950), pp. 150–1, 172–3.

CHAPTER XV

THE REVOLUTIONS OF 1848

ALTHOUGH the revolutions of 1848 were simultaneous and inspired by a common ideology, yet they were isolated phenomena. There was no international revolutionary organisation and the political refugees gathered together in France, Belgium, Switzerland and England were not the instigators of the revolutions in their countries. There was no plot and the revolutions were not concerted. Problems which were analogous in general took different forms in each state and produced conflicting results; the same vocabulary, the same programme, concealed dissimilar situations.

At the beginning of 1848 no one believed that revolution was imminent; yet the situation in many parts of Europe was such as precedes revolutions. In Italy the advent of Pius IX in June 1846, the general amnesty which he declared and the promises which he uttered, had created an atmosphere of wild excitement. There was unrest in Lombardy–Venetia which led to the declaration of a state of siege, there was the Sicilian insurrection of 12 January, and there was the grant or promise during February of constitutions at Turin, Florence and Naples. To a lesser degree a pre-revolutionary situation also existed in France. In the campaign of banquets to demand parliamentary and electoral reform the coalition of opposition parties had allowed the leadership to pass to the republicans, and Guizot's ministry barely survived the debate on the address on 12 February. In Germany[1] liberal and radical party congresses had drawn up definite programmes of reform. In Ireland,[2] general agreement had been reached on a programme of independence, and the supporters of Smith O'Brien and John Mitchel differed only on the means of attaining this end—by political agitation or by resort to force. In Switzerland the brief civil war[3] had, by December, given the radical centralist party complete power over the Catholic cantons of the *Sonderbund*. In Hungary the coalition of opposition parties was successful in the 1847 elections for the Diet, with a programme of minimal reforms. Furthermore, the famine of spring 1847 had almost everywhere led to 'hunger riots' and at the end of the year an economic crisis which involved large-scale unemployment, though unaccompanied by disturbances, affected almost all industrial districts.

Now were a revolution to break out at this juncture it would at once find a programme ready to hand, deriving ideologically from two sources

---

[1] Cf. ch. XIX, pp. 496–7.   [2] Cf. ch. IX, p. 217.
[3] *Ibid.* p. 223.

—the political situation and the social situation. But the varied opposition to the existing order, though provoked by concrete realities, confined itself to speculation; it was theoretical rather than practical; it did not reach the people. Indeed the 1848 revolutions were not revolutions of the masses; their leaders and instigators were intellectuals devoid of political experience, not men of action. Hence their extremist ideas and policies; imbued with the idealism of a generation that had grown up in a romantic atmosphere, they took little account of facts. Apart from a few exceptions in Hungary, Poland and Piedmont, they were bourgeois by origin; for the aristocracy, which in the eighteenth century supported policies of reform, had broken with liberalism after the French Revolution and linked its interests, and devoted its services, to monarchical conservatism. Their inspiration came not from America, which was little known and whose civilisation was regarded as materialist,[1] nor from England, which was influential only with economic doctrines and was discredited in continental eyes because of the power of its aristocracy and the wretchedness of its working classes, but from the teachings given to Europe by France. These consisted of three elements. There were, firstly, the fertile political schools of the Restoration, especially that of the individualist Benjamin Constant, whose theories were particularly welcomed in Switzerland and Germany, and of the *doctrinaires*, the teachers of the bourgeoisie of Spain, Germany and Italy. Secondly there was Lamennais, who with his liberal catholicism and *L'Avenir*[2] exercised a profound influence in Belgium, the Rhineland and Bavaria. Thirdly there was the Messianic republicanism which attracted so many republicans and young men after 1840 and led them to impose as a dogma the belief that France had a mission and a duty to spread and sustain liberty and nationality throughout Europe (cf. ch. IX, p. 218). The French republicans, for the most part, carried their doctrines to the point of demanding universal suffrage and a ministry answerable to parliament; absolute freedom of the press and of association; compulsory primary education and a tax on income. The political republicans and their organ, *Le National*, went no farther than this. But the social democrats who wrote in *La Réforme* also proposed social reforms, aiming at the organisation of labour, the establishment of producers' co-operatives and associations, and the nationalisation of the principal industries, including insurance and railways.

From all this the European liberals[3] had derived a simpler programme. It involved guarantee of the freedom of the individual, the reform of legal procedure and the introduction of the jury, freedom of the press, representative assemblies, a National Guard and the abolition of the confessional state and of the police regime. In addition some radicals affirmed

---

[1] For the influence of the U.S.A. upon some of the constitution makers of 1848–9 see, however, ch. VIII.　　　　[2] Cf. ch. IV, pp. 77–8.　　　　[3] Cf. ch. VIII.

that the representatives of the people should have full constituent powers and proclaimed the idea of the brotherhood of man.

Such, with nuances that differed according to different schools, were the programmes put forward by the Germans of the west and south and by the Italians, the one being more speculative in character, the other more matter-of-fact.

A further aspect of current political ideology was represented by the movement of nationalities (cf. ch. IX). There were two theories of nationality running parallel to each other; they were not yet in conflict, for their differences had not yet been made manifest. The French conception, deriving as it did from the rationalist doctrines of the eighteenth century and the Revolution, saw the nation as a spiritual community formed by the voluntary association of free men. The German conception, on the other hand, deriving from Herder's philosophy, from romanticism and from the philological, historical and legal studies of the universities, saw the nation as a natural, primitive organism, endowed with specific genius that found expression in language, customs and history. Spreading across western Europe, the French conception had inspired Italy and Ireland, just as it had inspired Poland and Greece. The German conception was successful in quite different regions, namely Germany and the Austrian empire, and where the young men attended German universities. The French was linked with the idea of and the claim to political liberty, the German inspired a will to power which might find fulfilment through means other than those of liberalism. In Germany in particular the two movements were so far distinct that liberalism, inspired by the French example, was virtually a counterpole to nationalism which was nurtured primarily on hatred of France. When, therefore, the liberal and nationalist demands reached their full development in 1848, they brought the whole structure of the European states into question and suggested an entirely new formula.

The social problem was less immediate, but because it concerned the masses possessed overwhelming significance. In three-quarters of Europe, where the feudal regime had not been abolished under Napoleonic rule, it affected peasants rather than working men. It involved the restriction of landed property to the nobility, the limitation of personal and property rights, the maintenance of tithes and forced labour service. The two necessities were to free the individual and to free the land. In Prussia the Patent of 1817 had halted Hardenberg's social reforms and in Germany in general the introduction of sugar-beet and agricultural machinery had sharpened the competitive struggle between the great landowners and the peasantry. In the three Polish territories the proletarianisation of the peasantry had proceeded apace since the beginning of the century. In the Austrian empire the landowning nobles who stood to gain by the increased demand for corn and meat had by legislation and economic measures sought to restrict the amount of free land and to substitute crippling rents for the former tenures. Everywhere, the growth of population that followed the Napoleonic wars aggravated the peasant's plight and forced him to seek to supplement his income by work in industry. In this way industry had its repercussions on the countryside.

But industry was still mainly represented, as in former days, by scattered craftsmen. The modern industrial regime[1] with its machinery, its rapid transport, capitalist organisation and liberal laws scarcely existed. England alone had gone through an industrial revolution. On the Continent industrial concentrations existed only in Belgium, in a few regions of France and Germany (the Rhineland, Thuringia, Saxony, Silesia and Berlin), and within the Austrian empire in Bohemia and Vienna. Such agglomerations of the proletariat were therefore exceptional, and nowhere save in England did they display the characteristics denounced by Engels. But this does not mean that the situation of the workers was not deplorable, for they had lost the protection of the old corporate state but could not yet benefit from the strength that lies in numbers and organisation. The many 'socialist' remedies put forward by theorists who, apart from Proudhon and some German communists, were intellectuals of bourgeois origin, lacked precision and showed little sense of reality or knowledge of economics.

These problems acquired an insistent urgency with the agricultural crisis of 1846, the financial crisis of early 1847, which checked investment and dried up credit for the whole year, and the industrial crisis and accompanying distress which followed in the autumn. The demands of serfs and unemployed workers for social reform were to come flooding through the breach which the political revolution was to open in the old structure.

The Paris Revolution of 24 February arose out of an incident that was, if not arranged in advance, at least deliberately exploited. In February neither the political and parliamentary leaders nor the republican journalists thought that they stood on the brink of a revolution. But a group of men, some young, all zealous, were determined that a revolution should be brought about. After organising a campaign against the regime through democratic banquets, they decided that a popular procession should accompany the guests to the final banquet held by the parliamentary opposition on 22 February. Though the government banned the meeting and the deputies withdrew their support, the organisers nevertheless let the demonstration go forward. Then on the 23rd, while the king, who had been disturbed by the readiness with which the bourgeois National Guard embraced the cause of reform, dismissed Guizot, they sustained the disturbances throughout the day in various eastern quarters of the city, and in the evening formed a long procession of demonstrators along the

[1] Cf. ch. II.

boulevards. When the anger of the people had been fanned by a bloody encounter between the mob and the troops outside the Ministry of Foreign Affairs, they exploited it to the full, raised the suburbs of Saint-Honoré, Saint-Martin and Saint-Antoine during the night, and armed the people by urging them to raid the gunsmiths' shops and *mairies*. By the morning of the 24th Paris was in revolt. The insurgents surrounded the central districts with barricades. While the palace and the politicians elaborated complex ministerial changes and issued conflicting orders that robbed Marshal Bugeaud, who was in command of the troops, of any chance of effective intervention, the rebels bore down on the Tuileries; and at half-past twelve the king, losing heart, meekly abdicated and made good his escape down the Champs-Elysées. An hour later the palace was taken and pillaged, while at the same time a few resolute men seized control of the main public services—the *mairie* of Paris, the Prefecture of Police, the Post Office. At the end of the morning the republican leaders were still closeted in the offices of *Le National*, seeking to give the riot a particular target and a central command—this, at a time when it had already won the day. But at least they were skilful enough to seize their opportunity in the Chamber. Brushing aside any discussion of a regency for the child Comte de Paris, they asked the crowd who had invaded the Chamber to assent by acclamation to the formation of a provisional government of seven 'radical' deputies, of whom the most important were Lamartine, Dupont de L'Eure, Ledru-Rollin and Marie. About five o'clock this government took possession of the Hôtel de Ville; about seven o'clock they were joined by four delegates from the advanced group linked with *La Réforme*; these included Louis Blanc and a workman, who were invited to participate in the government.

Thus in a few hours the Paris masses had swept away both the regime and the dynasty. If they had no more leaders than in 1830, they did far less damage, for the few outbreaks of violence were not serious. There was a further difference from 1830: they had no intention of allowing their victory to slip out of their hands. During the night they obliged the new government to proclaim the Republic without waiting for the nation's ratification. The next day they steered the republican regime in a social direction by extracting from the government a promise to ensure that all working men should get a living from their work and to guarantee employment to all citizens. Then, two days later, a 'Government Commission for Workmen' was formed. Before agreeing to join this commission the workers required that their working day should first be reduced by an hour and a half. Louis Blanc was the spokesman and formulator of these confused demands, but the same sincere desire to improve the lot of the working classes animated the entire government. Its deliberations were conducted under pressure from the people and before their eyes; processions, deputations, manifestations followed one another for some weeks. In this way, by one decree after another, a republic was gradually improvised based on universal suffrage, absolute freedom of the press and of association, and the abolition of the death penalty for political offences, of slavery, and of the debtor's prison. It was a republic that undertook social experiments of all kinds in order to regulate the organisation of labour— every description of workmen's trade unions, national workshops to occupy the unemployed in Paris and the principal cities, labour commissions in every department and in Paris at the Luxembourg, where Louis Blanc turned between six and eight hundred members—employers' representatives, workmen's representatives (twice the number), economists of every school—into a virtual parliament. There was not a breath of opposition. The provinces accepted the Paris Revolution without a murmur, even with delight; the clergy ostentatiously rallied to the new regime; the Legitimists were exultant.

One question occurred to every mind: what would be the effect on Europe? Would France now embark on the programme of disseminating freedom, which represented the gospel of republicanism? Lamartine and his colleagues feared the revolutionary chaos that would result from war, and the difficulty of establishing the regime if it were at odds with the coalition that the tsar and the king of Prussia were already endeavouring to establish. Lamartine put an end to this danger by giving Palmerston every assurance of his desire for peace (cf. ch. x, p. 261). He explained France's position in a manifesto that was approved by his colleagues on 2 March and published on the 5th. In this France proclaimed the principle of the sovereignty of the people and the right of each nation to determine its own fate, refused to recognise the peace treaties of 1815, declared herself the ally of every people who aspired to the same ideal, but accepted provisionally the present state of Europe and stressed her peaceful intentions. There were two other practical reasons that encouraged moderation: a disorganised army and an empty treasury. Indeed the revolution had turned the economic crisis into a catastrophe: panic ensued; bank deposits were withdrawn; the *bourse* slumped; all credit was stopped, and as a result workshops and factories were shut; the Treasury was exhausted and the Bank of France was threatened with liquidation. Over-riding all questions of principle the emergency demanded that paper money should be forced into circulation and a moratorium declared on all bills (18 March), discount banks be established to deal in commercial stocks and to advance loans on goods, the nine departmental banks be absorbed a little later into the Bank of France and the latter be given the monopoly of uttering paper money. Disaster was averted, but the financial and economic crisis, remaining acute until the summer, paralysed government initiative.

The news of events in Paris provoked an immediate upsurge of liberalism in those neighbouring countries which were a seed-bed for French ideas. In Italy the Paris Revolution justified and strengthened the process that was already under way, without setting new forces in motion (cf. ch. XXI, p. 562). In Piedmont the *Statuto* was promulgated on 5 March. The pope appointed a ministry with a lay majority on 11 March and granted a constitution on the 15th. These two constitutions, like those of Tuscany and Naples, represented a practical application of *doctrinaire* ideas and an adaptation of Louis Philippe's charter; nowhere did the masses intervene and nowhere did the reforms attain to democracy. In western Germany, from 1 to 12 March, following the example of the Grand Duchy of Baden, manifestations by bourgeois belonging both to the intelligentsia and the business world, coupled with great gatherings in the streets, led to the formation of parliamentary ministries and the concession of certain rights—in Hesse-Darmstadt, Hesse-Kassel, Nassau, Frankfurt, Württemberg, Brunswick and Thuringia. In the Hanseatic towns of the north peaceful revolutions turned the patrician regimes into democratic republics. In the Prussian Rhineland and Westphalia a vast petition was organised for representative institutions, and the bourgeoisie seized control of the municipalities and formed National Guards. Thus the contrast was sharpened between western Germany and the rest of the country. An apparent revival of the Peasants' Revolt, however, started a rising in the Neckar valley, the Black Forest and Odenwald—a splutter of age-old hatred and suffering, quickly suppressed by regular troops. Lastly, the question of national unity became so urgent that the Diet itself and the governments of Prussia, Bavaria and Württemberg, in late February and early March, began to consider a reform of the Confederation. On the initiative of a few liberals, some fifty politicians and writers met on 5 March in Heidelberg. They launched an appeal for the formation of a body representing all Germany, and a delegation of seven of them convoked everyone who had ever sat in a Diet or Chamber in order to fix an electoral law in a preparatory assembly. In all these movements in Italy and Germany there was no show of violence (apart from the peasant rising in the Neckar valley); they owed their success to the unanimous support of public opinion, their simultaneity, and the unreasoning fear of their governments, which were taken by surprise.

The revolution in central Europe came from another source, the very heart of the conservative system, Vienna itself. The Paris Revolution made itself felt by a collapse of the bank, aggravation of the industrial crisis in Bohemia and Vienna, an intensification of political intrigues in the court, and a general feeling of exaltation. This feeling was expressed in Vienna and Prague by a number of petitions from bourgeois and students, and in Pressburg, where the Hungarian Diet was meeting, by speeches demanding the suppression of the poll-tax and duty-labour and the formation of a government for Hungary based on national representation. The crisis culminated on 13 March, when the Lower Austrian Diet was to meet. As in Paris, peaceful demonstrators, consisting of bourgeois and students, clashed with the troops, and there followed an uprising in the suburbs. The court gave way in fear. Metternich fled. But the agitation continued till the 15th, when the emperor quietened it by promising a constitution, granting freedom of the press and forming a Council of Ministers. At Pressburg a passionate speech by Kossuth, in which he made much of events in Vienna and warned it against revolution, decided the Diet to approve the liberal programme, which was then taken by a delegation to Vienna for confirmation. A coalition ministry led by Count Batthyanyi was formed, and the state undertook to indemnify landowners for the abolition of feudal rights. During the three weeks that followed the Diet initiated several laws that were to give Hungary a wider autonomy. In Prague the petition organised by bourgeois and students acquired a wider scope, receiving working-class support and taking on a more national character. A delegation that was sent to Vienna on 19 March and returned on 1 April to voice its demands more vigorously, obtained a rescript on 8 April, which promised consideration of a common Diet for the Czech provinces at the coming Reichstag, granted political liberties, put the different languages on an equal footing and abolished seignorial administration of justice. The 'Charter of Bohemia' was to be defined and completed by the Austrian Parliament. In Prague and Budapest a group of young men and radicals had tried to enlarge this programme of moderate liberalism, but the group had been rapidly absorbed and had dissolved of itself. Apart from skirmishes in Vienna, the revolution had come about without violence, and neither in Bohemia nor in Hungary did the nationalist movements involve separatism. Its results, however, were to be seen more as promises than as achievements.

The moral effect was none the less immense. The fall of Metternich's regime entailed the immediate collapse of Austrian hegemony in Italy and the end of absolute monarchy in Prussia (cf. ch. XXI, pp. 562–3). As soon as news arrived, late on the 17th, of what had happened in Vienna, there was an outburst of fierce hatred against the Germans in Milan. Overriding all efforts at compromise, displaying a boldness that verged on folly, the people, despite their lack of arms, managed with the help of the neighbouring towns to drive out Radetzky and the Austrian garrison in five days of furious fighting. While the garrison took refuge on 31 March in the Quadrilateral, a provisional government took over the administration of Lombardy. Venice achieved its liberation with less effort: released from prison by the mob, Manin gave heart to his people by recalling the republic of St Mark, and secured by intimidation the surrender of the arsenal, the departure of the fleet and the capitulation of the governor. In a few days all the cities of Venetia, like those of Lombardy, had driven out the troops. On 21 and 26 March the three duchies similarly effected their liberation.

In the great industrial city of Berlin, where there was a serious wave of unemployment, the news from Vienna arrived on the 16th and provoked an agitation that grew swiftly in size as it was countered by military precautions. The brutality of the soldiery turned it into an insurrection on the 18th. Here the movement was spontaneous and violent. Rising against the army, the people seized control of the city and forced the king into humiliating surrenders, wringing from him successive political concessions by which he sought to assuage their anger. First he granted freedom of the press and the convocation of the Landtag, then the right of the Landtag to fashion an electoral law, then the principle of ministerial responsibility and the formation of a 'Rhine ministry' of liberals. His attempts to divert attention towards German unity succeeded only in committing him to a path along which he would be led much farther than he wished. Berlin's example provoked a burst of liberalism in all the towns of Prussia and a series of bloodless revolutions in all the monarchies of central Germany, Saxony and Hanover, from 17 to 30 March. At the same time a further step towards radicalism was marked by the emergence in western Germany of a republican party which, because of unemployment, gained support among the working class and expressed itself in a kind of municipal anarchy.

On the borders of Germany, Poles flocked into Posen, applauded by German public opinion, or waited for an invasion of Russian Poland. But Poland had rendered herself powerless as a result of the abortive rising of 1846, and the conflicting nationalism of Poles and Prussians soon broke up the unity of the liberal movement (cf. ch. IX, p. 228). No later than the middle of May, to the loud approval of these self-same Germans, the king of Prussia incorporated the Polish territories into his kingdom and thus into the confederation. On the other hand, the revolution carried the day in the Danish duchies, which proclaimed their independence on 18 March and chose a prince. German volunteers and the Prussian army flew to their assistance. At the end of April the Danish troops were thrown back across the Eider.

Taken all in all, these revolutions had been achieved at small cost. Violence had been limited to a few exceptional cases; it had been swift and merciful in Paris and Vienna, bloody and menacing in Milan and Berlin, the masses being aroused by some chance incident or an explosion of passionate hatred. Everywhere else, no more had been needed than bourgeois manifestations, sometimes supported by street demonstrations. In general, aims were moderate, and often results were incomplete or ill-defined. But in the few following weeks these revolutions consolidated their position. In Paris the republic, though struggling against the twin difficulties caused by revolutionary pressure and the economic crisis, strengthened its hold. Extremists, such as Blanqui and Barbès, who were the leaders of socialist clubs, had tried to prolong the questionable regime of direct government by the people of Paris and to obtain the postponement of elections by organising a '*journée*' on 16 April. But the government stood firm. The parties who were to fight the electoral campaign had taken shape. There were the conservatives, who invoked social order and religion; the democrats centred on the clubs and a central committee formed by Louis Blanc from the delegation of workers at the Luxembourg, who demanded a 'social republic'; and the republicans of *Le National*, who prided themselves on what had already been achieved and advocated liberalism in the widest sense. The elections were held on 23 April according to *scrutin de liste*, in an atmosphere that varied from calm to enthusiasm; and the results justified the hopes of the third group. Against the other two groups, who mustered about 180–200 deputies, they received a heavy majority out of the 900 seats.

In Italy the victory over the Austrians whetted nationalist feeling, and all over the country, even in Naples and Rome, legions of volunteers were formed to help the Lombards and Venetians. At first Charles Albert hesitated; he feared revolution and distrusted France; but on 25 March, borne on the tide of public opinion, he declared war on Austria, then crossed the Ticino and entered Milan. But so dilatory was his conduct of operations that it was not till early April that he made contact with the Austrians, winning a battle at Goito on 10 April.

The Berlin Landtag voted universal suffrage on 8 April. The governments opposed no obstacles to the meeting of deputies for the preliminary Parliament, which opened at Frankfurt on 31 March. It declared that all citizens, whatever their religion or social status, should vote in the election of the Constituent Assembly; but on 3 April it separated without attempting, in spite of the efforts of a few republicans, to sketch the first draft of a constitution; it merely nominated a committee of fifty to work to this end. In the second fortnight of April or the beginning of May elections were held everywhere, either for the National Assembly or for new Chambers.

In Austria, the imperial government, after some show of resistance, accepted on 11 April the extension of Hungary's autonomy through the grant of a unitary, liberal and parliamentary constitution. A fortnight afterwards it published the constitution for the rest of the empire, which had been promised on 15 March and was modelled on the liberal Charter of the Kingdom of Belgium (cf. pp. 191–2). On 9 May, yielding to the protests of the classes excluded by a restricted suffrage, it extended the vote to all citizens. Finally, after further demonstrations in Prague on 30 May Count Thun set up a National Council there on 30 May.

By the end of April a new Europe, which sought to organise itself according to the principles of democracy and nationality, had been born.

Yet by summer 1848 the tide had already begun to ebb. Though remaining liberal, Europe repudiated socialism and disorder. Here, too, it took its example from France. For in France the social experiment had been a disappointment and the advanced parties had shown themselves rash and maladroit. The Constituent Assembly, which met for the first time on 5 May, reorganised the government, entrusting executive power to a commission which appointed to its ministries men of the provisional government excluding the socialists. The socialists, angry at losing all share in power and relying on the clubs and the Workers' Committee from the Luxembourg, attempted a second revolution by a sudden attack on the Assembly on 15 May. They failed and were obliged to relinquish what posts they still held, such as the Prefecture of Police. Their leaders, Raspail, Blanqui, Barbès, Albert, were arrested. By this attack on national sovereignty democratic ideas themselves forfeited some credit. The persistent economic and financial crisis paralysed any democratic reform of taxes and the measures of nationalisation planned by Garnier-Pagès; it brought to nothing the trade unions and thwarted the national workshops. Émile Thomas, the director of the latter, had introduced welfare services and a club for civic education, and wished to incorporate the workshops into a vast scheme of industrial planning. But they had been disproportionately swollen by the growing number of unemployed and the continual influx of provincials. The total of workmen exceeded 115,000. There was insufficient work in Paris for a labour force of this size, and idleness led to demoralisation. Either the labour schemes were useless like those of the Minister of Public Works, or they demanded too lengthy preliminary study like those of the Department of Roads and Bridges (Ponts et Chaussées), or they raised political problems like Garnier-Pagès' repurchase of the railways. The Assembly grew uneasy at the heavy, futile expense. Moreover, the revolutionary parties looked to the workshops for an army, the lack of which had led to the fiasco of 15 May, and subversive propaganda of all kinds began to circulate. The conservatives, and the deputies who were opposed in principle to radical solutions for social problems, found it easy to denounce the danger; the government itself took alarm. It was planned to purge the workshops by sending home the provincials who had been improperly enrolled, and to reduce the number of workers in Paris by sending many of them to departments where great work-yards could be opened, as in Sologne. An attempt was made to select names and to form them into the necessary groups; but when, on 21 June, the young workers were informed that they must either leave for the provinces or, if they preferred, join the army, but that in any case they were dismissed from the workshops, the result was that revolt broke out the next day. It was a revolt not so much of men from the workshops (for the majority stood aloof), but of the mass of Parisian workers who were fighting for their ideal of a social republic and the organisation of labour, and, of course, of all the revolutionary elements. The civil war, conducted with relentless cruelty on either side, lasted from 22 to 26 June; the number of dead, though certainly large, cannot be computed. The repressive measures that followed involved the arrest, deportation or imprisonment of many thousands. Because of the crisis, all powers had necessarily been concentrated in the hands of General Cavaignac, and there was no return to the easy-going government that France had known before the 'June Days'. The executive power was reconstituted in the form of a President of the Council responsible to the Assembly. He closed down the clubs and the revolutionary papers and purged the civil service. The provinces, which had everywhere hastened to support the army of the forces of order, were relieved to feel themselves once more in the hands of a firm government.

The effect on Europe was tremendous. France's example had spurred on the social movement in industrial countries; now the victory of authority decided governments everywhere to attempt a reaction. In Germany the working-class movement had assumed many guises. Its first and most natural expression lay in the formation of political clubs for working men in Berlin, Breslau and Cologne; as the economic crisis deepened, their fortunes throve. Moreover, thanks to the new freedom of association, trade unions multiplied rapidly, and the idea of forming a central organisation occurred to some of their members; on 19 April the Central Committee of Working Men was founded in Berlin; imitated in Hamburg and Leipzig, it had as its mouthpiece the *Sozialpolitische Zeitung*; it appealed for the support of all working-class communities and it organised meetings. A far more original step was the attempt—curiously enough first made by artisans—to form a class organisation. As a result of an appeal which the working men's corporations of Leipzig launched on 22 April, meetings were held far and wide, issuing petitions against free enterprise. Then a Preparatory Congress in Hamburg (2–6 June) convoked a 'Social Parliament', which held sittings in Frankfurt from 15 July to 5 August and drew up a 'Charter for Artisans'. It demanded the organisation of trades on the basis of obligatory membership of corporations, with provincial Chambers and a general Chamber for all the trades of Germany; it also required that the number of trades should be limited and that privileges should be restored to the masters. Delegates and petitions came particularly from the textile centres of Silesia, Brandenburg and Westphalia. As a counterblast to this method of organising labour by returning to the medieval system, the factory workers in their turn arranged a 'General Congress of Workers' at Frankfurt in August, attended by 300 trade-union delegates, including Viennese, Hungarians and Bohemians. They adopted the principle that a workmen's league should be founded and that the social problem should be solved by the workers themselves. In this way the working class achieved representation independently of the political bodies, but this representation was characterised, and therefore weakened, by the two types of industrial economy into which Germany was divided. Moreover, just when the movement brought its dual claim before the Frankfurt Parliament, the credit of the working-class movement was compromised in the eyes of the Parliament by its connection, through another branch of the movement, with the revolutionary idea. As in France, the socialists, theorists and men of action could not conceive of the possibility of a social revolution without the accompaniment of a political revolution, and the communist group in Cologne in particular, which founded the *Neue Rheinische Zeitung* in June, sought to spur the working class on towards this goal. Against the bourgeois Parliament of Frankfurt a congress of the democratic committees that had been formed for the elections was set up under the presidency of a socialist. On 14 June it assembled 234 delegates from 66 towns, establishing a hierarchy of local committees and provincial congresses, with a central committee and a general congress set above them. Its programme entailed a democratic republic to ensure universal happiness, and the fraternity of all peoples. But authority no longer went in fear and trembling. Everywhere the local governments and the federal government suppressed popular agitation, in Berlin in June, in Silesia in July, and above all in Frankfurt and the west in the middle of September. As for the Frankfurt Parliament, it ignored the programmes of these proletarians and artisans. A few working men from Austria had given their support to the Germans, but they counted for little. Before the revolution they had neither attempted nor contrived to achieve any form of organisation; apparently they did not even understand the opportunity offered by this revolution in which they were taking part. They were content with unemployment relief and the public works which the government established. When the ministry, uneasy at the expense and encouraged by the outcome of the 'June Days' in France, cut down the wages paid for public work on 19 August, the Viennese workmen attempted to negotiate. Brawls on 23 August provided the occasion for bitter fighting in which they were overwhelmed by the National Guard.

In Austria (ch. xx, pp. 523–9), moreover, the struggle took place on the political, rather than the social, plane. The government was too weak to resist both popular demands and English pressure; for England, anxious to restore peace as soon as possible in Italy, persuaded it to cede Lombardy, under English mediation, to Piedmont in order to retain Venetia. Meanwhile conservative resistance centred in certain court circles and the army, in which the spirit of the old monarchy had taken refuge. From its ranks, without or in spite of the orders of the government, came the first movement towards a restoration of the old order. It was put into effect almost simultaneously by Windischgrätz in Bohemia and Radetzky in

Italy. Yet Bohemia, which was still patiently awaiting its statute from the imperial parliament, had proved its loyalty by refusing to send its representatives to the Frankfurt Parliament and by holding a congress of delegates from the various Slav peoples on 2 June (cf. ch. IX, pp. 232-3). This congress, while it proclaimed the solidarity of the Slavs and their desire for freedom and equality, represented a declaration of independence as against both Germany and Russia. On 12 June Windischgrätz's soldiers managed to provoke skirmishes with the Prague population, thus enabling the Marshal to overwhelm bourgeois, students and workers in a five-day battle and to establish a state of siege.

In Italy Austrian interests were served by the steady decay of the national movement. In an allocution of 29 April the pope had condemned the war. The enthusiasm of the volunteers came up against the apathy of the country people, the inertia of the authorities who did not bother to supply them, and the semi-hostility of the Piedmont army which did not trouble to embody or use them and abandoned them to local operations in which they gradually ceded Venetian territory before the technical superiority of the Austrians. They lost heart and deserted. King Charles Albert, a very mediocre strategist, pursued private ambitions. He neglected every suggestion made by the other sovereigns for the formation of a military alliance, and in spite of his undertakings he obtained the vote of the local populations for their annexation in June to Piedmont. Finally on 10 July he accepted the results of English mediation. But while he remained motionless, Radetzky was reorganising his troops and on 10 June seized Vicenza, refusing to heed his orders to obtain an armistice and ignoring the concessions that his government made as a result of English intervention. Then, while the smaller towns of Venetia fell one after the other, he took the offensive on 23 July. He routed the Piedmontese army at Custoza on the 25th and, reaching the Adige before its broken remnants, forced Charles Albert to abandon Milan on 5 August in spite of his formal engagements and to sign an armistice on the 9th, by which Lombardy, Venetia and the Duchies were evacuated. Apart from the fact that Venice, though blockaded, still held out, the situation that had existed before March was now restored. In Lombardy–Venetia Radetzky introduced a rule of iron, and occupied Ferrara. The king of Naples profited by this to prorogue the newly elected Chamber on 15 June, until such time as street-fighting with the Neapolitan workers should enable him—as it did in September—to restore power to the army and to a purged civil service. Hopes of a united Italy faded; the domain even of political liberty shrank to central Italy and Piedmont.

A similar drama had involved the Hungarian nation (ch. XX, pp. 523-9). The March movement had inspired the nationalists of other races who owed allegiance to the crown of St Stephen—Serbs from the borders, Roumanians from Transylvania, Slovaks, and especially Croats, who had been separatist from the first. At first the delegates of some of these movements had hoped that by negotiating with the autonomous government of Budapest they would obtain recognition of their political existence. But they found the Hungarians adamant, and in May their movement therefore took on a democratic, anti-Magyar complexion— the democratic trend being particularly marked with the Serbs and the Roumanians. In their assemblies at Karlovitz, Blassendorf and Zagreb they demanded and proclaimed their autonomy; they would be directly connected with Vienna, feudal rights would be abolished, and large properties would be broken up. The Croats, who knew from long experience how stubborn the Hungarians could be, supplied a leader for their joint enterprise, an officer from the frontier named Jellačić, who had been appointed Ban of Croatia by Vienna and on whom the Zagreb Assembly now conferred dictatorial powers (9 July). He organised Croatia into a separate province. Meanwhile the Hungarian Chamber, which differed little in its social composition from the former Diet, had met on 4 July and begun, on Kossuth's instigation, to build up a national army. Civil war was imminent. Vienna would have no difficulty in playing off these nationalist movements against one another. Victorious over the Italians, Vienna annulled the laws which had been voted by the Hungarians, who also lost the support of the Reichstag. Early in September the struggle began. From south-east, south and west, the Slav armies of the empire invaded the Hungarian provinces. Kossuth assumed the presidency of a 'Committee of Defence'; he enforced laws that lacked the emperor's approval; so that Hungary acted as though she were an independent state. When, on 23 September, the crowd murdered the Imperial High Commissioner, the possibility of conciliation faded. It was rendered still more remote by a further complication in Vienna. The radicals and workers planned to oppose the departure of troops for the Hungarian front, and, as the result of an insurrection that broke out on 6 October, the Minister of War was assassinated and the emperor and his ministers fled to Olmütz. But these popular elements could not stand against the army unaided. Windischgrätz marched on Vienna and in three days (29–31 October) he restored authority and subjected the city to a frenzy of repression. The submission of Hungary was only a matter of weeks.

In the international domain diplomacy reasserted its rights. England, for whom the freedom of the Sound was both a necessity and a tradition, could not allow German control at this point; she reacted vigorously to the Prussian action, mediated and imposed an armistice that forced Prussia to withdraw her troops and to submit the dispute to an international conference, held on 30 August (cf. p. 265).

Thus by the end of summer 1848 the revolution had everywhere been halted and often beaten back. Social revolution had been averted, and the advanced parties defeated. Public authority had been restored and sometimes—in the Kingdom of Lombardy–Venetia, in Vienna and Prague —even assumed by the military. The last months of the year were everywhere taken up in the elaboration of constitutions. Though liberal concessions were not yet repudiated, the experience of these critical months had led the constituent assemblies to organise the executive power on a firm footing. The French constitution was drawn up with care and discussed at length. Protracted debates examined in detail the great political problems, which were solved not so much by practical experience as by principles. The resulting Constitution of 14 November 1848 was entirely democratic in spirit: popular sovereignty was expressed in the election, by universal suffrage, both of the single Legislative Assembly and of the President of the Republic; all the rights of the individual and all freedoms, including freedom of education, were ensured and guaranteed; ministerial responsibility entailed a parliamentary regime, and the payment of parliamentary expenses meant that each and every man could become a representative. But after the experience of the 'June Days', decentralisation was abandoned for fear of anarchy, and the right to work for fear of socialism. The makers of the constitution had wished to establish a strong government and hoped to avoid all danger of personal power by limiting the President's functions to four years and by preventing his immediate re-election. The Assembly, deferring to the rights of the nation, put the new constitution into operation as soon as possible. The presidential election was immediately set under way; it took place on 10 December. The results were astounding. The progressive candidates received only a small number of votes—Raspail, the socialist, 40,000, Ledru-Rollin, the democrat, 400,000. The real fight was between General Cavaignac, the republican candidate, and Prince Louis Napoleon Bonaparte, a nephew of the great Napoleon. The prince who was unknown by the country and yet, thanks to the name he bore, had been elected deputy by several departments in June and September, received five-and-a-half million votes, while Cavaignac received less than a million and a half. Bourgeois, peasants, workers, had all voted for Louis Napoleon; the conservatives, who had made a pact with him for the defence of order and religion, supplied a ministry composed of men who were not Bonapartists, led by Odilon Barrot and Falloux. France, who nine months earlier had acclaimed the Republic, now entrusted her destiny to non-republicans. The Assembly, weakened and discredited, dared not continue with its task; it hurriedly passed a few laws and on 9 February decided to dissolve in the spring. The prince's election, which throughout Europe was regarded as an emphatic victory for the forces of order, spurred on governments to take resolute measures.

In Germany by contrast constitution-making was a novelty. Organic laws had to be given not only to the different states of the centre and the north, but to the German Federation, and often this task was carried out in an inconsistent and contradictory manner.

In the west, where the bourgeoisie was already familiar with the working of parliamentary government, the problem was easy: the regime had only to be guided towards democracy. In the centre and the east, on the other hand, the feudal and monarchical structure still stood firm and the state had always belonged to aristocratic classes who were determined to defend their interests. The Prussian Assembly met on 22 May. The left-wing parties were predominant. Popular agitation, which in June culminated in several days of insurrection, drove the Assembly to undertake democratic measures and to build the new state by demolishing the ideas and institutions of the *ancien régime*. But by July the right wing was reorganising its forces—the great landowners, Lutheran clergy, royal entourage and army, all deliberately looking for support in the countryside. The conflict broke out over the Chamber's desire to expel from the army those officers who were hostile to the new regime. Heartened by the example of Windischgrätz, the king entrusted the command of his Berlin troops to a determined general named Wrangel, who harshly suppressed the working-class agitations in September. Then he replied to a motion of sympathy with the Viennese, which was voted on 31 October, by appointing a reactionary ministry led by von Brandenburg and by transferring the Assembly to the provinces in the middle of November. The populace did not stir, and public opinion seemed favourable. The king therefore went further. On 5 December he pronounced the dissolution of the Constituent Assembly and himself granted a constitution guaranteeing these basic rights—equality before the law, universal suffrage, two legislative chambers, with the right of dissolution residing with the king, and the principle of permanent taxation. This constitution fulfilled the wishes of the country, as was shown by the January elections. The other German monarchies fell into line. Liberalism, if it had triumphed, triumphed only at the expense of democracy and popular sovereignty.

The Frankfurt Parliament, which opened on 18 May, was an assembly of about 800 members. It was in no way representative of the lower classes but was principally composed of intellectuals, who combined a conscientious earnestness and rigidity of purpose with a complete lack of political experience. Their complicated procedure still further delayed their work, which was held up by endless debates, at a time when the essential condition of success was to exploit immediately the nation's enthusiasm and the government's confusion. The Assembly broke up into a number of shifting parties. Not till 30 June did it decide to entrust the provisional government to an Imperial Vicar, the Archduke John, who did not in fact take over his functions till the end of July. The Assembly then began to publish its aims, formulating a policy which it lacked the means to put into practice. It wished to create a German army and fleet, to annex to the empire all countries where German was spoken, to exercise control over the separate governments, and by centralisation to give uniformity to the national institutions and economy. Only after this, on 19 October, did it begin to discuss those very institutions whose formation was its real purpose. The fundamental rights that would constitute the German common law were quickly decided on and promulgated at the end of the year without being submitted to the states for their approval. On 27 October the Parliament, carried away by its own nationalist fervour, declared that no part of the German empire could be joined to another state except by personal union. But in the meantime the victory of authority in Austria and Prussia meant that they had no intention of being either ousted or mastered, and was calculated to strengthen the resistance of governments whose attitude towards popular movements had already hardened. The imperial government in Vienna was in fact consolidating its position (cf. ch. xx, pp. 525–6). Troops from Moravia, Styria and Galicia, under Windischgrätz's command, flung back the Hungarians on 15 December, reoccupied Budapest on 4 January 1849 and won a final victory on 26 February. Meanwhile Prince Felix Schwarzenberg had, on 21 November, formed a ministry of men of real ability, such as Stadion and Bach. On the 27th he laid before the Reichstag his programme for the reconstruction of the state on a unified, though liberal, basis, and on 2 December he replaced the feeble emperor by young Francis Joseph. Like the king of Prussia, his government was confronted with a Reichstag which since 22 July had been prudently working its way towards the establishment of a federative, democratic constitution. Like the king, too, the government transferred the Reichstag from the insurrectionary capital, Vienna, to Moravia, and then pronounced its dissolution, granting a constitution on 4 March 1849 based at one and the same time on the unity of the empire, national equality and a form of representation. It was supplemented by decrees that regularised the abolition of feudalism, created municipalities and reformed the judicial system. At the same time the government made sure of Russia's diplomatic support.

Thanks to an unfortunate decision by Charles Albert, the Austrian government gained a further triumph in Italy. Incited by the democrats, the king of Piedmont had denounced the armistice on 12 March and recommenced hostilities. But the single battle of Novara on the 24th was enough to defeat his armies, force his abdication and impose a new armistice whose severity was only slightly mitigated by the efforts of French diplomacy.

In these conditions the Frankfurt Parliament was hardly likely to make its decisions unimpeded. The work of constitution-making, as it proceeded, raised the question of how the territory of the Reich should be defined and consequently whether all or part of Austria should be included. In February the parties regrouped into 'great Germans' and 'little Germans'. The majority resented the authoritarian tendencies shown by Austria, the negotiations that had already been begun with her by the governments of Bavaria and Württemberg, and her avowed intention of dominating the new Germany as she had dominated the old.

The great decisions on the country's institutions were taken at the end of January 1849 and in February, and on 27 March the constitution was completed. On 28 March King Frederick William was elected emperor of Germany by the votes of 290 out of the 538 deputies present. Prussia's supporters had won the day, exploiting a sudden catastrophe that seemed to overwhelm Austria. Galvanised by Kossuth, inspired with new vigour, the Hungarians had driven back the Austrians on three fronts, beaten Windischgrätz on 7 April and liberated their territory in a month. On 14 April the Chamber announced the deposition of the Habsburgs and proclaimed Hungarian independence. The whole recovery of Austria was in danger. Schwarzenberg did not hesitate; he appealed to the tsar. On 1 May he was able to make an official announcement of Russian support and in the course of the month three Russian armies marched into the empire. In Germany, too, Austrian fortunes had happily been restored: on 27 April Frederick William, faced by the choice between German liberalism and the Prussian tradition, had scornfully refused the crown offered him by the Frankfurt Parliament, dismissed his own Parliament and revised the electoral law.

All these simultaneous events—the election of a conservative majority in France, the rejection by the king of Prussia of the German crown, Schwarzenberg's appeal to the tsar, the collapse of Piedmont, the landing of French troops in the Roman state—showed that the revolution was on the wane. In some countries a few weeks were enough to mark its end. The Frankfurt Parliament emptied rapidly. First the Austrian deputies, then the Prussians, were recalled by their rulers, and the liberals returned home in discouragement. There remained only the republican minority, which vainly tried to put into operation a constitution that had been rejected by a king. Ever since the end of the year the democratic party had been forming 'March associations'; it now sought to enforce republican unity by means of a new revolution. But the risings in Saxony, the Palatinate and the Grand Duchy of Baden (early May) were crushed by the Prussian army, and the Parliament, which had taken refuge in Stuttgart, was dispersed on 18 June.

In Italy the disappointment of the nationalists and the inability of the liberal governments to grapple with the economic crisis had stirred the revolutionary movement to new life at the end of the year (cf. ch. XXI, p. 564). In Piedmont the electoral victory of the radicals had brought to office the governments of Gioberti and Rattazzi and resulted in the disastrous renewal of the Austrian war. In Rome a genuine revolution had led to the assassination of Rossi, the President of the Council, on 15 November 1848, and the pope, faced by further disorders, fled to Gaeta on the 24th. In Tuscany, while the radicals, with Guerrazzi, took over the reins of government, the grand duke similarly decided on flight. From all sides Mazzini's supporters flocked to this island of democracy in central Italy; they attempted to organise a common Constituent Assembly and finally proclaimed a republic in Rome and Florence. But the doom of these democracies was sounded at Novara. The Catholic powers discussed how best to restore the pope, while the latter appealed to Austria, which was beginning to occupy the Legations. Resolving to forestall and restrict Austrian action, the French government sent out an expeditionary corps, which reached Città-Vecchia on 25 April. A premature offensive by General Oudinot ended in failure, and Rome fell only on 1 July, after a three months' siege. Reinstated by Oudinot, the cardinals exacted reprisals which the French government was unable to mitigate. The Tuscan republic had been overthrown by Austrian troops at the end of May while the king of Naples reconquered Sicily in April and early May. The political revolution, like the nationalist, was over in Italy. Only Piedmont remained liberal. Shortly afterwards Hungary succumbed. The Russian and Austrian troops needed a campaign of only two-and-a-half months to bring about Kossuth's downfall and an unconditional surrender at Világos on 13 August. Venice, after being blockaded for six months and bombarded for a month and a half, yielded on 22 August. This series of victories enabled Schwarzenberg to drop the mask of liberalism: the Austrian constitution was suspended.

In France and Germany the revolution had come to a standstill. After lively disagreement with the government, the French Constituent Assembly had separated. The financial and economic crisis was over and the problem of unemployment had been solved, but business was still slack and would remain so till 1852. The republican party, bearing the responsibility for all these misfortunes, was severely defeated in the elections of 13 May: the party of order, which represented a coalition of conservatives, monarchists and Catholics, won 450 out of 750 seats. But the government party also lost ground to the left. In order to fight the presidential campaign the democratic elements had united to form a 'Mountain' party, which remained in existence and whose propaganda Barrot's ministry was unable to check. Receiving all the left-wing votes, they mustered about 200 seats in the new Chamber. In Paris they had been particularly successful; and encouraged by this result, their leaders were unwise enough to think that another '*journée*' in Paris would bring them back to power, and incautious enough to attempt a *coup de force* on 13 June. The people did not rise; the party was virtually decapitated by numerous arrests; Ledru-Rollin, Considérant and Félix Pyat joined Louis Blanc in England. Repressive laws followed as a matter of course—the suspension for a year of the right of association and the definition of new press offences. Shortly afterwards, on 31 October, the president freed himself from monarchist tutelage by forming a ministry composed of his own men; and, while sedulously keeping alive his popularity with the people and the army, he worked swiftly to secure the reins of government in his own hand (cf. ch. XVII, p. 444).

Meanwhile, with the Loi Falloux (15 March 1850)[1] the majority realised one of the principal points in their programme—freedom of education. This meant not so much a liberal reform, as that the church gained effective control of primary education and received a number of privileges in secondary education. The law combined with universal suffrage to give the clergy a political importance of the first order. Alarmed by the success of the Mountain party in the by-elections of March and April, the Assembly severely restricted universal suffrage: the law of 31 May 1850, by imposing rigorous residential conditions, reduced the number of electors by three million—or a third, and a press law of 16 July reintroduced caution-money and stamp-duty for newspapers. But the majority, though united in their struggle against the republicans, could not agree on the restoration of a monarchy. Louis Philippe's death on 26 August 1850 prepared the way for a reconciliation or 'fusion' between the two royal families, but the Comte de Chambord refused to grant any concession to liberal principles, and reconciliation was therefore postponed. Henceforward, what with Legitimists, Orleanists, Republicans and the growing party of the president, there was no effective majority. The comprehensive democratic regime of 1848 thus reverted to a regime of supervised liberty.

In Germany the initiative had passed from peoples to governments (ch. XIX, pp. 498–503). In Prussia the elections of August 1849 gave the right sufficient power to enable the king to alter the constitution at the end of the year and to re-establish entailed properties, and then, in 1850, to change the Upper House into a House of Lords. The organisation of municipalities, the recall of the provincial estates and a law on ministerial responsibility also marked a return to tradition. Following Bavaria's example, the other sovereigns prorogued or suspended their parliaments in order to have their hands free in dealing with the question of national organisation. Partly out of ambition and conviction, partly out of a desire to rally the support of his subjects, Frederick William was in fact trying to discharge on a governmental level the task that had defeated the representatives of the people. Strengthened by his vigorous repression of the 'Constitutional Campaign', he signed an agreement with Saxony and Hanover on 26 May, known as the Three Kings' Alliance. It laid before the other governments a plan for national unification that contained a number of the ideas of the Frankfurt Parliament, but in which princes and states replaced the executive and the second chamber. Bavaria and

[1] Cf. ch. IV, p. 80.

Württemberg, which were already conducting negotiations with Schwarzenberg, declined at once; the rest accepted in August; the heads of the liberal parties had given their support in June.

It was essential to act quickly in order to reap advantage from Austria's difficulties; but it was not till 15 October that the Administrative Council of the Union convoked the electors for 31 January 1850, in order to elect an assembly to which the constitution drafted on 20 March would be submitted. Austria was thus given time to prepare her riposte. She agreed with Bavaria and Württemberg to consider other suggestions for the reform of the Confederation; she organised a 'Munich Convention' on 27 February 1850; and she attempted to undermine Prussian influence with the other princes. In this way she gained the breathing-space necessary for her own internal reorganisation; debating-time was occupied by arranging for the Imperial Vicar to be replaced by a provisional Austro-Prussian commission, which took over its duties in December 1849. When elections to the Union Parliament were mooted, first the king of Saxony (on 25 October) and then the king of Hanover refused and withdrew from the Union. The Parliament, when it met, consisted merely of representatives of Prussia and twenty-six small satellites, and even then the constitution was not agreed on till late in April. Frederick William did not dare put it into operation. Profiting by these hesitations, Schwarzenberg went forward; he convoked according to ancient custom a plenary session of the Confederation and organised a 'Limited Committee' of the Diet until such time as it was reformed. The question suddenly became one of practical urgency on 1 September 1850, when a revolution in Hesse-Kassel brought about the expulsion of the elector from Kassel. The king of Prussia was by law entrusted with the task of restoring order to this state of the Union; the Diet Committee, on the other hand, decreed federal execution and requested Bavaria to undertake it. It seemed as though civil war were imminent. Schwarzenberg, relying on energetic Russian support and that of the other four German kings, presented Prussia with an ultimatum, and Frederick William had to suffer the cruel humiliation, at Olmütz on 29 November 1850, of accepting the evacuation of Hesse and Holstein and the dissolution of the shrunken Union. Austria consented only to discuss the reform of the Confederation at conferences of the princes which were held at Dresden from 23 December 1850 to 15 May 1851. As no results were reached, all agreed to revive the old institutions. The Diet recommenced its sittings on 23 August 1851. The German governments, freed from the fear of revolution, wished to hear no more of national unity.

By this date the French Republic, which was already the only survivor of the revolution, had only a few more months to live (ch. XVII, pp. 444–5). A conflict between the president and the Assembly, which had been latent since autumn 1850, was intensified in January 1851, when the president withdrew the command of the Paris troops from General Changarnier, a nominee of the royalist majority. With some skill the President had publicly accused the Assembly of impotence and reactionary tendencies. Public opinion, fearing a return to anarchy, was agreed that the president should be kept in power, but the Assembly refused on 19 July 1851 to revise the constitution in such a way as to allow for his re-election. From that moment Louis Napoleon's mind was made up: he would maintain his position by force. He got ready his weapons in the autumn, cleverly putting the Assembly in the wrong by proposing the restoration of universal suffrage, which it rejected on 13 November. During the night of 2 December 1851 a presidential decree dissolved the Assembly, provided for the arrest of its principal leaders, and submitted to the country a plebiscitary formula that gave him power to revise the constitution. In theory the Republic was to last until the proclamation of the Empire on 2 December 1852. But in fact, with the *coup d'état* and the constitution of 14 January 1852 it had already perished.

Sooner or later, in every country and in every respect, the revolution encountered failure. Yet the turmoil, brief though it had been, left the Europe of 1851 very different from the Europe of 1847.

Among the countries where the political question alone had arisen, the most obvious benefit was reaped by those states which did not undergo a revolution: Belgium gained a reduction of property qualifications for the franchise to their constitutional minimum and an administrative reform; the Netherlands gained a constitution reinforced by provincial autonomy; and both countries achieved a parliamentary regime. The monarchies of northern Europe became constitutional, Denmark by the constitution of 1849, Sweden by the transformation of the Diet in 1851. While keeping her title of Helvetic Confederation, Switzerland had become a federal state; memories of the civil war swiftly faded away, public opinion united in resisting foreign undertakings, and economic development was launched on an international scale: her national independence was thereby strengthened (cf. ch. IX, pp. 223–4). Switzerland had found a compromise solution between the democratic freedom of the cantons and the wider extension of the central power; she was to become a kind of laboratory for political experiments. Even in France, though the *coup d'état* of 1851 and the constitution of 1852 marked a step back from the liberal parliamentary regime of the July Monarchy, permanent gains were represented by universal suffrage and the principle of popular sovereignty. As for England (ch. XIII), the crushing of Chartism and of Irish agitation emptied the political arena; John Russell's efforts to bring about electoral reform were met by indifference, both among the public and in his own party; the country was absorbed by its economic, social and religious transformation. Throughout Europe political evolution was marking time; an aura of impropriety seemed to hang about the system of personal freedom and parliamentary government; everywhere the churches and the faithful had rallied to conservatism.

In the countries where the political question was complicated by nationalism, the results of the revolution varied.

In the Italian peninsula, the memory of a first concerted effort at liberation combined with accumulated hatred of the 'Tedeschi' to foster the myth of national unity. Clearly it was necessary to reconstitute the unsuccessful ideologies on new foundations, but the newly won experience was hard to assimilate, and Mazzini's ideas were destined for some time to be at odds with the aims of the Risorgimento. Political reaction was triumphant: in Naples, where it assumed a grotesquely cruel form, it relied on its own resources; in the Duchies and the Legations it was supported by Austrian garrisons; in Rome it was slightly tempered by the presence of French troops; and in Lombardy–Venetia it issued in military reprisals. Only in Piedmont, where Victor Emmanuel II had maintained the *Statuto*, did freedom find refuge. Piedmont became, in fact, the asylum for patriots and liberals; it was embarking on a period of economic modernisation; and, a fact of decisive importance, Cavour entered the ministry in May 1850. But these were still no more than hints of what the future had in store.

In Germany the national movement, after all its vicissitudes, died down until after the Crimean War (cf. ch. XIX). But unity had existed, and the memory of unity remained. It was plain, too, that unity might be achieved by other than parliamentary means, and certain circles of the Prussian army, humiliated by the capitulation of Olmütz, thought wistfully of unification centred on Prussia. All the states had become constitutional, and all recognised universal suffrage. But the principal novelty was that with the constitution of 1848 and 1850—a constitution that had been voluntarily granted from above—Prussia had ceased to be an absolute monarchy. She set an example in another respect: she limited the workings of universal suffrage by a class system and used the principle of a permanent tax cunningly to counterbalance the rights of Parliament. This system was imitated by the rest of Germany: by abolishing fundamental rights in December 1848 the Diet restored to governments the right to amend legislation and to set up exceptional courts; reaction had discovered a politico-religious philosophy.

The Austrian empire underwent still greater changes (cf. ch. XX). By its victory over Prussia and the support it received from the southern states, its external influence on Germany seemed to have increased considerably, while in Italy it possessed a strong hold on the centre of the country. Moreover, Austria was strengthened by her new internal structure. The constitution granted on 4 March 1849 had wholly ignored historic rights. Then the army was made directly dependent on the emperor's Cabinet, the ministers became responsible to the sovereign alone and, on 31 December 1851, the constitution was suspended. Schwarzenberg and his team had constructed a centralised state. It had a uniform administration based on Circles, which divided up the provinces and were dependent on ministries, and upon village municipalities. It could boast a uniform judicial system, which was independent of the civil service and was publicly administered. It was strengthened by its close understanding with the church, which received formal expression in the concordat of 1855. In short, it was a modern state such as Joseph II had dreamed of. Unfortunately Schwarzenberg, who had created it and could have given it permanence, died on 5 April 1852.

The positive results of the revolution in the social field were far more considerable. But the situation of the working class showed little improvement. Fear of socialism had checked the policy of social reform, while the transformation of the economic regime had not yet gone far enough to reveal its effects and the dangerous disequilibrium that would ensue. On all sides everything that might indicate or encourage socialism had been swept away; thus in France the right to work had, in particular, been eliminated. A policy of public assistance (that is, cheap accommodation, charitable societies, loans to trade unions) replaced a social policy. In Germany the Frankfurt Parliament was unable to provide a sequel to the two Labour Charters. In England a first piece of social legislation, the Ten Hours' Bill, had been passed in 1850. But the question-mark loomed up everywhere: inquiries were opened on working conditions in France and in England; Napoleon III was to give special thought to the position of the workers. The communists put forward the class struggle as their explanation and solution; but as yet they met with no response. The revolutionary legislation, however, had everywhere freed workers from the bondage of tradition; the corporations were destroyed; economic individualism, with the blessing of the law, would supply the new industrial regime with its necessary human material. In short, the 1848 revolution either set in motion or hastened the proletarianisation of the masses.

But the agrarian problem concerned a much larger number of men, and here the effect of the revolution was deeper and more beneficial. The different assemblies had abolished the feudal system, and the forces of reaction dared not return to it. This affected half Europe, for Russia remained apart. In Germany the reform was first established in the west and then, spreading to the centre and the east, was brought about almost automatically by the indemnification of landlords according to conditions determined by local laws. In Prussia the law that allowed for the cession and transfer of Silesian tenures did away with feudal dues. In the Austrian empire (p. 530) the task was the greater because it had not already been begun as in Prussia. No compensation was owing for personal servitude, and the indemnity for the redemption of dues from land was handled differently according to the separate provinces, though everywhere in a liberal manner. In Hungary, where the indemnity had been charged to the state by the revolutionary government, this charge was upheld. In Galicia money had been advanced by the province; in the rest of the kingdom the law of 4 March 1849 settled the principles of valuation and the method of payment; forced labour service was calculated as a third of a working day, while payments in kind were worked out on the land-survey assessment—half to be paid by the peasant and half by the province. No doubt the land problem—the dividing up of large properties into small peasant holdings—remained to be settled, in the Austrian empire, in central and southern Italy and especially in Brandenburg and Prussia. But at least the individual had been set free. 1848 did for Europe what 1789 had done for France. The abolition of serfdom and of all checks on individual freedom enabled both worker and peasant to move about at will; and emigration was now to become a perennial relief both against chronic over-population and temporary crises. Such was the beginning of that dissemination of Europeans which was to change the face of the earth.

If the 1848 revolution is considered in the light of these results, its meaning in the evolution of Europe becomes more easily comprehensible. It brought about the end of a world. Being the practical application of an ideology that sprang from the French Revolution and the First Empire, it can be said, by its failure, to have exhausted that ideology. Thus it is an end rather than a beginning, for subsequent events were the fruit of different ideas. To connect its convulsions with the later evolution of Europe is artificial and arbitrary. We must wait for the 1914–18 war before we see a Europe fashioned according to its plan of republican and parliamentary freedom and the universal principle of nationalities, and before we witness some attempt at that brotherly league of free peoples of which it dreamed. After the lapse of a generation Europe reassumed, by means of its legend, the role of guide and exemplar.

It would be false to attempt a systematic explanation of so complex a phenomenon, the survey of which has shown so many contradictions. An explanation that is purely political and ideological can account for the ideals that were pursued, the motives of those who began the revolution, and the reasons for its failure. But such an explanation is too narrow; it looks on social upheavals as surges of revolutionary extremism; it fails to take into consideration the huge social and economic structure that underlies political parties and is sometimes visible beneath all their commotions. An economic theory that explains everything by mass movements and places the revolution in the trough of a wave of depression, with its normal accompaniment of popular suffering, cannot tell us why countries like England and Belgium, where social reasons for revolution were strongest, had no revolution at all; it obscures the peculiar individual character of each revolution. Finally the Marxist doctrine, which conceives of the 1848 revolution as a first experiment in the class war and a first effort by the proletariat to cast off the bourgeois yoke, gives too general an interpretation to untypical, localised events (the 'June Days' in France, the Peasants' Revolt in Baden and the 'Constitutional Campaign' of 1849); it forgets that the revolution was everywhere the work of bourgeois intellectuals; above all, it anticipates future conditions by postulating an industrial proletariat, which in fact existed only in England and did not exist in Paris, which was the centre and source of the revolution. History cannot be content with systems; it demands richer, more complex patterns. A simple explanation is too simple to be true. To disentangle all the complex strands of the past, we need varying approaches, flexible attitudes, diverse analyses.

CHAPTER XVI

THE MEDITERRANEAN

I N this chapter it is not the intention to recapitulate the political history of the various Mediterranean countries—the unification of Italy, the French conquest and settlement of Algiers, the consolidation of the small Greek state, the reawakening of Egypt and the effort to conserve and reform the remains of the Turkish empire; or, again, to relate the diplomatic and military history of the international crises which these and other developments produced. Nor would it be easy, within this compass, to trace the influence of new ideas and habits which these countries shared in unequal degrees with the rest of Europe. Instead, an attempt will be made to define the common characteristics of the Mediterranean region in this period and to fasten upon some changes in the outward conditions of the region as a whole. The main key to these changes is the gradual advent of the steamship and, to a lesser extent, that of the railway, as carriers of the new industrial age into a still traditional pattern of life; if that is true, no apology is needed for focusing attention upon the Mediterranean considered internally as a network of communications and internationally as a through-route between Asia and the West. The political and strategical implications of these changes must be noticed, but not merely as part of the history of the several Mediterranean countries or of the two extra-Mediterranean powers, England and Russia, whose rivalry so much influenced the course of events within the region.

'The Mediterranean' is a name which has varied a little through the ages in meaning, and much more in its associations for its users. Whatever the geographer's definition may be, the historian will exclude the Black Sea; neither the poet Ovid in exile at Tomi nor the Empress Catherine II as conqueror of the Crimea could have any doubt that the Mediterranean was out of reach. The historian may still hesitate whether to stop, like the Admiralty's *Mediterranean Pilot*, at Gallipoli, but he will probably decide to reckon Constantinople among the Mediterranean ports and to regard the Bosporus instead as the gateway to a different world beyond. Even so, the extent is great. Constantinople and Port Said are each nearly 2000 sea miles distant from Gibraltar, and more than 1500 miles from Marseilles or Genoa by sea. Trieste is nearer than are the last two to Constantinople, but not much nearer to Port Said. (These distances compare with about 1300 sea miles from Gibraltar to London and less than 1900 from Glasgow to Newfoundland.) With this great extent, the Mediterranean is also a narrow sea, entered by narrow channels and pinched to several more or less narrow waists. The African coast is less than 90 miles from Sicily at one point (with the Island of Pantellaria in between), only 110 from Sardinia a little to the west and some 160 from Crete away to the east. The entrance to the Adriatic narrows to 40 miles. The Straits of Gibraltar are over 30 miles long and at one point less than 8 miles wide, while the Bosporus winds along for 16 miles, never more than 1 mile wide and sometimes much less. This extensive but land-locked and partially land-blocked sea is also a deep and salty sea, a nearly tideless sea, a sea with strong currents and finally a sea of sudden storms.

Where nature has provided so many channels, it is not surprising that the ancient world made use of slave-labour to cut more than one artificial canal; it is more surprising that the modern world waited so long to repeat the experiment on a larger scale. The advent of the machine provides only part of the explanation. Except in the last stages, the modern Suez canal was dug by Egyptian hand-labour, with comparatively little mechanical help; but it is true that without mechanical dredges the western approaches could hardly have been kept clear of silt from the Nile and that, but for the steamship, the project might never have matured.

The Mediterranean is more than a sea; the name means, too, all the coastlands for whose peoples this is the common sea, presenting them with a distinctive climate, similar natural products and a way of life which has for ages had recognisable similarities from end to end, and linking them together physically more than it separates them. Everywhere, the same rarity of frost or snow at sea-level, the same high average of sunshine, the same trees, the same olives and fruit and grain, and the same fish. Almost everywhere, too, in this period, the same still unexplained malarial fevers, the same fear of the plague and the same precautions against it. The value of these precautions was being questioned; in the 1830's Metternich vainly suggested a conference about the quarantine regulations, and one writer was soon arguing that most of them were unnecessary, since there had been no recent outbreaks at Marseilles, where the rules were less rigorously enforced, in spite of its busy trade with plague-stricken Egypt.[1] The suspicion was sometimes justified that the regulations were used by governments for searching letters and for obstructing politically unwelcome vessels and travellers. Such complaints were frequently made, for instance, about the quarantine station at the mouth of the Danube, in the main Sulina channel, during the period of Russian control there from the Treaty of Adrianople in 1829 to the Peace of Paris in 1856.

In the days of the leisurely Grand Tour, the discomforts and even hardships of Mediterranean travel might be softened by the wealth, or gilded by the poetical fancy, of the traveller; but steam navigation was

[1] J. Macgregor, *Commercial Statistics*, vol. 1 (London, 1844), pp. 1256 ff.

beginning to bring a new class, that of the 'tourist', who was full of practical and moral observations, and was apt to record his sufferings or his disapproval. One of the earliest, and one of the most tolerant, was Thackeray, who was commissioned, as the guest of a fast-developing shipping company, to popularise its new pleasure cruises.[1] But a cotton manufacturer on holiday in 1845, as a passenger in a succession of steamers, reiterated in his diary his complaints of dirt, fleas and bad food, and above all of the enforced delay of a fortnight in quarantine in the Lazzaretto on the Asiatic shore of the Bosporus.[2] Nevertheless, the habit spread, accompanied by a torrent of picturesque, romantic or optimistically utilitarian writings about the Levant, from which it is difficult to select reliable and comparable facts or even impressions.

Early in the nineteenth century much work was done in charting and surveying. A British naval officer, Rear-Admiral Smyth, who had done such work between 1810 and 1824, before the age of the steamship, wrote much later a kind of guide-book to the Mediterranean coasts, as a by-product of preparing nearly a hundred charts.[3] He began by quoting Dr Johnson's letter to Paoli: 'The grand object of travelling is to see the shore of the Mediterranean' from which came to us '...all our religion, almost all our arts, almost all that sets us above savages'. In the sequel he had little to say about this civilisation, but something to say about most of the ports. Much more systematic, and missing very little of the outward face of things, but generally barring politics, were the early series of guide-books which began with the steamships and the railways, and gave at least some reliable information, not only about the great cities and famous sites, but also about every little port which a traveller might now wish to visit, or find himself visiting in transit—John Murray's *Handbooks for Travellers* and Karl Baedeker's similar series. In addition, the age of commercial statistics was just beginning, bringing a mass of official and unofficial data. Such sources as these had the merit of asking much the same questions everywhere and of answering them in more or less common terms, so that a measure of statistical comparison is possible, however approximate and subject to hidden pitfalls.

A few very rough figures, almost all taken from one source, may give some indication of the relative activity of a number of ports in the first half of the period. These figures represent the tonnage of ships visiting each port in a year (that is, incoming plus outgoing, divided

---

[1] W. M. Thackeray, *Notes of a Journey from Cornhill to Grand Cairo...performed in the steamers of the Peninsular and Oriental Company* (London, 1846).

[2] Robert Heywood (Mayor of Bolton), *A Journey to the Levant in 1845* (privately printed, Cambridge, 1919).

[3] Rear-Admiral W. H. Smyth, *The Mediterranean: A Memoir Physical, Historical and Nautical* (London, 1854), refers mainly to conditions 30 years earlier. A more accurate, but later, source is *The Mediterranean Pilot*, compiled by the British Admiralty from its own and other surveys (1st edn, London, 3 vols., 1873–82).

by two).[1] The order of importance about 1870 is taken from another source.[2]

Order of impor-tance before 1850	Port	Ship-ping (in thou-sands of tons)	Order of impor-tance about 1870	Order of impor-tance before 1850	Port	Ship-ping (in thou-sands of tons)	Order of impor-tance about 1870
1	Constantinople	?	1	14	Nice	100	
2	Marseilles	500	2	15	Ancona	55	
3	Trieste	490	8	16	Venice	50	14
4	Leghorn	360	5	17	Palermo	45	7
5	Genoa	300	3	18	Fiume	40	16
6	Ionian Is. (all ports)	250		19	Salonica	40	15
7	Gibraltar	240		20	Beirut	40	
8	Barcelona	170	12	21	Cività-Vecchia	35	13
9	Messina	165	6	22	Crete (all ports)	35	
10	Malta	160		23	Piraeus	35	11
11	Alexandria	140	4	24	Naples	30	9
12	Smyrna	110	10	25	Cyprus (all ports)	30	
13	Syra	100		26	Patras	30	

The comparable figure for Cadiz was 165; for Odessa 160.

As to population, the figures are perhaps less unreliable, but they are even more deceptive. The commercial importance of a coastal town is not measured by the number of its inhabitants; some of the populous cities of Spain and south Italy, for instance, had poor harbours and compara-tively little trade. But such figures may serve to show the lines of change in fortune that political events or the economics of the steamship routes were bringing to the Mediterranean ports in this period. Those on page 420 are given, where possible, for two or three dates, one early in the period, one about the end of it and in some cases one about ten years later; the order is, approximately, that of the population about 1870. The order of importance in volume of shipping *before* 1850 (as suggested above) is shown as a figure before the name of each city. The figures are taken partly from earlier and later editions of Murray's *Handbooks* or McCul-loch's *Dictionary of Commerce*, and partly from *The Mediterranean Pilot* (1873–82).

A quick survey of the Mediterranean ports, gleaned from various sources and offered with all the necessary caution, may serve as a back-ground to the political and economic scene early in this period. Starting

[1] J. Macgregor, *Commercial Statistics*, vols. i and ii (1844), vol. v (1850). It is not always evident whether the tonnage of local coastwise shipping is included. No reliable figures could be found for Constantinople; it must have been among the first three, if not at the top. For Marseilles and Trieste, other sources had to be used.

[2] J. R. McCulloch, *A Dictionary of Commerce* (2nd edn, London, 1834; revised edn, 1871). McCulloch's data are not entirely comparable with Macgregor's, and he gives none for Gibraltar and Malta. Cf. also G. R. Porter, *The Progress of the Nation* (3 vols., London, 1836–43; 2nd edn, 1847; 3rd edn, 1851). All these made use of the British *Accounts and Papers*, which are well indexed.

Order of importance of shipping	Port	Population in thousands		
I	Constantinople	(no reliable figures, but probably at least half a million)		
24	Naples	(1845) 400	(1868) 450	(1881) 450
2	Marseilles	(1845) 170	(1870) 300	(1881) 318
11	Alexandria	(1847) 80	(1872) 212	(1881) 220
17	Palermo	(1847) 178	(1862) 187	(1881) 230
8	Barcelona	(1845) 140	(1869) 180	(1881) 243
12	Smyrna	(1840) 150	?	(1882) 180
5	Genoa	(1842) 114	(1871) 132	(1881) 168
?	Valencia	?	(1860) 108	(1881) 142
16	Venice	?	?	(1880) 130
?	Malaga	(1845) 51 ?	(1869) 110	(1881) 116
4	Leghorn	(1842) 60	(1861) 80	(1881) 100
	Toulon	(1845) 28 ?	(1869) 77	(1881) 77
3	Trieste	(1840) 57	(1871) 65	(1880) 90
?	Catania	(1846) 56	(1862) 64	(1881) 90
9	Messina	(1846) 58	(1861) 63	(1881) 70
19	Salonica	(c. 1840) 50 ?	(1872) 60	(1882) 65
23	Athens (with Piraeus)	(1840) 20	(1871) 60	?
14	Nice	?	(1870) 50	(1881) 50
20	Beirut	(1838) 20 ?	(1858) 45	(1881) 70
15	Ancona	(1843) 35	(1867) 30	(1880) 36
10	Malta (Valetta port)	?	(1873) 33 ?	(1878) 61
?	Cartagena	(1845) 30	(1869) 33	?
?	Alicante	(1845) 25	(1862) 32	(1881) 35
7	Gibraltar	(1840) 24	(1869) 25	?
26	Patras	(1840) 24	?	(1880) 26
13	Syra (Hermopolis port)	?	(1872) 16	(1881) 20
	Brindisi	(1853) 6	(1871) 14	(1881) 18
18	Fiume	?	(1871) 13	(1880) 20
21	Cività-Vecchia	(1843) 7	(1871) 12	?
	Port Said	—	(1875) 10	
	Pola	?	(1871) 6	(1881) 20

from Gibraltar, 'the great British depot for smuggling goods into the Peninsula' and therefore (as Thackeray went on to argue with an over-simplification characteristic of his age) the pioneer for the abolition of protective duties and of a chief reason for wars, we see in turn the cities of eastern Spain, more populous than busy, but getting busier as soon as they were all connected by railway with Madrid and with each other; Malaga, with its fine harbour badly silted up, but by 1870 inaugurating a screw steamship line direct to Boston, U.S.A.; Cartagena, decayed and neglected at first, but growing at the end; Alicante; Valencia, second only to Barcelona on this coast, with a port artificially much improved since 1792; Tortosa, reached with difficulty from the marshy delta of the Ebro; Tarragona, equally insignificant but with the walls of a large Roman city; and Barcelona itself, second city of Spain, 'the Manchester of Cata-lonia, which is the Lancashire of Spain'. Then Palma in Majorca, and the fine and healthy Minorcan harbour of Port Mahon, on which a British admiral could still cast a regretful and proprietary eye. Next, the French coast, from Cette (the port of Montpellier and exit of the old Languedoc canal) to Marseilles, a great city hard hit by the wars but quickly reviving, thanks to the steam packets and the new traffic with Algiers, and soon once more 'the best and busiest port of France' and of the whole Mediterranean too; Toulon with its naval arsenal but little commerce, and the huge roadstead of Hyères, where whole fleets could anchor safely. The 'commodious little port' of Nice, Italian until 1860, was becoming a prosperous health resort; and, beyond, the first wholly Italian city, Genoa, connected by rail with Turin and Milan and in 1870 just connected with Nice but not yet by a coastal line to the east. Genoa, with its old artificial harbour, formed by two great moles, had, well before 1870, steamships passing each way along the coast day by day, and was also the base of the small but select Piedmontese navy, whose admiral (in command about 1842) had been trained in the British naval service.

From this point onwards we hear much of 'pestilential exhalations' and prevailing coastal fevers. Tuscan Leghorn's spectacular growth, ascribed by some to its advantages as a free port and to religious toleration, was often contrasted with the comparative stagnation of Cività Vecchia, the port of Rome, whose fortifications had been designed by Michelangelo. Naples, for all its swarming population and its attractions for the traveller, was not so much a commercial port as a great city, set in a fertile plain, which happened to be on the coast; naval men were more interested in that 'little Gibraltar', the citadel of Gaeta, and commercial men paid more attention to the busy Sicilian ports of Palermo and, still more, Messina. The Adriatic coast had at first only Taranto, an ancient harbour long choked but still a big centre of fishery; Bari; and papal Ancona, now grown a little more active in trade than Venice in her decline, and allowing a complete toleration to its colony of several thousand Jews. Brindisi, still described in 1853 as a miserable and dilapidated haunt of malaria, had, fifteen years later, just become one of the ports of embarkation for Suez, but even in 1875 had little commerce apart from the 12,000 passengers who passed through in a year.

The outlook for the Austrian ports of the Adriatic seemed more promising. But Venice, in spite of the viaduct bridge of 4000 yards which connected it in 1845 by rail with the mainland, continued to lose ground to Trieste, which was quickly 'engrossing the entire trade of the Adriatic' and rising to the first rank among Mediterranean ports; once the difficult railway connection with Vienna was completed (after fifteen years' work on the final section from Laibach), full use could be made of the Austrian Lloyd shipping company, which had by 1871 one hundred steamships in direct connection not only with the Mediterranean but also with the Baltic and Atlantic ports of Europe and with the West Indies and the U.S.A. Pola, at first a fever-stricken and half-deserted town, was soon reviving as an Austrian naval arsenal, 'the Sebastopol of the Adriatic'; Fiume, though still in 1871 not connected by rail with the interior, was nevertheless 'the great seaport of the Kingdom of Hungary'. The lovely harbours of the Dalmatian coast (Lussinpiccolo, Zara, Sebenico, Spalato, Ragusa, Cattaro) were well protected, but hampered by lack of water and inland communications, and were of little more than local importance. Coming to the small ports of Albania and north-western Greece, the earlier accounts complained not only of fevers but, from this point onwards, of piracy too, with a belt of greater security in the British-occupied ports of the Ionian Islands, Corfu, Argostoli in Cephalonia (the best of these) and Zante.

Here the Levant began in earnest. The ports of Greece were, about 1840, beginning to recover from the disasters of the war of independence. Patras, at the mouth of the Gulf of Corinth, had been the chief outlet for the currant crop, but it never surpassed its older prosperity, and was giving way to a new rival, Piraeus (still known to many as Porto Leone). At the outset, Piraeus was merely 'a very convenient and sheltered port' though 'small and exporting little but oil'; by 1870 the steamships regularly called there. No longer were the tiny islands of Hydra and Spezzia (opposite Argos) 'the carriers of a large portion of the Levant Trade', and the population of Hydra fell from perhaps 40,000 in the 1820's to barely 12,000 in 1870. But the island of Syra was still enjoying a short-lived prosperity, due at first to its relative security for shipping during the troubles of the Greek revolt, and later as the chief entrepot for steamships distributing passengers and cargo all over the Aegean; in 1872 ten to twelve such ships called there each week, plying between Liverpool, Marseilles or Trieste and Smyrna or Constantinople, or locally to and from Piraeus, Crete (Candia) and the smaller islands. All this region was full of local activity; but Crete, though the giant among the islands, was repeatedly set back by the cycle of Turkish neglect, Greek revolts (1841, 1858, 1866) and Turkish reprisals. The roomy harbour of the island of Milo (Melos) was, in sailing days, 'frequented by almost all Levant shipping', including the naval squadrons of the powers, but it fell out of the race with the advent of steam. Of the islands off the coast of Asia Minor, Rhodes had long been in decay, with its two harbours almost choked; there was emigration from Samos and Lesbos (Mytilene), while Chios recovered in population and in agriculture, but not in commerce, from the massacre of 1822.

Of Smyrna, the only great port of Asia Minor, it was said in 1840 that 'she had ten times risen from her ruins with new splendour'; about half the population of 150,000 (rising to 180,000) were Turks, with some 40,000 Greeks, 10,000 Armenians and 15,000 Jews. Smyrna had a very long tradition of trade with western Europe, under the protection of a colony of some 5000 European merchants and their powerful consuls.

Still more cosmopolitan was Constantinople itself, with perhaps half a million people (and a great army of scavenging dogs) crowded within the huge extent of its old walls and spreading out into pleasant suburbs on the Bosporus and the Sea of Marmora. Already in 1840 a traveller might visit the newer activities of the naval arsenal, under an American director with Greek and Armenian artificers, the Military College and Military Hospital, the printing press of the *Moniteur Ottoman* (1831-), and the much older system of reservoirs which gave the city a plentiful water supply. Before 1870 there were many new developments, including Robert College (1863), promoted by the American Board of Protestant Missions and frequented not by Muslims but by Christians, especially by Bulgarians and Armenians. The commerce of Constantinople itself was perhaps not so great as that of Smyrna, but all the shipping from and to the Black Sea called there in passing, including the fast-growing traffic arising from the navigation of the Danube as an outlet for the exports (chiefly corn) of Hungary and the Balkan regions. There was no railway yet (except for the two short cuts from the Danube to the Black Sea, 100 and 120 miles north of the capital, for avoiding the river delta); but, by 1870, steamships of at least eleven nations were constantly putting in at Constantinople, including (among those carrying passengers) three English and three French companies, the Austrian Lloyd, more than one Russian line, one Turkish and one Egyptian company, and a number of small Greek enterprises. After Constantinople and Smyrna, the third port of Turkey was Salonica, growing fast and largely in the hands of prosperous Jewish families who had come long ago from Spain. Adrianople, though more populous than Salonica, was an inland city, only seasonally accessible for large boats by the navigable but much-silted river Maritza.

Turning southwards again from Smyrna, the traveller had little to notice along the southern coast of Asia Minor; Syria began with the 'unhealthy and dilapidated landing place' of Iskanderoon (Alexandretta), which had the only good anchorage off the Syrian coast and did a modest trade as the port for Aleppo; it was visited regularly by a French, and later by a Russian and an Egyptian, passenger-carrying steamer. Even in 1875 it had a population of only 1000 and a couple of jetties. In contrast, Beirut had a spectacular growth in trade, and its population trebled in the thirty years to 1868. The American mission, first established there in 1823, was followed by others and itself developed by 1866 into the Syrian Protestant College, ancestor of the American University of Beirut. The French had constructed a fine road to Damascus before 1870, and a London firm installed a water-supply a few years later, for this 'the commercial capital of Syria'. The other ports of Syria and Palestine were still inconsiderable; even Tripoli, Acre and Jaffa had little protection for more than small craft against the dangers of a lee shore during westerly gales.

Port Said, which had no existence until about 1860, had ten years later a population of 10,000, occupied entirely in maintaining the newly opened canal. At the other end, Suez, supplied with fresh water in 1863, was growing fast. In 1847 it had been described as 'a small and insignificant town, but not without interest...as the spot where the Israelites crossed the Red Sea'; yet it was then already necessary to describe it for the benefit of overland travellers to India. Until the canal was opened in 1869, Alexandria was the starting point of the overland route, which had been highly organised for some thirty years so as to transport passengers and mails via Cairo to Suez, first by river steamer and road and then (from 1854–8) by rail. Alexandria, already a busy cosmopolitan port of the Levant, grew from some 80,000 to more than 200,000 during the period; a quarter of the population consisted of foreigners, including about 20,000 Greeks, 14,000 Italians, 10,000 French, 5000 English and Maltese, and nearly 500 Germans or Austrians.

To come full circle, there remained only the inhospitable North African coast: Tobruk and Dernah, known only by name to European sailors; Benghazi, a small fortified town, with a good harbour but a narrow entry to it; Tripoli, from which a British naval survey officer in the 1820's had made some short journeys inland with a view to collecting information about the road to Timbuktu and the unmapped Niger river; then Tunis, with a fine anchorage and (in 1870) some 20,000 inhabitants; and, not far away, the Gulf of Bizerta, which sailors had already noticed as a potentially great harbour, naturally protected. The Algerian coastal towns were only precariously held by the French for many years after the first conquest in 1830, but grew in greater security from 1848 onwards. The city of Algiers itself had by 1870 a population of 70,000, and was in close contact with Marseilles, which regarded the whole colony almost as its own daughter. Finally, in nondescript Spanish Morocco, came Tetuan, with its 14,000 Moors and half as many Jews; Tangier, about half that size; and Ceuta, about as populous as Tetuan, but including a Spanish garrison of 3500 and some 2500 convicts.

These Mediterranean coastlands were in a sense more closely linked with each other by the sea than they were connected with their own hinterlands. The people of Marseilles shared experiences with those of Barcelona, and even of Alexandria, which they did not share with Paris; they had long been citizens almost of a republic within the kingdom of France, more interested in Africa and the Levant than in Versailles. Barcelona, too, had a seafaring tradition of its own, which owed little to Madrid. Of the other great ports, some, like Genoa and Venice, had been independent city states, while those of the Turkish Levant had often been able to ignore any native political authority above that of the local governor. There was never any question of a Mediterranean nationality, the very idea of which was excluded by traditional rivalries as much as by the religious cleavage in the Levant; but these were often the rivalries of sailors and traders, reflecting local differences of situation and interests, rather than the greater rivalries of dynasties or nations. For this reason there had usually been many cross-currents in Mediterranean politics and warfare.

Yet dynastic rivalries, too, had long entered into the pattern of Mediterranean politics, and were easily transformed into the rivalries of nations in the age of nationalities. To Colbert, and much more to Napoleon, Marseilles and Toulon were the commercial and naval springboards for great designs not locally conceived. To Madrid, Barcelona had been the link with Spanish Naples, and also with Habsburg Vienna via Leghorn, Milan and the Alpine passes. Genoa and Venice (though denied, as republics, the benefits of the doctrine of legitimacy and restoration in 1815) could not easily forget that they had been Mediterranean powers, and rivals on a large scale for the trade of the East. The Adriatic had been in a real sense a Venetian lake, its eastern coasts either Venetian or denied to rivals of Venice; this assumption was inherited, along with Venice and Trieste, by the Habsburg empire and in turn by the new Italian kingdom. In the Levant, the prestige of Venice had vanished with the loss of her commercial empire. Much more potent was the tradition of Byzantium, not only in the hearts of Orthodox Christians, but in the proud assumptions of the Turks themselves. The idea of Byzantium as mistress of the sea still survived at Constantinople, whenever the Ottoman navy sailed out to patrol the Aegean as far as Crete, or beyond to Syria and Egypt. The reality was now very different from the conception, but a revival did not seem impossible, for the Byzantine navy too had known times of humiliation followed by times of triumph. Equally, when a French naval squadron sailed into Greek waters in 1827, or to the coast of Syria a little later, the Latin empire of the thirteenth century was not entirely forgotten, whether by friend or enemy; and the name of France could still inspire more hopes and fears, either on traditional or on very modern grounds, than her presently reduced power seemed to justify.

The fact that from 1823 onwards the United States usually had a small naval squadron in the Mediterranean had no political importance at the time; but individual Americans made their mark, especially as philanthropists and missionaries, and 'American religion' became for a time the Levantine name for English-speaking Protestantism. Moreover, after 1848 the republics of America, both north and south, became the Mecca of many in search of a new start in life. This interest was reciprocal, and Mark Twain, in *The Innocents Abroad* (1870), shows the robustly Philistine American tourist beginning to be a little self-critical.

The sultan's command of the sea, and of the Levant generally, was now no longer challenged, within the Mediterranean, by Normans or Italians or Spaniards or even Frenchmen, but by his own insurgent subjects who dreamed, in Greece of a new Byzantium, or in Egypt of a new

Arab empire; and, from without, by that comparatively recent intruder, the British navy, or that other potential intruder from the new naval arsenals of Odessa and Sebastopol. Greece, Egypt, Britain, Russia—each spelt a different danger for the sultan.

The decision in 1830 to make the new Greece a small but independent kingdom, under the diplomatic guarantee of England, France and Russia as protecting powers, relieved both their own and the sultan's immediate anxieties. It recognised the presence on the stage of a new and unpredictable actor, representing hopes of future expansion and so of further changes; but, during the next forty years, the ambitions of the Greeks proved to be less disturbing to international affairs than to their own internal political stability. Neither the granting of a parliamentary constitution in 1843, nor the abdication of the Bavarian King Otto twenty years later in favour of Prince George of Denmark, nor again the British cession of the Ionian Islands to Greece on the same occasion, served at all to tip the balance of forces in favour of the Greeks. Their prospects in Crete, in Macedonia or in Asia Minor would depend, after 1878 as before, entirely upon their relations with each of the three protecting powers and upon the relations among these three from time to time (cf. ch. IX, p. 214).

Egypt was a second disturbing force, unpredictable and immediately much more alarming. The reappearance of North Africa in Mediterranean politics, as something more than a lair of 'Barbary pirates', began effectively with Napoleon I's expedition to Egypt, and the process could not be reversed by his ejection or by his final defeat. Mehemet Ali, the Albanian adventurer who ruled Egypt (1809–49) was no doubt a barbarian, but he was at least as intelligent as some of the rulers in Europe who were his contemporaries. His face was not turned only towards the Mediterranean, for he secured control of the Muslim Holy Places in Arabia and he was interested in the slaves and gold of the Sudan; but his position could never be secure while he was still only the sultan's viceroy. This made him deeply interested in the rivalries of the European powers at Constantinople, and at Cairo too; rivalries which he hoped to turn to his own advantage. If he preferred French to British soldiers, engineers and archaeologists, he also had a realistic respect for the British navy and desired to stand well with both France and England. In the Greek affair before 1830 he had been too deeply committed as the sultan's ally to withdraw without a show of fighting when England, France and Russia managed at last to agree on a joint intervention in favour of Greece; but he was careful to show these powers that he bore no malice for the destruction of his fleet, along with that of Turkey, at Navarino in October 1827, and that, while he kept Crete as the sultan's reward to him for his services, he was determined to rebuild his fleet and to prove to Europe that he would be a more reliable ally, and a more dangerous enemy, than the sultan himself. In the 'thirties, many Frenchmen believed that their old ally the sultan would do better for himself, and incidentally for France, by making large concessions to their new friend Mehemet Ali. Many, though not all, interested Englishmen took an opposite view; but both countries agreed in wishing to prevent the tsar from becoming the heir of the sultan.

Mehemet Ali refused in 1830 to be drawn into the French adventure which led to the conquest and settlement of Algeria. This enterprise, though less tempting to France than the historic lure of Egypt, was ultimately to prove more fruitful in opening up to her a great North African empire to offset her relative decline in Europe. The eastern and the western projects were closely linked in French minds at the start.[1] Polignac's first plan (September 1829) took up a recent suggestion by the French consul at Alexandria that Mehemet Ali should be induced to turn his eyes away from a lone adventure into Syria towards an attack upon Algiers in alliance with France. The viceroy pitched his terms so high (a loan of 20 million francs, free of interest, and a gift of four warships) that in January 1830 Polignac proposed instead a purely French attack on Algiers, with a loan of 10 million francs to Mehemet Ali if he would attack Tripoli and Tunis at the same time with 25,000 men. 'France would have reserved for herself the strategical points along the North African coast, and the viceroy, recognised as lieutenant of the king of France, would eventually, in spite of England, have carried French influence into the heart of Asia.'[2] But in February the viceroy decisively rejected even this more limited plan, on the grounds, partly that an enterprise against Muslim rulers, shared with a Christian power, would shake his prestige in the Muslim world, and partly that he was not prepared to face the known objections of England to such a plan. He told the British Consul at Alexandria that Turkey was finished, and that England should prepare to create a power in Asia to help her confront the Russians. Where could she find such a power but in Mehemet Ali and his son after him? With English friendship he could do anything, without it, nothing.[3] Consequently, France proceeded alone (June 1830) to capture the fortress of Algiers (and the treasure accumulated there by the Bey) at a moment when England was too much preoccupied to interfere. This first success was not undone by the fall of Charles X a month later; it was followed, under Louis Philippe, by a slow and costly struggle, whose final success came only on the eve of his own fall eighteen years afterwards. But, thereafter, with the decision in principle to treat Algeria, not as a colony but as an extension of France itself into Africa, develop-

[1] G. Douin, *Mohamed Aly et l'expédition d'Alger* (Cairo, 1930).
[2] Polignac, *Études historiques*, p. 227 (written after the fall of Charles X), quoted by G. Douin, *op. cit.* p. lviii.
[3] Consul Barker to Aberdeen, 8 March 1830, quoted by G. Douin, *op. cit.* p. xci.

ment went on steadily, not much affected by political revolutions in Paris, and nourished by the capital and the commercial enterprise of Marseilles and by settlers from the Mediterranean coastlands and the vineyards of southern France.

Mehemet Ali, having declined to be tempted by France in the west, was still determined to have Syria next, and believed that here at least he could play off France and England against each other, and both against Russia. France continued, indeed, to woo him as 'a Power naturally the friend of France and interested, like France, in the liberty of the Mediterranean';[1] but she wanted to use him as her tool against British preponderance, whereas his only object was to make use of any of the powers, or of the rivalries between them, for his own purposes. In England he had his advocates, but he was to have no success in his attempts to woo Palmerston, who was at this moment interested in the project of an 'alternative route' to the East through Syria and across the desert to the Euphrates, and thence down the river by steamboat to the Persian Gulf. Nevertheless, without any certainty of effective support even by France, or of acquiescence by England in a *fait accompli*, he proceeded alone into Syria (November 1831) and into Asia Minor a year later, rashly forgetting his own words of wisdom. The victory of his son Ibrahim at Konieh (21 December 1832) opened the road towards Constantinople, and converted an important but local issue into a major threat to the independence of Turkey, a threat coming not so much from Mehemet himself as from the Russians in their new role of patron-protectors of a feeble sultan (ch. x, pp. 251–2). Probably Mehemet was relieved to be halted by the obviously unanswerable argument of a Russian fleet and army inside the Bosporus; in the general alarm at that sight, he was able to obtain as much as he had ever expected from this campaign, namely the government of Syria, Acre and Damascus for himself, and that of Adana for his son, Ibrahim, the commander of his armies. Perhaps he would have been wiser not to insist upon so much.

The sultan was determined upon revenge. Palmerston was equally determined to undo the Russo-Turkish treaty of Unkiar Skelessi, to expel Mehemet Ali from Syria, and if possible force him to give up his system of state monopolies in trade. It appears that the secret article of this treaty of 8 July 1833 was not so alarming as was supposed, for the Russian government considered itself as much bound as the sultan to keep the Dardanelles closed to foreign warships, even Russian ones, in time of peace; but it was not so certain that this principle applied to the Bosporus under this treaty, and there remained the threat of an

[1] Sébastiani's instructions to Mimaut, the French Consul at Alexandria, 20 July 1832, quoted by G. Douin, *La Mission du Baron de Boislecomte: l'Égypte et la Syrie en 1833* (Cairo, 1927), p. 1.

apparent Russian 'protectorate' over Turkey.[1] The Anglo-Turkish Trade Convention of Balta Liman (16 August 1838), on the other hand, was equally believed by the Russians to have unfriendly political implications; if Mehemet Ali should refuse to recognise it as applying to Egypt, because that would involve giving up his monopolies, England might have a good legal case for coercing Mehemet Ali into submission on the sultan's behalf. For this reason, among others, he had been pressing for recognition of his independence, so that Egypt would not be affected by the Anglo-Turkish Convention. The sultan rashly played into his hands by initiating, without any ally, an attack on the Egyptians in Syria in the spring of 1839; in a single week his army was defeated at Nezib, his fleet deserted to the Egyptians, and he himself died (1 July) before the news of these disasters reached Constantinople.[2]

Mehemet Ali was not to enjoy the fruits of these successes. Since no one of the powers could hope alone to impose a settlement, all five endorsed the action of their ambassadors at Vienna (27 July 1839) in warning the Porte, at Metternich's instance, not to make hasty concessions to Mehemet Ali without their consent. The French did so with reserve, not wishing to see Mehemet Ali any more than the sultan humiliated, and refused to press upon him the terms which were suggested by Palmerston. Reassured as to the intentions of Russia on this occasion at least, Palmerston felt safe, after a struggle with his cabinet, in imposing a settlement without France, by means of the four-power Convention of London (15 July 1840), which envisaged, first the coercion of Mehemet if necessary, and secondly a reassertion of the principle of the closure of the Straits. Deceived by the bellicose attitude of his friends in France, Mehemet refused both stages of the offer made to him, and submitted to the powers only in December 1840, after a display of force against him by land and sea on the coast of Syria, and after the dramatic fall of Thiers' government in October. His reconciliation with Turkey, on the conditions imposed by the powers, was not complete until the end of June 1841; he secured a hereditary right to Egypt under the nominal suzerainty of the sultan, but had to restore everything else.

In July 1841 France came back into the fold by signing a five-power Straits Convention which provided that both the Dardanelles and the Bosporus should be closed to the passage of warships when Turkey was not at war. In spite of later denials, it was not intended that even a request by the sultan should justify entry in peace-time without the agreement of all the signatory powers. The principle was not new, but it now rested on a formal international pact, which was reasserted in 1856 and 1871 and never repudiated.

---

[1] P. E. Moseley, *Russian Diplomacy and the Opening of the Eastern Question in 1838 and 1839* (Harvard, 1934), ch. II and App. A.

[2] Cf. ch. X, pp. 254-8 for a fuller account of the Near Eastern crisis of 1839-41.

Thus, at the price of a serious but not insuperable rift in the Anglo-French *entente*, this settlement of Egypt put an end to the alarms occasioned by the ambitions of Mehemet Ali outside Egypt over the past twenty years. The French expedition to Syria in 1860 arose directly out of local massacres which Turkish misrule had failed to prevent; it was undertaken with the assent of the other powers in the midst of the Italian crisis, and was brought to an end within a year by the insistence of England, which suspected a revival of French ambitions in the Near East under Napoleon III. Anglo-French relations were again to be strained because of the strategical position of Egypt in relation to the Suez Canal, but that issue must be treated separately and it did not reach its climax until the British occupation of Egypt in 1882. The influence of France in the Levant, though often politically unpredictable, was strong and constant in sentiment and culture, based in Egypt on the impress of Napoleon and everywhere else on more traditional links. The French influence in these fields remained stronger on the whole than the British influence; yet it was far less radically different from the British than was that of Russia.

The other two forces mentioned above, England and Russia, cannot well be treated separately. It was the predominance, in any emergency, of British sea-power in the Levant and the pressure of Russian influence in the Levant, and the hostility between these two external powers, that gave a new and distinctive character to Mediterranean politics during the half-century 1828–78. It is true that the tension between the two was relaxed for more than ten years after the settlement of Egypt and the Straits in 1841, but to some people in both countries that seemed to be an unnatural interlude, and the advent of the Crimean War to be a recognition of the true situation created by the weakness of Turkey as a buffer between the despotic empire of Russia and the commercial empire of Great Britain. However natural the Russian interest in the Mediterranean might be, it was to most Englishmen a new and portentous thing, whereas their quarrels with France in this region seemed traditional, almost domestic.[1] The French, too, though unwilling to see Britannia ruling the waves, or British influence taking the lead over the French in the Levant, preferred the British fact to the Russian prospect. The other Mediterranean powers were really of the same mind; during the Crimean War, the Austrian government showed a very benevolent neutrality to France and England, and Cavour, in sending a Piedmontese contingent to the siege of Sebastopol, was not only seeking future favours with France and England for his designs in Italy, but also staking the claim of Italy as a future Mediterranean power, a claim which he knew could not be made good in opposition to Britain and one which Russia could do nothing to promote. A leading argument of the Piedmontese Cesare

[1] For the Crimean War, see ch. XVIII.

Balbo's *Hopes of Italy* (1843) had been that, once the Austrians should have withdrawn from Italy, they would find the Italians their natural allies in helping to stem and turn back the tide of the Slavs, especially in the Adriatic. The same anti-Slav note was heard in the early writings of Karl Marx. From one point of view, therefore, the Crimean War was almost a crusade of liberal and radical Europe, and indeed of Catholic Europe too, against 'the despot of the north' and the oppressor of the Poles, whose distinguished exiles, Slavs though they might be, were so vocal in the opposite camp (cf. ch. IX, p. 234).

This widespread and often exaggerated fear of Russia and the Slavs was one reason why the nations which bordered the Mediterranean acquiesced in the lesser evil of allowing the British to become a predominant influence in Mediterranean politics. A second compelling reason was the overwhelming strength of the British navy when it was exerted. It was too much to say that no changes could happen without British blessing, but at least any changes which happened without it could usually be rendered harmless to Britain by some counter-move. A third reason was the leading position of England in the manufacture and management of the new machines. Up to at least the middle of the century, most of the steamships, under whatever flag they sailed, were built either in England or under British direction, and British engineers often had a hand in operating them too; the same was true of the railways, starting a little later.

A few small ships began to use auxiliary steam in Italian coastal waters as early as 1818–19 (Sicily–Naples–Genoa–Marseilles, also Trieste–Venice). The British Admiralty's armed packets, which carried mails and a few passengers from Falmouth to Gibraltar and Malta, also began to use steam in 1830. By 1837 mails and passengers were being taken weekly to Gibraltar, fortnightly on to Malta and Corfu, and monthly on from Malta to Alexandria, whence they were transported by one of two rival agencies (both British) to Cairo and across the desert to Suez, and so carried monthly to Bombay by the new armed steamers of the Indian navy. This led Britain to occupy Aden as a coaling-station in 1839, and to see a new reason for confining the power of Mehemet Ali to Egypt alone. In 1837 the mail contract as far as Gibraltar was transferred to the Peninsular Steam Navigation Company, which was already operating six large steamers (500–900 tons). Two years later an arrangement was made with the French government for the eastern mails to be carried overland to Marseilles and thence by an Admiralty steam-packet to Malta and Alexandria; but Lord William Bentinck, for the East India Company, pressed for an all-British route, and in December 1840 the Peninsular *and Oriental* Steam Navigation Company was incorporated by royal charter on condition of establishing within two years a mail service to India, and a subsidiary service from Malta to Corfu.

By 1842 the P. and O. Company had absorbed two rivals (the East India Steam Navigation Company and the Eastern Steam Navigation Company), and secured the mail contract from Suez to Ceylon, Madras and Calcutta; this was extended in 1844–5 to Penang, Singapore and Hong Kong, and in 1851–2 from Singapore to Australia and New Zealand. Until 1854 the Company was obliged to leave the Suez–Bombay route to the East India Company's own service. In 1858 the discomforts of the overland portion were much reduced by completion of the railway from Alexandria to Suez, and in 1869 the official guests for the opening of the canal were brought in a P. and O. liner from Marseilles. By 1870, passengers could travel by rail to Brindisi, and thence by sea. The company launched services to Greece and Turkey in the 1840's, during the boom in Levantine trade which followed the British Trade Convention of 1838 with Turkey and the repeal of the Corn Laws in 1846. In 1844 the company advertised cruises for health and pleasure, which soon had the blessing of the *British Medical Journal*. Several other British companies began about the same time to operate regular steamship lines in the Mediterranean; but the chief rivals of the P. and O. were the French company which became the Messageries Maritimes (Messageries Impériales, 1852–70), and the Austrian Lloyd.

The Messageries, having begun as carriers by land, contracted in 1851–2 to carry the French mails from Marseilles to Italy and the Levant, adding the Algerian mails in 1854, new mail services to the Black Sea and also to South America in 1857, and to India and China in 1861. At first, most of their ships were built in England, but long before 1870 the Messageries had their own shipyards and had become much the largest carriers in the Mediterranean, with constant official support and no French rivals. The Austrian Lloyd Steam Navigation Company of Trieste, which started in 1833 as a shipping agency, began to own steamships in 1836 and provided the first regular service to Constantinople. It 'owed its origin chiefly to the conviction that the revival of Egypt, the emancipation of Greece... had caused a great revolution in trade and prepared its return to the ancient channel to Asia'.[1] Although this enterprise never reached the stature of the P. and O. or the Messageries, the revival of Trieste owed much to its growth. Genoa provided two Italian enterprises, the Società Sarda (1830) for Mediterranean traffic, and the well-known Società Rubattino (1840), which later came to specialise in eastern trade, launched a through-service to Bombay in 1857, acquired Assab as a coaling-station in 1869 (before it became an Italian colony in 1882) and eventually in 1881 amalgamated with the business of Florio (Palermo) which had started in 1849. The combined business, under the title 'Navigazione

---

[1] F. v. Raumer, *Italy and the Italians* (London, 1840), vol. I, p. 56. See p. 437, below. See also *Enciclopedia Italiana*, s.v. *Trieste;* and A. Tamaro, *Storia di Trieste*, 2 vols. (Rome, 1924), vol. II, ch. 37.

generale Italiana' was later still to obtain a large subsidy and for a time a virtual monopoly in Italy.

British supremacy in the Mediterranean was not very obtrusive. Gibraltar, which became a Crown Colony in 1840 (previously just a 'fortress'), was irritating to the Spanish customs and excise authorities, but did not give rise in this period to much public expression of Spanish resentment, or to any serious political incidents. Malta was not unprosperous, and Italians had more urgent tasks than to pay much attention to it yet. British influence in the Levant was devoted to the negative role of countering that of Russia at Constantinople and that of France at Cairo, and to ensuring that, while an active British control over the new routes to India would cost too much in political friction and perhaps in military effort, yet those routes should at least not be both developed and controlled by any rival European power.

British power was most evident in Palmerston's duel with Thiers over Syria in 1839–40 (see pp. 256–7); in his naval coercion of Greece in 1850 and 1854–6; and in the effect of benevolent neutrality towards Cavour's conquest of Sicily and Naples by means of the 'private enterprise' of Garibaldi in 1860 (cf. ch. xxi). The rebuff to Russia in 1856 was the work of France and England jointly, with the support of neutral Austria; but the character of the Crimean War, and the terms of the peace, reflect the share of British sea-power in the result. As a postscript to this period, British influence was seen again in Disraeli's peaceful assertion of an interest in the Suez Canal by the purchase of the Khedive's shares in 1875; in his denial to the Russians of the fruits of their victory in 1878 by another demonstration of sea-power, reinforced by the occupation of Cyprus as a symbol of that power for possible future use; and finally in the occupation of Egypt in 1882. But British supremacy was not pressed home except where major British interests appeared to be directly at stake. Moreover, it was not always entirely effective, as incidents at the beginning and at the end of the period showed. In 1830 and onwards no serious attempt was made to obstruct the French conquest and colonisation of Algeria, however suspicious the duke of Wellington, the Admiralty and the Colonial Office might feel about it. In 1870 Russia was able, during the crisis of the Franco-Prussian War, to denounce the neutralisation of the Black Sea, a provision which, however unreasonable and hard to enforce, had been regarded in England as a major achievement of the Peace of Paris (1856). Meanwhile, in the 'sixties, Britain had withdrawn, voluntarily and more or less gracefully, in favour of Greece, from half a century's uneasy protectorate in the Ionian Islands (cf. p. 242); and the Suez Canal had been completed by French enterprise, in the teeth of British political obstruction, but with vocal support, in the later stages, from important sections of British commercial opinion.

The economic and strategical consequences of the opening of the canal lie outside the scope of this chapter, and some of them were to affect the Atlantic nations and those of the East even more than the Mediterranean peoples themselves. The effect of the canal upon the latter might be compared, in a sense, to that of the construction of an arterial road or railway for through-traffic upon the towns and villages near which it passes, giving new economic activity to some, by-passing others, and in a way reducing the purely local importance of all. Yet the Mediterranean countries had the greatest share in the project and its execution, and the expected or imagined consequences are very relevant. This aspect of Mediterranean history in the period 1830–70 has a peculiar interest and deserves attention in some detail even at the risk of overemphasis. The early pioneers of the idea of a canal had an almost religious belief in the unlimited prosperity which it was to bring to the Mediterranean region by eliminating the British monopoly of trade with India and the Far East and bringing them into direct commercial contact with the Mediterranean. This hope was disappointed; for, although there was to be a rapid increase in the direct trade of the Mediterranean ports with India and beyond, and some relative decline in the British share, yet the British were to be the principal users of the canal from the first; and the next largest users in 1910 were to be, not the French or the Italians, but the Germans and the Dutch.[1] But, in the early days, it was this hope which fired imaginations in Marseilles, in Trieste, and also in Germany.

Ferdinand de Lesseps, while he was French vice-consul at Alexandria in 1832–3 at the age of 27, and then consul at Cairo for four years, read the report of Napoleon's engineer, Le Père, and, more important, made friends with Said, the future ruler of Egypt; but Le Père's report of a drop of 33 feet in level from the Red Sea to the Mediterranean was not disproved until 1847, and de Lesseps did not study the question very seriously until his diplomatic career had come to an end in 1849 as a result of his conduct of the French negotiations with Mazzini's Roman republic. He owed the missionary conception of the project to others, particularly to Michel Chevalier, Enfantin and the school of Saint Simon, by which he was himself influenced in a general way. Already in 1832 Chevalier had been arguing that, in the new and by nature pacific world of industrialists and bankers, a republican regime in France would lead

---

[1] C. W. Hallberg, *The Suez Canal: its history and diplomatic importance* (New York, 1931). The figures are taken from App. 1.

	No. of transits	Net tonnage (000)	Av. tonnage	No. of passengers (000)	British share of tonnage (%)
1870	486	436	under 1,000	27	71
1880	2,026	4,344	over 2,000	101	c. 80
1900	3,441	9,738	nearly 3,000	282 }	
1910	4,538	16,585	over 3,500	234 }	c. 70
1930	5,761	31,700	over 5,500	326	c. 56

only to war, which in turn could be waged only by stimulating the fever of democracy and so dissipating the newly accumulated wealth; but that this conflict could be avoided by the system of 'hierarchical association'. Moreover, it was no longer the Christian peoples only who were athirst for progress. The plan of pacification must therefore rest upon conciliation between the East and the West, in a system destined to regenerate the countries bordering on the Mediterranean, which 'will become the marriage bed of East and West'. In the material order, the railway was the most perfect symbol of universal association, turning what were at present great nations into no more than middling provinces. A future age might discover a motive power less complicated and less wasteful than the steam engine; but meanwhile steam would propel traffic by railways, navigable rivers and canals, between a Mediterranean port in each country and a different sea beyond; from Barcelona by way of the Ebro to Madrid and down the Tagus to Lisbon; from Marseilles up the Rhône to Lyons, by the Loire valley to Paris and down the Seine to Le Havre; or (in the reverse direction) from Amsterdam by the Rhine to Frankfurt, across to the Danube and so down by Belgrade either to the Black Sea or to Salonica; or again, from the Baltic up the Vistula and down the Russian river ways to the Black Sea and so on to Astrakhan and the Caspian; or finally from south Germany by railway over to Trieste and Venice. The material emblem of Italian unity would be the railway. The Adriatic would become the outlet by which Germany was destined to distribute over the Mediterranean region her own products and those of the Scandinavian countries. By another route, railways would connect Constantinople and Aleppo with the Euphrates and so with Baghdad and the Persian Gulf. In addition, the North African coast would be served by a continuous line from Ceuta to Alexandria. Finally, 'let us imagine that, to set in motion the double current which would flow to old Asia from Europe and from America, the two isthmuses of Suez and Panama are pierced, and then conceive, if we can, the delightful picture which the ancient Continent would soon present to our eyes'. All this might cost eighteen milliards of francs—no more, said Chevalier, than England had borrowed in sixty years for making war, and no more than the great nations were now spending in twelve years on the upkeep of armies and navies in time of peace. 'Such is our political plan....Combined with the moral achievement projected by our Supreme Father, this plan, which is the material aspect of the other, will one day ensure the triumph of our Faith.'[1]

Enfantin, the Supreme Father, conceived, while in prison (December

[1] M. Chevalier, *Politique industrielle et système de la Méditerranée* (Paris, 1832), reprinted from articles in the Saint-Simonian journal *Le Globe*, which ceased publication in April 1832. The argument summarised above comes from pp. 111–50 (January–February 1832). See also P. Lajard de Puyjalon, *L'influence des Saint-Simoniens sur la réalisation de l'isthme de Suez et des chemins de fer* (Paris, 1926).

1832–August 1833), the idea of a mission to Egypt, to promote education, and to study projects for a Nile barrage and above all for the canal which, he was convinced, could and would be achieved by himself and his friends. Enfantin and most of his fifty followers returned from Egypt in 1837, having made no progress in face of Mehemet Ali's scepticism or disinclination to offend the English. During 1839–40 French eyes were fixed on Syria rather than on Egypt; but in 1844 Chevalier reopened the question with an article in the *Revue des Deux Mondes*, and in 1845–6 Enfantin, now a director of the company which was building the Paris–Lyon–Méditerranée railway, launched his project, well-supported by French engineers and financiers and by the House of Orleans, but attempting also to enlist the co-operation of an Austro-German and an English group. The leaders of the French group consisted of Enfantin, the three brothers Talabot (all railway engineers) and Arlès-Dufour, a merchant of Lyons. Those of the Austro-German group were A. Dufour-Feronce, a Leipzig merchant and cousin of Arlès-Dufour, and L. Negrelli, chief engineer to the Austrian state railways (1842–8), who in turn had some influence with Baron K. L. von Bruck, a co-founder and director of the Austrian Lloyd Steamship Company at Trieste.[1] Metternich and A. von Humboldt had already shown a cautious interest both in this company and in the canal group and in June 1846 Negrelli presented a memorandum to the Austrian Finance Minister, claiming that opinion in England was beginning to see the political necessity of a canal for the safety of her rule in India, in spite of a purely commercial dread of losing her monopoly; 'on the day that the canal was opened, Vasco da Gama's discovery would lose its prime importance, the greatness of Venice and her younger Adriatic neighbours would revive, and the blessings of commerce would flow first over Austrian Italy, Tyrol, Carinthia and Carniola, and soon over the whole region of Austria to the neighbouring lands'. Negrelli suggested that, by means of two locks, the presumed flow from the Red Sea down to the Mediterranean could be controlled so as to scour the silt from the western approaches.

The English 'group' consisted merely of Robert Stephenson and his friend H. Starbuck, and it was never ardent or active. During the 'thirties, Lieut. Thomas Waghorn, R.N., had been promoting a business for conducting passengers and goods between Alexandria and Suez, and had merged with a competitor in 1841; but two years later Mehemet Ali granted the monopoly to an Egyptian Transit Company. In 1841 Arthur

---

[1] For the Austro-German activity, see Dr Georgi and A. Dufour-Feronce [grandson of the person mentioned in the text], *Urkunden zur Geschichte des Suez-Kanals* (Leipzig, 1913)—a valuable collection of letters concerning a little-known but significant episode. Negrelli's memorandum, pp. 21–6. For Negrelli, who died in 1858, see Wurzbach's *Biographisches Lexicon*. Bruck became Finance Minister in 1855, after two years as ambassador at Constantinople, where he met de Lesseps. If the role of the Austro-German group has often been underrated, it has been overrated by some German writers.

Anderson, a founder and director of the P. and O., had written to Palmerston, after a visit to Egypt, suggesting that the time had come to consider a canal; the viceroy's French engineer, Linant Bey, still assuming a difference in level between the two seas, was for a canal from Suez to Cairo, using the Nile on to Alexandria. But British interests, both individual and public, were opposed to it. Waghorn was publicly committed to the land transit, and soon Stephenson was to declare, on technical grounds, in favour of the much cheaper expedient of a railway by the same route. Palmerston was, for political reasons, more interested in the idea of an alternative route through Syria to the Euphrates and the Persian Gulf—a Syria which was therefore detached from French influence by his insistence in 1840 upon expelling the Egyptians and restoring it to Turkish rule.

From this point onwards the canal scheme was no longer specifically Saint-Simonian. On 30 November 1846 the three groups signed a form of agreement for a *Société d'Études du Canal de Suez*, with headquarters in Paris, each group undertaking to provide a consulting engineer and subscribers for 50,000 francs; provision was made for the eventual formation of a new society for executing any plan which should jointly be found practicable, with an agreed proportion of shares reserved for these founder-members and for the three engineers, Paulin Talabot, Louis Negrelli and Robert Stephenson. To Talabot was assigned a survey of the isthmus itself, and in 1847 his assistants proved that no difference in levels existed; but they were inclined, all the more, to fear silting at the western end, and joined with Linant Bey in preferring a canal from Suez to the Nile only. Negrelli's Austrian team, who studied the western approaches, reported that the cost of dredging would be formidable, but that no other obstacle existed. This group was now keener than any, particularly in Trieste, where the Austrian Lloyd Company, the Chamber of Commerce and the city itself became (with the Chamber of Commerce of Venice) subscribing members of the group. They hoped that Trieste would one day become the headquarters of the whole enterprise, and so outstrip Marseilles before her supremacy should be assured by completion of the railway to the French Atlantic ports and by the development of her great network of steamship lines; for this reason they were inclined to doubt the zeal of the French group.[1] They were also anxious to convert the British, by the argument, for instance, that, if Europe allowed the opening of an American transcontinental railway to California and a steamship line from there to China, and even the piercing of the American isthmus, to be completed before the Suez Canal, the centre of the world's business would soon be transferred from London to New York and from Europe to America; if America took the lead, England and Europe would

[1] *Urkunden zur Geschichte...*, Dufour-Feronce to Negrelli, 5. ii. 48 (pp. 107–8), 17. x. 50 (pp. 128–9).

be ruined, and Russia alone, resting on a different basis from that of central and western Europe, would found on their ruins a new Asiatic power.[1]

On the other hand, the English group's share of the expenses was borne by Stephenson alone; and he was already half a sceptic; asked to report on Suez and the Red Sea approaches, which presented no difficulty, he was able to make use of existing Admiralty charts without the expense of any special survey party, but still threw cold water on the scheme and recommended a railway instead. The other groups complained that he should have warned them and resigned from the society if he believed a railway and a canal to be incompatible, but it was their opinion that the railway would only prove the need of a canal also.[2] During the lull caused by the revolutions of 1848 and the illness and death of Mehemet Ali, the railway plan gained ground. Already in 1847 Palmerston was pressing it upon the viceroy and obtaining a promise from the sultan to favour it. In March 1849 Sir John Pirie, with some directors of the P. and O. Company, came to Egypt, offering to lend money to construct a railway for the Egyptian government, using British engineers. Mehemet Ali, who was always opposed to any project which he could not fully control, played off the British railway against the French canal and the canal against the railway, and said he would prefer to build a Nile dam before either; but, on his death in August 1849, the new viceroy, Abbas Pasha, accepted the new British argument that a railway, unlike a canal, was an internal project needing no permission from the sultan (a permission which he knew that England could deter the sultan from giving for a canal); and in July 1851 he signed with Stephenson a contract for the first section from Alexandria to Cairo. This was completed in 1854; another English firm obtained in 1855 the contract for the second section, Cairo to Suez, which was opened in 1858.

Meanwhile, de Lesseps had in 1852 tried in vain to win Abbas for the canal; the decisive turn in his favour came with the death of Abbas in September 1854 and his own dramatic intervention. Hurrying to Egypt, he obtained in November from his old friend Said, now viceroy, first a verbal promise and then a formal concession for ninety-nine years in favour of an international company under a director (de Lesseps), appointed by the Egyptian government which was to receive 15 per cent of the net annual profits. Of the remaining profits, 10 per cent was to go to the founder-members and 75 per cent to the company's shareholders, including the Egyptian government in respect of any shares that it might purchase. The international character was preserved by the provision

---

[1] *Urkunden zur Geschichte...*, Dufour-Feronce to Starbuck, 16. vii. 50 (pp. 127–8); to Negrelli, 14. v. 52 (pp. 141–2).

[2] *Ibid.* Enfantin to Dufour-Feronce, 7. ix. 51; Duveyrier to Dufour-Feronce (quoting Bruck), 21. xii. 51 (pp. 138–41).

that the tolls should be the same for the vessels of all nations, but there was no mention of the *Société d'Études*; the German group, at first delighted, soon began to take alarm and before long to question the good faith of de Lesseps.[1] This *coup*, for it was no less, had many repercussions. The whole scheme was still subject to ratification by the sultan. The French government, in alliance with England in the Crimea, hesitated to approve and, after an ominous delay, British official hostility was made known in the summer of 1855 by a dispatch to Paris and more publicly by the rebuffs which de Lesseps received in London from Palmerston and Clarendon. Nevertheless, he was able in January 1856 to announce, first that his own international commission had reported unanimously to the viceroy in favour of a direct canal, which would be both technically and financially practicable; and secondly that the viceroy had made a revised and more detailed concession to him in favour of his company. This contained a stipulation (relaxed in 1865) that most of the labourers should be Egyptians; it also fixed the maximum tolls for goods and passengers, made provision for possible renewal after ninety-nine years on terms more favourable to Egypt, and settled the constitution of the company, with its legal and administrative headquarters in Paris.

The fact that all the advocates of the canal in Egypt were French, or partisans of France, and that it now appeared more than ever as a French enterprise, had the effect of stiffening British opposition. De Lesseps had no success with the Peace Congress in Paris; and though he found influential supporters in London, Palmerston was adamant in the Commons (7 July 1857). In January 1858 the sultan was told that, if he consented, the British guarantee of Turkey would lapse, and in June a debate in the Commons ended with a big majority for the government (290 to 62). Yet in October de Lesseps launched his prospectus with reasonable success; more than 200,000 shares were at once taken up in France and some 100,000 in Turkey and Egypt. In April 1859 he actually began work at the future Port Said; he ignored two successive notes of veto from the sultan to the viceroy, and at last (26 October 1859) secured the open support of the French emperor. Hitherto, Napoleon III, though he had given an encouraging interview to Enfantin (10 April 1855)[2] and had left no room for doubting his personal interest, had never committed his government; but now he gave up any appearance of neutrality. In spite of Turkish manœuvres and a British memorandum reaffirming the 'insuperable objections of H.M. Government to the projected Suez Canal', de Lesseps kept the ear of the viceroy, who accepted in May 1860 the unsubscribed shares (113,642 in number) and soon started down the slope towards bankruptcy by borrowing from French banks at a high rate of

---

[1] *Ibid.* Arlès-Dufour to Negrelli, 20. xii. 54 (pp. 154–5); Dufour-Feronce to Enfantin, 19. ii. 55 (pp. 178–9), and to Negrelli, 5. iii. 55 (pp. 171–3).
[2] *Ibid.* Enfantin to Negrelli, 16. iv. 55 (pp. 174–6).

interest. On Said's death in January 1863 the troubles which had been accumulating over the supply of forced labour, and the ever-increasing costs of the work, came to a head; but the continued support of the new viceroy, Ismail, encouraged de Lesseps to ignore renewed Turkish threats. It appeared that England would no longer press her objections to the limit; on successive petitions from the directors (6 January 1864 and 4 February 1865), Napoleon III agreed, first to arbitrate on financial issues between the company and the viceroy, and then to use his influence with the sultan. Finally, on 19 March 1866 the sultan gave his consent, and de Lesseps reported his triumph to a meeting of shareholders in August. Palmerston had died a few months earlier.

The work itself, begun in April 1859, had moved slowly at first; early in 1862 the essential freshwater canal from the Nile reached Lake Timsah, and at the end of that year Mediterranean waters flowed into the lake. In the next two years very little progress was made, but from 1865 new life was given to the work by the greater use of machinery (made necessary by the abandonment of forced labour) and, still more, by the fading of political obstacles. By a channel of ninety miles, one-third of it through lakes, the waters of the two seas met in the Bitter Lakes in August 1869. In the opening procession of vessels on 17 November all the rulers of Europe were represented. It was the last day of glory for Napoleon III. Prosperity for the shareholders, mainly French, though long delayed was ultimately enormous. The cost, originally estimated by Linant in 1842 at less than 4 million francs, amounted in the end to 400 millions, and the prospect was at first so bleak that, in the eclipse of France, it was suggested in 1871, and again in 1874, that the company should sell the whole enterprise to the European powers jointly under international control; but no action was taken. When the Viceroy, now independent with the title of khedive, was forced by ruin to sell his shares in 1875 French interests failed to agree quickly enough upon finding the money; this alone gave Disraeli the opportunity to take what appeared to many Englishmen to be a serious risk. Commercially these fears were belied, but politically and strategically the canal was to bring for England almost as many troubles as advantages. The purchase of these shares gave her a voice, but not a controlling voice, in the management, and nothing short of an occupation of Egypt could make her feel secure.

The leading themes of this chapter have been the material developments of an expanding economy and their direct consequences. Nothing has been said of Italy, absorbed as she was in the struggle for unity, of the Roman question with its world-wide implications, of the civil wars in Spain, the growing-pains of Greece, or the processes of change, within the Muhammadan world from Constantinople all the way round to Morocco, which were mostly superficial as yet, but would issue before long in startling and apparently sudden transformations. These new movements and influences were not all due to material changes; they flowed as much from the infectious ideas of the American and French revolutions, and the restlessness of mind which the upheavals of the Napoleonic wars produced, as from any purely economic causes; but, among the carriers of the spirit of change, especially in the Islamic lands, were many men with commercial, military or political projects in their minds. These were all helped by the new ease and speed of communications, and some were inspired by a belief in limitless material progress. There is nothing peculiarly Mediterranean about the political and general thought of the age in this region.

CHAPTER XVII

THE SECOND EMPIRE IN FRANCE

IN France, the sequel to the revolution of 1848 seemed to mean more than the disappointment of the hopes of republicans. It seemed to mean, as well, an undoing of much of the progress towards liberal government that France had made prior to the outbreak of the revolution. For the *coup d'état* of 2 December 1851 inaugurated a more autocratic rule than France had known since the overthrow of Charles X, and inasmuch as one of the main purposes of this new absolutism was to safeguard the propertied classes and the church, its inception had the appearance of a return to the familiar pattern of political and social conservatism. Nevertheless, the Second Empire was not a mere retrogression, and the amiable adventurer who became Napoleon III was to earn the execration of reactionaries no less than of republicans. To the chagrin of both, time was to show that he was not insincere when he professed that the broad aim of his regime was to reconcile those whose watchword was 'progress' with those whose motto was 'order'. His success was to prove meagre, since this schism was to persist throughout his reign, and it was to issue again in bitter internecine strife when ultimately the Second Empire disappeared. Yet the endeavour was not quite vain. The empire was to endure as long as any regime in France since 1789, and in this period the nation was to experience a remarkable economic advance. Moreover, whatever the original intention of the emperor, France was to witness a gradual return to the practices of representative government, which were to be more firmly established at the close of his reign than ever before.

At the outset of the revolution of 1848, an astute observer would have had good reason to suppose that the new republican venture would be short-lived, but he would have been bold indeed if he had predicted that its demise would mean the accession of Louis Napoleon. In the spring of 1848, less than four years before he became master of France, the Bonapartist pretender was virtually unknown in his native land, and his partisans numbered no more than a handful of his personal henchmen. The son of Louis Bonaparte, that brother whom Napoleon I made king of Holland, and of Hortense de Beauharnais, the daughter of the Empress Josephine, Louis Napoleon was born in 1808, at the zenith of the meteoric career of his uncle.[1] But the nephew bore little remembrance of this age

---

[1] The question has been raised whether Louis Napoleon was legitimate, and various men have been named as his putative father. There is some room for doubt, since the estrangement between Louis and Hortense had become notorious even before Louis Napoleon was conceived, and later on Hortense was to bear a son, the future Duc de Morny, who was certainly illegitimate. However, there is no conclusive evidence to substantiate the charge that Louis Napoleon was also begotten out of wedlock.

of Napoleonic grandeur, since he was not yet eight years old when the empire crumbled into ruins. Thereupon his mother, who had separated from her husband, took up residence in Switzerland and Bavaria, where Louis Napoleon grew to manhood. He had early given an indication of his taste for political escapades, as well as an omen of his later entanglement in the Italian national movement, when he took a minor part in the insurrectionary movement in the Papal States in 1831, in which his elder brother died of fever. Soon thereafter, on the death of the duke of Reichstadt in 1832, he had found his vocation, when the political inheritance of his uncle devolved upon him. From then on he had made it his one purpose to restore the empire, with himself at its head, and he had never wearied or grown discouraged in the pursuit of this aim. With a blithe confidence that France would welcome him with open arms as soon as he set foot upon her soil and proclaimed his mission, he had made a first, foolhardy attempt to seize power in 1836, when he crossed the border into Strasbourg and strove to raise an insurrection in his favour. But the venture had been a fiasco, and, taken captive, he had been thrust back into exile. Subsequently he had settled in England, where he had attracted some notice in the fashionable world. In 1840 he had made a second attempt, crossing the Channel and landing at Boulogne, but again the enterprise miscarried. This time he had been imprisoned in the fortress of Ham, near the Belgian border. In 1846 he had escaped, taking refuge once more in England, where he had remained until the outbreak of the revolution of 1848 in his homeland.[1]

It was soon apparent that this revolution created a situation much more favourable to his cause than ever before. In his earlier ventures at the seizure of power, he had learned that the memories of grandeur which the name of Bonaparte evoked were not a strong enough magic to enable him to unseat Louis Philippe. The introduction of universal suffrage under the Second Republic, however, allowed the magic of his name to appeal to the middle-class and the peasant-proprietors, frightened by the threat of socialism, and gave him the overwhelming vote in the presidential election of 1848. Even the workers, disgusted by the bourgeois republic which had suppressed them in the 'June Days', were attracted to the Bonapartist programme. Immense as was this strategic advantage, however, his triumph at the polls did not assure Louis Napoleon of attaining that personal rule which was his ultimate purpose. In the first place, in seeking the office of president he had professed his acceptance of the republican regime, and his election did not give him a mandate to restore the empire. In the second place, the constitution of the republic provided that the president would hold office for a term of four years, and could not be re-elected. In the third place, he had to share power with a Legislative Assembly, elected in May 1849, in which he encountered

[1] For this revolution see ch. xv.

a suspicious resistance from both the republican minority and the loose coalition of conservatives who comprised the majority. These conservatives were far from won over to republicanism; most of them would have preferred a constitutional monarchy, with a parliament representative of the propertied classes, had it been possible to mend the rift between the Orleanists and the Legitimists. Failing this, they preferred to see the republic continue, as long as the legislature remained under their control.

Hence it was apparent that Louis Napoleon must either induce the conservatives to revise the constitution so as to allow him to prolong his tenure as president, or risk a *coup d'état*. At no time did he preclude the latter alternative, but now that he was so close to his goal, he evinced an unwonted hesitation at the prospect of a recourse to forcible means. For nearly three years he laboured assiduously to win the confidence and co-operation of the conservatives, and for a time he seemed likely to succeed. His readiness to dispatch an expedition to Rome (April 1849) to forestall Austria in defending the temporal power of the pope won him favour with the Catholics, as did his attitude towards the Falloux Law (15 March 1850),[1] which opened the way for the church to share in primary and secondary education, while his acquiescence in the electoral law of 31 May 1850, which disfranchised a large proportion of the urban populace, gave evidence of his willingness to aid the conservatives in preserving their preponderance in the Legislative Assembly. Once it became plain, in the summer of 1850, that there was no immediate hope of an agreement between the Orleanists and the Legitimists which would permit the candidate of either faction to take the throne, it seemed best, to some among the leaders of both camps, to permit Louis Napoleon to remain in office as president, since the Legislative Assembly would remain under their control. However, others remained unconvinced of the wisdom of such a move, believing that sooner or later Louis Napoleon would use his position to secure a personal rule in defiance of parliament. Their suspicions gained new substance when on 3 January 1851 he removed General Changarnier, who had avowed his determination to resist any move of the president to overpower the Legislative Assembly, from the command of the garrison and the National Guard of Paris. A sufficient number of conservatives therefore supported the republicans, when the issue of a revision of the constitution came to a vote in the Legislative Assembly (9 July 1851), to ensure that the proposal would not obtain the necessary three-fourths majority.

Thereafter Louis Napoleon had no choice but to prepare a *coup d'état*. In October 1851 he named as Minister of War General St Arnaud, who had agreed to share with him the risks of the bold gamble upon which he was now resolved, and as Prefect of Police, Maupas, who was also ready to become an accomplice. Meantime, with the intention of renewing

[1] Cf. ch. IV, p. 80 and ch. V, p. 107.

the dissensions between the republicans and the conservatives, so as to prevent them from forming a common front against him, the president proposed the repeal of the electoral law of 31 May 1850 (which he had originally approved) and a return to universal suffrage. As he expected, the conservative majority voted down the proposal, thus making it possible for him, when the time came to strike a blow against the Legislative Assembly, to pose as the champion of popular rights.

After several postponements, the night of 1–2 December 1851 was chosen for the *coup*. The operation was carried out with remarkable ease, under the supervision of St Arnaud, Maupas, and Morny—who took over the crucial post of Minister of the Interior. At the order of the president, the party leaders in the Legislative Assembly were arrested, the Assembly itself dissolved, and the personal rule of the president proclaimed. On 3 and 4 December some armed resistance developed in the republican quarters of Paris, but the army quickly and severely repressed this uprising, and though minor disturbances occurred in a number of localities in the provinces, nowhere did these attain grave proportions. They were enough, however, to confirm the widespread fear of anarchy as the year 1852 approached, when both president and legislature were due for renewal, and so to provide a justification for the *coup d'état*.

Forthwith the president proceeded to organise his dictatorship as a new government. On 14 December 1851 the nation was summoned to vote in a plebiscite endorsing the *coup d'état* and giving Louis Napoleon the right to promulgate a new constitution. The plebiscite registered more than seven million affirmative votes, as against less than one million in dissent. On 14 January 1852 the new constitution was issued, preserving the name of the republic but assuring an undisputed dominance to the president. Meantime, a campaign of political repression was set in motion, which was to be more systematic and comprehensive than any since the Terror of 1793–4. By an administrative order of 20 January 1852 special tribunals, known as 'mixed commissions', were instituted to take action against persons deemed dangerous to public order. These commissions, comprising the chief military and civil officials of each *département*, were authorised to proceed according to their own discretion, without necessarily observing the usual rules of judicial procedure, and were empowered to impose sentences ranging from detention to banishment, or to hand over accused persons to military courts for trial and possible execution. Eventually, actions were commenced against a total of about 26,000 persons. About 10,000 of these were set free or released under continued police surveillance, while another 10,000 were transported to Algeria.

For a year after the *coup d'état* France remained in a twilight zone, between the republic and the empire, while the prince-president tightened his grip upon the government, prepared public opinion for the ultimate step in his progress to the throne, and assured the diplomatic world that his reign would present no threat to the peace of Europe. Judging the time ripe at last, he summoned the nation to a second plebiscite on 21 November 1852, to sanction a restoration of the hereditary rule of the Bonaparte dynasty. Again, seven million voters gave their assent, as against about 250,000 in opposition, and on 2 December 1852 Louis Napoleon proclaimed himself emperor as Napoleon III. He styled himself Napoleon III on the ground that Napoleon I had abdicated in 1814 in favour of his son, later known as the duc de Reichstadt, and therefore, in the short interval before the allies restored Bourbon rule under Louis XVIII, this infant Bonaparte prince had been the lawful sovereign of France as 'Napoleon II', even though he had not actually reigned. However, Napoleon III explicitly acknowledged that the rule of the Bonaparte dynasty had legally lapsed with the accession of Louis XVIII, until his own assumption of the imperial rank in 1852. Recognising that, as the head of a new hereditary monarchy, he must renounce his bachelorhood, he proceeded to choose an empress. On 30 January 1853 he married Eugénie de Montijo, daughter of a Spanish nobleman who had fought on the French side in the Peninsular War. The empress, who had from her childhood cherished a romantic faith in the Napoleonic legend, was to prove well chosen for her role of presiding over the improvised splendours of a parvenu court. Moreover, she presently discharged her other obligation, bearing a son, known as the Prince Imperial, to provide a normal line of succession to the throne.

Though the restoration of the empire, when at last it was accomplished, afforded no more surprise than the reaping of a harvest, the inception of the new regime gave little indication of its attitude towards the basic problems of French national life. As president, Louis Napoleon had been regarded as the agent of the conservatives, but his *coup d'état* had been accomplished in defiance of their leaders, and the inauguration of the empire contradicted the hopes of the Orleanists and Legitimists, as well as of the republicans. To those who asked what was the sense of this new departure, the obvious answer was that it meant a renewal of Bonapartism. But no one could furnish a precise definition of what this signified, since the First Empire, which was its inspiration, had itself been an extemporisation. Before his rise to power Louis Napoleon had published a number of writings that expounded his conception of the tradition he represented. Notable among these were *Des idées napoléoniennes*, first published in 1839, and *De l'extinction du paupérisme*, which appeared in 1844. The former developed the familiar theme that Bonapartism meant the reconciliation of authority and liberty, and the more abstruse thesis that it meant a diplomacy dedicated to the preservation of peace. The argument was presented in such vague terms, however, as to give little clue as to the course the author would set in meeting the concrete problems now before him. The latter work was less remarkable than its title. It propounded a scheme for the resettlement of the urban poor, under the auspices of the government, on lands that had been allowed to pass out of cultivation. It bore witness to the concern of its author for the plight of the poor, but also to his desire not to arouse the trepidations of the rich.

In truth, Louis Napoleon had never had to make up his mind as to how he would solve the problems of his homeland. Having passed most of his adult life in exile, save for the six years of his imprisonment in the fortress of Ham, he had had little opportunity to gain a first-hand knowledge of the course of affairs in France, and because no large number of Frenchmen had ever rallied to his banner, he had never had to assume the responsibility for formulating the aspirations of a political party or directing a broad movement of popular opinion. His need, rather, had been to win friends however he could, while alienating as few as possible among those who might become his supporters, and thus the force of circumstances had abetted his own temperamental preference for dreaming of grandiose plans, instead of defining a precise programme.

Even after his election as president, he had remained a leader without a party. He had won a measure of support from the conservatives, since he served their need of a counterpoise to the republicans, but for the most part they thought of him as someone whom they could use for a while, then push aside. As president, he had begun to gather around him a number of individuals who had not been among his henchmen before the sudden improvement of his fortunes in 1848, but who now began to link their hopes of political advancement with his. Prominent among these were Rouher, Baroche, Billault, and Fould, who were to gain leading positions in the government of the empire. Though sometimes spoken of as the 'party of the Élysée', this loose consortium of place-seekers could hardly be considered a party in the full sense of the word, since they shared no common programme nor did they command a following among the public at large. Hence their presence in the entourage of the emperor neither determined nor indicated the course he would set.

Nor did the smaller circle of those whose attachment to the emperor was closer, for this inner council included persons whose views were so diverse as to show no common pattern. The Empress Eugénie, who soon gained and never relinquished a large personal influence upon the political decisions of her husband, made use of her position to urge him in the direction of a firm absolutism, coupled with an utter deference to the wishes of the church in respect to both domestic and foreign affairs. But her influence was offset by that of Persigny, who passed for a radical, and of the duc de Morny, who had ties with the Orleanists. No one had earned a better claim upon the emperor than Persigny, who had been his intimate friend and fanatical partisan since the bleak days of exile, while Morny, the illegitimate son of Queen Hortense, had won the trust of his half-brother by his share in planning and managing the *coup d'état* in 1851. So receptive was the emperor to the counsel of advisers who had no bond save their desire for place and influence, so erratic proved to be the course he set, that some observers concluded that he never had or developed a clearer sense of his purpose than to remain in power, or any more precise notion of how to do so than to take whatever action seemed opportune at the moment. More than one historian has concurred in this view, and dismissed Napoleon III as a man of mystery without a secret.

Yet it is possible to discern something more than sheer opportunism in his reign, or, at least, to discern a logic in his opportunism. For the emperor gave evidence that he believed himself capable of achieving that reconciliation of order and progress which he proclaimed to be his mission, and the measures he took at the outset of his reign gave reasonable promise of attaining his purpose. France, he believed, had no graver need than for a secure political order, and the Legitimists, Orleanists, and republicans, each in turn, had proved incapable of providing for this need. No alternative remained but the rule of a sovereign standing above these factions, who would give expression to the wishes of the mute mass of the nation, more desirous of the blessings of a stable government than of the triumph of any particular party. It would have been impossible for Napoleon III to wipe out by force the long-standing movements of opinion which were expressed in republicanism, Orleanism, and Legitimism, and it would have been neither feasible nor wise for him to seek to create a party of his own, to defend his cause in competition with the other parties already in the field. The only course open to him was to keep the reins of government in his own hands, while making sufficient concession to each party to blunt its opposition without becoming the captive of any one faction. Such a tactic was doubtless a kind of opportunism, but it was an opportunism serving the interests of France as well as of the emperor.

More would be required, however, than an autocratic rule combined with the dextrous balancing of one political faction against another. His regime would have to win the endorsement of the church, without which no regime could gain the acceptance of large sections of the rural populace or of the propertied classes in the cities and towns. Moreover, it must provide for the economic advance of the nation, which would at once give scope to the enterprise of the bourgeoisie and make possible an improvement of the condition of the urban masses. In such a view, there was no contradiction between serving the interests of the church and championing the cause of material progress, or between the defence of the propertied classes and solicitude for the poor.

Such seemed to be the logic in the mind of the emperor at the outset of his reign, and until 1859 the policies he pursued gave the appearance of a consistent programme. In this period he was to maintain an authoritarian personal rule, establish close and harmonious relations between the government and the church, and give vigorous aid and encouragement to business enterprise. During this interval, moreover, France was to show signs of accepting his governance with a minimum of dissension. From 1859 onward, however, the empire encountered grave vicissitudes, both at home and abroad, in response to which the regime was to take a new orientation. Under pressure from a number of sources, the emperor devolved more power upon parliament, until at length his regime became more liberal than autocratic, and his policies were to show a more eager desire to appease the left than to conciliate the right. Hence the reign of Napoleon III is divided into two periods, and if the policies he pursued at the outset represent a deliberate programme, those of the later years must be taken as a compromise of his principles.

At the start, the emperor made little or no attempt to disguise his personal rule. He delegated power only to subordinates who remained subject to his orders, or to agencies of government over which he retained a decisive influence, and he maintained so close a check upon the expression of political opinion that no opposition could overstep the bounds which he determined. For the surveillance of opinion, he relied in part upon the centralised apparatus of the administration, which previous regimes had utilised for the same purpose, receiving regular reports on the state of public sentiment throughout France from both the prefects and the *procureurs-généraux*. In part, he relied upon legislation adopted under the Second Republic for the regulation of political associations and the press. Thus, a law of 28 July 1848 required that all meetings for the discussion of political issues be open to the public and under the observation of an agent of the government, and no federation among political associations was permitted. Under press laws of 9–11 August 1848, renewed in 1849 and 1850 and rendered definitive by a decree of 17 February 1852, no newspaper might be published without the prior authorisation of the government, which meant that the publishers and editors must be persons of acceptable opinions, and the owners were required to put up a surety which might amount to as much as 50,000 francs. Within the government, the attribution of power which assured Napoleon's personal rule was determined by the constitution of 14 January 1852, which required only minor revision upon the proclamation of the empire.

This constitution made the emperor absolute master of the executive branch of the government, and also gave him a large share in the legislative process. As sovereign, he retained sole charge of foreign relations, including the right to wage war and sign treaties, as well as supreme command of the army and navy. He appointed and dismissed at his own discretion the ministers, and these were responsible to him as individuals, rather than as a corporate group. Hence the cabinet had the character of a committee of officials, not an autonomous organ of government capable of opposing a collective will to that of the emperor. For the adoption of the budget and the enactment of laws, other than those of a constitutional nature, the government was obliged to secure the assent of the *Corps Législatif*, the members of which were elected by universal suffrage for a term of six years. However, the *Corps Législatif* was not given the right to initiate legislation or to draw up the budget, or to amend either the budget or other bills without the permission of the *Conseil d'État*, a council composed of officials to which was entrusted the drafting of all legislation. Hence the elective chamber could only accept or refuse measures proposed by the nominated agents of the emperor. Indeed, the *Corps Législatif* was envisaged as a kind of consultative body, rather than as one shaping the fundamental policy of the government. Because it was to have only such a limited role, it was supposed to meet ordinarily for a session of only three months each year, and its members were to receive no remuneration. But in practice it was usually kept in session longer than three months, and eventually stipends, designated as 'indemnities', were paid to the deputies. The constitution also created a senate, comprising marshals, admirals, and cardinals, who held seats *ex officio*, and other members to a total of 150, appointed by the emperor for life. But at first the senate did not constitute an upper house, co-ordinate with the *Corps Législatif*. Its share in legislation was limited to registering imperial decrees having the character of constitutional provisions, which were not submitted to the elective chamber, and reviewing laws passed by the *Corps Législatif* to assure their conformity to the constitution.

Yet the empire was not as oppressive, even in the period of personal rule, as its constitution might give reason to suppose. Since those who were staunch partisans of his rule were never many, comprising little more than the circle of his personal intimates and the band of accomplices who had helped him execute his *coup d'état*, the emperor could not exclude from public life all who continued to prefer another kind of regime. He made no attempt to prevent the recognised leaders of the Orleanist and Legitimist parties from expressing in the press their views on political issues, or to shut them out of political office provided that they took the oath of allegiance. Though the government used its influence in elections to secure the return of a particular candidate in preference to others, as previous regimes had done, often it was obliged to make its choice from among a number of candidates, none of whom could be regarded as a reliable supporter of its policies. Much less latitude was permitted the republican opposition than the Orleanists and the Legitimists. Nevertheless, even republicans were allowed to seek election to public office, provided they acknowledged their acceptance of the empire *de facto*.

From the start, the emperor made plain his desire to win the endorsement of the church. He maintained the French garrison in Rome which had been sent to the aid of the pope in 1849, and he allowed a free hand to the church in its efforts to extend its role in primary and secondary education, which the Falloux Law of 1850 made possible (see also chs. IV and V, pp. 80 and 107). In particular, the church was indebted to his government for permitting the rapid growth of religious orders, the members of which provided the teaching personnel needed for this expansion, and for encouraging local authorities to take advantage of the provision of the Falloux Law which permitted them to entrust the teaching in public schools to members of religious orders.

Meantime, steps were taken to encourage the economic expansion which was to be the complement to political order. Notable among these were measures to make credit more readily available. The *Comptoir d'Escompte*, originally organised in 1848 under the auspices of the provisional government, had proved efficacious in meeting the demand for short-term discounts for the needs of commerce, and its charter was renewed and its operations broadened. But a pressing need still remained for banking institutions which would make long-term investments in new productive enterprises. To serve this need, the government gave charters in 1852 to two new institutions, the *Crédit Mobilier* and the *Crédit Foncier*. Under the management of the Péreire brothers, the *Crédit Mobilier* embarked upon a number of bold ventures in the financing of railways, shipping companies, gas-lighting companies, mining companies, and similar enterprises. The *Crédit Foncier*, which put its funds into mortgages on land-values, devoted most of its resources to investments in urban real estate, especially in Paris. It thus facilitated the rebuilding of the capital and other large cities, a work for which there was much need. It proved disappointing, however, in the other role envisaged for it—making long-term loans for the improvement of agricultural production.

Vigorous stimulation was also given to the building of railways. The construction of numerous small lines had begun in the reign of Louis Philippe, but the completion of the trunk lines had been held back because of inadequate financing and the slowness of the government to give leadership in developing plans and policies on a nation-wide scale. Construction was lagging on the routes planned from the capital to the south and south-west, and France, with about 3000 kilometres in service was much behind Britain and Prussia. From its inception, the government of Napoleon III took prompt and decisive action to bring about the merger of numerous small companies into six large enterprises, each of which was to develop and operate a regional network. By the Franqueville conventions of 1859, moreover, the government put their finances on a sound basis by signing contracts, replacing a welter of previous agreements, that guaranteed these companies a stipulated return on their investment, on condition of their operating specified branch lines where the traffic was not dense enough to be remunerative. By 1870, more than 17,000 kilometres of line were in use. Attention was also given to maritime transport. Subsidies were paid to the Messageries Maritimes (cf. p. 432) to assist the development of shipping service to Mediterranean ports, and to the Compagnie Générale Transatlantique for service across the North Atlantic.

As part of the same endeavour to stimulate economic advance, Napoleon III also took bold action to reduce the customs duties protecting French industry from foreign competition. Political as well as economic considerations entered into this decision, for the emperor was desirous of maintaining an *entente* with Britain, and he knew that such a move would win him the applause of the British advocates of free trade. But he was also persuaded—owing, in large measure, to the influence of the French economist Michel Chevalier—that a general lowering of tariffs would be beneficial to the French economy, both because it would permit the importation of industrial raw materials at lower prices, and because it would spur French manufacturers to adopt more modern methods of production, in order to lower their costs. With the approval of Napoleon III, Chevalier entered into discussions with Richard Cobden from which there issued the draft of a commercial treaty, which was ratified and put into effect in 1860. Its terms, involving a sharp reduction of French duties, provided the basis for similar agreements which the empire subsequently concluded with Belgium, the Netherlands, the German *Zollverein*, Sweden, Switzerland, Italy, and Spain (cf. p. 38).

As Napoleon III thus began to give substance to his vague promise of harmonising material progress with a conservative regime in politics, the empire began to win a wider and more positive public acceptance. Until 1859, indeed, it seemed not improbable that the issues which had so long divided the nation might gradually fade into oblivion, and ultimately Frenchmen might again discover how to work to a common purpose. For a decade after the *coup d'état*, the republican movement remained in a nearly total eclipse. Most of its leaders had been driven into exile before the disappearance of the republic, and with the inception of the new regime, most of the others were forced to flee or reduced to silence. Among the Orleanists, none of the former leaders rallied to the empire. Guizot, Thiers, and Odilon Barrot all passed into virtual retirement, though Thiers was later to re-emerge as the leader of a conservative opposition. But others, like Rouher, Baroche, and Billault, refused to remain in the shadows when the emperor offered them positions in his service, while the substantial bourgeois of the provinces, who were the backbone of the party, were not inclined to make a fetish of their allegiance to the Orléans family, once it became apparent that Napoleon III was capable of maintaining his seat on the throne and preserving order. The Legitimists were slower to make their peace, and the comte de Chambord gave express instructions that none of his partisans were to accept office under Napoleon III. Even without this ban, men of the extreme right were loth to come to terms with a Bonaparte. Yet not all who would have preferred the comte de Chambord to Napoleon III made the restoration of Bourbon rule their sole political desideratum. Most of them were no less concerned with the cause of the altar than of the throne, and few of these could remain irreconcilable foes of a sovereign who had so far proved so amenable to the wishes of the church as had Napoleon III.

No less significant seemed the response of disciples of two movements for social reform that were not identified with any of the three political parties antedating the empire. The Saint-Simonians comprised one of these. Although the Saint-Simonian organisation had dissolved in 1832, a number of its sectaries remained faithful to the ideas that had inspired the movement, and some of them saw in Napoleon III a man of their own persuasion, who had put an end to the sterile disputes among political factions and had begun that liberation of the forces of production which was the great task of the modern age. Prominent among these were the brothers Émile and Isaac Péreire, who took a leading role in organising and managing the *Crédit Mobilier* and in bringing about the mergers among railway companies from which emerged the six great regional networks, and Michel Chevalier, who was as enthusiastic an advocate of public works and of railways as he was a partisan of free trade.

For reasons quite unlike those which made the empire seem the realisation of the dream of Saint Simon, the new regime also gained approbation among the disciples of Frédéric Le Play. The doctrines of 'social peace' which this gentle-spirited mining engineer propounded placed no premium on the increase of riches as the means to the increase of human happiness, and in his view industrialism represented a menace to the well-being of mankind, rather than a blessing. The only efficacious social reforms were those which would preserve and strengthen the family, for only the family could provide for both the material needs of men and their hunger for the affection and respect of their fellows. The emperor soon perceived that a social gospel of this kind, which minimised the importance of the traditional issues of political debate, could prove useful to his purpose, and he was generous in his patronage of Le Play, who eventually was named a senator. Though Le Play never gained a large following, he commanded the attention of a considerable number of Catholic conservatives, and his acceptance of the empire afforded a kind of moral counterpart to the endorsement of the Saint-Simonians.

But time was to disprove the omens that seemed to augur the ultimate success of the emperor's design. His ill-starred participation in the War of Italian Liberation[1] marked the beginning of a new period in his reign, which saw an exacerbation of the dissensions within France over religious issues, as well as a reopening of the social and political cleavages he had striven to mend. As the decade of the 1860's wore on, it became obvious

[1] See ch. xxi.

that, instead of affording a new solution to the problems of France, the empire could only maintain an unsteady equilibrium, in the midst of strife among irreconcilable adversaries.

Foremost among the issues that revealed the dilemma of the empire were those involving the church. Napoleon III was well aware that his policy of deference towards the church would aggravate the opposition of that portion of the left which saw in the church the quintessence of reaction. But he expected that this opposition would be more than offset by the approval of Orleanists and Legitimists, who would endorse his policy either because of a sincere religious devotion or because the church seemed a bulwark of a conservative social order. It was his misfortune, however, that his reign coincided with that of Pope Pius IX, under whose leadership the church was to maintain a position of utter intransigence towards liberalism in both the arena of practical politics and the realm of ideas. It became apparent, as time passed, that if Napoleon were to continue in the course he had set he would be obliged, not only to sustain the temporal rule of the pope against Italian nationalism, but also to acquiesce in the sweeping condemnation of the spirit of the modern age enunciated in the Syllabus of Errors, and defer to the extreme expression of ultramontanism which was to come out of the Vatican Council of 1870 (see ch. IV, pp. 93–9). In so doing he would alienate not only the anticlerical republicans, but also those conservatives who, while dissociating themselves from the anticlericalism of the left, remained faithful to the traditions of Gallicanism. Yet if he were to draw back, he would suffer the imprecations of the ultramontanists. He had little choice, therefore, but to pursue a policy of trimming that would give a minimum of offence to either the ultramontanists or their adversaries, without satisfying either.

Apart from this renewal of religious quarrels, which he was powerless to avert, Napoleon III also encountered an opposition which was, in part, the consequence of his own endeavours to stimulate economic expansion. His measures to loosen credit and complete a nation-wide network of railways were well received. But the policy of lower tariffs inaugurated by the Anglo-French treaty of 1860 aroused widespread and forceful protests from business men, especially in the metallurgical and textile industries, which had hitherto been sheltered from British and Belgian competition, while the increased sales of French wines abroad, which was supposed to offset some of the disadvantages of foreign competition, proved less than had been hoped for. From the chorus of complaints it became evident that even if the emperor and his advisers were right in believing that foreign competition would provide a spur to the improvement of manufacturing processes in France, a substantial portion of the business world was far from eager to meet the challenge.

As industrialists were giving angered voice to their dissatisfaction, the urban working class also began to show signs of a renewed restiveness. In part, this represented a recrudescence of the Jacobinism endemic to the populace of the larger cities, which began to reappear as soon as the government relaxed the political repression instituted after the *coup d'état*. In part, it was a result of that same process of industrial advance which the emperor had striven to encourage. For the progress of the industrial revolution had, in France as elsewhere, the inevitable consequence of swelling the numbers of the industrial proletariat, while the improvement of business conditions brought a more rapid rise of prices than of wages. In response to this economic pressure, the trade-union movement began to gain new ground, in defiance of the legal prohibition upon the association of working-men for the purpose of securing higher wages. So far as the working-class gave indication of social aims broader than those of Jacobin republicanism, these owed their inspiration to the mutualist doctrines of Proudhon or Louis Blanc, and though Marx and Engels were elaborating the principles of 'scientific' socialism, their new creed remained almost unknown in France throughout the epoch of the empire. Nevertheless, the organisation in 1865 of a French section of the newly founded First International was the harbinger of a new and more formidable phase in the rise of the proletariat.

Time also brought a resurgence of the republicanism which appealed to some men of education among the middle classes. Few of those who had risen to prominence in 1848 as spokesmen for this kind of republicanism re-entered political life under the empire; most of them remained in exile, like Ledru-Rollin, or withdrew into private life, like Lamartine. But a new generation of leaders, dedicated to the same ideas, soon appeared. The elections of 1857 brought into the *Corps Législatif* a little band of five men, among whom were Émile Ollivier and Jules Favre, who, while accepting the empire *de facto*, were to become the nucleus of a republican opposition. Presently, other new names—Jules Simon, Léon Gambetta, Jules Ferry, Henri de Rochefort—were to be added to the group of republican adversaries of the regime.

The response of the emperor to these various pressures was to veer towards the left. One indication of this was a general amnesty accorded in 1859 to political offenders, most of whom were republicans. Then came a decree of 24 November 1860, by which the emperor accorded to both the *Corps Législatif* and the senate the right to vote a reply to the address which he made at the opening of each annual session of these chambers, and the right to publish verbatim accounts of their debates. By a decree of 19 January 1867 both houses were given the right to interpellate ministers; thereafter, the annual throne address was discontinued. By a decree of 14 March 1867 the senate was given a suspensive veto over bills passed by the *Corps Législatif*, as well as its previous right to review legislation as the guardian of the constitution; thus the senate became an upper house, comparable to a House of Peers. In 1868 the laws governing the press and public meetings were made less stringent. Taken together, these reforms did much to increase the prestige of parliament and to allow political leaders, other than the narrow circle of the emperor's associates and subordinates, freedom to express their views, even when these involved criticism of the government. However, the emperor still kept complete control of the executive (since the ministers remained responsible only to him) as well as sufficient influence over the legislature so that he could count upon the adoption of whatever bills his government might propose.

Other indications were also given of the new orientation towards the left. A concession of much importance to the working class was made in 1864, when working-men were given the right to strike, although penalties were still prescribed where men on strike sought to prevent others from working. Meantime, as Catholic publicists and high dignitaries of the church, after 1859, berated the emperor for abetting Italian nationalism at the expense of the temporal rule of the pope, the government showed less favour towards the expansion of the role of the church in education, and after the appointment of Victor Duruy as Minister of Education in 1863, this growth came to a stop.

Yet these moves did not suffice to appease the adversaries of the empire on the left and thus offset the Catholic criticism on the right. The elections of 1863 and 1869 saw successive increases in the number of republicans returned to the *Corps Législatif*, while Thiers, who returned to active political life in 1863, undertook to organise a conservative opposition, known as the 'Third Party', distinct from that of the republicans but likewise committed to an unremitting resistance to the policies of the government. Again, the response of the emperor was to make new concessions to the left. In January 1870 he called into his service Émile Ollivier, who had risen to prominence as a leader of the radical opposition in the *Corps Législatif*, and gave him a role which seemed tantamount to that of a prime minister. Under the provisions of a new constitution, submitted to a plebiscite on 8 May 1870, both the *Corps Législatif* and the senate were given the right to initiate legislation, as well as amend bills proposed by the government, to draw up their own order of business, and to pass resolutions of comment on the actions of the executive.

The plebiscite produced a favourable vote of a size not much less than that of 1852. But the significance of this ultimate revision of the constitution remained obscure. To some, it seemed to mean the beginning of a new regime—the 'Liberal Empire'—based upon parliamentary rather than autocratic government. However, the emperor still retained a number of important prerogatives. He continued to appoint the ministers, who remained accountable to him, and he kept command of the army and navy; moreover, he alone could propose a revision of the constitution, which would require a plebiscite but not the sanction of parliament. Hence he did not wholly commit himself to the principle of parliamentary supremacy, nor did he bind himself irrevocably, for he reserved sufficient power to re-establish his personal rule, if he should choose to risk another *coup* of the same kind as that which had established his dictatorship in 1851. But the likelihood of a return to absolutism seemed slight, for the emperor of 1870 was not the adventurer of 1851. Poor health had sapped his vigour, and even his interest in retaining a personal rule had seemed to ebb; he was now more anxious to preserve the empire for his son than for himself. In any event, questions as to what would be the subsequent evolution of the empire must remain unanswerable, since the regime was to disappear under the wave of foreign invasion only a few months after the promulgation of the new constitution.

But the sustained endeavour of Napoleon III to resolve the antithesis between authority and liberty in the realm of politics is not what gives his reign its principal importance in French history. The epoch is more significant for its remarkable economic advance, which was due to other circumstances as well as to the action of the government. In the slow process by which France modernised its economy in the nineteenth century, the phase coinciding with the Second Empire was of crucial importance, although it did not mark either the beginning of the industrial revolution in France or its ultimate peak.

The rapid development of land- and sea-transport was associated with a boom in the mining and metallurgical industries. The production of coal more than doubled, the smelting of iron shifted from the older methods using charcoal to the new technique using coke, in the 1860's both the Bessemer and the Siemens processes for the manufacture of steel were introduced into France, and the total production of iron and steel increased enough to place her in the second rank, behind Britain but ahead of Germany. Meanwhile, machine methods became widespread in the spinning and weaving of cotton goods, and, to a lesser extent, in the woollen industry, although the older handiwork methods did not disappear. A rough measure of the general level of industrial progress was the total horsepower of steam engines in manufacturing establishments, which increased about 500 per cent between 1850 and 1870. No less notable was the increase of foreign investment, which during the Second Empire rose from a total of about two billion francs to about twelve billions. Much of this investment was in foreign government bonds, but a large share went to finance the railway systems of Spain, Italy, and Austria-Hungary, and (see p. 440) the Suez Canal.

Agriculture made much less progress than the other branches of the national economy. Throughout the nineteenth century, indeed, French agriculture proved slow to change, owing partly to the reforms effected in the revolution of 1789, which strengthened the position of the tradition-bound small-holder. However, the construction of railways, which made it possible to ship produce to more remote markets, provided a stimulus to the operation of larger holdings, on a business basis rather than as homesteads.

It is difficult to establish what brought about the economic upsurge in this era. The phenomenon is not peculiar to France, for the 1850's and 1860's were a period of general economic advance in many other countries, notably Britain, Germany, and the United States. In some measure, the boom was probably influenced by the discovery of gold in California and Australia, which naturally had an inflationary effect throughout the world. It may have been due, in part, to the trend towards lower tariffs, particularly after the Anglo-French treaty of 1860, which made possible a freer flow of international trade. Another stimulus was the construction of railways, which represented the exploitation of new technological advances, for the railways not only created a new large-scale demand for iron and steel, as well as a mobile labour force, but also widened the area of the effective market for both agricultural produce and manufactures. To some degree, the expansion was doubtless a consequence of the wider use of incorporation with limited liability, which was facilitated in France by legislation of 1867, and of the growth of new credit institutions. Notable among these, besides the *Crédit Mobilier* and the *Crédit Foncier*, were the *Crédit Lyonnais* (1863) and the *Société Générale* (1864). It is still harder to assess the contribution of the government of the empire than to evaluate the importance of such other factors in the economic expansion. Clearly the government did not supply the whole impetus, but unquestionably it afforded encouragement to economic enterprise, and positive assistance at a number of points.

Associated with this business boom was the rise of the bourgeoisie to a position of unrivalled social pre-eminence. This process had, of course, begun much earlier, but not until the era of the Second Empire did the decline of the landed aristocracy become irreparable. This decline was due in part to the economic circumstances that gave business men command of new resources of wealth and prestige, but also to political, rather than economic factors. For the Legitimists, among whom were numbered most of what remained of the old nobility, largely boycotted political life, as well as the social life that centred in the court. They had pursued much the same policy under the Orléans monarchy and had already begun to suffer the effects of their self-imposed seclusion, but under the empire they prolonged their retirement into a third and fourth decade. The Orleanists, whose ranks included many country gentlemen as well as business men, did not adopt so intransigent an attitude, and many of them held positions of prominence. Yet clearly the characteristic figure of the Second Empire was the business magnate and stock promoter, whose wealth came from new industrial ventures, rather than landed estates.

Men such as these readily gained admittance to the circle about the emperor, and to them he accorded the highest patronage.

The process of industrialisation also wrought changes, though less pronounced, in the common people. An inevitable consequence of industrialism was that the proletariat gained in numbers and social importance. Nevertheless, throughout the period of the empire, the artisan remained the backbone of the working class. Paris was the only city in France in this era whose population surpassed one million, but not until a later date did it attain two millions. Its labouring populace still consisted preponderantly of skilled workmen, employed in small shops and producing luxury goods, together with a mass of unskilled casual labourers and domestic servants. Lyons, Marseilles, and Bordeaux—the next three largest cities, in that order—comprised among them a total population of less than one million. The new industrial proletariat arose mainly in the textile and metallurgical industries, and these developed in relatively small provincial cities, such as Lille and Roubaix, whose population ranged between 50,000 and 150,000. The rural population experienced even less change than the urban, since agriculture had only a minor share in the economic expansion of the period, nor was migration to the towns so rapid as to produce a marked rural depopulation. However, the empire showed much more solicitude for the peasants than any previous government since the revolution, and with the reign of Napoleon III we can perceive the beginning of that process of the wooing of the rural voter that was to become a characteristic of French political life under the Third Republic.

In the world of ideas there was no such accession of new vigour as was revealed in the world of economic enterprise. The debate went on between the champions of the church and the apostles of the rival religion of science, with little added to the argument save a more extreme dogmatism. On the one side, Veuillot remained the spokesman for those Catholics whose point of view was epitomised in the Syllabus of Errors (see ch. IV, pp. 90–4), while at the other pole, those who saw in the worship of science the new path to human salvation had their prophets in Auguste Comte and Littré, who became the principal expositor of the positivist tradition after the death of Comte in 1857. Yet France did not earn a clear pre-eminence in the work of enlarging the bounds of scientific knowledge. To be sure, this age witnessed the researches of Claude Bernard and Louis Pasteur, among others (see ch. III, pp. 50, 65–6). But the German universities remained the principal home of scientific research (cf. pp. 50–1, 114), if the progress of science be taken as depending upon the combined efforts of a large number of scholars, while Charles Darwin assured Britain of the honour of producing the scientific masterpiece of the period.

No one would question, however, the distinction which Paris held in the reign of Napoleon III as a cosmopolitan pleasure-resort. Long before this time, Europe had acknowledged the peculiar charm of *la Ville lumière*, but during the early nineteenth century, its lustre had somewhat dimmed. The Bourbon restoration had given Paris an austere atmosphere, especially under Louis XVIII, mingling a chastened piety with an embittered conservatism, that did not lend itself to gaiety. The reign of Louis Philippe had seen some relaxation, but the industrious making of money had been more honoured than the prodigal spending of it. Napoleon III set quite another example. In the rootless years of his youth he had acquired both a taste for pleasure and an attitude of indulgence towards dissipation, and until nearly the close of his life he retained some of the habits of a rake. As a matter of policy, moreover, Napoleon III gave encouragement to social ostentation by his lavish expenditures on the ceremonies and entertainments of the court, which he strove to make the centre of fashionable society. In his reign, Paris was largely rebuilt, the principal streets widened, and public services such as street-lighting and sanitation much improved. This work was carried out under the energetic supervision of Baron Haussmann as prefect of the Seine, but the initiative came from the emperor. In part, his motive was political, for the broadening of the boulevards made it difficult to erect barricades across them, and this provided a safeguard against popular insurrections such as had overthrown Charles X and Louis Philippe. But the intention was also to embellish the city and to furnish facilities commensurate with its growing size. Two of the architectural monuments of this rebuilding of Paris—the huge canopied shelter constructed for *les Halles*, or central market, and the new Opéra, begun in 1863 though not completed until 1875 (cf. p. 142)—were later imitated in numerous other cities, both in Europe and America.

The fashionable world that congregated in Paris constituted, to a larger degree than ever before, a world of new-rich. It became so in part because the old aristocracy chose to withdraw into seclusion, in part because the economic expansion gave unprecedented opportunities for men to rise to sudden wealth, and in part because a self-made emperor was not disposed to discriminate against others freshly risen to prosperity. Also noteworthy was the conspicuous role of the social milieu known as the *demi-monde*. This was a world of women who were regarded as not quite respectable, while not altogether disreputable, comprising courtesans who had risen to some affluence and had attained a measure of social grace, and women of better origin who had left their husbands, either because they had been discovered in too open a breach of their marital vows or because they had chosen a life of independence at the cost of their good name. It was by no means a new phenomenon for men of high position to maintain illicit relationships with women such as these, but there was some element of novelty in the general acceptance of this *demi-monde* as a kind of annexe to the more exclusive precincts of the social *élite*, and in the predominance of business magnates, rather than noblemen, among its *habitués*. The *demi-monde* did much to give the Paris of the Second Empire its reputation for raffish gaiety, a notoriety which the French capital was to keep into the twentieth century.

Of wider importance, however, were the results of Napoleon's ventures in foreign affairs. In his nebulous conception of his mission, the restoration of the diplomatic pre-eminence of France was to be the counterpart to the resolution of the embittered dissensions within the nation. As one means to this purpose, he strove to rebuild the French *imperium* overseas, which had shrunk to the verge of extinction after Napoleon I had abandoned Louisiana in 1803. For the most part, with the conspicuous exception of his intervention in Mexico, success attended his enterprises outside Europe, and to his initiative were due the beginnings of much of the huge colonial realm which was to become the pride of the Third Republic. France strengthened her hold upon Algeria, increased her political and economic influence in the eastern Mediterranean basin (see ch. XVI, pp. 427–30), established bases in Senegal and Somaliland, began penetration into Indo-China, and participated in the opening up of China (see ch. XXVI, pp. 692–6, 700–9).

But not until a later age was dominion overseas to become again a common measure of national grandeur, nor did Napoleon III himself regard this as the gauge of his diplomatic skill. In his view, the measure of his success would be the break-up of the coalition that had triumphed over Napoleon I, and the undoing of the territorial settlement negotiated at the Congress of Vienna. He sincerely believed in his uncle's prophecy from St Helena that 'the first ruler who calls upon the peoples of Europe will be able to accomplish anything that he wishes'. Nationality was the force of the future, and it must be harnessed to French interests, so as to restore a moral hegemony of France in Europe. To be sure, the league of the victors of Waterloo had begun to dissolve long before his accession. Britain had proved unwilling to sustain her partners in the Quadruple Alliance in their crusade against Spanish liberalism, and with the independence of Belgium, the bastion which had been entrusted to the Dutch, to serve as a barrier against French expansion towards the Rhine, had crumbled (see ch. x). Nevertheless, the reaction which had followed the revolutions of 1848 had once more seen Russia, Prussia, and Austria draw together, and the impotence of the Second Republic in face of this combination could not but remind France how powerless she was to determine the pivotal issues in the political organisation of Europe. Though far from agreed among themselves as to how these issues ought to be solved, the French were of one mind that Europe must be taught again to show a proper deference to the wish and will of France.

The first task confronting Napoleon III was to gain diplomatic recognition of his regime. In itself, this would be an open sign that France was no longer under the tutelage of the four powers which had accomplished her humiliation in 1815, since one of the articles in the Quadruple Alliance bound the signatories never to permit a Bonaparte again to reign in France. Despite the divergences that had since developed among the allies, the question remained as to whether the partners would countenance so bold a defiance. Indeed, Nicholas I, who had succeeded Metternich as the arch-champion of reaction, was disposed to take a firm stand, and, had Britain been willing to co-operate, he might have induced Prussia and Austria to follow his lead. However, Britain, which was desirous of good relations with Paris, in order to ensure French aid in thwarting the aggressive designs of Russia in the Near East, did not hesitate to recognise the new empire, whereupon Vienna, Berlin, and St Petersburg fell into line.

Trivial as the issue of recognition seemed, once Britain declared her position, the outcome of this crisis indicated the pattern of an Anglo-French *entente*, which was soon to assume much importance. Less than two years after the formal proclamation of the empire, France and Britain were at war as allies, defending the Ottoman empire against the armies of Nicholas I. The intricacies of the dispute which led to the Crimean War are discussed in the next chapter (pp. 468–78). Suffice it here to note that, though France had quite as much reason as had Britain to oppose the further extension of Russian influence at Turkish expense, she also had another interest in the war, apart from the particular issues at stake. For the outbreak of the Crimean War marked the close of the era, beginning with the Congress of Vienna, when the quarantine of France had provided one of the basic principles of the organisation of the European diplomatic structure. Two of the four powers once pledged to the Quadruple Alliance were now, for the first time, engaged in open warfare upon one another, while France was the partner of one of them. Nor was she merely a pliant instrument of her ally. Not only did Napoleon III share in the prestige of victory, but also he succeeded in impressing a mark of his own upon the peace settlement, since it was at his insistence, against the opposition of Austria and despite the reluctance of Britain, that the sultan was required to concede self-rule to Moldavia and Wallachia in such a way that these two Danubian provinces were able to unite in 1859, to form what was known as the Principality of Roumania.

But after this considerable success in re-establishing France as one of the arbiters of Europe, Napoleon III next embarked upon the venture— his alliance with Sardinia in war against Austria (see ch. xxi, pp. 571–2)— that was to prove the first in a series of blunders and mishaps, culminating in his own ruin and a new disaster for France. To be sure, his plan in launching this enterprise was not as improvident as the outcome would suggest. By destroying Austrian preponderance in Italy, he would gain a revenge upon another of the victors of 1814–15, while at the same time he would give substance to his reiterated professions of devotion to the principle of nationality. He had no thought of helping Sardinia to absorb the whole of Italy, since this would not only mean the abrogation of the temporal rule of the pope, which Catholic opinion in France would not accept, but would make France for ever after obliged to reckon with a strong neighbour on her south-eastern border. His intention was to help Sardinia wrest Lombardy and Venetia from the Austrians, then to bring about some kind of federation among the Italian principalities, over which the pope, who would retain his rule of the states of the church, would preside, while in return for assistance against Austria, Napoleon III would acquire Nice and Savoy from Sardinia. It was on this basis that the emperor reached agreement with Cavour at Plombières (July 1858), and that he entered upon the war which Cavour presently succeeded in provoking (April 1859). To the embarrassed surprise of Napoleon III, however, it proved impossible for him to restrain the force of the Italian national movement, once the French and Sardinians defeated the Austrians. Sensing his error, he brought the war to an abrupt stop (July 1859), permitting the Austrians to retain Venetia.[1] Nevertheless, within little more than a year Sardinia acquired rule of all the remainder of Italy save Rome, which remained under the control of the pope, thanks to the presence of the French garrison stationed there since 1849. As prearranged, Napoleon III took over Nice and Savoy, but France could hardly regard this slight extension of her borders as an adequate compensation for having made possible the new kingdom of Italy, especially as these annexations aroused deep hostility and suspicion in England. In respect to Rome, moreover, Napoleon III found himself confronted with a dilemma that defied solution. If he were to keep the French garrison in Rome, thus preventing the new Italian kingdom from making this its capital, he would sacrifice the goodwill he otherwise might claim as the champion of Italian nationalism, while if he were to withdraw the troops and countenance the dispossession of the pope from the remaining vestige of his temporal power, he would outrage Catholic opinion in France. Deeming it better to lose the gratitude of Italian nationalists than worsen the reproaches of the Catholics at home, he chose to keep the garrison in Rome, until a new corps of volunteer troops could be organised to defend papal rule. But this hope for a solution of the problem proved vain. Though the French troops were withdrawn for a short time in 1866, they were soon ordered back, remaining until shortly after the outbreak of the war of 1870 that marked the doom of the empire. Thus for the remainder of his reign Napoleon III was to find himself pitted against the Italian national movement he had done so much to reawaken, while the protection he continued to give the pope was insufficient to silence Catholic criticism.

[1] For the campaign, see ch. xii, pp. 323–4.

No more creditable to the emperor was the outcome of the French intervention in Mexico (see ch. xxv, pp. 677–8). France embarked upon this enterprise in 1861, in co-operation with Britain and Spain, when the three powers dispatched troops to Vera Cruz as a show of force in support of the European creditors of the bankrupt Mexican Republic. However, the French soon gave indication of broader aims, which involved giving extensive aid to those Mexican conservatives who were desirous of overthrowing the republican regime. Thus France would do a service to the Catholic Church, safeguarding its interests from the menace of the anticlerical policies which the Mexican republicans espoused, and would stand forth as the guardian of the Catholic and Latin peoples of the New World and their champion against the 'Anglo-Saxon' and Protestant influence of the United States. The British and Spaniards soon withdrew their expeditions. But the French persisted, and in alliance with the Mexican conservatives, set up in 1863 a Mexican empire, over which the Austrian Archduke Maximilian was induced to assume rule. Even with French help, however, Maximilian was unable to secure his hold upon Mexico, and his government soon demonstrated a hopeless ineptitude. The French began to lose interest, and as the Prussian challenge to Austria raised grave new issues in Europe, in which France was directly involved, they became anxious to rid themselves of their military commitments in the New World. Then, too, at the conclusion of the civil war in the United States, Washington, from the outset hostile to European intervention in Mexico, made clear its intention of aiding the leader of the Mexican republican guerrillas, Benito Juárez, in his struggle to unseat Maximilian. Thereupon in 1866 Napoleon III determined to liquidate his speculation, and ordered the withdrawal of the French expedition. Within a short time Juárez prevailed and put the hapless Maximilian to death.

Much more momentous in its consequences was the role of Napoleon III in the struggle which was beginning to develop between Prussia and Austria (see chs. XIX and XXII, pp. 517 and 577–8). No one had reason in 1862, when Bismarck became Minister-President of Prussia, to foresee the role he was soon to play in the unification of Germany. Nor was it plain in 1864, when he manœuvred Austria into an alliance with Prussia to despoil Denmark of the provinces of Schleswig and Holstein, that this was to lead to a decisive test of strength between Prussia and Austria. But it soon became obvious that this was the purpose towards which Bismarck was working. As tension developed between Berlin and Vienna, Napoleon III showed no grave concern. He was not unaware, to be sure, of the French interest in maintaining an equilibrium of forces between Prussia and Austria. But he did not assume—nor did he have reason to suppose—that in a clash of arms Prussia would win a speedy victory. Rather, he presumed that a new disturbance of the *status quo* would afford a fresh opportunity for intrigue to the advantage of France, and even if war should develop, he would have ample time to interpose as an arbiter. Hence he was susceptible to the shrewd manœuvres of Bismarck, when the latter, seeking to assure himself of French inaction in the event of war between Prussia and Austria, vaguely indicated his readiness to allow the emperor to realise his aspirations. Austria seemed no less amenable. Indeed, negotiations between Paris and Vienna issued in a definite engagement that, provided Napoleon III remain neutral in the war now brewing, Austria would assure him a voice in the settlement and would hand over to him the province of Venetia, which he would thereupon cede to Italy. But to the discomfiture of Napoleon III, the war of 1866 broke out before he had time to proceed farther with his own diplomatic preparations, and ended before he had a chance to influence its outcome.

After this rude shock, the emperor could not fail to recognise how serious was the problem before him, for no one supposed that Bismarck would rest content with the success he won in 1866, while France could never permit without a challenge the further progress of Prussia towards German unification. Yet the endeavours of the emperor to make ready for this eventuality revealed so little trace of the boldness he had so often shown in his earlier career, and so unwonted a disposition to temporise, as to suggest that the weariness of age and the ravages of poor health— he was suffering extreme pain from a stone in the urinary tract—had levied toll upon him. In a pitiful attempt to conciliate French public opinion by making at least some minor annexation to offset the aggrandisement of Prussia, he opened negotiations in 1867 for the purchase of Luxemburg from the king of the Netherlands (cf. ch. XXII, pp. 581-2). But nothing came of this wan hope. Meantime, taking heed of the unexpected strength Prussia had shown against Austria, he began to reorganise the French army. But so loud a clamour arose in parliament, when the government sought authority to increase the number of men under arms, that little was accomplished. No more success attended his efforts to conclude an alliance with Austria and Italy. The Italians were unwilling to co-operate unless the emperor withdrew the garrison from Rome, which he dared not promise, while the response of Vienna was indecisive. Discussions continued throughout 1869 and 1870, but no agreement was achieved before the fateful climax was reached in the diplomatic crisis, discussed in another chapter (pp. 586-99), out of which came the war of 1870.

Thus with no allies and its army ill prepared, the empire entered upon its decisive test of strength. The outcome was not long in doubt. In less than two months the German armies left French resistance a forlorn hope, and the emperor himself was taken prisoner in the battle of Sedan on 2 September 1870 (see ch. XII, pp. 325-7). Thereupon the Second Empire collapsed. As soon as the news of Sedan reached Paris, the republican opposition in the *Corps Législatif* proclaimed the overthrow of the empire and the establishment of a republican government of National Defence (4 September 1870). Utterly deserted, the empress escaped to England, where she was soon joined by the prince imperial and at the conclusion of the war by the deposed emperor. There Napoleon III lived out the last of his days in what he seemed to regard as a temporary but not wholly unwelcome retirement.

The collapse of the Second Empire was due to its inherent contradictions. Internally, it had proved impossible to reconcile the Bonapartist principle of authoritarian rule with the growth of industrialism and liberalism. In foreign policy, Napoleon III had misconceived the form which nationality would take. Instead of weak federal states under the patronage of France, it had produced powerful unitary states in Germany and Italy, which had completely altered the balance of power. Against his better judgment, which still inclined him even after Sadowa to be true to his principles and accept the *fait accompli*, he was driven by the pressure from his entourage and from French public opinion into a desperate policy of diplomatic gambling, in an attempt to retrieve the prestige of the regime.

Once the reign of Napoleon III was over, France seemed to repudiate all that was distinctive of his regime. Nevertheless, the empire did not disappear without leaving some mark upon the political life and institutions of France. Doubtless the ascendancy of parliament, which was one of the outstanding characteristics of the Third Republic, represented a return to the tradition of Orleanism, rather than an outgrowth of the grudging concessions Napoleon III made towards the close of his reign. However, universal suffrage, another of the hallmarks of the Third Republic, owed perhaps more to the empire than to the republican regime of 1848, for it was due, in large measure, to the long usage and reiterated praise of this institution under Napoleon III that the conservatives who drew up the constitution of 1875 dared not abolish it. In an opposite sense, Napoleon III was also responsible for another of the features of the Third Republic—the reluctance of the republicans to allow a man who showed signs of ambition for personal power to hold the office of President of the Republic, and their unwillingness to entrust the choice of the president to a popular election.

In the two decades after the war of 1914–18, when throughout Europe political movements arose that strove to establish authoritarian governments resting upon democratic principles, the Second Empire seemed to take on a new and broader meaning than had before been evident. To some observers it appeared that as a dictator ruling in the name of the people and consulting the popular will by means of plebiscites, Napoleon III was a precursor of such caesarian demagogues as Hitler and Mussolini. Yet the distinctions between his regime and theirs are perhaps greater than the similarities. For, in contrast to the later exponents of totalitarianism, Napoleon III made no attempt to create a single political movement dedicated to the support of his rule and to eliminate all other opinion than that which he expressed. He was too much a man of the mid-nineteenth century to conceive of what the German National-Socialists were to call *Gleichschaltung*—the regimentation of the entire life of the nation, public and private, under a single leader. Of all his inconsistencies, none was more excusable.

CHAPTER XVIII

THE CRIMEAN WAR

FOR nearly two centuries there was a war between Russia and Turkey about every twenty years. In October 1853 the ninth of this series began. But from the outset it was radically different from its predecessors; for Turkey felt confident of the armed support of Britain and France. By March 1854 they had joined her as allies. The Emperor Nicholas stood alone, deserted to his intense chagrin even by his young protégé, the Emperor Francis Joseph, whom he had saved from the Hungarians only five years before. Europe was ranged with the Muslim sultan against the Orthodox tsar.

Never before had the Ottomans had more than diplomatic support from the West, usually from France. Once, indeed, they had faced a momentary combination of Britain and France with Russia and had suffered the loss of their fleet at Navarino. The Habsburgs, their most ancient foe in Europe, had more than once been leagued with Russia against them, and, as recently as 1849, hand in hand with her, had quarrelled virulently with them over Hungarian and Polish refugees in Turkey. This last acute incident was a pointer to the future which gave much encouragement to the Turks and should have warned the Russians. Both France and Britain vigorously supported Turkey and sent their fleets to the Aegean. Stratford Canning, British ambassador at the Porte, even connived at the entry of Admiral Parker's squadron into the Dardanelles, despite the Straits Convention of 1841, and provoked justifiable remonstrances from St Petersburg.

In 1840–1 for the first time the problem of the Straits had been recognised as an European concern and regulated by the five powers (cf. ch. x, pp. 256–8). Nicholas and Nesselrode, his Foreign Minister, joined with surprising readiness in this settlement, because they judged it impossible to renew their very favourable treaty of Unkiar Skelessi and wished to use the second Mehemet Ali crisis to divide Britain from France. Now in 1853–4 the far greater question of the future of the Ottoman empire was raised by Russia's action and she was to find that it, too, must be regarded as the common concern of the powers, and no longer, as Nicholas and his predecessors had, in essentials, assumed, a matter to be determined by Russia with or without agreement with Austria. This new development in the relations of Europe with Turkey came to a head in the Crimean War. Herein, in large part, lies the importance of the war.

It was not brought about, as some have argued,[1] by the deliberate cun-

---

[1] For example, A. W. Kinglake, *The Invasion of the Crimea* (London, 1863–80), vol. I, *passim*.

ning of Napoleon III in using the dispute with Russia over the Holy Places to fortify his new position as emperor by a glorious appeal to arms, or to divide the victors over his uncle by luring Great Britain into partnership and Austria away from Nicholas's version of the Holy Alliance, or to engineer the collapse of the 1815 settlement and an appeal to nationalities for the benefit of the Italians and the Poles. Nor was the Crimean War caused, as others have argued,[1] by the machinations of Palmerston and Stratford de Redcliffe, bedevilling the pacific half-measures of Aberdeen and stirring up an ignorant and bellicose public opinion to 'back the wrong horse'. Still less was it brought about by British economic interests working to further their hold on Turkish markets and to avenge themselves upon Russia, their bugbear of high protection. War began because a nationalist and defiant Turkey would not yield to Russian demands which she held to be humiliating and threatening to the maintenance of her empire. France and Britain joined her, and Austria openly swung towards the allies because they were not prepared to allow Russia to settle her scores with Turkey by herself and to gain thereby complete ascendancy in the Balkans and Asia Minor.

The Russian demands upon Turkey arose out of the dispute over the Holy Places, which gradually became envenomed after the arrival in Constantinople (5 May) of a new French ambassador, the fiery and ambitious La Valette. The French position as protector of the rights of the Latins in the Holy Places in Jerusalem and Bethlehem had suffered through the increasing ascendancy of the Greeks during the previous half-century. This ascendancy was not unnatural since Orthodox pilgrims outnumbered the Catholic by a hundred to one.[2] Already at the end of Louis Philippe's reign France began to reassert her claims while the papacy and several Catholic orders displayed renewed activity. Louis Napoleon, anxious to conciliate Catholic opinion in France, took the matter much farther but he had no personal desire to make it a major issue such as might embroil him with Russia. In Constantinople, however, where the complicated negotiations were centred, intense rivalry developed between the French and Russian diplomats, encouraged by certain individuals in their respective Foreign Offices and certain newspapers. By October 1851 La Valette seemed on the point of success. Nicholas now intervened with a personal demand to the sultan for the maintenance of the *status quo*. The Porte, harried from both sides, addressed a note to France, in February 1852, which made concessions to the Latins and seemed to give full satisfaction to her. Almost immediately afterwards it secretly gave a firman to the Greeks which seemed to confirm their rights. But what might be promised, partly in writing and partly by word of mouth, in Constantinople might not be performed in Jerusalem, rent

[1] For example, P. de la Gorce, *Histoire du Second Empire* (Paris, 1894), vol. I, p. 201.
[2] Charles-H. Pouthas, *Démocraties et capitalisme, 1848–60* (Paris, 1948), p. 468.

by 'a continuance of desperate Irish rows between the diverse sections of the faithful'.[1]

There followed a succession of shuffling attempts by the Turkish authorities in Palestine to give something to each of the Christian contestants. Threats and counter-threats were bandied about: the French navy might blockade the Dardanelles or be sent to Syria, and it went in fact to Tripoli; the Russian embassy might leave Constantinople; the *Charlemagne*, a new battleship, after a hot tussle, was allowed through the Dardanelles, bringing La Valette back to the Golden Horn. The British, while Stratford de Redcliffe was on leave, were not yet engaged. By the end of 1852 the confusion was worse than ever. The Russians were prepared to help the sultan against the French if he carried out fully what he had promised, but they feared that the Grand Vizier, Mehemet Ali, and the Foreign Minister, Fuad Pasha, were tools of La Valette. Nesselrode attributed the worst designs to Napoleon III, as he had just become after the plebiscite of November. Nicholas, who had welcomed 'the man of 2 December', was now inveighing against him for pushing the Turks to extremes and had no welcome for a restoration of the empire. Indeed, erroneously believing that his brother monarchs in Vienna and Berlin would follow suit, he refused to recognise 'the dynastic numeral [*le chiffre dynastique*]'. Napoleon passed off the insult in Nicholas's form of address with a clever repartee and further showed his moderation by recalling La Valette on long leave (11 January). Still, the affair of 'the dynastic numeral' rankled on both sides.

By the new year Nicholas was contemplating drastic steps. The sultan had broken his word; he must be made to keep it and to give guarantees for the future. Fear had thrown the Porte into the arms of France; fear would bring the Porte back into the arms of Russia.[2] Nicholas recognised that Turkish resistance would probably lead to war, but was prepared to face that.[3] During January two corps on the southern frontier were openly put on a war footing. At the same time he decided to send a special envoy to Constantinople to demand both a satisfactory settlement of the question of the Holy Places and also a treaty or convention guaranteeing the future by making explicit the Russian claims, under the Treaty of Kutchuk Kainardji of 1774, in relation to the immunities and privileges of the Orthodox church.

The idea of a special mission had originated with Nesselrode (25 December 1852) probably to deflect his master from some more drastic step.

---

[1] Karl Marx, *The Eastern Question*, ed. E. M. and E. Aveling (London, 1897), p. 322; a reprint of letters written between 1853 and 1856 on the events of the Crimean War.

[2] Report of Nesselrode to the tsar, 20 December 1852/1 January 1853, in A. M. Zaionchkovskii, *Vostochnaya Voina 1853–1858* (St Petersburg, 1908), vol. I, pt. 2, p. 355.

[3] See minute of Nicholas on Brunnov's dispatch of 8/20 December 1852, *ibid.* vol. I, pt. 2, pp. 348–9.

The suggestion of a treaty or convention had been received from Reshid Pasha who was not then in office. Nicholas himself was pondering a sudden attack on Constantinople and, as his private notes show,[1] was scheming in expectation of the collapse of the Ottoman empire. He contemplated, as the least bad of all bad possibilities, an arrangement which would reduce the Ottoman empire to Asia, give the Principalities and northern Bulgaria to Russia, independence to the rest of Bulgaria and Serbia, the littoral of the Archipelago and of the Adriatic to Austria, Egypt and perhaps Cyprus and Rhodes to England, Crete to France, the Aegean isles to Greece, and make Constantinople a free city, with a Russian garrison on the Bosporus and an Austrian on the Dardanelles. Convinced that the death of 'the sick man' impended and that preparations for what should follow must be made in advance, Nicholas broached similar ideas in four conversations (9 January to 22 February 1853) with Sir Hamilton Seymour, the British ambassador in St Petersburg.

In December 1852 Aberdeen had become Prime Minister. Lord John Russell was Foreign Secretary until February 1853 when Clarendon succeeded him. Aberdeen had been Foreign Secretary in Peel's government in 1844 when Nicholas visited England and reached what he thought was agreement on the future of Turkey (see above, ch. x, pp. 259–60). Of this Nicholas had immediately reminded Lord John (16 December). In March 1854, when war had come, a British Blue Book published the Seymour conversations and part of the 1844 discussions with Aberdeen. It did much to stimulate or confirm the belief that the tsar was planning the dissolution of Turkey. Nicholas's object, now, as in 1844, was an understanding between gentlemen (his favourite diplomatic panacea) about what should follow the collapse of Turkey. It was especially important that each should know what the other would not allow. The British government, on the contrary, though it did not instruct Seymour to cease handling these hot coals until 5 April, from the first denied the tsar's assumption that the Ottoman empire was about to fall: any concert with Russia could only be to prevent collapse, not to hasten it by an agreement disposing in advance of the sultan's territory.

Both parties did, indeed, agree that they could not allow Constantinople to fall to any great power, a Byzantine empire to be set up or Greece to be substantially enlarged. The British further consented, much to Russia's satisfaction, not to make any other agreement, anticipating the fall of Turkey, without previous communication with St Petersburg. But they did not rise to Nicholas's bait of Egypt or Crete, and they could only view with alarm his suggestion that the Principalities, Serbia and Bulgaria might be independent states under his protection and, with still greater alarm his avowal that, while he would not establish himself in Constanti-

---

[1] The texts of these autograph notes by Nicholas, undated but evidently of December 1852, are printed in the original French in Zaionchkovskii, *op. cit.* vol. 1, pt. 2, pp. 357–8.

nople as proprietor ('*en propriétaire*'), circumstances might force him to do so as trustee ('*en dépositaire*').

As for France, Nicholas affected to disregard her and did not at this stage make any serious overtures to her. Austria, he declared, he could rely on (21 February)[1]—a fatal misconception that was not shared by Nesselrode. Two days later he wrote to the Emperor Francis Joseph promising him support, if necessary, in arms should his demands on Turkey about Montenegro be refused. While Russia was preparing to summon Turkey to give her satisfaction, Austria was taking action to foil a Turkish attempt to subdue the ever recalcitrant Montenegrins. She concentrated troops for a temporary occupation of Bosnia and Herzegovina, sent a military mission to warn Omer Pasha, the Turkish commander, to withdraw, and dispatched Count Leiningen to Constantinople with an ultimatum requiring the immediate cessation of hostilities and the settlement of certain frontier questions. Within a fortnight of his arrival the Turkish government gave in (14 February) and patched up peace with Montenegro.

Within another fortnight the Turks were faced with another special envoy, Prince Menshikov (28 February). Would they yield a second time to threatening demands from the giaour? Menshikov was a grandee and Minister of Marine, but he had not been Nicholas's first choice and was ill-fitted for his task. He arrived laden with voluminous instructions, which nevertheless gave him wide latitude, and accompanied by high naval and military officers, who openly reconnoitred even as far as Smyrna and Athens. Contemporaries blamed him for his intemperate and abusive behaviour, and some Russians for his dilatory lack of energy. His faults were exaggerated. Yet it is true that he began by insisting on the removal of the Foreign Minister, Fuad Pasha, and that he signally failed to settle matters, as Nicholas hoped, before the return of Stratford de Redcliffe. Menshikov was caught in the prevailing mizmaze of intrigue and Turkish delaying tactics and was victimised by rival dragomans and extremist counsellors in the embassy. 'The old Turks', the men of Unkiar Skelessi, were too old or unavailing and there were no other groups or individuals with the ear of the sultan who would stand out against the rising nationalist desire to resist Russian intimidation. This mood of defiance was typified by Mehemet Ali, the Grand Vizier, and Mehemet Rushdi, the Minister for War.

It hardened into determination the more the Turks felt that they would, in the last resort, receive French and British armed support. On 20 March, after news had reached Paris of the enforced resignation of Fuad Pasha and of the Russian military and naval preparations, the French fleet was ordered from Toulon to Salamis. Napoleon's decision was taken in

---

[1] See his notes on Russell to Seymour, 9 February 1853, communicated 21 February, *ibid*. vol. I, pt. 2, pp. 364–5.

isolation from the British government, who had stringently overruled Rose, chargé d'affaires at Constantinople, when he took it upon himself to summon the fleet from Malta. Napoleon, always prone to oscillate between extremes, seems to have swung far towards war as he almost at the same time swung in the opposite direction by sending de Lacour, a moderate man, with pacific instructions as his new ambassador to Constantinople. Although the British government did not send their fleet, they sent Stratford de Redcliffe. The Turks, like everybody else, feared him. But at this juncture his arrival (5 April) gave them hope that, if they stood firm, they would have his backing. 'If the Russians are in the wrong, as I believe they are,' wrote Stratford to his wife (27 April), 'my business is to make the wrong appear, and to stand by the Porte, or rather make the P. stand by me.'[1]

The Turks were further encouraged by the settlement of the immediate issue of the Holy Places on 22 April. This was brought about by amicable conversations between de Lacour and Menshikov with the assistance of Stratford de Redcliffe, who admitted that the Russians had had justifiable complaints. It cleared the ground for the main matter, a treaty or convention binding the sultan *vis-à-vis* Russia to the preservation of all the religious and spiritual immunities of the Orthodox church (the religious immunities included the upkeep of churches, religious buildings and pious foundations as well as the civil rights and exemptions of the Orthodox clergy; the spiritual immunities, included the right of the clergy to celebrate). Menshikov was empowered to offer the sultan a defensive alliance if he accepted the Russian proposals and incurred thereby the hostility of any of the powers. He did not, however, make the offer. It is difficult to suppose it could have succeeded. Stratford de Redcliffe would have exerted all his influence against it: if Turkey allied with any power it should be Britain, as he himself had proposed in 1849. Now he declared to the Russians that too close a friendship with the Turks would arouse as much suspicion in Europe as a rupture leading to war.

There was little likelihood of any friendship from the side of the Turks. They regarded Menshikov's draft treaty or convention as incompatible with their sovereign independence and tantamount to recognising Russia as arbiter in all matters relating to the Orthodox in Turkey, a view strongly supported by Stratford de Redcliffe and de Lacour and later shared by Clarendon and Drouyn de Lhuys. Although Menshikov greatly modified his original terms, deferred his departure and in the end proposed a note from the sultan to the emperor instead of a treaty or convention, he failed to obtain anything. Changes in the ministry (12 May) brought Mustapha Pasha to the Grand Vizieriate and Reshid Pasha to the Ministry of Foreign Affairs. Menshikov's brighter hopes were shattered when a Grand Council decided overwhelmingly to reject the Russian requirements

[1] S. Lane Poole, *The Life of Stratford Canning* (London, 1888), vol. II, p. 261.

(17 May). The final Turkish reply of 20 May referred only to the spiritual immunities and not in the binding form required. In consequence Menshikov left Constantinople on 21 May and diplomatic relations were broken off.

Both in London and Paris suspicions of Russia's intentions, already aroused by her military and naval measures, were deepened when only a part of Menshikov's instructions, and that the least important, was communicated to them. They concluded that the Turkish interpretation of Menshikov's demands was justified. Further, a Russian armed counter-stroke, probably in the shape of an occupation of the Principalities, seemed imminent. On 2 June the Aberdeen government ordered the Malta fleet to Besika Bay, just outside the Dardanelles, and Napoleon immediately followed suit. Palmerston was right when he said, in retro-spect, that this signal encouragement to the Turks meant 'the passing of the Rubicon'.[1]

The Emperor Nicholas felt, as he said, that his face had been slapped by the sultan. He did, indeed, make another abortive attempt to reach an arrangement with the Porte direct (19/31 May), but it was accompanied by a threat to occupy the Principalities and followed by a heated Russian circular (30 May/11 June) couched in terms especially wounding to France. Yet the day before, Nicholas had opened out to the French ambassador on the same lines as earlier to Seymour and had sought to get into personal touch with Napoleon III.

Ever since January the tsar had had an attack on Constantinople, either from the Bosporus or by land through the Principalities and Bulgaria, in mind. By May, in view of the French attitude, now supported by Great Britain, he decided on a half-measure—the occupation of the Principalities as a gage until Turkey satisfied his demands. At the same time he asked Austria[2] similarly to occupy Herzegovina and Serbia, an invitation that was declined. Nicholas did not intend to cross the Danube, but, if the Turks did not yield, the Principalities and Serbia might be declared independent. A general rising of the Christians would probably follow and 'the last hour of the Ottoman Empire strike'.[3]

Orders to cross the Pruth were given on 12/24 June and during July the Principalities and the line of the Danube were occupied by strong Russian forces. Nicholas publicly undertook to withdraw if the sultan accepted Menshikov's final note and the western fleets also withdrew. This last condition figured in another heated Russian circular (20 June/ 2 July) inveighing against western support of Turkey.

If Palmerston, then Home Secretary, had had his way western support

[1] E. Ashley, *The Life of...Palmerston, 1846–65* (London, 1877), vol. II, p. 45.
[2] Nicholas to Francis Joseph, 18/30 May 1853, extract in H. Schlitter, *Aus der Regierungszeit Kaiser Franz Joseph I* (Vienna, 1919), p. 93.
[3] Nicholas to Pashkievitch, 17/29 May 1853, Zaionchkovskii, *op. cit.* vol. I, pt. 2, pp. 437–8. Cp. A. P. Shcherbatov, *General Feldmarshal Knyaz Pashkievitch* (St Petersburg, 1888–1904), vol. VII, p. 54.

would have been still stronger. As the Russians crossed the Pruth, he was urging the dispatch of the combined squadrons to the Bosporus: a bold strong course was the safest way to maintain peace. This dubious recommendation, to which Stratford de Redcliffe was strongly opposed and Nicholas was not likely to have bowed,[1] was not put to the test. The cabinet went forward into the maze of negotiations which now took place in Paris, Vienna and Constantinople. Too many projects were afoot, but the main outcome was that the negotiators at Constantinople were displaced and that agreement was reached in Vienna. Great Britain, France, Austria and Prussia concurred in a note to be sent by the sultan to the tsar which should settle the questions at issue and lead to the evacuation of the Principalities. Known as the Vienna note, it was the handiwork in part of Napoleon and in part of Buol, the Austrian Foreign Minister. It was skilfully designed to harmonise the interests of Russia and France without apparently trenching upon the sovereign rights of Turkey. Its main importance lay in its being the joint product of the four powers. The fate of the Ottoman empire was, thus, in a sense, recognised as an European question. Moreover, far from backing up the Menshikov mission as Russia had backed up the Leiningen, Austria led the concert of the western powers and Prussia followed her. This step, though not regarded by Nicholas or Nesselrode as inimical, was none the less a sign that the alliance of the three eastern powers was ending. The Austrians were already telling the Russians that they were not prepared to join them in a policy based on the imminent collapse of Turkey in Europe.[2]

The draft note was sent to St Petersburg on 28 July and was promptly accepted, but in Constantinople it was received with vehement opposition. Nationalist and religious fervour had welled up on Russia's entry into the Principalities. The extremists pressed on military measures and used the Constantinople populace for their ends. Encouragement was given by news of British public opinion, heading strongly against Aberdeen and pacification, and immense enthusiasm was aroused by the arrival in mid-August of the Egyptian fleet with 15,000 troops. News of Russia's complaisance confirmed suspicions that the note was really her concoction. Stratford de Redcliffe did not believe in it—for it was not of his making—and he knew that his personal, as distinct from his official influence in favour of acceptance would have been disregarded. The utmost that could be salved was a reply requiring three amendments instead of plain rejection (20 August).

The amendments were designed to rule out any far-reaching Russian

---

[1] See Nicholas's instructions to Brunnov, 29 July/10 August, E. V. Tarle, *Krimskaya Voina* (Moscow, 1941), vol. I, p. 331.

[2] Francis Joseph to Nicholas, 21 July; cp. Francis Joseph to Nicholas, 7 January 1854; Schlitter, *op. cit.* pp. 94–5, 98. Meyendorff to Nesselrode, 15/27 July, reporting a conversation with Buol, *P. von Meyendorff: Politischer und Privater Briefwechsel, 1826–1863*, ed. O. Hoetzsch (Berlin, Leipzig, 1923), vol. III, p. 49. Cp. Tarle, *op. cit.* vol. I, pp. 324–5.

interpretation of the Treaty of Kutchuk Kainardji and any claim to protect the religious as well as the spiritual privileges of the Orthodox church. Nicholas was at first inclined to accept the Turkish modifications, but yielded to the unusual combination of the politic Nesselrode with national and Slavophile extremists. On 7 September he declared that the Vienna note must remain unmodified. Diplomatically he was in a strong position; for the other four powers, though not their representatives in Constantinople, were also still backing it.

Within a fortnight Russia's position was ruined by a confidential commentary, drawn up in her Foreign Office, on the note and its Turkish amendments. It so interpreted these as to give fair warrant for the belief that the 'old Nick policy of aggression and aggrandisement' was in full control. It leaked out into the press, being published in London on 22 September, and immediately produced deplorable results both in government circles and among the public at large in Great Britain and France. Simultaneously, in Constantinople war feeling was worked up by mass demonstrations. The weak and intimidated sultan and the Sheikh al-Islam swam with the tide and the belligerent Mehemet Ali, now Minister of War, and Omer Pasha the Croat renegade in command of a large army in Bulgaria, had everything their own way. By the end of September the issue was decided. On 4 October the sultan announced war if the Principalities were not evacuated within a fortnight. The Russians of course refused to go and on 23 October 1853 the Turks began hostilities on the Danube and a few days later near Batum. The Russians undertook, at any rate provisionally, to remain on the defensive north of the Danube, but said nothing about the Caucasus.[1]

These decisive events on the Golden Horn and the Danube confounded the diplomats' further attempts at negotiation. Nicholas failed, despite personal visits to Francis Joseph and Frederick William, to bind either by written promises to benevolent neutrality. He likewise failed in an overture for a personal agreement with Napoleon III who held fast to Britain. The French, indeed, took the lead in pressing for the two fleets to be sent up from Besika Bay to the Bosporus, and on 23 September joint instructions were sent for the passage of the Dardanelles. Following Turkish requests, the French and British fleets moved, in part, into the Dardanelles and, in part, up to Constantinople itself. But Stratford de Redcliffe deferred full compliance with the instructions of 23 September until he received the British cabinet's peremptory orders of 8 October to bring the fleet up to the Bosporus. British public opinion, as even Aberdeen privately confessed, would not allow the abandonment of Turkey. By 15 November the British and French fleets were concentrated at Constantinople.

[1] Circular of Nesselrode, 19/31 October; Nicholas to Menshikov, 9/21 October, texts in Zaionchkovskii, *op. cit.* vol. II, pt. 3, p. 170.

The British government had refused a French proposal to enter the Black Sea; for that would have made war inevitable, as Nesselrode wrote to Brunnov, his ambassador in London.[1] On the contrary, Britain told Russia that she would not enter the Black Sea as long as the Russians did not cross the Danube and did not attack any Black Sea port; but she could not abandon the Turks to their fate by undertaking to remain neutral. Nicholas's immediate reaction was that this meant war.[2] Nevertheless, he issued orders that Turkish ships were not to be attacked in port but only at sea.[3] The Turks, not the Russians, first crossed the Danube. They won two minor successes before, on 18/30 November, at Sinope, a Russian squadron wiped out a Turkish flotilla and two transports believed to be bound for the Caucasus front. Sinope demonstrated the devastating effect of the new Paixhans naval shells against wooden vessels (cf. ch. XI, p. 281). Still more devastating was the effect of Sinope in the west.

This perfectly legitimate operation was denounced as a 'massacre', an infamous and cruel act of treachery and an unpardonable insult to national honour. The entire British press called for war, and public sentiment, which during the autumn had grown more and more anti-Russian, now ran beyond control. The news of Sinope coincided with the resignation of Palmerston (14 December) on the ground of opposition to a reform bill proposed by Lord John Russell. It was said to be really due to his disagreement with Aberdeen, the queen and the Prince Consort on armed support to Turkey. There was a howl for the return to power, or at least to office, of the strong man who would vindicate Britain against the tsar, and on 25 December Palmerston returned as Home Secretary. There was a prolonged outcry against the Prince Consort, popularly suspected of working for Russia against Palmerston, and the wildest rumours gained credence.

In the France of the Second Empire there could be no such ebullitions, but the effect of Sinope was strong. A £2,000,000 loan to Turkey was immediately settled. Napoleon was insistent that the two fleets must enter the Black Sea and that the Russian fleet must take no action against Turkey. This demand was jointly made to St Petersburg (22 December) and was followed on 3 January by the two fleets entering the Black Sea. After some delay Nicholas answered (4/16 January) with an inquiry whether the French and British admirals had also orders to stop Turkish action against Russia; if the reply was negative, his ambassadors were

---

[1] Nesselrode to Brunnov, 5/17 October 1853, Tarle, *op. cit.* vol. I, p. 368.

[2] See Nicholas's minute: 'Ainsi c'est la guerre. Soit!' on Brunnov to Nesselrode, 26 October/7 November 1853; F. F. Martens, *Recueil des traités et conventions conclus par la Russie* (St Petersburg, 1898), vol. XII, pp. 330–1.

[3] See Menshikov, commanding in the Crimea, to Admiral Kornilov, 6/18 November, transmitting the imperial orders but interpreting them in as limiting a sense as possible. Zaionchkovskii, *op. cit.* vol. II, pt. I, p. 300.

to leave Paris and London at once. Although Napoleon was now cherishing hopes of a peaceful outcome through a personal letter to Nicholas and would have preferred not to give an immediate reply, he yielded to British pressure and identical answers were given on 1 February. These were not satisfactory to Nicholas, and on 6 February Brunnov and Kiselev left London and Paris respectively, and a fortnight later Seymour and Castelbajac left St Petersburg.

The two western powers did not declare war until 28 March, but it was certain once they decided to deny the Black Sea to Russian but not to Turkish naval operations. Already on 12 March they had signed an alliance with Turkey and on 19 March the first French troops left for the Dardanelles. Britain and France signed a similar alliance with each other only on 10 April. Meanwhile their armies had begun to land on the Gallipoli peninsula and at Scutari where a subsidiary camp was pitched. The allies expected Russia to repeat the rapid advance on Adrianople and Constantinople effected in 1829. The Russo-Turkish war had now become a quadripartite struggle and Russia stood alone. She could not count on Austria even for neutrality. Orlov, sent by the tsar on a special mission to Vienna (28 January to 9 February), failed both in last-minute peace proposals and in securing any definite pledge from Austria.

The military operations were slow to develop. The Russians, dividing their forces between Europe and Asia, left themselves too weak for a quick decisive stroke and settled to the siege of the Danubian town of Silistria. Omer Pasha in Bulgaria would not risk another engagement. The British and French commanders-in-chief, Lord Raglan and Saint-Arnaud, were instructed to defend Constantinople and, while it was not immediately threatened, concentrated on the administrative task of transporting and encamping their armies, postponing strategic decisions. In May the allies moved up to the Bulgarian port of Varna, still undecided between a defensive concentration or an offensive to relieve Silistria and liberate the Principalities. Before the decision was made the Russians withdrew from the Principalities and the allies had no further military objective in the Balkan Peninsula. This was the work of Austria.

Buol's immediate object was to safeguard the lower Danube basin against Russia. His policy was so far anti-Russian and his position was strong. Russia was vulnerable to Austria all the way from south Poland to Bessarabia. Throughout the war part of her forces were kept on this frontier to meet possible Austrian hostilities. By May Austria had so deployed her forces as to threaten Russia's position in the Principalities. Her third army was mobilised behind the Turco-Hungarian border, her fourth stationed in Galicia and an emergency levy of 95,000 men authorised. Already on 20 April Buol had signed an alliance with Prussia which gave Austria the right to call on her for 200,000 men and bound her to join in pressure upon Russia to evacuate the Principalities. This pressure Prussia in vain tried to make impartial by a simultaneous summons to the allies to evacuate the Black Sea. Buol addressed his demand to Russia on 3 June and Prussia endorsed it (12 June). On 14 June he signed a convention with Turkey which allowed Austria to occupy the Principalities for the duration of the war, and, in the event of disorders there, Herzegovina and Albania. On 23 June Russia raised the siege of Silistria. Her reply (29 June) partially yielded to the Austrian summons because Nicholas underestimated Buol's anti-Russian disposition and overestimated Frederick William's capacity to restrain Austria. He hoped, however, to gain some equivalent and meanwhile retained Moldavia. But he presumed too far on Austria's loyalty. Buol had already sounded Paris about an alliance. He now prepared to concert measures with the allied commanders against the Russians in Moldavia. He agreed, also, on conditions of peace which Austria would support the allies in exacting. These were the four points, accepted by Francis Joseph (8 August) in a mood of impatience at Russia's hesitations. Prince Gorchakov, however, had already arrived in Vienna with Russia's promise to complete the evacuation. Buol did not now finish the negotiation with the west even when Russia rejected the four points (26 August). The Russian evacuation and the Austrian occupation, which began on 22 August, gave Austria all Buol then dared take. Her best insurance against a renewal of Russia's threat to the lower Danube would be a western victory with which she was associated. But Buol dared not risk the association until the victory was sure enough to make Russian counter-measures against Austria improbable.

When the evacuation of the Principalities lifted the threat from Constantinople, the Crimea became the new theatre of war. English rather than French, the choice probably reflected a sea-power's instinct to exploit the command of the Black Sea, recently demonstrated by the bombardment of Odessa. The object was to capture the forts which sheltered the Russian fleet, and to destroy, at Sebastopol, an accessible concentration of Russian war material. The commanders in the field accepted the plan after a reconnaissance (19 August) which failed to reveal the number of Russian troops in the Crimea or to convince them that they could supply the expedition after it had landed. But a move had become essential; for cholera had begun to ravage the armies, the French by the beginning and the British by the end of July.

In the new campaign both sides fumbled (see also ch. XII, pp. 322–3). The Russians did not attack while the allied armies were vulnerable during the five days of landing on the beaches of Eupatoria. Their effort to block the allies' march south at the River Alma (20 September) was defeated, owing to the irresponsibility of Menshikov, now the Russian commander, as much as to the solidity of the British infantry. On the other hand, the allies gained little, since they allowed Menshikov to escape with his army intact. Yet he wasted this advantage, letting the allies make a wide detour to the east unmolested, and take up positions (26 September) south of Sebastopol. Again the allies missed an opportunity. For six days they outnumbered the garrison and Todleben's defences were unfinished, but they did not summon Sebastopol to surrender nor, even after the first bombardment (17 October), attempt an assault. At Balaclava (25 October) Menshikov was defeated in an attempt to cut off the British port of supply both from Sebastopol and from the French positions near Kamiesh to the west. But the allied victory was costly and hollow. Lucan had failed to manage the British cavalry as a whole so that, whereas the charge of the heavy brigade was an effective piece of generalship, that of the light brigade was extravagant heroism. The Russians, moreover, were left in command of the only metal road which connected the port with the British camp on the plateau. Divided counsels had again prevented pursuit and decisive victory.

Yet the allies had done enough to embolden Buol. Austria reopened negotiations in Paris (3 October), instructed her commander in the Principalities to let the Turks pass through into Russian Bessarabia and put her whole army on a war footing for a campaign in the following spring. Prussia, in alarm, made unavailing efforts to induce Austria to promise only to negotiate together with herself and the Germanic Confederation. She then turned to Russia whom she pressed to accept the four points. Russia had professed herself ready to negotiate on them when events in the Crimea sharply checked Buol. Preparations for an assault on Sebastopol on 17 November had exposed the allies to Menshikov's field army, now reinforced from the Russian Danube army. He took the British by surprise on Inkerman ridge on 5 November. This was an infantry battle, reduced to a series of desperate encounters between small numbers by the character of the ground and by the fog and rain. The Russians were defeated but Sebastopol was saved. Thus a military decision was postponed and the armies condemned to a winter of disease and privation on the Chersonese plateau. Buol dared pursue his anti-Russian policy no farther. On 20 November Francis Joseph cancelled the general mobilisation order. The point when Austria might have declared war on Russia was now passed.

This was not at once evident. On 26 November Austria induced Prussia to extend to the Principalities the guarantee of her territory given by the April alliance and on 2 December she signed the Franco-British alliance. Buol, however, took this last step expecting it to be ineffective. Austria bound herself to declare war if Russia failed to accept the four points by the end of the year, but four days earlier Gorchakov, Russian ambassador in Vienna, had been officially told to negotiate on them. Furthermore, its significance was almost as much anti-Italian as anti-Russian. Austria was rewarded by Napoleon's guarantee, in the convention of 22 December,[1] of the territorial *status quo* in the Italian peninsula until the eastern complications were settled. Buol, in seeking to protect what he believed to be Austrian interests, tried to get advantages from all sides. It was an over-ambitious policy which left on both neutrals and belligerents the impression of duplicity and timidity.

Although the tripartite alliance did not alter Austria's policy towards Russia, diplomatically it marked the opening of a new phase; for it became the starting-point of fresh negotiations with Russia. A series of conferences began in Vienna on 15 March. Nobody believed that they would in fact produce peace. Indeed, during the winter both France and Britain were stirred to a more military temper. Napoleon's desire to fight to an effective finish was reflected in his decision to go himself to the Crimea from which Clarendon with difficulty dissuaded him. In Britain, an outcry against the mismanagement of the war and Roebuck's parliamentary motion for an inquiry brought down the coalition government. Palmerston became Prime Minister, reforms were undertaken, and, after the resignation of Gladstone and his fellow Peelites (22 February), the new cabinet braced itself for its military responsibilities. The Cobdenite peace party had decisively failed and the working-class regarded the war as in a sense its own. Prince Albert's visit to Boulogne (September 1854), ministerial visits to Paris (November) and Napoleon's visit to Windsor (April 1855) eased the working of the Anglo-French alliance. Meanwhile on 2 March Nicholas had died and the inexperienced Alexander II come to the throne. The removal from the picture of Nicholas's legendary ambition and temperamental rigidity encouraged the allies to hope that a decisive victory in the field might really produce a sound peace. Palmerston deprecated negotiation 'in the middle of a Battle' with the fate of Sebastopol still undecided.[2] The British plenipotentiary, Lord John Russell, was more hopeful but failed to gain the preliminary alliance with Prussia which he regarded as essential. Turkey was evasive. Buol regarded the negotiations chiefly as a means of concealing his hand from both sides. Russia was dilatory—one of Gorchakov's many references home suspended discussion for three weeks (27 March to 17 April)—yet wished to avoid a breakdown. The hope of Drouyn de Lhuys, the French plenipotentiary, that a rupture of negotiations would oblige Austria to come in on the side of the allies was unrealisable; since Buol's influence was waning and Francis Joseph's tightening control produced a stricter and more candid neutrality. Thus the negotiators muddled on with 'deceptive amiability'[3] until the conferences were intermitted on 26 April and finally broken off on 4 June.

---

[1] See F. Valsecchi, *L'alleanza di Crimea* (Milan, 1948), p. 479 for the text.

[2] Palmerston to Clarendon, 11 March, 16 April 1855, private Clarendon papers, Bodleian Library, Clar. dep. c. 31, fos. 49, 126.

[3] E. Hammond to his wife, 23 March 1855, private Hammond papers, Public Record Office, F.O. 391/31. Hammond acted as secretary to Russell.

Yet they carried the powers some way towards the peace terms ultimately laid down. Russia conceded point one of the four points, that the protectorate of the Principalities should belong to the powers jointly, and point two, that international measures should be taken to improve the navigation of the Danube and assure its freedom. Point four, however, that Russia's special relationship to the Orthodox should cease and their privileges be guaranteed by the powers jointly, was postponed. Contention had fastened on the third point providing for the revision of the Straits Convention of 1841. Whereas it was agreed that this implied a European guarantee to Turkey and recognition that a conflict between the Porte and any one great power was the concern of them all, divergence persisted on the naval arrangements themselves. The opening, or the partial opening, of the Straits, and a system of counterpoise to keep the rule of closure, but to admit so many western ships into the Black Sea as would offset any increase in the Russian fleet, and to allow Turkey to call up help at need, were all discussed. The outcome indicated that an arrangement to keep the Straits closed and to neutralise the Black Sea—an idea of French origin—was the only one likely to be both acceptable to the allies and imposable upon Russia. The repudiation by the French and British governments of their representatives' acceptance of the counterpoise proposal removed both Drouyn de Lhuys and Lord John Russell from office. Finally, the conferences saw a decline in Austria's influence. In the struggle against Russia, Britain now set the pace and the British pull upon Napoleon III grew stronger at the expense of the Austrian. It became increasingly plain that Austrian neutrality denoted the weakness of isolation and not the strength of an arbiter.

Military operations during 1855 were also moving towards a decision. The year had begun badly despite the improvements in the British auxiliary services and the arrival of considerable reinforcements. A bombardment of Sebastopol (9–19 April) was again fruitless and the plan to cut Russia's sea communications by taking the Kerch peninsula was abandoned. Improvement began only when Napoleon's proposed visit had been staved off and the fastidious Canrobert replaced by the bolder Pélissier. The Kerch expedition now succeeded (21 May), while the Sardinians, under General La Marmora, arrived at Balaclava to take up positions to the east of the British. The June assault on Sebastopol failed, but was the last failure. Raglan's death (28 June) meant a change in the British command too and General Simpson's arrival coincided with a renewal of confidence. On 16 August the French and Sardinians defeated the Russian field army at the Tchernaya. Next day the bombardment of Sebastopol was resumed, the final assault followed and on 9 September the Russians abandoned the town. The Russians had been defeated but were not overwhelmed. An objective of some local value had been taken, but the allies might well hesitate to advance into Russia while no one knew what resources she had for her defence. A real victory meant another campaign: peace at this point a virtual repetition, in the Turkish question, of the terms discussed at the Vienna conferences. The course of events in 1855 had, however, introduced extra questions.

Cavour's political and the allies' military needs had brought in Sardinia and the Italian question (see ch. xxI, p. 569). At first the Italians had seen the war as a contest between the liberal west and absolutist Russia with her traditional allies. In December 1853 the activities of Baron de Brenier, a Napoleonic emissary, in Turin lent plausibility to this interpretation. But it did not outlast Austria's desertion of her ally. The first English soundings about Italian assistance (April 1854) consequently failed. Cavour, however, under pressure from the king, finally carried a policy of supporting the West, despite opposition, despite the French guarantee to Austria of 22 December and although the real value of any arrangements with the allies could not be written into them. On 10 January 1855 Sardinia adhered to the Franco-British alliance and on 26 January signed military and financial conventions with Britain and France. Whatever Cavour's immediate motives (see p. 569), the risk he took in placing Sardinia temporarily in the same camp as Austria afterwards appeared as the measure of his statesmanship. All he had obtained was that Sardinia was an ally and not a subordinate (allié et non serviteur), that her army of 15,000 men should act as an independent force, and representation at the peace congress. But events proved him right in judging that Austria's association with the West would be as barren as Sardinia's might be fruitful.

Both Napoleon and Palmerston, in different ways, were thinking beyond Turkey in Europe. Napoleon hoped the war might restore Finland to Sweden and give liberty to Poland. France made advances to Sweden and Drouyn de Lhuys discussed Poland with Clarendon in London on his way to the Vienna conferences (April 1855). Later Napoleon spoke openly of changes in Italy and on the left bank of the Rhine. The English court and the Peelites suspected Palmerston of similar plans.[1] Napoleon was too wavering and Palmerston too sceptical to lay real plans to turn the coming congress into the liberal counterpart of the Congress of Vienna. Yet Palmerston was prepared to seek widely dispersed securities against Russia: in Clarendon's phrase to build 'a long line of circumvallation' around her.[2] He looked first to the Baltic, where Napier's fleet had made an impressive, if fruitless, entry. Sweden had a dispute with Russia on the Norwegian–Finnish frontier and seemed a likely ally. But King Oscar disliked the Scandinavian liberals' enthusiasm for the western allies and

[1] D'Azeglio to Cavour, 9 February 1855, Cavour e l'Inghilterra (Bologna, 1933), vol. I, p. 40.
[2] Clarendon to Magenis (Stockholm), 18 October 1855, F.O. 73/269, quoted by P. Knaplund, 'Finmark in British Diplomacy 1836–55', American Historical Review (April 1925), vol. xxx, p. 499.

in December 1853, in conjunction with Denmark, issued a declaration of neutrality. Then, as western military prospects improved and Palmerston showed some eagerness, Sweden took courage, and the king of Denmark declared he would follow her in any measure against Russia. Eventually, after the fall of Sebastopol had released forces for the renewal of naval operations in the Baltic, Canrobert succeeded in concluding a treaty (21 November 1855) which pledged Britain and France to assist Sweden if she was faced with Russian pretensions or aggression. Palmerston saw herein the means of 'preventing Russia from establishing a great naval station...on the Coast of Norway' or elsewhere in the Baltic.[1] This advantage he would drive home by the destruction, proposed as early as March 1855, of the fortifications on the Aaland Islands.

Palmerston looked secondly to the Caucasus. In April 1855 he pronounced for Circassian independence from both Russia and Turkey. Early in the war Russia had invaded Turkey from Circassia, seized Bayazid, which commanded the British trade route into Persia, and now threatened Kars. General Williams, as British commissioner with the Turkish army, and a few British officers organised its defence. But on 28 November 1855 Kars fell. The 'vital Importance'[2] which Palmerston attached to Kars and to Circassia now began to be shared by an angry British public. Outside the Black Sea, Greece, if she could be made a stable kingdom loyal to the West, might be a further bulwark against Russia. But her instability proved incurable. Moreover, in the spring of 1854 King Otto had prepared to invade Turkey with Russia, who, under the treaty of 1832, was a protecting power like Britain and France. Allied troops then occupied the Piraeus (26 May). Though Palmerston refrained, reluctantly, from using the troops to compel reform, he hoped to do something by agreement with Russia as well as France when peace came to be made.

In the autumn of 1855 Palmerston was planning a new campaign to capture Cronstadt and drive the Russians out of Georgia and Circassia, but Napoleon, despite nationalist language about Italy and Poland, was bent on peace. The fall of Sebastopol satisfied the French public and still let Napoleon hope that moderate terms might permit him to repair his relations with Russia without losing the British alliance. The Paris Exhibition, with its foretaste of peace, provided cover for informal soundings by German emissaries. They carried peaceable assurances to St Petersburg as well as to Frankfurt. In December, Seebach, Nesselrode's son-in-law and Saxon Minister in Paris, sounded St Petersburg on Napoleon's behalf, and Gorchakov in Vienna approached the duc de Morny.

Buol had resumed his part of mediator and already agreed with Bour-

---

[1] Palmerston to Clarendon, 26 July 1855, private Clarendon papers, Clar. dep. c. 31, fo. 358.
[2] Palmerston to Clarendon, 3 August 1855, *ibid.* fo. 381.

484

queney, French ambassador in Vienna, on a memorandum of terms to be presented to Russia (14 November). Britain had no share in these negotiations and, when the memorandum was presented for her acceptance, rejected it with some asperity. She even talked of continuing the war alone with Turkey and Sardinia. A more acceptable memorandum was, however, drafted (24 November) with the assistance of Seymour, now ambassador in Vienna. But it was not until late December that Austria could present the terms to St Petersburg as an ultimatum expiring on 18 January. Alexander II was ready for peace lest worse befall. The Swedish treaty, Napoleon's language about Poland and Britain's interest in Circassia led him to fear lest another campaign might end in territorial losses. Financial strain, difficulties in the recruitment and training of soldiers and rumblings of peasant discontent were also discouraging.[1] On the other hand, the success at Kars permitted Russia to accept peace without humiliation. Alexander, however, disliked the Austrian mediation and still more the fifth point of the memorandum, which allowed the allies to make such demands additional to the four points as the fortunes of war justified. This Alexander rejected. Russia's hesitation was Prussia's opportunity. Throughout the conflict, although she had an army of 400,000 men, Prussia had played the part of a second-class power. She was weakened by divergences of view in government circles in Berlin, Manteuffel's lack of mastery and, above all, the confused but restless activity of Frederick William. Yet the king never allowed Prussia to be dragged at the heels of Austria nor seriously endangered her relations with Russia. Thus Alexander welcomed her intervention as minimising the appearance of yielding to Austria. Buol needed support and at once proposed to include Prussia in allied deliberations on further measures if Russia rejected the ultimatum. Prussia accordingly supported the terms with the tsar (30 December and 6 January) and gained from Austria a promise to back her claim to admission to the peace congress. There followed Russia's acceptance of the Austrian ultimatum (16 January), the choice of Paris as the place of the congress (23 January), the recording of the terms agreed upon in principle in the protocol of 1 February, the assembly of the congress and the declaration of an armistice (25 February) for land operations to last until 31 March.

Many of the results of the war had already appeared. The casualties had been relatively heavy. The French sent to the Crimea over 309,000 men, recruited under the conscription law of 1832. Of these 11,000 were killed or died of wounds and 21,000 died of sickness. The British sent out over 96,000 men, raised by voluntary enlistment. Of these 2755 were killed in action, 11,848 died of wounds and 17,799 died of sickness. The returns of the Russian medical department from July 1853 to July 1856 give their

[1] See E. V. Tarle, *Krimskaya Voina* (Moscow, 1945), vol. II, pp. 406–11, for the discussion in the councils of 20 December 1855/1 January 1856 and 3/15 January 1856.

losses as 500,000.[1] This figure seems too high considering that Russia, although she had an army of one million men on paper, in September 1855 had only 150,000 men in the Crimea and about 60,000 in the army operating in Asia.[2] The Turkish casualties are not known. It was widely known that much loss could have been prevented and that there had been, especially in the British army, much avoidable distress. Press correspondents attached to the armies and, after 1855, using the submarine cable from Balaclava to Varna to telegraph their news, gave full and quick publicity to mismanagement. In Britain one consequence of the war was the reorganisation of army administration. Its several sections were brought together under the Secretary for War and the commander-in-chief. The militia, army clothing, the commissariat, the ordnance, with the engineers and the artillery, were transferred to the War Office or the Horse Guards from other departments or from autonomous positions. The Secretary for War lost his colonial business (1854) and took on the duties of the Secretary at War, whose office was eventually abolished by statute (1863). Of the auxiliary services, the Land Transport Corps was raised in 1855, the Director-General of the Army Medical Department was given extra powers, and the functions of the Purveyor General, controlling army hospitals, were defined. The Army Medical School, new surgical techniques, including the use of chloroform, new hospital techniques, with the modern nursing profession as shaped by Florence Nightingale, were all legacies of the Crimean War. Improvements in barracks, the development of training camps, after Aldershot had been bought (1853), and the extension of the government arms factories were incidental features of the modernisation of the British army. These changes were consistent with the wider movement towards a civil service freed from patronage and geared to efficiency begun in 1849 and carried forward during Gladstone's first spell as Chancellor of the Exchequer. Finance was less affected than administration; for the cost of the war was small in proportion to the growing wealth of the country. Business was active throughout, there was capital for investment, and the munition industries provided extra employment. Gladstone, who prepared the two budgets of 1854, met the costs mainly by taxation; Sir G. C. Lewis in 1855 rather by borrowing. Of the £70 millions which the war cost about £38 millions were met by taxation, and the rest by loan. War finance meant in effect retention and increase of the income tax, which survived the date when it was due to end, 1860, to become a permanent part of the British taxing system.

The French administration bore the additional demands of the war well and the Ministry of War showed adaptability in devising arrange-

---

[1] M. I. Bogdanovich, *Vostochnaya Voina 1853–1856* (St Petersburg, 1877), vol. IV, pp. 413–15.
[2] *Ibid.* pp. 184, 192.

ments for calling up the reserve and in accepting inventions in preserving food for the provisioning of the troops. The government was chiefly concerned with the effect of the war on the loyalty of the investing classes and the industrial worker. The war was financed by loans, three being raised, in March 1854 and January and July 1855. Each was larger than the last and more readily taken up. As they were put up directly to public subscription their success seemed proof of confidence in the regime. Yet Napoleon was disinclined to try the financial strength of France too far and by the autumn of 1855 seems to have feared the bursting of the bubble. He was also nervous about the urban industrial worker; for the bad wine and corn harvests of 1853 and 1854 had sent food prices up and industrial depression, except in the ports of embarkation for the Crimea and favoured industries, caused unemployment. But on the whole the war revealed the unexpectedly good economic and social health of France.

Defeated Russia, by contrast, was affected to the point of revolutionary change, for the Crimean War brought to a head her immense internal problems. Within the framework of the tsarist regime a social and economic revolution took place. The 'great reforms' of the 'sixties, centring on the emancipation of the serfs of 1861 and the codification and modernisation of the law (see above, ch. xiv, pp. 369–80), all owed something to the consequences of defeat.

The unique alliance of Britain and France with Turkey brought more Europeans behind the Ottoman curtain and probably caused a more realistic Turkish approach to reform and westernisation. On the other hand, its cost had caused a fall in the value of the paper money, which had largely displaced coin, and so a steep rise in prices, distress and restiveness. No measures were taken to remedy the worsening financial mismanagement until 1859 when a council of finance was created. But it failed to check the arbitrary personal expenditure of the sultan and to produce a regular budget. Meanwhile immediate needs were met by foreign loans. Two loans were raised in 1854 and 1855 which were guaranteed by France and Britain. Turkey was to contract a dozen more before the next eastern crisis. From this time the European bond-holders became a new force with an interest in Turkish reform and their guaranteed rights opened the possibility of interference in Turkish internal affairs in case of default.

The congress opened in Paris on 25 February. Britain and Russia were the leading opponents. Clarendon and Cowley, the British representatives, felt isolated; for a *rapprochement* had already begun between France and Russia, and Walewski, the first French representative, was dubbed by Clarendon the third Russian plenipotentiary. Prince Orlov, supported by Brunnov, proved a good negotiator for Russia by his skill, courtesy and plain dealing. Britain fought for a system of securities which might prevent or postpone a renewal of Russian aggression upon Turkey. Her most substantial gain was the transference of southern Bessarabia from Russia to Turkey and its incorporation in Moldavia. The Treaty of Paris, 30 March 1856, thus pushed Russia back from the Danube mouths (articles XX and XXI). Palmerston attached great importance to this and vigorously combated the assertion that it was an Austrian rather than a British interest.[1] The arrangement was, however, short-lived, lasting only until 1878. The treaty, in the second place, ended Russia's claim to act in a special relationship to Turkey and her practice based on the claim. Europe, not Russia, was recognised as the protector of the Roumanian Principalities and the Orthodox Christians (articles XXII and IX). Europe guaranteed Turkish integrity and independence (article VII) and henceforward any power or powers in conflict with Turkey were to seek the mediation of a third party before resort to arms. A separate tripartite treaty, signed on 15 April, by Britain, France and Austria reinforced the guarantee. Thirdly, Russian naval preponderance over Turkey was ended; for the Black Sea was neutralised (article XI) and ceased to be a Russian lake. The Straits Convention of 1841 was replaced by a new convention which maintained the rule of closure, while the Porte was at peace. These naval arrangements were an especially sharp blow to Russian pride. Neutralisation and closure together were an effective restraint upon Russia, but there was nothing to prevent Turkey from keeping a squadron in the Straits or in the Sea of Marmora, and in time of war she could call up an ally through the Straits, who would find Russia unarmed and vulnerable. The neutralisation, however, lasted barely fifteen years. The Treaty of London in March 1871 sanctioned Russia's denunciation of November 1870.

The Roumanian Principalities, reformed and contented, under Turkish suzerainty, were to provide a fourth barrier to Russian aggression. Arrangements for their reformed government were to be devised by a European commission which was to consult Moldavian and Wallachian wishes through their elected representatives (articles XXII to XXVII). These plans were confused by the raising of the question of Roumanian unity and independence. Napoleon suggested unity already in January 1856 and, although Palmerston deprecated it as difficult to execute and likely to provoke Austria as well as to weaken Turkey, Walewski proposed it on 6 March in the congress. The question being left open, in August 1858 the two Principalities acquired a modicum of administrative unity and in 1859 a common governor, but at the expense of Anglo-French amity and by no means to the discomfiture of Russia. Next, the treaty sought to strengthen Turkey herself by improving relations between the sultan and his Christian subjects. Palmerston had hoped to induce him to legislate both on this and on the Principalities under the advice of the ambassadors

---

[1] Palmerston to Clarendon, 16 January, 25, 27, 29 February and 2 March 1856, private Clarendon papers, Clar. dep. c. 49, fos. 27, 134 and ff.

in conference at Constantinople before the congress met.[1] But Stratford de Redcliffe, who was becoming increasingly independent and a growing liability through his quarrels with the French, was an uncooperative negotiator. The sultan, however, was induced to issue a *hatti-humayun* on 21 February. The treaty then took note of this action and of the sultan's intention to communicate the document to his fellow signatories, who renounced interference, singly or collectively, in Turkish internal affairs. The *hatti-humayun* declared Christian and Muslim equal before the law, in access to public office, in freedom of religion and the right to maintain churches and schools, and admission to the army. The congress, therefore, admitted the sultan to 'the public law' of Europe and to the family of European powers. This provision, although it arose from the discussion of the relations between the sultan and his Christian subjects, in the treaty prefaced the guarantee of Turkish integrity and independence. Lastly, in the Baltic, Russia was obliged, by a separate Anglo-Russian treaty, to demolish the forts on the Aaland Islands.

These arrangements did not represent the full realisation of Palmerston's policy. From 17 February, when Clarendon arrived in Paris, until 8 March Britain was struggling to gain a wider programme and was defeated by Russia. She wanted the neutralisation of the Sea of Azov and the dismantling of the shipbuilding yards at Nicolaieff. The protocols recorded Russia's assurance that she would use these places only for the small ships still admitted to the Black Sea, but they were not neutralised. Further, Britain was defeated over Circassian independence, though she gained the restoration of Kars to Turkey and a slight modification of the Russo-Turkish Asiatic frontier. Clarendon rather played down Palmerston's Circassian project. Practicability apart, it was difficult to press when Russia took her stand on the terms of the Treaty of Adrianople of 1829 and, with French encouragement, on those of the February protocol which had not included it. He fought harder for a larger cession of Bessarabia. But Clarendon was a bad pleader for Napoleon's support against Russia. On 8 March he gave way as the alternative to something very like a rupture with France[2] after fighting Orlov single-handed for nearly a fortnight. The frontier was to be drawn as Russia wanted it, but still, Palmerston consoled himself, kept her from the 'flotilla-bearing' lower Pruth.[3]

Austria had little reason to consider that the treaty fully safeguarded her interests in the Danube basin. She was obliged to evacuate the Principalities on the conclusion of a Russo-Turkish peace and did so in

---

[1] See Clarendon to Stratford, 11, 18, 21, 25 January, 1 February 1856, private Clarendon papers, Clar. dep. c. 135, pp. 66, 102, 124, 150, 193.

[2] Clarendon to Palmerston, 8 March 1856, private Clarendon papers, Clar. dep. c. 135, p. 363.

[3] Palmerston to Clarendon, 9 March 1856, private Clarendon papers, Clar. dep. c. 49, fo. 164.

March 1857. The Bessarabian cession was a substantial gain, but the way opened to Roumanian unity and independence much lessened her satisfaction with the arrangements for the Principalities. The treaty set up an international commission for the improvement of the navigation of the Danube. This, too, was a gain, but she would have preferred the exclusion of the upper river and a riverain to an international commission. On both points she yielded to Britain.

Prussia entered the Paris negotiations after their crisis was passed. Her title to be represented was the revision of the Straits Convention of 1841, and her participation was strictly limited to its discussion. She was defeated in a 'vaudeville travesty'[1] of a negotiation to avoid record in the treaty of this restriction.

France gained prestige but few tangible advantages from the congress and treaty. Napoleon was more interested during the congress in improving his relations with Russia than in taking precautions to confine her ambition. But at the same time he wished to maintain the alliance with Britain. His commitments both in the general treaty and the tripartite treaty of 15 April (from which at the last moment he sought to free himself)[2] were undertaken rather as the means of preserving the alliance with Britain than the Ottoman empire. Nor had he much reason to be satisfied with the treatment of the broader questions in which he was interested.

After the treaty had been signed, the congress turned to these questions. Napoleon and Clarendon had already addressed Orlov about Poland. In November 1855 Napoleon had threatened to make Polish liberty a *sine qua non* condition of peace. Now, he and Clarendon sought only a public assurance of a change in Russia's Polish policy and finally gave up even this. On Greece, Palmerston unsuccessfully tried to persuade France and Russia to join Britain in pressure on King Otto to improve his government. Italian nationalism fared little better than Polish and Greek liberty. Earlier schemes to give Parma and Modena to Sardinia, and to dispatch one of their rulers to govern the Roumanian Principalities, evaporated in the realities of the congress atmosphere. In the end, the Italian question was raised in speeches deploring generally the unsettled condition of Europe, and Clarendon's indictment of Austrian, papal and Neapolitan misgovernment was toned down for the protocol. Finally, Britain, in the 23rd protocol signed on 14 April, gained a record of opinion in favour of resort to the mediation of a third power before recourse to war. This came from Clarendon off his own bat and foreshadowed the trend of his 1869 disarmament proposals (see p. 585) as well as reflecting

---

[1] Clarendon to Palmerston, 22 March 1856, private Clarendon papers, Clar. dep. c. 135, p. 438.
[2] See Clarendon to Palmerston, 31 March 1856, private Clarendon papers, Clar. dep. c. 135, p. 486.

the Cobdenite pacifism of the 'fifties. Another British idea for a resolution in favour of free trade in foodstuffs and raw materials was still-born. On the last day, 16 April, the Declaration of Paris on maritime law was signed. Britain made a virtue of necessity and accepted the principle that the flag covers the goods, gaining in return the formal abolition of privateering.

In diplomatic history the Crimean War acted as a solvent, and much that had been accepted as diplomatically normal disappeared. The policy of Nicholas and Nesselrode had presupposed Russo-Austrian co-opera-tion. But Russia could no longer count on Austria. Austria's attitude during the war, the help she gave in exacting the Bessarabian cession and the tripartite treaty she signed with Britain and France and valued chiefly as a bond of union were clear signs of this. Both Austria and Russia, moreover, had suffered a diplomatic decline. The ghost of 'the gendarme of Europe' had been laid. Russia like Austria was, in future, to be 'the colossus with feet of clay'. Russia like Austria turned to France. 'All our efforts', wrote Nesselrode, 'must be directed to the retention of Napoleon's goodwill' as the only safeguard against the renewal of a hostile coalition.[1] Yet though both Austria and Russia turned to France, the reversal of alliances of 1756 could not be repeated in 1856. Within three years Austria was at war with her new ally of 1854 and 1856, and Prussia, who had begun to mobilise during the war of 1859 on his behalf, seemed to Francis Joseph his only loyal friend. Alexander too had found France a difficult partner. From the beginning he had feared to be drawn in the wake of Napoleon's ambition. Yet the treaty which he signed with Napoleon on 3 March 1859 promising neutrality in a possible Austro-French war came dangerously near to entangling him both in Napoleon's support of nationalities and in his operations to upset the Vienna settle-ment. Alexander too was to remember Prussia and that she alone of the great powers had not been hostile during the war. In 1863 the Russo-French friendship foundered on the Polish rock and the Russo-Prussian association was revived. Thus the Crimean War had broken up the eastern pattern of European relations only so that it might reappear, but as a group pivoting upon Prussia or Germany rather than one turning upon the Russo-Austrian axis.

Similarly the war had reshaped the eastern question. It had postponed the collapse and partition of Turkey and set up a defensive wall round her empire, in which the tripartite alliance and, more especially, the Franco-British alliance should have been the reinforcing steel. The struggle would never again lie simply between the Russian tsar, greedy for territory, and the sultan his defenceless victim, still less between Orthodox and Muslim. Yet western sentiment would in future be stirred by the struggle of Roumanian, Serb or Bulgar for freedom from an alien rule and for

---

[1] Nesselrode to Orlov, 5 April 1856, Tarle, *op. cit.* vol. II, pp. 453–4.

administrative safeguards or constitutional rights against arbitrary oppression. In Russia imagination would respond to the bond between Slav and Slav; for the war had destroyed the treaty of Kutchuk Kainardji and rendered tsarist paternalism towards orthodox Christians out of date. Moreover, the essential antagonisms of interest remained and Russo-British hostility was unabated. It was nowhere expected that the arrangements of 1856 would be permanent. Alexander II set himself to reverse the Bessarabian and Black Sea concessions. Gorchakov, Foreign Minister from 1856, was confident of success and made a habit of speaking of the treaty as 'a screen full of holes'.[1] For Palmerston and Clarendon it was 'defective' in leaving Russia too formidable, but they thought 'the future must take care of itself'.[2] Nor had they any confidence in the tripartite treaty, which had originated after all with Austria, and still less in the alliance with France. In Palmerston's phrase 'a summer season's' partnership,[3] its value was exhausted by 1860 while the tripartite alliance was to prove a dead letter. The conflict then between Britain and Russia had been broken off but not settled. In a new eastern crisis Britain might find herself alone and faced with a dilemma: the old anti-Russian course would entail opposition to nationalist and constitutionalist causes with which she sympathised, and a new liberal course would involve an anti-Turkish policy of allowing Russia a free hand which was against her interests. Never again could Turkey rely upon the support in arms of Britain or France or Austria against Russia. If the new starting-point, made in the declaration of the common concern of the great powers in the Turkish question, meant anything at all, it would mean concern to agree among themselves on such modifications of Turkish integrity and independence as might stop up the antagonism between Britain and Russia and the parallel antagonism, foreshadowed in the Crimean War, between Austria and Russia.

[1] See for example Buchanan to Granville, 20 November 1870, private Granville papers, P.R.O. 30/29/97.
[2] Palmerston to Clarendon, 7 March 1856, private Clarendon papers, Clar. dep. 49, fo. 155.
[3] Palmerston to Clarendon, 9 January 1856, *ibid.* Clar. dep. 49, fo. 15.

CHAPTER XIX

PRUSSIA AND THE GERMAN PROBLEM, 1830–66

THE problem of the form of German unification was raised by the nature of the settlement of Germany made at the Congress of Vienna in 1815. This had failed to satisfy the hopes of those who had wanted to see some form of German national unity emerge from the turmoil of the Napoleonic wars; nor had the expectation of constitutional reforms in the individual states been fulfilled to any great extent. The German Confederation as established at Vienna was to prove an unsatisfactory—and unworkable—compromise. In Prussia much of the work of the period of reforms after 1808 was undone, and Austria under Metternich provided a pattern of reaction that, since 1819, had been followed by the majority of the other German states. For a decade after the Carlsbad decrees of 1819 political discussion, whether of constitutional reform or of German unification, was difficult, and political action almost impossible.

The French Revolution of July 1830 gave the signal for a revival of liberalism throughout Germany. The actual outbreaks of violence were few, and their effects small. In Brunswick an unpopular duke was replaced by his brother; the elector of Hesse, hated for his arbitrary rule and his extravagant mistress, was forced to grant a constitution that was to be repeatedly broken. There were smaller disturbances in Saxony, Bavaria and elsewhere, while some months later, at Göttingen in the kingdom of Hanover, members of the university seized the town-hall. The Polish national revolt in 1831 was almost as important as the July Revolution in arousing liberal enthusiasm in Germany, and Polish representatives took part in the gathering of liberals held at Hambach in the Bavarian Palatinate in May 1832. This '*Hambacher Fest*' was a manifestation by liberal intellectuals—professors, students, lawyers, writers—expressing the reviving movement in favour of constitutional government and German unity. Inevitably it recalled the Wartburg festival of 1817, and indeed its political results were similar. Metternich and the Austrian government were already contemplating federal action against the liberal revival, and the Hambach demonstration was sufficient to overcome the hesitations of some of the other states. Accordingly, in June the majority of the German governments accepted six articles asserting monarchical principles that recalled the Carlsbad decrees of 1819. The 'Metternich system' seemed as firmly established as ever in spite of the example of the July Revolution in France. As the principles embodied in the Six

Articles and similar measures were put into practice, the list of liberal martyrs grew. In Prussia, for example, the works of the exiled Heine and other writers of the 'Young Germany' movement were banned in 1835, while in Hanover in 1837 seven Göttingen professors who protested against the violation of the constitution by the new king (the former duke of Cumberland) were expelled from their chairs.

Even more important than the revived discussion of political problems, both as they affected the organisation of the individual states and of Germany as a whole, were the economic developments inaugurated by the creation of the German Customs Union (*Zollverein*) in 1834. The establishment thereby of the economic unity of the greater part of Germany under Prussian leadership improved trade, encouraged industry and led to the construction of the first sections of the German railway system. (The first railway in Germany, from Nuremberg to Fürth, was opened in December 1835.) Although the states of north-east Germany, Hanover, Oldenburg, Brunswick and the Hansa cities, relying on their maritime connections and English support, remained outside the *Zollverein* in a rival organisation, the Tax Union (*Steuerverein*), the advantages of the Prussian system were too clear for them to keep aloof from it for long. Brunswick joined the *Zollverein* in 1844, Hanover in 1851 and Oldenburg in 1852, only Hamburg and Bremen surviving as free-trade ports until 1888.

Yet, in spite of the *Zollverein*, Germany remained a predominantly agricultural country until after the foundation of the empire. Nevertheless improvement of communications and industrial development soon had a political effect. The increase of population and its greater mobility contributed to the growth of new industrial areas, notably in the Ruhr and the Rhineland, and these in turn served as the basis of a new liberalism in Prussia. New leaders from the mercantile world joined the intellectuals who had hitherto formed the liberal party. David Hansemann and Ludolf Camphausen, for instance, made fortunes in industrial and railway development and brought to their political activities a practical spirit and practical demands. Removal of restraints on trade, participation of the middle class in government and administration, and the weakening of the power of the old Prussian nobility, these were to be the main points of their political programme, and by 1840 it looked as though some of them might be realised, since it was widely expected that the new king, Frederick William IV, who ascended the Prussian throne in that year, would inaugurate a period of political change.

By 1840 the Prussian state had consolidated the gains of 1815. Although in the Rhineland and Posen a quarrel with the Roman Catholic church over such topics as the education of the children of mixed marriages had culminated in 1837 with the arrest of the archbishops of Cologne and Posen, the new reign saw a reconciliation between the Prussian state and the Roman church. The new king had a romantic feeling for Catholicism (he showed great interest in the Oxford Movement in England), and his sympathy was demonstrated by the part he played in the refounding of Cologne Cathedral in 1842 (cf. ch. VI, pp. 139–40). At the same time the memories of the French administration on the Rhine had been obliterated, although the population had won their struggle to preserve the advantages of the legal code that the French had introduced. The successful assimilation of the new provinces was demonstrated in the international crisis of 1840, when there was great popular enthusiasm for the 'Watch on the Rhine' (a phrase originating in the title of a song by Max Schneckenburger), and new slogans were added to the repertoire of German nationalism—among them Hoffman von Fallersleben's song *Deutschland, Deutschland über Alles*, and Nicolas Becker's *Sie sollen ihn nicht haben, den freien deutschen Rhein*.

The successful absorption of the new Prussian provinces, like the making of the *Zollverein*, was the work of the Prussian officials who had made the Prussian administrative system, and especially the educational system, the envy of liberals throughout Europe. This idealised view was not just based on memories of the reforms of Stein and Hardenberg. The Prussian bureaucracy was producing a new class of enlightened paternal administrator to reinforce the traditional Junker ruling caste, and the efficiency and loyalty of the Prussian administrative class was to make it an essential basis of any future unified Germany. A sense of unquestioning obedience to the promptings of duty derived from the Kantians, and of the paramount nature of the state's claims derived from Hegel, produced the ideal organ for an enlightened autocracy. Hegel was the predominant intellectual influence of the period, but if his writings could inspire the servants of the Prussian state, they could also inspire revolution. The doctrine that the state was the embodiment of reason could be turned into a doctrine that if the existing state did not embody reason, it should be overthrown. Thus the 'Young Hegelians' helped to inspire the Revolution of 1848, and their influence was considerable among the Rhenish liberals, one of whose newspapers, the *Rheinische Zeitung*, was edited for a short time in 1842 by Karl Marx, himself a notable product of the Young Hegelian School.

The 'Metternich system', for all its apparent stability, was being weakened not only by intellectual and economic developments. In Austria and Prussia there were new monarchs less likely to uphold the existing system than their predecessors. In Austria the Emperor Ferdinand, who came to the throne in 1835, was feeble-minded, and Metternich's position became less strong as the influence of his rivals increased. In Prussia the accession of Frederick William IV began a new phase, socially and politically. The new king had grown up in the atmosphere of the conservative romantic revival with its enthusiasm for what it believed to be the ideas and institutions of the Middle Ages. His pathological fantasy and vanity were nourished on the doctrines of the Swiss conservative political philosopher, Karl Ludwig von Haller, who preached the ideal of the 'Christian-patrimonial state' in which an ordered system of estates and corporations was united under the authority of a benevolent Christian king ruling by the Grace of God. His enthusiasm for a romantic German past made many people hope that he would take practical steps to achieve a greater measure of German unity. Yet his feeling for tradition and for medieval institutions also led him to accept the supremacy of the Habsburgs as the 'Arch-House' in Germany, so that the relations between the two German great powers were not in fact immediately troubled.

Nevertheless, his accession was widely welcomed by all who hoped for a German national policy that would lead towards political unity. There were signs, too, that he would be prepared for certain liberal measures in internal policy. For instance, the old War Minister of the War of Liberation, Boyen, returned to office; the censorship was relaxed; men who had suffered for their liberal opinions like Ernst Moritz Arndt were rehabilitated. Hegel's old opponent Schelling was brought back to a chair at Berlin University. It was hoped that the king would at last grant the representative institutions promised by his father in May 1815. Disappointment with his policy soon began to be expressed. The relaxing of the censorship only made demands for further reform more widespread. In 1841 the Diets of the individual Prussian provinces met for the first time in four years and the publicity given to their debates revealed a demand for constitutional change which increased during their subsequent sessions, now held regularly at two-yearly intervals. In East Prussia demands for freedom of the press were vigorously expressed by Johann Jacoby; in Posen the Poles criticised Prussian rule; and in the Rhineland the new liberal party led by Camphausen, Hansemann, Hermann von Beckerath and Gustav Mevissen constantly called for the fulfilment of the constitutional promises that had been made by Frederick William III in 1815.

However, the king's ideas of a 'patrimonial state' were very far removed from the constitutional plans of his liberal subjects, and he postponed action as long as he could, while trying to content liberal demands by the formation of a joint committee of the Provincial Diets. He temporised until 1847, but at last on 3 February of that year summoned a United Diet composed of representatives of the provincial Diets; this met in Berlin in April. How far the king was out of touch with the demands of the time is shown by Metternich's comment on the speech with which he opened the Diet: 'Nothing was in stronger contrast to the present style in political matters than the deep personal pathos which ran through the whole speech, the pretentious accent laid on the illustrious speaker's subjective convictions, the polemics against the ideas of the day.'[1] Under

---

[1] Veit Valentin, *Geschichte der deutschen Revolution von 1848–9* (Berlin, 1930), vol. I, p. 67.

these circumstances it is not surprising that the United Diet dispersed at the end of a few months, the hopes of its liberal members unsatisfied, without even having secured an undertaking from the king that it would be regularly summoned in future.

But the growing discontent was not limited to Prussia. The economic difficulties of the 'forties and the example of successful agitation abroad combined with the growing movement for national unity to produce a desire for change. In the industrial areas of Prussia and Saxony, employers and apprentices were anxious to be rid of the surviving medieval restrictions; the peasant proprietors of the south-west wanted the abolition of the remaining feudal obligations; in all the small states the middle class—officials, lawyers, professors—were demanding a larger field for political activity in the shape of a more closely unified Germany. The local political situation varied. In some states, the two Mecklenburgs for instance, the old order had survived unchanged from the Middle Ages, with the sovereign's power curbed by Estates composed of the nobility and gentry, and the other classes too weak to threaten the existing system. In others, such as Hesse-Kassel and Brunswick, the demands were for the most elementary constitutional guarantees against a despot. In Baden and Württemberg, where a genuine if limited parliamentary system existed, the liberals were agitating for an extension of the franchise and, above all, for German unity. In Bavaria the prevailing political issue of clericalism versus liberalism was obscured by the controversy about the relations between the king and the dancer known as Lola Montez.

Whatever the political and constitutional situation in the individual states, the demands that led to the revolutionary situation of 1848 were demands of a numerically small but active middle class wanting a share in political life. Only occasionally (as in the disturbances among the weavers of Silesia in 1844 and 1845) did new social forces make themselves felt in a savage form. Indeed, when there were outbreaks of real social unrest (in Baden in April 1848 or in Dresden in May 1849), the liberal middle classes combined with the conservatives and the regular armies in order to suppress radical revolt.

It only needed the example of the February Revolution in Paris to bring all these discontents into the open, and in March 1848 the German revolution began, the story of which is told elsewhere in this volume (see ch. xv).

By the beginning of 1849 it was plain that the revolutions had had no marked effect on the position of the reigning dynasties in Austria and Prussia. On 2 December 1848 the Emperor Ferdinand abdicated in favour of his eighteen-year-old nephew, Francis Joseph. The first stage of the war in Italy had ended in an Austrian victory four months before and the Piedmontese were finally defeated at the battle of Novara in March 1849.

Although the Hungarian revolt was not finally suppressed until the summer, the immediate threats to the integrity of the monarchy had been met. Moreover, the empire now had in Prince Felix zu Schwarzenberg a minister with a positive policy, great diplomatic gifts and a firm will.[1] Until his death he conducted a great attempt to reassert Austria's position in Germany and in the Austrian empire itself. The first step was to restore political order inside the monarchy; in March a new centralised constitution that treated the Austrian empire as a single whole was promulgated, and Schwarzenberg was ready to pursue an independent policy in Germany (see ch. xx, p. 526).

In Prussia, too, the revolution had failed by the end of 1848. The king had rapidly lost any sympathy he might have felt in March with the moderate liberals. The temper of the Berlin Assembly had grown more radical and the position of the moderate liberals had grown weaker. Although men like Camphausen were still politically active (Camphausen had ceased to be Prime Minister, but was still Prussian representative at Frankfurt), it was the conservatives who were becoming increasingly powerful, and exercising more and more influence over the unstable king. On 2 November a new ministry was formed under Count Brandenburg, the son of King Frederick William II by a morganatic marriage. On 5 December the Assembly was dissolved and a new constitution promulgated by royal command; the concessions to liberal ideas which the constitution contained were soon nullified by the restoration in May 1849 of the old restricted franchise. The constitution was amended after much discussion during the following year, and was published in its final form in January 1850. Although the basic rights of the individual appeared to be guaranteed, the king retained the right to nominate and dismiss ministers and, as the years 1862–6 were to show, it was perfectly possible to carry on government without the support of the Diet.

The appointment of the Brandenburg ministry, the dismissal of the Assembly, and the new constitution, all showed how far the king was listening to conservative advisers. Indeed, the real power now lay with a group of noblemen whose ideas found expression in the *Kreuzzeitung* and whose aim was the restoration of absolute rule and the revival of Prussian particularism. Otto von Bismarck-Schönhausen, who was beginning to make a name as one of the most brilliant speakers of this group, was full of enthusiasm for 'specific Prussian qualities' (*spezifisches Preussentum*) and spoke with suspicion and contempt of the movement for national unity as 'the German swindle'.[2] In November 1850 Otto von

[1] For a rather different estimate see p. 529.
[2] Erich Eyck, *Bismarck* (Zürich, 1941), vol. I, p. 115. The account of Bismarck's career and policy in the following pages is necessarily largely based on Dr Eyck's definitive biography of Bismarck. The author would like to acknowledge his deep indebtedness to Dr Eyck and his masterly work, the conclusions of which are summarised in English in Eyck, *Bismarck and the German Empire* (London, 1950).

Manteuffel became Prime Minister, and with him the conservative 'Camarilla', inspired by the brothers Ludwig and Leopold von Gerlach, entered on a period of undisputed power, and Prussia on an era of complete reaction against the liberal ideas of 1848.

The success of the counter-revolution in Prussia and Austria meant that the Frankfurt Assembly had to take these two states into account: that is, German unity could be achieved only with the active support of one or other government. In January 1849 the new liberal constitution for a united Germany had passed its first reading in the Frankfurt Assembly, so that the question of the sovereign and frontiers of the new German state was becoming urgent. The last months of the Frankfurt Assembly (January–April 1849) were spent discussing this problem and ended in the decision to elect a hereditary emperor and the offer of the imperial crown to Frederick William IV on 28 March. The king himself was constantly wavering in his policy, torn between his romantic loyalty to the House of Habsburg and his personal vanity ('Our master's head is organised differently from that of other men',[1] Brandenburg complained). The Prussian ministers, however, were ready to give moderate approval to a scheme for uniting Germany under Prussian leadership and excluding Austria. (This was later known as a 'little German' (*Kleindeutsch*) solution of the German problem.) The publication of the new Austrian constitution in March meant that there was no longer any chance of detaching the German-speaking provinces of Austria for inclusion in a united Germany, since Austria was now to be treated as a unified single state. Schwarzenberg's aim was to secure Austria's entry as a whole into the German Confederation, and this would inevitably involve the Austrian emperor in assuming the lead in Germany. 'His Majesty is as Emperor the first German prince. This is a right sanctified by tradition and the march of the centuries, by the political power of Austria, by the text of treaties on which the as yet undissolved federal system rests. His Majesty is not disposed to renounce this right.'[2]

Such unqualified assertions of Habsburg claims were bound to lose the support of those liberals who at Frankfurt had favoured keeping the German-Austrian provinces inside a united Germany (the 'great German' (*Grossdeutsch*) solution), and the field was clear for the advocates of Prussian leadership. On 28 March therefore the king of Prussia was elected hereditary emperor at Frankfurt by 290 votes against 248 abstentions. But when Eduard Simson, the President of the Assembly, travelled to Berlin to offer him the crown, the king made it quite clear that he regarded himself as a king by divine right who could only accept a crown offered him by the German princes; in private he spoke with

[1] Heinrich Friedjung, *Oesterreich von 1848 bis 1860* (Stuttgart and Berlin, 4th edn, 1918), vol. I, p. 180.
[2] Schwarzenberg to Trautmannsdorff, 24 January 1849, *ibid.* vol. I, p. 182.

32-2

contempt of a 'pig's crown' that did not come by the grace of God but by the grace of 'master bakers and butchers'.[1] This refusal was in effect the end of the Frankfurt Assembly and its constitution. Although the constitution had been accepted in principle by many of the smaller states, the king of Prussia's refusal of the imperial crown prevented any further effective action. As the spring and summer passed the members of the Assembly and the provisional government at Frankfurt resigned, were recalled or simply went away. The last risings of the left in Baden and Saxony were suppressed by Prussian troops; the Assembly, reduced to a radical rump, was removed to Stuttgart at the end of May, and in June was finally dispersed by order of the king of Württemberg. The revolution of 1848 was at an end.

The failure of the Frankfurt Assembly to produce a new political framework for Germany meant that the initiative passed to the governments of the individual states. Constitutionally, an 'interim' arrangement was proclaimed in September 1849 under which Prussia and Austria assumed joint responsibility for the affairs of Germany until May 1850 when a definitive constitutional system was to be introduced. This formal compromise, however, served only to provide the setting for a bitter struggle between Austria and Prussia, in which the other German governments looked nervously on.

Prussia now, in the summer of 1849, began at last to have a clear German policy to oppose to that of Schwarzenberg. This was due to the growing influence of General Joseph Maria von Radowitz. From May onwards he was largely responsible for Prussian policy, although he did not actually become Foreign Minister until September 1850. He was a Catholic who derived his political ideals from the same sources as Frederick William, so that his views were in fact a more consistent and balanced version of those of the king. Bismarck later called him 'Property man to the king's medieval fantasy',[2] but he had a more practical policy than the epigram implies. A passionate conservative and opponent of revolution, he differed from the Prussian nobles of the Gerlach school who were his colleagues—and most bitter opponents—in believing that to prevent revolution concessions must be made to the national demands that had found expression in 1848. An attempt must be made to see 'whether our government could be led along a path which will not make the so-called German party its most bitter enemies at a time when a life and death struggle against the democratic party is beginning',[3] he wrote to his wife in April 1849. His immediate object was to make the most of the opportunity provided by the failure of the Frankfurt assembly, and he determined to assert Prussian leadership and win support from moderate liberal

[1] Valentin, *op. cit.* vol. II, p. 380.
[2] Otto, Fürst von Bismarck, *Gedanken und Erinnerungen* (Stuttgart, 1898), vol. I, pp. 64–5.
[3] Friedrich Meinecke, *Radowitz und die deutsche Revolution* (Berlin, 1913), p. 236.

opinion by going some way to satisfy the desire for national unity, if possible with Austrian agreement, if not, without it. His first step, once it was clear that Schwarzenberg would not co-operate, was to secure the support of the two states adjacent to Prussia, Hanover and Saxony, and on 26 May an 'Alliance of the Three Kingdoms' was signed which agreed to an attempt to form a union of north German states. Radowitz next needed to secure some popular support, and in June a meeting of many former members of the Frankfurt Assembly was held at Gotha in a mood 'of the most painful resignation, of patriotic renunciation'.[1] Here those right-wing liberals who had supported at Frankfurt the idea of Prussian supremacy agreed to Radowitz's plans—though only after considerable hesitation because of the conservative nature of the project and its sponsor. But Radowitz's real difficulties were with his Prussian colleagues; for both his national aims and his Catholicism were suspect to the Protestant supporters of 'specific Prussian' particularism. It was only after much opposition in the Prussian Diet, headed by Ludwig von Gerlach and Bismarck, and with the support of the king that Radowitz succeeded in arranging for a Diet to meet at Erfurt in March 1850, to be composed of representatives from the north and central German states who were to form the new union.

The autumn and winter therefore were devoted to a diplomatic battle in which Schwarzenberg endeavoured to detach Prussia's supporters. For Austria too had a positive policy that went beyond the mere assertion of traditional Habsburg supremacy in Germany, and the new programme had an economic as well as a political side. The Austrian Minister of Commerce, Karl Ludwig von Bruck, had definite ideas about regaining for Austria the economic initiative that had been lost with the formation of the *Zollverein* (cf. ch. xx, p. 530). He was born in the Prussian textile town of Elberfeld and had made a fortune in the Austrian port of Trieste; he dreamed of an empire of 70 million people, a vast economic unit in central Europe under Austrian leadership that would unite the *Zollverein* with the Austrian economic sphere in the Danube basin. He was doomed to disappointment at every turn, but his ideas were sufficiently grand to win a certain amount of liberal support that would not have been given to Schwarzenberg's hard-headed diplomacy alone.

However, this diplomacy was successful during the winter of 1849–50 in breaking up Radowitz's union project even before the assembly of the Erfurt Congress. Hanover withdrew before the meeting, and the governments of Saxony, Württemberg and Hesse-Kassel were already losing interest. Moreover, the Austrians had in February 1850 agreed to support a plan for the amendment of the Federal Constitution put forward by Brunswick, Württemberg and Saxony. The constitutional basis of the

---

[1] A. Stern, *Geschichte Europas von 1848 bis 1871* (Stuttgart and Berlin, 1916), vol. VII, p. 402. See also Eyck, *op. cit.* vol. I, p. 137.

Austrian attack on the Prussian project was that the German Confederation was still in being and that it was illegal to attempt constitutional change without the approval of the Federal Diet. To give point to the criticism, the Federal Diet was summoned for 10 May when the interim arrangement was due to end. As the smaller states wavered and Frederick William himself began to be worried lest Radowitz's plans were too liberal, the Erfurt congress came to nothing. On the other hand, Schwarzenberg succeeded in persuading the Federal Diet in May to threaten sanctions against any state that attempted to break away from the Confederation.

The crisis came in the autumn of 1850. In two states, Hesse-Kassel and Holstein, the liberals were desperately trying to defend some of the ground won in 1848, and in both the sovereigns, the elector of Hesse and the king of Denmark, were hoping for the support of Austria and the Federal Diet against their subjects. It was principally the case of Hesse that provoked the crisis; indeed, Schwarzenberg deliberately exploited the elector's appeal to the Federal Diet in the hope of finally destroying the Prussian Union. On 12 October the emperor of Austria met the kings of Bavaria and Württemberg and they issued a declaration that they would maintain the Confederation and intervene in Hesse if necessary. On 15 October the elector appealed for military help.

Prussia's interest in Hesse was mainly strategic; Hessian territory divided the Prussian kingdom, and the Prussians had the right to use certain main military roads (the *Etappenstrassen*). At the same time it was essential for Radowitz's policy that Prussian predominance over the neighbouring small states should be retained. Both Austria and Prussia sent troops into Hesse, the former to help the elector, the latter to safeguard the military roads. War appeared imminent and on 8 November there was a skirmish. Meanwhile, however, the Prussian government had already decided to negotiate. They had failed to get the support of the tsar (see ch. x, p. 265), while the king was losing his nerve and was genuinely appalled at the thought of a civil war between Germans. Radowitz and the heir to the throne, the prince of Prussia, were ready to challenge Austria, but Brandenburg and Manteuffel preferred to give way rather than break what they regarded as the natural solidarity of the conservative powers, and the traditional co-operation of Austria and Prussia against liberalism. Radowitz resigned on 3 November, his union project already defeated; Brandenburg died suddenly on 6 November and was succeeded by Otto von Manteuffel, at this period the spokesman of the extreme conservatives. Manteuffel soon began negotiations, and, with the help of Russian mediation, met Schwarzenberg and reached agreement with him at Olmütz on 29 November 1850. The union project was to be abandoned and the revision of the Federal Constitution referred to the free decision of the German princes.

War was averted, at the price of a diplomatic defeat of Prussia which was far more serious than the actual terms of the Olmütz agreement. For many Prussians the 'humiliation of Olmütz' remained a symbol of shame until it was obliterated by the victory of Königgrätz in 1866. In fact the compromise reached at Olmütz by which the federal constitution was to be freely revised at a meeting of the German princes at Dresden from December 1850 to March 1851 left nobody wholly satisfied.

The decision taken at Dresden was that the 1815 Federal Constitution should be restored. Under the circumstances, this was a victory for Manteuffel and the Prussian conservatives, who wanted to restore the system under which Prussia and Austria jointly defended a conservative, traditional Germany against revolution. Yet for many Prussians, whether they had believed in the liberal ideals of 1848 or in the constructive conservatism of Radowitz, this was a deeply unsatisfactory arrangement; the efforts of the past three years had been vain and the 'humiliation of Olmütz' seemed more important than the restoration of the old Confederation. Schwarzenberg, too, achieved less than he had hoped. He wanted Austria to dominate the new Confederation; he planned that there should be a strong executive power which Austria would control, and that Austria as a whole should enter the Confederation. Schwarzenberg's desire to exclude the smaller states from the central executive enabled Manteuffel, in the negotiations preceding the final settlement, to pose as their champion. Eventually therefore Schwarzenberg had to abandon his more ambitious aims and content himself with a return to the position of Metternich (cf. ch. xx, p. 538). Even more serious, perhaps, than the failure of Schwarzenberg's constitutional hopes was Austria's failure to use the political advantages won at Olmütz to gain admission to the *Zollverein*. Bruck had not succeeded in winning the middle states of Germany for his idea of a central European economic sphere, and he failed at the time of the Dresden Conference to remould the *Zollverein*—which was due for renewal in 1853—so as to include Austria. Such remoulding as did occur was to Prussia's advantage, for Hanover and the remaining states of the *Steuerverein* joined the Prussian system in 1851 or soon after, and Austria remained excluded from Germany just when the German economy was starting the first phase of its rapid expansion.

But if Prussia was smarting from defeat at Olmütz, and Schwarzenberg was unable to realise the whole of his plans for Austrian supremacy, it was the liberals throughout Germany who were most disappointed by the re-establishment of the old system. In 1848 German unity had not, after all, been won; even the *pis aller* that Radowitz's plans had offered had not been achieved; Bruck's plans for a vast German economic sphere had come to nothing. In the individual states, as in Germany as a whole, the gains of the past years were being lost. In most states the constitutions were being revised in a conservative sense, in accordance with the recommendations of a Federal Committee appointed in August 1851 to remove the 'filth of the year of shame',[1] as the king of Prussia put it. Many liberals and radicals had been forced to emigrate, or decided to leave Germany of their own free will—some, like Karl Marx, to continue political agitation abroad, others to make a new career in America, like Carl Schurz, who later became Secretary of the Interior in the United States.

In Austria the government attempted to create a centralised system run by a German bureaucracy, and followed a clerical policy that gave the Roman Catholic church more power than it had had since before the reign of Joseph II (see ch. xx, p. 533). In Prussia, too, the Manteuffel ministry expressed the same mood. An unimaginative, bigoted and inflexible government based on an efficient bureaucracy reintroduced a measure of political censorship and a political police. The king's personal advisers, especially the brothers Gerlach, represented an even more extreme conservatism than Manteuffel himself, a conservatism based on a narrow Protestant piety and on a refusal to accept any of the ideas of even such mild liberals as had succeeded in getting themselves elected to the Prussian Diet. Prussian politics in the next decade, therefore, remained obstinately conservative and provincial, and held out little hope for those people in Prussia and the rest of Germany who wanted a positive lead towards national unity or constitutional reform.

This despair explains the change of atmosphere in the German liberal movement in the 'fifties. An increasing number of writers began to realise that the liberals of 1848 had paid too little attention to the importance of power in politics. 'To be sovereign means to exercise power and only he who possesses power can exercise it. This direct connection between power and sovereignty is the fundamental truth and the key to the whole of history.'[2] This quotation from a pamphlet published in 1853 with the significant title 'Foundations of Political Realism' ('*Realpolitik*'—it seems to be the first use of the word) is typical. Moreover, power in this connection meant primarily power as embodied in a strong united German national state. 'The German nation', Julius Froebel said in 1859, 'is sick of principles and doctrines, literary existence and theoretical greatness. What it wants is Power, Power, Power! And whoever gives it power to him will it give honour, more honour than he can imagine.'[3] This mood, coupled with an increased respect for the facts of political life, was to produce the National Liberalism of the 1860's and the enthusiastic support for Bismarck's policy of forcible unification of Germany under Prussian leadership.

[1] Erich Brandenburg, *Die Reichsgründung* (2 vols., Leipzig, 1916), vol. i, p. 363.
[2] A. L. von Rochau, *Grundsätze der Realpolitik, angewendet auf die staatlichen Zustände Deutschlands* (1853) quoted in Friedrich Meinecke, *Die Idee der Staatsräson* (Munich, 1925), p. 493.
[3] Quoted in Heinrich, Ritter von Srbik, *Deutsche Einheit* (Munich, 1935), vol. iii, p. 5.

Yet the 'fifties were not just years of political stagnation. They were also years of economic development. The railway network was developed and completed: coal production rose, so that by 1860 Germany had outstripped both France and Belgium. The urban population in the industrial areas of the Ruhr, Silesia and Saxony increased, so that the growing industrial working class began to have political importance. Workingmen's Associations were being founded by the end of the decade: economists like J. K. von Rodbertus or Hermann Schulze-Delitsch were suggesting new forms of organisation—state socialism on the one hand, producers' and consumers' co-operatives on the other—and the way was being prepared for the great socialist agitation begun by Ferdinand Lassalle. Germany was sharing in the general increase of capital in Europe that resulted from the opening up of new sources of supply of gold, and in 1857 over-speculation led to a financial crisis that increased dissatisfaction with the existing political system.

This economic development was to the advantage of Prussia and the *Zollverein*, while Austria's economic position grew weaker. Bruck had resigned in May 1851 (although he returned to office as Minister of Finance in 1855), and the most his successor had been able to achieve was a commercial treaty with Prussia in 1853 that he described as a 'not very advantageous armistice'.[1] It was, in fact, increasingly hard to find a compromise between Prussia, whose expanding economy was accompanied by a movement for increasing freedom of trade, and Austria, whose backward industries and state monopolies still required protection, and in 1862 a treaty between Prussia and France gave France the 'most favoured nation' treatment till then enjoyed by Austria under the 1853 treaty. Moreover, Austria's foreign policy imposed a growing strain on her finances: during the Crimean War the army was mobilised and forces were stationed on the Austro-Russian frontier, while the war with Italy in 1859 added to the burden. Throughout the years preceding the war of 1866, therefore, Austria was struggling with a growing deficit and increasing financial difficulties while the position of Prussia and the *Zollverein* was improving (cf. ch. xx, pp. 538–9).

It was not until 1859 that the political reaction began to be challenged, both in Prussia and in Germany as a whole. In that year the war between France and Austria in Italy was to raise a host of questions about the solidarity of the German Confederation, its military organisation and its responsibility for the non-German parts of the Austrian empire. At the same time the success of the movement for Italian national unity aroused the envy of German nationalists. The Crimean War in 1854–5 had already shown how difficult it was for the German Confederation to follow a common and consistent policy. While Austria had mobilised to force Russia to evacuate Moldavia and Wallachia, Prussia had remained strictly

[1] W. O. Henderson, *The Zollverein* (London, 1939), p. 225. See also ch. xx, p. 535.

neutral (see ch. XVIII, *passim*). However, as Austria finally was not involved, the question of the whole relationship between Prussia and Austria and of the structure of the Confederation did not arise.

In 1859 the situation was very different. When the war began not only was the leading member of the Confederation directly involved, but also public opinion in Germany was deeply stirred and divided. Many saw the cause of Italian national unity as one with which German patriots and liberals were bound to sympathise; for them Austria was, in Arnold Rüge's phrases, the 'Hangman of Italy' and the 'Oppressor of Germany'. This view was commonest among the north German liberals and radicals, and was held, for instance, by Lassalle. Others, however, saw in the war an opportunity for demonstrating German national solidarity against the hereditary enemy, France. This view was commonest among the south German liberals who still hoped for the unification of a greater Germany under Austrian, not Prussian, leadership.

But the war did more than revive popular political discussion. It raised the whole question of Austro-Prussian relations in an acute form, and was to test the system of dual control established at Olmütz and Dresden. The Austrian government was naturally anxious to secure support from the whole Confederation, and above all the assistance of the Prussian army, but diplomatic negotiations failed to secure either. The Archduke Albert visited Berlin in April and tried vainly to persuade the Prussians to form a joint Austro-Prussian force on the Rhine; following Prussia's example, the Confederation as a whole never mobilised. The most that Prussia was prepared to do was to mobilise six army corps on 14 June (ten days after the battle of Magenta and ten days before Solferino), but rather with a view to armed mediation than with the intention of supporting Austria.

This conspicuous lack of solidarity between Austria and Prussia was partly due to the influence of Bismarck. After a successful career as Prussian representative with the Federal Diet at Frankfurt, Bismarck had just been appointed Prussian ambassador at St Petersburg, where he had arrived at the end of March. At Frankfurt he had shown himself a skilled and ruthless diplomat who, in spite of his friendship with the Gerlachs and other pro-Austrian Prussian conservatives, had established clearly the independence of Prussian policy. At the same time he had come to realise how unsatisfactory the existing machinery of the Confederation was, and was already considering how it should be changed to Prussia's advantage.

Prussia's neutrality was a blow to Austria and to the Confederation as reconstructed in 1850–1. Francis Joseph proclaimed publicly, after the peace of Villafranca had ended the war, that he had been abandoned by his nearest and most natural allies. But the war of 1859 not only revealed the impossibility of producing a common policy acceptable to both Austria and Prussia; it also led to an examination of the machinery of the German Confederation. It was, indeed, clear that, even if Prussia had decided to support Austria, the Federal arrangements for joint action by the various states were quite inadequate. These arrangements dated from 1821, and they had never been tested. No Federal commander could be appointed until the war had actually started; the contingents from the middle and smaller states were combined in mixed corps within which there was no unity of organisation or method—for instance, within the VIII Corps, which included regiments from Württemberg and Baden, the field signal for retreat in the Baden army was the signal for attack in the army of Württemberg.

One of the consequences of the events of 1859 was therefore that the next five years were spent in proposals and arguments about the reform of the Federal constitution. These discussions were not just the concern of the individual governments. They were made the more urgent by the renewed popular activity that started in 1859. The habit of holding congresses with representatives from all over Germany was reviving; a congress of economists was held in 1858 and one of jurists in 1860. The centenary of Schiller's birth in the autumn of 1859 also provided an opportunity for a demonstration of romantic loyalty to a German national ideal. The most important practical step, however, was the formation, in September 1859, of the German National Association (*Deutsche Nationalverein*).

The *Nationalverein* was the first national political movement that could claim to have a real organisation in most of the German states (although it was occasionally forbidden as being too liberal, for instance in the two Mecklenburgs, the most medieval of all the German states). It had a royal patron in Prince Ernest of Saxe-Coburg, and the support of the most prominent liberal politicians of central and north Germany, men who were to be prominent over the next thirty years, and to contribute much to the creation of the empire, such as the Hanoverians Rudolf von Bennigsen and Johannes Miquel (who had begun as a friend of Karl Marx and was to end as an extreme conservative Prussian minister). It included economists like Hermann Schulze-Delitsch, the pioneer of the co-operative movement in Germany, while many of its aims were furthered by political propagandists from the academic world like the young historian from Saxony, Heinrich von Treitschke, who was to become the most eloquent advocate of Prussia's right to rule in a united Germany, though remaining a critic of many of the *Nationalverein's* methods. By 1862 the *National-verein* had 25,000 members, mostly in north and central Germany. For it was the chief organ of those liberals who had now come to believe in the 'little German' solution of the German problem, by which Austria should be excluded from Germany and the new Germany united under Prussian leadership. Although some liberals were prepared to make any sacrifice of liberal ideals of constitutional government in order to win national unity—'Better the stiffest Prussian military rule than the wretchedness of the small states',[1] a leader of the liberals in Hesse-Darmstadt is reported to have said—the *Nationalverein's* tacit acceptance of the principle of Prussian leadership inevitably made Prussia's internal politics a matter of concern to liberals all over Germany.

For Prussia the years between 1858 and 1862 were years of political crisis. Frederick William IV's capriciousness, conceit, sensibility and fantasy had slowly turned into madness, and in the autumn of 1858 he was too ill to continue to rule. His brother, the prince of Prussia, thereupon became regent. The future Emperor William I was then a man of 61. He was a complete contrast to his imaginative and unreliable brother, and in his caution, practical sense and sound unpretentious judgment he was much more like his unspectacular father. He had been brought up as a Prussian officer, and as a boy he had fought in the Napoleonic wars; all his life his main interest was in the army and in military matters. On the other hand he had been hostile to the advisers of his brother and, though a believer in conservative monarchy and the existing territorial settlement in Germany, had never forgotten the 'humiliation of Olmütz'. It was therefore expected that he would appoint a new ministry to replace that of Manteuffel, who was now disliked and mistrusted by everybody, including his former colleagues of the extreme conservative party. Moreover, William's wife was the granddaughter of the duke of Weimar, Goethe's patron, and reputed to sympathise with the liberal ideals of the romantic period; his son, too, had married Victoria, the English Princess Royal and the favourite daughter of the Prince Consort. With these liberal influences in his family and with the necessity of finding a new ministry, the prince regent's assumption of power was hailed by Prussian liberals as inaugurating a 'new era' of constitutional government.

When looking for an alternative government to that of Manteuffel and the extreme conservatives of the *Kreuzzeitung* party, the regent turned to the party known, also from its newspaper, as the *Wochenblatt* party. While the *Kreuzzeitung* represented the views of the old Protestant Prussian nobility east of the Elbe, the *Wochenblatt* was the organ of some of the aristocrats of Westphalia and the Rhineland and of a large number of senior officials and diplomats. It was only by the standards of Prussia in the 'fifties that such a party could be regarded as 'liberal', but at least it stood for a monarchy genuinely subject to a constitution, and for a parliament with certain powers, however limited. Accordingly, a ministry was formed out of members of the *Wochenblatt* group and a few very moderate liberals, under the nominal presidency of a member of the younger branch of the royal house, Prince Anton of Hohenzollern-Sigmaringen; Rudolph von Auerswald, an old friend of the regent who had held office

---

[1] Eyck, *op. cit.* vol. i, p. 337.

with Camphausen and Hansemann in 1848, was Minister without Portfolio and effective Prime Minister.

But the liberals' hope that the 'new era' had begun was soon disappointed. The regent had been uneasy at their acclamations, and the government entered on office with a declaration of conservative principles and a statement on its German policy limiting Prussia to 'moral conquests'.[1] The regent's own interests were restricted to military reforms, and the mobilisation in the summer of 1859 had revealed weaknesses in the Prussian military machinery that, in his view, made such reforms urgent. In December 1859 he appointed General Albrecht von Roon War Minister, and early in 1860 Roon announced his proposals for reforms. He was one of those Prussian officers who lived only for the army: early left an orphan, he had grown up as a member of the Prussian officer corps and served the army with austere devotion, thinking only of military efficiency and little of the ends which it was to serve. He soon became the minister to whom William paid most attention, and could be sure of royal support for his military reforms.

These were embodied in a bill placed before the Diet early in 1860 with a request that the credits necessary for their execution be voted. Some of Roon's proposals were purely technical: the whole army was to be re-equipped with new types of weapon, for instance. The two most important changes, however, had serious political repercussions. Roon's main aims were to rejuvenate the army, to increase the number with the colours at any given moment, and to increase the power of the professional officer corps. To achieve the first aim he proposed that each recruit should serve the full term of three years with the colours instead of the two years that had become customary. To achieve the other two aims he planned to abolish the independence of the Reserve Army (the *Landwehr*) by calling up its younger members to the regular army on mobilisation, and by embodying the reserve officers in the regular officer corps.

These proposals were bound to arouse opposition from even moderate liberals, however loyal they were to the ideal of an efficient Prussian army. The *Landwehr* was a treasured possession of the middle class, full of romantic memories of the war of liberation and the reforms that accompanied it. The loss of its independence and the subordination of its officers was a bitter blow both to the liberal ideal of a nation in arms and to the members of the middle class whose highest social ambition was to become officers of the Reserve. At the same time the proposed change

---

[1] 'Moralische Eroberungen in Deutschland durch eine weise Gesetzgebung bei sich, durch Hebung aller sittlichen Elemente und durch Ergreifung von Einigungselementen, wie der Zollverein es ist....' Regent's speech on 8 November 1858. Johannes Ziekursch, *Politische Geschichte des neuen deutschen Kaiserreiches* (Frankfurt-am-Main, 1925), vol. I, *Die Reichsgründung*, p. 11. See also, for example, Heinrich von Sybel, *Die Begründung des deutschen Reiches durch Wilhelm I* (Munich, 1889–94), vol. II, pp. 220–1.

lengthening compulsory service was unpopular and its social implications clear; three years of military discipline were, it was felt by William and his advisers, more likely to produce loyal subjects than two.

The opposition to the bill shocked the regent, for he felt that the 'new era' ministry had entitled him to the gratitude of the liberals of various shades who now were a serious force in the Diet. The opposition, indeed, was prepared to make far-reaching concessions; they were not opposed to military reforms as such and eventually limited their opposition to the extension of the period of service. In 1860 a compromise was reached that gave the government what it wanted for its immediate programme; the military budget was voted provisionally because of the threatening European situation. In 1861 the conflict was renewed and led to a prolonged period of constitutional struggle. In the spring a compromise military budget was voted by a majority of only eleven, and soon after, a new liberal party was formed by men who saw the importance of the principle of parliamentary control over military expenditure, and who also wanted Prussia to pursue a more active German policy. The new party was called the German Progressive Party (*Deutsche Fortschritt-partei*); its leaders were Max von Forckenbeck, a lawyer, later to become Mayor of Breslau and Berlin, and Leopold von Hoverbeck, a nobleman from East Prussia, who was prepared to oppose the other members of his class and found a party that was to rely for support on the urban middle class. It also included radicals of an older generation like Johann Jacoby from Königsberg. Its objectives included the establishment of the 'firm unity of Germany which cannot be thought of without a strong central power in Prussian hands and without a common German popular representation'.[1] Thus the aims of the *Nationalverein* were finding support in a strong and influential party inside Prussia that appeared to be making a real stand for the preservation of a parliamentary constitution.

In the elections to the Diet at the end of 1861 the Progressive party had a surprising success; although the limited and indirect franchise prevented the creation of a mass party, the new party had shown that it commanded considerable middle-class support. The king (for Frederick William had died in January 1861) and Roon prepared for a hard struggle; among senior officers there was talk of a *coup d'état*. In March 1862 the ministry of the 'new era' was dismissed and new elections were ordered, in the hope of destroying the majority won by the Progressives and old liberals in the previous December. However, in spite of every official effort to influence the elections, the new house again contained a liberal majority committed to rejecting the military budget needed to finance Roon's reforms. Throughout the summer the king tried to find a government that would solve the dilemma by winning parliamentary

[1] L. Parisius, *Deutschlands politische Parteien* (Berlin, 1878), p. 36, quoted Eyck, *op. cit.* vol. I, p. 371.

support. None of the ministers he selected was able to find an answer. The name of Bismarck was often mentioned. In May he had been in Berlin, and it was widely expected that he would be asked to assume office. However, the king was still suspicious of his friendship with the Gerlachs and the *Kreuzzeitung* group, and mistrustful of his forceful and independent methods; and he had been transferred to the Prussian embassy in Paris.

By September the king's position was desperate. His ministers refused to take the responsibility of governing without the vote of a budget and he talked of abdication. Then Roon finally accepted the idea of a government that would ignore the opposition in the Diet, and on 18 September telegraphed to Bismarck to hasten his return to Berlin. Even the king now saw that Bismarck was the only man with the strength of character and political skill to govern without the parliamentary support required by the constitution. Bismarck arrived in Berlin on 20 September 1862 and two days later agreed to take office.

Bismarck was now a man of 47, of great physical vigour and with a vast appetite for food and drink. His energy and penetrating intelligence made an instantaneous impression on all who met him, even on his opponents. Yet this intense nervous vitality occasionally in moments of crisis found relief in outbursts of tears or violent rage. Bismarck had met his wife in the pietist circles of the Prussian Protestant nobility, and from her friends he had acquired religious beliefs that were strongly held, although without any influence on the morality of his public conduct. He could exercise great charm when he chose and his letters to his wife sometimes reveal a poetic sensibility. Although his diplomatic experience had made him intellectually far removed from the young Junker who had come to Berlin to take his seat in the United Diet of 1847, he never lost his feeling for his Prussian estates and his origins in the north German plains; nor did he ever lose his Junker's contempt for the landless middle classes of the cities. Yet his Junker background never prevented him from taking political action that conflicted with the views of his aristocratic compatriots if he thought it would serve his wider aims. It was this freedom from prejudice and utter lack of scruple that gave him his strength. He was contemptuous of 'tedious humanitarian babblers' and 'the vague and changeable concept of humanity'; he was absolutely ruthless in the persecution of his enemies. And he was as free from political inhibitions as he was from moral ones; when he came to power he talked with equal scorn of the 'nationality swindle' of the liberals and the 'sovereignty swindle'[1] of the rulers of the smaller states. It was on 29 September 1862, however, at his first appearance before the Finance Committee of the Prussian Diet as head of the government, that he revealed for a moment his political programme and methods in the most famous of all his

[1] Eyck, *op. cit.* vol. I, p. 373. See also A. O. Meyer, *Bismarck* (Leipzig, 1944), p. 153.

phrases: 'Germany is not looking at Prussia's liberalism, but at her power ...Prussia must preserve her power for the favourable moment, that has already several times been passed. Prussia's frontiers are not suited to a healthy national life. The great questions of our time will not be decided by speeches and majority decisions—that was the mistake of 1848–9—but by Blood and Iron.'[1]

Bismarck had been summoned to deal with the Prussian constitutional conflict and to carry through the army reforms. Yet inevitably he found himself involved with the 'German question', and the two problems— the Prussian constitutional conflict and the German national struggle— became inextricably involved until they were both resolved after, and indeed by means of, the war of 1866. The diplomatic manœuvres and the popular agitation begun in 1859 both demanded that Prussia should adopt a positive policy towards the problem of German unity. The middle states had made various proposals for constitutional reform of the Confederation, chiefly at the instigation of Count Friedrich von Beust, the Saxon Prime Minister and the most energetic champion of the independence of the middle and small states. These plans had not come to anything because of the divergent interests of the states concerned and the suspicions (especially in Bavaria) that prevented them from wholeheartedly supporting Austria. Beust and Ludwig von der Pfordten, the Bavarian Minister, still believed, indeed, in a 'Third Germany' that would hold the balance between the two great powers.

Meanwhile the Austrian government began its last attempt to assert Austrian preponderance in Germany and to compensate Austria in Germany for her defeat in Italy. The constitutional reorganisation in the winter of 1860–1 gave some faint grounds for hope that the monarchy might become slightly more liberal. Popular support for the idea of a 'Greater Germany' including Austria and under her leadership was organised by the Reform Association (*Reformverein*) founded in Munich in October 1862 to counteract the influence of the pro-Prussian, 'little German' *Nationalverein*. Its leader was a veteran of the left wing of the Frankfurt Assembly of 1848, Julius Froebel, who had taken part in the Vienna rising of October 1848; now, however, his advice began to filter through into the channels of the Austrian bureaucracy. Count Rechberg, Austrian Foreign Minister from 1859 to 1863, genuinely believed in a policy of peaceful dual control of Germany, with Prussia and Austria each dominating its own sphere of influence. Other Austrians, however, like Anton von Schmerling, the Minister of the Interior, and Ludwig von Biegeleben, the official in charge of German affairs in the Foreign Ministry, believed in some form of 'Greater Germany' with Austria predominant.

---

[1] W. Böhm (ed.), *Fürst Bismarck als Redner: Vollständige Sammlung der parlamentarischen Reden Bismarcks* (Berlin and Stuttgart, n.d.), vol. II, p. 12.

By the summer of 1863 the various influences favouring a positive Austrian policy in Germany had led the emperor to propose a Congress of Princes at Frankfurt to discuss Austrian suggestions for the reform of the Confederation. The hopes of the south German liberals were high; yet the difficulties in the way of the Habsburg monarchy giving any satisfaction to popular and national demands were clearly pointed out in a poster displayed by the *Nationalverein* during the Frankfurt meeting in answer to propaganda urging Francis Joseph to become German emperor:

...Francis Joseph German Emperor? Yes, if he will, with complete abandon, become wholly nothing but a German Emperor. Yes, if, placing himself confidently at the head of the nation, he at once recognises the immutable constitutional rights of 1849. Yes, finally, if he also achieves peace and reconciliation with the other races of his Empire so that they stand gladly by us against every foe from East or West. Say 'Yes', Francis Joseph, and the whole great people dedicates to you property and possessions as the glorious restorer of Germany.[1]

Quite apart from Austrian difficulties in satisfying popular demands, however, the Frankfurt Congress of Princes failed because the king of Prussia, without whose assent any reform of the Confederation was unthinkable, was not present. Bismarck had taken up office determined to assert Prussia's right to be treated as a great power and the equal of Austria. At the same time, he was ready to co-operate with Austria provided Prussia's position as paramount power in, at least, north and central Germany was recognised. (On 5 December 1862 the Austrian Minister in Berlin reported that Bismarck was urging Austria to abandon her German policy and to transfer the monarchy's centre of gravity to Hungary.) Bismarck realised, however, that differences between the German states might provide the occasion for a European crisis and, especially, for French intervention. One of his first diplomatic acts, therefore, was to make sure that he could count on the goodwill of Russia. His championship of neutrality during the Crimean War, his period of office at the St Petersburg embassy and his conservatism had already made him a figure trusted by the Russian government. In January 1863 the revolt in Russian Poland enabled him to give practical help to the Russians, and in February General von Alvensleben went to St Petersburg and signed an agreement allowing for exchange of information about Polish activities, promises of armed help if necessary and permission to chase fugitives inside Prussian territory. When the convention became known it made the liberals in the Prussian Diet (to say nothing of public opinion abroad) more hostile to Bismarck and his policies than ever.

As yet, however, there was little reason to suppose that relations between Prussia and Austria would become so strained as to provoke a European crisis. Bismarck could still obtain his ends by diplomatic means. The

---

[1] Srbik, *op. cit.* vol. IV, p. 65.

most important of these ends in 1863 was to defeat Austria's renewed attempt to reform the Confederation in her own interest. This was achieved by Prussia's absence from the Frankfurt Congress, although this absence was secured only with difficulty. Early in August Francis Joseph visited King William at Gastein and invited him to attend the Frankfurt meeting later in the month. However, the invitation was refused and the Congress assembled without Prussia. The princes at Frankfurt (all the other sovereigns of the Confederation had accepted except the king of Denmark and the rulers of three of the smallest states) decided to make another attempt to persuade the king of Prussia to come. The king of Saxony went in person to deliver the invitation. All William's instincts of conservative and monarchical solidarity were aroused: 'a king as courier from thirty ruling princes'[1] made the invitation hard to refuse. Bismarck, however, after a struggle eventually persuaded him to stay away; it was the first of a series of such struggles in which the minister had to fight bitterly to overcome the monarch's prejudices.

With this refusal the Austrian reform plan was doomed. The popular support of the south German liberals was soon lost; as one of them, Bluntschli, had remarked in the previous year: 'With their hearts many people believe in a "great Germany", with their heads they believe it to be impossible and so become "little Germans" from necessity.'[2] After 1863 the Austrian cause had little positive appeal. Bismarck immediately attempted to capture popular support by his counter-proposals. These included a division of power between Austria and Prussia, and, most important of all, the establishment of 'a true national representation based on the direct participation of the whole nation...'.[3] It was, however, still too soon for the liberals to trust Bismarck sufficiently to receive such a programme from him; nor were the governments of the several states prepared for such a radical measure.

In the autumn of 1863 it was the Schleswig-Holstein question that occupied the attention both of diplomats and liberal leaders. The Danish war in 1848 had shown how dearly German liberals were attached to the idea of separating the two duchies from the Danish crown and incorporating them both fully into Germany (cf. ch. IX, p. 219). Now in 1863 the king of Denmark had promulgated laws that would separate Schleswig from Holstein and assimilate Schleswig to the rest of the Danish kingdom under a centralised constitution. The Federal Diet had already decided to take action against Denmark when, on 15 November 1863, the situation was further complicated by the death of the Danish king. This added a controversy about the succession to that about the constitution, for the

---

[1] Bismarck's *Gedanken und Erinnerungen*, vol. I, p. 340.

[2] Bluntschli during a meeting of deputies from the various German parliaments at Weimar in 1862. W. Mommsen, 'Zur Beurteilung der deutschen Einheitsbewegung', in *Historische Zeitschrift*, 3rd series, vol. 138 (1928), p. 528.

[3] H. Schulthess, *Europäische Geschichtskalender* (Nordlingen, 1863), p. 78.

succession laws in the Duchies differed from those in the kingdom of Denmark. The candidate on whom the hopes of the liberal and national movement in Germany were set was Frederick, prince of Augustenburg. He was an inexperienced politician, but he was reputed to be liberal in sympathy and had the support of the Prussian crown prince. He had immediately proclaimed himself the lawful heir to the duchies and asked for federal help in establishing his claim. By the beginning of 1864 negotiations between the Diet, Prussia, Austria and Denmark had broken down. Federal contingents had entered Holstein in December 1863, and on 16 January 1864 Prussian troops followed them; on 1 February an Austro-Prussian force crossed into Schleswig and war with Denmark began.

Bismarck was conscious of the dangers of the situation; France, England and Russia might intervene; he was still facing a hostile majority in the Prussian Diet which refused to vote funds for the war. He had therefore been careful to associate Austria with every step against Denmark and a formal alliance was signed on 17 January. Russia, although the duke of Oldenburg was her candidate for the throne of the duchies, was inhibited by the Polish revolt and the Alvensleben Convention (cf. ch. IX, p. 236); Napoleon III allowed himself to be contented with vague hints of a general territorial rearrangement in Europe, while in England Palmerston and Russell were unable to execute the menaces which they had freely employed. The lack of any common policy among the great powers meant that their attempt to solve the problems raised by the war by means of a conference in London came to nothing; by August 1864 the war was over, Denmark defeated, and the preliminaries of peace had been signed, King Christian of Denmark renouncing his right to Schleswig-Holstein.

Bismarck's policy had been equally successful at home. He had told the Prussian Diet in April 1863 that he would get money where he could find it, and had boasted 'We are going to wage war with or without your consent'.[1] Moreover, he made the most of Article 109 of the constitution, which laid down that taxes once voted continued to be levied until actually repealed by the Diet. Money therefore was raised by indirect taxation, from the postal services and from the income of the considerable state property, especially mines and forests. Roon's reforms had been put into operation, and his administration and Moltke's operational planning tested in a victorious war. Inevitably, Prussia's success in a national war, in which she had played the largest part, strengthened the feeling that national unity under Prussian leadership was the only possible solution of the German problem. In spite of the continued hostility of the Progressive party in Prussia, individual liberal leaders began to support Bismarck's policy, while between the Danish war and the war of 1866 he made contact with liberal leaders outside Prussia, such as Oetker in Hesse-Kassel and, eventually, Miquel and Bennigsen in Hanover.

[1] Böhm, *Fürst Bismarck als Redner*, vol. II, p. 101.

Many Prussian conservatives, too, including the king, were given renewed confidence in Bismarck's policy by the Prussian successes in the storming of the Duppel lines and the battle of Alsen. Neither they nor Bismarck, however, felt any enthusiasm for Augustenburg and the liberal and national forces which supported him. As early as 31 December 1863, when the war was just about to break out, Bismarck had admitted in the intimacy of his family circle that annexation of the duchies to Prussia was his ultimate aim. At the end of the war they were in joint Austro-Prussian occupation pending the Confederation's decision about their future, and therefore any solution involving their subordination to Prussia alone was bound to lead to a conflict with Austria.

Prussia was in a strong position, since Austria had no real interest in Schleswig-Holstein and no desire to annex territory in north Germany. The most that Francis Joseph and Rechberg hoped was that they might use the promise of withdrawal from the duchies to persuade the Prussians to yield them territory in Silesia and to guarantee Austria's remaining Italian possessions. The two victorious monarchs and their ministers had met at Schönbrunn in the summer of 1864 and established a temporary working arrangement for the occupation of the conquered territory. Rechberg had gained little—neither territorial compensation nor guarantee of Austria's non-German possessions—and within a few months he had to resign his office. Support for Augustenburg had diminished owing to Bismarck's opposition and his own tactlessness. The other members of the Confederation were being forced to withdraw their forces, leaving Austria and Prussia in occupation. The Prussians moved their naval base from Danzig to Kiel in March 1865. Under the circumstances popular support for Prussia's claim to the duchies grew.

Throughout 1865 Bismarck seems to have pursued a policy that could be executed by either peace or war. His aim was to annex Schleswig-Holstein and eliminate Austria from north Germany. If Austria could be persuaded to renounce her German policy peacefully this would have the advantage of avoiding international complications, in which the policy of the powers, and especially of France, would be uncertain. In May, therefore, he restrained the king and some of the other Prussian ministers who apparently wanted to precipitate a crisis with Austria at once.[1] In August another meeting of the emperor of Austria and the king of Prussia and their ministers led to the Convention of Gastein—a 'papering over of the cracks'[2] as Bismarck called it—by which the administration of the duchies was provisionally divided, Austria governing Holstein and

---

[1] See especially Rudolf Stadelmann, *Das Jahr 1865 und das Problem von Bismarcks deutscher Politik* (*Beiheft* to *Historische Zeitschrift*, 1933). For an account in English of the diplomatic background of the war of 1866 see Chester W. Clark, *Franz Joseph and Bismarck before 1866* (Cambridge, Mass., 1934). See also the excellent account in A. J. P. Taylor, *The Struggle for Mastery in Europe 1848–1918* (Oxford, 1954), ch. VIII.

[2] *Fürst Bismarcks Briefe an seine Braut und Gattin* (Stuttgart, 1900), p. 567.

Prussia Schleswig. Their ultimate destiny was left uncertain, but, by accepting the Prussian proposals for a division of power, Austria not only abandoned the principle of working solely in the name of the Confederation, but also left Bismarck room for further diplomatic manœuvres when it suited him.

By the end of 1865 Bismarck was ready for the next stage. The Gastein convention had given him the opportunity of picking a quarrel with Austria, and it had also been a defeat for those Austrians who wanted Austria to take a bold lead in the national movement. Prussian criticism of the Austrian administration in Holstein increased; in January 1866 a liberal meeting tolerated by the Austrian authorities gave grounds for a formal protest to Vienna. Finally on 28 February a crown council in Berlin decided that Prussia was ready for war for the possession of Schleswig-Holstein and supremacy in Germany. Two conditions seemed necessary for success: a favourable European situation and popular support inside Germany. Bismarck had met Napoleon III at Biarritz in the previous autumn, apparently without obtaining any definite promises; right up to the outbreak of the war Napoleon's attitude was vacillating and uncertain. He wanted territorial advantages, and at one moment Bismarck, although he subsequently denied it vehemently, seems to have been ready to hint at concessions west of the Rhine. At no stage before the outbreak of war, however, was Napoleon ready to intervene decisively; only at the last minute did he gamble on an Austrian victory and sign a treaty with Francis Joseph by which, in return for French neutrality, Austria would cede Venetia at the end of the war. Bismarck had gambled on French neutrality and his gamble was justified.

The most important decision taken at the crown council of 28 February was to offer an alliance to Italy. Negotiations began almost at once and an offensive and defensive alliance was signed on 8 April, with an understanding that the treaty would lapse if there were no war within three months. (Italy was not the only one of Austria's enemies whom Bismarck was prepared to mobilise against her, for early in June he made contact with some of the leaders of the Hungarian revolutionary movement.) Bismarck now had the Italian alliance, the hesitant approval of the king and the sanction of Roon and Moltke for his war policy. The Prussian conservatives (with the honourable exception of his old friend Ludwig von Gerlach, for whom Bismarck's unscrupulousness and readiness to abandon conservative principles were too much) were prepared to follow his lead, even if with some misgivings. He still had to win popular support.

On 9 April a special meeting of the assembly of the Confederation was summoned, and Bismarck astonished everyone by proposing that a German Parliament elected by universal suffrage should meet to discuss constitutional reform. By this move he hoped both to win liberal support and to make reform of the Confederation rather than territorial ambitions in Schleswig-Holstein the issue on which the final breach with Austria should come. Liberal suspicions were still too strong for these proposals to receive a whole-hearted welcome, although they coincided with liberal demands. Moreover, Bismarck himself seems to have believed that universal suffrage would be a measure that would strengthen rather than weaken conservative influence; for, he thought, the votes of loyal peasants would outweigh those given to the middle-class liberals of the towns.

Yet Bismarck's proposal sufficed to achieve his purpose of wrecking the federal constitution and bewildering both liberals and conservatives in the smaller states by his readiness to enlist the forces of revolution on his side. Individual members of the Progressive party and the followers of Lassalle came out in favour of war. A meeting of liberals at Frankfurt under the presidency of Rudolph Bennigsen declared itself in favour of neutrality. Inside Prussia, too, Bismarck was trying to get liberal support. He had attempted a compromise on the question of the army reforms in the previous year without success; relations with the Diet had soon deteriorated again as the result of prosecution of deputies for what was said in the chamber. Now Bismarck promised the new Finance Minister, August von der Heydt, that he would seek a vote of indemnity for his period of rule without parliamentary support. Karl Twesten, the leading champion of parliamentary freedom of speech earlier in the year, stated his readiness to move a vote of indemnity in return for a promise of constitutional behaviour in the future. Bismarck was prepared for this step, and it was prevented only by the personal opposition of the king.

Thus with the degree of support he could expect both at home and abroad still uncertain, but with Italy and the Prussian army firmly on his side, Bismarck proceeded to break up the Confederation and declare war. From the end of April onwards mobilisation began in Italy and Austria; Prussia mobilised in the first week of May. Each side accused the other of warlike preparations. Last attempts at mediation were made—by General Anton von Gablenz, brother of the Austrian governor of Holstein, and himself a Prussian officer whose family was scattered in the service of several of the middle and small states, who proposed the creation of a separate duchy of Schleswig-Holstein under a Prussian prince, and the division of military leadership in Germany between Prussia and Austria; and by Napoleon III who proposed, as usual, a European conference. Neither was successful. Francis Joseph and his ministers had genuinely tried for peaceful collaboration with Prussia, and had gone to the limit of concession, but they were confident that they could beat Prussia if war came, a view that was shared by most of the rest of Europe.

The middle and small states were in a difficult position. Many of the smaller states of the north and centre already had military conventions with Prussia, and, in any case, support of Prussia or neutrality were the only strategically possible alternatives for them. In all the states dynastic quarrels and the opposition of the liberals to the nobility made a coherent policy difficult. Although Hanover and Hesse-Kassel were geographically so placed as to make resistance almost impossible, their rulers were ready to march against Prussia, while the opposition were ready to welcome a Prussian victory. Bavaria and Saxony were the only kingdoms large enough to be militarily important. Pfordten and Beust, however, had delayed till the last moment the construction of a common front with Austria. When war came, Saxon troops fought well on Austria's side, but Bavarian policy was hindered by the personality of the young king Ludwig II; he was to end insane and already preferred the romantic solitude of his mountain castles and the company of actors and artists to the affairs of government. To the popular movements in the south Austria now had little to offer save the idea of loyalty to the Federal Constitution which had already proved unworkable, and which Austria herself had neglected in the provisional settlement of the Schleswig-Holstein question in 1865.

On 14 June the last full meeting of the Federal Diet took place at Frankfurt. Prussian troops had entered Holstein a week previously and diplomatic relations between Berlin and Vienna had already been broken off. At Frankfurt a motion, introduced by Bavaria, to mobilise the contingents other than those of Prussia and Austria was carried by nine votes to six, Luxemburg, the Mecklenburgs and three groups of the small states of the north and centre going with Prussia. The Prussian representative thereupon walked out. On the night of 15/16 June Prussian troops crossed the frontiers of Hanover, Saxony and Hesse-Kassel.

The military history of the war has been fully and finally told in Friedjung's *Struggle for Supremacy in Germany*.[1] The Hanoverian army was defeated on 27/28 June at the battle of Langensalza after an initial success, and capitulated on 29 June. The elector of Hesse had already been taken prisoner. One Prussian army advanced through Nassau and Frankfurt into Bavaria, while another concentrated against the Austrian and Saxon forces in Bohemia. On 3 July the Austrians were decisively defeated at Königgrätz (Sadowa). The struggle for supremacy was over.

Within two months of this victory Bismarck had settled the pattern of German unification and ended the constitutional conflict in Prussia. While the Prussian army was still advancing towards Vienna the possibility of French intervention remained, and a peace settlement became urgent. Bismarck succeeded in combining acceptance of French mediation with the imposition on Austria and the southern states of the terms of peace he wanted. A preliminary peace was signed at Nikolsburg on 26 July; the final Peace of Prague followed on 23 August. Bismarck's

[1] For a brief examination in this volume see ch. XII, pp. 324–5.

hardest struggle had been with the Prussian military leaders and with the king himself, who combined a legitimist reluctance to dethrone dynasties with a conqueror's desire to gain territory from Austria, Saxony and Bavaria. Bismarck, on the other hand, with the support of the crown prince, realised that, by limiting the new Confederation to north Germany and leaving the southern states intact, he would lessen the resentment of the defeated peoples, who in due course would be prepared to join the north in a united Germany, ready to march against France if necessary. Thus in the final settlement, Bavaria, Württemberg, Baden and Hesse-Darmstadt paid indemnities, but lost no territory; at the same time they signed treaties of alliance with Prussia by which their armies came under Prussian command in the event of foreign war. The rulers of Hanover and Hesse-Kassel were deposed and their territories, together with Schleswig-Holstein and the free city of Frankfurt, annexed to Prussia. The other states north of the River Main, and Saxony, joined the new North German Confederation. Austria lost Venetia, paid an indemnity and was formally excluded from any voice in German affairs. The way in which the 'German Question' would be solved had become clear.

But it was not only Austria's position in Germany and the 'great German' idea that were destroyed at Königgrätz and in the peace settlement. Conservatives and clericals all over Germany suffered a defeat at the hands of the popular national forces that Bismarck was now able to exploit. In Prussia this new alignment of political forces was seen in the way in which the constitutional conflict was ended. The Diet had been dissolved on 9 May, and the final stage of the elections took place on the day of Königgrätz, 3 July. The Progressive party, which opposed the war, suffered a severe defeat in the atmosphere of patriotic enthusiasm. On 1 September Bismarck himself introduced a bill into the new Diet asking for an indemnity for the years in which government had been carried on without parliamentary support. On 3 September the indemnity was voted by 230 votes to seven with a number of abstentions. The government had won its case; and the limited value to the liberals of the indemnity law was shown by the king's comment on his policy in the preceding years: 'I had to act in that way, and I shall always act thus if similar circumstances arise again.'[1]

The formation of the North German Confederation, the indemnity law and the decision that the new north German parliament should be elected by universal suffrage gave Bismarck a fresh basis of political support. The old conservative party split; for many of the Junkers felt that their principles had been flouted by Bismarck's apparent concessions to parliament and his alliance with the popular and national movements, while as old-fashioned legitimists they were bound to condemn the 'theft of the crowns' of Hanover and Hesse-Kassel. A new party of Free

[1] M. Philippson, *Max von Forckenbeck* (Leipzig, 1898), cit. Eyck, *op. cit.* vol. II, p. 305.

Conservatives emerged to become Bismarck's loyal supporters, while the old conservatives remained his constant critics. Even more serious was the effect of the new developments on the Progressive party. A large section of the party and many of its ablest leaders, including Forckenbeck and Twesten, now bound themselves to Bismarck's national policy and voted for the indemnity law. Soon they were to join with liberals outside Prussia to form the National Liberal party under Bennigsen, and it was with their support that the new empire was to be founded. Caught in the dilemma of all nineteenth-century liberals between their political morals and national ideals, they had chosen the national ideals.

CHAPTER XX

THE AUSTRIAN EMPIRE AND
ITS PROBLEMS, 1848–67

I T is customary to divide the history of the Austrian monarchy in the
mid-nineteenth century into periods: the *Vormärz*, during which the
forces (chiefly national ones), impatient of the system established under
the Emperor Francis and prolonged under Ferdinand, took shape and
gathered strength; the revolution, when those forces actively challenged
and temporarily overthrew the regime; the reaction, the violent repression
of the revolution by those forces still at the disposal of the old order;
and the gradual emergence of a new system, based on a compromise
between the various elements.

The first two of these periods are touched upon elsewhere (see vol. XI
and this volume, ch. XV), so that the present chapter need concern itself
only with the readjustment which followed the revolution. Yet it is
difficult to know where to begin. The scheme described above, while
convenient when taken broadly, is difficult to apply in detail. Neither
the political nor the chronological distinctions are clear cut. There
were in the Austria of the *Vormärz* a full dozen national movements,
each with aims which involved changes in the existing order, while the
regime itself was fundamentally hostile to any nationalism; but so conflicting were the ambitions of the different nationalities that many of
them saw their chief hope in a strengthening of the central authority of
the crown as a protection against their stronger neighbours; and conversely, the crown felt obliged to seek the alliance of this or that nationality,
against some more dangerous common enemy. The chosen ally was then
a loyal supporter of the regime while the third party was a revolutionary;
but these definitions were political rather than juridical, and often short-
lived, as was well shown by the case of Baron Jellačić, described by the
crown in a close succession of documents as a trusted servant, a rebel,
and a true man again. The Hungarians maintained through more than
a decade that the political changes introduced by them in March 1848,
having been duly enacted by the Diet and sanctioned by the crown, were
entirely legal; it was the crown which committed the illegality in later
cancelling them unilaterally; and in 1865 the crown tacitly admitted the
truth of this contention. As for chronology: the revolution really broke
out in 1846 among the peasants of Galicia, and the crown promptly made
of them its most dependable supporters. After this, March 1848 may,
from a pragmatical standpoint, be regarded as the beginning of the
revolutions—a word by all means to be used in the plural and not in the

singular. But by the end of April everything was over in Galicia, after the socage peasants had been emancipated on the 25th and a rising of the Polish nobility in Cracow put down the next day. Thereafter the government could use the Polish political class or ignore them exactly as suited its purpose, encouraging or repressing the peasants and the primitive Ruthene intelligentsia accordingly; while not needing in practice to take either factor much into consideration. When on 9 August Charles Albert accepted the Armistice of Vigevano the Italian provinces equally passed out of the immediate revolutionary picture. A proportion (not a very high one) of the armed forces had to be kept in Italy to prevent a recurrence of disorder, but since it was generally agreed that whatever happened to the Italian provinces, they would not be integrated into the rest of the Austrian dominions, they formed only a small and occasional factor in the general equation being worked out by 'revolution' and 'reaction', the answer to which was to constitute the future form of Austria.

As significant factors in that equation, beside the court and its direct supporters, there remained, in the west, the Germans and the Czechs, and in the east, the Hungarian regime, as remodelled by the April Laws (ch. xv, p. 398), on the one side, and the Croats, the Serbs of the south, the Transylvanian Roumanians and, to a lesser extent, some of the other 'nationalities', on the other. Here the decisive step taken by the court was when, on 4 September, heartened by the news of Radetzky's victory at Custoza, it reinstated Jellačić in the position and dignities from which it had solemnly deposed him on 10 June. Just what form the future Hungary was to take was still obscure; but in any case, its existing government ranked henceforward as rebels.

Of the two protagonists in the western provinces, the Czechs had always been the less dangerous, since that small people could never become a disruptive force within Austria unless utilised for that purpose by Russia, and Tsar Nicholas was defending Austria, not attacking it. Palacký expressed the point of view which, under the circumstances, Czech nationalism was bound to adopt towards Austria, as such, on his famous rejection of the invitation to Frankfurt (pp. 238–9), in April 1848. The question which remained was whether the Czechs' claims within Austria could be satisfied without driving the German-Austrians into rebellion. In fact, the Czechs' early demand for recognition of the 'rights of the Bohemian crown'— that is, for a Czech-dominated federal unit, consisting of Bohemia, Moravia and Silesia, within Austria—had been one of the things which had most exacerbated the German-Austrians. But Windischgrätz's ruthless suppression of the Prague riots of June (the motives of which had been as much social as national) sobered the Czech leaders (one of them confessed afterwards: 'We should never have gone to Vienna [that is, to the Constituent] but for Windischgrätz') and made them, for the time, generally anxious to reach a constructive agreement with the German-Austrians.

Strong elements among the latter (who were much less united than any other nationality in the monarchy) remained genuinely revolutionary throughout the summer and autumn of 1848, in the hope that a solution would emerge at Frankfurt which satisfied their national and social ideals; alternatively, or in connection therewith, that the Hungarian government would be able to maintain itself, with the twofold consequence of keeping the Slavs down and of establishing constitutional and liberal institutions in the monarchy. But the hopes from Frankfurt faded out, then those from Hungary, and in October Windischgrätz crushed the radicals of Vienna as he had crushed those of Prague in June. Now the German-Austrians, too, ceased to be a revolutionary element; thrown back on 'Austrianism', they could hope only to achieve the best terms possible, within fairly narrowly defined limits.

And those terms would be granted to them, not taken by them of right.

When the new Schwarzenberg ministry was formed in November and the Diet moved to Kremsier the 'reaction' was really firmly in the saddle west of the Leitha, and there was no longer any prospect that, whatever plan the Diet evolved, it would be that on which Austria was governed in the immediate future. If the results of its deliberations nevertheless remain not only interesting but also important, this is partly because portions of them were taken over by the government in its own subsequent productions, partly because the people's representatives themselves, when allowed to meet again in 1861, took up their argument much where they had laid it down in March 1849. Above all, two fundamental principles survived nearly all the changes of the next eighteen years, to reappear almost *verbatim* in the 'Fundamental Laws' of 1867: the first laying down the equality of all citizens before the law, the second declaring that: 'All peoples [*Volksstämme*] of the empire are equal in rights. Each people has an inviolable right to preserve and cultivate its nationality in general, and its language in particular. The equality of rights in the school, administration and public life of every language in local usage [*landes-üblich*] is guaranteed by the State.'[1]

For the rest, the debates showed that of the 'Austrian' peoples, only the unimportant Slovenes really desired the radical solution of scrapping the 'historic units' in favour of a new organisation of Austria on an ethnic basis; the Czechs, it is true, made a similar proposal, but only after their first, more ambitious, demand had been again put forward and rejected, and even so, in connection with a wider plan (which went beyond the Diet's terms of reference) to redivide the whole monarchy, attaching the Slovak areas of Hungary to the Czech. They did not really want Bohemia and Moravia partitioned: they wanted them kept undivided, and under Czech hegemony. The Poles, quite simply, stood for an undivided Galicia, dominated by themselves, but although in this sense

[1] The Law of 1861 substituted 'recognised' for 'guaranteed'.

federalist, they would not form a solid front with the Czechs, never being quite certain whether they could not strike a better bargain with the Germans. The Ruthenes, out of fear of the Poles, were solid centralists. The Germans, as the strongest single element, and one represented in almost every Land, stood for giving the maximum authority to the central government and the minimum to the Lands. At the same time, since their own Lands, although small, were numerous, they supported the retention of the 'historic units', combined with the principle that each of these should be equal in rights with every other; an arrangement which gave results much more favourable to them than the repartition of the monarchy on ethnic lines, when they would have emerged as the largest single group, but only one of a number, and excluded from that control over the other peoples which they had so long exercised and would not willingly renounce.

The resultant compromise retained the historic units (except that Vorarlberg was to be merged in the Tirol) but provided that those of mixed nationality should be divided into *Kreise*, delimited on an ethnic basis. The Lands were 'equal in rights' and each sent six delegates to the upper house; but where the Land was divided into *Kreise*, each *Kreis* also sent a representative. It was an arrangement possessing considerable merits, especially for the Germans, for although the respective competencies of the central Reichstag and of the Lands were not exactly defined, the tendency was indubitably centralist.

Meanwhile, the Diet had owed even its continued existence only to the fact that Hungary was still undefeated. Moreover, it was the uncomfortable fact that the April Laws on which the Hungarian government rested had really been sanctioned by Ferdinand, Hungary's legally crowned king. On 2 December Ferdinand was induced to abdicate, not because he was feeble-minded (although such was the case), but because he was bound by the April Laws. He was now succeeded by his young nephew, henceforward known as Francis Joseph. A manifesto in which the new sovereign addressed his peoples announced his intention of 'uniting all Lands and peoples of the monarchy in one great state', and although these words were ambiguous, the presence of Jellačić and Windischgrätz at the ceremony of abdication made his meaning clear. It was, of course, at once understood by the Hungarian Diet, which, on Kossuth's motion, refused to admit the abdication of Ferdinand as legal; it could recognise no other sovereign until he had been crowned and taken the oath to the constitution.

The court then showed its hand plainly. On 19 December an imperial Patent restored the institutions of a Serbian patriarch and voivode and promised to regularise their position 'on the principle of the equality of rights of all Our peoples'. The same day Jellačić crossed the Austrian frontier into Hungary at the head of the imperial forces. Windischgrätz followed behind him, having been invested by the young emperor with plenipotentiary powers to reduce the country. Other armies advanced from the north, and in the south the Serbs again took up arms. Greatly outnumbered, the Hungarians retreated; Buda fell on 4 January 1849. The Austrian forces then suffered a temporary set-back, but won another heavy victory at Kápolna on 27 February. The war now seemed over, and on 4 March Schwarzenberg issued a new constitution, applicable to the entire monarchy (except the Italian provinces, whose position was reserved for later settlement). On 7 March the Diet of Kremsier was dissolved on the ground that it had failed to complete its constitutional task; actually its constitutional committee had ended its labours with demonstrative self-congratulations on 2 March.

The March constitution, which was mainly Count Stadion's work, took over a large part of the proposals of the Kremsier Diet. For the 'West Austrian Lands' it restored the 'historic units', with the modification that Galicia was divided into two Crownlands (an innovation personally introduced by Stadion, who had been Statthalter in Lvow and a warm patron of the Ruthenes, whom, indeed, he was accused by the Poles of having 'invented' as a nation). Again there was to be a central parliament of two houses, and Landtags; but this time the competencies of the latter were exactly defined and were relatively limited. The list of civic liberties promised to the people was not ungenerous. It was, indeed, largely taken over from that compiled by their own representatives, and the equality of rights of all 'peoples' and the inviolable right of each to preserve and cultivate its language was expressly reaffirmed. A fairly extensive communal autonomy was promised, and enacted by an order of 11 March. Elected assessors were to assist the professional *Kreis* and *Bezirk* authorities. An addition which time was to prove important was that the *Staatsrath*, the advisory body to the crown which in one form or another had existed since the sixteenth century and whose off-shoot, the privy conference, had really ruled Austria for Ferdinand, was preserved in altered form. Its new version, the *Reichsrath*, was to consist of twenty-one members, nominated by the emperor, but, since the introduction of ministerial responsibility, it was destined for a role not larger than that of the British Privy Council.

But the importance of the constitution lay elsewhere. Francis Joseph's proclamation expressly declared his decision to apply it to 'the single and undivided Empire of Austria'. In future 'Austria' was to be a unity, both political and economic. The monarch would be crowned only as emperor of Austria; there would be only one citizenship; and laws would apply equally throughout the entire territory.

Complete uniformity was not, indeed, envisaged: Lombardy and Venetia were to receive a special statute, and it was stated that: 'The constitution of the kingdom of Hungary remains in force, with the reservation that those of its provisions which are contrary to the present imperial constitution are abrogated, and that equality of rights is assured to every nationality and every locally current language in all fields of public and civic life; a special statute will regulate these questions.' The practical effect of the proclamation was, however, to wipe out the Hungarian constitution; the more so since the Patent enumerated the 'Crownlands' which made up the Austrian empire. The kingdom of Hungary was one of them; Croatia-Slavonia, with Fiume, another; Transylvania with the *Partium*[1] another, both being entirely independent of Hungary. The rights of the 'Serbian Voivodina' were confirmed; whether it would be attached to 'another province' was reserved for discussion, as was the union of Dalmatia with Croatia. The Military Frontier[2] retained its old status.

The proclamation was thus a flat defiance alike to the Austrian constitutionalists, to Italy and to Hungary: to everyone, in fact, except Jellačić, and to him it gave much less than he had expected. The inhabitants of the Austrian provinces, to do them justice, took the whole thing without a murmur loud enough to cause the authorities anxiety, and the business of government went on exactly as it had before: by enactment by the appropriate authority, pending the end of the 'state of emergency'.

Not so elsewhere. In Italy Charles Albert denounced the armistice and resumed hostilities: but on 23 March Radetzky inflicted on him, at Novara, a defeat so crushing that he abdicated (see ch. XII, pp. 321–2). His successor, Victor Emmanuel, ended by recognising Austria's possessions in Italy. Lombardy and Venetia were, however, kept under strict military control and thus remained outside the general picture. The promised special status could not yet be granted them; on the other hand, the general measures of the government (except some in the economic field) were not applied to them.

In Hungary, on the contrary, the government meant to achieve the most speedy and complete integration of the whole area comprising the 'Lands of the Holy Crown' with the Austrian dominions. Windischgrätz, who himself possessed estates in Hungary and had many friends among the landowning class there, was indeed at first inclined to interpret the imperial proclamation by restoring the pre-1848 constitution in the conquered parts of the country, leaving the amendment of it until later; and a certain collaboration towards this end developed in west Hungary between him and the Hungarian magnates, who now constituted themselves as an 'Old Conservative' Party, with the programme of a restoration of the old constitution—to which, indeed, they admitted no amendment, except that they accepted as *fait accompli* the emancipation of the

---

[1] That is, such parts of eastern Hungary, not recognised as forming part of historic Transylvania, as had been at one time or another united administratively with Transylvania.
[2] See vol. VII, p. 402.

socage peasants. But the country was, of course, not behind them. The Hungarian government answered the proclamation of 4 March by a counter-proclamation, dated 14 April, which declared Hungary, with all its annexes (Transylvania, Croatia, etc.) a completely independent state, and deposed from the throne of it 'the perjured House of Habsburg-Lorraine'. Pending the final settlement of the form of state, Kossuth became 'Governor' or 'regent'.[1] Bach, at that time Minister of Justice in the Austrian government, promptly argued that this proclamation 'rendered the Hungarian constitution null and void' so that the government's hands were now free. Schwarzenberg himself could not share Windischgrätz's views; he was dictatorial, not feudal, and already on 12 April had got Windischgrätz replaced by General Welden, as provisional head both of the military operations and of the civilian administration. On 30 May Welden in his turn was replaced as commander-in-chief by Haynau, to whom was attached, as civilian commissioner, Baron Geringer. Bach, who had now personally taken over the Ministry of the Interior from Stadion (whose reason had given way) invested Geringer with plenipotentiary powers to introduce the new order. The blue-print for this was issued on 4 July. What was left of Hungary was to be divided into five districts, each under a high commissioner; and the districts were brought into being as the armies advanced. Simultaneously work began on implementing the emancipation of the socage peasants and on introducing equality of usage for all 'local' languages. Austrian civilian commissioners were even attached to the Russian armies to realise the desired measures behind their battlefields also.

On 13 August Görgey surrendered to the Russian armies at Világos. On 1 September Haynau issued a proclamation declaring the rebellion at an end, and summoned all soldiers, officials and members of the Diet to appear before the authorities for screening. The day before, the ministerial council in Vienna had withdrawn from Haynau the power to pass sentence of death. Nevertheless, the famous 'martyrs of Arad' suffered the supreme penalty on 6 October; well over 1000 persons were condemned by court martial to imprisonment or fortresses. Minor offenders were conscripted into the army, in such numbers that the authorities could not cope with them and they had to be discharged. On 17 October a 'provisional administrative system' was introduced for the whole country, and on 1 November the March constitution was extended to Hungary, without the earlier reservations, it being again argued that the Hungarian Diet's own actions had rendered the constitution null and void. The five districts were now definitely constituted, delimited, as far as

[1] The statement often made that on this occasion Hungary proclaimed herself a republic is incorrect. The title assumed by Kossuth (*Kormányzó*) means literally 'one who governs' or 'rules' and was that borne from 1920 to 1944 by Admiral Horthy, in whose case it was invariably translated 'regent' and during which period the fact that Hungary was a monarchy, although one which temporarily lacked a king, was not disputed.

possible, to place the Magyars in a minority; the old administrative subdivisions were retained, but all the officials were now government employees, and the majority of them—the host popularly known as the Bach Hussars—were non-Hungarians, German-Austrians, Poles, and above all, Czechs. The civilian authorities were assisted by the new gendarmerie, a large body, the organisation of which was one of the regime's most urgent tasks.

Transylvania, enlarged as had been promised, was organised on rather similar lines. The Saxons were the most favoured of the local elements, but very considerable linguistic and cultural concessions were made to the Roumanians, in accordance with the principle of national equality. Here too, however, the ultimate control was vested in Vienna.

The settlement of the Southern Slav areas presented great difficulties since the new Serb Patriarch, Rajačić, who was the Hungarian Serbs' real leader (the first elected Voivode, Colonel Šuplykać, had died, and his successor, Stratimirović, had only been given the title of Vice-Voivode), proved to be more of a Serb nationalist than a Yugoslav. He now asked for the Voivodina to be made an independent Crownland and claimed for it, besides the county of Bács-Bodrog, the Bánát, the adjacent areas of the Frontier, and the Slavonian counties. Haynau had meant to keep the Bánát as a separate command, but finally, to pacify the Serbs, he added its three counties (but not the Frontiers) to that of Bács-Bodrog and two districts of Szerem to form the 'Serb Voivodina and Bánát of Temesvár'—an area in which the Serbs now formed only about one-fifth of the population, barely outnumbering the Germans and easily outnumbered by the Roumanians. Jellačić got the rest of Szerem and the other two Slavonian counties for his Croatia; also Fiume and the Muraköz, detached from Hungary, but Dalmatia was still withheld from him, as were the Croat Frontier districts. And to the disgust of both Serbs and Croats, they both came under the same centralised rule as Hungary or the Austrian provinces: Austrian administrators ruled them by order-in-council, and non-Croat officials, Germans or Slovenes, sat in the local offices.

For good or ill, the politically and economically unitary empire was now established. All the ministerial threads now ran together in the hands of Bach, who definitively took over Stadion's portfolio in June, yielding that of Justice to Schmerling. Schwarzenberg, who in any case was mainly occupied with foreign affairs, was no great light; but Bach, Schmerling, Krausz (Finance), Bruck (Trade) and Thun (Education) formed a vigorous team, each eager to press forward with the reforms which he thought necessary, and none anxious to be hampered by the popular will. Indeed, Bach soon cancelled the steps which Stadion had taken in the direction of popular representation. Immediately on taking over the Ministry of the Interior he suspended the Communal Autonomy Law, and in March 1850, dropped the *Kreis* and *Bezirk* assessors.

The measures initiated during this period cut off much old wood, the disappearance of which had been long overdue. The most grandiose among them were those which gave practical effect to the emancipation of the peasants—a large-scale and most complex operation in which (counting Hungary) over three million persons received land, while nearly 100,000 had to cede it. In the German-Austrian and Bohemian Lands one-third of the compensation was paid by the state, one-third by the Land and one-third by the recipient. In Galicia and Hungary no payment was required of the peasants, but even in the other Lands the payment was low, since the land was assessed for the purpose at only about one-third of its real value. The compensation to the ex-owner was correspondingly meagre.

The patrimonial jurisdiction of the landlords having been abolished, the whole judicial system had to be recast, and a new system of *Bezirk* courts was established, with higher instances at the Land centres and a Supreme Court of Appeal, as final instance for both Austria and Hungary. The changes introduced here were by no means all retrogressive, as the old system of depositions taken privately and in writing gave way to a public procedure based on the oral examination of witnesses. The jury system was introduced for all crimes and serious misdemeanours.

The railways were taken over by the state and expanded, notably by the construction of the *Südbahn*; communications were greatly improved, the merchant fleet expanded, the postal services reorganised. Chambers of Trade and Industry were founded and vigorous attempts made both to expand industry and to push exports. It was Bruck's dream to make the new combined Austro-Hungarian economic territory the leading economic factor in Europe, and especially in central Europe. With this aim, a more liberal trade policy was adopted and tariffs reduced.

Even Thun's ministry enacted during this period a number of measures most of which were technically admirable and many of them definitely liberal in spirit. The *gymnasia* were reformed, freedom of instruction and learning was introduced in the universities, the students given freedom to change their universities and technical instruction greatly developed.

The new system even brought some cultural and national satisfaction, on the lower levels, to the less advanced nationalities of the monarchy, particularly in Hungary and Galicia. The principle was laid down that in elementary schools, instruction should be given in the pupil's mother tongue, and accordingly, a considerable number of schools began to give elementary instruction in Slovak, Ruthene and Slovene. In secondary and higher education, too, Slovaks were no longer instructed in Magyar, nor Ruthenes in Polish, and they began to receive a certain measure of instruction in their languages in such establishments.

Similarly, the instructions first issued to officials (for Hungary) provided that no 'linguistic compulsion' was to be applied in church or school;

that the locally current languages were to be placed on an equal footing; that all official notices were to be issued in the languages locally current; that dealings with the public were to be in the locally current languages; and that communications should be accepted, and answered, in those languages. Similar enactments appeared for other Lands.

Very soon, however, the all-important rule was laid down that German was to be the sole language of the 'inner service', that is, of communications between one government office and another, throughout the entire monarchy, so that every public servant had to know it. It was also the 'language of service' in the army. It became the sole official language in Silesia and Bukovina, and the language of the courts, not only in the higher instances but in many lower courts in non-German areas. Education followed. In Ruthene Galicia, higher instruction was at first given 'provisionally' in German, since no qualified Ruthene teachers were available; but although this could not be said of the Poles, the ancient Jagiellon University of Cracow was entirely Germanised in 1854, as were many of the higher educational establishments in Hungary. Czech was abolished outside the elementary schools, except for religious instruction, in 1853: and two orders, of 16 December 1854 and 1 January 1855 respectively, decreed that in all *gymnasia* throughout the empire, Lombardy-Venetia excepted, German must be an obligatory subject and instruction should be given 'mainly' in that language, at least in the higher classes. Thus administration, justice and education alike were, except on the lowest levels, in German, and instruments of Germanisation.

In 1850 and 1851 all these measures were still, officially, provisional, being enacted by order-in-council pending the termination of the 'emergency'. It is still not certain how far Bach, the ex-liberal, the 'Minister of the Barricades', had shed his earlier ideas, and he may well have been driven forward by fears that if he did not reform from above, others would not reform at all. Schwarzenberg, and other members of Francis Joseph's entourage, on the other hand, disliked, not Bach's methods, but his deeds. It was probably more in the hope of bridling Bach, than with any other purpose, that they early began to press on Francis Joseph, not to restore constitutional institutions, which they disliked heartily, but to make himself sole and absolute ruler. The moving spirit in this connection was von Kübeck, who was beyond any doubt one of the most upright and intelligent servants of the old regime but also one to whom effective conservation now seemed to be far more important than any kind of innovation. He it was who had been largely responsible for organising the abdication of Ferdinand and the succession of Francis Joseph; and he was close in the secrets of the imperial family. On 5 December 1850 Kübeck was nominated president designate of the *Reichsrath* and when that body was called into existence in the following April, being the only one of Stadion's proposed institutions to achieve that distinction, he found himself Francis Joseph's special adviser-in-chief. He at once began to press on his young master the desirability of abolishing ministerial responsibility, and vesting all responsibility in the monarch alone. The *Reichsrath*, as the supreme advisory body, would replace the ministerial council, the ministers relapsing into the position of departmental chiefs (this being roughly the relationship which had existed before 1848 between the *Staatskonferenz* and the various *Hofstellen* and *Hofkanzleien*).

It was not difficult to convert to these ideas the young Francis Joseph, who was as firmly convinced as any of his family of his divine right and mission to rule, for his subjects indeed, but not with them. On 20 August 1851, three days after Kübeck had expounded his views to the emperor in a long, reasoned memorandum, Francis Joseph issued a rescript relieving the ministers of all responsibility, except to himself. The abolition of the March constitution was now only a matter of time. It had never, perhaps, been more than that since Schwarzenberg's diplomatic victory over Manteuffel at Olmütz in November 1850 had seemed— although later developments were to prove the appearance deceptive—to decide in Austria's favour the diplomatic struggle for hegemony in Germany, and had thus freed her from the need to *ménager* the opinion of the secondary kings and princes of Germany. There had, however, still remained the fear that fresh unrest might perhaps break out in France and spread thence to the rest of Europe. Louis Napoleon's successful *coup d'état* of 2 December 1851, in Paris, removed this fear also. The way was now clear. On 31 December the so-called 'Sylvester Patent' or proclamation of New Year's Eve (*Sylvesterabend*) revoked the March constitution, confirming, however, that the laws enacting the equality of citizens before the law and the emancipation of the socage peasants remained valid. The emperor now assumed sole and exclusive political responsibility. The principles on which the state was to be administered were listed in a document addressed to Schwarzenberg, and really composed by Bach. The system was one of complete absolutism, exercised through the bureaucracy, and close centralisation. Of self-governing institutions, only the remnants of the communal autonomy survived, but the existing elected councillors, etc., became government servants, and there were to be no further elections. 'Advisory' committees, representative chiefly of the landed nobility, were to be constituted in each Crownland, *Kreis* and *Bezirk*; these, in the event, never came into being. The 'historic units', as remodelled, survived, but the functions of the Land Offices were reduced, the chief weight now falling on the smaller unit, the *Gemischter Bezirksgericht*, so called because it united political and judicial functions. Many functions were carried out by *Hofkommissionen*, whose members were appointed by and directly responsible to Vienna.

With the Patent the return to pre-revolutionary political conditions, and indeed, far beyond them, was complete and political absolutism could go no farther. The next seven years saw in fact no major change in the political machine: only small readjustments and a steady increase in Germanisation; tempered for the population by the successive proclamation in most Crownlands of the end of the state of emergency. The system gravitated more and more into the hands of Bach, for Schmerling had resigned in January 1851, Bruck in May, and Krausz followed soon after; their successors were unimportant. When Schwarzenberg died suddenly, in April 1852, Francis Joseph appointed no new prime minister: Count Buol, a pupil of Metternich, took over the conduct of foreign affairs. The *Reichsrath* proved ineffectual and, when Kübeck died in 1853, it ceased to have any importance whatever.

One other important move was made: to renew the old alliance which had so long linked the Habsburg dynasty and the Holy See. The prime movers here were Francis Joseph's old tutor, von Rauscher, who in 1853 became cardinal-archbishop of Vienna, and Thun; but Bach was a strong ally, as were Francis Joseph himself and his family. Even in 1850 the powers and privileges of the Roman Catholic bishops had been considerably enlarged; in June 1851 the Jesuits, whose activities in Austria had been suspended in May 1848, were reinstated. In April 1852 negotiations were opened for a concordat, and this was concluded in August 1855. It put the church of Rome in an extraordinarily powerful and privileged position. The Catholic church was placed under the especial protection of the state. The pope could communicate freely with the bishops, clergy and people, without consulting the lay authorities. The bishops had full charge over all Catholic education. The ecclesiastical courts were restored. The property of the church was declared sacred and inviolable, and the funds derived from Joseph II's dissolution of the monasteries were transferred to its keeping. A secret agreement went farther still, including, for example, a promise that Austria would not alter any confessional or inter-confessional laws without the previous consent of the Holy See.

The conclusion of the concordat may be taken as the farthest point reached by the Austrian government in its march back from 1848. It was followed by a year or two of standstill: then the slow gathering became perceptible of the forces of opposition; and from 1859 onward the government was steadily forced back until a new resting point was reached in 1867–8. Its retreat was reluctant, and the path of it anything but direct; but this is due not so much to the inconsistency and impulsiveness for which Francis Joseph was often blamed as to the fact that those forces which were pressing him backwards, and with which he was obliged, in the end, to 'compromise'—Hungarian nationalism and Viennese finance —were precisely those for which he and his nearest advisers had the least natural sympathy. And this explains why the much-abused Compromise, when it was reached at last, could justify itself historically by continuing to exist for half a century—a remarkable term of life for any political settlement in central Europe: because it gave satisfaction to the strongest forces in the field.

The peoples of the western half of the monarchy accepted the re-introduction of absolutism with the best grace imaginable. It must be remembered that a substantial proportion of them were ex-socage peasants, who had benefited greatly by the liberation. It is true that some of them were disagreeably surprised to find that the state now expected them to pay taxes, and there were some riots in Galicia and the Bukovina; but in any case, they were not having the landlords back. The industrial workers did not count politically; a combination of full employment and close police supervision kept them quiet. The real intellectual ferment of the revolution, among both German-Austrians and Czechs, had been supplied by a very small class of intellectuals, and of these the Germans, on the whole, felt amply compensated for the loss of united Germany by the prospect now reopened to them of fulfilling their 'Germanic mission' by running the affairs of the other nations of the monarchy, including the Hungarians: a prospect which was not only ideologically, but also materially satisfactory, since the enormously enlarged bureaucracy offered careers to as many young middle-class German-Austrians as wanted them. The Viennese ex-politicians and *literati* made sarcastic jokes, which their later historians dutifully anthologised as evidence of 'resistance', but real resistance was negligible. The Czechs did not receive the small national satisfaction from the new regime which came to the Germans, but obtained as many practical benefits. Every middle-class Czech spoke German well enough to become a Bach Hussar, in which body the Czechs formed the largest contingent. The few devoted nationalists among them were embittered but isolated. When Havlíček, the most wholehearted of them all, returned to Prague in 1855 from the residence in Brixen which had been the penalty imposed on him by the regime (such was the measure of the terrorism of that day) his most painful impression was that 'the reaction was and is in ourselves—and chiefly in ourselves'![1]

This appeasement was greatly facilitated by the fact that, for the common man, material existence was more than usually easy during the early 'fifties. The emancipation of the peasants gave a great impetus both to agriculture and to economic life generally. The peasants worked for themselves as for decades they had not worked for their masters, produced much more than before and entered the economic field as consumers with purchasing power. Bruck did all he could to foster free exchange: the

[1] T. G. Masaryk, *Karel Havlíček*, p. 153, cit. B. Bretholz, *Geschichte Böhmens und Mährens* (Reichenberg, 1921–5), vol. IV, p. 129.

trade barriers with Hungary and Lombardy-Venetia were in any case abolished and he now sought to provide the freest possible exchange with Germany. The system of import prohibitions was changed to one based on tariffs, as low as he could make them; after him, Buol in 1853 concluded a commercial treaty with Prussia based on the 'most favoured nation' clause which proved very advantageous to the consumers and to many industries, which gained more by the extension of markets than they lost through the lowered protection (but cf. ch. XIX, p. 505). The new Chambers of Commerce and Industry did good work, and the large public works—railways, etc.—provided employment and lucrative contracts; so, for that matter, did the equipment of the army, which was conducted in an incredibly wasteful fashion.

The industrial boom which resulted from all this (and which chiefly benefited Vienna and Bohemia) was made possible largely because now, for the first time, industry began to operate largely or mainly on a credit basis: in other words, because finance came to dominate industry. In the *Vormärz* the Austrian National Bank had dealt almost exclusively with the state. Of private bankers, the house of Rothschild stood alone; the remainder were dwarfs, and their operations largely clandestine. Now the whole system expanded suddenly. Very large credit transactions were undertaken first by the *Crédit Mobilier*, a Jewish concern with headquarters in Paris. Then in 1853 an Austrian group founded the first important Austrian private bank, the *Eskompte-Gesellschaft*, and in 1855 the Viennese Rothschilds founded the great *Creditanstalt*, with the specific design of driving the *Crédit Mobilier* out of the field.

These institutions really helped Austrian industry to maintain itself and expand: even more, they brought many fortunes to speculators, for an extraordinary wave of speculation accompanied, in particular, the foundation and first operations of the *Creditanstalt*. This enriched not only the Jews in the *Leopoldstadt* of Vienna, and an enormous number of little men who came into lucky possession of some booming shares in one of the numerous new shareholding companies, but also many of the great aristocrats, whose resentment against the new liberalism was thereby perceptibly softened. The founders of the *Creditanstalt* included the names, not only of Rothschild and Laurels, but also of Schwarzenberg, Fürstenberg, Auersperg, Chotek and others of the first families of Austria.

The other side of the medal was represented by the constantly growing state expenditure. The complicated administration, the extravagant army, the grandiose public works and the compensation of the landowners swallowed enormous sums, and although the Austrian system of taxation was extended to Hungary, and a new income-tax introduced, the budgets —in spite of the windfall from the Sardinian war indemnity—could never be balanced. The state borrowed from the National Bank, or sold crown property. The mobilisation during the Crimean war (see ch. XVIII, pp. 478–80), in particular, was extremely expensive, and after this nearly all the state railways, which comprised two-thirds of all railways then existing in Austria, were sold, on terms extremely unfavourable to the exchequer, to an international group in which the *Crédit Mobilier* held the leading position.

This done, the state had to meet its deficits by floating loans. Since, however, the situation was extremely profitable from the point of view of the buyer, either of the state properties or of the loans, so long as the state did not go bankrupt; and since the threat of bankruptcy had not yet appeared, finance continued to smile on the regime, and industry still sunned itself in the smiles of finance.

It was otherwise in Hungary. Here alone, outside the Italian provinces, had the hand of the 'reaction' been, of necessity, really heavy; but here alone it proved impossible to relax the pressure in any essential respect. There were a large number of amnesties and acts of grace and the whole political system was left 'provisional' for a year after the Sylvester Patent, in the hope that some political compromise might be reached; but all the efforts made in this direction by the Old Conservatives proved unsuccessful, and in January 1853 a 'Definitivum' was issued, which confirmed the previous territorial and political arrangements and initiated an era of still more systematic rule from above.

Even in Hungary there were, of course, collaborators, chiefly among the local Swabians, but the great mass of the middle and small nobility, who previously had controlled every aspect of the national existence, now stood frigidly aloof. Even had he wanted it otherwise, Bach would have been thrown back on foreigners for the conduct of his new regime. He had reckoned with this; but where his calculations, like those of others before and after his day, went wrong, was in underestimating the hold possessed on the country by its traditional leaders. The German-Austrian, Czech and Polish officials arrived in their thousands, armed with the most enlightened instructions. Unacquainted with the language, the conditions and the mentality of the local inhabitants, they could do nothing with them. Detested as they were by the local population, they were no happier than their victims. One of them has described his experiences vividly and with humour. The day he arrived in the village assigned to his charge, he found a queue awaiting him. This proved to consist of persons condemned to imprisonment for sedition; but there were no prisons for them, so every day they drew a sum in lieu of rations, and spent it in the local public-house. The police reported ruefully that the population stood squarely behind its old leaders. The peasants persisted in maintaining that Kossuth, not Bach, had liberated them, and that against the will of 'Vienna'.[1] The emancipation had even bridged the gulf between

[1] In 1935 there were still Hungarian villages which voted for the opposition because the government still meant 'Vienna' to them.

the social classes, uniting them against 'Vienna'. Even the Jews took the side of the Hungarian government, whose almost last act at Debrecen had been to remove the restrictions on them; restrictions which the new regime had reimposed.

Some of the Slovak intellectuals took the side of the regime, petitioning for territorial autonomy within a federated Austria, but they were few; the two northern districts of Hungary, delimited to give Slovak and Ruthene majorities respectively, were only a little less disaffected than the central ones.

Moreover, the new Crownlands created with the special aim of forming a counterweight to Hungary were in hardly better state. In Transylvania the Roumanians, although pleased to be free of the Magyar yoke, found the German hardly more bearable. They did not combine with the local Magyars, but like them they opposed the regime. The Croats were thoroughly disgruntled at finding Dalmatia, and even the Military Frontier, still kept apart from them and Croatia merely a Crownland—under centralised rule and administered, no less than Hungary, by non-natives— instead of the centre of a Triune kingdom. The 'Definitivum' divided Croatia into six *Regierungsbezirke*, each under a chief nominated from Vienna. A commission arrived to screen the officials. Those found not up to standard were dismissed, if the reason was political, or sent to school to learn German, and the Bach Hussars descended on Croatia as mercilessly as on Hungary. Jellačić was given the post of *Statthalter*, but immersed himself in those poetical labours for which, to tell the truth, he showed more aptitude than for either politics or strategy. The remark made by a Croat leader to a Hungarian friend is famous: 'What you have got as punishment, we have been given as reward.'

The Serb Voivodina was a shambles from the first. The Roumanians of the Bánát always resented being included in it. The Germans (not to mention the Bunyevci[1] and the local Magyars) protested vigorously against being put under the Serbs. The Serbs complained at the non-inclusion of the Frontiers; worse still, their loyalty became something more than suspect, particularly after relations between Austria and Russia cooled, at the time of the Crimean War. In the end, the Voivodina also was put under centralised control, supervised on the higher levels chiefly through Germans.

There were two aspects of the Hungarian situation which were particularly serious. One was the financial: the bureaucratic administration, ineffectual as it was, proved exceedingly expensive, while on the other side, the Hungarians displayed an unexampled ingenuity in failing to pay

---

[1] The descendants of immigrants believed to have come from the Herzegovina at the end of the seventeenth century. Their language was a dialect of Serb written in Latin characters, but their religion was Roman Catholic. Politically they usually sided with the Hungarians rather than the Serbs. Their chief centre was Szabadka and its environs.

taxes. The attempt to rule Hungary against her will was costing the government enormous sums annually. The second danger was the foreign-political. The bulk of the nation still looked to Kossuth as its leader, and Kossuth, fertile of brain and golden of tongue, was touring the world, and sending his emissaries about it, everywhere stirring up hostility to the Habsburgs and plotting their downfall. Thus the dissatisfaction in Hungary encouraged Austria's enemies, for it was to be anticipated that in the event of war Hungary would rise against the government.

That prospect grew steadily nearer. Austria had reached the peak of her apparent power at Olmütz in November 1850; but her very success had rallied the other powers against her, in a fashion of which Prussia was able to take advantage. At the Dresden Congress in March 1851 Schwarzenberg had been forced finally to drop the demand that the whole unitary Austrian state, German and non-German areas alike, should be admitted into the *Bund* and see that body restored as it had been constituted in 1815, with the anomalous result that half the new unitary state was inside the *Bund* and half outside it. Austria was now back in her old position of a rival with Prussia for the leadership in Germany; and as each year went by the balance shifted farther in Prussia's favour. In the Crimean War Austria followed a clumsy and hesitant policy which cost her the tsar's friendship and brought her nothing in exchange (see ch. XVIII). Cavour's skilful diplomacy, on the other hand, brought Piedmont a large addition in prestige, so that the *status quo* in Italy was no longer secure. Moreover, Louis Napoleon had now found his feet, and was openly espousing the principle of nationality. An alliance between France and Piedmont, directed against Austria, had cast its shadow before, even before the Plombières meeting of 20 July 1858 (see pp. 271 and 463).

These events kept alive the hopes of the Hungarian irreconcilables, and meanwhile the situation at another nerve-centre had changed. Bruck, brought back as Finance Minister in 1855, tried to restore order by a return to orthodoxy which included heavy increases in taxation. Then in 1857 the great stock-exchange crash, travelling from England and America, via Germany, reached Vienna. The bubble was pricked. Stock-exchange speculators found themselves beggars. Credits to industry were called in. Now the newly (and most expensively) constructed *Südbahn* had to be sold, and the Tisza railway. The *Creditanstalt* itself suffered heavily. The holders of existing loans turned against any further borrowing, as dangerous to the security of the earlier issues. From this moment onward finance and business generally began to press for economy in state expenditure, concentrating their attacks particularly on Bach's bureaucracy and on the army. It is not irrelevant that the circles which led

¹ (Cf. p. 503.) The wording of the note left the position of the Italian provinces ambiguous.

these attacks were particularly antagonistic to the Concordat and to all its implications.

It was the worst possible moment to economise on the army, for by now it was an open secret that France and Sardinia were preparing to attack Austria in Italy, and Prussia's attitude, too, was threatening. Francis Joseph could not bring himself to buy Prussia's support at her price. War came in April 1859. Austria, by her ultimatum, was the technical aggressor, but not the real one; the war was the work of Louis Napoleon and Cavour (see ch. XXI, pp. 571–2). Francis Joseph simply advanced the outbreak of hostilities in the hope of a quick victory which would spare him a long and costly campaign, or the hardly less costly process of keeping a large force under arms.

For the threat of this war brought to a head Austria's difficulties from the two sides which, as we said, constituted, in their different but interlocking ways, serious threats to the regime. 150,000 troops had to be left in Hungary, partly to prevent a rising, partly to collect taxes, which the wretched Bach Hussars were quite unable to get in. In Vienna, the National Bank was obliged, four days before the outbreak of war, to suspend payments in currency and to collect an emergency tax by simply docking the coupons of the state loans. A fresh loan, although issued at 70 and at 5 per cent, found hardly any subscribers; banks, consumers and private taxpayers were simply ordered to take it up, and the state took advances from the National Bank to the tune of 133 million *gulden*. Finally, an extraordinary surcharge on the direct taxes was ordered by imperial decree.

The quick victories failed to materialise, partly owing to the gross incompetence of the Austrian commander-in-chief, Gyulai, and his advisers—a weakness for which Francis Joseph, who had dispensed with a Minister of Defence and taken personal charge of the army and its affairs, was personally responsible—partly owing to political disaffection: while German and Czech troops were kept in Hungary, Hungarians were sent to Italy, and not only they and the Italian soldiers but—more ominous still—the trusted Croats deserted in large numbers. Sardinia won the battles of Magenta and Solferino largely because the soldiers of the Austrian army deserted or surrendered.

It was on the morrow of Solferino that Francis Joseph began his retreat from absolutism. Buol had already resigned when the emperor sent his ultimatum to Sardinia, being replaced as Foreign Minister by Rechberg. Now, in July, Rechberg took over the duties of Minister President; but the important change was that Bach was dismissed in favour of a new minister whose appointment came, indeed, as a surprise to everyone, including himself: Count Goluchowski, a Polish aristocrat, previously *Statthalter* in Galicia. 'But I am a Slav', he is said to have exclaimed when the emperor told him of his new appointment: to which Francis Joseph replied: 'The Slavs are my most loyal subjects.' It was a fact that at the time they were causing him far less anxiety than either the Germans or the Magyars.

But it was not to them that the first concessions were made; nor, indeed, was Goluchowski a true representative of the federalist nobility which was soon again to raise its voice. 'The Laxenburg Manifesto' of 23 August 1859, which set out the new government's programme, began with the promise that all government expenditure, civil and military, should be submitted to 'effective control', adding assurances that the non-Catholic religions should be allowed autonomy and freedom of worship and that 'the position of the Israelites should be regulated along modern lines, but taking into account local and provincial conditions'. A measure of communal autonomy was to be restored, and a 'substantial part' of the duties at present performed by the bureaucracy transferred to autonomous bodies; whereafter 'bodies representing the Estates' were to be called into being 'in the various Crownlands'.

The word 'constitution' was not mentioned in the manifesto, which did not imply that Francis Joseph had become a convert to constitutionalism, or to democracy; only that certain concessions, to certain interests, had become simply unavoidable. Even they came slowly: it was only on 21 December that a state debt commission was appointed—a measure the reception of which by the business and financial interests showed that they regarded it as totally inadequate.

Meanwhile, the Italian war having ended on terms unexpectedly favourable to Austria—who lost Lombardy, but retained Venice and the Quadrilateral—the most important political problem was that of Hungary. Typically, Francis Joseph was still unwilling to negotiate with the real forces in that country, the lesser nobility who stood by 1848; but the Old Conservatives now again came forward as mediators. Even they demanded more than the government was willing to give, for the essential of their claim was the restoration of the pre-1848 constitution, but they were prepared to see this amended by giving larger powers to the crown as a counterweight both to Kossuth's separatism and to his liberalism. Throughout the autumn of 1859 Rechberg was engaged in private conversations with the Old Conservative leaders, and it was largely on their suggestion that on 5 March 1860 Francis Joseph issued the so-called 'March Patent'. The *Reichsrath* was to be enlarged and, while remaining, in the last instance, only advisory, given a quasi-representative character by adding to its twenty-one original members thirty-eight more from the various Landtags. Pending the constitution of the latter, the monarch himself would appoint the new members. This body, the 'Reinforced *Reichsrath*', was convoked for 31 May; a portion of its members were drawn from the higher Viennese bourgeoisie, the remainder from the various Lands, these being in nearly every case high aristocrats or prelates.

The six Hungarian members were all Old Conservatives (to do the government justice, it suggested other names also, but the nominees rejected the invitation). Even so, they proved distressingly Hungarian. Their leaders, Counts Széczen and Emil Dessewffy, proved themselves much the most skilful and experienced politicians among all those present. In effect, they took charge of the whole proceedings. They welded the aristocratic representatives from the Lands into a 'United Party of the Federalist Nobility', which outnumbered the centralists and their allies, and then turned the proceedings into something resembling those of a constituent assembly.

Of the highest importance was the attitude taken up by the Hungarians towards their colleagues from Bohemia and Galicia. Seeing their chief enemy in Viennese centralism—whether absolutist, bureaucratic or liberal —they were prepared to ally themselves with any of its opponents, and supported, not only the claim of the Polish aristocrats for a special status for Galicia but also that which the Bohemian leaders (the chief of whom was Count Clam-Martinitz) were emboldened to put forward for recognition of the rights of the Lands of the Bohemian crown. This was not merely a tactical move, made during the session, for Eötvös, the brains of the Hungarian aristocracy, endorsed the same claim in his *Garantien der Macht und Einheit Oesterreichs* (1859).

In return, the Bohemian aristocrats, as well as the Poles, supported the Hungarians' demands for the restoration of their constitution. This meant that the Slovaks were abandoned; the Transylvanian Roumanians and, still more, the Serbs of the Voivodina were quite obviously marked out as future sacrifices to Hungary. Even the Croats received relatively little consideration. Thus a new alignment of political forces came into being, or rather an old one returned in more definite form. The Czech nationalist intellectuals abandoned, in the interests of the larger claim, such community of action as they had hitherto maintained with German liberalism, while the German nationals were driven to seek again the friendship of the Hungarian liberals.

Led by the Hungarians, the united nobility secured the adoption by the Reinforced *Reichsrath*, by a majority (the Croats voting with the majority, but all the German bourgeois representatives, the Serbs, Roumanians and Ruthenes against), of a report recommending that the monarchy should be reconstructed on a new system which should take into account 'the historic-political individualities of its various components' and should 'link up with the formerly existing historic institutions'. Communal autonomy and the local institutions of Hungary should be restored; in the other Lands, where no institutions analogous to the Hungarian existed, they should be created. All the Diets should be convoked, and the Lands should be guaranteed real autonomy. The report admitted the equality, in principle, of all Lands of the monarchy.

While these negotiations and debates were going on, quite a number of concessions of real political value had been made to Hungary. The quinquipartite division of the country was given up. Field-Marshal Benedek, himself a Hungarian, was made governor-general. Yet another amnesty was issued, and the predominance of the German language in education greatly reduced. (In this respect, parallel concessions to the Polish language were made in Galicia.) None of these appeased public opinion, particularly since in September 1859 Thun had issued a 'Protestant Patent', regulating the position of the Protestant churches, which the latter regarded as grossly violating their rights.

Francis Joseph was now in haste to reach a settlement; on 21 October he had to meet the tsar and the prince regent of Prussia in Warsaw, and did not want to come to the meeting with half his dominions in almost open revolt against him. Széczen, it is said, assured him, in the course of a conversation in a railway train, that a settlement on the lines of the Reinforced *Reichsrath*'s majority report would be accepted in Hungary. A document to the effect was hurriedly drafted, and appeared, in the form of the so-called 'October Diploma' on 20 October 1860. In fact, it closely followed the recommendations of the Majority Report. The crown would in future exercise its legislative powers 'with the co-operation of the Landtags, legally assembled, and of the *Reichsrath*, to which the Landtags have to send members in a number fixed by Us'. The *Reichsrath* was to deal with questions affecting the monarchy as a whole (these were enumerated), the Landtags with all others; 'in the Kingdoms and Lands belonging to the Hungarian crown in the sense of their earlier constitutions, and in the other Kingdoms and Lands constitutionally, in the sense of and in accordance with their Statutes'. The organs of local self-government in Hungary were to be reinstated immediately, and similar institutions created elsewhere. Communal elections were to be carried through immediately. The *Reichsräthe* of the non-Hungarian Lands were to meet without the Hungarians when questions were under discussion of the type which had long been 'handled and decided' for them as a unit.

Simultaneously with the Diploma, a large number of rescripts were issued. Francis Joseph reaffirmed the assent given by his ancestors in the seventeenth and eighteenth centuries to certain laws relating to the Hungarian Estates, the effect of this being, broadly, to re-establish the constitutional *status quo ante* 1848 in Hungary. In connection therewith, the Hungarian Court Chancellery was re-established, Baron Vay, until recently in prison for sedition, being appointed chancellor. The chancellor was to be a member of the central government, into which Széczen also was taken, as Minister without Portfolio. The validity of those laws of 1848 which dealt with the emancipation of the peasants was recognised, although no others. Magyar was restored as the central official language and that of the 'inner service', as of higher education, but adequate facilities were to be given to non-Magyars to use their languages in local administration and elementary education. Immediate elections were to be held in the county and municipal diets, whereafter the old system of autonomous local government would be resumed. The Diet was to be convoked in 1860, to submit further proposals for recasting the relationship between Hungary and the crown.

Similarly, the Transylvanian Court Chancellery was restored and the Transylvanian Diet, in its old shape, summoned to meet and, after hearing the representatives of all local nationalities, religions and classes, to submit proposals for the realisation of the principle of the equality of all citizens. The Ban of Croatia was instructed to convoke the local diet in order to submit proposals for a new internal constitution, and also for the relationship between Croatia and Hungary. A commission was to be sent to the Voivodina to report on the wishes of the local peoples as to their future. In Cis-Leithania the government was to elaborate statutes for the various Lands, assuring to them 'representation adapted alike to their historic development, their present requirements, and the interests of the Empire'.

The ministries of the Interior, Justice and Cults were abolished.

The Diploma was ill-received almost everywhere. It did not even satisfy the Czechs, who had expected more. Practically all the Germans were against it: the bureaucrats *à la* Bach, because they saw Hungary slipping out of their hands; the nationalists, who saw the Sudeten Germans left at the mercy of Czech majorities under the new federalism; the liberals, who saw the federalists and clericals installed as the rulers of Austria; the moneyed interests, to whom the Diploma offered no real satisfaction. The three last-named groups were able to form a loose common front, united by the slogan that 'Austria must be treated as favourably as Hungary'. That is, if Hungary had a central, constitutional parliament, Austria must have one too. Broadly, then, the Diploma had already prepared the Germans of Austria for dualism.

The protests, which a relaxation of the censorship allowed to be more vocal, grew louder when Goluchowski began publishing his *Landesstatute*: in every case exceedingly conservative instruments which left the land-owning aristocracy and the prelates in a dominating position. Then came fresh financial difficulties: von Plener, who had become Finance Minister after the suicide of Bruck, had to propose an uncovered issue of paper money to the tune of 50 million *gulden*, in anticipation of taxes. But the greatest disappointment came from Hungary. Széczen himself had not reckoned on this sudden issue of the relevant enactments by ukase, without any previous preparation of public opinion. And in any case, it immediately became clear that the magnates had entirely misjudged opinion in their own country. It was true that Hungarian public opinion towards the Habsburgs was not completely negative.

Kossuth's name was still, sentimentally, the most popular in the country, but after the armistice of Villafranca it looked as though Kossuth's grandiose schemes for mustering Europe against Austria were doomed to failure; nor were his projects for Danubian federation at all universally popular in Hungary. Much of the nation was prepared to come to terms with the Habsburgs, but their idea of acceptable terms was not that of the Old Conservatives.

Increasingly, Hungarian opinion had been falling into line behind the man who now emerged as the country's leader, Francis Deák. This quiet, unassuming country gentleman, a leader before 1848 of the movement for social and political reforms in Hungary, had entered the 1848 government as Minister of Justice, but had not accompanied it to Debrecen in January 1849. He had thus not participated in the deposition of the Habsburgs, of which he disapproved. On the other hand, he maintained with complete firmness that the April Laws were legal and that all measures taken by the crown, from the issue of the March constitution onward, were legally null and void. Not even the most generous concessions by the crown would be acceptable if issued unilaterally, without previous consultation with Hungary's lawful Parliament. As interim tactics, during the 'fifties, he had advocated passive resistance; and the nation had become increasingly converted to this idea, which spared it bloodshed and kept its money in its pockets (since the resistance was mainly to the tax-collectors) and was showing its practical effectiveness by forcing the crown, step by step, into retreat. Under Deák's leadership, Hungary unhesitatingly rejected the October Diploma, and the first results of its accompanying concessions were, accordingly, discouraging enough to the government; for the counties celebrated the restoration of their Diets by electing to those bodies such persons as Kossuth, Cavour and Louis Napoleon. Under the influence of these demonstrations, and of the loudly voiced dissatisfaction of the Viennese tax-payers and financiers, Francis Joseph, on 14 December, dismissed Goluchowski in favour of Anton von Schmerling.

Schmerling was a man on whom, for some years past, the liberals of Vienna, the civil servants and the Sudeten Germans had united in fixing their hopes. He represented at once German nationalism, centralism and constitutionalism, and was correspondingly unpopular among the feudalists and the Slavs. Strangely enough, his candidature was supported and indeed actually proposed by the Hungarian Old Conservatives, who believed that he would effectively carry through the concessions granted to Hungary in October, and it was popular among the Hungarian 1848 Party, who thought that he would pave the way towards the dualism —a centralised constitutional Austria balancing a centralised, constitutional Hungary—which most of them still felt, as they had felt in 1848, to be the ultimate solution best guaranteeing their own position.

In fact, a few days after Schmerling's appointment, the Voivodina was reincorporated in Hungary and, soon after, the Muraköz restored to it. Francis Joseph was not blind to the real situation in Hungary, for he called Eötvös and Deák to private audiences, which left personal good impressions on both sides. Schmerling, however, was not, in reality, a pro-Hungarian at all. He was as much of a centralist as Bach, but had not yet drawn the logical conclusion, to which he was afterwards driven, that if centralisation could be carried out at all, this could only be by force. On 26 February the 'February Patent', which embodied his ideas, appeared. Nominally a development of the October Diploma, this contrived radically to modify the spirit of the earlier document. The *Reichsrath* remained; it was to consist of 343 deputies, delegated, in fixed numbers, by the Diets of the 'Lands' (among which Transylvania and Croatia were listed separately). The respective competencies of the *Reichsrath* and the Lands (all of which, from Hungary to the Bukovina, still ranked as equals) were exactly defined, those of the former being very extensive. An elaborate electoral geometry weighted the electoral colleges in the Austrian Lands heavily in favour of the Germans, with a small curia of landed proprietors holding the balance in Bohemia and Moravia. A 'narrower *Reichsrath*', not attended by the deputies from the Hungarian Lands and Venetia, was to sit alone when subjects of exclusive interest to Austria were being discussed. There was also an Upper House.

Simultaneously with the issue of the Patent, all Landtags were convoked for 6 April, in order that they should send their representatives to the *Reichsrath*.

The Patent was received almost as ill as the Diploma, although the objections came, of course, from different quarters. The Slav nationalists, the feudal aristocracy and also the German clericals protested strongly; there were turbulent scenes in the Landtags of Prague and some other centres. When, finally, the 203 *Reichsrath* representatives from Cis-Leithania were ready to assemble, three groups numbering 130 deputies and composed almost entirely of German bourgeois, with the Ruthenes, were prepared, some of them with considerable reservations, to support the Patent; the German clericals, Poles, Czechs and Slovenes—in all, seventy deputies—formed the opposition. Meanwhile, the Venetians boycotted the elections altogether and a large party in Hungary favoured the same course. Deák, however, advised that the Hungarian parliament should meet. The elections practically swept away the Old Conservatives, and not one deputy who was returned now accepted the Patent. The two houses, after listening non-committally to a speech from the throne, divided into two parties who agreed precisely on the substance of what they should demand—recognition of the 1848 Laws, to which they were then prepared to agree certain modifications—and differed only on whether they should couch their demands in the form of a reply to the address, which would have implied recognition that the address itself, made in the name of a sovereign who had not yet been crowned king of Hungary, was legal, or of a resolution, which, it could be presumed, would come to Francis Joseph's notice. Deák, for once compromising with his strict principles, advised the latter course, which was adopted by a very narrow majority; but the demands formulated in the 'Reply' were so uncompromising that Schmerling simply returned an ultimatum summoning the Diet to send its representatives to the *Reichsrath* forthwith. When this was rejected, he dissolved the Diet and reintroduced the absolutist regime of the preceding decade.

The deadlock was renewed, and Schmerling was confident that time was on his side; but he was wrong. One of the few decisions taken by the Diet was to set up a committee which should work out an equitable and satisfactory nationalities law. Although the majority of this committee was firm in refusing the demands of the Serb and Slovak minority leaders for any derogation, on either a territorial or a personal-national basis, of the unity of the state, they agreed, on Eötvös' motion, to enunciate the principle of complete national equality, from which no derogation was permissible except in the practical field of the use of the different languages, and that only in so far as necessitated by the practical requirements of administration. This formula in fact satisfied many of the 'nationalities'. The Diet also enacted the equality of rights for the Jews, and the abolition of the remaining obligations of the socage peasantry.

Deák also approached the Croats, offering them a 'blank sheet' on which to write the conditions under which they would return to their old association with Hungary; further conceding their claim to the disputed Slavonian countries. The Croats, too, were deeply hostile to the Patent, and further irritated by the régime's continued hesitation to attach Dalmatia to Croatia. In July their Diet resolved, by 120 votes to 3, to enter into a closer constitutional relationship with Hungary if their independence was recognised; a few days later, they resolved not to send their delegates to the *Reichsrath*. In November the Croat Diet also was dissolved. Only in Transylvania did things go somewhat better for the government. The Saxons and Roumanians presently appeared in the *Reichsrath*; but the Hungarians remained completely hostile.

Meanwhile in Vienna the opposition of the Czechs and Poles grew increasingly violent. The Poles concentrated on their own demand, for a special status for an undivided Galicia; the Czechs not only revived the claim for the rights of the Lands of the Bohemian crown, but maintained that the whole *Reichsrath* was unconstitutional, while the Hungarians absented themselves. Schmerling was thus ruling against Slavs and Hungarians at once, and his system came more and more to resemble that of Bach, with its political repression and its weakness on both sides of the financial ledger: expensive administration and decreasing resources, since the Hungarians had returned to passive resistance and to non-payment of taxes. Now the tax-payers and the banks in their turn grew restive again, and showed their discontent in a way particularly disagreeable and also dangerous to Francis Joseph: over 40 per cent of the state's annual expenditure now went on the national debt, and large sums were required also for repayment of advances from the National Bank. The moneyed circles declared these to be sacrosanct, and in their attacks on the government, which were often more violent than those made by the opposition itself, demanded reductions of administrative, and also of military expenditure.

Of the various opponents of the regime, it was the Hungarians whom Francis Joseph first brought himself to approach. Deák's position was, after all, not anti-Habsburg or unreasonable. He took his stand quite strictly on certain fundamental documents agreed between the crown and Hungary: on the Pragmatic Sanction of 1722, amending and extending the Succession Law of 1687, and itself extended and amended by the assurances given by Leopold II on his succession in 1791. Under these the crown was bound to govern Hungary according to her own laws and customs, agreed with the Diet, and not *ad normam aliarum provinciarum*, and no Austrian authority had anything whatever to say in Hungary. But by the same instruments Hungary had recognised the legal right of the Habsburgs to succeed to the throne (provided they accepted coronation, swore the coronation oath and subscribed to the Diploma), had admitted that Hungary was united *indivisibiliter atque inseparabiliter* with the Habsburgs' other dominions and even admitted the existence of certain affairs (foreign policy, defence and the finance entailed thereby) of common interest to Hungary and those dominions. And since he also accepted the view, strongly maintained by Kossuth, that a constitutional regime in Hungary such as the 1848 Laws had established could not count on survival while the Austrian regime was autocratic, he necessarily admitted some sort of consultation, in these matters, with the constitutional representatives of Austria.

This offered a basis of agreement, which had become urgent in 1864 since the international situation had again grown dangerous and Austria was threatened alike by France, Italy and Prussia. Francis Joseph could not bear to divide his opponents by buying one of them off; Rechberg, who would have compromised with Prussia, was dismissed on 27 October in favour of Mensdorff-Pouilly, who with Hofrat Biegeleben, now the real director of foreign policy, favoured a forward policy. In December Francis Joseph than began secret private negotiations, through an intermediary, with Deák, who insisted that the union of Transylvania could not be abandoned, nor could Croatia be detached from the Holy Crown. Francis Joseph must be crowned king of Hungary and undertake the appropriate obligations. But he explained how far he was ready to go in the matter of common institutions, and promised that Croatia should have adequate autonomy, and the nationalities treatment in the sense of the 1861 draft. By arrangement, he published these views on the basis of a possible compromise in a series of newspaper articles which appeared in the spring of 1865; whereupon Francis Joseph suddenly travelled to Pest, where he promised publicly 'to do everything possible to satisfy the peoples of my Hungarian Crown'. On 27 July, when the session of the narrower *Reichsrath* closed, Schmerling and nearly all his ministers, except Mensdorff, the Hungarian Chancellor, Majláth, and Count Maurice Esterházy, Minister without Portfolio, were dismissed. On 20 September a manifesto appeared suspending the operation of the October Diploma and February Patent. These were to be submitted to the Hungarian and Croat Diets. The result of the negotiations, if satisfactory at all, was afterwards to be laid before legal representatives of the Cis-Leithanian Lands, convoked later for that purpose. Pending this, the government would take the indispensable measures by the exercise of emergency powers.

Thus, in Francis Joseph's view, the negotiations with Hungary were proceeding along a direct line. That they did not do so was because, to succeed Schmerling (but with competencies extending only to Cis-Leithania), he appointed Count Belcredi, a member of the Bohemian landed aristocracy, feudal, federalist and Slavophile. The appointment was made on the suggestion of Esterházy, himself an Old Conservative, who still thought in the terms of the 1861 alignment of forces and drew the natural conclusion from the support which the German-Austrians had cheerfully given to Schmerling's renewed larger centralism; also, apparently, believing, with his class-colleagues, that Hungary would accept a central *Reichsrath* if not over-powerful. But the effect was very different. In the west, the Slavs were jubilant and revived their plans for federalising Austria. The Germans were correspondingly embittered, and the turn of events now raised to influence the German-Austrian autonomists, a small party led by Kaiserfeld, whose main strength lay in Styria. This party had continued to advocate the old idea that the German-Austrians should make terms with the Hungarians and Poles, thus freeing their hands to deal with the Czechs and Slovenes; since 1862 they had had a working agreement with the Hungarian liberals, and this was now intensified. When the Hungarian parliament met in December, the Old Conservatives' calculations again proved faulty. Francis Joseph said that he no longer disputed the legality of the 1848 Laws (and in token thereof enacted the reunion of Transylvania) but wanted them revised in the light of the later instruments. The Hungarians politely but firmly refused to recognise either Diploma or Patent, or to enter any central *Reichsrath*; but they would consider simultaneous meetings of representatives from their own parliament and of those of the Habsburgs' other dominions when the monarch wished to discuss matters admitted under the Pragmatic Sanction to be of common interest to Hungary and to those dominions; and they would set up a parliamentary committee to discuss modalities.

Meanwhile in Austria the Landtags met and wrangled: things were at a deadlock until the Hungarian question was settled. In the middle of this, the Austro-Prussian war broke out, to end in a few weeks with crushing defeat for Austria (see chs. XII and XIX, pp. 325 and 519).

Again voices were raised in Hungary that Austria's difficulty was Hungary's opportunity, but this was not Deák's view, nor that of Count Gyula Andrássy, who now came forward to take a part second only to Deák's own in the negotiations. Far shallower in mind than Deák, Eötvös or even Széczen, Andrássy combined the advantages of exceptional personal charm, a most persuasive tongue, and a lineage which made him *hoffähig*. A native of the Slovak north Hungary, Andrássy was more alive than Deák to the Slav danger, and certain movements among the local Slovaks and Ruthenes, coinciding with indiscreet utterances by Palacký, deepened his conviction that the only safety for Hungary lay in a connection with Austria, and at that, an Austria not dominated by the Slavs.

In a memorandum which he submitted to Francis Joseph in 1866 he argued that 'an artificial reconstruction of the Bohemian crown and a grouping of the Slav provinces round it would only begin in Austria a work which would necessarily end outside it'. In private audience he is said to have summed up dualism in the words: 'You look after your Slavs and we will look after ours.' The autonomists' programme in Austria offered a foundation on which this structure could be built, while Bismarck's similar conviction that the maintenance of Austria was a European necessity, in view of the Russian danger—the conviction which led him to impose such generous peace terms after Königgrätz—made it possible to fit this inner Austrian programme into an international one.

It was Andrássy who in 1866 persuaded Francis Joseph to drop federalism for Austria. The chief obstacle to dualism was now Belcredi's government, most of whose members, like himself, were federalists and Slavophiles. This was overcome after the introduction into the government of the Saxon, Beust, who also advocated dualism—not out of wish for a final reconciliation with Prussia, but for the opposite reason that he hoped, by favouring the German-Austrian liberals, to regain for Austria the sympathies of the secondary German states, preliminary to reopening the struggle for the hegemony in Germany. But the immediate effect was the same. Beust established contact both with the Hungarian liberals and with their Austro-German sympathisers. A Hungarian ministry was formed, under Andrássy, on 17 February 1867. The Austrian Landtags had been dissolved on 2 January, and new elections ordered, after which an extraordinary *Reichsrath* was to debate the settlement with Hungary.

These were carried through on Schmerling's franchise: nevertheless, their results foreshadowed a small federalist majority in the *Reichsrath*. Beust urged that this would mean the breakdown of the settlement with Hungary, and Andrássy came from Pest to support him and to insist that the representatives of Austria were not entitled to approve or disapprove Hungary's relations with her king. Francis Joseph gave way, and a new Patent, of 4 February, cancelled that of 2 January, transforming the extraordinary *Reichsrath* into an ordinary one. Belcredi now resigned; Beust took over, and secured for the *Reichsrath* a centralist majority by buying off the Poles, who, after at first demanding complete autonomy for Galicia, accepted in the end a special status, under a *Landesminister*, which gave them the reality of their wishes. Left now in the minority, the Czech leaders vented their anger by making a 'Pilgrimage to Moscow', where they hailed Russia as 'the sun of the Slav community'. Needless to say, this gesture strengthened German centralism in Austria.

The final agreement with Hungary was now reached with relative ease. Very briefly, Hungary was reinstated, April Laws and all, as a constitutional monarchy, governed by her own laws and free from any control by Austria over her internal affairs. Nevertheless, foreign affairs, defence, and the finance necessary to carry on those two activities were recognised as matters of common interest to Hungary and to the crown's other possessions, and a machinery was devised for debating these through parliamentary delegations so ingeniously shaped that no man could say whether it was square or circular. Each side voted its quota towards the common expenses, this quota being fixed anew every ten years. A customs union was concluded, also renewable every ten years. On 8 June Francis Joseph was crowned king of Hungary. Next year the negotiations with Croatia were successfully concluded. Croatia received an autonomy which did full justice to her historic rights, and a nationalities law reaffirmed, and laid down the practical application of, the 1861 formula.

The *Reichsrath*, from which the Czechs absented themselves, duly 'took note' of the Compromise and then proceeded to enact a revision of the Austrian constitution which made it at once more centralised and more liberal; many of the formulae produced at Kremsier, including the famous statement on the national and linguistic question, reappeared. The status of Galicia was regulated in the manner agreed.

So the long struggle ended. When in 1870 Francis Joseph was toying with the idea of revenge on Prussia, the project arose once again of revising the constitution in a federal and Slavophile direction. It was again Andrássy who prevailed on Francis Joseph to drop the project, so that Austria-Hungary remained a state based internally on the supremacy of the Germans in the west and of the Magyar-feeling Hungarians in the east; with the corollary that in foreign policy she was bound to Germany. It is true that since the balance in Austria was a very delicate one, the German element was thereafter often in a minority west of the Leitha, but the Slavs were never again, so long as the monarchy survived, in a position to overthrow the fundamental principles on which it had been placed in 1867.

CHAPTER XXI

ITALY

FEW people in 1830 believed that there might exist an Italian nation. There were eight several states in the peninsula, each with distinct laws and traditions. No one had had the desire or the resources to revive Napoleon's partial experiment in unification. The settlement of 1814–15 had merely restored regional divisions, with the added disadvantage that the decisive victory of Austria over France temporarily hindered Italians in playing off their former oppressors against each other. Austria now owned Venetia as well as Lombardy, and indirectly controlled the central duchies, Tuscany, Lucca, Modena and Parma; and Austrian forces were at hand to quell the insurrections of Naples and Piedmont in 1821. Italians who, like Foscolo and Rossetti, harboured patriotic sentiments, were driven into exile. The largest Italian state, the Bourbon Kingdom of the Two Sicilies with its eight million inhabitants, seemed aloof and indifferent: Sicily and Naples had once formed part of Spain, and had always been foreign to the rest of Italy. The common people in each region, and even the intellectual *élite*, spoke their mutually unintelligible dialects and lacked the least vestiges of national consciousness. They wanted good government, not self-government, and had welcomed Napoleon and the French as more equitable and efficient than their native dynasties.

In the forty years after 1830 the peninsula was to be unified under a single government. This *risorgimento* of Italy did not follow any preconceived plan, and many various ideological, political and economic forces aided it, directly or indirectly. A strong movement for economic and governmental reform already existed among the ruling classes of the *ancien régime*, particularly among the military and civilian officials who had served under the French. Secret societies had grown up whose type was the *carboneria*, their members pledged to revolt with signatures written in blood. Everywhere the peasants were watching for an opportunity to rise and better their lot. Many merchants wanted a wider national market and the removal of internal trade barriers (of which there were twenty-two along the River Po alone); in their eyes the new railway age demanded an interlocking system of communications, and standardisation of the different measures and currencies which caused so much delay, error and fraud. Progressive landowners as well as tradesmen and manufacturers were attracted to the idea of an Italian *Zollverein*, and to a general adoption of the metric system. All these many incentives towards change contributed to the administrative, political, social and economic revolution which accompanied the making of Italy. Deeper still there was a cultural movement which diffused a common literary language, as recently refined by Manzoni, and promoted a habit of retrospection in history and fiction to the past greatness of Italy, to folk memories of the Lombard League and the Guelphs fighting against German invaders. An educated minority was thus at hand to concentrate present grievances behind the struggle first for individual freedom, then for independence of the foreigner, and finally for national unity.

The external context of this struggle was the conflict between France and Austria. Tangled diplomatic situations needed bold statesmanship for their exploitation, and also the armed force of a state prepared to annex its neighbours and so aggregate a greater Italian kingdom. Such a nucleus was Sardinia and Piedmont, a state which was largely French in language and culture and contained but one-fifth of Italy's population. King Charles Albert, who ruled at Turin from 1831 to 1849, at first flouted his destiny by linking Piedmont with the reactionaries against the liberals, making a close alliance with Austria against France. In time, however, circumstances compelled him to quarrel with Austria, the predominant Italian power. In 1814, instead of obtaining further territory in France or Switzerland as hoped, Piedmont had almost casually picked up the Italian coastal province of Liguria: henceforward a southern outlet through Genoa and Savona at last made her a maritime, industrial, and essentially Italian state. The unification of Liguria with Sardinia, Piedmont and Savoy was, too, a distinct step towards the defeat of regional particularism, that primary obstacle to Italian unity. The radical merchants of Genoa had protested angrily against subjection to Turin; but before very long their liberal and national ideas were to engulf the narrow court aristocracy of the capital.

The French revolution of 1830 detonated a train of small insurrections in 1831 up and down Italy. If they failed, it was because they were inspired by too many uncoordinated aims and interests. At one extreme the ambitious Francis IV, duke of Modena, had hoped that revolution might be used for enlarging his own domain. At the other, the silk merchant Menotti had had visions of national unity based on Rome. The only practical outcome was a brief displacement of several governments in central Italy. Francis fled from Modena in February, Marie Louise from Parma, and the papal pro-legate from Bologna. Many other cities also raised the tricolour flag and formed provisional governments. But instead of joining a common front, their instinctive municipalism came uppermost: Piacenza remained loyal out of rivalry with Parma, Reggio was suspicious of Modena, Genoa of Turin, and Sicily of Naples. The new dictator of Modena forbade extension of the revolution to Massa and Carrara, cravenly hoping to win Austrian favour by a pacific policy, and for the same reason Bologna argued that 'the affairs of Modena are not our concern'. In March 1831 the Austrians crossed the Po to restore the three former governments; but when Zucchi retreated from Modena, he and his 700 rebels were disarmed as 'foreigners' by the provisional government of Bologna. In this latter town, deputies from Ancona, Perugia, Ravenna and Ferrara had meanwhile met and formed themselves into 'The United Italian Provinces'. By the end of March, however, the last rebels had surrendered at Ancona. Their capitulation, though ratified by the Legate *a latere*, was then abrogated by Pope Gregory XVI on the grounds that pardon had been granted under duress.

The revolution of 1831 proved that the 'legitimate' governments lacked the firm loyalty of the people and continued only because of Austrian support. It also indicated the existence of some liberals with a rudimentary political programme, and threatened the prospect of epidemic disorder until they had been appeased. For the moment, however, the counter-revolution had won decisively; the concept of Italy as a nation receded once again; Menotti was executed by his former collaborator, Francis IV, and many future national leaders fled into exile from Modena and Piedmont.

For fifteen years or more the *ancien régime* was reprieved. Francis and Gregory both ruled until 1846, Marie Louise and Charles Ludovic of Lucca until 1847, Leopold II of Tuscany and Ferdinand II of Naples until 1859. The cruel administration of Canosa in Naples and Cardinal Bernetti in the Papal States was criticised even by Metternich, who advocated moderation and legality so as to avoid further revolution. By comparison, the government of Austrian Lombardy and Venice was liberal. Tuscany, also, was ruled by a relatively enlightened despot: exiles from other Italian states could feel at home at Florence; progress was made there in popular education and land reclamation; and the legal system was in some respects more liberal than the *code Napoléon* itself. At Rome, on the other hand, if government was not consistently intolerant, it was always inefficient, corrupt, arbitrary and slow. There were no published accounts to serve as a check on the administration, and there was both an ecclesiastical and political censorship as well as the police and the Holy Office to curb dissentient opinions. In the Roman countryside a counter-revolutionary force of irregulars, the *centurioni*, violated the law with impunity. Only the presence of French troops in Ancona after 1832—to parry that of the Austrians in Bologna—recreated that equipoise whose absence had cramped the revolutions of the previous year; and on this slender thread of Franco-Austrian rivalry the future of Italy depended.

In Piedmont, Charles Albert as king had renounced his juvenile friendship for the liberals. He acted rather to impress the conservatives by an exaggerated legitimism, and at his accession refused to include in the usual amnesty his accomplices in the liberal movement of 1820–1.

Mazzini urged him in vain 'to be the Napoleon of Italian liberty'. To Mazzini, prophet of the new age, the goal was national unity and independence, not the partial liberties demanded by the *carbonari* and *federati*. Mazzini had bitter words for the ineffectual Italian resistance against Austria in 1831, and concluded that discipline and a self-conscious nationalism were urgently required. In July 1831 he therefore gathered forty other exiles at Marseille and formed his new society of the *Giovine Italia*, intending it to be not just a regional body, but national, an integrating and initiating force (see also ch. IX, p. 224). Its first test came in the 'sergeants' conspiracy' of 1833 in Piedmont, when a soldiers' brawl accidentally betrayed his plans. Charles Albert reacted with excessive severity by comparison with the Austrians, who had spared General Zucchi. Twelve people were executed. Mazzini was condemned to death *in absentia*, so was Garibaldi in 1834 (he went to take service with the Bey of Tunis), and the Abbé Gioberti was among those exiled.

Some historians have argued that Charles Albert continued to be one of the chief obstacles to the *risorgimento*.[1] His persecution of the radicals in 1833–4 certainly fits in with his Austrian alliance of 1831 and his attempt to drag an unwilling Metternich into war against Orleanist France. He still had territorial claims upon France,[2] and actively supported the legitimist duchesse de Berry against Louis Philippe. He also backed with arms and money the legitimist claimants Don Carlos in Spain and Don Miguel in Portugal, thus gratuitously antagonising Britain as well. His wife was a Habsburg, and in 1842 he married his son Victor Emmanuel to another; and his Austrian sympathies were such that, on the occasion of this marriage, the Austrian General Radetzky referred to the Piedmontese army as the 'advance guard of the Imperial forces'.

Eventually Charles Albert changed sides. He had failed to gain ground from France, and his hopes of annexing a canton of Switzerland were to collapse in 1847 with the defeat of the *Sonderbund*. Instead he turned his attention to the fertile plain of Lombardy, for a long time a distant object of dynastic ambition. Austrian intervention in central Italy was upsetting the balance of Italian power against him, and her separate railway system was diverting the trade of central Europe from Genoa to Trieste. By 1840 even his ultra-conservative Foreign Minister, Solaro della Margherita, was wondering whether revolutions in Hungary and Bohemia might not break up the Austrian empire and so give Piedmont a free hand in Lombardy. Only the king's own character prevented him trying to hasten this consummation. As the French ambassador wrote in 1846, he 'will listen with pleasure to dreams about the future of Italy which promise

---

[1] See the argument between L. Salvatorelli, *Pensiero e azione del Risorgimento* (Turin, 1944), pp. 100–1; and L. Bulferetti, *Questioni di storia del Risorgimento...*, ed. E. Rota (Milan, 1951), pp. 130ff.

[2] P. Silva, *Figure e momenti di storia italiana* (Milan, 1939), p. 148.

him a great role in history. But at the moment of action it will all fade away.'[1]

In his internal policy, Charles Albert, although politically absolutist, repaired some of the deficiencies which made his kingdom one of the most backward states of Europe. Several different currencies still circulated in its component provinces, and internal customs stations curtailed the freedom of traffic. Duties had multiplied by four times between 1815 and 1830, with grave damage to revenue as well as trade. Accordingly, many restrictive tariffs were lifted after 1835. A start was made with constructing railways, irrigation canals, and new port installations at Genoa. There was a half-hearted attempt to break the shackles of feudalism in Sardinia. A reform of the legal codes in 1838–40 brought a partial return to the Napoleonic system which Charles Albert's predecessors had inconsiderately abandoned after 1814. Then in the early 1840's permission was given for an Agricultural Society, which came to have a deep liberalising influence through its two thousand members. Like other similar societies in Lombardy and Tuscany it helped to inaugurate an agricultural revolution, by experimenting with new breeds of farm animals, introducing machinery, attacking plant diseases, and trying to improve the quality and transportability of wine.

This reforming spirit was a sign of the times and not peculiar to Piedmont. It was in Naples that there appeared the first Italian steamboat, as well as the first iron bridge and the first railway; and as early as 1833 Ferdinand II had talked of making a league among the various Italian states. For the chief example of political tolerance one must probably look to Parma; for the most liberal tariffs and laws, to Tuscany; for efficient government, to Lombardy. Only in Florence could non-Catholics attend the university, and only in Parma could Jews hold jobs in the public administration (in Piedmont the Jews had to live in ghettoes and were not allowed to own land).[2] Undoubtedly it was Austrian Lombardy which showed the greatest prosperity and the greatest advance in industrialisation. Lombardy boasted the finest system of communications in continental Europe, and it was not Austrian obscurantism so much as the municipal jealousies of Bergamo and Treviglio which held up the Milan–Venice railroad. The Austrian rulers were far ahead of other Italian sovereigns in educational development. Their taxes, though heavy, were less than those of their predecessors or successors. Their press laws allowed the existence of more than twice as many newspapers as in Piedmont or Tuscany. Cattaneo's '*Politecnico*' freely advocated revolutionary liberal reforms, and the '*Annali di Statistica*' possessed distinguished correspondents all over Italy who could not publish at home. Apparently the people of Lombardy remained content and loyal, at least

[1] G. F.-H. Berkeley, *Italy in the Making, 1815 to 1846* (Cambridge, 1932), p. 256.
[2] For the position of the Jews generally see ch. IX, p. 243.

until 1840. So far were they from feelings of Italian unity that the Milan Chamber of Commerce advocated joining the German *Zollverein* as a means to greater prosperity. In 1841 Metternich was planning a close economic union of Austria with the states of Italy as an antidote to Italian nationalism. He might well have succeeded, for even among the radicals there were some, like Cattaneo, who thought there was more to be gained from Austria than from Piedmont. Where Metternich failed was in preventing single campaigns against individual abuses from gradually developing into a larger scheme of renovation: and when the movement for reforms reached a certain point, it became political.

This imminent political revolution frightened Charles Albert quite as much as it frightened Metternich, and with reason. Solaro was politically more reactionary than preceding ministers before 1835, and even persuaded Gregory XVI in 1841 to restore the ecclesiastical privileges which in Austria and Tuscany had been abolished for fifty years. His censorship allowed no talk of pope or king; the word 'country' had to be substituted for 'nation' or 'Italy', the words 'liberal' and 'constitution' were impermissible, and 'revolution' had to be replaced by 'anarchy' or 'government by violence'. Cavour once described Turin as an intellectual hell, and D'Azeglio left for twelve years in 1831 to publish his novels in the freer atmosphere of Milan.

Charles Albert himself was by temperament insincere, given to concealing his opinions even from friends, and deliberately misleading them. His diary shows him distrusting everyone and habitually playing off one minister against another; and foreign ambassadors remarked on his love of mystification, his changefulness of view, and his thinly concealed ambition. Metternich agreed that he was 'ambitious as well as vacillating; he is a despot, and requires from the liberals only the incense which the *litterati* burn to him; he detests not only France, but also Austria which bars him from the throne of Italy'.[1] For a long time Charles Albert misinterpreted ideas of national independence as being merely a disguise for hostility to throne and altar. His intimate correspondence with Francis IV then shows his views altering as he began to fear that other sovereigns might outdo him by posing as national leaders; and as he claimed that he himself and the pope were the sole legitimate rulers in Italy, he ultimately found conservative and Catholic reasons for himself exploiting nationalism in a dynastic war against Austria.

The necessary intellectual stimulus for this first war of liberation was provided by the neo-Guelph writers, who in the early 1840's made political liberalism almost obligatory for men of culture, and helped to associate Catholicism with the national movement. Even though they

---

[1] C. Spellanzon, *Storia del risorgimento e dell'unità d'Italia* (Milan, 1936), vol. III, pp. 453–4.

disagreed on details and formed no organised party, they collectively provided a respectable if distorted version of Mazzini's ideas, and then linked it up with previous traditions of thought. Manzoni, Rosmini and Tommaseo had begun to develop the idea of a liberal Catholicism. Others tried to involve the pope historically by showing how the medieval papacy had fought the Germans. Of these neo-Guelphs, Farini and Minghetti became ministers of Pius IX after 1847, Capponi was to be Prime Minister of Tuscany, and Balbo, Gioberti and D'Azeglio were each in time to become Prime Minister of Piedmont. But already, before 1847, even if their books had to be published abroad, they had acquired a profound influence throughout Italy.

Silvio Pellico's *Le mie prigioni* had appeared as early as 1832, describing his ten years in Austrian prisons. Although written in a spirit of religious resignation, with little if any patriotic intent, its great success almost accidentally labelled Austria as the great oppressor of the peninsula. At Brussels in 1843 Gioberti produced his *Del primato morale e civile degli Italiani*, dedicated to Pellico (see also ch. IX, p. 225). Here he argued that there existed an Italian race which was united in blood, religion and language, even if political unity was unattainable; and its natural leader was the pope. Although Gioberti had little faith in papal politics, he hid his deeper thoughts because he was aiming at an audience of priests, and he carefully excised from his manuscript all criticism of Austria and the Jesuits. He thus passed the censor with a scheme which reconciled religion and country: patriotism suddenly became orthodox and a matter for public discussion instead of for hole-and-corner conspiracy. Later on, Gioberti openly attacked the narrow Catholicism of the Curia; but it was his earlier appeal to papal leadership which was remembered, and his theme of Italian 'primacy' helped to give his countrymen the necessary self-confidence for political revolution.

Another influential work was Balbo's *Delle speranze d'Italia*, dedicated to Gioberti and published in 1844. Balbo agreed that a federal state was the obvious goal, because the various peoples of Italy were so distinct that they needed different forms of government. Unlike Gioberti, however, he concentrated less on general principles than on practical points, and he developed the idea that sometime Austria would voluntarily expand eastwards into the Balkans and leave Italy more free. As a good Piedmontese, he envisaged Charles Albert, not the pope, as leader of the future Italian confederation. In 1846 Durando's *Della nazionalità Italiana* actually proposed to take away most of the pope's temporal possessions, and redivide Italy between three secular, federated kingdoms.

Meanwhile, almost every year, insurrections occurred somewhere. Their inspiration, though not always their direction, came from Mazzini, who wanted not a federation of monarchies but a single republic, not an imposition from above but an autonomous self-determination from below.

To Gioberti's objections that local insurrections were wasteful and dis-heartening, Mazzini replied that only thus could you rouse the people, and without the people a revolution would be vitiated and would deserve to fail. Mazzini thus generated a very powerful force with which (and subsequently for which) the royalists were driven to compete. We see this in 1845, when Charles Albert told D'Azeglio to assure people that, if only they abandoned agitation, circumstances might one day permit his army to deliver them. A further stage was reached towards conflict with Austria when, in 1846, the repudiation of an agreement on the salt trade brought in retaliation a prohibitive duty on Piedmontese wines entering Lombardy. Although the Austrophile Solaro continued in office until 1847, the hypo-thesis of an eventual war was several times mentioned, without any material preparations being made. The Piedmontese had long been con-vinced that they would sometime supplant Austria in Milan, and now that both neo-Guelphs and Mazzinians were making public confession of national sentiment, popular excitement was shortly to make this convic-tion one of the many explosive forces in Italy.

Just when the patriots were uncertain what their next move should be, a reputedly liberal pope was elected in June 1846. Pius IX was not in fact a liberal, but he was sincerely anxious to relax the tension which had grown up under Gregory between the papal government and its subjects. His amnesty of some thousand prisoners and exiles, although only a customary act of clemency and fully approved in advance by Metternich, was at once read as adhesion to the neo-Guelph programme of liberty and independence. Wild scenes of enthusiasm greeted the act, and Pius, who was no politician but was most susceptible to popularity and applause, was led on to make other concessions. The myth of a liberal and patriotic pope was only the fantasy of an excited populace. Pius's statement of November in favour of railways and his decree announcing a *consulta di stato* in April 1847 can both be connected with popular demonstrations in Rome, but were taken to signify his conversion to Gioberti's ideas. Concessions were made to local self-government, and a proposal was advanced for a customs union with other Italian states. The Jews were also allowed outside the Ghetto, and no longer received in carnival with the formal kick which had symbolised their servile status. Metternich began to take alarm, as he saw Pius unwittingly raise up a monster which might prove uncontrollable; the revolutionaries could now march under the slogan of '*viva Pio nono*'; the Guelph party was growing up again, but this time with no Ghibellines to contain it.

The year 1847 saw the sovereigns of Italy in retreat, especially as the bad harvest of 1846 brought food riots and forced them to concede liberal economic reforms. The people were feeling their power, and the revolution had effectively begun. Charles Albert tried to hold out against the current, supported by the evident lack of enthusiasm for political reform among both peasants and nobility in Savoy-Piedmont[1]—it was forbidden at Turin to read the newly emancipated newspapers of Tuscany and Rome, or to celebrate the pope's anniversary. But a new situation emerged when Austrian troops entered Modena on the death of Francis, and when in July 1847 Metternich unwisely defied papal protests and occupied Ferrara. As well as further upsetting the balance of power against Piedmont, this lost Austria her position as the guardian of legitimacy; it also impelled the pope still more towards the liberals, and gave Charles Albert the excuse for a war which could be justified as defensive and in aid of the Holy See. The king let fall covert hints of his desire for national independence. In October, after a warning from Balbo that Leopold and Pius were outbidding him for the moral leadership of Italy, he suddenly dismissed Solaro and introduced liberal provisions for local government and a looser censorship. This, he hoped, would be enough, and he reiterated his solemn promise to concede no more. But it was the thin end of a wedge. Balbo and Cavour brought out a new journal, significantly entitled *Il Risorgimento*, to advocate further political changes, arguing that even the best laws would not work under an absolute government. When demonstrations took place at Genoa in December, the king first thought they were an attempt to restore Genoese independence with English help, and ordered the troops to suppress them. None the less, they frightened him with visions of republicanism, especially when his soldiers fraternised with the demonstrators and the city administration of Turin joined in the request for a constitution.

In southern Italy, if people were less patriotic than in the north, they were more revolutionary because they were far poorer and had less to lose. Ferdinand realised the necessity for cheaper corn and salt, but bureaucratic inefficiency always held up action. His weakest point was Sicily, where even the upper classes of society were incensed against his recent fusion of the Sicilian and Neapolitan administrations. Although the more moderate Sicilians followed D'Azeglio's advice in renouncing the weapon of insurrection, the radicals had no such scruples; hence Mazzini's ideas again won precedence over those of the neo-Guelphs. A rumour spread in Palermo that on 12 January 1848 they would challenge the authorities with a demonstration: somewhat hesitantly, a few bold men set the example; by degrees the demonstration became an insurrection; finally, when after two days it had established itself, the well-to-do took over and made it a movement for restoring the aristocratic constitution of 1812. The price of success in Palermo was a hundred dead. Unrest then spread to Naples, and Ferdinand was forced in February to grant a constitution as a 'spontaneous' and 'irrevocable' proof

---

[1] Letter of Massari to Minghetti, 19 November 1847, M. Minghetti, *Miei Ricordi* (4th edn, Turin, 1889); and G. Prato, *Fatti e dottrine economiche alla vigilia del 1848* (Milan, 1921), p. 238.

of his good intentions. This abject surrender forced the hand of Leopold of Tuscany, Charles Albert and even Pius IX, all of whom had to follow suit in March by conceding more or less liberal constitutions.

Until the last minute Charles Albert had maintained that such an act was irreconcilable with his conscience; but finally his ministers persuaded him to receive episcopal absolution from his oath, and a *statuto* was published which was to remain the fundamental law, first of Piedmont then of Italy (cf. ch. VIII, pp. 200–1). Only he carefully kept it a conservative document, reserving to himself foreign policy and the conduct of war, as well as all executive power and nomination to the upper house. Since ministers remained answerable to him and not to parliament he neither intended nor foresaw that parliamentary government would develop under his successors.

Another significant advance was the pope's proposal to form a customs league. Remarkably enough, Piedmont had not yet anticipated such a compact as a way to exclude Austria and win leadership in Italy. In August 1847 Tuscany and the Papal States had arranged to form an economic league together, but Charles Albert proved reluctant to lower his tariffs to the Tuscan level, and only agreed in principle several months later. Early in 1848 Piedmont again held up formation of a defensive alliance among Italian states. Charles Albert rather followed Balbo in wanting to defeat Austria first, so as then to be able to dominate a subsequent federation. Hence the widespread distrust of his ambition. According to Farini, other Italian states were sometimes more afraid of him than of Austria. Only when the Piedmontese realised that they could not win without help did they later become more interested in an alliance.

Some liberals like Petitti and Cattaneo now began to think a war of independence unnecessary and even undesirable, since war might halt the great advances already being made towards liberty and prosperity. But the forces of change were too strong and multifarious for a peaceful outcome: Sicily had not yet won formal independence; Mazzini was quite unsatisfied by moderate reforms; the Austrians were in Ferrara, and the Austrian embargo on Piedmontese wine was a crying grievance; food production had not been sufficiently increased by partial abandonment of protection; and there was still no constitution in Venice and Lombardy. Existing railway schemes did not link up across state boundaries, but were intended less for trade than for royal pleasure. The *Annali di Statistica* complained that, although man could travel 25 miles an hour, it took eight weeks for goods to traverse the 200 kilometres from Florence to Milan.[1] The same paper had hoped that 'the steamship lines between Bombay and Suez, Alexandria and Marseille have reversed the terms of the problem which was solved by Vasco da Gama when he passed the

---

[1] R. Ciasca, *L'origine del programma per l'opinione nazionale italiana del 1847–8* (Turin, 1916), p. 358.

Cape of Good Hope': but so far there were no material results to show. Such grievances were magnified by the intellectual revolution which, particularly in Lombardy, had organised a new public opinion against the *ancien régime*. All-Italian scientific congresses had met at Pisa in 1839, Turin in 1840, and subsequently at Florence, Padua, Milan, Naples and Genoa, all stressing the unity of Italy in culture and geography, and showing how its several states were interdependent.

In March 1848 a long-suppressed rebellion broke out in Milan and finally precipitated war. For some months there had been clashes with the police. The Milanese had learnt from the Boston tea-party to abstain from smoking, and tension had mounted with the spread of such passive resistance and boycott. When petitions were submitted for reforms and autonomy, more repressive measures were the only response, because for Austria to yield in Italy would have detonated all the other oppressed peoples of her ramshackle empire. Finally the Paris revolution of 25 February precipitated revolt in Vienna itself on 13 March (see ch. xv, pp. 395–6). This news reached Milan and Venice when both were surging with insubordination. Casati, the mayor of Milan, tried to restrain people, but over a thousand barricades were soon blocking the streets, and he had to head a provisional government in order to contain the revolt within limits and give it some direction. During the heroic 'five days' at Milan the insurgents lost 300 men, almost all of them lower-class town artisans; but Radetzky was compelled to evacuate the city. Milan, like Sicily, had justified Mazzini's obstinate faith in popular initiative.

Subsequent legend made out that Charles Albert had only been waiting for this revolt before himself attacking Austria. In fact it caught him quite unawares, having made no preparations for an offensive war; and he had just given assurances to Austria of his pacific intentions.[1] The 'five days' found his troops on the distant French frontier, ready only to fight against the revolution. Though he had lately sent arms to the reactionaries in Switzerland, he could send none to Milan. He even halted the volunteers who tried to cross the frontier into Lombardy. He was waiting to see, first if a popular rising could really defeat the Austrians, and secondly whether his own intervention would serve the Piedmontese monarchy or just help to establish a Milanese republic. This delay deprived him of the gratitude due to a saviour, and invited the charge of playing at politics. Cavour had to warn him that, if he did not intervene now the Austrians were being defeated, both the dynasty might fall and Lombardy be lost for ever to Piedmont—already he had been anticipated by Leopold of Tuscany. Accordingly, after many hesitations, he accepted the tricolour flag and crossed the Ticino, to aid the revolt but also to

---

[1] Spellanzon, *op. cit.* vol. III, p. 628; also A. Omodeo, *La leggenda di Carlo Alberto nella recente storiografia* (Turin, 1940); and the opposite view held by N. Rodolico, *Carlo Alberto negli anni 1843–9* (Florence, 1943), vol. II, p. 325.

forestall republicanism. His ambassador at Vienna was ordered to explain this step as designed to prevent the further spread of revolution. His generals were instructed to advance circumspectly, and Radetzky was thus left unhampered in his hasty retreat through hostile country.

Obviously, without the Piedmontese army the Austrians could hardly be defeated before they could regroup in their quadrilateral of fortresses beyond Lake Garda. Hence even Mazzini now gave grudging allegiance to the king. But Charles Albert was as frightened of the radicals as of Austria. He refused Garibaldi's offer of collaboration. He was horrified that Venice should think to revive its republic and appeal for French intervention. Other political disagreements arose with the Tuscans, who were uneasy about Piedmontese intentions and were themselves bent on annexing Massa and Carrara; also with the Papacy, which was expected to incorporate Modena and Parma. Still more serious, many of the Lombards were lukewarm, whether suspicious of Piedmont or afraid of social convulsion, and preferred rather to confide in Austria for the maintenance of order and enlightened government. Cattaneo heatedly denounced Charles Albert as 'the man who betrayed the patriots of 1821 and shot those of 1833'; and he added, 'I should prefer the Austrians to recapture Milan than see a traitor in command of Lombardy'. When, instead of postponing political questions until after the war, the king requested a vote for immediate union of Lombardy with Piedmont, some of the Lombards objected that this would divide people at a critical moment and make other Italian sovereigns frightened of Piedmontese aggrandisement. Plebiscites were taken notwithstanding, but they included a proviso for the union of northern Italy to be followed by an assembly to choose a new constitution. This in its turn infuriated the loyal monarchists of Turin as being rank ingratitude by the Lombards to their deliverer. But, for about ten days, Piedmont, Lombardy and Venice became a single state.

Meantime, as Cattaneo said, 'while Charles Albert was collecting votes, Radetzky was collecting men'.[1] Bonaparte, with no larger army than that of Piedmont, had cut through northern Italy like a knife and organised Lombard forces from nothing. Charles Albert, however, was unwilling to build up a potentially dangerous Lombard army. A later commission of inquiry established that, for all his vaunted hostility to Austria, even his commanding officers had no maps of Lombardy, no study had been made of Austrian fortifications, and the railway had not yet been built from Turin to Alessandria; food, tents and medical supplies were deficient; lack of horses immobilised the artillery; troops had not been instructed in the new percussion musket; while the officers, having mostly been

---

[1] Cattaneo's strictures on Piedmontese policy and strategy have mostly been borne out by the documents: see P. Pieri in *Studi sul risorgimento in Lombardia*, ed. A. Monti (Milan, 1949), pp. 9–45.

appointed by family connection, did not know the basic words of command. Charles Albert valorously insisted on directing operations at the front; but his chronic indecision and pre-Napoleonic ideas of generalship invited personal responsibility for what followed.

The initial slowness of advance, and the failure to watch the Alpine passes whence Radetzky obtained supplies, gave the Austrians two months for consolidation and for a relief column to reach Verona.[1] In May the Tuscans were checked at Curtatone and the Romans at Vicenza; in July the Piedmontese were defeated at Custoza. Radetzky then offered a compromise which would have confirmed the independence of Milan; but Charles Albert, while ready to renounce Venice, relied on English mediation to give him all Lombardy, and feared that anything less would provoke a republican rising. Instead of accepting a truce, he retreated, although no defences had been built on either the Oglio or the Adda; and, against his generals' advice, he divided his forces and fell back on Milan instead of Piacenza. He there promised the Milanese to make a desperate stand, but in fact abandoned the city at once, and in a way which suggested that his primary interest had been to prevent Milan saving herself again and calling in the French. The national war was becoming a dynastic war. Despite the counsel of his warlike Casati–Gioberti ministry to invoke French help, he believed the French to be more dangerous than the Austrians, and so General Salasco signed an armistice on 9 August. Instead of being a deliverer, the king withdrew from Lombardy under accusation of treachery.

The first eighteen months of constitutional government at Turin saw eight successive premiers. No minister was very keen to implement the 'unconstitutional' Salasco armistice. It was not only the radical majority after the elections of January 1849 which wanted to resume hostilities, but moderate conservatives like Cavour regarded war as 'the only means of re-establishing order in the interior'.[2] England and France would surely guarantee that, even if defeated, Piedmont could only lose the price of an indemnity. When war reopened in March, the army was as unprepared as ever: the king and his generals had been so discredited that a Polish commander-in-chief was employed, but he knew nothing of the terrain. Senior officers even confessed to the Austrians that they fought indifferently because opposed to the war[3]—and so confirmed that the Piedmontese were not yet educated to lead a national movement. Strategical errors brought complete defeat at Novara after only a three days' campaign. One general was subsequently shot for disobedience. Meanwhile the Lombards remained passive.

---

[1] For an account of Radetzky's operations see ch. XII, pp. 321–2.
[2] C. Cavour, Nouvelles lettres inédites, ed. A. Bert (Rome, 1889), p. 222.
[3] A. Colombo, Gli albori del regno di Vittorio Emanuele II, secondo nuovi documenti (Rome, 1937), p. 41; A. Anzilotti, Gioberti (Florence, 1922), p. 232.

By this time the revolution had collapsed in southern Italy. Separation from Naples was the chief aim of Sicilians; and when they refused the reconciliation offered by the new constitutional government at Naples, even the Neapolitan liberals rallied to preserve the Bourbon dominion. A parliament met at Palermo, but the deputies had other interests than those which had first moved the common people to man the barricades. Likewise in Naples a *jacquerie* split the unsatisfied peasants from the liberal intellectuals, whose object was jobs and influence. In May 1848, after bombarding the city, Ferdinand altered the spirit of his 'irrevocable' constitution: its evident unworkability had been a reflection on the political immaturity of the liberals as well as on the king's bad faith. A papal allocution of 29 April had also disowned the Austrian war, so proving that constitutional government was impracticable where the sovereign was sole interpreter of a higher law. Later in the year the pope fled to Gaeta, leaving Mazzini to become virtual dictator of a Roman republic for three months in 1849. Mazzini made some attempt to free trade, abolish serfdom and break up the large estates; but at Rome, too, there developed a stultifying cleavage between moderates and radicals. Pius henceforth abjured all compromise with the liberals who had abused his good nature and credulity. The Catholic powers were summoned to restore his temporal dominion, and four armies bore down on Garibaldi and Mazzini. Against the liberal Catholicism of Rosmini and Gioberti, the Jesuits triumphantly asserted that liberalism derived from the Protestants and was incompatible with true religion. Henceforward the *risorgimento* was left to the anticlericals, with corresponding disadvantages for both church and state. The Roman republic fell to the French in July 1849, and thereafter maintenance of the temporal power required despotic government and a foreign garrison. Sicily had been overrun by King 'Bomba's' Swiss mercenaries in May; and when Manin's Venetian republic collapsed in August, the Italian revolution was over. The peninsula became occupied territory even more than before, Austrian forces holding Tuscany and Modena, and the French remaining in Rome.

Evidently the moderates and neo-Guelphs had been more interested in their own individual liberties than in national independence. The Neapolitan liberals had turned against Sicily, the Messinese against the rival city of Palermo, and even some of the Palermitan liberals had changed sides when the revolution touched their personal property. With certain notable exceptions there had been insufficient readiness to make sacrifices. When starving Venice appealed for aid, she received from the rest of Italy (said Tommaseo) but one day's supply. Far from the revolution cementing *italianità*, internal animosities had been sharpened, and D'Azeglio's unworthy jeers at the defenders of Rome were heartily reciprocated. Charles Albert's policy of *Italia farà da se* had been revealed as absurd, and disillusioned politicians had to admit that the making of

Italy demanded the active interest of some other European state. D'Azeglio concluded that centuries must elapse before Italy learnt constitutional practice and became a great power. Gioberti gave up his myth of Italian 'primacy', and put his faith rather in republican France: the only hope, he thought, was for Piedmont to overcome its provincialism and make terms with democracy; and the pope would have to forfeit his temporal authority.

Immediately after Novara, Charles Albert abdicated, and shortly died at Oporto. After seventeen years combating liberalism and nationality, he had not been able in a moment to set aside his past. Posthumous legends notwithstanding, he was a weak character with a weak intellect, and his more amiable qualities could not obliterate the double-dealing which both friend and foe describe.[1] The flattering tales of an 'Italian Hamlet' and the 'martyr of Oporto' came later, manufactured by the very people who had helped bring Piedmont to disaster.

Another political myth described how Victor Emmanuel II, after succeeding his father, compelled Radetzky to moderate the Vignale armistice and stoutly resisted Austrian attacks on the *statuto*.[2] Radetzky was not in fact out to humiliate Piedmont, but prudently offered favourable terms to avoid French intervention and to bolster up royalty against Piedmontese radicalism. In return, Victor Emmanuel promised he would override the radical majority in parliament. He ignored that majority in appointing a conservative general as premier, while another general bombarded radical Genoa into submission. He also ratified the treaty with Austria, despite the fact that elections in July 1849 confirmed the parliamentary opposition against it. By the notorious 'proclamation of Moncalieri' in November he personally warned the electorate to endorse this action, explaining his determination 'to save the nation from the tyranny of parties': the implication was that, if parliament did not confirm his treaty, he would revoke the constitution.

Victor Emmanuel thus succeeded in partially re-establishing royal authority. If his remained a more limited monarchy than that of Naples or Prussia, this was because Custoza and Novara had seriously damaged the prestige of royalty in both Piedmont and Italy. He sometimes ruled arbitrarily and raised taxes by royal decree, but other Italian rulers behaved far worse, and it should be remembered that probably Piedmont was more or less indifferent to its form of government provided that it was in fact governed.[3] The *statuto* and the tricolour flag at least were

[1] See the illuminating remarks of his devoted friend, Count de Sonnaz, *Mes souvenirs sur le Roi Charles-Albert*, ed. A. Omodeo (Turin, 1940).

[2] Cf. W. R. T. Thayer, *The Life and Times of Cavour* (London, 1911), vol. I, pp. 104, 208; and Howard McGaw Smyth in vol. VII of *The Journal of Modern History* (1935, Chicago) pp. 141–182.

[3] Report of the French Minister at Turin, 21 November 1949, P. Matter, *Cavour et l'unité italienne* (Paris, 1925), vol. II, p. 134.

still in being, and henceforward the *risorgimento* was represented by a regular government instead of merely by prophets and conspirators.

With wise moderation, the king chose D'Azeglio of the right centre as premier. D'Azeglio, in his ministry of 1849–52, did as much as honesty and cautious good sense could do to restore confidence in the monarchy and recommence a policy of reforms. One of his principal measures concerned the Piedmontese church, which after 1814 had been reimbursed thoroughly for confiscations under the revolution, and whose separate courts and rights of sanctuary were incompatible with that equality before the law decreed in the *statuto*. In 1850, therefore, the Siccardi laws abolished ecclesiastical jurisdiction, limited the number of recognised holy days, and prohibited ecclesiastical corporations from acquiring land in mortmain without permission. Archbishop Franzoni forbad his clergy to comply with these laws, and tried to coerce the cabinet by withholding absolution and religious burial from those responsible. But since the church was now in full opposition to the liberal movement, this was a test of strength, and it was not worth while for the laity to offer a compromise.

D'Azeglio was supported in this policy by Count Cavour, who, after being defeated in his first election, joined the ministry in 1850. At various times in the next eighteen months Cavour held the departments of finance, naval affairs, agriculture and industry. He was a rationalist in religion, a radical-conservative in politics; he had been a soldier and journalist by profession, and was now a highly successful agriculturist as well as a director of the Bank of Turin and the Turin–Genoa railway. A most able and ambitious man, he had already considered whether to join the opposition and overthrow the D'Azeglio cabinet,[1] and he continued in relations with both Balbo on the right and Rattazzi on the left until he could contrive a new parliamentary majority of his own. As he was primarily a financier, Cavour had to find the money for the 1848–9 campaigns and the Austrian indemnity; he had to pay for railways, for very necessary army reforms, and for reviving the scheme to build a naval base at Spezia so that Piedmont 'should not be inferior to any other Italian power'. Heavy increases in taxation over ten years eventually raised the annual revenue from 80 to 146 million *lire*, but the public debt grew sixfold in the same period. Cavour could never balance the budget, but he did succeed in increasing the country's productive capacity. He had the loyal support of a growing middle class educated in the principles of classical economy, who disliked existing economic restrictions the more as they grew in wealth. Commercial treaties were therefore negotiated in 1850–1 with France, England and Austria, and a policy of freeing trade enriched the nation and won the grateful friendship of England.

Owing to D'Azeglio's war-wound, Cavour soon became leader of the house, and set about using his position to supplant his chief. D'Azeglio

---

[1] L. Salvatorelli, *Prima e dopo il quarantotto* (Turin, 1948), p. 179.

was not a tactician or a debater. He was an amateur in politics, an artist by profession, an aristocrat by upbringing, and a politician only by accident. If he was the finer character, Cavour was easily the finer politician, and the times needed a man who could appreciate that honesty was not always the best policy. Cavour first required a personal clientele in parliament; and as his preference for the conservatives was hampered by religious scruples[1] and by their loyalty to the existing premier, he secretly made an alliance or *connubio* with Rattazzi and the left centre (February 1852). Only one other minister was with him in this, and yet, without warning, he suddenly committed the government in public to a breach with its conservative wing, thus leaving D'Azeglio more isolated. He did not even offer his resignation after this until forced by the king, and until he adjudged that it was bound to bring down the rest of the cabinet sooner or later. The *connubio* set a durable tradition for Italian politics, which henceforth tended to revolve round a loose centre coalition as later in France, instead of round two more or less sharply opposing parties as in England; and Italian historians have tried to justify it accordingly. Here as elsewhere, Cavour was in fact trying to model himself on English practice, for he thought that a similar alliance of Disraeli and Palmerston was in course of formation. Of all his political actions, he was most proud of this one, and it did not fail to carry him eventually into power.

D'Azeglio finally resigned in November 1852, when the king declined to approve his bill for introducing civil marriage. Victor Emmanuel had first intrigued with 'the king's friends' in the senate to quash the bill, but then found that Cavour, hoping to obtain office, would not support D'Azeglio in resisting this arbitrary act of prerogative. Only when Cavour was more securely entrenched in power did he essay further anticlerical legislation and persuade the king to dissolve the monasteries.

As Cavour admitted publicly, Piedmontese laws still lagged behind those of the other Italian states, and it was therefore the more remarkable a task of reform which he accomplished in his eight years as Prime Minister. He had often to withstand personal as well as political opposition from the king. He had to overcome considerable unpopularity among the common people for his conservative past and his swingeing taxes. He had to fight aristocratic opposition in the senate, as well as a bench of bishops which contained some of the wealthiest prelates in Europe. The methods he used in this struggle were novel and rigorous: often he overrode his cabinet; he applied the secret funds to bribe the press at home and abroad, and once to employ a lady of birth in seducing the emperor of the French; over controversial measures he set the tradition of taking

[1] He told De la Rive: 'Je n'aurais pas mieux demandé que de gouverner par le centre droit...mais il m'a été impossible de m'entendre avec lui sur les questions religieuses', W. De la Rive, *Le comte de Cavour* (Paris, 1862), pp. 302–3.

action first and then asking parliament for retrospective consent; unlike D'Azeglio, he freely employed the civil service to secure election of government candidates to parliament,[1] and used measures he knew to be illegal for suppressing opposition newspapers.[2] He could always claim that a liberal end justified illiberal means. And yet he was never tempted to abolish parliament, because he realised how strong it made him if correctly manipulated. He always preferred to disarm opposition peaceably wherever possible, presenting an issue frankly and accepting suggestions and amendments.

In foreign politics, while Mazzini kept Italian discontent alive before European opinion, Cavour even forewarned Austria in 1853 against the Mazzinian insurrection at Milan. Although in consequence the radicals accused Cavour of being *piemontesissimo*—putting Turin before the rest of Italy—he was but biding his time. The only real advances, he used to say, were those which were slow and wisely ordered. He was determined to isolate the Italian question from any chance association with democracy and social revolution, for only thus could he attract the one class which could solve it successfully. This did not prevent him making a dignified protest when, in 1853, Austria sequestrated the possessions of Lombards living in Piedmont. On the other hand, his intervention in the Crimean War in 1855 was not the brilliant *coup* once thought,[3] but rather the indirect result of a royal conspiracy with the French ambassador to supplant him by the conservatives. Victor Emmanuel liked battles just as he liked a hunting party, and because in war he could cast off constitutional trammels. He also wanted to distract the patriots and radical *italianissimi* from the danger zone of Lombardy. Far from Cavour making a courageous and far-sighted decision, he was reluctantly indulging a royal whim to avoid being dismissed. Only one minister wanted to join in the war, for it meant alignment with the national enemy Austria and the expenditure of frail resources on a distant battlefield where no national interests were at stake. It was not an example of Piedmont's initiative at long last, but rather another instance of the instability of her constitution. It merely showed how clever Cavour was at making the best of a very bad job.

The Crimean War ended before the small expeditionary force of 15,000 men had been able to exert itself beyond a minor engagement. Unwillingly Cavour went in 1856 to the peace conference, still expecting to be the scapegoat for a useless war, but half hoping that he might win one of the duchies for his pains. The only positive achievement at Paris was a short statement by Lord Clarendon that the present state of Italy was unsatisfactory (cf. ch. XVIII, p. 490). Cavour was disappointed with this.

---

[1] Carteggi di Cavour, *La liberazione del mezzogiorno* (Bologna, 1949), vol. I, p. 122.
[2] L. Chiala, *Lettere di C. Cavour* (Turin, 1887), vol. VI, p. 130.
[3] Cf. F. Valsecchi, *L'alleanza di Crimea* (Milan, 1948), pp. 346–417, with the old view as given in A. J. Whyte, *The Political Life and Letters of Cavour* (London, 1930), pp. 122–51.

But Manin and other republican exiles in Paris took note that he could speak as an Italian and might possibly be induced to advance from the aggrandisement of Piedmont to the making of Italy. Cavour said privately that their talk of Italian unity was 'a lot of nonsense';[1] but later in 1856 he secretly offered encouragement to Manin's National Society on two conditions: that they abandoned republicanism and he could disown them if necessary. Thus, once again, he skilfully divided his opponents and won a valuable new source of strength, still without committing himself beyond recall. He was quite ready to champion the idea of unity, but only when public opinion was ready for it, and only if it did not compromise the monarchy or the interests of Piedmont. He also explained that, as he could never flout the wishes of Napoleon III, Naples might have to become an appanage of Lucien Murat, the son of its former king, Joachim. Fortunately, Murat was not brave enough to press his claims. Fortunately, too, public opinion in Piedmont was meanwhile being educated in *italianità*, as numerous Italian immigrants rose to important positions in the Turin press and university.

It was a severe reverse when the 1857 elections doubled the clerical opposition. In 'normal times', Cavour admitted, this would have forced a ministerial crisis. But by now he had made himself indispensable, and was able to find a pretext for annulling some of the opposition elections. He also forced the resignation of the anticlerical Rattazzi whose friendship had become a liability. Rattazzi, as Minister of the Interior, had been implicated with Mazzini in 1856 over a rising in Lunigiana, and had also failed to prevent a republican outbreak at Genoa in June 1857. The *connubio* thus ended in divorce, and Cavour decided to move towards the right as evidence to convince Louis Napoleon that Piedmont was a safe bulwark against revolution. Mazzini, therefore, was again condemned to death. The opposition to what he called Cavour's 'Prussian policy' was failing, as repeated insurrections foundered on popular apathy. Mazzini offered to collaborate, but Cavour needed him in opposition so as to frighten the conservatives at home and abroad into aiding his own more orthodox brand of revolution. In any case, for Cavour, Mazzini was more an enemy than Francis Joseph himself. There was a deep incompatibility between the democrat and the liberal conservative, the mystic and the rationalist, the prophet and the sceptical politician. While both were necessary for the making of Italy, it was Cavour who now called the tune.

In January 1858 an attempt on Napoleon's life was made by an Italian, Orsini. As French support was essential, Cavour urgently prosecuted the revolutionary party, and when juries proved recalcitrant, passed a bill

---

[1] G. E. Curàtulo, *Garibaldi, Vittorio Emanuele, Cavour* (Bologna, 1911), p. 127. Significantly enough, the phrase was left out in Chiala's semi-official edition of Cavour's letters (vol. II, p. 372).

to amend legal procedure. More than a hundred suspected agitators were expelled, and Mazzini's paper, *Italia del Popolo*, which had already had at least 150 issues confiscated, was altogether and tyrannically suppressed. Fortunately Napoleon wanted Piedmont as an ally against Austria: he needed to stop Austrian influence spreading in Italy, as well as to acquire renown and break up the humiliating settlement of 1815, and to obtain as the price of his help certain frontier rectifications and a marriage into the oldest dynasty of Europe (cf. ch. XVII, pp. 462–3). Cavour therefore embarked confidently on a diplomatic duel with Count Buol. In 1856–7 the Austrians had tried to woo the Lombards with the promise of partial autonomy under the Archduke Maximilian: a number of exiles, despairing of any other solution, even began to return to Milan. Cavour countered this with French support, picking a quarrel and inducing Buol to try and restore Austrian prestige by breaking off diplomatic relations. Then he set about widening the breach and hurrying Napoleon into war against Austria for Italy's benefit.

Cavour's journey to arrange matters with Napoleon was taken without the approval or even the knowledge of his cabinet. At Plombières in July 1858 it was loosely arranged that Cavour should provoke war in the following spring, when the 'people' of Massa-Carrara would appeal for annexation. Victor Emmanuel should then revive the old Napoleonic kingdom of northern Italy down as far as Bologna, while there was to be a separate kingdom of central Italy, perhaps under Napoleon's cousin. In January 1859 a formal treaty confirmed that France should take Nice and Savoy in compensation. Cavour meanwhile applied himself to make Austria declare war and give his ally an excuse to intervene as a defender of the oppressed. Lombards were ostentatiously enlisted in his army so that Austria would pose as a bully and demand their extradition; and the king, on Napoleon's suggestion, spoke provocatively to parliament of the 'cries of grief' from the downtrodden subjects of other Italian states. England was horrified that Cavour, 'unassailed by any foreign power, and with no point of honour at stake', should thus deliberately seek war, and Malmesbury frightened Napoleon into backing down and demanding Piedmontese disarmament. Cavour, prostrate with grief, had to submit. But Austria, although financially and militarily unprepared, again made Lombardy a test for the viability of her multi-national empire; and Buol foolishly seized on Napoleon's withdrawal as the opportunity to crush an isolated Piedmont (cf. ch. XX, p. 539). Too late did his military advisers grasp what he was doing. In April, Cavour was saved by the Austrian idea of a preventive war.

By another stroke of fortune, the Austrian forces delayed several weeks a few hours' march from Turin, so giving Napoleon time to intervene. (For some account of the campaign see ch. XII, pp. 323–4.) Early in June the French defeated the Austrians at Magenta and forced them out of

Lombardy. Another victory followed at Solferino. Then in July, as Mazzini had accurately foretold, Napoleon suddenly stopped short, and concluded an armistice at Villafranca which left Venetia and even the quadrilateral of Lombard fortress towns in Austrian possession. Cavour was thunderstruck, and desperately advised Victor Emmanuel to continue fighting alone. But the king had taken the occasion of war to gather the conduct of policy into his own hands, and was realistic enough to reject this advice. France had won her prestige victory, and feared that northern Germany might rally to Austrian aid on the Rhine; nor did Napoleon want Piedmont too strong in the Italian federation he aimed to create. He had discovered that Cavour, instead of working for a separate kingdom of central Italy as agreed at Plombières, had surreptitiously sent agents to prepare annexation of the duchies to Piedmont. Napoleon therefore felt justified in deserting his ally, provided that he dropped the French claim to Savoy and Nice. Cavour resigned. He had already provoked one angry scene lately with Victor Emmanuel when he had accused the king's mistress of infidelity. In July there was another scene over Villafranca. Being neither a soldier nor a sporting man, nor a courtier, Cavour had never been one of the king's favourites; and so the more courteous and courtly Rattazzi took office with an interim ministry. In November the peace of Zürich confirmed that Tuscany and Modena as well as Venice should return to their old rulers.

French intervention had at least won most of Lombardy for Piedmont; and before long the settlement was to be further modified in her favour. In January 1860 Lord John Russell persuaded the French to concede the principle of non-intervention in central Italy, so that the duchies and the Romagna could choose their own future. Baron Ricasoli in Florence, and Farini in Modena, Parma and Bologna, had both formed provisional governments and asked for annexation. Protestant Britain was not averse to a diminution in papal territory; nor was Napoleon, judging from the officially authorised pamphlet *Le Pape et le Congrès*. Cavour returned to power in January with a plan to offer Savoy and Nice again to Napoleon if he would allow the annexation of central Italy. A bargain was concluded in March. Before parliament had been informed what was happening, French troops marched in to 'arrange' plebiscites in ratification of the accomplished fact, and by a remarkable *tour de force* Cavour then convinced the deputies that Nice was really more French than Italian. In the same month the union of Tuscany and Emilia with Piedmont was peacefully effected: out of 427,512 votes registered in Emilia, 426,006 were for annexation, and the remainder were declared null and void.[1] The kingdom of Sardinia had thus more than doubled its size in one year, and now included almost half the population of Italy.

Cavour continued to try to win Bourbon Naples as an ally and equal

[1] G. Del Bono, *Cavour e Napoleone III, 1859–60* (Turin, 1941), p. 289.

partner in this settlement. He had no plans for unifying Italy, but hoped to consolidate his position in the north, and then in a few years' time assist in another European war which his northern kingdom could use for the acquisition of Venice. He thought it undesirable that another insurrection should break out in the south, for only if he remained strictly moderate and conservative would France either help win Venice or withdraw her garrison from Rome.

Mazzini, on the contrary, believed with religious earnestness that Italy must be unified, and by her own exertions, not by the condescension of interested foreigners, or else some deep moral corruption would curse her beyond hope of redemption. He had long considered that a revolutionary situation existed in the south, which he could use to regain the initiative. Once again, Sicily proved the ignition point. Enmity against Naples and peasant vendettas were two highly tensed forces in Sicily, and Mazzini's agents touched off both of them in April 1860. Garibaldi, moreover, though he had had his own disagreements with Mazzini, was so incensed by Cavour bartering away his home town of Nice that he, too, was in rebellious mood. After being twice expelled from Piedmont, Garibaldi had become a brilliant guerrilla leader in his South American exile. He had returned in the hour of national emergency, but in 1848 and 1859 had been given a poor share in the Lombard wars, for the regular officers despised and feared his volunteers. In May 1860 he took the bit between his teeth and led his famous thousand filibusters to Sicily. Cavour did all he dared to stop him, but then had to fall back on a policy of wait-and-see: 'if the insurrection is put down', Cavour explained to the French ambassador, 'we shall say nothing; if it is victorious, we shall intervene in the name of order and authority'.[1] The cabinet even seems to have decided on Garibaldi's arrest; but Cavour personally was in two minds, because elections were being held, the cession of Nice was causing a serious ministerial crisis, and he feared that the king was sympathetic to Garibaldi and wanted the excuse to appoint a new premier.

Before Cavour could decide, Garibaldi had astonished everyone by capturing Palermo. A widespread peasants' revolt was disrupting the Bourbon administration and had helped to terrify a large army into submission. Cavour seized his chance and sent commissioners to annex Sicily. But Garibaldi believed, no doubt rightly, that Cavour wished to stop him short of Naples, and so refused to surrender the base which he needed for further operations on the mainland. This worried Cavour, for 'the king could not accept the crown of Italy at the hands of Garibaldi',[2]

[1] C. Maraldi, *Documenti francesi sulla caduta del regno meridionale* (Naples, 1935), pp. 30–1.
[2] 'Le Roi ne peut tenir la couronne d'Italie des mains de Garibaldi: elle chancellerait trop sur sa tête....Pour un Prince de la Maison de Savoie mieux vaut périr par la guerre que par la révolution....Son sort est scellé à jamais si on la traîne dans un ruisseau': Cavour to Nigra, *Il carteggio Cavour–Nigra* (Bologna, 1929), vol. IV, pp. 122–3.

and if the rebels continued to advance they might clash with the French at Rome. So he now stopped supplies going to help the revolution. While pretending to negotiate an alliance with Francis of Bourbon, his Neapolitan legation instigated a rival conspiracy to forestall Garibaldi, and succeeded in bribing the more important generals and ministers. But his agents had completely misinformed him about public opinion at Naples, and when the city fell to Garibaldi in September, he had to adopt a yet bolder project. Garibaldi's extraordinary success had so quickened enthusiasm for immediate unification, that Cavour at last announced his conversion to this Mazzinian heresy: 'incidents' were manufactured on the papal frontier, Umbria and the Marches conquered from the pope to 'save them from the revolution', and thence Naples invaded. Garibaldi had to yield; and the Piedmontese victory over the papal mercenaries at Castelfidardo was magnified by official apologists in order to try and reduce the glamour of his own previous victories. The usual plebiscites were supervised by the occupying forces, and the inevitable huge majorities declared their unconditional wish for annexation.

The word 'annexation' was used deliberately, for although a Kingdom of Italy was now proclaimed, it was to be essentially a graft upon the former Kingdom of Sardinia, and the king's title remained Victor Emmanuel the Second. This gesture to themselves by the Piedmontese helped to sweeten for them the task of organising—and, at first, governing—the rest of Italy. But the necessary process of 'Piedmontisation' was naturally irksome to the other conquered and annexed states. Many Sicilians had been fighting for independence of Naples, and had only sought a Piedmontese alliance as a means to self-government. Many Neapolitans had wrongly understood that annexation would be combined with local autonomy, and now had to watch the loss of business, administrative jobs and prestige to the smaller and less 'Italian' city of Turin. Some of the radicals had been fighting for a republic. Garibaldi himself was disgusted at the meanness shown to his volunteers and at having to stop them short of Rome. Tommaseo and Cattaneo represented a group of die-hards who had wanted an Italian federation, not a centralised government under which such a discrete body of peoples would be ruled in uniformity by unsympathetic bureaucrats in distant Turin. As for the peasants who formed 90 per cent of the population, few of them knew what the word 'Italy' meant; they had lent their powerful aid to the rebellion in the blind hope of obtaining land and economic security, but now discovered that the *ancien régime* had been their friend against the rapacious middle classes and landlords whom they had unwittingly and unwillingly helped into power. The more sincere Catholics were appalled that Cavour should have defied excommunication by making war on the Holy See, taking most of its territory and extending there the anticlerical legislation current in the north. Furthermore, the sudden and unconsidered extension of free trade from Piedmont to backward provinces extinguished or depressed local industries, and converted large areas from relatively prosperous cattle-breeding to uneconomic cereal production—since geographic situation and poor communications put the south at an immediate disadvantage when protection was discarded. Even at Turin the court aristocracy strongly resented the process of dilution by un-pedigreed southerners. D'Azeglio recommended that Naples should at once be separated off again, because evidently the plebiscites had not the remotest correspondence with public opinion.

Although many people protested and even continued to deny the existence of an Italian nation, a miracle had somehow happened. The skill and noble ambition of a few brave men, a fortuitous moment in European diplomacy, the obstinate convictions of a growing class of intellectuals, and a sudden wave of enthusiasm which equated unity with everything that was noble and profitable, all these in fortunate combination realised Mazzini's utopian dream just when Mazzini himself was utterly disillusioned and forced out again into the bitterness of exile. Deputies from all over Italy were elected to the parliament which opened at Turin in February 1861. Unluckily the session was marred by an unseemly brawl between Garibaldi and Cavour. Little enough had been done to seal the union when, in June, Cavour was taken with a severe fever: the doctors bled him half a dozen times or more until his last resistance was sapped; then Fra Giacomo charitably defied an ecclesiastical interdict and accorded him the last rites. He died when still some months before his fifty-first birthday. It was the greatest misfortune that he did not live to turn his mind to the baffling problems of reconstruction.

In twelve years Victor Emmanuel had had but three prime ministers, now he had one a year: Ricasoli in 1861, Rattazzi in 1862, Farini and then Minghetti in 1863, General La Marmora in 1864, then Ricasoli and Rattazzi again, General Menabrea in 1867, and Lanza in 1869. Politics were fickle and disorganised, partly because there was so little clear difference of opinion. Cavour no more than D'Azeglio had encouraged formation of a parliamentary opposition, and when out of office in 1852 and 1859 had merely left Turin to await a favourable moment for re-capturing power. After his death, many small personal groups jostled somewhat aimlessly for place, for they had been brought up to an unhealthy dependence on a single man.

There was general agreement on the problems to be solved: the acquisition of Venice and Rome, the levelling out and assimilation of diverse laws and customs, the suppression of counter-revolution, and the achievement of financial equilibrium. This last problem can be illustrated by the fact that, in some years, expenditure was half as much again as revenue. To remedy this the currency was debased and ecclesiastical property nationalised, and taxes were raised on food until many people fell to starvation level. One major source of expense was that sixty battalions of troops had to be sent almost at once to quell a civil war which dragged out for four years in the south. Bourbonists and papalists exploited the wish for local autonomy and the hatred of northern conscription and taxes, while the economic discrimination of government and landlords kept the peasantry a revolutionary instead of a conservative force. Martial law had to be applied also in Sicily, where the annual quota of military recruits mostly contrived to disappear into the hills and expand the veritable army of outlaws. On one occasion a separatist government actually came into being at Palermo. The casualties in this wasting war were to outnumber those in all the battles for national independence put together; for in all the regular campaigns between 1848 and 1870, the total price of independence and unity was estimated at some 6000 dead and 20,000 wounded[1]—a small cost for such an achievement.

Venice was won in 1866. The Austrians had first offered to surrender it without fighting, to avoid a war on two fronts, but Italy needed the prestige of an armed victory and refused. The resultant war concluded ingloriously when Italy, despite superior numbers, was defeated at Custoza again, and on sea at Lissa. But as her ally Prussia won an overwhelming victory (cf. ch. xix, p. 519), Austria ceded Venice to Napoleon, who passed it on. Rome was more difficult, for the pope was less amenable than the Austrian emperor, and negotiations repeatedly came to nought. Garibaldi made another attempt to march on Rome in 1862, having been encouraged to think that Rattazzi would stand aside ready to exploit his success or failure. Instead, the royal troops wounded and captured him at Aspromonte. Much the same happened again in 1867, when Menabrea unwillingly found himself in a position where he had to try to help the French defeat Garibaldi's volunteers at Mentana. Most people—D'Azeglio being a notable exception—felt that, without Rome, Italy would not be Italy: quite apart from sentimental considerations, other regions were increasingly loth to allow precedence to Turin or any other merely provincial centre. Finally, in 1870, the unexpected victory of Prussia over France brought a withdrawal of the French protecting garrison, and, at the moment when papal infallibility was proclaimed, the Italians marched into Rome against merely token resistance. This was not quite Mazzini's idea of national redemption by popular initiative; but what to Mazzini seemed but the ghost or the corpse of Italy, to others appeared real enough. A 'geographical expression' had come to life. With the acquisition of Rome, the *risorgimento* seemed, for the time being, to be complete.

[1] Fortunato's figures: E. Tagliacozzo, *Voci di realismo politico dopo il 1870* (Bari, 1937), p. 118.

CHAPTER XXII

THE ORIGINS OF THE FRANCO-PRUSSIAN WAR AND THE REMAKING OF GERMANY

FOR many years the legend flourished that Bismarck, by a masterly *coup*, tricked France into declaring war on Prussia in July 1870. No one was more assiduous in fostering this story than Bismarck himself, in moods of mischief or vainglory; many historians found evidence to support him, and carried the tale of his deceit of the French back several years before 1870. The truth is far more complicated. Bismarck certainly bears his share of responsibility for the outbreak of war, but cannot claim the whole of it; the question even of when he began to desire war remains obscure, as does the question of exactly what results he hoped would follow from it.

Among its other results one, the shift in Europe's diplomatic centre of gravity from Paris to Berlin, had been among his few long-term objectives from the start of his career in office in 1862. He had always meant, if he could, to turn Berlin into the directing centre of a Europe controlled by a Prussianised Germany. The events of the rest of the 'sixties were dominated by his determination to remake Germany on terms of his own choosing. This determination soon became evident, and the four powers strong enough to stand up to Prussia had to decide what to do about it. Great Britain and Russia were, for divers reasons, indifferent. The British deliberately pursued a policy of isolation. The Russians, emerging from the retirement in which they had been plunged by the Crimean War (ch. x, pp. 268–9), found themselves rivals with Austria in south-east Europe, and therefore looked more with favour than otherwise on any distraction to be provided for the Habsburgs in Germany. Austria's active hostility was defeated, as the last chapters have shown. France, too, was hostile: but no opportunity for French intervention in the German civil war was found, and the victors of Königgrätz (which the French called Sadowa) could not be challenged lightly.

During the next four years the struggle for control of German unity took on something of the character of a duel between Bismarck and Napoleon III, and one profound and simple difference between them must be noted from the start: Napoleon did not know his own mind, and Bismarck did. Napoleon hesitated perpetually, like Buridan's ass (the comparison is borrowed from Eyck's *Bismarck*), between dynastic, religious, and military advantages, between advantages in foreign and advantages in internal policy; he suffered from too fertile a political imagination, and too often pursued incompatibles. Many accounts of his activities suppose that he pursued one aim consistently at a time: this was not so. But Bismarck started, like a successful general, by defining his object: a limited Germany unified under the control of the Prussian ruling class in which he had been born. He saw all the potential advantages which perplexed Napoleon in regular proportion to each other and to his object, and did not try to secure too many at once.

Both in France and in Prussia there was a strong 'militarist' group, close to the throne, of professional soldiers anxious to exercise their profession; in both countries a system of conscription had habituated a large number of men to the use of arms (see ch. XII, p. 312); the pacifist sentiments which could get some slight hearing in Cobden's England were of little importance in France and of none in Prussia. After the wars of 1859 and 1866 each country was confident of its own prowess, and ready one day to accept a war with the other. The name of Napoleon had created much glory for France, but the nephew had not the genius in the field, nor the powers of leadership, nor the strength of character, of the uncle; and Bismarck proved more successful both in holding the soldiers in check at moments politically inapt for war, and in providing them with the victory they sought.

On the day after the disaster of Königgrätz Francis Joseph ceded Venetia to Napoleon by telegraph, and asked him to arrange an armistice. The emperor of the French was surprised by the Austrian collapse; he seems to have expected the Austrians to win the war, and at all events had taken no steps to hedge against the Prussian victory that now confronted him. He had not mobilised his army; and now that some of his ministers pressed him to do so, while Austria's army was still on a war footing, he found there was no time left to do so usefully. Besides, he was ill; and the splendid opportunity that for a moment seemed to lie under his hand slipped by. It took him ten days to compile proposals, markedly favourable to Francis Joseph; but Bismarck accepted them readily, for he had no wish to trample on Austria—he only wanted to get her out of the way of Prussian power (preliminaries of Nikolsburg, 26 July, and peace treaty of Prague, 23 August 1866). Venetia was to pass to defeated Italy, though this was a loss more in prestige than in strength: some contemporaries saw that it was really to Austria's advantage to surrender this hostile population. To victorious Prussia Austria had to cede no territory at all, and had only to pay a small cash indemnity; and though she left the superseded Germanic Confederation, the North German Confederation (*Norddeutscher Bund*) that was to succeed it was to be restricted mainly to Protestant states, and not to extend south of the River Main.

Bismarck was chiefly occupied, till June of the following year, in settling the new Confederation's constitution. North of the Main he arranged that Prussia should recoup herself by much severer terms for Austria's German allies, several of which were absorbed into the Prussian state by frontier revisions that added four-and-a-half millions to Prussia's population and gave her for the first time one continuous boundary from the Meuse to the Memel. One of the vanished states, Hanover, provided Prussia with abundant secret-service money for a generation to come, while the knotty political problem of the demarcation between its former ruler's private and public fortunes remained unsolved.

In a preliminary tussle with the Prussian parliament, Bismarck secured a significant tactical success. The opposition which the Progressive party had maintained to his unconstitutional action, more than thirty months before, in making war on Denmark without parliamentary financial sanction was suddenly deprived of support by a public opinion which greeted with enthusiasm the victory over Austria. The liberal majority in the new parliament, elected on the day of Königgrätz, dared not risk another dissolution which would have swept it away; and on 3 September 1866 a bill of indemnity for the illegal spending on the Danish war was voted by a majority of over three to one. The vote, cast with the glories of the immediate past in mind, was heavy with consequences for the future: it marked the defeat of liberalism in Germany, for it provided a convenient precedent to which later governments could appeal, and so secured the independence of the executive from parliamentary control.

Bismarck further weakened his parliamentary enemies by devising for the new Confederation an executive branch with real administrative powers, which the old had never had. A lower house (*Reichstag*) was to be elected by universal suffrage—an arrangement that even the West-minster parliament had just feared to make—but its powers were advisory only, not even including the power of the purse that Prussian experience had just shown to be ineffective, except for some control over the size of the army; and the peasant mass of the electorate was soundly conservative. The new Confederation had the king of Prussia for its President; and the predominance in it of Prussia was secured by an ingenious trick. To the four Prussian votes in the upper chamber of the old Confederation were added the thirteen votes which had belonged to the states newly declared part of Prussia; and fourteen votes in the new upper house (*Bundesrat*) were to be enough to reject any constitutional amendment.

Throughout the constitutional discussions and debates, private and public alike, Bismarck had the unintended assistance of Napoleon III, who played the part of bogey-man to Bismarck's entire satisfaction, whenever the spectre of a foreign danger to German soil was called for. Napoleon had proposed the Main frontier to ensure that the German states remained divided. He envisaged three German groupings, one centred on Prussia, and one on Austria; the third and weakest, the four states bounded by the Main, the Rhine, Austria, and Bohemia, would, he hoped, look to himself for guidance. To these four states the Treaty of Prague promised an independent international existence, but even before it was signed Bismarck had persuaded them secretly to sign away part of their independence.

An increase in Prussian strength necessarily required, in the eyes of French public opinion and by the practice of French diplomacy, an increase in French strength also. To secure this Napoleon had sent Benedetti (1817–1900), his shrewd Corsican ambassador at Berlin, down to see Bismarck in the field to demand extensions of French territory in the Palatinate, at the expense of Bavaria, Luxemburg, and Prussia herself. Bismarck was short with Benedetti; but managed to extract from the ambassador (after both had returned to Berlin) a draft treaty in Benedetti's own hand, containing fresh proposals under which France would take Belgium and Luxemburg, in return agreeing to the union of all Germany but Austria and an offensive and defensive Franco-German alliance. Of this project, put forward on Napoleon's instructions, Bismarck made spectacular use four years later: it appeared, undated, in *The Times* of 25 July 1870. More immediately, he was able to denounce the various Napoleonic designs to the south-German diplomats in his capital. Convinced of France's bad faith, Württemberg, Baden, and Bavaria made secret treaties with Prussia in mid-August by which they entrusted their armies to Prussian command in the event of a Franco-Prussian war.

Napoleon could find no support in Europe for his plans to expand. Austria was helpless, Prussia hostile, Russia aloof; England, in the throes of a change of government, expressed her usual anxieties for Belgium; Italy, aggrieved by the way in which Venetia came to her, had no wish to offer him her weak support. He had to suffer the humiliation of withdrawing his demands unmet; but he did not forget them. For the rest of his reign one of the dominating influences on his foreign policy was this unassuaged desire to compensate France for Prussia's gains.

From this time onward peace was insecure. Napoleon convinced himself, or was convinced by his more hectic advisers, that he could not afford to see a unified Germany, and must be ready to fight to prevent one from coming into existence. He parted at once with his Foreign Minister, Drouyn de Lhuys, who now regarded German unity as inevitable and was not sorry to go: 'I have seen two dynasties fall', he said to Goltz, the North German envoy, 'and I know the signs.'[1] Just as a man running dares not stop suddenly, lest he lose his balance and fall, Napoleon could retain his balance at home only if he ran from victory to victory abroad. His Mexican venture was already a defeat: he withdrew the last of his troops, under pressure from the United States, in March 1867. Simultaneously, he tried to make friends with Russia, but bungled the

[1] H. Oncken, *Die Rheinpolitik Kaiser Napoleons III...* (Stuttgart, 1926), vol. II, p. 41.

negotiation. Russia wanted France's support in the Levant, where a Cretan revolt seemed to offer a chance of reopening the eastern question; but France's current eastern interests were commercial rather than political, and Russia could not be persuaded to take a suitable interest in Rhineland problems. Napoleon needed to find some triumph that would strike the imagination of his subjects, and show them that he protected French interests by securing a due equivalent for Prussia's new gains. Early in 1867, during his talks with Russia, he seemed to find what he was looking for when he revived his proposal to obtain Luxemburg.

For fifty years the city of Luxemburg had contained a Prussian garrison, as a fortress of the Germanic Confederation, intended with several others to hinder a French advance into central Europe. The new North German Confederation did not include Luxemburg: therefore, it could be argued, the garrison ought to go. Moreover, William III of the Netherlands, owner of the grand duchy of Luxemburg, which the creation of Belgium had separated from the rest of his kingdom, was short of money. In March 1867 Napoleon agreed with him secretly to buy the grand duchy outright, for cash down; having previously, as he thought, arranged with Bismarck that there would be no Prussian objection. But the secret was not well enough kept, and when it leaked out the German press—with Bismarck's connivance—protested strongly against the proposed transfer. Bismarck chose this moment to publish the secret treaties which he had made with the south German states in the previous August.

Napoleon suddenly found himself faced with the prospect of having to pay for Luxemburg, if he wanted it, with men as well as money; and he could no more easily find allies to help him to get it than he had been able to find them the year before. True, Bismarck was equally unsuccessful in creating an alliance to work against him: the inexperienced but stolid British Foreign Secretary, Stanley (1826–93), refused to be frightened by Prussian hints that Napoleon really cherished designs on Belgium, and the Austrian Foreign Minister Beust (1809–86), a recent recruit to Habsburg service from Saxony, tartly rejected Bismarck's professions of amity. With some German patriotism, he also refused an offer of alliance from Napoleon, since it envisaged a war against Prussia that would not appeal to the Germans in Austria. He put forward an idea of his own, that Luxemburg should be handed over to Belgium and that France should receive instead two Belgian fortresses surrendered in 1815: a proposal detested in Brussels and peremptorily forbidden in London. France and Prussia embarked on various precautionary measures preliminary to mobilisation. But the resources of diplomacy were not yet exhausted; nor were the leaders on either side yet determined on a war. Bismarck thought —or so he said in an expansive moment four years later—that Prussia by herself was probably not strong enough to defeat France in single combat, and that the cement of her alliances with the south German states had not yet set. He was able to suggest to Napoleon through the Prussian ambassador in Paris, who had the ear of the empress, that the question of a Luxemburg straw was not worth debating in arms.

Advantage was taken of a friendly and disinterested suggestion by the tsar to summon a conference of the European powers' representatives in London. As with most successful nineteenth-century conferences, previous concert between the disputants settled what it was to decide. Napoleon, appreciating that he was isolated, and unwilling to bring on a war, changed his tune: instead of baying for compensations, he chanted for a while praise of peace and France's reverence for international engagements; and his minister Rouher arranged with Goltz what the settlement was to be. The Prussian garrison was to leave Luxemburg, the fortress was to be dismantled, and the grand duchy was to be guaranteed neutral by the powers. Thanks to Prussian pressure on Stanley, these provisions were included in the Treaty of London which concluded the short conference on 11 May 1867.

Soon afterwards a curious interpretation of the phrase 'collective guarantee' in this treaty was put before the Westminster parliament by Stanley and by his father and Prime Minister, Derby. Their doctrine appeared to mean that if any guaranteeing power invaded the guaranteed territory, none of the co-guarantors would be called on to take any action in its defence: a puzzle for lawyers. Otherwise the incident served its turn in English politics, by strengthening a minority government in some awkward debates over parliamentary reform, and in Prussian by hastening the conclusion of the north-German constitutional debate. The French rejoiced that the garrison was to go, and the Germans were glad to have kept the French from succeeding to it. (Indeed Bismarck, not wishing at the moment to exacerbate the French further, fended off in September a request from Baden to join the new Confederation.) An exhibition at Paris provided a more attractive scene for the conduct of international relations than a green table in Downing Street. But the tsar, who came to see it with many other royalties—including the king of Prussia—was shot at by a young Pole; and the gaieties were still more effectively spoiled by the news which reached Europe at the end of June. The Mexican affair was over: Maximilian had been executed at Queretaro (cf. chs. xxiv and xxv, pp. 641, 677–8).

Two months later Napoleon and Eugénie paid a visit of condolence to Francis Joseph at Salzburg. On his way there Napoleon remarked, almost casually, at Munich railway station that if the south German states were to join Bismarck's new Confederation in a way that angered France, he would have to go to war with them. The Austrian emperor was attended by several of his ministers; the emperor of the French relied on his own sagacity. Neither advice nor inspiration produced any definite compact; and Napoleon was left with the hope that his engaging manners had made some impression on the man whose empire he had so often, in the past eight years, attacked. For three years more he followed the mirage of the Austrian alliance: yet it may be doubted whether Francis Joseph was ever ready to come to terms with the man but for whom his brother would not have stood before a firing squad.

One of the inducements to Napoleon to ally himself with the Habsburg monarchy was that Austria-Hungary was predominantly Catholic; the alliance would therefore be popular with Catholics in France. On the other hand, to pursue a consistently Catholic policy would necessarily put him at odds with Italy; almost Italy's only remaining national ambition was to secure what territory round Rome still remained in the temporal power of the pope. Having failed to ingratiate himself with the Italians by the present of Venetia in July 1866, Napoleon at least withdrew that December the French garrison at Rome. The Italian government was emboldened in consequence to wink at, or even to encourage, revolutionary raids on the papal enclave; by the end of September 1867 these raids had attained strength formidable enough to alarm the pope, the more so as Garibaldi appeared on the spot to lead them.

This faced Napoleon with a difficult decision, the more difficult because his advisers were so much divided. He could support the Italian claims to papal territory, and thus both secure an ally that he believed to be of weight, and complete the part that he had played ever since the Plombières meeting as patron of united Italy. But to do this he would have to combine with anti-clerical and revolutionary forces: which he dared not do. His own regime depended too much on the violent repression of unrest and on the loyalty of Catholics. To Catholics—and his wife was an ardent Catholic—there could be no question of France's duty: it must be to support the pope, whatever the cost. In the end, Napoleon preferred the ally at home to the ally abroad, and let a small French expeditionary force sail for the Tiber; although characteristically he hesitated even beyond the last minute, trying to recall it by semaphore just as it was leaving French territorial waters.

It arrived in the nick of time to help defeat the Garibaldini at Mentana, only a dozen miles from Rome, on 3 November: a check that the Italians were reluctant to forgive. Nor did they find acceptable Rouher's pronouncement in the French parliament a few days later, that imperial France would never allow the new Italian kingdom to possess itself of Rome.

Secretly, Napoleon continued to coax Francis Joseph, hoping to expand the understanding to which he fancied they had come at Salzburg into a fully fledged alliance; and this policy eventually brought him up against the consequences of having replaced his garrison in Rome. The talks with Austria-Hungary were at first very secret: Napoleon's own ambassador in Vienna, Gramont, knew nothing of them till he became Foreign

Minister in 1870. Francis Joseph displayed his usual perfect manners, but courtesy concealed a reluctance to commit himself. Beust would not accept Napoleon's renewed proposal for an active alliance aimed at Prussia; not only because it was unacceptable to the German-speaking half of the monarchy, but because some of the leading Magyars, whose position had just been strengthened by the *Ausgleich* (cf. ch. xx), were positively hostile to France. Napoleon would not accept Beust's innocent-seeming counter-proposal, that the two powers should take no diplomatic action without previous accord, since that might deprive him of his initiative. Austria, in fact, felt too weak to move alone, and on her proposition Italy was brought in to make a third; and this brought the negotiation to a standstill after a year. If Austria would not stir without Italy, Italy would not stir without having Rome; and Austria supported her in this—fearing that Prussia might offer Italy, as the price of an alliance, not only Rome but also the Trentino. Now Rome, as we have seen, was not something that Eugénie's husband was prepared to give up. Eventually, in September 1869, there was an exchange of letters between Napoleon and Francis Joseph, and Napoleon and Victor Emmanuel. The Austrian and Italian monarchs assured the emperor of the French, in the warmest terms, of their affection for him and of their determination to come to his aid in war; but this in personal letters, not in formal diplomatic documents. Napoleon placed a pathetic trust in these worthless assurances. 'He made his preparations languidly,' said Acton, 'like a man in whom pain has extinguished resolution and activity and hopefulness, and took so much time that he never concluded.'[1]

All through these ineffectual negotiations the French army authorities were trying to improve their forces, and to meet the doubts which had crept into their minds since Sadowa about whether theirs still was the best army in the world. Napoleon took a keen interest in problems of army organisation and armament. Niel (1802–69), who had been promoted marshal on the field of Solferino, became his Minister of War early in 1867, and took charge of a large reform. After prolonged preparation, a law was passed in January 1868 which extended the length of conscript service from seven years to nine, the last four of these in reserve. The transfer from the old system to the new was still in progress when war broke out in 1870; nor was the new as effective as its founders had hoped—partly because of changes made during its passage through parliament, where many deputies were anxious to reduce military spending. But at least Niel saw before he died the whole army equipped with a good breech-loading rifle, named after its inventor Chassepot (cf. ch. XII, p. 305). Some early models of the Chassepot had 'worked wonders' (*ont fait merveille*) at Mentana, according to a dispatch from the French commander there, conspicuously lacking in tact, which was published to annoy

[1] Acton MS. 4928, f. 108.

the Prussians and succeeded in wounding the Italians. Outside France Niel's reforms were thought to be important. In northern Germany army reform went on also, with less opposition and more efficiency: the armies of the rest of the new confederation were assimilated as far as could be to Prussia's.

During these changes, neither France nor Prussia wanted to fight; the French because they were not ready, and the Prussians because each year's postponement of the war would add 100,000 trained soldiers to their army. Yet the French gave the impression to the rest of Europe that they were *mauvais coucheurs*, dissatisfied with their surroundings. For example, in the winter of 1868-9 a French railway company—in debt to the French government—tried to buy two Belgian ones. The Belgians took fright, and in February passed a law forbidding Belgian railways to sell their lines to foreigners. The French government at once took umbrage—so sharply indeed as to create a presumption that it had been privy to the deal from the start, and having failed to secure a political advance towards the lower Rhine was now seeking an economic one. A firm protest from Clarendon, who had again become the British Foreign Secretary in December, brought the scare to an abrupt close.

After the war, some Frenchmen said that they had sensed it coming; that the atmosphere was heavy with menace. In fact, this would have been more true of the spring of 1869 than of 1870.

On the second day of 1870 the Ollivier ministry was formed in France, with Clarendon's friend Daru as Foreign Minister (cf. ch. iv, p. 97). Ollivier was known to be a supporter of German unity; and one of Daru's first acts was to demand, with success, that Napoleon should cease another of his secret negotiations, in which he had engaged after the September exchange of letters on the projected triple alliance. He had sent Fleury, one of his military entourage, as ambassador to St Petersburg; while holding the putative triple alliance in play, he had launched inquiries about the price that Russia would charge for becoming his ally instead. As soon as Fleury's activities were curtailed, Daru embarked on an equally secret project, equally devoid of result. He got Clarendon to take up with Bismarck, as if from himself and not from Daru, the question of reduction of large standing armies. The secret of these talks was really well kept: they almost eluded even Acton's attention, and little about them appeared in print until a life of one of the ambassadors concerned—Lord Newton's *Lord Lyons*—was published forty-three years later. Nothing came of them at all. Bismarck no doubt divined that Clarendon's proposals had originated in Paris; he deployed against them arguments, some ludicrous and some evasive, curiously like the arguments for refusing to reduce the German navy put forward by his successors in the years before 1914. He never spoke of his real reason for refusing to treat: he did not trust the French, and so could take no risks. He already foresaw that if a French attack was made, and failed, it might be the occasion for completing his version of German unity. Clarendon died of overwork on 27 June, soon after the failure of these talks, at the moment when Europe had most need of him.

Napoleon as usual did not enter with his whole heart into his ministers' projects. In March, while the disarmament talks were still going on in Berlin, he was engaged in military discussions in Paris with an Austrian archduke, intended to put more reality into his triple alliance plans. Daru resigned in April, on a difference with his colleagues on an internal point, and was replaced on 15 May by the duc de Gramont (1819–80), a career diplomat conspicuous for his dislike of Bismarck, whose appointment was evidently intended to show that Napoleon like most monarchs of his day intended to keep control of foreign affairs in his own hands. In June the emperor sent Lebrun, another military confidant, to Vienna, without even telling his ministers that he was doing so; Lebrun got satisfactory assurances of military help from Francis Joseph, except that they were verbal assurances only. Gramont urged on Napoleon the futility of searching for allies in advance: if there was war with Prussia, he said, other powers would come tumbling over each other in their eagerness to join victorious France; or if *per impossibile* France was not victorious, what good could allies do? It was with this counsellor at his elbow that Napoleon approached the final crisis of his reign.

Though he had extended France's south-eastern frontier in 1860, and had tried in vain to extend her north-eastern frontier since July 1866, Napoleon never seems to have directed any covetous glances towards Spain: partly since the Pyrenees form so natural a frontier; partly since his wife was a patriotic Spaniard; partly since he recalled how the invasion of Spain had helped to ruin his uncle. However, it was from this neglected quarter that the crisis in which his empire fell developed.

The reign of Isabella II of Spain had drawn to an animated close in September 1868, when her corrupt despotism broke down under the weight of its own inefficiency and the attack of two military politicians, Serrano and Prim (1814–70). (Prim had commanded the Spanish troops in Mexico, where he had learned no love for France.) Those who seek to find the hidden hand of Bismarck in all the transactions of these years which turned out to France's disadvantage have fancied they can detect him at work here. If Bismarck is credited with venomous foresight over a period of years, this conjecture is a possible one; but there is no evidence of any kind for it, and the weight of probabilities tells against it. Isabella fled to Paris; and her successors at once began search for a monarch to preside over the constitutional regime which they set up. Eyck has drawn an engaging sketch of Prim thumbing over the *Almanach de Gotha* for a prince of the necessary impeccable breeding and Catholic religion;[1] but

[1] E. Eyck, *Bismarck* (Zürich, 1941), vol. II, p. 438.

the possible choices were few. It was widely recognised at the time, in the press as well as in 'diplomatic circles', that the only probable starters were Isabella's child Alfonso, Ferdinand of Portugal, the dukes of Montpensier, Aosta, and Genoa, and some prince of the Catholic branch of the Hohenzollern family, whose Protestant head was king of Prussia.

From the domestic Spanish point of view there was little to choose between these candidates, save that Alfonso was disliked; but other powers had other views. England might be expected to oppose Montpensier on traditional grounds, for he was Louis Philippe's son. Austria would not look kindly on an Italian, nor France on a German; and France under a Bonaparte would equally oppose Montpensier. For Prussia, the Hohenzollern candidate had an obvious strategic advantage, should he succeed: when the war with France which almost everyone in Berlin took for granted as inevitable broke out, he would compel the French to keep glancing backward over their shoulders: a point somewhat lightly touched on by the many historians who have sought to present this candidature solely as a trick of Bismarck's intended to precipitate the war.

That Bismarck was concerned to promote the Hohenzollern candidature there can now be no doubt, though his motives for taking it up are still not all of them clear. The subject had come to his attention as far back as November 1866;[1] and he took a close interest in the Spanish situation, sending out to Spain in May 1869 two confidential emissaries, Bernhardi and Versen (1833–93), whose eventual task—facilitated by the disposal of over £50,000 in cash—was to accustom the army and the church in Spain to the idea of a Hohenzollern ruler.[2] Strategy apart, there is no need to presume any other motive for his actions, at first, than a desire to cause France the embarrassment either of accepting a Hohenzollern king of Spain, or of undertaking a troublesome diplomatic campaign to prevent this candidate's success. The fact that Prince Leopold of Hohenzollern (1835–1905), on whom Prim's choice came to rest, was more nearly related, through his Murat grandmother, to Napoleon III than to William I was used by Bismarck as an excuse for expressing surprise at French protests at his candidature: the chancellor knew that Hohenzollern family loyalty was entirely engaged on the Prussian side. Leopold's father, Karl Anton, Prussian Prime Minister in 1858, was a personal friend of his distant cousin the king.

Another family connection of importance to Leopold was that he had

[1] This fact, like many others of importance to this subject, was first revealed in R. H. Lord's *The Origins of the War of 1870* (Harvard, 1924), an analysis of part of the German archives. Many of the conclusions proved by Lord from documents were divined thirty years earlier by Acton's historical insight, but Lord seems not to have used Acton's papers; nor were all the German files available to him. Those hidden from him were published by G. Bonnin, *Bismarck and the Hohenzollern candidature for the Spanish throne* (London, 1957). These two books, and vol. XXVIII of the French government's *Origines diplomatiques de la guerre de 1870–1871* (Paris, 1931), which covers the period 1–15 July 1870, are the cardinal printed sources.   [2] Acton MS. 4928, f. 162; Bonnin, appendix A.

married Ferdinand of Portugal's daughter, so that those in Spain who advocated a united Iberian kingdom could hope that Leopold's children might one day obtain it by succession if Leopold became king of Spain. However, a more direct means to this end would lie in making Ferdinand himself, or his son Luiz the king-regnant of Portugal, king of Spain; and Princess Leopold was most reluctant to stand in their way. It was not until both Ferdinand and Luiz, and one of the Italians, had refused his offers that Prim first made a formal approach to Leopold in September 1869.[1] This approach may possibly have been encouraged from Berlin. In any case, it failed: neither Leopold nor his father liked the look of the Spanish throne, and both feared French opposition. Prim accordingly opened negotiations with the duke of Genoa, then a boy at Harrow; but early in 1870 the duke's uncle, the king of Italy, forbade him to stand. Prim therefore really had no choice but to approach some lesser princeling, which would be repugnant to Spanish pride; or to make Spain a republic, which would be repugnant to Spanish sentiment; or to antagonise France and England at once by an offer to Montpensier; or to turn once more to the Hohenzollerns.

Late in February 1870 Prim's messenger Salazar set off again for Germany, this time with entreaties to Bismarck as well as to the king of Prussia and to Leopold. Prim enjoined extreme secrecy on Leopold, though his previous negotiations had been more or less open: this argues anxiety lest French opposition should be fatal to the scheme, and also may have been encouraged from Berlin, where Bismarck now took up, and pressed most earnestly, the Hohenzollern candidature. In a powerful paper of 9 March he urged on his reluctant monarch the importance of the strategic reasons for control of Spain, and added ingeniously, though not quite fairly, that if no Hohenzollern stood a Bavarian Wittelsbach might succeed, and provide a sure if distant rallying-point for elements hostile to the new Germany Bismarck was constructing.[2]

In the Prussian capital it was pretended by the few people in the know at the time, when they came to be questioned afterwards, that Salazar's visit was a purely family affair. Nevertheless on 15 March William held in his palace a dinner party which was attended by his chancellor, his Minister for War, his chief of staff, and three lesser advisers, besides Karl Anton and Leopold and the king's own heir. Bismarck now with all his colleagues urged on the prince the duty and indeed the necessity of

[1] Late in March 1869 a Spanish diplomat visited Berlin, and was suspected by Benedetti—probably wrongly—of discussing the Hohenzollern candidature then. Benedetti both warned his government of his suspicions and raised the point with Thile (1812–89), Bismarck's deputy at the Prussian foreign office; Thile firmly denied the possibility of the candidature. In May Bismarck lectured Benedetti on the insecurity of the Spanish throne—presumably with his tongue in his cheek, as he had only just sent Bernhardi out there.

[2] This document was carefully hidden, in the 1920's, both from Lord and from the editors of *Die Grosse Politik*. It was first published in 1931, and can now be seen, with the king's honourable and reluctant marginalia, in Bonnin, *op. cit.* pp. 68–73.

standing; but the king was reluctant to force the young man's hand, and left it to him to decide. Leopold, after a few days' consideration, refused. His father had by now conceived some enthusiasm for being the father of a king, and sent at once for Leopold's surviving younger brother Friedrich (Anton had died of wounds at Königgrätz), but Friedrich also after some delay refused the doubtful honour, and the whole plan was abandoned.

It was revived in an unexpected way, by Versen. This thirty-six-year-old cavalry major disliked the dropping of a scheme on which so much of his time had been spent, and by dexterous management persuaded the Prussian crown prince, Karl Anton, and Bismarck to co-operate—behind the king's back—in begging Leopold to change his mind. Prim of course supported this forlorn hope; Salazar returned once more to Germany; and Leopold at last, on 19 June, wrote to the king of Prussia for formal leave to accept. This leave was wrung from an angry William on the 21st; and two days later still Salazar was able to leave for Madrid with the all-important letter of acceptance.

At this point a curious incident intervened. Salazar sent home a cipher telegram, through Prussian channels, announcing his success, and saying that he would return on 26 June. Through what a secret inquiry later showed to be an error by a cipher clerk at Madrid, the Prussians there passed this date on as 9 July. The change had results that reached far. Madrid was already unbearably hot; and Prim, not wishing to exasperate Parliament by prolonging its sitting for a fortnight for an object he could not yet reveal, prorogued it until October. Salazar, on the move, knew nothing of this, and when he reached Madrid he did not conceal from his friends the news he brought with him. The Catholic Hohenzollerns were hardly more discreet. It is not therefore surprising that on 2 July a rumour of Leopold's acceptance appeared in a Paris newspaper; and Prim that same evening had to make what explanation of the affair he could to an infuriated French ambassador. On Sunday 3 July, the fourth anniversary of Sadowa, the news was all over Paris.

No earlier than the previous Thursday, Ollivier had said in answer to a parliamentary question that his government was in no way disturbed; at no time had the continued peace of Europe seemed more stable to it. English readers will know better the remark made to Granville, the new Foreign Secretary, by the permanent head of the British Foreign Office on 5 July; he had never known so great a lull in foreign affairs. In Prussia, the appearance of calm had been equally complete: Bismarck at Varzin, his remote Pomeranian estate; the queen at Coblenz, the king taking the waters at Ems near by; Benedetti left Berlin on 1 July for a cure at Wildbad, leaving Le Sourd in charge of his embassy. The calm vanished in a flash; within a fortnight, France and Prussia were at war. The curious reader can trace the details of this fortnight's doings, which are summarised below, in Lord's book and the French documents, and in many books of memoirs, all more or less misleading, in which participants in the conflict have sought to clear their own and blacken their opponents' characters. (No memoirs by Napoleon or by Prim survive.)

The news of Leopold's acceptance was received in France with nervous anger. The Paris newspapers wrote of it in almost unanimous execration, regarding the project as intended to weaken French security and no less rightly protesting, though in the strongest possible terms, at the secrecy in which it had so far been shrouded. In court and government circles there were no two opinions, though the reasons for hostility were some-times more elaborate. After the disaster, Napoleon said that the insecurity of the Spanish throne had weighed heavily with him, since it seemed to point to Prussian intervention to prop Leopold up against a revolution in a few years' time. (Indeed the next king of Spain ruled for barely two years before his reign dissolved in anarchy.) At the moment, Napoleon agreed with his entourage—a counter-attack must go in at once. This was made the more urgent when the reassembly of the Spanish parliament to elect Leopold formally was, on 7 July, announced for the 20th. But the French opened their campaign in so bad a temper that they made two capital mistakes. One was to direct it exclusively against Prussia. Had the Prussian government merely been asked to use its good offices to discourage Leopold from putting himself forward, and to join in a French protest at Madrid against Prim's choice, it would have been hard indeed for it to refuse. As it was, Le Sourd was sent (4 July) to put a brusque question to Thile, who gave him an even brusquer reply. 'In Berlin', said Ollivier in retrospect, 'they slammed the door in our face, and laughed at us.'[1]

The second mistake was worse. On the afternoon of 6 July Gramont closed a brief reply to a parliamentary question, a reply which asked the Chamber not to press for a debate at so delicate a moment, with this highly coloured passage:

But we do not believe that respect for a neighbouring people's rights compels us to suffer a foreign power, by putting one of its princes on the throne of Charles V, to disturb the present balance of strength in Europe to our disadvantage (Keen applause from many quarters) and to endanger the interests and the honour of France. (More applause: continuous cheering.) We sincerely hope that this event will not take place. To prevent it, we rely alike on the wisdom of the German, and the friendship of the Spanish peoples. (Friendly interruption.) Should it turn out otherwise, strong in your support, gentlemen, and in the nation's (another friendly interruption), we shall know how to do our duty without wavering or weakness. (Prolonged applause—repeated cheering. Some disturbance and protests on the left.)[2]

---

[1] *L'Empire libéral*, XIV, 35. It is to be remembered that this volume of Ollivier's apologia did not appear (at Paris) till 1909.

[2] Corps Législatif, 6 July 1870; *Journal Officiel de l'Empire Français*, 7 July, p. 1189, c. 2.

The delight with which the Assembly received this statement was so great that the sitting had to be suspended for a while; and Ollivier, who had helped to draft it, defended it to the end of his days as an excellent declaration. In fact it was, though popular, disastrous. Not only was its tone objectionable, with its deliberately invidious distinction of Prussia, as near a neighbour as Spain, as a 'foreign power' instead of a 'neighbouring people'; not only was Gramont moving ahead of the evidence available to him, and contradicting the formal denials of Thile, when he accused Prussia of having engineered the plot. His closing words clearly threatened war if his demands were not met. They were fatal. If the further ineptitudes of Gramont's and Napoleon's diplomacy had not a few days later plunged France into war, there would still have been this speech to explain; and as Bismarck more than once remarked in the ensuing week, he was ready to demand an explanation of it so humiliating that France could be relied on to fight instead.

Bismarck, half a day's journey from his capital, had not so far taken a prominent part; though as early as 29 June a telegram from Salazar, with whom he had remained in constant touch, warned him that things were coming to a head. Advantage of his absence was taken by Gramont, who knew that William I, though slow and sometimes obstinate, lacked his chancellor's determination. At the start of the crisis, on the afternoon of 4 July, Gramont and Ollivier saw Werther the Prussian ambassador in Paris—an honest diplomat, ignorant of the inside history of the candidature—and persuaded him to carry to Ems, whither he had long intended to travel on the next night but one, news of the extremely painful impression made on the French government by Leopold's acceptance. They appealed, through Werther, to William's good nature and love of peace, and made it plain that they hoped William would forbid Leopold to go on. Werther, who reached Ems early on 6 July, rather toned down what they had said to him, but at least made clear to the king the tenseness of official nerves in Paris and the widespread talk there of war.

William was sensibly impressed; and that same afternoon—ironically enough, the afternoon of Gramont's irretrievable speech—he wrote to Karl Anton. The king warned his cousin of the degree of French excitement—he enclosed a copy of Werther's report to himself—and put forward various suggestions for appeasement. Leopold, meanwhile, had vanished. Much ink has been wasted on attempts to account for his movements; there seems little doubt that his family told the truth—that he had gone for a walking tour in a remote part of the Austrian Alps, leaving no address, and did not happen to look at a newspaper until 13 July, when of course he left at once for home. So far as he knew when he started on the 1st, his fate would not be decided till October; and he had had recent strain enough to deserve a holiday.

For the greater part of the next week William, worried and confused, tried to follow a policy of his own that would succeed in persuading his cousins to withdraw Leopold's name without any sacrifice of the honour of Hohenzollern, either through bad faith to Spain or through an appearance of unseemly concession to the threats of France. Gramont's speech much annoyed him, but Werther's account of the mood in Paris convinced him that there was genuine danger of a war, which he did not himself want to provoke. The junior diplomat Abeken, whom the chancellor had posted with him, constantly urged on him, at Bismarck's distant dictation, an attitude of firmness and a policy of no concessions; but his wife, with whom he was in daily correspondence and who sometimes came over to visit him, urged on him with no less weight the importance of preserving peace. His court officials were most of them more or less bellicose, but he was exposed on the other hand to the good manners and the adroit persuasiveness of Benedetti, who reached Ems late on 8 July—journeying at his own suggestion—with the task of coaxing William into advising Leopold to withdraw, if he could not get him to order the prince to do so.

Other forces were at work in the interests of peace. William himself suggested to Bismarck that an appeal might be made to the good offices of some friendly power, on the lines laid down in the Treaty of Paris; the speed with which Bismarck advised against this helps to show how determined he was to leave the French to fall into the pit they were digging for themselves. Gramont had already appealed to other powers. The tsar disapproved of Leopold's acceptance, but was not inclined to protest at it; he had had a friendly interview with his uncle King William at Ems at the beginning of June, at which nothing seems to have been said of the candidature, and though he thought that Hohenzollern pretensions went rather farther than was courteous to France, it was not at that time a Russian interest to enhance French power against Prussian, and he took no action. Austria did not take any effective measures for the support of either side. Francis Joseph's ambassador in Paris could see too clearly how some of the ruling circles there had determined to force a war on Prussia. As early as 6 July he had found the empress 'strongly in favour of war' and 'ten years younger at the prospect of a political victory or a war'.[1] Beust counselled moderation to Gramont, and sent an envoy specially from Brussels to urge it on him and on Napoleon; but both refused him an interview until too late. In England Gladstone's cabinet was at sixes and sevens over its Irish land policy—a subject that is now known to have come near to destroying it—and so much occupied with domestic matters that it only noticed with reluctance what was happening across the Channel.

For in France from the first the militarists had seized the initiative. Fortified by the almost unanimous support of the press, they urged on the emperor all the advantages of an immediate war. Every year that

[1] Metternich to Beust, 8 July 1870 (from *English Historical Review*, vol. XXXVIII, pp. 92–3).

passed saw Germany's population rise in relation to France's; every year that passed saw the states of Germany draw closer together in military alliance. Temporarily the French army had the advantage in equipment, for the Chassepot was a better rifle than the needle-gun, and devastating results were expected from a new and fearsome weapon, the *mitrailleuse*, ancestress of the machine guns that were to dominate the battlefields of 1918 (cf. ch. XII, p. 307). The problem that was raised by this apparent superiority was grave. Every reasonable man and woman, in France and Germany alike, would have agreed in 1870 that war, considered by itself, was an evil. Yet a plausible, self-consistent case could be put forward to show that there were worse things than war, that one of those worse things would be the eclipse of French culture by Prussian efficiency, that Bismarck's Prussia had shown by its underhand arrangements with Spain that it was working for such an eclipse, and that therefore it would be treacherous folly for any French statesman to fail to grasp the opportunity which these arrangements had placed in his hand to make use against Prussia of France's temporary and probably transient military predominance. Moreover, not all the spokesmen of militarism in France could at this time be described as reasonable. The 'patriot' sheets urged immediate mobilisation, preparatory to a declaration of war; and though the soldiers did not press matters quite so fast to a conclusion, they took a number of precautionary measures. These did not fail to attract the attention of the north German embassy at Paris, and reports of them started as early as 9 July, when Benedetti's mission had hardly begun.

On the Prussian side there was no need for military precautions. Thile wired to Abeken on the evening of the tenth that an officer 'assured me that on the General Staff *everything is ready*' ('*versicherte mir, dass auf dem Generalstabe* Alles bereit sei'). Moltke and Roon were enjoying a few days at their country houses, resting in the knowledge that every step worth taking—yet—had been taken already. Bismarck of course was much more busy. Not only was he conducting the critical work of his Foreign Office from Varzin, and carrying on constant exchanges by telegram with the king; he was also supervising a campaign of vitriolic intensity in the Prussian newspapers, whose denunciations of France and all things French were matched for venom and ill temper only by the simultaneous onslaughts in the Parisian journals on Prussia and all things Prussian. He was not fully informed, nor promptly, of all the steps that his monarch was taking in daily interviews with Benedetti and in communications by messenger with Karl Anton; but he knew enough to realise that the decisive moment was approaching, when either French or Hohenzollern patience would give way. He left Varzin on 12 July for Ems—a journey necessarily made through Berlin.

He reached the capital that evening. On the way from the station his carriage crossed Gorchakov's; the two chancellors shook hands and exchanged a few amiable words. Gorchakov, who was on holiday, retired from the scene. Bismarck went on to his office—and was rudely shaken by what he found there: a telegram from Abeken which told him that Leopold had withdrawn. Other messages with it explained that the with-drawal had been secured, in part at least, by pressure from William on Karl Anton, that William was contemplating announcing it himself to Benedetti, and that feeling in Paris was if possible even more feverishly anti-Prussian than in the previous days. Bismarck cancelled his onward journey, and stayed in Berlin to contemplate how French diplomacy had achieved a resounding success, one that the aged Guizot called the most splendid of his lifetime.

The tactic of working on William in Bismarck's absence had been superb. William, without telling—perhaps without daring to tell—Bismarck what he proposed, had sent Colonel Strantz of the General Staff to Karl Anton, charged with messages that have never been published but of which the purport was made clear by Karl Anton's actions. Moreover, Napoleon had privately arranged with the Spanish ambassador in Paris to send Karl Anton another envoy likely, for family reasons, to be listened to: Strat, the agent in Paris of Karl Anton's son Karl, prince of Roumania. Strat was not only charged with a plea to the old prince to preserve peace by making his son Leopold withdraw his name, but also brought an implied threat, that if he did not, his son Karl's tenure of the throne of Bucharest would be abbreviated by French intrigue. Strat and Strantz both arrived late on 11 July, and talked to Karl Anton far into the night. Ambition for Leopold struggled in the old man's mind with ambition for Karl; a sense of duty to the head of his house with a sense of honour that made him reluctant to withdraw a word once given. In the morning, Karl and duty won; he sent a telegram to Prim, with a copy to the Spanish ambassador in Paris (neither in cipher), renouncing in Leopold's name any claim to the throne of Spain. William was also told, and received the news with simple delight that a wearisome difficulty had been overcome.

The reaction in Paris was different. Of course the renunciation was welcomed; but French opinion was by now so excited that Karl Anton's telegram by itself did not seem enough. Could the father's word even be regarded as binding on the son? Everyone remembered, or was at once reminded, that only six years before another German prince, an Augusten-burg claiming the throne of Denmark, had refused to abide by his father's renunciation of it on his behalf; the adventurous journey, as worthy of light opera as of high politics, by which Leopold's own brother had picked his way across enemy territory to his Roumanian crown was even fresher in memory. More weight attached to the diplomatic argument that France had received an insult from Prussia, as well as Spain, through the form in which the candidature had been sprung on her suddenly and secretly, although her diplomats had never left any doubt in the mind of anyone who had consulted them that France would never agree to a German king of Spain.

This diplomatic argument was no doubt uppermost in the minds of Gramont and Ollivier when in the early afternoon of 12 July they together saw Werther, who had returned to Paris; though they cannot have forgotten that their own government's tenure was precarious, for the chambers were full of ambitious men ready to pounce on them if they did not present a brutally firm attitude to Prussia. Gramont had only heard of the renunciation a couple of hours before—the post-office authorities sent him a copy of Karl Anton's telegram at the same time as they delivered it to the Spanish ambassador, who called to inform Gramont of it at the beginning of the interview with Werther; Gramont cannot have been acting on mature reflection or with the advice of his emperor. He proposed to Werther that the incident should be closed by a letter of apology to Napoleon III from William I, in which the Prussian king should say that he was sorry for the trouble his cousins had caused and that he was animated by feelings of respectful friendship for France. Werther ruined his own career by undertaking to put this request before his monarch; but the making of it unsettled more than an elderly gentleman's standing in the Prussian diplomatic service. By insisting on getting something more than the renunciation out of Prussia, Gramont brought on war.

Though he acted at first on impulse, carrying with him by personal and social force the agreement of Ollivier—such a provincial lawyer was not inclined to argue with a duke in this atmosphere of crisis and peril— Gramont went out that evening to the palace of St Cloud to report what he had done to Napoleon. He carried into the calm of the suburbs the passions that agitated the centre of Paris, and seems to have had no trouble in convincing the emperor that he had done right. Indeed, the two of them, under Eugénie's influence, decided that a further and equally wounding request should be made of the king of Prussia. At seven o'clock Gramont telegraphed to Benedetti to secure from William an assurance that his permission, as head of the Hohenzollern family, would never again be given to Leopold to put himself forward for the Spanish throne. Gramont renewed this order, in different words, at midnight; but omitted in either telegram to mention to Benedetti his conversation with Werther in the afternoon. He did, however, impress on the ambassador the need for an answer quickly, in order to appease the violence of Parisian feeling. These telegrams, which Ollivier called 'the crazy improvisation [*la folle improvisation*] of St Cloud', were decisive: they destroyed the second empire. Foolish as they were, it took a day for them to achieve their effect: Wednesday, 13 July 1870.

At eight that morning William set out for his usual two hours' constitutional in the park at Ems; a walk interrupted by several exchanges with Benedetti through an aide-de-camp, at the end of which the ambassador managed to place himself in the king's path. After a few minutes' talk about the renunciation, of which both had just seen an account in the local newspaper, Benedetti pressed on the king the need for a promise never to let Leopold's name come up again. He did not manage his business as dexterously as usual; William, surprised at the request and rather offended at the urgency of the Corsican's tone, said emphatically that he could never make such a promise, raised his hat, and walked on.

Later in the day he let Benedetti know, through an aide, that he had now heard in writing of the renunciation (Strantz had got back to Ems at midday), and that he approved of it; but to the ambassador's almost frantic appeal for a further interview he returned, in the evening, a firm refusal. This refusal was certainly motivated by the receipt, in the late afternoon, of Werther's dispatch which gave Gramont's demand for a letter of apology: a demand which the king not unnaturally found impertinent, and which, though wrongly, he imagined Benedetti was also charged to put before him.

It is to be noted that Benedetti had not yet received this snub when, soon after luncheon, Abeken wrote the celebrated telegram to Bismarck in which he gave an account, largely in the king's words, of what had happened in the park that morning. This telegram[1] put Benedetti's proposal and William's dealings with him in a rather sterner light than the facts warranted. A possible explanation of its tone might lie in something as simple as the summer afternoon climate of Ems, which can be almost intolerably stuffy. It included a rather unusual final paragraph, giving Bismarck authority to reveal the incident to the press as well as to the Prussian embassies if he so wished.

Bismarck had spent a bad night and a tantalising day in Berlin, without reliable news of how the renunciation had been received at Paris. At about four in the afternoon he saw Lord Augustus Loftus, the slow and solemn British ambassador, to whom he made no secret of his hatred of the French; he went so far as to compare Napoleon's government to a 'band of robbers', in the justified hope that Loftus would repeat the wounding phrase later that day and so help sting the French beyond endurance. For there is no doubt that after hearing of Leopold's withdrawal Bismarck was determined to seize the opportunity of precipitating a war, preferably so that France appeared the aggressor. He hoped that French pride and French folly would find the withdrawal insufficient, and make some fresh demand that would make war certain. Failing that, he was ready to take Prussia over to the offensive, and demand an explanation of Gramont's speech—that fatal speech of a week before—which would achieve the result that by now he ardently desired. He said almost as much to Loftus;

---

[1] Enciphered by 3.10 p.m.; dispatched 3.50 p.m.; received at Berlin 6.09 p.m. Text in Lord, *Origins of the War of 1870*, pp. 220–1; translation in (for example) C. Grant Robertson, *Bismarck* (London, 1918), pp. 496–7.

the rest can be inferred from the telegrams he wrote in the following hours, and from the delight with which he used to recount in later years how, that evening, he had bamboozled the French into seeming to bring on the war for which he now longed.

There has never been any secret about Bismarck's desire for war at the end; he was fond of retelling its outbreak as the great triumph of his life. Whether he had desired war all along is not so certain, and his defenders from that charge must make what play they can with his previous retirement to Varzin when he knew the crisis was near explosion point, and his subsequent conduct as the arbiter of European peace. His forcing on of the Hohenzollern candidature in spite of France's known susceptibilities, and his attitude in the closing stages of the crisis, create a strong presumption that war had never been far from his mind; though only an uncannily keen eye for the fleeting opportunity enabled him to secure its outbreak.

Roon and Moltke dined with him that evening. He always used to say that they arrived in low spirits, but in fact the three of them were in good enough heart to telegraph to the king suggesting that an ultimatum be sent to France demanding that she account for her conduct. Meanwhile Abeken's message describing the morning's incidents at Ems was being deciphered. At first Bismarck and his guests were much depressed by it; but they saw possibilities in the permission to publish. Bismarck rapidly drew up a revised draft of the message, much shorter and very much ruder; his companions were delighted with it; and within a couple of hours it was being distributed, free, on the streets of Berlin.[1] It was also telegraphed to the north German representatives at most of the European capitals except Paris.

It reached Paris soon enough. The condensed version made it appear that Benedetti had discourteously pressed an unreasonable demand on William, and had, with equally decided discourtesy, been rebuffed.

Bismarck's condensation has always popularly been taken as the efficient cause of the Franco-Prussian war; but that is only partly true. It provided indeed the necessary state of mind among the inhabitants of each country for making the war popular; the French and the Prussians each felt that they had received an intolerable insult and that satisfaction for it must be sought in arms. But neither France nor Prussia was a democracy, and it is necessary to trace briefly the steps by which the rulers of each hurried what had started as a diplomatic incident to the end that diplomacy is popularly supposed to avert.

The French cabinet spent the afternoon of 14 July in session at the Tuileries, in Napoleon's presence, and arrived at two decisions: to mobi-

[1] Text in Lord, *op. cit.* pp. 231–2; translation in (for example) Grant Robertson, *loc. cit.* The original condensation, in Bismarck's hand, on the decipher from Ems can be seen in PRO:GFM 21/47.

lise the army reserves, and to appeal to a congress of the powers. It was not until after this meeting that the unhappy Werther was able to see Gramont and explain that he had been instructed to go on leave at once. He so managed his explanation as to make it clear that the Prussian government had disavowed him: this incident heightened Gramont's impression that Prussia was going to stick at nothing. In the evening, among the dense crowds on the boulevards shouting for war as fiercely as the crowds had shouted in Berlin the night before, ministers appreciated that their two decisions were self-contradictory; and they met again at St Cloud after dinner. Napoleon's incapacity to make up his mind continued to dog and depress him, but plenty of people were now ready to make it up for him: above all his wife, who attended the meeting, and passionately urged war. Among many items of bad news, the worst was that Bismarck's version of the Ems telegram was being circulated by Prussian legations abroad. It seemed clear to the French cabinet that Prussia was intent on forcing a war on France: they therefore decided that the country's safety demanded an immediate mobilisation, and that it was best to press ahead and seize such military advantages as could be culled from rapid action. The Minister of War, Lebœuf, assured them that the army was at the peak of preparedness; Gramont practically shouted the emperor down when Napoleon glanced at the idea of a congress. (Mere mention of the word to him by Vitzthum next evening 'threw the duke into an indescribable rage'.[1]) War was determined on, and next morning a final cabinet met to settle details. Napoleon remarked a few days later to an English friend: 'France has slipped out of my hand. I cannot rule unless I lead. . .I have no choice but to advance at the head of a public opinion which I can neither stem nor check'[2]—a strange echo of the famous utterance, once attributed to Ledru-Rollin, in the troubles of 1848–9.[3]

Benedetti, who had travelled overnight from Ems, saw Gramont and Ollivier just after this cabinet on the morning of the 15th; he gave his account of what had actually passed on the promenade at Ems, and may have mentioned how the king had shaken his hand as he left Ems station, murmuring 'Au revoir à Berlin';[4] his report left the two ministers un-shaken in their belief that Prussia desired war. (Benedetti's own accounts stop with his departure from Ems.)

On Friday afternoon, 15 July, Ollivier and Gramont presented to parliament their request for money to cover mobilisation costs, couched in such terms as to amount to a declaration of war. Ollivier carried the lower house with him by the overwhelming majority of 245 votes to ten.

---

[1] Note by Vitzthum, probably in 1873, quoted in Oncken, *Rheinpolitik Napoleons*, vol. III, p. 443.

[2] To F. C. Lawley, *Daily Telegraph*, 25 July 1870.

[3] 'I am their leader, I have to follow them.'   [4] Acton MS. 4928, f. 180.

Only Thiers and Favre made effective speeches in opposition; Gambetta spoke with them, but voted for war. A few hours later William, who had spent the day travelling to Berlin, took his own decision to mobilise, after an hour's talk with Bismarck in the train and ten minutes' consideration of inaccurate news from Paris in a crowded waiting-room of the Potsdam station; and passed through dense and cheering crowds to his palace. The formal French declaration of war reached Berlin four days later (19 July 1870).

The only serious attempt by a neutral to avert the war, Granville's appeal to France and Prussia to have recourse to the friendly offices of England, was made too late—late on 14 July—to have the least chance of success: events had moved too fast for any serious notice of it to be taken by either side. Moreover, the British cabinet had been consistently ill-informed; as Acton put it in a note, cruel but true, 'their exhortations, tainted with ignorance of the central transactions of the last five months and not penetrating to the marrow of affairs, carried neither authority nor conviction'.[1]

The immediate origins of the war of 1870 may be traced to short temper and excitement on the part of the peoples and the statesmen of both belligerent nations: insensate bellowings for war in both capitals; the recklessness of Gramont, pitted against the calculation of Bismarck; the protracted irresolution of Napoleon III, and the hasty irresolution of William I.

The course of the war is summarised in another chapter (ch. XII, pp. 325–7). This one may conclude by touching on some of the political events which accompanied the military ones, and indeed were often dictated by them. It was fear of France, for instance, that originally moved the states south of the Main to enter the war on Prussia's side: their governments and peoples felt alike, with an alarm that had sound foundations in memories of the first French empire but was needless viewing the inefficient mobilisation of the second, that French armies would pour across the Rhine and that any decisive battle would be fought on its eastern bank. Prudence seemed to dictate compliance with the legal obligation under which the states lay, under the once secret treaties of August 1866, to put their armies under Prussian command if Prussia were attacked by France; and no patriotic German doubted that she had been.

Napoleon, having failed to bring his allies to the sticking point, paid the penalty. Fear of Russia, whence clear indications were given that Austrian intervention would invite attack—Russia had promised as much to Prussia as far back as March 1868—sufficed to keep Austria-Hungary neutral. Personal assurances of high respect continued to pass between Francis Joseph and Napoleon, but not a cartridge came from Vienna to help the French. Once more France requested Italian aid; once more

[1] Acton MS. 5519.

Italy named Rome for capital as the price; once more Napoleon refused to pay. By the time the war had gone on for a month it was clear that a French army, even under a Bonaparte commander, was not invincible; and France fought on as she had begun, alone.

England, suspicious for a decade, was especially alienated by the publication of the Benedetti project (see p. 580 above). Under pressure from England, France agreed—late, and making difficulties—to an extra treaty reinforcing the neutrality of Belgium: a treaty to which Prussia gave immediate assent, for the Prussian general staff knew that it would not need to send troops across Belgian territory to bring Napoleon down.

He surrendered at the beginning of September, and his empire fell with him. The temporal power of the pope survived the Second Empire by sixteen days; on 20 September 1870 Italian troops entered Rome.

The regime which succeeded Napoleon in France would have been ready to conclude peace at once, had Bismarck's terms not demanded such harsh retribution for a war for which the Government of National Defence felt it was not responsible. Bismarck insisted, on military advice, on the cession of territory on the eastern frontier of France, which had been in French hands for more than a century; the cession was not one that the new French government felt it could honourably make until it had tried its fortunes in the field. Long afterwards, Bismarck sometimes spoke of the annexation of Alsace and northern Lorraine, which in Woodrow Wilson's words 'unsettled the peace of the world for fifty years', as if he had always disapproved of it. He might have been able to prevent it, but did not wish to do so. He did not merely shelter, at the time, behind arguments that a German frontier on the Vosges was strategically indispensable, or that his elderly and obstinate monarch insisted on some tangible spoils of victory. He devoted all his outstanding diplomatic talent to securing this annexation, and succeeded (preliminaries of Versailles, 26 February, and Treaty of Frankfurt, 10 May 1871). Gladstone worked with righteous but ineffective indignation to arrange a European protest against this proposal, and had to satisfy himself with securing a reduction of the large cash indemnity demanded of beaten France.

Meanwhile Bismarck had been busy in two other fields as well. The Russian denunciation of the clauses in the Treaty of Paris which forbade a Russian Black Sea fleet is discussed elsewhere (see vol. XI, ch. on International Relations). A final word needs to be said here of the settlement of the German question by the establishment of the German second empire.

Military necessity was its mainspring: in July and August, faced as they thought with imminent danger from France, the south German states turned to Prussia for protection; and in the autumn, when Prussian military genius had secured victory after victory, they continued to turn to Prussia from a no less human desire, having found themselves on the winning side, to stay there.

Bismarck had felt for many years that a spring tide of popular feeling in Germany would be needed to secure German unity under Prussia; he saw and seized the opportunity that victory provided. But he knew the kind of unity he wanted, and took great care not to let popular feeling get out of hand. Apart from the one fatal error of excess on France's eastern frontier, he limited the territory of the new state to what Prussia could conveniently digest; he settled, in fact, for a *kleindeutsch* (small German) state, and never desired to bring into it either Austria itself or any of the millions of Germans in the Austro-Hungarian or Russian empires.

Moreover, Bismarck limited the newly made Germany constitutionally as well as territorially. At Versailles, where the Prussian headquarters were by then established, he worked in the autumn of 1870 with the representatives of Baden, Bavaria, Hesse and Württemberg—separately, not in conference—on the framework of a German empire. The existing constitution of the North German Confederation was used, and the changes were for the most part verbal—even the extensive concessions that appeared to be made to Bavaria either were made on matters of no real importance, or never in later practice left the plane of formality. It was still possible for Prussia, alone, to forbid any constitutional change. The administration was still strong *vis-à-vis* the parliament, and the federal authority *vis-à-vis* the component states; the armed services were still directly under the monarch, and virtually not subject at all to parliamentary control; the chief of the civil executive, the imperial chancellor (*Reichskanzler*)—Bismarck himself, of course—was still 'responsible' (*verantwortlich*), and with a pregnant full stop the new constitution like the old did not say to whom. No concessions to the public were made, save in the creation of a 'Germany'.

Bismarck succeeded perfectly; but the final struggle was painful. It centred round the person and title of the monarch. William I, a patriotic Prussian all through, born in a royal house and thoroughly used to being a king, did not want to be an emperor, least of all with the title of 'German Emperor' (*Deutscher Kaiser*), and not 'Emperor of Germany' (*Kaiser von Deutschland*), which Bismarck insisted he should take—both because it had a more popular ring, and because it did not imply territorial sovereignty, and so spared the feelings of the subordinate rulers. As usual, William gave way to Bismarck in the end; but it called for one more effort of Bismarckian industry and intrigue to get for him the necessary letter of invitation from the senior of the other German ruling houses, the Wittelsbach king of Bavaria. A more popular form of invitation would have been abhorrent to Bismarck and to all the rulers concerned. Ludwig II, who was only 25, despised the Hohenzollerns as parvenus, and had no desire to place himself under a Hohenzollern emperor. But he was not much interested in politics: architecture and music—he was Wagner's patron—were his two avowable passions, and he was already showing signs of the madness that led him fifteen years later to suicide in the Starnberger See. He had already begun the series of gigantic castles of the romantic decadence which have made his permanent mark on his kingdom; and in the fastness of Hohenschwangau he was persuaded by his court chamberlain, Holnstein, to copy out and sign a suitable letter to William which Bismarck had drafted himself. Holnstein used two arguments on him: one political, that the new monarchy was to be elective, 'Hoh[enzollern] today, Wittelsbach tomorrow';[1] the other, more potent, material. For the rest of his life Ludwig received an additional £15,000 a year, provided by Bismarck out of the funds of Ludwig's former ally George of Hanover. This made further extravagances of castle-building feasible, and postponed for a decade Ludwig's financial catastrophe. Holnstein took 10 per cent.

In this inelegant fashion the German empire was founded. It was proclaimed on the 170th birthday of the kingdom of Prussia, 18 January 1871, at a spot which was to figure in German history again forty-eight years later: the Galerie des Glaces in the palace of Versailles.

[1] Acton MS. 5387, f. 33.

CHAPTER XXIII

NATIONAL AND SECTIONAL FORCES IN THE UNITED STATES

THE years between 1830 and 1870 were marked, in the western world, by the triumph of nationalism in three important areas—Italy (chs. IX and XXI), Germany (chs. IX and XIX) and the United States. In Italy, nationalism could not achieve its fulfilment until it overcame the obstacles of universalism—the universalism of both church and empire. In Germany, Bismarckian nationalism reached its goal by breaking down the forces of German particularism and by sacrificing the democratic values of 1848. In America, the alignment of forces was different: the ideals of nationalism and democracy were fused and the force which resisted nationalism was sectionalism within the United States. The sequence of development was also different, for nationalism seemed to gain a quick and easy triumph in America during the first three decades of the nineteenth century, and then belatedly encountered the disruptive force of sectionalism which grew in strength until the tension between the two forces culminated in the Civil War of 1861–5.

At the time when Andrew Jackson came to the American Presidency in 1829, Italy was still split into minor principalities, largely under the domination of the Habsburgs, and Germany as yet remained a loose confederation of thirty-eight autonomous states. By contrast, the triumph of nationalism in the United States already appeared, at least outwardly, to be complete. During the forty years of the republic's existence, no other country had grown so rapidly and no other people were so proud of their national growth. The population, which stood at 12,800,000 in 1830, was more than three times as great as in 1790. The area of the country had more than doubled, reaching a total of 1,754,000 square miles. The western frontier had been pushed from the Mississippi River to the Rocky Mountains, and the southern limits, which had originally lain along the Georgia–Florida boundary, now extended to the Gulf of Mexico. The union of thirteen states had increased to twenty-four.

These physical gains, moreover, had been accompanied by political developments that seemed steadily to augment the strength of the central government. For twenty-eight years political control had been in the hands of a party which was theoretically committed to the states-rights philosophy of its founder, Thomas Jefferson, but in operative terms Jefferson's followers had swung over to measures of a kind previously advocated by that arch-nationalist Alexander Hamilton. Among such measures were the acquisition (through the Louisiana Purchase in 1803) of an immense area under national rather than state authority, the waging of a nationalist war against Great Britain in 1812, the chartering of a national financial institution (the Second Bank of the United States) in 1816, the adoption of a protective tariff as a measure of economic nationalism in 1816, the construction at Federal expense of a national highway to link east and west (the Cumberland Pike, completed 1818), and the bold enunciation in 1823 of a foreign policy (the Monroe Doctrine) which claimed an entire hemisphere for national guardianship by the United States. While these strides towards nationalism were being taken by Congress and the Executive, John Marshall, as Chief Justice of the Supreme Court, was giving a strongly national character to the constitutional law of the United States by a series of decisions holding that acts of the states were void whenever they encroached upon the sphere of action assigned by the constitution to the central government; it was Marshall who declared in 1821 that 'the United States form, for many and for most important purposes, a single nation'.

In economic terms, also, the republic was becoming more genuinely a unit. In colonial times, adjoining colonies had often been quite isolated from one another, while ocean-borne trade—the only significant form of commerce—had bound them closely to their markets across the Atlantic. But the development of turnpikes, the construction of canals, and the advent of the steamboat had all contributed to the growth of a domestic commerce which created closer ties between the states and eventually overshadowed foreign trade. While this was happening, the potentialities of economic nationalism had received political recognition. Henry Clay of Kentucky had advocated an 'American System', which would encourage agriculture in the west by providing roads or other transport facilities (known as 'internal improvements') for taking crops to market, and would encourage industry in the east by means of a protective tariff. As Clay planned it, industrial areas would serve as markets for western agriculture, and the western farming regions would provide a market for eastern industry. Each would supplement the other economically and support the other politically, and a national economy would result. Although such measures of economic nationalism continued to encounter opposition for reasons which will appear presently, the fact was that a national economy was growing rapidly by 1830, supported by the banking and tariff and highway legislation mentioned in the preceding paragraph.

To modern students of nationalism, however, neither the physical growth of the United States nor the political and economic manifestations of national development will count for as much as the essential, underlying homogeneity of the American people, who were bound together by a common culture, common ideals, and common institutions. By all these criteria the Americans appeared to be very much one nation. Their religious and moral tradition was overwhelmingly Protestant; their Old

World origin still remained primarily British; and their speech, for all its regional variations, did not vary as much as did dialects within the mother country. But even when they came of diverse stocks with diverse tongues, their economic and social origin was fairly uniform, for most Americans originated from a class in the Old World that had lived by manual labour applied to cultivation of the earth. In their New World environment they still practised a large measure of self-sufficiency in their economy and held to a strong belief in the necessity and dignity of work. Personally, they were committed to ideals of individual self-reliance, and socially to ideals of equalitarianism. Finding these ideals embodied in the American political and legal system, with its broad suffrage, its easy access to education, its freehold tenure in land, and its emphasis upon equality before the law, they took immense and invidious pride in their 'institutions'. Apparently no people in the world were more patriotically devoted to their country than the Americans.

But though this nationalism seemed triumphant, there remained two serious obstacles to its continued ascendancy. One of these was the unresolved discrepancy between democracy as Jefferson had planned it and nationalism as Hamilton had planned it. Hamilton had visualised the national government as an anti-democratic device for protecting the interests of the *élite* and keeping the populace in order; while Jefferson, fearing just such a central authority, had looked to the states to resist national power and to protect democracy at the local level. So long as these philosophies prevailed, with their implication that the American people must choose between nationalism and democracy, the future of nationalism remained in doubt. A second obstacle lay in the physical, economic, and social diversities between various sections within the United States, which were potentially so strong that, if developed, they might offset the features in common which bound all the American people together, and might elevate the section rather than the nation to a supreme position as the focus of loyalty. Both of these obstacles came conspicuously into evidence during Jackson's administration and it was at that time, therefore, that the history of American nationalism entered a new phase.

In some respects Jackson himself seemed to represent southern and western sectional interests. As a slaveholder and cotton planter, he showed a Southerner's respect for the rights of the states. As a fighting Westerner, whose own life was a long, bitter struggle against a privileged social and political inner circle, he was instinctively hostile to the Federalist concept of nationalism. He won the election of 1828 by carrying every state (except Maryland) west of the Delaware and the Hudson and losing every state east of these rivers. But in other ways he was the very symbol of nationalism. As a Tennessee frontiersman he shared the devotion of the west to the Union; as hero of the battle of New Orleans he embodied national military glory; as the invader of Florida he had been the aggressive champion of American territorial growth. But despite the complexities of his position a close scrutiny of his attitude on any given question will usually show that his stand was nationalistic in substance, even when not consistent with the overt forms of nationalism. Thus, when Georgia began to remove the Indians from state lands in violation of Federal treaties with the tribes, Jackson approved, but his approbation rested upon a belief that Indian removal was sound national policy, even though being pursued through the instrumentality of the state. Similarly, when Congress voted Federal funds for the construction of a turnpike between Maysville and Lexington in Kentucky, Jackson vetoed the measure (1830), and thus gave great comfort to the advocates of states-rights; yet his action was based not so much upon opposition to Federal support for a national transportation system as upon the conviction that the Maysville project was essentially local. Other more thoroughly national projects, such as the extension of the Cumberland Pike and the building of roads in the territories, received his firm support.

The distinctive character of Jackson's nationalism, however, showed most clearly in the two major struggles of his administration—the contest over the recharter of the Bank of the United States and the conflict with South Carolina on the issue of Nullification. The first of these struggles involved the reconciliation of nationalism and democracy, the second involved the problem of nationalism and sectionalism.

The bank was a corporation chartered by the United States but owned and controlled by private stockholders. It served as the sole bank of deposit for the government, and thus was exclusively privileged to use the Federal funds. Also, it was authorised to issue notes which were acceptable in payment of government obligations, and which thus enjoyed a governmental sanction as money. It did not hold an exclusive power to issue notes, for many banks were chartered by the states with this power, and a substantial volume of the state banks' notes was in circulation. But the Bank of the United States exercised immense influence over other banks, for the large scale of its operations enabled it to accumulate the notes of any state bank and to present these notes for redemption in specie if it distrusted the policies of the bank in question. Thus the Bank of the United States held controlling authority over almost all other banks, and while the existence of such a co-ordinating power may have been desirable, the wisdom of vesting it in a privately controlled corporation was far less clear. Alexander Hamilton had deliberately chosen to create an alliance between government and the monied interests by conferring such a power upon the First Bank of the United States and this kind of alliance still persisted in the successor bank, whose charter was due to expire in 1837. The president of the bank, Nicholas Biddle of Philadelphia, a proud and somewhat overbearing aristocrat, let himself be persuaded to press for a renewal of the charter before the presidential election of 1832. Henry Clay sponsored the measure in Congress, and easily secured the passage of a bill to recharter. Thus the question came squarely before Andrew Jackson.

Without hesitation, Jackson vetoed the bill. His opposition rested partly upon a states-rights denial of the constitutional power of the central government to charter a bank, and partly upon western resentment against the stringent credit policies of the bank (though Jackson was by no means a champion of loose credit policies). But, above all, he disliked the privilege inherent in a grant of public power to private beneficiaries. He believed that the power alternately to expand and to contract credit could be used by financial manipulators to expropriate the value of the earnings of productive workers. To his mind the government ought to divorce itself from any such operations, and ought to conduct its own financial transactions with 'hard money'. Thus it would help to protect honest earnings by promoting a monetary system based upon specie and therefore safe from manipulation. In short, his opposition rested upon democratic grounds and he appealed to the democratic masses to support him. Unlike the democracy of Jefferson, his democracy was not primarily one of farmers, for it embraced all the productive classes and thus it marked a vital step in the adjustment of democratic philosophy for a republic which was already ceasing to be agrarian.

Jackson's veto precipitated the kind of political battle in which he was at his best. His adversaries first attempted to override the veto, and failing in this, united in choosing Clay as the candidate to oppose him for the Presidency in 1832. Both sides appealed strenuously to the people, and Jackson won by heavy majorities. Having beaten off the attack he now assumed the offensive at once, and instead of waiting for the bank's charter to expire he caused the Secretary of the Treasury to withdraw all Federal funds without further delay.

This destroyed the power of the bank and seemed to complete Jackson's triumph. But it soon became apparent that he had not devised any satisfactory alternative to the bank, and his only recourse was to deposit the funds in various state-chartered banks which became known as 'pet banks'. With new funds in hand and with no central bank to restrain them, the pet banks expanded their credit recklessly, departing farther and farther from the President's hard-money ideals. When Jackson, too late, attempted to curb their inflationary practices by placing the sale of public lands on a specie basis, the only result was to precipitate a panic (1837) in which most of the banks failed and the government lost its deposits. By this time, Jackson's term was over, but his successors now adopted the policy of keeping government funds in an 'independent treasury', and leaving the banks to their own devices. The result was that from this time until the Civil War the circulating medium of the country consisted primarily of miscellaneous bank-notes, issued by many different state-chartered banks and varying in the extent to which their exchange value deviated from their face value. In short, the monetary system was almost completely decentralised.

In a formal sense, Jackson's policy seemed an absolute negation of nationalism. He had denied the national power to charter a bank, and by destroying the only central banking institution in the country he left the United States for a generation without a national financial system or a national monetary supply. Yet, paradoxically, it was during the bank contest that Jackson gave to American nationalism the strength through popular support which it had previously lacked.

The very alignment of forces in the bank contest itself contributed to nationalism, for this was the first time that a public issue had been carried directly to the voters for a decision by the American people collectively. Also, Jackson's bold policy began to transform the nature of the presidential office. Jackson conceived of himself not as the chairman of an administrative organ, but as a tribune of the people; hence he used the neglected power of veto with vigour for the first time, and by appealing directly to public opinion to sustain him against Congressional opposition, he imparted to his office a function of national leadership which had previously been lacking in the American political system. The modern American Presidency, as an office of power, originated with Andrew Jackson. Moreover, the fierceness of the bank controversy fostered the development of two highly organised political parties—Democratic and Whig—and the fact that these national parties maintained local organisations in each of the states tended to nationalise American politics.

Over and above these concrete developments loomed the general fact that Jackson had begun to fuse nationalism and democracy by asserting the protection of democratic values as an objective of national policy. By his support of universal, free manhood suffrage, rotation in office, nomination of candidates by party convention rather than by Congressional caucus, and the general principle of popular rule, he, more than anyone else, established government by the people in place of government by a class of recognisable gentlemen. With a concept of national power very unlike that of the Federalists, he asserted that the 'true strength' of the general government 'consists in...making itself felt, not in its power but in its beneficence; not in its control, but in its protection'.[1] This insistence that national strength would increase more by being placed upon a democratic basis than by the sheer exercise of power freed nationalism of its Federalist stigma and brought into conjunction for the first time the twin forces of nationalism and democracy. A generation later Abraham Lincoln brought the country successfully through the crisis of

[1] Message of Andrew Jackson to Congress, 10 July 1832, in James D. Richardson (ed.), *A Compilation of the Messages and Papers of Presidents* (1900), vol. I, p. 322.

Civil War by his steadfast insistence that the maintenance of this conjunction transcended all other goals.

Thus, Jackson successfully cleared away the first of the two major obstacles to nationalism. The second major obstacle—the sectional obstacle—also came to the fore during his administration, in the form of Nullification, and Jackson dealt with it also, but not with such conclusive success.

The Nullification crisis arose from the opposition, in the South, and especially in South Carolina, to protective tariff legislation, which had first been adopted in 1816 without clear-cut sectional opposition and which had been reinforced by subsequent acts in 1824 and 1828. During the decade of the 'twenties South Carolina suffered a prolonged economic depression for which she blamed the tariff, and when relief was not forthcoming under a new tariff act in 1832 she invoked a constitutional defence which had been developed by her senator, John C. Calhoun. Calhoun, who was to rank as the great spokesman of the South and the foremost American political theorist of his generation, had worked out a defensive theory known as the doctrine of Nullification. Beginning with the generally accepted premise that the states had originally been co-parties in an agreement (the constitution) which limited the central government to certain functions, Calhoun argued that when, in the judgment of one of the states, the central government exceeded its powers, the state in question, as one of the co-parties, could restrain the agent of the co-parties (that is, the central government) by suspending or 'nullifying' the exercise of the disputed function, and could maintain this suspension until the dispute had been resolved by constitutional amendment. In short, he regarded the individual state as the final arbiter of the limits of constitutional power and denied such a role to the Supreme Court on the ground that, as a branch of the central government, it could not legitimately decide the limits of power of the government of which it was a part. He did not advocate the withdrawal of states from the Union—indeed he insisted that his corrective would prevent disunion—but his theory of the unimpaired sovereignty of the states provided a basis for the later doctrine of secession.

South Carolina brought Calhoun's doctrine into play by calling a state convention which in 1832 adopted an Ordinance of Nullification to suspend the collection of duties. Jackson responded by warning the people of South Carolina in a solemn address that 'The laws of the United States must be executed', and that 'Disunion by armed force is treason', and he secured the adoption of a Force Act, giving him authority to use the army and the navy to enforce the laws. Conflict appeared imminent, but the crisis was averted. The nullifiers agreed to suspend their ordinance pending the reconsideration of the tariff by Congress; Congress promptly adopted a measure, introduced by Clay, for the gradual reduction of duties; South Carolina thereupon repealed her ordinance, and though she defiantly 'nullified' the Force Act, the controversy subsided. Carolina claimed a victory, but when Jackson left the Presidency in 1837 he remained, in the eyes of the American people, a triumphant champion of the Union.

Jackson owed his success in dealing with Nullification partly to the firmness of his own Unionism and partly to the prompt redress of Carolina's grievances. He deferred the sectional crisis until a time when the Union would be better able to meet it, and he provided an encouraging example for later Unionists. But the compromise of 1833 did not go to the roots of sectional unrest, and the only reason that Jackson was able to control the situation was because other Southern states, although sharing Carolina's opposition to the tariff, were not prepared to support her extreme measures. In short, sectional solidarity had not yet developed.

In fact, the sectional pattern was so complex that its background requires some examination. As early as the seventeenth century, conspicuous contrasts had developed between the colonies from Pennsylvania northward and those from Maryland southward. The Southern colonies were physically distinctive in their rich soil, their warm climate with its long growing season, and their low coastal plain which was penetrated by tidal rivers. All of these factors proved favourable to an economy of staple crops (tobacco in Virginia and Maryland, rice and indigo in Carolina), and these crops, in turn, were conducive to the development of the plantation as the unit of production and to the utilisation of negro slaves as labour. Such an economy also entailed a large export trade and a reliance upon overseas markets both as an outlet for crops and as a source of supplies. Plantation slavery produced a patriarchal type of society, with a markedly conservative temper and with a well-articulated stratification of social classes. Also, the rather formal Anglicanism of the planters did not interfere with a certain hedonism in their way of life.

The New England and middle Atlantic colonies, on the other hand, lacked the physical conditions which would support staple crops, and they adopted a basic economy of subsistence farming, but the middle colonies escaped the restrictions of pure subsistence by producing grain for the southern and West Indian markets, while New England developed extensive fisheries and ocean-borne commerce. Where the sources of wealth were largely commercial, the merchant, rather than the planter, became the dominant social figure, and free workers rather than slaves were needed in the labour force. The chronic shortage of export products with which to buy imports prompted the Northern colonies to practise the crafts and to diversify their production. Extremes of wealth were less conspicuous than in the South and social demarcations were less sharp. Society was more competitive and more responsive to change. The Puritanism of New England and the Quaker influence in Pennsylvania produced a stronger emphasis upon piety in everyday life.

These striking contrasts between North and South were clearly recognised at the time, and they were the basis for a certain amount of antagonism. Therefore some later historians have depicted the two sections as seats of irreconcilable civilisations, destined from the beginning to clash in inevitable war.[1] Yet, with full allowance for the reality of this cleavage, there was another sectional dualism in America which at times seemed more basic than the North/South dichotomy. This was the antagonism between older, more or less densely populated, economically mature, socially stratified settlements along the coast, on the one hand, and the newer, sparsely populated, economically undeveloped, socially undifferentiated settlements in the interior, on the other. In sectional terms, these differences tended to polarise on an East-versus-West or seaboard-versus-frontier axis. The position of the West as a region of insufficient capital, prone to fall into a debtor status and susceptible to economic exploitation, led to a chronic situation of conflict beginning as early as Bacon's Rebellion in Virginia in 1676 and continuing as late as the Populist movement of the 1890's. Frequently this East/West cleavage seemed to overshadow the North/South dualism, and to become the primary sectional demarcation. Throughout the eighteenth and early nineteenth centuries the physically isolated, politically under-represented, economically debt-ridden subsistence farmers in the Shenandoah valley of Virginia and the up-country of Carolina seemed to have far more in common with the similarly circumstanced settlers in the interior of Massachusetts and the backwoods of Pennsylvania than either group had with the grandees of the coastal area—whether merchant princes in Boston or planter aristocrats along the James and the Ashley.

At the beginning of the nineteenth century, the Western districts had not only developed points of contrast with and antagonism to the Eastern areas; they had also given promise of growing until they would overwhelm the distinctively Northern and Southern coastal districts. Neither the rice and tobacco culture of the Southern tidewater areas nor the maritime commerce of the Northern coastal strip seemed likely to penetrate very far into the interior, and it appeared that all of the frontier settlements, which were pushing out so rapidly toward the west, would remain, north and south alike, regions of subsistence agriculture, populated by an increasing body of small farmers whose rapid growth would confine both the mercantile society of the northern coast and the plantation society of the southern coast within petty local enclaves. The geographical unity of the Mississippi valley, and the economic ties provided by the river system would enhance the homogeneity of the West and would further promote the solidarity of the agrarian interest. This was, in a sense, what

[1] For example, Edward Channing, *A History of the United States* (New York, 1925), vol. vi, pp. 3–4; James Truslow Adams, *The Epic of America* (Boston, 1931), pp. 250–5.

Thomas Jefferson had foreseen as the basis of American democracy, and his dream had seemed in the process of fulfilment when, in 1804, the interior districts overthrew Federalist control in every north-eastern state except Connecticut, and when the non-slaveholding farmers of the up-country districts in the South challenged the political power of the planters and even questioned the institution of slavery within their own states. In 1831 the western counties forced a serious debate on slavery in the Virginia legislature.

Thus the deepening division between East and West became, for a time, the major sectional cleavage. But at its very height, when it seemed destined to overshadow and localise the distinctions between North and South, a double transformation began to take place—a transformation in both North and South—which altered the factors of sectional alignment and re-established the primacy of the dualism between North and South. This transformation, occurring over a period of several decades, had begun prior to Jackson's presidency but had not developed far enough to make the sectional crisis of 1832 acute. Between 1830 and 1860, however, its further development made the problem of harmony between the sections increasingly difficult.

In the North, this transformation resulted from the rapid growth of industry and the development of a vast domestic market. Historically, the north-east, with its diversified economy, had long engaged in a limited amount of handicraft production. But the extensive development of industry had been inhibited by the free influx of British goods, by the absorption of New England's capital in oceanic trade, and most of all by the lack of a sizeable market—a lack resulting both from the physical inaccessibility of many districts, especially in the west, and from the inability of subsistence farmers to purchase goods. During the period of Jefferson's embargo and the war of 1812, however, the paralysis of the merchant marine forced north-eastern capitalists to seek new forms of enterprise, and at the same time the stoppage of imports from Britain created a lively demand for native manufactures. These circumstances hastened the growth of industry, but the determining factor in its long-term development was the revolution in transportation which made the American domestic market the largest unobstructed field of commerce in the world. A whole series of developments—the successful operation of steamboats after 1807, the adaptation of the steamboat to Mississippi River traffic in 1817, the Federally financed construction of the Cumberland Pike across the Alleghenies in 1818, the state-financed digging of the Erie Canal to link the Great Lakes with New York in 1825, and the privately financed development of railroads after 1828—all made it possible to create an exchange economy in which industrial north and agricultural west would reciprocally serve as markets and as sources of supply, each for the other. The development of this East/West alliance was the basis of Clay's American System as early as 1824 and of Abraham Lincoln's support of both the free homestead policy and the protective tariff as late as 1860. So effectively did the new, artificial ties of turnpike, canal, and railroad do their work, that the north-west was economically drawn almost entirely away from her natural, geographical orientation toward the mouth of the Mississippi and was linked instead to the north-east. In 1852 the volume of grain which passed eastward from the Mississippi valley through Buffalo to eastern ports was two-and-a-half times as great as that which went down the river to New Orleans. The upper valley and the north-eastern states had subordinated their differences, by 1860, to so great an extent that in the sectional crisis they constituted practically a single North.

While this economic revolution was in progress in the North, a parallel revolution, which followed upon Eli Whitney's invention in 1793 of the cotton gin, was giving new vigour to the southern plantation economy. Whitney's invention made economically practicable the cultivation of a new staple crop, more profitable than rice or tobacco. Unlike them, cotton could be cultivated under varied soil conditions, and in large units or small. But like them, it could make profitable use of the gang labour of slaves. Hence cotton gave slavery a new lease of life; the plantation system quickly expanded out of the coastal districts and into the interior; the plain farmers of the southern uplands turned from their subsistence economy to the staple economy of cotton; and in less than five decades after Whitney's invention, cotton advanced a thousand miles across the lower south, all the way to the Brazos River bottoms of Texas, drawing slavery and the plantation with it. At the termination of this advance the new crop had become king for a South whose former internal differences were now sunk in the fact that it was 'the land of cotton'.

This newly homogeneous South presented sharper contrasts than ever before to the newly homogeneous North. As the South became committed to a plantation pattern of life and to slave labour, it placed increasing stress upon the values of social stability and conservatism, upon the maintenance of a stratified society, and upon the ideals of leisure and honour that are associated with a gentry class. (Much of the South, still remaining in a raw and boisterous frontier phase, fell absurdly short of these ideals, but all of the South accepted them to some degree as ideals.) As the North grew steadily more urban and more heavily involved in industrial enterprise, it embraced the values of 'progress' and social change, insisted upon the importance of social mobility, and upheld middle-class ideals of prudence, hard work, and practicality.

These developments not only accentuated the dissimilarities between the sections but also destroyed the equilibrium which had existed in 1790 when the two regions were roughly equal in wealth and population. This disparity itself placed the Union under severe strains, for the North naturally expected its increasing physical preponderance to be reflected by a predominant share in the political control, while the South tenaciously insisted upon the maintenance of a sectional equilibrium in government as its right under the constitution.

Clearly sectional problems were an acute reality, and yet it remains very important to distinguish between sectional dissimilarities and sectional antagonisms. Despite the deterministic assumption of many historians that sectional diversities would automatically lead to sectional conflict, history presents many instances of diverse regions that are bound together in national unity because their diversity leads to reciprocal dependence. In fact, national self-sufficiency rests upon internal diversity.[1] To explain sectional animosities, therefore, it is not enough merely to demonstrate the existence of diverse ways of life; specific issues of conflict must arise, and the more completely the division on these issues follows sectional lines, the more likely is acute sectional hostility to result.

At the time when industry and commerce were creating a new, more closely articulated North, and cotton was diminishing the former tidewater-versus-frontier divisions within the South, a number of matters of public policy arose on which North and South came, to some extent, into conflict. One of these was the question how far the Federal government should go in subsidising internal improvements. The North, in general, desired maximum support for projects which would link north-eastern industry with north-western agriculture, while the South jealously resisted a development which might nullify the natural orientation of the whole Mississippi valley southward to the port of New Orleans, and which could not effectively include South Atlantic ports because of the existence of an Appalachian mountain barrier between seaboard and interior. A second issue on which alignments were to a considerable extent sectional was that of the central bank which Jackson destroyed. The north-east, as the centre of capital, was also the centre of ownership of bank shares; in addition, its preoccupation with commerce made it aware of the advantages of a firmly controlled monetary system. Hence it tended to support the bank. The South, by contrast, with its agrarian and debtor status, responded with hostility to an institution which was operated in the creditor interest for the advantage of owners in another region.

A third issue which tended to become sectional was that of the opening to settlement of lands owned by the government. Eastern industrial interests opposed any distribution of public lands which would make such property cheap enough to draw workers away from the factory at a time when expanding industry needed a supply of labour. The South and West, with their growing commitment to agriculture, were far more ready to encourage rapid distribution of lands as a stimulus to agricultural

---

[1] This point has been well analysed by James G. Randall in 'The Civil War Restudied', *Journal of Southern History* (1940), vol. VI, pp. 441–9.

expansion. This clash of interests, which recurred constantly during the 'thirties and 'forties, led to a famous debate in the Senate in 1830 in which Robert Y. Hayne of South Carolina put forward the doctrine of Nullification and Daniel Webster of Massachusetts delivered a classic oration in defence of national union.

Still a fourth issue, full of dangerous sectional potentialities which the Nullification crisis had exposed, was that of the tariff. The North regarded a protective system as essential to the development of industry, which was vitally needed to secure the prosperity, the national self-sufficiency, and the economic independence of the republic. The South, selling its cotton on the world market, resented restrictions which prevented it from buying in the same market, and felt that it, as a section, was being forced to subsidise the economy of a rival section. Since the South could not make its purchases abroad, it was forced to sell twice—first to sell its cotton for foreign credits, and then to sell its foreign credits in the northern money market. Constant losses through this process embittered the South against the tariff.

An important factor of safety, however, operated to prevent sectional tension from reaching a breaking-point on any of these issues. This factor was the absence of complete sectional unity on any one of the questions which were being contested. True, the South opposed a restrictive land policy and internal improvements, but some planters already perceived that cheap land would give small farmers an advantage over slaveholders in the race to occupy new areas, and backwoods Alabama and Mississippi were as eager as backwoods Indiana and Illinois for Federal aid in overcoming their frontier isolation. Conversely, while the North as a whole favoured these policies, Northern farmers refused to be guided by Northern industrialists on the land question, and a city like Boston resisted measures which were designed to aid her commercial rivals like New York and Philadelphia.

It was the same with the bank and the tariff. Working-class elements in New York and Pennsylvania went against their section to oppose the bank, while mercantile interests in Charleston went against theirs to support it. Though Northern industry demanded a protected market, Yankee merchants fought a vigorous rear-guard action to safeguard their ocean-borne trade; though Southern cotton demanded a free market, ambitious men in the South dreamed of a Southern textile industry which would need protection. As late as 1816 Calhoun had been the foremost advocate of a tariff measure and Webster had been its leading opponent. As late as 1832, South Carolina, attempting to unite the South on this issue, had found herself unsupported and alone under the banner of Nullification.

The fact that alignments on these questions did not totally coincide with geographical boundaries was of great importance in restraining the disruptive forces of sectionalism. So long as the protectionist and the free-trader, or the supporter of the bank and the advocate of hard money, lived in the same community, personal contact inhibited them from forming stereotyped or unreal images of one another, while local political leaders felt the necessity of seeking common ground for both. Sectionalism, therefore, could not assume a wholly egocentric form. But once sectional demarcation became complete, there was then no check upon the exaggeration and hostility with which men of one section might picture the other—no restraint upon the invective with which the politician might denounce those outside his district in order to woo those within it. It was the nature of sectionalism that as it became complete it would become egocentric. It had not done so on other issues, but negro slavery presented an issue on which it was to become complete.

Until the late eighteenth century, the institution of slavery had not presented sectional contrasts either legally or in terms of moral attitudes. The chattel status of the slave was established in all of the thirteen colonies which formed the original Union, and though the slave population of the Northern colonies was small, Yankee enterprise in the slave trade had been conspicuous. As for moral scruples, these were confined to the Quakers. Then, when the Enlightenment came, it brought a reaction against slavery in North and South alike. The great Virginians—Washington, Jefferson, and many others—regarded slavery as an evil, which ought to be eradicated. But the magnitude of slavery was of an entirely different order on the two sides of the Mason and Dixon line. Less than 6 per cent of the slave population in 1790 lived north of this line, while 94 per cent lived south of it. North of the line, one person in forty-nine was a slave; south of it, one in three. These proportions gave an entirely different value to slavery in the two sections both as an economic interest and as a system of social control over the negroes, many of whom were not far advanced beyond the African tribal condition.

Because of this great discrepancy, the forces working against slavery operated most unevenly. In the South, they produced acts of private manumission, state measures to abolish the African slave trade before the Federal prohibition of it went into effect in 1808, proposals to restrict the domestic trade, and support for an American Colonization Society (1817) which sought the manumission of slaves and their repatriation in Africa. In the North, by contrast, state after state, between 1774 and 1804, either abolished slavery outright, or provided for gradual abolition, so that by 1846 the last vestiges of the institution had ceased to exist north of Maryland and Delaware.

At first, the presence of contrasting groups of 'slave states' and 'free states' had seemed not to indicate any real cleavage but merely a difference in timing, for the South could not emancipate so readily because of its larger slave population. But by 1830 it became clear that the attitudes of the two sections were swinging towards opposite poles. In the South, the growth of the cotton economy sent the price of prime field-hands steadily up from $300 in 1795 to $11,00 in 1820. Consequently, slavery, which had seemed in process of becoming an anachronism, attained a new economic vitality. At the same time, episodes or threats of violence, such as the gory slave insurrections in Santo Domingo (1792), the discovery of a major insurrection plot in Charleston (1822), and the murder of fifty-five whites by a band of revolting slaves in Virginia (1831), prompted frightened Southerners to adopt a more repressive attitude. Southern masters who had previously dallied with the American Colonization Society became increasingly defensive as Northern denunciation of their institution increased. After 1830 the South wholly abandoned its earlier condemnation of slavery, and put forward America's only fully articulated defence of a status society. Thomas R. Dew, James H. Hammond, Calhoun, and others argued that chattel slavery was more humane than wage slavery, that a separate working class, destined to toil, had always been necessary as a basis of civilisation, that the negro was biologically inferior and unfit for freedom, and that slavery was ordained of God. In short, as Calhoun affirmed, slavery was not an evil, but 'a good, sir, a positive good'.[1]

If this view had been confined to slaveholders, it could not have controlled Southern policy, for two-thirds of the Southern whites were of families that held no slaves at all, and only one-sixth were of families that held more than five slaves (1850). But though the great majority of free people in the South had no economic stake in slavery, they accepted the pro-slavery argument with remarkable unanimity. As members of the dominant caste, they fully shared the slaveholders' fears of what would happen to social order and to white supremacy if the negroes should be freed. Consequently, the South united to defend slavery as an institution of social control, as well as an economic institution.

In the North, meanwhile, conditions were ripening for a militant anti-slavery movement. The North shared fully in the world-wide techno-logical change by which the labour of machines was being substituted for the labour of unskilled humans, so that slavery was rendered economi-cally obsolete, and society could, for the first time, afford to treat the use of involuntary labour as a moral and not an economic question. In the North, the powerful emotional drives of evangelical Protestantism, com-bined with the natural-rights doctrine of the equality of all men, had produced a profound and pervasive belief in the dignity of the human individual. This belief appeared, for instance, as the major theme in the writings of the foremost American thinker of the period, Ralph W. Emerson. It encouraged a faith in progress and the perfectibility of the

---

[1] Speech in the Senate, 6 February 1837. Cit. Richard K. Crallé (ed.), *Works of John C. Calhoun* (New York, 1851–67), vol. II, pp. 631–2.

individual, and this faith, in turn, stimulated a series of reform movements which became one of the most characteristic features of the age. Prison reform, dress reform, reforms in the care of the insane and of the blind, temperance reform, the adoption of universal manhood suffrage, the crusade for women's rights, the pacifist movement, and various utopian colonies, all reflected the vigour of this humanitarian drive. But slavery, with its palpable violations both of the principle of equality as taught by the Enlightenment and of the principle of human brotherhood as taught by the evangelical churches, attracted more attention from reformers than any other evil. These reformers, deeply influenced by the abolition movement in England, emulated it in demanding legislative action, and accordingly turned from their earlier programme of persuasion, with its goal of voluntary, gradual manumission, and began both to denounce the sinfulness of the slaveholder and to clamour for mandatory and immediate abolition. In 1830 William Lloyd Garrison launched his weekly, *The Liberator*, with the declaration that he did not propose 'to think or speak or write with moderation'. In 1831 Theodore Dwight Weld, an evangelist of intense fervour, began a crusade that ultimately led to the training of seventy missionaries who carried their burning denunciation of slavery throughout the North. In 1833 the American Anti-Slavery Society was established; by 1840 two thousand auxiliary societies had been organised to accommodate a membership of between 150,000 and 200,000 people.

Thus the issue of slavery, constantly intensified by the agitation of the abolitionists, provided, as did no other question, a division on which the alignment was almost wholly sectional. Thereby the slavery question opened the way for each section systematically to misunderstand and misrepresent the other. More and more the Yankee began to typify the Southerner as a sadistic, degraded slave-driver, the Southerner to typify the Yankee as a ranting, fanatical abolitionist. Around these false and lurid stereotypes, all the diverse and complex factors of sectional rivalry polarised, and thus sectionalism entered its most dangerous stage—the egocentric phase.

Even with the fullest recognition of the importance of the slavery issue, however, it is a mistake—one made by many historians—to regard the whole period from 1830 to 1860 as a mere extended prologue to the Civil War. From some accounts, one might suppose the American people were exclusively concerned with the slavery question, morning, noon, and night, ceaselessly for thirty years. But in fact these years were much occupied with the broadening of democracy, the continued growth of the area, population, and wealth of the country, and the constant drive to develop or exploit natural resources. Thirty thousand miles of railroad were constructed, thousands of new corporations were chartered, 4,900,000 immigrants poured in from the Old World, and the annual value of American manufactures reached a total of $1,885,000,000. All this activity lay entirely outside the orbit of the slavery controversy, though the more rapid growth of the North tended to increase the self-consciousness of the South as a minority section.

It is also a common mistake—made by Southerners at the time and by some historical writers since then—to suppose that the Northern people collectively embraced abolitionism. In fact, the influence of the abolitionists, though great, was highly paradoxical. They never polled a formidable vote in any national election, they never captured control of a major party, and they never emancipated any slaves, except a few fugitives. It may be argued that their significance was greater in the South, where they unintentionally created a violent sectional revulsion against Northern opinion, than in the North, where they failed in their intention to stimulate violent action against the Southern institution. By their preaching to the Northern people, they succeeded in arousing moral sympathy for the wrongs of the slave, but failed to overcome moral scruples concerning the legal rights of the slaveholder. The American people, still in a federal stage of political organisation, had been nurtured in the belief that each state retained, under the constitution, a right to decide the slavery question for itself. A few abolitionists like Garrison boldly followed this logic to the conclusion of denouncing the constitution as 'a covenant with death and an agreement with hell'.[1] But most Northerners, restrained by their dread of any policy which might endanger the Union and by their respect for legal rights, were content to satisfy their moral scruples by abolishing slavery in their own states and their constitutional scruples by leaving it alone in other states.

But while these legal scruples continued to inhibit any impulse toward direct action, the immense power of anti-slavery feeling gradually brought the majority of Northerners to the conviction that slavery must ultimately be eliminated from American society—that it must be placed 'in the course of ultimate extinction',[2] with whatever consequences this might imply for the South. Meanwhile, during the period when they were waiting for the opening of a legal path toward this goal, the vast psychological force of the anti-slavery impulse, which had been deflected from a direct assault upon slavery itself, found an outlet in an intensive contest over certain peripheral matters, such as the status of slavery and the slave trade in the District of Columbia, the return of fugitive slaves, and most of all, the position of slavery in newly settled territories, possessing political organisation, but not yet admitted as states.

Because of this indirectness, the territorial question, so-called, became,

[1] This characterisation of the constitution was placed on the masthead of *The Liberator* in 1843 and continued thereafter.

[2] Abraham Lincoln at Springfield, Illinois, 16 June 1858 (the 'House Divided' speech), in Roy P. Besler (ed.), *The Collected Works of Abraham Lincoln* (New Brunswick, 1953), vol. II, p. 461.

for forty years, the most inflammable issue in American politics. By a supreme paradox, sectional rivalry centred upon slavery not in the areas where it involved the bondage of four million human beings, but in those where no slaves were to be found. Physically, most of the territories did not present conditions favourable to the introduction of slavery. Thus, it has been said, the Union was needlessly wracked by a struggle over 'an imaginary negro in an impossible place'.[1] If one assumes literally that this territorial contest was really concerned with what it purported to be concerned with, it would seem to follow either that the political leaders of the time were hopelessly unrealistic in precipitating such a concrete crisis over such an abstract question, or else that the contention was fundamentally a rivalry for sectional power—a struggle in which the North was more concerned to create additional states into which it could expand and which would vote with it in the Senate, than it was to help the poor slaves in the South. Both of these views have been widely held by historians.[2] From another standpoint, however, it may appear that the territories became focal because the anti-slavery forces were compelled to make their attack at a point where slavery was constitutionally vulnerable rather than at a place where it enjoyed constitutional sanction.[3] But no matter which of these views is adopted, it is incontestably true that whenever a new area was opened, sectional crisis invariably ensued.

At the time when Andrew Jackson left the Presidency in 1837, the legal basis for determining the status of slavery appeared to be settled throughout the area of the United States. In the states themselves, power lay exclusively with these states, thirteen of which sanctioned slavery while thirteen others forbade it. East of the Mississippi, one territory, Florida, had been acquired from Spain with slavery already established, and another, Wisconsin, was closed to slavery under an ordinance adopted in 1787 by the Congress under the Articles of Confederation. In the area west of the Mississippi, acquired by the Louisiana Purchase in 1803, slavery was explicitly excluded from all territory north of 36° 30' and implicitly permitted south of this line. This division along a line of latitude had been adopted as part of the 'Missouri Compromise' in 1820, after a violent flare-up over the admission of Missouri as a slave state.

So long as the area of the country remained unchanged, therefore, it appeared that the slavery issue could not arise as a Federal question.

[1] Attributed to an unnamed Congressman from the South in James G. Blaine, *Twenty Years of Congress...* (Norwich, Conn., 1884), vol. I, p. 272.

[2] For the view that the participants were unrealistic see, for example, G. F. Milton, *The Eve of Conflict: Stephen A. Douglas and the Needless War* (Boston, Mass., 1934); Avery O. Craven, *The Repressible Conflict* (Baton Rouge, La.,1939); James G. Randall, *Lincoln, the President* (New York, 1945), vol. I. For the view that the struggle was one for power cf. Charles A. and Mary R. Beard, *The Rise of American Civilisation* (London, 1927), vol. I, ch. XVII.

[3] David M. Potter and Thomas G. Manning, *Nationalism and Sectionalism in America 1775-1877* (New York, 1949), pp. 215-16; Arthur M. Schlesinger Jr., 'The Causes of the Civil War', in *Partisan Review*, vol. XVI (1949), pp. 469-81.

But any further territorial expansion would again drag the question into the political arena, for the Missouri Compromise applied only to the area of the Louisiana Purchase, and not to future acquisitions. And the forces of territorial expansion, never dormant for very long, had begun to work again in the region known as Texas.

Historically, Texas was part of Mexico, but during the 1820's the Mexican government had encouraged immigration from the United States. Cotton-planting Southerners, carrying their slaves with them, had responded by pouring into the rich Texas river bottoms and had quickly proved restive under Mexican control. When the Mexican government, taking alarm, had tardily attempted to assert its authority, the settlers had risen in revolution, proclaimed an independent republic (1836) and overwhelmed a large Mexican army at the battle of San Jacinto. Soon after, they sought admission for Texas as a state.

To Northerners, who favoured expansion but who feared the sectional power of slavery, Texas presented a dilemma, and strong Northern opposition to annexation developed. Andrew Jackson recognised the delicacy of the question, and left it entirely to his successor, Martin Van Buren (1837–41). Van Buren, too, avoided decisive action, and when defeated by the Whigs in 1840, he passed the problem on to William Henry Harrison (who died after a month in office, 1841), and to Harrison's successor, John Tyler of Virginia (1841–5). Unlike his predecessor, Tyler was willing to press actively for annexation. The fact, however, that Tyler's Secretary of State, John C. Calhoun, openly linked the Texas question with the defence of negro slavery further antagonised Northerners, who were increasingly convinced that the Texas revolution had been a pro-slavery plot and that annexation would lead to war with Mexico. In 1844, after Texas had been a republic for eight years, the Senate overwhelmingly defeated a treaty of annexation. Sectional animosity was blocking national expansion.

By this time, however, the forces of expansion were beginning to operate in a larger theatre. American pioneers were pushing west across the continent, to the shores of the Pacific. They were migrating in considerable numbers to the Columbia River valley of Oregon, which was claimed by both Great Britain and the United States and which had been left open, under a treaty in 1818, to settlers from both countries. Other venturesome Americans were going to California, and were quick to note how tenuous were the bonds that held this remote province to Mexico. Expansionists perceived that American farmers were winning the race against British fur-traders in Oregon; they recognised the feebleness of Mexican control in the region from Texas to the Pacific; and they began to dream of a great republic stretching from sea to sea.

In 1844 the Democratic party suddenly seized upon this national impulse toward expansion and found a way to get around each section's fear of aggrandisement by the other. The Democrats proposed to balance expansion for the North with expansion for the South by a programme which called euphemistically for 'the reoccupation of Oregon and the reannexation of Texas'. With this slogan, they triumphantly elected James K. Polk to the Presidency (1845–9). His victory led Congress to vote the annexation of Texas as a slave state even before he came to office, and upon his accession he promptly notified Britain of the termination of the treaty of 1818 for Oregon and proposed to Mexico the purchase of the entire south-west.

At this point the widespread support of the expansionist programme seemed to mark the triumph of nationalism over sectionalism, but subsequent developments quickly brought the sectional issue again into the ascendant. Instead of making good the Democrats' promise to secure the boundary '54° 40', or fight', Polk agreed with Britain to divide Oregon at the 49th parallel. While thus abandoning part of what he had promised to Northern expansionists, he gave full measure to Southern expansionists by asking Congress to declare war on Mexico (1846) after a clash between American and Mexican patrols along the Rio Grande (cf. ch. xxv, pp. 674–5).

In the twenty-month war that followed, American armies marched to California, to Monterrey, and to Mexico City itself. From their overwhelming victory a peace ensued by which the United States acquired the entire south-west (Treaty of Guadalupe Hidalgo, 1848). Nationalist aspirations now achieved realisation as the United States became a transcontinental republic and a power in two oceans. Less than seventy years after the Declaration of Independence the country had grown from its precarious beginnings to possess the area and resources which would enable it in the twentieth century to occupy a position of world power.

Yet the climax of national fulfilment was also, paradoxically, the prelude to sectional crisis, for it brought the territorial question to the centre of the political arena. From the beginning of the Mexican war, Northern Congressmen had attempted to retaliate for the compromise which sacrificed part of their claim in Oregon, by demanding the exclusion of slavery from any territory won from Mexico (Wilmot Proviso). For four years, while the status of slavery in the Mexican Cession remained in doubt, and while Congress battled over the question, the crisis mounted. It reached an acute stage by 1849, when Zachary Taylor (1849–50), a Whig who had succeeded Polk in the Presidency, recommended that both California and New Mexico be admitted as free states. By this time, Southern leaders were threatening to secede rather than be excluded from areas 'purchased by the common blood and treasure of the whole people', and a convention of nine Southern states was being planned to meet at Nashville to consider whether the South ought to remain in the Union.

This emergency brought about the most famous and elaborate agreement in the long series of major compromises which, almost like international treaties, had traditionally been invoked to settle acute sectional disputes. The three-fifths compromise on the counting of slaves for purposes of representation, adopted in the Constitutional Convention in 1787, the Missouri Compromise of 1820, and the tariff compromise of 1833, all furnished precedent for another great compromise. Henry Clay, who had been instrumental in both of the latter two settlements, now came forward again with measures for conciliation. The death of President Taylor in 1850 and the succession of Millard Fillmore (1850–3) to his post enabled Clay to secure Presidential support. When Daniel Webster gave his venerable blessing and Senator Stephen A. Douglas of Illinois his vigorous and resourceful backing, passage was assured and in the autumn of the year of Taylor's death the Compromise of 1850 was adopted.

This compromise attempted to provide a comprehensive settlement for all aspects of the slavery question. It included legislation to secure the return of fugitive slaves. It guaranteed slavery but abolished the slave trade in the District of Columbia. It admitted California as a free state. Most important of all, it provided a new formula for the rest of the area ceded by Mexico: this whole region, which now constitutes four states, was organised into two territories, Utah and New Mexico, with no provision whatever about slavery except that 'when admitted as a state, the said territory or any portion of the same shall be received into the Union with or without slavery, as their constitution may prescribe at the time of their admission'.

Here was a formula which seemed almost magical in its effectiveness: eliminate the slavery question from national politics by invoking the unchallenged democratic principle of local self-government. If the people of Massachusetts and Virginia were entitled to settle the slavery question for themselves, without Congressional interference, then the people of Utah and New Mexico, it was argued, were entitled to a similar autonomy. Yet behind the façade of 'popular sovereignty', with its unassailable democratic premise, there lurked a fatal, and perhaps intentional ambiguity. To Southern leaders, the absence of restriction meant that Congress was now abandoning any pretended power to exclude slavery during the territorial period, and was conceding the right of slaveholders to carry slaves into all territories until the time of admission to statehood, at which time popular sovereignty would come into operation. To some moderates, it meant that the courts would determine the question for the territories, in the light of Mexican and American law. But to Douglas and the Northern Democrats, it meant that the territorial legislatures would take control of the question as soon as they were organised. In short, agreement on the principle of local control masked a disagreement as to the stage of political advancement at which local control would come into play.

Two years later Franklin Pierce (1853–7) and the Democrats won the heaviest majority in any presidential election since 1820, on a platform which proclaimed the 'finality of the Compromise'. Optimists now supposed that the dangers of sectional strife were safely past. But since the 'popular sovereignty' formula really concealed a disagreement rather than adjusting it, dissension was in any case likely to break out again. It did break out, more bitterly than ever, in connection with the Kansas–Nebraska question and the case of Dred Scott.

The Kansas–Nebraska area, which was part of the Louisiana Purchase north of 36° 30', lay athwart the line of a proposed railway between Illinois and the Pacific coast. To expedite this project, territorial organisation was necessary, and Stephen A. Douglas took the lead in arranging it. Douglas recognised that Southern support would be essential, and he attracted such support by proposing to repeal the anti-slavery restriction of the Missouri Compromise and to apply popular sovereignty, thus opening Kansas and Nebraska to a race between Northern and Southern settlers. Supported by Southern votes and applying extreme pressure, he drove this measure through (1854). But outraged anti-slavery men protested that popular sovereignty in the Louisiana Purchase was a wholly different thing from popular sovereignty in the Mexican Cession: they were being cheated of the promise they had received years before when they admitted Missouri as a slave state and they angrily prepared to resist any further concessions.

The Kansas–Nebraska Act repealed a territorial compromise but did not impair the Congressional power to compromise. Three years later, however, the Dred Scott decision (1857) deprived Congress of this power. The Supreme Court, ruling in the case of a negro who claimed freedom by virtue of former residence in free territory, held that Congress had no power to exclude slavery from any territory. Not only had the Missouri Compromise been void from the beginning, but it also followed that if Congress lacked power to exclude slavery, it could not confer such power upon a territorial legislature. This meant that the Northern theory of popular sovereignty for the territories was also void, and that all these areas were wide open to slavery. Only within the states could slavery be prohibited. The full implication of the Dred Scott case was not widely understood at first, but an Illinois lawyer, Abraham Lincoln, did much to expose the significance of the decision when he met Stephen A. Douglas in a series of debates arising from a senatorial election in 1858.

Thus by 1857 the long-standing structure of compromise lay smashed to fragments. The removal of what had been, at best, a frail barrier now opened the way for a direct clash of sections. The South was determined to secure the rights which the Supreme Court accorded to it as guarantees under the constitution; the North, deprived both of the line 36° 30' and of the popular sovereignty principle, came increasingly to the conclusion that it might as well abandon half-way measures, and, despite the Supreme Court, exclude slavery from all territories. In a larger sense, the South was committed to the belief that the loose federation formed in the eighteenth century should be maintained against the transforming economic forces of the nineteenth century, and that the constitution, as a legal absolute, could be preserved intact against evolutionary change. The North, exulting in its rapid progress and its growing power, was resolved that political adjustment to this transformation should not be blocked either by a numerical minority or by a literal interpretation of the constitution. Slavery, viewed in this context, was but one aspect of the opposition between two societies—one static and oriented to the past, the other dynamic and committed to the future.

While these diametrically opposite attitudes were crystallising, a series of developments marked the growth of bitterness and the deterioration of Union sentiment. The immense success of the sensational anti-slavery novel, *Uncle Tom's Cabin*, in 1852, the caning of Senator Sumner in 1856, the adoption of Personal Liberty laws by Northern states to prevent the enforcement of the Fugitive Slave act, the dramatic attempts by large mobs in the North to rescue fugitives who were being returned, and the chronic guerrilla warfare between pro-slavery and anti-slavery settlers in 'Bleeding Kansas', all marked the extremism of the forces now at work. In 1859, when the abolitionist John Brown was captured and sentenced to hang, after attempting to start a slave insurrection by means of a raid upon Harper's Ferry, Virginia, the outpouring of sympathy for him in the North caused deep alarm and a major alienation of Unionist sentiment in the South.

'The cords that bind the States together', Calhoun had said in 1850, 'are not only many, but various in character. Some are spiritual or ecclesiastical; some political; others social.'[1] Disunion, he predicted, could not be brought about at one stroke, but must come gradually, as one by one these cords were broken. Even before he spoke, both the Methodist church and the Baptist church had divided into separate Northern and Southern branches, and the Presbyterians were locked in constant sectional dissension. During the 'fifties, Southern students began to leave Northern schools, Southern vacationists to absent themselves from their customary Northern resorts, and Southern patriots to wear homespun rather than cloth from Northern factories. One by one the cords of Union were snapping.

The most important nationalising institutions that remained were the political parties. Both Whigs and Democrats had consistently maintained a party clientèle in both sections and had sought to take national rather than sectional positions on public questions. Northern and Southern

---

[1] Speech in the Senate, 4 March 1850. Cit. Crallé (ed.), *Works of Calhoun*, vol. IV, pp. 556–8.

leaders had consulted together in party councils and worked together toward party goals. But in the 'fifties, even these pillars of nationalism began to crumble. In the Whig party, strife between 'Conscience Whigs' and 'Cotton Whigs' led to disintegration, with most of the Northern members going ultimately into the newly formed Republican party, and with Southern members drifting into the Democratic ranks. By 1856 the Democratic party was the only major national party remaining. In that year it nominated James Buchanan (1857–61) for the Presidency, and won the election by carrying five free states and all of the fifteen slave states except Maryland (which went for a nativist group called the American, or Know-Nothing party). Buchanan's principal opposition came from the Republicans, who denounced slavery as a 'relic of barbarism' and carried eleven free states, but secured only 1200 votes in the entire South. The Democratic party was now the only national party, and it too became sectionalised in 1860 when the Douglas Democrats, still supporting popular sovereignty, and the administration Democrats, demanding free access for slavery in all the territories, split and nominated separate candidates (Douglas and John C. Breckinridge). The Constitutional Unionists, as successors to the Whigs, nominated John Bell of Tennessee. The Republicans nominated Abraham Lincoln on a platform promising the complete exclusion of slavery from all the territories.

Lincoln received only 39 per cent of the popular vote, but it was so concentrated in the free states that he would have been elected even against a united opposition. He carried seventeen of the eighteen free states, and part of the eighteenth; the fifteen slave states went overwhelmingly against him. The polarisation of the sections was now virtually complete and the final crisis was not long to await.

History has clarified Lincoln's position as a man of more than national stature, everlastingly just in according to the slaveholders all the legal rights they claimed except the territorial right, and wise in his realisation that the slavery problem was too big for quick or simple solutions. But in 1860 his victory presented a bleak prospect to the South, which pictured him as a rank, incendiary abolitionist. The situation as it appeared to Southerners was that discriminatory and exploitative policies had already caused the South to fall far behind the North in wealth and population (in 1860 the free inhabitants of the free states numbered 18,800,000, those of the slave states 8,030,000); the South had long since lost its former status of equality in the House of Representatives, and Congress had passed into the hands of a party which openly proposed to defy the decisions of the Supreme Court; now the Presidency was also about to pass into this same hostile control. Many Southerners felt that no true union remained, but only a sectional domination, and that at this juncture it behoved the Southern states, which had always insisted upon the retention of their sovereignty, to resume their sovereign capacity.

For more than a decade a faction of ardent secessionists, or 'fire-eaters', led by William L. Yancey of Alabama, Barnwell Rhett of South Carolina, and Edmund Ruffin of Virginia, had urged disunion, and this group now found a widespread Southern response to its warning that the South could escape subjugation to an alien North only by seceding at once. This programme of immediate secession was vigorously resisted by moderates who urged delay either to seek guarantees from the North or to assure effective joint action among the Southern states. These moderates were, for the most part, lovers of the Union, who wanted to preserve it on a voluntary basis. In this sense, Unionism in the South still remained a powerful force, almost strong enough to check the drift towards secession. But there were almost no unconditional Unionists who believed in the power of the Federal government to coerce a state, and in this sense Unionism was extremely weak. As the crisis developed, attempts at compromise failed, and the moderates found that they could not ride out the storm.

Between December and March 1860–1 South Carolina, Georgia, Florida, Alabama, Mississippi, Louisiana, and Texas held conventions, and each convention separately adopted an Ordinance of Secession. Almost simultaneously, these states formed a Southern union—the Confederate States of America—and installed Jefferson Davis of Mississippi as President on 22 February 1861. Yet despite Confederate boasts of a united South, eight other slave states declined to follow them, and remained in the old Union. Such was the continuing strength of American nationalism in the South as late as the eve of war.

When Lincoln became President on 4 March he found not only a fully formed Southern republic but also a very tense situation at two Federal forts in the South—Pickens in Florida and Sumter in South Carolina. Federal garrisons, holding these places, were regarded by the Confederates as invaders and were threatened with military force. There is strong evidence that Lincoln did not expect nor want war, but desired a period of inaction, during which Southern Unionism (to which he had appealed in his inaugural speech) might reassert itself. But he was not willing to withdraw the garrisons or to let them be starved out. Accordingly he sent a relief expedition to Fort Sumter in April. The Confederates, in anticipation of its arrival, bombarded and captured the fort. Thereupon Lincoln called for 75,000 troops; Virginia, North Carolina, Tennessee, and Arkansas went over to the Confederacy rather than meet this request; and American nationalism moved into the phase of supreme crisis which was resolved only by four years of Civil War.

Historians have found a favourite topic for controversy in the question whether the Civil War might have been averted, or whether it was the inevitable result of deterministic forces—an 'irrepressible conflict'. Some writers have found a deterministic answer in their analysis of basic social and economic factors. Others, stressing the artificiality of the territorial question, the large part played by violent emotions, and the damage caused by the folly of extremists in both the abolitionist and the secessionist camps, have argued that the 'irreconcilable' differences were more fictitious than real, and that the crisis was artificial.[1] There is probably no way of resolving this controversy conclusively, one way or the other, but two considerations in connection with it may be noted. First, it seems safe to say that psychological and emotional forces and the rise of extremists to positions of leadership may be quite as 'real' in their impact and quite as inevitably determined in their origins as the most basic social and economic conditions. Second, it appears certain that the disparity in the rate of Northern and Southern growth had destroyed the equilibrium between the sections, but that the South would never accept the political consequences of this change without a crisis. Whether the crisis had to take the form of armed conflict, and whether this phase of armed force had to occur precisely when it did, or might have come a month, or a year, or a decade sooner or later, would seem to be open to endless speculation.

The American Civil War lies outside the limits of the present chapter,[2] but this discussion of the interplay of nationalism and sectionalism would hardly be complete without some indication of the final resolution of the conflict between these opposing forces.

From the beginning of the Civil War, the more immediate question was whether the Union could attain victory, but the more fundamental question was whether victory, if won, could restore an American nation. Could the triumph of one section and the defeat of another section abate the intensity of sectionalism, especially when the Republicans were already adopting measures such as the Morrill Tariff, the National Bank Act, and the Pacific Railroad Act to secure Northern sectional ends? Could the process of coercion produce a spirit of voluntary loyalty which is the very essence of Union?

It was fortunate for the United States that, although most men in public life were either unable or unwilling to understand this problem, Abraham Lincoln saw it with perfect clarity. Throughout the fighting, he was constantly alert to uphold the maintenance of the Union as the grand object of the war, and, like Andrew Jackson before him, to infuse the concept of American nationalism with a broadly democratic philosophy. Hence he refused to make the abolition of slavery an objective, and waited almost two years before issuing an Emancipation Proclamation which freed all slaves in areas which were still in rebellion but did not interfere with slavery in the loyal slave states of Delaware, Maryland, Kentucky, and

[1] See *ante* pp. 611 and 620.
[2] For an account of it see ch. XXIV.

Missouri. His refusal to act until he was convinced that 'slavery must die that the nation might live' incurred violent denunciation from the abolitionists, but the forbearance which they deplored enabled him to strike slavery a more deadly blow than they could ever deliver. By his patience in waiting until the principle of Union and the principle of emancipation converged, he was able, as J. G. Randall has said, 'to fuse the cause of nationalism with the cause of freedom'.[1]

Lincoln came near the beginning of a period, not yet ended, of extreme and ruthless nationalism that often sacrifices the individual in the name of the state and repudiates democracy as inconsistent with national power. The other great nation-builders of his century—Napoleon, Cavour, Bismarck—seemed ready to subordinate human welfare in general to the fulfilment of French, or Italian, or German destiny. It was a distinctive contribution therefore of Lincoln's that he based his defence of the Union not upon the exaltation of the American state, but upon the universal cause of democracy, to which the survival of the American Republic seemed essential. In a supreme moment at Gettysburg, he did not mention the word American, but spoke of the war as a test whether any nation conceived in liberty and dedicated to the proposition that all men are created equal could long endure. The vital issue was not the survival of one nation, more or less, but the survival of a nation committed to the principle that government of the people, by the people, and for the people should not perish from the earth.

Because of his deep awareness of the importance of voluntary loyalty as a basis of national union, Lincoln was prepared to restore the Southern states to the Union on the most conciliatory terms possible, and for this purpose he was even prepared to sacrifice some of the sectional advantage which the North might gain by victory. In general, the Republican party did not share this purpose with him, and after his assassination control passed into the hands of a faction which imposed a sterner programme of 'Reconstruction' on the South. Whatever else may be said of this policy, it certainly did not diminish sectional bitterness in either North or South, and at the end of twelve years of reconstruction, the spirit of nationalism seemed weaker than at the beginning of the war. The restoration of nationalism by political means, therefore, must be said to have failed, and it remained for a gradual social process, a kind of folk reconstruction, to restore the bonds of Union. It was in this final phase that the essential forces of nationalism—never extinguished, though for a long while latent —again came into play. The basic homogeneity of the American people, their common speech, their common descent from British stock, their common acceptance of the Protestant ethic, their common historical experience in the American revolution and on the frontier, their common commitment to ideals of democracy, liberty, and individualism, generated

[1] *Journal of Southern History* (1940), vol. VI, pp. 441–9.

an emotional longing for reconciliation within the old Union. This yearning expressed itself in a thousand forms such as the poem of Francis Miles Finch honouring both 'The Blue and the Gray' in 1867, the funeral of General Grant, at which distinguished Southern generals, wearing the grey sash of the Confederacy, served as pall-bearers in 1885, and the Spanish-American War in which Southern troops rushed to enlist voluntarily under the flag of the Union in 1898. By the end of the century folk reconstruction had accomplished what political reconstruction failed to achieve, and a spontaneous American nationalism had again sprung up within the framework of Union which the Civil War had preserved.

CHAPTER XXIV

THE AMERICAN CIVIL WAR

IN the perspective of military history the Civil War is the first modern war.[1] It marked a transition from the older warfare, which involved principally the fighting forces, to the modern which affects in varying degree every group of society and which would demand ultimately a totalisation of national life. The Civil War was a war of material as well as of men. It witnessed the innovation or employment of mass armies, railroads, armoured ships, the telegraph, breech-loading and repeating rifles, various precursors of the machine-gun, railway artillery, signal balloons, trenches, and wire entanglements.[2] It was a war of ideas and therefore of unlimited objectives. One side or the other had to win a complete victory: the North to force the South back into the Union, the South to force the North to recognise its independence. There could be no compromise, no partial triumph for either. In contrast to the leisurely, limited-objective wars of the eighteenth century, the Civil War was rough, ruthless and sometimes cruel.

It was the first great military experience of the American people and their greatest historical experience. The drama, the agony, the valour of the years 1861–5 became a permanent part of the national consciousness. So did a profound realisation of its significance. In American history the Civil War is the great pivotal event, comparable to the revolution of 1789 in France. It settled certain differences, and it settled them permanently. It destroyed slavery, and assured the ascendancy of industrial capitalism. Furthermore, it preserved the Union and stabilised, if it did not indeed create, the modern American nation. Although Americans have continued to argue about some of the problems it left, its great result—the endurance of the Union—has been accepted by all elements in the nation. Since 1865 no party, class, or section has even contemplated the possibility or desirability of dividing the nation.

On the eve of the war it was not certain that the North would win. True, all the great material factors were on its side. The twenty-three states of the North, or the United States, had a greater population and hence

---

[1] For a brief account of the military course of the war see ch. XII, pp. 327–30.

[2] Cf. ch. XII, pp. 305–6, 310. Although breech-loaders and repeaters were employed in the war, the basic weapon of the infantry soldier was the Springfield rifle, a muzzle-loading, one-shot gun. Capable of killing at half a mile, it was most accurate at 250 yards. Rifled artillery guns with ranges of up to five miles came into use, but the standard artillery weapon was the 'Napoleon', a 12-pound brass smooth-bore. It could fire a mile, was accurate at half that distance, and was murderous at 250 yards. The Springfield and the Napoleon invested Civil War armies with greater range, accuracy, and firepower than previous American armies had possessed.

a larger manpower reservoir than the eleven states of the South, the Confederate States. The population of the North was approximately 22,000,000; that of the South something over 9,000,000. But in comparing the human potential, several qualifying factors have to be taken into account. The Northern total includes the four slave states that had refused to secede (Maryland, Delaware, Kentucky, Missouri), which furnished thousands of volunteers to the Confederacy, and the Pacific coast states (California, Oregon), which sent no troops to the main theatres of conflict. Both sections contained minority groups opposed to the war: the Peace Democrats in the North and the mountain people in the South. The two groups were perhaps approximately equal in size. Included in the Southern total are some 3,500,000 slaves, leaving a white population of about 6,000,000. Although the slaves were not directly available for military service, it would be a mistake to discount them. Indirectly they provided an important source of strength. Many served as military labourers, acting as teamsters and cooks in the armies and constructing fortifications. The great majority remained at home on the plantations where they performed a vital function in agricultural production. If they had not been present to plant, care for, and harvest the crops, white men would have had to do this work. In short, the slaves freed a large number of whites for military service.

When all the factors in the manpower situation are measured, however, it is evident that the North possessed a definite superiority and was capable of raising larger forces than the South. But this advantage was not decisive. Wars are not won by numbers alone. Furthermore, the North did not attain a clear numerical superiority until the last year and a half of the war. The Confederacy, by resorting early to conscription, mobilised a large proportion of its manpower rapidly. The Confederate armies increased in size until 1863, and then steadily declined. Before 1863 the Union armies were usually larger than those of their opponents, but not vastly larger. At the battle of First Manassas (1861) the two armies were approximately equal in size, 30,000 each. The same was true at Shiloh (1862), where each army numbered 40,000 on the first day. In the fighting in the Seven Days before Richmond (1862) the Federals committed 100,000 troops and the Confederates 85,000. Other battles in which the odds favoured the Federals but not greatly were Stone's River (1862), 45,000 to 38,000; Gettysburg (1863), 90,000 to 75,000; and Chattanooga (1863), 56,000 to 46,000. At Chickamauga (1863) the Confederates had an advantage of 70,000 to 58,000. There were a few engagements, notably Fredericksburg (1862) and Chancellorsville (1863), in which the odds were greater, approaching two to one, but it was not until the closing months in 1865, when the Confederate armies were depleted by defeat and desertion, that they reached the five-to-one ratio remembered by later generations of Southerners. It was well within the realm of possibility that the Confederacy, during the first two years of the war, might have won its independence by victory on the battlefield.

More important than the manpower differential was the superior potential of the Northern economic system. This became increasingly significant as the conflict settled into a sustained and long struggle. It was apparent in both agricultural and industrial production. At the outset both sides possessed the capacity to produce enough food for their ordinary civilian needs. As the war continued, the North was able to expand its productive capacities to meet the new war demands, while Southern agricultural production declined under the strain of war. The North swelled its production, even though thousands of farm-boys joined the armies, by an increased employment of labour-saving machines like the reaper, thresher, and drill. In the South the food-producing area was steadily reduced by Federal occupation or devastation; and the agricultural labouring force was decreased by the tendency of the slaves to flock to the camps of the invading armies. But even with damaged facilities, the South continued to produce, at least until 1864, sufficient foodstuffs for its minimum needs. Most of the shortages during the last two years of the war were due primarily to inadequacies in the railway system, which could not move supplies where they were needed.

The North's greater potential was most strikingly apparent in industrial production. On the eve of war the North possessed approximately 110,000 factories, representing a capital investment of $850,000,000, employing 1,131,000 workers, and turning out annually products valued at $1,500,000,000. For the South, the figures were: establishments, 20,000; capital, $95,000,000; workers, 110,000; value of products, $155,000,000. Both sides strove to expand their facilities, but inevitably the North, with its initial pre-eminence and its greater knowledge of industrial techniques, far outstripped the South. In the vital arms industries, for example, the thirty-eight largest gun factories in the North by 1862 could produce 5000 rifles a day; the maximum for Southern plants, which because of labour and supply shortages was not often achieved, was only 300 a day.

Northern industrial supremacy meant that the Northern armies, after the economic system had been geared to war production, would have more of everything than the Southern. In the first year of war both sides purchased large supplies, particularly arms, in Europe. But by 1862 the North was able to provide practically all its material, and dependence on Europe ceased. By contrast, the South, while labouring frantically to expand its facilities, throughout continued to rely on Europe, importing what goods it could run through the Northern naval blockade. Confederate industrial deficiency affected almost every phase of the war effort. Although the ordnance department, headed by the brilliant Josiah Gorgas, accomplished wonders, Confederate firearms were inferior to Northern weapons, and the firepower of a Confederate army was rarely equal to that of its enemy. The Southern economy was unable to provide its military forces with uniforms, shoes, medical supplies—and it was unable to furnish ordinary consumer goods to its civilian population. Its failure hurt the Southern will to fight. After 1863 morale sagged seriously, and one reason was the popular realisation that the South had exhausted its resources, while those of the enemy seemed limitless.

In transport the North possessed a marked advantage. It had more and better inland water transport, more surfaced roads, and more wagons and animals. But its greatest superiority was in its railways. The Civil War was one of the first in which railways played an important role. They carried raw materials to factories and finished goods to military distribution centres. They transported recruits to training camps and trained soldiers to army camps. They moved troops long distances from one theatre to another and with unprecedented speed. In 1862 the main Confederate field army in the west was shifted from northern Mississippi via Mobile to Chattanooga, Tennessee, a distance of 800 miles. In 1863 a Federal corps was moved from the eastern to the western theatre in the then unheard-of time of eight days. The North had approximately 20,000 miles of railways; the South, with an equal land-area, had only 10,000 miles. Furthermore, many of the Southern lines, having been built to connect two specific towns, were short; there were long gaps between key points; and the lines had not been built according to a uniform gauge. The few through-lines, like the connections between Richmond and Memphis and between Richmond and the Carolinas, ran close to the land or sea frontier, and hence were vulnerable. Before the war the South had purchased its rolling stock from Northern factories or from Southern plants that during the war were concentrating on armaments. The result was that, when stock was destroyed or worn out, it could not be replaced. The railway system steadily deteriorated, and by 1864 it was almost in a state of collapse. Some historians think that the railway breakdown was a major cause of defeat.[1]

The North possessed the great weapon of sea-power. In 1861 the Federal navy was small, numbering only ninety ships of all types and 9000 sailors. Rapid expansion soon made naval power a major factor. By 1864 the navy included some 670 ships and 51,000 men. No average total for the Confederate navy can be given because of the frequent destruction of its vessels; its personnel, however, reached only 4000. Northern sea-power performed two important functions. First, it established a blockade. The mission of sealing off the long Southern coastal line was difficult to execute, and even after the navy attained maximum size, it

[1] For example, Charles W. Ramsdell, *Behind the Lines in the Southern Confederacy* (Baton Rouge, 1944), pp. 94–5; Robert C. Black III, *The Railroads of the Confederacy* (Chapel Hill, 1952), pp. 294–5.

could not maintain a completely effective blockade. Blockade runners continued to operate throughout the war. Although the effects of the blockade in depriving the South of supplies have been exaggerated,[1] it did, nevertheless, hurt the Confederacy. It hindered the Confederacy from importing bulky goods (the blockade runners were necessarily light ships), it prevented Confederate cruisers from using Southern ports as bases, and it gave the Southern people a feeling of being cut off from the outside world. The second function of sea-power was to aid Federal land forces to subjugate the vast western region between the Appalachian Mountains and the Mississippi River. Here the larger rivers were navigable to gunboats and transport ships. Some of the largest operations in the west were joint land and naval movements. Without the employment of sea-power on the western rivers, it is doubtful whether the Federals could have occupied the west.

Some historians,[2] impressed by the North's material advantages, have concluded that the Southern struggle was doomed from the start. Actually, the odds were not as overwhelming as they appear. As previously indicated, the Confederacy might have won a military decision up to 1863. Not all the advantages were with the North. The South, for the most part, fought on the defensive in its own country and commanded interior lines. The invaders had to maintain long lines of communication and garrison occupied areas. And because this was a civil war, the North had to do more than capture the enemy capital or even defeat enemy armies. It had to conquer a people and convince them that their cause was hopeless. Perhaps the Confederacy's best chance, after the opportunity for a military decision had passed, was psychological. The South was fighting for one simple objective, its independence; it had no aggressive designs against the North. The North, on the other hand, was fighting an aggressive war to maintain two somewhat abstract principles: the permanence of the Union and, later, the emancipation of the slaves. At any moment the North could have peace and its own independence simply by quitting the war. If the South had been able to convince the North that it could not be beaten, it might, even after 1863, have won its freedom. There would be times, notably in the summer of 1864, when it seemed that the North was discouraged enough to abandon the struggle.

Thoughtful Southerners realised the importance of the North's superior economic potential. They believed, however, that Southern military leadership and valour would be able to overcome the North's material

---

[1] The impact of the blockade, and the conflicting views of scholars on its influence, are analysed in J. G. Randall, *The Civil War and Reconstruction* (Boston, 1937), pp. 650-1. For a criticism of its effectiveness, see Frank L. Owsley, *King Cotton Diplomacy* (Chicago, 1931), pp. 268, 273-4, 285.

[2] For example, Francis B. Simkins, *The South Old and New* (New York, 1948), pp. 137-8; Charles A. and Mary R. Beard, *The Rise of American Civilization* (New York, 1939), vol. II, pp. 52-4.

advantages. But even if the human factor failed to outweigh economics, there was still an almost certain promise of success—Europe would intervene on the side of the South. The intervention argument, which convinced even the most realistic Southerners, ran as follows: the economic systems of England and France depended on their textile industries, which had to have Southern cotton; England and France, therefore, would force the North to stop the war and concede Southern independence. Diplomacy thus became a major element in Confederate statecraft. The South hoped to receive recognition as a nation, to secure material aid, and to persuade Great Britain and France to break the blockade and force mediation on the North. The United States, believing that it could handle its inner troubles if unhampered by outside interference, strove to prevent recognition and intervention.

In the diplomatic narrative the key nations are England and France. They were the only nations who were capable of interfering in the American struggle, and who felt that their interests might be affected by the outcome. England and France, allied in the Crimean War, continued to act together in many areas, one of their understandings being that questions concerning the United States fell within the sphere of British influence. The French emperor, Napoleon III, would not therefore intervene unless England moved first. The third power of Europe, Russia, like the United States a rising nation, also felt that its aspirations were blocked by England. Because of this supposed community of interests, Russia openly sympathised with the North. In 1863 Russia dispatched two fleets, one to New York and the other to San Francisco. The actual reason for their appearance was a threat of war with England over Poland: Russia wanted to get her navy into position to attack British commerce. But in America it was widely believed that the Russians had come out of friendship for the United States, and a long-lasting legend began that the Russian squadrons had offered support should Britain and France attempt to break the blockade.

When the conflict began, the sympathies of the ruling classes of England and France were for the Confederacy. Although some were motivated by a feeling of cultural kinship with the planter aristocracy of the slave states, they reacted as they did primarily because they disliked the ideal and the reality which the United States represented. European liberals, pressing for a broader popular basis for government, had delighted to hold up the United States as a successful example of democracy in a populous country. It was an argument that conservatives were hard put to answer. John Bright, the great English liberal, eloquently described the nature of American influence: 'Privilege has beheld an afflicting spectacle for many years past. It has beheld thirty millions of men, happy and prosperous, without king, without the surroundings of a court, without nobles except such as are made by eminence in intellect and virtue.

...Privilege has shuddered at what might happen to old Europe if the great experiment should succeed.'[1] But the great experiment seemed to be breaking up, and its failure promised to discredit democracy everywhere. Also for many years past the dominant groups in England and France had beheld with uneasiness the growing strength of the American Republic. In an independent Confederacy they saw a check to the young power rising in the west. A divided America would mean that no single powerful nation existed in the western hemisphere. Once started, the process of division might continue. An independent South might be followed by an independent west, and the various American republics would have to seek the support of England or France and would thus fall under European influence. Even anti-slavery liberals in England and France tended to favour the Southern cause. For reasons of domestic politics, the Northern government at first maintained that it was waging war to restore the Union but not to destroy slavery. Many liberals concluded that the South was fighting for the honoured liberal principle of self-determination.

But British and French opinion was never solidly in sympathy with the South. From the beginning some members of the upper classes, particularly in England, spoke out for the North. Liberals like Bright and Richard Cobden foresaw that no matter how the Northern government defined the purposes of the war, it would have to become ultimately a war to destroy slavery. To their working-class followers, they described the American conflict as a struggle between free and slave labour. This seemed plausible to the politically conscious but unenfranchised labourers. Whatever the conservative leaders of the nation might think, the English workers identified the Northern cause with their own. They expressed their sympathy in mass meetings, in resolutions, and, through the speeches of Bright and other liberals, in Parliament itself. When President Lincoln issued the Emancipation Proclamation (1 January 1863), they felt that their impression of the war as a struggle for free labour had been confirmed. The proclamation, making emancipation an official objective of Northern war aims, had an enormous influence in turning liberal opinion in Europe against the Confederacy.

At the outbreak of hostilities the British government issued a proclamation of neutrality which recognised the Confederacy as a belligerent. France and other nations followed suit. In the United States the British action was deeply resented. The Northern government contended that it was not fighting a war but repressing an insurrection, and that granting belligerency status to the Confederacy was an unneutral act. Nevertheless, England had proceeded in conformity both with accepted practices of neutrality and with the realities of the situation. No matter how the United States officially defined the conflict, it was actually fighting a war,

[1] *Speeches of John Bright on the American Question* (Boston, 1865), p. 177.

as Lincoln himself conceded in his proclamation establishing the blockade. The North was convinced, however, that England did not intend to remain neutral and that recognition of belligerency would be followed by recognition of independence.

Yet neither England nor France or any European nation extended diplomatic recognition to the Confederacy. Nor did England and France, although on several occasions they discussed mediation, ever seriously consider intervention. Several factors influenced the final outcome of the diplomatic struggle. The personnel of the Northern diplomatic corps was, in general, superior at all levels to that of its rival. Judah P. Benjamin, the Confederacy's Secretary of State for the greater part of the war, was clever and able, but he failed to present the Southern cause in terms that would appeal to European governments and opinion. His counterpart in the North, William H. Seward, after some initial sabre-rattling blunders (at first he seemed to think his principal duty was to insult Britain), became an outstanding secretary of state. The North was fortunate in being represented in London by a skilled and distinguished minister, Charles Francis Adams, whose father and grandfather had occupied the Presidency. He easily outshone the Confederate representative, James M. Mason, a genial Virginia country squire of bucolic manner. The Southern diplomats in Europe, reflecting the cultural isolation in which the South had long lived, betrayed an ignorance of European thought; in particular, they underestimated the intensity of the anti-slavery sentiment in most European nations.

Cotton diplomacy failed to exert the decisive influence which the South had envisaged. When the war began, English textile manufacturers possessed a surplus supply of cotton, having imported in 1860 some 2,580,000 bales from the United States. The immediate effect of the shortage created by the war and the blockade was to enable the operators to dispose of their remaining finished goods at high prices. By 1862, when only 70,000 bales were imported, the supply was becoming scanty, and the effects were felt in England and France. Many mills had to close, and in Britain over 500,000 workers were thrown out of employment. The English and French operators managed, however, to bring in enough cotton from Egypt and India to avoid a complete collapse. Perhaps the most significant feature was that the English textile workers, even those without jobs, continued to support the North.

Other economic forces proved stronger than the cotton shortage. A succession of crop failures in England reduced the domestic production of wheat to a point where large amounts had to be imported annually from the United States: King Wheat momentarily seemed more powerful than King Cotton. Important English economic interests found they were making money out of the war. Sales to the American contestants swelled profits in the munitions, textile, linen, and other industries. As Confederate commerce destroyers, some of them built in Britain, harried American commerce from the sea, England took over the carrying trade of her principal mercantile rival. Political and military factors also operated to restrain English intervention. The Emancipation Proclamation caused English opinion to shift markedly in favour of the North. As the greatest naval power, and hence the leading exponent of the weapon of blockade, England hesitated to interfere with the Northern blockade for fear of setting a dangerous precedent. Finally, neither England nor France, even if they had wished to act, could risk intervening unless the Confederacy seemed close to victory; otherwise they would have to fight a North capable of striking back. The South never developed a certainty of victory. There was a brief time in the closing months of 1862 when Southern success seemed assured—and when England and France might have acted —but this moment passed with Union victories at Antietam and Stone's River and never returned.

During the war three incidents strained relations between the United States and Britain; one assumed the proportions of a crisis and might have resulted in war. The first and most dangerous, known in American history as the *Trent* affair, occurred late in 1861. The Confederate government appointed two commissioners, James M. Mason and John Slidell, to England and France. Slipping through the blockade to Havana, the commissioners embarked for England on the British steamer *Trent*. In Cuban waters was a United States frigate (the *San Jacinto*), commanded by Captain Charles Wilkes, who, knowing Mason and Slidell were aboard the *Trent*, decided, with no authorisation from his superiors, to capture them. Intercepting the *Trent* after she left Havana, he compelled her captain to hand over the diplomats, and bore them off to Boston. The Northern public hailed him as a national hero: he had arrested the rebel commissioners and humiliated unneutral Britain. Actually, he had placed his government in a delicate position. Denouncing Wilkes's act as a violation of international law, the English government prepared a demand for the release of the prisoners, reparation, and an apology. As originally drafted, the document was almost an ultimatum, which the United States probably would have rejected. But before it was sent off, the language was toned down, primarily at the urging of the Prince Consort, in order to allow the American government a loophole through which to back out. Lincoln and Seward realised that the North could not afford to become involved in a foreign war; they knew also that the Northern public would be infuriated if the diplomats were released immediately. They spun out negotiations until opinion had cooled, and then returned Mason and Slidell with an indirect apology which satisfied England. Ironically, in the course of the incident both governments had contended for policies which historically they had opposed: Britain for the rights of a neutral and America for the rights of a belligerent. Incidentally, when Mason and Slidell proceeded to their respective posts, they accomplished nothing for their country. Mason was never received officially in London, and in 1863 he left for France convinced that England favoured the North. In France Slidell associated on friendly terms with the emperor, but he too failed to secure recognition or intervention. They were far more valuable to the Confederacy when they languished in a Northern prison.

The second episode intensified American suspicions that England did not mean to observe a proper neutrality. Early in the war the Confederate government, in order to weaken the blockade, decided to buy or have built in Europe fast destroyers to prey on Northern sea commerce. (The Confederate naval department thought that the North would detach ships from the blockade to hunt the destroyers.) Six vessels, of which the most famous was the *Alabama*, were built or purchased in England, and sailed from English ports to begin their work. Although the United States minister in London, Adams, regularly informed the British government of the projected departure of each ship, the government took no effective action to detain them, usually claiming that it did not possess satisfactory evidence that the raiders were intended for the Confederacy. Before 1863 the United States, for fear of provoking intervention, dared not object too strongly; it limited its protest to charges that permitting the destroyers to be constructed contravened rules of neutrality. After the war these protests formed the basis for the so-called '*Alabama* damage claims', which the United States served on England—and which England paid.

The third incident, in reality a continuation of the second, was the affair of the Laird rams. In 1863 the Confederacy was beginning to feel the pinch of the blockade; although the commerce raiders had almost swept the Northern merchant marine off the sea, the Federal government had refused to weaken its naval cordon. In a bold move to destroy the blockade, the Southern government placed an order with the Laird shipbuilding company for two powerful ironclads. These rams constituted a potential menace that the North could not ignore: the loss of its commerce it could absorb but the blockade had to be maintained. Furthermore, now that the war was turning in its favour, the United States could speak more firmly. Seward instructed Adams to inform the British government that if the rams, or any other vessels intended for the Confederacy, were allowed to leave British ports, there would be danger of war. Adams delivered the message, but even before it was received the government had detained the rams. In fact, the cabinet some months previously had decided to stop the practice of English shipyards building vessels for the Confederacy. The new policy was apparent to the United States; Adams's dramatic warning was meant to ensure its maintenance. Suddenly England had realised that for a naval power she had been imprudent. The assistance which she had permitted the South to secure might bring a similar form of retaliation against her in future wars. Hastily she conceded her error before any dangerous precedents were created.

Napoleon III, if he could have followed his inclinations, would have intervened in the American struggle. Forced to follow Britain's lead, he could only express sympathy for the South and permit it to secure commerce destroyers in France. Primarily he desired a Southern victory because of his ambition to re-establish French colonial power in the western hemisphere; if the United States was split into two nations, neither would be strong enough to block his designs. He seized the opportunity created by the war to set up a French-dominated empire in Mexico. Before the war Mexico had borrowed $80,000,000 from English, French, and Spanish bankers. When the government, nearly bankrupt, suspended payments on the debt, the creditors appealed to their governments for redress and the three powers agreed to send a land and naval force to Mexico. Late in 1861 they occupied several coastal towns, whereupon Mexico proposed to settle her obligation and the invaders began to differ as to their objectives. England and Spain withdrew from the enterprise in April 1862, but the French occupied Mexico City, and in 1863, with the support of one native political faction, proclaimed a new government to be headed by an Austrian archduke, Maximilian, as emperor. Napoleon's move clearly violated the Monroe Doctrine, but the United States, afraid of provoking French intervention and fully occupied at home, dared only to register a formal protest. Not until after the Civil War had ended could it bring enough pressure to force Napoleon to withdraw his troops (1866–7). Then Maximilian's government fell, and he was executed by his subjects. The Confederacy, hoping for French aid, voiced official approval of the new satellite state. Southern opinion, however, tended to condemn the French venture as an infringement of the Monroe Doctrine, thereby posing an interesting historical question. If the South had won independence, which American nation would have owned and enforced the doctrine? Or, in such case, could it have been upheld?

The exploits of the Northern economic system, heralding the rise of a new industrial giant, were not lost on European observers. Both industry and agriculture expanded their productive capacities. The Northern economy performed the same enormous feat that the national economy would in the two great wars of the twentieth century. It both supplied the immense demands of modern war and enlarged the national wealth; it created goods faster than war could destroy them. The vast expansion was largely a result of the war, of huge purchases by the government of all kinds of goods. Although the government did not actually intervene in the modern sense to mobilise the economy, its activities stimulated almost every segment of the economic system.

The greatest expansion occurred in industry. Those industries which supplied the needs of the armed forces experienced the most spectacular increase in output: iron and steel, textiles, boots and shoes, arms and munitions, railways, and coal. The annual production of coal jumped from a peacetime figure of 13,000,000 tons to 21,000,000, the annual consumption of wool from 85,000,000 pounds to over 200,000,000. Some railways enlarged their traffic by as much as 100 per cent, and the inland waterways recorded an even greater increase. In part this stupendous expansion was accomplished by remodelling old factories or building new ones, in part by using machines and processes which had been introduced before the war but only sparingly utilised. The Howe–Singer sewing machine enabled the textile industry to meet the demands for uniforms, creating in the process a new business, ready-made suits for men. A similar device in the making of shoes, machine-stitching of soles to uppers, revolutionised the shoe industry. In arms manufacturing, the principle of interchangeable parts was employed with startling results. Before the war the combined output of the two largest arsenals had been only 22,000 weapons a year; by 1862 one alone was turning out 200,000 rifles annually.

Similar feats of production were recorded by Northern agriculture. In addition to satisfying the normal civilian needs, the farmers were called upon to supply foodstuffs to the army and to alleviate the wheat shortage in England. With hardly a sign of strain, the agricultural system was able to meet both domestic and foreign demands. Wheat production leaped from 142,000,000 bushels for the whole country to 191,000,000 bushels from the North alone, and the amount exported increased threefold. Wool production rose from 60,000,000 pounds to 142,000,000 pounds. As in industry, the expansion was partly the result of enlarged facilities— new land brought under cultivation in the west—and partly of the employment of machines introduced before the war but never widely used. Forced into mass-production by the demands of the war, the farmers now resorted to labour-saving machinery: the mower, the thresher, and the reaper. By the end of the war, 250,000 reapers were employed on Northern farms. They were largely responsible for the tremendous expansion in wheat production.

Another stimulus to economic expansion was the legislation enacted by the Republican party during the war. In an economic sense, the Republicans represented the aspirations of Northern business and agriculture; they advocated the old Federalist–Whig doctrine that the national government should foster the economy with subsidies and beneficent laws. With Southern opposition removed from Congress, they proceeded to satisfy the economic expectations of the groups that had put them in power. Most of the laws benefited business and finance, an indication that the eastern wing of the party was acquiring an ascendency over the western-agricultural wing.

The chief gains of the western faction were the Homestead Act (1862) and the Morrill Land Grant Act (1862). By the first, any citizen or any alien who had declared intentions of citizenship could register claim to a quarter section of public land (640 acres), and, after furnishing evidence that he had lived on it for five years, receive title on payment of a nominal fee. After the war thousands of settlers in the west would thus claim 'free' farms. The Morrill Act answered a western demand for Federal aid for agricultural education. It provided that each state should receive 30,000 acres of public land for each of its Congressional representatives, the proceeds from the land to be used for instruction in agriculture, engineering, and military science. After the war, the measure provided the basis for the great growth of the so-called Land Grant colleges.

The business wing of the party scored significant gains in tariff, railway, and immigration legislation. In 1861 the Morrill Tariff Act provided a moderate boost in existing rates. Later measures (1862, 1864) raised the average of duties to 47 per cent, double the level of the pre-war rates, and gave industry the protection it demanded from European competition. The promoters of a transcontinental railway (from a point in the Mississippi valley to the Pacific coast) persuaded Congress to enact legislation (1862, 1864) creating two corporations, the Union Pacific and the Central Pacific, to construct a line between Omaha, Nebraska, and San Francisco, California. The government was to aid the companies by advancing them loans and making grants of public lands. Work on the line was not commenced until after the war, when other promoters sought and secured similar legislative support. Most of the western railways were built with Federal subsidies. Here were internal improvements on a scale hardly envisaged by the Federalists or the Whigs. When immigration from Europe fell off sharply in the first years of the war, threatening a labour shortage, Congress came to the rescue with a contract labour law which authorised employers to import labourers, paying the costs of their transport, the future wages of the migrants being mortgaged to repay the costs. Largely because of this measure, over 700,000 immigrants entered the country during the war.

The most important legislation affecting business and finance was the National Bank Act (1863, amended 1864) which created a new financial complex, the National Banking System, that endured until 1913. In its inception, the measure was envisaged partly as a long-range reform of banking arrangements and partly as a solution to the immediate money needs of the government. Its architects, one of whom was the Secretary of the Treasury, Salmon P. Chase, presented it as a law to restore control of the currency to the Federal government (on the eve of the war 1500 state-chartered banks were issuing notes of widely varying values). They argued that the country needed a uniform banknote currency and that national supervision of the banking system would enable the government to market its bonds more economically. The act outlined a process by which a 'banking association' could secure a Federal charter and become a National Bank. Each association was required to possess a minimum capital and to invest one-third of its capital in government bonds. It could issue banknote currency up to 90 per cent of the current value of the securities. To ensure a standard currency and to impel state banks to join the system, Congress placed a prohibitive tax on notes of state banks. By the end of the war the system included 11,582 banks which were circulating notes amounting to over $200,000,000. Although some bankers disliked the regulatory features of the law, the system ultimately benefited primarily the financial and creditor classes; the east continued to have a banknote circulation far in excess of the other sections. Historically, the National Banking System marked a return to the Federalist–Whig idea of a connection between the government and the financial community, the concept which the Jacksonian Democrats had sought to destroy.

With its vast reservoirs of wealth, the North possessed ample resources to sustain the huge costs of modern war. Northern war financing was not, however, particularly efficient. The failure of the governmental and monetary leaders to exploit adequately the existing resources can be ascribed largely to national inexperience in financing anything that was very expensive. It was hard for a people who paid scarcely any taxes to grasp the realities of a war that came to cost $2,000,000 a day. The North financed the war from three principal sources: taxation, which yielded $667,000,000; loans, which brought in $2,600,000,000; and paper currency, of which $450,000,000 was issued.

When the war began, Chase, who thought it would be short, failed to recommend a programme of new taxes. Both he and the legislators thought that the war should be financed mainly from loans. The principal measure enacted in 1861 was a modest income tax, the first in the nation's history. Not until 1862 did Congress pass an adequate tax bill, the Internal Revenue Act, which placed moderate duties on practically all goods and most occupations. Although the government's programme did not fully exploit the taxable resources of the country, the war taxes marked a new departure. Through their medium the hand of the government was coming to rest on thousands of individuals who had never paid levies to the central government. The United States was acquiring a national internal revenue system, one of the many unexpected nationalising results of the war. From loans the government secured three times as much revenue as from all other sources combined. The process of selling bonds was, however, hampered by clashes between Chase and the bankers, the Secretary favouring short-term issues at low interest and the financiers holding out for long-term loans at high interest. Both had to compromise. Chase's most original contribution to bond-selling was in seeking a broad popular subscription to government stocks. The Treasury sold $400,000,000 of bonds to small purchasers, one of the first examples of mass financing of war in modern history. The government resorted to the issue of paper money early in 1862 when tax receipts were small and bonds were selling slowly. The Legal Tender Act authorised the printing of paper currency, which, because of its colour, came to be known as 'greenbacks'. Because the greenbacks were not supported by specie and depended for redemption on the good faith of the government, they fluctuated violently in value, ranging in relation to a gold dollar from $0·39 to $0·69. They were an easy answer to the government's need for quick funds, but, by inflating prices, they increased the costs of the war. They had, however, an enduring effect on the economy. Together with the notes of the National Banks, they constituted a large part of the nation's circulating money supply. The United States was also acquiring a national currency.

A substantial part of the war revenues went to support the large Northern armies. At the beginning of the war, the regular army numbered only 16,000. President Lincoln, without constitutional sanction, authorised increases and called for volunteers for national service. When Congress met in July 1861 it provided, at Lincoln's recommendation, for enlisting 500,000 volunteers to serve for three years. In the first days of the war, when the country was moved by an outburst of patriotism, the volunteer system brought out enough men to fill up the armies. But after the first flush of enthusiasm the number of enlistments dwindled alarmingly. Finally the government realised it would have to resort to conscription, and in March 1863 Congress enacted the first national draft law in American history, whereby all able-bodied males between twenty and forty-five if unmarried and twenty and thirty-five if married were liable to military service for three years. Although few exemptions were authorised (high government officials and men who were the sole support of dependants), a conscript could escape service by hiring a substitute or by paying the government a fee of $300. These loopholes were bitterly criticised as examples of special privilege, and the cash commutation was repealed.

Actually, the law did not directly draft men; the purpose behind it was to stimulate enlistments by threatening to draft. Each state was assigned at intervals a quota. If it could, by offering cash bounties or other inducements, meet its allotment, it escaped the draft completely; only if it failed to fill its quota did the national government move in to invoke conscription. Despite the peculiar working of the measure, it filled up the armies. The Federal forces increased steadily, reaching a maximum in 1865. Because of the vague statistics kept during the war, no accurate statement of the numbers raised is possible. It is estimated that 1,500,000 served for three years. The casualty rate was enormous, and if the Confederate casualties are reckoned in the total, the Civil War is the most costly American war. The total deaths in the Northern armies numbered 360,000 and in the Confederate armies, 258,000. Of the Northern total, 110,000 were battlefield deaths; the remainder died of sickness and disease.

Before the war the American people had hardly felt the weight of government in their daily lives. Conscription came as a strange and irritating control. Although the great majority submitted to its discipline, opposition was widespread, particularly from labourers, immigrants, and advocates of peace. In some places, notably New York City, it erupted into violence and riots. Some state governors challenged the authority of the central government to conscript, but the Lincoln administration continued to force men into the army. The impact of war was destroying state rights in the North as surely as the war's result would destroy the Southern concept of state sovereignty.

In its President the North had a leader who was determined to maintain American nationality. Abraham Lincoln possessed the qualities of states-manship—intellectual and moral strength, a deep understanding of the spirit of his age and of popular thought, superb political skill—and the will to employ those qualities to accomplish his purpose. Lincoln's task, the most difficult ever confronted by an American statesman, was to preserve a nation. He had to restore the Union, to direct a civil war, and at the same time to sustain a basic unity of purpose among his own people. As Professor Allan Nevins has emphasised,[1] Lincoln was able to perform his great task because he had another element of statesmanship, passion. Lincoln's passion was for democracy, for the world's greatest example of democracy, the American Union, for what he called 'the last, best hope of earth'.[2]

When Lincoln assumed the Presidency he was regarded by most people in Washington as a humble man who realised that he was not big enough for the post. Actually, he was well aware of his great inner powers, and superbly confident in his abilities. His assurance was revealed in his choice of a cabinet, which included four men who had been his rivals for the Republican nomination. The general level of ability was above average, and three of the members, Seward, Chase, and the Secretary of War, Edwin M. Stanton, were first-rate men. Although several of the Secretaries thought they were abler than Lincoln, he managed them all for his own purposes. Lincoln's confidence was also demonstrated by his bold exercise of his war powers. He had an expansive view of the wartime role of the President: in order to achieve his objectives he even violated provisions of the constitution, stating that he would not lose the whole for fear of disregarding a part. He summoned troops to suppress 'the rebellion', which was equivalent to a declaration of war; illegally increased the size of the regular army; and proclaimed a naval blockade of the South.

The exercise of presidential war powers that stirred the greatest resent-

---

[1] In *The Statesmanship of the Civil War* (New York, 1953), pp. 5–6, 8–9, 17–18.
[2] Roy P. Basler (ed.), *The Collected Works of Abraham Lincoln* (New Brunswick, 1953), vol. v, p. 537.

ment was the suspension of civil law in areas where resistance to the war appeared. Two groups opposed the war effort: Southern sympathisers in the loyal slave states and the Peace Democrats. Among the Democrats there were three fairly definite factions. The War Democrats, a minority, accepted office and were practically absorbed into the Republican organisation. The great majority of the party, who may be designated the Regular Democrats, gave general support to the war, but retained their separate identity and reserved the right to criticise the administration. Operating within the framework of the main party was the third faction, the Peace Democrats or 'Copperheads', who constituted the strongest organised opposition to the war. Centred in the western states and representing the old agrarian tradition, they feared that agriculture and state rights were being sacrificed to industry and nationalism. They advocated an armistice, the convocation of a convention to which the South would be invited, and amendments to the constitution to preserve state rights. Inasmuch as the Peace Democrats favoured maintenance of the nation, even if by an unpractical and impossible method, they were Unionists. But they were themselves divided. Some supported the formation of a western confederacy, and some organised secret societies which allegedly engaged in treasonable activities. Against opponents of the war Lincoln used the weapon of military arrests. At first he suspended the right of *habeas corpus* only in specified areas, but in 1862 he proclaimed that all who discouraged enlistments, resisted the militia draft, or engaged in disloyal practices would be subject to martial law. An estimated 13,000 persons were arrested and imprisoned. The arbitrary seizures shocked many Americans, including supporters of the war, but, considered historically, they only symbolised the impulse to enforced unity that modern war demands.

The Republican party also had its factions—the Radicals and the Conservatives. In fundamental agreement on most issues, they differed violently on the policy towards slavery to be adopted as a result of the war. The Radicals, of whom Congressman Thaddeus Stevens of Pennsylvania was a typical representative, wanted to abolish slavery immediately. The Conservatives, led by Lincoln, feared the effects of a sudden, violent change in race relations; they favoured a gradual compensated emancipation to be accomplished over a period of years. In the struggle between the two factions the Radicals won, not so much by their own efforts as by the logic of the war situation. The Conservatives, in proposing that the war should be fought to save the Union but not to destroy slavery, were asking the people to fight and sacrifice to preserve the institution that most people believed was the cause of the war. The longer the war continued the more certain Northern opinion was to demand the destruction of slavery. It was moving rapidly in that direction by the summer of 1862. In July the Radicals pushed through Congress a

Confiscation Act which declared free the slaves of all persons aiding and supporting the insurrection.

Lincoln, always a superb reader of public opinion, saw the signs of the times. He realised that in order to achieve his larger purpose of preserving the American nation he would have to yield his lesser objective of preventing the sudden striking down of slavery. To save the nation he had to keep the support of the Radicals, who were the unconditional Unionists; and if a majority of the Northern people wanted emancipation as a war aim, he could not afford to divide opinion by resisting their will. He decided, in July 1862, to place himself at the head of the antislavery movement by issuing an executive proclamation freeing slaves in the Confederacy. His decision, resting on the sound principle that a needed change should be made at the right time, was in the best tradition of English-American pragmatism.

Lincoln withheld announcement of his purpose until a favourable turn in the war. On 22 September 1862, after the battle of Antietam, he issued a preliminary proclamation stating that on 1 January 1863 he would declare free the slaves in all states then in rebellion. As no state returned to its allegiance by that date, he published the final Emancipation Proclamation. This declared forever free the slaves in most areas of the Confederacy. Not included were the state of Tennessee, most of which was under Federal control, and western Virginia and southern Louisiana, which were also held by Federal troops; presumably these areas were excepted because they were not enemy territory and hence were not subject to the war powers. The proclamation did not, of course, apply to the four loyal slave states, nor did it abolish slavery as an institution in the region where it did apply. Immediately the proclamation freed no slaves; its enforcement would have to wait until Federal armies conquered the South. But its promulgation meant that the war had taken a new turn—it had become a war to destroy slavery as well as to save the Union. And once the antislavery process was started it could not be reversed. Early in 1865 Congress sent to the states for ratification the Thirteenth Amendment to the Constitution, which freed slaves everywhere and abolished slavery as an institution.

In 1864 the United States faced a presidential election, the first to be held during a war. This election is one of the few in the history of democratic governments when a people were offered the choice of continuing a war or abandoning it—and voted for war. After the Congressional elections of 1862, in which the Democrats scored substantial gains, the Republicans attempted to strengthen their organisation by turning it into a coalition of all groups who supported the war. Seeking particularly to attract the War Democrats, they changed the party name from Republican to Union. Lincoln was the Union candidate in 1864, although many Radicals would have preferred a less conservative leader, and Andrew

Johnson, a War Democrat, was the nominee for Vice-President. In the summer it seemed that the Republicans would be defeated in the November election. Lincoln himself expected to be beaten. War weariness gripped the Northern people; they seemed ready to concede that the South could not be conquered. This depressed mood would, of course, reflect itself in votes for the Democrats. Oddly, the North appeared ready to give up the struggle at a moment when the exhausted South no longer had the resources to achieve a military decision. Some of the Radical leaders, convinced that Lincoln would drag the party down to defeat, planned to prevent his nomination and to substitute one of their men in his place.

Before they could move against Lincoln, the political picture suddenly changed. The Democrats met in convention and nominated the former general George B. McClellan, whom the Radicals feared and hated. The peace faction got a plank in the platform denouncing the war as a failure and calling for a truce and a national convention. Although McClellan repudiated the plank, the Democrats stood before the country as the peace party. The peace plank and McClellan's nomination had the effect of causing the Radicals to close ranks behind Lincoln. At the same time Northern armies scored several important victories, notably the capture of Atlanta, Georgia, which rejuvenated popular morale and raised Republican hopes.

When the votes were counted in November, Lincoln had 212 electoral votes to only twenty-one for McClellan. Lincoln's popular majority, however, was only 400,000; a slight shift of votes in the big states would have changed the result. But a Democratic victory would not have changed the outcome of the war. Even if McClellan had decided to comply with the peace plank, he would not have taken office until March 1865 and by then the South was at the point of collapse.

The Southern nation that came into existence as a result of the secession movement, the Confederate States of America, was a confederation of sovereign states. Delegates from the first seven states to secede met at Montgomery, Alabama, in February 1861, framed a constitution and chose the executive officers. (The four states that seceded later accepted the Montgomery constitution.) State sovereignty was specifically recognised in the constitution. The powers delegated to the central government were fewer than those in the constitution of the old Union, and the reserved powers of the states were greater. The Southern principle of the concurrent voice, the power of a minority to check the majority, appeared frequently in the document. To enact various types of legislation—to admit a new state, to pass an appropriation bill—a two-thirds vote of the two-house legislature was required. Any three states could demand and force the convocation of a convention of all the states to amend the constitution. The right of a state to secede was implied, but, significantly, was not expressly stated. Like the government of the Union, the

Confederate government was divided into three branches: an executive consisting of a President and Vice-President, a two-house Congress, and a National Judiciary.

The government-makers at Montgomery were anxious to avoid any impression that they represented a rash, revolutionary movement. As President they selected Jefferson Davis of Mississippi, a moderate secessionist, and as Vice-President, Alexander H. Stephens of Georgia, who believed passionately in the right of secession but doubted there was much cause for its exercise. The choice of Davis was fateful. In contrast to his rival at Washington, whose task was to preserve a nation, Davis's was to make one. He failed, largely because he lacked many of the elements of statesmanship. He had integrity and intelligence, and he was an excellent administrator. Over-conscious of his intelligence, he was sensitively proud of his opinions and could not brook criticism or contradiction. Over-aware of his administrative skill, he spent too much time on small routine items, and in political thinking rarely rose above the level of a cabinet secretary. He believed in the Southern cause intellectually, but felt no passion for it. His state-papers were logical and correct—and completely unmoving. Perhaps his greatest defect as a leader of a revolutionary cause was his refusal to realise that it was a revolution. He proceeded on the assumption that the Confederacy was an established, recognised nation. When the situation demanded ruthless zeal, he tied himself up in legal red tape. It is a curious fact that Lincoln, heading an established government, displayed more revolutionary vigour than Davis.

Davis's cabinet was, at the best, an assemblage of only average ability. Several of the members were capable administrators but nothing more. The ablest was Judah P. Benjamin, who held three different positions, finally becoming Secretary of State. He confined his energies to his particular department and never tried to influence Davis in large matters of policy. The personnel of the cabinet changed frequently. There were three Secretaries of State, two of the Treasury, five of War, and four Attorneys-General. The shifting nature of the body indicates Davis's reluctance to delegate power. The secretaries were, in effect, his clerks. Many of them recognised their status and resigned.

While the Northern economy expanded, the South underwent a period of shortages, suffering and sacrifice. Subjected to the strain of war, the static Southern economic system almost collapsed. The South lacked factories, machines, production managers, skilled labourers, and the resources to create new wealth. Whereas the North created new resources, the resources of the South were quickly consumed by the demands of the military machine. Moreover, the war, and specifically the blockade, cut off the South's principal source of revenue, the sale of its agricultural products in Europe. The conditions of Southern economic life posed hard problems for the men who had to finance the Confederacy's war efforts.

Because surplus capital had usually been invested in slaves and land, the amount of short-term assets held by banks or individuals was small. Southern banks, except in New Orleans, the South's only urban centre, were fewer and smaller than those in the North. The only specie possessed by the government was the $1,000,000 seized at the beginning of hostilities in the United States mints in the South.

The Confederacy drew its war revenue from three sources: taxation, loans, and paper money. Like its Northern counterpart, the Confederate Congress was reluctant to impose rigorous duties on a people unaccustomed to heavy taxes. The first measure, passed in 1861, failed really to tax. It provided for a direct tax on property to be levied by the states; if a state preferred, it could, instead of taxing its people, pay its quota as a state. Most states assumed the tax, which they met by issuing bonds. In 1863 Congress enacted an internal-revenue tax; a unique feature of the measure was the 'tax in kind', which required every planter and farmer to contribute one-tenth of his produce to the government. The returns from the various war taxes were slight. Because of difficulties in fixing the value of the farm-produce received, the exact amount cannot be calculated, but it has been estimated that the Confederacy raised only 1 per cent of its total income by taxes. The government issued bonds in such large amounts that the people came to suspect its ability to redeem them. Some of the loans were in the form of produce, subscribers being permitted to deposit commodities, or the promise of commodities, with the government in exchange for bonds. Often the promises were not fulfilled or the goods were spoiled or destroyed by the enemy. One reason why the government accepted taxes and loans in produce was its desire to escape its own currency. The government started issuing paper notes in 1861, partly because it needed ready-money, partly because this form of currency seemed an easy way to finance the war. Once started, it could not stop. By 1864 a total of $1,000,000,000 had been issued. The inevitable result was depreciation and an astronomical inflation of prices. It was an index of the unstable currency system that Federal greenbacks circulated in the South at a higher premium than Confederate notes. Hit particularly hard by the inflated prices were people with fixed incomes and town-dwellers, who depended on others for their food. They suffered real privation and in the process lost much of their faith in Confederate victory. To protect the government from the effects of its own currency, Congress enacted the Impressment Act, which authorised departments to fix their own purchase price. One result was to cause producers to avoid selling to the government.

The Confederacy first attempted to recruit its armies from volunteers. In 1861 several hundred thousand men enlisted, the great majority for twelve months. Once the initial enthusiasm had waned, volunteering dropped off, and the Confederacy seemed threatened by a manpower crisis. The most ominous feature was that the twelve-months men, the veterans, were not re-enlisting. Accordingly, in April 1862 Congress adopted a Conscription Act declaring that all able-bodied white males between eighteen and thirty-five were liable for three years military service. The twelve-months soldiers were retained in the army but required to serve only two years more. Later measures in 1862 and 1864 extended the age-limits to seventeen and fifty. The original act and those that followed provided for numerous exemptions. It was realised that some men had to be left at home to perform the productive functions. Consequently, many occupational deferments were permitted. The framers erred in allowing too many group-exemptions and in excusing individuals—editors, teachers, printers, and others—who were not engaged in vital work. These exemptions aroused wide resentment on the part of groups not excluded, who felt they were being discriminated against. Some provisions seemed to favour the rich. A conscript could escape service by employing a substitute (eventually this clause was repealed), and one white man on each plantation with twenty or more slaves was deferred. The so-called 'twenty-nigger law' angered ordinary folk, moving them to say it was a rich man's war and a poor man's fight.

Conscription filled up the armies until the end of 1862. As 1863 opened, some 500,000 men were serving. Thereafter the forces steadily decreased in size. Military reverses, war weariness, and the occupation of large areas by Federal armies combined to dry up the manpower sources. At the close of 1863, 465,000 men were carried on the army rolls, but only about 230,000 were present for duty. The situation worsened in 1864–5, when an estimated 100,000 desertions occurred. When the end came, all Confederate armies in the field numbered only about 100,000. As with the Union forces, the exact total of men in service is difficult to determine. An approximately accurate estimate is that 900,000 served for three years.

At the outbreak of war the Southern people were almost united in their desire to achieve independence. The only organised opposition to the war came from the mountain areas, particularly in western Virginia and eastern Tennessee, whose people constituted less than 10 per cent of the Southern population. Southerners were united in wishing to win the war, but they divided bitterly on how it should be conducted. Some of the differences almost tore the government to pieces. In part, the divisions were the clashes normal in any popular government: people criticised Davis for making faulty decisions or Congress for enacting unwise laws. Other controversies reflected the conditions of Southern culture. Most upper-class Southerners—and men from this caste held most of the high offices—were proud, sensitive, imperious individuals. Perhaps because they were masters of a subject race, they took offence easily when opposed or criticised. They were accustomed to giving orders, but did not submit readily to discipline. Many of the fierce quarrels between President Davis and Congress can be explained by the personalities of the parties involved. In contrast with Lincoln, who vetoed only three bills, Davis vetoed thirty-eight and saw thirty-seven of them repassed.

But the great divisive force was, ironically, the principle of states rights. Southerners had talked so much about states rights that it had become a cult with them, to a point where they resented any kind of control. The supporters of states rights possessed sufficient cohesiveness to be known as a party—the states rights party, headed by Vice-President Stephens. They stood first for state sovereignty and then for a national Southern state. They desired an independent South, but if to achieve that goal states rights had to be sacrificed, they preferred defeat. Passionately devoted to their quixotic principles, they fought almost every attempt of the government to impose centralised controls. They attacked the Davis administration on two main issues: (1) they denied that the government could suspend *habeas corpus* or conscript soldiers; and (2) they alleged that the administration was refusing opportunities to negotiate peace. Davis, faced by opposition to the war in the mountain areas, asked Congress for authority to dispense with civil law (instead of suspending it himself, as Lincoln did). He received permission to suspend for only a limited time or in a limited place; a bill giving him general authorisation was defeated by the states-righters, who accused him of seeking to establish a dictatorship. Their opposition to conscription was equally violent and, because state officials could hinder its execution, more effective. By the terms of the draft act, governors could certify state militia troops as exempt, and some governors, notably Joseph Brown of Georgia and Zebulon M. Vance of North Carolina, kept thousands of men out of service. In 1864, with Federal armies striking deep into the South, Brown defied the government to enforce conscription in Georgia. The states-righters were fascinated by the idea of a negotiated peace, and brought constant pressure on Davis to make overtures to the North. They never made it absolutely clear whether they wanted a settlement based on independence or on a return of the South to the Union. At different times they urged both alternatives. The evidence seems plain enough that in the later stages of the war they would have accepted a peace without victory, with whatever control over race relations they could have persuaded the North to grant.

An assessment of the Southern failure would have to give weight to several factors—the South's lack of industrial resources, the inadequacy of its transport system, the collapse of its financial system. Ranking high on any list would be the nature of its political arrangements. The Confederacy was founded on a principle, states rights, that made failure almost inevitable. It is highly doubtful whether a confederation of sovereignties can win a modern war. If it could, it is even more doubtful that such a government could survive in the modern world.

At the outset of the war neither government had a general strategic plan. Strategic designs were worked out in the heat of conflict and in the light of what the planners learned about the military situation. Because the policy of the North was to restore the Union by force, Northern strategy had to be offensive. Federal armies had to invade the South, defeat Confederate armies, and occupy the entire section. The policy of the South was to establish its independence by force. Therefore the government determined on a defensive strategy. This decision was forced on the South partly by the nature of Northern strategy, and partly because a strategy of defence seemed logical for a power that wanted only to be let alone and that harboured no aggressive intentions. With equal logic, the South might have demonstrated that it was too strong to be conquered by going over to the offensive and winning victories on Northern soil.

Geography influenced profoundly the strategic planning of both sides and the nature of the war. The physical features of the South, in which most of the battles would be fought, divided the war into three theatres: the eastern, the western, and the trans-Mississippi. The great Appalachian Mountain barrier, extending from Maryland to Georgia, made impossible any unified conduct of operations east of the Mississippi. The area between the mountains and the sea-coast became the eastern theatre, and the vast region between the mountains and the Mississippi became the western theatre. West of the river, the states of Arkansas, Louisiana, and Texas constituted the trans-Mississippi theatre.

Most of the fighting in the eastern theatre occurred in Virginia, where the chief Northern objective was to capture Richmond, which became the Confederate capital after Virginia seceded, and to defeat the defending Southern army. The movements of both armies were largely controlled by the proximity of the rival capitals, separated by a marching distance of only 130 miles. For the Northern invaders, the most obvious route was to strike from Washington or a base in northern Virginia straight southward to Richmond. Once, in 1862, they attempted, unsuccessfully, another possible invasion road, moving on the waterways east of the capital. In western Virginia was a secondary route between the capitals, the Shenandoah valley, running the length of the state and reaching to the Potomac River. Either side could use it for an offensive or for a diversionary movement to deceive the other. The Confederates were particularly adept in manœuvring their valley forces in a manner to create illusions that they meant to threaten Washington. Not until 1864–5 did the Federals crush Confederate resistance in Virginia and grasp Richmond.

In the western theatre the first strategic objective of the Federals was to seize the line of the Mississippi, thereby splitting the Confederacy into two. To achieve this they moved, with land and sea forces and from north and south, against Confederate strong-points on the river. When they found a particular place too strong to attack, they moved on streams parallel to the Mississippi, thus outflanking the Confederates. By the summer of 1863, with the fall of Vicksburg, the Federals had possession of the river line. They then started operations to secure their next objective, the line of the Tennessee River. This stream, flowing across Tennessee and part of Alabama to the Ohio, was an obvious invasion path into the heart of the South. On the Tennessee the key position was Chattanooga. If the Federals could capture the city, they would have a base from which they could again split the Confederacy. They occupied Chattanooga in 1863, and from it in 1864 General W. T. Sherman moved in the great march that carried him by the end of the war to North Carolina.

Action in the trans-Mississippi area was minor in comparison with the campaigns elsewhere. Neither side committed large forces in this region. Federal forces operating from Missouri occupied the northern half of Arkansas. In 1862 a Northern naval and land expedition seized New Orleans, which with the southern part of Louisiana was held for the remainder of the war. Several plans were broached to occupy the rest of Arkansas and Louisiana and to send a column into Texas, but the Federal high command was unwilling to supply sufficient troops to execute them. It was unnecessary, after the fall of Vicksburg, to conquer the states west of the Mississippi. The Federals, merely by holding the river line, could contain the entire theatre and isolate it.

The strategy of the Confederacy, largely formulated by Davis, was to meet each Northern offensive, to hold every threatened point. It has been called a dispersed defensive. An alternative programme for the side with the inferior forces would have been to guard shorter lines enclosing the most defensible areas or those containing important resources. In deciding to defend the entire South, Davis was partly influenced by practical political considerations. For the new Southern government to abandon any part of its territory would seem an admission of weakness and might deprive it of popular support. But Davis seemed to think almost instinctively in defensive terms; with him the holding of places, many of which turned out to be traps for their garrisons, became an *idée fixe*. On the few occasions when Southern armies did undertake offensive movements, the thrusts failed—largely because they were made with insufficient strength—because the government refused to add available defensive units to the attacking forces. But Davis and his advisers should not be criticised for adopting a defective strategy. Their military thinking was necessarily limited by the influences of their culture. As Clausewitz said, a nation's social system will determine the kind of war it fights. The principle of the Southern system was states rights, and the South fought a states-rights war. Southern political leaders were unable to install centralisation in the conduct of government, and Southern military directors failed to establish a unified strategy or a centralised command.

The Confederate command throughout the war consisted mainly of

President Davis. For a brief period early in 1862 Davis appointed General Robert E. Lee to act under his direction as commander of all Confederate armies. But Lee, a man of brilliant abilities, was not called upon, except at rare intervals, to formulate strategy; he acted as a mere adviser, providing counsel when Davis asked for it. In the summer of 1862 Lee assumed field command, and Davis did not replace him. Not until February 1864 did he take another adviser, Braxton Bragg, who had failed in field command. Early in 1865 Congress, in a move designed to clip Davis's powers, created the position of general-in-chief; it was expected that Davis would have to give the post to Lee, the South's greatest general, and that Lee would take over the direction of military affairs. Davis did appoint Lee, announcing at the same time that he was still commander-in-chief, and Lee accepted the office on this basis. The war ended before the new arrangement had a chance to prove itself. It is doubtful whether Lee could have commanded a field army and also directed other armies. Nor is it certain that Lee, who thought primarily in terms of his native Virginia, could have altered his strategic thinking to include national concepts.

The United States entered the war with an archaic and inadequate command system. Command arrangements in the small peacetime army were performed by an agency loosely referred to as 'the staff', which consisted of the general holding appropriate rank in the army and the heads of the War Department bureaux, and which was not a staff in the modern meaning of the word. It held no joint meetings and discussed no common problems. No member or section was charged with formulating strategy. Each official—the quartermaster-general, the head of ordnance, the adjutant-general—administered his department much as he pleased. The senior general at the beginning of the war was seventy-five-year-old Winfield Scott, who, with the exception of John E. Wool, another aged veteran, was the only officer to have commanded troops in numbers sufficient to be called an army. (Scott's army in the Mexican War numbered 14,000.) None of the younger officers, who would command the field armies in the war, had directed as large a unit as a brigade.

At the head of the military organisation was the constitutional commander-in-chief, the President. Lincoln had a completely civilian background; he had no military education, and, except for an inconsequential militia interlude, no military experience. Yet Lincoln became a great war-President; as a director of war he was superior to Davis, who had received a professional military education and served in the regular army. Lincoln illustrates the truth of Clausewitz's statement that an acquaintance with military affairs is not the principal qualification for a war director but that a superior mind and moral strength are better qualifications. Because of his mental and moral powers, Lincoln developed into a superb strategist. Recognising that numbers were on his side, he mobilised the maximum manpower resources of the North, and urged his generals to exercise constant pressure on the strategic line of the Confederacy until a weak spot was found. Better than his first generals, he realised that the true objective was to destroy the Confederate armies and not to occupy places. Lincoln has been criticised for interfering with his generals, but most of his interventions were designed to force hesitant or timid officers to act aggressively. And most of his interferences had salutary effects. In contrast with Davis, who interfered with his generals to make a faulty defensive strategy more defensive, Lincoln acted to implement a sound offensive strategy.

During the first three years of the war, Lincoln performed many functions that would now be handled by the chief-of-staff. He framed strategic plans and even directed tactical movements. He assumed an active role because of the inadequacies of the existing command system and because the various officers he appointed as general-in-chief—Scott, George B. McClellan, Henry W. Halleck—either would not or could not execute their responsibilities. Early in 1864, with Lincoln and Congress as chief architects, the nation finally received an efficient, modern command system. Thereafter Lincoln exercised fewer command functions, although he continued to supervise the general operations of the military machine.

Under the new arrangements, Ulysses S. Grant, who had emerged as the North's ablest general, was named general-in-chief by Lincoln, with the rank of lieutenant-general created by Congress. Grant was charged with planning strategy for all theatres of the war and directing the movements of the seventeen Federal armies on all fronts. He proved to be the general for whom Lincoln had long searched. He possessed, as did no other general on either side, the ability to see the war as a whole and to devise over-all strategy. Although Lincoln gave him a relatively free hand, Grant always submitted the general features of his plans to the President for approval. Halleck, who had been general-in-chief, now became 'chief-of-staff', a post in which he acted as a channel of communication between Lincoln and Grant and between Grant and the departmental commanders. The 1864 system of commander-in-chief to form policy and indicate grand strategy, general-in-chief to frame battle strategy, and chief-of-staff to co-ordinate information was, with the possible exception of the Prussian General Staff, the most efficient then in existence. It was one of the principal reasons why the North won the war.

The Civil War determined many things, both immediately and in its ultimate effects on national and world history. It decided that the United States would remain one nation. It unified that nation as it had never been unified before and placed it on the way to become a great world power. By destroying slavery and by demonstrating that a popular government could preserve liberty during an internal conflict, it vindicated and vitalised the democratic concept everywhere. Lincoln saw the significance of this aspect of the struggle. After the election of 1864 he said: 'It has demonstrated that a people's government can sustain a national election in the midst of a great civil war. Until now it has not been known to the world that this was a possibility.'[1] Some of the immediate results of the war were unfortunate and malefic. The nation had to chart a course through the painful ordeal of reconstruction, which was not dealt with on a very high level of statesmanship, and through the booming economic expansion after the war, when material standards seemed to transcend all others. But even then the great idealistic critics of American life saw the war in a long and proper perspective and believed that its results would endure. Revolutions in the interest of society, wrote Emerson, are always remembered: 'These are read with passionate interest and never lose their pathos by time.' If the American people marching with 'a careless swagger to the height of power' could recover and regulate the spirit which had enabled them to win the war, the United States could become 'the new nation, the guide and lawgiver of all nations'.[2] And Walt Whitman, who, deeply touched by the impact of the war, understood its meaning and his country better than most, seeing in 1871 many things in America that he did not like, could write: 'Today, ahead, though dimly yet, we see in vistas, a copious, sane, gigantic offspring.'[3]

[1] Roy P. Basler (ed.), *The Collected Works of Abraham Lincoln*, vol. VIII, p. 101.
[2] *The Complete Writings of Ralph Waldo Emerson* (New York, 1929), vol. II, pp. 1185, 1188, 1193–4.
[3] 'Democratic Vistas', in Mark van Doren (ed.), *Walt Whitman* (New York, 1945), pp. 389–90.

CHAPTER XXV

THE STATES OF LATIN AMERICA

THE wars of Spanish American independence virtually ended in 1824. Between the Great Lakes and Cape Horn European dominion in the New World had been reduced to a chain of islands in the West Indies, to the British settlement of Belize in Central America, and to the three colonies of British, French and Dutch Guiana in South America. In the Caribbean sea the old French colony of Saint Domingue had established its rule, as the new republic of Haiti, over the old Spanish colony of Santo Domingo. Brazil had separated from Portugal. And from the viceroyalties, captaincies-general, and presidencies of Spain on the mainlands of North and South America seven new republics had been formed—Mexico, the United Provinces of Central America, Colombia, Peru, Chile, Paraguay, and those Provinces of the Río de la Plata which were to become at last Argentina. To these new states four others were added by 1830. The provinces of Upper Peru, the former Presidency of Charcas, became in 1825 the Republic of Bolivia. Uruguay, in 1828, was born of war between the United Provinces of the Río de la Plata and Brazil; and Ecuador and Venezuela, in 1830, both seceded from Colombia. Territorial changes were yet to come. Other republics would be brought to birth. But already in 1830 the political map of South America had more or less assumed its modern form.

The largest of these thirteen successor states to the former dominions of Spain and Portugal, and the most fortunate in its history, was the empire of Brazil. Long years of war and civil disorder had destroyed the prosperity, undermined the stability, and disrupted the economic life of most of the new republics of Spanish America, and for them, untutored in the art of self-government, the bitter fruit of independence was political collapse. Politically at least, these states were not the adult heirs of imperial Spain; they were her orphan children. In most there was little cohesive force, little sense of *communitas*, to weld into a whole the diverse elements of which society was composed; and while the masses were sunk in poverty and ignorance, the dominant social class had yet to learn to govern itself before it could govern others. 'Is it conceivable', the future liberator of northern South America, Simón Bolívar, had asked in 1815, 'that a people but recently freed from its chains can ascend into the sphere of liberty without melting its wings like Icarus and plunging into the abyss?'[1] And fifteen years later, nearing his tragic end, he wrote in anguish

---

[1] Vicente Lecuna (ed.), *Cartas del Libertador* (10 vols., Caracas, 1929–30; vol. xi, New York, 1948; vol. xii, ed. M. Pérez Vila, Caracas, 1959), vol. i, p. 196.

42-2

and despair: 'For us America is ungovernable. He who serves a revolution ploughs the sea.'[1]

The independence of Brazil was cast in a different mould. In this vast and empty land, whose whole population at the beginning of the nineteenth century was less than four millions, but whose every province was as big as a European state, the transition from dependent to independent status had been a gradual process. Colony became kingdom, kingdom empire. There was no abrupt break with the colonial past, no violent struggle for control of the instruments of government, no prolonged and desolating civil war. Independence was achieved almost without bloodshed. The heir to the crown of Portugal himself became the emperor of Brazil, endowed the country with its constitution, and secured its entry into the family of nations; and the throne thus peacefully established was to survive for more than sixty-five years.

The prestige of the Braganza dynasty preserved the unity and integrity of the old viceroyalty of Brazil. But by 1830 the personal popularity of the young Prince Pedro, who had raised, in 1822, the famous cry of 'Independence or Death!', had vanished. As the price of their recognition of Brazilian independence, he had been compelled to sign unpopular treaties both with Britain and with Portugal. He had fought, and certainly had not won, an inglorious war with the United Provinces of the Río de la Plata. He had remained, in Brazilian eyes, improperly concerned with Portuguese affairs; and as his foreign policy had been discredited, so also had his domestic policy. Too absolutist in tone, too dissolute in manners, and too much under the influence of the Portuguese element in the country for the liking of the plantation aristocracy of Brazil, he had never known how to become 'entirely and truly a Brazilian'.[2] On 7 April 1831 he was forced to abdicate; and with that event the transference of power in Brazil from a Portuguese to a native aristocracy was at last completed.

'Brazil will belong to Brazilians, and will be free.' So wrote Evaristo da Veiga, the brilliant editor of the Rio de Janeiro journal *Aurora Fluminense* in a proclamation issued by the senators and deputies of the empire on 8 April.[3] But would Brazil, under a succession of regencies—for the new emperor, Dom Pedro de Alcantara, was not yet six years old—continue to exist at all? Would the monarchy, and not only the monarchy but the unity of the country, of which the crown was the symbol, survive? So violent was the reaction from royal absolutism, so rapid the political disintegration, and so chaotic the economic condition of the country after the exile of the first Pedro, that the answers to both these questions were

---

[1] Vicente Lecuna (ed.), *Cartas del Libertador*, vol. IX, p. 376.
[2] John Armitage, *The History of Brazil* (2 vols., London, 1836), vol. II, p. 104.
[3] H. Handelmann, *Historia do Brasil* (Rio de Janeiro, 1931), p. 932. Handelmann's work was first published in German in 1860.

doubtful. As in the new states of Spanish America, there were continual outbursts of disorder, barrack-room conspiracies, and military risings. Pará, in the far north, was the scene of revolutionary disturbances for four years, Rio Grande do Sul, in the extreme south, defied the authorities at Rio de Janeiro for ten. And while the integrity of Brazil was itself threatened, under the Acto Addicional to the constitution, promulgated in 1834, which substituted a single regent for a triple regency but substituted also provincial legislatures for provincial councils, the unitary monarchy almost, but not quite, became a federal republic.

But the experience was conclusive. Moderate opinion rallied behind the child emperor, and Brazil was fortunate to find statesmen of high ability to devote themselves to the tasks of preserving the monarchy, maintaining the supremacy of civil government, and reconstructing authority. The Acto Addicional was itself modified in 1840 in a sense unfavourable to the provincial legislatures, and in the same year, for the sake of internal peace and unity, Dom Pedro was declared of age. A year later he was crowned, though not till 1847 did he begin to rule as well as reign, and the times were still troubled. Rio Grande do Sul was not pacified till 1845, and there was a last revolutionary protest from Pernambuco in 1848. But thereafter, and for forty years, Brazil enjoyed, under the benevolent rule of her scholar-emperor, a peace and prosperity rarely known to most of her Spanish American neighbours.

At the time of the first census in 1872 the population of Brazil was still only ten millions. In the 'fifties it was no more than eight. Of the inland provinces Minas Geraes alone was relatively populous, and, for the rest, civilisation was barely more than a coastal fringe. The bulk of the population was illiterate. More than a third was in slavery, and, north and south, a landed aristocracy—the sugar and cotton planters of the north-east, the cattle proprietors of the inland provinces and of Rio Grande do Sul, the coffee-planters of the south-east—dominated both social and economic life.

But a new Brazil was already emerging. Though slavery remained to cast its dark shadow over the empire, the slave-trade had ceased. The efforts made to suppress it under the Anglo-Brazilian convention of 1826 and an anti-slave-trade law of 1831 had indeed failed, and while Brazilian opinion had been outraged by the high-handed methods employed by Great Britain to sweep the seas of slavers, particularly after the passing of the Aberdeen Act of 1845, perhaps a million slaves had entered the country between 1831 and 1851. But in 1850, at long last, the trade was outlawed and, within a few years, it ended. To Rio Grande do Sul, Santa Catarina and Paraná the thin flow of German immigrants, who were to help in later years to turn southern Brazil into a true zone of expanding settlement, was increasing. Though Bahia and Pernambuco still retained their old pre-eminence, based on cotton and sugar, the expansion of the coffee industry in the south-east—in São Paulo, Minas Geraes and Rio de Janeiro—already foreshadowed the days when coffee would be king. And in the 'fifties and 'sixties a silent transformation was in progress. Banks, railways, factories, steamships, telegraph lines, appeared. The great 'Union and Industry' highway to link Rio de Janeiro with Minas Geraes was begun in 1853, the Dom Pedro Segundo railway in 1855, the famous Santos–São Paulo line in 1860. In 1851 Ireneu de Souza, best known as the Baron of Mauá, founded the Mauá Bank; and Mauá, who built the first railway and introduced gas-light to Rio de Janeiro and the steamboat to the Amazon, and whose operations were conducted on an international scale, was the forerunner of a new age and of a generation whose interests would lie in industry, commerce and finance, as well as in land, and whose rise would help to undermine the rule of the *fazendeiro* or landowner.[1]

It was, however, the *fazendeiro* who made the empire and who dominated its political life as he dominated its social and economic life. But above him stood the emperor. The basis of the political system was an oligarchy so small that under the constitution given by Dom Pedro I to the nation in 1824 only a tiny fraction of the population ever exercised the suffrage. Its form was that of the parliamentary government of England. A prime minister selected his colleagues. A cabinet was dependent upon a majority in the Chamber of Deputies. An upper house—the Senate, whose members were appointed for life—won an enviable reputation for the gravity and distinction of its debates. Two parties—the Liberals and the Conservatives—rotated in office. The press was free. Yet whatever the panoply of constitutionalism, and whatever the apparent limitations on the imperial prerogative, in the last analysis supreme power rested with the emperor. His executive and so-called 'moderative' functions, his appointing and dismissive powers, ensured that in the end what Dom Pedro wished would prevail.

Full of interest and fertile in experience, the system worked for two reasons. In the first place, for the greater part of Dom Pedro's reign the interests of the monarchy and the interests of the oligarchy were identified. Secondly, the system worked because Dom Pedro wished it to work. Parliament, in his view, was to assume the political direction and administration of the country; it was his task to exercise a general supervision and to ensure, if he could, the honesty of officials and the correct observance of constitutional practices. Errors, no doubt, he made, and as his reign progressed criticism of his 'personal' power became increasingly marked. But Dom Pedro was the schoolmaster of the nation: it was not the least of his services that he gave to Brazil a political education.

The empire reached its full height by the middle 'sixties. Trade and revenues were expanding, foreign investment—principally British invest-

---

[1] *Fazenda*—estate, ranch or plantation. Hence *fazendeiro*.

ment—was increasing. Until the 'eighties, indeed, and at a time when the export of British capital was playing an increasingly important role, Brazil remained the area in Latin America most favoured by the British investor, and between 1852 and 1875 one Brazilian loan after another was floated in London by N. M. Rothschild and Sons, rightly named 'the bankers of the empire'.[1]

But though the prosperity of the empire continued to increase, the prestige of the monarchy steadily declined, and the decade which opened with the entry of Brazil into the greatest of all South American wars, the Paraguayan War of 1864–70 (see p. 673), revealed, for the first time, the signs of fissure in the imperial structure. The Liberals, in and out of parliament, campaigned for the curtailment of Dom Pedro's 'personal power'. The Republican party, though it was long quite uninfluential, was born in 1870. The question of negro slavery became more insistent, for Brazil, after Lincoln's emancipation proclamation of 1863, was now the only great slave state in the world; and though, in 1871, the famous Rio Branco law, which created an emancipation fund and provided that all children henceforth born of slave mothers should be free, seemed to relegate the subject to the background, nine years later the abolition movement was in full swing. Just as the rise of the republican idea in the only monarchy in the New World was sooner or later inevitable, so, moreover, with the rise of ultramontanism in Europe, was a clash between church and state, and a struggle which began in 1873 over the question of freemasonry seriously affected both the prestige of the monarchy and the loyalty to Dom Pedro of a large section of the Brazilian clergy. The Paraguayan war itself, the one great, though not the only military struggle of the empire—for Brazil, always interested in the politics of the Río de la Plata basin, had assisted in the overthrow of the Argentine dictator, Rosas, in 1852—was not only long and costly; it engendered friction between civil and military authorities, and it left a sinister legacy of military discontent, a contempt, among soldiers, for the ways of the civilian. And, finally, amidst social and economic change, the pre-eminence of the *fazendeiro* who had made the empire was already being undermined. The empire was to survive till 1889. But by the 'seventies it had already begun to wane.

A slave state among free states, a monarchy amidst republics, the empire of Brazil was a unique phenomenon in Latin America; and, of the states formed from the old dominions of Spain, Chile alone, in the years after 1830, experienced a comparable evolution. Geography imposed a natural unity on Chile. The country was an island. The mountains and the desert, the sea and the forest, hemmed it in on every side. As Copiapó marked the limit of settlement to the north, so Valdivia and Chiloé were outposts of civilisation in the south. But, between the rim of the desert

[1] J. F. Normano, *Brazil. A Study of Economic Types* (Chapel Hill, 1935), p. 155.

of Atacama and the Bío-Bío river, which formed the northern limit of the Indian territory of Araucania, settled Chile was a region somewhat smaller than England and Scotland. Its whole population in 1830 was little more than a million, European and Indian in origin but distinguished by an increasing racial homogeneity. And the key both to its social and to its economic structure lay in an inherited system of landownership which had made the *hacienda,* or landed estate, the fundamental territorial, social and economic unit—to which the peasant was bound by contract or custom—and had endowed Chile with a landed gentry conservative by instinct, habit and conviction.

The *fazendeiro* made the empire of Brazil. The *hacendado* made the 'aristocratic republic' of Chile. And as, in Chile, the dislocation wrought by the wars of independence was less severe than in most of the other republics of Spanish America, so also the period of political experimentation and disorder was shorter. In 1830, after seven turbulent years during which the country had been torn between competing theories of government and rival aspirants to govern, the conservative oligarchy closed its ranks. In Diego Portales, a member of the business house of Portales, Cea and Company, and the architect of a new order, the oligarchy found a leader and Chile a master, and under a constitution which, after prolonged debate, was finally promulgated in 1833 the state was at last organised on solid and lasting foundations.

The constitution of 1833 exactly corresponded with the ideas and habits of the Chilean aristocracy and with the structure and traditions of Chilean society. It revived the law of entail, which had been under attack; excluded from the suffrage the illiterate and the propertyless—that is, the greater part of the population; allied the church to the state; and married local to central government. Within the central government it endowed the president with powers so extensive that he could, and did, become virtually an autocrat, an autocrat, however, who was less a personal ruler than the leader of the party to which he owed his power. And for forty years the system thus established was little changed. During these years internal peace was only three times seriously disturbed and Chile knew only four presidents—Joaquín Prieto, Manuel Bulnes, Manuel Montt, and José Joaquín Pérez—each of whom ruled for two successive terms. And though by the 'sixties a new order was already arising, for half a century longer, but under very different conditions, the constitution of 1833 continued to be the institutional framework of Chilean political life. It survived the civil war of 1891, which marked the downfall of the presidential system and its replacement by a parliamentary regime, and it was not finally abandoned till 1925. No instrument of government in Latin America proved more successful; only one other was to have so long a life.

With the establishment of political stability in the 'thirties, the way was opened for the slow unfolding of the country's economic life. A war designed to break up a confederation, newly established, between Peru and Bolivia—the creation of the then dictator of Bolivia, General Andrés Santa Cruz, and potentially an over-mighty neighbour to the north—retarded this development indeed, and occasioned, in 1837, the murder of Portales by mutinous soldiers. But in the 'forties the pace of change was quickened. New discoveries of mineral wealth—copper and silver in the north, coal in the south; the orderly conduct of the national finances, and the restoration of confidence in Chilean credit by an honest endeavour to meet obligations incurred under the London loan of 1822; a rising foreign trade, the greater part with Britain; all spelt a new prosperity. There was no Chilean Mauá. But what Mauá did for Brazil, William Wheelwright, a native of Massachusetts, in part did for Chile—founding in 1840 the Pacific Steam Navigation Company, whose ships were to link the ports of Chile to those of Peru and Panama and Europe, introducing the electric telegraph, building the first railway, from Copiapó to the copper port of Caldera, which was opened in 1851, and promoting the line between Santiago and Valparaíso, which another United States citizen, Henry Meiggs, completed in 1863. The foundation first of Fort Bulnes and then, in 1847, of Punta Arenas marked the beginnings of pioneer advance to the far south and the effective occupation of the Straits of Magellan, while in a region less remote, but which was still 'not Chile, but Chilean territory', German immigrants, farmers and peasants were encouraged in the late 'forties and 'fifties to find new homes in the forests and glades of Valdivia. Meanwhile the creation in 1842 of the University of Chile, with the great Venezuelan, Andrés Bello, as its first rector, of the first Teachers' Training College, presided over by the Argentine exile, Domingo Faustino Sarmiento, and of the short-lived Literary Society, reflected and encouraged an intellectual awakening soon to be mirrored in political life itself.

Chile was a one-party state. But it was also a changing state. Its cities were growing. A generation was arising which knew not Portales, and already in the late 'forties a new Liberal party appeared to fight for political freedom, to challenge conservative rule, and, in 1851, to challenge it indeed by force of arms. The struggle was short, bloody, and decisive, and for the next ten years Manuel Montt, against whose election to the presidency the Liberals had revolted, maintained a political control as rigid as that of Portales himself. Yet the famous *decenio Montt* (1851–61), progressive in almost every field except the political, revealed a gradual weakening in the power of the oligarchy. A stern disciplinarian and a firm believer in the 'government of the masses by the classes',[1] Montt himself delivered a body blow against the entrenched power of privilege by abolishing, in 1852, the law of entail, thus facilitating the division of the

[1] M. H. Hervey, *Dark Days in Chile* (London, 1891–2), p. 305.

great estates. He was led, moreover, into a sharp conflict with the church, in its origins trivial enough, but destroying, as a result, the harmony which had hitherto generally existed between the ecclesiastical and the civil authorities. And as his administration had begun with an outburst of violence, so, as it drew to an end, the threat of violence was renewed. The extreme Conservatives, resenting Montt's liberalism, made common cause with the extreme Liberals, who resented his absolutism, and when, in 1859, his devoted follower and *alter ego*, Antonio Varas, was put forward to succeed him, civil war followed. As in 1851, the struggle was short. But Varas withdrew his name, and in the elections of 1861 it was a compromise candidate, José Joaquín Pérez, who was elected.

The election of Pérez—the last president to serve for two consecutive five-year terms—marked the beginnings of a progressive liberalisation of politics, the end of the 'autocratic' and the beginning of the 'liberal' republic. There was no sudden change. But Pérez invited the co-operation of the Liberals; and the increasing importance of the legislature, the organisation of a Radical party, the enactment of a law permitting freedom of worship, and the passage of a constitutional amendment, in 1871, forbidding the president to succeed himself, were all signs of the times, the reflection of social as well as of economic change. Chile in 1871 was still a small and 'modest' republic.[1] The aristocracy still ruled, but it was an aristocracy far wider than the oligarchy which had constructed the constitution of 1833. And a new era was about to begin, both in political and economic life. The country had fought in the 'sixties one foreign war. A dispute between Spain and Peru had culminated in 1864 in the seizure by a Spanish naval squadron of the Chincha Islands, with their rich guano deposits, in the bay of Pisco. The islands were returned, on humiliating terms, a few months later. But American sentiment had been aroused. There were protests from Chile, demonstrations in Santiago, prolonged diplomatic interchanges, and, at the last, the Spanish admiral proclaimed, in September 1865, a blockade of the coast of Chile, and Chile replied with a declaration of war against Spain, in which Peru, Bolivia and Ecuador later joined. Its major incidents were the suicide of the admiral after the capture of one of his schooners by a Chilean sloop, and the outrageous bombardment of Valparaíso, followed by that of Callao, in 1866. Not till 1871, however, was a truce signed; and another, and greater, war was soon to begin. Its field was the Desert of Atacama where, for more than a quarter of a century, Chile and Bolivia had disputed each other's territorial claims, and where, with Chilean workers and Anglo-Chilean capital, the nitrate industry had begun its rapid rise. The stage was already set for that War of the Pacific (1879–83) in which Chile was to deprive Bolivia of her Pacific littoral and Peru of her southernmost pro-

[1] The epithet is that of President Balmaceda, in 1890. *Diario Oficial* (Santiago), 2 October 1890.

vinces, and from which she emerged, enriched with new sources of wealth, the dominant power on the west coast of South America.

To turn from the history of Chile to that of Bolivia is to enter a different world, the Andean and Indian world of tropical South America. Bolivia herself was a state in little more than name, without political, social or geographical cohesion. Her vast amorphous territory stretched from the barren shores of the Pacific to the tropical jungles of the basin of the Amazon. But the bulk of her population of little more than a million was confined among those lofty heights where the Andes reach their greatest breadth. Here the city of La Paz had lain on one of the great trade-routes of the Spanish empire, from Lima to Buenos Aires. Here also the Villa Imperial de Potosí had won for itself the name of the most famous mining town in history. But these were memories of the past. The trade-route had been disrupted. The mining industry lay in ruins. A prisoner of her mountains even before the loss of her maritime territory to Chile in the War of the Pacific, her native Indian peoples half-barbarous, her small white minority and her more numerous body of *mestizos* untrained to rule and unequal to the heavy burden of administration, Bolivia was long doomed to stasis or decay. And though for ten years (1829–39) an able *mestizo* soldier with imperial ambitions, Andrés Santa Cruz, maintained control and even succeeded in uniting Bolivia and Peru in a short-lived federal state, the Confederación Peru-Boliviana (1836–9) (see p. 665), thereafter, with but brief intervals, the country's annals became a sombre story of anarchy, misery and tyranny, culminating in the grotesque rule of an illiterate half-caste and habitual drunkard, Mariano Melgarejo (1864–71), whose career has been fittingly described as compounded of 'treason and crimes, progressively more vile and detestable'.[1]

No South American state faced more paralysing problems than Bolivia. But the praetorian politics of Peru and the perennial instability of Ecuador —the former Presidency of Quito, which had been incorporated between 1822 and 1830 in the neighbouring republic of Great Colombia—reflected, at least in part, the same deep-seated ills. These countries faced the sea. They could respond more easily to the new currents of foreign trade. But they, also, were Indian as well as Andean lands. The aboriginal stock and, in smaller proportion, *mestizos*, formed by far the largest elements in their relatively scanty populations. Their highland and lowland peoples lived in worlds apart. They had emerged exhausted from the long struggle for independence. For statehood they were ill-equipped: military traditions had been fastened upon them; regional rivalries divided them; and while, in each, personal, local and sectional loyalties tended to take precedence over general and national, each oscillated between anarchy and despotism. Autocracy was the norm of government, revolution the method of changing it. Ecuador's tragic history was written in the strife between her

[1] Alcides Arguedas, *Historia General de Bolivia, 1809–1921* (La Paz, 1922), p. 252.

mountain capital of Quito and her Pacific port of Guayaquil as well as in the struggle for power of rival *caudillos*, of whom the most remarkable, the stern and theocratic Gabriel García Moreno, the dominant figure from 1860 till his assassination in 1875, turned to the church and the discipline of religion—but turned in vain—to supply that unifying force which the state could not provide. Peru found a master in Ramón Castilla (1845–51; 1855–62), a soldier of part Indian descent, 'brave as a lion, prompt in action, and beloved of his men';[1] and, while Castilla secured an order hitherto unknown, the European demand for the guano deposited on the islands and headlands of a rainless shore, as well as for the nitrate of soda which abounded in the southernmost province of Tarapacá, restored the country's shattered finances and opened golden vistas of prosperity. Both to dig the guano and to work on the sugar and cotton plantations of the coastal valleys thousands of Chinese labourers were imported between 1849 and 1874, though more particularly after 1861—the notorious coolie traffic which Castilla himself opposed. But wealth so easily won only served to corrupt the state at the moment of its possible regeneration, and within ten years of Castilla's retirement—years marked by a brief war with Spain (see p. 666) and by a recrudescence of political disorder—the country had been brought to the verge of bankruptcy. The financial and economic crisis which paralysed Peru in the 'seventies was precipitated by reckless expenditure on public works—above all on the building of railways, miracles of construction, to link the coast to the interior—financed, at enormous cost, by extravagant loans. But it was the result also of a long demoralisation of public life. And the final price for these years of waste and irresponsibility had yet to be paid. In the War of the Pacific (p. 666), which found Peru unprepared and left her ravaged, exhausted and dismembered, it was exacted to the full.

Colombia and Venezuela, the most northerly of the Andean and tropical republics of South America, were *mestizo* rather than Indian states. The pure Indian strain was here less marked. The mixed races outnumbered whites and Indians alike, as also a further element, more pronounced in Venezuela than in Colombia, the negro element. But the lines of caste and class were deeply cut. Poverty and ignorance were the common lot, and so terrible had been the havoc wrought by the revolutionary wars that in Venezuela a third of the population had perished. The two countries had been temporarily linked, with Ecuador, in a single state, Great Colombia, of which Bolívar himself was the principal founder. But Great Colombia had already dissolved into its component parts when Bolívar died in 1830, and each, thereafter, went its separate way. In Venezuela a small civilian oligarchy, supporting and supported by Bolívar's old lieutenant, the great guerrilla leader, José Antonio Páez, succeeded in maintaining a comparatively stable regime over a period of sixteen years

[1] C. R. Markham, *Travels in Peru and India* (London, 1862), p. 297.

(1830–46). But thereafter the country knew little peace till the advent of the long dictatorship of Guzmán Blanco (1870–88). Colombia, known in turn as New Granada (1832), the Granadine Confederation (1858), the United States of Colombia (1861), and the Republic of Colombia (1886), had a more distinctive history. The state owed much to the organising genius of its 'man of laws', Francisco de Paula Santander (1832–7), and it enjoyed in the decade of the 'forties what seemed, in retrospect, to be an almost golden era of prosperity. But the promise of these years was unfulfilled. And though it may be true that in Colombia men 'fought for ideas'[1] and that here, more than in most Spanish American countries, political parties represented a genuine opposition of competing principles, nevertheless the strife of centralists and federalists, clericals and anti-clericals, conservatives and liberals, held back the country's economic development and disrupted its political life. Dictatorship was less endemic in Colombia than in the other Andean states, but stability was no less difficult to maintain.

Disorderly as was the course of the northern, Andean and tropical republics of South America, that of the United Provinces of the Río de la Plata and of Uruguay in the temperate lowlands of the south was equally turbulent. Embracing one of the greatest of the great plains regions of the Americas, the territory of the United Provinces of the Río de la Plata extended from the Atlantic to the Andes and from the windswept plateaux of Patagonia to the mountain walls of Bolivia. But, apart from Indian tribes yet unsubdued, the country contained in 1830 less than three-quarters of a million people. Immense distances and empty spaces separated its scattered centres of population. On the waters of the Río de la Plata, Buenos Aires was the gateway from the pampas to the sea, the link between Europe and the plains; and Buenos Aires, like its great province of the same name, had grown and flourished on foreign trade. But the interior cities had been reduced to poverty. The inland provinces resented the economic hegemony of the maritime province. The country at large had rejected the political supremacy of Buenos Aires. And in the bitter struggles between centralists and federalists, town and country, Buenos Aires and the provinces, the United Provinces had become by 1830 little more than a 'chain of petty republics',[2] the prey of rival *caudillos*, those rural chieftains who, supported by their *gaucho* hordes, the 'men on horseback' of the Argentine pampas, had bent the interior cities to their wills and governed the provinces as their private fiefs.

Only a *gaucho* could control the *gauchos*, and, in December 1829, the installation of Juan Manuel de Rosas, a federalist, a landowner, and a stock-farmer, skilled in *gaucho* arts and *gaucho* ways, as governor of

[1] F. García Calderón, *Latin America: its Rise and Progress* (London, 1913), p. 201.
[2] The phrase of Juan Manuel de Rosas. Ernesto Quesada, *La Época de Rosas* (Buenos Aires, 1923), p. 230.

Buenos Aires province heralded the approach of a new age and the establishment of one of the most savage and unbridled of Latin American despotisms. The years between 1829 and 1852 were the Age of Rosas, an age which is still, in some respects, 'the most obscure'[1] as well as the most complex in Argentine history. Not till 1835, after a troubled interval during which Rosas had retired from the governorship and had enhanced his prestige by a victorious campaign against the Indians on the southern frontiers, did a reluctant legislature grant to the great dictator those absolute powers for which he asked. But thenceforth Rosas governed absolutely, and, the master of Buenos Aires province, made himself also the chief of the various *caudillos* who dominated the other Argentine provinces. The constitutional organisation of Argentina, during these years, was in abeyance. Her economic life, except in the one province of Buenos Aires, stagnated, and even in this province, though Rosas had at first represented the interests of his fellow landowners and cattle-breeders, extending the frontiers of the province and facilitating the whole-sale transfer of land from public to private hands, in the end he represented no interests but his own. And while the country's intellectual life was 'never more vigorous',[2] it flowed, not within the nation's boundaries, but outside them. It was in Uruguay or Chile that the great exiles, Juan Bautista Alberdi, Bartolomé Mitre, Domingo Faustino Sarmiento, and many another, waged their ceaseless war against the tyrant.

Nor was the Age of Rosas one of peace. It proved, on the contrary, to be an era of almost constant war, within the 'Argentine Confederation' and with other states. Rosas went to war with Bolivia in 1837. He persisted in regarding the small republic of Uruguay, which had won its independence in 1828 as a buffer state between Argentina and Brazil and in which rival chieftains, leaders of the 'Reds' and 'Whites', contended for power, as no more than a dissident Argentine province, and while his exiled opponents supported one faction, Rosas supported the other, the struggle culminating in the long siege of Montevideo, the 'new Troy', from 1843 to 1851. Meanwhile a quarrel with France had precipitated a French blockade of Buenos Aires (1838–40) and an alliance between the blockading force and the enemies of Rosas in Uruguay and in the littoral provinces; and this blockade was followed by another in 1845, when France and Britain jointly intervened to safeguard both the independence of Uruguay and their own especial interests.

The sequel was a triumph for Rosas. The British blockade was lifted in 1847, the French in 1848. An Anglo-Argentine treaty followed in 1849 and a Franco-Argentine in 1850. But the economic effects of the blockade had been serious. And whatever the success of Rosas in the field of diplomacy, the fact remained that the political and economic problems

---

[1] Quesada, *op. cit.* p. 41.
[2] F. A. Kirkpatrick, *A History of the Argentine Republic* (Cambridge, 1931), p. 160.

of Argentina were still unsolved. For two decades Rosas had indirectly served the cause of Argentine unity by asserting his own authority over that of the lesser *caudillos* of the provinces. To Buenos Aires, moreover, he had given a relatively honest and efficient administration. But Rosas had no constructive political programme. He had too long sacrificed the economic interests of the interior provinces to those of Buenos Aires, and even in Buenos Aires the price of his leadership proved too heavy. In May 1851 one of his own henchmen, Justo José de Urquiza, the governor of Entre Ríos province, 'pronounced' against him, obtaining the support both of Uruguay and of Brazil, and on 3 February 1852, at Monte Caseros, no great distance from Buenos Aires, the dictator was overthrown. Taking refuge on board a British warship, he was carried to England—to end his days in exile near Southampton.

Urquiza had pledged himself to secure the constitutional organisation of Argentina. But ten more years were to pass before this pledge was fully redeemed. In 1852 a Constituent Assembly indeed met at Santa Fe, and this assembly promulgated, on 25 May 1853, the constitution of the Argentine Confederation. It owed much to a little book hastily written and published in Chile by the distinguished exile J. B. Alberdi,[1] and strongly reflected the influence of the constitution of the United States. But Buenos Aires, jealous of her own pre-eminence, and fearful lest the mantle of Rosas should fall on Urquiza, had refused to be represented at the Congress and declined to recognise the constitution. After a vain attempt at coercion, she was left to go her own way, drew up, in 1854, the constitution of the 'State of Buenos Aires', and remained *de facto* independent.

There were now two governments, that of Buenos Aires and that of the Argentine Confederation, whose temporary capital was formed at Paraná. Urquiza, by signing identical treaties with Britain, France and the United States, ensured that the inland waterways should be open to foreign shipping, and, reorganising federal finances, he tried also to encourage immigration and to improve communications. But Buenos Aires continued to monopolise the bulk of foreign trade and, consequently, the customs' revenues. A tariff war between the rival powers was soon in progress, and this culminated, in 1859, in open hostilities. Her army defeated at the battle of Cepeda, Buenos Aires was at last constrained to join the federal republic. But she would do so permanently only on her own terms. The conflict was renewed in 1861; and this time, at Pavón (17 September), the verdict of Cepeda was reversed. The national government at Paraná was overthrown, to be reconstituted with a new congress at Buenos Aires; and in October 1862 Bartolomé Mitre, the victor at Pavón and the governor of Buenos Aires, became the first constitutional president of the undivided state.

[1] J. B. Alberdi, *Bases y Puntos de Partida para la Organización Política de la República Argentina* (Valparaíso, 1852).

Mitre built on the foundations which Urquiza had laid, and though the constitutional problems of Argentina were not yet completely solved, with the establishment of political unity in 1862 the way was opened for the full and natural development of the country's economic life. In 1862 the republic contained less than fifty miles of railway. Only 373 square miles of land were under cultivation. The prairie Indians were unsubdued. Sheep counted for more than cattle. And at the time of the first census in 1869 the recorded population was still under two millions. But the rims of steel pushing their way out from Buenos Aires, the construction of the Central Argentine Railway from Rosario to Córdoba between 1863 and 1870, the Baring loan of 1866, and the small but mounting statistics of immigration, were all signs of the great economic revolution which was to come. Argentina had entered her modern age, and the transformation of her pampa had already begun.

Mitre's presidency, however, closed in 1868 amidst a great catastrophe. Its scene was the small republic of Paraguay, a sub-tropical land whose boundaries marched with those of Argentina and Brazil as well as of Bolivia, and whose singular history as an independent state had been little more than the history of three men, each in turn the absolute ruler of a subject people.

The first, and most remarkable, of these dictators, Dr José Gaspar Rodríguez de Francia, had established his despotism between 1811 and 1814 on the determination of the creoles of Paraguay to be independent of Buenos Aires, had consolidated it by terror, and reigned thereafter in solitary omnipotence, but reigned, it must be added, with the broad consent of the native Guaraní and *mestizo* peasantry, whose interests he in part subserved. Austere, capricious, merciless, and embodying in his own person both the state and the law, Francia isolated Paraguay from the rest of the world, preserved her independence, made her self-sufficient, and gave her peace; and on his death in 1840, almost without disturbance, and with merely a brief interval, one despotism was succeeded by another. Under Carlos Antonio López, who was proclaimed Consul in 1841 and President-Dictator in 1844, the state remained a police state, the system of espionage invented by Francia continued to flourish, and the Paraguayans were drafted into an army which was finally to become the most powerful in South America. Ruling with less rigour than Francia, however, López also abandoned Francia's isolationist system, inviting foreigners to enter the country, opening the rivers, encouraging foreign trade, and even building a railway. His army was for defence, his wish for peace. But, dying in 1862, he bequeathed, in effect, the presidency to his son, Francisco Solano López, and whatever his services to his country, undid them by that act.

For Paraguay was now 'a potential Prussia'. A 'powerful war machine, despotically controlled', had appeared in South America,[1] and its master

[1] P. H. Box, *The Origins of the Paraguayan War* (Urbana, Illinois, 1930), p. 289.

was a pinchbeck Napoleon, vain, cruel and unprincipled, seeking a place in the sun. The origins of the Paraguayan War of 1864–70, in which the humble peasants of Paraguay held at bay, with invincible heroism, the forces of the Triple Alliance of Argentina, Brazil and Uruguay, were complex. But, for its outbreak and continuance, the prime responsibility rests with López. Paraguay had boundary disputes both with Argentina and Brazil; but neither of these need have led to war had not López willed it. In the unstable politics of Uruguay, where the wars of the 'Reds' and the 'Whites' still continued, and where the 'Reds' looked for support now to Argentina and now to Brazil, herself not without imperial ambitions, the materials for an explosion in the Río de la Plata basin were always present. But it would not have occurred had not López sought an opportunity, in his own words, to 'make his voice heard in the affairs of the Río de la Plata',[1] to gratify his own ambition and to assert his own power. He found it in Brazilian intervention in Uruguay in 1864, challenged first Brazil and then Argentina, and led his people along a road of serfdom, blood and terror which ended only with the near-extinction of the Paraguayan nation. When López fell in 1870, the population of Paraguay had been reduced from more than a half to less than a quarter of a million. Only women, old men and children survived. Such was the price of despotism, and such the fate of the nation which Francia had founded.

The war of the Triple Alliance and the War of the Pacific (see p. 666), which followed it in 1879, were the last great international conflicts in nineteenth-century South America. With one exception—the war waged by Spain in the 'sixties not only with Chile but with Peru, Bolivia and Ecuador as well (see p. 666)—these conflicts had lain between the South American states themselves. Nor had the political independence or the territorial integrity of any South American state been seriously menaced except by another South American state. Britain, it is true, had occupied the Falkland Islands, dispossessing an Argentine garrison, in 1832–3. But the Falkland Islands were far distant from the American mainland and their ownership was disputable. France in 1838–40, and France and Britain together in 1845, had forcibly intervened in the war between Rosas and Uruguay (see p. 670). But these interventions, however dangerous in principle and however contrary to the spirit of the Monroe Doctrine, proclaimed in 1823, certainly disguised no territorial aims, nor did they in fact threaten Argentine independence. As for Spain's Pacific aberration, it could have but one end—a humiliating withdrawal.

In Mexico, in Central America, and in the Caribbean Sea the story was a different one. And here, indeed, peril from abroad, both from Europe and from the United States, and the danger which the authors of the Monroe Doctrine had themselves foreseen, that an unstable or disintegrating area might provoke competitive intervention and the extension

[1] *Ibid.* p. 211.

to the western hemisphere of the European principle of the balance of power, assumed a more threatening aspect.

Mexico, at the time of the establishment of her independence in 1821, was a country half the size of Europe with a population no greater than that of contemporary Ireland. Here, in 1810, the great insurrection led by Miguel Hidalgo y Costilla, a rising, only with difficulty suppressed, of the dispossessed against the possessing classes, had shown what dangerous forces revolution might unleash. But here also independence, when it came, had taken the form of a conservative reaction. Mexico alone among the old colonies of Spain began her independent life not as a republic but as a monarchy. But her first ruler, Agustín de Iturbide, an ambitious and unscrupulous creole soldier, was not of the stuff that the founders of empires are made of, and a military conspiracy soon destroyed him. Empire, in 1823, gave way to republic, and the intellectual leaders of the creole aristocracy, themselves divided, substituted for the centralised institutions of government, which they had always known, a federal system of which they knew nothing.

The empire had been a temporary expedient and an embittering experiment. The republic, whose constitution, modelled on that of the United States, represented a triumph of theory over experience and of local over metropolitan interests, seemed to spell permanent disaster. From 1823 to 1827 stability was indeed maintained. But thereafter revolts, *pronunciamientos* and barrack-room revolutions were countless. The federal system, so soon as it had taken root, was itself abrogated in 1835, to be restored, nominally at least, some years later. But, federal government or unitary government, the result was the same. Presidents, deputy-presidents and acting-presidents followed one another in bewildering succession. In thirty years the executive office changed hands forty-six times, and throughout that period the dominant figure in Mexican politics was a cynical opportunist, 'in diplomacy, an unsustained Talleyrand; in war, a sorry Napoleon',[1] Antonio López de Santa Anna.

To preserve the territorial integrity of Mexico was, in these conditions, a nearly hopeless task. A Spanish invasion from Cuba in 1829, aimed at the reconquest of the country, was indeed effectively repelled. But separatist movements rapidly developed. Yucatán seceded from the federation in 1839 and long remained apart from it. More serious still, Texas, a periphery province colonised from the United States, revolted in 1835, proclaimed her independence in 1836, and maintained it by force of arms, the Texans, after a desperate struggle, finally capturing Santa Anna himself. Nine years later, in 1845, the 'Lone Star Republic' was annexed to the United States, and that event precipitated a war between the United States and Mexico which resulted in the occupation of Mexico City by General Winfield Scott and in the surrender to the United States, by the

[1] H. H. Bancroft, *History of Mexico* (6 vols., New York, 1883–8), vol. v, p. 802.

Treaty of Guadalupe Hidalgo in 1848, not only of Texas, but of California and of all the territory between them (cf. ch. XXIII, pp. 621–2). Mexico had been reduced to less than a half of her original size.

For the secession of Texas in 1836 Mexico had chiefly herself to blame. And though responsibility for the war between Mexico and the United States was divided, sooner or later, in the imperial sweep of the United States from the Atlantic to the Pacific, California and New Mexico must have been lost by a country which could neither settle nor administer them. But the chief threat to the independence and territorial integrity of Mexico came, not from without, but from within. A country which could produce the conservative historian and politician Lucas Alamán, the veteran champion of liberalism Valentín Gómez Farías, or even Santa Anna himself, was not devoid of talent. Nor was the strife for power between federalists and centralists, liberals and conservatives, wholly selfish. The trouble lay far deeper. A small landed aristocracy; a vast mass of illiterate and poverty-stricken peasants; a church, itself the largest landowner in the country, whose property could not be alienated, whose clergy claimed exemptions from the jurisdiction of civil courts, and whose influence was almost wholly illiberal; an army of idle officers and ignorant men, amenable only to military law; a country divided by caste and class, and between province and province: these were not the foundations on which a successful republican government could be erected. The demoralisation and disorganisation of the age of Santa Anna, the financial chaos, the fraudulence and corruption, were not the signs of an imperfect democracy. They were the evidences that, unless the society which produced such evils could be reconstructed or dominated, government itself must cease to function.

The movement of reformation began in mid-century, and a revolt occurring in 1854 at the little town of Ayutla in the state of Guerrero marked the beginning of a new, though a still more violent, age. What was, in its origins, scarcely more than a *putsch* of politicians directed against the last autocracy of 'His Most Serene Highness', Santa Anna, rapidly became a general, almost a national, movement. It looked backward, to the thwarted aspirations of the Mexican *mestizos* and to reforms attempted, but attempted in vain; it looked forward, to the establishment of a new Mexico fashioned in the image of nineteenth-century liberalism; it substituted for the strife of parties a conflict of principles; and it carried to cabinet office and finally to the presidency a Zapotec Indian of stern integrity and indomitable tenacity, Benito Juárez.

Now came a series of drastic innovations—the *Ley Juárez*, in November 1855, which reorganised the judicial system and limited the legal immunities, or *fueros*, of the clergy and the military; the suppression of the Jesuit order; the *Ley Lerdo*, or *Ley de Desamortización*, in June 1856, which forbade civil and ecclesiastical corporations to hold real property

43-2

save for the purpose of public worship, and provided, not for the confiscation, but for the forced sale, on generous terms, of lands immobilised in mortmain by the dead hand of the church; the limitation of clerical fees; and, finally, in February 1857, the promulgation of a new constitution. Structurally this was similar to the old federal constitution of 1824. It provided, however, for a unicameral legislature; it pointedly ignored the existence of the Roman Catholic church as a state church; and it embodied, together with a long bill of rights, both the *Ley Juárez* and the *Ley Lerdo*.

The liberal constitution, in years to come, was easily to be manipulated to serve the purposes of presidential autocracy. The *Ley Lerdo*, which was partly intended to encourage a wider distribution of property, was to assist, not the spread of peasant proprietorship, but the rise of a new aristocracy. As re-enacted in the constitution, moreover, it was to strike a blow also at the communal ownership of land by townships and villages, in general to the still further impoverishment of the Mexican Indian. And, together, the *Ley Juárez* and the *Ley Lerdo* violently antagonised the privileged classes, both clerical and lay. The pope had already condemned the new legislation. The archbishop of Mexico threatened with excommunication all who should swear allegiance to the constitution, and in December 1857 a *coup d'état* in Mexico City, the culmination of a long series of armed revolts, swept away the new order and restored the old. A military dictatorship, installed in January, hastened to undo the work of the reformers, while Juárez, on whom the presidency had constitutionally devolved, fled to the provinces, there to organise resistance and finally to re-establish the liberal government in the country's chief sea-port, Vera Cruz.

The war thus begun lasted for three years, was waged with a singular intensity, and prostrated Mexico. In its midst Juárez, in July 1859, proclaimed yet more sweeping reforms—the disestablishment of the church, the confiscation of its property, the suppression of the monasteries, and the institution of civil marriage—and proposed also plans for the division of the great estates, the reform of taxation, the promotion of education, and the encouragement of immigration. He had already obtained recognition by the United States and, by his control of Vera Cruz, he deprived the military government in Mexico City of the much-needed customs' revenue. Not till 1860, however, did his cause begin to triumph, nor was it till January 1861 that he at last returned to his capital—to dismiss the Spanish minister and the papal nuncio, who had been warm supporters of the fallen regime, to expel the archbishop and some other ecclesiastics, and to carry into effect his laws of reform. But guerrilla warfare still continued; the finances of the country were in chaos; and in July, shortly after Juárez had been 're-elected' to the presidency, he took the grave step—he could do no other—of suspending for two years all payments on the external national debt.

The effect was disastrous. Four months earlier, Britain had recognised the Juárez government on condition that it accept liability for damages sustained by British subjects at the hands of successive Mexican regimes. Some of these claims were new. The government recently displaced had, for example, robbed the British legation in Mexico City of a large sum of money, and its opponents had seized a silver train which was the property of foreign merchants. Others were old, and, under a convention signed in 1851, Mexico had appropriated a proportion of her customs' revenue to their settlement. Mexico, moreover, was heavily indebted to British bondholders on account of her first sterling loans, raised in the 'twenties. And not only had she now suspended payments on her funded debt; she had repudiated, if only temporarily, her international obligations under agreements which had been signed, not with Britain alone, but also with Spain and France; and at this point 'the long policy of patience pursued by the European powers in dealing with Mexico' gave way to a policy of action.[1] By the Convention of London, signed in October 1861, the three powers agreed to enforce payment of their debts by military occupation of parts of the Mexican coast, but agreed also not to infringe either the territorial integrity of Mexico or her political autonomy. In December a Spanish army landed at Vera Cruz, to be joined in January 1862 by French troops and British marines. The threat of foreign intervention long overhanging Mexico had become a reality.

So far as Spain and Britain were concerned the episode was soon over. Their forces were withdrawn in April. For, intervention begun, it rapidly became clear from the actions of the French officials—including the support of a peculiarly dishonest and scandalous financial claim—that French designs were very different from those agreed upon in the Convention of London. Napoleon III, indeed, deceived by the specious reasoning of Mexican exiles, by his own representative in Mexico, and by other interested persons, had allowed himself to believe that a French army would be welcomed in Mexico as an army of liberators (cf. chs. XVII, XXIV and pp. 464 and 641). He had seen himself as the saviour of an oppressed people and as the defender of the Latin world against the might of the United States, now herself torn by civil strife. He was convinced that Mexico was ripe for monarchy, and in the Archduke Maximilian of Austria he had already selected the prince who should reign over the regenerated country. His armies, heavily reinforced, pushed forward in the face of determined resistance, and in May 1863 Juárez, the symbol now not of Mexican liberalism alone, but of national independence, once more left the capital. Under French dictation an assembly of notables offered the crown to Maximilian. Assured of Napoleon's support, Maximilian accepted it, and in June 1864 entered Mexico City. The story of intrigue, ambition, illusion and deception had reached its climax.

[1] Dexter Perkins, *The Monroe Doctrine, 1827–1867* (Baltimore, 1933), p. 354.

The end was tragedy. Tolerant, romantic, well-intentioned, but strangely deficient in the most ordinary common sense, Maximilian had not the slightest real knowledge of the country, convulsed by passion and drenched with blood, which he had come to rule. The clericals and conservatives, who had suffered much but learnt nothing, were soon alienated by his liberal inclinations and by his refusal to restore to the church nationalised property now in private hands. The Papacy deserted him. Juárez, a fugitive, maintained a stubborn resistance. And, at the last, Napoleon betrayed his puppet. The empire rested on foreign bayonets; and when in 1866 those bayonets began to be withdrawn, its fall was inevitable. The American civil war had ended, and Napoleon, subjected to increasing pressure from the United States, and anxious also to escape from a costly, an unpopular and a seemingly endless adventure, abandoned Maximilian to his fate. The last French soldiers left in March 1867, and as they left the forces of Juárez closed in upon the doomed emperor. In May he surrendered, and in June he paid with his life for his own folly and for the deceits of others.

The war and the empire ended together. For Juárez, now once again the undisputed President of Mexico, there remained five years of life in which to undertake the immense task of reconstructing the war-torn country, and when he died, in 1872, his hopes were unfulfilled. Political life was still punctuated by revolts and disorders; schools were few; the masses were sunk in poverty. But amidst a disunited people the slow unfolding of a national consciousness had begun. And as Juárez had saved the country, so after 1876 one of his old lieutenants, Porfirio Díaz, was now to master it, to modernise it, and, at long last, to give it peace.

From first to last the Napoleonic adventure in Mexico had been a sustained challenge to the Monroe Doctrine in the name of the balance of power, and a deliberate attempt to set bounds to the rising influence of the United States. The Monroe Doctrine, indeed, commanded little respect in Europe and little confidence in Latin America. And just as France challenged that doctrine, in frank hostility, in Mexico, so Britain repudiated it, though not without some regard for the susceptibilities of the United States, in Central America, and Spain ignored its application in the West Indies.

Central America, the narrow strip of land which links Mexico to the isthmus of Panama, was so named from the United Provinces of Central America, a federation established in 1823 as the political heir of the Spanish captaincy-general of Guatemala, which had been annexed in 1822 to the empire of Iturbide. Never united except in name, the United Provinces consisted of five states—Guatemala, El Salvador, Honduras, Nicaragua, and Costa Rica—whose total territory was little larger than that of Spain and whose combined population was under two millions, composed, for the most part, of illiterate Indians and scarcely less illiterate *mestizos*. And barely had the new state been launched than it was plunged into strife, political, regional and ecclesiastical, from which there emerged by 1829 the figure of Francisco Morazán, of Honduras, briefly to dominate an anarchic scene, to launch a full-scale attack on the power and property of the Roman Catholic church, to transfer the federal capital from Guatemala City to San Salvador, and to maintain the semblance of a federation till 1838. In that year, however, it collapsed; and although the middle group of states—Nicaragua, El Salvador and Honduras, which had more affinities with each other than with either Guatemala or Costa Rica—attempted from time to time to revive it, these efforts were always vain.

From 1838, therefore, the history of Central America became the history of five turbulent and quarrelsome republics, each of which felt free to intervene in the affairs of its neighbours. The strongest, the predominantly Indian republic of Guatemala, remained till 1865 under the almost uninterrupted control of a superstitious and reactionary half-caste, Rafael Carrera, at once the master of a conservative and clerical aristocracy and a tool in its hands. The most isolated, Costa Rica, was also the most enlightened. But in all of these states 'authority established and upheld by force was the only authority which was recognised or respected'. In all, there was 'no recourse against bad government, except revolution'. And in all, civil war 'thus became an indispensable part of the political system'.[1]

Not all of the Central American area, however, was in the possession of the Central American republics. On its Caribbean shores, and fronting the Gulf of Honduras, lay the British settlement of Belize, a settlement which traced its origins to the seventeenth century and over which British sovereignty had long effectively been exercised though never officially proclaimed. And the Belize settlers had gradually extended their activities of mahogany cutting far to the west and far to the south of the boundaries allotted to their settlement in treaties signed between Great Britain and Spain. Eastwards from Cape Honduras, moreover, and then southwards to the San Juan River, the 'Mosquito coast' was the territory of the 'Mosquito Indians'—a strangely mixed and semi-nomadic people who had consistently resisted the authority of Spain, and over whom, in the eighteenth century, Britain had exercised a vague protectorate.

British connections with the Mosquito Indians had never been entirely abandoned. It had been the custom, for example, for the Mosquito king to be crowned in Jamaica and in 1824 he was crowned at Belize. And in the 'thirties, mainly through the energetic action of the superintendent of Belize, these connections were extended and consolidated. Not only did Britain revive old and extremely tenuous claims to the island of Ruatan, the largest of the Bay Islands group in the Gulf of Honduras, which was occupied in 1838–9, but she revived also the Mosquito Protec-

[1] D. G. Munro, *The Five Republics of Central America* (New York, 1918), p. 31.

torate. A British Resident on the Mosquito shore was appointed in 1844. The territory was locally renamed Mosquitia, and the Mosquito king was presented with a flag which bore a marked resemblance to the Union Jack. Three years later Britain announced that this territory, which was under the protection of the British crown, was bounded to the south by the San Juan River, and in 1848 the Nicaraguan authorities at the port of San Juan were dispossessed in the name of the local monarch and the town itself was renamed Greytown, in honour of the governor of Jamaica.

In all this, British designs were far more limited than contemporaries were apt to suppose. Nor were the claims of any Central American state to exercise dominion over the Mosquito coast plain and indisputable. But Greytown had an interest all its own. It was the key to what appeared to be one of the most practicable routes for the construction of an inter-oceanic canal by way of the San Juan River and the great lake of Nicaragua; and, at the moment of the annexation of Greytown, this route, and the problem of transisthmian communications generally, took on a new impor-tance. For not only had the United States now acquired California, but also, in January 1848, California was found to be a land of gold; and the inevitable result was a gold-rush across Central America. Already, in 1846, the United States had signed a treaty with the Republic of New Granada guaranteeing to American citizens a right-of-way across the isthmus of Panama, and here the Panama Railway, undertaken by Ameri-can capital, was opened in 1855. In 1849, however, a canal company was formed in the United States for the construction of a ship canal across Nicaragua with one terminal at Greytown; and no sooner had a contract been signed between this company and Nicaragua than Britain served notice that the San Juan River belonged to the Mosquito kingdom and could not be disposed of without the consent of the Mosquito king, and, of course, of his protector, the British government.

The diplomatic controversy which followed, urbanely conducted in London and Washington but carried on with intense bitterness between British and United States representatives in Central America, resulted in the signing, on 19 April 1850, of the Clayton–Bulwer Treaty, and by this instrument Britain and the United States agreed that the proposed canal should be constructed under their joint protection, that neither party would seek any exclusive control over it, and further, that neither party would 'occupy, or fortify, or colonise, or assume, or exercise any dominion over Nicaragua, Costa Rica, the Mosquito coast, or any part of Central America'.

The Clayton–Bulwer treaty was designed to effect a compromise between British and American points of view, and, in effect, to neutralise the Central American area. But the language of this self-denying ordinance, and of its explanatory declarations, was ambiguous. The treaty, in Britain's view, did not affect the status of the Mosquito protectorate as an independent but protected kingdom, though Greytown, it was admitted, must ultimately be evacuated and the boundaries of the protectorate defined. Nor did it at all concern either the Belize settlement or Ruatan; and in 1852 Ruatan and its neighbouring islands were erected into the colony of the Bay Islands.

This precipitated fresh controversy and lively demands from Washington that Britain should withdraw not only from the Bay Islands and the Mosquito Protectorate but from the more recently occupied parts of the Belize settlement also. Meanwhile, in Central America itself, events moved towards a crisis. Greytown, where there was trouble between the municipality and the Accessory Transit Company—Cornelius Vanderbilt's Atlantic and Pacific Ship Canal Company, now engaged in transporting passengers across the isthmus by way of the San Juan River—was bombarded and destroyed by an American warship in 1854. In the following year an American 'filibuster', William Walker, who had already led raids on Mexican territory, arrived in Nicaragua, then in the throes of civil war, captured the town of Granada, and in 1856 was 'elected' president. Recognised by the United States, but antagonising the Transit Company and faced by a coalition of the other Central American republics, he was indeed driven out in 1857, but twice attempted to return, and finally met his death in Honduras in 1860.

Such a state of affairs was intolerable. But Britain had no wish to risk a war with the United States. Nor did she hold strong views about the necessity of checking American advance in Central America; and in 1856 both governments made a further and most serious effort to settle the differences between them. That failing, it seemed possible that the United States might abrogate the Clayton–Bulwer treaty altogether, a step which could only accentuate difficulties in Central America. And to avert this danger Britain decided to attempt to reach a settlement on the general lines of that treaty, but this time by direct negotiations with the Central American republics themselves.

Eventually, in 1859 and 1860, the problem was solved. By the Anglo-Honduran Treaty of 1859 the Bay Islands were surrendered to Honduras, and Honduran claims were recognised to a part of the Mosquito coast. By the Anglo-Nicaraguan treaty of 1860, Nicaraguan sovereignty was admitted over the rest of the celebrated shore, though the Mosquito Indians were to retain a measure of autonomy within specified boundaries, and Greytown became a free port. And by the Anglo-Guatemalan treaty of 1859—which was itself to be the foundation of prolonged dispute between its signatories—the frontiers of the Belize settlement, as they were deemed to have existed at the time of the Clayton–Bulwer treaty, were redefined in accordance with the claims long advanced by the Belize settlers. Three years later the settlement was formally erected into the colony of British Honduras.

The Central American question was the stormiest episode in the history of Anglo-American relations in Latin America between the promulgation of the Monroe Doctrine in 1823 and the crisis which was to arise over the dispute between Britain and Venezuela in 1895. Its settlement was a triumph, not of the Monroe Doctrine (of which the Clayton–Bulwer treaty was later to be regarded as a violation), but of good will and good sense. It was not from Britain, moreover, but from the United States, that the greater threat had arisen to the security and independence of the Central American republics themselves. But in the 'sixties this threat also was removed. The United States was now involved in the bitter tragedy of civil war. And while, for this and other reasons, expansionist sentiment within the United States declined, so also did interest in interoceanic communications across Central America.

In one other region there was to be a clash between the principles implicit in the Monroe Doctrine and the actions of a European power. Its scene was the island which Columbus had named Española. Here, in 1822, the negro republic of Haiti, under the rule of an educated mulatto, Jean-Pierre Boyer, had annexed the neighbouring Spanish colony of Santo Domingo. Haitian independence had been recognised by France (on onerous financial terms) in 1825. And from the decade of the 'twenties to that of the 'forties Boyer ruled in comparative peace. But the negro population of Haiti, leavened and governed by a small élite of *gens de couleur*, was semi-barbarous. The land was a land of poverty-stricken peasants. And when, in 1843, a 'revolution of the intellectuals' overthrew Boyer, political and economic decline proceeded *pari passu*. A restoration of black supremacy culminated in the long and savage dictatorship of an illiterate negro, who, as the Emperor Faustin I, created four princes and fifty-nine dukes but reduced the country to financial and economic chaos. On his fall, in 1859, the republic was restored. It was even, in 1862, at last recognised by the United States. But its annals remained tragic, and Froude's harsh description of it in 1888 as a 'caricature of civilisation'[1] certainly reflected contemporary opinion.

Meanwhile, Santo Domingo had revolted, to establish its independence as the Dominican Republic in 1844. For twenty-two years the country had endured a tyrannical occupation deliberately designed to Haitianise its Spanish-speaking population, whites, mulattoes and negroes. The use of the Spanish language had been discouraged. Negroes had supplanted whites. Landowners had emigrated. And, independence won, such weak hopes as might reasonably have been entertained for the stability of the new state were soon shattered. Distracted by domestic strife and in constant fear of reabsorption by its black neighbour, it appealed for protection, or annexation, to France, the United States, and Britain—all of which, though suspicious of each other's intentions, endeavoured to curb

[1] J. A. Froude, *The English in the West Indies* (London, 1888), p. 343.

Haitian ambitions. Finally, in 1861, its then president persuaded Spain to reassume her ancient dominion. Spanish troops arrived from Cuba. The Spanish flag replaced the Dominican. And the ex-president of the republic became the new Spanish governor-general.

With the possible exception of Britain's occupation of the Falkland Islands in 1832–3, this event was notable as the sole example of the re-assertion of European sovereignty over former colonial territory in the New World. But the experiment was brief. Spanish rule proved to be as incompetent as Dominican and as odious as Haitian. It could be maintained only by force and at great expense; and in 1865 the mother country abandoned her thankless task. Four years later the revived republic signed an annexation treaty with the United States. The United States Senate, however, failed to ratify it, and the Dominican Republic, like Haiti, was left, in conditions which steadily deteriorated, to work out her salvation alone. Side by side, a predominantly black and a pre-dominantly mulatto republic, unable to share their small island in peace, followed a course which was to lead, almost inevitably, to that momentous event in their history—their temporary occupation by the United States.

'Many tyrants will arise upon my tomb', wrote Bolívar in 1826;[1] and the prophecy was fulfilled. *Caudillismo*, the rule of the military chieftain, the strong man, the local leader, was a phenomenon common to all the Latin American states. More than the praetorian legacy of the revolutionary wars, it was deeply rooted in the structure, the character, and the traditions of Spanish American society. In vain the architects of a new order had attempted to establish a rational pattern of freedom in constitutions which, too often, borrowed eclectically from abroad, and conformed too rarely to political and social realities at home. The constitutionalists were 'swept away before the winds of personalism'.[2] Authority revived, not in the impersonal state, but in the person of the *caudillo*. And for half a century after the close of the wars of independence most of the new states of Latin America—Brazil and Chile were the chief exceptions—were scourged, now by tyranny, now by anarchy. Few peoples had set out upon a career of independent nationhood with such initial disabilities. Nowhere did the reconciliation of freedom with order prove more difficult to achieve.

Yet, even in those countries whose political, social and economic development was most retarded, time did not stand still, nor were men's minds inactive. The temper of politics slowly changed; the cruder forms of military despotism began to vanish, civilian oligarchies took control and a new type of presidential autocrat arose. And though 'the twilight

---

[1] Lecuna, *Cartas del Libertador*, vol. v, p. 292.
[2] R. M. Morse, 'Toward a Theory of Spanish American Government', *Journal of the History of Ideas*, vol. xv (1954), pp. 79–80.

of the *caudillos*' lasted long, in the decade of the 'seventies the states of Latin America stood upon the threshold of a new age, in which the distinctions between them became more marked, and in which the rise of Argentina and Mexico was at last to emulate the earlier but continuing rise of Chile and Brazil. The mounting figures of trade, investment and immigration told their own tale. For fifty years Latin America had been open to the trade of the world. Yet the flow of European capital investment, after the first flush of excitement in the 'twenties, had been generally held back, and the immigrant stream from the Old World to the New had set, not to the southern, but to the northern hemisphere. But already in the 'fifties and 'sixties there were signs of change, and by 1876 the amount of British capital alone invested in Latin America amounted to nearly one hundred and eighty million pounds sterling. It was to reach nearly one thousand millions in 1913. And with a migration of people as well as of capital, a quickening of economic activity, and a greater political stability, a new chapter in the economic and political history of Latin America began, and a chapter, also, closely related to the economic history both of England and Europe.

CHAPTER XXVI

THE FAR EAST

At the beginning of the second quarter of the nineteenth century the central area of the Far East, comprising China, Korea and Japan, with approximately half the population of Asia and a quarter of the population of the world, was still almost inaccessible to the travel and commerce of Western nations and virtually impervious to Western cultural influences. In particular, the vast empire of China, under the Ch'ing dynasty set up in Peking by the Manchus in 1644, remained untouched by the internal disintegrations and external encroachments which had overtaken the more westerly of the major Asian powers since the end of the seventeenth century. The Mogul empire had disappeared and over most of India had been replaced by the direct or indirect rule of the British East India Company; the Ottoman empire had lost territory to Russia and had been weakened by the secession of Egypt and the national revolt of the Greeks; Persia also had lost territory to Russia and had been curtailed in the east by the new realm of Afghanistan. But China had not merely suffered no loss of territory since 1700, but had extended her borders by the incorporation of the central Asian empire of the Kalmuk Mongols including Tibet. This massive political organism, reaching from the Pacific to the Pamirs, was loosely, but effectively, controlled by a central government in Peking; it inherited a tradition of imperial unity closely associated with the teaching of the Confucian scholar class and going back to an age contemporary with the Roman empire of Augustus. In 1830 the traditional structure of the empire seemed as strong as it had ever been, and the ruling class, in which Manchu barbarism had been assimilated to Chinese civilisation, was wrapped in a complacent ethnocentric self-sufficiency, with no idea of the disasters and transformations that were soon to befall it.

The Chinese were not aware of the existence of any neighbours who could either threaten their independence or challenge their way of life. The nomadic peoples of the northern steppes who in former times had been such a menace to the Middle Kingdom were now under the sway of a Chinese government which had derived its strength in the first place from those same peoples. Farther north, the empire included much of what is now eastern Siberia as far as the Sea of Okhotsk, holding a frontier fixed by the Treaty of Nerchinsk in 1689 with the Russians, who were still too few in numbers and too deficient in overland communications with their homeland to be a considerable power east of the Yenisei. To the west, high mountain ranges provided the Manchu-Chinese empire with strong natural frontiers, and beyond Tibet the Himalayas set a barrier which, after the defeat by the Chinese of the Gurkha invasion of Tibet in 1792, was not again to be pierced until the British expedition to Lhasa in 1904. To the east and south China held a vague suzerainty over a group of relatively small states which paid ceremonial tribute to the Chinese imperial monarchy—Korea, Luchu, Annam, Siam and Burma. Farther to the east, self-contained in their own islands, were the Japanese, who paid no tribute to China, but under the rule of the Tokugawa shogunal dynasty (in control of Japan since 1600) no longer sent forth the corsair fleets which had been the scourge of the coasts of China during the fifteenth and sixteenth centuries. From the seas to the south the merchants of Western nations carried on a trade with China which from 1757 was confined by law to the single port of Canton; these peoples, collectively known to the Chinese as *Hsi-yang jên* or 'men of the Western Ocean' and classified under the general heading of *i* or 'barbarians', had acquired territorial power in parts of South-east Asia—the Spanish in the Philippines, the Dutch in Indonesia, the British in Arakan, Tenasserim and at Singapore—but none of these areas was immediately adjacent to China, and no Western power yet possessed a *point d'appui* on the coast of China, except for the Portuguese, who had received the grant of Macao in 1557 in return for services in the suppression of piracy. Yet it was from one of these maritime nations trading to the Far East from remote Europe that the Chinese empire was soon to receive a blow not only profoundly humiliating for its prestige, but destined to have consequences decisive for the whole course of its subsequent history.

The Chinese imperial government did not have any conception of international relations corresponding to the Western idea of permanent diplomatic intercourse within a system of equal sovereign states. In Confucian philosophy China was the unique source of true civilisation for mankind and the emperor of China was the sole legitimate representative of Heaven in mundane affairs; he was ideally a world ruler and the relations of other monarchs to him could only be those of vassal to suzerain. This vassalage was expressed by the payment of tribute together with various ceremonies which acknowledged the supremacy of the Chinese emperor. The tribute was not burdensome in amount and was valued by the Chinese court not for its economic importance but for the enhancement of prestige which it brought to the reigning dynasty; the tributary was usually well rewarded with privileges of trade with China, and, as the system involved no direct control by the Chinese government over the internal affairs of the tributary, it gained voluntary acceptance from a number of peoples who did not regard such acts of formal submission to a power so much larger and stronger than themselves as derogatory to their dignity. It sometimes happened, however, that political necessity drove the Chinese government to have dealings with foreign rulers who declined to conform to the Chinese idea of their proper status, and in these cases Chinese officialdom had to make exceptions from the rule. Thus in the Treaty of Nerchinsk, which defined the frontier between the Chinese and Russian empires, there was no acknowledgement of the inferiority of the tsar to the Chinese emperor. But such concessions, enforced by the necessity of terminating hostilities and agreeing on a land frontier, were to be kept to a minimum, and there did not seem to be any reason for having diplomatic relations on a non-tributary basis with distant nations which merely traded with China by sea and had no common boundary by land with the Middle Kingdom. The Peking court permitted merchants from Europe and North America to trade at Canton under regulations laid down unilaterally by the local Chinese authorities, but saw no reason for entering into diplomatic relations with the governments of these foreign merchants' home countries. The foreigners in Canton, therefore, had no support or protection for their interests from diplomatic or consular representatives of their own nations, and their only means of appeal to the Chinese authorities for redress of grievances was by way of humble petition presented through the Co-hong, an association of Chinese merchants officially licensed for carrying on foreign trade.

Among the Western nations the British had by far the largest share in the total volume of the trade at Canton. Their business was conducted either by the East India Company or by 'country' merchants from India operating under its licence, so that the company's representatives in Canton could act on behalf of the whole British commercial interest involved in the trade. The company, however, was unable to obtain any improvement in the unsatisfactory conditions of trade at Canton or permission to trade at any places other than Canton. The British government in 1793 sent a mission headed by Lord Macartney to Peking to negotiate an agreement directly with the Chinese government; the embassy was courteously received, but the boats and carts in which the envoys were conveyed to the capital bore flags inscribed 'Bearers of tribute from England', and none of the requests made for the revision of existing practice at Canton or the opening of new ports were granted by the Chinese. A second embassy headed by Lord Amherst in 1816 was similarly without effect, and the trade at Canton continued on the same terms as before. Despite the irksome conditions, it was too profitable for the foreign merchants to abandon, and the Chinese saw no reason to alter the system as long as the foreigners, however reluctantly, submitted to it. During the 'thirties, nevertheless, two new developments combined to produce a crisis between the British at Canton and the local Chinese authorities. The first of these was the increase in the traffic in opium as an element in the Canton trade. During the eighteenth century the East India Company's problem had been to find goods which could be sold in China to pay for the tea and other Chinese products purchased there; for a long time the balance of trade was against the Europeans and the deficit had to be made up with specie. But towards the end of the century the adverse balance was being reduced by exports of opium from India. The drug had previously been carried by the Portuguese from Goa; the British first entered the trade in 1773, but at that time the total sales were still small. In 1729 the emperor Yung Chêng had issued an edict against the smoking of opium, which had become a fashionable addiction in China, but it could be legally imported as a medicinal drug until 1800, when it was absolutely prohibited by an edict of the emperor Chia Ch'ing. Henceforth it was no longer carried by the East India Company's own ships, but country ships brought it from Bengal and sold it over the side to boats in the Canton river, the buyers paying bribes to the local officials to turn a blind eye to the traffic. The sales continually increased during the first three decades of the nineteenth century, and spasmodic attempts of the Chinese authorities to enforce the law only led to the opium being transferred to storeships stationed outside the estuary of the river; from these storeships the opium was smuggled ashore at various points on the coast. French, Dutch and American, as well as British, traders dealt in opium, but except for small quantities from Persia and Turkey, it was all supplied from India on British account, and the Chinese held Britain responsible. As the volume of the illicit trade grew, the central government in Peking became increasingly concerned, not only because of the effects of the opium-smoking habit—which had become widespread in the official class —but also because of the outflow of silver from China due to the reversal of the balance of foreign trade and the prevalence of a corruption which lined the pockets of Canton officials but brought nothing to the customs revenue. Finally in 1838 the emperor Tao Kwang appointed an imperial high commissioner, Lin Tse-hsü, with special powers to go to Canton and enforce the legal prohibition.

This action was bound to produce a crisis in the relations between the Chinese authorities and the foreign merchants at Canton, but it would probably not have led to any armed conflict if the British trading interest had then still been represented by the East India Company. But since 1834 the situation had been radically altered by a second factor which contributed no less than the growth of the opium trade to the increase of tension. In 1834 the British East India Company's monopoly was terminated by Act of Parliament and the China trade was thrown open to free competition on the British side; at the same time Lord Napier was appointed Superintendent of Trade to go to Canton and perform there the functions previously vested in the supercargoes of the Company. But, whereas the senior British merchant in Canton was recognised by the Chinese as a 'taipan' competent to represent an association of private individuals, the new superintendent came as a representative of his government claiming to deal directly with Chinese officials. He was instructed by Lord Palmerston to notify his arrival by letter to the Canton viceroy. But the Chinese refused to receive the letter, declaring that he must observe the regulation whereby foreigners could only communicate with the provincial administration by petition through the Hong merchants' association. The viceroy instructed the Hong merchants to inform Napier that, though he might be forgiven for being 'unaware of the necessity of conforming to the laws of the Celestial Empire', he must leave Canton immediately. As he did not do so, orders were issued stopping all trade and forbidding Chinese to sell provisions to the British merchants. Napier's reply to this was to order up two British frigates, which forced their way up the river under fire and landed marines for the protection of the British factory. But the factory was surrounded by a strong force of Chinese troops, supplies were short, and finally Napier yielded and left for Macao, where he died of fever a fortnight later. His successor as superintendent adopted a policy of 'absolute silence and quiescence' pending fresh instructions from London.

The British government was in no hurry to take further decisions in the matter in view of the flat refusal of the Chinese bureaucracy to enter into any kind of official relations. Napier had reported that it was an 'idle waste of time' to negotiate with the Chinese without adequate 'means of compulsion', but such means—over and above two or three warships—were not yet available in the China Seas. Meanwhile the trade at Canton had been resumed, and continued, in spite of the deadlock over the status of the superintendent, until the arrival of Commissioner Lin in Canton in March 1839 to enforce the opium prohibition law. Lin's method was to surround the foreign factories with troops and announce that nobody would be allowed to leave until all the opium in the storeships had been brought up the river and handed over. Under this pressure more than 20,000 chests of opium were surrendered and destroyed, and Lin then gave permission for normal trade to be reopened. But Captain Elliot, who was now superintendent, ordered all the British merchants to leave Canton and go to Macao, until guarantees against a repetition of such collective duress should be given them. As the British would not return to Canton, Lin ordered the Portuguese governor to expel them from Macao, and they moved in their ships to the anchorage of Hong Kong on the other side of the estuary. The situation was further complicated by an incident which involved the whole question of jurisdiction over foreigners on Chinese soil. Some sailors ashore at Kowloon had been involved in a brawl in which a Chinese was killed; at a trial held on board a British ship under the authority of the superintendent it was found impossible to determine who had struck the fatal blow. The Chinese authorities, dissatisfied with this result, demanded that all the sailors involved in the fight should be handed over to them for investigation, but this was refused in accordance with what had become the British practice—not to hand over men accused of homicide, because of the Chinese use of judicial torture to extract confessions of guilt.

On 25 October 1839 Commissioner Lin issued an order that the British ships must within three days either come up to Canton or depart from the coast of China; this was coupled with a renewed demand for surrender of the sailor guilty of the Kowloon murder. Elliot ignored these demands, and on 3 November a clash took place between two British frigates and a fleet of twenty-nine Chinese war junks. Four of the latter were sunk and the rest put to flight—an action which for the first time clearly demonstrated the extreme disparity in fighting power between European warships and the antiquated naval armaments of China. The first Anglo-Chinese war had begun.

The British government now decided to send an expeditionary force from India and to carry on hostilities with the aim not merely of restoring the former state of affairs at Canton but of revising the basis of British commerce with China. Operations were undertaken, not only in the Canton area, but northwards along the coast as far as Chusan Island, which was occupied; warships were sent on to the mouth of the Peiho requesting the appointment of a Chinese plenipotentiary for negotiations. The imperial government, alarmed at the apparently irresistible power of the 'rebellious barbarians' on the sea and the effects of naval blockade in both the Canton and Yangtse estuaries, sent Kishen, the viceroy of Chihli, to negotiate with British envoys at Canton. The British demanded direct official intercourse on equal terms with the provincial administration for the settlement of disputes arising out of the trade at Canton, the payment of an indemnity, and the cession of the island of Hong Kong. Kishen accepted these terms, but the cession of Chinese territory caused an outcry in all quarters in China; Kishen was sent in chains to Peking and condemned to death (though he was reprieved and later pardoned), while the war was renewed, but with consequences disastrous to the Chinese. Colonel Sir Henry Pottinger, who had served in India, was now sent out from England as plenipotentiary, and naval and military reinforcements were dispatched to strengthen his hand. Amoy and Ningpo were taken; the invaders also forced their way up the Yangtse and captured Chinkiang at the intersection of the river with the Grand Canal. When Nanking was invested, China again came to terms, and the Treaty of Nanking, the first to be concluded by China with a western maritime nation, was concluded on 29 August 1842. The fighting had shown that the Chinese imperial army, in spite of the prestige it still retained from its victory over the Gurkhas in 1792, was hardly any better able to cope with Western armed forces on land than were the Chinese war junks at sea. The army at this time consisted of two distinct categories of troops—the forces of the Eight Banners, who were Manchus (with Mongol and Manchurian Chinese contingents) and garrisoned the capital and principal strategic points of the empire, and the Green Standard soldiers, who were Chinese and were already in the eighteenth century reckoned to be more efficient than the Manchus. It was difficult to combine these separate military formations against a foreign foe, and by 1840 both of them were too degenerate in leadership and too antiquated in equipment to be able to stand in the field against the troops of a Western power. Divided and decentralised in organisation, led by officers who were selected by tests in archery and weight-lifting, demoralised by a corruption so far-reaching that in some units only a small fraction of the soldiers on the payroll actually existed, armed only with obsolete matchlocks, spears and bows, and suffering from the contempt of a people accustomed to give all its respect to the civilian scholar-official, the Chinese army was quite un-prepared to sustain the task of national defence in the era of stress and strain which the empire had now to face. China's actual strength, indeed, provided no adequate support for the provocative international preten-sions of the Confucian *literati*, who sought to keep the Middle Kingdom closed to outer barbarians and at the same time to carry on a considerable foreign trade unregulated by any form of equal diplomatic intercourse with other nations. The Chinese view was that the trade at Canton was merely permitted by favour of the emperor, that the foreigners who came there had no rights as against the imperial officials and that they were free to stay away if they did not like the conditions laid down. Such an interpretation of sovereign rights was theoretically consonant with Western international law, which could not justify refusal by foreign residents to submit to the jurisdiction of an independent state within whose borders they were living or to invoke the protection of their own national armed forces whenever they felt aggrieved. On the other hand, in Western international law the recognition of the territorial jurisdiction of a sover-eign state was closely linked with the system of official international relations through diplomatic envoys and consuls on a basis of equality between states for the negotiated settlement of disputes, and the refusal of the Chinese government to enter into such relations was itself the greatest grievance of the Western merchants and the governments sup-porting them. In the absence of any direct contacts with Chinese official-dom the tendency was for disputes to lead to armed clashes, especially as the British, who were the principal Western trading nation in the China Sea, were also by this time the masters of India, and did not find it easy to make the transition from imperial grandeur in Calcutta to downtrodden humility in Canton. With such basically different conceptions of inter-national intercourse and with so much pride on both sides an outbreak of war was bound to occur sooner or later in the situation which existed at Canton after 1834, and it was inevitable that the British, if victorious, would use their power to open wider the door which had hitherto been kept almost shut against the foreigner on China's shores. The Chinese could not continue their policy of exclusion unless they were strong enough to enforce it, and they were not.

The Treaty of Nanking provided for the cession of the island of Hong Kong to Britain in full sovereignty and for the opening to foreign trade of four more ports in addition to Canton, namely Amoy, Foochow, Ningpo and Shanghai. At all the ports licensed for trade, consuls were to be appointed with the right of direct communication on a basis of equality with Chinese officials of the same rank. Extra-territorial jurisdiction was not explicitly conceded by the treaty, but it was introduced by a supplementary agreement, which provided for the application of English law to British subjects charged with crimes in China, the law to be administered by consular courts. The British claim for extra-territorial jurisdiction was due to their unwillingness to submit their nationals to the procedure of Chinese courts and implied an assertion of the inferiority of the Chinese judicial system, but at the outset this was by no means the most contested part of the peace settlement, for it had from the point of view of the Chinese authorities the compensating advantage that the British government assumed responsibility for sailors going ashore from their ships and thus assisted the inadequate Chinese police of the treaty ports in the maintenance of order. It was only at a later date, when the adverse economic and political consequences of the system for China had become manifest, and familiarity with Western conceptions of sovereign rights had made the Chinese aware of the inferior international status which it involved, that extra-territoriality came to be regarded as the most galling feature of the 'unequal treaties', and its removal the supreme objective of nationalist agitation. It is one of the ironies of history that agreements denying China equality with the nations of the West were imposed on China while the West was still striving to gain from the court of Peking recognition of equal rank for its rulers with the Son of Heaven.

In concluding the Treaty of Nanking the British disclaimed any intention of seeking for themselves in China rights and privileges which would not be available to other nations, and the United States and France hastened to follow where Britain had led the way in negotiating similar treaties for their nationals. The Americans, not having taken part in the war with China, could not claim the appointment of imperial commissioners specially to make a treaty with them, but Kiying, who had been one of the two Chinese plenipotentiaries at Nanking, had now been sent to Canton with power to handle foreign affairs, and agreed to enter into negotiations with Caleb Cushing, who was sent to China as American plenipotentiary and arrived at Macao early in 1844. Kiying at first tried to make the American envoy accept a status of inferiority to China by the form of official correspondence which he adopted, but Cushing insisted on the same formal equality which had already been conceded to Britain, and finally got his way. The first Sino-American treaty was signed at

Wanghia on 3 July 1844, and three months later a French envoy, Théodose de Lagrené, obtained a treaty for France. The French introduced a new issue by pressing for repeal of the prohibition of Catholic Christianity enacted in China in 1724, and succeeded in obtaining an edict of toleration for the Catholic faith, which was later extended to Protestantism after the representatives of the latter had claimed equality of treatment. The agreement of the imperial government to tolerate the Christian religion was brought about by Kiying and he was never forgiven for it by the Confucian conservatives, who pursued him with bitter hatred for his alleged subservience to foreigners; he was degraded on the accession of the emperor Hsien Feng in 1850 and after a brief and unsuccessful re-appearance in diplomacy during the Tientsin negotiations of 1858 was condemned to death.

The most important immediate consequence of the treaties of 1842–4 was the phenomenal growth of Shanghai as a commercial port. Hitherto Canton had been the sole outlet for foreign trade of the produce of the Yangtse valley which more naturally moved down this great navigable river to a mart at or near its mouth; thus, as soon as Shanghai was opened to foreign trade, it began an economic development which soon made it a more important trading centre than Canton. In 1844, forty-four foreign ships entered the port; in 1855 the number was 437. Parallel with the expansion of trade went the increase in the number and prosperity of the foreign merchants in Shanghai. In 1845 the British consul made an agreement with the local Chinese authorities for a piece of ground outside the old walled city to be set aside for British residence, the land being acquired by individual contracts with the Chinese owners. Subsequently a British-American dispute arose because the American consul raised his flag within this area; the conflict was resolved by an agreement to share the ground, and this was the origin of the famous International Settlement of Shanghai. At the outset there was no question of a relinquishment of Chinese administrative authority over the area, but its new residents were persons enjoying extra-territorial rights and determined to create the public utilities and services of a European city. A 'Committee of Roads and Jetties' was set up, which soon developed into a kind of municipal administration. In 1854, when Shanghai was involved in a Chinese civil war and the authority of the Chinese government was at a low ebb, the foreign residents obtained rights of police and taxation in their settlement, which could further be defended from any incursions from without by a volunteer corps reinforced in case of need by marines from warships in the river. The International Settlement thus became in effect an independent city-republic with its own laws and administration; its prosperity drew into it a large Chinese population who far outnumbered the foreign residents, but did not share in the municipal franchise.

The treaties of 1842–4 thus made great inroads into China's seclusion, but on two essential points they left the traditional Chinese position intact. China had not yielded on the question of opening regular diplomatic relations with foreign powers; there were now indeed official dealings with foreign government representatives, but these were to be conducted by a commissioner in Canton, who for most of the time concurrently held the office of viceroy there, and there was still no direct contact with the imperial government. Further, there was still no right of travel for foreigners outside the five treaty ports and small surrounding areas— reckoned to extend to a radius of thirty miles—where they were permitted to make excursions for recreation. The capital and the whole interior of the country remained barred to the foreign visitor. For the Chinese seclusionist it was of the greatest importance to maintain these restrictions and keep the barbarian intruders penned up in the settlements assigned to them; as a result of defeat in war, it had not been possible to preserve the old system of controlling foreigners, but not an inch more than was strictly required by the treaties should now be conceded. The Western nations, on the other hand, were far from content with what they had gained; they were resolved to press demands both for diplomatic representation in Peking and for freedom of travel throughout China. The opportunity for negotiations to this end was afforded by a clause in the American and French treaties of 1844 which stated that they might be revised at the end of twelve years; by virtue of the most-favoured-nation principle Britain was held also to have the right to propose revision of her treaty. The time for claiming revision would fall in 1856. Meanwhile, the application of the existing treaties brought about endless friction, which greatly increased after the recall of Kiying from Canton in 1848. Kiying during his period of office there pursued a policy of conciliation, which he defended on the ground that it was useless to expect the Western barbarians to conform to the usages of civilisation; as he explained in a memorial to the emperor: 'If we restrained them by the ceremonial forms used for dependent tribes, they would certainly not consent to retire and remain in the status of Annam and Luchu, since they do not accept our calendar or receive imperial investiture.'

The most acute conflict of these years was over the so-called 'right of entry' into the walled city of Canton. After 1842 the foreigners were no longer cooped up in the narrow area of the factories, as they had been before the war; they were now permitted to ramble about in the countryside, but the Chinese still refused to allow them to pass through the gates of the walled city. The foreign consuls claimed that the treaties gave foreigners the right to do so, but the Chinese denied it, and by the Chinese texts of the treaties they appear to have been in the right. The issue was peculiar to Canton; at Shanghai and the other new treaty ports, where foreigners had been unknown before 1842, entry within the walls was accepted as part of the new order of things—which was locally popular as having ended the former commercial monopoly of Canton—but at Canton, where the population remembered the lowly status of the foreign merchants in the old days, the idea of their having freedom to walk about the city as they pleased was quite intolerable. The Cantonese felt they could retain their self-esteem as long as foreigners could be stopped at the gates; the foreigners, on the other hand, felt that they lost face in the eyes of the Chinese if they did not insist on their alleged right. Under strong pressure from the consuls Kiying at last, in January 1846, agreed to allow entry, but this produced such violent rioting in the city that he was driven to reverse his decision. His successors maintained the refusal, with support from Peking, the unalterable aversion of the people of Canton to the presence of foreigners within their walls being given as the reason for the prohibition. The consuls protested, but for the time being no steps were taken to enforce the claim.

The activities of western missionaries, both Catholic and Protestant, in the interior of China provided a further source of conflict over the interpretation of the treaties. The Chinese government maintained that no foreigners were entitled by the treaties to travel or reside in any part of the empire outside the five ports and their immediate neighbourhood. The Christian missionaries, on the other hand, claimed that the toleration edict of 1844 implied a right of propagating the various forms of the Christian faith throughout the country, and in any case they were not disposed to be diverted from their calling by any opposition from the heathen rulers of China. They were protected by the principle of extra-territoriality against the operations of Chinese law, and all that Chinese officials could do in accordance with the treaties was to arrest a missionary, when found in the interior, and send him under escort to the nearest treaty port, where, having committed no offence under the laws of his own country, he was released and promptly dived once more into the forbidden territory. The missionaries were not, however, immune from mob violence, which the officials were generally not too anxious to check; and where the reputation of western guns might avail to safeguard the lives of the missionaries, their Chinese converts and those who facilitated their residence could be subjected to persecution. The attitude of the Confucian scholar class towards Christianity varied; some were impressed by the austerely dedicated lives of the pioneer missionaries and were interested in, without being converted to, their teaching. But the great majority of the literati regarded the new religion not merely as a foreign faith which was being propagated in China under the protection of aggressive foreign powers, but also as a doctrine which could not, like Buddhism and Taoism, be fitted into the traditional pattern of Chinese culture, but was subversive and destructive of the ancestral way of life. These forebodings received apparent confirmation from the course of the Taiping rebellion when a movement calling itself Christian not only rose in arms against the reigning dynasty but also showed the most ruthless intolerance towards other forms of religious belief wherever it established its power. For Confucianism as a state religion the distinction between heresy and treason had never been very sharp, and strong anti-Christian feeling was aroused in areas endangered or ravaged by the Taipings. Sporadic persecution culminated in the martyrdom of the French Catholic priest Chapdelaine, who was tortured and beheaded by the magistrate of Hsilin in Kwangsi in February 1856, his converts also being executed or imprisoned. Redress for this action was demanded by the French consul from the Canton viceroy, and the latter's refusal to grant it provided the *casus belli* for the French participation with Britain in the war of 1856.

If the activity of foreign missionaries under the protection of extra-territorial rights seemed to the Chinese an encroachment on the internal jurisdiction of the empire, a no less serious curtailment of it arose from the practice of foreign registration of Chinese-owned shipping which grew up after 1842. Foreign registration brought Chinese ships under the protection of foreign navies, and the prevalence of piracy along the coasts of south China, particularly after the imperial authority had been weakened by the Taiping rebellion, made this a great advantage for Chinese merchants. But if it thus gave security to commerce, Chinese as well as foreign, during a period of administrative breakdown in China, it also meant that Chinese police were precluded from boarding ships which flew a foreign flag, even in quest of Chinese criminals or to prevent smuggling. Attempts by the Chinese authorities to interfere with foreign-registered Chinese ships led to sharp clashes with the foreign consuls. In 1854 a vessel flying the American flag was held up in the harbour of Shanghai and her crew removed on suspicion of smuggling ammunition to rebel forces; an American frigate intervened and enforced a salute to the American flag by a Chinese warship by way of redress. Two years later, a British-registered ship, the *Arrow*, was boarded in the harbour of Canton by Chinese soldiers, who removed several of her crew on a charge of piracy. The British consul then made various demands on the Canton viceroy, Yeh Ming-ch'en, and when full satisfaction for the incident was not received, began naval operations against the river forts and the city of Canton itself.

China was thus for a second time at war with Britain, but no longer as the united, though loosely administered, empire that had confronted the Western 'barbarians' in 1839. The great upheaval of the Taiping rebellion had been tearing the country apart for the last five years. This insurrection, beginning after the Ch'ing dynasty had just completed over two hundred years of rule over China, drew much of its inspiration from the anti-Manchu sentiment which had persisted underground in south China from the time of the conquest; it was also an effect of the increasing pressure of population on the land which has occurred with every prolonged period of internal peace and order in China and has periodically produced great outbursts of revolt and changes of dynasty. An important contributory factor, however, was the discredit which had fallen on the house of Ch'ing because of its humiliating defeats at the hands of the Western barbarians; the Treaty of Nanking was felt as a disgrace for which the imperial dynasty must bear the responsibility and in accordance with historical precedents it was expected that the *t'ien ming* or Mandate of Heaven, the divine authority to rule over China, would soon be bestowed elsewhere. In another way, too, the Western impact was now affecting the course of events within China. Movements of revolt against the established social and political order in China had traditionally been associated with heretical religious teachings of Buddhist or Taoist origin; now Christianity was added to the already existing elements of subversive thought. Hung Hsiu-ch'uan, a native of Kwangtung, of peasant stock, born in 1813, was one of the many Chinese of those times who after receiving a regular classical education was unsuccessful in the competitive public examinations which were the gateway to an official career; during an illness following his second failure in 1837 he had visions which he later interpreted in the light of certain Protestant Christian tracts he had picked up in Canton, and eventually he became convinced that he had received a divine commission to regenerate China. Having failed to enter the civil service, he had become a village schoolmaster; in 1844 he began to preach his new doctrine of salvation, admitting converts by a ceremony of baptism. The members of the sect, who called themselves the Shangti Hui (Shangti being the Chinese name adopted by the Protestant missionaries for God), denounced not only the Buddhist and Taoist cults, but also the honours paid to the tablet of Confucius. Hung thus ranged himself against all the existing religions of China, and as he soon lost his ordinary pupils, he was compelled to wander about to make a living as an itinerant seller of writing materials. In this way, however, he spread his teaching to other districts, and in 1847 he revisited Canton, studying there for two months under an American missionary called Roberts. After this his preaching against idolatry became more violent, and his followers began to destroy images in public temples to the great annoyance of the unconverted, whose complaints led to judicial action against some of them. Up to now the movement had been a purely religious one without political aims, but the collisions with the secular authorities in which the Shangti Hui was involved by its acts of violence inevitably raised the question whether officials who opposed the revealed will of God were not themselves part of the evil from which China was to be cleansed. At last, in the autumn of 1850, matters were brought to a head by an attempt of the provincial police to arrest Hung: he was forcibly rescued by his followers, and from that moment found himself at the head of an armed force committed to open rebellion against the existing government. Soon afterwards he assumed the title of T'ien Wang or Heavenly King and proclaimed the founding of a new dynasty under the name of T'ai P'ing or Great Peace, whence his followers became known to foreigners as Taipings. To the Ch'ing government they were known as Ch'ang Mao Tsei or Long-haired Bandits because they rejected the wearing of the queue which had been the sign of submission to the Manchus in China.

A series of military expeditions dispatched by the government against the Taipings failed to crush them; their fanaticism under the skilful military leadership of one of Hung's converts made them a formidable fighting force, while the troops of the imperial government were at an even lower ebb of efficiency than at the time of the Opium War. The Taiping army was besieged in Yunganchow in Kwangsi, but broke out and made its way through Hunan to the Yangtse, then descended the river in boats, capturing one city after another and finally taking Nanking in March 1853. Nanking was declared the capital of the new dynasty and for a moment it seemed that Hung had China at his feet. Had he advanced immediately in full strength on Peking he might easily have made an end of the Manchu dynasty, for the imperial armies were demoralised by the Taiping successes, and the Ch'ing court, under the weak and incompetent emperor Hsien Feng, who had succeeded to the throne in 1851, seemed incapable of acting with energy or decision in its own defence. But Hung settled down in Nanking to enjoy the fruits of victory and sent only a section of his army northward to attack Peking. It reached a point within twenty miles of Tientsin, but was there defeated by a force which included a strong contingent of Mongol cavalry, the Taiping army being composed almost entirely of infantry. The tide of fortune began to turn, and after some further fighting the Taipings withdrew south of the Yellow River. The weaknesses of the new regime now became apparent. The regime retained, except for Nanking itself, the mobile guerrilla character with which it had emerged from the highlands of Kwangsi; it failed to establish a regular civil administration in the conquered provinces and raised revenue by plundering expeditions hardly to be distinguished from banditry. The peasants, who had been attracted by a radical programme of redistribution of land in accordance with the vaguely egalitarian economic principles of Taiping teaching, were alienated by the ruthless foraging. The army, though relatively well disciplined, was divided by quarrels among the generals which developed after the failure of the expedition against Peking, and in 1856 the Tung Wang or Eastern Prince, one of the five chiefs created as the immediate subordinates of the T'ien Wang himself, began to dispute the authority of his master by claiming also to be receiving direct divine revelations; he was put to death together with his family and adherents, and the Taiping power was greatly weakened by the slaughter.

Much more serious, however, for the fate of the Taiping cause was the hostility aroused by the religious fanaticism of the movement. Everywhere the Taipings destroyed temples and pagodas; irreparable damage was done to the architectural heritage of China, and Christianity was presented to the Chinese as a violent and persecuting faith. The popular anti-Manchu secret societies of south China, which were the natural allies of the Taipings against the Manchu dynasty but had Buddhist or Taoist associations, were alienated by the Taiping intolerance, or their offers of co-operation were rejected by Hung as long as they remained heathen. But it was among the Confucian scholars that the most intense and politically effective antagonism to the Taiping revolution developed. A successful rebel leader who paid due honour to Confucius and showed respect for the Confucian tradition would have had no difficulty in winning over this class and providing himself with civil servants of the type which had governed China under every dynasty for two thousand years. Even the uncouth Manchus in the seventeenth century, despite the romantic loyalties of some Confucians for the lost cause of the Ming, had been able to find enough scholar-officials to provide a civil administration of the traditional kind for their military dominion. How much more should a new native Chinese dynasty have been able to do so after having broken the spell of Manchu military might and being in a position to offer to Chinese not only the offices which they held under the Ch'ing, but also those reserved for a culturally assimilated, but still alien, people! But the anti-Confucianism of the Taipings made it virtually impossible for them to obtain the services of the *literati*, and this was the main cause of their failure to establish a civil administration in the provinces they overran. Nor was the Confucian opposition confined to non-cooperation with the new regime; it came to assume the form of an armed counter-revolution—a movement owing little or nothing to the direction of the Peking court to which it nominally gave its allegiance, but springing directly from the provincial gentry and *shen shih* or 'girdled scholars'—holders of literary degrees without public office who wielded great influence in the localities where they lived. The two most important leaders of this reaction against the Taipings were Tseng Kuo-fan in Hunan and Li Hung-chang in Anhui. Both of them raised provincial militia armies to fight against the Taipings and these forces proved far more efficient and better disciplined than the old Manchu Banner and Green Standard troops who had been repeatedly routed by the rebels. As a result of their campaigns the Taipings were cleared out of the greater part of the territory which they had overrun and confined by the beginning of 1860 to a narrow tract along the lower Yangtse in Anhui and Kiangsu. Nanking was encircled and the revolt was all but at an end, when the Taipings succeeded in breaking out to the east in the direction of Shanghai and thereby added to their story a supplementary chapter in which other nations as well as Chinese were involved (see pp. 705–6).

At the time of their capture of Nanking in 1853 the attitude of the Western treaty-port residents towards the Taipings was generally one of hopeful expectation. Since the revolt had developed in the interior and not in the vicinity of the ports, little was known of it, but the fact that its leaders professed Christianity aroused sympathy for them and it was hoped that they would be more ready than the existing regime to open the country and enter into commercial and diplomatic relations with foreigners. Further, they appeared to be winning the civil war and it seemed expedient, without taking sides in the struggle, to make friendly contact with the probable future rulers of the empire. The governor of Hong Kong, Sir George Bonham, therefore ascended the Yangtse to Nanking in a small naval vessel and sought an audience of the T'ien Wang. This did not take place, however, because Bonham was told that 'God the Heavenly Father has sent our sovereign down on earth as the only true sovereign of all nations in the world' and that he must acknowledge himself a subject of the T'ien Wang; as an official representative of Her Britannic Majesty, Queen Victoria, he was unable to do this and so had to sail away again without making personal contact with the Taiping leader. It was indeed simply a repetition of the situation which had confronted Lord Napier in 1834. The claim to universal supremacy as asserted by the Ch'ing dynasty had been abated in consequence of defeat in war by the Treaty of Nanking, but was now being revived by the founder of a new dynasty who had had no experience of European gunfire; the T'ien Wang had come to restore the rights of China which the degenerate Manchus had been unable to maintain and his conviction of a divine commission from the Christian God had merely reinforced the idea of the proper status of a Chinese emperor which he had been brought up to accept.

Until 1860 the Taipings did not advance farther east than Chinkiang; thus they did not come into any direct contact with the rising foreign mercantile community of Shanghai. Had they advanced to Shanghai immediately after their capture of Nanking they would probably have captured the Chinese city without serious opposition and thereafter controlled the main part of China's foreign trade. As it was, the foreign community tended to be drawn indirectly into China's internal struggle; in spite of declarations of strict neutrality by the consuls, Shanghai became the centre of a traffic in arms and western adventurers took service in the armies of both sides. Rumours of international intrigue were in the air; the American commissioner, Humphrey Marshall, reported to his government that the British were about to give support to the Taipings in return for the opening of the Yangtse to their trade and that the Manchu court was seeking help from Russia. Then in September 1853 the Small Sword Society, one of the numerous secret societies of south China, broke out in revolt and seized Shanghai. The Small Swords were independent of the Taipings, who condemned their heathen practices; theirs was one of a number of insurrections which were touched off by the Taiping upheaval without being under Taiping control. Desultory fighting went on in and around Shanghai for a year and a half and foreigners were involved in clashes with both Chinese parties. In April 1854 plundering in the foreign settlement by imperial troops led to the battle of Muddy Flat, when British and American volunteers reinforced by naval landing parties drove them from the settlement area. In December French forces combined with imperial troops to recapture the Chinese city from the Short Swords, having become involved in the fighting through measures to protect a Catholic mission. Meanwhile, the Western consuls and merchants had taken steps to preserve some kind of administrative order in the port, where trade continued in spite of the political chaos which prevailed. The imperial customs-house having been destroyed and the customs officials dispersed, there was nobody to collect the customs payments due to the Chinese government on the foreign trade. An agreement was therefore made with the highest local Chinese official (who was a refugee in the foreign settlement) that the dues should be collected by foreign inspectors nominated by the consuls and working in the service of the Chinese government. This was the origin of the foreign-administered Inspectorate of Maritime Customs, which was later extended to all treaty ports and became the main source of revenue available to the Chinese government as security for foreign loans.

From the spring of 1855 to the spring of 1860 conditions in the Shanghai area were comparatively peaceful, but in 1856, as already related (p. 696), Anglo-Chinese hostilities broke out at Canton over the Chinese boarding of a British-registered ship. For a time the warfare was indecisive in character, for it was impossible to capture Canton with the forces locally available, and reinforcements were long in arriving; the Indian government was busy with the war in Persia and afterwards with the Indian Mutiny, and some troops sent out from Britain for the campaign in China were also diverted to India to take part in the suppression of the Mutiny. But by the autumn of 1857 Britain had been joined by France—on account of the Chapdelaine case—in belligerency against China, or at least against the Canton viceroy Yeh Ming-Chen, and between them the two allies were able to muster enough strength for an assault on the city. The attackers broke in after a heavy naval bombardment and captured Yeh, who had gone into hiding; he was deported to Calcutta, where he died a year later.

Lord Elgin and Baron Gros, who had been appointed plenipotentiaries by Britain and France respectively for the revision of the treaties with China, now decided to sail north with their fleets to Shanghai and invite the imperial government to send representatives to a conference there; if there was no satisfactory outcome of this procedure, it was planned to go on to the Peiho and advance towards the capital. American and

Russian envoys now joined the British and French, though without actual belligerency. Reed, the American plenipotentiary, was himself in favour of American participation in the war and told the Secretary of State that 'the powers of Western civilisation must insist on what they know to be their rights and give up the dream of dealing with China as a power to which any ordinary rules apply'.[1] The American government, however, did not give him leave to commit American armed forces; he was instructed merely to take advantage on the most-favoured-nation principle of any concessions forcibly extorted from China by the British and French, leaving them to do whatever fighting was needed. The Russian position was different. Russia was not one of the nations trading by sea with China; on the contrary, she was expressly excluded from the maritime trade on the ground that she already conducted an overland trade through Kiakhta on the Mongolian border. Count Putyatin, who joined the envoys of the maritime powers in Hong Kong towards the end of 1857, was instructed to obtain for Russia the right of commerce by sea, as well as by land, with China; much more important for Russian interests, however, were the territorial demands being made at the same time on China (through the military governor of northern Manchuria) by Count Muraviev, the Russian governor-general of eastern Siberia (cf. ch. XIV, pp. 384–5). The Russo-Chinese frontier north of the Amur had remained nominally as fixed by the treaty of 1689, but during the 1850's Muraviev had taken advantage of the weakening of the Chinese empire by the Taiping rebellion to plant Russian settlements along the Amur. With all its available forces engaged in coping with an insurrection which threatened the overthrow of the dynasty, the Peking government was in no position to resist these encroachments in a remote and thinly inhabited northern territory, and nothing was done to stop them. But now Russia was demanding formal cession of all Chinese territory north of the Amur and east of the Ussuri and stronger pressure was required to compel Peking to yield. The war being waged against China by Britain and France served well the purpose of reducing further the Chinese capacity or will to resist in the north, and Putyatin's mission was to increase the joint Western pressure on Peking, while at the same time avoiding belligerency, so that Russia was left free to befriend China against Britain and France if circumstances made it expedient— as they were to do two years later.

The scheme for negotiations at Shanghai came to nothing, as the envoys of the four Western powers were told to return to Canton and deal there with a new commissioner for foreign affairs who had been appointed to replace the deported Yeh. The envoys refused, however, to go back to Canton; instead, they set sail for the Peiho and sent notes ashore demanding a conference with imperial plenipotentiaries to be held either at Tientsin or Peking; the replies being deemed unsatisfactory, the Taku

[1] J. W. Foster, *American Diplomacy in the Orient* (Boston and New York, 1904), p. 234.

forts were attacked and captured by the British and French admirals and the envoys moved up the river to Tientsin. The Peking government now consented to appoint plenipotentiaries and after brief negotiations treaties were signed with each of the four Western powers. Meanwhile, ten days after the capture of the Taku forts, Muraviev concluded separately the Treaty of Aigun whereby all Chinese territory north of the Amur was ceded to Russia and the territory east of Ussuri was to be subject to a Russo-Chinese condominium.

The Tientsin treaties provided not only for the opening of eleven more treaty ports—three of them up the Yangtse River, whose navigation was now permitted to Western shipping—but also conceded the two points on which the imperial court had most stubbornly resisted Western pressure—the right of travel in the interior and the right of diplomatic representation in Peking. Toleration for the profession and propagation of the Christian religion was also written into the treaties. The main objectives of Western policy were thus attained. But, as the treaties had been extorted by force from an unwilling government, and as there was an active and powerful extremist element which reproached the government for having yielded, it was only to be anticipated that there would be further trouble before the treaties could be put into effect, and so indeed there was. The imperial court took the opportunity of post-treaty negotiations on customs tariffs to appeal to Britain to refrain from exercising the right conferred by the Tientsin treaty to maintain a permanent diplomatic mission in Peking. The British government agreed that its representative in China should reside elsewhere than in Peking, provided that he would be admitted to the capital on special occasions. But one such occasion was required in the immediate future—the meeting for exchange of ratifications of the recently concluded treaties. The British, French and American envoys sailed to Taku for this purpose and arrived there on 20 June 1859, only to find the river barred to their entry. Admiral Hope, commanding the British naval escort, then attacked the Taku forts, but this time the garrisons, which had been re-equipped since the capitulation of the previous year, put up an effective resistance, and the attack was beaten off. Following this set-back, the British and French envoys returned to Shanghai; Ward, the American representative, however, being officially a neutral in the Anglo-French war against China, detached himself from his colleagues, and landing at Peitang, farther up the coast, was allowed to come to Peking, where the Russian envoy, Ignatiev, had already exchanged ratifications. Ward arranged for an audience with the emperor for the purpose of delivering a letter from the president of the United States, but cancelled it on learning that the *kotow* or ceremonial prostration would be required of him.

The British and French governments meanwhile decided to resume belligerent action against China and went north again with increased forces in the summer of 1860. The Taku forts were taken and Tientsin occupied after some hard fighting. Faced with the imminent prospect of a march on Peking, the Chinese government entered into negotiations, but the parley was wrecked by the pressure of a court faction which was in favour of continued resistance and brought about a treacherous attack on the British and French negotiating representatives and their escorts travelling under a flag of truce. Of the two truce parties, eighteen persons were made prisoners and twenty-one killed; the captives included Harry Parkes, who had been British consul in Canton, and Lord Elgin's private secretary. An attempt to use the prisoners as hostages was unsuccessful; the Anglo-French army resumed its advance, demanding their unconditional release. The emperor and his entourage fled to Jehol, leaving his younger brother, Prince Kung, to negotiate with the invaders. The prisoners were set free, but as a punishment for the killing of the other members of the truce parties Lord Elgin ordered the destruction of the imperial summer palace of Yuenmingyuen, which had already been looted by the British and French vanguards. A few days later the ratifications of the British and French treaties of 1858 were exchanged in Peking, and a supplementary convention was concluded, imposing fresh indemnities on China, opening Tientsin to foreign trade and reasserting the right of diplomatic residence in the capital.

During the critical days after the flight of the emperor, when Chinese officials were in a state of panic, the Russian envoy Ignatiev acted as a neutral go-between for negotiations, and as a reward for his services—which he did not fail to exaggerate—in assuaging the wrath of the Western belligerents induced the Chinese to cede to Russia outright the territory east of the Ussuri which had been placed under a Russo-Chinese condominium by the Treaty of Aigun. Thus, without firing a shot, Russia not only gained by the operation of the most-favoured-nation principle all the commercial and diplomatic rights forcibly extorted from China by Britain and France, but also acquired a large slice of Chinese territory whereby the frontier of the Russian empire in Asia was extended southward along the Pacific coast to the border of Korea. At that time, indeed, the trans-Ussuri territory was reckoned of little value, being only very thinly inhabited by primitive hunting tribes, but within a year of the cession the Russians founded at its southern extremity a new town to which they gave the name of Vladivostok (cf. p. 385).

It was Prince Kung who negotiated the agreements of 1860 and terminated a war which had turned to utter disaster for China; the imperial court, having departed from the capital on an 'autumn inspection tour' remained in Jehol watching developments from a safe distance. A whole year elapsed before the emperor returned to Peking and then it was no longer the same emperor. Hsien Feng, a feeble ruler whose policy had been continually swayed by court intrigues, fell ill in Jehol and died there in August 1861. He was succeeded by his only son, aged five, whose mother was an imperial concubine named Yehonala, the empress consort having failed to produce a male heir. During the lifetime of Hsien Feng Yehonala had already acquired great influence, but while the emperor lay dying a conspiracy of her enemies in the palace was organised to exclude her from the regency for her son's minority. The emperor on his death-bed was induced to sign an edict appointing a board of eight regents nominated by the anti-Yehonala clique. She, however, had taken possession of the dynastic seal required for the validity of the edict, and her supporters repudiated the authority of the regents. The conflict was decided by a *coup d'état*; the regents were arrested on the return of the court to Peking and either executed or degraded. Their powers were henceforth vested jointly in the former empress-consort and Yehonala. The latter assumed as an honorific title the name by which she is better known to history; as the Empress Dowager Tzu Hsi she was to be the dominant figure in Chinese politics for the next forty-seven years. Her co-regent was willing that she should in effect conduct affairs of state on her sole authority and the various organs of government looked to her for decisions which she did not fail to give. Deficient as she was in knowledge of the world outside the palace walls, she was nevertheless superlatively skilful in the arts of political manipulation, and succeeded for nearly half a century in preserving a badly shaken regime which a less able hand would soon have brought to final ruin.

The first and most notable achievement of the new reign was the definitive suppression of the Taiping rebellion and reunification of the empire under the Ching dynasty. The rebellion had remained in being during the whole period of external warfare from 1856 to 1860, but it was never again a threat to the seat of the central government as it had been in 1854. The operations of Tseng Kuo-fan's forces had indeed almost achieved the suppression of the revolt by the beginning of 1860; food supplies to Nanking were cut off and the recapture of the city seemed to be within sight. But the Taipings broke out eastward and succeeded in overrunning the greater part of the Soochow–Shanghai area, which had hitherto remained immune from the ravages of the civil war. This vigorous, but strictly localised, revival of Taiping insurgency interrupted trade in the hinterland of Shanghai and seriously affected the interests of the foreign as well as the Chinese merchants of the rapidly expanding commercial port. The neutrality which the Western powers had hitherto maintained in relation to the struggle going on in the interior of China now gave way to intervention on behalf of the Peking government against the Taipings. In recent years, with the growth of a romantic cult of the Taipings as the pioneers of nationalism and social revolution in China, it has become common to represent this intervention as the outcome of motives far transcending the local interests of Shanghai trade; it is attributed to the jealousy of Christian missionaries for a form of their religion independent of their guidance and to fears of Western governments that a victorious Taiping dynasty established in Peking would make China too strong to be coerced by Western power. But the Taipings in 1861 were not a force advancing to victory; they had conspicuously failed to overturn the Manchu dynasty and had lost nearly all the territory they had controlled six years previously. Only in the Shanghai area were they now formidable, and there they appeared to foreign observers no longer as a power disputing with the Ching emperor for possession of the celestial empire, but as a mere predatory nuisance despoiling a rich and fertile province. The desire of the Shanghai merchants was to see peace and order restored in China, so that trade might revive; had there been any prospect of the Taipings becoming the effective government of China, the foreign business community would have been the first to advocate recognition of the new regime, but as there was no such prospect they were in favour of co-operation with the imperial authorities to put an end to the disastrous insurrection as quickly as possible. Thus British and French forces helped to defend Shanghai against Taiping attacks even while their fellow-countrymen were carrying on hostilities against the Chinese central government on the Peiho, and later on, after peace had been restored in north China, the aid given to the local Chinese officials in Kiangsu for repelling the Taiping incursion had the blessing of the Peking court, which, however little it liked the Western barbarians, considered it only right and proper that they should fight on behalf of the Son of Heaven instead of warring against him. Some of the fighting was indeed done by British and French regular forces, but operations were left more and more to a foreign-officered Chinese army, financed by Shanghai merchants and commanded originally by the American Frederick Ward, whose status was that of a mercenary general in Chinese service. Ward achieved some striking initial successes, but he was killed in action in September 1862. After a period of disorganisation his army was placed under the command of Major Charles Gordon, who was authorised by the British government to take service under the Chinese government. Gordon won a series of victories over the Taipings, operating in combination with the Chinese militia armies under Tseng Kuo-fan and Li Hung-chang. By the spring of 1864 the end of the insurrection was in sight, but Gordon did not remain to take part in the final act; he was recalled to British army service and his troops—the so-called 'Ever-victorious Army'—disbanded. Nanking was besieged by Tseng without foreign aid and fell in July, the Tien Wang having committed suicide.

The collapse of the Taiping rebellion restored the authority of the Ching dynasty throughout China from Peking to Canton, and China could once more face the world as a unified state. There were still, however, areas of revolt in the western parts of the empire, though these had nothing to do with the Taipings and did not threaten to take over the central government. The disruption of the imperial authority during the Taiping rebellion had given an opportunity for local independence to followers of the other monotheist faith which challenged the norms of Chinese traditional civilisation: the Chinese Muslims known as Panthays in Yunnan and as Tungans in Kansu and Shensi rose in revolt and set up regional governments of their own. The revolt of the Panthays began in 1855, that of the Tungans in 1862. The Tungan rising had repercussions in Chinese Turkestan, where the bulk of the population was also Muslim, though Turkish and not Chinese in language; an adventurer from Ferghana named Yakub Beg made himself master of Kashgar and the Tarim basin, while Russia took advantage of the confusion in 1871 to occupy Kulja. For a while it seemed that the western borderlands of the Manchu-Chinese empire might be broken away by a group of Muslim states. Reconquest was difficult because of the remoteness and inaccessibility of the centres of insurrection, but after the suppression of the Taipings the task of crushing the Muslim rebels was undertaken and carried out gradually, but persistently, in a series of military campaigns. The Panthays held out until 1873, the Turkestan rebels until 1878, but the revolts were in the end everywhere crushed, often with great cruelty, and the authority of Peking was again extended westward to the Pamirs and south-westward to the borders of Burma. The recovery was completed when, after a diplomatic crisis with a threat of war, Russia restored Kulja to China in 1881.

The restored empire, however, was no longer the China of 1839 or even of 1859. The seclusion of Chinese society had been fatally breached; China had been compelled to enter into diplomatic relations on a basis of equality with Western states and to grant Western merchants and missionaries free access to all her territory. The question was no longer whether China's rulers would be able to prevent the influx of the West, but how they would adapt themselves to the new conditions. They could seek to make themselves stronger by acquiring the Western technology and administrative organisation by which they had been defeated, or they could do their best to ignore the unpleasant contemporary reality and obstruct in every way possible the forces which they no longer dared openly to oppose. In the main they took the latter course, though there were certain adaptations which they had to make and which were to have far-reaching consequences. The treaties of 1858 required that China should set up a regular Foreign Ministry to deal with foreign diplomatic missions instead of leaving foreign relations to provincial viceroys or special commissioners, and this meant also that some officials of high rank must have a knowledge of foreign languages instead of relying on menial interpreters; a College of Foreign Languages was therefore created in Peking in 1862. It was further decided that something must be done to modernise the military and naval forces, and for this purpose in the following year a school was instituted in Shanghai, attached to the Kiang-nan arsenal, where Western sciences and mathematics were taught by foreign instructors. But it was not until the 'seventies that students were sent abroad for training, and the intellectual contamination involved in thus exposing young minds to alien thought was the cause of much misgiving to the more conservative mandarins, and the same fears were undoubtedly at the back of the government's reluctance to send its own diplomatic missions abroad even after foreign legations had been established in Peking. A Chinese legation was not set up in any Western capital until 1877; in the meantime, China relied largely on friendly foreigners to negotiate for her in foreign countries, the most famous of them being the ex-minister of the United States in Peking, Anson Burlingame, who told an American audience in 1868 that the day was at hand when 'this great people [would] extend its arms towards the shining banners of Western civilisation'.[1] In China, however, at this date the most powerful elements in society were still taking thought to devise means of holding Western civilisation in check. Unfortunately, since the Christian missionaries who were the principal propagators of this civilisation in China —the much more subversive cultural effects of Western secular education had not yet become apparent—were under the protection of the treaties, the only way of removing them or interfering with their work was by mob violence, and this became a constant feature of Chinese–Western relations during the last four decades of the nineteenth century, culminating in the great Boxer outbreak of 1900. The 'girdled scholars' were generally behind the attacks on missionaries and their converts; an inflammatory propaganda against Christianity was carried on by means of posters, and at some point the incitement had its effect in arson, assault or murder. A particularly violent riot took place in Tientsin in 1870, when two Catholic priests, ten Sisters of St Vincent de Paul, nine other Europeans and a number of Chinese Christian converts were killed. The officials were placed in an equivocal position by these outbursts; they were responsible for the protection of foreigners against lawless violence, but they usually themselves shared in the hatred of the foreign religion and were afraid of occurring popular odium by zeal on its behalf. Hence they were often suspected of actually conniving at anti-foreign outrages and almost every incident was followed by demands from the Western legations for the punishment of local officials for neglect of their duty. The disturbances thus involved China in continual trouble in her foreign relations without achieving the ulterior purpose of the agitation, for the missionaries were not driven out, but arrived in increasing numbers, and their schools became the most important means of diffusion of Western education in China.

The defeats and humiliations of China as the traditional supreme power

[1] F. W. Williams, *Anson Burlingame...* (New York, 1912), p. 119.

of the Far East inevitably had their sequels in the lesser Asian countries to the south and east. In 1855 Sir John Bowring, the British Superintendent of Trade in China, was sent to negotiate a treaty with Siam, and with the lesson of the British compulsion of China to reinforce his arguments, he obtained terms—including the right of extra-territorial jurisdiction—on the model of the treaties which China had concluded with the Western powers. Three years later France extended her policy towards China to cover Annam, where the Catholic religion, introduced by French missionaries during the eighteenth century, had been subjected to persecution during the first half of the nineteenth. Just as France, in accordance with the Second Empire policy of combining patronage of the Catholic church with an active promotion of French economic and strategic interests overseas, had joined in the second British war against China in order to exact retribution for the execution of the French missionary Chapdelaine, so also in Annam the naval force which had taken part in the Peiho operations of 1858 was used in combination with a Spanish expedition from Manila to enforce the toleration of Christianity. This enterprise was successful, but the reward of victory was not only religious; France also annexed the three eastern provinces of Cochin China, including the city of Saigon, and thus laid the foundations for her empire of Indo-China. In 1863 she established a protectorate over Cambodia, suzerainty over which was in dispute between Annam and Siam; in 1867 the rest of Cochin China was also annexed. By 1870 the French were thus firmly established in the delta of the Mekong, though they had as yet no control over Annam proper or Tongking.

A similar French attempt in 1866 to subdue Korea after the execution of nine French priests there was less successful. A naval expedition under Admiral Roze was sent against Korea, but as no landing forces, were available and the Koreans could not be brought to negotiation by blockade or naval bombardment alone, nothing was accomplished. Korea, indeed, was the Far Eastern country which, by taking advantage of its relatively out-of-the-way position, succeeded in holding out longest against Western demands for diplomatic and commercial relations and toleration of missionaries, and thereby fully earned the title of the 'Hermit Kingdom'. After the repulse of the French expedition Korea rebuffed German, Russian and American attempts to open diplomatic relations and did not conclude a treaty with any foreign power until 1876. Then it was not with a Western nation, but with Japan, and the fact that it was Japan which then took the lead in opening Korea after having been herself until recently an exponent of seclusionism in its most extreme form was significant of an entirely new factor in Far Eastern affairs—the initiative of an Asian country which was not passively resisting or accepting the pressures of the West, but actively and freely adapting itself to them.

Up to 1853 Japan had maintained the system of the *Sakoku* or 'closed country' as it had been established in the seventeenth century after the early period of commercial contacts with Western nations and the propagation of Christianity in Japan. Under the seclusion policy no foreigners were allowed to come to Japan except for Chinese and Dutch merchants, who were allowed a small and carefully regulated trade confined to the single port of Nagasaki, and no Japanese was permitted to go abroad; the construction of ocean-going ships was forbidden and the teaching or practice of Christianity strictly forbidden. There were in Japan a few individuals who acquired a knowledge of the Dutch language and from Dutch books formed some conception of the world outside Japan, but they were not in a position to influence national policy, and the attitude of Japan's effective government, that of the Tokugawa family who held the office of shogun or generalissimo under the nominal sovereignty of the emperor, remained unchanged through the first half of the nineteenth century. In 1825 instructions were given to coastguards to fire on any foreign ships approaching the shores of Japan; these were later modified to allow provisions and water to be given to shipwrecked sailors, but such involuntary visitors must be compelled to depart as soon as possible.

The pressure from the West for opening Japan was in the early days much less than that for developing trade with China. The British had no existing commercial stake in Japan such as they already had at Canton before 1839 and the Dutch were not strong enough to contemplate using force in Japan; moreover there was no Japanese export comparable in importance to Chinese tea, and for the European maritime nations—and also for the Americans before the middle of the century—Japan was the most remote of the Far Eastern lands. But with the settlement of the American Pacific coast and the establishment of a shipping route between San Francisco and Shanghai, Japan was brought into a new relation geographically to Western oceanic enterprise and the United States came to have an interest in opening Japan, particularly in order to get a coaling station on the long trans-Pacific sea-route to Shanghai. Thus it happened that Japan was compelled to abandon her seclusion policy, not by Britain or France, but by America. The fact that this was accomplished by the threat of force, but without actual warfare, was mainly due to Japanese knowledge of the fate that had already befallen China from Western ships and guns.

Commodore Perry with four American warships arrived off Uraga—not far from Yedo, the modern Tokyo, at that time the seat of the shogunate government—in July 1853. He bore a letter from the President of the United States and declared that unless it were received and answered, he would not be accountable for the consequences. The letter having been received, he sailed away, announcing that he would return for the answer the following year. The shogun, thoroughly alarmed at this menacing visit, summoned a council of feudal lords who debated the question whether to resist or submit to the American demands. There was a strong party in favour of defying the enemy, but the decisive argument was that Japan had no fleet and that the coastal defences were inadequate to withstand bombardment by Western naval guns; it was decided that, for the time being at least, discretion was the better part of valour, and that Perry should be given a conciliatory answer. The result was the Treaty of Kanagawa, signed on 31 March 1854, which was the first step in the opening of Japan. This treaty did not, it is true, provide for diplomatic relations or extra-territoriality and the only ports opened to trade were Shimoda and Hakodate. But it was the thin end of the wedge, and, as in China, there was soon pressure to drive the wedge in deeper. Britain and Russia at once followed the United States in extracting treaties from Japan; both of them obtained the opening of Nagasaki to their ships, and Russia successfully claimed extra-territorial jurisdiction for her nationals. By 1858 the shogunal government had become convinced that the seclusion policy must be radically revised, and the news of what was happening to China only confirmed them in their view of the necessity for Japan to accept without resistance the new order of things that was being violently imposed on China. But the Yedo administration now found itself in a dilemma. A strong opposition to any further concessions was developing in the country and it found leadership in the imperial court in Kyoto. The basis of the rule of the house of Tokugawa, which had held the office of shogun since 1603, was threatened by the unpopularity incurred by a policy of apparently supine submission to foreign demands. On the other hand, defiance of the Western powers might lead to the same kind of violent compulsion which had overwhelmed China.

In the Japanese political system of the Tokugawa period the imperial dynasty had never been divested of its formal sovereignty; constitutionally governing power had merely been delegated to the shoguns as perpetual prime ministers. In practice the imperial court was excluded from any share in the administration of the country, and the emperors lived in a seclusion verging on imprisonment with the performance of certain religious rites as their only state function; to the outer world the shogun in Yedo appeared to be the only ruler of Japan and was often referred to at this time as 'the emperor'. But the shoguns could only maintain the subordination of the ancient imperial dynasty as long as effective force was on their side and the existing state of affairs was regarded by Japanese national sentiment as normal and proper. In 1858 neither of these conditions was any longer fulfilled. Since the eighteenth century a romantic literary movement springing from the study of early Japanese literature and the Shinto religion, in contrast to the Chinese and Confucian studies patronised by the shogunate, had spread far and wide the idea that authority in Japan rightly belonged to the imperial dynasty and that the power of the shogun could be revoked at any time by the *de jure* sovereign. This moral undermining of the Tokugawa regime might not by itself have been fatal, but it coincided with a revival of old antagonisms against the Tokugawa among a group of feudal families and their retainers—notably those of the fiefs of Satsuma in south-western Kyushu and Choshu fronting the Straits of Shimonoseki, the western entrance to the Japanese Inland Sea. With its prestige disastrously lowered by its surrenders to foreign demands, the shogunate was now no longer able effectively to control either the imperial court or the disaffected elements of the feudal nobility.

In an endeavour to cover itself against criticism the Yedo government sought the emperor's sanction for a new treaty negotiated with Townsend Harris, the American consul in Shimoda who had established quasi-diplomatic relations with the shogun. But the imperial consent was refused and the treaty was signed without it. The Harris treaty of 1858 went far beyond the previous agreements of foreign powers with Japan; it provided for diplomatic representation in Yedo, the opening of additional ports, rights of permanent residence and freedom of travel. But the shogun was now faced with a widespread assertion that this, and corresponding treaties subsequently negotiated with Britain, France and Russia, were not binding on patriotic Japanese because they lacked the emperor's sanction. The anti-foreign agitation led to a series of murderous attacks, not only on foreigners in the ports, but also on the Western diplomatic missions when they were established in Yedo; meanwhile, the emperor, supported by Satsuma, Choshu and other disaffected fiefs, began to issue orders to the shogun, culminating in January 1863 in a command that he proceed to 'drive out the barbarians' forthwith. The shogun, who was better informed about the strength of the barbarians than the cloistered courtiers of Kyoto, could do nothing to carry out this directive, and was denounced by the anti-Tokugawa faction as a traitor and a coward. He was summoned to Kyoto and finally induced to inform the foreign envoys that Japan would revert to the policy of seclusion. The Western diplomats refused even to discuss such an idea, and the Yedo government reported to Kyoto that it was impossible to enforce the imperial order. The lord of Choshu, however, took it on himself to enforce it in the Straits of Shimonoseki, using coastal batteries and small warships to prevent the passage of foreign ships. He thus involved himself in a private war against the Western world, as a result of which his batteries were bombarded and destroyed by a joint British-French-Dutch-American naval expedition. The lord of Satsuma in the meantime had had his fief capital, Kagoshima, bombarded by a British squadron in reprisal for the murder of an Englishman by his retainers. The inability of either Choshu or Satsuma to offer effective opposition to Western gunfire now convinced the feudal supporters of the Kyoto court that expulsion of the barbarians was not a practical proposition; the Western powers for their part, having come to realise that their treaties were invalidated by the lack of imperial ratification, determined to obtain this ratification, and moved their naval squadrons to Osaka Bay. There was no way out for the emperor, and the ratifications were given.

Logically, with the imperial consent to the treaties, the enemies of the Tokugawa were deprived of the cause by exploiting which they had embarrassed and discredited the shogun. But the very fact that the Western powers had now formally recognised the emperor as the legitimate ruler of Japan completed the downfall of the shogunate. In November 1867 the last Tokugawa shogun, Yoshinobu, resigned his governing power to the fifteen-year-old emperor Mutsuhito, better known to history by his reign title of Meiji. The surrender came too late to avert a civil war between a group of fiefs led by Satsuma and Choshu and those remaining loyal to the Tokugawa, but the struggle was of brief duration, and after its conclusion the imperial court was moved from Kyoto to Yedo, now renamed Tokyo, where it took over the existing apparatus of the shogunal administration.

The men who now came to the fore, advising and acting in the name of the young emperor, were for the most part retainers of Satsuma and Choshu who were prepared for radical innovations for the sake of national strength and independence. Having been persuaded by events that it was impossible to oppose Western power without learning the secrets of its success, they had become advocates of unrestricted intercourse with the West, and in the 'charter oath' which they induced the emperor to take in the presence of an assembly of feudatories in April 1868 was inserted a clause that 'knowledge shall be sought all over the world'. In their purpose of acquiring the knowledge which would make their country strong, these men were able by the peculiar circumstances of their rise to power to combine to a remarkable degree a revolutionary spirit and a traditionalist loyalty. They had overturned an *ancien régime* by invoking a yet more ancient tradition which, because it had been so long in eclipse, was relatively free from implication in the vested interests of a privileged ruling class. Their *coup d'état* had been at once a revolution and a restoration. Whereas in China Taiping Christianity had attacked and antagonised the main traditional forces of society, the Meiji Restoration and the reforms that followed it were carried out in the name of the original gods of Japan and of the oldest national institutions. Moreover, the Meiji reformers, drawn from a military caste, were fully persuaded of the need for change by the argument of military defeat, in contrast to the dominant scholar-officials of China for whom the potency of barbarian gunfire was no proof of the inadequacy of Confucian culture. The success of Japan's adaptation to the Western challenge in the years after 1868 was due to the concentration of will with which her rulers applied themselves to the building of national power. They had their reward. Within forty years, while China remained weak, passive and inert, Japan, emerging victorious from the ordeal of war against Russia, was accepted by the West as a great power.

INDEX

Aaland Islands, 484, 489
Aargau, anti-clerical measures in, 223
Abbas Pasha, viceroy of Egypt, 438
Abd-el-Kader, amir of Mascara, 320
Abeken, Heinrich, Prussian diplomat, 592, 593, 596
Aberdeen Act (1845), 661
Aberdeen, George Hamilton Gordon, 4th earl, 122, 259, 471, 474
Abyssinian campaign (1868), 305
Académie des Beaux Arts, 144
Académie Française, 213
Académie de Peinture et de Sculpture, 144
Academy of Science, St Petersburg, 50
Accessory Transport Co., 681
Acids
  carbolic, 52, 64, 73
  mineral, 52
  acetic, 65
  tartaric, 65
Acid towers, waste from, 51
Acre
  invested by Egyptian troops, 251
  as a port, 423
  government by Egypt, 428
Act of Union (1707), church patronage of, 83
Act of Union (1801), abolishes Dublin parliament, 217
Acto Addicional, 661
Acton, John Emerich, 1st Baron
  condemns nationalism, 12
  on The General Council, 95
  on theory of nationality, 214
  nationality retrograde step, 245
  British Cabinet ill-informed, 599
Adams, Charles Francis, American minister in London, 638, 640
Adams, John Quincey, sixth president of U.S.A., 203
Aden, occupied as coaling station, 431
Adrianople, 423
  Treaty of (1829), 241, 417, 489
Adriatic, 421, 425
Afghanistan, 685
Aftonbladet, 127
Agamemnon (1852), 279
Agassiz, Louis, scientist, 51, 71, 120
Agence générale pour la défense de la liberté religieuse, 78
Agnosticism, spread of, 9
Agriculture
  extension of markets, 5, 25
  increasing productivity of farms, 23

enclosure, 24
use of fertilisers, 24
animal diseases, 24
drainage, 24–5
improvement in three stages, 24–5
tenant farmers' capital needs, 25
spread of sugar beet, 27
science in, 52
technical revolution in, 65
employment in, 332
effects of revolution on, 413
Aigun, Treaty of, 703, 704
Ak-merchet (renamed Perovsk), 387
Aksakov, I. S., writer, 368
Aksakov, K. S., writer, 368
Alabama, 615, 627, 655
Alabama damage claim, 640
Alamán, Lucas, historian and politician, 675
Alaska, ceded to U.S.A. (1867), 384
Albania, 422, 479
Alberdi, Juan Bautista, 670, 671
Albert, Archduke of Austria, visit to Berlin (1859), 506
Albert, French socialist, arrested, 399
Albert, Prince, Prince Consort of Queen Victoria
  on science, 52
  interest in technical institutes, 113
  suspected of working for Russia, 477
  visit to Boulogne, 481
  and the *Trent* affair, 639
Alcohol, composition and synthesis of, 65
Aldershot, purchase of, 486
Aleppo, 423
Alexander I, tsar of Russia, death of, 358
Alexander II, tsar of Russia
  greater intellectual freedom under, 233
  attitude towards Peace of Paris, 269
  assassination, 358
  and reform, 369
  emancipation of serfs, 370
  and liberalisation of Finland, 376
  attempted assassination of, 378, 582
  becomes tsar, 481
  and Bessarabia and Black Sea concessions, 492
  and Hohenzollern candidature for Spanish throne, 592
Alexandretta, 423
Alexandria
  volume of shipping, 419
  population of, 420, 424
  mail service to, 431
  communications to Suez, 432, 436–8

715

Algebra, 56
Algeria
  French conquest of, 7, 320, 416, 427, 433
  an extension of France, 427
  transportation to, 445
  France strengthens hold on, 461
Algerian campaign (1838), use of rifled
  musket, 304
Algiers
  traffic with Marseilles, 421
  population, 424
Alicante, 420
Alizarin, synthesis of, 64
Alkalis, 52
Allgemeine Zeitung
  Heine's contribution barred, 125
  circulation, 126
Alliance Israélite Universelle, 244
Alsace
  discovery of potassium salts (1852) in, 24
  cotton spinning mills using water power,
  28
Alsace and Lorraine, surrendered by
  France, 17, 600
Alsen, battle of, 516
Alvensleben Convention, 515
Amari, Michele, historian, 225
Amazon, river, steamboats on the, 662
America, South, xix–xx, 659–73
  Rothschild influence, 3
American Anti-Slavery Society, 618
American Board of Protestant Missions, 423
American Civil War, xix, 631–58
  casualties, 19, 654
  use of breech-loading weapons, 304
  electric telegraph, 310
  Jomini's teachings, 316
  general course of events, 327–30
  war of material and unlimited objectives,
  331
  formation of Confederate States, 627
American Colonization Society, 616, 617
American Journal of Education, 117
American System (Henry Clay), 604
Amherst of Arracan, William Pitt Amherst,
  Earl, leads trade mission to Peking, 687
Amiel, Henri Frédéric, Swiss thinker, com-
  ments on Tocqueville, 12
Ammonia, 52
Amoy
  captured by British, 690
  a treaty port, 692
Ampère, Jean Jacques Antoine, historian, 115
Amur river, 384, 702, 703
Anaesthesia and anaesthetics
  introduction of, 51, 72–3
  see also Ether, Chloroform
Ancona
  French army of observation in, 251

volume of shipping, 419
population, 420
allows toleration to Jews, 421
French troops in, 554
Anderson, Arthur, Director of P. and O., 437
Andrássy, Count Gyule, Hungarian states-
  man, 549–50
Angelis, Cardinal de, 96
Anglo-Argentine Treaty (1849), 670
Anglo-Brazilian convention (1826), 661
Anglo-Chinese war, 690, 696
Anglo-French Commercial Treaty (1860),
  37, 454, 458
Anglo-Guatemalan Treaty (1859), 681
Anglo-Honduran Treaty (1859), 681
Anglo-Nicaraguan Treaty (1860), 681
Anglo-Turkish Trade Convention of Balta
  Liman (1838), 429
Animal products, increase in, by 1870, 26
Annali di Statistica, 556, 561
Annam
  pays tribute to China, 686
  missionary activity in, 709
  toleration of Christianity, 709
Annapolis, naval academy established in, 293
Anthracite, American, 31
Anti-Corn Law League, 342–3
Antietam, battle of, 639
Antioch College, U.S.A., 119
Antiseptics, 64, 73
Antonelli, Cardinal Giacomo, papal secre-
  tary of state, 97
Antwerp
  a centre of academic art, 151
  bombardment by Anglo-French forces, 250
Aosta, prince Amadeus, duke of, 587
Apostolical succession, doctrine of, 83
Apprentices, shortage of in Prussia, 43
April Laws, sanctioned by Ferdinand, 523
Arad, martyrs of, 528
Arakan, British influence in, 686
Aralsk, 387
Architecture, vii, 135–43
  Britain leads Europe in eighteenth cen-
  tury, 134
  Russian Byzantine revival, 142, 363
  rebuilding of Paris, 460
  destruction of Chinese, 699
Argentina
  war with Bolivia, 670
  fall of Paraná government, 671
  becomes undivided state, 671
  tariff war with Buenos Aires, 671
  Constituent Assembly (1852), 671
  Constitution (1853), 671
  Paraná becomes capital, 671
  railways, 672
  population, 672
  the Baring loan (1866), 672

Argostoli, 422
Arkansas, 627, 654, 655
Arlès-Dufour, Jean-Barthélemy Arlès, merchant of Lyons, 436
Armenians, 422–3
Armies, xi, 302–30
  reform, 14
  reorganisation in the British army, 356, 486
  role of the British, 356
  the Russian army, 369, 379
  Land Transport Corps, 486
  auxiliary services, 486
  purchase of Aldershot, 486
  Roon's reforms of Prussian army, 509–10
  the Chinese army, 690–1
Armstrong, Sir William George, engineer, 51, 284
Army Medical School, 486
Arndt, Ernst Moritz, liberal and nationalist, 227, 496
Arnim, Count Heinrich von, Prussian foreign minister
  plans for a united Germany, 261
  approach to France for alliance, 262
Arnim, Ludwig Achim von, poet, 172
Arnold, Edwin, journalist, 122
Arnold, Matthew, scholar and poet, 105, 109, 110, 112, 115, 116, 158, 178
Arnold, Thomas, Headmaster of Rugby, 113
Art, vii, 134–5, 143–55
Asia, Russia in, 382–8
Asia Minor, 422–3
  invaded by Egypt (1832), 428
Aspirin, 64
Aspromonte, Garibaldi captured at, 576
Assab, acquired as coaling station, 432
Atacama, Desert of, 666
Atelier, L', 123
Athens, 420
Atlanta, capture of, 649
Atlantic and Pacific Ship Canal Company, 681
Atomic theory
  revival by Dalton, 60
  consolidation of, 60
Atomic weights, table of, compiled, 61, 62
Attwood, Thomas, banker, currency reformer, 347
Auchterarder, 83
Auersperg family, 535
Auerswald, Rudolph von, Prussian Minister-President, 508
Augsburger Allgemeine Zeitung, 94
Augustenburg, Prince Frederick Charles of, claimant to Schleswig-Holstein, 515–16
Aurora Fluminense, 660
Ausgleich of 1867, 185, 209, 229, 234, 240

Australia
  wool supplies, 27
  railways, 34, 350
  telegraph link with Britain, 36, 350
  federated Dominion, 211
  immigration grants, 353
  systematic colonisation, 353
  goldfields in, 355, 458
  population, 355
  constitutional development, 355
  mail service, 432
Austria, xvi–xvii, 522–51
  Lombardy, 88, 401, 535, 540, 552, 569
  relations between State and Church, 107, 413, 504, 533, 557
  press, 125, 238
  constitutions, 185, 197, 408, 499, 526, 532
  federalism, 197, 209
  the Diet, 197, 239, 524, 526
  the monarchy, 199, 406, 497, 499, 532
  period of reaction, 204
  local government, 207
  reasons for failure of democratic way of life, 208
  Hungarian affairs, 209, 239–40, 398, 406, 522, 526, 528–9, 535
  relations with Russia, 229, 407, 469
  and German affairs, 237, 268, 412, 512
  literature and scholarship, 238
  language problems, 239, 531
  Germanisation, 240
  enforces Prussian capitulation at Olmütz, 265
  occupies Republic of Cracow, 267
  occupies Tuscany, 408, 565
  relations with Prussia, 410, 505, 520
  ministerial responsibility, 412
  centralisation, 413
  judicial system, 413, 530, 533
  neutrality in Crimean War, 430, 481, 482, 538
  defeat by France, 463
  Venetia, 463, 520, 535, 552, 576
  the Balkans, 469, 472, 475, 479
  and Crimean War peace negotiations, 480, 485
  interest in Danube basin, 489
  diplomatic decline, 491
  and the *Zollverein*, 501, 503
  police, 504, 534
  censorship, 504
  finance and economics, 505, 535
  commercial treaties, 505, 535
  Schleswig-Holstein question, 514–15
  Königgrätz, defeat at, 519
  Modena, 560, 565
  Ferrara, 560
  Magenta, defeat at, 571
  Solferino, defeat at, 571

Avenir, L' (Lamennais), 77–9, 123, 390
Avogadro, molecular theorist, 60, 63

Baader, Francis Xavier, theologian, 78
Bach, Alexander von, Austrian statesman, 406, 528, 529, 533, 539
Bacon's Rebellion (1676), 611
Bács-Bodrog, county of, 529
Bacteria, theory of, 50
Baden, Grand Duchy of
    unrest in, 395, 407, 497
    risings suppressed, 500
    indemnity to Prussia, 520
    secret treaty with Prussia, 580
    and the new Confederation, 582
Bagehot, Walter, economist and writer
    the course of the English novel, 157
    on the English Constitution, 193
    at London University, 206
Bahamas, 356
Baines, Edward, journalist and politician, 85
Bakunin, Michael, Russian revolutionary, 367, 374
Balaclava, allied victory at, 480
Balance of payments, mid-nineteenth century, 39
Balbo, Count Cesare, Italian patriot, 200, 225, 430–1, 558
Ballot, secret, 185, 347
Baltic, the, 489
Baltimore Sun, 129
Balzac, Honoré de, novelist, 21, 124, 159, 161, 162
Bánát, the, 529, 537
Bancroft, George, U.S. secretary to the Navy, 293
Bank Charter Act (1844), 42
Bank für Handel und Industrie, 41
Banks and Banking
    influence of Saint-Simonian school, 3
    co-operative, 23
    bank failures in 1815 and 1825, 40
    private, 40
    Joint stock, 40, 344
    Bank of England, 40
    functions of, 40
    provincial branches, 40
    the Bank Rate, 41, 42
    control of note issue, 41–2, 345
    sole bank of issue, 42
    relations with other joint-stock banks, 344
    in France, 41–2, 394
    in Russia, 379–80
    in U.S.A., 604, 606–7, 614, 643–4, 645
    in Confederate States, 651
    in Brazil, 662
Bank Charter Act (1844), 344–5
Barbados, 356
Barbès, Armand, socialist, 397, 399

Barbizon, painters of, 147
Barcelona, 420, 424–5
Bari, 421
Barnard, Henry, 117
Barnes, Thomas, editor of *The Times*, 122
Baroche, Pierre Jules, French minister of Interior, 447
Barrett, Elizabeth, poet, 177
Barrot, Odilon, French statesman, 14–15, 404, 452
Barry, Charles, architect, 138
Barye, Louis, sculptor, 143
Baths, public, 72
Batthyanyi, Count Ludwig, Austrian minister, 396
Batum, 476
Baur, Ferdinand Christian von, historian, 102
Bavaria, 390, 395, 407
    and The Vatican Council, 95
    negotiations with Schwarzenberg, 409–10
    change of ruler, 497
    King meets Francis Joseph, 502
    Prussian troops invade, 519
    indemnities to Prussia and treaty of alliance, 520
    secret treaty with Prussia, 580
Bay Islands, Honduras, 681
Bayazid, 484
Baudelaire, Charles-Pierre, art critic and poet, 147, 148, 149, 159, 172, 173, 178–80
Bazaine, François-Achille, Marshal, 306, 326
Beaconsfield, Benjamin Disraeli, 1st earl of, *see* Disraeli, Benjamin
Beale, Dorothea, 118
Becker, Nicolaus, poet, 227, 495
Beckerath, Hermann von, liberal leader, 496
Beer
    grain production for, 26
    brewing of, 64
Beirut, 419–20, 423
Beirut, American University of, 423
Belcredi, Count Richard, Austrian minister of state, 548, 550
Belgian National Assembly, elects Leopold of Saxe-Coburg, 249
Belgium, 389, 390, 392
    emergence of, 16
    grain production, 26
    the Cockerill plant, 29
    output of steel, 30
    condition of roads in, 31
    railway routes in 1844, 33
    public ownership of railways, 33
    repeals Corn Laws, 38
    a refuge for French *émigré* journalists, 127–8

Belgium (*cont.*)
government reforms (1831), 189
sovereignty of the people, 191
franchise, 192, 411
Liberals come to power (1847), 202
intervention by Britain, 214
separation from Holland, 221
Treaty of XXIV Articles, 221
loss of East Limburg, Maestricht and Luxemburg, 221
linguistic difficulties, 221–2
the 'Flamingants', 222
rising in 1830 against forced union with Holland, 247
independence of, 248–50
neutrality of, 7, 600
Belinskii, Y. V. (1811–47), publicist, 367, 368
Belize, 679, 681
Bell, Sir Charles, surgeon, work on sensory and motor nerves, 66
Bell, John, sculptor, 143, 626
Bell, The (Herzen), 128, 370, 371
Bello, Andrés, rector, Chile university, 665
Benedek, Ludwig von, Field Marshall, 324, 542
Benedetti, Count Vincent, French diplomat
sees Bismarck, 580
at Wildbad, 589
at Ems, 592, 593
instructed to obtain assurances from William I, 595
the episode at Ems, 595–6
sees Gramont and Ollivier, 598
Bengal, export of opium, 688
Benghazi, 424
Benjamin, Judah P., Confederate secretary of state, 638, 650
Bennett, James Gordon, American newspaperman, 129
Bennigsen, Rudolph von, Hanoverian statesman, 507, 515, 518, 521
Bentham, Jeremy, Utilitarian philosopher, 7, 53, 82, 109, 157, 193, 352
Bentham, Sir Samuel, Brigadier General, 284
Bentinck, Lord William, Governor-general of India, 431
Benzene, ring-formula of, 62
Benzol, 52
Berchet, Giovanni, poet, 225
Berlin, 43
revolution of 1848, 261, 397, 400–1
unemployment in, 397
meeting of United Diet, 496–7
replaces Paris as diplomatic centre of gravity, 577
Berlin Academy for Officers, 317
Berlin Academy of Science, 50

Berlioz, Hector, composer, 144
Bermuda, 356
Bernard, Claude, physiologist, 50, 65, 66, 459
Bernetti, Tommaso, Cardinal, papal secretary of state, 554
Bernhardi, Theodor, confidential agent, 587
Bernoulli, Jean, mathematician and physicist, kinetic theory of gases, 60
Berry, Caroline, duchesse de, 555
Berthier, Louis-Alexandre, Marshal, 314
Berthollet, Comte Claude-Louis, chemist, 115
Bertin family (*Journal des Débats*), 123
Berzelius, Johann Jakob, Swedish chemist, completes table of atomic weights, 61, 62, 64, 65
Bessarabia, 480
ceded to Turkey, 488
Bessemer, Sir Henry, civil engineer and inventor, 30, 51
Bessemer process (1856), 4, 30, 65
Beust, Count Ferdinand Friedrich von, Saxon statesman, 512, 519, 549–50, 581, 584, 592
Beyle, Marie-Henri (Stendhal), writer, 159, 162, 163, 164
Biarritz, meeting between Bismarck and Napoleon III (1865), 517
Bibikov, Dmitri, Russian governor-general, 362
Bible
Lyell's theories of age of earth and antiquity of man, 9
Darwin's theory of evolution, 9
Old Testament chronology, 75
Gospel authenticity, 75
historical criticism of, 102
biblical chronology, 102
Biddle, Nicholas, President, First Bank of U.S.A., 606
Biegeleben, Ludwig Maximilian von, Austrian Foreign Office official, 512, 547
'Bildungsroman', The, 161–2
Billault, Auguste, French statesman, 447
Birkenhead, H.M.S., lost at sea, 281
Birmingham
manufacture of machine tools, 29
stronghold of domestic industry, 42
Birmingham Political Union, 347
Bismarck, Otto, Count von
comes to power, 16
achievements aided by Russo-British preoccupation, 17
interest in the General Council, 95
and the press, 121, 127
bill of indemnity, 188, 199, 520, 579
borrowed from American Constitution, 195

Bismarck (*cont*.)
  crushes Progressive Party, 199
  creation of a united Germany, 199, 504, 577, 601
  theoretical knowledge of federalism, 210
  effects of Olmütz on, 210
  influence of Motley and of Mohl, 211
  and Schleswig-Holstein, 211, 220, 245, 516–17
  challenge to Austrian primacy, 268, 324
  clashes with Moltke, 311
  becomes minister-president of Prussia, 464
  outmanœuvres Napoleon III, 465
  a brilliant speaker, 498
  and Radowitz, 500, 501
  lack of solidarity between Prussia and Austria, 506
  character of, 511–12, 599
  'Blood and Iron' speech, 512
  secures Russia's goodwill, 513
  finance for Danish war, 515
  alliance with Italy (1866), 517
  contact with Hungarian revolutionaries, 517
  meeting with Napoleon III at Biarritz, 517
  and universal suffrage, 518
  breaks up the Confederation and declares war, 518
  publishes Benedetti's draft treaty, 580
  and Hohenzollern claim to Spanish throne, 588, 594, 596
  distrust of French, 585
  at Varzin, 589, 593, 597
  readiness for war, 596–7
Bitzius, Albert ('Jeremias Gotthelf'), Swiss pastor and writer, 166
Bizerta, Gulf of, 424
Black Forest, 395
Black Sea
  British and French navies enter, 477
  Prussia summons allies to evacuate, 479
  neutralisation of, 488
  admission of small ships, 489
Blake, William, poet and painter, 1, 135
Blanc, Louis, socialist, 393, 394, 398, 408
Blanco, Guzmán, dictator of Venezuela, 669
Blanqui, Louis-Auguste, revolutionary, 397, 399
Blassendorf Assembly, 403
Blast furnaces, 51, 342
Bluntschli, J. K., jurist and liberal, 514
Bohemia, 392
  in 1848, 187, 395–6, 398, 401–2
  scheme for autonomy, 210
  Prussian troops invade, 519
  Czech domination in, 523, 524

  aristocratic leaders, 541
  electoral colleges, 546
Bohemia, Charter of, 396
Boileau, L.-A., architect, 140
Bokhara, 386, 388
Bolivar, Simón, founder of Colombia, 659, 668
Bolivia
  becomes republic (1825), 159
  loss of territory to Chile, 666
  population, 667
  mining industry, 667
  brief union with Peru, 667
Bologna, 553, 554, 571, 572
Boltzmann, Ludwig, physicist, 56
Bolyais, the brothers, mathematicians, 56
Bone dust, use as fertiliser, 24
Bonham, Sir George, governor of Hong Kong, 700
Bonn University resists decrees of the General Council, 100
Books of the Polish Nation, 237
Boole, George, mathematician, 56
Bosnia, 472
Boston, U.S.A., opens library, 120
Boston Liberator, 130
Bouguereau, William, painter, 153
Boulogne, Prince Albert at, 481
Bourbon monarchy, close relationship with church, 76
Bourcet, Pierre-Joseph, engineer, 314, 316
Bourqueney, François-Adolphe, comte de, French ambassador, 484–5
Boussingault, Jean Baptiste, physiological chemist, 65
Bowles, Samuel (*Springfield Republican*), 130
Bowring, Sir John, linguist, superintendent of Trade in China, 709
Boxer rebellion (1900), 708
Boyen, Hermann von, Prussian adjutant-general, returns to office, 496
Boyer, Jean-Pierre, President of Haiti, 682
Boyle, Robert, physicist, 60
Bradford, 43
Bragg, Braxton, Confederacy adviser, 656
Brandenburg, 400, 414
Brandenburg, Count Friedrich Wilhelm von, Prussian prime minister, 405, 498, 502
Brazil
  landowners power in, 3
  separation from Portugal, 659
  independence, 660
  population, 660, 661
  war with Rio de la Plata, 660
  illiteracy, 661
  slavery in, 661, 663
  German immigrants, 661
  cotton, 661
  sugar, 661

Brazil (*cont.*)
  coffee, 661
  railways, 662
  introduction of gaslight, 662
  steamboats on the Amazon, 662
  constitution under Pedro, 662
  free press, 662
  British investment in, 662
  clash between church and state, 663
  freemasonry, 663
  prestige of monarchy, 663
  republican party in, 663
Brazos river, 613
Bread
  grain production for, 26
  scarcity in 1838–42, 26
  price of, 74
Breckinridge, John C., Confederate general, 626
Bremen
  prosperity aided by steamboats, 4
  free-trade port, 494
Brenier, Baron de, French emissary, 483
Brentano, Clemens, poet and romanticist, 172
Breslau, 400
Brett, John, painter, 152
Bright, John, statesman
  opposes Ecclesiastical Titles Act, 85
  and the Anti-Corn-Law League, 342–3
  and the American Civil War, 636–7
Brindisi, 420–1
Britannia, H.M.S., 292
British Association for Advancement of Science, 50
British and Foreign School Society, 85
British Guiana, slavery in, 341
British Honduras, 681
British Indian Telegraph Company, 350
British Jews, Board of Deputies of, 244
British Medical Journal, 432
British North America Act (1867), 211, 354
British Public Health Act (1848), 72
'British Society', first state grant to, 110
British Trade Convention (1838), 432
Brontë, Emily, writer, 163
Brown, Ford Madox (1821–93), painter, 151–2
Brown, John, American abolitionist, 203, 625
Brown, Joseph, governor of Georgia, 653
Brown, Robert, botanist, 67
Browning, Robert, poet, 177, 216
Bruck, Baron Karl Ludwig von, Austrian minister
  on Mediterranean trade, 432
  interest in Suez Canal, 436
  Austrian economic initiative, 501
  resignation, 505, 533
  minister for Trade, 529

  Finance Minister, 538
  suicide, 543
Brunel, Isambard Kingdom, engineer, lays down first iron liner, 281
Brunnov, Baron Ernst Philipp von, Russian Ambassador to Great Britain
  calls on Palmerston, 256–7, 264
  leaves for Paris, 478
  at Congress of Paris, 487
Brunswick
  government reforms (1832), 189
  uprisings in, 395, 497
  duke of replaced by brother, 493
  in the Tax Union, 494
  amendment of Federal constitution, 501
Brussels, Palais de Justice, 142
  University, 107
Bryce, James, M.P., professor of civil law, 129
Buchanan, James, fifteenth president of U.S.A., 203, 626
Buchez, Philippe, theorist of catholic democracy, 101, 213
Büchner, Georg, dramatist, 184
Buda, fall of, 526
Budapest
  Houses of Parliament, 140
  reoccupied by Windischgrätz, 406
Buenos Aires
  the link with Europe, 669
  blockade by Britain and France, 670
  defeat at battle of Cepeda, 671
  victory at battle of Pavón, 671
  Congress (1861), 671
  administration of, 671
  constitution of, 671
Bugeaud de la Piconnerie, Thomas-Robert, Marshal, 320–1, 393
Builders' Union, 346, 347
Bukovina, 531, 545
Bulgaria
  nationalism in, 242–3
  development of education, 242
  demand for independent church, 243
Buller, Charles, liberal politician, 352
Bulnes, Fort (Chile), 665
Bulnes, Manuel, President of Chile, 664
Buloz, François, editor *Revue des Deux Mondes*, 123, 128
Bulwer, Edward George Lytton (Bulwer-Lytton, 1st Baron Lytton), 122
Bunsen, Robert Wilhelm, chemist, 58
Bunyevci, 537
Buol, Count Karl Ferdinand von, Austrian statesman
  his part in the Vienna note, 475
  anti-Russian policy, 478
  alliance with Prussia, 478
  over-ambitious policy, 481

Buol, Count (*cont.*)
as mediator, 484
conduct of foreign affairs, 533
resigns, 539
diplomatic duel with Cavour, 571
Burckhardt, Jacob, historian, 12
Burdett-Coutts, Baroness, 139
Buren, Martin Van, eighth president of U.S.A., 621
Burlingame, Anson, American minister in Peking, 708
Burma, 351, 686
Burne-Jones, Edward, painter, 153
Buss, Frances Mary, 118
Butler, Dom Cuthbert, 93
Butter, 64
Butterfield, William, architect, 138
Buxton, Sir Thomas Fowell, reformer, 341
Byron, George Gordon, 6th Baron, poet, 146, 172

Cabanel, Alexandre, painter, 153-4
Cables, submarine, influence on shipping, 5
Cadiz, 419
Cairo, 424, 431
Calcutta
telegraph service with London, 36
mail service from Suez, 432
Caldera, 665
Calderon de la Barca, Pedro, dramatist, 182
Calhoun, John C., American statesman
death of, 203
Nullification crisis, 609
advocates tariff measures, 615
on slavery, 617
the Texas question, 621
California, 203, 632
gold discovered in, 458, 680
settlers in, 621
admission to Union, 622
American troops in, 622
surrendered to U.S. by Mexico, 675
Callao, 666
Cambodia, 709
Cambridge, colleges opened to non-Anglicans, 87
Cambridge Camden Society, 138
Camphausen, Ludolf, industrialist, 494, 496, 498
Canada
rebellion (1837), 19, 193, 353
railways, 34, 350
federated Dominion, 211
reunion of Upper and Lower, 354
loses preferential treatment for corn in United Kingdom market, 354
imposes tariff on British goods, 355
purchases Hudson Bay territory, 355
new Province of Manitoba, 355

Canada Act (1791), 353
Canning, Stratford, *see* Stratford de Redcliffe, 1st Viscount
Canosa, Antonio, Prince of, his cruel administration of Naples, 554
Canrobert, François-Certain, Marshal
replaced by Pélissier, 482
treaty with Sweden, 484
Canton
port for foreign trade, 687
East India Company (British) at, 687
traffic in opium, 687
Chinese view of trade at, 691
right of entry into walled city, 694-5
Cape Colony
sea communications with Australia, 350
constituent developments, 355
Capital
investment in agriculture, 25
raising of, by corporate enterprise, 39
Capponi, Gino A. G. G., Marchese, prime minister of Tuscany, 558
Captain, H.M.S. (1867), 280
Capuchins of Aix, religious community of, 78
Cardwell, Edward, Viscount, secretary for war, 356
Carlile, Richard, journalist, 121
Carlos, Don, pretender to Spanish throne, 253, 555
Carlsbad Decrees, 493
Carlton Club (Conservative), 339
Carlyle, Thomas, historian and essayist, 10, 11, 21, 68, 158
Carnot, Sadi, engineer, motive power from heat, 59
Carolina, North, 330, 627, 634, 653, 655
Carolina, South
secedes from Union, 207
Nullification issue, 606, 609
economic depression, 609
calls state convention, 609
the Force Act, 610
Carpeaux, J. B., sculptor, 143
Carrara, 553, 563, 571
Carrel, Armand (*Le National*), 123
Carrera, Rafael, Guatemalan dictator, 679
Cartagena, 420
Casati, Gabrio, Conte, mayor of Milan, 562
Cassagnac, Granier de, journalist, 125
Castelbajac, Barthélemy, Marquis de, French ambassador to Russia, 478
Castelfidardo, defeat of papal forces at, 574
Castilla, Ramon, president of Peru, 668
Castlereagh, Robert Stewart, Viscount, 267, 270
Catalysis, 63
Catania, 420

Catherine II, empress of Russia, and the Mediterranean, 416
Catholic Congress (1863), 89
Cattaneo, Carlo, writer
  pro-Austrian views, 557
  and Italian independence, 561, 574
  denounces Charles Albert, 563
Cattaro, 422
Cattle, transport by rail, 25
Cauchy, Augustin Louis, mathematician, 56
Cavaignac, Louis Eugène, General, French minister of war, 263, 400, 404
Cavour, Camillo, Count di
  the secret pact of Plombières, 16
  a free church in a free state, 76
  alliance with Napoleon III, 88
  on the press, 121
  Risorgimento, 128
  Italian liberals' support, 188
  defeats Napoleon III, 209
  enters ministry (1850), 412, 567
  sends contingent to Sebastopol, 430
  policy of support to the West, 483
  skilful diplomacy, 538
  on Turin, 557
  warning to Charles Albert, 562
  alliance with Rattazzi, 568
  dissolution of the monasteries, 568
  use of secret funds to bribe press, 568
  warns Austria of Mazzini's insurrection in Milan, 569
  goes to peace conference (1856), 569
  Napoleon III not to be opposed, 570
  diplomatic duel with Count Buol, 571
  return to power, 572
  desire for alliance with Naples, 572
  resignation, 572
  death, 575
Celluloid, 64
Central America, United Provinces of, 678–81
  republic, 659
  population, 678
  capital transferred to San Salvador, 679
  attack on power and property of Roman Catholic church, 679
Central Committee of Working Men, 400
Central Pacific Railroad, 643
Cepeda, battle of, 671
Cette, 421
Ceuta, 424
Ceylon, 350, 432
Cézanne, Paul, painter, 135
Chaadaev, Peter Yakovlevich, Russian essayist, 366
Chadwick, Sir Edwin, reformer, 337, 341
Chalmers, Thomas, D.D., Scots divine, 83
Chambers of Commerce
  in Austria, 535
  in Milan, 557
Chambers of Trade and Industry, in Austria, 530
Chambord, Henri, Comte de, 409, 452
Chancellorsville, battle of, 632
Changarnier, Nicolas-Anne-Théodule, General, removed by Louis Napoleon, 444
Chapdelaine, Auguste, Roman Catholic priest, 696, 701, 709
Charles X, king of France, dethroned, 14, 427
Charles XV, king of Sweden, 220
Charles of Hohenzollern, Prince, 242
Charles Albert, king of Piedmont-Sardinia
  defeated at Custoza and Novara, 186
  liberates Lombardy, 200
  the *Statuto* of, 200
  abdication, 322, 527, 566
  declares war on Austria, 398
  character of, 402, 557
  abandons Milan, 402
  unfortunate decision, 406
  accepts armistice of Vigevano, 523
  denounces armistice, 527
  defeat by Radetzky, 527
  alliance with Austria and France, 553
  renounces friendship for liberals, 554
  his Austrian connections, 555
  supports duchesse de Berry against Louis Philippe, 555
  supports Don Carlos and Don Miguel, 555
  Metternich's opinion of, 557
  correspondence with Francis IV of Modena, 557
  dismisses Solaro, 560
  forced to grant a constitution, 560
  crosses the Ticino, 562
  military unpreparedness, 562
  refuses Garibaldi's offer of collaboration, 563
  policy and strategy, 563–4
  retreat to Milan, 564
  accused of treachery, 564
  reliance on England and France, 564
  proclamation of Moncalieri, 566
  death, 566
Charles, Jacques Alexandre César, physicist, 60
Charles Ludovic, duke of Lucca, 554
Charleston, U.S.A.
  mercantile interests, 615
  insurrection plot (1822), 617
'Charter for Artisans', 400
Chartist Movement
  the Six Points, 185, 347
  April fiasco, 186
  increasing agitation, 193

Chartist Movement (*cont.*)
  discredited, 196
  London demonstrations, 202
  need for solidarity, 345
  failure of, 346
  the petition, 347–8
Chase, Salmon P., secretary, U.S. Treasury, 643, 644, 646
Chassepot, Antoine Alphonse, inventor, 304
  rifle, 305–6, 593
Chattanooga, battle of, 632
Cheese, America dominates English import market, 26
Chekhov, Anton, dramatist, 182
Chernaev, Michael, General, 388
Chernyshevskii, Nicholas, socialist, 370–1
Chevalier, Michel, political economist, 434, 436, 452
Chia Ch'ing, emperor of China, prohibits import of opium, 688
Chickamauga, battle of, 632
Child, banking firm of, 40
Child-labour, restricted by Act of 1833, 44, 83, 341
Childers, Hugh, First Lord of the Admiralty, 300
Chile
  republic, 659
  influence of geography, 663
  institution of parliamentary regime, 664
  revival of law of entail, 664
  alliance of church and state, 664, 666
  power of president, 664
  area, 664
  population, 664
  constitution (1833), 664
  a one-party state, 665
  abolishes law of entail, 665
  German immigration, 665
  University of, 665
  Teachers' Training College, 665
  introduction of telegraph, 665
  railways in, 665
  discovery of copper and silver, 665
  discovery of coal, 665
  London loan (1822), 665
  guano deposits, 666
  declares war against Spain, 666
  increases her territory, 666
  religious freedom, 666
  civil war in, 666
Chiloé, 663
Chimkent, 387–8
China
  Taiping rebellion, 8, 384, 695–701, 705–6
  missionary work in, 79, 707, 708
  under Manchu emperors, 186
  opium trade, 384, 688
  carriage of mails, 432

opening up of, by France, 461
incorporation of empire of Kalnuk mongols, 685
trade with western world, 686
diplomatic intercourse, 686–7, 691, 694, 703, 707
ceremonial tribute from small states, 686
Canton, port of foreign trade, 686, 688
tea trade, 687
balance of trade, 688
disparity of fighting power between Chinese and European forces and warships, 688, 690
appointment of consuls, 692
religious toleration, 693, 695, 703
right of travel for foreigners, 694, 703, 707
extra-territoriality, 695
attitude of Confucian scholars, 695
destruction of Chinese architecture, 699
imperial custom house destroyed, 701
capture of Taku forts, 703–4
treaties with Western powers, 703
indemnities imposed on, 704
diplomatic residence in capital, 704
flight of emperor to Jehol, 704
attack on party under flag of truce, 704
use of prisoners as hostages, 704
effect on trade of Taiping rebellion, 705
reunification under Ching dynasty, 705
death of Hsien Feng, emperor, 704–5
regency of Tzu Hsi, 705
authority of Ching dynasty restored, 706
Foreign Ministry set up, 707
College of Foreign Languages, 707
modernisation of military and naval forces, 707–8
Boxer rebellion (1900), 708
incitement to mob violence, 708
riots in Tientsin (1870), 708
students for training abroad, 708
Legations in Western capitals, 708
Chincha Islands, 666
Chinkiang, captured by British, 690
Chios, 422
Chloroform, 52, 64, 72, 486
Cholera, 44, 72, 479
Choshu, 712
Chotek family, 535
Christian IX, king of Denmark, 220, 575
Christina, widow of Ferdinand II, regent of Spain, 253
Chronograph, Bashforth electric, 51
Church, Eastern Orthodox
  supports rising of Hungarian Croats, 240
  immunities and privileges, 470, 473, 476
  Russia's special relationship to, 482
Church of England
  schools, 87
  supports 'Ten Hours' Bill (1840), 342

Church of England (*cont*.)
supports factory legislation, 343
Church, Protestant
comes to terms with Darwinism, 71
study of scriptural language, 71
attitude to science, 74
General Assembly of Church of Scotland, 83, 84
patronage, 83
Free Church of Scotland, 84
civil equality for Nonconformists, 85
beginnings of Congregational movement, 87
Methodist church, 87, 625
beginnings of Baptist movement, 87, 625
disestablishment of Irish church, 100–1, 218
disestablishment of Welsh church, 101
in Hungary, 542
Church, Roman Catholic, vi, 13, 76–85, 87–101
and education, 107, 409, 444, 456
in Austria, 413, 504, 533
in France, 444, 448–51, 454, 456
in Prussia, 494–5
in Piedmont, 567
in Mexico, 675–6
in Honduras, 679
in China, 693, 695–6, 708
in Annam, 709
in Korea, 709
Church Temporalities Act (1833), 100
Chusan Islands, occupation of, 690
Civil Service
in France and Prussia, 206, 495
recruitment, 206, 338
need for larger in Britain, 337
reform, 338, 486
in Italy, 569
Civil Service Commission, 338
Civiltà Cattolica (Jesuit magazine), 89, 90, 94
Città-Vecchia
French forces dispatched to, 408
shipping and population, 419–20
port of Rome, 421
Clam-Martinitz, Count, Bohemian leader, 541
Clarence, William, duke of, Lord High Admiral, 290
Clarendon, George, 4th earl of
views on papal infallibility, 95
British mediation, 272
becomes Foreign secretary, 471
British representative at Congress of Paris, 487, 489
indictment of Austrian, papal and Neapolitan misgovernment, 490
mediation by a third power before recourse to war, 490

interest in Polish liberation, 490
on Bessarabia and Black Sea, 492
opinion of Italy, 569
Foreign Secretary, 585
death of, 586
Clausewitz, Karl von, General, military strategist and thinker, 302, 313, 316–20, 655, 656
Clausius, Rudolph Julius Emmanuel, physicist, 51, 59, 60
Clay, Henry, American statesman
his 'American system', 604, 613
recharter of Bank of U.S.A., 607
as candidate for presidency, 607
issue of Nullification, 609
Compromise of 1850, 623
Clayton–Bulwer treaty, 680–1, 682
Clergy
assume new character, 76
political importance of, 409
legal immunities of, in Mexico, 675
Clifton Suspension Bridge, 136
Clippers, American
for quick passage, 35
use in Crimean war, 35
Clothing, a domestic industry, 42
Coal and coal-mining
output, 30–1, 333, 505
prices, 31
famine of 1869–73, 31
American anthracite, 31
American bituminous, 31
working deeper seams, 31
becomes less hazardous, 31
increase in employment between 1841 and 1871, 43
for steamships, 279
export of, 333
employment of women and girls, 342
in Chile, 665
Coal-gas, 52
Coaling stations
Aden, 431
Assab, 432
Coal-tar, 52
Cobbett, William, radical journalist, 121
Cobden, Richard, statesman
Treaty with France (1860), 38, 349, 452
on foreign policy, 270
and the Corn Laws, 342
and American Civil war, 637
Cochin-China, 7, 709
Coffee, in Brazil, 661, 663
Coke, 29
Coke-ovens, 51
Coleridge, Samuel Taylor, poet, 157, 172
Coles, Captain Cowper, R.N., 280, 286
Collège de France, 115

Collodion, 52
Cologne
  refounding of cathedral, 139, 495
  in 1848, 400, 401
  arrest of archbishop of, 494
Colomb, Sir John, 356
Colombia, 659, 669
Colonial Laws Validity Act (1865), 355
Colonial policy, changes in British, leading
  to self-government, 20, 349, 352–6
Colonies, sources of raw materials and
  markets for British goods, 350
Columbia, District of, U.S.A.
  return of fugitive slaves, 619
  slave trade in, 623
Combination Laws, 45, 345
Committee for the Defence of Religious
  Freedom, 79
Commons, House of, property qualification
  for membership, 335
Communist Manifesto (Marx and Engels), 3,
  11, 188
'Community of the Polish People in Eng-
  land', 234
Compagnie Générale Transatlantique, 452
Compromise of 1850, 623
Compromise Tariff (U.S.A.) of 1833, 37, 609
Comte, Auguste, French philosopher, 54,
  55, 109, 459
Concordat with Austria (1855), 107, 533
Confederate States of America
  formation of, 627
  see also American Civil war
Confiscation Act, 648
Congregation of Rites, approve summoning
  a General Council, 93
Congress (U.S.A.)
  abolishes flogging, 298
  strides towards nationalism, 604
  votes funds for Maysville turnpike, 606
  and renewal of Charter of First Bank of
    U.S.A., 607–8
  reduction of tariff, 609
  votes annexation of Texas, 622
  and the Mexican War, 622
  and slavery, 622–4, 626, 647–8
  legislation during the Civil War, 642–5
  of the Confederacy, 650–3
Conscience, Hendrik, novelist, 221
Conscription
  in France, 578, 584
  in Prussia, 578
  in U.S.A., 645
  in Confederacy, 652
Conseil Académique, 80
Conseil d'État, 450
Conseil Royal de l'Université, 80
Conseil Supérieur de l'Instruction Publique,
  80

Conservative Party, formation of English,
  339
Considérant, Victor-Prosper, socialist thin-
  ker, 408
Constable, John, painter, 135, 146
Constant, Benjamin, author and politician,
  162, 390
Constantine Pavlovitch, Grand Duke of
  Russia, 361
Constantinople, 423, 425, 476, 478
Convicts, transportation of, 353
Cook, John Douglas, editor, *Saturday
  Review*, 123
Cooper, James Fenimore, novelist, 167
Co-operative movement, 345, 346, 348, 507
Co-operative societies
  in agriculture, 25
  Rochdale, 46
Co-operative Wholesale Society, 46, 348
Copernican cosmology, 71
Copiaco, 663, 665
Copley, John Singleton, painter, 134
Copper, in Chile, 665
Corfu, 422, 431
Corn
  duties, 343
  supplies from Russia, Germany and
    North America, 344
Corn Laws
  assume common pattern, 26
  Peel's amendment (1844), 26
  repeal of, 26, 27, 122, 334, 338
  effect of Irish famine, 38
  effects of repeal, 432
Cornelius, Peter von, painter, 144
Corot, Jean Baptiste Camille, painter, 135,
  144, 147, 148, 149
Corps Législatif
  functions of, 450
  subject to veto by senate, 455
  increased return of republicans, 456
  right to initiate legislation, 456
  proclaims overthrow of Empire, 465
Costa Rica, 678, 679, 680
Costilla, Miguel Hidalgo y, Mexican revolutionary, 674
Cotman, John Sell, painter, 147
Cotton
  yarn-making revolutionised, 28
  output and labour costs, 28
  introduction of power looms, 28
  French and Belgian mills, 28
  American output of 1830–60, 28
  India and Egypt become exporters, 28
  mercerisation of, 64
  exports of, 332
  industry linked with overseas trade, 333
  imports from U.S.A., 333
  employment in, 333

Cotton (*cont.*)
essentially a factory industry, 333
more profitable than tobacco or rice, 613
invention of cotton gin, 613
effect of American Civil war, 4, 638
purchases from Egypt and India, 638
in Brazil, 661, 663
Council of Constance, 94
Courbet, Gustave, painter, 148–50, 151, 152
Cousin, Victor, philosopher, 109, 115, 241
Cowley, Henry Wellesley, 1st earl, diplomat, 487
Cowper–Temple clause (Forster Education Bill), 86
Cracow
no longer a free city, 16
incorporated in Austria, 235, 267
rising of Polish nobility, 523
University of, 531
Crédit Foncier, 25, 451, 458
Crédit Lyonnais (1863), 458
Crédit Mobilier (1852), 34, 41, 451, 453, 458, 535, 536
Creditanstalt, 34, 535, 538
Crémieux, Adolphe, French minister of Justice, 244
Crete
suggested for German immigration, 228
local shipping service, 422
given to Mehemet Ali, 426
revolt in, 581
Crimean War, xv, 468–92
no local struggle, 15
complex diplomacy of, 16
power of new weapons, 16, 306
use of clippers, 35
revelation of inefficiency, 122, 241, 322, 481, 486
destroyed conditions which had maintained peace, 267
effect on balance of power, 268–9
ships mostly under sail, 279
use of telegraph, 309, 486
medical services, 323
weakness of Turkey, 430
events leading up to, 462, 469
policy of German Confederation, 505
and Austro-Prussian relations, 506
Croatia
as a separate province, 403
a Crownland, 537
relations with Hungary, 543, 547
hostility to the February Patent, 545–6
Croce, Benedetto, political thinker, 209
Crome, John, painter, 135
Cronstadt, Russian naval base, 484
Crystal Palace, 136

Cullen, Paul, Cardinal, archbishop of Dublin, 100
Cumberland, iron-ore deposits in, 29
Cumberland, U.S. sloop, 285
Cumberland Pike, The, U.S.A., 604, 606, 612
Cunard Steamship Line
establishes Liverpool–Boston service in 1840, 36
Liverpool–New York service, 36, 332
founded, 332
Curtatone, 564
Cushing, Caleb, American plenipotentiary to China, 692
Custine, Astolphe, marquis de, traveller, 18, 357 n.
Customs, amendments of 1842, 26, 46, 53, 60
Custoza, battle of, 186, 263, 321, 402, 523, 564, 576
Cuvier, Georges, palaeontologist, 68, 115
Cuza, Alexander, prince of Roumania, 241–2
Cyprus
suggested for German immigration, 228
shipping, 419
occupation of, 433
Czartoryski, Prince Adam-George, Polish politician and general, 234
Czech Repeal Association, 238
Czechs
nationalism of, 238, 523
demand for Czech-dominated federal unit, 523–4
officials in Hungary, 529, 536
language restrictions, 531
practical benefits received under absolutism, 534
nationalist intellectuals, 534, 541
troops in Hungary, 539
opposition in and to *Reichsrath*, 545–6, 550
'pilgrimage to Moscow', 550

Daily News
price—one penny, 122
reports on Franco-Prussian war, 122
Daily Telegraph
the Levy Lawson family, 121
first London penny paper, 122
Dairy produce prices, 27
Dale, R. W., Congregationalist divine, opposes Forster Education Bill, 86
Dalmatia
future undecided, 527
attachment to Croatia, 546
Damascus
water supply, 423
government by Egypt, 428

Dana, Charles A., New York editor, 130
Danube, river
  navigation of the, 7, 482, 490
  steamboats on Middle, 32
  dredging by international commission, 32
  Russian control of, 417
  Turkish forces cross the, 477
Danzig, chief outlet for Vistula farms, 26
Dardanelles
  closure to warships, 252, 256, 429
  Admiral Parker's squadron enters, 468
  regulated by the five powers, 468
Dartmouth, Royal Naval College, 293
Daru, Comte Napoléon, French statesman
  and the General Council, 97
  Foreign minister, 585
  resignation, 586
Darwin, Charles, biologist
  theory of evolution, 9, 67, 102
  impact on biological studies, 49
  hypothesis of natural selection, 56
  Origin of Species, 67–70
  agnostic, 71
  generally accepted by scientists, 71
  influence of, 75
  arouses controversy, 348
Darwin, Erasmus, physician and poet, 69
Das Kapital (Marx), 55, 188, 205
Daumier, Honoré, caricaturist, 147, 149, 151
Daunt, W. J. O'Neil, protagonist of disestablishment, 100
Davaine, Casimir-Joseph, doctor, 24
David, Jacques-Louis, painter, 144
Davis, Jefferson, president of Confederate States of America, 627, 650
Davy, Sir Humphry, chemist, discovered electrolysis, 63
Day, Benjamin, American newspaperman, 129
D'Azeglio, Massimo, Italian patriot and statesman
  in Milan, 557
  jeers at defenders of Rome, 565
  views on Italy as a power, 566
  prime minister of Piedmont, 567
  resignation, 568
  use of civil service to ensure election of government candidates, 569
  illegal suppression of newspapers, 569
  separation of Naples, 575
De Ecclesia
  claims for spiritual power an authority over the temporal, 97
  leakage to the press, 97
Deák, Francis, Hungarian politician, 544, 545–6, 547, 549

Death penalty, for political offences, 394
Death-rate
  stability of, 74
  compared with France and Belgium, 74
Degas, Edgar, painter, 154
Del Primato morale e civile degli Italiani (Gioberti), 199–200, 558
Delacroix, Eugène, painter, 144, 145–7, 148, 149
Delane, John Thadeus, editor of The Times, 122
Delaroche, Paul, painter, 151
Delaware
  slavery in, 616, 628
  refuses to secede, 632
Della nazionalità Italiana (Durando), 558
Delle speranze d'Italia (Balbo), 200, 558
Delvigne, Henri-Gustave, inventor, work on expanding bullet, 304
Demmler, Georg Adolph, architect of the Schwerin palace, 142
Democracy in America (Tocqueville), 12, 186, 191
Democratic Party (America)
  joined by Northern Whigs, 626
  factions in, 647
  Congressional gains in 1862, 648
Denmark
  large landlords as agricultural producers, 23
  net exporters of grain, 26
  German 'crusade' against, 187
  bullied by Prussia and Frankfurt National Assembly, 198
  constitution (1849), 203, 411
  Schleswig-Holstein problem, 203, 220, 265, 464
  death of the king, 203, 514
  Liberal Nationalists involve country in war, 219
  the question of succession, 219
  study of folk-lore, 219
  nationalist German influences, 219
  assimilates Schleswig under a centralised constitution, 514
  absent from Congress of Frankfurt (1863), 514
  defeated by Prussia and Austria, 515
Deportation to Siberia, 372
Derby, Edward Geoffrey, 14th earl of, prime minister, 582
Derby, Edward Henry, 15th earl of, British foreign secretary, 581
Dernah, 424
Des Progrès de la révolution et de la guerre contre l'église (Lamennais), 77
Descent of Man (Charles Darwin), 70
Dessewffy, Count Emil, Hungarian federalist, 541

Devastation, H.M.S., 286–7
Development of Revolutionary Ideas in Russia (Herzen), 358
Dew, Thomas R., Confederate politician, on slavery, 617
Diaz, Porfirio, president of Mexico, 678
Dicey, A. V., jurist, 205
Dickens, Charles, novelist, 11, 152, 162, 165
Dictionary of Commerce (McCulloch), 419
Diderot, Denis, philosopher and critic, 183
Diesterweg, F. A. W., head of Berlin College, 113
Digitalis, in medicine, 72
Dillon, Captain Sir William (R.N.), equerry to Duke of Sussex, 289
Diploma of 1860, 185, 209
Disarmament
  European recommended (1831), 251
  discussions (1870), 585–6
Disease, germ theory of, 66, 73
Disestablishment
  Oxford Movement on, 83
  of Church of Ireland, 100–1
  of Church of Wales, 101
Disraeli, Benjamin, earl of Beaconsfield
  Sybil, quoted, 1, 10, 165
  Tancred, quoted, 10
  Reform Act (1867), 206
  purchase of Suez Canal shares, 433, 440
Dissenters' Chapels Act (1845), 86
Dobrolyubov, Nikolai A., writer, 371
Doherty, John, trade-union leader, 346
Döllinger, Johann Josef Ignaz, theologian, 78, 94, 100, 101
Dominican Republic
  appeals for protection or annexation, 682
  Spain reassumes her ancient protection, 683
  occupation by U.S.A., 683
Donelson, Andrew Jackson, American minister to Prussia, 194
Dostoevsky (Dostoevskii), Feodor, writer, 21, 157, 159, 163, 166, 168–9, 365
Douglas, Stephen A., U.S. senator, 623, 624, 626
Dover (1840), first iron ship in Royal Navy, 281
Drainage
  as a means of increasing soil fertility, 24
  cost of, 25
Dred Scott decision (1857), 624
Dresden
  Opera House, 141
  State Gallery, 141
  unrest in (May 1849), 497
  meeting of German princes (1850–1), 410, 503
Dresden, Congress of, 538

Dreyse, Johann Nikolaus, 304
Droste-Hülshoff, Baroness Annette Elizabeth von, poet, 175–6
Drouyn de Lhuys, French plenipotentiary
  opinion of Menshikov's draft treaty, 473
  hopes of Austrian intervention, 481
  Black Sea proposal, 482
  discusses Poland with Clarendon, 483
  leaves the ministry, 580
Du Concile général et de la paix religieuse (Maret), 94
Du Devoir des catholiques dans la question de la liberté d'enseignement (Montalembert), 79
Duc, J.-L., architect, 142
Duff, Alexander, Rev., 118
Dufour, Guillaume-Henri, General, Swiss commander, 223
Dufour-Feronce, A., merchant, 436
Dumas, Alexandre, père, novelist, 124, 164
Dumas, Jean Baptiste André, chemist, 62
Du Mont, Joseph (*Kölnische Zeitung*), 126
Dupanloup, Félix Antoine, bishop of Orléans, 79, 80, 92, 93, 95
Dupont de l'Eure, Jacques-Charles, 393
Dupuy de Lôme, Stanislas, French *Directeur du Matériel*, 278–9
Durando, Giacomo, Italian statesman, and pope's temporal possessions, 558
Dürer, Albrecht, painter, 151
Durham, John, 1st earl of, statesman, 20, 260, 352, 353–4
Durham Report (1839), 20, 193
Durham University
  founded by Dean and Chapter, 82
  colleges opened to non-Anglicans, 87
Duruy, Victor, French minister of Education, 115, 118, 456
Dutacq, journalist, 124, 125
Dyes, aniline and vegetable, 52, 64
Dysentery, 44

Earth, age of, 68
East Anglia, drainage of fen land, 24
East India Company (British)
  end of government in India by, 8, 356
  Civil Service of, 206
  iron gunboats, 281
  carriage of mails, 431, 432
  replaces rule of Mogul empire, 685
  trading at Canton, 687
  tea shipping, 687
  Chinese monopoly terminated, 688
East India Steam Navigation Company, 432
East Limburg, Belgium loses, 221
Eastern Steam Navigation Company, 432
Ecclesiastical Titles Act, 85
Ecclesiologist, The, 138
École des Beaux Arts, 144

École Centrale des Arts et Manufactures, 113
École Libre, Paris, 78, 79
École Normale Supérieure, 115
École Polytechnique, 51, 115
École Pratique des Hautes Études, 115
Economists, Congress of (1858), 507
Ecuador, strife between capital and port, 667–8
Education, vi, 104–20
  growing demand for 'modern', 6
  Nonconformists concentrate on, 85
  first governmental grant, 85, 110
  education department formed (1856), 85
  voluntary schools, 86
  increased state grants, 86
  board schools, 86
  in France, 51, 78, 79, 104–18 passim
  in Great Britain, 85, 86, 104–19 passim
  in Germany, 104–16 passim
  in Italy, 104, 115
  in Russia, 104, 106, 119, 363, 378–9
  in Poland, 106
  in Switzerland, 106, 110, 113, 114
  in Belgium, 107, 112
  in Denmark, 107, 110, 119–20
  in Holland, 107–8, 109, 112
  in Austria, 109, 111, 114
  in Finland, 110
  in Norway, 110
  in Sweden, 110
  in Hungary, 111
  in United States of America, 116–17, 119, 120
  in Australia, 117
  in Canada, 117
  in Colonies, self governing, 117
  in India, 117–18
  in New Zealand, 117
  in South Africa, 117
  in Dutch East Indies, 118
Edwards, Edward, first librarian, Manchester library, 120
Eggs, import of, 25
Egypt
  becomes exporter of cotton, 28, 638
  army under Ibrahim invests Acre, 251
  invades Syria and Asia Minor, 251, 428
  prevalence of plague, 417
  railways in, 424
  a disturbing force, 426
  destruction of fleet at Navarino (1827), 426
  strategical position of, 430
  occupation by Great Britain, 430, 433
  fleet sails to Constantinople, 475
Eichendorff, Joseph Freiherr von, poet, 175–6
Eichhorn, Johann Gottfried, theologian, 102
Eider, river, 219, 397

Eighteen Articles, Treaty of, 221
Elbe, river, steamboats on, 32
Elberfeld, 501
Elections, cost of contesting, 335, 336
Electricity, consumption of power in 1870, 57
Electrolysis, discovery by Davy, 63
Elgin, James Bruce, 8th earl of, governor-general of Canada, 354, 701, 704
Eliot, Charles W., president of Harvard, 117
Eliot, George (Mary Ann Evans), novelist, 159, 162
Eliot, T. S., poet, 178
Elliot, Captain, Superintendent of Trade, 689, 690
Emancipation Proclamation (U.S.A.), 628, 639
Emerson, Ralph Waldo, author, 120, 167, 179, 180, 617, 658
Emigration
  of Europeans to America, 2
  of Russians to Siberia, 2, 382–4
  of skilled workers, ban on, 28
  from Great Britain, 332
Emilia, union with Piedmont, 572
Empire and Commonwealth, new conception of, 20
Enclosures
  in England, 24
  in Germany, 24
Energy
  exactly defined concept of, 59
  conservation of, 59
  conversion of, 59
Enfantin, Barthélemy Prosper, reformer, 434, 435–6
Enfield rifle, 304
Engels, Friedrich, socialist, 3, 55, 392
Engineering, employment in, 333
Engines, marine
  manufacture in Glasgow, 29
  compound, 36
English Constitution, The (Bagehot), 193
englische Verfassungs- und Verwaltungsrecht, Das (Gneist), 193
Entail, law of, in Chile, 664, 665
Enzymes, discovery of, 65
Eötvös, Joseph, Baron, Hungarian leader, 545, 546, 549
Ère nouvelle, L' (Lacordaire), 101
Erfurt, meeting of Diet (March 1850), 501
Ericsson, Captain John, designer of the Monitor, 278
Erie Canal, 32, 612
Ernest of Saxe-Coburg, Prince, 507
Ernest Augustus, king of Hanover
  violation of constitution, 106, 494
  the constitutions of, 189–90
Eskompte-Gesellschaft, 535

Essay on Population (Malthus), 1
Esterházy, Count Maurice, 548
Esterházy, Prince, 254
Estonia, 231
Ether, introduction by Morton and Wells, 72
Eugénie (de Montijo), empress of the French
  married to Napoleon III, 446
  influence in political decisions, 447, 582, 595, 598
  ardent catholic, 447, 583
  escape to England, 466
Eupatoria, 479
Evolution
  British contribution to science, 50
  mechanism and philosophy of, 69
  see also Darwin, *Origin of Species*
Ewart, William, M.P., work for libraries and museums, 120
'Ewart's Act' (1850), establishment of libraries and museums, 120
Excellent, H.M.S., 283
Explosives, 52
Extra-territorial jurisdiction
  under Nanking Treaty, 692
  in China, 695, 696
  in Siam, 709
  in Japan, 711

Factory Acts, 44, 83, 341–2
Factory inspectors
  appointed by Act of 1833, 44, 341
  in Prussia, 45
  in France, 45
Falkland Islands occupied by Britain, 673, 683
Fallersleben, Hoffman von, musician, 495
Falloux, Frédéric, Comte de, 404
Falloux Law, see *Loi Falloux*
Faraday, Michael, chemist, 51, 53, 56–7, 58, 71
Farias, Valentin Gómes, Mexican liberal, 675
Farini, Luigi Carlo, minister of Pius IX, 558, 560, 572
Farm produce, increase of
  in Hungary, 23
  in Roumania, 23
  in South Russia, 23
Farming
  employment in 1870, 24
  improvement in equipment, 25
  high overheads of West European, 25
Farragut, David, United States Naval commander, 328
Fathers and Children (Turgenev), 374
Favre, Jules, statesman, opposes war with Prussia, 455, 599

February Patent, 545, 548
Fellenberg, Philipp Emanuel von, teacher, 108
Ferdinand, emperor of Austria
  ascends throne (1835), 495
  feeble minded, 495
  abdication, 497, 531
Ferdinand II, of Naples
  rule of, 554
  thoughts of a league of Italian states, 556
  compelled to grant a constitution, 560
  alterations to constitution, 565
Ferdinand of Saxe-Coburg-Gotha, King Consort of Maria II of Portugal, 587, 588
Ferdinand VII, king of Spain, death of, 253
Fermentation, 65
Ferrara, 402, 554, 560, 561
Ferry, Jules, French statesman, 455
Fertilisers, 24, 65
Feudal system, Germanic world still subject to, 15
Fichte, Johann Gottlieb, philosopher, advocate of economic self-sufficiency, 227
Figaro, 125
Fillmore, Millard, thirteenth president of U.S.A., 203, 623
Finch, Frances Miles, poet, 630
Finland
  the *Kalevala* epic, 231
  the Grand Duchy of, 231
  superficial liberalisation, 376
  Napoleon III's interest in restoration to Sweden, 483
First Bank of the United States, 606
'First International', French section formed, 455
First Manassas, battle of, 632
Fisheries, New England, 610
Fitzgerald, Edward, poet, 177
Fiume, 419–20, 422
Five Power Conference (1851–2), 266
Flaubert, Gustave, writer, 148, 159, 161, 162, 165, 170
Flax, wet spinning process, 28
Fleury, General, ambassador to St Petersburg, 585
Fliegende Blätter, 131
Flogging, abolished in U.S. navy, 298
Florence, 389, 556
Florida, 603, 606, 620, 627
Fly Sheet Controversy (1844–8), 87
Foley, J. H., sculptor, 143
Follen, Karl, revolutionary, 194
Foochow, treaty port, 692
Foodstuffs, duties on imported, 343
Foot rot, 24
Footwear, a domestic industry, 42

Forbes, Archibald, war correspondent, reports on Franco-Prussian war, 122
Force Act, 609–10
Forckenbeck, Max von, lawyer, 510, 521
Ford, John, dramatist, 159
Forster's Education Act (1870), 86, 107, 111, 337
Forsyth, Rev. Alexander, chemist, 303
Foscolo, Ugo, writer, in exile, 552
Fossils, 68
Foucault, Jean Bernard Léon, physicist and mechanician, 58
Fould, banking family of, 41
Fould, Achille, politician and financier, 447
Foundries, 342
Four Kings Alliance, 410
Fourier, François Charles Marie, socialist, 109
France, xiv–xv, 442–67
    trade and commerce: agriculture, 26, 457–8; iron and steel, 29–30, 457; coal, 31, 357; jealousy of British prosperity, 254; effect of Crimean war, 487
    communications: roads, 31, 451, 458; railways, 333; maritime, 452
    architecture: Gothic revival, 40; constructional use of iron, 140; Neo-Renaissance, 141–2; the *Beaux Arts* style, 142; design in two dimensions, 143
    literature: novel replaces the drama, 156; exploratory character, 158; realism, 159–60; genius of Victor Hugo, 164; the historical novel, 165; the realism of Flaubert, 170; poetry predominantly 'romantic', 171–3; superb workmanship of Baudelaire, 179
    painting and sculpture: most important in Europe during nineteenth century, 143; revival of the Academy, 144; work of Delacroix, 145–7; realism in, 147; the school of Barbizon, 147; the work of Courbet, 148–9
    religion, church and state: anti-clerical character of 1830 Revolution, 77; freedom of worship, 77; pope repudiates liberal catholicism, 78; revival of religious communities, 78; missionary enterprise, 79; use of Roman Liturgy enforced, 79; freedom for Catholic education, 79, 80; passing of the *Loi Falloux*, 80; Syllabus of Errors, 90–2; the General Council, 93–8; right of the papacy to censure actions of civil power, 97–8; papal infallibility, 98; Liberal Catholics weakened by division, 100
    warfare, military and naval: the work of Paixhans, 276–7, 283, 284; screw propeller, 278–9; the work of Labrousse, 278, 284; the steam battleship, 279, 285; use of armour, 282; shells replace roundshot, 283; the *Levée permanente*, 299; improvements in bullet design, 303–4; the Chassepot rifle, 305–6, 593; Napoleon III's private arsenal, 307; the *Mitrailleuse*, 307, 593; conscription, 312; writings of Jomini, 313–16; use of railways, 323
    treaties and alliances: most-favoured nation treatment to Britain, 38; efforts to reach understanding with Austria, 259; with Russia, 491; with Piedmont, 538; with China, 693, 703–4; with Turkey, 487; *rapprochement* with Russia, 487
    China war: the Chapdelaine affair, 696, 701, 709; joins British forces at Canton, 696, 701; Baron Gros appointed plenipotentiary, 701; capture of Taku forts, 702–4; Tientsin treaties, 703; action resumed against China, 704; ratification of treaties of 1858, 704; defence of Shanghai, 706; French policy to include Annam, 709
    Italian War of Independence: army of observation, 251; notable development in means and methods, 323; use of railways, 323; Jomini's advice sought, 323; battle of Magenta, 323, 324, 571; introduction of rifled cannon, 323; battle of Solferino, 325, 571; forces at Cività-Vecchia, 408; receives Nice and Savoy, 463; Catholic powers summoned to restore pope's temporal dominions, 565; Roman republic falls to French troops, 565; forces remain in Rome, 565; pact of Plombières, 571; armistice of Villafranca, 572; concedes principle of non-intervention in Central Italy, 572; withdrawal of Rome garrison, 572
    Franco-Prussian war: controversial origins, 16; surrender of Alsace and Lorraine, 17; declaration of war, 98, 598–9; cavalry shattered at Sedan, 305; effectiveness of Prussian artillery, 306; battle of Gravelotte–Saint Privat, 306; the *Mitrailleuse*, 307; strategic pattern, 325–7; mobilisation, 597; appeal for Italian aid, 599; terms of peace, 600
    in Africa: conquest of Algiers, 7, 424, 461; transportation to Algiers, 445; bases in Senegal and Somaliland, 461
    in Cochin-China, 7, 709
    in Syria, 430
    in Indo-China, 461
    in Mexico, 464, 580, 641

France (*cont.*)
in Korea, 709
and the Crimean war: war not of France's seeking, 469; French position as protector of Latins in Holy Places, 469; arrival of La Valette, 469; navy at Tripoli, 470; La Valette goes on leave, 470; movements of the Fleet, 472–3, 474, 476–7; Napoleon's part in the Vienna note, 475; arrival of Egyptian forces, 475; loan to Turkey, 477; war declared, 478; dispatch of troops to Dardanelles, 478; Napoleon's visit to Windsor, 481; Canrobert replaced by Pélissier, 482; discussions on Finland and Poland, 483; treaty signed with Sweden, 484; terms of peace, 485; casualties, 485; cost and finance, 486–7; peace conference, 487–8
and the Mexican war: Convention of London (1861), 677; troops landed at Vera Cruz, 677; Maximilian with French support assumes the crown, 677; Maximilian abandoned, French troops withdrawn, 678; execution of Maximilian, 678
Francia, José Gaspar Rodríguez de, president of Paraguay, 672
Francis IV, duke of Modena
hopes for revolution, 553
flees from Modena, 553
execution of Menotti, 554
rule of, 554
Francis Ferdinand, Archduke, revival of federalism planned, 210
Francis Joseph, emperor of Austria
obtuseness of, 209
meets tsar Nicholas, 252
assumes supreme command of army, 323
meeting with kings of Bavaria and Württemberg, 502
proposes a Congress of Princes, 513
visits William of Prussia, 514
belief in divine right of kings, 532
ministers responsible solely to him, 532
inconsistency and impulsiveness, 533
meeting with tsar and prince regent of Prussia in Pest, 548
legality of 1848 laws, 548
crowned king of Hungary, 550
Franco-Prussian War, *see under* France
Franco-Russian secret treaty (1859), 271
Frankfurt, 395
preliminary parliament meets at, 398
General Congress of Workers at, 400
Congress of Princes (1863) at, 513, 514
Free City annexed by Prussia, 520

Frankfurt National Assembly
crusade against Denmark, 187, 198
urged to follow America's Federal Union, 195
constitution of, serves Weimar republic, 196
and Schleswig-Holstein, 219
votes for independence of Poland, 228
offers imperial crown to Frederick William IV, 264, 499–500
composition of, 405
dispersal, 500
Frankfurt, Treaty of (1871), 600
Frankfurter Zeitung, 126
Frankland, Edward, F.R.S., chemist, 62
Frantz, Constantin, writer, 211
Franzoni, Luigi, archbishop of Turin, 567
Frederick VII, king of Denmark, abolishes absolutism, 219
Frederick Charles, prince of Prussia, 325
Frederick William III, king of Prussia, his indecision, 247
Frederick William IV, king of Prussia
refuses to accept leadership of new federal *Kleindeutschland*, 195
character of, 209, 485, 495–6, 508
talks with Stratford Canning, 262
threatens abdication, 262
offer of imperial crown, 264, 407, 500
political concessions forced from, 397
dissolves Constituent Assembly, 405
becomes king of Prussia (1840), 494
interest in Oxford movement, 495
refounding of Cologne Cathedral, 495
Metternich on, 496
disappointment with policy of, 496
appalled at thought of civil war, 502
death of, 510
Fredericksburg, battle of, 632
Freemasonry in Brazil, 663
French Organic Law of 1842 (railways), 33
French Society for Elementary Instruction, 110
Freytag, Gustav, novelist, 166
Friedrich, Johann, professor of theology, excommunicated, 100
Frith, William P., painter, 150
Froebel, Friedrich Wilhelm August, educationist
Kindergarten banned in Prussia, 106
influenced by Pestalozzi, 108
Froebel, Julius, political writer, 504, 512
Fuad Pasha, Turkish Foreign minister
suspected of French sympathies, 470
enforced resignation of, 472
Fugitive Slave Act, 625
Fulton, Robert, engineer, 277

'Fundamental Laws' (1867), 524
Fünen, Danish Island, protection by Sweden (1848), 220
Fur trade, in Oregon, 621
Fuseli, Henry, painter, 135

Gablenz, Anton von, Prussian general, 518
Gaeta, 408, 421, 564
Gagern, Max von, German liberal, 261
Gainsborough, Thomas, painter, 135
Gaj, Ljudevit, philologist, 238
Galicia, 234–6, 406, 478
    emancipation of peasants, 414, 523
    Polish domination, 524
    division into two Crownlands, 526
    special status for, 546
Gallait, Louis, painter, 151
Gallatin, Albert, U.S. statesman, 203
Gallipoli, 478
Gambetta, Léon Michel, French statesman
    anti-clericalism, 76
    the Baudin trial, 125
    opposition to the empire, 455
    in favour of war with Prussia, 599
Gangrene, prevalence of, 73
Garibaldi, Giuseppe
    expedition to Sicily, 88
    march on Rome, 201, 433, 576
    condemned to death *in absentia*, 555
    offers collaboration to Charles Albert, 563
    expulsion from Piedmont, 573
    captures Palermo and Naples, 573–4
    brawl with Cavour, 575
    Aspromonte, 576
    defeat at Mentana, 583
    leads raids on papal enclave, 583
Garnier, Charles, architect, 142
Garnier-Pagès, Étienne, politician, 399
Garrison, William Lloyd, newspaperman and abolitionist, 130, 618, 619
Gärtner, Friedrich von, architect, 140, 141
Gases, kinetic theory of, 56
Gaskell, Mary (Mrs), novelist, 11, 160
Gas-light industry, 52
Gastein, meeting of Francis Joseph and William I, 514
Gastein, Convention of, 516–17
Gasworks, 51, 65
Gatling, Richard, inventor, 306
    gun, 306–7
Gau, Franz Christian, architect, 140
Gauguin, Paul, painter, 146
Gauss, Karl Friedrich, mathematician, 56, 114
Gautier, Théophile, French poet and journalist, 125, 146, 173
Gavarni, Paul, painter and lithographer, 147

'General Assembly's College', Calcutta, 118
General Council (Vatican Council)
    superior authority of, 94
    summoning of, 94–5
    proceedings, 96–9
    political aftermath unfavourable, 99
Genoa, 553, 560, 562, 570
    shipping and population, 419–20, 431
    naval base, 421
    eastern trade, 425, 432
    trade diverted to Trieste, 555
    port installations, 556
    bombardment of, 566
Genoa, duke of, 587, 588
Geology, assigns the earth's age, 68
Geometries, based on non-Euclidean postulates, 56
George, prince of Denmark, succeeds to throne of Greece, 426
Georgia (Transcaucasia), 372
Georgia (U.S.A.)
    march of Union forces through, 329
    removal of Indians, 606
    conscription in, 653
Gerbet, Olympe-Philippe, bishop of Perpignan, 77, 89
Gerhardt, Karl Friedrich, chemist, 62
Géricault, Théodore, painter, 144, 146
Geringer, Karl Gabriel, Baron, Austrian Civil Commissioner, 528
Gerlach, Leopold von, general, 499, 504, 511
Gerlach, Ludwig von, politician, 499, 501, 504, 511, 517
Germany, xv, xvi, xviii, 493–521, 577–602
    trade and commerce: railways, 4, 41, 308, 494, 505; a principal manufacturing country, 4, 51; first co-operative bank, 23; landlords as agricultural producers, 23; extension of enclosure, 24; potash deposits, 24; chemical fertilisers, 24, 65; the *Landschaften*, 25; the *Zollverein*, 26, 37, 228, 494, 501, 503, 505; grain production, 26; introduction of spinning machinery, 28; production of iron, 29–30; coal production, 31, 505; banks and banking, 41; child labour, 45; in field of science, 50–1, 57–60, 62, 65–7; need for maritime commerce, fisheries and colonies, 228; predominance of agriculture, 494; population, 494, 505; co-operative movement, 507
    constitutional developments: growth of nationalism, 17, 198, 226–9; 'Radical' unions, 46; Prussia dominant power in, 100, 185, 494, 499; constitutions for lesser states, 189; American influence

Germany (*cont.*)

on constitution of 1849 and 1867, 195; creation of German Empire, 199, 210, 602; return to autocracy, 204; humiliation of Olmütz, 204, 210, 410, 412, 502, 503, 508; Lassalle's 'Workers Programme', 205; reasons for failure of democracy, 208; constitutions of 1867 and 1871, 210, 211, 520, 578–9; Confederation of 1815, 210, 226, 493, 518; question of reform of, 496–7, 502–3, 507, 512–14, 517; demand for a Greater Germany, 227, 512; revolution of 1848, 389–415 *passim*, 497; rising in Berlin (March 1848), 397, 497–8; Frederick William IV refuses imperial crown, 407, 499; Three Kings' Alliance, 409–10; all states now constitutional, 412; participation of middle class in government and administration, 494; Prussia and Austria assume joint responsibility for German affairs, 500; France as hereditary enemy, 227, 506

relations between church and state, 100, 107

education: relations with state and church, 105–7; work of Froebel, 108; high standard of, 109; gymnasiums, 111; technical schools and universities, 111, 113–14

press: development of, 125–7, 131; freedom of, 125–6, 397; comparative position of, 131; Wolff news agency, 132

architecture, 139–40

art, 143, 150

literature: the romantics, 158, 174; the 'Bildungsroman', 161; comparative immaturity, 166–7; poetry, 174–6

warfare: the needle gun, 304–5; cavalry becomes obsolete, 306; breech-loading artillery, 306; use of railways, 308–9; electric telegraph, 310; conscription, 312; reforms by Roon, 509, 515; Kiel becomes naval base, 516

Schleswig-Holstein and the Danish war (1864), 211, 219, 220, 311, 514–16

Austro-Prussian war (1866), 16, 305, 308, 310, 324–5, 517–19, 578

Franco-Prussian war (1870), *see under* France

see also under individual states

Gettysburg, battle of, 328, 632

Giacomo, Fra, 575

Gibbs, Josiah Willard, American scientist, 51

Gibraltar

shipping and population, 419–20

smuggling, 420

Admiralty packet service from Falmouth, 431

becomes a Crown colony (1840), 433

Gide, André, writer, 181

Giessen, the laboratory of Liebig, 50

Giessener Schwarzen, 194

Gioberti, Vincenzo

and the neo-Guelphs, 199–200

supports Victor Emmanuel, 201

favours federal solution, 225

exiled, 555

little faith in papal politics, 558

and the Jesuits, 565

and pope's temporal power, 566

Giovine Italia (Mazzini), 555; *see* 'Young Italy'

Girardin, Émile de, of Paris *Presse*, 121, 124

Girardin, Saint-Marc, writer in *Journal des Débats*, 123

Girtin, Thomas, painter, 135

Giusti, Giuseppe, poet, 225

Gladstone, William Ewart

reduces import duties, 38

opposes Ecclesiastical Titles Act, 85

University Tests' Act 1871, 87

interest in General Council, 95

and Irish disestablishment, 100, 101, 218

campaign against Neapolitan prisons and Bulgarian atrocities, 202

resignation, 481

budgets (1854), 486

and the Alsace-Lorraine annexation, 600

Glasgow, 29, 43

Glass-works, 342

Globe, Le, 130

Glycerine, 66

Glycogen, 66

Gneisenau, Neithardt, Count, Prussian marshal and reformer, 310

Gneist, Rudolph von, author, 193, 207

Goa, 688

Godkin, E. L., New York editor, founder of the *Nation*, 130–1

Goethe, Johann Wolfgang von, poet and philosopher, 139, 161, 172, 176

Gogh, Vincent van, painter, 135

Gogol, Nikolai, novelist and dramatist, 165, 182, 368

Goito, battle of, 398

Gold

new sources of supply of, 505

in Australia, 355, 458

in California, 458, 680

Golovnin, Alexander V., minister of education, 379

Goltz, Robert, Graf von der, diplomat, 582

Goluchowski, Count Agenor, Austrian statesman, 539, 543, 544
Gorchakov, Alexander, Prince, Russian statesman
  succeeds Nesselrode, 16, 269
  chairman, State Council, 360
  chancellor, 387
  conquest of Khiva, 388
  negotiations in Vienna, 479–81
  approach to duc de Morny, 484
  Black Sea concessions, 492
Gordon, Charles, Major, 706
Görgey, Arthur, Hungarian general, 528
Görres, Johann Josef von, nationalist writer, 78, 227
Goschen, George Joachim, First Lord of the Admiralty, 300–1
Gotthelf, Jeremias, 166, *see* Bitzius, Albert
Göttingen, 106, 493, 494
'Government Commission for Workmen', 393
Government of India Act (1853), 337
Graham, Sir James, First Lord of Admiralty, 278, 295, 299, 300
Grain
  European production, 23, 26
  American, 65, 613
Gramont, Alfred, duc de, French foreign minister, 583, 586, 590–1, 595, 599
Granada, New, treaty with U.S.A., 680
Grand National Consolidated Trades Union, 346–7
Grant, Ulysses, General, American commander, 316, 328–9, 330, 630, 657
Granville, George Leveson Gower, 2nd earl, 589, 599
Grassman, Hermann Gunther, mathematician, 56
Gravelotte–Saint Privat, battle of, 306, 326
Gravitation, doctrine of universal, 49
Gray, Sir John, 100
Great Britain, xi–xii, 331–56
  trade and industry: beginnings of factory system, 4; domestic industries, 4, 42; import of livestock, 25; grain production, 26, 683; textiles, 27–8, 333, 342, 638; Corn Laws, 27, 38, 122, 334, 342; iron, 29, 333; steel, 30, 333; coal and coal-mining, 30–1, 279, 333, 342; canals, 30; roads, 31; railways, 32–3, 332; shipping, 36; postal service, 36, 332; telegraph, 36–7; Navigation Laws, 38, 334, 351; income tax, 38; banks and banking, 39–41, 334–5; employment of children, 44, 83, 341–2; trade unions, 45–6, 346–7; immigration, 332, 353; competition from Germany and U.S.A., 334; overseas investment, 334, 350; balance of trade, 334;

factory inspection, 341; Factory Acts, 341–2, 413; Contribution Act, 345; dependence on overseas trade, 353
agriculture, 24–5, 332, 342
diplomatic alignments and events: 'most favoured nation' terms to France, 38; independence of Belgium, 214, 249, 461; cedes Ionian Islands to Greece, 242, 246; withdrawal from continental issues, 269–70, 272; Mediterranean policy, 431, 433; recognition of Second Empire, 462; alliance with Turkey, 468; occupation of Falkland Islands, 673; Ruatan and Mosquito Protectorate, 679
religion, church and state: repeal of Test and Corporations Act, 76; Catholic emancipation, 77, 100; Oxford movement, 81–3, 100; missionary enterprise, 83; Scottish church, 83–4; Roman Catholic church in, 84–5, 87; Nonconformists, 85–7; the Church of Ireland, 100–1; Christian Socialism, 101
education: universities, 87, 116, 119, 206; the role of the state, 106; Lancasterian system, 110; state grants, 110–11; Forster's Education Act (1870), 111, 337; the public school system, 113; the pupil teacher system, 114; Mechanics' Institutes, 119, 120; libraries, 120
press: family proprietorship, 121; changes in law of libel, 121; paper duty and stamp tax, 121–2; increase in number of newspapers, 123; growth of illustrated press, 131; news agencies, 132–3
architecture, 134, 136–43, 154–5
sculpture, 143
painting, 150–5
literature: general characteristics, 156–60; the novelists, 162–3, 165–8; poetry, 172, 174, 176–8; drama, 181–2; *see also under individual authors*
administrative institutions and reform: franchise, 185, 192, 204, 336; pocket boroughs, 185, 192, 336; Chartist Movement, 193, 202; civil service, 206, 337–8; Local Government Board (1871), 207; police, 337; Poor Law administration, 337; Reform Acts (1832), 189, 192, 289, 334–6, 338, 345; (1867), 206, 211, 236; Municipal Reform Acts (1835), 207, 334; (1841), 337; Representation of the People Act (1867), 334
warfare, naval and military: instrument of national policy, 274, 282–3; armament, 275–6, 280, 284–7; patronage and promotion, 289–90, 292; recruitment, 291–2, 293–5; reserve service, 296, 299; cavalry, 302, 305; de-

Great Britain (*cont.*)
velopments in firearms, 302–6; use of electric telegraph, 309–10; army reorganisation, 356, 486
and the China wars: Taiping rebellion, 8, 384, 695–6, 697, 698–9, 700, 705, 706; campaigns of 1856–60, 701–4
and the Crimean War: complex diplomacy of, 16; power of new weapons, 16, 306; revelations of inefficiency, 122, 241, 322, 481, 486; effect on balance of power, 268–9; medical services, 323; events leading up to, 462, 469; movements of allied fleets, 472, 474–7; Palmerston's attitude, 474–5; recall of ambassadors and declaration of war, 478; the war on land, 478–84; terms of peace, 485; casualties, 485; cost and finance, 486; peace conference, 487–8
and the Mexican war (1861), 677
Great Exhibition (1851), 6, 25, 52, 53, 203
Great Lakes, U.S.A., 32
Greece, 391
emergence as a kingdom, 16
intervention by Britain, 214
ports recovering from effects of war of independence, 422
currant crop, 422
parliamentary constitution (1843), 426
King Otto succeeded by Prince George of Denmark, 426
receives Ionian Isles, 426
government of King Otto, 490
Greeley, Horace (of *New York Tribune*), 120, 129–30, 188, 206
Gregory XVI (Mauro Capellari), Pope, 78, 554, 557
Grey, Charles Grey, 2nd earl, 248
Greytown, 680
Grillparzer, Franz, dramatist, 182, 237
Gros, Baron, French plenipotentiary in China, 701
Grundtvig, Nikolai Frederik Severin, Danish bishop, 107, 114, 119
Guadalupe Hidalgo, Treaty of (1848), 622, 675
Guardians, Board of, 337
Guatemala, 678, 679
Guayaquil, 668
Guéranger, Dom, abbot of Solesmes, 79
Guerazzi, Francesco Domenico, 408
Guéronnière, de la, French journalist, 125
Guibert, Jacques Antoine Hippolyte, Comte de, eighteenth-century military thinker, 314
Guizot, François, French statesman, 105, 115, 190, 259, 389, 392, 452
Gun-cotton, 64
Gutta-percha, 53

Gutzkow, Karl Ferdinand, novelist, 166
Guyot, Raymond, 254
Gwatkin, H. M., ecclesiastical historian, 81
Gyulai, Count Franz, Austrian general, 539

Habeas Corpus Act
suspended in Ireland, 217
suspended in U.S.A., 647, 653
Haiti, 682
Hakodate, Japanese trade port, 711
Halleck, Henry Wager, general, 316, 657
Haller, Karl Ludwig von, writer, 496
Hals, Frans, painter, 135
Ham, British import market, 26
Hambach, *Hambacher Fest* (1832), 493
Hamburg, 4, 26, 400, 494
Hamburg–Berlin Railway, 308
Hamilton, Alexander, U.S. statesman, 603, 605, 606
Hamilton, Hugh, professor of natural philosophy, 56
Hamilton, William, painter, 134
Hammond, James H., abolitionist, 617
Handbooks for Travellers (John Murray), 418, 419
Hanover
constitution of 1833, 189
constitution of 1840, 190
revolution of 1848, 397
in the Tax Union, 494
with Prussia and Saxony forms alliance of the Three Kingdoms, 409, 501
quits Prussian Union, 410, 501
joins the *Zollverein*, 503
defeat at battle of Langensalza, 519
annexed to Prussia, 520
finances German secret service, 579
Hansemann, David, industrialist, 494, 496
Hardenberg, Karl August von, prince, 391
Hardy, Sir Thomas Masterman, admiral, 278
Harper's Ferry, raid on, 625
Harris, Townsend, American consul at Shimoda, 712
Harris Treaty (1858), 712
Harrison, William Henry, ninth president of U.S.A., 621
Harvesters, 25
Harz Mountains, Germany, 24
Haussmann, Baron, Prefect of the Seine, 142, 460
Havas Agency, 5, 132
Havlíček, Karel, nationalist, 238, 534
Hawthorne, Nathaniel, novelist, 167
Haxthausen, August, Baron von, 18, 357 n.
Hayman, Francis, painter, 134
Haynald, Ludwig, cardinal and archbishop of Kalocsa, 100
Haynau, Baron Julius Jacob von, Austrian commander in chief, 528

Hayne, Robert Y., American Senator, 615
Health, Board of, 337
Heat, physics of, 59
Hebbel, Friedrich, dramatist, 182, 183, 184
Hebrew faith of polytheist origin, 102
Hefele, C. J., historian of the Roman church, 94, 100
Hegel, Georg Wilhelm Friedrich, philosopher, 55, 183, 184, 227, 495
Heidelberg, 395
Heine, Heinrich, poet, 17, 126, 174–5, 494
Held, F. W. A. (*Die Lokomotive*), 125
Helmholtz, Hermann von, physiologist, 59, 60, 66
Helvétius, Claude-Adrien, philosopher, 53
Herbart, Johann Friedrich, philosopher, 108
Herder, Johann Gottfried, philosopher, 216, 226
Hérédia, José-Maria de, poet, 173
Hertz, Heinrich, physicist, 58
Herzegovina, 472, 474, 479, 537 n.
Herzen, Alexander, political writer, 10, 13, 128, 216, 245
Hesse-Darmstadt, 395, 520
Hesse-Kassel, 395
  revolution (1850), 410
  evacuated by Prussia, 410
  Radowitz's union project, 501
  elector seeks help of Federal Diet, 502
  elector taken prisoner, 519
  annexed by Prussia, 520
Hetherington, Henry (*Poor Man's Guardian*), 121–2
Heydt, August von der, Prussian finance minister, 518
Hierta, Lars (*Aftonbladet*), 127
Hill, Sir Rowland, 332
Hirsch, Max, German trade unionist, 46
Histoire des Girondins (Lamartine), 216
History of Israel (Wellhausen), 102
History of the Jews (Milman), 102
History of the People of Israel (Edwold), 102
Hoare, banking firm of, 40
Hoe, Richard, inventor, 131, 132
Hoff, van t', Jacobus Hendrikus, chemist, 63
Hofmann, August Wilhelm von, chemist, 52, 62
Hoffmann, E. T. A., writer and musician, 179
Hohenlohe-Schillingsfuerst, Chlodwig, Prince von, 228
Hohenschwangau, 602
Hohenzollern, Leopold, prince of
  candidate for Spanish throne, 587–92
  withdrawal of, 594–6
Hohenzollern-Sigmaringen, Prince Karl Anton of, 508, 587, 593–4
Holland
  drainage of peat bogs in, 24

net importers of grain, 26
  franchise, 192
  death of king of, 203
  Treaty of XVIII Articles, 220–1
  sends armies into Belgium, 249
  surrenders Antwerp to Belgium, 250
  influence in Indonesia, 686
Holnstein, Count, Bavarian Court Chamberlain, 602
Homestead Act (1862), 642
Honduras, 678–9, 681
Hong Kong, 432, 689, 690, 692
Hong merchants' association, 689
Hooker, Sir Joseph Dalton, M.D., naturalist, 71
Hope, banking family of, 41
Hope, James, admiral, 703
Hopes of Italy (Balbo), 200, 431
Hortense (de Beauharnais), queen of Holland, 442–3, 447
Hospitals, 72
Hottingucr, banking family of, 41
Housing, 43–4
Hoverbeck, Leopold von, leader, German Progressive Party, 510
Howe–Singer sewing machine, 642
Hsien Feng, Chinese emperor, 698, 704–5
Hübner, Joseph Alexander von, Baron, Austrian agent, 263
Hudson Bay Company, 355
Hughes, John, Christian Socialist, 118
Hugo, Victor Marie, French poet and dramatist, 13, 80, 144, 164, 165, 174, 181, 190
Humboldt, Alexander von, Baron, 436
Hung Hsiu-ch'uan (Tien Wang), leader of the Taipings, 697–8, 706
Hungary
  large landlords as agricultural producers, 23
  Magyars ban federalism, 209
  independence of Austria, 264, 407, 528
  coalition of opposition parties succeed in election (1847), 389
  revolution of 1848–9, 390, 402–3, 406, 408
  indemnity to landowners for abolition of feudal rights, 396
  Statute of Hungary, 396
  Kossuth becomes regent, 528
  ineffectual administration of, 537
  tax evasion, 537–8, 547
  emancipation of peasants, 542
  Magyar restored as official language, 542
  Court Chancellery re-established, 542
  elections to be held and Diet convoked, 543
  April laws, legality of, 544
  passive resistance in, 544, 547
  a constitutional monarchy, 550
Hunt, Holman, painter, 151, 153

Hunter, Robert T., lawyer, statesman, 195
Huskisson, William, statesman, 38
Hutton, R. H. (*Spectator*), 123
Huxley, Thomas Henry, naturalist, 71, 112
Hydrodynamics, 51
Hyères, 421

Ibrahim, son of Mehemet Ali, Pasha of
  Egypt, 251, 428
Ibsen, Henrik, dramatist, 184
Ignatyev, Count Nicholas Pavlovitch,
  Russian ambassador at Constantinople,
  234, 703, 704
Illinois, 615, 624
Illustrated London News, 131
Illustration, L', 131
Illustrierte Zeitung, 131
Illustrious, H.M.S., 292
Immaculate Conception, doctrine of, 85
Immerman, Karl Lebrecht, novelist, 166–7
Imperial, the Prince, 446, 466
Impressment Act, 651
India
  establishment of rule under viceroy, 8
  western type educational system intro-
    duced, 8, 117–18
  export of cotton, 28, 638
  railways, 34, 350
  missionary work, 79
  newspapers, 131
  overland route to, 255
  Civil Service, 337, 352
  telegraphic communication, 350
  penal code, 352
  direct rule by the crown, 356
  mail service, 431–2
  the British East India company, 685
  opium trade, 688
Indian Mutiny, causes crisis in banking,
  42
Indiana, 194, 615
Indigo, 64, 610
Indo-China
  missionary work in, 79
  penetration by France, 461, 709
Indonesia, 686
Induction, electrical, 56
Industrial and Provident Societies Acts
  (1852 and 1862), 348
Industries, domestic, 42, 341
Ingres, Jean A.-D., painter, 144, 145
Inspectorate of Maritime Customs (China),
  701
Institut de France, 144
Institutions Liturgiques (Guéranger), 79
*Instruction pastorale sur diverses erreurs du
  temps présent*, 89
Instrument makers, scientific, 53
Internal Revenue Act (U.S.A.), 644

International Postal Union (1874), establishment of, 36
International Working Mens' Association, 7
International Working Mens' Movement,
  205
Ionian Islands
  ceded by Britain to Greece, 242, 426
  shipping, 419, 422
Iowa, 189, 203
Ireland
  lack of industries, 2–3
  emigration, 3, 218, 344
  potato blight, 24
  affairs of Roman Catholic church in, 100,
    217
  disestablishment, 100, 161
  'cabbage-garden revolution', 202, 217
  nationalism in, 217–18, 391
  Act of Union (1801), 217
  Habeas Corpus Act suspended, 217
  decline in population, 331
  programme of independence, 389
Irgiz, 387
Irish Confederation, 217
Irish Republican Brotherhood (Fenians),
  218
Irkutsk, 383
Irving, Washington, novelist, 167
Iron
  production of, 3, 29, 30, 43, 333
  in shipbuilding, 4
  conversion of cast into wrought, 29
  ore deposits, 29
  price of, 29
  output increased by use of coke, 30
  Pittsburgh industry, 31
  employment in, 43
  use in architecture, 136, 140, 142
  export of, 333
Isabella II, queen of Spain, 586
Ismail, viceroy of Egypt, 440
Isomers, optical, 63
Italia del Popolo (Mazzini), 571
Italy, xvii, 552–76
  religion, church and state: Cavour's
    maxim, 76; secularisation of ecclesi-
    astical property, 88, 575; control of
    education, 93; king and government of
    Italy under ban of church, 99; treat-
    ment of Jews, 243, 556, 559; ecclesiasti-
    cal censorship, 554; toleration for non-
    Catholics, 556; election of Pius IX,
    559; Jesuit attitude to liberalism, 565;
    the Siccardi laws, 567; dissolution of
    monasteries, 568; civil marriage, 568
  treaties and alliances: Pact of Plombières
    (1858), 16, 209, 271, 463, 538, 571; with
    Napoleon III (1859), 88; with Prussia
    (1866), 271

Italy (*cont*.)
    education, 111, 115
    press, 128, 560
    architecture, 140
    Charles Albert, *see under* Charles Albert
    Victor Emmanuel II, succession of, 209, 566
    First Austrian war: battle of Custoza, 186, 263, 402, 523, 564; battle of Novara, 263; peace treaty (1849), 264; armistice, 322; declaration of war, 398; battle of Goito, 398; renewal of war, 407; finance, 567
    Second Austrian war (1859): use of railways, 309; battle of Magenta, 323, 571; French troops support Piedmont, 323, 462–3; battle of Solferino, 323, 571; Armistice of Villafranca, 572
    Third Austrian war: second battle of Custoza, 576; naval defeat at Lissa, 576
    see also under individual states
Iturbide, Agustin de, emperor of Mexico, 674

Jackson, Andrew, general, seventh president of U.S.A., 605–10
Jacoby, Johann, radical, 496, 510
Jaffa, 423
Jahn, Friedrich Ludwig, publicist, 227
Jamaica, 356, 679
Japan
    diplomatic relations with Western states, 7, 712
    Meiji Restoration (1867), 211, 713
    constitution (1889), 212
    creation of army and navy, 212
    seclusion policy, 709–10
    Christianity in, 710
    trade, 710–11
    foreign travel, 710, 712
    shogunate of the Tokugawa family, 710–13
    defences in 1853, 711
    treaties with Western powers, 711–13
    bombardment of Kagoshima, 712
    naval squadrons at Osaka Bay, 713
    civil war, 713
    court moves to Tokyo, 713
    accepted by West as a great power, 713
Japelli, Giuseppe, architect, 140
Jassy, Academy of, 241
Jefferson, Thomas, third president of U.S.A., 603, 605, 612
Jellačić, Joseph, Count, Ban of Croatia, 403, 522, 523, 525, 537
Jesuits
    in Switzerland, 81, 223
    support doctrine of Immaculate Conception, 88
    reinstated in Austria (1851), 533
    Gioberti on, 565

incompatibility of liberalism with true religion, 565
suppression of in Mexico, 675
Jews
    population, 243
    debarred from professions, 243
    suppression of Yiddish, 243
    settlements in Palestine, 244
    emigration to U.S.A., 244
    support Hungarian government, 537
    in public services, 556
    in France, 243
    in Germany, 243
    in Italy, 243, 556, 559
    in Netherlands, 243
    in Poland, 243
    in Principalities, 243
    in Russia, 243
    in Spain, 243
    in Switzerland, 243
    in Turkey, 244
    in Hungary, 537
    in Austria, 540
John, Archduke, of Austria, 405, 410
Joint-stock companies, promotion of, 39
Jomini, Baron Henry, military thinker, 302, 313–16, 323
Joseph II, Holy Roman emperor, 533
Joule, James Prescott, physicist, 57, 59
Journal des Débats, 123
Journalists
    convicted for inciting disturbances in England, 121
    French *émigré* attacks on Napoleon III, 128
Joyce, James, writer, 157
Juárez, Benito, Mexican republican leader, 464, 675–6, 678
Jurists, congress of (1860), 507

Kaiserfeld, German-Austrian autonomist leader, 548
Kanagawa, Treaty of (1854), 711
Kankrin, Count Jegor, Russian finance minister, 364
Kansas, 203, 624
Kansas–Nebraska Act (1854), 624
Kápolna, battle of, 526
Karlovitz Assembly, 403
Karlsruhe Conference (1860), 62
Kars, 484, 489
Kashgar, 385, 707
Katkov, Michael, editor, 129, 234, 376
Kavelin, Constantin, lawyer and agrarian reformer, 375
Kay-Shuttleworth, Sir James (Dr Kay), 109, 114
Kazimullah, Caucasian leader, 385–6
Keats, John, poet, 172

Keble, John, divine, 82, 83, 100
Kekulé von Stradonitz, August, chemist, 62
Keller, Gottfried, novelist, 161
Kentucky, 628, 632
Kerr, Robert, professor, architect, 138
Ketteler, Freiherr Wilhelm Emmanuel von, bishop of Mainz, 101
Keyser, Nicaise de, painter, 151
Khiva, 386, 387, 388
Khokand, 386, 387–8
Khomyakov, Alexis Stepanovitch, writer, 367
Kiel, naval base at, 516
Kiev, university of, 363
Kindergarten schools, 108
Kingsley, Charles, Christian socialist, 118
Kirchhoff, Gustav Robert, chemist, 58
Kireevskii, I. V., writer, 367
Kiselev, Count Paul Dimitrievich, statesman and diplomat, 361, 478
Kishen, viceroy of Chihli, 690
Kiss, August, sculptor, 143
Kiying, Chinese plenipotentiary at Nanking, 692, 693, 694, 695
Kladderadatsch, 131
Klenze, Leo von, architect, 141
Koch, Robert, professor of hygiene, 24, 66
Kogalniceanu, Michael, statesman, 242
Kohn, Professor Hans, historian, 233
Kold, Kristen, educational leader, 110, 120
Kollar, Jan, scholar, 232
Kölliker, Rudolf Albert von, zoologist, 71
Kölnische Zeitung, 126
Kolokol, see *Bell, The*
Konieh, battle of, 428
Königgrätz (Sadowa), battle of, 310, 325, 519, 578
Kopal, 387
Korea
  Russia extends her borders to, 7
  pays tribute to China, 686
  policy of seclusion, 709
Kossuth, Lajos (Louis), Hungarian statesman
  and subject nationalities, 239–40
  seeks independence from Austria, 264
  warning against revolution, 396
  builds up army, 403
  downfall of, 408
  regent of Hungary, 528
  seeks support against Austria, 538, 544
Kowloon incident, 689–90
Krasinski, Zygmunt Napoleon, Count, poet, 234, 237
Krausz, Baron Philip von, Austrian minister of finance, 529, 533
Kremsier
  Draft Constitution of (1849), 197–8
  Austrian Diet at, 524, 526
Kreuzzeitung party, 14, 498, 508, 511

Kübeck, Karl Friedrich, Freiherr von, adviser to Emperor Francis Joseph, 531–3
Kuenen, Abraham, professor of Hebrew, 102
Kugler, Franz Theodor, writer on fine arts, 150
Kulja, 707
Kung, Prince, brother to emperor of China, 704
Kutchuk Kainardji, Treaty of (1774), 470, 476

Laboulaye, Édouard-René, political scientist, 207
Labrousse, Nicolas-Hippolyte, French naval officer, 278
Labrouste, Henri, architect, 140
La Convention du 15 septembre et l'encyclique du 8 décembre, 92
Lacordaire, Jean-Baptiste-Henri, Dominican preacher, 77, 78, 89, 101
Lacour, Edmond de, French ambassador to Turkey, 473
Lafayette, Marquis de, general, 194
La Gloire, French frigate, 279, 282, 285
Lagrené, Théodose de, French envoy to China, 693
Laird, shipbuilding company, 640
Lamarck, Jean Baptiste, zoologist, 68, 69
La Marmora, General, Sardinian commander, 482, 575
Lamartine, Alphonse de, author and statesman, 21, 173, 216, 261, 393, 394, 455
Lamennais, Félicité de, abbé, 77–8, 79, 101, 123, 216, 390
Lancashire, drainage of moss lands, 24
Land and Liberty (Ogarev), 373
Landschaften, Prussian, 25
Landseer, Sir Edwin, painter, 153
Landwehr, the Prussian, 509
Langensalza, battle of, 519
Lanskoi, Count, Russian minister of interior, 375
Lanterne, La, 125
La Paz, 667
Laplace, Pierre-Simon, Marquis de, astronomer and mathematician, 55
La première entente cordiale (Guyot), 254
Lassalle, Ferdinand, socialist, 127, 205, 505, 506
Latin Monetary Union (1865), 218
Latreille, A. Pierre André, historian, 76
Latvia, 231
Laurent, Auguste, chemist, 62
La Valette, Charles-Jean-Marie-Félix, marquis de, French ambassador to Turkey, 469, 470
Laveleye, Émile de, publicist, 245
Lavoisier, Antoine Laurent, chemist, 61
Lavrov, P., publicist, 375
Lawes and Gilbert (Rothamsted), 24

Laws of Thought (Boole), 56
Laxenburg Manifesto (1859), 540
Le Bel, Achille, chemist, 63
Leben Jesu (D. F. Strauss), 75, 102
Lebœuf, Edmond, Marshal, 598
Lebrun, Barthélemy Louis Joseph, general, aide-de-camp to Napoleon III, 586
Leconte de Lisle, Charles, poet, 173
Le Creusot, 30
Ledru-Rollin, Alexandre-Auguste, Republican journalist and politician, 393, 404, 408, 455
Lee, Robert Edward, Confederate general, 328, 329, 330, 656
Leeds Mercury, 44
Lefuel, H.-M., architect, 142
Legal Tender Act, 645
Leghorn, 419–21, 425
Legitimists, French, 444, 446, 448, 450, 452, 454
Legnago, 321
Leiningen, Count, Austrian emissary, 472
Leipzig, 400
Lelewel, Joachim, historian, 234
Le mie prigioni (Pellico), 558
Lenau, Nikolaus, poet, 176
Lenin (Vladimir Ilyich Ulianov), revolutionary, 358
Leopardi, Giacomo, Count, poet, 172
Leopold I, king of Belgium, 190, 249
Leopold II, Holy Roman emperor, 547
Leopold II of Tuscany, 554, 560
Le parti libéral, son programme et son avenir (Laboulaye), 207
Le Père, Jean-Baptiste, architect, 434
Le Play, Frédéric, social reformer, 452
Le Plongeur, French submarine, 287
Lermontov, Michael, novelist, 162
Lesbos, Island, 422
Le Sourd, Georges, acting French chargé d'affaires in Berlin, 590
Lesseps, Ferdinand de, engineer, and Suez Canal project, 434, 438–9
Lessing, Gotthold Ephraim, critic and dramatist, 183
L'État et ses limites (Laboulaye), 207
Levant, The, 418, 422, 424–5, 430, 433
Levy, J. M., controller of *Daily Telegraph*, 122
Levy Lawson family, of the *Daily Telegraph*, 121
Lewis, Sir George Cornewall, chancellor of exchequer, 486
Ley Juárez, 675–6
Ley Lerde, 675–6
Li Hung-Chang, leader of reaction against the Taipings, 699, 706
Liberator, The (W. L. Garrison), 618
Libraries
free lending in England and U.S.A., 120

Liebig, Justus, Baron von, chemist, 24, 50, 51, 62, 65, 114
Life of Frederick the Great (Kugler), 150
Liguria, 553, 570
Lille, 43, 139, 459
Limited liability companies, 40
Lin Tse-hsü, 688–90
Linant Bey, engineer to Mehemet Ali, 437
Lincoln, Abraham, sixteenth president of U.S.A.
    assassination of, 132
    support for protective tariffs, 613
    becomes president, 626–7
    Emancipation proclamation, 628, 637
    importance of voluntary loyalty, 629
    unconstitutional acts, 645, 646–7
    bold exercise of power, 646
    suspension of civil law and right of *habeas corpus*, 647
    superb strategist, 656
    interference with generals, 657
Lincolnshire, draining of fen lands, 24
Linen, wet spinning of flax, 28
Linnaeus, Carl, naturalist, 68–9
Linnean Society, 67
Lion of Flanders (Conscience), 221
Lissa, naval battle of, 576
List, Friedrich, economist, 227, 228, 308
Lister, Joseph, Lord, founder of antiseptic surgery, 24, 73
Lithography, 131
Lithuania
    Russian repression in, 230, 236
    the *Populists*, 236
Liverpool, 43
Liverpool–Manchester Railway, 32
Livingstone, David, explorer, 351
Lobatchevsky, Nicolas Ivanovitch, mathematician, 56
Locke, John, philosopher, 53
Locomotives, manufacture of, 29
Loftus, Lord Augustus, British ambassador in Prussia, 596
Loi Falloux (1850), 80, 86, 107, 409, 444
Lokomotive, Die (F. W. A. Held), 125
Lombardy
    in revolt against Austria, 262–3
    unrest in, 389
    provisional government, 396
    ceded to Piedmont, 401
    to receive special statute, 526
    good government and communications, 556
    promised autonomy by Austria, 571
London
    manufacture of machine tools, 29
    university of, 50
    Albert Memorial, 143
    St Pancras Station, 149

London Conference, regarding Belgian provinces, 248
London Convention (1840), 429
London, Treaty of (1852), 219
London, Treaty of (1867), 582
London, Treaty of (1871), 488
London Working Mens' Association, 347
López, Francisco Solano, president of Paraguay, 672–3
Lord, R. H., historian, 590
Lord Campbell's Libel Act (1843), 121
Lord High Admiral, office of, 290
Lord Lyons (Lord Newton), 585
Lords, House of, 335
Louis Napoleon (Charles Louis Napoleon), prince
  coup d'état (1851), 187, 416, 451
  elected president, 404, 443
  parentage, 442
  imprisonment at Ham, 443
  constitutional difficulties, 443
  part in insurrection of the *Carbonari*, 443
  sole purpose to restore the empire, 443
  early attempts to seize power, 443
  hesitation in resorting to force, 444
  attitude to Falloux Law, 444
  and the electoral law, 444, 445
  writings of, 446
  proclaimed as Napoleon III, 446
  concern for the poor, 447
  a leader without a party, 447
  see also Napoleon III
Louis Philippe, king of France
  fall of, 124
  ridiculed in press, 131
  seeks accommodation with eastern powers, 247
  intrigues for Belgian throne, 249
  dislike of Anglo-French *entente*, 254
  abdication, 393
  death of, 409
  and Algerian campaign, 427
Louisiana, 627, 655
Louisiana Purchase (1803), the, 461, 603, 620, 621, 624
Loutherbourg, Philipe Jacques de, painter, 134
Louvain University, 107
Lovett, William, chartist, 110, 346, 347
Lowe, Robert, leader-writer, *The Times*, 122
Lowell, James Russell, poet, 179
Loyal National Repeal Association, 217
Lucan, George Charles Bingham, 3rd earl of, 480
Lucca, 552
Lucerne, Switzerland
  Constitution of 1841, 81

Great Council of, 81
  and the Jesuits, 223
Luchu, pays tribute to China, 686
Ludwig II, king of Bavaria, 519, 601–2
Ludwig, Karl Friedrich Wilhelm, physiologist, 51, 66
Ludwig, Otto, novelist and dramatist, 166
Lunéville, peace of, 313
Lussinpiccolo, 422
Luxemburg
  Belgium loses, 221
  dispute of 1867, 272
  under guarantee of the Powers, 272
  supports Prussia in Federal Diet, 519
Lyceum movement (U.S.A.), 120
Lyell, Sir Charles, geologist, 9, 68, 69, 71, 102
Lyon, Mary, educationist, 119
Lyons, 42, 43, 435

Macao, 686, 689, 692
Macartney, George, 1st earl, 687
Macaulay, Thomas Babington, Lord, 117, 352
Macaulay, Zachary, philanthropist, 341
McClellan, George, B., U.S. general, 649, 657
McCormick, Cyrus Hall, inventor, 25
Macedonia, 426
Machine tools, manufacture of, 29
Machinery
  wrecking of, in uprisings (1830), 25
  improvement in, 27
  ban on export of, 28
MacMahon, Marie-E.-P.-M., marshal of France, 306, 326
Madder, synthesis of, 64
Madras, 432
Madrid, 420, 424–5, 435, 589
Maestricht, 221
Magellan, Straits of, 665
Magendie, François, physiologist, 66
Magenta, battle of (1859), 323, 506, 539, 571
Mahmud II, sultan of Turkey
  defeat by Mehemet Ali, 251
  appeals to Russia for aid, 252
  reopens hostilities against Mehemet Ali, 254–5, 429
  death of, 256, 429
Mahogany, 679
Mails
  penny post, 332
  carriage of Mediterranean, 431
  carriage of Indian, 432
Majláth de Székhely, George, politician, 548
Malaga, 420
Malaria, 72
Malines, 33, 77, 89, 90, 107
Mallarmé, Stéphane, poet, 178, 179, 180
Mallet *frères*, bankers, 41

Malmesbury, James, 3rd earl of, British foreign secretary, 571
Malta, 160–1, 431, 433
Malthus, Thomas Robert, political economist, 1, 54, 69
Mameli, Goffredo, poet, 225
Manchester, 10, 29, 43, 120, 206
Manchester and Liverpool railway, 332
Manchester Guardian, The, 121, 123
Manchu empire, 384, 685
Manchuria, 385, 702
Manchus, 690–1, 698–700
Manet, Édouard, painter, 154
Manila, 709
Manin, Daniel, Venetian leader, 201, 396, 565
Mann, Horace, secretary Massachusetts state Board of Education, 109, 111, 117
Manning, B. L., historian, 86
Manning, Henry Edward, Cardinal, 83, 87, 93, 95
Manteuffel, Otto von, Prussian statesman, 485, 498–9, 502, 503, 532
Mantua, 321
Manumission of slaves, 616
Manzoni, Alessandro, Count, writer, 225, 553, 558
Maori Wars (1857–70), 355
March Patent (5 March 1860), 540
Maret, Mgr, dean of theological faculty of the Sorbonne, 94–5, 101
Margarine, 64
Maria, queen of Portugal, 253
Marie, Alexandre Thomas, politician, 393
Marie Louise, duchess of Parma, 553, 554
Marinoni, Hippolyte (Presse), 132
Marnoch, 83
Marrast, Armand (Tribune), 123
Marriage, civil
  in Piedmont, 568
  in Mexico, 676
Marryat, Frederick, captain, naval officer and novelist, 295
Marseilles, 422, 431–2, 434–5
  prosperity aided by steamboats, 4, 421
  quarantine regulations at, 417
  volume of shipping, 419
  population, 420
  connections with Algiers, 421, 424, 428
  revival, 421
  importance to Napoleon, 425
  Mazzini at, 555
Marshall, Humphrey, American Commissioner in China, 700
Marshall, John, U.S. chief justice, 604
Marx, Karl, socialist
  Communist Manifesto, 3, 43
  determinism, 6, 55
  theory of class war, 10
  edits Rheinische Zeitung, 125, 495
  human relationships within capitalism, 160
  applauds 'crusade' against Denmark, 187
  incisive criticism of liberals, 188
  received in London, 202
  Das Kapital, 205
  anti-Slav writings, 431
Maryland, 605, 610, 626, 628, 632
Mason, James M., Confederacy representative, 638, 639–40
Massa, 553, 563, 571
Massachusetts, 34, 45, 185, 611, 623
Massenbach, Christian von, colonel, 310
Match industry, 342
Mauá Bank, 662
Mauá, Ireneu de Souza, Baron of, Brazilian financier and industrialist, 662
Maupas, Charlemagne-Émile de, prefect of police, 444, 445
Maurice, Frederick Denison, divine and Christian Socialist, 101, 118, 152
Mauritius, slavery in, 341
Mayer, Julius Robert von, physicist, 59, 60
Maximilian, emperor of Mexico (archduke of Austria), 208, 464, 582, 641, 677–8
Maxwell, James Clerk, physicist, 49, 57–8, 60
Maysville turnpike, 606
Mazzini, Giuseppe (1805–72), Italian patriot
  Young Italy, 128, 224, 555
  collaboration with Piedmont-Sardinia, 198, 563
  favours unitary republic, 199
  supports Victor Emmanuel, 201
  on British nationality, 213
  exile in London, 215
  belief in natural frontiers, 224
  distrust of France, 225
  forms Young Europe, 225
  in 1848–9, 408, 412, 565
  objective national unity, 555
  condemned to death, 555, 570
  and rising in Lungiana, 570
Meat prices, 27
Mechanics Institutes, 119, 120
Mecklenburg, 497, 519
Medicine, 71–2
Medill, Joseph, Chicago Tribune, 130
Mediterranean, xiii–xiv, 416–40
  comparative distances, 416
  climate, 417
  quarantine regulations, 417
  relative activity of ports, 418–19
  ports, population of, 420
Mediterranean Pilot (1873–82), 419
Mehemet Ali, viceroy of Egypt
  invests Acre, 251
  retains Syria, etc., 252, 428
  threatens to declare independence, 254

Mehemet Ali (*cont.*)
  sultan's desire to crush, 257
  interest in slavery, 426
  presses for recognition of his independence, 429
  attitude to canal project, 436
  urges Nile dam, 438
  death of, 438
  Grand Vizier, 470, 472
  minister of war, 476
Mehemet Rushdi, Turkish minister for war, 472
Meiggs, Henry, citizen of U.S.A., 665
Meiji Restoration, the, 211, 713
Meissonier, Jean Louis Ernest, painter, 147, 150
Melbourne, William Lamb, 2nd viscount, 202
Melgarejo, Mariano, president of Bolivia, 667
Melville, Henry Dundas, 1st viscount, First Lord of Admiralty, 277
Melville, Hermann, novelist, 164, 167
Memphis, 634
Mendel, Gregor, Abbot of Brünn, 56, 70
Mendeléef, Dmitri Ivanovitch, chemist, 63
Menotti, Ciro, patriot, 553, 554
Mensdorff-Pouilly, Count Alexander, general, 547, 548
Menshikov, Alexander Sergeievich, prince, 472, 473–4, 479, 480
Mentana, battle of (1867), 305, 583, 584
Menzel, Adolf, painter, 150, 151, 152
Méon, Mgr de, archbishop of Malines, 77
Mercerisation, 64
Mercury, use in venereal disease, 72
Meredith, George, novelist, 163
Mérimée, Prosper, writer, 125, 164
Merrimac, Confederate armoured ship, 285–6
Messageries Maritimes, 432, 452
Messina, 419–21
Metal trade, employment in, 333
Metal wares, a domestic industry, 42
Metric system, 552
Metternich-Winneburg, Clement, Prince von, statesman
  effect of his Six Acts, 13
  on accession of Pius IX, 87
  close watch on press, 125
  checks further constitution-granting, 189
  dismissed from office, 200, 203
  received in London, 202
  Swiss revisionist proposals of early 1830's, 222
  and the *Sonderbund*, 223
  fear of Russia's Near Eastern policy, 247
  and Belgian provinces, 248

  determination to restore order in Italy, 250–1
  supports Russia in dealing with Polish rebels, 251
  and Near East crisis of 1839–40, 255–8
  and occupation of Cracow, 267
  leaves Vienna, 396
  and Mediterranean quarantine regulations, 417
  interest in Suez canal, 436
  influence of rivals, 495
  on a speech by Frederick William IV, 496
  criticism of administration in Italy, 554
  opinion of Charles Albert, 557
  plan for economic union of Austria and Italy, 557
Mevissen, Gustav, liberal leader, 496
Mexico
  abandons unitarism for federalism, 186
  exiles Santa Anna, 203
  reverts to centralism (1836), 208
  federal constitution (1857), 208, 676
  federal republic restored (1867), 211
  French intervention in, 464, 677–8
  Britain, France and Spain occupy coastal regions, 464, 677
  the empire of Maximilian, 464, 677–8
  revolt of Texas, 621, 674
  territorial losses under treaty of Guadalupe Hidalgo (1848), 622, 675
  war with U.S. (1846), 622, 674
  occupation by General Winfield Scott, 622, 674
  suspends payment of her debts, 641, 676
  Maximilian's government, 641
  republic formed, 659, 674
  independence attained, 674
  population, 674
  Spanish invasion from Cuba, 674
  separatist movements, 674
  relations between church and state, 675, 676
  demoralisation under Santa Anna, 675
  judicial system under Juárez, 675
  coup d'état (1857), 676
  liberal government re-established at Vera Cruz, 676
  relations with Britain, 677
  foreign debts, 676–7
  reverts to republic, 678
Meyer, Victor, chemist, 63
Michael Obrenovich, Prince of Serbia, 242
Michelet, Jules, historian
  a new view of history, 11
  dismissal of, 105
  at the *Collège de France*, 115
  Latin co-operation, 218
  advocate of Roumanian liberals, 241
Mickiewicz, Adam, poet, 105, 215, 237

Microscopy, 67
Middlesbrough, iron ore deposits, 29
Mieroslawski, Ludwig, general, 235
Miguel, Dom, Portuguese pretender, 253, 555
Milan
  in 1848, 201, 321, 396–8, 402, 562
  communications, 421, 425
  and the German *Zollverein*, 557
  Cavour warns Austria of insurrection (1853), 569
Mildert, Bishop van, 82
Mill, James, economist, 109, 352
Mill, John Stuart, philosopher, 12, 53–5, 205, 206, 214, 352, 353
Millais, John Everett, painter, 151, 153
Millaud, Moïse (*Petit Journal*), 125
Millet, Jean François, painter, 147–8, 149, 151
Milman, Henry Hart, dean of St Paul's, 102
Milo, island of, 422
Milton (Blake), 1
Milyutin, D. A., Russian minister of war, 379
Milyutin, N., Russian deputy minister of Interior, 371, 375
Minas Geraes, 661, 662
Mines Act (1842), 342
Minghetti, Marco, minister of Pius IX, 558
Minié, captain, French army officer and inventor, 304
Minnesota, 203
Miquel, Johann, Prussian minister of Finance, 507, 515
Mirari Vos, encyclical of Gregory XVI, 78
Missions and missionary work
  in Africa and the East, 8
  in Asia, 79, 695–6
  expansion by non-Roman churches, 103
  in U.S.A., 103
  British and French in Tahiti, 259
  American at Beirut, 423
Mississippi river, 31, 34, 328–9, 603, 611, 613–14, 620, 635, 654–5
  steamboats on, 32, 612
Mississippi state, 615, 627, 634
Missouri, 194, 620, 629, 632
Missouri Compromise (1820), 620, 621, 623, 624
Mistral, Frédéric, poet, 175
Mitchel, John, Irish nationalist, 217, 389
Mitrailleuse, the, 307, 593
Mitre, Bartolomé, governor of Buenos Aires, 670, 671
Modena, 209, 250, 553, 560, 565, 572
Mohl, Hugo von, botanist, 67
Mohl, Robert von, politician and political thinker, 67, 211

Möhler, J. A., church historian, 94
Moldavia, 479, 488; *see also* Principalities
Molecular theory, 60–2
Molesworth, Sir William, politician, 353
Moltke, Helmuth Karl, Graf von, chief of German General Staff
  interest in military use of railways, 308–9, 310–11
  disciple of Clausewitz, 320
  the Seven Weeks war, 310–11, 324, 517
  the Franco-Prussian war, 310, 325, 326, 593
Monarchy
  limited in Belgium, 191, 194
  limited in Great Britain, 192
  under Kremsier draft constitution, 198
  relations with ministers, 340
  Haller's ideas of, 496
  Chinese view of, 686
Monasteries, dissolution of
  in Austria, 533
  in Piedmont, 568
  in Mexico, 676
Monet, Claude, painter, 149, 154, 155
Moniteur Officiel, 125
Moniteur Ottoman, 423
Monitor, Confederate armoured ship, 285–6
Monroe Doctrine, 604, 641, 673, 678, 682
Montalembert, Charles Forbes, comte de, writer and politician, 77, 78, 79–80, 89, 107
Montefiore, Sir Moses, philanthropist, 244
Montenegro, 241, 472
Monterrey, American troops in, 622
Montevideo, 670
Montez, Lola, dancer, 497
Montgomery, Alabama, meeting of Southern delegates, 649–50
Montgomery Constitution, 649
Montpensier, Antoine, duc de, 259, 587
Montt, Manuel, president of Chile, 664, 665
Moral and Civil Primacy of the Italians (Gioberti, 1843), 225
Moravia, 309, 523, 524
Morazán, Francisco, Honduran leader, 679
Moreno, Gabriel Garcia, president of Ecuador, 668
Mörike, Eduard, poet, 175, 176
Morny, duc de, illegitimate son of queen Hortense, 445, 447, 484
Morrill Land Grant Act (1862), 642–3
Morrill Tariff Act (1861), 628, 643
Morris, William, designer and socialist, 154–5, 178
Mortara, Edgar, Jewish child, 244
Mortimer, J. H., painter, 134

Mortmain, lands held in
  in Piedmont, 567
  in Mexico, 675–6
Morton, William Thomas Green, and Wells, Horace, introduction of ether, 72
Moscow, 36, 365, 368, 373, 381
Moscow News (Katkof), 129
Moskvityanin, Slavophile review, 230, 368
Mosquito coast, 679–80
Motley, John Lothrop, historian, 210–11
Mount Holyoke, American school, 119
Muddy Flat, battle of, 701
Mulhouse, textile mills, 43
Muller, Adam H., nationalist, 227
Müller, Johann, physiologist, 66, 114
Multiplices Inter, encyclical of Pius IX, 95
Münchengrätz, Treaty of (1833), 13, 253, 365
Munich
  Lamennais, Lacordaire and Montalembert at, 78
  university resists decrees of General Council, 100
  architecture in, 140–1
Munich Convention (1850), 410
Munro, Alexander, sculptor, 143
Muraköz, the, 529, 545
Murat, Prince Lucien, 570
Muraviev, Count, Russian governor-general of East Siberia, 236, 384–5, 702, 703
Muri, 81
Muridism, 385
Museums, under 'Ewart's Act' (1850), 120
Musset, Alfred de, poet, 173, 174, 181–2
Mussolini, Benito, 99, 201
Mustapha Pasha, grand vizier, 473
Mutiny Bill (1868), 270
Mutsohito, emperor of Japan, 211, 713

Nagasaki, 710, 711
Nägeli, Karl Wilhelm, botanist, 67
Nanking, 690, 698, 706
Nanking, Treaty of, 690, 692, 697
Napier, William John, Lord, Superintendent of Trade at Canton, 688–9
Naples
  university, 115
  proclaims Spanish constitution (1812), 199
  constitution (1848), 389, 395
  raises volunteers to aid Lombardy, 398
  king prorogues the Chamber, 402
  Austrian garrison in, 412
  shipping and population, 419–21, 431
  falls to Garibaldi, 433, 574
  cruel administration, 554
  possible claim of Lucien Murat, 570
Naples, Ferdinand II, king of, 402

Napoleon III, emperor of the French
  pact of Plombières, 16, 463, 571
  character, 19, 448, 454, 460, 577–8, 598, 599
  Anglo-French commercial treaty, 37
  influence of Pasteur, 50
  alliance with Cavour, 88
  Franco-Prussian tension, 95
  collapse of his regime, 99
  press support for, 125
  annexation of Nice and Savoy, 201, 463, 572
  desire to keep Italy weak, 209
  sympathy with nationalism, 241, 462
  seeks advice of Jomini, 323
  thought for the workers, 413
  suspected ambitions in Near East, 430
  interest in Suez Canal, 439–40
  broad aim of his regime, 442
  marriage, 446
  powers as sovereign, 449
  relations with church, 450–1, 454
  measures for availability of credit, 451
  tariffs, 452, 454
  general amnesty, 455
  veers towards the left, 455
  poor health, 457, 465, 578
  rebuilding of Paris, 460
  importance of diplomatic recognition, 461
  undoing of Vienna settlement, 461
  war with Austria, 462–3, 571–2
  garrison in Rome, 463, 465, 573, 583–4
  Mexican affair, 464, 580, 677–8
  project to acquire Luxemburg, 465, 580–2
  reorganisation of French army, 465, 584
  surrender at Sedan, 465, 600
  joins the empress in England, 466
  affair of 'the dynastic numeral', 470
  and the Crimean War, 472–5, 477, 480–5
  interest in restoration of Finland to Sweden, 483
  and better relations with Russia, 484, 489–91
  and the Principalities, 488
  and Polish liberty, 490
  signs treaty with Austria, 517
  and Schleswig-Holstein, 518
  attempt on his life, 570
  fails to seize opportunity in 1866, 571
  receives Venetia, 576, 578
  proposals for regrouping German states, 579
  expansionist designs, 580–2
  overtures to Austria, 582–4
  projected triple alliance, 584–6
  and Hohenzollern candidature, 587, 590–2, 595–9
  see also Louis Napoleon
Nashville, 622
Nassau (Germany), 395, 519

Nation, The, Irish weekly, 131, 217
National, Le, 123, 390, 393
National Association for protection of Labour, 346
National Bank Act (1863 and 1864), 628, 643
National Committee (Poles), 234
National Guard, 214, 390, 392, 395
National Mechanics' Institute, 82
National Society (Manin), 114, 570
'National Society for promoting the education of the poor', 85
Nationalverein, 510, 513
Natural selection, 69
Naval Discipline Act, 297
Naval power: navies, 274–301
   use of in the Crimean war, 279, 283, 433
   expenditure on British, 356
   armed packets, 433
   French navy, 276, 281, 283, 284, 298, 299, 300
   United States navy, 276, 277, 278, 298, 425
   Russian navy, 281, 284, 287
   Turkish navy, 281, 284
   Austrian navy, 286
   Italian navy, 286
   German navy, 516
   Chinese navy, 688
Navigation Laws, abolition of, 38, 334, 344, 351
'Navigazione generale Italiana', 432–3
Near Eastern Crisis (1839–40), 254–8, 429, 433
Nebraska, 624, 643
Neckar valley, rising in, 395
Negrelli, Louis, chief engineer, Austrian State Railway, 436, 437
Neilson, Clydeside iron worker, hot-air process, 29
Nekrasov, Nikolai, Russian poet, 180
Nemesis, gunboat, 281
Nemours, Louis-Charles, duc de, candidate for Belgian throne, 249
Neptune, discovery of planet, 49
Nerchinsk, Treaty of (1689), 384, 685, 687
Nerval, Gérard de, poet, 173
Nesselrode, Karl Robert, Count von, Russian statesman, 248, 260, 265, 269, 470, 476, 477
Neue Freie Presse, Austria, 126
Neue Preussische Zeitung, 126
Neue Rheinische Zeitung, 401
Nevelskoi, G. I., explorer, 385
Nevins, Professor Allan, historian, on Lincoln, 646
New Brunswick, 353
Newcastle upon Tyne, 29
New England, 610

Newlands, John Alexander, chemist, 63
Newman, John Henry, cardinal, 81–4, 92, 100, 156
New Mexico, 622–3
New Orleans, 613–14, 651
   battle of, 605
New York, 36, 141, 206, 636, 646
New York Associated Press, 133
New York Herald (Bennett), 121, 129, 188
New York Sun (Day), 129, 130
New York Times (Raymond), 129
New York Tribune (Greeley), 129
New Zealand, 8, 350, 355, 432
New Zealand Company, 353
News agencies, 5, 132
Ney, Michel, marshal of France, 313
Nicaragua, 678–9, 680, 681
Nice
   shipping and population, 419–20
   health resort, 421
   ceded to France, 463, 571, 572, 573
Nicholas I, tsar of Russia
   Near Eastern policy, 1825–50, 247, 252, 256, 258–60, 266, 468
   and Belgium, 247
   and Poland, 251
   meets Francis of Austria at München-grätz, 252
   proposed Quadruple Alliance, 258, 270
   isolation of France, 258
   visits England (1844), 259–60, 359, 471
   and revolutions of 1848, 260, 394
   and Prussian union plan, 264–5, 502
   supports existing treaties, 265, 269
   succession, 358
   reign, xii, 358–69
   death, 358, 369, 481
   character, 358–9, 361, 363, 462
   trust in army officers, 361
   Committee of December 1826, 361
   deserted by Austria (1854), 468
   snub to Napoleon III, 470
   and the crisis leading to the Crimean War (1852–3), 470, 471, 474–6
   and the Crimean War, 476–9
Nicolaieff, shipbuilding yards at, 489
Niel, Adolphe, marshal of France, army reforms of, 584–5
Nietzsche, Friedrich, philosopher, 157, 158, 170
Nightingale, Florence, reorganisation of British army medical services, 72, 486
Nikolaevsk, 385
Nikolsburg, preliminary peace of (1866), 519
Ningpo, 690, 692
Nitrate industry in Chile and Peru, 666, 668
Nitrates, Chilian, use as fertiliser, 24, 65

Nitrogen in soil, 65
Northcote, Sir Stafford, statesman, 337
Northern Star, 347
Norton, Captain, British army officer, 304
Norway
    constitution, 189
    franchise, 192
    study of folk-lore, 219
Notes from the Fatherland, 368
Novara, battle of, 186, 263, 406, 497, 564
Nullification
    issue of, 606, 609, 615
    Ordinance of, 609

Oastler, Richard, reformer, 44, 347
Oberlin College, U.S.A., 119
Oblomov (Goncharov), 169–70, 369
O'Brien, Bronterre, Chartist, 347
O'Brien, Smith, Irish political leader, 389
O'Connell, Daniel, Irish political leader, 217
O'Connor, Feargus, newspaperman and re-
    former, 347
October Diploma (1860), 542, 543, 544, 548
Odenwald, 395
Odessa, 26, 479
Oersted, Hans Christian, scientist, 53, 56
Oetker, liberal leader in Hesse-Kassel, 515
Ohm, Georg Simon, scientist, 57
Oidium, effect on French vintage, 24
Oken, Lorenz, philosopher and morpho-
    logist, 50
Old Catholic schism, 100
Old Testament, historical criticism of, 102
Oldenburg, 494
    duke of, 515
Ollivier, Émile, politician, 92, 97, 455, 456,
    585, 589, 591, 595
Olmütz
    emperor and ministers flee to, 403
    meeting of Schwarzenberg and Manteuf-
    fel, 502, 532
Olmütz Punctation (1850), Prussia's humi-
    liation, 204, 210, 265, 410, 412, 503, 508
Omer Pasha, Turkish commander, 472, 476,
    478
Opium, 72, 687–8, 689
Oporto, death of Charles Albert at, 566
Oregon, 203, 621–2, 632
Orenburg, 386
Origin of Species (Darwin), 67–8, 70–1, 102,
    348
Orleanists, 444, 446–8, 450, 452, 454, 458
Orlov, Alexis Feodorovitch, prince, diplo-
    mat, 478, 487
Orsini, Felice, revolutionary, attempt on life
    of Napoleon III, 570
Osaka Bay, 713
Osborne, Royal Naval College, 293
Oscar I, king of Sweden, 483

Ostrovsky, Alexander Nicholaevitch, dra-
    matist, 182
Otto I, king of Greece, 484, 490
Ottoman empire
    fate of, a concern of all the powers, 16
    decay of, 186
    nationalism of Balkan Christian subjects,
    240–3
    control of administration by Phanariot
    Greeks, 240
    threatened by Mehemet Ali, 251
    see also Turkey
Oudinot, Charles-Nicholas, marshal of
    France, 408
Overbeck, Friedrich, painter, 151
Owen, Richard, naturalist, criticism of
    Darwin, 71
Owen, Robert, socialist reformer, 110, 194,
    341, 342, 345, 346, 348
Oxford colleges opened to non-Anglicans, 87
Oxford Movement, 81–3, 100, 495
Ozanam, Antoine-Frédéric, writer, 101

Pacca, Bartolomeo, cardinal, papal pro-
    secretary of state, 78
Pacific Railroad Act, 628
Pacific Steam Navigation Company, 665
Pacific, War of the, 666, 668
Padua, 140, 562
Páez, José Antonio, guerrilla leader, 668
Paixhans, Henri Joseph, inventor, 276–7,
    284, 477
Palacký, František, historian, 238, 523, 549
Palaeontology, 68
Palermo
    the port of, 420–1
    insurrection in, 560
    parliament at, 565
    capture by Garibaldi, 572
    separatist government, 576
Palma, 420
Palmerston, Henry John Temple, 3rd Vis-
    count, statesman
    popularity of, 216
    cession of Ionian Islands, 242
    policy of co-operation with France, 246
    and the Belgian provinces, 248–9
    and Treaty of Unkiar Skelessi, 252, 255–6,
    428
    Near East policy, 252, 258
    the balance of power, 257, 258, 264, 267
    reply to Nicholas I regarding isolation of
    France, 258
    return to Foreign office, 259
    Anglo-Russian relations, 260
    and the Second French Republic, 261
    mediation in Italy (1848), 262–3
    warns Prussia against aggression, 262
    the Schleswig-Holstein problem, 265

Palmerston (*cont.*)
  interpretation of 'non-intervention', 270
  dismissal of, 340
  and Mehemet Ali, 428–9
  imposes settlement on Turkey and Egypt, 429
  naval coercion of Greece, 433
  and Cavour's conquest of Sicily and Naples, 433
  Suez Canal, 435–40
  Home Secretary, 474, 477
  Prime Minister, 481
  deprecates premature negotiations, 481
  and King Otto's government of Greece, 490
  on Bessarabia and Black Sea, 492
  instructions to Lord Napier, 689
Panama railway and canal, 435, 680
Pan-Scandinavian movement, 220
Pan-Slav Conference (1867), 234
Pan-Slav Congress (1848), 187, 232–3, 402
Pan-Slavism, 232–4
Panthays, Chinese Muslims, 707
Papacy
  papal infallibility, 13, 81, 93–4, 96, 98–9
  temporal power, 13, 565, 583, 600
  attitude to science, 71
  apostolic succession, 83
  and the Immaculate Conception, 88
  authority of General Council over the, 94
  right to censure civil power, 97–8, 99
Papal states
  extinction of, 88
  reform in administration of, 88
  insurrection of the *Carbonari*, 443
  arbitrary government under Gregory XVI, 554
  the *centurioni*, 554
  Jews allowed outside the ghetto, 559
  economic league with Tuscany, 560
  designs on Modena and Parma, 563
Paper, wood-pulp, 64
Paraguay, 659, 672–3
Paraguayan war (1864–70), 663, 673
Paraná, 671
Paris
  archbishops of, 89
  architecture in, 140–2, 460
  Académie des Beaux Arts, 142
  in 1848, 392–5, 397–8, 399–400, 415
  population, 459
  largely rebuilt by Napoleon III, 460
  role of *demi-monde* in, 460–1
Paris, comte de, 393
Paris, Congress of (1856), 128, 235, 241, 268, 487–91
Paris, Declaration of (1856), 299, 491
Paris Exhibition of 1867, 29
Paris–Lyon–Méditerranée railway, 436

Paris, Treaty of (1856), 32, 269, 271, 433, 462, 488–90, 600
Parisis, Mgr Pierre-Louis, bishop of Langres, 79
Parkes, Harry, British consul in Canton, 704
Parma, 209, 552–3, 572
  Jews in administration, 556
  political tolerance, 556
Paroles d'un croyant (Lamennais), 78, 216
Parsonstown, 58
Pasteur, Louis, chemist, 24, 51, 63, 65–7, 73
Pastor Aeternus, 98
Patmore, Coventry, poet, 178
Patras, 420, 422
Pavia, 321
Pavón, battle of, 671
Paxton, Joseph, horticulturist, 136
Peabody Trust, the, 139
Pecchi, Count Gioacchino Vicenzo, bishop of Perugia, 89
Pedro I, emperor of Brazil, 660
Pedro II, emperor of Brazil, 661–3
Peel, Sir Robert, statesman, 26, 38, 202, 259, 339, 343
Peiho river, 690
Pélissier, Aimable-Jean-Jacques, Marshal, 482
Pellico, Silvio, writer, 558
Penang, 432
Peninsula Steam Navigation Company, 431
Peninsular and Oriental Steam Navigation Company, 431–2
Pennsylvania, 31, 610–11, 615
Penny Magazine (1832), 122
Peoples' High School Movement (Denmark), 119
Péreire, Émile and Isaac, founders of the *Crédit Mobilier*, 453
Pérez, José Joachín, president of Chile, 664, 666
Périer, Casimir, French statesman, 249
Periodic Law, 63
Perkin, Sir William Henry, chemist, 52
Pernambuco, 661
Perovskii, Count Basil Alexeievich, governor-general, Orenburg, 387
Perrone, Giovanni, professor of Collegium Romanum, 88
Perry, Commodore, U.S. naval commander, 710
Persia, 685
Persigny, Victor Fialin, duc de, 447
Personal Liberty Laws (U.S.A.), 625
Peru, 659, 666–8
Perugia, 554
Peschiera, 321
Pestalozzi, Johann Heinrich, teacher, 104, 108
Pesti Hirlap, 238
Petit Journal, 125, 132

Petitti di Roreto, Carlo Ilarione, economist and philanthropist, 561
Petöfi, Alexander, poet, 238
Petrashevskii-Butaševič, Michail Vasilevič, politician, 365
Pfordten, Ludwig von der, Bavarian minister, 512, 519
Philadelphia Public Ledger, 129, 131
Philipon, Charles (*Caricature* and *Charivari*), 131
Philippines, 686
Phosphates, 65
Phosphorus, 30
Photius, Archimandrite, religious extremist, 360
Photography, 52
Photosynthesis, 65
Phylloxera, 24, 66
Piacenza, 321, 553, 564
Pickens, Fort, Florida, 627
Pie, Louis François, bishop of Poitiers, 90
Piedmont-Sardinia, kingdom of
   religion, church and state: secularisation of ecclesiastical property, 88, 575; control of education, 93; aggression against papal states, 93; religious toleration, 243, 556, 559; ecclesiastical censorship, 554; defeat of papal forces at Castelfidardo, 574
   political and constitutional developments: *Statuto* (1848), 128, 185, 198, 200–1, 395, 412; succession of Victor Emmanuel II, 209, 566; failure of Young Italy's revolution, 225; abdication of Charles Albert, 322, 406, 527, 566; alliance with France, 538; acquires Liguria, 552; reform of legal code, 556; disagreements with Tuscany and Rome, 563; parliament at Turin (1861), 575; prime ministers, 575
   press: freedom of, 128, 557, 560
   war with Austria: battle of Custoza, 186, 263, 402, 523, 564; attacks Austria in Lombardy, 200; battle of Novara, 263, 406, 527, 564; peace treaty (1849), 264; use of railways, 309; armistice, 322, 406; battle of Magenta, 323, 571; battle of Solferino, 323, 571; support of French troops, 323, 462–3; declaration of war, 398; battle of Goito, 398; renewal of war, 407; naval bases, Genoa, 421, Spezia, 569; rules all Italy save Rome, 463; armistice of Villafranca, 572; naval defeat at Lissa, 576
   trade, commerce and economics: expansion, 209; communications, 323, 556; customs, 556; agriculture, 556, 559; currencies, 556, 575; a backward state, 556; finance of war, 567; the Crimean War, 569

Pierce, Franklin, fourteenth president of U.S.A., 203, 624
Pigot, John, Irish patriot, 217
Piracy
   in the Levant, 422
   in China, 696
Piraeus, 419–20, 422, 484
Pirie, Sir John, Bart, shipowner, 438
Pisa, 562
Pius IX, Giovanni Mastai-Ferreti, pope
   Syllabus of Errors, 9, 89–94
   opposition to modern trend of civilisation, 71
   restores territorial hierarchy, 84
   accession, 87, 185, 389, 559
   under protection of French troops, 88
   amnesty for political prisoners, 88, 389
   flight to Gaeta, 88, 408, 564
   declines to censure Montalembert, 90
   calls General Council, 93
   relations with Victor Emmanuel, 95
   gives priority to definition of infallibility, 98
   places king and government of Italy under ban, 99
   surrender to Austrians, 200
   appoints ministry, 395
   grants a constitution, 395
   condemns war, 402
   appeals to Austria, 408
   intransigence towards liberalism, 454
   susceptibility to popularity, 559
   conversion to Gioberti's ideas, 559
   forced to grant a constitution, 560
   condemns Mexican legislation, 676
Place, Francis, Radical, 345, 347
Plague and the black rat, 72
Plating, electro-, 13
Plener, Ignatius von, Hungarian finance minister, 543
Pletkov, Russian writer, 213
Plombières, Pact of (1858), 16, 209, 271, 463, 538, 571
Poe, Edgar Allan, writer, 167, 179
Poelaert, Joseph, architect, 142
Pogodin, Michael Petrovitch, historian and politician, 232, 368
Pola, 421
Poland
   Frankfurt Assembly votes for independence of, 228
   emigration of 1830–1, 234, 237
   Cracow incorporated in Habsburg empire, 235
   general amnesty by Alexander II, 235
   Agricultural Society, 235
   Warsaw Academy of Medicine, 235
   administration and educational reforms, 235

Poland (*cont.*)
  demands return of eastern borderlands, 235
  Russian becomes official language, 236
  religious instruction forbidden, 236
  end of vestiges of self-government, 236
  becomes the 'Vistula Territory', 236
  risings of: (1830–1), 21, 186, 248, 362; (1846), 234–5, 397; (1863), 21, 128, 186, 230, 236–7, 513
  repressive measures, 252–3
  the 'Arnim' plan for reconstruction of, 262
  serfdom in, 372
  in 1848, 390, 391, 397
  discussed at Congress of Paris, 490
Polignac, Jules, prince de, 427
Political economy, 6, 53
Politecnico (Cattaneo), 556
Polk, James Knox; eleventh president of U.S.A., 622
Polytechnikum, Zürich, 106
Poor Law Amendment Act (1834), 337
Poor Law Commissioners, 337
Poor Man's Guardian (Henry Hetherington), 121
Pope and the Council (Janus), 94
Populist movement
  in Russia, 375
  in U.S.A., 611
Port Mahon, 420
Port Said, 420, 424
Portales, Diego, Chilean political leader, 664, 665
Portugal, 253, 686, 688
Posen, Grand Duchy of, 228, 234, 397, 494
Postal service, British reform of 1840, 36
Postl, Carl (Charles Sealsfield), Austrian writer, 194
Potassium salts, 24
Potatoes, 24, 26, 343
Pottery industry, 342
Pottinger, Sir Henry, colonel, 690
Prague, 100, 402, 523
Prague, Treaty of (1866), 220, 519, 520, 580
Prague News, 238
Précis de l'art de la guerre (Jomini), 314–15
Pre-Raphaelite Brotherhood, 151–3
Press, vii, 14, 121–33, 409, 449, 486, 496
  in Austria, 126, 127, 504
  in Belgium, 127
  in Denmark, 127
  in Norway, 127
  in Sweden, 127
  in Switzerland, 127
  in Italy, 128, 560, 569
  in Egypt, 131
  in India, 131
  in Japan, 131

Press Association, 132
Pressburg, 395, 396
Presse, Die, 126
Presse, La, Paris, 121, 124
Prévost-Paradol, writer, *Journal des Débats*, 123
Prieto, Joaquín, president of Chile, 664
Prim, Juan, statesman and general, 586, 588, 594
Prince Albert, H.M.S., 286
Princeton, U.S. naval vessel (1842), 281
Principalities, The, 204
  growth of national consciousness, 241
  Russia withdraws from, 478
  occupation by Austria, 479
  now Roumania, 488
  evacuated by Austria, 489
Principles of Geology (Lyell), 68, 102
Privateering, formal abolition, 491
Prix de Rome, 144
Prospective Review, 156
Protestant Dissenting Deputies, The (B. L. Manning), 86
'Protestant Patent', 542
Proudhon, Pierre-Joseph, socialist, 149, 392
Prussia, xv–xvi, 493–521
  the army: reforms, 16, 509–10, 515; the General Staff, 310–11; recruitment and organisation, 311–12; Prussian Army Law (1814), 312; Prussian War School, 317; the *Landwehr*, 509
  struggle for German supremacy, 16; dominant power in Germany, 100; progress towards unification, 465; Prussia and Austria assume joint responsibility for German affairs, 500; Bismarck establishes independence of Prussian policy, 506
  treaties and alliances: the Olmütz Punctation, 210, 265, 410, 412, 503; agreement with Saxony and Hanover, 409; Austrian Commercial Treaty (1853), 505; French Commercial Treaty (1862), 505; Alliance with Austria (1864), 515; Alliance with Italy (1866), 517; Peace of Prague (1866), 220, 519; secret treaty with Württemberg, Baden and Bavaria, 580
  trade, commerce and economics: imports of grain, 26; shortage of apprentices and journeymen, 45; child labour, 45; improved by *Zollverein*, 494, 503; railways, 505; population, 579
  constitutional development: Constitution of 1850, 109, 409, 498; democratic institutions, 189; Patent of 1817, 391; changes in 1848, 397–8, 405, 498; reaction in 1849, 407, 409, 498; demands for change, 496; meeting of United

Prussia (*cont.*)
Diet, 496–7; conflict of 1860–6, 510–12, 515, 517–20; formation of National Liberal Party, 521
monarchy: mildly limited, 185; right to amend constitution, 409; no longer absolute, 412; right to nominate and dismiss ministers, 498; divine right of kings, 499
administration: local government, 206–7; administrative system, 495
religion: reconciliation with Roman Catholic church, 494–5
education, 107–9, 111–13, 495
press, 125–7, 131–2
navy, 516
and the Franco-Prussian war (1870–1): controversial origins, 16, 597–9; acquires Alsace and Lorraine, 17, 600; declaration of war, 78; superiority of Chassepot rifle, 305; use of breech-loading artillery, 306, 325; battle of Gravelotte–Saint Privat, 306, 326; victory of Sedan, 306, 327; nullification of the *Mitrailleuse*, 307; use of telegraph, 310; initiative of subordinate commanders, 310; strategy, 325–6; superior deployment, 325; battle of Wörth, 326; battle of Vionville, 326
Schleswig-Holstein and war with Denmark (1848 and 1864): independent states, 219; dispatch of Prussian troops (1848), 219, 265; provision for plebiscite, 220; candidature of prince of Augustenburg, 515, 516; war with Denmark (1864), 515; Bismarck's objective, annexation, 516
and the Seven Weeks War (1866): value of Prussian needle gun, 305; Prussia achieves initial advantage, 308; use of railways, 308–9, 324; movements directed from Berlin, 310; Moltke's strategy, 324–5; arrival of crown prince's army, 325; defeat of Austria at Königgrätz, 325, 519; diplomatic relations broken off, 519; Peace of Prague, 519
Public health, little progress before 1870, 44
Pugin, A. W. N., architect, 136, 137
Punch, 131
Punta Arenas, 665
Pusey, Edward Bouverie, divine, 83
Pushkin, Alexander, poet, 172, 182, 368
Putyatin, Count, Russian admiral, 385, 702
Pyat, Félix, politician and dramatist, 408

Quadruple Agreement (1840), 257, 429
Quadruple Alliance (1815), 462; (1834), 253–4, 462

Quakers in U.S.A., 610, 616
Quanta Cura, encyclical of Pius IX, 1864, 90
Queretaro, Maximilian executed at, 582
Quinet, Edgar, writer, 216, 241
Quinine, 64, 72
Quito, 668

Radetzky, Count Joseph, Austrian field-marshal, 321–2, 396, 402, 523, 562–4
Radiations, study of, 58
Radowitz, General Josef Maria von, Prussian minister of foreign affairs, 264, 500–2
Raglan, Fitzroy Somerset, 1st Baron, British army commander, 322, 478, 482
Ragusa, 422
Raiffeisen, Friedrich Wilhelm, 23
Railways
competing with other forms of transport, 4, 26, 33
Britain and Belgium lead in, 30
boom periods, 32, 332
the Manchester–Liverpool railway, 32, 332
operating mileage, 32, 332
speed of travel, 32, 33
amenities, 33, 141
as common carriers, 33
fares, 33
expansion by 1859, 34
military use of, 308–9, 323, 324, 325, 328, 329
development of the telegraph, 332
finance, 334
in Argentina, 672
in Australia, 34, 350
in Austria, 530, 535, 536
in Belgium, 33
in Brazil, 662
in Canada, 350
in Egypt, 432
in France, 33
in Germany, 494, 505
in Holland, 34
in India, 34, 350
in Italy, 34, 556, 561
in Peru, 668
in Russia, 34
in Spain, 34, 420
in the U.S.A., 34, 612, 618, 624, 643
Rajačić, Serbian patriarch, 529
Ram Mohan Roy, Hindu thinker, 118
Randall, J. G., historian, on Lincoln's emancipation proclamation, 629
Rankine, William John Macquorn, physicist, 59
Raspail, François, chemist and politician, 399, 404

Rat, black, 72
Rattazzi, Urbano, Piedmontese statesman, 568, 570, 572, 576
Rauscher, Joseph Othmar von, cardinal, tutor to Francis Joseph, 533
Ravenna, 554
Rawlinson, Sir Henry Creswicke, Bart, major-general, 388
Raymond, Henry J., American newspaper-man, 129–30
Raznochintsi, the, 106
Reaping by machine, 25
Rechberg, Count Johann Bernard, Austrian foreign minister, 512, 514, 539, 547
Reciprocity Treaty, Anglo-American (1854), 354
Red Cross Society founded, 7
Redlich, Josef, jurist and historian, on the Kremsier draft constitution, 197
Reed, Sir Edward James, naval architect, 286
Reed, William Bradford, lawyer, diplomat, 702
Reeve, Henry, leader-writer, *The Times*, 122
Reffye, J. B. A. Verchère de, artillery officer, 307
Reform Association (*Reformverein*), 512
Reform Club, London (Liberal), 138, 339
Réforme, La, 124, 390, 393
Reggio, 553
Reichsrath, the Austrian, 533, 540, 541, 545, 546, 550
Reichstadt, duc de, son of Napoleon I, 443, 446
Reichstag (North German Confederation), 579
Religion, vi, 76–103
  missionary enterprise, 8, 79, 83, 423, 695–7, 708–9
  papal infallibility, 13, 81, 93–4, 96, 98–9
  repeal of Test and Corporations Act, 76
  religious orders in France, 78, 451
  in Palestine, 469
  dissolution of monasteries, 81, 676
  Jesuits, 81, 88, 223, 523, 565, 675
  Oxford Movement, 81–3, 100
  Apostolic Succession, 83
  disestablishment, 83, 100–1, 218, 676
  Syllabus of Errors, 89–94, 454, 459
  papal right to censure civil power, 97–9
  Jewish, 243–4, 540
  Orthodox, in the Holy Places, 470, 473
  Nonconformists in U.S.A., 625
Religion of Israel (Kuenen, 1869), 102
Renan, Ernest, historian and essayist, 9, 102
Renoir, Auguste, painter, 154
Renwick, James, architect, 141
Report on the Affairs of British North America (Durham), 353

Report on the Organisation of the Permanent Civil Service (Trevelyan and Northcote), 337
Representation of the People Act (1861), 338; (1867), 334, 338
Republican party (U.S.A.)
  formation of, 626
  and Lincoln's terms to the South, 629
  factions within, 647–9
Researches into Early History of Mankind (Tylor), 102
Reshid Pasha, Turkish minister of foreign affairs, 471, 473
Reuter's news agency, 5, 132
Revue des Deux Mondes, 123, 128, 436
Rheinische Zeitung, 125, 495
Rhett, Barnwell, secessionist, 627
Rhine, river, 32, 228, 326, 495, 506, 579, 585, 599
Rhineland, the, 390, 392, 494–6, 508
Rhodes, Island of, 228
Ricasoli, Baron Bettino, Italian statesman, 572, 575
Rice in Maryland, 616
Richmond, Virginia, Confederate capital, 327, 328, 330, 634, 654
Riemann, Georg, mathematician, 56
Rietschel, Ernst, sculptor, 143
Rimbaud, Arthur, poet, 171, 172, 179, 180
Rio Branco Law (1871), 663
Rio de Janeiro, 661–2
Rio de la Plata
  republic, 659, 669
  see also Argentina
Rio Grande do Sul, disturbances in, 661
Rise of the Dutch Republic (Motley), 211
Risorgimento, Il (Balbo and Cavour), 560
Roads, macadamised, 31
Robert College (Constantinople), 423
Roberts, Issachar Jacob, missionary to China, 697
Rochdale Co-operative Manufacturing Society, 348
Rochdale Equitable Pioneers Society, 46, 348
Rochefort, Henri (*La Lanterne*), 125, 455
Rodbertus, J. K. von, economist, 505
Roebuck, John Arthur, politician, 481
Roenne, Friedrich von, representative in U.S.A. of Frankfurt government, 195
Romagna, the, 572
Rome
  Lamennais advocates his cause, 78
  republic in, 88, 198, 565
  French troops in, 88, 95, 444, 465, 565, 573–4, 576, 583
  Italian troops take possession, 98
  Victor Emmanuel II, monument to, 142
  Garibaldi's march on, 201

Rome (*cont.*)
fall of, 408
papal rule in, 463, 554, 559–60
Italian troops enter, 600
Roon, Albrecht, Count von, Prussian states-
man and general, 324, 509, 517, 593, 597
Rosas, Juan Manuel de, Argentine dictator,
663, 669–71
Rosmini-Serbati, Antonio, theologian and
philosopher, 558, 565
Rosse, William Parsons, earl of, astrono-
mer, 58
Rossetti, Dante Gabriel, poet and painter,
151, 152, 153, 177, 178, 225
Rossetti, Gabriele, poet and liberal, 552
Rossi, Count Pellegrino, diplomat and
economist, assassination of, 408
Rostovtsev, Jacob, civil servant, 371
Rothschild, house of, 34, 243, 535, 663
Rotteck, Karl Wenceslas von, historian, 193,
194
Rouault, Georges, painter, 146
Roubaix, 459
Rouher, Eugène, politician, 447, 582, 583
Roumania
creation of, 229, 241, 462, 488
Roumanians in Hungary, 239–40, 402–3,
523, 529, 537, 541, 546
see also under Principalities
Rousseau, Théodore, painter, 147
Royal Agricultural Society journal, 23
Royal Commission
on Irish Church revenues (1832), 100
on Universities (1850), 50
Royal Institute of British Architects, 139
Royal Naval College, Portsmouth, 291–2
Roze, Pierre Gustave, admiral, 709
Ruatan, island of, 679, 681
Rubber, 52, 53
Rude, François, sculptor, 143
Rudin (Turgenev), 369
Ruffin, Edmund, agriculturist, publisher
and secessionist, 627
Rüge, Arnold, philosopher and liberal, 506
Ruggiero, Guido de, political thinker, 209
Ruhr
coal mines, 30
new industrialism, 494
population, 505
Ruskin, John, art critic and writer, 68, 137,
178
Russell, Alexander (*Scotsman*), 123
Russell, Lord John
'open letter' to bishop of Durham, 85
on Britain's ties with Europe, 267
Queen Victoria's memorandum to, 340
failure to form a government, 343
and Canadian constitution, 353
and electoral reform, 411, 477

foreign secretary, 471
at Vienna conferences of 1855, 481–2
principle of non-intervention, 572
Russell, Lord Odo, British representative in
Rome, 95
Russell, William Howard, war correspondent, *The Times*, 122
Russia, xii–xiii, 357–88
territorial changes: advances her borders
to Korea, 7; conquest of central Asian
khanates, 381–2, 386–8; cedes Alaska
to U.S.A., 384; obtains Amur river
province and Sakhalin, 385, 704; occupation and restoration of Kulja, 707
rebellion: risings in Poland, 13, 229, 234,
237, 251, 362, 376; secret society in
Ukraine, 231
trade and industry: exports, 26, 364, 380;
productivity, 364, 380; pig-iron production, 364, 381; tariff policy, 364,
380; currency, 364; domestic industries,
364; textile industry, 364, 380; railways,
365, 380, 381, 382, 385, 386; co-
operative institutions, 371, 373; Bank
of Russia, 379–80; financial reforms,
379; harvests, 380, 381; joint-stock
companies, 380; taxation, 382; coal,
388
education: state control of, 106, 230,
362–3, 379; universities, 106, 230, 363,
365, 378; ministry of, 360; Academy of
Science, 363; secondary and primary,
378; science teaching, 379
social structure: educated class with no
assured position, 106; emancipation of
serfs, 204, 370–2, 380–2, 487; need for
internal reforms, 268; the nobility, 360,
369; public sale of serfs, 361; 'free'
peasants, 361; right to buy freedom,
362; army principal field of personal
advancement, 369; commutation of
labour services, 369; serfdom in
Siberia, Poland and Transcaucasia,
372; slavery, 383, 387; forced immigration in Far East, 385
administrative institutions: District Councils (*Zemstva*), 111; police administration, 359; the Chancellery, 359, 360,
361; Third Department, 359, 361;
Ministry of Education, 360; Council
of Ministers, 360, 379; State Council,
360, 377; provincial government, 361;
press, 128–9, 230, 368, 370–1; censorship,
128, 359–60, 365, 368, 376, 378
architecture, 139, 142, 363
literature, 165–6, 168–9, 182, 366–9
Crimean War, xv, 468–92: results, 241;
Russian navy in, 279, 281; Russian
military defects, 322

Russia (*cont.*)
Army: conscription, 236, 379; in Crimean war, 322–3; prestige of, 369; corruption in, 369; chief field of personal advancement, 369; size of, 369; universal military service, 379
treaties: Unkiar Skelessi (1833), 252, 255–6, 428, 468; Münchengrätz Agreement (1833), 252–3, 365; Franco-Russian (1859), 491; Paris (1856), 269, 488–90, 600; Kutchuk Kainardji (1774), 470, 476
religion: conversions to Orthodoxy, 231; Bible Society dissolved, 360; authority of tsar, 363
administration of justice: Chancellery decrees, 360; codification of laws, 363, 487; deportation, 372; new judicial system, 377–8; the bar, 378
the monarchy: divine right of tsar, 363
Russian America Company, 384
Ruthenes, 525, 530, 537, 541, 549
Rutherford, Mark (William Hale White), 158

Sacconi, Giuseppe, architect, 142
Sadowa, *see* Königgrätz
Šafarik, Josef, scholar, 232
Said Pasha, viceroy of Egypt, 438, 439, 440
Saigon, 709
Saint Arnaud, Armand Leroy de, marshal of France, 444, 445, 478
Saint Domingue, becomes Haiti, 659
Saint-Simon, Comte Claude Henri de, philosopher, 109
Saint Simonian school
influence on development of railways and banks, 3
influence on de Lesseps, 434–5
support for Napoleon III, 453
St Vincent de Paul, Society of, 78, 101, 708
Sainte-Beuve, Charles-Augustin, critic, 125, 149
Sakhalin, island of, 384, 385
Sala, G. A., journalist, 122
Salasco, Carlo di, Piedmontese general, 564
Salazar y Mazarredo, Spanish Councillor of State, 588, 589
Salic law in Denmark, 219
Salonica, 419–20, 423
Salt trade, Austro-Piedmontese, 559
Salvador, El, 678
Salzburg meeting of Napoleon III and Francis Joseph, 582
Samarin, George, reformer, 375
Samarin, G. F., administrator, 368
Samos, Island of, 422

San Francisco, 636, 643
San Jacinto, battle of, 621
San Jacinto, U.S. frigate, 639
San Juan river, 679, 680, 681
San Salvador, capital of United Provinces of Central America, 679
Sanctuary, in Piedmont, right of, 567
Sand, George (Aurore Dupin, baronne Dudevant), novelist, 124, 165
Santa Anna, Antonio Lopez de, general and politician, 203, 208, 674
Santa Cruz, Andrés, general, dictator of Bolivia, 665, 667
Santander, Francisco de Paula, Colombian patriot, 669
Santo Domingo, 617, 682
São Paulo, 661
Sarmiento, Domingo Faustino, Argentine exile, 665, 670
Satsuma, 712–13
Saturday Review, 123
Savannah, 329
Savigny, Friedrich Karl von, jurist, 227
Savoy, ceded to France, 463, 572
Saxony, 392
condition of roads in, 31
government reforms (1831), 189
risings in, 397, 407, 500
industrial unrest, 497
alliance of the Three Kingdoms, 501
plan to amend Federal Constitution, 501
urban population, 505
king of, offers imperial crown to William I of Prussia, 514
invaded by Prussia (1866), 519
joins North German Confederation, 520
Scharnhorst, Gerhard Johann David von, general and reformer, 310, 317
Schele de Vere, Maximilian, Swedish observer at Frankfurt in 1848, 195
Schelling, Friedrich Wilhelm von, philosopher, 78, 496
Schiller, Johann Friedrich von, poet and dramatist, 134
Schinkel, Karl Friedrich, architect, 139, 140
Schlegel, August Wilhelm, critic, 139, 172
Schlegel, Friedrich, critic, 158, 171
Schleiden, Matthias Jakob, botanist, 67
Schleswig-Holstein, 219–20, 265, 464, 514–18, 520
Schmerling, Anton Baron von, Austrian statesman
and German unity, 194
attempt to restore local autonomy, 207
belief in a Greater Germany, 512
minister of Justice, 529
resignation, 533
replaces Goluchowski, 544

Schmerling, Anton (*cont.*)
a centralist, 545
and the Hungarian Diet, 546
dismissed, 548
Schneckenburger, Max, poet, 227, 495
Schönbrunn, Francis Joseph meets William I
at (1864), 516
School Boards (U.K.), set up in 1870, 337
Schools and Universities on the Continent
(Arnold), 115
Schopenhauer, Arthur, philosopher, 183, 184
Schültze, Max Johann Sigismund, professor
of anatomy and physiologist, 67
Schulze-Delitsch, Hermann, economist, 505,
507
Schurz, Carl, Republican politician (U.S.A.),
206
Schwann, Theodor, physiologist, 66, 67
Schwarzenberg, prince Felix von, Austrian
statesman
dissolves Diet and suspends constitution,
197, 408
champion of Austrian hegemony, 203,
499, 503
forces restoration of German Confederation, 210
repressive measures in Lombardy, 263
ultimatum to Prussia, 265
forms ministry, 406, 524
appeals for Russian aid, 407
negotiations with Bavaria and Württemberg, 409–10
makes Austria a centralised state, 413
death of, 413, 533
qualities of, 498
seeks admission of all Austria into *Bund*,
499, 538
exploits appeal from elector of Hesse-
Kassel, 502
failure of his constitutional hopes, 503
issues new constitution (March 1849),
526
replaces Windischgrätz, 528
dislike of Bach, 531
signs the Olmütz Punctation, 532
Schwarzenberg, Friedrich, Prince von,
Austrian prelate, defers publishing decrees of General Council, 100
Schwerin Palace, 142
Scotland
draining of moss-lands, 24
church in, 83–4
nationalism in, 217 n.
population, 331–2
franchise, 335
Scotsman, The, 123
Scott, Sir George Gilbert, architect, 136,
138, 145, 149
Scott, Sir Walter, novelist, 157, 165

Scott, Winfield, general, soldier and pre-
sidential nominee
Lincoln's criticism of, 657
occupies Mexico City, 674
Screw-propeller, perfection of, 278
Scutari, 478
Sebastopol, siege of, 306, 322–3, 479, 480, 482
Sebenico, 422
Secession, Ordinances of (U.S.A., 1860–1),
627
Secret Societies
Saints Cyril and Methodius (Ukraine), 231
in Poland, 234
in Bulgaria, 243
during American civil war, 647
in China, 699, 700
Sedan, battle of (1870), 305, 306, 327, 465
Sedgwick, Adam, geologist, criticism of
Darwin, 71
Seebach, Saxon minister in Paris, 484
Semipalatinsk, 386
Semper, Gottfried, architect, 141
Senegal, 461
September Convention (1864), 88
Seraing, proximity of coal and ore, 30
Serbia, 240–2, 474
Serfdom, abolition of
in Austrian empire, 6, 413–14, 523, 530
in Russia, 6, 370–2
Serno-Solovevich, S., revolutionary, 373
Serrano, Dominguez Francisco, Duke of La
Torre, 586
Seton-Watson, R. W., historian
on the Kremsier draft constitution, 197
on the Crimean war, 260
Sewage disposal, 72
Seward, William Henry, American states-
man, 638, 646
Seymour, Sir George Hamilton, diplomat,
British ambassador, 471, 478, 485
Shaftesbury, Anthony Ashley Cooper, earl
of, 83, 341
Shamyl, Caucasian guerrilla leader, 386
Shanghai
becomes international settlement, 7, 693
a Treaty Port, 692
growth of, 693
seized by the Small Sword Society, 700–1
trade affected by Taiping rebellion, 705
British and French forces in defence of,
706
school for teaching Western sciences and
mathematics, 708
Shaw, Richard Norman, architect, 154–5
Sheffield, 42, 43
Sherman, William T., general, 316, 329–30,
655
Shevyrev, Stepan Petrovich, literary critic,
368

Shiloh, battle of, 632
Shimoda, trade port, 711, 712
Shinto religion, 711
Shipbuilding, employment in, 333
Shipping, 25–6
  carriage of foodstuffs on lakes and rivers, 4, 32, 35
  transatlantic, 36, 332
  British tonnage, 332–3
  colonies linked to Britain by, 349
  tonnage visiting Mediterranean ports, 419–20
  mail services to Mediterranean and beyond, 431–2
  pleasure cruises, 432
  San Francisco–Shanghai service, 710
Short Outline of Croat-Slovene Orthography (Gaj), 238
Siam
  missionary work in, 79
  Britain's treaty with, 709
Siberia
  emigration and deportation to, 2, 358, 372, 384
  serfdom in, 372
  Russian consolidation in, 382
  administration, 383
  population, 383, 384
  frontiers, 384–6
Siccardi laws (1850), 567
Sicily
  British-type constitution (1812), 199, 560
  insurrection (1848), 389, 560, 562, 565
  population, 552
  administrative fusion with Naples, 560
  Garibaldi in, 573
  martial law, 576
Siècle, Le, 124, 125
Siemens, Werner von, industrialist and pioneer of electric-telegraphy, 51, 53
Silesia, 392, 401, 413
  textile industry, 400, 497
  population, 505
  Czech domination in, 523
Silistria, siege of, 478, 479
Silk
  industry in Lyons, 42
  substitutes for, 64
Simon, Jules, politician, 455
Simpson, Sir James Young, Bart, 64, 72
Simpson, General Sir James, Crimean commander, 482
Simson, Eduard, president, Frankfurt Assembly, 499–500
Singapore
  cable service, 350
  mail service, 432
  British influence in, 686

Singulari Nos, encyclical of Gregory XVI, 78
Sino-American treaty (1844), 692–3
Sinope, defeat of Turkish fleet, 281, 477
Six Articles, The (Germany), 493–4
Slav Congress (1848), 232–3
Slave trade
  restrictions, 6
  African measures to abolish, 616
  in Brazil, 661
Slavery
  campaign for abolition, 83
  British Empire, abolition in, 341
  compensation to slave-owners, 341
  conditions conducive to in U.S.A., 610
  debate in Virginia legislature, 612
  effect of spread of cotton cultivation in the South, 613, 617
  manumission, 616
  in Southern States of America, 616, 632
  insurrections, 617
  defence of, 617
  abolitionist movement, 618–19
  return of fugitives, 619, 623, 625
  legal basis, 620–4
  emancipation proclaimed, 639, 648
  Confiscation Act, 648
  Thirteenth Amendment to the Constitution, 648
Slavophiles
  in Russia, 230, 232–3, 366–8, 370–1, 375
  in the Austrian empire, 548–50
Slidell, John, Confederate States' representative to France, 639, 640
Slovaks, 240, 524, 530, 537, 541, 546, 549
Slovenes, 402, 524, 529–30, 545
Slowacki, Julius, poet, 237
Small Swords Society, The, 700–1
Smiles, Dr Samuel, author, 51
Smith, Adam, economist, 342, 344
Smith, Sir Francis Pettit, engineer and inventor, development of screw propeller, 278
Smyrna, 419–20, 422
Smyth, W. H., Rear-Admiral, 418
Snider, Jacob, inventor, 305
Soane, Sir John, architect, 136
Soap industry, 64
Società Rubattino (1840), 432
Società Sarda (1830), 432
Société d'Etudes du Canal de Suez, 437
Société Générale (1864), 458
Society of Arts, 134
Sociology, 54, 55
Sodium salicylate, 64
Soil fertility, 24, 52
Solar system, 59
Solaro della Margherita, Clemente, Piedmontese foreign minister, 555, 557, 560

Solesmes, Benedictine abbey of, 79
Solferino, battle of, 323, 539, 571
Solingen, domestic industries, 42
Sologne, 399
Somaliland, French bases in, 461
Sonderbund war (1847), 81, 107, 196, 223
South Africa, 27, 117, 211
South African Campaign (1852), 304
South Carolina, 196, 207, 329, 606, 609–11, 615, 627, 634
Souza, Ireneu de, *see* Mauá, Baron of
Sozial-politische Zeitung, 400
Spain
   continuous disorders in, 186
   constitution of 1812, 189
   franchise under constitution of 1812, 192
   anarchy and chaos, 204
   excludes Jews, 243
   railways in, 420
   influence in Philippines, 686
Spalato, 422
Spectator, The, 123
Spectroscopy, 58
Spectrum analysis, 58
Spencer, Herbert, philosopher, 69, 109, 112
Speranskii, Count Michael, statesman, 363, 383
Spezia, naval base, 567
Spielhagen, Friedrich, novelist, 167
Spinners, General Union of Operative, 346
Spirits, duty on, 38
Spoleto, council at (1849), 89
Sprengel, Kurt Polycarp Joachim, physician and botanist, 65
Springfield (Mass.), *Republican*, 130
Staatslexikon (Rotteck and Welcker), 193
Stadion, Count Francis, statesman, 406, 526, 528
Staël [Holstein], Germaine, Baroness de, writer, 172
Standard, The, price one penny, 122
Stanley, Edward Geoffrey Smith, 14th earl of Derby, statesman, 341
Stanley, Edward Henry, 15th earl of Derby, statesman, 581, 582
Stanton, Edwin M., American secretary for war, 646
Starbuck, H., member of English Suez Canal 'group', 436
Starnberger See, suicide of Ludwig II, 602
Stassow, Vassili Petrovich, architect, 139
Statuto of 1848, *see under* Piedmont-Sardinia
Steamship, the
   as ocean-going transport, 4, 36
   factor in building Suez canal, 4
   extends markets, 5
   for haulage of barges, 32
   as lake and river transport, 32, 35, 424

on the Mississippi, 32, 612
   improvements in, 35–6, 278, 281, 420–1
   transatlantic crossing, 36, 332
   in navies, 277–80
   used for towing, 277
   colliers, 279
   in the Mediterranean, 418, 420–4, 431–2
   British construction of, 431
   on the Amazon, 662
Steel
   Bessemer process, 4, 30, 457
   world output of, 30
   exports of, 30, 333
   the making of, 333
   Siemens process in France, 457
Stendhal, *see* Beyle, Marie-Henri, 159, 162–3, 166
Stephens, Alexander H., Vice-President of the Confederacy, 650, 653
Stephens, Frederic George, art critic, 151
Stephens, J. R., Chartist, 347
Stephenson, Robert, civil engineer, 436, 437, 438
Sterckx, Engelbert, cardinal, 89
Stethoscope, invention of, 72
Steuerverein, 494, 503
Stevens, Alfred, sculptor, 143
Stevens, Thaddeus, Congressman, 647
Stifter, Adalbert, writer, 161, 165
Stirling, Edward, leader-writer, *The Times*, 122
Stone's river, battle of, 632, 639
Stow, David, educational writer and pioneer, 114
Strachan, Bishop John, 117
Straits Convention (1841), 258, 429, 468
   revision of, 482, 490
   replaced, 488
   denounced by Russia, 488
Strantz, Colonel von, Prussian officer, 594, 596
Strat, J., Roumanian agent in Paris, 594
Stratford de Redcliffe, Stratford Canning, 1st Viscount, British ambassador to Turkey, 262, 270, 468, 470, 472, 473, 475, 476, 489
Stratimirović, 529
Strauss, David Friedrich, theologian (*Leben Jesu*), 75, 81, 102
Strickland, William, architect, 141
Strossmayer, Mgr George, Croatian prelate, 100
Stuart, James, pioneer of adult education, 119
Stubbs, George, painter, 135
Stuttgart, 407
Styria, 548
Succession, Hungarian Law of (1687), 547
Sudeten Germans, 544
Suez Canal, 4, 424, 433–40

Suffrage, universal manhood
  in Belgium, 192
  in France, 192, 204, 404, 409, 411, 443, 445, 446
  in Great Britain, 192, 204, 336, 343 347
  in Holland, 192
  in Norway, 192
  in Spain, 192
  in Sweden, 192
  in Switzerland, 196, 204
  in Piedmont, 200
  in Germany, 204, 210, 398, 498, 518, 579
  in U.S.A., 204-5
  in Hungary, 398
  in Brazil, 662
  in Chile, 664
Sugar, 27, 38, 65
Sugar-beet, 27, 391
Sulivan, Captain Thomas B., naval officer, 289
Sumner, Charles, U.S. Senator, caning of, 625
Sumter, Fort, 627
Sun Tzu, Chinese military thinker, 317
Šuplykać, colonel, Hungarian Serbs' voivode, 529
Supreme Court (U.S.A.), 624, 625
Surgery, 72-3
Sussex, H.R.H., Augustus Frederick, duke of, 290
Sweden
  franchise under constitution of 1809, 192
  and Scandinavianism, 220
  transformation of Diet (1851), 411
  frontier dispute with Russia, 483
  Britain and France sign treaty with, 484
Swinburne, Algernon Charles, poet, 178, 216
Swine fever, 24
Switzerland
  trade, industry and economics: spinning, 28; industrial chemistry, 29; condition of roads, 31
  chaos of economic arrangements, 222
  education: reform of primary schools, 80; training colleges, 80, 224; technical university of Zürich, 80, 106, 113; university of Berne, 80, 114; and the Jesuits, 81, 223; von Fellenberg's schools, 108; made compulsory, 110; university of Basle, 114
  religion: rivalry of Protestant and Catholic cantons, 80-1; dissolution of monasteries, 81; the Jesuits, 81, 223; reconciliation of church and state, 81; Old Catholic schism, 81, 100; Jews, 243; see also under Sonderbund war
  constitutional developments: in Liberal cantons, 80; in Lucerne, 81, 223; the

Federal Pact (1815), 81, 222-3; victory of the Radicals, 81, 223, 389; Constitution of 1848, 81, 185-6, 196, 223, 411; a real democracy, 186; Federal Tribunal (1874), 196; political laboratory, 196, 411; constitutional reform (1867), 211; complete national independence, 223-4, 411; suppression of 'Young Europe', 225
Sybil (Disraeli), quoted, 1, 10
Syllabus of Errors (Syllabus Errorum), 89-94, 454, 459
'Sylvester Patent', 532, 538
Syra, Island of, 419-20, 422
Syria
  missionary work in, 79, 423
  Mehemet Ali in, 427-9
  French expedition to (1860), 430
Syrian Protestant College, 423
Széczen, Count Anton, statesman, 541, 542
Szerem, 529

Tahiti, missionaries in, 259
Taiping rebellion, 8, 384, 697-700, 705, 706
Taku forts, capture of, 703-4
Talabot, the brothers, French railway engineers, 436, 437
Talleyrand-Périgord, Charles Maurice de, prince of Benevento, diplomat, 247-9
Tamworth Manifesto of 1834 (Peel), 339
Tancred (Disraeli), quoted, 10
Tangier, 424
Tao Kwang, emperor of China, 688
Taranto, 421
Tarapaca, 668
Tariff of Abominations (1828), 37
Tariff Compromise (1833), 623
Tarim basin, Turkestan, 707
Tarragona, 420
Tashkent, 387, 388
Tasmania, 353, 355
Taunton Commission, 113
Tax Union, see Steuerverein
Taxation
  meets part cost of Crimean war, 486
  income tax, 486
  in Austria, 538
  in Piedmont, 567
  and American Civil war, 651
  in Shanghai, 693
Taylor family, of Manchester Guardian, 121
Taylor, John Edward, founder of the Manchester Guardian, 132
Taylor, Zachary, twelfth president of U.S.A., 622-3
Tea
  duty on, 38
  trade with China, 687

Tegetthoff, Wilhelm von, Admiral, Austrian naval commander, 286
Telegraph, electric
  service to Continent and America, 36, 57
  development of, 53
  taken up by railways, 57, 332
  use in Crimean war, 309, 486
  British India Telegraph Company, 350
Telescope, reflecting, 58
Tellkampf, Johann Louis, German professor, 194
Temps, Le, 125
Tenasserim, British influence in, 686
Tennessee, 605, 626–7, 634, 648
Tennessee, river, 655
Tennyson, Alfred, Lord, poet, 174, 176–7
Test and Corporation Acts, repeal, 76
Tetuan, 424
Texas
  cotton in, 613
  proclaimed independent republic (1836), 621, 674
  annexed to U.S.A., 622, 674–5
  secedes, 627
  theatre of civil war, 654–5
Textile industries
  decline of domestic industry, 4, 42, 333
  development of machinery, 27–9
  British cotton, 333
  employment in British, 333
  Factory Acts relating to, 341–2
  in Russia, 364, 380
  in France, 457, 459
Thackeray, William Makepeace, novelist, 162, 163, 165, 418, 420
Thermometer, clinical, invention of, 72
Thierry, Augustin, historian, 11
Thiers, Louis-Adolphe, statesman and historian
  and the *Loi Falloux*, 80
  goes into opposition, 190
  and the Near East crisis (1840), 256–7, 433
  fall of his government, 429
  in virtual retirement, 452
  return to politics, 456
  opposition to war with Prussia, 599
Thomas, Pierre-Émile, director of French national workshops, 399
Thomson, Sir William, later Lord Kelvin, scientist, 50, 53, 58, 59
Thoreau, Henry David, American writer, 167
'Three Kings Alliance' (1850), 409
Threshing machinery, destroyed in uprisings, 25
Thun-Hohenstein, Count Leo, Austrian Minister of Education, 529, 542
Thuringia, 392, 395
Tibet incorporated in China, 685

Ticino, river, 321, 398
T'ien Wang, *see* Hung Hsiu-Ch'uan
Tientsin
  Admiral Putyatin at, 385
  opening to foreign trade, 704
  occupied by British forces, 704
  treaties, 703, 707
Tiflis, 386
Timbuktu, 424
Times, The, 14, 121, 122, 131, 132, 342, 580
Tithe
  payment by Irish catholics, 100
  in Europe, 391
Tobacco
  English duty on, 38
  in Virginia, 610
Tobolsk, 383
Tobruk, 424
Tocqueville, Alexis de, statesman and publicist, 1, 10, 186, 193
Todleben, Franz Eduard Ivanovich, Russian general, at Sebastopol, 480
Tokyo, 710, 713
'Tolpuddle Martyrs', 346–7
Tolstoi, D., Russian minister, 379
Tolstoy, Lyof, Count, writer, 160, 163, 165, 169, 182
Tommaseo, Niccoló, writer and politician, 558, 574
Tortosa, 420
Toulon, 420–1, 425
Townsend, Meredith (*Spectator*), 123
Trade and commerce
  American development increased by immigration, 2, 332
  command of sea-routes indispensable, 3, 349
  impact of railways and steamboat, 4, 25–6, 32, 33–4
  increased farm productivity for, 23, 27
  new agricultural implements for sale, 25
  sources of capital for trade and industry, 25, 458
  customs duties, 25–7, 37–8, 254, 342–4, 364, 452, 458, 535, 604, 609–10
  international grain trade, 26–7
  importance of textiles, 27–8, 333, 381
  the age of iron, 29–30
  coal, 30–1, 333
  customs unions, 37, 494–5, 561
  international trade policies, 37
  need for increased capital, 39
  banks and banking, 40–2, 334–5, 451, 458, 535
  British and French competition, 254
  Chartered companies, 281, 353, 355, 431, 432, 685, 687–8
  growing competition from Germany and U.S.A., 334

Trade and commerce (*cont.*)
British overseas capital investment, 334, 350
trade unions, 346, 455–6
co-operative movement, 348
commercial treaties, 349, 452, 505, 535, 567
quest for new markets, 349, 351
colonial markets, 350–2
British monopoly in India and Far East, 434
trade with China, 461, 686–8
see also under separate countries
Trade Unions
early growth, 45
as friendly societies, 46
arbitration machinery, 46
in America, 46
in Great Britain, 345–7
Trades Union Congress, formation of, 347
Traité des grandes opérations militaires (Jomini), 313
Transatlantic cable, 133
Transcaucasia
resistance movement in, 369, 385
assimilation of, 382
railways, 386
Transportation of convicts, 353
Transylvania, 402, 529, 537, 543, 545–7
Trappists form community at Milleray, 78
Travellers' Club, London, 138
Treasury
U.K., approval for municipal loans, 337
U.S.A. forms independent, 607
Treaty ports, Chinese, 692, 703
Treitschke, Heinrich von, historian and publicist, 210, 218, 507
Trent affair, the, 639
Trevelyan, Sir Charles, Bart, governor of Madras, 118, 337
Treviglio, 123
Tribune, 123
Trieste, 18, 420, 421, 425, 432, 501, 555
Trinity College, Dublin, represented in Commons, 335
Tripartite Alliance (1854), 481
Tripoli (Libya), 424
Tripoli (Syria), 423
Trollope, Anthony, novelist, compared with German contemporaries, 166
Trollope, Mrs Elizabeth, writer, 191, 194
Troy, American school, 119
Troya, Carlo (1784–1858), Italian historian, 225
Tseng Kuo-fan, leader of reaction against the Taipings, 699, 705, 706
Tung Wang, a Taiping leader, 698
Tungans, Chinese Muslims, in revolt, 707
Tunis, Bey of, Garibaldi takes service with, 555
Tupper, J. L., contributor to *The Germ*, 152

Turgai, 387
Turgenev, Ivan, novelist, 166, 168, 180, 182, 368
Turin, 392
all-Italian scientific congress, 562
parliament (February 1861), 575
Turin, Luigi Franzoni, archbishop of, 567
Turkestan
cotton, 381
Russian conquest of, 382, 386–8
annexation of Tashkent, 388
Turkey
and the Crimean war, xv, 468–92
Balkan nationalism, 229, 240–3
weakness of, 241, 430
and Mehemet Ali, 251–2, 254–7, 427–9
Treaty of Unkiar Skelessi, 252, 255–6, 428, 468
ports of, 422–3
destruction of fleet at Sinope, 281, 284, 426, 468
at Navarino, 426
massacres in Syria, 430
Turner, J. M. W., painter, 135, 150
Tuscany, 552
education, 115, 554
elects Victor Emmanuel II, 209
union with Piedmont, 209, 572
republic proclaimed, 408
enlightened rule in, 554, 556
agricultural societies, 556
press, 556, 560
tariffs, 556, 561
abolition of ecclesiastical privilege, 557
grant of constitution, 561
economic league with papal states, 561
designs on Massa and Carrara, 563
forces checked at Curtatone, 564
occupied by Austrian forces, 565
return to former rulers, 572
Twain, Mark (Samuel Langhorne Clemens), humorist, 167
Twenty-four Articles, Treaty of, 221
Twesten, Karl, Prussian politician, 518, 521
Tyler, John, tenth president of U.S.A., 621
Tylor, Edward Burnett, anthropologist, 102
Typhus, 44, 72
Tyutchev, Fedor Ivanovich, poet, 232
Tzu Hsi, empress dowager of China, 705

Ullathorne, William Bernard, Roman Catholic bishop of Birmingham, 87
Ultramontanism, 79, 81
Uncle Tom's Cabin, 625
Union Pacific Railroad, 643
Unitarians, 86, 87
United Diet (Prussia), meeting in Berlin, 496–7
United Italian Provinces, 554

'United Party of the Federalist Nobility', 541

United States of America, xviii–xix, 603–30
  social structure: immigration, 2, 618, 643; population, 2, 22, 603, 626, 642; slavery, 203; suffrage, 204–5
  trade and commerce: domestic market, 5; grain production, 7, 642; with Great Britain, 26, 612; cotton, 28; iron and steel, 29, 30, 31; coal and coke, 30, 31, 642; gold, 35; shipping, 36, 280; interstate free trade, 37; tariffs, 37; banks and banking, 41, 607, 643; trade unions, 46; income tax, 644
  agriculture: import of machinery, 25; grain production, 27, 642; cotton, 28
  communications: canals, 31, 612, 680; railways, 32, 34, 141, 612, 618, 624, 643; highways, 35, 604, 606, 612
  finance: banks and banking, 41, 607, 643; federal funds withdrawn from First Bank of U.S.A., 607; formation of independent Treasury, 607; decentralisation of, 608; for roads and railways, 612; tariffs, 643; income tax, 644
  education, 50, 116–17, 119–20
  science, 51, 72
  press, 129–33
  architecture, 140–1
  literature, 164, 167, 179–81
  constitutional developments: held as model to Frankfurt National Assembly, 195; suffrage, 204–5; South Carolina secedes, 207; Louisiana Purchase (1863), 603, 620, 621, 624; Indians on state lands, 606; Nullification crisis, 606, 609, 613; the Force Act, 609, 616; Missouri Compromise (1820), 620, 621, 623, 624; Thirteenth Amendment, 648
  Civil war, xix, 631–58: place in American history, 19; casualties, 19, 654; John Brown's raid, 203; breech-loading weapons, 304; general course of operations, 327–30; formation of Confederate States, 627
  navy, 277–8, 285–7, 298–9, 425
  army, 304–5, 310, 316, 328
  and Mexico, 464, 580, 622, 674
  judicial system, 604, 609
  and China, 692–4, 700–3, 708
  and Japan, 710–12

United States of Europe, concept of a, 7

Univers, L' (Veuillot), 79, 80, 123

Universal Postal Union (1874), 7

Universities
  University College London founded, 77
  open to non-Anglicans, 87
  Free-Church colleges, 87
  admission of women, 119

University Extension Movement, 119
  reform of curriculum, 206
  foundation of new, 206
  Vilna, closed by Russia, 230
  parliamentary representation of Oxford and Cambridge, 335
  of Russia, 106, 119
  of Belgium, 107
  of Austria, 114, 530
  of Germany, 114, 116, 459
  of Sweden, 119
  of U.S.A., 119

University Tests Act (1871), 87

Unkiar Skelessi, Treaty of (1833), 252, 255–6, 428, 468

Upjohn, Richard, architect, 141

Ural river, 386

Urea, synthesis of, 62

Urquiza, Justo José de, governor of Entre Ríos province, 671

Uruguay, 659, 670

Ussher, James, archbishop of Armagh, 102

Ussuri river, 385

Utah, 203, 623

Utilitarianism (Mill), 205

Uvarov, Count Sergei Semenovich, Russian minister for Education, 230, 362, 365

Vacuum tubes, Faraday's work on, 58

Valdivia, 663, 665

Valencia, 420

Valency, theory of, 62

Valetta, 420

Valparaiso, bombardment of, 666

Vance, Zebulon M., governor of North Carolina, 653

Vanderbilt, Cornelius, steamship and railroad promoter, 681

Varas, Antonio, politician, 666

Varna, 478, 481

Vassar College, U.S.A., 119

Vatican Council (1870), 454; see also General Council

Vay, Baron, Hungarian Chancellor, 542

Veiga Evaristo da, editor, 660

Venelin, George (1802–39), Russian historian of Slovak origin, 242

Venereal disease, use of mercury, 72

Venezuela, 668–9

Venice
  in revolt with Lombardy, 262
  achieves liberation, 396
  blockaded, 408
  population, 420
  toleration of Jews, 421
  promised to France by Austria, 464
  to receive special statute, 526

Venice (*cont.*)
  collapse of Manin's republic, 565
  return to former rulers, 572
  ceded to Napoleon III by Francis Joseph, 578
Vera Cruz, French, British and Spanish troops at, 464, 677
Verdi, Giuseppe, composer, 184, 225
Verlaine, Paul Marie, poet, 179
Verona, 321
Versailles, 601, 602
Versen, Max von, Prussian general staff officer, 587, 589
Veto, American presidential power of, 608, 653
Veuillot, Louis, publicist, 79, 80, 123, 459
Vicenza, 321, 402, 564
Vicksburg, capture of, 328, 655
Victor Emmanuel II, king of Italy
  guarantees Rome to the papacy (1864), 88
  not invited to General Council, 95
  Rome withheld from, 95
  elected king of Italy, 209
  and armistice of Vignale (1849), 322, 566
  maintains the *Statuto*, 412, 566
  recognises Austrian possessions in Italy (1849), 527
  partial re-establishment of royal authority, 566
  and D'Azeglio, 567–8
  and Cavour, 568–9, 571–3
  and the Crimean war, 569
Victoria, Princess Royal of England, 508
Victoria, queen of England
  purchases pictures by Frith, 154
  knights Landseer, 154
  memorandum about Palmerston, 340
  attitude to ministers, 340
  and Tsar Nicholas I, 359
Victoria and Albert Museum, London, 154
Vie de Jésus (Renan), 102
Vienna, 18, 125
  banking in, 41, 535, 539
  theatres in, 182–3
  revolution in, 261, 321, 395–6, 403, 524
  communications with, 425
  industrial boom, 535
  stock-exchange crash, 538
Vienna, Congress of (1815), 266, 462, 493
Vienna Note (1853), 475–6
Vienna Settlement (1815), 16, 191, 247, 260, 266, 272
Vigevano, Armistice of, 523
Vigny, Alfred de, poet, 171, 173
Világos, Hungarian surrender at, 408, 528
Villafranca, armistice of, 506, 544, 572
Villemessant, Hippolyte de (*Le Figaro*), 125
Vionville, battle of, 326

Virchow, Rudolph, Prussian doctor and politician, 67
Virginia, 185
  in the Civil War, 327–8, 627, 648, 652, 654
  tobacco, 610
  Bacon's Rebellion (1676), 611
  subsistence farming in, 611
  legislature debates slavery, 612
  slaves revolt in (1831), 617
Visconti, Louis Tullius Joachim, architect, 141
Vistula, river, 26, 32
Vladivostock, founding of, 385, 704
Voivodina (Serbian), 527, 529, 537, 541, 543
Vom Kriege (Clausewitz), 317
Vorarlberg, to be merged in the Tirol, 525
Vossische Zeitung, 126

Wackenroder, Wilhelm Heinrich, Romantic writer, 139
Waghorn, Thomas, lieutenant R.N., promoter of the overland route to India, 436
Wagner, Wilhelm Richard, composer, 184
Waitangi, Treaty of, 353
Wakefield, Edward Gibbon, colonial statesman, 352, 353
Walewski, Alexandre, comte, French politician, minister of Napoleon III, 487
Walker, William, American adventurer, 681
Wallace, Alfred Russell, traveller and naturalist, 69
Wallachia, 462, 505; *see also under* Principalities
Walter, Thomas U., American architect, 142
Walters family of *The Times*, 121, 122
Wanghai, 693
Wappers, Gustaf, Baron, painter, 151
Ward, Frederick, American adventurer, 706
Ward, John Elliott, American lawyer, politician, diplomat, 703
Warrior, H.M.S. (1860), 279, 285
Wartburg festival, 493
Washington, 141, 142, 328
Water, provision of pure supply, 72
Water power in spinning mills, 28
Waterways, 30
Watts, George Frederick, painter, 153
Wealth of Nations (Adam Smith), 342
Webster, Daniel, American statesman, 195, 203, 615, 623
Wehrli, Johann Jakob, pioneer in education, 113
Weimar Republic, 208
Weld, Theodore Dwight, abolitionist, 618

Welden, Baron Franz Ludwig von, Austrian general, replaced by Haynau, 528

Wellhausen, Julius, evangelical theologian and orientalist, 102

Wellington, Arthur Wellesley, 1st Duke of, 202, 248, 433

Werther, Karl von, Baron, Prussian ambassador in Paris, 591, 592, 595, 598

Wesselenyi, Baron, member of Hungarian parliament, 240

West Indies, slavery in, 341

Western Associated Press, 133

Western Union Telegraph Company, 133

Westminster, Statute of, 355

Westphalia, 400

Wette, Wilhelm Martin Leberecht de, evangelical theologian, 102

What is to be done? (Chernyshevskii), 374

Wheat
  Russian, 26
  American, 27

Wheatstone, Sir Charles, physicist, 53

Wheelwright, William, promoter of enterprises in Latin America, 665

Whistler, James MacNeill, painter, 155

Whitehead, Robert, industrialist, inventor, 287

Whitman, Walt, American poet, 2, 167, 180–1, 658

Whitworth, Sir Joseph, engineer, 284

Wiegmann, Arend Friedrich August, German naturalist, 65

Wielopolski, Alexander, Marquis, Polish statesman, 235

Wilberforce, Samuel, bishop, 71

Wilkes, Captain Charles, commanding U.S. frigate *San Jacinto*, 639

Willard, Emma, pioneer in women's education, 119

Willems, Jan Frans, poet, philologist, 221

William I, king of Holland, 221

William IV, king of Great Britain and Hanover, 189, 190

William I, king of Prussia
  army conflict dominates early reign of, 16
  becomes regent, 508
  character of, 508
  absent from Frankfurt Congress of Princes, 513–14
  reluctance to dethrone dynasties, 520
  exchanges with Benedetti at Ems, 595–6
  decides to mobilise, 599
  irresolution of, 599
  form of title as emperor, 601

William III, king of Holland, 581

Williams, Sir William Fenwick, 'of Kars', general, British commissioner with Turkish army, 484

Wilmot Proviso, 622

Windischgrätz, Alfred, Prince von, Austrian Field-Marshal
  disperses Pan-Slav Congress, 187, 402
  restoration of old order in Bohemia, 401–2, 523
  restores authority in Vienna, 403, 524
  reoccupies Budapest, 406
  defeated by Hungarians, 407
  at abdication of Ferdinand, 525
  given power to reduce Hungary, 525–6
  replaced by General Welden, 528

Windsor, Napoleon III visits, 481

Wine
  duty on, 38
  export of French, 454
  Piedmontese, 556, 559, 590

Wisconsin, 189, 203, 620

Wiseman, Nicholas, Roman Catholic archbishop of Westminster, 84, 87

Wochenblatt party, 14, 508

Wöhler, Friedrich, chemist and professor of medicine, 62

Wolff, Bernhard, founder of German press agency, 5, 132

Wood, Sir Charles, 1st Viscount Halifax, politician, 118

Woodhull, Victoria Claflin, reformer, candidate for U.S. presidency, 206

Wool
  European, 23
  Russian, 26
  price increase, 27
  supplies from outside Europe, 27
  combing by machinery, 28
  introduction of power loom, 28
  cotton and wool textiles, 28

Wool, John Ellis, major-general, American army veteran, 656

Woolner, Thomas, sculptor, 143

Workhouses, 337

Working-men's Associations, in Germany, 505; *see also under* International

Wörth, battle of (1870), 326

Wrangel, Friedrich, Graf von, Prussian general, 405

Württemberg
  formation of parliamentary ministry, 395
  negotiations with Schwarzenberg, 407–10
  agitation for extended franchise, 497
  amendment of Federal constitution, 501
  army, 507
  pays indemnity, 520
  secret treaty with Prussia, 520, 580
  and making of German empire, 601

Württemberg, king of
  disperses rump of Frankfurt Assembly, 500
  meets Francis Joseph, 502

Wurtz, Charles Adolphe, chemist, 62
Wyatt, Sir Matthew Digby, architect and writer on art, 143
Wyoming, 206

Yakub Beg, ruler of Kashgar, 707
Yancey, William L., secessionist, 627
Yangtse river, open to Western shipping, 703
Yeh Ming-ch'en, Canton viceroy, 696, 701
Yehonala, *see* Tzu Hsi
York
  meeting of British Association, 50
  burns effigy of pope, 85
'Young Europe', 225
'Young Italy' (Mazzini), 128, 224, 225, 555
Yucatán, secession of, 674
Yuenmingyuen, burning of imperial palace of, 704

Yung Chêng, emperor of China, edict against opium smoking (1729), 688
Yunganchow, Taipings besieged in, 698

Zagreb Assembly, 403
Zaichnevskii, Peter Grigorievich, revolutionary writer, 373
Zang, August (*Die Presse*), 126
Zante, island of, 422
Zara, 422
Zasulich, Vera, revolutionary, 378
Zoffany, Johann, painter, 135
Zola, Émile, novelist, 148
Zollverein, the German, 26, 37, 38, 228 494–5, 501, 503, 505
Zucchi, Carlo, general, 554, 555
Zug, canton of, 81
Zürich, 80–1, 106, 114
Zürich, Peace of (1859), 572
Zwirner, Ernst Friedrich, master builder, 140